COMPREHENSIVE STRUCTURED

COBOL

SECOND EDITION

L. Wayne Horn
Gary M. Gleason

Pensacola Junior College

 boyd & fraser publishing company
Danvers, Massachusetts

Credits

Vice President & Publisher	Thomas K. Walker
Senior Acquisitions Editor	James H. Edwards
Production Coordinator	Patty Stephan
Marketing Manager	Christopher Will
Manufacturing Director	Dean Sherman
Cover Photograph	Mark Tomalty/Masterfile
Cover Design	Mike Fender Design
Text Design	Sandra Rigney
Production Service	The Book Department
Composition	Graphic Typesetting Service

© 1992 by boyd & fraser publishing company
A Division of South-Western Publishing Company
Danvers, Massachusetts 01923

Manufactured in the United States of America

COBOL is an industry language and is not the property of any company or group of companies, or of any organization or group of organizations. No warranty, expressed or implied, is made by any contributor or by the CODASYL Programming Language Committee as to the accuracy and functioning of the programming system and language. Moreover, no responsibility is assumed by any contributor, or by the committee, in connection therewith. The authors and copyright holders of the copyrighted material used herein, FLOW-MATIC (trademark of Sperry Rand Corporation), Programming for the UNIVAC® I and II, Data Automation Systems copyrighted 1958, 1959, by Sperry Rand Corporation; IBM Commercial Translator Form No. F 28-8013, copyrighted 1959 by IBM; FACT, DSI27A5260-2760, copyrighted 1960 by Minneapolis-Honeywell, have specifically authorized the use of this material in whole or in part, in the COBOL specifications. Such authorization extends to the reproduction and use of COBOL specifications in programming manuals or similar publications.

Names of all products mentioned herein are used for identification purposes only and may be trademarks and/or registered trademarks of their respective owners. South-Western Publishing Company and boyd & fraser publishing company disclaim any affiliation, association, or connection with, or sponsorship or endorsement by such owners.

Library of Congress Cataloging-in-Publication Data

Horn, Lister Wayne.
    Comprehensive structured COBOL / L. Wayne Horn, Gary M. Gleason. —
    2nd ed.
      p. cm.
    Includes index.
    ISBN 0-87835-857-9
    1. COBOL (Computer program language) 2. Structured programming.
  I. Gleason, Gary M. II. Title.
  QA76.73.C25H673 1992
  650′.0285′5133—dc20   91-33959
                                               CIP

2 3 4 5 6 7 8 B 5 4 3 2

CONTENTS

10. THE STRUCTURED PROGRAMMING ENVIRONMENT — 387

11. INTERACTIVE PROGRAMS AND CHARACTER STRING MANIPULATION — 431

12. SEARCH PROCEDURES — 477

DIRECTORY OF PROCEDURES

DIRECTORY OF PROGRAMS

[1]Program requires Report Writer which is not implemented in the RM/COBOL-85 compiler supplied with this text.

[2]This program uses features that are specific to RM/COBOL-85 and may have to be modified to run in any other environment.

PREFACE

ABOUT THIS BOOK

The purpose of *Comprehensive Structured COBOL, Second Edition* is to teach structured programming concepts and practices in the context of ANSI-74 and ANSI-85 COBOL. This text is the result of years of classroom experience. The reading and conceptual levels are closely matched with the abilities of average college students. The programming examples and exercises are based on realistic business applications. The text and instructor's manual have been carefully designed and include many pedagogical features to simplify the teaching and learning processes.

Comprehensive Structured COBOL, Second Edition satisfies the requirements of a one- or two-semester course in COBOL programming, such as that described by the Data Processing Management Association (DPMA) in its Model Computer Information Systems Curriculum CIS '86, Courses CIS86-3 and CIS86-4 (Introduction to and Intermediate Business Application Programming), or its Associate-level Model Curriculum, Courses COMP.4 and COMP.5 (Programming Language I and II).

Since the publication of the first edition of this text, several events have occurred which have had profound effects on computer-related education. Microcomputers have become more powerful with a much broader array of software available for them. The first steps toward true integration of corporate and institutional computer resources have been taken with the widespread use of networks and micro- to mainframe links. IBM has adopted COBOL as a standard programming language as part of its effort to create a uniform computing environment spanning the entire range of its product line. The COBOL world has seen the final adoption of the COBOL-85 Standard amid much controversy. Some application developers are beginning to use COBOL-85, particularly for new projects. Use of fourth generation software development tools (which often generate COBOL source code) has increased. None of these events has decreased the importance of COBOL in the curriculum of Computer Information Systems or similar programs of study, and yet the world in which students will work in the 1990s is quite different from the world in the mid-1980s.

NEW FEATURES IN THIS EDITION

This edition builds on the strengths of the first edition and also reflects the contemporary scene in computing, especially in COBOL education. Following are some of the most important changes in this edition:

Increased Coverage of the COBOL-85 Standard

Most chapters include a section entitled "COBOL-85 Update" which covers features of the COBOL-85 Standard related to that chapter. Included are many programs illustrating the power of COBOL-85 language features. Emphasis is on those COBOL-85 topics which educators say they find most useful and are most likely to cover with their classes. Appendixes contain the complete COBOL-74 and COBOL-85 Standards. By using this text, it is possible to create a course that is COBOL-74 or COBOL-85 oriented.

Inclusion of Ryan McFarland COBOL Compiler

COBOL has traditionally been taught in a mainframe environment. At many colleges, this continues to be the mode of instruction. In other cases, however, access to a mainframe is limited or perhaps nonexistent. Using microcomputers in COBOL instruction has been hampered by the high cost of good COBOL compilers. Adopters of this text are entitled to a license for a high-quality COBOL development system—Ryan McFarland's RM/COBOL-85—for the MS DOS environment (IBM PC/PS 2 or compatible). This software includes an editor as part of the project management system RM/CO*. Students can develop and test programs on any available microcomputer without mainframe access. This brings down the cost of COBOL instruction. It also increases student achievement by making it possible to write more programs and versions of programs than was previously possible. Though the Ryan McFarland compiler is available, the text and its sample programs cover standard COBOL, thereby making it possible to use the book in any computing environment with any compiler. Appendixes B and H cover specific details of RM/COBOL-85. The remainder of the text covers standard COBOL.

Increased Emphasis on Proper Structured Programming Practices

This edition continues the practice of presenting each major program example by means of a statement of the problem, an analysis of the problem with pseudocode, and a solution to the problem. Standards for naming and numbering paragraphs are developed and illustrated throughout the book. Paragraph names use the *verb object* form whenever possible. In addition to sequence, paragraph numbers reflect the hierarchy of the paragraph in the control structure—1000 at the highest level; 2000, 2100, etc., at the second level; and so forth. Structure diagrams, which are included for most programs, now include the paragraph number as well as the paragraph name.

Expanded Coverage of Indexed and Relative Files

The chapters on indexed and relative files are improved with fuller coverage and many more program examples. This reflects the increased importance of these types of files in the development of systems for both the micro- and mainframe environments.

Revised Program Examples

All programs in the text have been rewritten. Many are illustrated with sample data and output, often with annotation. A Student Disk with the source code for all program examples is included. Students may test and modify existing programs without retyping code—a useful activity for enhancing understanding of language features and program logic.

Enhanced Glossary

The glossary includes definitions of terms from the ANSI-85 COBOL Standard as well as from the text itself.

Improved Teaching/Learning Aids

Most programming assignments have been revised to include a detailed description of the file to be processed. An Instructor's Resource Disk with sample test data for most programming assignments is included with the Instructor's Manual. The Instructor's Manual includes both the Student's and Instructor's Resource Disks, a test bank, and new transparency masters. These tools will help the instructor with the tasks of preparing lectures and evaluating student achievement. MicroSWAT III, a computerized test-generating program, is also available to adopters of the text.

OTHER FEATURES

This edition of the text incorporates those features of the first edition that teachers and students found to be most helpful including the following:

Systems Approach

The first half of the text (Chapters 1 through 9) is oriented toward the fundamentals of COBOL and the basic techniques of top-down program design and structured programming. The second half (Chapters 10 through 16) stresses a broader systems approach. The focus in the second half is on the relationship of individual programs to a complete data processing system. This provides students with an understanding of a program as an element of a whole system rather than as an isolated entity. The student is asked to consider the impact of an applications program on the information system itself by considering various trade-offs between functionality and availability of computing resources. Topics such as establishing audit trails, backup files, transaction logs, and error recovery procedures are covered. This text helps bridge the gap between the student's first exposure to a programming language (which of necessity focuses on the details of syntax and semantics of the language and program logic) and the broader considerations of the environment in which the resulting programs will be used.

Batch and Interactive Concepts

Both batch and interactive concepts and techniques are covered. The importance of interactive systems is often ignored or insufficiently addressed in many competing COBOL texts. This text not only presents the traditional batch-oriented concepts but also includes a discussion of techniques, such as menus and prompts that are appropriate for interactive programs. Many interactive program examples are also included.

Early Introduction of Programming

A limited but logically complete subset of COBOL is introduced early in the text so students can begin writing programs almost immediately. Seeing the results of their efforts helps motivate students to keep learning as topics are expanded using a spiral approach in later parts of the text.

Emphasis on Program Debugging

Most chapters include a section titled "Debug Clinic" which contains detailed debugging techniques, caution notes, style recommendations, and discussion of potential problems and possible solutions. These sections help students become more efficient and professional in their approach to programming and help to avoid some of the frustrations experienced by students learning a new programming language.

Self-Test Exercises

Each chapter contains "Self-Test Exercises" which test vocabulary, basic skills, and understanding of programming techniques. They enhance the learning process by providing students immediate feedback; all Self-Test answers appear in a separate section at the end of the book.

Variety of Programming Assignments

Each chapter contains a variety of business-oriented programming assignments enabling instructors to meet the needs of students with varying interests and levels of ability. For those instructors who prefer to have students write programs which use the same data or are part of the same data processing system, this text includes three such sets of assignments. The programming assignments and data sets in Appendix E ("Personnel System") or Appendix F ("Sales Accounting System") can serve as the basis for all programming assignments needed for Chapters 1 through 9. The third system in Appendix G ("Subscription System") can be used for Chapters 10 through 16. These appendixes may be used in place of, or in addition to, the regular end-of-chapter programming assignments.

ACKNOWLEDGMENTS

Comprehensive Structured COBOL, Second Edition has been designed as a complete teaching and learning system. Systems of any sort must be "fine tuned," and many people have helped in this process. We are indebted to all who have contributed to the success of this effort. Deserving of special thanks and praise are those who reviewed drafts of the manuscript and whose comments and suggestions were invaluable. Among them are Steve Deam, Milwaukee Area Technical Institute; Robert Harris, Appalachian State University; James Kennedy, St. John's River Community College; Robert Landrum, Jones County Junior College; Susan Lisack, Purdue University; George Novotny, Ferris State University; Paul W. Ross, Millersville University; and Walter Witschey, Tulane University.

Finally, we extend our thanks to the editorial and production staffs at boyd & fraser: Tom Walker, Vice President and Publisher, for conceiving this book, encouraging us to write it, and sticking by us over the years; James Edwards, Senior Acquisitions Editor, who helped give specific direction to the second edition; Patty Stephan, Production Coordinator; Christopher Will, Marketing Manager; and Margaret Kearney and the staff at The Book Department, who did an outstanding job of copyediting, preparing the material for typesetting, laying out pages, and creating the artwork.

L. Wayne Horn

Gary M. Gleason

1. COMPUTERS, DATA PROCESSING, AND PROGRAMMING

1.1 WHAT IS A COMPUTER?

From astronomy to zoology, from business to medicine, from art to engineering, computers have become very important tools in almost all areas of human endeavor. Since the first primitive automatic computing machines were devised in the 1940s, computers have undergone steady improvement. Each substantial improvement yielded more computing power and greater reliability at less cost, resulting in a greater number of applications for which the computer could be cost effective. Presently, computers are available in sizes ranging from the microcomputer, the smallest of which is the size of a briefcase, to mainframes that fill a large room. Computer prices range from about one thousand dollars for a microcomputer, to several million dollars for a large mainframe. In between, computers are available in a wide range of sizes, shapes, and prices (with an equally wide variety of capabilities). Today it is possible to choose a computer for almost any application at a reasonable cost.

What do such diverse devices have in common that enables us to classify them all as computers? All computers execute sequences of instructions called **programs**. Programs are written to solve specific problems; they are placed in the computer's memory, which recalls the programs when they are needed. Thus, the same computer can solve different problems simply by changing the program it executes.

As shown in Figure 1.1, all computers share a basic logical organization composed of five logical components called **units**:

- input unit
- output unit
- memory unit
- control unit
- arithmetic/logic unit

The **input unit** transfers data from some external medium, such as a keyboard or magnetic tape, into the computing system. The **output unit** transfers data from the system onto some external medium, such as paper or magnetic tape. Data is stored in the **memory unit**. The memory unit also stores the sequence of instructions (the program) required to manipulate the data to produce the desired results.

Memory is composed of storage locations, each of which has an **address**. The content of any location is made available to other units of the computing system by specifying to the memory unit the address of the desired data. Data is stored in a location by specifying to the memory unit

1

Figure 1.1   Organization of a computer

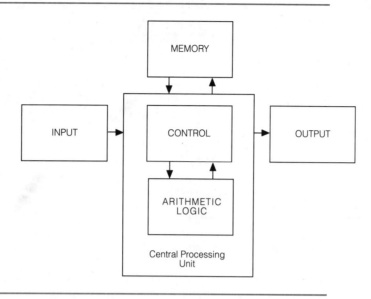

the content and the address of the location into which the data is to be placed. The commands that order data to be placed, moved, or used in various ways are given to the computer in programs discussed at length in later chapters.

The **control unit** executes each program one instruction at a time. When the program requires data, the control unit activates the input unit. When a program instruction requires that data be written out, the control unit activates the output unit. When a program requires that computations be performed, the control unit activates the **arithmetic/logic unit**, which performs all the arithmetic and logical operations. The control and arithmetic/logic units are often referred to collectively as the **central processing unit**, or **CPU.**

The hardware for these components varies greatly among computing systems. The central processing unit ranges from an electronic chip called a **microprocessor** (Fig. 1.2) in a microcomputer system (Fig. 1.3), to larger units in other computers called minicomputers (Fig. 1.4), as well as in the more powerful mainframes.

Input and output devices are available for a great variety of input and output media. A commonly used input/output device is the **computer terminal**, which contains a typewriterlike keyboard by which data is entered into the computing system. Terminals have a video screen (also called a **cathode ray tube** or **CRT**) on which information is displayed to the operator. Some terminals have the capability of printing data on paper using an attached printer. Terminals allow the user to enter data and receive information; they serve as both input and output devices.

Printed output is an almost universal requirement in applications of computing systems. To accommodate the need for **hard copy** (output printed on paper by a printer), a variety of types of printers are used. Printers such as the one shown in Figure 1.5 can produce output at rates varying from 300 to 1600 lines per minute; these printers are usually found in minicomputers and mainframe-based systems. Microcomputer systems usually utilize a dot matrix printer (Fig. 1.6), which measures speeds in

Figure 1.2   CPU for a microcomputer
Courtesy International Business Machines Corporation

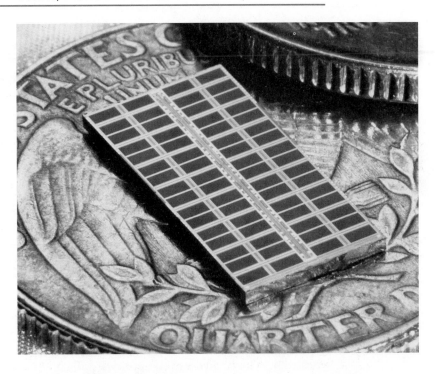

Figure 1.3   An IBM Microcomputing system (the IBM PS/2)
Courtesy International Business Machines Corporation

Figure 1.4   IBM AS/400 Product Family
Courtesy International Business Machines Corporation

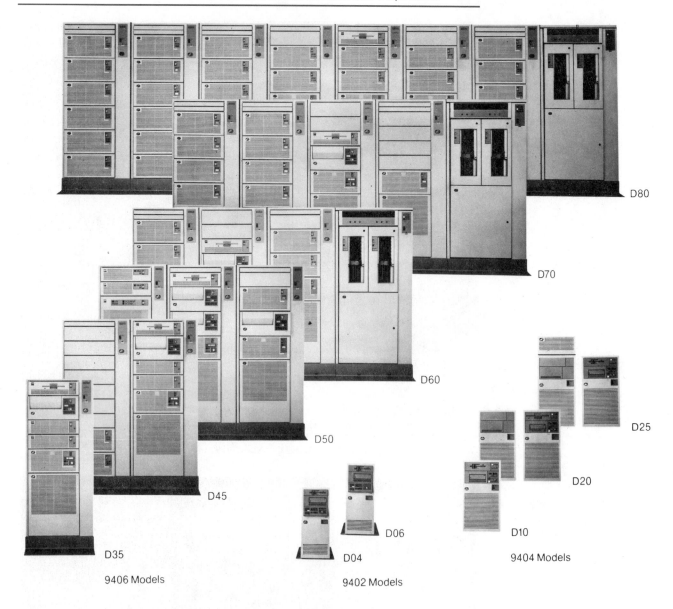

D80

D70

D60

D50

D45

D35

9406 Models

D06

D04

9402 Models

D25

D20

D10

9404 Models

characters per second, or a laser printer (Fig. 1.7), which has the capability of printing several pages per minute. Larger (and faster) versions of laser printers are also used in minicomputers and mainframe systems.

Most computing systems have mass storage devices capable of storing many millions of characters in a form that can be readily accessed by the computer. The two most common types of mass storage devices are **magnetic tape drives** (Fig. 1.8) and **disk drives**. Tapes are most often used for long-term storage of large volumes of data; they are used primarily in minicomputers and mainframe systems (although tape drives are available for use with microcomputers). Mini- and mainframe computers often use disk drives (Fig. 1.9) which store data on removable disk packs. Microcomputers commonly use disks with limited storage capacity called **floppy**

Figure 1.5 A high-speed printer
Courtesy International Business Machines Corporation

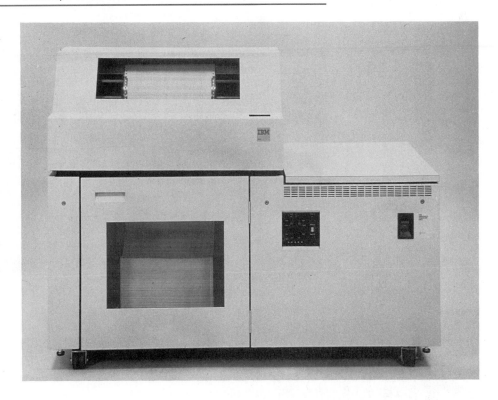

Figure 1.6 A dot matrix printer
Courtesy International Business Machines Corporation

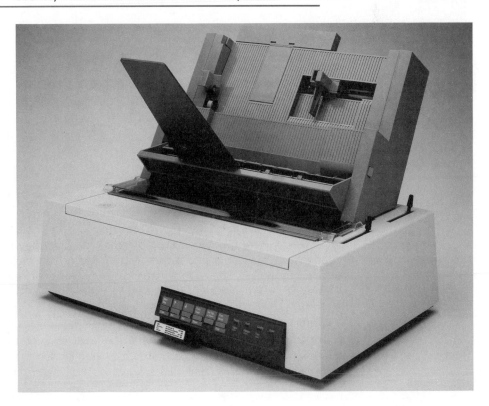

Figure 1.7   A laser printer
Courtesy International Business Machines Corporation

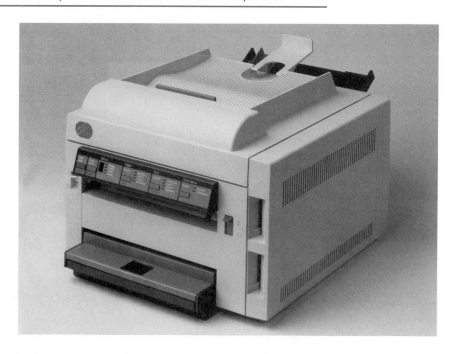

Figure 1.8   Magnetic tape drives
Courtesy International Business Machines Corporation

Figure 1.9   Disk drives
Courtesy International Business Machines Corporation

disks (Fig. 1.10) for long-term storage of data and disks with larger capacity called **hard disks** (Fig. 1.11) for storage of information required by the ongoing day-to-day operation of the system.

Both disks and tapes have the capability of reading and writing data on a magnetic medium (disk or tape) and reading the information at a later time; hence, they function as both input and output units in a computer system. Disk drives are equipped with movable read/write heads that make it possible to access any piece of data on demand. (Such access is

Figure 1.10   Floppy disks come in a variety of sizes.
Courtesy Mike Broussard/Ken Russo

Figure 1.11   A hard disk such as the one shown in this photo is
often used in microcomputer systems.
Courtesy International Business Machines Corporation

impossible with tapes because of the linear nature of the recording
medium.) Because of their random-access capability, disks are indispen-
sable in providing the direct access to data required in an interactive computing environment.*

1.2 COMPUTER PROGRAMMING LANGUAGES

The term **hardware** refers to the physical devices which make up a computing system. The devices pictured in Figures 1.3 through 1.11 are examples of computer hardware. The programs and their supporting documents required to make the hardware function are referred to as **software**.
Computer hardware is completely useless without software.

There are two basic types of software: **system software** and **application software**. System software consists of programs that control the operation of the computer, perform routine tasks needed by computer users,
and provide facilities for the development of programs. Application software consists of programs that are designed to help the user solve problems and perform data processing tasks related to specific needs.

Computer programs must be expressed in a language the computer
hardware can read and use. Each central processing unit "understands"
programs in **machine language**. Machine language is numerical (binary)—
that is, the operation to be performed and the data to be operated on are
expressed numerically. Machine languages tend to be very different from
one computer to another, depending on the design of the CPU; programs

*At one time the punched card was used for communicating with computing systems,
and it still may be found in some installations.

written in machine language for one particular computer usually cannot be executed by a computer built by a different manufacturer. It is very hard to write programs in machine language because every detail must be turned into a coded expression built of numbers.

As there are a great many disadvantages to machine language, other languages (generally called **high-level languages**) have been devised for constructing programs. Programs written in high-level languages use words and symbols to represent both the operations to be performed and the addresses of data items to be operated on. **COBOL**, an acronym for *CO*mmon *B*usiness *O*riented *L*anguage, is one example of a high-level language. Other commonly available programming languages include:

- BASIC (*B*eginners' *A*ll-purpose *S*ymbolic *I*nstruction *C*ode)
- FORTRAN (*FOR*mula *TRAN*slation)
- RPG (*R*eport *P*rogram *G*enerator)
- Pascal (named for French mathematician Blaise Pascal)
- WATBOL (*WAT*erloo CO*BOL*)
- C (developed by AT&T for use on UNIX-based systems)
- Ada (developed by the Defense Department)

A program written in a high-level language must be translated into machine language before it can be executed. Programs called **compilers** perform this task. A COBOL program, called a **source program**, is submitted to the COBOL compiler, which automatically translates the program into an equivalent machine language program called the **object program.** The object program then can be executed by the computing system. In addition to translating the program into machine language, the compiler also produces a listing of the source program and checks its content for correctness.

There are many advantages to writing programs in high-level languages. The languages are symbolic rather than numeric in nature, thereby enabling the programmer to formulate a problem solution in somewhat familiar terms. The more a language resembles ordinary speech, the faster the programmer can work. The details of the exact form of machine language are handled by the compiler; the programmer can be concerned only with the logic of the program. Furthermore, programs written in a high-level language tend to be transportable (i.e., they can be used on machines of many different designs and manufacturers), whereas machine language programs are specific to individual types of machines.

1.3 COMMUNICATING WITH THE COMPUTER

The computer user must communicate the program and data to be processed to the computing system. As noted earlier, no two computing installations are totally the same in all particulars, so it is impossible to provide complete details of all that the user will need to know in order to enter a program and data for processing at an installation. All installations have manuals or handouts that explain procedures to be followed at that installation; the user must secure these instructions before attempting the first program. The following is a brief survey of common types of systems encountered in academic computing centers.

On Line/Off Line

The term **on line** means that a device is in direct communication with a computing system; **off line** means that a device is acting on its own without direct communication with a computing system. Most computer terminals are on line; all data and instructions entered by the user are communicated directly to the system. Printers are typically turned off line for an operator to adjust the paper and then turned on line to receive output from the computer.

The term **batch computing** implies that data is collected for some period of time before being submitted for processing; **interactive computing** implies that the computer and user engage in a dialogue in which the user enters commands and/or data for immediate processing by the system. Punched card and some diskette systems are batch systems. The user must completely prepare the program and data files to be processed utilizing off-line devices. (A **file** is a collection of records. Each record contains a collection of data items pertaining to one entity—person, an inventory item, a bank transaction, or a program statement.) Only when the program and data are completed can the system accept the program for compilation and execution.

Systems utilizing terminals usually offer interactive computing. A program called an **editor** enables the user to build a file containing the program to be executed. When satisfied with the program, the user can give commands to execute the compiler and, if there are no errors, execute the program itself. The program can process data from a data file (which has been created utilizing the editor) or from the user who enters data at the terminal in response to messages from the program. If errors are encountered by the compiler or during execution, the user can use the editor to modify the program file and/or data file and repeat the compilation-execution process.

In an interactive computer system, the entire program development process typically is carried out by the computer and user while the user is sitting at a terminal. In a batch system, the user typically prepares the program and data at one station, submits the task to the computer at a second station, and then waits for the output to be produced at a third station. Some systems combine interactive and batch processing. Such systems generally have an interactive terminal for the user to enter a program and data; however, once the program and data are entered, the tasks of compiling and executing the program are treated as in batch computing (i.e., the user must wait until the system can perform the tasks and produce the desired output).

Single-User/Multiuser Systems

Some computing systems, particularly smaller systems, are **single-user systems** because they can communicate with only one user at a time. Other systems are classified as multiuser systems because they can engage in simultaneous communications with several users. **Multiuser systems** behave as though each person is the sole user of the system; however, in most systems the computer is engaged in **timesharing** (i.e., allocating a small slice of time to each of many users, usually on a rotating basis).

Most multiuser systems require that each user be assigned an account number and a password before being allowed to utilize the system. The purpose of the account number is to enable the computing system to keep track of who uses which resources and in what quantity. The password protects one user's files from others, so it must be kept secret. Both the account number and the password must be entered using a **sign on** (or **log on**) procedure when a user initiates communication with the computer. There are also **sign off** (or **log off**) procedures required when the user terminates communication. Details of these procedures are quite specific to individual computing systems.

1.4 OVERVIEW OF DATA PROCESSING

In the preceding sections we have used the terms *data* and *information* virtually synonymously. In everyday usage this is quite common; however, there is an important technical distinction between the two terms. Generally, **data** refers to the symbols that represent some event or idea. For example, the letters that make up a person's name, the digits that form a Social Security number, the serial number on an appliance, and the amount of a sale would be classified as data. **Information** is the meaning that is attached to data. A roster listing all of the students in a class in alphabetical sequence would constitute information for a teacher. A report showing a summary of each salesperson's sales for a day or week would be information for a sales manager. Information must be meaningful; that is, it must enable someone to accomplish a goal. The class roster is useful because it enables the teacher to maintain student records. A sales summary report is useful because it helps the sales manager to spot potential problems and reward salespeople who have produced well.

Information is derived from data by a variety of means. The task of processing data to derive information is as old as human history, because the need for information is inherent in most human activities. The following is a list of activities by which people process data:

- *Storage.* Data is stored for later use. People use file cabinets for storing data in printed form; computers use disks and tapes for the same purpose.

- *Retrieval.* Data must be retrieved for use when needed. Alphabetical storage systems are often used to facilitate this retrieval of data; computer-based systems usually use codes to provide for unique identification required for electronic retrieval of data.

- *Recording.* Data must be recorded on some medium. Historically, people used paper-and-pencil techniques; in many computer applications, data is captured electronically by means of bar code readers and similar devices.

- *Calculation.* Some information can be derived from data by performing calculations. Examples include the amount of sales tax due on a sale or a student's average grade.

- *Categorization.* Data is often placed in categories based on some criteria, for example, items that are exempt from sales tax and students who either pass or fail a course.

- *Summarization.* Information which attempts to summarize some aspect of all of the data is often needed; for example, the total sales for a day or the number of students who fail a course.

- *Sorting.* Data is rarely recorded in a useful order; the process of rearranging data is called **sorting**. Data is routinely sorted by account number or name in order to increase its usefulness.

- *Reporting.* Information is useless unless it is presented to people who need it. Creating layouts for the presentation of information in either printed or screen form is a very important part of a data processing system.

These activities can all be accomplished manually with the aid of machines such as calculators and typewriters or with the aid of a computer. In this text we focus on the development of computer programs that perform one or more of the data processing steps outlined above.

1.5 ORGANIZATION OF DATA

In a computing environment, data is organized into logical units of increasing size to facilitate the data processing task. From the smallest to the largest, the units are as follows:

- **Character**: the smallest unit of data. Characters may be either numeric (0, 1, 2, . . . , 9) or alphabetic (A, . . . , Z; a, . . . , z). Other characters such as the period, comma, or apostrophe may also be used when appropriate.
- **Data item (data field)**: a group of related characters. A person's name, an account number, and the amount of a sale are examples of data fields.
- **Record**: a group of related fields or items. Usually a record relates to a single person, product, transaction, or event. For example, a record related to a person might contain the person's name, Social Security number, and date of birth.
- **File**: a group of related records. Usually all of the records in a file have the same layout—that is, each record has the same sequence of fields. For example, a file might contain records regarding all of the sales for a given period of time or all of the students enrolled in a class or school.
- **Data base**: a group of related files. Data bases are typically maintained by special data base software that manages data related to multiple files.

The relationships among basic units of data are summarized in Figure 1.12. In this example, the data base is made up of two files: Employee File and Department File. The records in Employee File are composed of five fields:

Social Security Number	(9 numeric characters)
Name	(20 alphabetic characters)
Sex	(1 alphabetic character)
Marital Status	(1 alphabetic character)
Date of Birth	(6 numeric characters)

The records in Department File are made up of three fields:

Department Number	(3 numeric characters)
Social Security Number	(9 numeric characters)
Rate of Pay	(4 numeric characters)

Figure 1.12 Example of relationships among characters, fields, records, files, and data bases

Personnel Data Base

Employee File

Social Security Number	Name	Sex	Marital Status	Date of Birth
111111111	JONES JOHN	M	S	050867
222222222	SMITH MARY	F	M	030752
333333333	DOE HARRY	M	M	020170
444444444	BLACK JOHN	M	S	070371

Department File

Department Number	Social Security Number	Rate of Pay
001	111111111	0567
001	555555555	0789
002	222222222	0978
002	888888888	0734
002	333333333	1045
003	444444444	0823

Note that data files usually do not contain editing symbols such as hyphens in a Social Security number, slashes in a date, or a decimal point in dollars and cents. These symbols are added by a processing program to help clarify the meaning of the data.

COBOL is often characterized as a file-oriented language. That is, everything that the program does to data starts with the file in which the data is contained. The program first specifies the file and its characteristics, such as the device associated with the file, the name of the file known to the operating system, and the physical organization of the file. Next, the program describes the record(s) associated with each file by listing the fields in order. Each field is defined by describing its length (the number of characters which make up the field) and its type (numeric, alphabetic, or other).

Because COBOL was developed prior to the use of data bases, the language makes no use of the data base level of organization of data. Most companies that market data base systems also provide an enhancement to the COBOL compiler, enabling programs written in COBOL to access data maintained in the data base. Unfortunately, there is no standard for these enhanced language features.

Where does data come from? We have seen that one of the basic steps in computer data processing is data recording—collecting data and storing it in a form suitable for processing by the computer. Data comes from documents on which the data is written, or it may be captured mechanically or electronically. In any case, we usually assume that the data is in place, and we proceed to write programs which process that data in a variety of ways. As a student, you will be working on programming projects that are essentially hypothetical in nature (although they are based on situations that occur in the real world.) Thus, the data that your programs will process will also have to be created by a somewhat artificial means. Generally, you should attempt to create a sample data file that will contain sufficient data to test all of the aspects and special features of a program in order to verify that a program is functioning correctly. Some instructors will provide sample data for some or all of the programming assignments. Other instructors prefer students to create their own sample data to test their own programs. In this case you will receive instruction in the use of an editor which can be used to create such files. (In an actual program development situation, sample data to be used in testing programs may be the responsibility of the programmer, or the responsibility may be given to a person or group specializing in program testing and verification.)

1.6   REPORTS

Before beginning the programming task, the programmer must know the layout of the files to be processed and the specifications for the information to be produced by the program. The programmer should know which data is to be included in a report and any other information the report must contain. Creating attractive and useful reports is a fundamental part of the programmer's job.

Most reports have at least four elements in common:

- **Page heading**. The page heading, printed at the top of each page of the report, should identify the company or organization and the purpose of the report. The date the report was produced and page numbers are also very useful.
- **Column headings**. Below the page heading there are column headings showing the meaning of the data items listed in the main body of the report. The column headings are printed on each page of the report.
- **Body**. Following the column headings is the body of the report, which contains the detailed data from one or more files. Often one line in the body of the report corresponds to one record in a data file.
- **Summary line(s)**. At the end of the report there may be summary information regarding all of the data in the report. Totals, averages, and counts are often included here.

Consider the personnel file illustrated in Figure 1.12. Suppose that the management of XYZ Company, Inc. (the fictious company that we will use for purposes of illustration) wishes to have a listing of the data contained in the file. A report such as the one shown in Figure 1.13 is the desired end product.

To produce such a report, the programmer should lay out on a worksheet called a **printer spacing chart** the information that the report is to contain (Fig. 1.14). The exact placement and content of headings are included. Fields that will be filled with data are sketched in with 9's (for numeric fields) or X's (for alphabetic or other types of fields). Comments can be added as needed to clarify the meaning of the layout. Often several variations of a report will be designed before one is finally chosen for implementation.

The programs that you will be writing initially will not contain all of the elements of a complete report listed above. We will start with programs that have no page heading, column headings, or summary lines. You will gradually add elements to your reports as you become more familiar with

Figure 1.13 Example of a report

```
Page Heading ——|  7/12/90                    XYZ COMPANY, INC.
                                             PERSONNEL LIST                    PAGE     1

Column Heading ——| SOCIAL SECURITY                        SEX   MARITAL    DATE OF
                       NUMBER          NAME               CODE   STATUS     BIRTH

                   |   111 11 1111    JONES JOHN           M       S       05/08/67

   Body ——        |   222 22 2222    SMITH MARY           F       M       03/07/52

                   |   333 33 3333    DOE HARRY            M       M       02/01/70

                   |   444 44 4444    BLACK JOHN           M       S       07/03/71


Page Heading ——|  7/12/90                    XYZ COMPANY, INC.
                                             PERSONNEL LIST                    PAGE     2

Column Heading ——| SOCIAL SECURITY                        SEX   MARITAL    DATE OF
                       NUMBER          NAME               CODE   STATUS     BIRTH

                   |   555 55 5555    WHITE JOAN           F       S       12/03/68

   Body ——        |   666 66 6666    SMITH SUE            F       M       11/23/72

                   |   888 88 8888    GREY SUSAN           F       S       09/09/67

Summary Line ——|                     TOTAL NUMBER OF PERSONNEL      7
```

Figure 1.14 Example of a printer spacing chart showing the layout for a report

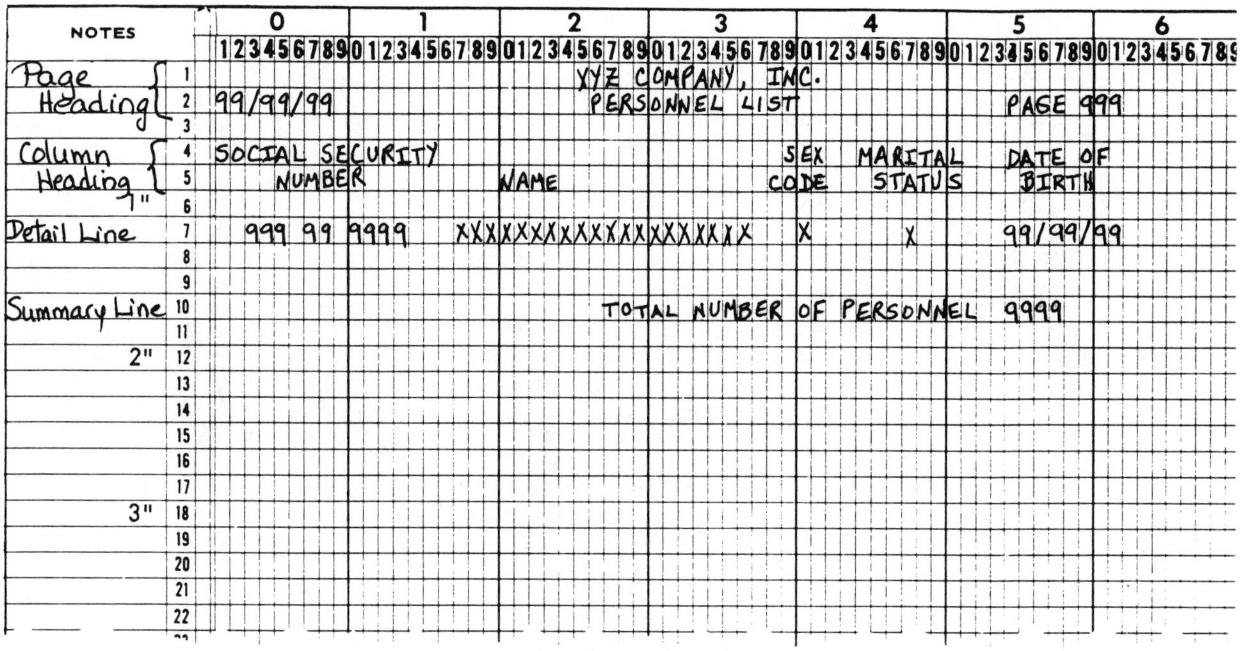

Figure 1.15 A summary of program flowchart symbols

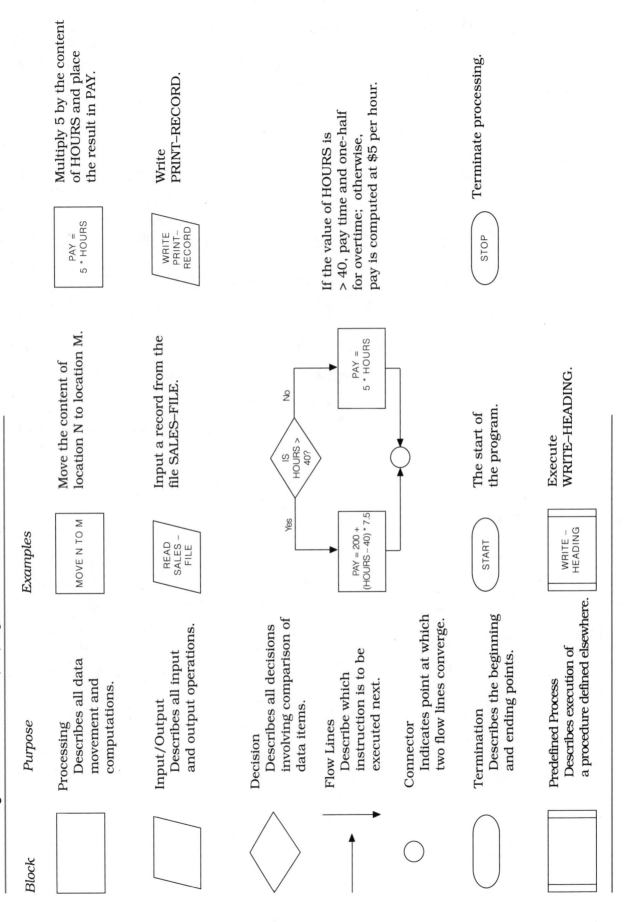

Block	Purpose	Examples	
	Processing Describes all data movement and computations.	MOVE N TO M	Move the content of location N to location M.
		PAY = 5 * HOURS	Multiply 5 by the content of HOURS and place the result in PAY.
	Input/Output Describes all input and output operations.	READ SALES–FILE	Input a record from the file SALES–FILE.
		WRITE PRINT–RECORD	Write PRINT–RECORD.
	Decision Describes all decisions involving comparison of data items.		If the value of HOURS is > 40, pay time and one-half for overtime; otherwise, pay is computed at $5 per hour.
	Flow Lines Describe which instruction is to be executed next.		
	Connector Indicates point at which two flow lines converge.		
	Termination Describes the beginning and ending points.	START	The start of the program.
		STOP	Terminate processing.
	Predefined Process Describes execution of a procedure defined elsewhere.	WRITE–HEADING	Execute WRITE–HEADING.

Decision example flowchart:

IS HOURS > 40?

Yes → PAY = 200 + (HOURS – 40) * 7.5

No → PAY = 5 * HOURS

COBOL so that eventually you will be writing programs that produce professional quality reports. Regardless of the size or complexity of a report, however, it is a good idea to start with a printer spacing chart that you can use as a guide in coding the program.

1.7   PROGRAM FLOWCHARTS

A program is a sequence of instructions describing actions to be taken by the computer. A **program flowchart** is a visual representation of these steps. Each type of instruction is represented in a flowchart by a different type of symbol called a **block**. Inside each block, the programmer writes a description of the instruction to be executed. Figure 1.15 illustrates types of instructions and their corresponding blocks.

An oval-shaped symbol is used to describe the beginning and ending points in a flowchart. The instruction START typically denotes the beginning, and the instruction STOP or END denotes the ending point.

Flowlines such as $\rightarrow$ describe the direction of flow—that is, which instruction is to be executed next. All blocks in a flowchart are connected by flowlines.

A parallelogram-shaped symbol is used to describe input and output operations. The instruction READ is used to denote an input operation; the instruction WRITE is used for output. The name of the file may also be used in the block to define the file to which the instruction pertains. For example, a flowchart for a program to read a record from the file INPUT-FILE would be:

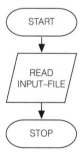

A rectangle is used to describe processing, such as movement of an input record, as in the flowchart which follows:

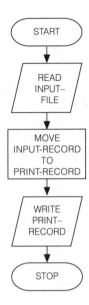

A program flowchart to compute pay at $5 per hour for an employee is as follows:

In this flowchart, note the use of the asterisk to denote multiplication in the computation of PAY. The following symbols are usually used to denote arithmetic operations:

+   addition

−   subtraction

*   multiplication

/   division

A diamond-shaped symbol is used to denote decisions. Decisions involve relations such as greater than (>), less than (<), and equal to (=) between data items. If the relation is true, the "yes" path from the decision block is followed to determine the next instruction. If the relation is false, the "no" path from the decision block is followed. For example, suppose we wish to pay time and a half for overtime hours worked by an employee. If the value of HOURS is less than 40, we will pay the employee at $5 per hour. If the value of HOURS is more than 40, we will pay the employee $5 times 40, or $200, plus $7.50 per hour for all hours in excess of 40. This program could be illustrated by the following flowchart:

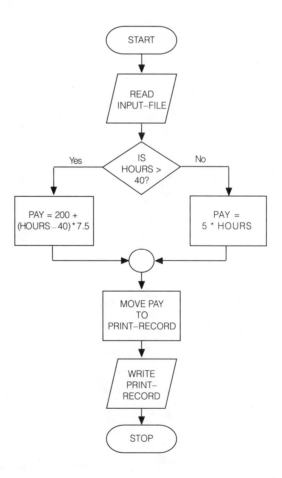

In this flowchart, note the use of the circle (called a connector block). This symbol is used when two or more flow lines converge.

In some flowcharts it is useful to draw separate flowcharts for some complicated procedures and to indicate that the procedures are to be executed using the predefined process block:

For example, let's construct a separate procedure called COMPUTE-PAY to take care of the details of determining the appropriate value of PAY based on HOURS. The following procedure is incorporated in a predefined process block.

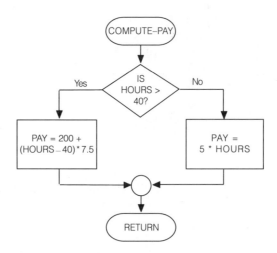

Note that the termination block is used with the procedure name to note the entry to the procedure and the statement RETURN to note the end of the procedure.

Using this procedure, the program to compute an employee's pay can now be written as:

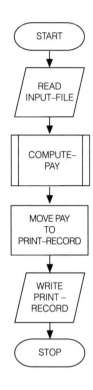

Program flowcharts are a useful means of describing a program in a rough form prior to writing the program in a programming language. They are also used as a form of documentation to enable a person unfamiliar with a program to understand how it works.

1.8 PSEUDOCODE

Pseudocode (from *false* code) is an alternative program preparation technique that has become a very important tool for COBOL programmers. Pseudocode is an informal language that omits many of the details required in a real programming language but expresses the procedure to be implemented in a useful preliminary form. The syntax of pseudocode is nonstandard; each programmer uses a version with which he or she is comfortable. For example, the following pseudocode expresses a procedure for computing an employee's pay at $5 per hour:

Pay employee

```
Read input file
Pay = 5 * hours
Move pay to print record
Write print record
Stop
```

A different programmer might express the procedure in a different form. The important point when using pseudocode, however, is that the overall logical flow be correct, not the exact syntax or even the level of detail included.

Decisions are expressed in pseudocode using an If/Else structure that has the general form:

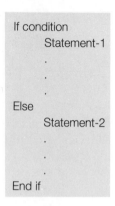

```
If condition
        Statement-1
            .
            .
            .
Else
        Statement-2
            .
            .
            .
End if
```

For example, suppose pay is computed at $5 an hour for hours less than or equal to 40 but $7.50 an hour for hours over 40. This procedure can be expressed in pseudocode as

```
If hours > 40
        Pay = 200 + (hours − 40) * 7.5
Else
        Pay = 5 * hours
End If
```

The procedure *Pay employee* would now appear as:

```
Pay employee
        Read input file
        If hours > 40
                Pay = 200 + (hours − 40) * 7.5
        Else
                Pay = 5 * hours
        End If
        Move pay to print record
        Write print record
        Stop
```

Note the use of indentation to delineate two statements visually, one of which will be carried out if the condition hours > 40 is true and the other of which will be carried out if hours > 40 is false. Note also, the use of the words "End If" to specify the end of the statements controlled by the If statement.

Execution of another procedure is signified in pseudocode using the Do statement with the general form

```
Do procedure name
```

This statement signifies that the named procedure should be carried out, and at its end, control should return to the statement following the Do statement. For example, the payroll procedure described above could be specified as two procedures:

Pay employee
>Read input file
>Do Compute pay
>Move pay to print record
>Write print record
>Stop

Compute pay
>If hours > 40
>>Pay = 200 + (hours − 40) * 7.5
>
>Else
>>Pay = 5 * hours
>
>End If

Within the general outlines given above, you are at liberty to express program specifications in pseudocode using any syntax you desire. Often pseudocode specifications undergo many transformations between the first rudimentary document and the final design for a program. Remember to include only essential elements of a procedure in pseudocode; leave as many details of the final program as possible to the program itself. The purpose of pseudocode, like flowcharting, is to enable the programmer to express the overall problem and its proposed solution in a form more expressive and convenient to use than actual programs.

1.9 PROGRAM DEVELOPMENT

The task of developing a program involves much more than simply writing COBOL code, although this is a necessary step. In practice, more time is usually spent analyzing the problem at hand before writing the program, and testing the actual program usually requires more time than coding it. The task of developing a program may be viewed as a seven-step process:

1. *Define the problem.* What is the purpose of the program? What data is to be processed? What output is desired? What input is available? How will the program accomplish the desired goals?

2. *Design test data.* Only if the program is executed with an adequate amount of test data and the output produced is compared to the output desired can the programmer be reasonably sure that a program is correct. At this step, test data that will thoroughly test all aspects of the program should be designed.

3. *Design the program.* Decide on names for all files, records, and fields that will be needed in the program. Draw a flowchart or write the pseudocode for the procedure required.

4. *Code the program.* Write the COBOL equivalent of the program designed in step 3 above.

5. *Compile the program.* Submit the program for compilation and correct any syntax errors.

6. *Test the program.* Run the program with the test data from step 2 above. If the output produced is not correct, revise the program and return to step 5. This process is referred to as **debugging** the program.

7. *Document the program.* A properly written COBOL program has a great deal of built-in documentation; however, other forms of documentation such as structure diagrams, record layouts, printer

spacing charts, and user manuals also may be needed. Documentation is actually an ongoing process, with portions of the final package produced at earlier stages in the program development process.

1.10   WHY STRUCTURED PROGRAMMING?

When computers were first put into use, the users tried to make them as efficient as possible to justify costs and prove the value of the systems. From the beginning, however, people who bought computers had to deal with not only the cost of using the hardware to solve a problem (hardware costs), but also the cost of preparing programs for the machine to execute (program development costs). At first, hardware costs were much greater than program development costs. The emphasis on machine efficiency often forced programmers to use complicated logic and programming tricks that resulted in very efficient programs, but the programs were difficult to debug and difficult for any other programmer to modify. **Documentation** (detailed explanations supplied with a program) provided a partial solution to the problem, but the documentation was often incomplete and sometimes incorrect.

In recent years hardware costs have become much lower than program development costs, and there has been a corresponding shift in programming philosophy. Programmer productivity has become a higher priority than the machine efficiency of the programs written. Programmers are now encouraged to develop straightforward solutions to problems and to concentrate on building programs in such a way that debugging, additional coding, and future enhancements will require minimal effort.

Structured programming is a way of writing programs which, if followed carefully, will result in programs that are easy to read, understand, debug, and modify. A structured program can be understood clearly not only by its author but also by anyone else who needs to understand or change it. Structured programming decreases programming costs, particularly when applied to large programming projects. This cost decrease is apparent not only in the initial programming stages but also in the later stages when the programs must be modified to suit new requirements. In addition, there tend to be fewer detected and undetected logical errors in structured programs, so testing, debugging, and maintenance times are reduced. Structured programming, in short, has gained wide acceptance as a standard programming technique.

1.11   WHAT IS STRUCTURED PROGRAMMING?

Structured programming, a general approach to the programming task, has gained a considerable following during the past decade. The concept of structured programming can be traced to the work of Bohm and Jacopini in the 1960s. The early emphasis in the movement was on program modularity. Edsger Dijkstra, a pioneer in the field, wrote a letter, "Go To Statement Considered Harmful," which was published in a 1968 issue of *Communications of the ACM.* In this letter, Professor Dijkstra observed that program complexity is largely a function of the use of GO TO statements. He recommended that the GO TO statement be eliminated from programming languages in the interest of forcing programmers to develop simpler program designs. There is, however, much more to structured programming than modularity and the elimination of GO TO statements. Concepts of program control structures, programmer productivity aids, program design techniques, and techniques for enhancing maintainability have been incorporated under the general framework of "structured programming."

One of the first large-scale implementations of this philosophy was made by IBM in developing a data processing system for the *New York Times.* The project was widely reported as a success because of the unusually low error rate in the programs making up the system. Gradually, structured programming concepts and practices have emerged from theory and experimental use to become standards for the industry.

Although some of the problems associated with designing and developing software have yet to be solved, structured programming offers significant advantages over previous practices. Programming systems designed and written according to these methods tend to be not only error-free but also easy to maintain by subsequent programmers, who must make minor modifications to accommodate changes in the systems.

A fundamental proposition of structured programming is that program design is the single most important aspect of the program development process. A well-designed program will be easy to code, debug, and maintain. A poor program design cannot result in a "good" program, no matter how much effort goes into subsequent program development steps.

In programming, "structure" refers to the way in which statements are related to one another. Only three program structures are needed for program development:

- Sequence
- If/Then/Else (Decision)
- Iteration (Loop)

In fact, in structured programming, only these three structures are permitted.

In a **sequence structure**, each statement is executed in succession. A sequence structure is shown as:

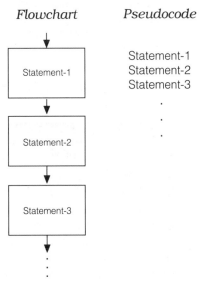

Flowchart   *Pseudocode*

Statement-1
Statement-2
Statement-3

After statement 1 is executed, statement 2 is executed, followed by the execution of statement 3, and so on.

The If/Then/Else structure, also called a **decision structure**, describes a test condition and two possible resulting paths. Only one path is selected and executed, depending on the evaluation of the given test condition. The decision structure is shown as:

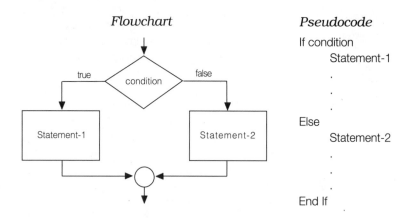

The **iteration structure** causes the repetition of one or more statements until a given condition is met. The iteration structure is shown as:

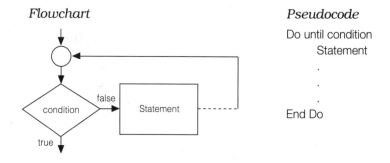

Structured programming has come to mean much more than simply programs that use only the three basic structures. In a COBOL environment, concepts of top-down program design and standards for program coding are usually considered to be part of the overall concept referred to as "structured programming."

1.12   SELF-TEST EXERCISES

1. Matching

1. program	a. computer and user engage in a dialogue
2. input unit	b. communicates directly with a computing system
3. output unit	c. program which enables user to build and modify files
4. memory unit	d. procedure used to identify a user to a computing system
5. control unit	e. device used to communicate with computing system in an interactive mode
6. arithmetic/logic unit	f. carries out arithmetic and logical instructions
7. CPU	g. program written in machine language
8. microcomputer	h. central processing unit
9. CRT	i. general term for computing machinery
10. terminal	j. collection of records
11. floppy disk	k. program written in a high-level language
12. line printer	l. computer based on an electronic chip
13. hardware	m. carries out instructions which transfer data from outside into memory
14. software	n. video terminal
15. high-level language	o. data is accumulated over a period of time before processing
16. source program	p. high-speed printed output device
17. object program	q. stores currently active programs and data
18. compiler	r. computer engages in communication with more than one user
19. on line	s. carries out instructions which transfer data from memory to the outside world
20. batch computing	t. symbolic language such as COBOL
21. interactive computing	u. set of instructions for a computer
22. file	v. executes each program instruction
23. editor	w. general term for computer programs
24. timesharing	x. small disk often used in academic computing systems
25. sign on	y. program which translates a source program into an object program
26. mass storage	z. magnetic tape and disk

2. Matching

1.

2.

3.

4.

5.

6.

a. termination
b. decision
c. input/output
d. connector
e. processing
f. predefined process

3. List three structures that are sufficient for any program and that are the only structures used in a structured program. Draw a program flowchart for each one.

4. List the seven steps of program development.

5. List eight activities involved in processing data.

6. Give an example to illustrate the relationships among characters, fields, records, files, and data bases.

7. What purpose is served by a printer spacing chart?

REFERENCES

Bohm, C., and G. Jacopini. "Flow Diagrams, Turing Machines and Languages with Only Two Formation Rules." *Communications of the ACM* 9, no. 5 (May 1966): 366–71.

Dijkstra, Edsger. "Go To Statement Considered Harmful." *Communications of the ACM* 11, no. 2 (Feb. 1968): 147–48.

Stevens, W. P., G. J. Meyers, and L. L. Constantine. "Structured Design." *IBM Systems Journal* 13, no. 2 (1974).

Yourdon, E., and L. L. Constantine. *Structured Design.* Englewood Cliffs, N.J.: Prentice-Hall, 1979.

2. INTRODUCTION TO COBOL

2.1 ORIGIN AND DEVELOPMENT OF COBOL

The origin of COBOL lies in the development in the late 1950s of programming systems that were better suited to commercial applications than the algebraic languages then in use. Much of the early work was carried out by Dr. Grace Hopper, a commander in the navy. Beginning in 1959, a series of meetings among concerned individuals of the Department of Defense, academic institutions, and computer manufacturers resulted in the organization of CODASYL (COnference on DAta SYstems Languages). The avowed purpose of this group was the development and standardization of a commercial programming language.

CODASYL has developed several versions of the COBOL language. The earliest version was known as COBOL-60. This was superseded by COBOL-68 and then by COBOL-74, in 1968 and 1974, respectively. Because the American National Standards Institute formally adopts standards for the language, these versions of the language are often referred to as ANSI-68 and ANSI-74, respectively. A new standard, ANSI-85, has recently been adopted. At this time, COBOL-74 remains the most widely used version of the language; however, COBOL-85 compilers have become commercially available from several sources, and this version of the language is gaining some converts.

The original intent in the development of COBOL was to design a language that was

- naturally suited to commercial data processing,
- self-documenting (anyone should be able to read and understand a COBOL program), and
- extensible (the language should be designed so that new features could be added to later versions without fundamental change in the structure or syntax of the language).

The first objective was attained by organizing every COBOL program around the data files which are to be processed. The files, records within files, and fields within records are described very explicitly. The second objective was met by allowing very long data-names to describe data items, by allowing operations (such as ADD and SUBTRACT) to be specified verbally rather than in symbolic form, and by insisting on a paragraph/sentence structure for each program segment. The third objective was met by the original designers because COBOL has been redesigned and extended to include a multitude of features never envisaged by the original group, yet the fundamental organization and structure of COBOL programs remain the same now as in the beginning.

2.2 ORGANIZATION OF A COBOL PROGRAM

All COBOL programs are organized into major subordinate parts called DIVISIONs. Four DIVISIONs are required in a COBOL program:

- IDENTIFICATION DIVISION
- ENVIRONMENT DIVISION
- DATA DIVISION
- PROCEDURE DIVISION

Each division begins with a division header consisting of the division name, the word DIVISION, and a period.

Some divisions are divided into SECTIONs. A section is preceded by a section header which consists of the section name, the word SECTION, and a period. For example, the ENVIRONMENT DIVISION is divided into two sections:

- CONFIGURATION SECTION
- INPUT-OUTPUT SECTION

The DATA DIVISION is divided into two sections:

- FILE SECTION
- WORKING-STORAGE SECTION

Another basic unit of subdivision is the **paragraph**. A paragraph is preceded by a paragraph header which consists of a paragraph-name followed by a period. In the IDENTIFICATION and ENVIRONMENT DIVISIONs, the paragraph headers are specified by the COBOL syntax; in the PROCEDURE DIVISION, the programmer names the paragraphs.

The next lower unit of subdivision is the **sentence**. A sentence consists of a series of COBOL clauses followed by a period. A clause may be as simple as one entry specifying a name for the program or programmer in the IDENTIFICATION DIVISION or as complex as a series of commands describing how data is to be processed in the PROCEDURE DIVISION.

COBOL programs are made up of two basic types of entries: **COBOL reserved words**, which have a specific meaning in the language, and **programmer-defined entries**, which are made up by the programmer. A list of COBOL reserved words is printed inside the front and back covers of this text. Reserved words are included for DIVISION, SECTION and paragraph headings, commands, and various other entries. Reserved words may not be used for programmer-defined entries. The programmer defines names for files, records, data items, the program name, and various other entries.

Programmer-defined entries are subject to the following additional restrictions:

- The maximum length is 30 characters.
- Uppercase alphabetic characters (A, B, . . . , Z), numeric characters (0, 1, . . . , 9), and the hyphen (-) can be used.[1] No other characters or spaces can be used.
- The hyphen (-) cannot be the first or last character.
- At least one character must be alphabetic.[2]

---

[1] In COBOL-85, lowercase alphabetic characters (a, b, . . . , z) can also be used.

[2] Exceptions to this rule include paragraph-names, section names, and level numbers, which may be composed entirely of numeric characters.

These rules are the same for all types of programmer-defined words, whether they are the names of files, records, or data items. For example, the following are some valid programmer-defined entries:

DATA-FILE ⎫
DATA-RECORD ⎭   It is a good idea to use the word FILE or RECORD in names of files and records.

CUSTOMER-NAME-DR ⎫
BALANCE-DR ⎭   The suffix DR might indicate that these items are a part of DATA-RECORD.

2000-WRITE-HEADING ⎫
9000-READ-DATA-FILE ⎭   Paragraph-names in the DATA DIVISION are often preceded by a number which indicates the sequence of the paragraphs in the program.

The following are some invalid programmer-defined identifiers:

-A	Begins with a hyphen
A-NUMBER-	Ends with a hyphen
A.B	Contains a period
A-VERY-LONG-PROGRAMMER-WRITTEN-WORD	Contains too many characters
ADD	A COBOL reserved word

Technically, a programmer can assign any name to a program, a file, a record, or a data item. Provided the name is used consistently in the program, the program will function correctly. However, using arbitrary names for things should be avoided because this practice tends to make a program difficult to read. Standards for naming programs, files, records, and fields should be adopted and followed carefully. Some of the standards that we recommend are illustrated in the following program example.

Program Example

Let us write a COBOL program to print a copy of the content of a file. The program will process two files, which we shall call DATA-FILE and REPORT-FILE. These names are arbitrary; a programmer can use any suitable names for files. The records associated with each file will also require names; we will call the records DATA-RECORD and REPORT-RECORD; these names are also programmer defined. The program will read a record from DATA-FILE and write it on REPORT-FILE, repeating the process until all records from DATA-FILE have been processed.

The IDENTIFICATION DIVISION for this program is shown in Figure 2.1. The purpose of the IDENTIFICATION DIVISION is to identify the program, its author, and other related information.

Figure 2.1   IDENTIFICATION DIVISION for file list program

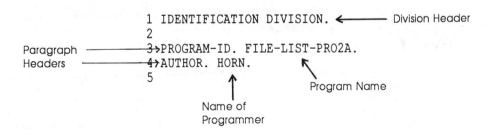

Line 1 contains the division header. Line 2 is a blank line inserted to enhance readability of the program. Most compilers allow the programmer to insert blank lines in programs for this purpose; such lines have no effect on the function of the program.[3] Line 3 contains a name (FILE-LIST-PRO2A) that is assigned to the program; this name is determined by the programmer and will change from program to program.[4] The program name is preceded by a paragraph header PROGRAM-ID. This entry will be present in every COBOL program. Line 4 contains an entry that is used to specify the name of the programmer. The programmer's name is preceded by the paragraph header AUTHOR.

The ENVIRONMENT DIVISION for the file list program is shown in Figure 2.2. The purpose of the ENVIRONMENT DIVISION is to identify the computing "environment" in which the program will function.

Figure 2.2   ENVIRONMENT DIVISION for file list program

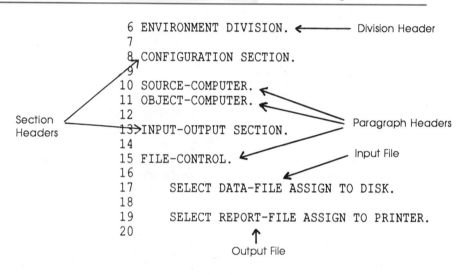

Line 6 contains the division header. Line 8 contains the section header for the CONFIGURATION SECTION. The CONFIGURATION SECTION contains two paragraphs: SOURCE-COMPUTER (line 10) and OBJECT-COMPUTER (line 11). The SOURCE-COMPUTER entry specifies the computer that will be used to compile the program; the OBJECT-COMPUTER entry specifies the computer that will be used to execute the program. In most instances, the entries in these paragraphs will be the same. The exact entry required in these paragraphs varies from computing system to computing system, and often the entry can be omitted altogether. You will need to determine what entry is required in your system for these paragraphs. In the programs of this text, these paragraphs have been included, but the computer name entries have been omitted.

Line 13 contains the section header for the INPUT-OUTPUT SECTION. This section is used to describe the data files that the program is going to process. It contains one paragraph: FILE-CONTROL. Line 15 contains the

---

[3] In compilers which do not allow this practice, the programmer may place an asterisk (*) in position 7 of an otherwise blank line. This addition turns the line into a comment which the compiler includes in the program listing but otherwise ignores.

[4] In our examples, the last sequence of characters (PRO2A in this case) is the name of the file containing the program on the available disk. The first part of the name describes the function of the program.

paragraph header FILE-CONTROL. One sentence, beginning with the reserved word SELECT, is required for each file the program is going to process. Line 17 contains the SELECT entry for DATA-FILE; line 19 contains the SELECT entry for REPORT-FILE. The words ASSIGN TO are COBOL reserved words. The words DISK and PRINTER signify the devices in the system that will be associated with the file. These entries will change depending on the requirements of individual computing systems.

The DATA DIVISION for the file list program is shown in Figure 2.3. The purpose of the DATA DIVISION is to describe the data records and other data items the program will require.

Figure 2.3   DATA DIVISION for file list program

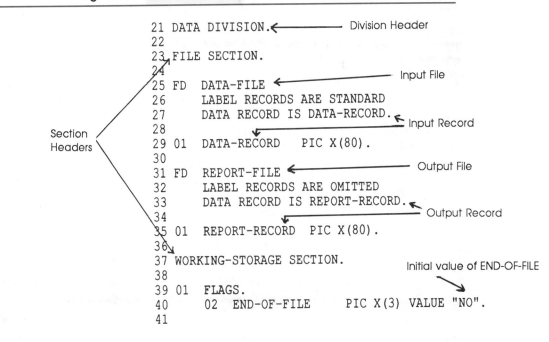

Line 21 contains the division header. The DATA DIVISION is divided into two sections: FILE SECTION (line 23) and WORKING-STORAGE SECTION (line 37). The FILE SECTION is used to describe the files the program will process and their associated data records. Each file must be described by an FD entry (an abbreviation for *File Description*) which consists of the characters FD followed by the name of the file and various clauses that describe the file. The FD entry constitutes a sentence that begins with FD and ends with a period. The FD entry for DATA-FILE begins with line 25 and ends on line 27. Most COBOL sentences may be coded on one or more lines as desired. Often each clause of a sentence is placed on a separate line to improve readability. Line 26 contains the LABEL RECORDS clause for the DATA-FILE. LABEL RECORDS ARE STANDARD will be the most common entry here, although for files assigned to certain devices (e.g., printers), the entry LABEL RECORDS ARE OMITTED may be required. Line 27 contains the DATA RECORD clause, which is used to specify the name of the data record (DATA-RECORD) associated with DATA-FILE.

Line 29 contains a description of DATA-RECORD. This entry consists of a level number (01) followed by the data-name (DATA-RECORD), the reserved word PIC (which is an abbreviation for PICTURE), and the picture codes X(80). The code X signifies that the record contains alphanumeric data (any combination of alphabetic and numeric characters); the number 80 signifies the length of the record. The length 80 is quite common for a record, but each file in a system will have a record length determined by the nature of the data contained in the file and/or the requirements of the operating system.

Lines 31 through 33 contain the FD entry for REPORT-FILE. Note the similarity of this entry to the FD entry for DATA-FILE. Line 35 contains the record description for REPORT-RECORD, which closely resembles the description for INPUT-RECORD. Remember that the purpose of this program is to create a listing of DATA-FILE, so this resemblance would be expected.

Line 37 contains the section header WORKING-STORAGE SECTION. The purpose of the WORKING-STORAGE SECTION is to define data items that are required in the program but which are not a part of the records the program will process. In this case the program will need a data item to signify that all of the data from DATA-FILE has been read. We will call the item END-OF-FILE, define it to contain three alphanumeric characters (PIC X(3)), and specify that its initial value will be "NO" because initially the end of the file has not been reached. This task is carried out in lines 39 and 40. Line 39 contains an 01 entry setting up a data-name FLAGS. This is a **group item** that encompasses all of the subsidiary data items that immediately follow it. In this case, only one subordinate entry is required (02 END-OF-FILE...), but in general other entries of the same type could also be included here. Line 40 contains the entry defining the data item END-OF-FILE. Note that the 02 entry is indented below the 01 entry of which it is a part. The VALUE clause is used to establish the initial value of the data item (VALUE "NO"). During the execution of the program, the value of the item will be changed to "YES" when the end of DATA-FILE is encountered.

END-OF-FILE is classed as an **elementary item** because it is not further subdivided. Elementary items are always declared with a PIC clause. By contrast FLAGS is a group item. It can be subdivided into several elementary items. Group items are never declared with a PIC clause.

The purpose of the PROCEDURE DIVISION is to describe the processing steps required to accomplish the objective of the program. In developing a program it is usually beneficial to have a preliminary description of the tasks that the PROCEDURE DIVISION must accomplish before attempting to code this portion of the program. Either a program flowchart or pseudocode can be used for this preliminary plan. The plan for this program is shown in Figure 2.4. You will probably prepare only one of these types of plans; both are shown here for reference. The actual PROCEDURE DIVISION for this program is shown in Figure 2.5.

Line 42 contains the division header. The PROCEDURE DIVISION is divided into two paragraphs: 1000-MAIN-CONTROL (lines 44–54) and 2000-PROCESS-DATA (lines 56–61). In the PROCEDURE DIVISION, **paragraph-names** are defined by the programmer. It is customary to use names that begin with a sequence of numeric digits (1000 and 2000 in this case) to signify the actual sequence of the paragraphs in the program. In a short program this may not appear to be necessary, but in a long program this practice aids the reader in locating a paragraph. The rest of the paragraph-name chosen should be as descriptive as possible of the task that will be accomplished in that paragraph.

Lines 46 and 47 contain the OPEN statement for the files to be processed by the program. The OPEN statement requires that the OPEN mode

Figure 2.4   Plan for file list program

Pseudocode

> *Main control*
>> Open files
>> Read data file
>> Do Process data until
>>> End of file
>> Close files
>> Stop
>
> *Process data*
>> Move data record to report record
>> Write report record
>> Read data file

Program Flowchart

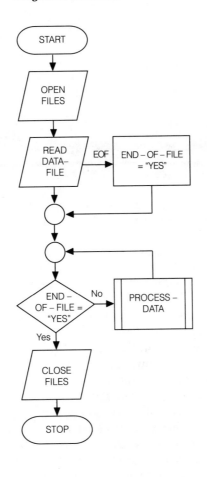
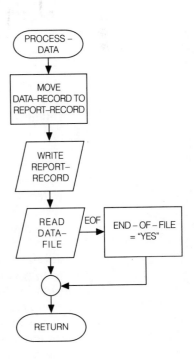

Figure 2.5   PROCEDURE DIVISION for file list program

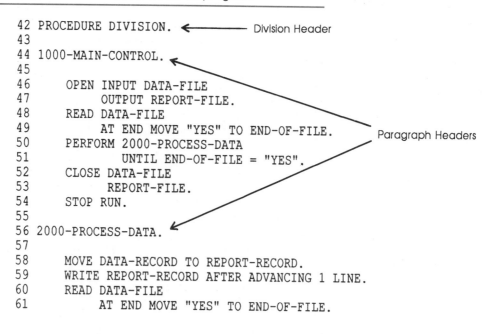

```
42 PROCEDURE DIVISION. ◄───────── Division Header
43
44 1000-MAIN-CONTROL.
45
46    OPEN INPUT DATA-FILE
47        OUTPUT REPORT-FILE.
48    READ DATA-FILE
49        AT END MOVE "YES" TO END-OF-FILE.
50    PERFORM 2000-PROCESS-DATA
51            UNTIL END-OF-FILE = "YES".
52    CLOSE DATA-FILE
53        REPORT-FILE.
54    STOP RUN.
55
56 2000-PROCESS-DATA.
57
58    MOVE DATA-RECORD TO REPORT-RECORD.
59    WRITE REPORT-RECORD AFTER ADVANCING 1 LINE.
60    READ DATA-FILE
61        AT END MOVE "YES" TO END-OF-FILE.
```

Paragraph Headers

for a file be specified (INPUT or OUTPUT). Thus, DATA-FILE is opened in INPUT mode, and REPORT-FILE is opened in OUTPUT mode. Note that the OPEN statement is one sentence but is contained on two lines for readability. A file must first be opened before it can be processed by a COBOL program.

Lines 48 and 49 contain a READ statement for DATA-FILE. The READ statement addresses the file by name and includes the AT END clause, which specifies the action to be taken when no more data is contained in the file. In this case we specify MOVE "YES" TO END-OF-FILE when this occurs. This means that the content of data item END-OF-FILE will be replaced by "YES" (remember that we initially defined this item to contain "NO").

Lines 50 and 51 contain the PERFORM statement that causes the program to enter a loop and continue its work until all the data from DATA-FILE has been processed. The paragraph 2000-PROCESS-DATA will be executed repeatedly until the condition END-OF-FILE = "YES" becomes true. Initially, this condition is false (if there is any data in DATA-FILE).

Lines 52 and 53 contain the CLOSE statement for the files processed by the program. This statement consists of the reserved word CLOSE followed by a list of the files to be closed. These are placed on separate lines to improve readability. Line 54 contains the STOP RUN statement, which terminates the execution of the program.

Line 56 contains the paragraph header for 2000-PROCESS-DATA. This paragraph handles the details of processing the record from DATA-FILE that has just been read by the program and reading the next record from DATA-FILE. The processing steps involve moving data from DATA-RECORD to REPORT-RECORD (line 58) and writing that record to the file (line 59). Note that the WRITE statement addresses the record associated with a file, not the file itself. Lines 60 and 61 contain the READ statement to cause the

Program 2a

```
 1 IDENTIFICATION DIVISION.
 2
 3 PROGRAM-ID. FILE-LIST-PRO2A.
 4 AUTHOR. HORN.
 5
 6 ENVIRONMENT DIVISION.
 7
 8 CONFIGURATION SECTION.
 9
10 SOURCE-COMPUTER.
11 OBJECT-COMPUTER.
12
13 INPUT-OUTPUT SECTION.
14
15 FILE-CONTROL.
16
17     SELECT DATA-FILE ASSIGN TO DISK.
18
19     SELECT REPORT-FILE ASSIGN TO PRINTER.
20
21 DATA DIVISION.
22
23 FILE SECTION.
24
25 FD  DATA-FILE
26     LABEL RECORDS ARE STANDARD
27     DATA RECORD IS DATA-RECORD.
28
29 01  DATA-RECORD   PIC X(80).
30
31 FD  REPORT-FILE
32     LABEL RECORDS ARE OMITTED
33     DATA RECORD IS REPORT-RECORD.
34
35 01  REPORT-RECORD  PIC X(80).
36
37 WORKING-STORAGE SECTION.
38
39 01  FLAGS.
40     02  END-OF-FILE      PIC X(3) VALUE "NO".
41
42 PROCEDURE DIVISION.
43
44 1000-MAIN-CONTROL.
45
46     OPEN INPUT DATA-FILE
47         OUTPUT REPORT-FILE.
48     READ DATA-FILE
49         AT END MOVE "YES" TO END-OF-FILE.
50     PERFORM 2000-PROCESS-DATA
51             UNTIL END-OF-FILE = "YES".
52     CLOSE DATA-FILE
53         REPORT-FILE.
54     STOP RUN.
55
56 2000-PROCESS-DATA.
57
58     MOVE DATA-RECORD TO REPORT-RECORD.
59     WRITE REPORT-RECORD AFTER ADVANCING 1 LINE.
60     READ DATA-FILE
61         AT END MOVE "YES" TO END-OF-FILE.
```

next record from DATA-FILE to be read. The same AT END clause that was used earlier is repeated; when there is no more data in the file, the value of END-OF-FILE is replaced by the characters "YES" so that the condition END-OF-FILE = "YES" on the PERFORM statement will become true, and processing of records from DATA-FILE will terminate.

Program 2a displays the completed program. Although this program is very simple, it contains all of the requirements for a complete COBOL program and can serve as a model when you write your own programs.

2.3 A REPORT PROGRAM

A file which is part of an accounting system contains records for each customer's account. Each record is 84 characters in length and has the following fields:

Positions	Content
1–9	Account number
10–19	Customer last name
20–29	Customer first name
30	Customer middle initial

Other record positions contain data that is not used in this problem.

A report listing the content of this file is desired. Figure 2.6 contains a printer spacing chart showing the desired positions of the various fields on the output report

Figure 2.6   Printer spacing chart for Program 2b

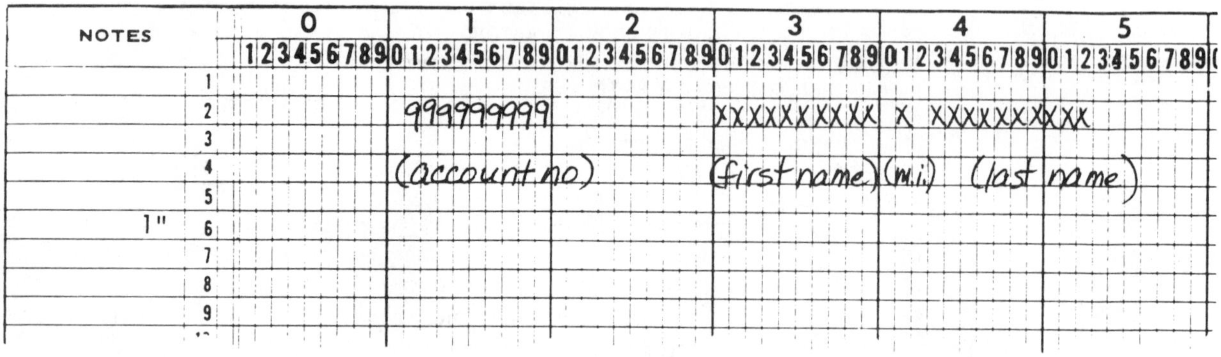

Problem Analysis

The required program must process a data file, which we call ACCOUNT-FILE, to produce a printed report that we call REPORT-FILE. ACCOUNT-FILE will be contained on disk, and REPORT-FILE will be assigned to a printer. The program will require a flag that can be used to control the processing loop in much the same way as was needed in Program 2a. This flag will be defined in the WORKING-STORAGE SECTION of the DATA DIVISION. In this case, the form of the output record is different from the form of the input record, so it will be necessary to move individual fields from the input record into related fields on the output record. Many positions on the output record are not used; therefore, it is necessary to move spaces

Figure 2.7   Plan for Program 2b

Main control

    Open files
    Move spaces to report record
    Read account file
    Do Process data until end of file
    Close files
    Stop

Process data

    Move fields to report record
    Write report record
    Read account file

into the record before moving individual data items into the record. Otherwise, undesired characters may be printed in these unused areas. The procedure for solving this problem is summarized in Figure 2.7.

Problem Solution

Program 2b produces the desired report. Lines 29 through 34 contain the description of ACCOUNT-RECORD. Note that each data-name in ACCOUNT-RECORD uses the suffix AR. This convention makes it possible to determine quickly where a given data item is defined. For example, note that the name of each field in REPORT-RECORD is given the suffix RR. ACCOUNT-RECORD contains one numeric field (the account number) and three alphanumeric fields (the parts of the name). A numeric field is defined using the picture code 9. In this case, ACCOUNT-NUMBER-AR is defined as PIC 9(9). This means that the field consists of nine (the number in parentheses) numeric digits (signified by the picture code 9). An alternative way to represent this picture is

```
02 ACCOUNT-NUMBER-AR PIC 999999999.
```

Lines 40 through 49 contain the description of REPORT-RECORD. This description is coded directly from the printer spacing chart shown in Figure 2.6. A numeric field is described using the picture code 9; alphanumeric fields are described using the picture code X. The unused positions within the record are described using the reserved word FILLER in place of a programmer-defined data-name. Such entries are commonly given alphanumeric picture codes. In describing a record, positions that will not be explicitly referenced by name within a program are assigned the data-name FILLER. For example, in this program the description of ACCOUNT-RECORD contains the entry

```
02 FILLER PIC X(54).
```

to represent the 54 unused positions in the record. It is important that a record description describe all of the positions of the actual input or output record. In this case, the record in the file to be processed contains 84 characters; therefore, the program must account for all 84 characters. The output record for the printer contains 132 characters (which is a common record length for printers); thus, the record description for this file accounts for all 132 positions. The record length for printers varies

Program 2b

```
 1 IDENTIFICATION DIVISION.
 2
 3 PROGRAM-ID. CUSTOMER-LIST-PRO2B.
 4 AUTHOR. HORN.
 5
 6 ENVIRONMENT DIVISION.
 7
 8 CONFIGURATION SECTION.
 9
10 SOURCE-COMPUTER.
11 OBJECT-COMPUTER.
12
13 INPUT-OUTPUT SECTION.
14
15 FILE-CONTROL.
16
17     SELECT ACCOUNT-FILE ASSIGN TO DISK.
18
19     SELECT REPORT-FILE ASSIGN TO PRINTER.
20
21 DATA DIVISION.
22
23 FILE SECTION.
24
25 FD  ACCOUNT-FILE
26     LABEL RECORDS ARE STANDARD
27     DATA RECORD IS ACCOUNT-RECORD.
28
29 01  ACCOUNT-RECORD.
30     02 ACCOUNT-NUMBER-AR        PIC 9(9).
31     02 LAST-NAME-AR             PIC X(10).
32     02 FIRST-NAME-AR            PIC X(10).
33     02 MIDDLE-INITIAL-AR        PIC X.
34     02 FILLER                   PIC X(54).
35
36 FD  REPORT-FILE
37     LABEL RECORDS ARE OMITTED
38     DATA RECORD IS REPORT-RECORD.
39
40 01  REPORT-RECORD.
41     02 FILLER                   PIC X(11).
42     02 ACCOUNT-NUMBER-RR        PIC 9(9).
43     02 FILLER                   PIC X(10).
44     02 FIRST-NAME-RR            PIC X(10).
45     02 FILLER                   PIC X.
46     02 MIDDLE-INITIAL-RR        PIC X.
47     02 FILLER                   PIC X.
48     02 LAST-NAME-RR             PIC X(10).
49     02 FILLER                   PIC X(79).
50
51 WORKING-STORAGE SECTION.
52
53 01  FLAGS.
54     02  EOF-FLAG       PIC X(3)  VALUE "NO".
55
```

Program 2b *(concluded)*

```
56 PROCEDURE DIVISION.
57
58 1000-MAIN-CONTROL.
59
60     OPEN INPUT ACCOUNT-FILE
61         OUTPUT REPORT-FILE.
62     MOVE SPACES TO REPORT-RECORD.
63     READ ACCOUNT-FILE
64         AT END MOVE "YES" TO EOF-FLAG.
65     PERFORM 2000-PROCESS-DATA
66             UNTIL EOF-FLAG = "YES".
67     CLOSE ACCOUNT-FILE
68         REPORT-FILE.
69     STOP RUN.
70
71 2000-PROCESS-DATA.
72
73     MOVE ACCOUNT-NUMBER-AR     TO ACCOUNT-NUMBER-RR.
74     MOVE FIRST-NAME-AR         TO FIRST-NAME-RR.
75     MOVE MIDDLE-INITIAL-AR     TO MIDDLE-INITIAL-RR.
76     MOVE LAST-NAME-AR          TO LAST-NAME-RR.
77     WRITE REPORT-RECORD AFTER ADVANCING 1 LINE.
78     READ ACCOUNT-FILE
79         AT END MOVE "YES" TO EOF-FLAG.
```

depending on the actual hardware in use at a particular installation. You must check the documentation for your system to determine the record length of the printer available to you.

The PROCEDURE DIVISION of this program resembles the PROCEDURE DIVISION of Program 2a in many respects. The primary difference in this program is the processing steps required to produce the desired output. Before any other data is moved to OUTPUT-RECORD, it is necessary to ensure that the entire record contains blanks. This task is accomplished by the MOVE statement at line 62:

    MOVE SPACES TO REPORT-RECORD.

The word SPACES is called a **figurative constant**. (Other types of constants are numeric constants such as 1 and alphanumeric constants such as "NO".) This MOVE statement will move the number of spaces required to fill the REPORT-RECORD. Any content that previously occupied these locations will be destroyed. If this statement is omitted, undesirable characters may be printed in the positions described in the output record as FILLER, representing the contents of memory in these locations at the time the program was executed. Moving spaces into the entire record prior to filling up individual parts of it is similar to wiping a chalkboard clean prior to writing on it; the purpose is to ensure that the previous contents do not detract from the new.

The statements at lines 73 through 76 cause the individual fields from ACCOUNT-RECORD to be moved to corresponding fields in REPORT-RECORD. Note that, except for the suffixes, data items holding the same information are assigned the same names. Thus, the field that will hold the first name is called FIRST-NAME-AR in ACCOUNT-RECORD and FIRST-NAME-RR in REPORT-RECORD. Note also that the order of the fields can be

Figure 2.8   Sample data and output from Program 2b

Sample Account File

```
111111111JONES          JAMES           A
222222222SMITH          MARY            S
333333333DOE            JOHN            J
444444444WHITE          SAM             Q
555555555BLACK          ARNOLD          W
```

Sample Output from Program 2b

```
111111111               JAMES           A  JONES
222222222               MARY            S  SMITH
333333333               JOHN            J  DOE
444444444               SAM             Q  WHITE
555555555               ARNOLD          W  BLACK
```

changed in moving data to the output record. In this case, `ACCOUNT-RECORD` contains data in this order: last name, first name, middle initial. The output record has data in this order: first name, middle initial, last name. The program can process all or any part of an input record in any order required to produce the needed output. Compare the data in a sample account file with the output produced by the program as shown in Figure 2.8.

2.4 PREPARING A COBOL PROGRAM FOR COMPILATION

A COBOL program may be prepared and entered into the computer in a variety of ways. Regardless of the method used, a COBOL program initially may be written on coding sheets such as the one shown in Figure 2.9. Each line of the coding sheet represents one input record. Each line is divided into fields used in entering COBOL statements. Positions 1 through 6 were originally used for a sequence number. The first record could be numbered 001010, the second record would then be 001020, and so on. In most systems today, sequence numbers are not keyed by the programmer. Many compilers add sequence numbers to each statement in the program listing for ease of reference, but sequence numbers are not part of the original program.

Positions 73 through 80 were intended for an identification sequence. The programmer may enter the program name here or choose to leave these positions blank. Position 7 is used in the continuation of a nonnumeric literal from one line to another (see Chapter 5, Section 5.7 for details). If the character * is entered in position 7, the entire line is treated by the compiler as a comment (i.e., the line is listed on the program listing but is not translated into machine language). Comments are useful to provide documentation regarding the function and purpose of the program. If position 7 is not used for either of these purposes, it is left blank. Most compilers allow the insertion of blank records into the program to provide for visual separation of various groups of statements in the final program listing; if this is not permitted, the programmer may place an asterisk in position 7 of a blank line.

Figure 2.9   Sample COBOL coding sheet

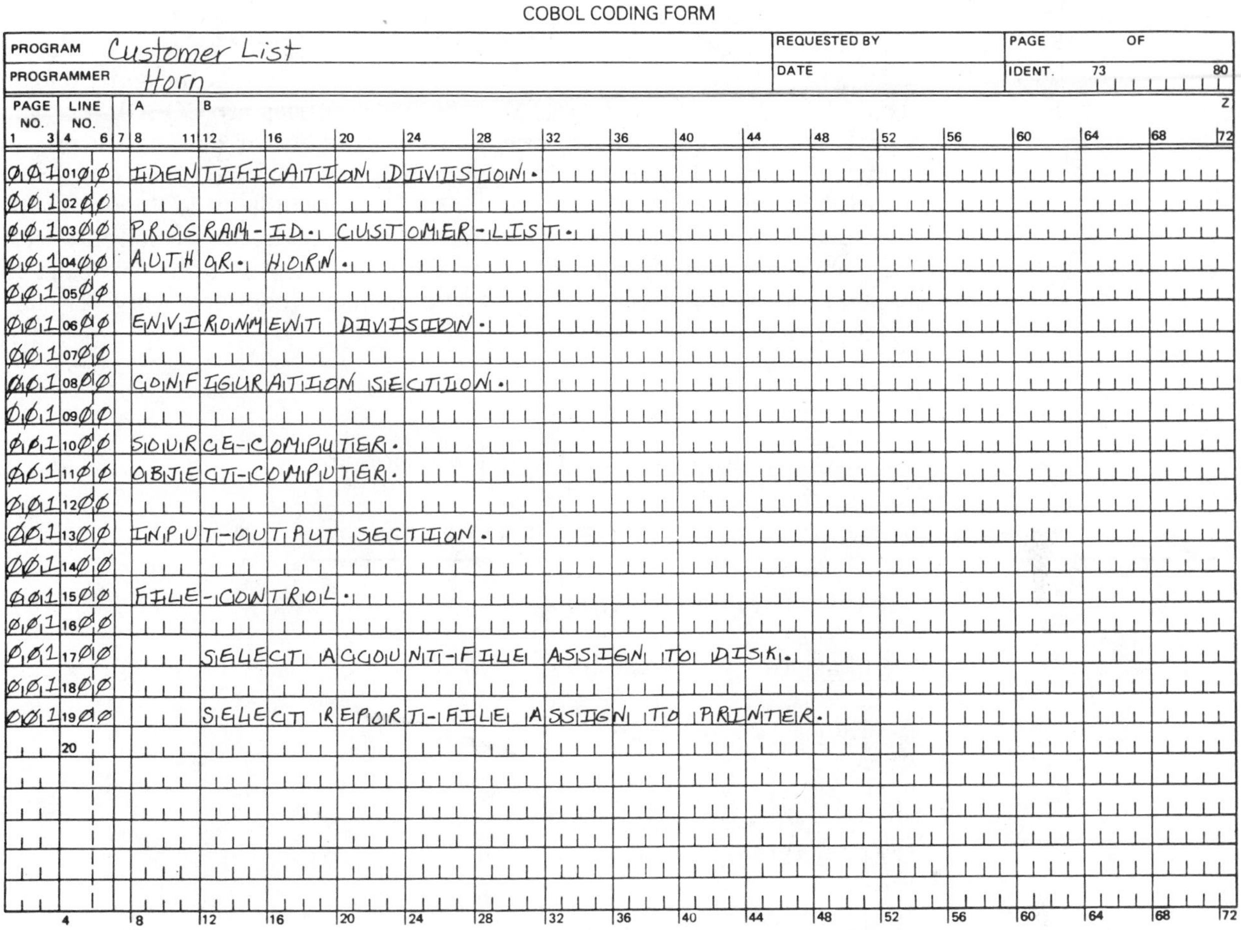

COBOL CODING FORM

| PROGRAM | Customer List | | | REQUESTED BY | | PAGE | OF |
| PROGRAMMER | Horn | | | DATE | | IDENT. | 73   80 |

```
001 0010  IDENTIFICATION DIVISION.
001 0020
001 0030  PROGRAM-ID. CUSTOMER-LIST.
001 0040  AUTHOR. HORN.
001 0050
001 0060  ENVIRONMENT DIVISION.
001 0070
001 0080  CONFIGURATION SECTION.
001 0090
001 0100  SOURCE-COMPUTER.
001 0110  OBJECT-COMPUTER.
001 0120
001 0130  INPUT-OUTPUT SECTION.
001 0140
001 0150  FILE-CONTROL.
001 0160
001 0170      SELECT ACCOUNT-FILE ASSIGN TO DISK.
001 0180
001 0190      SELECT REPORT-FILE ASSIGN TO PRINTER.
    0200
```

Positions 8 through 72 are used for the content of the COBOL statement. Two margins (A and B) are delineated on the coding form. Some COBOL statements must begin in Margin A (positions 8–11), and others may not begin before Margin B (positions 12–71).

The following entries begin in Margin A:

DIVISION headers
SECTION headers
paragraph-names
FD entries
01 entries

All other entries begin in Margin B. It is a good idea to begin Margin A entries in position 8 and Margin B entries in position 12, even though the compiler will accept Margin A entries anywhere between positions 8 and 11 inclusive and Margin B entries anywhere to the right of position 12.

Note the placement of COBOL statements in Programs 2a and 2b. The rules for placement of statements permit a statement that may begin in Margin B to be placed anywhere on the line after position 12. In particular, record description entries (levels 02-49) may begin anywhere on the line. However, it is common practice to show the breakdown of data records by indenting subordinate items as shown in Programs 2a and 2b.

2.5 IDENTIFICATION DIVISION ENTRIES

The general form of the IDENTIFICATION DIVISION is shown in Figure 2.10. This format is used throughout the text to represent the general form for COBOL program elements. All capitalized entries are COBOL reserved words. Entries that are underlined, if used, must be present as shown. All punctuation marks such as the hyphen (-) and the period (.) must be present as shown. Any entry that is capitalized but not underlined may be included at the programmer's discretion. Any entries described in lower-case characters are supplied by the programmer. Any entry enclosed in brackets ([]) is an optional entry. For example, a complete IDENTIFICATION DIVISION might be:

```
IDENTIFICATION DIVISION.
PROGRAM-ID. SAMPLE.
```

All other paragraphs in the division are optional.

Figure 2.10   General form of the IDENTIFICATION DIVISION

```
IDENTIFICATION DIVISION.

PROGRAM-ID. program-name.

[AUTHOR. [comment-entry] . . . ]

[INSTALLATION. [comment-entry] . . . ]

[DATE-WRITTEN. [comment-entry] . . . ]

[DATE-COMPILED. [comment-entry] . . . ]

[SECURITY. [comment-entry] . . . ]
```

Various operating systems place restrictions on the program name specified in the PROGRAM-ID paragraph. Check locally available documentation for further details.

Ellipses (. . .) used on the general format specifications indicate that more than one element of the preceding type may be present. Note, for example, that all of the paragraphs except for PROGRAM-ID may contain as many sentences as desired.

The general purpose of the IDENTIFICATION DIVISION is to identify the program, the programmer, when and where the program was written, and the purpose for writing the program.

- The PROGRAM-ID paragraph specifies a name for the program.
- The AUTHOR paragraph specifies the name(s) of the programmers.
- The INSTALLATION paragraph specifies where the program was written.
- The DATE-WRITTEN paragraph specifies the date on which the program was written.

Figure 2.11   Completely coded IDENTIFICATION DIVISION for Program 2b

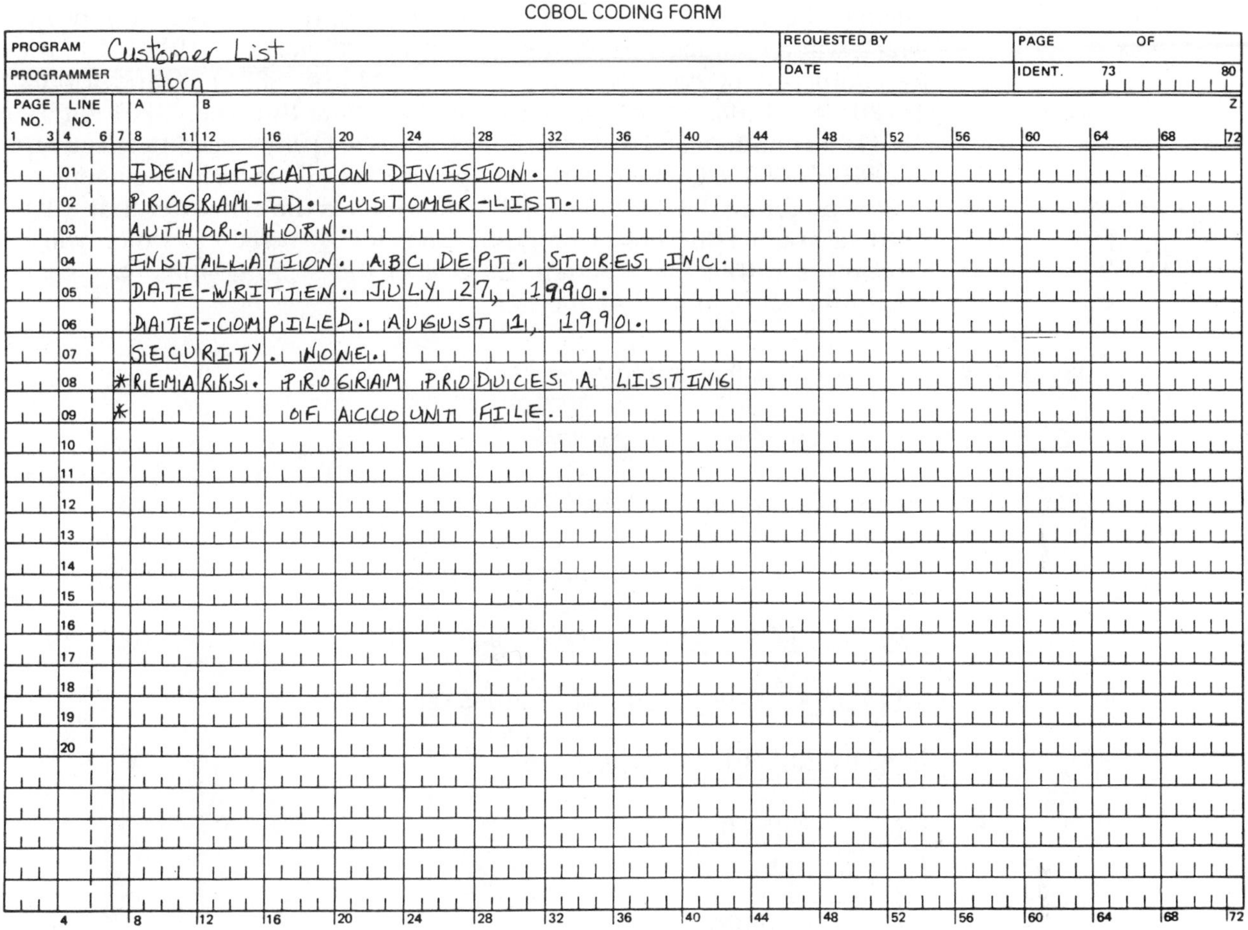

COBOL CODING FORM

PROGRAM	Customer List
PROGRAMMER	Horn

REQUESTED BY

DATE

PAGE   OF

IDENT.   73   80

```
01   IDENTIFICATION DIVISION.
02   PROGRAM-ID.  CUSTOMER-LIST.
03   AUTHOR.  HORN.
04   INSTALLATION.  ABC DEPT. STORES INC.
05   DATE-WRITTEN.  JULY 27, 1990.
06   DATE-COMPILED.  AUGUST 1, 1990.
07   SECURITY.  NONE.
08  *REMARKS.  PROGRAM PRODUCES A LISTING
09  *         OF ACCOUNT FILE.
```

- The DATE-COMPILED paragraph specifies when the program was compiled. Most compilers will insert an appropriate date into this paragraph, replacing whatever entry was made by the programmer.
- The SECURITY paragraph is used in sensitive application areas to specify the security level required for personnel to have access to the program.

Figure 2.11 illustrates a completely coded IDENTIFICATION DIVISION for Program 2b. Note the inclusion of an additional "paragraph" in this example. The REMARKS paragraph is actually a comment because of the asterisk placed in column 7. ANSI-68 COBOL provided for a REMARKS paragraph at this point; the specification was omitted in later versions of COBOL.

The REMARKS comments may be used for any purpose the programmer desires. They are typically used to describe in general terms the purpose served by the program. This paragraph may also be used to document changes made by subsequent programmers.

2.6 **ENVIRONMENT DIVISION ENTRIES**

The ENVIRONMENT DIVISION describes the computing system and the files which will be required by the program. The ENVIRONMENT DIVISION may be composed of two sections, CONFIGURATION SECTION and INPUT-OUTPUT SECTION, as shown in Figure 2.12. Note that the INPUT-OUTPUT SECTION is optional.[5] The CONFIGURATION SECTION is used to specify the SOURCE-COMPUTER, which is the computer that will be used to compile the source program; the OBJECT-COMPUTER, which is the computer that will be used to execute the object program; and SPECIAL-NAMES, which will be recognized within the program. Entries in these paragraphs vary somewhat from one compiler to another.

Figure 2.12   General form of the ENVIRONMENT DIVISION

```
ENVIRONMENT DIVISION.

CONFIGURATION SECTION.

SOURCE-COMPUTER. computer-name.

OBJECT-COMPUTER. computer-name.

[SPECIAL-NAMES. special-names-entry.]

INPUT-OUTPUT SECTION.

[FILE-CONTROL.
    SELECT select-entry . . .]

[I-O-CONTROL.
    i-o-control-entry . . .]
```

All data to be processed and all output produced by a COBOL program must be organized into sets of data records called files. The FILE-CONTROL paragraph of the INPUT-OUTPUT SECTION is used to describe the files which the program will process. There will be one SELECT entry for each file. For example, refer to the SELECT sentences defining the files in Programs 2a and 2b. The I-O-CONTROL paragraph of the INPUT-OUTPUT SECTION is used to describe special procedures to be used by the program in processing files.

The only entry that will be found in the ENVIRONMENT DIVISION of most COBOL programs will be the FILE-CONTROL paragraph of the INPUT-OUTPUT SECTION. Each file to be processed must be described in a SELECT sentence.The general form of the most useful parts of the SELECT sentence is

SELECT file-name ASSIGN TO system-name.

[5] COBOL-85 and some other compilers also allow the CONFIGURATION SECTION to be omitted.

where the **file-name** is the name of the file that will be used within the COBOL program, and the **system-name** is a description of the file that is communicated to the operating system. The general form of system-names varies from one computer installation to another; the manual for your installation will contain details.

2.7 DATA DIVISION ENTRIES

Data items that will be required in a program must be described in the DATA DIVISION. Generally, programs require three distinct types of data items:

- Input: items that are part of an input record description.
- Output: items that are part of an output record description.
- Working: items that are required temporarily by the program but are not on an input record or an output record.

When a record from a file is read, data from the file is placed in the input record area. Before a record can be written onto an output file, that data must be placed in the output record. All other items needed by the program will be classified as working items.

File Section

The general form of the DATA DIVISION is shown in Figure 2.13. The FILE SECTION contains a description of each file to be processed and a description of each type of record in the file. In Programs 2a and 2b, an input file description is followed by a description of the input record, and an output file description is followed by an output record description. The WORKING-STORAGE section contains a description of working data items. For example, in Program 2b a control variable (EOF-FLAG) is defined in WORKING-STORAGE. (Subsequent programs will require more extensive entries in WORKING-STORAGE.)

Figure 2.14 shows the general form of the most useful entries of the FD (*File Description*) entry. The use of braces { } indicates that one and only one of the entries contained within may be chosen.

Figure 2.13   General form of the DATA DIVISION

```
DATA DIVISION.

   ⎡ FILE SECTION.                                        ⎤
   ⎢ ⎡ FD file-description-entry            ⎤             ⎢
   ⎢ ⎣    record-description-entry . . .    ⎦  . . .      ⎥
   ⎢ ⎡ WORKING-STORAGE SECTION.             ⎤             ⎥
   ⎣ ⎣ [record-description-entry . . .]     ⎦             ⎦
```

Figure 2.14   General form of the FD entry. Note: The recording
mode clause is an extension not included in ANSI
standards specification.

```
FD file-name

    [RECORDING MODE IS {V/F}]

    [RECORD CONTAINS integer CHARACTERS]

    LABEL {RECORD IS / RECORDS ARE}  {OMITTED / STANDARD}

    [DATA {RECORD IS / RECORDS ARE}  record-name-1  [record-name-2 . . .]].
```

The RECORDING MODE clause is an IBM extension of ANSI COBOL
standards; it is required only by IBM compilers and may not be allowed by
other compilers. The most common entry is RECORDING MODE IS F, which
designates **fixed-length records**. Each record in a file having fixed-length
records contains the same number of characters as all other records. (The
entry V would designate **variable-length records**.) The RECORD CONTAINS
clause is used to describe the length of the record(s) associated with this
file; the clause is optional. If the RECORD CONTAINS clause is omitted, the
compiler will assume a record length equal to the total length of the elementary items specified in the record description that follows.

The LABEL RECORDS clause usually is required; it was originally
intended to describe to the COBOL compiler the way in which the program
should process the first record in a tape file. If the LABEL RECORD IS
STANDARD was specified, the first record in the file was assumed to be a
label record containing a file identification, expiration date, file description, access keys, and other such information. Label records are used to
control access to a file to ensure that files are not destroyed by mistake
and that unauthorized programs do not have access to the file. If LABEL
RECORDS ARE OMITTED is specified, the first record on a file is assumed to
be a data record. In most COBOL compilers today, the LABEL RECORDS
clause is meaningful only for tape files. Files stored on disk are accessed
by the operating system via directories that contain the name of the file
and pointers to the actual location on the disk for the content of the file.
The LABEL RECORDS clause is a required clause in COBOL-74. Because the
clause is not as useful as it once was, it is designated as optional in
COBOL-85. The DATA RECORD clause specifies the name of one or more
records that will be found in the file. A detailed description of each type of
record must follow the FD entry.

A **record-description-entry** has the form shown in Figure 2.15 where
level-number is a two-digit number in the range 01 to 49, **data-name** is the
name that identifies with the item, and **picture** is a description of the number and type of characters that will make up the item. The level-number
01 is classed as the highest level, 02 is the next highest level, and so forth.
Level-numbers 02, 03, . . . , 49 are used on data items that are subordinate to items with higher level-numbers. In Program 2b the input record is given the overall name ACCOUNT-RECORD and is subdivided into
items (also called fields) which include ACCOUNT-NUMBER-AR, LAST-NAME-

Figure 2.15   General form of the record-description-entry

$$\text{level-number} \begin{Bmatrix} \text{data-name} \\ \underline{\text{FILLER}} \end{Bmatrix} \begin{Bmatrix} \underline{\text{PICTURE}} \\ \underline{\text{PIC}} \end{Bmatrix} \text{IS picture} \quad [\underline{\text{VALUE}} \text{ IS literal}].$$

AR, and so forth. The reserved word FILLER is used as the data-name for a field that does not need to be referenced by any subsequent part of the program. The input record may be visualized as a sequence of characters as follows:

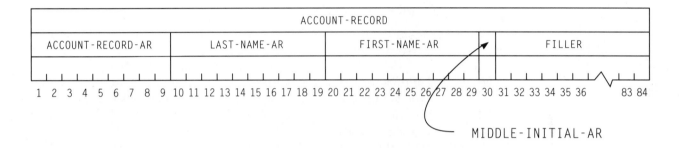

Any reference to the data-name ACCOUNT-RECORD refers to the entire 84 characters; a reference to ACCOUNT-NUMBER-AR or LAST-NAME-AR refers to a specific subset of these characters. A record description entry which contains a PICTURE clause is an elementary item; a record description entry which does not contain a PICTURE clause is a group item. Group items must be subdivided; elementary items may not. ACCOUNT-RECORD is a group item; ACCOUNT-NUMBER-AR and LAST-NAME-AR are elementary items.

A requirement of structured programming is that data-names be as descriptive as possible to aid the reader in understanding a program. Fields that will contain the same data at some point in the program are customarily assigned essentially the same name. A suffix (or prefix) is used to provide unique data-names and to indicate which record contains the field. For example, in Program 2b the data item ACCOUNT-NUMBER is present both on ACCOUNT-RECORD and REPORT-RECORD. The data-name ACCOUNT-NUMBER-AR is used for the field on ACCOUNT-RECORD (AR is an abbreviation for ACCOUNT-RECORD), and ACCOUNT-NUMBER-RR is used for the field on REPORT-RECORD.

A picture clause is made up of a sequence of characters called **picture codes**, which are used to describe the length of the field and the type of data contained in the field. The picture code 9 is used to describe a numeric character; the picture code X is used to describe an alphanumeric character. (An alphanumeric character is any representable character [digit, letter, or other]; a numeric character is any digit 0 through 9.) The total number of 9's or X's used in the picture defines the length of the field. Thus, in Program 2b, the field ACCOUNT-NUMBER-AR with a picture 9(9) is described as a nine-digit numeric item; the field LAST-NAME-AR with a picture X(10) is a ten-character alphanumeric field. All of the FILLER entries are given alphanumeric pictures of varying lengths. A repetition factor enclosed in parentheses may be used in a picture. When the repetition factor is used, the preceding character is repeated the specified number of times. For example, the entry PIC 9(4) is equivalent to PIC 9999.

Working-Storage Section

Entries in the WORKING-STORAGE SECTION are data items that are used in the program but not specifically included in an input record or an output record. The VALUE clause may be used to establish an initial value to a data item in the WORKING-STORAGE SECTION. (Its use for this purpose is restricted to elementary items in the WORKING-STORAGE SECTION. It may not be used in the FILE SECTION.) For example, the initial value of EOF-FLAG in Program 2b is specified to be "NO". The value of an item may be specified as any one of the following:

- numeric constant (e.g., VALUE IS 0)
- alphanumeric constant (e.g., VALUE IS "NO")
- figurative constant (e.g., VALUE IS SPACES)

Numeric constants are written as a sequence of digits (e.g., 0, 123); alphanumeric constants are written as a sequence of characters enclosed in quotes (e.g., "NO", "YES"); and figurative constants are COBOL reserved words that represent a specific value such as ZERO and SPACES. (See Fig. 4.15 in Chapter 4 for a complete list of figurative constants.) In some systems alphanumeric constants are enclosed in single quotes (') rather than the double quotes (") used in this text. The user must check locally available documentation to find out which character is accepted by a particular compiler.

Examples of Valid Constants

123	Numeric constant
"JOE JONES"	Alphanumeric constant
ZERO	Figurative constant

Examples of Invalid Constants

A1	Alphabetic character cannot be part of a numeric constant
"A	Additional quotes are required on the right

2.8 PROGRAM EXAMPLE

Problem Statement

Records in a file contain the following fields:

Positions	Description
1–6	Old balance (2 decimal places implied)
9–15	Deposit amount (2 decimal places implied)

A program is needed to produce a report showing the new balance for each account. The new balance is computed by adding the old balance and deposit amount. Headings are required in the report as shown in Figure 2.16.

Problem Analysis

This program is required to process a file on disk, which we will call ACCOUNT-FILE, to produce a file on the printer, which we will call REPORT-FILE. There are three primary differences between this program and Program 2b:

Figure 2.16   Printer spacing chart for Program 2c

NOTES		0 1234567890	1 1234567890	2 1234567890	3 1234567890	4 1234567890	5 123456789
Head Line	1	OLD BALANCE	DEPOSIT AMOUNT	NEW BALANCE			
Detail Line	2	9999.99	9999.99	9999.99			
	3						
	4						
	5						
1"	6						
	7						
	8						
	9						
	10						
	11						

- Headings must be printed.
- Arithmetic operations must be performed.
- Numeric data contains an implied decimal point and must be edited for output.

The appropriate time to produce headings is after files have been opened and before processing the first data record. As part of the processing of each record, the value of the old balance must be added to the deposit amount, and the result must be placed on the output record. Appropriate editing of the output must be performed to ensure that an actual decimal point is printed, even though the input data contained only an implied decimal point. That is, an input item such as

$$0 \quad 1 \quad 2 \quad 3 \quad 4 \quad 5$$

in which the implied position of the decimal point is between the 3 and the 4, representing a value 123.45, must be printed as

$$0 \quad 1 \quad 2 \quad 3 \quad . \quad 4 \quad 5$$

A plan for this program is shown in Figure 2.17.

Figure 2.17   Plan for Program 2c

Main control

  Open files
  Write heading
  Read account file
  Do Create report until end of file
  Close files
  Stop

Create report

  Move input fields to output record
  Compute new balance
  Write detail line
  Read account file

Problem Solution

The required program is shown in Program 2c. A sample of the output produced by the program is shown in Figure 2.18. Note the use of the V picture code in the descriptions of the numeric fields OLD-BALANCE-AR and DEPOSIT-AMOUNT-AR (lines 30 and 32). Each of these fields is six digits in length with two implied decimal positions. The picture code V is used to represent the position of the implied decimal point. Thus a picture code such as

    PIC 9999V99

describes a field containing six characters. The V does not represent a character in the field. When computation is performed on numeric items,

---

Program 2c

```
 1 IDENTIFICATION DIVISION.
 2
 3 PROGRAM-ID. BALANCE-PRO2C.
 4 AUTHOR. HORN.
 5
 6 ENVIRONMENT DIVISION.
 7
 8 CONFIGURATION SECTION.
 9
10 SOURCE-COMPUTER.
11 OBJECT-COMPUTER.
12
13 INPUT-OUTPUT SECTION.
14
15 FILE-CONTROL.
16
17     SELECT ACCOUNT-FILE ASSIGN TO DISK.
18
19     SELECT REPORT-FILE ASSIGN TO PRINTER.
20
21 DATA DIVISION.
22
23 FILE SECTION.
24
25 FD   ACCOUNT-FILE
26      LABEL RECORDS ARE STANDARD
27      DATA RECORD IS ACCOUNT-RECORD.
28
29 01   ACCOUNT-RECORD.
30      02 OLD-BALANCE-AR     PIC 9999V99.
31      02 FILLER            PIC XX.
32      02 DEPOSIT-AMOUNT-AR  PIC 9999V99.
33      02 FILLER            PIC X(66).
34
35 FD   REPORT-FILE
36      LABEL RECORDS ARE OMITTED
37      DATA RECORD IS REPORT-RECORD.
38
39 01   REPORT-RECORD       PIC X(132).
40
```

Program 2c   *(concluded)*

```
41 WORKING-STORAGE SECTION.
42
43 01  FLAGS.
44      02  EOF-FLAG        PIC X(3)   VALUE "NO".
45
46 01  HEAD-LINE.
47      02 FILLER          PIC X(3)     VALUE SPACES.
48      02 FILLER          PIC X(11)    VALUE "OLD BALANCE".
49      02 FILLER          PIC X(3)     VALUE SPACES.
50      02 FILLER          PIC X(14)    VALUE "DEPOSIT AMOUNT".
51      02 FILLER          PIC X(3)     VALUE SPACES.
52      02 FILLER          PIC X(11)    VALUE "NEW BALANCE".
53
54 01  DETAIL-LINE.
55      02 FILLER            PIC X(5)     VALUE SPACES.
56      02 OLD-BALANCE-DL    PIC 9999.99.
57      02 FILLER            PIC X(11)    VALUE SPACES.
58      02 DEPOSIT-AMOUNT-DL PIC 9(4).99.
59      02 FILLER            PIC X(7)     VALUE SPACES.
60      02 NEW-BALANCE-DL    PIC 9(4).99.
61
62 PROCEDURE DIVISION.
63
64 1000-MAIN-CONTROL.
65
66     OPEN INPUT ACCOUNT-FILE
67         OUTPUT REPORT-FILE.
68     MOVE HEAD-LINE TO REPORT-RECORD.
69     WRITE REPORT-RECORD AFTER ADVANCING PAGE.
70     READ ACCOUNT-FILE
71         AT END MOVE "YES" TO EOF-FLAG.
72     PERFORM 2000-CREATE-REPORT
73             UNTIL EOF-FLAG = "YES".
74     CLOSE ACCOUNT-FILE
75           REPORT-FILE.
76     STOP RUN.
77
78 2000-CREATE-REPORT.
79
80     MOVE OLD-BALANCE-AR TO OLD-BALANCE-DL.
81     MOVE DEPOSIT-AMOUNT-AR TO DEPOSIT-AMOUNT-DL.
82     ADD OLD-BALANCE-AR DEPOSIT-AMOUNT-AR GIVING NEW-BALANCE-DL.
83     MOVE DETAIL-LINE TO REPORT-RECORD.
84     WRITE REPORT-RECORD AFTER ADVANCING 1 LINES.
85     READ ACCOUNT-FILE
86         AT END MOVE "YES" TO EOF-FLAG.
```

COBOL automatically aligns decimal positions to take into account implied decimal positions within a field.

This program requires that two different types of output lines be printed—a heading line and detail lines. This requirement is handled by defining a "dummy" output record for the printer files called REPORT-RECORD, consisting of 132 undifferentiated characters and defining areas in WORKING-STORAGE for the actual records to be used. This strategy is

Figure 2.18   Sample execution of Program 2c

Sample input file for Program 2c

```
001000   002000
030000   004400
055000   002000
067890   001367
120000   100000
003478   001210
```

Sample output from Program 2c

```
OLD BALANCE      DEPOSIT AMOUNT      NEW BALANCE
    0010.00          0020.00          0030.00
    0300.00          0044.00          0344.00
    0550.00          0020.00          0570.00
    0678.90          0013.67          0692.57
    1200.00          1000.00          2200.00
    0034.78          0012.10          0046.88
```

useful because it allows us to define the actual records using the VALUE clause to establish the content of the record. (Recall that the VALUE clause cannot be used for this purpose in the FILE SECTION of the DATA DIVISION.) In this program two records are defined in WORKING-STORAGE:

HEAD-LINE (lines 46–52)
DETAIL-LINE (lines 54-60)

Note that in both records the VALUE clause is used to establish the initial value of all areas except those that will be filled from input fields (OLD-BALANCE-DL and DEPOSIT-AMOUNT-DL) and the field that will be computed (NEW-BALANCE-DL). To actually print the contents of a WORKING-STORAGE record, it is necessary to move it to REPORT-RECORD before writing REPORT-RECORD. This is done in Program 2c at lines 68 through 69 for HEAD-LINE and at lines 83 through 84 for DETAIL-LINE. Note that the use of the clause AFTER ADVANCING PAGE in the WRITE statement at line 69 causes this output to be produced at the top of a new page, a desirable break for the headings being printed at this point in the program.

In order to print an actual decimal point, the edit picture code "." is used in the description of output fields. For example, in line 56 the field OLD-BALANCE-DL is described as

PIC 9999.99.

The 9's represent numeric positions as before. The decimal point represents an actual printed decimal point taking up one position in the field. Thus, this field requires seven positions within the output record. When numeric data is moved into a field described using the edit picture code ".", the decimal point is inserted in place of the implied decimal point. Note, however, that the new field is not numeric. Arithmetic computations cannot be performed on a field described using edit picture codes. An edited item can be used to receive the result of a computation if that result is not needed in further computations as is the case in Program 2c.

The requirement that the two fields from the input record be added is accomplished by the ADD statement at line 82:

```
ADD OLD-BALANCE-AR DEPOSIT-AMOUNT-AR GIVING
    NEW-BALANCE-DL.
```

This statement will cause the computer to add the content of two fields and place the result in the location specified in the GIVING clause, in this case into NEW-BALANCE-DL.

2.9 SUMMARY OF PROCEDURE DIVISION ENTRIES

The PROCEDURE DIVISION describes the processing of the data files. It is the "action part" of any COBOL program. The PROCEDURE DIVISION of Program 2c has two paragraphs: 1000-MAIN-CONTROL and 2000-CREATE-REPORT. Each sentence in the PROCEDURE DIVISION is made up of one or more statements. A statement begins with a COBOL reserved word describing the operation to be performed. Statements used in Program 2c include:

```
OPEN       PERFORM
MOVE       CLOSE
WRITE      STOP RUN
READ       ADD
```

The OPEN statement causes the designated files to be opened (i.e., readied for processing). A file must always be opened before any READ or WRITE operations may be performed on it.

The MOVE statement causes data to be copied from one data item (the sending item) to another (the receiving item). A MOVE replaces the contents of the receiving item but does nothing to the sending item.

The WRITE statement causes the specified output record to be written onto the appropriate file. The AFTER clause designates the vertical spacing of paper for a printer file. A general form of the WRITE statement with the AFTER clause is shown in Figure 2.19.

Figure 2.19   General form of the WRITE/AFTER statement

$$\underline{\text{WRITE}} \text{ record-name} \left[\underline{\text{AFTER}} \text{ ADVANCING} \left\{ \begin{matrix} \text{integer} \\ \underline{\text{PAGE}} \end{matrix} \left[\begin{matrix} \text{LINE} \\ \text{LINES} \end{matrix} \right] \right\} \right]$$

When the AFTER clause is used, PAGE is used to skip to the top of a new page; 0 is used to skip no lines before printing; 1 is used to skip one line before printing (the equivalent of single spacing in typing); 2 is used to skip two lines before printing (the equivalent of double spacing in typing); 3 is used to skip three lines before printing; and so forth.

The READ statement causes a record to be read from the specified file. When the record is read, a check is made to determine if it is the system end-of-file record. The purpose of the system end-of-file record is to mark the end of the data records so that a program will not inadvertently process data belonging to another file. When the end-of-file record is read, the statement(s) in the AT END clause of the READ statement will be executed. For example, in Program 2c the READ statement

```
READ ACCOUNT-FILE
    AT END MOVE "YES" TO EOF-FLAG.
```

will cause the contents of the data item END-OF-FILE to be set to "YES" when the end-of-file record for the file INPUT-FILE is read.

The PERFORM statement causes the sentences of the designated paragraph to be executed if the condition given in the UNTIL clause is *not* met. For example, the statement

```
PERFORM 2000-CREATE-REPORT
    UNTIL EOF-FLAG = "YES".
```

will cause a test of EOF-FLAG to be made. If EOF-FLAG = "YES", the next statement will be executed. If EOF-FLAG ≠ "YES", the paragraph 2000-CREATE-REPORT will be executed. After execution of the paragraph, the condition is tested again, and the procedure is repeated. In Programs 2a, 2b, and 2c, this logic is used to process each record of the input file and to stop processing when the end-of-file record has been read.

The CLOSE statement is used to terminate processing of designated files. Any file that is opened should always be closed before the program stops execution. The STOP RUN statement is used to terminate execution of the program. The ADD statement is used to perform the arithmetic operation of addition on designated data items and place the results in a location specified in the GIVING clause. For example,

```
ADD OLD-BALANCE-AR DEPOSIT-AMOUNT-AR GIVING
    NEW-BALANCE-DL.
```

will cause the sum of OLD-BALANCE-AR and DEPOSIT-AMOUNT-AR to be placed in NEW-BALANCE-DL.

The elements of a complete COBOL program are summarized in Figure 2.20.

Figure 2.20   Summary of a simple COBOL program

```
IDENTIFICATION DIVISION.
```

The program, author, and other identifying information is given.

```
ENVIRONMENT DIVISION.
```

The computing system(s) to be used and the files to be processed are specified.

```
DATA DIVISION.
FILE SECTION.
```

The input and output files and the records for these files are described.

```
WORKING-STORAGE SECTION.
```

Other data items required by the program are described.

```
PROCEDURE DIVISION.
```

The files are opened. Each record of the input file is processed, and the appropriate line of output is written. When all the records have been processed, the files are closed and the execution of the program is terminated.

2.10 DEBUG CLINIC

It is almost inevitable that there will be errors in COBOL programs when they are first submitted for compilation. Errors may be classed as either syntax errors or logical errors. A **syntax error** is an error in constructing a COBOL statement. The compiler will alert the programmer that syntax errors have been made by printing appropriate messages as part of the program listing. A **logical error** is an error in the logic of the program; the program does not perform the desired function. These errors become apparent as the programmer examines the output produced from the processing of sample data. **Debugging** is the process of removing syntax errors and logical errors from programs.

Syntax Errors

Program 2d is an example of a program with syntax errors. It represents what might be an intermediate stage in the development of Program 2c.[6] In this listing, the error messages produced by the compiler follow the statement that contains the error.[7] Usually the messages immediately follow the line of code that contains the actual error, but occasionally other lines of code may intervene. One error may produce one error message or several error messages. Common sources of syntax errors are omission of periods, omission or misspelling of reserved words, and misspelling of data-names.

─────── Example ───────

The error message following line 52 in Program 2d was caused by the omission of the reserved word `PIC` in line 52:

```
02 FILLER    X(11) VALUE "NEW BALANCE".
```

─────── Example ───────

Line 59 is in error because the period was omitted at the end of the line:

```
02 FILLER    PIC X(7) VALUE SPACES
```

This error caused the error messages listed after line 60. Because the period is missing on line 59, the compiler tried to interpret line 60 as a part of the statement which began on line 59.

─────── Example ───────

The error message at the end of the program listing is produced because the paragraph referred to in line 72 does not exist. The cause of this error is the misspelling of the paragraph-name in line 78.

─────── Example ───────

The error message following line 82 is caused by the omission of the period in line 59. Because of this error, the data-name `NEW-BALANCE-DL` was never defined in the program.

─────────────────────────

[6] This output was produced using the Microsoft COBOL compiler. Users of the Ryan McFarland compiler may refer to Appendix H, Figure H.3, to see the results of compiling Program 2d using RM COBOL-85.

[7] Some compilers gather all error messages and print them at the end of the program listing.

Program 2d

```
 1 IDENTIFICATION DIVISION.
 2
 3 PROGRAM-ID. BALANCE-PRO2D.
 4 AUTHOR. HORN.
   .
   .
   .
46 01  HEAD-LINE.
47     02 FILLER          PIC X(3)     VALUE SPACES.
48     02 FILLER          PIC X(11)    VALUE "OLD BALANCE".
49     02 FILLER          PIC X(3)     VALUE SPACES.
50     02 FILLER          PIC X(14)    VALUE "DEPOSIT AMOUNT".
51     02 FILLER          PIC X(3)     VALUE SPACES.
52     02 FILLER             X(11)     VALUE "NEW BALANCE".
```
233-S***************************   (0)**
**   Unknown data description qualifier
```
53
54 01  DETAIL-LINE.
55     02 FILLER          PIC X(5)     VALUE SPACES.
56     02 OLD-BALANCE-DL   PIC 9999.99.
57     02 FILLER          PIC X(11)    VALUE SPACES.
58     02 DEPOSIT-AMOUNT-DL PIC 9(4).99.
59     02 FILLER          PIC X(7)     VALUE SPACES
60     02 NEW-BALANCE-DL   PIC 9(4).99.
```
** 27-S******   (2)**
**   Number too large
```
61
62 PROCEDURE DIVISION.
63
64 1000-MAIN-CONTROL.
65
66 OPEN INPUT ACCOUNT-FILE
67         OUTPUT REPORT-FILE.
68    MOVE HEAD-LINE TO REPORT-RECORD.
69    WRITE REPORT-RECORD AFTER ADVANCING PAGE.
70    READ ACCOUNT-FILE
71        AT END MOVE "YES" TO EOF-FLAG.
72    PERFORM 2000-CREATE-REPORT
73         UNTIL EOF-FLAG = "YES".
74    CLOSE ACCOUNT-FILE
75         REPORT-FILE.
76    STOP RUN.
77
78 2000-CREATE-REPRT.
79
80    MOVE OLD-BALANCE-AR TO OLD-BALANCE-DL.
81    MOVE DEPOSIT-AMOUNT-AR TO DEPOSIT-AMOUNT-DL.
82    ADD OLD-BALANCE-AR DEPOSIT-AMOUNT-AR GIVING NEW-BALANCE-DL.
```
** 12-S*** (2)**
**   Operand is not declared
```
83    MOVE DETAIL-LINE TO REPORT-RECORD.
84    WRITE REPORT-RECORD AFTER ADVANCING 1 LINES.
85    READ ACCOUNT-FILE
86        AT END MOVE "YES" TO EOF-FLAG.
87
*     2000-CREATE-REPORT
```
348-S****************   (2)**
**   Procedure name 2000-CREATE-REPORT undeclared

Note that the OPEN statement at line 66 begins in Margin A rather than in Margin B. This compiler did not treat this as an error; however, another compiler might call attention to this error. Unfortunately there are no standards for error messages; each compiler uses a different set. Usually a programmer's guide containing detailed information about the error messages is available for the COBOL compiler used at a given computer center.

Logical Errors

Even if a program is compiled without syntax errors, logical errors in the program may remain. The programmer must devise one or more sets of test data and execute the program with the test data in order to ensure that the program correctly performs the function(s) specified for it. It is a good idea to design the test data very early in the program development process; when the expected output with a set of test data is known in advance, the output actually produced by the program can be analyzed easily.

2.11   STANDARDIZATION OF COBOL

This text describes the version of the language generally called COBOL-74 (currently the most widely available implementation) and the most useful extensions in COBOL-85. Even though the language is standardized, each implementation of COBOL is somewhat different. Differences that exist among implementations are of three varieties.

- Different requirements in areas specified in the COBOL standard as implementor-defined. (Example: the entry in the ASSIGN clause of the SELECT entry in the ENVIRONMENT DIVISION.)
- Additional clauses required by certain compilers but not by others. (Example: IBM compilers require the RECORDING MODE clause in an FD entry in the DATA DIVISION.)
- Different levels of implementation of standard COBOL. The ANSI standard describes the language as a Nucleus that contains the minimum set of functions required of a COBOL compiler and a set of functional processing modules:

Table Handling	Segmentation
Sequential I-O	Library
Relative I-O	Debug
Indexed I-O	Inter-Program Communication
Sort-Merge	Communication
Report Writer	

Within each module are two or more levels of implementation. The standard defines a minimal implementation of COBOL as low levels of the Nucleus, Table Handling, and Sequential I-O. A full implementation includes a high-level Nucleus and all of the functional processing modules. A subset implementation includes any level of the Nucleus and any combination of functional processing modules from a minimal implementation to a full implementation. Most implementations of COBOL are subset implementations.

Because of the wide variety of implementations of standard COBOL, users must have access to the implementor's reference manual for the

COBOL compiler with which they will be dealing. This text will describe full ANSI-74 and ANSI-85 COBOL. Not all of the features described here will work on all systems. Minor modifications to the programs in this text will probably be required to make them run on a particular computing system. Your best guide is the reference manual.

2.12 COBOL-85 UPDATE

The ANSI-85 COBOL standard includes a number of changes and enhancements that are designed to make the task of the programmer less tedious and to improve the readability of programs. Among these changes are the following:

- Lowercase as well as uppercase letters can be used in writing COBOL programs. For example, instead of REPORT-FILE the programmer can write report-file or Report-File.
- The CONFIGURATION SECTION in the ENVIRONMENT DIVISION is optional and can be omitted if desired.
- The word FILLER is optional in specifying an elementary item in the DATA DIVISION. For example, instead of

```
    02 FILLER    PIC X(3).
```

the programmer can write

```
    02      PIC X(3).
```

- The LABEL RECORDS clause is optional in the FD entry.

These changes are illustrated in the context of a complete program in Program 2c85. This program is equivalent to Program 2c, but it is written in a COBOL-85 style. We have adopted the practice of using both upper- and lowercase letters in writing programmer-defined words, while retaining all uppercase letters for COBOL reserved words. (This choice is a matter of taste but was chosen to improve the readability of the program. Compare Program 2c85 with Program 2c to assess the extent to which readability is improved.) We have omitted the CONFIGURATION SECTION in the ENVIRONMENT DIVISION since this section contains no useful information. We have omitted the word FILLER wherever possible. We have omitted the LABEL RECORDS clause in all the FD entries since they are unnecessary in the particular system we are using.

Program 2c85

```
 1 IDENTIFICATION DIVISION.
 2
 3 PROGRAM-ID. Balance-Pro2c85.
 4 AUTHOR. Horn.
 5
 6 ENVIRONMENT DIVISION.
 7
 8 INPUT-OUTPUT SECTION.
 9
10 FILE-CONTROL.
11
12     SELECT Account-File ASSIGN TO DISK.
13
14     SELECT Report-File ASSIGN TO PRINTER.
15
16 DATA DIVISION.
17
18 FILE SECTION.
19
20 FD   Account-File
21      DATA RECORD IS Account-Record.
22
23 01   Account-Record.
24      02 Old-Balance-AR     PIC 9999V99.
25      02                    PIC XX.
26      02 Deposit-Amount-AR  PIC 9999V99.
27      02                    PIC X(66).
28
29 FD   Report-File
30      DATA RECORD IS Report-Record.
31
32 01   Report-Record        PIC X(132).
33
34 WORKING-STORAGE SECTION.
35
36 01   Flags.
37      02   EOF-Flag         PIC X(3)   VALUE "NO".
38
39 01   Head-Line.
40      02                 PIC X(3)    VALUE SPACES.
41      02                 PIC X(11)   VALUE "OLD BALANCE".
42      02                 PIC X(3)    VALUE SPACES.
43      02                 PIC X(14)   VALUE "DEPOSIT AMOUNT".
44      02                 PIC X(3)    VALUE SPACES.
45      02                 PIC X(11)   VALUE "NEW BALANCE".
46
47 01   Detail-Line.
48      02                     PIC X(5)     VALUE SPACES.
49      02 Old-Balance-DL      PIC 9999.99.
50      02                     PIC X(11)    VALUE SPACES.
51      02 Deposit-Amount-DL   PIC 9(4).99.
52      02                     PIC X(7)     VALUE SPACES.
53      02 New-Balance-DL      PIC 9(4).99.
54
```

Program 2c85 *(concluded)*

```
55 PROCEDURE DIVISION.
56
57 1000-Main-Control.
58
59     OPEN INPUT Account-File
60         OUTPUT Report-File.
61     MOVE Head-Line TO Report-Record.
62     WRITE Report-Record AFTER ADVANCING PAGE.
63     READ Account-File
64         AT END MOVE "YES" TO EOF-Flag.
65     PERFORM 2000-Create-Report
66             UNTIL EOF-Flag = "YES".
67     CLOSE Account-File
68         Report-File.
69     STOP RUN.
70
71 2000-Create-Report.
72
73     MOVE Old-Balance-AR TO Old-Balance-DL.
74     MOVE Deposit-Amount-AR TO Deposit-Amount-DL.
75     ADD Old-Balance-AR Deposit-Amount-AR GIVING New-Balance-DL.
76     MOVE Detail-Line TO Report-Record.
77     WRITE Report-Record AFTER ADVANCING 1 LINES.
78     READ Account-File
79         AT END MOVE "YES" TO EOF-Flag.
```

2.13 SELF-TEST EXERCISES

1. Matching

    1. CODASYL
    2. ANSI
    3. DIVISION
    4. ENVIRONMENT
    5. DATA
    6. IDENTIFICATION
    7. PROCEDURE
    8. sequence number
    9. continuation
    10. Margin A
    11. MOVE
    12. PROGRAM-ID
    13. CONFIGURATION SECTION
    14. INPUT-OUTPUT SECTION
    15. SOURCE-COMPUTER
    16. OBJECT-COMPUTER
    17. SELECT
    18. FILE SECTION
    19. WORKING-STORAGE SECTION
    20. FD
    21. level-number
    22. FILLER
    23. OPEN
    24. PERFORM
    25. CLOSE
    26. AFTER

    a. assigns name to a COBOL program
    b. entry used in FILE SECTION of the DATA DIVISION
    c. used on WRITE statements addressed to printer
    d. computer used to compile the program
    e. largest unit of subdivision of a COBOL program
    f. column 7
    g. column 8
    h. assigns a file to a system component
    i. columns 1-6
    j. Conference on Data Systems Languages
    k. terminates processing of a file by a COBOL program
    l. section of DATA DIVISION in which records associated with files are defined
    m. division of a COBOL program which defines data to be processed
    n. American National Standards Institute
    o. statement which readies a file for processing
    p. computer used to execute the program
    q. identifier used to indicate levels of subdivision of data
    r. division of a COBOL program which identifies the program and the programmer
    s. division of a COBOL program which specifies the computing environment in which the program will function
    t. instruction used to copy data from one memory location to another
    u. reserved word used to define unused positions of a record
    v. command used to execute a COBOL paragraph
    w. portion of the DATA DIVISION used to define data not directly a part of an input or output record
    x. portion of ENVIRONMENT DIVISION used to define the computing system
    y. division used to describe the processing of data
    z. portion of ENVIRONMENT DIVISION used to define files to be processed

2. Write a complete IDENTIFICATION DIVISION for Program 2c.

3. Draw a program flowchart for Program 2c.

4. List entries which must begin in Margin A.

5. Classify each of the following data-names as valid or invalid:
    a. INPUT-REC
    b. 100-32
    c. 300 -PARA
    d. PARA-
    e. INPUT-DATA-TO-BE-PROCESSED-BY-THIS
    f. INPUT REC

6. The following list of items was taken from Program 2c. Match each item with the applicable items from the list of descriptive terms below.

   1. HEAD-LINE
   2. PROCEDURE DIVISION
   3. MOVE
   4. ACCOUNT-FILE
   5. INPUT-OUTPUT SECTION
   6. DEPOSIT-AMOUNT-DL
   7. 1000-MAIN-CONTROL
   8. ASSIGN
   9. EOF-FLAG
   10. "OLD BALANCE"
   11. 1
   12. SPACES
   13. X(5)
   14. 9999.99
   15. FILLER
   16. ADD
   17. AUTHOR

   a. division header
   b. section header
   c. paragraph header
   d. group data name
   e. elementary data name
   f. alpha-numeric constant
   g. figurative constant
   h. numeric constant
   i. reserved word
   j. picture
   k. file name

7. Write DATA DIVISION entries to define a record containing the following fields:

Positions	Content
1-20	Customer name
21-35	Street address
36-45	City
46-47	State
48-52	Zip code
53-80	Unused

8. Classify each file-name, record-name, and data-name defined in Program 2c using the following table:

   Where Defined in DATA DIVISION

Type of Item	FILE SECTION		WORKING-STORAGE SECTION		
	Used for Input	Used for Output	Used for Input	Used for Control	Used for Output
File					
Record					
Field					

9. In Program 2c, the column headings are not perfectly centered over the columns in the body of the report. What changes to the program are necessary to improve the appearance of the report?

10. List four changes made in COBOL-85 that contribute to program readability.

2.14 PROGRAMMING EXERCISES

1. Each record in a file contains the following fields:

Positions	Content
1–20	Customer name
21–35	Street address
36–45	City
46–47	State
48–52	Zip code
53–57	Current balance (2 decimal places implied)

   Write a program to list the content of this file. The report should contain appropriate headings as shown in the printer spacing chart in Figure 2.21.

Figure 2.21 Layout for report in Exercise 1

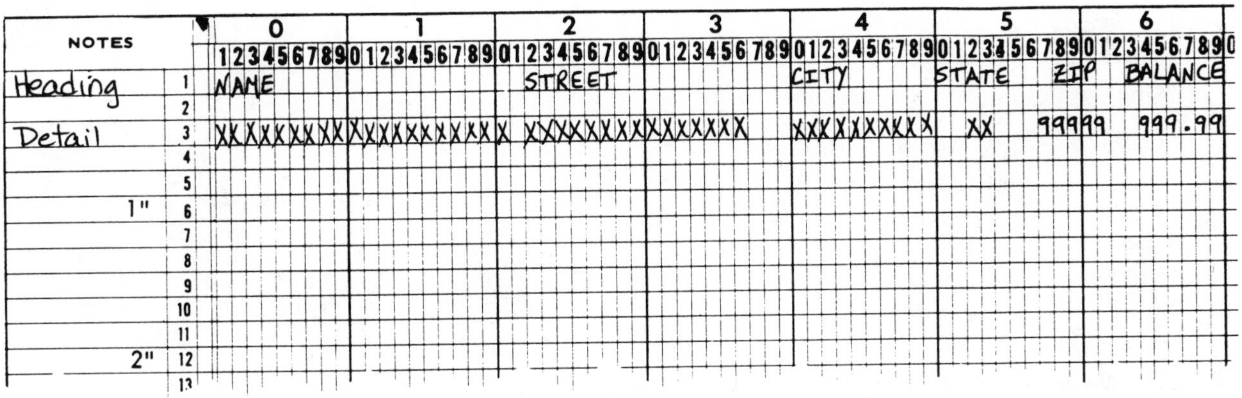

2. Write a program to produce address labels from the input data defined in Exercise 1 above. Output should be of the form:

   Name
   Street Address
   City   State   Zip

   Skip three lines before beginning each label.

3. Write a program to process a file containing records as follows:

Positions	Content
3–4	Grade-1
6–7	Grade-2
10–11	Grade-3

   Compute the sum of the grades and list them with appropriate headings.

4. Jones Furniture Company maintains four warehouse facilities. Inventory records show the quantity of a given item on hand in each

facility. The format for each record is

Positions	Content
1–5	Inventory number
6–15	Item description
16–17	Quantity on hand warehouse 1
18–19	Quantity on hand warehouse 2
20–21	Quantity on hand warehouse 3
22–23	Quantity on hand warehouse 4

Produce a report showing the total quantity of each item on hand. Include appropriate headings.

3. STRUCTURED PROGRAMMING IN COBOL

3.1 STRUCTURED PROGRAMMING GOALS AND STRATEGIES

One of the most onerous problems in utilizing computer-based data processing systems is the cost of developing and maintaining software for the system. Most development and maintenance costs are labor related because programming is highly labor intensive. Other costs result from errors in the system's programs that may cause lost productivity or lost opportunity. A primary goal of structured programming is to decrease the overall costs of developing and maintaining a system. Structured programming methodology has been demonstrated to be a successful tool for

- reducing initial development costs and time by increasing programmer productivity,
- producing programs that are virtually error free, and
- simplifying the tasks of program maintenance and reducing the associated costs.

A variety of strategies, some of them new and some adapted from engineering and other disciplines, are used to achieve these goals. A primary strategy of structured programming is to create programs that are simple and easy to comprehend. A program with a simple overall design is of much greater value than one with a complex design, because the person who must maintain the program will spend less time learning the mechanics of the program in order to determine where changes must be made. Also, the original programmer is less likely to make logical errors if the design is simple, and errors that do occur should be easier to correct. The virtual elimination of the GO TO statement, as recommended by Dijkstra, and the implementation of only a selected set of program structures contribute greatly to program simplicity.

A structured program must be readable. Readability makes the job of debugging and maintenance easier by reducing the time spent learning what the program is doing and how the task is being accomplished. Readability is achieved by using descriptive data and procedure names and by using rules for alignment and indention of program elements. A side benefit of readability is that the program becomes largely self-documenting, reducing the need for most other forms of documentation.

A structured program should be designed and coded in a modular fashion. A **program module** is a segment of code having a well-defined purpose and a single entry and single exit point. A complex task is decomposed into a set of modules; a structured program is a set of modules linked together by a control structure that determines the order in which the modules are executed. If a program is divided into well-thought-out modules, the debugging process is easier because errors are readily traced to a particular module. Maintainability is also enhanced because the maintenance programmer can readily locate the particular section of the program which must be changed by matching the required change to the program module "responsible" for that function.

The general thrust in data processing over the past few years has been toward developing a professionalism among programmers, analysts, and other data processing personnel. Calling programmers "software engineers" emphasizes the parallel between developing computer programs and developing mechanical or electronic systems. Many practices that have long been associated with engineering, including well-defined methodology, emphasis on product design, standards for product testing, and modular decomposition of complex systems, have increasingly been adopted by data processing professionals. The day of brilliant but eccentric programmers who develop programs in total isolation, using their own unique methods, is largely in the past. Current programming techniques emphasize simplicity, readability, modularity, and program maintainability. The resulting program may not have the hallmark of creativity that characterized programs of the past, but the programs work well, are easy to read and maintain, and help hold down the cost of developing and maintaining computing systems.

3.2   TOP-DOWN PROGRAM DESIGN

Structured programming is really a programming discipline. It encompasses techniques used to develop program logic and standards for the actual coding of the program. The technique used for program development is generally referred to as **top-down program design.** In top-down program design, a program is specified as a set of procedures to be executed in some chosen sequence; a procedure may be relatively simple (opening a file) or complex (accumulating the sum of a sequence of data items). A complex procedure will, in turn, be broken down into a sequence of simpler procedures until at last the COBOL code for the program can be written.

3.3   PROGRAM EXAMPLE

Problem Statement

A data file contains records with a field in positions 10 through 14 representing a whole number quantity (no decimal places). A program that will list these quantities and calculate their total is needed. A printer spacing chart for the desired report is shown in Figure 3.1.

Problem Analysis

The entire program could be summarized as one high-level procedure:

    Compute the sum of a set of data items

This statement amounts to little more than a restatement of the problem

Figure 3.1   Printer spacing chart for Program 3a

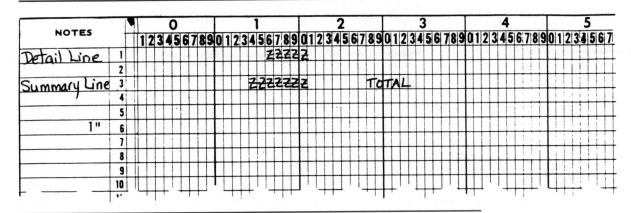

to be solved. In order to design a suitable program, it is necessary to re-specify the program as a sequence of simpler procedures:

```
Open files
Read the first data record
Do until no more data
        Accumulate to sum of each data item
End do
Write the sum
Close files
Stop
```

At this point it is apparent that the procedure "Accumulate the sum of each data item" is still fairly high level and may be respecified as follows:

```
Add the data item to the sum
Read the next data record
```

Thus the complete program now has the form:

```
Open files
Read the first data record
Do until no more data
        Add the data item to the sum
        Read the next data record
End do
Write the sum
Close files
Stop
```

Upon examination of this procedure, we realize that an important require-ment of the program specification has been omitted—the program should produce a list of the items read. During the processing of each record, the value of the data item should be written on the printer. Because the COBOL program requires that the actions controlled by the DO-UNTIL structure be coded as separate procedures, we should revise the design one more time as follows:

Main control

    Open files
    Read the first data record
    Do Process data until end of file
    Write the sum
    Close files
    Stop

Process data

    Add data item to sum
    Write data item
    Read the next record

This plan is now sufficiently complete for the programmer to begin writing the actual program. The process by which this plan was derived is an example of top-down program design. At each successive stage in the process, one or more complex tasks are broken down into a series of simpler tasks. At some stage the plan is expressed in simple enough terms that the program can be written.

This problem requires the use of a programming technique called **accumulation** in order to compute the required total. In accumulation, a data item is used to store a running total; that is, each new value is added to the accumulator, and the results replace the old value. The accumulator must have the initial value of zero before any values are added to it. An easy way to accomplish this task is to use the VALUE IS ZERO clause when the accumulator is defined in WORKING-STORAGE. (ZERO is another figurative constant; the clause VALUE IS 0 would be equivalent.)

Problem Solution

A solution to this problem is shown in Program 3a. This program processes an input file called AMOUNT-FILE and produces a printed report on PRINT-FILE. As in Program 2c, the two different output records are defined in WORKING-STORAGE: DETAIL-LINE (lines 48–50) and SUMMARY-LINE (lines 52–56). Prior to printing either of these records, the record is moved to PRINT-RECORD, which is the record defined in the FILE SECTION for PRINT-FILE. (See, for example, lines 69–70 and 79–80.)

The accumulator in this program is called GRAND-TOTAL and is defined in WORKING-STORAGE as follows (lines 45–46):

```
01  TOTALS.
    02 GRAND-TOTAL        PIC 9(7) VALUE ZERO.
```

The item GRAND-TOTAL is a numeric field with initial value zero. It is defined as being subordinate to the group item TOTALS so that if a subsequent programmer wishes to add other accumulators to the program, all of them will be grouped together for easy reference.

The actual task of accumulating the total is carried out by the ADD statement at line 77:

```
ADD NUMBER-AR TO GRAND-TOTAL.
```

This statement causes the value of NUMBER-AR to be added to GRAND-TOTAL and the result to replace GRAND-TOTAL. The statement is equivalent to the following ADD statement:

```
ADD NUMBER-AR GRAND-TOTAL GIVING GRAND-TOTAL.
```

Program 3a

```
 1 IDENTIFICATION DIVISION.
 2
 3 PROGRAM-ID. ACCUMULATION-PRO3A.
 4 AUTHOR. HORN.
 5
 6 ENVIRONMENT DIVISION.
 7
 8 CONFIGURATION SECTION.
 9
10 SOURCE-COMPUTER.
11 OBJECT-COMPUTER.
12
13 INPUT-OUTPUT SECTION.
14
15 FILE-CONTROL.
16
17     SELECT AMOUNT-FILE ASSIGN TO DISK.
18
19     SELECT PRINT-FILE ASSIGN TO PRINTER.
20
21 DATA DIVISION.
22
23 FILE SECTION.
24
25 FD  AMOUNT-FILE
26     LABEL RECORDS ARE STANDARD
27     DATA RECORD IS AMOUNT-RECORD.
28
29 01  AMOUNT-RECORD.
30     02 FILLER              PIC X(9).
31     02 NUMBER-AR           PIC 9(5).
32     02 FILLER              PIC X(66).
33
34 FD  PRINT-FILE
35     LABEL RECORDS ARE OMITTED
36     DATA RECORD IS PRINT-RECORD.
37
38 01  PRINT-RECORD           PIC X(132).
39
40 WORKING-STORAGE SECTION.
41
42 01  FLAGS.
43     02 EOF-FLAG            PIC X(3) VALUE "NO".
44
45 01  TOTALS.
46     02 GRAND-TOTAL         PIC 9(7) VALUE ZERO.
47
48 01  DETAIL-LINE.
49     02 FILLER              PIC X(15) VALUE SPACES.
50     02 NUMBER-DL           PIC ZZZZZ.
51
52 01  SUMMARY-LINE.
53     02 FILLER              PIC X(13) VALUE SPACES.
54     02 GRAND-TOTAL-SL      PIC ZZZZZZZ.
55     02 FILLER              PIC X(7) VALUE SPACES.
56     02 FILLER              PIC X(5) VALUE "TOTAL".
57
```

Program 3a   *(concluded)*

```
58 PROCEDURE DIVISION.
59
60 1000-MAIN-CONTROL.
61
62     OPEN INPUT AMOUNT-FILE
63          OUTPUT PRINT-FILE.
64     READ AMOUNT-FILE
65          AT END MOVE "YES" TO EOF-FLAG.
66     PERFORM 2000-PROCESS-DATA
67             UNTIL EOF-FLAG = "YES".
68     MOVE GRAND-TOTAL TO GRAND-TOTAL-SL.
69     MOVE SUMMARY-LINE TO PRINT-RECORD.
70     WRITE PRINT-RECORD AFTER ADVANCING 2 LINES.
71     CLOSE AMOUNT-FILE
72           PRINT-FILE.
73     STOP RUN.
74
75 2000-PROCESS-DATA.
76
77     ADD NUMBER-AR TO GRAND-TOTAL.
78     MOVE NUMBER-AR TO NUMBER-DL.
79     MOVE DETAIL-LINE TO PRINT-RECORD.
80     WRITE PRINT-RECORD AFTER ADVANCING 1 LINE.
81     READ AMOUNT-FILE
82            AT END MOVE "YES" TO EOF-FLAG.
```

For example, suppose AMOUNT-FILE contains the following data:

```
00034
00100
00002
00400
```

At the beginning of execution of Program 3a, the content of memory is as follows:

Comment	NUMBER-AR	GRAND-TOTAL
Beginning of execution	?	0

After the first record has been read and processed, the first value (34) will be added to the current value of GRAND-TOTAL (0) so that the new value of GRAND-TOTAL will be 34:

Comment	NUMBER-AR	GRAND-TOTAL
After first record	34	34 (0 + 34)

When the second record is read, the value of NUMBER-AR will be replaced by 100. When this record is processed, 100 will be added to the current value of GRAND-TOTAL:

Comment	NUMBER-AR	GRAND-TOTAL
After second record	100	134 (100 + 34)

Processing of the remaining records is summarized as follows:

Comment	NUMBER-AR	GRAND-TOTAL
After third record	2	136 (134 + 2)
After fourth record	400	536 (136 + 400)

When all of the data has been processed, GRAND-TOTAL contains the total of all of the values of NUMBER-AR. The output from Program 3a with this sample data is shown in Figure 3.2.

Figure 3.2 Sample output from Program 3a

```
   34
  100
    2
  400

  536         TOTAL
```

It is imperative that GRAND-TOTAL be a numeric item in order for this computation to be carried out. That is why a separate entry in the DATA DIVISION is required for both GRAND-TOTAL and GRAND-TOTAL-SL, the field used to store that value on the SUMMARY-LINE. GRAND-TOTAL-SL is defined as an edited field and, therefore, is nonnumeric. The content of GRAND-TOTAL-SL could not have arithmetic operations performed on it. Prior to moving SUMMARY-LINE to PRINT-LINE for printing, the content of GRAND-TOTAL is moved to GRAND-TOTAL-SL (line 68).

In this program the edit picture code Z is used to provide editing of numeric output fields. The picture code Z causes suppression of leading nonsignificant zeros. Thus, instead of output such as

$$\lfloor 0 \, 0 \, 0 \, 1 \, 2 \, 3 \rfloor$$

which would result using a picture such as 9(6), we are able to produce output such as

$$\lfloor \quad \quad \quad 1 \, 2 \, 3 \rfloor$$

by using a picture Z(6). The leading zeros are replaced by spaces in the edited field.

3.4 STRUCTURED PROGRAMMING STYLE

A major goal of structured programming is readability and ease of understanding. Unstructured programs sometimes get too complicated to be readable; one reason for this is the use of the unconditional branching statement GO TO. The GO TO statement causes a branch to a specified location within a program *with no provision for returning.* By contrast, the PERFORM statement causes a branch to a specified location, but when the paragraph is completed, control returns to the PERFORM statement. In a structured program, virtually all branching will be controlled by the PERFORM and IF statements. The GO TO statement, if used at all, is used in a very restricted and controlled manner, as described later in this book. In fact, it is possible to write any program using only three structures—sequence, decision, and iteration; none of these structures requires the GO TO statement in COBOL implementation. For this reason, structured programming is sometimes referred to as "go-to-less" programming; avoiding the use of the GO TO statement is an important principle of structured programming.

The goals of readability and ease of understanding lead to certain restrictions and practices in the coding of a structured COBOL program. For example, it is important to use meaningful names for data items, paragraphs, and other names defined by the programmer. In COBOL, data-names and paragraph-names may range in length from one to thirty characters, thus giving the programmer a wide latitude in the assignment of names. In a particular program, for example, a programmer might choose to call two data-names X and Y, or the programmer might choose PAY-RATE and HOURS-WORKED. It is obvious that the latter choice is more descriptive and would aid in understanding the type of data stored in each data-name. In a similar fashion, the names of paragraphs should describe the functions performed in each paragraph. For example, in Program 3b the paragraph-names

```
1000-MAIN-CONTROL
2000-INITIALIZE-DATA
2100-PROCESS-DATA
2200-END-PROGRAM
3000-ACCUMULATE-SUM
3100-WRITE-DETAIL-LINE
9000-READ-AMOUNT
```

were chosen to aid the reader in understanding the program. The paragraph numbers 1000, 2000, and so on, help the reader to locate the paragraph quickly and serve as an aid to locate the level of the paragraph in the structure of the program. (See Section 3.8 for more information about the level of a paragraph.)

Comprehension and readability are enhanced considerably by the use of short, single-function paragraphs in a program. For example, Program 3a is rewritten in Program 3b to contain a number of short, single-function paragraphs. Note that Program 3a contains only two paragraphs, while Program 3b contains seven paragraphs. Which program is easier to read and understand? In this simple example you may prefer Program 3a. However, as programs become longer and more complex, the practice of coding reasonably short, single-function paragraphs can result in a more understandable and readable program. A rule of thumb is that no paragraph should be longer than one page of print or one screen on a CRT display, whichever is appropriate. There is nothing to prevent paragraphs from being shorter to increase readability and understandability.

The discussion above suggests that there are good ways and not-so-good ways to write a correct COBOL program. Style is important in programming, as it is in writing reports, letters, or novels. A good program is distinguished by more than correctness; the style in which it is written determines whether people can read and understand the program with ease. A well-written program is far more valuable than a program which, although it performs the same task, is written in a way that makes it unreadable and difficult to understand.

We cannot set down an exhaustive list of rules regarding style for writing a structured COBOL program, as there are no universally agreed-

Program 3b

```
 1 IDENTIFICATION DIVISION.
 2
 3 PROGRAM-ID. ACCUMULATION-MODULAR-PRO3B.
 4 AUTHOR. HORN.
 5
 6 ENVIRONMENT DIVISION.
 7
 8 CONFIGURATION SECTION.
 9
10 SOURCE-COMPUTER.
11 OBJECT-COMPUTER.
12
13 INPUT-OUTPUT SECTION.
14
15 FILE-CONTROL.
16
17     SELECT AMOUNT-FILE ASSIGN TO DISK.
18
19     SELECT PRINT-FILE ASSIGN TO PRINTER.
20
21 DATA DIVISION.
22
23 FILE SECTION.
24
25 FD  AMOUNT-FILE
26     LABEL RECORDS ARE STANDARD
27     DATA RECORD IS AMOUNT-RECORD.
28
29 01  AMOUNT-RECORD.
30     02 FILLER              PIC X(9).
31     02 NUMBER-AR           PIC 9(5).
32     02 FILLER              PIC X(66).
33
34 FD  PRINT-FILE
35     LABEL RECORDS ARE OMITTED
36     DATA RECORD IS PRINT-RECORD.
37
38 01  PRINT-RECORD           PIC X(132).
39
40 WORKING-STORAGE SECTION.
41
42 01  FLAGS.
43     02 EOF-FLAG            PIC X(3) VALUE "NO".
44
45 01  TOTALS.
46     02 GRAND-TOTAL         PIC 9(7) VALUE ZERO.
47
48 01  DETAIL-LINE.
49     02 FILLER              PIC X(15) VALUE SPACES.
50     02 NUMBER-DL           PIC ZZZZZ.
51
52 01  SUMMARY-LINE.
53     02 FILLER              PIC X(13) VALUE SPACES.
54     02 GRAND-TOTAL-SL      PIC ZZZZZZZ.
55     02 FILLER              PIC X(7) VALUE SPACES.
56     02 FILLER              PIC X(5) VALUE "TOTAL".
57
```

Program 3b   *(concluded)*

```
58 PROCEDURE DIVISION.
59
60 1000-MAIN-CONTROL.
61
62     PERFORM 2000-INITIALIZE-DATA.
63     PERFORM 2100-PROCESS-DATA
64            UNTIL EOF-FLAG = "YES".
65     PERFORM 2200-END-PROGRAM.
66     STOP RUN.
67
68 2000-INITIALIZE-DATA.
69
70     OPEN INPUT AMOUNT-FILE
71          OUTPUT PRINT-FILE.
72     PERFORM 9000-READ-AMOUNT.
73
74 2100-PROCESS-DATA.
75
76     PERFORM 3000-ACCUMULATE-SUM.
77     PERFORM 3100-WRITE-DETAIL-LINE.
78     PERFORM 9000-READ-AMOUNT.
79
80 2200-END-PROGRAM.
81
82     MOVE GRAND-TOTAL TO GRAND-TOTAL-SL.
83     MOVE SUMMARY-LINE TO PRINT-RECORD.
84     WRITE PRINT-RECORD AFTER ADVANCING 2 LINES.
85     CLOSE AMOUNT-FILE
86           PRINT-FILE.
87
88 3000-ACCUMULATE-SUM.
89
90     ADD NUMBER-AR TO GRAND-TOTAL.
91
92 3100-WRITE-DETAIL-LINE.
93
94     MOVE NUMBER-AR TO NUMBER-DL.
95     MOVE DETAIL-LINE TO PRINT-RECORD.
96     WRITE PRINT-RECORD AFTER ADVANCING 1 LINE.
97
98 9000-READ-AMOUNT.
99
100     READ AMOUNT-FILE
101        AT END MOVE "YES" TO EOF-FLAG.
```

upon standards for style. You will find a number of programs in this text which, though imperfect, are written in "good" structured programming style. If you discover ways in which you can improve on our style, feel free to practice your improvements in your own programs. Any organization such as a large business which uses structured COBOL programming extensively will have a style book outlining rules and practices expected in coding programs at that installation.

In summary, the following rules form the bases for structured programming:

- Use top-down program design techniques.
- Use only the sequence, decision, and iteration structures.
- Use unconditional branching (the GO TO) with restraint, if at all.
- Follow standards of program readability and understandability.

By following the examples of structured COBOL programs in this text and applying the major rules above, you can become adept at writing structured COBOL programs. Although structured programming may place an added burden on you initially because you have to learn rules for structure as well as rules for COBOL language, the benefits of the structured approach far outweigh the disadvantages.

3.5 THE PERFORM STATEMENT

The PERFORM statement causes a program to execute a paragraph and, when the paragraph is completed, to return either to the PERFORM statement itself or to the statement following the PERFORM statement. A general form for the PERFORM statement is

PERFORM paragraph-name [UNTIL condition]

Note the use of brackets in this general form. Brackets mean that the enclosed portion of the statement is optional. Remember that capitalized words are COBOL reserved words and lowercase words specify elements to be supplied by the programmer. Reserved words that are underlined are required; those not underlined are optional at the discretion of the programmer.

If the UNTIL clause is omitted, the PERFORM statement causes the specified paragraph to be executed, and upon completion of that paragraph, control returns to the statement following the PERFORM statement. For example, in the partial program illustrated in Figure 3.3, the statement

PERFORM 2000-WRITE-SUMMARY-LINE.

in the paragraph 1000-MAIN-LOGIC causes the paragraph 2000-WRITE-SUMMARY-LINE to be executed. The three sentences in the paragraph will be executed in sequential order; then, the statement immediately following the PERFORM statement will be executed. The flowchart form of this structure is shown in Figure 3.3.

The result would be the same if the statements in the executed paragraph were inserted in place of the PERFORM statement. For example, consider the statement PERFORM 3000-ACCUMULATE-SUM at line 76 of Program 3b. The statement (line 90)

ADD NUMBER-AR TO GRAND-TOTAL.

is the only statement in 3000-ACCUMULATION-SUM. It could be inserted in place of the statement PERFORM 3000-ACCUMULATE-SUM to give the same results. In general, if you wish to cause the execution of a paragraph one time, you will use the PERFORM statement without the UNTIL option.

If, however, you desire to cause the execution of a paragraph to be repeated a number of times until some condition is satisfied, you must include the UNTIL clause in the PERFORM statement. In this case the con-

Figure 3.3   Example of the use of the PERFORM statement

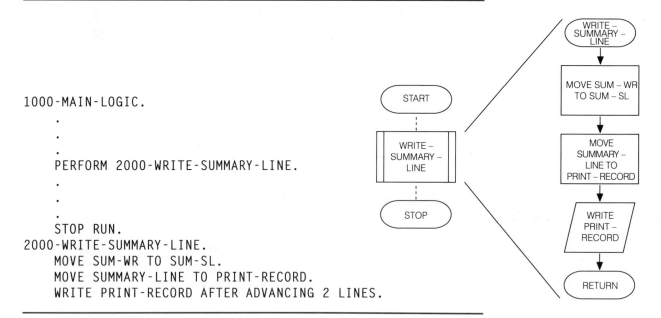

```
1000-MAIN-LOGIC.
    .
    .
    .
    PERFORM 2000-WRITE-SUMMARY-LINE.
    .
    .
    .
    STOP RUN.
2000-WRITE-SUMMARY-LINE.
    MOVE SUM-WR TO SUM-SL.
    MOVE SUMMARY-LINE TO PRINT-RECORD.
    WRITE PRINT-RECORD AFTER ADVANCING 2 LINES.
```

dition is tested before execution of the paragraph. If the condition is not met (the condition is false), the named paragraph is executed (PERFORMed). After the paragraph has been executed, the condition is tested again; if the condition now is met, the statement following the PERFORM is executed. Otherwise, execution of the paragraph is repeated.

Figure 3.4 illustrates the use of this version of the PERFORM statement. The condition being tested involves the value of a data-name called EOF-FLAG. A data-name such as this is sometimes called a "program switch" because it has two values—"NO" and "YES"—in much the same way as a light switch has two positions—off and on. The value "NO" corresponds to the switch being set in the "off" position; the value "YES" represents the "on" position. Program switches are used as communications links among paragraphs of a program.

The program switch in Figure 3.4 is used to detect when the last record from the input file has been read. As long as the last record has not been read, the switch remains in the "off" position. When the last record is read, the switch is turned to the "on" position. The occurrence of the reading of the last record is in the paragraph 2000-PROCESS-DATA; the fact that the last record has been read is communicated to the paragraph 1000-MAJOR-LOGIC via the setting of the program switch EOF-FLAG. The statement

```
PERFORM 2000-PROCESS-DATA
        UNTIL EOF-FLAG = "YES".
```

will cause control to be passed to the paragraph 2000-PROCESS-DATA as long as the switch is "off" (i.e., it has value other than YES). The switch is in the "off" position in the WORKING-STORAGE SECTION where the data item is defined:

```
01  EOF-FLAG PIC XXX VALUE "NO".
```

The switch is turned to the "on" position in the paragraph 2000-PROCESS-DATA in the AT END clause of the READ statement. Figure 3.5 illustrates in

Figure 3.4 PERFORM/UNTIL program example

```
WORKING-STORAGE SECTION
01  EOF-FLAG PIC XXX VALUE "NO".
    .
    .
    .
PROCEDURE DIVISION.
1000-MAJOR-LOGIC.
    .
    .

    PERFORM 2000-PROCESS-DATA
         UNTIL EOF-FLAG = "YES".
    .
    .

    STOP RUN.
2000-PROCESS-DATA.
    .
    .

    READ INPUT-FILE
        AT END MOVE "YES" TO EOF-FLAG.
```

flowchart form the logic of this use of the PERFORM statement. In general, any paragraph executed by a PERFORM/UNTIL statement must modify the condition being tested or the program will enter an infinite loop. An **infinite loop** is formed when a sequence of statements is executed repeatedly with no possibility for the program to exit the sequence. Most computing systems contain a provision for terminating programs after a reasonable period of time to protect the system from programs that are caught in an infinite loop.

Figure 3.5 Flowchart of the PERFORM/UNTIL in Figure 3.4

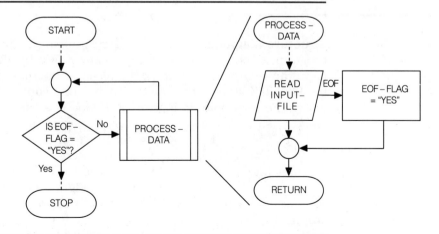

3.6   A MODULAR EXAMPLE

Recall that Program 3a lists and calculates the sum of a sequence of values that are contained in a data file where each record in the file contains one value. Program 3a illustrates the process of accumulation, which is used to compute the sum of a sequence of data items. As mentioned earlier, the process essentially is one of maintaining a "running" total (i.e., adding one data item at a time into the total). In the beginning, a data item (GRAND-TOTAL) to be used to contain the total is assigned an initial value of zero; a data item used in this way is called an **accumulator**. When each data record is read, the data item from that record is added to the accumulator in the statement (line 77):

```
ADD NUMBER-AR TO GRAND-TOTAL.
```

When all records have been read, the accumulator holds the accumulated sum of the values.

Program 3b contains Program 3a redone in an expanded modular form. Note that the PROCEDURE DIVISION of Program 3a contains two paragraphs, and Program 3b contains seven paragraphs. The 2100-PROCESS-DATA paragraph of Program 3b calls upon other paragraphs to do various functions, whereas in Program 3a instructions for these functions are written into the paragraph 2000-PROCESS-DATA. For example, in place of the statement ADD NUMBER-AR TO GRAND-TOTAL (line 77 of Program 3a), we find PERFORM 3000-ACCUMULATE-SUM (line 76 of Program 3b). The content of the paragraph 3000-ACCUMULATE-SUM is the statement ADD NUMBER-AR TO GRAND-TOTAL (line 90 of Program 3b).

The modular style used in Program 3b is the style preferred among most programmers. Each paragraph is concise and carries out a single well defined function; the name assigned to the paragraph is descriptive of the paragraph's function. The art of writing "good" structured programs begins with breaking down the task at hand into a manageable set of tasks, each of which can be implemented in a COBOL program by a paragraph of reasonable size and complexity. The remainder of this text contains many examples of structured programs which the reader may use as models.

3.7   STRUCTURE DIAGRAMS

Structure diagrams represent the relationships among paragraphs in a program. Each paragraph is represented as a block in the diagram; the paragraph-name is written in the block. If one paragraph is executed via the PERFORM statement from another, a line connecting the two blocks is drawn. For example, in Figure 3.6, PARA-B is executed (PERFORMed) from PARA-A, so a line in the structure diagram connects the block labeled PARA-B. The structure diagram for Program 3a is shown in Figure 3.7.

For a program such as this with a very simple structure, the diagram provides little new insight into the program. However, consider the structure diagram for Program 3b shown in Figure 3.8. In this case, because of the numerous paragraphs, the diagram shows at a glance which paragraphs are used primarily to control the functioning of the program and which paragraphs carry out the operations (such as input, output, and computation) required by the program.

Figure 3.6   Example of structure diagram

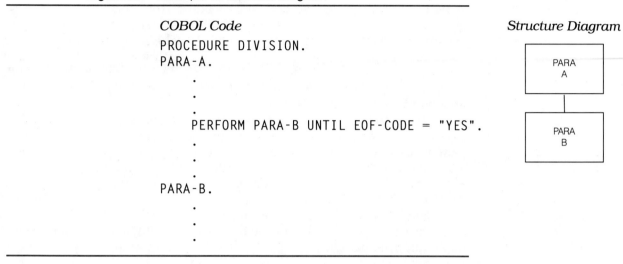

COBOL Code

```
PROCEDURE DIVISION.
PARA-A.
     .
     .

     .
     PERFORM PARA-B UNTIL EOF-CODE = "YES".
     .
     .
     .
PARA-B.
     .
     .
     .
```

Structure Diagram

Figure 3.7   Structure diagram for Program 3a

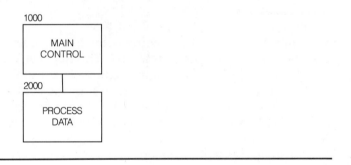

Figure 3.8   Structure diagram for Program 3b

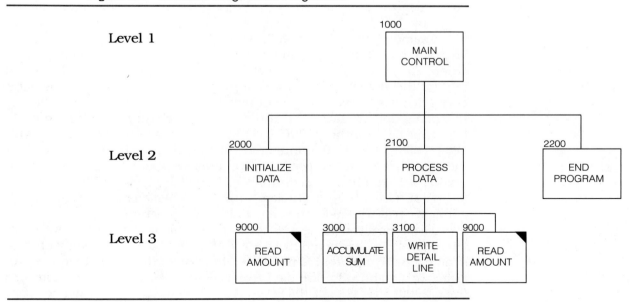

Paragraphs which function primarily to provide control appear in the structure diagram with several lines leading from them to other paragraphs. In this case, 1000-MAIN-CONTROL and 2100-PROCESS-DATA are examples of control paragraphs. Paragraphs which function primarily as operations appear in the structure diagram with few or no lines leading from them. In this case, 2000-INITIALIZE-DATA, 3000-ACCUMULATE-SUM, 3100-WRITE-DETAIL-LINE, 9000-READ-AMOUNT, and 2200-END-PROGRAM are operational paragraphs.

A structure diagram clearly shows the hierarchy into which paragraphs of a program are divided. A paragraph which is executed from a paragraph directly via a PERFORM statement, or indirectly by way of a paragraph which is PERFORMed, is *subordinate* to that paragraph. Thus, in Figure 3.8 it is clear that all other paragraphs are subordinate to 1000-MAIN-CONTROL, and 3000-ACCUMULATE-SUM, 3100-WRITE-DETAIL-LINE, and 9000-READ-AMOUNT are subordinate to 2100-PROCESS-DATA.

The triangular shading in the blocks labeled 9000-READ-AMOUNT signifies that this paragraph is PERFORMed from more than one place in the program.

3.8   NUMBERING AND NAMING PARAGRAPHS

We will adopt a standard convention for numbering and naming paragraphs in the programs in this text. The number will serve two functions: It will denote the sequence of paragraphs in the PROCEDURE DIVISION, and it will denote the level of the paragraph in the control structure of the program. In so far as possible, the name should describe the type of operation a paragraph is going to carry out and what that operation is going to be carried out on.

Using paragraph numbers to denote the sequence of paragraphs in a program has a very pragmatic purpose. When a programmer is debugging or revising a program, it is important to be able to locate a paragraph quickly. Knowing, for example, that a paragraph numbered 2100 comes between paragraphs 2000 and 2200 will be a considerable help, particularly when the programmer is working with extremely long and complex programs.

Examination of Figure 3.8, which shows the structure diagram of Program 3b, will help you understand the concept of the level of a paragraph. The paragraph at the top of the chart (1000-MAIN-CONTROL) is said to be at the first level. The first digit in the number assigned to this paragraph denotes a level-one paragraph. Paragraphs that are controlled by this paragraph are said to be at the second level; they are assigned numbers that begin with 2 (2000-INITIALIZE-DATA, 2100-PROCESS-DATA, 2200-END-PROGRAM). Continuing in this fashion, we have paragraphs at the third level that are controlled by level-two paragraphs; these paragraphs are numbered accordingly (3000-ACCUMULATE-SUM and 3100-WRITE-DETAIL-LINE). A problem with this scheme occurs when a paragraph is performed more than one time in the program.

Theoretically, a paragraph of this type could occur at two or more different levels in the hierarchy. We will use numbers beginning with 9 to denote a paragraph that is performed from more than one point in a program. In Program 3b, the paragraph 9000-READ-AMOUNT is performed from 2000-INITIALIZE-DATA and 2100-PROCESS-DATA; hence, it is assigned a number beginning with 9. Because the number also denotes the order of the paragraphs, these paragraphs always occur at the end of the listing of the PROCEDURE DIVISION.

The words in a paragraph name should reflect what the paragraph does in the program. As we have said, a good program module should carry out a well-defined function. It is usually possible to assign a name of the form *verb-object* to describe the function being carried out. The verb specifies the action, and the object specifies what is being acted on. For example, in Program 3b, the paragraph that accumulates the sum of the input data is called ACCUMULATE-SUM; ACCUMULATE is the verb and SUM is the object. The paragraph that reads a record from AMOUNT-FILE is named READ-AMOUNT. The verb is READ (the type of operation that is going to happen), and the object is AMOUNT (what is going to be read). It is not always easy to give paragraphs names that conform strictly to this rule. In particular, the purpose of the paragraph at level one is to control the execution of all the other paragraphs in the program. For paragraphs at this level, we have chosen names such as MAIN-CONTROL, which are descriptive but do not conform completely to the verb-object format that is our ideal.

3.9 COUNTING

We have seen that accumulation can be used to compute the sum of a sequence of data items. A variation of this technique (called **counting**) can be used to compute the frequency of occurrence of specific items. This is accomplished by adding 1 to the accumulator each time an item is encountered; an accumulator used in this fashion is called a **counter**. This process is illustrated in the following example:

Problem Statement

Modify Program 2c to include totals for each column (Old Balance, Deposit Amount, and New Balance) and a line at the end of the report specifying the number of accounts processed. A printer spacing chart for the required report is shown in Figure 3.9. There should be a blank line between the

Figure 3.9   Printer spacing chart for Program 3c

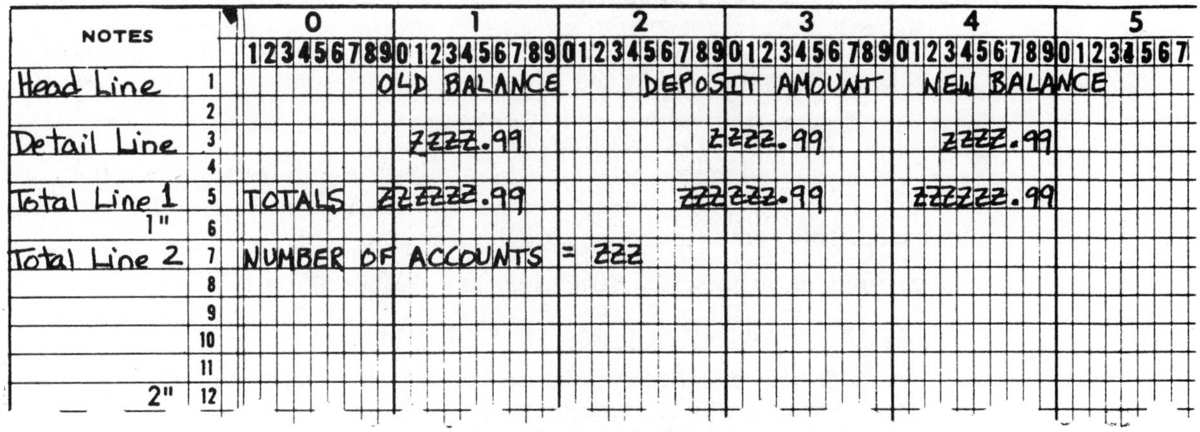

column headings line and the body of the report. All fields should be edited with zero suppression.

Problem Analysis

Accumulation will be required to compute the sum of each of the data elements. Since there are three separate sums, three different accumulators will be required. (Let us call these accumulators TOTAL-OLD-BALANCE, TOTAL-DEPOSIT, and TOTAL-NEW-BALANCE.) A counter will also be required (NUMBER-OF-ACCOUNTS); the program will add 1 to this item each time a record from ACCOUNT-FILE is processed. All of these items must be initialized to 0. A plan for this program is as follows:

Main control

    Open files
    Read account file
    Do Create report until end of file
    Write totals
    Stop

Create report

    Compute new balance
    Write detail line
    Compute totals
    Add 1 to number of accounts
    Read account file

Problem Solution

A solution to this problem is shown in Program 3c. A sample of the output produced by the program is shown in Figure 3.10. A structure diagram for the program is shown in Figure 3.11.

Recall that in Program 2c, the content of NEW-BALANCE-DL was computed by the statement

```
ADD OLD-BALANCE-AR DEPOSIT-AMOUNT-AR GIVING
    NEW-BALANCE-DL.
```

In this program it is necessary to use the computed value in a later computation, so it is necessary to declare a different item to receive the result of the computation. This is done at lines 46 and 47:

```
01  COMPUTED-AMOUNTS.
    02 NEW-BALANCE        PIC 9(4)V99 VALUE 0.
```

Note that NEW-BALANCE is *not* edited; the editing is carried out when NEW-BALANCE is moved to NEW-BALANCE-DL, which is defined at line 71 as

```
02 NEW-BALANCE-DL        PIC Z(4).99.
```

This additional step is made necessary by the requirement that the content of NEW-BALANCE be used in a computational statement after it is computed. This computation is carried out at line 118:

```
ADD NEW-BALANCE TO TOTAL-NEW-BALANCE.
```

Note that the following statement would be invalid:

```
ADD NEW-BALANCE-DL TO TOTAL-NEW-BALANCE.
```

Program 3c

```
 1 IDENTIFICATION DIVISION.
 2
 3 PROGRAM-ID. BALANCE-TOTALS-PRO3C.
 4 AUTHOR. HORN.
 5
 6 ENVIRONMENT DIVISION.
 7
 8 CONFIGURATION SECTION.
 9
10 SOURCE-COMPUTER.
11 OBJECT-COMPUTER.
12
13 INPUT-OUTPUT SECTION.
14
15 FILE-CONTROL.
16
17     SELECT ACCOUNT-FILE ASSIGN TO DISK.
18
19     SELECT REPORT-FILE ASSIGN TO PRINTER.
20
21 DATA DIVISION.
22
23 FILE SECTION.
24
25 FD  ACCOUNT-FILE
26     LABEL RECORDS ARE STANDARD
27     DATA RECORD IS ACCOUNT-RECORD.
28
29 01  ACCOUNT-RECORD.
30     02 OLD-BALANCE-AR     PIC 9999V99.
31     02 FILLER            PIC XX.
32     02 DEPOSIT-AMOUNT-AR  PIC 9999V99.
33     02 FILLER            PIC X(66).
34
35 FD  REPORT-FILE
36     LABEL RECORDS ARE OMITTED
37     DATA RECORD IS REPORT-RECORD.
38
39 01  REPORT-RECORD       PIC X(132).
40
41 WORKING-STORAGE SECTION.
42
43 01  FLAGS.
44     02 EOF-FLAG         PIC X(3)  VALUE "NO".
45
46 01  COMPUTED-AMOUNTS.
47     02 NEW-BALANCE      PIC 9(4)V99 VALUE 0.
48
49 01  ACCUMULATORS.
50     02 TOTAL-OLD-BALANCE   PIC 9(6)V99 VALUE 0.
51     02 TOTAL-DEPOSIT       PIC 9(6)V99 VALUE 0.
52     02 TOTAL-NEW-BALANCE   PIC 9(6)V99 VALUE 0.
53
54 01  COUNTERS.
55     02 NUMBER-OF-ACCOUNTS PIC 999     VALUE 0.
56
```

```
57 01  HEAD-LINE.
58     02 FILLER            PIC X(8)    VALUE SPACES.
59     02 FILLER            PIC X(11)   VALUE "OLD BALANCE".
60     02 FILLER            PIC X(5)    VALUE SPACES.
61     02 FILLER            PIC X(14)   VALUE "DEPOSIT AMOUNT".
62     02 FILLER            PIC X(3)    VALUE SPACES.
63     02 FILLER            PIC X(11)   VALUE "NEW BALANCE".
64
65 01  DETAIL-LINE.
66     02 FILLER            PIC X(10)   VALUE SPACES.
67     02 OLD-BALANCE-DL    PIC ZZZZ.99.
68     02 FILLER            PIC X(11)   VALUE SPACES.
69     02 DEPOSIT-AMOUNT-DL PIC Z(4).99.
70     02 FILLER            PIC X(7)    VALUE SPACES.
71     02 NEW-BALANCE-DL    PIC Z(4).99.
72
73 01  TOTAL-LINE-1.
74     02 FILLER               PIC X(8)    VALUE "TOTALS  ".
75     02 TOTAL-OLD-BALANCE-TL PIC Z(6).99.
76     02 FILLER               PIC X(9)    VALUE SPACES.
77     02 TOTAL-DEPOSIT-TL     PIC Z(6).99.
78     02 FILLER               PIC X(5)    VALUE SPACES.
79     02 TOTAL-NEW-BALANCE-TL PIC Z(6).99.
80
81 01  TOTAL-LINE-2.
82     02 FILLER               PIC X(21) VALUE
83         "NUMBER OF ACCOUNTS = ".
84     02 NUMBER-OF-ACCOUNTS-TL  PIC ZZZ.
85
86 PROCEDURE DIVISION.
87
88 1000-MAIN-CONTROL.
89
90     PERFORM 2000-INITIALIZE-REPORT.
91     PERFORM 2100-CREATE-REPORT
92          UNTIL EOF-FLAG = "YES".
93     PERFORM 2200-WRITE-TOTALS.
94     CLOSE ACCOUNT-FILE
95          REPORT-FILE.
96     STOP RUN.
97
98 2000-INITIALIZE-REPORT.
99
100    OPEN INPUT ACCOUNT-FILE
101        OUTPUT REPORT-FILE.
102    MOVE HEAD-LINE TO REPORT-RECORD.
103    WRITE REPORT-RECORD AFTER ADVANCING PAGE.
104    MOVE SPACES TO REPORT-RECORD.
105    WRITE REPORT-RECORD AFTER ADVANCING 1 LINES.
106    PERFORM 9000-READ-ACCOUNT-FILE.
107
```

Program 3c *(concluded)*

```
108 2100-CREATE-REPORT.
109
110     ADD OLD-BALANCE-AR DEPOSIT-AMOUNT-AR GIVING NEW-BALANCE.
111     MOVE OLD-BALANCE-AR     TO OLD-BALANCE-DL.
112     MOVE DEPOSIT-AMOUNT-AR TO DEPOSIT-AMOUNT-DL.
113     MOVE NEW-BALANCE        TO NEW-BALANCE-DL.
114     MOVE DETAIL-LINE        TO REPORT-RECORD.
115     WRITE REPORT-RECORD AFTER ADVANCING 1 LINES.
116     ADD OLD-BALANCE-AR      TO TOTAL-OLD-BALANCE.
117     ADD DEPOSIT-AMOUNT-AR   TO TOTAL-DEPOSIT.
118     ADD NEW-BALANCE         TO TOTAL-NEW-BALANCE.
119     ADD 1                   TO NUMBER-OF-ACCOUNTS.
120     PERFORM 9000-READ-ACCOUNT-FILE.
121
122 2200-WRITE-TOTALS.
123
124     MOVE TOTAL-OLD-BALANCE TO TOTAL-OLD-BALANCE-TL.
125     MOVE TOTAL-DEPOSIT      TO TOTAL-DEPOSIT-TL.
126     MOVE TOTAL-NEW-BALANCE TO TOTAL-NEW-BALANCE-TL.
127     MOVE TOTAL-LINE-1       TO REPORT-RECORD.
128     WRITE REPORT-RECORD AFTER ADVANCING 2 LINES.
129     MOVE NUMBER-OF-ACCOUNTS TO NUMBER-OF-ACCOUNTS-TL.
130     MOVE TOTAL-LINE-2        TO REPORT-RECORD.
131     WRITE REPORT-RECORD AFTER ADVANCING 1 LINES.
132
133 9000-READ-ACCOUNT-FILE.
134
135     READ ACCOUNT-FILE
136         AT END MOVE "YES" TO EOF-FLAG.
```

Figure 3.10   Sample output from Program 3c

	OLD BALANCE	DEPOSIT AMOUNT	NEW BALANCE
	10.00	20.00	30.00
	300.00	44.00	344.00
	550.00	20.00	570.00
	678.90	13.67	692.57
	1200.00	1000.00	2200.00
	34.78	12.10	46.88
TOTALS	2773.68	1109.77	3883.45
NUMBER OF ACCOUNTS =	6		

Any field used in performing a calculation must be strictly numeric; the field used to receive the result of a calculation may be numeric or edited. When a calculated result is not needed for further calculations, it is acceptable to place the result directly in the edited field, as was done in Program 2c. When a calculated result *is* needed for further calculation (as in this program), it is necessary to declare a numeric field as a temporary

Figure 3.11   Structure diagram for Program 3c

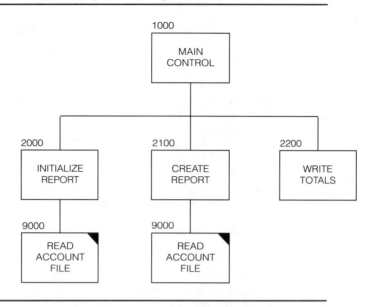

repository for the value. This field is used in later calculations and can be moved to an edited field for output if this is a requirement of the program.

You will note that all of the numeric items declared in WORKING-STORAGE are initialized with the VALUE clause. It is imperative that accumulators and counters be initialized with the value zero, but a field that will be used to receive the result of a computation does not absolutely have to be initialized, because whatever value is contained in the field will be replaced by a new value. We adopt the practice of initializing *all* fields defined in WORKING-STORAGE to simplify the tasks of testing and debugging the program. For example, if the program does not perform the required calculation for any reason, the field will have a predictable value. (If a field is not initialized, the value contained in the item is unpredictable and may vary with each execution of a program—a fact that can make the debugging process a bit more difficult than need be.)

The process of counting is carried out in line 119:

```
ADD 1 TO NUMBER-OF-ACCOUNTS.
```

After the first record is read, the content of NUMBER-OF-ACCOUNTS will be 0 + 1 = 1. After the second record is read, the value will be 1 + 1 = 2; after the third record is read, the value will be 2 + 1 = 3, and so forth.

One of the requirements of the program was to print a blank line below the column headings. This is accomplished at lines 104 and 105 by moving SPACES to REPORT-RECORD and by writing the record using the clause AFTER ADVANCING 1 LINES. (This technique can be used any time you need to write a single blank line on a report.)

Notice that the Z picture code is used in describing all numeric fields on output records. This results in suppression of leading (nonsignificant) zeros and in a substantial improvement in the appearance of the report (compare Figs. 2.18 and 3.10).

3.10 DEBUG CLINIC

The PERFORM Statement

A fundamental restriction on the use of the PERFORM statement is that no paragraph may PERFORM itself. The following code would be invalid:

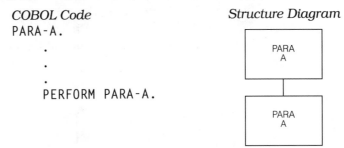

COBOL Code
```
PARA-A.
    .
    .
    .
    PERFORM PARA-A.
```

Structure Diagram

In general, COBOL compilers will not detect violations of this rule; however, when the program is executed, an infinite loop will result.

A more general restriction on the PERFORM statement is that no paragraph may PERFORM another paragraph that results in a PERFORM of the original paragraph. For example, consider the following code:

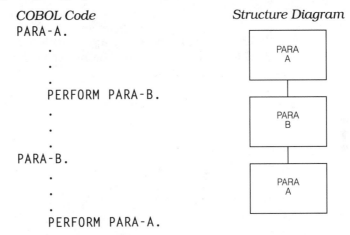

COBOL Code
```
PARA-A.
    .
    .
    .
    PERFORM PARA-B.
    .
    .
    .
PARA-B.
    .
    .
    .
    PERFORM PARA-A.
```

Structure Diagram

PARA-A PERFORMs PARA-B, which in turn PERFORMs PARA-A. As before, this code results in the creation of an infinite loop during execution. The error is perhaps more obvious from the structure diagram than from the COBOL code itself. This does not mean that a given paragraph may not occur several times in the structure diagram. For example, in Figure 3.8, 9000-READ-AMOUNT occurs twice. The first time it is subordinate to 2000-INITIALIZE-DATA; the second time it is subordinate to 2100-PROCESS-DATA. However, note that in Figure 3.8, no paragraph is subordinate to itself.

Program Structure

As we discussed earlier, constructing "good" structured programs is as much an art as a science; however, certain guidelines should be observed. We have already discussed some of them: use of three fundamental structures, use of descriptive data-names and paragraph-names, and segmentation of the program into control and operational paragraphs. The segmentation of a program has been the subject of a great deal of research, with the result that there is now general agreement on two principles: (1) the span of control for each paragraph should be limited and (2) the overall number of levels in the structure should be limited. Both of these have close analogs in organization theory.

In an organization, a manager should not be responsible for too many subordinates. The manager's "span of control" reaches an optimal limit; it is counterproductive to ask a manager to control more than that limit. In a similar way, a control paragraph in a COBOL program has a maximum "span of control." There is a limit to the number of subordinate paragraphs that a given paragraph should control directly. A structure diagram such as

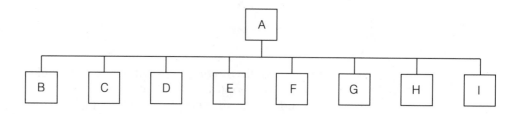

probably represents a paragraph with too many subordinates; its span of control is too large. It would be better to substitute an organization such as

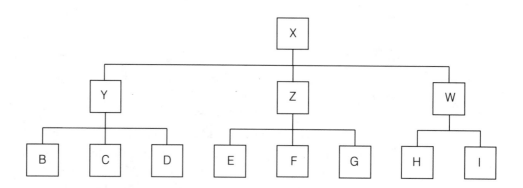

in which each control paragraph has a more restricted span of control.

There is no general agreement as to the number of paragraphs that represents an appropriate span of control in a COBOL program. It seems clear that ten subordinates are probably too many, but where the line is drawn is a matter of personal opinion.

In a management hierarchy, levels range from the chief executive officer at the top through various levels of middle management to the lowest level employee. As the number of levels of bureaucracy grows, problems of communication and control may develop. In a similar way, problems of communication and control may develop within a COBOL program which has too many levels of subordination. Thus, a structure such as

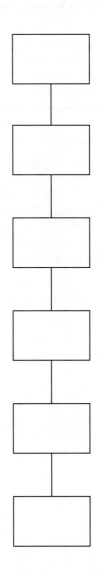

which has six levels, should probably be redesigned to have fewer levels. A structure such as

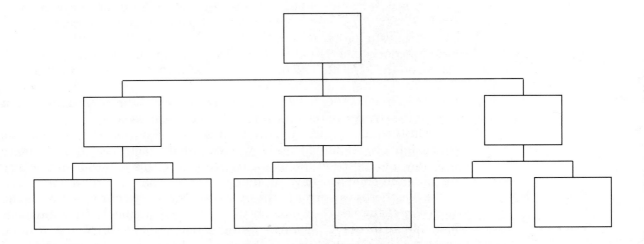

which has only three levels, is preferable to the six-level structure.

COBOL programmers should analyze the structure diagrams of programs they write to determine if each control paragraph has an appropriate span of control and if there are an appropriate number of levels of subordination within the program. It is usually possible to redesign any program that fails either of these tests.

Loop Control

In a structured program, loops are created by the iteration structure implemented in COBOL by the PERFORM/UNTIL statement. Recall that PERFORM/UNTIL causes execution of the specified paragraph until a condition is met. Three possible errors may occur: the paragraph is never executed at all, the paragraph is executed exactly one time, or the paragraph is executed continuously without a proper end, creating an infinite loop. Consider the PERFORM/UNTIL statement from Program 3b (lines 63 and 64):

```
PERFORM  2100-PROCESS-DATA
         UNTIL EOF-FLAG = "YES".
```

In flowchart form this would appear as

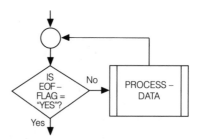

In one instance, suppose analysis of output from the program showed that the paragraph 2100-PROCESS-DATA was never executed at all. What would be the probable cause? The only reason is that EOF-FLAG is equal to "YES". This could happen in one of two ways: either the initial value of EOF-FLAG was specified to be "YES" in WORKING-STORAGE, or the program has caused the value of EOF-FLAG to become "YES" prior to execution of the PERFORM/UNTIL statement. A probable cause of this latter condition is that there were no records in the file so that when 9000-READ-AMOUNT is PERFORMed in 2000-INITIALIZE-DATA (Program 3b, line 72), the AT END clause on the READ statement causes the value "YES" to be moved to EOF-FLAG. In the first case, the programmer should rewrite the definition of EOF-FLAG in WORKING-STORAGE; in the second case, the programmer must ensure that there are records in the file to be processed.

On the other hand, suppose analysis of the output showed that the paragraph 2100-PROCESS-DATA was executed exactly one time. If there was only one record in the file being processed, this is obviously the way the program should behave. If, however, there was more than one record in the file, there is an error in the program. One likely source of error is the omission of the UNTIL clause on the PERFORM statement. The statement PERFORM 2100-PROCESS-DATA would cause 2100-PROCESS-DATA to be executed exactly one time. If the UNTIL clause is in its proper place, another cause for this error would be a statement within 2100-PROCESS-DATA which sets the value of EOF-FLAG to "YES" by mistake.

Or, suppose analysis of the output from the program led us to believe that the program had entered an infinite loop. For example, the program has been terminated because of excessive elapsed time or because a message has been produced indicating that an attempt has been made to read past end-of-file (i.e., an attempt to read more records than the file contains). If the value of EOF-FLAG never becomes "YES", the PERFORM/UNTIL statement will cause 2100-PROCESS-DATA to be executed forever.

There are two possible causes for this condition: either the READ operation has been omitted with 2100-PROCESS-DATA, or the AT END clause on the READ statement does not set EOF-FLAG equal to "YES". Omission of the READ operation within the loop will cause the program to appear to process the first record again and again. This is the most probable cause if the program terminates because of excessive time used. Failure of the program to set EOF-FLAG to "YES" when end-of-file is reached will generally result in an attempt to read past end-of-file.

3.11   COBOL-85 UPDATE

Two very significant changes that were incorporated into ANSI-85 COBOL are the inclusion of scope delimiters and an alternate form of the PERFORM statement called the "in-line" PERFORM.

COBOL statements are classed as either imperative or conditional. An **imperative statement** is a single action that is, in a sense, self-contained. Imperative statements include OPEN, ADD, MOVE, and CLOSE. By contrast, **conditional statements** may encompass other statements as part of the action being specified. The READ statement is an example of a conditional statement because of the AT END clause. The statements that are part of this clause are performed conditionally, only when the end of the file is reached. If the end of file is not read, the statement(s) in the AT END clause are not executed. The statements included in the AT END clause are said to be within the scope of the READ statement because they are controlled by that statement.

In COBOL-74, the only way to define the scope of a conditional statement is with the period; that is, the end of the sentence also terminates the statement. In COBOL-85, specific statements are included for all conditional statements that specify the termination of the scope of the statement; these are called **scope delimiters.** For the READ statement, the scope delimiter is

```
END-READ
```

Consider the following READ statement taken from Program 3a:

```
READ AMOUNT-FILE
    AT END MOVE "YES" TO EOF-FLAG.
```

The period following the AT END clause terminates the statement and the sentence.

In COBOL-85, the statement could be written as*

```
READ Amount-File
    AT END MOVE "YES" TO EOF-Flag
END-READ
```

The END-READ entry serves one of the functions of the period in the COBOL-74 program statement: It terminates the READ statement by telling the compiler where the AT END clause is finished. In COBOL-74, the READ statement with an AT END clause must be in a separate sentence; in COBOL-85, this is still possible but is not mandatory. When the END-READ entry is included, the READ statement could be embedded in a sentence containing other statements since it is no longer necessary for the end of the sentence to coincide with the end of the statement.

A general form for the READ statement in COBOL-85 is shown in Figure 3.12. Note that the END-READ entry is optional; a period can still be used to terminate the statement if desired.

Figure 3.12   General form of READ statement in COBOL-85

```
READ file-name
    AT END
            statement ...
END-READ
```

One characteristic of both COBOL-74 and COBOL-85 is that a sentence can be made up of any number of imperative statements. The only requirement is that a paragraph must contain at least one sentence. Because of the lack of scope delimiters in COBOL-74, it is customary to code each statement as a separate sentence whether this is technically necessary or not. Because of the presence of scope delimiters in COBOL-85, this practice is no longer necessary; in fact, some programmers adopt the standard of making each paragraph only one sentence and including the scope delimiters for each conditional statement (whether they are absolutely necessary or not). This practice can make a program easier to update at a later time if necessary.

Consider the following paragraph coded in COBOL-74 style:

```
2000-INITIALIZE-DATA.
    OPEN INPUT DATA-FILE
        OUTPUT REPORT-FILE.
    READ DATA-FILE
        AT END MOVE "YES" TO EOF-FLAG.
    MOVE HEADING-LINE TO REPORT-RECORD.
    WRITE REPORT-RECORD AFTER PAGE.
```

The paragraph is composed of four sentences. Because READ is a conditional statement, it must be terminated by a period. (If the period were omitted, the MOVE statement would be part of the scope of the READ; the only time the MOVE statement would be executed would be when the end of file was reached.) In COBOL-85 style, this paragraph could be coded as

---

*Remember that in COBOL-85 both upper- and lowercase characters can be used. In this text we follow the convention of capitalizing COBOL reserved words and capitalizing the first letter of programmer-defined elements.

```
2000-Initialize-Data.
    OPEN INPUT Data-File
        OUTPUT Report-File
    READ Data-File
        AT END MOVE "YES" TO EOF-Flag
    END-READ
    MOVE Heading-Line TO Report-Record
    WRITE Report-Record AFTER PAGE.
```

This paragraph contains one sentence made up of four statements, one of which is a conditional statement (READ).

In COBOL-74, the PERFORM statement always specifies a paragraph to be executed and is classified as an imperative statement. This version of the PERFORM statement is, of course, still available in COBOL-85, but the new standard includes a significant extension, sometimes referred to as an "in-line" PERFORM statement. This statement contains a clause that includes those statements to be executed and a scope delimiter (END-PERFORM) to specify the end of the range of statements controlled by the PERFORM statement. A general form for this statement is shown in Figure 3.13.

Figure 3.13   General form of in line PERFORM statement in COBOL-85

```
PERFORM [UNTIL condition]
        statement ...
END-PERFORM
```

Consider the following coding segment from Program 2a:

```
                    .
                    .
                    .
        PERFORM 2000-PROCESS-DATA
            UNTIL END-OF-FILE = "YES".
                    .
                    .
                    .
    2000-PROCESS-DATA.
        MOVE DATA-RECORD TO REPORT-RECORD.
        WRITE REPORT-RECORD AFTER ADVANCING 1 LINE.
        READ DATA-FILE
            AT END MOVE "YES" TO END-OF-FILE.
```

Using an in-line PERFORM statement, a programmer could write this segment in the following manner:

```
            .
            .
            .
     PERFORM UNTIL End-Of-File = "YES"
        MOVE Data-Record TO Report-Record
        WRITE Report-Record AFTER ADVANCING 1 LINE
        READ Data-File
           AT END MOVE "YES" TO End-Of-File
        END-READ
     END-PERFORM
            .
            .
            .
```

Program 3a85 is a revision of Program 3a which makes use of the COBOL features previously covered. Note that it is now possible to code that entire program as one module expressed as one sentence in one paragraph. Using the in-line PERFORM statement makes it possible to write larger paragraphs—that is, program modules that accomplish more work. It is no longer necessary to break a program into paragraphs each time a PERFORM statement is used simply because of the demands of the syntax of the language. On the other hand, unlimited use of this feature can make paragraphs that are too complex and violate the spirit of program modularity, an important part of structured programming.

Program 3a85

```
51 PROCEDURE DIVISION.
52
53 1000-Main-Control.
54
55     OPEN INPUT Amount-File
56          OUTPUT Print-File
57     READ Amount-File
58         AT END MOVE "YES" TO EOF-Flag
59     END-READ
60     PERFORM UNTIL EOF-Flag = "YES"
61             ADD Number-AR TO Grand-Total
62             MOVE Number-AR TO Number-DL
63             MOVE Detail-Line TO Print-Record
64             WRITE Print-Record AFTER ADVANCING 1 LINE
65             READ Amount-File
66                 AT END MOVE "YES" TO EOF-Flag
67             END-READ
68     END-PERFORM
69     MOVE Grand-Total TO Grand-Total-SL
70     MOVE Summary-Line TO Print-Record
71     WRITE Print-Record AFTER ADVANCING 2 LINES
72     CLOSE Amount-File
73           Print-File
74     STOP RUN.
```

3.12 SELF-TEST EXERCISES

1. What is a switch? Why are switches used?
2. What is an accumulator? Why are accumulators used?
3. What is a counter? Why are counters used?
4. The following is a procedure to copy the content of Old File onto New File:

   Main logic

       Open files
       Read old file
       Do Build file until end of file
       Close files
       Stop

   Build file

       Move old record to new record
       Write new record
       Read old file

   Modify the COBOL program segment shown in Figure 3.14 so that the program will function correctly. (This program could be used to make a duplicate of a file for backup purposes.)

Figure 3.14   Program with logical errors

```
Line
1       PROCEDURE DIVISION.
2
3       1000-MAIN-LOGIC.
4
5           PERFORM 2000-INITIALIZE-DATA.
6           PERFORM 2100-BUILD-FILE.
7           PERFORM 2200-CLOSE-FILES.
8           STOP RUN.
9
10      2000-INITIALIZE-DATA.
11
12          OPEN INPUT OLD-FILE
13              OUTPUT NEW-FILE.
14          PERFORM 9000-READ-OLD-FILE.
15
16      2100-BUILD-FILE.
17
18          MOVE OLD-RECORD TO NEW-RECORD.
19          WRITE NEW-RECORD.
20
21      2200-CLOSE-FILES.
22
23          CLOSE OLD-FILE
24              NEW-FILE.
25
26      9000-READ-OLD-FILE.
27
28          READ OLD-FILE
29              AT END MOVE "YES" TO EOF-FLAG.
```

5. What purpose is served by numbers used with paragraph-names? Are the numbers required by COBOL syntax, or are they part of structured programming style?

6. Classify each of the following paragraph-names as "desirable" or "undesirable":

```
READ-DATA-FILE
ANSWER
DO-COMPUTATIONS
DATA-MOVEMENT
ZZYZX
```

For each undesirable paragraph-name, suggest a more desirable alternative.

7. What is a structure diagram? Why are structure diagrams useful?

8. Rewrite the PROCEDURE DIVISION of Program 2c in the modular form described in this chapter. Draw the associated structure diagram. Classify each paragraph as providing a control or an operational function.

9. Draw the structure diagram of the program shown in Figure 3.14.

10. What is the difference between an imperative statement and a conditional statement? Give examples of each type of statement.

11. What is a scope delimiter? What is the basic scope delimiter used in COBOL-74? What scope delimiters were added in COBOL-85?

12. What is an in-line PERFORM statement? What effect does the use of this statement have on the structure of a program?

3.13 PROGRAMMING EXERCISES

1. A file contains daily sales records for a small retail business. The format for each record is

Positions	Content
1–4	Department number
5–10	Date
11–15	Amount of sale (999V99)

Write a program to list these records with appropriate headings. Compute the total of the sale amounts and print a line at the conclusion of the report containing this total. (A printer spacing chart for the desired report is shown in Figure 3.15.)

2. A real estate office maintains a file containing a record for each property it handles. The records have the following format:

Positions	Content
1–10	Multiple Listing Service Number (MLS Number)
11–18	Sale price (in dollars - PIC 9(8))

Write a program to compute and print the total price for the properties and the total number of properties.

Figure 3.15 Printer spacing chart for Exercise 1

NOTES		0 1234567890	1 1234567890	2 1234567890	3 1234567890 1
Column Heading	1	DEPARTMENT		SALE	
	2	NUMBER	DATE	AMOUNT	
	3				
Detail Line	4	9999	99/99/99	ZZZ.99	
	5				
Total Line 1"	6		TOTAL	ZZZZ.99	
	7				
	8				
	9				
	10				
	11				
2"	12				

3. Modify the program you wrote for Exercise 1 in Chapter 2 (Section 2.14) to compute the total of the current balances, and print the number of customers in the file.

4. Modify the program you wrote for Exercise 2 in Chapter 2 (Section 2.14) to print the number of mailing labels printed.

5. Modify the program you wrote for Exercise 3 in Chapter 2 (Section 2.14) to compute and print the totals of all grade-1, grade-2, and grade-3 values. Also print the number of records in the file as the last line of the report.

6. Modify the program you wrote for Exercise 4 in Chapter 2 (Section 2.14) to compute and print totals of items for each warehouse. Also compute and print the number of inventory items represented in the file.

4. INPUT, OUTPUT, AND DATA MOVEMENT

4.1 PROGRAM EXAMPLE

Problem Statement

The ABC Department Store maintains an inventory file showing the stock number, description, quantity on hand, and unit cost for each item it stocks. The salesclerks need a listing of the file so they can ascertain quickly the availability of items. The purchasing agent needs a listing of the file to aid in making decisions on which items should be reordered. The president of the store has expressed curiosity about the total number of different items carried by the store; he feels the information could be used in an advertising campaign he is planning. Figure 4.1 shows a printer spacing chart for the desired report.

Problem Analysis

Note that the report is made up of the following elements:

> Page headings
> Column headings
> Detail lines
> Summary line

As we have seen, this organization is quite typical of most reports written for business purposes. Page headings and column headings must be written before any detail lines are produced. The report requires one detail line for each record in the file being processed. The summary line is printed

Figure 4.1   Printer spacing chart for Inventory Report

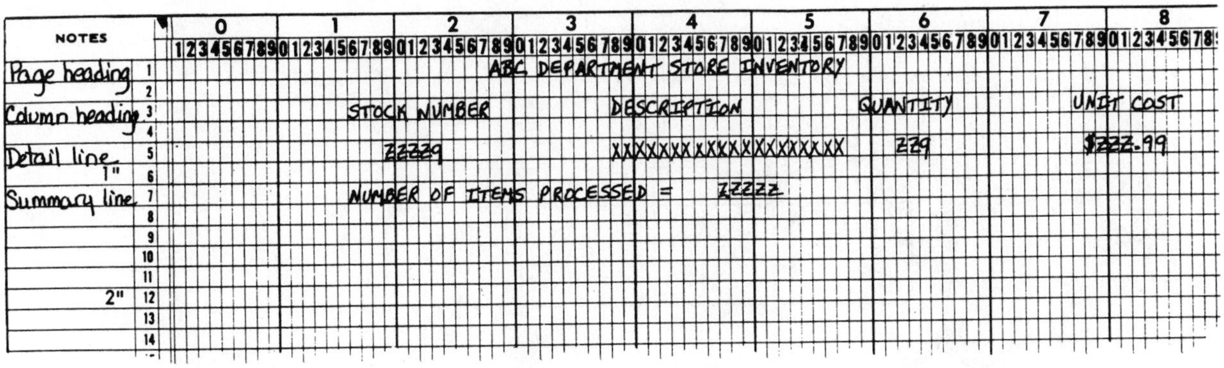

Figure 4.2 Plan for Inventory Report Program

Main control

  Open files
  Write headings
  Read product file
  Do Process data until end of file
  Write summary line
  Close files
  Stop

Process data

  Add 1 to number items processed
  Move input fields to detail line
  Write detail line
  Read product file

after all records in the file have been processed. A plan for this program is shown in Figure 4.2.

Problem Solution

A program for the problem is shown in Program 4a. Figure 4.3 shows the structure diagram for this program. Note that the routines (`3000-CREATE-DETAIL-LINE` and `3100-WRITE-DETAIL-LINE`) involve several statements. Structuring these routines as separate paragraphs aids in keeping the paragraphs containing the primary logic of the program (`1000-MAIN-CONTROL` and `2100-PROCESS-DATA`) simple, short, and easy to understand. A sample of the output produced by the program is shown in Figure 4.4.

Figure 4.3 Structure diagram for Program 4a

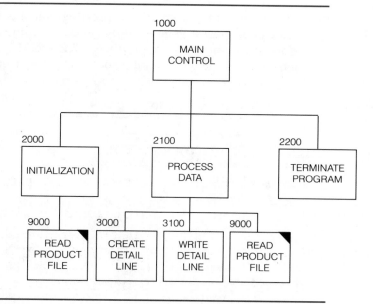

Figure 4.4   Sample output from Program 4a

```
                          ABC DEPARTMENT STORE INVENTORY
   STOCK NUMBER           DESCRIPTION            QUANTITY           UNIT COST
      11111               WIDGET                    1             $   2.00
      22222               GADGET                    3             $   9.00
      33333               RATCHET                   4             $  11.11
      44444               CUTTER                   20             $300.00
      55555               SPADE                   100             $   7.00
      66666               CLUB                     99             $  56.90
              NUMBER OF ITEMS PROCESSED =           6
```

4.2   THE SELECT AND FD ENTRIES

Every file to be processed by a program must also be defined in a SELECT statement in the FILE-CONTROL paragraph of the INPUT-OUTPUT SECTION of the ENVIRONMENT DIVISION. The purpose of the SELECT statement is to associate the file with a particular type of physical device. The general form of the SELECT statement is

```
SELECT file-name ASSIGN TO system-name.
```

For example, in Program 4a, the file PRODUCT-FILE is associated with a disk file in the statement (line 17)

```
SELECT PRODUCT-FILE ASSIGN TO DISK.
```

The system-names associated with particular devices vary from one compiler to another. Check with your instructor or with the local system manual to find out what system-names to use.

One FD entry is required in the FILE SECTION of the DATA DIVISION for each file to be processed. A general form for the FD entry is

```
FD   file-name
          ⎰ RECORD IS  ⎱  ⎰ STANDARD ⎱
     LABEL ⎱ RECORDS ARE⎰  ⎱ OMITTED  ⎰
     ⎡      ⎰ RECORD IS  ⎱                              ⎤
     ⎢ DATA ⎱ RECORDS ARE⎰  data-name-1 [ data-name-2] . . . ⎥ .
     ⎣                                                  ⎦
```

Program 4a processes two files, so two FD entries are required—one for the file PRODUCT-FILE (lines 25–27) and one for the file REPORT-FILE (lines 36–38). A record description must be provided following the FD entry. The record description may be quite simple, such as the description of the record PRINT-RECORD (line 40), a sequence of 132 characters, or quite complex, such as the description of the record PRODUCT-RECORD (lines 29–34), which is subdivided into a number of fields.

In general, a record will contain several fields. If the description of these fields is not written in the FILE SECTION, then it is written as a part of WORKING-STORAGE. This approach is used with the file REPORT-FILE in Program 4a. There are four different types of output records for this file. The description of these records—MAJOR-HEADING (lines 50–53), MINOR-HEADING (lines 55–63), DETAIL-LINE (lines 65–73), and TOTAL-LINE (lines 75–80)—is placed in the WORKING-STORAGE SECTION. The program moves the appropriate record to the output record before writing a record on the file PRINT-FILE (for example, lines 96, 98, and 125). Note that these descriptions make use of the VALUE clause to specify the content of a number of fields. The VALUE clause may *not* be used in a record-description-

Program 4a

```
 1 IDENTIFICATION DIVISION.
 2
 3 PROGRAM-ID. INVENTORY-PRO4A.
 4 AUTHOR. HORN.
 5
 6 ENVIRONMENT DIVISION.
 7
 8 CONFIGURATION SECTION.
 9
10 SOURCE-COMPUTER.
11 OBJECT-COMPUTER.
12
13 INPUT-OUTPUT SECTION.
14
15 FILE-CONTROL.
16
17     SELECT PRODUCT-FILE ASSIGN TO DISK.
18
19     SELECT REPORT-FILE ASSIGN TO PRINTER.
20
21 DATA DIVISION.
22
23 FILE SECTION.
24
25 FD  PRODUCT-FILE
26     LABEL RECORDS ARE STANDARD
27     DATA RECORD IS PRODUCT-RECORD.
28
29 01  PRODUCT-RECORD.
30     02 STOCK-NUMBER-PR      PIC 9(5).
31     02 DESCRIPTION-PR       PIC X(20).
32     02 QUANTITY-PR          PIC 9(3).
33     02 UNIT-COST-PR         PIC 999V99.
34     02 FILLER               PIC X(47).
35
36 FD  REPORT-FILE
37     LABEL RECORDS ARE OMITTED
38     DATA RECORD IS PRINT-RECORD.
39
40 01  PRINT-RECORD            PIC X(132).
41
```

Program 4a *(continued)*

```
42 WORKING-STORAGE SECTION.
43
44 01  FLAGS.
45      02 EOF-FLAG              PIC X(3) VALUE "NO".
46
47 01  TOTALS.
48      02 RECORDS-IN            PIC 9(5) VALUE ZERO.
49
50 01  MAJOR-HEADING.
51      02 FILLER               PIC X(27) VALUE SPACES.
52      02 FILLER               PIC X(30) VALUE
53        "ABC DEPARTMENT STORE INVENTORY".
54
55 01  MINOR-HEADING.
56      02 FILLER       PIC X(4)  VALUE SPACES.
57      02 FILLER       PIC X(12) VALUE "STOCK NUMBER".
58      02 FILLER       PIC X(11) VALUE SPACES.
59      02 FILLER       PIC X(11) VALUE "DESCRIPTION".
60      02 FILLER       PIC X(10) VALUE SPACES.
61      02 FILLER       PIC X(8)  VALUE "QUANTITY".
62      02 FILLER       PIC X(10) VALUE SPACES.
63      02 FILLER       PIC X(9)  VALUE "UNIT COST".
64
65 01  DETAIL-LINE.
66      02 FILLER               PIC X(8) VALUE SPACES.
67      02 STOCK-NUMBER-DL      PIC ZZZZ9.
68      02 FILLER               PIC X(14) VALUE SPACES.
69      02 DESCRIPTION-DL       PIC X(20).
70      02 FILLER               PIC X(4) VALUE SPACES.
71      02 QUANTITY-DL          PIC ZZ9.
72      02 FILLER               PIC X(13) VALUE SPACES.
73      02 UNIT-COST-DL         PIC $ZZZ.99.
74
75 01  TOTAL-LINE.
76      02 FILLER               PIC X(15) VALUE SPACES.
77      02 FILLER               PIC X(27) VALUE
78        "NUMBER OF ITEMS PROCESSED =".
79      02 FILLER               PIC X(4) VALUE SPACES.
80      02 RECORDS-IN-TL        PIC Z(5).
81
```

Program 4a   *(concluded)*

```
 82 PROCEDURE DIVISION.
 83
 84 1000-MAIN-CONTROL.
 85
 86     PERFORM 2000-INITIALIZATION.
 87     PERFORM 2100-PROCESS-DATA
 88           UNTIL EOF-FLAG = "YES".
 89     PERFORM 2200-TERMINATE-PROGRAM.
 90     STOP RUN.
 91
 92 2000-INITIALIZATION.
 93
 94     OPEN INPUT PRODUCT-FILE
 95          OUTPUT REPORT-FILE.
 96     MOVE MAJOR-HEADING TO PRINT-RECORD.
 97     WRITE PRINT-RECORD AFTER PAGE.
 98     MOVE MINOR-HEADING TO PRINT-RECORD.
 99     WRITE PRINT-RECORD AFTER ADVANCING 2 LINES.
100     PERFORM 9000-READ-PRODUCT-FILE.
101
102 2100-PROCESS-DATA.
103
104     ADD 1 TO RECORDS-IN.
105     PERFORM 3000-CREATE-DETAIL-LINE.
106     PERFORM 3100-WRITE-DETAIL-LINE.
107     PERFORM 9000-READ-PRODUCT-FILE.
108
109 2200-TERMINATE-PROGRAM.
110
111     MOVE RECORDS-IN TO RECORDS-IN-TL.
112     WRITE PRINT-RECORD FROM TOTAL-LINE AFTER ADVANCING 2 LINES.
113     CLOSE PRODUCT-FILE
114           REPORT-FILE.
115
116 3000-CREATE-DETAIL-LINE.
117
118     MOVE STOCK-NUMBER-PR   TO   STOCK-NUMBER-DL.
119     MOVE DESCRIPTION-PR    TO   DESCRIPTION-DL.
120     MOVE QUANTITY-PR       TO   QUANTITY-DL.
121     MOVE UNIT-COST-PR      TO   UNIT-COST-DL.
122
123 3100-WRITE-DETAIL-LINE.
124
125     MOVE DETAIL-LINE TO PRINT-RECORD.
126     WRITE PRINT-RECORD AFTER ADVANCING 2 LINES.
127
128 9000-READ-PRODUCT-FILE.
129
130     READ PRODUCT-FILE
131           AT END MOVE "YES" TO EOF-FLAG.
```

entry in the FILE SECTION; its use is restricted to definitions of data items in the WORKING-STORAGE SECTION. If you wish to define a record which will contain constant data, employ the technique used with the file REPORT-FILE in Program 4a:

1. Define the data-record as an elementary item of appropriate length in the FD entry.
2. Define records and their content in the WORKING-STORAGE SECTION.
3. Move data to the data-record defined in the FD entry before processing.

This procedure is usually followed for output files, as they are likely to contain records having constant data.

4.3 THE OPEN AND CLOSE STATEMENTS

Before any file in a program can be processed, it must be opened. The OPEN statement causes the computing system to perform various initialization procedures required before the file can be processed. The general form of the OPEN statement is

```
OPEN    {INPUT  file-name-1    [file-name-2] . . .} . . .
        {OUTPUT file-name-3    [file-name-4] . . .}
```

The programmer must specify whether a file is being opened as an INPUT or an OUTPUT file. It is permissible to READ records from a file opened as an INPUT file, and it is permissible to WRITE records onto a file opened as an OUTPUT file. It is *not* permissible to WRITE a record onto a file opened as INPUT or to READ a record from a file opened as OUTPUT. An attempt to perform either of these operations will result in an execution-time diagnostic message, and the program will be canceled.

——————— Examples ———————

To open INCOME-FILE as an INPUT file, use the statement

```
OPEN INPUT INCOME-FILE.
```

To open the file PRINTED-REPORT-FILE as an OUTPUT file, use the statement

```
OPEN OUTPUT PRINTED-REPORT-FILE.
```

More than one file at a time may be opened by an OPEN statement. For example, the statement

```
OPEN OUTPUT PRINTED-REPORT-FILE NEW-MASTER-FILE.
```

will cause the files PRINTED-REPORT-FILE and NEW-MASTER-FILE to be opened as OUTPUT files.

The CLOSE statement causes a file to become unavailable for further processing. Any file which is opened in a program should also be closed before the program terminates. The general form of the CLOSE statement is

```
CLOSE file-name . . .
```

One or more files may be closed in a CLOSE statement. Consider, for example, the following CLOSE statements:

```
CLOSE INPUT-FILE OUTPUT-FILE. (2 files are closed)
CLOSE PRINTED-REPORT-FILE. (1 file is closed)
```

Any file that has not been opened is assumed to be closed. A file may be opened and closed any number of times in a program. However, a file must be closed before it can be opened. In a typical file processing program, such as the one shown in Program 4a, files are opened (2000-INITIALIZATION) and processed (2100-PROCESS-DATA). After all inputs and outputs have been performed, the files are closed (2200-TERMINATE-PROGRAM).

4.4 THE READ STATEMENT

A READ statement causes the computer to read one record from a specified file. The contents of the record are placed in the record area specified in the FD entry for the file. A general form for the READ statement is

```
READ file-name [INTO data-name] AT END statement. . .
```

The file addressed in a READ statement must be currently opened as an INPUT file. When the end-of-file record is read, the statement or statements at the AT END clause of the statement are executed. For example, the statement

```
READ DATA-FILE
      AT END CLOSE DATA-FILE
            STOP RUN.
```

will cause the statements CLOSE DATA-FILE and STOP RUN to be executed when end-of-file is reached on DATA-FILE. In a structured program, a switch is often set when the end-of-file record is read. (A **switch** is a data item which has only two possible values, e.g., "1" and "0", "yes" and "no", "on" and "off".) A typical READ statement in a structured program would be

```
READ DATA-FILE
      AT END MOVE "YES" TO EOF-FLAG.
```

The contents of the switch (in this case, EOF-FLAG) can be tested in subsequent instructions to determine whether the record should be processed (if not end-of-file) or whether processing should be terminated (if end-of-file has been reached). See, for example, the paragraph 1000-MAIN-CONTROL in Program 4a.

When the INTO clause is included on a READ statement, data is placed in the record area specified in the FD entry for the file and also into the specified data-name. This feature is often used to allow the placement of a detailed description of an input record in the WORKING-STORAGE section. For example, in Program 4a, the FD entry for the file PRODUCT-FILE could be rewritten as

```
FD  PRODUCT-FILE
     LABEL RECORDS ARE STANDARD
     DATA RECORD IS PRODUCT-RECORD.
01  PRODUCT-RECORD PIC X(80).
```

The following entries (which define the fields contained on the record) could be added to the `WORKING-STORAGE` section:

```
01   PRODUCT-RECORD-DESCRIPTION.
     02  STOCK-NUMBER-PR    PIC 9(5).
     02  DESCRIPTION-PR     PIC X(20).
     02  QUANTITY-PR        PIC 9(3).
     02  UNIT-COST-PR       PIC 999V99.
     02  FILLER             PIC X(47).
```

With these changes, the `READ` statement at lines 130 through 131 in Program 4a would be changed to

```
READ PRODUCT-FILE INTO PRODUCT-RECORD-DESCRIPTION
     AT END MOVE "YES" TO EOF-FLAG.
```

Data would be placed into the input-record `PRODUCT-RECORD` and into `PRODUCT-RECORD-DESCRIPTION`.

Your instructor may want you to follow this practice in the programs you write.

4.5 THE MOVE STATEMENT

The `MOVE` statement causes the copying of data values from one location in memory to another. The general form of the `MOVE` statement is

```
MOVE data-name-1 TO data-name-2 . . .
```

The data at the location from which the information is moved (the sending item) is not changed; the data at the target location (the receiving item) is replaced by new data. For example, suppose `FLDA` and `FLDB` are as shown in Figure 4.5. After execution of the statement

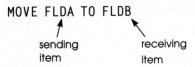

the contents of `FLDA` are unchanged; the contents of `FLDB` are the same as `FLDA`. More than one item may be designated as a receiving item. In this case, the contents of the sending item are moved to each of the receiving

Figure 4.5   Results of the execution of `MOVE FLDA TO FLDB`

Contents before `MOVE`

FLDA   FLDB

| J | O | E | | | | X | Y | Z | W | |

Contents after `MOVE`

FLDA   FLDB

| J | O | E | | | | J | O | E | | |

items. For example, the statement

```
MOVE FLDA TO FLDB FLDC FLDD.
```

will cause FLDB, FLDC, and FLDD to receive identical data from FLDA.

4.6   THE WRITE STATEMENT

The WRITE statement causes one record to be written onto an output file. A general form of the WRITE statement is shown in Figure 4.6. Remember that the WRITE statement always addresses a record, while a READ statement addresses a file. The record-name used in the WRITE statement must be the same as the record declared in the FD entry for the file. The contents of the record are transferred to the appropriate file. The file addressed in a WRITE statement must currently be open as an output file.

If the printer is the device assigned to the file, the BEFORE/AFTER clause is used to specify the vertical spacing of the printed output line. The AFTER option causes vertical spacing to be performed prior to writing a new line. The BEFORE option causes the line to be written first, and then the vertical spacing is performed. In either case, the PAGE entry will cause the advancement of paper to the top of a new page; the use of an integer (such as 0, 1, 2, 3) causes the printer to skip the specified number of lines.

Data to be written onto a file must be present in the output record area before the WRITE statement is executed. In Program 4a, four types of output lines are defined in the WORKING-STORAGE SECTION: MAJOR-HEADING (line 50), MINOR-HEADING (line 55), DETAIL-LINE (line 65), and TOTAL-LINE (line 75). Prior to the WRITE operation for the first three types of lines, the contents of each appropriate output line are moved to the output record area. For example, in lines 96 and 97 you find

```
MOVE MAJOR-HEADING TO PRINT-RECORD.
WRITE PRINT-RECORD AFTER PAGE.
```

Use of the FROM clause can simplify output operations of this type. When the FROM clause is included, the contents of the designated data-name are automatically moved to the output record area before the WRITE operation is performed. The two statements above could be combined as follows:

```
WRITE PRINT-RECORD FROM MAJOR-HEADING AFTER PAGE.
```

The contents of MAJOR-HEADING are moved to PRINT-RECORD before the output record is written. The FROM clause is used in Program 4a in writing the TOTAL-LINE (line 112):

```
WRITE PRINT-RECORD FROM TOTAL-LINE AFTER ADVANCING 2 LINES.
```

Figure 4.6   General form of the WRITE statement

```
WRITE record-name          [FROM identifier-1]
   ⎡ ⎧ BEFORE ⎫                ⎧ ⎧⎧ identifier-2 ⎫      ⎡ LINE  ⎤⎫⎫
   ⎢ ⎨ AFTER  ⎬  ADVANCING     ⎨ ⎨⎨ integer      ⎬      ⎢ LINES ⎥⎬⎬
   ⎢ ⎩        ⎭                ⎪ ⎩⎩              ⎭      ⎣       ⎦ ⎪
   ⎢                           ⎪ ⎧ mnemonic-name ⎫                ⎪
   ⎣                           ⎩ ⎩ PAGE          ⎭                ⎭
```

4.7 DATA TYPES

Any field may be classified as numeric, alphanumeric, numeric edited, or alphanumeric edited, depending on the type of picture codes used in the PICTURE clause associated with the field.

Numeric fields are used for computational purposes—that is, the contents of a numeric field can have arithmetic operations performed on it. An **alphanumeric field** contains a series of characters; no arithmetic operations are permitted. **Edited fields** are used to change the appearance of data, usually for output purposes. A **numeric edited field** is used to edit numeric data, while an **alphanumeric edited field** is used to edit alphanumeric data. (You have used numeric edited fields to insert a printed decimal point and to suppress leading nonsignificant zeros in numeric data.) Following is a detailed discussion of each of these data types and the associated picture codes.

A numeric field may contain only numeric data. A numeric field is defined using the picture codes 9, V, P, and S. The 9 specifies a numeric digit (i.e., a single number), V specifies the position of the decimal point, P shows the position of a digit assumed to have value zero, and S specifies that the item is to be signed (i.e., may become negative).

─────── **Examples** ───────

```
03 SAL-CODE PIC 9.
```

SAL-CODE is a one-digit numeric field. For instance, this field could be used if the salary paid for a particular project is coded as a single-digit.

```
03 SALARY PIC 999V99.
```

SALARY is a five-digit field such as 423.78 (representing dollars). The decimal point is assumed to be placed between the third and fourth digits. Note that such salaries cannot be negative because the S code is not included in the description of the field. In Program 4a, STOCK-NUMBER-PR (line 30), QUANTITY-PR (line 32), UNIT-COST-PR (line 33), and RECORDS-IN (line 48) are unsigned numeric items.

```
01  AMOUNT PIC S9(4)V9(3).
```

AMOUNT is a seven-digit field. The decimal point is placed between the fourth and fifth digits. The item may become negative since the S is present. (If an S is not present in the picture codes of a numeric item, then the item is assumed always to be positive.) If used, an S must precede other codes used in describing the item.

An alphanumeric field may contain any string of numeric, alphabetic, or special characters. Alphanumeric fields may be defined in two ways:

1. All group items are considered as alphanumeric regardless of the definition of the elementary items in the group. Recall that a group item is an item which is subdivided into one or more elementary items. The specification of group items does not contain a PICTURE clause. For example, in Program 4a, MAJOR-HEADING, MINOR-HEADING, DETAIL-LINE, TOTAL-LINE, PRODUCT-RECORD, FLAGS, and TOTALS are group items and, therefore, are classed as alphanumeric.

2. Fields defined using the picture code X are alphanumeric. The X represents an alphanumeric character. In Program 4a, DESCRIPTION-PR (line 31), PRINT-RECORD (line 40), EOF-FLAG (line 45), and all of the FILLER entries are alphanumeric because of the picture code X.

Fields defined using the picture codes Z, $, *, and so on, are numeric edited items. The purpose of these codes is to prepare a numeric item for readability on a report. For example, in Program 4a, the items STOCK-NUMBER-DL (line 67), QUANTITY-DL (line 71), UNIT-COST-DL (line 73), and RECORDS-IN-TL (line 80) are given numeric edited pictures and, therefore, are nonnumeric items. The Z provides for the substitution of a blank for a nonsignificant leading zero. The decimal point is inserted in place of the assumed position of the decimal point. The $ is printed to label items which represent dollar amounts.

Alphanumeric edited fields are used to edit alphanumeric fields for output. Picture codes used to specify an alphanumeric edited field include X, B (for blank insertion), 0 (for zero insertion), and / (for slash insertion).

Arithmetic operations can be performed only on numeric-type data items. Arithmetic operations, therefore, cannot be performed on data which is alphanumeric, numeric edited, or alphanumeric edited.

A summary of the relationship between picture codes and the type of data defined is shown in Figure 4.7. All of these codes will be described in detail later in this chapter.

4.8   DATA MOVEMENT

Data processing involves a lot of data movement. Sometimes you have to move alphanumeric data from one data item to another; more often you have to move numeric data to a numeric edited field. All would be easy enough if the receiving fields always had as many characters (or elements or numbers or letters) as the data, but that does not always happen. For instance, a check-writing program in a major Blue Cross plan does not have very many spaces assigned for the name of the person receiving the check. So instead of the person's full name, which the computer has in its subscriber file—properly spelled and listed by name, address, and policy number—Alphonse Hornswogger will get a check made out to HORNS, A. Clearly, the data item in the check-writing program has fewer spaces than the name in the input file it is processing.[1] The rules for fitting data into spaces too large or too small depend on the kind of data you are using, as detailed below.

When alphanumeric data is moved from one field to another, characters are moved from left to right. If the sending field and receiving field have exactly the same length, the receiving field becomes an exact duplicate of the sending field.

---

[1] Hornswogger endorses his check by writing HORNS, A. first; then, underneath the endorsement he writes his full and correct name. Can truncating (cutting off) a name lead to confusion? No, because the Blue Cross computer is really reading the subscriber account number, for which there are always enough data spaces. The computer does not pay much attention to Mr. Hornswogger's name.

Figure 4.7   Summary of picture codes

Data Class	Code	Meaning
Alphanumeric	X	Alphanumeric character
Numeric	9	Numeric digit
	V	Implied position of decimal point
	S	Signed field
	P	Scaling
Alphanumeric Edited	X	Alphanumeric character
	B	Blank insertion
	/	Slash insertion
	0	Zero insertion
Numeric Edited	9	Numeric digit
	.	Decimal point
	Z	Zero suppression
	,	Comma insertion
	$	Dollar sign (fixed or floating)
	+	Plus sign (fixed or floating)
	−	Minus sign (fixed or floating)
	*	Asterisk (check protection)
	DB	Debit insertion
	CR	Credit insertion
	B	Blank insertion
	/	Slash insertion
	0	Zero insertion

───────── **Example** ─────────

```
MOVE FLDA TO FLDB.
```

| A | B | C | D | | A | B | C | D |

FLDA PIC X(4)   FLDB PIC X(4)

If the receiving field is longer than the sending field, blanks are added to the rightmost positions of the receiving field

───────── **Example** ─────────

```
MOVE FLDA TO FLDB.
```

These blanks are inserted because FLDB is longer than FLDA.

| 1 | A | 3 | B | | 1 | A | 3 | B | | |

FLDA PIC X(4)   FLDB PIC X(6)

If the receiving field is shorter than the sending field, the *rightmost* characters are truncated.

—————— Example ——————

```
MOVE FLDA TO FLDB.

1 A 3 B              1 A

FLDA PIC X(4)     FLDB PIC XX
```

The JUSTIFIED RIGHT clause can be used in the definition of an alphanumeric item in the DATA DIVISION to cause data moved to the field to be right justified with truncation and padding on the left.

—————— Example ——————

```
MOVE FLDA TO FLDB.

1 A 3 B                    1 A 3 B

FLDA PIC X(4)     FLDB PIC X(6) JUSTIFIED RIGHT

MOVE FLDA TO FLDB.

1 A 3 B              3 B

FLDA PIC X(4)     FLDB PIC X(2) JUSTIFIED RIGHT
```

The rules for alphanumeric data movement are summarized by the examples in Figure 4.8.

Figure 4.8   Examples of alphanumeric data movement: MOVE FLDA TO FLDB

FLDA		FLDB		Comment
Definition	*Content*	*Definition*	*Content After* MOVE	
PIC XXX	A B C	PIC XXXX	A B C	Data is left justified with blanks inserted on the right.
PIC XXX	A B C	PIC XX	A B	Rightmost characters are truncated.
PIC XXX	A B C	PIC X(4) JUSTIFIED RIGHT	A B C	Data is right justified with blanks inserted on the left.
PIC XXX	A B C	PIC XX JUSTIFIED RIGHT	B C	Leftmost characters are truncated.
PIC XXX	A B C	PIC XXX JUSTIFIED RIGHT	A B C	When fields have the same width, the JUSTIFIED RIGHT clause has no effect.

Numeric Data

When numeric data is moved to a numeric-type data item, the digits to the left of the decimal point are moved from right to left. If the receiving field is too short, truncation of excess *leftmost* digits will be performed. If the receiving field is too long, zeros will be inserted in the unused leftmost digits.

─────── **Example** ───────

```
MOVE FLDA TO FLDB.
```

| 0 | 1 | 2 | 3 | 4 | | 0 | 1 | 2 | 3 | 4 |

FLDA PIC 99999   FLDB PIC 9(5)

| 0 | 1 | 2 | 3 | 4 | | 0 | 0 | 0 | 0 | 1 | 2 | 3 | 4 | Extra zeros were inserted because FLDB is longer than FLDA.

FLDA PIC 99999   FLDB PIC 9(8)

| 0 | 1 | 2 | 3 | 4 | | 2 | 3 | 4 | Truncation occurred because FLDB is shorter than FLDA.

FLDA PIC 99999   FLDB PIC 999

Digits to the right of the decimal point are moved from left to right. If the receiving field is too short, truncation of excess *rightmost* digits will be performed. If the receiving field is too long, zeros will be inserted in the unused rightmost digits. In the following examples, the caret symbol represents the assumed position of the decimal point.

─────── **Example** ───────

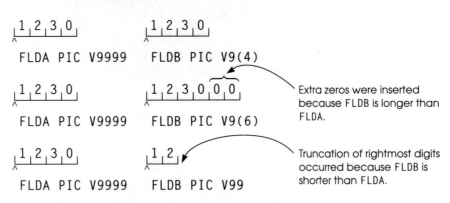

```
MOVE FLDA TO FLDB.
```

| 1 | 2 | 3 | 0 | | 1 | 2 | 3 | 0 |

FLDA PIC V9999   FLDB PIC V9(4)

| 1 | 2 | 3 | 0 | | 1 | 2 | 3 | 0 | 0 | 0 | Extra zeros were inserted because FLDB is longer than FLDA.

FLDA PIC V9999   FLDB PIC V9(6)

| 1 | 2 | 3 | 0 | | 1 | 2 | Truncation of rightmost digits occurred because FLDB is shorter than FLDA.

FLDA PIC V9999   FLDB PIC V99

Decimal points in two numeric fields are aligned before transferring digits in the MOVE operation. Transfers of digits to the left and to the right of the decimal point are carried out independently.

─── **Example** ───

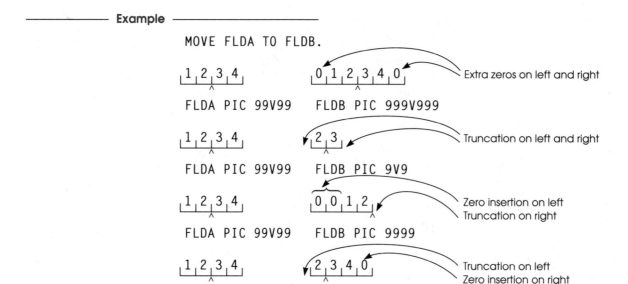

Internally, the sign of a data item is expressed as a code in the right-most digit of the item. For purposes of illustration in this book, we will show the sign by a raised − or + above the rightmost digit.

─── **Example** ───

```
  ‾
1,2,3,4,5
      ^
FLDA PIC S999V99     The value of FLDA is negative.
          +
0,0,1,2,3
      ^
FLDB PIC S999V99     The value of FLDB is positive.
```

If a signed data item is moved to an unsigned data item, the sign is lost. The value of the resulting field is unsigned and, therefore, positive.

─── **Example** ───

```
MOVE FLDA TO FLDB.
      ‾
1,2,3,4,5              1,2,3,4,5
      ^                       ^
FLDA PIC S999V99       FLDB PIC 999V99
```

If an unsigned data item is moved to a signed item, the resulting value is assumed to be positive.

——————— Example ———————

```
MOVE FLDA TO FLDB.
                                    +
 1 2 3 4 5         1 2 3 4 5
|_|_|_|_^_|        |_|_|_|_^_|

FLDA PIC 999V99    FLDB PIC S999V99
```

P Picture Code

The P picture code can be used to scale numeric data read from a data-record. The P takes the place of a decimal digit with assumed value zero.

——————— Example ———————

Suppose a record has a three-digit field representing the population of a city in thousands. An appropriate description of such a field would be

```
03 POPULATION PIC 999PPP.
```

For example, if the content of the field were

```
 1 2 3
|_|_|_|
```

the value of the item POPULATION would be 123,000 for purposes of computation and data movement.

——————— Example ———————

Suppose a record has a two-digit field representing a measurement in units of hundred-thousandths. An appropriate description would be

```
03 MEASUREMENT     PIC VPPP99.
```

Thus, if the content of the field was

```
 1 2
|_|_|
```

the value would be .00012.

When data is moved to or from a scaled field, the digits represented by P are used to align the decimal points prior to the movement of the data.

——————— Example ———————

```
MOVE FLDA TO FLDB.
 3 4                0 3 4 0 0 0
|_|_|               |_|_|_|_|_|_|

FLDA PIC 99PPP      FLDB PIC 999999.
```

For computational purposes, the value of FLDA and FLDB will be the same: 34,000.

The movement of numeric data is summarized in Figure 4.9.

Figure 4.9   Examples of numeric data movement: MOVE FLDA
TO FLDB
Note: the symbol ∧ is used to show the implied position of
the decimal point.

FLDA		FLDB		*Comment*
PICTURE	*Content*	PICTURE	*Content After* MOVE	
9999	0 1 2 3∧	999999	0 0 0 1 2 3∧	Extra zeros inserted on left.
9999	0 1 2 3∧	99	2 3∧	Truncation of leftmost digits.
99V99	0 1∧2 3	999V999	0 0 1∧2 3 0	Extra zero on left and right.
99V99	0 1∧2 3	9V9	1∧2	Truncation on left and right.
S99V99	0 1∧2 3̄	99V99	0 1∧2 3	Sign lost due to unsigned receiving field.
99V99	0 1∧2 3	S99V99	0 1∧2 3⁺	Unsigned data becomes positive.
99PP	1 2	9999V99	1 2 0 0∧0 0	The value of FLDA is 1200.
9(6)	1 2 3 4 5 6∧	999PPP	1 2 3	Scaling truncates rightmost digits but value is not changed.
V9(6)	∧0 0 0 1 2 3	VPPP99	1 2	Scaling truncates leftmost digits.

4.9   EDITING

The only time numeric data is moved into a nonnumeric field is for purposes of editing the data for output. The receiving field is described using
numeric edited picture codes. Numeric edited picture codes such as Z, $,
and period (.) react with the numeric digits moved into the field, resulting
in an appropriately edited character string.

Decimal Point Insertion (.)

The use of the decimal point (.) in a numeric edited picture causes the
decimal point to be inserted in the indicated position in the item. The
implied position of the decimal point in the numeric sending item is
aligned with the indicated position in the numeric edited receiving item.
Zeros will be inserted into the resulting field on the left or right if the
receiving item is longer than the sending item. Digits may also be truncated on the left or right if the receiving item is too short to receive all of the
digits of the sending field.

──────── **Example** ────────────

```
MOVE FLDA TO FLDB.
```

0	1	2	3	4

FLDA PIC 999V99   FLDB PIC 999.99

0	1	2	3	4

FLDA PIC 999V99   FLDB PIC 9999.9 ← Extra zero on left
Truncation on right

0	1	2	3	4

FLDA PIC 999V99   FLDB PIC 9.999   Truncation on left
Extra zero on right

If a V is used in an edited picture, the decimal point is *not* included in the receiving field, although it is used to align the implied decimal positions between the sending and receiving fields.

──────── **Example** ────────────

```
MOVE FLDA TO FLDB.
```

FLDA PIC 999V99   FLDB PIC 9V999

If FLDB is printed, only the characters 2340 would appear on the page.

Zero Suppression (Z)

The character Z in a numeric edited picture will cause substitution of blanks for leading zeros in the sending item. When a nonzero digit is encountered, that digit and all subsequent digits (zero or nonzero) are moved to the receiving field.

──────── **Example** ────────────

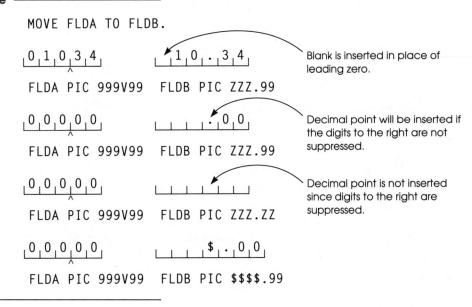

```
MOVE FLDA TO FLDB.
```

FLDA PIC 999V99   FLDB PIC ZZZ.99   Blank is inserted in place of leading zero.

FLDA PIC 999V99   FLDB PIC ZZZ.99   Decimal point will be inserted if the digits to the right are not suppressed.

FLDA PIC 999V99   FLDB PIC ZZZ.ZZ   Decimal point is not inserted since digits to the right are suppressed.

FLDA PIC 999V99   FLDB PIC $$$$.99

Figure 4.10 Examples of decimal point insertion and zero
suppression: `MOVE FLDA TO FLDB`

FLDA		FLDB		Comment
Definition	*Content*	*Definition*	*Content After* `MOVE`	
`PIC 999V99`	`0 1 2 3 4`	`PIC 999.99`	`0 1 2 . 3 4`	Decimal point insertion.
`PIC 999V99`	`0 1 2 3 4`	`PIC 99.999`	`1 2 . 3 4 0`	Digits truncated on left and padded on right.
`PIC 999V99`	`0 1 0 3 4`	`PIC ZZZ.99`	`1 0 . 3 4`	Blank inserted in place of leading zero.
`PIC 999V99`	`0 0 0 0 0`	`PIC ZZZ.ZZ`	` `	If value is zero, the field contains blanks.
`PIC 999V99`	`0 0 0 0 2`	`PIC ZZZ.ZZ`	`. 0 2`	If value is not zero, the decimal point is not suppressed.

The use of the decimal point and Z picture codes is summarized in Figure
4.10.

Dollar Sign Insertion ($)

The character $ used as the first character in a numeric edited picture will
cause the dollar sign to be the first character in the receiving item.

────── **Example** ──────

```
MOVE FLDA TO FLDB.
```

`0 1 0 3 4`   `$   1 0 . 3 4`

`FLDA PIC 999V99`   `FLDB PIC $ZZZ.99`

If more than one dollar sign is used in the edited picture, the character will
cause zero suppression in each position in which it occurs, and the dollar
sign will be inserted immediately in front of the first nonsuppressed
character.

────── **Example** ──────

```
MOVE FLDA TO FLDB.
```

`0 1 0 3 4`   `$ 1 0 . 3 4`

`FLDA PIC 999V99`   `FLDB PIC $$$$.99`

`0 0 0 0 0`   `$ . 0 0`

`FLDA PIC 999V99`   `FLDB PIC $$$$.99`

Check Protection (*)

The character * used in a numeric edited picture will cause the asterisk to be inserted in place of each leading zero or other suppressed character. The asterisk is used chiefly in prefacing the dollar amount on checks.

───── Example ─────

```
MOVE FLDA TO FLDB.
```

```
|0,0,0,1,2,3,4|        |*,*,*,1,2,.,3,4|
          ^
FLDA PIC 99999V99   FLDB PIC *****.99
```

```
|1,2,3,4,5,6,7|        |$,1,2,3,4,5,.,6,7|
          ^
FLDA PIC 99999V99   FLDB PIC $*****.99
```

```
|0,0,0,0,0|            |$,*,*,*,.,*,*|           The decimal point is not
        ^                                        suppressed.
FLDA PIC 999V99     FLDB PIC $***.**
```

The comma is used in a numeric edited picture to cause a comma to be inserted in the appropriate position in the receiving field if the character immediately preceding is not a suppressed zero.

───── Example ─────

```
MOVE FLDA TO FLDB.
|0,0,1,2,3,4,5|            |0,.,0,1,2,.,3,4,5|
FLDA PIC 9(7)             FLDB PIC 9,999,999

|0,0,1,2,3,4,5|            |      1,2,.,3,4,5|
FLDA PIC 9(7)             FLDB PIC Z,ZZZ,ZZZ

|0,0,0,0,1,2,3|            |          1,2,3|
FLDA PIC 9999999         FLDB PIC Z,Z(3),Z(3)

|0,0,0,1,2,3,4|            |        1,.,2,3,4|
FLDA PIC 9999999         FLDB PIC Z,ZZZ,ZZZ

|0,0,1,2,3,4,5,6,7|        |    $,1,2,.,3,4,5,.,6,7|
            ^
FLDA PIC 9(7)V99         FLDB PIC $$,$$$,$$$.99

|0,0,1,2,3,4,5,6,7|        |$,*,*,*,1,2,.,3,4,5,.,6,7|
            ^
FLDA PIC 9999999V99      FLDB PIC $*,***,***.99
```

Figure 4.11   Examples of the dollar sign, asterisk, and comma for numeric editing: MOVE FLDA TO FLDB

FLDA		FLDB		Comment
Definition	*Content*	*Definition*	*Content After* MOVE	
PIC 999V99	0 1 0 ₃ 3 4	PIC $$$$.99	$ 1 0 . 3 4	Single dollar sign acts as an insertion character.
PIC 999V99	0 0 1 3 4	PIC $$$$.99	$ 1 . 3 4	Multiple dollar signs will float.
PIC 9(5)V99	0 0 0 1 2 3 4	PIC *****.99	* * * 1 2 . 3 4	Asterisk replaces leading zeros.
PIC 9(5)V99	0 0 0 0 0 0 0	PIC *(5).**	* * * * * . * *	Asterisk replaces all suppressed characters except decimal point.
PIC 9(7)	0 0 1 2 3 4 5	PIC 9,999,999	0 , 0 0 1 2 , 3 4 5	Comma inserted in each position.
PIC 9(7)	0 0 1 2 3 4 5	PIC Z,ZZZ,ZZZ	1 2 , 3 4 5	Comma is suppressed if digit to right is suppressed.
PIC 9(7)V99	0 0 1 2 3 4 5 6 7	PIC $$,$$$,$$$.99	$ 1 2 , 3 4 5 . 6 7	Comma may be used with $.
PIC 9(7)V99	0 0 1 2 3 4 5 6 7	PIC $*,***,***.99	$ * * * 1 2 , 3 4 5 . 6 7	Comma may be used with *.
PIC 9(3)V99	1 2 3 4 5	PIC $$$.$$	$ 2 3 . 4 5	Note suppression of leading digit.
PIC 9(3)V99	0 0 0 0 0	PIC ZZZ.99	. 0 0	

Figure 4.11 *(concluded)*

FLDA		FLDB		*Comment*
Definition	*Content*	*Definition*	*Content After* MOVE	
PIC 9(3)V99	0 0 0 0 0 ∧	PIC ZZZ.99 BLANK WHEN ZERO		Value moved to FLDB has value zero; hence, field is replaced by spaces.

Use of the dollar sign, asterisk, and comma for editing is summarized in Figure 4.11.

Sign Insertion (+ and −)

The character "−" used as the first or last character in a numeric edited picture will cause the minus sign to be inserted in the appropriate position of the receiving field if the sending item is negative. If the sending field is positive or unsigned, a blank is inserted.

─────── **Example** ───────

MOVE FLDA TO FLDB.

1 2 3 4 5̄ ∧   − 1 2 3 . 4 5

FLDA PIC S999V99   FLDB PIC −999.99

0 1 2 3 4̄ ∧   1 2 . 3 4 −

FLDA PIC S999V99   FLDB PIC ZZZ.99−

1 2 3 4 5̇⁺ ∧   1 2 3 . 4 5

FLDA PIC S999V99   FLDB PIC ZZZ.ZZ−

The character "+" may be used in exactly the same way as the character "−" except that the plus sign will be inserted whenever the sending item is positive or unsigned, and the minus sign will be inserted if the sending item is negative.

——————— **Example** ———————

```
MOVE FLDA TO FLDB.
        +
 1 2 3 4 5                    + 1 2 3 . 4 5
      ^
 FLDA PIC S999V99            FLDB PIC +ZZZ.ZZ

        _
 0 1 2 3 4                    -   1 2 . 3 4
      ^
 FLDA PIC S999V99            FLDB PIC +ZZZ.ZZ

 0 0 0 1 2                          . 1 2 +
      ^
 FLDA PIC 999V99             FLDB PIC ZZZ.99+
```

The use of more than one minus sign (or plus sign) as the first characters in an edit picture will cause zero suppression. It will also give you the appropriate sign preceding the first nonsuppressed character.

——————— **Example** ———————

```
MOVE FLDA TO FLDB.
            _
 0 0 0 1 2 3 4                    - 1 2 . 3 4
        ^
 FLDA PIC S99999V99          FLDB PIC -(6).99

            _
 0 0 0 0 0 1 2                      - . 1 2
          ^
 FLDA PIC S99999V99          FLDB PIC ++++++.99
```

The characters CR and DB used as the last two characters in an edit picture will cause CR or DB to be inserted in the receiving field if the sending field is negative. Otherwise, blanks will be inserted.

——————— **Example** ———————

```
MOVE FLDA TO FLDB.
        _
 0 1 2 3 4                     1 2 . 3 4 C R
      ^
 FLDA PIC S999V99            FLDB PIC ZZZ.99CR

        +
 0 1 2 3 4                     1 2 . 3 4
      ^
 FLDA PIC S999V99            FLDB PIC ZZZ.99CR

        _
 0 0 0 1 2                       $ . 1 2 D B
      ^
 FLDA PIC S999V99            FLDB PIC $$$$.99DB
```

Further examples of editing numeric data are shown in Figure 4.12.

Figure 4.12 Examples of editing numeric data: MOVE FLDA TO FLDB

FLDA		FLDB		Comment
Definition	*Content*	*Definition*	*Content After* MOVE	
PIC S999	$\overline{0\ 1\ 2}$	PIC -ZZZ	- 1 2	Sending field is negative; minus sign is inserted.
PIC S999	$\overset{+}{0\ 1\ 2}$	PIC ZZZ-	1 2	Sending field is positive; minus sign is suppressed.
PIC S999	$\overline{0\ 1\ 2}$	PIC ZZZ+	1 2 -	Sending field is negative; plus sign is replaced by minus.
PIC S999	$\overset{+}{0\ 1\ 2}$	PIC +ZZZ	+ 1 2	Sending field is positive; plus sign is inserted.
PIC S9(6)	$\overline{0\ 0\ 0\ 1\ 2\ 3}$	PIC -(7)	- 1 2 3	Minus may float.
PIC S9(6)	$\overline{0\ 0\ 0\ 1\ 2\ 3}$	PIC ++++,+++	+ 1 2 3	Plus may float.
PIC S999V99	$\overline{0\ 1\ 2\ 3\ 4}$	PIC ZZZ.99CR	1 2 . 3 4 C R	Sending field is negative; CR is inserted.
PIC S999V99	$\overset{+}{0\ 1\ 2\ 3\ 4}$	PIC $$$$.99BCR	$ 1 2 . 3 4	Sending field is positive; CR is suppressed. B acts as insertion character.
PIC S999V99	$\overline{0\ 1\ 2\ 3\ 4}$	PIC $ZZZ.99BDB	$ 1 2 . 3 4 D B	Sending field is negative; DB is inserted.
PIC S999V99	$\overset{+}{0\ 1\ 2\ 3\ 4}$	PIC $$$$.99DB	$ 1 2 . 3 4	Sending field is positive; DB is suppressed.
PIC S999V99	$\overline{0\ 1\ 2\ 3\ 4}$	PIC $$$$.99-	$ 1 2 . 3 4 -	Sending field is negative; minus sign is inserted.

Blank Insertion (B)

The character B used in an edit-type picture will cause a blank to be inserted in the receiving field.

─────── Example ───────

```
MOVE FLDA TO FLDB.
```

| 1 | 2 | 3 | 4 | 5 | 6 | 7 | 8 | 9 | | 1 | 2 | 3 | | 4 | 5 | | 6 | 7 | 8 | 9 |

FLDA PIC 9(9)   FLDB PIC 999B99B9999

| 0 | 1 | 2 | 3 | 4̄ | | | | 1 | 2 | . | 3 | 4 | | | C | R |

FLDA PIC S999V99   FLDB PIC ZZZ.99BCR

Alphanumeric, as well as numeric, data can be edited using the code B.

─────── Example ───────

```
MOVE FLDA TO FLDB.
```

| A | B | C | D | | A | B | | | C | D |

FLDA PIC X(4)   FLDB PIC XXBBXX

FLDB in this case is classed as an alphanumeric edited field.

Slash Insertion (/)

The character "/" used in an edit-type picture will cause the slash to be inserted in the receiving field. The primary use for this code is for editing date fields.

─────── Example ───────

```
MOVE DATE-IN TO DATE-OUT.
```

| 0 | 3 | 0 | 5 | 9 | 2 | | 0 | 3 | / | 0 | 5 | / | 9 | 2 |

DATE-IN PIC 9(6)   DATE-OUT PIC 99/99/99

The slash can be used to edit alphanumeric, as well as numeric, data.

─────── Example ───────

```
MOVE FLDA TO FLDB.
```

| A | B | C | D | | A | / | B | / | C | D |

FLDA PIC XXXX   FLDB PIC X/X/XX

Zero Insertion (0)

The character "0" in an edit picture will cause zero to be inserted in the receiving field. Zero insertion can be performed on numeric and alphanumeric fields.

────────── **Example** ──────────

```
MOVE FLDA TO FLDB.
```

|1|2|3|4|ᴧ |1|2|0|0|3|4|

```
FLDA PIC 9(4)    FLDB PIC 990099
```

```
MOVE FLDA TO FLDB.
```

|A|B|C|D| |A|0|B|C|D|

```
FLDA PIC X(4)    FLDB PIC X0XXX
```

Further examples of the use of the picture codes B, slash, and zero are shown in Figure 4.13.

A summary of all possible cases of data movement is shown in Figure 4.14. The result of a data movement operation in those cases described as

Figure 4.13   Examples of B, slash, and zero: MOVE FLDA TO FLDB

FLDA		FLDB		Comment
Definition	*Content*	*Definition*	*Content*	
PIC X(4)	|A|B|1|2|	PIC XXBXX	|A|B| |1|2|	Insertion of blank in alphanumeric field.
PIC X(4)	|A|B|1|2|	PIC XXXX0	|A|B|1|2|0|	Insertion of zero in alphanumeric field.
PIC X(4)	|A|B|1|2|	PIC XX//XX	|A|B|/|/|1|2|	Insertion of slash in alphanumeric field.
PIC 999999	|0|1|2|0|8|6|	PIC 99/99/99	|0|1|/|2|0|/|8|6|	Slash insertion in numeric field.
PIC 9(9)	|1|2|3|4|5|6|7|8|9|	PIC 999B99B9(4)	|1|2|3| |4|5| |6|7|8|9|	Blank insertion in numeric field.
PIC 999	|1|2|3|	PIC 999000	|1|2|3|0|0|0|	Zero insertion in numeric field.

Figure 4.14   Summary of data movement by type

		Receiving Field Type			
		Alphanumeric	Numeric	Numeric edited	Alphanumeric edited
Sending Field Type	Alphanumeric	Characters moved left to right with truncation and padding on right except when JUSTIFIED RIGHT is used with receiving field.	Not permitted.	Not permitted.	Appropriate characters are inserted in receiving field.
	Numeric	Same as alphanumeric to alphanumeric.	Decimal points in fields are aligned. Digits right of decimal point are moved left to right. Digits left of decimal point are moved right to left. Truncation/padding of leading/trailing digits in receiving field.	Same as numeric to numeric, except editing of numeric digits is performed.	Not permitted.
	Numeric edited	Same as alphanumeric to alphanumeric.	Not permitted.	Not permitted.	Not permitted.
	Alphanumeric edited	Same as alphanumeric to alphanumeric.	Not permitted.	Not permitted.	Not permitted.

"not permitted" depends on the system in use. In most cases, the compiler will treat such MOVE instructions as syntax errors. In any case, these types of moves are most likely logical errors because the result will be of no value to the program. While the movement of a numeric field to a field described as alphanumeric is permitted and handled in the same way as an alphanumeric to alphanumeric move, this type of movement is rarely performed in practice. Numeric data is usually moved to another numeric field or to a numeric edited field in preparation for output.

4.10   FIGURATIVE CONSTANTS

The COBOL language provides a number of **figurative constants** which are assigned reserved word names (Fig. 4.15). Any of these figurative constants may be used in any place the corresponding nonfigurative constant

Figure 4.15   Figurative constants

Reserved Word	Value
ZERO ZEROS ZEROES	0
HIGH-VALUE HIGH-VALUES	the largest value which can be represented in the computer
SPACE SPACES	one or more blanks
LOW-VALUE LOW-VALUES	the smallest value which can be represented in the computer
ALL "character"	a string of appropriate length consisting entirely of the specified character
QUOTE QUOTES	quotation mark(s)

would be appropriate. Examples of using the figurative constants ZERO and SPACES are abundant in Program 4a.

─────── Example ───────

The following are equivalent:

```
03 DATA-A PIC X(5) VALUE ALL "*".
03 DATA-A PIC X(5) VALUE "*****".
```

In both cases the content of DATA-A will be

```
  *  *  *  *  *
 |__|__|__|__|__|

 DATA-A
```

─────── Example ───────

Suppose you desire to describe the character string "XYZ" for inclusion on an output line. The following code could be used:

```
02 DATA-B.
   03 FILLER PIC X       VALUE QUOTE.
   03 FILLER PIC XXX     VALUE "XYZ".
   03 FILLER PIC X       VALUE QUOTE.
```

The content of DATA-B will be

```
 "  X  Y  Z  "
 |__|__|__|__|__|

 DATA-B
```

Use of the figurative constant QUOTE is a convenient way to specify the character (") in the string since quotes are used in coding nonnumeric constants in COBOL.

The following statements are equivalent:

```
MOVE 0      TO FLD.
MOVE ZERO   TO FLD.
```

The figurative constants HIGH-VALUE(S) and LOW-VALUE(S) are used in certain instances for passing values between a program and the operating system.

4.11   SIGNED NUMBERS

As noted earlier, the picture code S must be the first code in the picture of any data-name which may be negative. For example, the following DATA DIVISION declarations specify FLD-A and FLD-B as signed variables:

```
01   REC-DESC.
     03 FLD-A      PIC S9999.
     03 FLD-B      PIC S9V99.
     03 FILLER     PIC X(73).
```

Suppose REC-DESC specified in the preceding example is the description of a data-record. FLD-A and FLD-B may be positive or negative. If a value is entered in a field in the ordinary fashion, it is stored as an unsigned (positive) value. But what about a negative quantity? There are two ways to enter negative data: (1) enter the sign as a part of the rightmost digit in the field and (2) enter the sign as a separate character.

Sign in Rightmost Digit

As discussed in Section 4.8, the sign of a value is associated with the right-most digit in the field. This practice originated at a time when punched cards were used as input. When punched cards were used, the sign was punched in conjunction with the rightmost digit in the field. An 11 zone, together with the digit in the rightmost position, is used for a negative value. A 12 zone and the appropriate digit are used for a positive value.

If a data card containing the characters

record position	1 2 3 4 5 6 7 8 9	80
	0 0 3 M 4 0 A	

were read using the record description above, the content of FLD-A and FLD-B would be

```
           ‾
 0 , 0 , 3 , 4 ,            4 , 0 , 1 ,
              ^              ^
   FLD-A                   FLD-B
```

The absence of any zone punch will also signify a positive value. When output is produced for a signed field, the character equivalent of the punch combination will be used. For example, if the content of FLD-A and FLD-B were printed without editing, the output would appear as

$$\underline{|0\,|0\,|3\,|M\,|} \qquad \underline{|4\,|0\,|A\,|}$$

FLD-A   FLD-B

The appearance of alphabetic characters in the rightmost position of the fields is caused by the inclusion of zones in the output. (M uses the code 11–4 and A uses the code 12–1.) The movement of a signed field to an edited field is necessary to suppress this inclusion of a sign zone along with the digit in the rightmost position.

─────── Example ───────

MOVE FLDA TO FLDB FLDC.

$$\overset{+}{\underline{|0\,|3\,|4\,|}}_{\land} \qquad \underline{|0\,|3\,|4\,|}_{\land} \qquad \underline{|\,\,|3\,|4\,|}$$

FLDA PIC S999   FLDB PIC 999   FLDC PIC ZZZ

Those who use terminals and disks to enter data must perform the logical equivalent of supplying a 12 zone or an 11 zone in the rightmost position of a signed numeric word. It is done by the character equivalent of the punch combination (Fig. 4.16). Thus, in order to enter FLDA and FLDB with values −34 and +4.01, respectively, the terminal or disk user would enter

0 0 3 M   4 0 A
─────────   ───────
  FLDA   FLDB

Note that characters representing $\overset{+}{0}$ and $\overset{-}{0}$ are omitted from the list in Figure 4.16. Details as to how these characters are to be entered vary from one system to another. The reader must check the user's manual or other local documentation to determine the appropriate procedure.

The SIGN IS Clause

The sign of a data item may be entered as a leading or trailing character in the field if the item is defined using the SIGN IS clause, which has the following general form:

SIGN IS $\left\{ \begin{matrix} \underline{LEADING} \\ \underline{TRAILING} \end{matrix} \right\}$ [$\underline{SEPARATE}$ CHARACTER]

When this clause is used in the definition of the item, the S picture code, which must be present, is counted as a position in the field.

─────── Example ───────

A field A is four characters in length, and the user desires to enter the sign of the field as a leading character. The field would be defined by

A PIC S999 SIGN IS LEADING SEPARATE CHARACTER.

If the characters $\underline{|-\,|1\,|0\,|2\,|}$ are entered on the input record, the value of A will be −102. If the characters $\underline{|\,\,|\,\,|-\,|3\,|}$ are entered, the value of A will be −3.

Figure 4.16   Representation of signed data

Punched Card Code	Character	Meaning for Signed Data
12–1	A	$+1$
12–2	B	$+2$
12–3	C	$+3$
12–4	D	$+4$
12–5	E	$+5$
12–6	F	$+6$
12–7	G	$+7$
12–8	H	$+8$
12–9	I	$+9$
11–1	J	-1
11–2	K	-2
11–3	L	-3
11–4	M	-4
11–5	N	-5
11–6	O	-6
11–7	P	-7
11–8	Q	-8
11–9	R	-9

───── Example ─────

A field B is six characters in length; the user will enter the sign in the right-most character of the field. The field would be defined by

    B PIC S99999 SIGN IS TRAILING SEPARATE CHARACTER.

If the characters 0 0 1 0 2 − are entered on the input record, the value of B will be −102.

4.12 QUALIFICATION AND MOVE CORRESPONDING

We have stated that it is a good practice to give related names to related data items. The practice that we have adopted is to use a suffix to help the user determine the location of the definition of an item.[2] For example, to define a record that is associated with the file DATA-FILE that contains two items—a name and an address—we could use the following program segment:

```
01   DATA-RECORD.
     02 CUSTOMER-NAME-DR      PIC X(20).
     02 ADDRESS-DR            PIC X(30).
```

To define a record that will print out this data, we use a different suffix but retain the same basic name:

```
01   REPORT-RECORD.
     02 CUSTOMER-NAME-RR      PIC X(20).
     02 FILLER                PIC X(5).
     02 ADDRESS-RR            PIC X(30).
```

Within the PROCEDURE DIVISION, it is necessary to write two MOVE statements to move the data from DATA-RECORD to REPORT-RECORD:

```
MOVE CUSTOMER-NAME-DR      TO CUSTOMER-NAME-RR.
MOVE ADDRESS-DR            TO ADDRESS-RR.
```

In a program that processes very long and complex data-records, having to write one MOVE statement for each field can become quite burdensome.

The COBOL compiler does not actually require that every data-name written in the DATA DIVISION be unique, although it is quite common for a programmer to make each one unique. It is possible, however, to use the same data-name as many times as desired to define different data items. If the programmer does reuse the same data-names, any reference to a data item must be made unique by qualification. The general form of a qualified reference is

$$\text{data-name-1} \left\{ \begin{array}{c} \text{IN} \\ \text{OF} \end{array} \right\} \text{data-name-2}$$

where data-name-1 is defined as subordinate to data-name-2. The words IN and OF can be used interchangeably.

For example, we could refer to CUSTOMER-NAME-DR in the example above as

```
CUSTOMER-NAME-DR IN DATA-RECORD
```

or

```
CUSTOMER-NAME-DR OF DATA-RECORD
```

Of course, since CUSTOMER-NAME-DR is unique anyway, nothing can be gained from using a more elaborate qualified reference. Qualification is

---

[2] The only exception to the use of suffixes is for computational and control fields defined at the beginning of WORKING-STORAGE.

used only when it is necessary to create a unique field reference. For example, suppose we rewrite the definitions of DATA-RECORD and REPORT-RECORD as follows:

```
01   DATA-RECORD.
     02 CUSTOMER-NAME      PIC X(20).
     02 ADDRESS            PIC X(30).
     .
     .
     .
01   REPORT-RECORD.
     02 CUSTOMER-NAME      PIC X(20).
     02 FILLER             PIC X(5).
     02 ADDRESS            PIC X(30).
```

It is now necessary to qualify both CUSTOMER-NAME and ADDRESS to create a unique reference. To move the data from DATA-RECORD to REPORT-RECORD we could write

```
MOVE CUSTOMER-NAME IN DATA-RECORD TO
     CUSTOMER-NAME IN REPORT-RECORD.
MOVE ADDRESS IN DATA-RECORD TO
     ADDRESS IN REPORT-RECORD.
```

In a program with many fields to be moved, the necessity for adding qualifiers makes the whole task even more of a chore for the programmer and tends to make the PROCEDURE DIVISION lengthy and complicated.

Why, then, would anyone wish to use duplicate data-names? The answer lies in the MOVE CORRESPONDING statement. This statement always addresses a group data item and will move the content of subordinate fields which have the same data-names. Subordinate fields that do not have the same names are not affected. The general form of the statement is

$$\underline{\text{MOVE}} \left\{ \begin{array}{l} \underline{\text{CORRESPONDING}} \\ \underline{\text{CORR}} \end{array} \right\} \text{ data-name-1 } \underline{\text{TO}} \text{ data-name-2}$$

For example, with the alternate definitions of DATA-RECORD and REPORT-RECORD, we could write

```
MOVE CORRESPONDING DATA-RECORD TO REPORT-RECORD.
```

In this example, the fields happen to be in the same order in the two records, although this is not necessary for the MOVE CORRESPONDING statement to function properly. It is also not necessary that all of the fields correspond. The MOVE CORRESPONDING statement will move *only* those fields with the same data-name. If none of the fields had the same data-name, the MOVE CORRESPONDING statement would have no effect on the receiving fields. In a program that must process many fields in this manner, the MOVE CORRESPONDING statement can result in much simpler code in the PROCEDURE DIVISION. One MOVE CORRESPONDING statement can do the job of any number of MOVE statements that might otherwise be required.

The MOVE CORRESPONDING statement has been the object of considerable criticism over the years. The original designers of the language thought that it would be a very useful statement for the reasons just outlined. However, use of the statement requires that all references to items be qualified in other statements; this condition can be a considerable burden on the programmer who must code not only the data-name of the elementary item, but also the data-name of the record in which the item is defined. The result is twice as much work and twice as many opportunities to make a mistake. Also, statements in which qualification is used are much longer and, therefore, less readable. For these reasons (and other more theoretical ones), most style manuals prohibit giving data items like names; without like-named items, the MOVE CORRESPONDING statement is useless. In the programs that we will write as examples in this text, we will not use this facility, and we advise you not to use it in your own programs.

4.13 DEBUG CLINIC

File, Record, Field References

A very common mistake made by beginning programmers is to reference a file, record, or field by two different names in the same program. It is important to remember that all references to the same file, record, or field must use the same data-name.

For example, consider the screened lines in Program 4a. Note that the name PRODUCT-FILE is used in the SELECT entry, FD entry, OPEN statement, READ statement, and CLOSE statement. Also note that the name PRODUCT-RECORD is used in both the DATA RECORD clause and the following 01 entry. Failure to use the same file, record, or field name in each reference will be treated by the compiler as a syntax error.

Mixing WRITE/BEFORE and WRITE/AFTER

Care must be exercised in utilizing both options of the WRITE statement in the same program. Recall that the BEFORE option causes lines to be printed prior to advancing the paper (WRITE . . . BEFORE ADVANCING) and the AFTER option causes paper to be advanced prior to writing the line (WRITE . . . AFTER ADVANCING).

In a given program, if WRITE/BEFORE is used for all WRITE statements, the printer normally will be on a new line for each output. The same observation is true if WRITE/AFTER is used for all WRITE statements. If a program uses a WRITE/AFTER followed by a WRITE/BEFORE, the WRITE/AFTER leaves the paper on the line printed. The following WRITE/BEFORE causes another line to be printed, and then the paper is advanced. The second line of print will be printed on top of the first one! To avoid problems of this kind, most COBOL programmers employ only WRITE/AFTER in a given program.

Editing

When performing editing of numeric data, make sure the receiving field contains a sufficient number of positions for all digits in the sending field. Remember that when a numeric field is moved to an edited field, the decimal points are aligned. Leading and trailing digits are truncated or padded with zeros, depending on the number of positions in the edited field.

Suppose the instruction

```
MOVE FLDA TO FLDB.
```

is executed.

$$\underset{\wedge}{1\,|\,2\,|\,3\,|\,4\,|\,5} \qquad 2\,|\,3\,|\,.\,|\,4\,|\,5\,|\,0 \qquad \text{Note truncation on left and padding on right.}$$

FLDA PIC 999V99.   FLDB PIC ZZ.999

In this case, FLDB contains too few digits on the left to accommodate all digits of FLDA, resulting in truncation of the leading digit. FLDB contains more digits to the right of the decimal point than FLDA; hence, FLDB is padded on the right with a zero.

$$\underset{\wedge}{1\,|\,2\,|\,3\,|\,4\,|\,5} \qquad \$\,|\,1\,|\,2\,|\,3\,|\,.\,|\,4\,|\,5 \qquad \text{Note leading space.}$$

FLDA PIC 999V99   FLDB PIC $$$$$.99

FLDB contains space for four digits to the left of the decimal point. Since FLDA has only three digits left of the decimal point, FLDA is padded on the left with a zero. Because of the editing function, the leading zero is then suppressed.

$$\underset{\wedge}{1\,|\,2\,|\,3\,|\,4\,|\,5} \qquad \$\,|\,2\,|\,3\,|\,.\,|\,4\,|\,5 \qquad \text{Note truncation.}$$

FLDA PIC 999V99   FLDB PIC $$$.99

FLDB contains space for only two digits left of the decimal point because the dollar sign uses one space and is never suppressed. This results in the truncation of the leading digit of FLDA.

The programmer must be careful to construct edit pictures which are sufficiently long to accommodate all digits of the field to be edited.

Signed Fields

Recall that a field which will be signed (i.e., may become negative) must be described in the DATA DIVISION by a picture which contains the picture code S as its first character. Thus, if the data 032J is read into a field described as S9999, the resulting value is -321. Suppose signed data is entered into a field which is not described using the S picture code. For example, the data 032J is read into a field described as 9999. In this case, the value stored will be 321—a positive value! In order for a field to store a negative value it *must* be described using the S picture code.

Remember also that when a signed field is specified without the SIGN IS SEPARATE CHARACTER clause, S is *not* counted as a part of the number of characters in the field. If the SIGN IS SEPARATE CHARACTER clause is used, the S *is* counted as a character in the field.

```
Q PIC S999.
```

The size of the field is three.

```
R PIC S999 SIGN IS LEADING SEPARATE CHARACTER.
```

The size of the field is four.

4.14 COBOL-85 UPDATE

As you will note by examining Figure 4.14, one operation that is prohibited in COBOL-74 is the movement of a numeric edited field to a numeric field. This restriction is lifted in COBOL-85; it is permitted to move the content of a numeric edited field to a numeric field and thereby preserve the value contained in the data item. The operation is called **de-editing**; it is the inverse of the editing that is performed when a numeric field is moved to a numeric edited field.

——————— Example ———————

Consider the following fields:

```
 0 1 3 4 5 6 7                                        
|_|_|_|_|_|_|_|      |_|_|_|_|_|_|_|_|_|_|_|      |_|_|_|_|_|_|_|_|
        ^
FLDA PIC 99999V99    FLDB PIC $ZZ,ZZZ.99        FLDC PIC 99999V99
```

We assume that the initial value of FLDA is 1345.67. After the instruction MOVE FLDA TO FLDB is executed, the content of FLDB will be an edited version of the value 1345.67:

```
 0 1 3 4 5 6 7       $    1 , 3 4 5 . 6 7
|_|_|_|_|_|_|_|      |_|_|_|_|_|_|_|_|_|_|_|      |_|_|_|_|_|_|_|_|
        ^                                                ^
FLDA PIC 99999V99    FLDB PIC $ZZ,ZZZ.99        FLDC PIC 99999V99
```

Now, suppose the instruction MOVE FLDB TO FLDC is executed. In COBOL-74, this instruction would be invalid because FLDB is numeric edited and FLDC is numeric. In COBOL-85, however, the statement would result in placing the value 1345.67 in FLDC:

```
 0 1 3 4 5 6 7       $    1 , 3 4 5 . 6 7       0 1 3 4 5 6 7
|_|_|_|_|_|_|_|      |_|_|_|_|_|_|_|_|_|_|_|    |_|_|_|_|_|_|_|
        ^                                               ^
FLDA PIC 99999V99    FLDB PIC $ZZ,ZZZ.99        FLDC PIC 99999V99
```

When a move of numeric edited to numeric type is executed, the decimal point in the sending field is aligned with the decimal point in the receiving field, the same way as in the performance of a numeric-to-numeric move. Truncation and padding take place on the left and right of the receiving field. Insertion characters, such as the dollar sign ($), comma (,), and asterisk (*), are ignored. The sign of the numeric edited field can be indicated by a plus sign (+), minus sign (–), credit (CR), or debit (DB). In any case, the result will be an appropriate sign in the receiving field if, of course, there is provision for a sign in the receiving field.

─────── Example ───────

Consider two items FLDD and FLDE defined as follows:

| $ 1 , 0 0 0 . 0 0 C R | | |

FLDD PIC $$$,$$$.99BCR   FLDE PIC S99999V99

After the instruction MOVE FLDD TO FLDE is executed, the content of the items will be

| $ 1 , 0 0 0 . 0 0 C R | | 0 1 0 0 0 0 0 |

FLDD PIC $$$,$$$.99BCR   FLDE PIC S99999V99

The value contained in FLDE will be −1000.00, which is the numeric equivalent of the content of FLDD.

───────────────────────────

This form of data movement is likely to prove useful in program maintenance. If the programmer must perform an arithmetic operation on a field that has already been edited, the edited field can be moved temporarily to a numeric item. The operation can be performed on the numeric item, and then the result can be moved back to the numeric edited field. With this facility, it is unnecessary for the programmer to search through the program to find the place(s) at which the value contained in the field was computed prior to being moved into the numeric edited field—an operation that can be very tedious for a long program.

4.15 SELF-TEST EXERCISES

1. Consider the following information about a file:

   File-name: SALES-FILE
   Device type: disk
   Record-name: SALES-RECORD

   a. Write an FD entry for the file.
   b. Write an OPEN statement for the file.
   c. Write a READ statement for the file.
   d. Write a CLOSE statement for the file.

2. Consider the following information about a file:

   File-name: PAYROLL-FILE
   Device type: printer
   Record-name: PAYROLL-RECORD

   a. Write an FD entry for the file.
   b. Write an OPEN statement for the file.
   c. Write a WRITE statement for the file.
   d. Write a CLOSE statement for the file.

3. Show the result of the statement MOVE ITM1 TO ITM2 for ITM1 and
   ITM2 as shown below:

   a. |_1_|_2_|_3_|_4_|_5_| |___|___|___|___|___|
                  ^
      ITM1 PIC 999V99   ITM2 PIC 9(5)

                                    |___|___|___| |___|
                                    ITM2 PIC 9(3)   ITM2 PIC 9PP

                                    |___|___|___|___|___|___|___|___|
                                    ITM2 PIC 9(8)

                                    |___|___|___|___|___|___|___|
                                               ^
                                    ITM2 PIC 999V9999

                                    |___|___|___|___|___|___|___|
                                                ^
                                    ITM2 PIC 9999V999

   b. |_0_|_1_|_2_|_3_|_4_|_5_|_0_| |___|___|___|___|___|
                  ^
      ITM1 PIC 9(4)V999   ITM2 PIC ZZZZZ

                                    |___|___|___|___|___|___|___|___|
                                    ITM2 PIC $$$$$$.99

                                    |___|___|___|___|___|___|
                                    ITM2 PIC ****.9

   c. |_4_|_3_|_2_|_1_| |___|___|___|___|___|___| |___|___|___|___|___|___|
      ITM1 PIC X(4)   ITM2 PIC X(6)   ITM2 PIC X(6) JUSTIFIED RIGHT

                                   |___|___| |___|___|
                                   ITM2 PIC XX   ITM2 PIC XX JUSTIFIED RIGHT

   d. |_0_|_0_|_1_|_2_|_3_|_4̄_| |___|___|___|___|___|___|___|___|
                  ^
      ITM1 PIC S9(4)V99   ITM2 PIC −(5).99

                                   |___|___|___|___|___|___|___|___|
                                   ITM2 PIC +(5).++

                                   |___|___|___|___|___|___|___|___|___|___|
                                   ITM2 PIC Z(5).99CR

                                   |___|___|___|___|___|___|___|___|___|___|___|
                                   ITM2 PIC $Z,ZZZ.99BDB

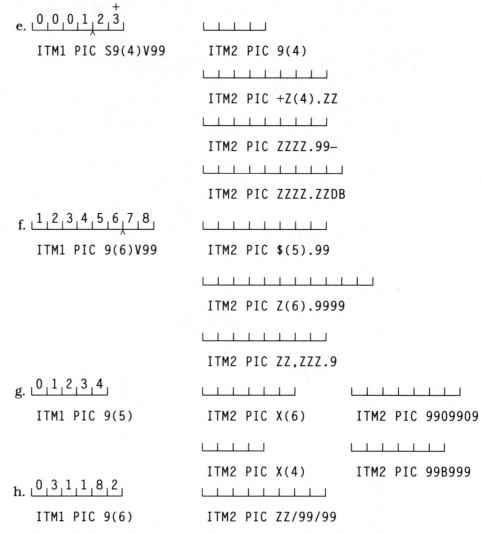

e. |0|0|0|1|2|3̂⁺|

ITM1 PIC S9(4)V99   ITM2 PIC 9(4)

|_|_|_|_|_|_|_|_|_|
ITM2 PIC +Z(4).ZZ

|_|_|_|_|_|_|_|_|_|
ITM2 PIC ZZZZ.99−

|_|_|_|_|_|_|_|_|_|_|
ITM2 PIC ZZZZ.ZZDB

f. |1|2|3|4|5|6|7|8̂|

ITM1 PIC 9(6)V99   ITM2 PIC $(5).99

|_|_|_|_|_|_|_|_|_|_|_|
ITM2 PIC Z(6).9999

|_|_|_|_|_|_|_|_|
ITM2 PIC ZZ,ZZZ.9

g. |0|1|2|3|4|

ITM1 PIC 9(5)   ITM2 PIC X(6)   ITM2 PIC 9909909

|_|_|_|_|
ITM2 PIC X(4)   ITM2 PIC 99B999

h. |0|3|1|1|8|2|

ITM1 PIC 9(6)   ITM2 PIC ZZ/99/99

4. Draw a program flowchart for the paragraph of Program 4a which will terminate the processing of the loop. What will cause this termination?

5. List types of output lines found in most reports.

6. In each cell of the following table classify each type of move as permitted or not permitted. Use the ANSI-74 standard.

		Receiving Field			
		Alphanumeric	Numeric	Numeric edited	Alphanumeric edited
Sending Field	Alphanumeric				
	Numeric				
	Numeric edited				
	Alphanumeric edited				

7. What is qualification? When is qualification necessary?

8. What are some advantages and disadvantages to the use of the MOVE CORRESPONDING statement?

9. What is de-editing? Why might this operation be useful?

4.16 PROGRAMMING EXERCISES

1. Each record in a file contains the following data:

Positions	Content
1–9	Account number
10–25	Customer name
26–31	Account balance (2 decimal places)
32	Sign (− indicates credit balance)
33–38	Date of last payment (*mmddyy*)

Write a report listing this data with appropriate headings and editing as specified in the printer spacing chart shown in Figure 4.17. Include the total of all balances and the number of accounts in the report. To perform the required editing:

Insert a space between digits 3 and 4 and between digits 5 and 6 of Account number.
Print a fixed $ for Account balance.
Suppress leading zeros in printing Account balance.
Print CR if the value of Account balance is negative.
Edit the date with slashes (*mm/dd/yy*).
Use a floating $ to print the total balance.
Print CR if the total balance is negative.

Figure 4.17 Printer spacing chart for Exercise 1

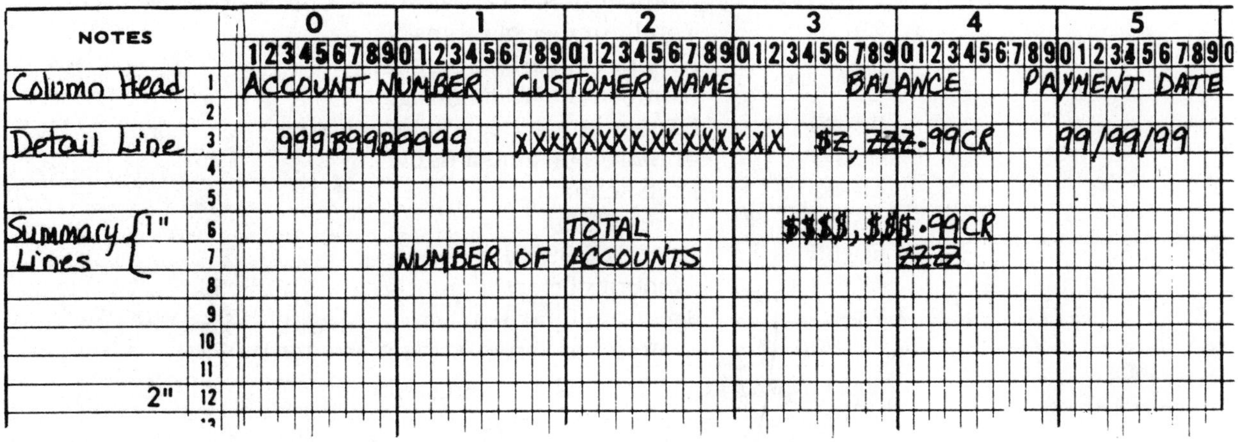

2. Write a program to produce an appropriately edited report listing each item from data records in the following format:

Positions	Content
1–20	Name
21–34	Street address
35–48	City
49–50	State
51–55	ZIP code
56	Marital status code
57–64	Yearly salary (two decimal places implied)

Write a line at the conclusion of your report specifying the total number of records processed.

3. Write a program to process a file containing records in the following format and produce a report listing sales in each department. Two decimal places are implied in each sales amount. The last line of the report should contain the totals for each column of the report.

Positions	Content
1–6	Date (*mmddyy*)
10–19	Sales in shoe department
20–29	Sales in ladies' clothing
30–39	Sales in men's clothing
40–49	Sales in children's clothing
50–59	Sales in jewelry department

4. A real estate company maintains the following records for each listed property:

Positions	Content
1–8	Multiple listing number
9–10	Zone
11–25	Address
26	Number of bedrooms
27–28	Number of baths (9V9)
29	Total number of rooms
30	Number of cars in carport
31	Number of cars in garage
32–39	Elementary school name
40–47	Junior high school name
48–55	High school name
56–59	Taxes (9999)
60–66	Price (9999999)
67–73	Amount of existing mortgage (9999999)
74–77	Amount of payment on existing mortgage (9999)
78–80	Interest rate on existing mortgage (V999)

Write a program to list this file using a format similar to the following:

```
MULTIPLE LISTING NUMBER xxxxxxxx ZONE xx
ADDRESS xxxxxxxxxxxxxxx PRICE $xxxxxxx
ROOMS x BEDROOMS x BATHS x.x
CARPORT x GARAGE x
        .
        .
        .
etc.
```

5. The managers of Burgers, Inc., which operates a franchise system of hamburger restaurants, are concerned with the profitability of a number of the company's outlets. They have requested a report showing basic data about each store. The format for the input records is:

Positions	Content
1–10	Franchise number
11–25	Location
26–40	Manager's name
41–49	Previous year's profits (S999999V99)
	(Field could be negative if the store lost money; use SIGN IS TRAILING SEPARATE CHARACTER.)

6. The manager of the computer at ABC Furniture, Inc. prepares a record in the following format for each supply requisition she makes:

Positions	Content
1–6	Date (*mmddyy*)
7–25	Description
26–31	Amount (9999V99)

   At the end of each month, she collects all the requisitions and runs a program to list each requisition and the total for the month. Write a program for the manager to use for this task.

5. ARITHMETIC STATEMENTS

Arithmetic statements are used to perform computations in a COBOL program. Two types of arithmetic statements can be used. One type uses the verbs ADD, SUBTRACT, MULTIPLY, and DIVIDE to specify the arithmetic operation to be performed. The other type uses the verb COMPUTE and allows the programmer to specify arithmetic operations using the symbols + (for add), − (for subtract), * (for multiply), / (for divide), and ** (for exponentiation). The programmer may choose whichever type of statement would be most advantageous.

5.1 THE ADD STATEMENT

The ADD statement is used to perform addition of numeric data items. Figure 5.1 shows a general form for the ADD statement. Any number of data items may be added; the result is placed in data-name-n. If the TO option is used, the item participates as an addend. If the GIVING option is used, the calculated sum is moved to the receiving item which does not participate in the addition.

Figure 5.1 General form of the ADD statement

$$\underline{\text{ADD}} \begin{Bmatrix} \text{data-name-1} \\ \text{constant-1} \end{Bmatrix} \cdot \cdot \cdot \begin{Bmatrix} \underline{\text{TO}} \\ \underline{\text{GIVING}} \end{Bmatrix} \text{data-name-n}$$

─────── **Example** ───────

Add credit to present balance to get new balance.

    ADD CREDIT BAL GIVING NEW-BAL

    0 3 2 0 0   0 0 4 0 0 0̄   0 0 0 8 0 0̄

    CREDIT PIC 999V99   BAL PIC S9999V99   NEW-BAL PIC S9999V99

Calculation: 32.00 + (−40.00) = −8.00

─────── **Example** ───────

Add the constant 3.2 to the values contained in X and Y to get Z. In this case, suppose X = 23.0 and Y = 123.

```
ADD 3.2 X Y GIVING Z
```

| 2 3 0 | 1 2 3 | 0 1 4 9 2 |
| X PIC 99V9 | Y PIC 999 | Z PIC 9(4)V9 |

Calculation: 3.2 + 23.0 + 123 = 149.2

─────── Example ───────

Add 1 to the present value of the data item KOUNT.

```
ADD 1 TO KOUNT
```

Before Execution   *After Execution*

| 0 0 3 | 0 0 4 |
| KOUNT PIC 999 | KOUNT PIC 999 |

─────── Example ───────

Add the constant 3.2 and the contents of X and Y to Z, whose values in this case are 23.0, 123, and 149.2.

```
ADD 3.2 X Y TO Z
```

Before Execution

| 2 3 0 | 1 2 3 | 0 1 4 9 2 |
| X PIC 99V9 | Y PIC 999 | Z PIC 9(4)V9 |

After Execution

| 2 3 0 | 1 2 3 | 0 2 9 8 4 |
| X PIC 99V9 | Y PIC 999 | Z PIC 9(4)V9 |

Calculation: 3.2 + 23.0 + 123 + 149.2 = 298.4
Note that this example could be rewritten as

```
ADD 3.2 X Y Z GIVING Z.
```

The results would be exactly the same.

─────────

When the computer executes the ADD (and also the SUBTRACT) instruction, data items are adjusted to align decimal positions; the operation is performed, taking into account the sign of the field (if any); the result is placed in the receiving fields. In all arithmetic instructions (as in the MOVE instruction), data is moved to the receiving field from the decimal point to the right and also from the decimal point to the left. **Truncation** occurs on the leftmost digits of the integer portion and on the rightmost digits of the fractional portion if the receiving field is too short. Padding with zeros occurs on the left and right if the receiving field is too long.

─────── Example ───────

Add the regular hours (40) to overtime hours (6.5) to get total hours. The regular and overtime hours may contain fractions, but total hours does not.

ADD REG-HR OV-HR GIVING TOT-HR

4	0	0		0	6	5		0	4	6

REG-HR PIC 99V9   OV-HR PIC 99V9   TOT-HR PIC 999

Calculation: 40.0 + 6.5 = 46.5 ← Truncated when result is moved to TOT-HR.

—————— Example ——————

Add regular sales (30.40) to special sales (245.00) to get total sales.

ADD REG-SALES SPECIAL-SALES GIVING TOTAL-SALES

0	3	0	4	0		2	4	5	0	0

REG-SALES PIC 999V99   SPECIAL-SALES PIC 999V99

| 0 | 0 | 0 | 2 | 7 | 5 | 4 | 0 | The first three zeros pad out the field of whole dollars.
|---|---|---|---|---|---|---|---|

TOTAL-SALES PIC 9(6)V99

5.2   THE SUBTRACT STATEMENT

The SUBTRACT statement is used to perform subtraction of numeric data items, as shown in the general form in Figure 5.2. The result is placed in the last data-name specified. The GIVING clause is optional when the subtrahend (the value subtracted from) is specified as a data-name but required when it is specified as a constant.

Figure 5.2   General form of the SUBTRACT statement

$$\underline{\text{SUBTRACT}} \begin{Bmatrix} \text{data-name-1} \\ \text{constant-1} \end{Bmatrix} \cdots \underline{\text{FROM}} \begin{Bmatrix} \text{data-name-n} & [\underline{\text{GIVING}}\ \text{data-name-m}] \\ \text{constant-n} & \underline{\text{GIVING}}\ \text{data-name-m} \end{Bmatrix}$$

—————— Example ——————

Subtract FICA tax (26.00) from pay (400.00) to get net pay.

SUBTRACT FICA FROM PAY GIVING NET-PAY

0	2	6	0	0		0	4	0	0	0	0		0	3	7	4	0	0

FICA PIC 999V99   PAY PIC 9999V99   NET-PAY PIC 9999V99

Calculation: 400.00 − 26.00 = 374.00

——————— Example ———————

Subtract FICA tax (26.00) from pay (400.00).

```
SUBTRACT FICA FROM PAY
```
Before Execution

```
 0 2 6 0 0              0 4 0 0 0 0
```

FICA PIC 999V99   PAY PIC 9999V99

After Execution

```
 0 2 6 0 0             0 3 7 4 0 0
```

FICA PIC 999V99   PAY PIC 9999V99

Any number of items may be subtracted. The sign (if any) is considered in the operation.

——————— Example ———————

Subtract 3.2 and X (−1.2) from Y (.32) to get Z.

```
SUBTRACT 3.2 X FROM Y GIVING Z
```

```
        –                    +                   –
 0 1 2 0           0 0 3 2          0 1 6 8
```

X PIC S99V99   Y PIC S99V99   Z PIC S99V99

Calculation: .32 − 3.2 − (−1.2) = −1.68

When you subtract from a constant, the GIVING clause *must* be specified, since it is not permissible to store a different value in a constant.

——————— Example ———————

Subtract contents of Field A (20) from 25. The following statement is *invalid:*

```
SUBTRACT FLDA FROM 25.
```

The following statement is *valid:*

```
SUBTRACT FLDA FROM 25 GIVING FLDB
```

```
 2 0 0 0              0 5 0 0
```

FLDA PIC 99V99   FLDB PIC 99V99

5.3 THE MULTIPLY STATEMENT

The MULTIPLY statement is used to perform multiplication of two numeric items (Fig. 5.3). The result is placed in the last data-name specified.

Figure 5.3   General form of the MULTIPLY statement

$$\underline{MULTIPLY} \begin{Bmatrix} \texttt{data-name-1} \\ \texttt{constant-1} \end{Bmatrix} \underline{BY} \begin{Bmatrix} \texttt{data-name-2 [\underline{GIVING} data-name-3]} \\ \texttt{constant-2 \quad \underline{GIVING} data-name-3} \end{Bmatrix}$$

—————— Example ——————

Multiply pay (400.00) by the constant .075 to get FICA tax. (Note that you are multiplying by a constant, so the GIVING clause is required.)

```
MULTIPLY PAY BY 0.075 GIVING FICA
```

| 0 4 0 0 0 0 | | 0 0 3 0 0 0 |
|-------------| |-------------|

PAY PIC 9999V99   FICA PIC 9999V99

Computation: 400 × .075 = 30.00

—————— Example ——————

Multiply price (20.00) times percent (25%) to get sale price. (Note that most sales are based on a percent-off figure, not on a direct percent as in this example.)

```
MULTIPLY PRICE BY PCT GIVING SALE-PRICE
```

| 0 2 0 0 0 | | 2 5 0 | | 0 0 5 0 0 |
|-----------| |-------| |-----------|

PRICE PIC 999V99   PCT PIC V999   SALE-PRICE PIC 999V99

Computation: 20.00 × .250 = 5.00

—————— Example ——————

Multiply the contents of FLDA (12.3) by the contents of FLDB (2.3), and store the results in FLDB.

```
MULTIPLY FLDA BY FLDB
```

Before Execution

| 1 2 3 | | 0 2 3 |
|-------| |-------|

FLDA PIC 99V9   FLDB PIC 99V9

After Execution

| 1 2 3 | | 2 8 2 |
|-------| |-------|

FLDA PIC 99V9   FLDB PIC 99V9

Computation: 12.3 × 2.3 = 28.29 ← This last digit will be truncated when the result is moved to FLDB.

5.4 THE DIVIDE STATEMENT

Recall the terminology used in arithmetic division:

$$\begin{array}{r} 2 \leftarrow \text{Quotient} \\ \text{Divisor} \rightarrow \quad 7)\overline{15} \leftarrow \text{Dividend} \\ \underline{14} \\ 1 \leftarrow \text{Remainder} \end{array}$$

The DIVIDE statement has two formats as shown in Figure 5.4. When the INTO option is specified, the divisor is specified first and the dividend is specified next. If the GIVING clause is omitted, then the quotient replaces the dividend.

Figure 5.4   General form of the DIVIDE statement

Format 1

DIVIDE $\left\{ \begin{array}{l} \text{data-name-1} \\ \text{constant-1} \end{array} \right\}$ INTO data-name-2

Format 2

DIVIDE $\left\{ \begin{array}{l} \text{data-name-1} \\ \text{constant-1} \end{array} \right\} \left\{ \begin{array}{l} \underline{\text{INTO}} \\ \underline{\text{BY}} \end{array} \right\} \left\{ \begin{array}{l} \text{data-name-2} \\ \text{constant-2} \end{array} \right\}$ GIVING data-name-3 [REMAINDER data-name-4]

——————— Example ———————

Divide KOUNT (20) into TOTAL (100) to get AVERAGE.

DIVIDE KOUNT INTO TOTAL GIVING AVERAGE

          Divisor   Dividend   Quotient

   2 0   0 1 0 0   0 5

KOUNT PIC 99   TOTAL PIC 9999   AVERAGE PIC 99

——————— Example ———————

Divide the contents of FLDA (12.3) into FLDB (4.6).

DIVIDE FLDA INTO FLDB

        Divisor   Dividend Quotient

Before Execution

  1 2 3   0 4 6

FLDA PIC 99V9   FLDB PIC 99V9

Computation: 4.6 ÷ 12.3 = .3

After Execution

  1 2 3   0 0 3

FLDA PIC 99V9   FLDB PIC 99V9

When the BY option is specified, the dividend is specified first and the divisor is specified next. The GIVING clause *must* be used in this case.

─────────── Example ───────────

Divide TOTAL (100) by KOUNT (20) to get AVERAGE.

```
DIVIDE TOTAL BY KOUNT GIVING AVERAGE
         ↑         ↑              ↑
      Dividend   Divisor       Quotient

   0 1 0 0          2 0           0 5
  └─┴─┴─┴─┘        └─┴─┘         └─┴─┘
  TOTAL PIC 9999   KOUNT PIC 99   AVERAGE PIC 99
```

If the REMAINDER option is included, the remainder after the division will be placed in the specified data-name. The remainder is computed by subtracting the product of the quotient and divisor from the dividend.

─────────── Example ───────────

Given a number of ounces, compute the number of pounds and ounces. For example, 20 ounces is equal to 1 pound, 4 ounces. The number of ounces left over is equal to the remainder after dividing by 16 and subtracting the number of ounces in 1 pound.

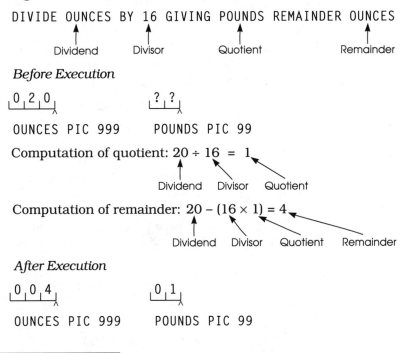

```
DIVIDE OUNCES BY 16 GIVING POUNDS REMAINDER OUNCES
         ↑         ↑            ↑              ↑
      Dividend   Divisor     Quotient      Remainder
```

Before Execution

```
   0 2 0           ? ?
  └─┴─┴─┘         └─┴─┘
  OUNCES PIC 999   POUNDS PIC 99
```

Computation of quotient: 20 ÷ 16 = 1
                          ↑   ↑   ↑
                      Dividend Divisor Quotient

Computation of remainder: 20 − (16 × 1) = 4
                          ↑   ↑   ↑   ↑
                      Dividend Divisor Quotient Remainder

After Execution

```
   0 0 4           0 1
  └─┴─┴─┘         └─┴─┘
  OUNCES PIC 999   POUNDS PIC 99
```

─────────── Example ───────────

Divide the dividend (62.8) by the contents of FLDA to get FLDB, and place any remainder in FLDC.

```
DIVIDE 62.8 BY FLDA GIVING FLDB REMAINDER FLDC
         ↑       ↑           ↑             ↑
      Dividend Divisor    Quotient      Remainder
```

Before Execution

$$\underset{\wedge}{\underline{\lfloor 0 \mid 1 \mid 3 \rfloor}} \qquad\qquad \underset{\wedge}{\underline{\lfloor ? \mid ? \mid ? \rfloor}} \qquad\qquad \underset{\wedge}{\underline{\lfloor ? \mid ? \rfloor}}$$

FLDA PIC 9V99   FLDB PIC 999   FLDC V99

Computation of quotient: $62.8 \div .13 = 483$

                     Dividend   Divisor   Quotient

Computation of remainder: $62.8 - (.13 \times 483) = .01$

                     Dividend   Divisor   Quotient   Remainder

After Execution

$$\underset{\wedge}{\underline{\lfloor 0 \mid 1 \mid 3 \rfloor}} \qquad\qquad \underline{\lfloor 4 \mid 8 \mid 3 \rfloor} \qquad\qquad \underset{\wedge}{\underline{\lfloor 0 \mid 1 \rfloor}}$$

FLDA PIC 9V99   FLDB PIC 999   FLDC PIC V99

5.5   THE COMPUTE STATEMENT

The COMPUTE statement is used to perform any desired sequence of arithmetic operations. The symbols used for operations are

+ Add
− Subtract
* Multiply
/ Divide
** Exponentiation

The general form of the COMPUTE statement is

> <u>COMPUTE</u> data-name = expression

The value of the expression is placed in the location specified by the data-name. An **expression** is either a constant, a variable, or any valid combination of constants and/or variables linked by arithmetic operations and parentheses. Arithmetic operation symbols and the equal sign must be preceded and followed by at least one blank.

──────── **Examples** ────────

Move the value 42 to FLDA.

     COMPUTE FLDA = 42

Place the value of FLDA into FLDB.

     COMPUTE FLDB = FLDA

Multiply content of FLDA by 3 and place the result in FLDC.

     COMPUTE FLDC = 3 * FLDA

Divide the TOTAL by KOUNT and place the result in AV.

     COMPUTE AV = TOTAL / KOUNT

Add A and B; subtract C from the result.

```
COMPUTE VALUE = A + B - C
```

Multiply A times itself three times to get the cube of A or A^3.

```
COMPUTE X = A ** 3
```

Parentheses may be used to control the order in which operations are carried out. Expressions within parentheses are evaluated first. For some compilers a left parenthesis must be preceded by a blank, and a right parenthesis must be followed by a blank or a period.

─────────── Example ───────────

Add 3 to the contents of FLDB. Then multiply the sum by 6.

Note the absence of blanks in these positions.

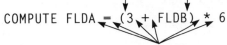

```
COMPUTE FLDA = (3 + FLDB) * 6
```

Note the presence of blanks in these positions.

Once 3 is added to FLDB, the result is multiplied by 6.

As many sets of parentheses as are necessary may be used.

─────────── Example ───────────

Compute the result of adding Z to Q; subtract that sum from Y; then multiply what is left by 6.

```
COMPUTE X = (Y - (Z + Q)) * 6
```

The expression in the innermost set of parentheses is evaluated first.

An expression is evaluated by performing operations in order of precedence (Fig. 5.5). Operations with equal precedence (such as multiplication and division or addition and subtraction) are performed in a left-to-right order.

Figure 5.5   Precedence of arithmetic operations

Expressions in parentheses		High precedence
**	Exponentiation	
*/	Multiplication and division	
+ −	Addition and subtraction	Low precedence

─────────── Example ───────────

Compute B × C first. Then add A.

```
COMPUTE X = A + B * C
```

Multiplication has higher precedence than addition; therefore, B and C are multiplied first, and only then is the result added to A.

─────── Example ───────

Compute the power 2^3 first. Then divide the result into the product of 4×2.

    COMPUTE FLDA = 4 * 2 / 2 ** 3

Exponentiation has the highest precedence; hence, the first operation to be performed is 2^3. Then, because multiplication precedes division, and they are both of the same order of precedence, the next operation is 4×2. Finally, division is performed, giving 1 as the value of the expression.

─────── Example ───────

Compute 3×2 and add it to 4. Then compute $3 \times 3 \times 3$ and multiply that result by 2. Subtract the last answer from the first (3×2 plus 4). (Your answer will be -44.)

    COMPUTE A = 4 + 3 * 2 - 3 ** 3 * 2

This is equivalent to

    COMPUTE A = (4 + (3 * 2)) - ((3 ** 3) * 2)

5.6 THE ROUNDED OPTION

The ROUNDED option may be used with any of the arithmetic statements. When it is specified, rounding of the computed result will be performed by the computer before it places the value in the receiving field. Rounding is performed by adding 5 to the digit immediately following the rightmost decimal digit to be stored, and then truncating excess decimal digits as usual.[1] For example, suppose the calculated result for an arithmetic operation is 12.347, and this value will be stored in a location with picture 99V99. Rounding will be performed as follows:

12.347   If this last digit is 0, 1, 2, 3, or 4, rounding has no effect on the value
+   5   stored. If this digit is 5, 6, 7, 8, or 9, rounding causes a carry of 1 into the
12.352   next position and does affect the value stored.
            2 is lost due to truncation.

    1 2 3 5
      ^
PIC 99V99

─────────────

[1] Negative quantities are rounded by first taking the absolute value of the field, then performing the rounding operation, and finally making the resulting field negative. For example,

12.347   absolute value   12.347
12.35   result is negative   +   5
                                 12.352

    1 2 3 5
      ^
PIC S99V99

If the receiving field had picture 99V9, the rounding would result in

12.345   This digit is less than 5; rounding has no effect on the value stored.
+   5
12.3~~95~~ ←—— 95 is lost due to truncation.

```
| 1 | 2 | 3 |
         ^
PIC 99V9
```

The placement of the ROUNDED option in each of the arithmetic statements is shown in the general formats in Figure 5.6.

Figure 5.6   General form of arithmetic statements

$$\underline{\text{ADD}} \begin{Bmatrix} \text{data-name-1} \\ \text{constant-1} \end{Bmatrix} \ldots \begin{Bmatrix} \underline{\text{TO}} \\ \underline{\text{GIVING}} \end{Bmatrix} \text{data-name-n} \quad [\underline{\text{ROUNDED}}]$$

$$\underline{\text{SUBTRACT}} \begin{Bmatrix} \text{data-name-1} \\ \text{constant-1} \end{Bmatrix} \ldots \underline{\text{FROM}} \begin{Bmatrix} \text{data-name-n } [\underline{\text{GIVING}} \text{ data-name-m}] \\ \text{constant-n} \quad \underline{\text{GIVING}} \text{ data-name-m} \end{Bmatrix} [\underline{\text{ROUNDED}}]$$

$$\underline{\text{MULTIPLY}} \begin{Bmatrix} \text{data-name-1} \\ \text{constant-1} \end{Bmatrix} \underline{\text{BY}} \begin{Bmatrix} \text{data-name-2 } [\underline{\text{GIVING}} \text{ data-name-3}] \\ \text{constant-2} \quad \underline{\text{GIVING}} \text{ data-name-3} \end{Bmatrix} [\underline{\text{ROUNDED}}]$$

$$\underline{\text{DIVIDE}} \begin{Bmatrix} \text{data-name-1} \\ \text{constant-1} \end{Bmatrix} \underline{\text{INTO}} \text{ data-name-2} \quad [\underline{\text{ROUNDED}}]$$

$$\underline{\text{DIVIDE}} \begin{Bmatrix} \text{data-name-1} \\ \text{constant-2} \end{Bmatrix} \begin{Bmatrix} \underline{\text{INTO}} \\ \underline{\text{BY}} \end{Bmatrix} \begin{Bmatrix} \text{data-name-2} \\ \text{constant-3} \end{Bmatrix} \underline{\text{GIVING}} \text{ data-name-1 } [\underline{\text{ROUNDED}}]$$
$$[\underline{\text{REMAINDER}} \text{ data-name-4}]$$

$$\underline{\text{COMPUTE}} \text{ data-name } [\underline{\text{ROUNDED}}] = \text{expression}$$

———— **Example** ————

Add 6.2, 4.52, and 7.892 to get an answer rounded to the nearest whole number.

```
ADD 6.2 4.52 7.892 GIVING X ROUNDED
```

Computation:
```
          6.2
          4.52
       +  7.892
         18.612
       +     5
         19.112
```

After Execution

```
| 1 | 9 |
         ^
X PIC 99
```

─────── Example ───────

Multiply the contents of FLDA (12.3) times the contents of FLDB (3.4), and round the answer to tenths.

```
MULTIPLY FLDA BY FLDB ROUNDED
```

Before Execution

1	2	3

FLDA PIC 99V9

0	3	4

FLDB PIC 99V9

Computation:

$$
\begin{array}{r}
12.3 \\
\times\ 3.4 \\
\hline
492 \\
369 \\
\hline
41.82 \\
+\quad 5 \\
\hline
41.87 \\
\end{array}
$$

After Execution

4	1	8

FLDB PIC 99V9

─────── Example ───────

Add 4.2 to 8.97 and round the answer to tenths.

```
COMPUTE XYZ ROUNDED = 4.2 + 8.97
```

Computation:

$$
\begin{array}{r}
4.2 \\
+8.97 \\
\hline
13.17 \\
+\quad 5 \\
\hline
13.22 \\
\end{array}
$$

1	3	2

XYZ PIC 99V9

5.7 PROGRAM EXAMPLE

Problem Statement

The XYZ Company requires that a payroll register, showing gross pay and net pay for its employees, be constructed. Input consists of records that contain the following fields:

Employee number
Employee name
Regular hours worked
Overtime hours worked
Pay rate
Federal withholding rate
Other deductions

The program must calculate and print:

> Gross pay
> Amount of federal income tax to withhold
> Amount of FICA taxes to withhold
> Net pay

The program must also accumulate and print appropriate totals. The printer spacing chart for the required report is shown in Figure 5.7.

Problem Analysis

This problem requires that a data-file, called PAY-FILE, be processed to produce a printed report called PAY-REGISTER. The processing of each record entails the computation of four amounts—withholding, FICA, gross pay, and net pay. It will be necessary to define numeric fields for these amounts (in addition to the edited fields on the output record) because they are involved in further computations. Totals must be accumulated for five different fields; therefore, five accumulators will be needed.

   The overall structure of this problem resembles those examples presented previously. The primary difference in this program is the number of computations required. A plan for this program is shown in Figure 5.8.

Figure 5.8   Plan for payroll register program

Main control

   Open files
   Write headings
   Read pay file
   Do Process data until end of file
   Write total line
   Close files
   Stop

Process data

   Compute amounts for detail output
   Accumulate totals
   Write detail line
   Read pay file

Problem Solution

Program 5a makes extensive use of the arithmetic statements described in this chapter, particularly in the paragraph 3000-COMPUTE-PAY (lines 191–203). A structure diagram for this program is shown in Figure 5.9. The program also illustrates several new COBOL features and structured programming practices.

Continuation of Nonnumeric Literals

Lines 68–69 illustrate a common situation that arises when defining long nonnumeric literals in the DATA DIVISION. The string of characters is too long to fit on one line in the usual fashion. Two solutions to the problem are possible. One solution is to bring the entire character string to a second line, an approach used in Program 5a. An alternative solution is to

Figure 5.7   Printer spacing chart for payroll register

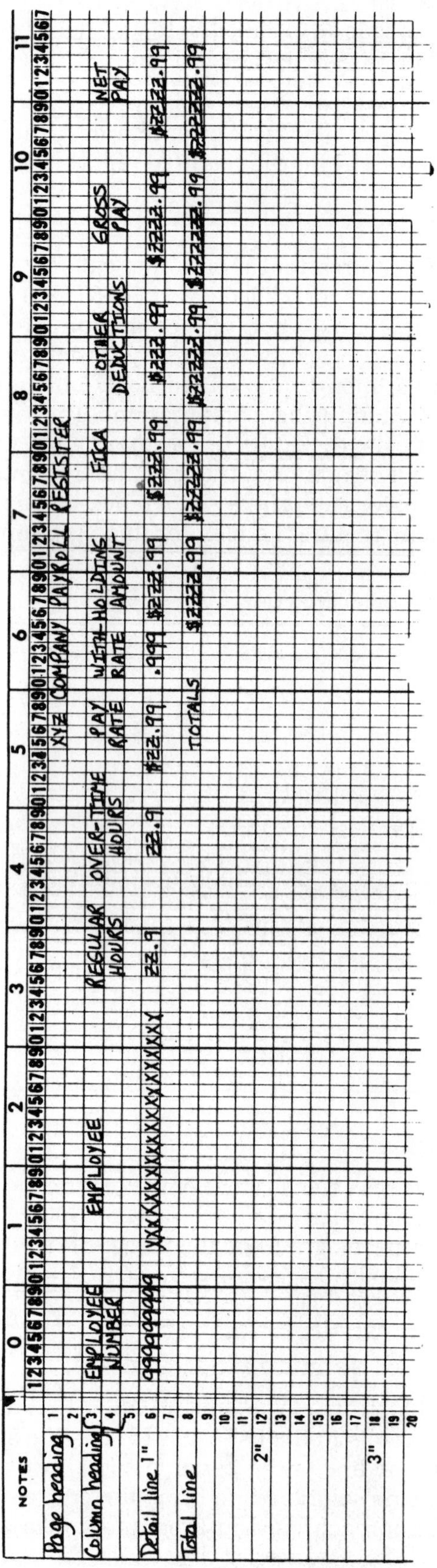

Figure 5.9   Structure diagram for Program 5a

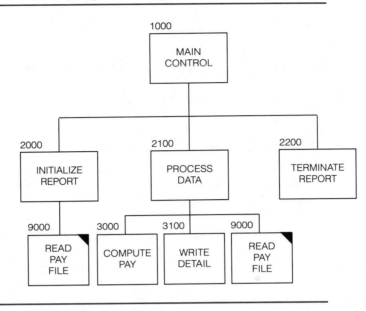

continue the literal from the first line to the second, as shown in Figure 5.10.

As shown in Figure 5.10, the literal XYZ COMPANY PAYROLL REGISTER is broken into two parts: The first part on line 1 extends from positions 61–72; the second part is on line 2, positions 13–28. The two parts are connected by placing a hyphen (−) in position 7 and quotes in the B margin (position 12) of the continuation line. In general the placement of a hyphen in position 7 of a line will cause the content of that line to be treated as a continuation of the preceding line. When using this mechanism to continue nonnumeric literals,[2] the remaining characters of the literal must be preceded by a quote in the B margin. Note that there are no quotes following the literal on the first line; all of the characters from the opening quote through position 72 are treated as part of the literal.

Figure 5.10   Continuation of nonnumeric literals

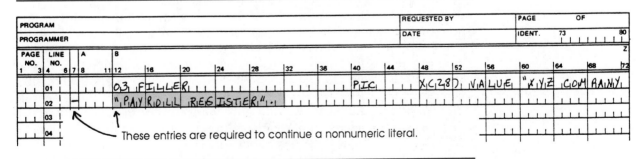

---

[2] Although other COBOL elements, including data-names, numeric-constants, and reserved words, can be continued by use of a dash in position 7, the continuation facility is recommended only for nonnumeric literals.

Grouping of Related Fields in WORKING-STORAGE

A number of data-names in addition to the usual output records are defined in WORKING-STORAGE. All of the data-names could be defined as 01 items; however, current structured programming practice requires that related items be grouped under 01 items that describe the relation. Thus, under COMPUTED-AMOUNTS, the items WITH-AMT, NET-PAY, GROSS-PAY, and FICA are defined; under TOTALS, all the data-names used as accumulators are defined. This practice makes the program easier to read.

VALUE Clause for all Data-names

In Program 5a, the data-names listed under TOTALS are all accumulators. The VALUE clause is used to ensure that the initial value of each data-name is zero so that the accumulation process will function properly. The data-names listed under COMPUTED-AMOUNTS are also initialized to zero. This is not a requirement of the logic of the program since the value in each of them is replaced by appropriate statements in 3000-COMPUTE-PAY (see lines 191–203).

All elementary numeric items defined in WORKING-STORAGE should be given an initial value. The reason for this practice lies not in an absolute requirement for logical correctness but in making the program easier to debug and update. Suppose, for example, that a programmer omits the initialization of some data-name such as FICA-AMT. Suppose further that the statement computing FICA-AMT is omitted in the PROCEDURE DIVISION. In this case, the first reference to FICA-AMT usually will cause the program to terminate because of invalid data. The source of such an error is usually difficult to locate. However, if FICA-AMT had been initialized, the reference to the data-name would have been processed with a value zero, and the program would have continued in a normal fashion. When it was noted that the value of FICA-AMT was zero on the same output, the programmer could surmise that the computation in the PROCEDURE DIVISION was either incorrect or omitted. Thus, the debugging process is simplified considerably.

This practice also results in programs that are easier to update. If a subsequent revision of the program results in the deletion of the statement that computes a value for the data-name, the remaining statements can be left unaltered because the content of the data-name will have no effect on the computations.

Constants in WORKING-STORAGE

Consider the data item FICA-FACTOR defined in line 51 of Program 5a. This value is used in the computation of the FICA withholding amount at line 196. The practice of defining constants such as this in WORKING-STORAGE makes programs easier to change when the value of the constant changes. If this practice is followed, a programmer performing maintenance has to make only a single change in a well-defined, easily located WORKING-STORAGE entry. Otherwise, the maintenance programmer must search through the PROCEDURE DIVISION and change every instance where the constant is used. This is a particular burden if the constant is used more than once. There is always the chance that one value will be changed but another will not be, resulting in a potentially difficult debugging problem.

Program 5a

```
 1 IDENTIFICATION DIVISION.
 2
 3 PROGRAM-ID. PAYROLL-REGISTER-PRO5A.
 4 AUTHOR. HORN.
 5
 6 ENVIRONMENT DIVISION.
 7
 8 CONFIGURATION SECTION.
 9
10 SOURCE-COMPUTER.
11 OBJECT-COMPUTER.
12
13 INPUT-OUTPUT SECTION.
14
15 FILE-CONTROL.
16
17     SELECT PAY-FILE ASSIGN TO DISK.
18
19     SELECT PAY-REGISTER ASSIGN TO PRINTER.
20
21 DATA DIVISION.
22
23 FILE SECTION.
24
25 FD  PAY-FILE
26     LABEL RECORDS ARE STANDARD
27     DATA RECORD IS PAY-RECORD.
28
29 01  PAY-RECORD.
30     03 EMPLOYEE-NUMBER-PR      PIC 9(9).
31     03 EMPLOYEE-NAME-PR        PIC X(20).
32     03 REG-HRS-PR              PIC 99V9.
33     03 OT-HRS-PR               PIC 99V9.
34     03 PAY-RATE-PR             PIC 99V99.
35     03 WITH-RATE-PR            PIC V999.
36     03 OTHER-DEDUCTIONS-PR     PIC 999V99.
37     03 FILLER                  PIC X(33).
38
39 FD  PAY-REGISTER
40     LABEL RECORDS ARE OMITTED
41     DATA RECORD IS PAY-REGISTER-RECORD.
42
43 01  PAY-REGISTER-RECORD        PIC X(132).
44
45 WORKING-STORAGE SECTION.
46
47 01  FLAGS.
48     02 EOF-FLAG                PIC X(3) VALUE "NO".
49
50 01  CONSTANTS.
51     02 FICA-FACTOR             PIC 9V9999 VALUE 0.0750.
52
53 01  COMPUTED-AMOUNTS.
54     03 WITH-AMT                PIC 999V99  VALUE ZERO.
55     03 NET-PAY                 PIC 9999V99 VALUE ZERO.
56     03 GROSS-PAY               PIC 9999V99 VALUE ZERO.
57     03 FICA                    PIC 999V99  VALUE ZERO.
```

Program 5a   *(continued)*

```
 58
 59 01  ACCUMULATED-TOTALS.
 60     03 TOTAL-NET                PIC 9(6)V99 VALUE ZERO.
 61     03 TOTAL-WITH               PIC 9(4)V99 VALUE ZERO.
 62     03 TOTAL-OTHER              PIC 9(5)V99 VALUE ZERO.
 63     03 TOTAL-FICA               PIC 9(5)V99 VALUE ZERO.
 64     03 TOTAL-GROSS              PIC 9(6)V99 VALUE ZERO.
 65
 66 01  HEADING-LINE.
 67     03 FILLER                   PIC X(54) VALUE SPACES.
 68     03 FILLER                   PIC X(28) VALUE
 69        "XYZ COMPANY PAYROLL REGISTER".
 70
 71 01  SUB-HEAD-1.
 72     03 FILLER                   PIC X     VALUE SPACES.
 73     03 FILLER                   PIC X(8)  VALUE "EMPLOYEE".
 74     03 FILLER                   PIC X(6)  VALUE SPACES.
 75     03 FILLER                   PIC X(8)  VALUE "EMPLOYEE".
 76     03 FILLER                   PIC X(11) VALUE SPACES.
 77     03 FILLER                   PIC X(7)  VALUE "REGULAR".
 78     03 FILLER                   PIC X(2)  VALUE SPACES.
 79     03 FILLER                   PIC X(9)  VALUE "OVER-TIME".
 80     03 FILLER                   PIC X(3)  VALUE SPACES.
 81     03 FILLER                   PIC X(3)  VALUE "PAY".
 82     03 FILLER                   PIC X(2)  VALUE SPACES.
 83     03 FILLER                   PIC X(12) VALUE "WITH-HOLDING".
 84     03 FILLER                   PIC X(5)  VALUE SPACES.
 85     03 FILLER                   PIC X(4)  VALUE "FICA".
 86     03 FILLER                   PIC X(5)  VALUE SPACES.
 87     03 FILLER                   PIC X(5)  VALUE "OTHER".
 88     03 FILLER                   PIC X(6)  VALUE SPACES.
 89     03 FILLER                   PIC X(5)  VALUE "GROSS".
 90     03 FILLER                   PIC X(7)  VALUE SPACES.
 91     03 FILLER                   PIC X(3)  VALUE "NET".
 92
 93 01  SUB-HEAD-2.
 94     03 FILLER                   PIC X(2)  VALUE SPACES.
 95     03 FILLER                   PIC X(6)  VALUE "NUMBER".
 96     03 FILLER                   PIC X(9)  VALUE SPACES.
 97     03 FILLER                   PIC X(4)  VALUE "NAME".
 98     03 FILLER                   PIC X(14) VALUE SPACES.
 99     03 FILLER                   PIC X(5)  VALUE "HOURS".
100     03 FILLER                   PIC X(5)  VALUE SPACES.
101     03 FILLER                   PIC X(5)  VALUE "HOURS".
102     03 FILLER                   PIC X(4)  VALUE SPACES.
103     03 FILLER                   PIC X(4)  VALUE "RATE".
104     03 FILLER                   PIC X(2)  VALUE SPACES.
105     03 FILLER                   PIC X(4)  VALUE "RATE".
106     03 FILLER                   PIC X(2)  VALUE SPACES.
107     03 FILLER                   PIC X(6)  VALUE "AMOUNT".
108     03 FILLER                   PIC X(12) VALUE SPACES.
109     03 FILLER                   PIC X(10) VALUE "DEDUCTIONS".
110     03 FILLER                   PIC X(4)  VALUE SPACES.
111     03 FILLER                   PIC X(3)  VALUE "PAY".
112     03 FILLER                   PIC X(8)  VALUE SPACES.
113     03 FILLER                   PIC X(3)  VALUE "PAY".
114
```

Program 5a *(continued)*

```
115 01   DETAIL-LINE.
116        03 FILLER                     PIC X    VALUE SPACES.
117        03 EMPLOYEE-NUMBER-DL         PIC 9(9).
118        03 FILLER                     PIC X(2) VALUE SPACES.
119        03 EMPLOYEE-NAME-DL           PIC X(20).
120        03 FILLER                     PIC X(3) VALUE SPACES.
121        03 REG-HRS-DL                 PIC ZZ.9.
122        03 FILLER                     PIC X(6) VALUE SPACES.
123        03 OT-HRS-DL                  PIC ZZ.9.
124        03 FILLER                     PIC X(3) VALUE SPACES.
125        03 PAY-RATE-DL                PIC $ZZ.99.
126        03 FILLER                     PIC X(2) VALUE SPACES.
127        03 WITH-RATE-DL               PIC .999.
128        03 FILLER                     PIC X    VALUE SPACES.
129        03 WITH-AMT-DL                PIC $ZZZ.99.
130        03 FILLER                     PIC X(3) VALUE SPACES.
131        03 FICA-DL                    PIC $ZZZ.99.
132        03 FILLER                     PIC X(3) VALUE SPACES.
133        03 OTHER-DEDUCTIONS-DL        PIC $ZZZ.99.
134        03 FILLER                     PIC X(3) VALUE SPACES.
135        03 GROSS-PAY-DL               PIC $Z(4).99.
136        03 FILLER                     PIC X(3) VALUE SPACES.
137        03 NET-PAY-DL                 PIC $Z(4).99.
138
139 01   TOTAL-LINE.
140        03 FILLER                     PIC X(54) VALUE SPACES.
141        03 FILLER                     PIC X(6)  VALUE "TOTALS".
142        03 FILLER                     PIC X(4)  VALUE SPACES.
143        03 TOTAL-WITH-TL              PIC $Z(4).99.
144        03 FILLER                     PIC X    VALUE SPACES.
145        03 TOTAL-FICA-TL              PIC $Z(5).99.
146        03 FILLER                     PIC X    VALUE SPACES.
147        03 TOTAL-OTHER-TL             PIC $Z(5).99.
148        03 FILLER                     PIC X    VALUE SPACES.
149        03 TOTAL-GROSS-TL             PIC $Z(6).99.
150        03 FILLER                     PIC X    VALUE SPACES.
151        03 TOTAL-NET-TL               PIC $Z(6).99.
152
153 PROCEDURE DIVISION.
154
155 1000-MAIN-CONTROL.
156
157        PERFORM 2000-INITIALIZE-REPORT.
158        PERFORM 2100-PROCESS-DATA
159             UNTIL EOF-FLAG = "YES".
160        PERFORM 2200-TERMINATE-REPORT.
161        STOP RUN.
162
163 2000-INITIALIZE-REPORT.
164
165        OPEN INPUT PAY-FILE
166             OUTPUT PAY-REGISTER.
167        WRITE PAY-REGISTER-RECORD FROM HEADING-LINE AFTER PAGE.
168        WRITE PAY-REGISTER-RECORD FROM SUB-HEAD-1 AFTER 2.
169        WRITE PAY-REGISTER-RECORD FROM SUB-HEAD-2 AFTER 1.
170        MOVE SPACES TO PAY-REGISTER-RECORD.
171        WRITE PAY-REGISTER-RECORD AFTER 1.
172        PERFORM 9000-READ-PAY-FILE.
```

```
173
174 2100-PROCESS-DATA.
175
176     PERFORM 3000-COMPUTE-PAY.
177     PERFORM 3100-WRITE-DETAIL.
178     PERFORM 9000-READ-PAY-FILE.
179
180 2200-TERMINATE-REPORT.
181
182     MOVE TOTAL-WITH   TO TOTAL-WITH-TL.
183     MOVE TOTAL-FICA   TO TOTAL-FICA-TL.
184     MOVE TOTAL-OTHER  TO TOTAL-OTHER-TL.
185     MOVE TOTAL-GROSS  TO TOTAL-GROSS-TL.
186     MOVE TOTAL-NET    TO TOTAL-NET-TL.
187     WRITE PAY-REGISTER-RECORD FROM TOTAL-LINE AFTER 2.
188     CLOSE PAY-FILE
189           PAY-REGISTER.
190
191 3000-COMPUTE-PAY.
192
193     COMPUTE GROSS-PAY ROUNDED = REG-HRS-PR * PAY-RATE-PR +
194                                 OT-HRS-PR * PAY-RATE-PR * 1.5.
195     MULTIPLY WITH-RATE-PR BY GROSS-PAY GIVING WITH-AMT ROUNDED.
196     MULTIPLY FICA-FACTOR BY GROSS-PAY GIVING FICA ROUNDED.
197     SUBTRACT WITH-AMT FICA OTHER-DEDUCTIONS-PR
198         FROM GROSS-PAY GIVING NET-PAY.
199     ADD WITH-AMT             TO TOTAL-WITH.
200     ADD FICA                 TO TOTAL-FICA.
201     ADD OTHER-DEDUCTIONS-PR  TO TOTAL-OTHER.
202     ADD GROSS-PAY            TO TOTAL-GROSS.
203     ADD NET-PAY              TO TOTAL-NET.
204
205 3100-WRITE-DETAIL.
206
207     MOVE EMPLOYEE-NUMBER-PR   TO EMPLOYEE-NUMBER-DL.
208     MOVE EMPLOYEE-NAME-PR     TO EMPLOYEE-NAME-DL.
209     MOVE REG-HRS-PR           TO REG-HRS-DL.
210     MOVE OT-HRS-PR            TO OT-HRS-DL.
211     MOVE PAY-RATE-PR          TO PAY-RATE-DL.
212     MOVE WITH-RATE-PR         TO WITH-RATE-DL.
213     MOVE OTHER-DEDUCTIONS-PR  TO OTHER-DEDUCTIONS-DL.
214     MOVE WITH-AMT             TO WITH-AMT-DL.
215     MOVE FICA                 TO FICA-DL.
216     MOVE GROSS-PAY            TO GROSS-PAY-DL.
217     MOVE NET-PAY              TO NET-PAY-DL.
218     WRITE PAY-REGISTER-RECORD FROM DETAIL-LINE AFTER 1.
219
220 9000-READ-PAY-FILE.
221
222     READ PAY-FILE
223         AT END MOVE "YES" TO EOF-FLAG.
```

5.8 THE ON SIZE ERROR OPTION

The `ON SIZE ERROR` option causes the program to test for errors and to take appropriate action when one of the following two types of errors is found during execution of an arithmetic statement:

- Division by a divisor having value zero.
- A receiving field that is too small to accept all the significant digits to the left of the decimal point of the calculated result.

The programmer is responsible for specifying data items that are sufficiently large to hold any valid results. The programmer also needs to ensure that the computer is not asked to attempt the impossible operation of dividing by zero. However, such errors do occur because of errors in data and/or programmer oversight. The `ON SIZE ERROR` option allows the program to take appropriate action when such errors are detected during execution of a program. If the `ON SIZE ERROR` option is included in the arithmetic statement, the statement in that clause will be executed if either of the errors is detected. The general form of the clause is

```
ON SIZE ERROR statement . . .
```

Any number of statements may be included in an `ON SIZE ERROR` clause. The clause is placed after the main body of each of the arithmetic statements.

───────── **Example** ─────────

Add X (78.3) and Y (87.2) to get Z; also, if a size error occurs, write an appropriate message.

```
ADD X Y GIVING Z
    ON SIZE ERROR
        WRITE OUTLINE FROM ERROR-MSG-LINE AFTER 1.
```

Before Execution

| 7 | 8 | 3 | | 8 | 7 | 2 | | 1 | 2 | 3 |

X PIC 99V9   Y PIC 99V9   Z PIC 99V9

Computation:

$$78.3$$
$$+\ 87.2$$

Size error ──────→ 165.5
detected

Because a size error has occurred, the `WRITE` statement will be executed; that is, the program will now print a message explaining that the answer field is too small.

After Execution

| 1 | 2 | 3 |

Z PIC 99V9

The content of `ERROR-MSG-LINE` will be written on the printer. An appropriate message would be `ARITHMETIC OVERFLOW HAS OCCURRED`.

─────── Example ───────

Divide the contents of FLDA (2.3) by the contents of FLDB (0) to get FLDC. Also, if a size error occurs, move both FLDA and FLDB to a report line that explains the error.

```
DIVIDE FLDA BY FLDB GIVING FLDC
    ON SIZE ERROR
        MOVE FLDA TO FLDA-OUT
        MOVE FLDB TO FLDB-OUT
        WRITE OUT-LINE FROM ERR-LINE AFTER 1.
```

Another option for this statement would be

```
DIVIDE FLDA BY FLDB GIVING FLDC
    ON SIZE ERROR
        PERFORM ERROR-MESSAGE-OUTPUT.
```

The paragraph ERROR-MESSAGE-OUTPUT would contain the required statements to produce the error message.

Before Execution

| 0 | 2 | 3 | | 0 | 0 |

FLDA PIC 99V9   FLDB PIC 99

Since the value of the divisor is zero, the statements in the ON SIZE ERROR clause will be executed; the division will not be performed.

───────────────────────

In each of the above examples, the sentence following the arithmetic statement will be executed next after the ON SIZE ERROR statements have been executed. In flowchart form, the ON SIZE ERROR option is shown as

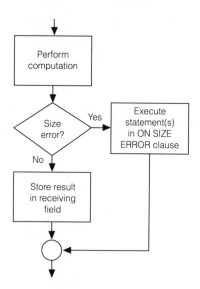

If a division by zero is attempted by a statement and the ON SIZE ERROR clause is not a part of the statement, the program is halted by the operating system, which prints an appropriate error message. If a receiving field is too small to accept the significant digits to the left of the decimal

point and the ON SIZE ERROR clause is not a part of the statement, the results are moved to the receiving field, and the leftmost digits will be truncated.

Example

Add the content of a data item X to another, Y, to get the result Z.

```
ADD X Y GIVING Z
```

Before Execution

7	8	3

X PIC 99V9

8	7	2

Y PIC 99V9

?	?	?

Z PIC 99V9

Computation:

$$\begin{array}{r} 78.3 \\ +87.2 \\ \hline 165.5 \end{array}$$

After Execution

7	8	3

X PIC 99V9

8	7	2

Y PIC 99V9

leftmost digits of receiving field have been truncated →

6	5	5

Z PIC 99V9

One area in programming in which size errors are particularly prevalent is in the accumulation of totals. The programmer has little control over the number of records the program will process or the size of the values that fields will contain. Inflation, which causes values to increase, is a partial cause of this problem. A program which performed adequately in the past may be faced with an overflow in accumulation of totals because of newly inflated values.

One way in which the programmer can warn the user of a report in which overflow has occurred is by placement of flags beside fields in which there has been overflow. For example, suppose the TOTAL-LINE from Program 5a (lines 139 through 151) is replaced with the following:

```
01   TOTAL-LINE.
     03  FILLER              PIC X(54)      VALUE SPACES.
     03  FILLER              PIC X(6)       VALUE "TOTALS".
     03  FILLER              PIC X(4)       VALUE SPACES.
     03  TOTAL-WITH-TL       PIC $Z(4).99.
     03  ERROR-IN-WITH-TL    PIC X          VALUE SPACES.
     03  TOTAL-FICA-TL       PIC $Z(5).99.
     03  ERROR-IN-FICA-TL    PIC X          VALUE SPACES.
     03  TOTAL-OTHER-TL      PIC $Z(5).99.
     03  ERROR-IN-OTHER-TL   PIC X          VALUE SPACES.
     03  TOTAL-GROSS-TL      PIC $Z(6).99.
     03  ERROR-IN-GROSS-TL   PIC X          VALUE SPACES.
     03  TOTAL-NET-TL        PIC $Z(6).99.
     03  ERROR-IN-NET-TL     PIC X          VALUE SPACES.
```

Each accumulated total has been provided with a field into which an appropriate character such as "*" can be placed if overflow occurs. The statements which compute these totals in the PROCEDURE DIVISION (lines 199 through 203) can be replaced by

```
ADD WITH-AMT TO TOTAL-WITH
    ON SIZE ERROR MOVE "*" TO ERROR-IN-WITH-TL.
ADD FICA TO TOTAL-FICA
    ON SIZE ERROR MOVE "*" TO ERROR-IN-FICA-TL.
ADD OTHER-DEDUCTIONS-PR TO TOTAL-OTHER
    ON SIZE ERROR MOVE "*" TO ERROR-IN-OTHER-TL.
ADD GROSS-PAY TO TOTAL-GROSS
    ON SIZE ERROR MOVE "*" TO ERROR-IN-GROSS-TL.
ADD NET-PAY TO TOTAL-NET
    ON SIZE ERROR MOVE "*" TO ERROR-IN-NET-TL.
```

If a size error occurs in any of the accumulation statements, the character "*" will be moved to the appropriate output field. Output from this program might appear as

```
TOTALS $1129.30 $304.00 $3222.19 $5241.14*$1035.91*
```

in which overflow has occurred in accumulation of the last two items-- TOTAL-GROSS and TOTAL-NET.

5.9 DEBUG CLINIC

Computation with Nonnumeric Items

Note that in Program 5a, several data items appear to be defined twice. For example, consider GROSS-PAY (line 56). GROSS-PAY is defined as a numeric item (PIC 9999V99), and GROSS-PAY-DL is defined as numeric edited (PIC $Z(4).99). This dual definition is necessary because after GROSS-PAY is computed (line 193), it is required for further computations (lines 195 through 203). In general, a computation statement may place results in a numeric edited field. For example,

```
COMPUTE GROSS-PAY-DL ROUNDED =
    REG-HRS-PR * PAY-RATE-PR +
    OT-HRS-PR * PAY-RATE-PR * 1.5.
```

would be a valid statement. The result would be computed, and the value would be edited when placed in GROSS-PAY-DL. But GROSS-PAY-DL is a nonnumeric item because of the editing process. Because it is nonnumeric, it cannot be part of a numeric operation. Thus, a statement such as

```
ADD GROSS-PAY-DL TO TOTAL-GROSS.
```

would be invalid.

Items used as accumulators are used both as the receiving field and as a part of the computation, so accumulators must be defined as numeric fields as well as edited output fields. In preparation for output, the numeric field that has acted as an accumulator is moved to an appropriately edited output field. Any other item that will be used in further computations after a value is placed in it must be defined both as a numeric field and as a separate edited field. Remember:

> Computations cannot be performed on numeric edited data items.

Testing Programs

As programs become longer and more complex, the job of providing adequate test data becomes more demanding. In fact, it may be necessary to test programs with more than one set of data records to make sure that the program will function properly in all sets of circumstances. A common practice is to test each program at least three times: once with no data (that is, with an input file that contains no data records); again with "good" data (data that results in no error conditions); and finally with "bad" data (data that tests the program's ability to handle error conditions). The development of a set of data records that provides a thorough test of a program's logic should be started early in the program-development cycle. This task is one that beginning programmers often do not perform adequately because it can be tedious and time-consuming. However, the success or failure of a programming project often hinges as much on thorough testing of the finished product as it does on imaginative program design or meticulous coding. Placing a program into production before it has been adequately tested surely will be embarrassing for the programmer and perhaps expensive for the organization. The old engineering maxim "There is never time to do it right but always time to do it over" often applies to programming.

5.10 COBOL-85 UPDATE

As we have noted in our discussion of the ADD statement, there are two basic forms: ADD . . . TO and ADD . . . GIVING. In COBOL-85, it is permissible to use the word TO in the GIVING format of the ADD statement. A general form is as follows:

$$\underline{\text{ADD}} \left\{ \begin{array}{l} \text{data-name-1} \\ \text{constant-1} \end{array} \right\} \cdots \underline{\text{TO}} \left\{ \begin{array}{l} \text{data-name-n} \\ \text{constant-n} \end{array} \right\} \underline{\text{GIVING}}\ \text{data-name-m}$$

The word TO is optional and has no effect on the execution of the statement. That is, during execution of the program, the content of operands 1 through n are added, and the result is placed in data-name-m, the identifier following the GIVING clause. In particular, the content of data-name-n is not changed.

──────── Example ────────

The following statements are equivalent in COBOL-85:

```
ADD X Y TO Z GIVING W.      ADD X Y Z GIVING W.
```

In each case, only the value of W will be changed.

One of the major changes in COBOL-85 is the addition of scope delimiters to all conditional statements. We have already discussed END-READ and END-PERFORM, both of which can be used to terminate the READ and PERFORM statements. In COBOL-85, each of the arithmetic statements may have a scope delimiter if desired. The new reserved words are

```
END-ADD
END-SUBTRACT
END-MULTIPLY
END-DIVIDE
END-COMPUTE
```

These reserved words are useful when the ON SIZE ERROR clause is included as part of one of the arithmetic statements. This clause makes what would otherwise be an imperative statement into a conditional statement because the statement(s) in the SIZE ERROR clause are executed only if the size error condition is detected during the computation. (In COBOL-74, the SIZE ERROR clause must be terminated by a period; using the new scope delimiters makes this practice unnecessary in COBOL-85.)

──────────── **Example** ────────────

```
ADD X Y TO Z GIVING W
    ON SIZE ERROR
            WRITE Outline FROM Error-Msg-Line AFTER 1
END-ADD
```

In this example, it is not necessary to conclude the ADD statement with a period unless it is the last statement in a paragraph.

A second modification to the arithmetic statements that was introduced in COBOL-85 is the inclusion of the NOT ON SIZE ERROR clause as an optional part of each of the arithmetic statements. Statements in the NOT ON SIZE ERROR clause are executed if the size error condition does *not* occur—that is, if the arithmetic operation is completed normally. A general form for the new construct is as follows:

```
[ON SIZE ERROR statement-1]
[NOT ON SIZE ERROR statement-2]
```

The following flowchart shows the effect of the two clauses during execution of the statement:

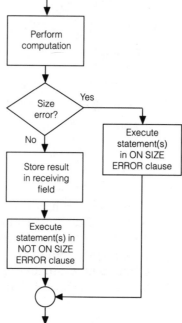

——————— Example ———————

Add the value of A to B. If size error occurs, move zero to B-Out and an asterisk to B-Error-Out; otherwise, move B to B-Out and move a space to B-Error-Out.

```
ADD A TO B
    ON SIZE ERROR
        MOVE ZERO TO B-Out
        MOVE "*" TO B-Error-Out
    NOT ON SIZE ERROR
        MOVE B TO B-Out
        MOVE SPACE TO B-Error-Out
END-ADD
```

Paralleling the inclusion of NOT ON SIZE ERROR in COBOL-85 is the introduction of NOT AT END, which can be included in the READ statement. A general format for this clause is as follows:

```
READ file-name
     [AT END statement-1]
     [NOT AT END statement-2]
[END-READ]
```

During execution of the program, if the read operation detects the end of the file, statement-1 is executed; otherwise, statement-2 is executed. The following flowchart shows the execution of this statement.

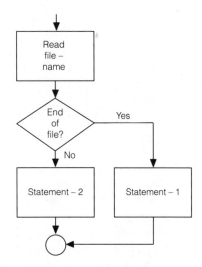

This form of the READ statement can be used to simplify the logic of the PROCEDURE DIVISION of many programs. Previously, we have always read an input file at two points in a program—once prior to entering the processing loop and again as the last action in the loop. (The task we must accomplish is to process each record in the file and stop when all records have been processed.) Consider the following program segment:

```
PERFORM UNTIL Eof-Code = "YES"
    READ Data-File
        AT END
            MOVE "YES" TO Eof-Code
        NOT AT END
            PERFORM Process-Data
    END-READ
END-PERFORM
```

If this statement is used as the basic loop control mechanism in a program, it is unnecessary to read the first record from `Data-File` prior to entering the loop, and it is unnecessary to read successive data records from the file as the last task accomplished in `Process-Data`. All reading of the file can take place at this one point in the program since control returns to the `READ` statement after execution of `Process-Data`, as shown in the following flowchart:

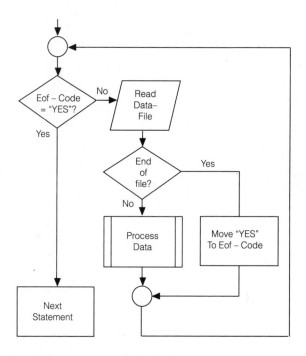

Program 5a85 shows this technique applied to Program 5a. Note that we have omitted the paragraph `9000-Read-Pay-File`, which would have been necessary using our previous loop control mechanism. Compare the paragraph `2100-Process-Data` with the similar paragraph in Program 5a. In this program, the paragraph does exactly what you would expect it to do given its name; it processes the data from one data-record and has nothing to do with reading the next record from the file (which technically is unrelated to processing the data from the preceding record). Also compare `2000-Initialize-Report` with the similar paragraph in Program 5a. This paragraph contains tasks that must be accomplished prior to reading the first record in the file; it does not read the first record. All records are read as part of `1000-Main-Control`.

This technique can be adapted for use with any COBOL program. However, it is most appropriate when using a COBOL-85 compiler because it makes effective use of statements that are supported only by COBOL-85.

Program 5a85

```
  1 IDENTIFICATION DIVISION.
  2
  3 PROGRAM-ID. Payroll-Register-Pro5a85.
  .
  .
  .
138 01  Total-Line.
139     03                              PIC X(54) VALUE SPACES.
140     03                              PIC X(6)  VALUE "TOTALS".
141     03                              PIC X(4)  VALUE SPACES.
142     03 Total-With-TL                PIC $Z(4).99.
143     03 With-Error-TL                PIC X     VALUE SPACES.
144     03 Total-FICA-TL                PIC $Z(5).99.
145     03 FICA-Error-TL                PIC X     VALUE SPACES.
146     03 Total-Other-TL               PIC $Z(5).99.
147     03 Other-Error-TL               PIC X     VALUE SPACES.
148     03 Total-Gross-TL               PIC $Z(6).99.
149     03 Gross-Error-TL               PIC X     VALUE SPACES.
150     03 Total-Net-TL                 PIC $Z(6).99.
151     03 Net-Error-TL                 PIC X     VALUE SPACES.
152
153 PROCEDURE DIVISION.
154
155 1000-Main-Control.
156
157     PERFORM 2000-Initialize-Report
158     PERFORM UNTIL Eof-Flag = "YES"
159             READ Pay-File
160                 AT END
161                     MOVE "YES" TO Eof-Flag
162                 NOT AT END
163                     PERFORM 2100-Process-Data
164             END-READ
165     END-PERFORM
166     PERFORM 2200-Terminate-Report
167     STOP RUN.
168
169 2000-Initialize-Report.
170
171     OPEN INPUT Pay-File
172          OUTPUT Pay-Register
173     WRITE Pay-Register-Record FROM Heading-Line AFTER PAGE
174     WRITE Pay-Register-Record FROM Sub-Head-1 AFTER 2
175     WRITE Pay-Register-Record FROM Sub-Head-2 AFTER 1
176     MOVE SPACES TO Pay-Register-Record
177     WRITE Pay-Register-Record AFTER 1.
178
179 2100-Process-Data.
180
181     PERFORM 3000-Compute-Pay
182     PERFORM 3100-Write-Detail.
183
184 2200-Terminate-Report.
185
186     MOVE Total-With  TO Total-With-TL
187     MOVE Total-FICA  TO Total-FICA-TL
188     MOVE Total-Other TO Total-Other-TL
189     MOVE Total-Gross TO Total-Gross-TL
190     MOVE Total-Net   TO Total-Net-TL
191     WRITE Pay-Register-Record FROM Total-Line AFTER 2
192     CLOSE Pay-File
193           Pay-Register.
```

Program 5a85   *(concluded)*

```
194
195  3000-Compute-Pay.
196
197        COMPUTE Gross-Pay ROUNDED = Reg-Hrs-PR * Pay-Rate-PR +
198                                    Ot-Hrs-PR * Pay-Rate-PR * 1.5
199             ON SIZE ERROR
200                   MOVE 0 TO Gross-Pay
201        END-COMPUTE
202        MULTIPLY With-Rate-PR BY Gross-Pay GIVING With-Amt ROUNDED
203             ON SIZE ERROR
204                   MOVE 0 TO With-Amt
205        END-MULTIPLY
206        MULTIPLY FICA-Factor BY Gross-Pay GIVING FICA ROUNDED
207             ON SIZE ERROR
208                   MOVE 0 TO FICA
209        END-MULTIPLY
210        SUBTRACT With-Amt FICA Other-Deductions-PR
211           FROM Gross-Pay GIVING Net-Pay
212           ON SIZE ERROR
213                   MOVE 0 TO Net-Pay
214        END-SUBTRACT
215        ADD With-Amt              TO Total-With
216           ON SIZE ERROR
217                   MOVE "*" TO With-Error-TL
218        END-ADD
219        ADD FICA                  TO Total-FICA
220           ON SIZE ERROR
221                   MOVE "*" TO FICA-Error-TL
222        END-ADD
223        ADD Other-Deductions-PR   TO Total-Other
224           ON SIZE ERROR
225                   MOVE "*" TO Other-Error-TL
226        END-ADD
227        ADD Gross-Pay             TO Total-Gross
228           ON SIZE ERROR
229                   MOVE "*" TO Gross-Error-TL
230        END-ADD
231        ADD Net-Pay               TO Total-Net
232           ON SIZE ERROR
233                   MOVE "*" TO Net-Error-TL
234        END-ADD.
235
236  3100-Write-Detail.
237
238        MOVE Employee-Number-PR    TO Employee-Number-DL
239        MOVE Employee-Name-PR      TO Employee-Name-DL
240        MOVE Reg-Hrs-PR            TO Reg-Hrs-DL
241        MOVE Ot-Hrs-PR             TO Ot-Hrs-DL
242        MOVE Pay-Rate-PR           TO Pay-Rate-DL
243        MOVE With-Rate-PR          TO With-Rate-DL
244        MOVE Other-Deductions-PR   TO Other-Deductions-DL
245        MOVE With-Amt              TO With-Amt-DL
246        MOVE FICA                  TO FICA-DL
247        MOVE Gross-Pay             TO Gross-Pay-DL
248        MOVE Net-Pay               TO Net-Pay-DL
249        WRITE Pay-Register-Record FROM Detail-Line AFTER 1.
```

5.11 SELF-TEST EXERCISES

1. Write COBOL statements for each of the following:
   a. Add A and B.
   b. Subtract EXPENSE from INCOME and store result in BALANCE.
   c. Store the product of A and D in A.
   d. Divide SALES by 12 and store the quotient in MONTHLY-AVERAGE.
   e. Compute the volume of a sphere ($V = 4/3\ \pi\ r^3$).
   f. $I = P \times R \times T$
   g. $a = 25\%$ of b
   h. $A = P(1+r)^n$

2. Show the contents of each data item after execution of each of the following statements:

   a. ADD A B GIVING C ROUNDED

0 2 3	0 4 5 6	
A PIC 99V9	B PIC 99V99	C PIC 99

   b. SUBTRACT A FROM C GIVING B

0 3 2̄	1 7 0̄	
A PIC 99V9	C PIC S99V9	B PIC 99

   c. MULTIPLY C BY B

0 3 2 1 (+)	0 4 2̄
C PIC S99V99	B PIC S999

   d. DIVIDE C BY B GIVING A ROUNDED REMAINDER D

0 6 0̄	1 2 0 (+)		
C PIC S99V9	B PIC S999	A PIC S99V9	D PIC S99

   e. COMPUTE A = B ** 3

0 3̄	
B PIC S99	A PIC S999

   f. COMPUTE A ROUNDED = C + B * A ON SIZE ERROR MOVE 0 TO A

0 5	1 2 3	1 6
C PIC 99	B PIC 99V9	A PIC V99

   g. COMPUTE A = A + (B − C) / B
          ON SIZE ERROR
              MOVE 0 TO A.

3 2 0	0 0	0 1 2
A PIC 99V9	B PIC 99	C PIC 999

   h. MULTIPLY A BY B GIVING C ROUNDED

3 2 0̄	0 1 0 2	
A PIC S99V9	B PIC 99V99	C PIC 99

i. DIVIDE A INTO B

$$\overline{3\,|\,2\,|\,0\,}_{\wedge}\qquad\overset{+}{\underline{6\,|\,4\,|\,0}}_{\wedge}$$

A PIC S99V9   B PIC S99V9

3. Identify each paragraph in Program 5a as a control or operation paragraph.

4. With respect to the operation of Program 5a, what purpose is served by each of the following:
   a. line 53
   b. the VALUE clause on line 54
   c. line 51
   d. the ROUNDED option on line 193

5. Given a date in the form *mmdd*, compute the equivalent approximate Julian date. Julian date refers to the day of the year. Jan. 1 has Julian date 1; Dec. 31 has Julian date 365; and so on. Hint: Each month has approximately 29.7 days.

6. List scope delimiters that can be used in COBOL-85 arithmetic statements.

7. Consider the COBOL-85 statement

   ADD P TO Q GIVING R.

   Which data item(s) will receive a new value?

8. Construct the structure diagram for Program 5a85. Compare it to the structure diagram for Program 5a shown in Figure 5.9. Which program structure is simpler?

5.12 PROGRAMMING EXERCISES

1. Write a program to produce an end-of-year sales summary for a retail store. Input consists of records containing the following fields:

Positions	Content
1–10	Department name
11–15	Department number
16–22	Amount of sales in first quarter
23–29	Amount of sales in second quarter
30–36	Amount of sales in third quarter
37–43	Amount of sales in fourth quarter

   Output should consist of all input data and the total sales for each department as well as the total sales for the store as shown in the printer spacing chart in Figure 5.11. If overflow occurs in the computation of any item, print an asterisk beside the field in the report, and move zero to the item.

2. Write a program to compute the amount of money one will earn investing P dollars at an interest rate R for N years with interest compounded daily. The formula required is:

   $$A = P \times (1 + R/365)^{365 \times N}$$

Figure 5.11 Layout for report required in Exercise 1

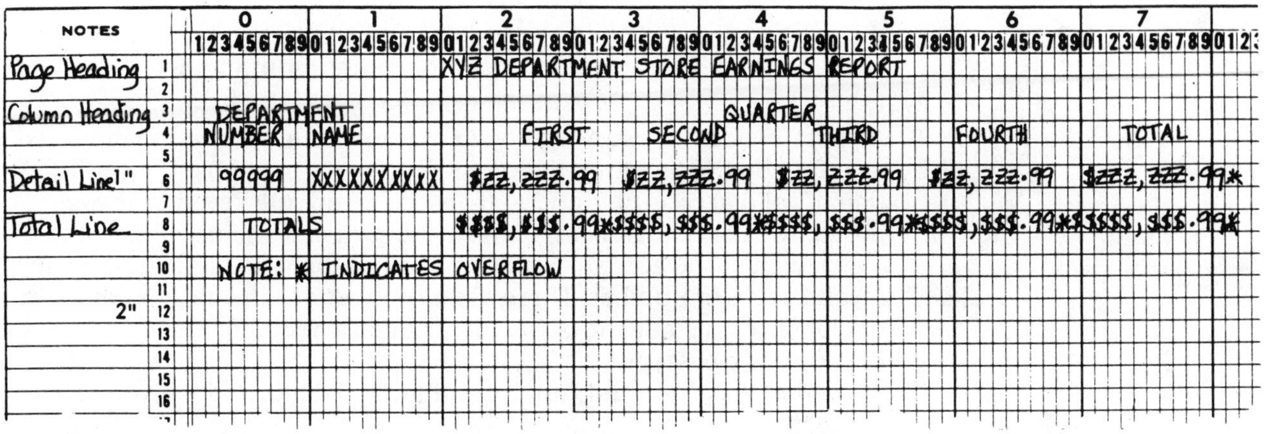

Each record in the file to be processed by the program contains the following data:

Positions	Content	
1–8	Principal	(P) 999999V99
9–11	Rate	(R) V999
12–13	Time	(N) 99

3. Write a program that could be used by a department store to determine the value of items in stock. Input consists of records containing the following fields:

Positions	Content
1–9	Item number
10–20	Description
21–25	Unit cost (999V99)
26–28	Number on hand

Output should consist of all data read in and the value of each item (quantity * unit cost) as well as the total value of all items in stock.

4. An inventory file contains records in the following format:

Positions	Content
1–6	Item number
7–20	Description
21–26	Cost (9999V99)
27–32	Selling price (9999V99)

A sale is planned with progressive discounts from selling price of 10%, 15%, and 20%. Write a program to list all of the input data and the three discounted selling prices.

5. A daily sales file contains records with the following fields:

Positions	Content
1	Department number (1, 2, 3, or 4)
3–8	Date (mmddyy)
10–20	Item description
25–30	Selling price for each item (9999V99)

35–40	Cost of each item 9999V99
42	Quantity

Write a program to list all input data, and compute total amount of sale and profit for each sale. Accumulate and print totals of sales and profits.

6. A check digit is an extra digit of an account number that is computed as a function of the other digits. Its purpose is to enable the verification of valid account numbers. If any digits are miskeyed or transposed, the check digit computed by the program will not match the check digit of the account number, thus enabling identification of an invalid account number. There are a number of schemes for computation of check digits. One of the most effective methods uses the following sequence of steps:

   a. Suppose the account number contains 5 digits and a sixth check digit:

   $$d_1 d_2 d_3 d_4 d_5 d_{ck}$$

   b. Compute $S = d_1 + 2 \times d_2 + 3 \times d_3 + 5 \times d_4 + 7 \times d_5$. (The multipliers are purposely chosen to be prime numbers; this system has been shown to yield very good error detection capabilities.)

   c. The check digit d_{ck} is the units digit of S.

   Write a program to input a sequence of account numbers and compute the check digit. The account number is in positions 1–5 of the records to be processed by the program. For example, suppose the account number is 23576.

   $$S = 2 + 2 \times 3 + 3 \times 5 + 5 \times 7 + 7 \times 6 = 100$$

   The units digit of 100 is 0, hence $d_{ck} = 0$. The complete account number is 235760. Suppose that in the transcription process two digits of the account number are transposed (a very common error); for example, 237560 is entered instead of 235760. The check digit computation for 235760 is $S = 2 + 2 \times 3 + 3 \times 7 + 5 \times 5 + 7 \times 6 = 96$; hence, the check digit for this account number would be 6, not 0. The erroneous account number would be detected.

7. Write a program to generate seven-digit account numbers beginning with 1000001 using the method of check digit computation described in Exercise 6. Often the check digit is inserted as a middle digit in the account number: e.g., 1001000. Modify your program to list the account numbers in this fashion.

8. Write a program to list the number of bills of each denomination required to make up the pay envelopes for a payroll. Input consists of the net amount to be paid in dollars. Output should consist of the number of twenties, tens, fives, and ones required for that amount. Compute and list the total number of bills of each denomination which will be required. For example, $273 would be made up of

13 twenties	= $ 260
1 ten	= $ 10
0 fives	= $ 0
3 ones	= $ 3
	$ 273

Each record in the file to be processed by this program contains the net amount in positions 10–12.

9. Write a program to calculate the amount of monthly payment required to pay a mortgage based on the following input data:

Positions	Content
1–6	Principal (*P*) 999999
10–12	Interest rate (*R*) V999
15–16	Time in years (*T*) 99

The required formula is $\dfrac{P \times \dfrac{R}{12}}{1 - \left[\dfrac{1}{1 + \dfrac{R}{12}}\right]^{(T \times 12)}}$

Example

P	R	T	Expected Value of Monthly Payment
$ 10,000	.08	20	$ 83.64
$ 65,000	.16	30	$ 874.09
$105,000	.175	25	$1551.41

Note: Your computed values may vary slightly from those shown because of internal differences among computers.

6. IF STATEMENT AND CONDITIONS

6.1 PROGRAM EXAMPLE

A company maintains a personnel file, each record of which contains the following items:

> Employee identification number
> Employee name
> Sex code (*M* = male, *F* = female)
> Employee date of birth *(mmddyy)*
> Date employee was hired *(mmddyy)*

The personnel manager needs a list of employees who were hired after 1989 and wants to know how many of them there are. A printer spacing chart for the required report is shown in Figure 6.1.

Figure 6.1 Printer spacing chart for Employee Report Program

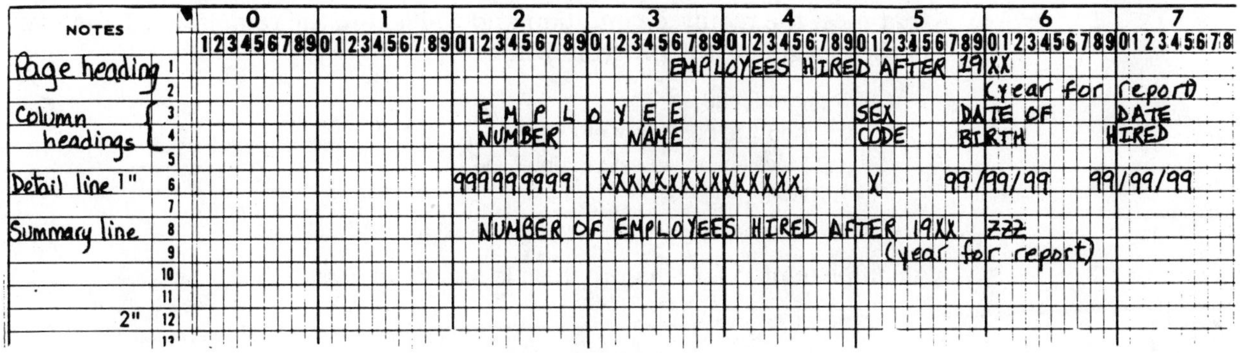

Problem Analysis

The required report contains page and column headings, a detail line, and a summary line. The page and column headings must be written as part of initialization prior to entering the loop which will process each record in the file. The summary line must be written after all records in the file have been processed. In order to place the required information on the summary line, it is necessary to count the records that meet the specified condition; this will require a counter initialized to zero (NUMBER-EMPLOYEES). Each time an employee who was hired after 1989 is encountered, the value of NUMBER-EMPLOYEES will be increased by one.

So far, the program required for this problem resembles other programs that process a data file and produce a report. The major difference in this program is that not all records in the file are to be counted; only records for employees who were hired after 1989 are of interest. This task requires the selection program structure. In pseudocode, selection is expressed using the following form:

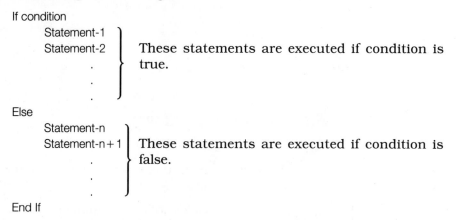

When no actions are to be taken because the condition is false, the Else clause can be omitted:

```
If condition
        Statement-1
        Statement-2   These statements are executed if condition is true.
                .
                .
                .

    End If
```

This form suits the present problem because we wish to process records that meet the required condition and will ignore the remainder. Thus, part of the design for this program will be

```
If year hired > 89
        Add 1 to number of employees
        Move employee data to detail line
        Write detail line
    End If
```

A complete plan for this program is shown in Figure 6.2.

Problem Solution

The program for this problem is shown in Program 6a. The structure diagram for this program is shown in Figure 6.3. The IF statement in lines 133 through 135 implements the selection structure required in the plan. The syntax for the COBOL IF statement resembles the syntax of the pseudocode. The reserved word IF is followed by a condition, which is followed by the actions to be carried out if the condition is true at the time the statement is executed. In this case, the IF statement appears as

```
IF YEAR-HIRED-PR IS GREATER THAN YEAR-FOR-REPORT
    ADD 1 TO NUMBER-EMPLOYEES
    PERFORM 3000-WRITE-DETAIL-LINE.
```

Figure 6.2   Plan for employee report

Main control

    Open files
    Write headings
    Read employee file
    Do Process data until end of file
    Write summary line
    Close files
    Stop run

Process data

    If date hired > 89
        Add 1 to number employees
        Move employee data to detail line
        Write detail line
    End If
    Read employee file

Figure 6.3   Structure diagram for Program 6a

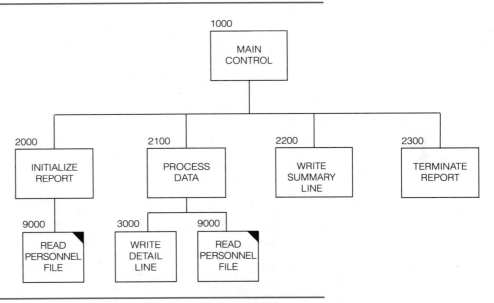

The condition

    YEAR-HIRED-PR IS GREATER THAN YEAR-FOR-REPORT

will be true when YEAR-HIRED-PR has a value of 90, 91, etc., because the value of YEAR-FOR-REPORT is set to 89 via the VALUE clause in WORKING-STORAGE (see line 49). Note that the IF statement is terminated by a period. This period corresponds to the "End If" line in the pseudocode. The period determines the scope of the IF statement. All of the statements following the condition and preceding the period will be carried out when the condition is true. (In this case there are two statements in this clause, but in general there could be many.) A more complete description of the IF statement is presented in the next section.

Program 6a

```
 1 IDENTIFICATION DIVISION.
 2
 3 PROGRAM-ID. RECENT-HIRE-REPORT-PRO6A.
 4 AUTHOR. HORN.
 5
 6 ENVIRONMENT DIVISION.
 7
 8 CONFIGURATION SECTION.
 9
10 SOURCE-COMPUTER.
11 OBJECT-COMPUTER.
12
13 INPUT-OUTPUT SECTION.
14
15 FILE-CONTROL.
16
17     SELECT PERSONNEL-FILE ASSIGN TO DISK.
18
19     SELECT EMPLOYEE-REPORT-FILE ASSIGN TO PRINTER.
20
21 DATA DIVISION.
22
23 FILE SECTION.
24
25 FD  PERSONNEL-FILE
26     LABEL RECORDS ARE STANDARD
27     DATA RECORD IS PERSONNEL-RECORD.
28
29 01  PERSONNEL-RECORD.
30     03 ID-NUM-PR       PIC 9(9).
31     03 NAME-PR         PIC X(15).
32     03 SEX-PR          PIC X.
33     03 BIRTH-DATE-PR   PIC 9(6).
34     03 DATE-HIRED-PR.
35        05 MONTH-HIRED-PR    PIC 99.
36        05 DAY-HIRED-PR      PIC 99.
37        05 YEAR-HIRED-PR     PIC 99.
38     03 FILLER          PIC X(43).
39
40 FD  EMPLOYEE-REPORT-FILE
41     LABEL RECORDS ARE OMITTED
42     DATA RECORD IS EMPLOYEE-REPORT-RECORD.
43
44 01  EMPLOYEE-REPORT-RECORD      PIC X(132).
45
46 WORKING-STORAGE SECTION.
47
48 01  YEAR.
49     02 YEAR-FOR-REPORT PIC 99 VALUE 89.
50
51 01  FLAGS.
52     02  EOF-FLAG       PIC X(3) VALUE "NO".
53
54 01  COUNTERS.
55     02 NUMBER-EMPLOYEES PIC 999 VALUE 0.
56
```

Program 6a   *(continued)*

```
57 01   HEAD-LINE.
58         03 FILLER               PIC X(35) VALUE SPACES.
59         03 FILLER               PIC X(24) VALUE
60            "EMPLOYEES HIRED SINCE 19".
61         03 YEAR-FOR-REPORT-HL PIC 99.
62
63 01   SUB-HEAD-1.
64         03 FILLER               PIC X(21) VALUE SPACES.
65         03 FILLER               PIC X(15) VALUE "E M P L O Y E E".
66         03 FILLER               PIC X(13) VALUE SPACES.
67         03 FILLER               PIC X(3) VALUE "SEX".
68         03 FILLER               PIC X(5) VALUE SPACES.
69         03 FILLER               PIC X(7) VALUE "DATE OF".
70         03 FILLER               PIC X(5) VALUE SPACES.
71         03 FILLER               PIC X(4) VALUE "DATE".
72
73 01   SUB-HEAD-2.
74         03 FILLER               PIC X(21) VALUE SPACES.
75         03 FILLER               PIC X(6) VALUE "NUMBER".
76         03 FILLER               PIC X(5) VALUE SPACES.
77         03 FILLER               PIC X(4) VALUE "NAME".
78         03 FILLER               PIC X(13) VALUE SPACES.
79         03 FILLER               PIC X(4) VALUE "CODE".
80         03 FILLER               PIC X(4) VALUE SPACES.
81         03 FILLER               PIC X(5) VALUE "BIRTH".
82         03 FILLER               PIC X(6) VALUE SPACES.
83         03 FILLER               PIC X(5) VALUE "HIRED".
84
85 01   DETAIL-LINE.
86         03 FILLER               PIC X(19) VALUE SPACES.
87         03 ID-NUM-DL            PIC 9(9).
88         03 FILLER               PIC X(2) VALUE SPACES.
89         03 NAME-DL              PIC X(15).
90         03 FILLER               PIC X(5) VALUE SPACES.
91         03 SEX-DL               PIC X.
92         03 FILLER               PIC X(5) VALUE SPACES.
93         03 BIRTH-DATE-DL        PIC 99/99/99.
94         03 FILLER               PIC X(3) VALUE SPACES.
95         03 MONTH-HIRED-DL       PIC 99.
96         03 FILLER               PIC X VALUE "/".
97         03 DAY-HIRED-DL         PIC 99.
98         03 FILLER               PIC X VALUE "/".
99         03 YEAR-HIRED-DL        PIC 99.
100
101 01   SUMMARY-LINE.
102        02 FILLER                   PIC X(22) VALUE SPACES.
103        02 FILLER                   PIC X(34) VALUE
104           "NUMBER OF EMPLOYEES HIRED SINCE 19".
105        02 YEAR-FOR-REPORT-SL       PIC 99.
106        02 FILLER                   PIC X VALUE SPACES.
107        02 NUMBER-EMPLOYEES-SL      PIC ZZZ.
108
```

Program 6a   *(concluded)*

```
109 PROCEDURE DIVISION.
110
111 1000-MAIN-CONTROL.
112
113     PERFORM 2000-INITIALIZE-REPORT.
114     PERFORM 2100-PROCESS-DATA
115             UNTIL EOF-FLAG = "YES".
116     PERFORM 2200-WRITE-SUMMARY-LINE.
117     PERFORM 2300-TERMINATE-REPORT.
118     STOP RUN.
119
120 2000-INITIALIZE-REPORT.
121
122     OPEN INPUT PERSONNEL-FILE
123          OUTPUT EMPLOYEE-REPORT-FILE.
124     MOVE YEAR-FOR-REPORT        TO YEAR-FOR-REPORT-HL.
125     MOVE HEAD-LINE              TO EMPLOYEE-REPORT-RECORD.
126     WRITE EMPLOYEE-REPORT-RECORD AFTER PAGE.
127     WRITE EMPLOYEE-REPORT-RECORD FROM SUB-HEAD-1 AFTER 2.
128     WRITE EMPLOYEE-REPORT-RECORD FROM SUB-HEAD-2 AFTER 1.
129     PERFORM 9000-READ-PERSONNEL-FILE.
130
131 2100-PROCESS-DATA.
132
133     IF YEAR-HIRED-PR IS GREATER THAN YEAR-FOR-REPORT
134         ADD 1 TO NUMBER-EMPLOYEES
135         PERFORM 3000-WRITE-DETAIL-LINE.
136     PERFORM 9000-READ-PERSONNEL-FILE.
137
138 2200-WRITE-SUMMARY-LINE.
139
140     MOVE NUMBER-EMPLOYEES TO NUMBER-EMPLOYEES-SL.
141     MOVE YEAR-FOR-REPORT  TO YEAR-FOR-REPORT-SL.
142     WRITE EMPLOYEE-REPORT-RECORD FROM SUMMARY-LINE AFTER 2.
143
144 2300-TERMINATE-REPORT.
145
146     CLOSE PERSONNEL-FILE
147           EMPLOYEE-REPORT-FILE.
148
149 3000-WRITE-DETAIL-LINE.
150
151     MOVE ID-NUM-PR             TO ID-NUM-DL.
152     MOVE NAME-PR               TO NAME-DL.
153     MOVE SEX-PR                TO SEX-DL.
154     MOVE BIRTH-DATE-PR         TO BIRTH-DATE-DL.
155     MOVE MONTH-HIRED-PR        TO MONTH-HIRED-DL.
156     MOVE DAY-HIRED-PR          TO DAY-HIRED-DL.
157     MOVE YEAR-HIRED-PR         TO YEAR-HIRED-DL.
158     MOVE DETAIL-LINE           TO EMPLOYEE-REPORT-RECORD.
159     WRITE EMPLOYEE-REPORT-RECORD AFTER 2.
160
161 9000-READ-PERSONNEL-FILE.
162
163     READ PERSONNEL-FILE
164         AT END MOVE "YES" TO EOF-FLAG.
```

6.2 THE IF STATEMENT

The general form of the IF statement is shown in Figure 6.4. If the condition is true, only the statement(s) before the ELSE clause will be executed. If the condition is false, the statements following ELSE will be executed; the statements preceding ELSE will *not* be executed. When the statement(s) either before the ELSE clause or in the ELSE clause are completed, control is given to the sentence following the IF statement. A flowchart of the IF statement is shown in Figure 6.5.

Figure 6.4 General form of the IF statement

```
IF condition
    {statement-1...}
    {NEXT SENTENCE }
[ELSE
    {statement-n...}
    {NEXT SENTENCE } ] .
```

Figure 6.5 Flowchart of the IF statement

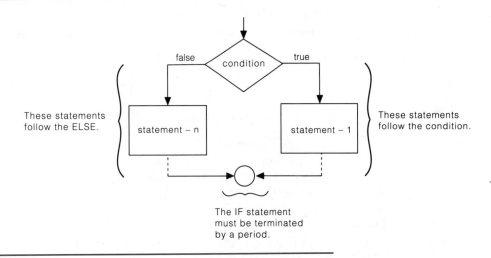

These statements follow the ELSE.

These statements follow the condition.

The IF statement must be terminated by a period.

———— Example ————

If the value of HOURS is greater than 40, execute OVERTIME-PAY; otherwise, execute REGULAR-PAY.

```
IF HOURS > 40
    PERFORM OVERTIME-PAY
ELSE
    PERFORM REGULAR-PAY.
```

———— Example ————

If A = B, execute COMPUTE-PROC and OUTPUT-1 sequentially; then execute the next sentence. If A ≠ B, perform OUTPUT-2; then execute the next sentence.

```
IF A = B
    PERFORM COMPUTE-PROC
    PERFORM OUTPUT-1
ELSE
    PERFORM OUTPUT-2.
```

If no action needs to be taken because a true (or false) condition is encountered, the statement NEXT SENTENCE can be used to pass control to the sentence following the IF statement.

────────────── Example ──────────────

If the value of the variable KODE is equal to 0, the next sentence is executed; otherwise, 1 is added to KOUNT, OUTPUT-ROUTINE is executed, and the next sentence is executed.

```
IF KODE EQUAL 0
    NEXT SENTENCE
ELSE
    ADD 1 TO KOUNT
    PERFORM OUTPUT-ROUTINE.
```

The above example is equivalent to adding 1 to KOUNT and executing OUTPUT-ROUTINE when the value of KODE is *not* equal to 0. The following statement is thus equivalent to the preceding sentence:

```
IF KODE NOT EQUAL 0
    ADD 1 TO KOUNT
    PERFORM OUTPUT-ROUTINE
ELSE
    NEXT SENTENCE.
```

The ELSE clause of the IF statement is optional. If the ELSE clause is omitted and the condition is false, the sentence following the IF statement is executed. (The statements following the condition are executed only when the condition is true.)

────────────── Example ──────────────

If AGE is greater than 25, move AGE and NAME to an output record and write the output record.

```
IF AGE IS GREATER THAN 25
    MOVE AGE TO AGE-OUT
    MOVE NAME TO NAME-OUT
    WRITE OUT-REC AFTER 1.
```

────────────── Example ──────────────

If the value of KODE is not equal to 0, add 1 to KOUNT and execute OUTPUT-ROUTINE.

```
IF KODE NOT EQUAL 0
    ADD 1 TO KOUNT
    PERFORM OUTPUT-ROUTINE.
```

This program segment is equivalent to

```
IF KODE NOT EQUAL 0
      ADD 1 TO KOUNT
      PERFORM OUTPUT-ROUTINE
ELSE
      NEXT SENTENCE.
```

The rules of COBOL syntax do not require that each statement in an IF statement be placed on a separate line, nor that the word ELSE be aligned with IF as shown in the above examples. However, this placement does aid in readability, and it is a recommended structured programming practice.

6.3 RELATIONAL CONDITIONS

The preceding examples contain many examples of the use of relational conditions. Relational conditions are used to compare two entities (see Fig. 6.6). Note that the relation being tested may be expressed either symbolically, using the symbols $<$, $>$, or $=$, or verbally as LESS THAN, GREATER THAN, or EQUAL TO. (The use of the words THAN and TO in the verbal expressions is optional.) The meanings of the symbols are as follows:

Symbol	Verbal Expression
$<$	LESS THAN
$>$	GEATER THAN
$=$	EQUAL TO

When writing a condition, a programmer may choose either a symbol or the corresponding verbal expression; the meaning of the resulting condition will be the same.

─────── Example ───────

The following conditions are equivalent:

```
HOURS > 40
HOURS GREATER THAN 40
HOURS GREATER 40
```

The word IS may be included in a condition at the option of the programmer; the purpose of the word is to aid in readability.

Figure 6.6 General form of relational conditions

$$
\left\{ \begin{array}{l} \text{data-name} \\ \text{literal} \\ \text{arithmetic-expression} \end{array} \right\} \quad \text{IS [\underline{NOT}]} \left\{ \begin{array}{l} < \\ > \\ = \\ \underline{\text{LESS}} \text{ THAN} \\ \underline{\text{GREATER}} \text{ THAN} \\ \underline{\text{EQUAL}} \text{ TO} \end{array} \right\} \left\{ \begin{array}{l} \text{data-name} \\ \text{literal} \\ \text{arithmetic-expression} \end{array} \right\}
$$

─────── **Example** ───────

The following conditions are equivalent to each other and to those in the previous example:

```
HOURS IS > 40
HOURS IS GREATER THAN 40
HOURS IS GREATER 40
```

To negate any of the relations, write NOT before the type of relation. For example, the condition

```
HOURS IS NOT GREATER THAN 40
```

is true when the value of HOURS is 0, 1, 2, 3, . . . , 38, or 40 and false if HOURS has value of 41 or larger.

─────── **Examples** ───────

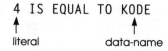

This condition will be true when the value of KODE is 4 and false otherwise.

NAME-FIELD NOT EQUAL SPACES

    ↑   ↑

data-name   literal

This condition will be false when all the characters in NAME-FIELD are blanks and true otherwise.

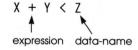

The value of the expression X + Y will be computed, and this value will be compared to the value in Z.

Occasionally, it is necessary to write conditions of the form A ≤ B (A less than or equal to B) or A ≥ B (A greater than or equal to B). This can be done easily by using the NOT option. The COBOL equivalent of A ≤ B is

```
A NOT GREATER THAN B
```

or

```
A NOT > B
```

─────── **Example** ───────

If the value of SALES is 600 or greater, compute COMMISSION as 10% of SALES.

```
IF SALES NOT LESS THAN 600
    MULTIPLY 0.10 BY SALES GIVING COMMISSION.
```

The values 600, 601, 602, . . . satisfy the condition SALES NOT LESS THAN 600.

6.4 NESTED IF STATEMENTS

In many instances, actions will depend on conditions being satisfied. For example, suppose we want to count the number of males and females in a set of data that contains a SEX-CODE having value M for males and F for females. If the value of SEX-CODE is neither M nor F, the data record contains an error, and we perform an error routine to take appropriate action. This error routine is performed when the sequence of conditions SEX-CODE = "M" and SEX-CODE = "F" are both false. The flowchart for this task would be:

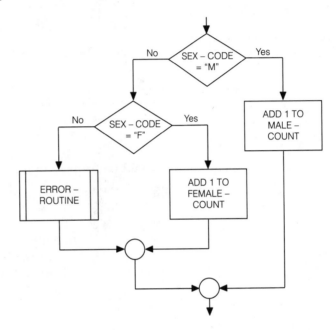

The following program segment could be used to perform this task:

```
IF SEX-CODE = "M"
     ADD 1 TO MALE-COUNT
ELSE
     IF SEX-CODE = "F"
          ADD 1 TO FEMALE-COUNT
     ELSE
          PERFORM ERROR-ROUTINE.
```

Note that the terminal connector blocks in the above flowchart correspond to the period that terminates the IF statement in the COBOL code. In this example, the ELSE clause of the IF statement which tests the condition SEX-CODE = "M" contains another IF statement which tests the condition SEX-CODE = "F". If both of these conditions are false, then ERROR-ROUTINE will be executed. This is an example of an IF statement that contains another IF statement. Statements of this sort are called **nested** IF statements. This example also shows a useful way to test conditions that exclude one another; a person is either male or female, not both. When an IF statement is nested, an ELSE clause may be included for each IF. For example, suppose we wish to obtain a list of the names of males and females who are over 20 years of age, together with the notation OVER 20 and MALE or FEMALE. The flowchart for this task would be:

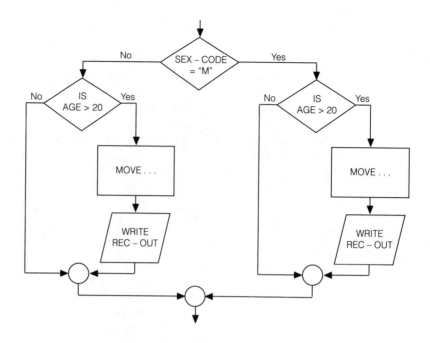

This flowchart would be translated into COBOL as

```
IF SEX-CODE = "M"
    IF AGE > 20
        MOVE "OVER 20" TO AGE-OUT
        MOVE NAME TO NAME-OUT
        MOVE "MALE" TO SEX-OUT
        WRITE REC-OUT AFTER 1
    ELSE
        NEXT SENTENCE
ELSE
    IF AGE > 20
        MOVE "OVER 20" TO AGE-OUT
        MOVE NAME TO NAME-OUT
        MOVE "FEMALE" TO SEX-OUT
        WRITE REC-OUT AFTER 1
    ELSE
        NEXT SENTENCE.
```

Note the importance of the ELSE clause after the first WRITE REC-OUT AFTER 1. If this clause were omitted, the next ELSE clause would have been associated with the test on AGE rather than the test on SEX-CODE. The preceding coding could be simplified (and improved) as follows:

```
IF AGE > 20
    MOVE "OVER 20" TO AGE-OUT
    MOVE NAME TO NAME-OUT
    IF SEX-CODE = "M"
        MOVE "MALE" TO SEX-OUT
        WRITE REC-OUT AFTER 1
    ELSE
        MOVE "FEMALE" TO SEX-OUT
        WRITE REC-OUT AFTER 1.
```

The flowchart for this code would be:

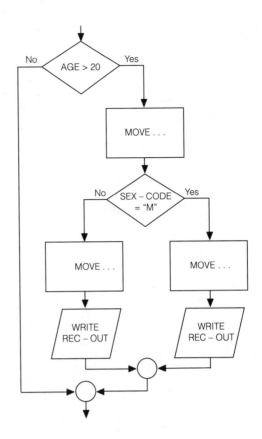

In the preceding example, the statement `WRITE REC-OUT AFTER 1` occurs in both clauses of the `SEX-CODE` test. We might wonder if this could be simplified by placing the common statement after the `IF` statement, so that no matter which branch of the test is taken, the common statement will still be executed. This is not the case at all because, after either clause of an `IF` statement is concluded, the following *sentence* is executed next. In the above example, the output is to be performed only if `AGE` is greater than 20. If the output statement followed the entire `IF` statement, it would be produced for all values of `AGE`. If the logic of a problem makes this type of structure necessary, the entire sequence of statements should be placed into a separate paragraph. The preceding program segment could be written as

```
IF AGE > 20
    PERFORM OVER-20-ROUTINE.
.
.
.
OVER-20-ROUTINE.
    MOVE "OVER 20" TO AGE-OUT.
    MOVE NAME TO NAME-OUT.
    IF SEX-CODE = "M"
        MOVE "MALE" TO SEX-OUT
    ELSE
        MOVE "FEMALE" TO SEX-OUT;
    WRITE REC-OUT AFTER 1.
```

6.5   SIGN AND CLASS CONDITIONS

Thus far, all conditions used in our examples have been relational. Such tests as

```
IF KOUNT IS GREATER THAN 13. . .
IF AMOUNT < 0. . .
IF SEX-CODE = "M". . .
```

use conditions of this type. Remember that alphanumeric as well as numeric tests may be made with the relational condition. Two additional types of conditions may be used: the sign condition and the class condition.

Sign Condition

The sign condition is a convenient way to test the sign (positive, negative, or zero) of a data-name or expression. The general form of this condition is shown in Figure 6.7.

Figure 6.7   General form of the sign condition

$$
\begin{Bmatrix} \text{data-name} \\ \text{expression} \end{Bmatrix} \quad \text{IS [\underline{NOT}]} \quad \begin{Bmatrix} \underline{\text{POSITIVE}} \\ \underline{\text{ZERO}} \\ \underline{\text{NEGATIVE}} \end{Bmatrix}
$$

Example

```
IF KODE IS ZERO. . .
PERFORM PARA-X UNTIL A + B IS POSITIVE. . .
IF AMOUNT-DUE NEGATIVE. . .
IF BALANCE IS NOT NEGATIVE. . .
```

Note that NOT NEGATIVE is equivalent to testing for greater than or equal to zero, and NOT POSITIVE is equivalent to testing for less than or equal to zero. If a field tested for sign has not been defined using the S picture code, it will never be negative.

Class Condition

The class condition is used to test whether a data-name contains alphabetic data or numeric data. Figure 6.8 shows the general form of this condition. The numeric test can be performed on fields with numeric or alphanumeric pictures. If the data-name contains any characters other than 0, 1, 2, . . . , 9, then the numeric test will be false.

Figure 6.8   General form of the class condition

$$
\text{data-name} \quad \text{IS [\underline{NOT}]} \quad \begin{Bmatrix} \underline{\text{NUMERIC}} \\ \underline{\text{ALPHABETIC}} \end{Bmatrix}
$$

─── **Example** ───────────

```
IF IN-FLD IS NUMERIC. . .
ELSE. . .
```

1	2	3	4

```
IN-FLD PIC X(4)
```

Numeric test is true.

	1	2	3

```
IN-FLD PIC X(4)
```

Numeric test is false because the field contains a blank—a nonnumeric character.

When testing signed fields with the numeric test, the condition will be true if the field contains a valid sign and numeric digits.

─── **Example** ───────────

```
IF FLDA IS NUMERIC. . .
ELSE. . .
```

0	1	2	3⁺

```
FLDA PIC S9(4)
```

0	1	2	3	−

```
FLDA PIC S9(4) SIGN IS TRAILING
              SEPARATE CHARACTER
```

In both cases the numeric test is true.

The alphabetic test may be performed on fields with alphanumeric or alphabetic pictures. If the field contains only characters A, B, C, . . . , Z, or a blank, then an alphabetic test will be true; otherwise, it will be false.

─── **Example** ───────────

```
IF NAME IS ALPHABETIC. . .
ELSE. . .
```

J	O	H	N		J	O	N	E	S					

```
NAME PIC X(15)
```

Alphabetic test is true.

J	.		J	O	N	E	S							

```
NAME PIC X(15)
```

Alphabetic test is false because of the period.

J		J	O	N	E	S		3	R	D				

```
NAME PIC X(15)
```

Alphabetic test is false because of the "3".

```
 J o h n   J o n e s
```

NAME PIC X(15)

Alphabetic test is false because of the lowercase characters in the field.

As should be clear after studying these examples, the usefulness of the alphabetic test is limited to those fields which may legitimately contain only alphabetic uppercase characters and spaces. For example, using it to test the content of a field containing a person's name would cause many names (which may correctly contain periods, lowercase characters, and numbers) to be treated erroneously as containing invalid data.

Fields that should contain only numeric characters but do not, and fields that should contain only alphabetic characters or spaces but do not, may occur because of error in data preparation or entry. It is important that data processing systems be provided with error-free data. The class condition is a useful tool to enable the COBOL program to take alternate action when it encounters data containing errors.

6.6   COMPLEX CONDITIONS

All of the conditions described to this point—relational, sign, and class—are called **simple conditions**. The logical operations NOT, AND, and OR may be used to construct **complex conditions** based on simple conditions.

NOT

The NOT operation acts on a single condition with the general form

> NOT condition

The resulting complex condition is true when the condition is false and false when the condition is true.

Example

Write a condition that will be true when the value of HRS is not greater than 40.

NOT HRS > 40

```
 3 2
```

HRS PIC 99 Since HRS > 40 is false, NOT HRS > 40 is true.

Example

Write a condition which will be true when NET-PAY is nonnegative (i.e., greater than or equal to zero).

```
NOT NET-PAY IS NEGATIVE
 0 0 3 6 0 0
        ∧
NET-PAY PIC S9999V99
```

The condition NET-PAY IS NEGATIVE is true; therefore, NOT NET-PAY IS NEGATIVE is false.

AND

The AND operation connects two conditions with the general form

> condition-1 **AND** condition-2

The resulting complex condition is true only when both condition-1 and condition-2 are true. It is false in all three other cases (that is, it is false if condition-1 or condition-2 or both are false).

────── Example ──────

Write a condition which will be true when both A < 10 and B = 4.

```
A < 10 AND B = 4
 0 6           0 3
    ∧             ∧
A PIC 99     B PIC 99
```

The condition A < 10 is true but B = 4 is false; therefore, the complex condition is false.

────── Example ──────

Write a condition that will check the validity of HRS and RATE, both of which are numeric fields.

```
HRS IS NUMERIC AND RATE IS NUMERIC
```

Both HRS and RATE must be numeric for the complex condition to be true.

OR

The OR operation, which connects two conditions, has the general form

> condition-1 **OR** condition-2

The resulting complex condition is true when condition-1 or condition-2 or both are true (three cases), and false only when both condition-1 and condition-2 are false.

────── Example ──────

Write a condition that will be true when either A < 10 or B = 4 or both.

```
A < 10 OR B = 4
 0 6           0 3
|___|^        |___|^

A PIC 99     B PIC 99
```

The complex condition is true, even though B = 4 is false.

—————— Example ——————

Write a complex condition that will be true if either HRS or RATE is not numeric.

```
HRS IS NOT NUMERIC OR RATE IS NOT NUMERIC
```

For both the AND and the OR operations, there are four possible combinations: both conditions being true, either one being false, or both conditions being false. These operations, together with the value of resulting complex conditions, are summarized in Figure 6.9. The operation NOT acts only on one condition; hence, there are only two possibilities—the condition is either true or false. The value of the resulting compound condition is summarized in Figure 6.10.

Figure 6.9   Summary of logical operations AND and OR

condition-1	condition-2	condition-1 AND condition-2	condition-1 OR condition-2
true	true	true	true
true	false	false	true
false	true	false	true
false	false	false	false

Figure 6.10   Summary of the logical operation NOT

condition	NOT condition
true	false
false	true

Complex conditions may be used in either IF statements or the PERFORM statement. For example, suppose we wish to repeat execution of a routine continually until either of two conditions is met. The following code illustrates the use of a complex condition in the PERFORM statement to accomplish this objective:

```
PERFORM ROUTINE
    UNTIL CONDITION-1-FLAG = "YES" OR CONDITION-2-FLAG = "YES".
```

Similarly, if repetition of a routine is desired until both of two conditions are true, the following code could be used:

```
PERFORM ROUTINE
    UNTIL CONDITION-1-FLAG = "YES" AND CONDITION-2-FLAG = "YES".
```

Suppose, for example, we wish to modify Program 6a to produce a listing of male employees who were hired after 1989. Lines 133–135 in Program 6a could be rewritten as

```
IF SEX-PR = "M" AND YEAR-HIRED-PR > YEAR-FOR-REPORT
    ADD 1 TO NUMBER EMPLOYEES
    PERFORM 3000-WRITE-DETAIL-LINE.
```

If more than one logical operation is present in a complex condition, the order in which the operations are evaluated will determine the value of the condition. The same problem arises in the evaluation of arithmetic expressions containing more than one arithmetic operation. Recall that arithmetic operations are assigned precedence. In evaluating an arithmetic expression, arithmetic operations with higher precedence are performed before operations with lower precedence. In a similar fashion, logical operations are assigned precedence to control the order of evaluation in complex conditions. Figure 6.11 gives the rules of precedence for logical operations.

Figure 6.11 Precedence for evaluation of complex conditions

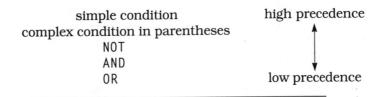

For example, suppose a data item A has a value of 6, and B has a value of 3. Consider the complex condition:

```
NOT A < 10 AND B = 4
```

As NOT has higher precedence than AND, the condition NOT A < 10 is evaluated before the condition involving AND. The entire condition will be evaluated as follows:

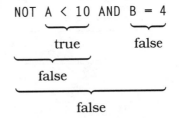

In evaluating a complex condition, the simple conditions, which may be relational, class, or sign conditions, are evaluated first. In this example, the simple conditions are A < 10 and B = 4, which are evaluated as true and false, respectively. Then the logical operation with the highest precedence is evaluated. In this case, NOT has highest precedence, so the NOT condition is evaluated next. Finally, the next highest operation is evaluated—in this case an AND condition that results in the final value of the entire condition.

——————— Example ———————

Consider the following condition with the values of fields as shown:

```
A < 10 OR B = 4 AND A IS NOT POSITIVE
```

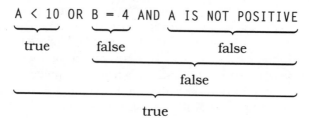

A PIC 99   B PIC 99

The above condition is evaluated as follows:

A < 10 OR B = 4 AND A IS NOT POSITIVE

 true   false   false

         false

       true

The AND condition is evaluated before the OR condition because AND has higher precedence than OR.

If two or more operations with equal precedence are present (two or more ORs, for example), the conditions are evaluated in order from left to right.

——————— Example ———————

Consider the following condition with the values of fields as shown:

```
AGE < 29 AND YRS-EXPERIENCE > 5 AND DEPT-CODE = 3
```

AGE PIC 99   YRS-EXPERIENCE PIC 99   DEPT-CODE PIC 9

The above expression is evaluated as follows:

AGE < 29 AND YRS-EXPERIENCE > 5 AND DEPT-CODE = 3

 true   true   false

     true

      false

If you want to write a logical expression that requires an order of evaluation different from the normal order, use parentheses. Conditions within parentheses are evaluated before conditions outside parentheses. Parentheses may, of course, be used to improve the readability of a complex condition even when the normal order of evaluation is appropriate for the condition.

——————— Example ———————

Consider the following condition with contents of fields as shown:

```
NOT (A < 10 AND B = 4)
```
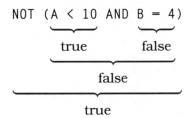
```
A PIC 99    B PIC 99
```

The above expression is evaluated as follows:

```
NOT (A < 10 AND B = 4)
        ⌣          ⌣
       true       false
          false
           true
```

In this case, note that the AND condition is evaluated before the NOT condition because of the parentheses.

--- Example ---

Consider the following condition with the contents of fields as shown:

```
AGE < 29 AND (YRS-EXPERIENCE > 5 OR DEPT-CODE = 3)
```
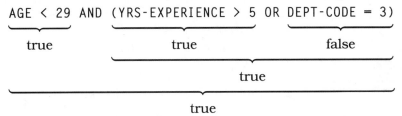
```
AGE PIC 99    YRS-EXPERIENCE PIC 99    DEPT-CODE PIC 9
```

The above expression is evaluated as follows:

```
AGE < 29 AND (YRS-EXPERIENCE > 5 OR DEPT-CODE = 3)
    ⌣                ⌣                    ⌣
   true             true                false
                         true
                        true
```

--- Example ---

The XYZ Department Store has decided to give a Christmas bonus to its employees. The amount of the bonus is subject to the following considerations:

- Employees with less than one year of experience will be given a flat $100 bonus.
- Employees with one to three years of experience will receive $100, plus 10 percent of their monthly paycheck for each year of experience.
- Employees with three to twenty years of experience will receive 20 percent of their monthly paycheck, plus 5 percent of the monthly pay for each year of experience.
- Employees with more than twenty years of experience will receive the same bonus as twenty-year employees.

Let us assume that data records are to be processed containing the following fields:

```
YEARS          number of years experience
MONTHLY-PAY    amount of monthly pay
```

The routine required to compute the amount of the Christmas bonus is shown in Figure 6.12. Notice that by use of complex conditions, it is possible to perform the computations without the use of nested IF statements, which would otherwise be required.

Figure 6.12   Christmas bonus computation

```
IF YEARS = 0
    COMPUTE BONUS = 100.
IF YEARS > 0 AND YEARS NOT > 3
    COMPUTE BONUS = 100 + YEARS * 0.1 * MONTHLY-PAY.
IF YEARS > 3 AND YEARS NOT > 20
    COMPUTE BONUS = 0.2 * MONTHLY-PAY +
                    YEARS * 0.05 * MONTHLY-PAY.
IF YEARS > 20
    COMPUTE BONUS = 1.2 * MONTHLY-PAY.
```

6.7   NAMED CONDITIONS

Named conditions are useful in documenting the meaning of a programmer-written test. Suppose, for example, that data being processed contains a code having value M if sex is male and F if sex is female. The PROCEDURE DIVISION statement

```
IF KODE = "M"
    PERFORM MALE-ROUTINE
ELSE
    IF KODE = "F"
        PERFORM FEMALE-ROUTINE
    ELSE
        PERFORM ERROR-ROUTINE.
```

could be used for differentiation in the processing of males and females. The meaning of the tests KODE = "M" and KODE = "F" is not apparent from the statement of the condition itself. It is possible to assign a name to the conditions KODE = "M" and KODE = "F". The 88 level used in the DATA DIVISION defines these names as follows:

```
03 KODE PIC X.
    88 SEX-IS-MALE VALUE "M".
    88 SEX-IS-FEMALE VALUE "F".
```

The condition SEX-IS-MALE is true if KODE has a value of "M" and false otherwise. The condition SEX-IS-FEMALE is true when KODE has a value of "F" and false otherwise. The PROCEDURE DIVISION code above could now be rewritten as:

```
IF SEX-IS-MALE
    PERFORM MALE-ROUTINE
ELSE
    IF SEX-IS-FEMALE
        PERFORM FEMALE-ROUTINE
    ELSE
        PERFORM ERROR-ROUTINE.
```

The general form of the 88-level entry is shown in Figure 6.13. Any number of 88-level entries may follow an elementary data item definition in the DATA DIVISION.

Figure 6.13   General form of the 88-level entry

$$88 \quad \text{condition-name} \left\{ \begin{array}{l} \underline{\text{VALUE}} \text{ IS} \\ \underline{\text{VALUES}} \text{ ARE} \end{array} \right\} \text{literal-1} \left[\left\{ \begin{array}{l} \underline{\text{THROUGH}} \\ \underline{\text{THRU}} \end{array} \right\} \text{literal-2} \right]$$

$$\left[\text{literal-3} \left[\left\{ \begin{array}{l} \underline{\text{THROUGH}} \\ \underline{\text{THRU}} \end{array} \right\} \text{literal-4} \right] \right] \dots \; .$$

─── Example ───

A common usage of named conditions is in end-of-file testing. For example, in Program 6a, suppose the definition of EOF-FLAG at lines 51–52 is replaced by

```
01   FLAGS.
     02 EOF-FLAG    PIC X(3) VALUE "NO".
        88 END-OF-FILE    VALUE "YES".
```

Then the code at lines 114–115, which is currently

```
PERFORM 2100-PROCESS-DATA
    UNTIL EOF-FLAG = "YES".
```

can be replaced by

```
PERFORM 2100-PROCESS-DATA
        UNTIL END-OF-FILE.
```

The latter code is more readable and is equivalent to the first code because END-OF-FILE is a name for the condition

```
EOF-FLAG = "YES".
```

Note that more than one value can be included in a VALUE clause.

─── Example ───

Suppose a company has numbered its stores 1, 2, 3, 7, 10, and 20. The program that checks the validity of the store-number on an input record could use the following code:

```
03 STORE-NUMBER    PIC 99.
   88 VALID-STORE-NUMBER VALUES ARE 1 2 3 7 10 20.
```

The condition VALID-STORE-NUMBER will be true when the value of STORE-NUMBER is 1, 2, 3, 7, 10, or 20. The definition of the named condition VALID-STORE-NUMBER enables the program statement

```
IF  STORE-NUMBER =  1  OR
       STORE-NUMBER =  2  OR
       STORE-NUMBER =  3  OR
       STORE-NUMBER =  7  OR
       STORE-NUMBER = 10 OR
       STORE-NUMBER = 20
   PERFORM PROCESS-DATA
ELSE
   PERFORM INVALID-STORE-NUMBER.
```

to be replaced by the much more readable and compact code

```
IF VALID-STORE-NUMBER
    PERFORM PROCESS-DATA
ELSE
    PERFORM INVALID-STORE-NUMBER.
```

This mechanism also makes the task of program maintenance easier, as new store numbers can be added or existing numbers deleted by making a simple change in the DATA DIVISION only. It is not necessary to make modifications to the PROCEDURE DIVISION.

The THROUGH clause is useful for including a sequence of values. For example, the above 88-level entry could also be written as:

```
88 VALID-STORE-NUMBER VALUES ARE 1 THROUGH 3 7 10 20.
```

The clause 1 THROUGH 3 is equivalent to 1, 2, 3.

─────────────── Example ───────────────

The following code could be used to define a condition INVALID-STORE-NUMBER which would include all possible values of STORE-NUMBER except 1, 2, 3, 7, 10, and 20:

```
03 STORE-NUMBER PIC 99.
    88 INVALID-STORE-NUMBER
        VALUES ARE 0 4 THRU 6 8 9 11 THRU 19 21 THRU 99.
```

6.8 ABBREVIATED RELATIONAL CONDITIONS

Relational conditions are made up of three parts: subject, relation, and object. For example, in the relational condition

```
A + B < 32
```

the subject is A + B, the relation is <, and the object is 32. When relational conditions are linked by AND or OR to form complex conditions, it is possible to abbreviate the condition when the subject, or the subject and the relation, are the same. Abbreviation is accomplished by omitting the common subject or subject and relation in subsequent relations. Figure 6.14 gives the general form of an abbreviated complex condition.

Figure 6.14 General form of the abbreviated complex condition

$$\text{relation-condition} \left\{ \begin{Bmatrix} \underline{\text{AND}} \\ \text{OR} \end{Bmatrix} \text{[\underline{NOT}] [relation] object} \right\} \quad \dots$$

—————— **Example** ——————

Nonabbreviated Form	Abbreviated Form	Comment
A < B AND A < 3	A < B AND 3	Both the subject and relational operator are omitted in abbreviated form.
A > 16 OR A NOT < C	A > 16 OR NOT < C	Subject is omitted in abbreviated form.
A < B AND A < C OR A > D	A < B AND C OR > D	Subject and relation are omitted for the first abbreviation; only the subject is omitted in the second abbreviation.

It is *not* possible to omit objects in forming abbreviations. For example, the correct abbreviation for A < B OR A = B is A < B OR = B, not the common mistake A < OR = B.

Using abbreviated conditions can be false economy. It takes only a moment longer to write A < B AND A < C OR A > D than to write A < B AND C OR > D; but the first condition is immediately understandable, whereas it takes a moment or two to interpret the second condition. Therefore, the first (nonabbreviated) condition contributes to program maintainability.

6.9 DATA VALIDATION

Errors can enter a data processing system in many ways. Wrong values for data fields can be entered at the source of the data. For example, a clerk sells an item for $10 but writes $9 on the sales ticket. Errors can also occur when someone prepares a machine-readable document that will ultimately be processed by the computing system. The data entry person could make any number of errors in keying the data: digits within a field could be transposed, an alphabetic character could be entered in what should be a numeric field, or a numeric character could be entered in what should be an alphabetic field, to list a few examples. A well-written program will attempt to test the data it processes to detect as many errors as possible in the data items.

Data fields that contain characters of an inappropriate type (i.e., a numeric field that contains an alphabetic character or an alphabetic field that contains a numeric character) are said to contain invalid data. The class test is a convenient means for checking the validity of input data

Figure 6.15   Simple data validation program

```
1000-MAIN-CONTROL.

    PERFORM 2000-INITIALIZE-REPORT.
    PERFORM 2100-PROCESS-DATA
            UNTIL EOF-FLAG = "YES".
    PERFORM 2200-TERMINATE-REPORT.
    STOP RUN.

2000-INITIALIZE-REPORT.

    . . .

2100-PROCESS-DATA.

    PERFORM 3000-VALIDATE-DATA.
    IF ERROR-FLAG = "YES"
        PERFORM 3100-PROCESS-INVALID-DATA
    ELSE
        PERFORM 3200-PROCESS-VALID-DATA.
    PERFORM 9000-READ-DATA-FILE.

2200-TERMINATE-REPORT.

    . . .

3000-VALIDATE-DATA.

    MOVE "NO" TO ERROR-FLAG.
    IF EMP-NUM-DR IS NOT NUMERIC
        MOVE "YES" TO ERROR-FLAG.
    IF EMP-NAME-DR IS NOT ALPHABETIC
        MOVE "YES" TO ERROR-FLAG.
    IF HRS-WORKED-DR IS NOT NUMERIC
        MOVE "YES" TO ERROR-FLAG.
    IF PAY-RATE-DR IS NOT NUMERIC
        MOVE "YES" TO ERROR-FLAG.

3100-PROCESS-INVALID-DATA.

    . . .

3200-PROCESS-VALID-DATA.

    . . .

9000-READ-DATA-FILE.

    . . .
```

fields. Each data item on an input record can be checked using the appropriate class test. If the item does not contain the correct type of data, an error message concerning the record can be written, and processing of the data can be bypassed. For example, consider the following record description:

Figure 6.16 Structure diagram of a simple data validation program

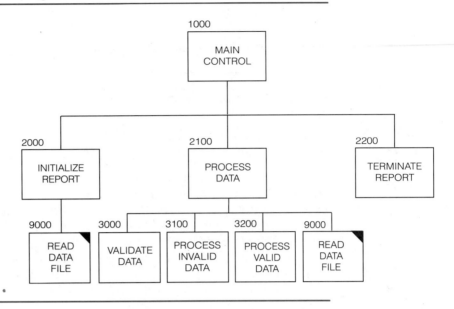

```
01    DATA-RECORD.
      03 EMP-NUM-DR          PIC 9(9).
      03 EMP-NAME-DR         PIC X(20).
      03 HRS-WORKED-DR       PIC 99V99.
      03 PAY-RATE-DR         PIC 99V99.
```

Part of a program to check the validity of the data in this record is shown in Figure 6.15. The structure diagram for this program is illustrated in Figure 6.16.

In this program, note the use of the switch ERROR-FLAG. The switch is set to value "NO" or "YES" in 3000-VALIDATE-DATA. It is then used by 2100-PROCESS-DATA to determine the appropriate action to take for the record. Note that in this program, it is necessary to initialize ERROR-FLAG in the procedure 3000-VALIDATE-DATA. This initialization is necessary because the value of ERROR-FLAG may have been reset during the processing of the preceding record.

Data validation also may take the form of checking that data in fields is within valid ranges. For example, suppose the maximum and minimum pay-rates are defined in WORKING-STORAGE as

```
01    PAY-RATES.
      03 MAXIMUM-RATE        PIC 99V99 VALUE 30.00.
      03 MINIMUM-RATE        PIC 99V99 VALUE 4.25.
```

To detect a field outside this range, the following statements could be added to the 3000-VALIDATE-DATA paragraph:

```
IF PAY-RATE-DR > MAXIMUM-RATE OR PAY-RATE-DR < MINIMUM-RATE
   MOVE "YES" TO ERROR-FLAG.
```

Another means by which this range check can be accomplished is to add a named condition INVALID-PAY-RATE to the description of DATA-RECORD as shown on the following page:

```
01   DATA-RECORD.
     03  EMP-NUM-DR        PIC 9(9).
     03  EMP-NAME-DR       PIC X(20).
     03  HAS-WORKED-DR     PIC 99V99.
     03  PAY-RATE-DR       PIC 99V99.
         88  INVALID-PAY-RATE VALUES ARE 0 THRU 4.24
                                        30.01 THRU 99.99.
```

It would now be possible to add the following statement to 3000-VALIDATE-DATA:

```
IF INVALID-PAY-RATE
   MOVE "YES" TO ERROR-FLAG.
```

The use of a simple two-value switch will result in a record being flagged as an error, although no indication will be given as to which field is in error or the type of error that may be present. It is indeed possible to write a complete description of the errors encountered in a data-record; it is also possible to generate a code that would indicate which fields are in error and what type of error was encountered. For example, in this case, there are four items to be tested, so let's assume that ERROR-CODE is a four-digit number. The first digit would indicate an error in the first field, the second digit would indicate an error in the second field, and so on. Assume that "1" in a given position would indicate that the wrong type of data is present. A "2" would mean that the value of the data item is out of range. (If there were more types of errors, we could easily extend the list of codes.) 3000-VALIDATE-DATA could now be coded as:

```
3000-VALIDATE-DATA.
    MOVE 0 TO ERROR-CODE.
    IF EMP-NUM-DR NOT NUMERIC
       ADD 1000 TO ERROR-CODE.
    IF EMP-NAME-DR NOT ALPHABETIC
       ADD 100 TO ERROR-CODE.
    IF HRS-WORKED-DR NOT NUMERIC
       ADD 10 TO ERROR-CODE.
    IF PAY-RATE-DR NOT NUMERIC
       ADD 1 TO ERROR-CODE
    ELSE
       IF PAY-RATE-DR > MAXIMUM-RATE
          ADD 2 TO ERROR-CODE
       ELSE
          IF PAY-RATE-DR < MAXIMUM-RATE
             ADD 2 TO ERROR-CODE.
```

Naturally, the out-of-range test does not apply to alphabetic information. Therefore, if PAY-RATE-DR is NOT NUMERIC, the testing for an out-of-range value should not be performed. Thus, if EMP-NUM-DR is not numeric and the pay rate is out of range, the ERROR-CODE generated would be 1002. The value of ERROR-CODE could be written out along with the data in 3100-PROCESS-INVALID-DATA. A programmer-prepared guide for the user (commonly called an operations manual) could explain the meaning of the code used in the flag. In the following example more detailed descriptions of errors are produced.

6.10 PROGRAM EXAMPLE

Problem Statement

At the XYZ Gas Company, data gathered by meter readers is loaded into a file called GAS-USAGE. Each record in this file contains

> Account number
> Customer name
> Previous meter reading
> Present meter reading

This data will ultimately be used to compute monthly bills. However, first the data must be validated to prevent the production of erroneous bills. In particular, data records with any of the following conditions are suspect and should not be processed:

- Nonnumeric data in a numeric field.
- Nonalphabetic data in a customer-name field.
- An unreasonable high amount of gas used (> 100,000).

A program is needed to process the data in the file GAS-USAGE and prepare a report showing all suspect records. Any record which is not suspect should be written to a file VALID-GAS-USAGE which will be used to produce the actual bills. Specific descriptions of each error encountered in a record are to be written in a report format shown in Figure 6.17.

Figure 6.17 Printer spacing chart for Program 6b

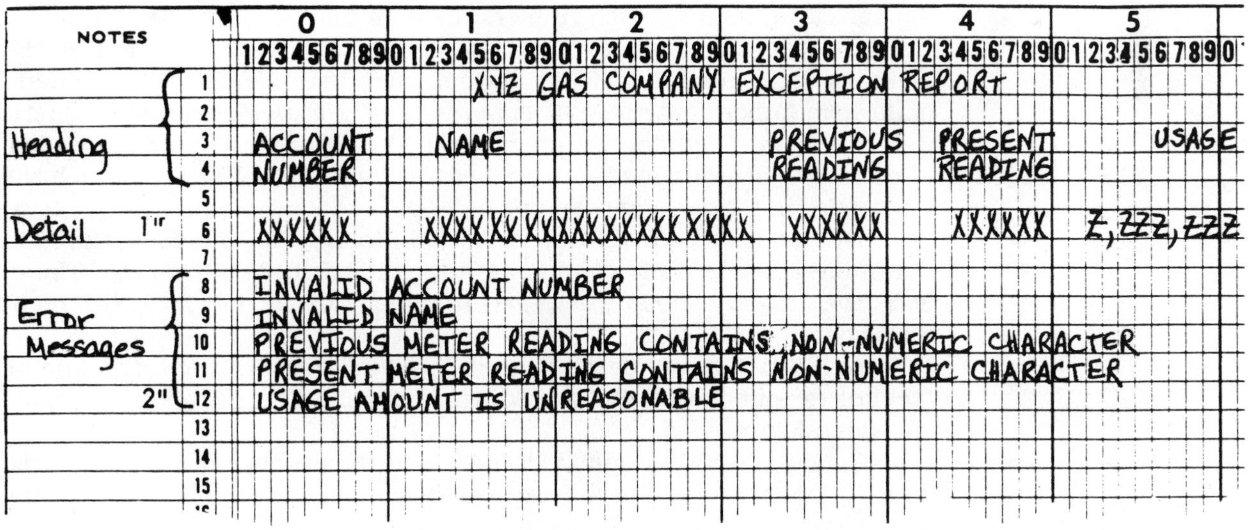

Problem Analysis

Programs encountered thus far in this text have almost always processed two files—an input file and an output file. This is not, however, a general rule. In this problem, the program processes three files—one input file and two output files. In general, a program may process any number of input and/or output files.

The computation of the amount of gas used in this problem is not as straightforward as we might initially expect. At first glance there is a temptation to compute the amount of usage by subtracting the previous reading from the present reading. This procedure is fine most of the time; however, meters count only up to some maximum (999999 in our example) before they *roll over* and begin again at zero. If this happens, the present reading will actually appear to be less than the previous reading. For example, suppose the previous reading was 999980 and the present reading is 000020. The amount of usage is actually 40. To handle this case, the formula for computing usage is

Usage = (present reading + 1000000) − previous reading.

For the above data the computation would yield

Usage = (20 + 1000000) − 999980
      = 1000020 − 999980
      = 40

The procedure for computing usage can be expressed as

If previous reading < present reading
      Usage = present reading − previous reading,
Else
      Usage = (present reading + 1000000) − previous reading
End If

When nonnumeric characters are present in a numeric field, the computer will use the numeric equivalent of the character in any computations with that field. The numeric equivalent is based on the internal representation of the character. When the field is edited for output by usual methods, the content of the field will appear to be numeric. This problem can be solved by treating each numeric field as both numeric and alphanumeric, because each character is preserved in an alphanumeric field. By defining each numeric field as a group item with a numeric elementary data item subordinate to it, it is possible to work with an alphanumeric field (the group item) or a numeric field (the elementary item) as needed. (Recall that all group items are classed as nonnumeric.) This approach will be needed in the present program.

When one of the reading fields contains an invalid character, the computation of usage is of no value because the basic data is flawed. Therefore, the program should compute the value of usage only if the two readings contain valid data.

At this point, and based on the preceding considerations, it would be helpful to summarize the procedure required to solve this problem as shown in Figure 6.18.

Notice that we have not yet addressed the problem of controlling the production of the report—a detail line is to be included in the output only if one or more errors are found in a record. The error messages must occur *after* the related detail line. For a given record, a number of error messages may be written.

A simple way of carrying out this task is to use five flags, one for each possible error:

```
INVALID-ACCT-NUMBER-FLAG
INVALID-NAME-FLAG
INVALID-PREVIOUS-FLAG
INVALID-PRESENT-FLAG
INVALID-USAGE-FLAG
```

Figure 6.18   Plan for data validation program (Program 6b)

Main control

Open files
Write headings
Read gas usage file
Do Process data until end of file
Write summary line
Close files
Stop

Process data

Move "NO" to all error flags.
Do Validate account number
Do Validate name
Do Validate previous reading
Do Validate present reading
If previous reading and present reading valid
    Do Compute usage
Else
    Move 0 to usage
End If
Do Validate usage
If record is invalid
    Add 1 to number of invalid records
    Do Write invalid data
Else
    Do Write valid data
End If
Read gas usage file

Compute usage

If previous reading < present reading
    Usage = present reading − previous reading
Else
    Usage = (present reading + 1000000) − previous reading
End If

Write invalid data

Write detail line
Write appropriate error messages

Write valid data

Move gas usage record to valid gas usage record
Write valid gas usage record

For each record, all of the flags are set to "NO". Then, the various validity tests are performed on the data. Each test procedure can change the appropriate flag to "YES" if an error is found. After all tests are completed, the program writes the detail line if any of the flags are set to "YES"; if all of them remain set to "NO", there are no errors in the record. If the record contains invalid data, the program then tests each of the flags in succession to write the appropriate set of error messages.

Problem Solution

The program for this problem is shown as Program 6b; the structure diagram is shown in Figure 6.19. A sample data file and the report produced by Program 6b is shown in Figure 6.20. Note the technique used to secure alphanumeric and numeric data names for the same data item. For example, at lines 33–34 the field for account-number is defined as

```
02  ACCOUNT-NUMBER-AN-GUR.
    03  ACCOUNT-NUMBER-GUR PIC 9(6).
```

Because `ACCOUNT-NUMBER-AN-GUR` is a group data item, it is classed as alphanumeric. When this field is moved to the output line at line 228, the alphanumeric item is moved to an alphanumeric field. This is necessary so that any alphabetic characters in the field will not be printed using the numeric equivalent. (This would have happened had the numeric item `ACCOUNT-NUMBER-GUR` been used for output purposes.)

The pseudocode statement

If record is invalid. . .

is implemented in the program at lines 169–173:

```
IF    INVALID-ACCOUNT-NUMBER
    OR INVALID-NAME
    OR INVALID-PREVIOUS
    OR INVALID-PRESENT
    OR INVALID-USAGE
```

This is a complex condition that will be true if any one of the named conditions which make it up is true. Each of these named conditions will be true if the associated error flag is equal to `"YES"` (see lines 59–68).

The pseudocode statement

Move "NO" to all error flags

is implemented at lines 155 through 159:

```
MOVE "NO" TO INVALID-ACCOUNT-NUMBER-FLAG
             INVALID-NAME-FLAG
             INVALID-PREVIOUS-FLAG
             INVALID-PRESENT-FLAG
             INVALID-USAGE-FLAG.
```

Recall that when multiple receiving fields are specified in a `MOVE` statement, the sending field value is moved to each of the receiving fields.

Summary of Data Validation Concepts

In this chapter we have discussed several of the most common types of data errors and related validation procedures designed to detect those errors.

Error	Validation technique
An inappropriate character is in a field.	Use numeric and alphabetic tests.
Coded item contains nonrecognizable value.	Use named condition listing all valid codes.
Data item or computed item contains unusually large or small value.	Check for reasonable range of values.

Program 6b

```
 1 IDENTIFICATION DIVISION.
 2
 3 PROGRAM-ID. DATA-VALIDATION-PRO6B.
 4 AUTHOR. HORN
 5
 6 ENVIRONMENT DIVISION.
 7
 8 CONFIGURATION SECTION.
 9
10 SOURCE-COMPUTER.
11 OBJECT-COMPUTER.
12
13 INPUT-OUTPUT SECTION.
14
15 FILE-CONTROL.
16
17     SELECT GAS-USAGE-FILE ASSIGN TO DISK.
18
19     SELECT INVALID-DATA-REPORT  ASSIGN TO PRINTER.
20
21     SELECT VALID-GAS-USAGE-FILE ASSIGN TO DISK.
22
23
24 DATA DIVISION.
25
26 FILE SECTION.
27
28 FD  GAS-USAGE-FILE
29     LABEL RECORDS ARE STANDARD
30     DATA RECORD IS GAS-USAGE-RECORD.
31
32 01  GAS-USAGE-RECORD.
33     02 ACCOUNT-NUMBER-AN-GUR.
34        03 ACCOUNT-NUMBER-GUR    PIC 9(6).
35     02 NAME-GUR                 PIC X(20).
36     02 PREVIOUS-READING-AN-GUR.
37        03 PREVIOUS-READING-GUR  PIC 9(6).
38     02 PRESENT-READING-AN-GUR.
39        03 PRESENT-READING-GUR   PIC 9(6).
40     02 FILLER                   PIC X(42).
41
42 FD  INVALID-DATA-REPORT
43     LABEL RECORDS ARE OMITTED
44     DATA RECORD IS PRINT-LINE.
45
46 01  PRINT-LINE          PIC X(132).
47
48 FD  VALID-GAS-USAGE-FILE
49     LABEL RECORDS ARE STANDARD
50     DATA RECORD IS VALID-GAS-USAGE-RECORD.
51
52 01  VALID-GAS-USAGE-RECORD    PIC X(84).
53
```

```
 54 WORKING-STORAGE SECTION.
 55
 56 01   FLAGS.
 57      02 EOF-FLAG                      PIC X(3) VALUE "NO".
 58         88 END-OF-FILE               VALUE "YES".
 59      02 INVALID-ACCOUNT-NUMBER-FLAG  PIC X(3) VALUE "NO".
 60         88 INVALID-ACCOUNT-NUMBER VALUE "YES".
 61      02 INVALID-NAME-FLAG            PIC X(3) VALUE "NO".
 62         88 INVALID-NAME             VALUE "YES".
 63      02 INVALID-PREVIOUS-FLAG        PIC X(3) VALUE "NO".
 64         88 INVALID-PREVIOUS         VALUE "YES".
 65      02 INVALID-PRESENT-FLAG         PIC X(3) VALUE "NO".
 66         88 INVALID-PRESENT          VALUE "YES".
 67      02 INVALID-USAGE-FLAG           PIC X(3) VALUE "NO".
 68         88 INVALID-USAGE            VALUE "YES".
 69
 70 01   VALIDATION-LIMITS.
 71      02 UPPER-USAGE-LIMIT            PIC 9(6) VALUE 100000.
 72
 73 01   COMPUTED-AMOUNTS.
 74      02  AMOUNT-USED            PIC 9(7) VALUE ZERO.
 75      02  NUMBER-INVALID-RECORDS PIC 999  VALUE ZERO.
 76
 77 01   HEADING-LINE-1.
 78      02 FILLER         PIC X(14) VALUE SPACES.
 79      02 FILLER         PIC X(32) VALUE
 80         "XYZ GAS COMPANY EXCEPTION REPORT".
 81
 82 01   HEADING-LINE-2.
 83      02 FILLER         PIC X    VALUE SPACE.
 84      02 FILLER         PIC X(7)  VALUE "ACCOUNT".
 85      02 FILLER         PIC X(4)  VALUE SPACES.
 86      02 FILLER         PIC X(4)  VALUE "NAME".
 87      02 FILLER         PIC X(16) VALUE SPACES.
 88      02 FILLER         PIC X(17) VALUE "PREVIOUS   PRESENT".
 89      02 FILLER         PIC X(6)  VALUE SPACES.
 90      02 FILLER         PIC X(5)  VALUE "USAGE".
 91
 92 01   HEADING-LINE-3.
 93      02 FILLER         PIC X    VALUE SPACE.
 94      02 FILLER         PIC X(6)  VALUE "NUMBER".
 95      02 FILLER         PIC X(25) VALUE SPACES.
 96      02 FILLER         PIC X(17) VALUE "READING   READING".
 97
 98 01   DETAIL-LINE.
 99      02 FILLER                 PIC X      VALUE SPACE.
100      02 ACCOUNT-NUMBER-DL      PIC X(6).
101      02 FILLER                 PIC X(4)  VALUE SPACES.
102      02 NAME-DL                PIC X(20).
103      02 FILLER                 PIC X(2)  VALUE SPACES.
104      02 PREVIOUS-READING-DL    PIC X(6).
105      02 FILLER                 PIC X(4)  VALUE SPACES.
106      02 PRESENT-READING-DL     PIC X(6).
107      02 FILLER                 PIC X(2)  VALUE SPACES.
108      02 USAGE-DL               PIC Z,ZZZ,ZZZ.
109
```

Program 6b   (continued)

```
110 01   ERROR-MESSAGES.
111      02 MESSAGE-LINE-1          PIC X(23) VALUE
112         " INVALID ACCOUNT NUMBER".
113
114      02  MESSAGE-LINE-2         PIC X(13) VALUE
115         " INVALID NAME".
116
117      02  MESSAGE-LINE-3         PIC X(55) VALUE
118         " PREVIOUS METER READING CONTAINS NON-NUMERIC CHARACTER".
119
120      02  MESSAGE-LINE-4         PIC X(54) VALUE
121         " PRESENT METER READING CONTAINS NON-NUMERIC CHARACTER".
122
123      02  MESSAGE-LINE-5         PIC X(29) VALUE
124         " USAGE AMOUNT IS UNREASONABLE".
125
126 01   SUMMARY-LINE.
127      02 FILLER                      PIC X(14) VALUE SPACES.
128      02 FILLER                      PIC X(26) VALUE
129         "NUMBER OF INVALID RECORDS ".
130      02 NUMBER-INVALID-RECORDS-SL   PIC ZZZ.
131
132 PROCEDURE DIVISION.
133
134 1000-MAIN-CONTROL.
135
136      PERFORM 2000-INITIALIZE-DATA.
137      PERFORM 2100-PROCESS-DATA
138              UNTIL END-OF-FILE.
139      PERFORM 2200-WRITE-SUMMARY.
140      PERFORM 2300-TERMINATE-REPORT.
141      STOP RUN.
142
143 2000-INITIALIZE-DATA.
144
145      OPEN INPUT GAS-USAGE-FILE
146          OUTPUT INVALID-DATA-REPORT
147                 VALID-GAS-USAGE-FILE.
148      WRITE PRINT-LINE FROM HEADING-LINE-1 AFTER PAGE.
149      WRITE PRINT-LINE FROM HEADING-LINE-2 AFTER 2.
150      WRITE PRINT-LINE FROM HEADING-LINE-3 AFTER 1.
151      PERFORM 9000-READ-GAS-USAGE.
152
```

```
153 2100-PROCESS-DATA.
154
155     MOVE "NO" TO INVALID-ACCOUNT-NUMBER-FLAG
156                 INVALID-NAME-FLAG
157                 INVALID-PREVIOUS-FLAG
158                 INVALID-PRESENT-FLAG
159                 INVALID-USAGE-FLAG.
160     PERFORM 3000-VALIDATE-ACCOUNT-NUMBER.
161     PERFORM 3100-VALIDATE-NAME.
162     PERFORM 3200-VALIDATE-PREVIOUS-READING.
163     PERFORM 3300-VALIDATE-PRESENT-READING.
164     IF INVALID-PREVIOUS OR INVALID-PRESENT
165         MOVE ZERO TO AMOUNT-USED
166     ELSE
167         PERFORM 3400-COMPUTE-AMOUNT-USED.
168     PERFORM 3500-VALIDATE-USAGE.
169     IF     INVALID-ACCOUNT-NUMBER
170        OR INVALID-NAME
171        OR INVALID-PREVIOUS
172        OR INVALID-PRESENT
173        OR INVALID-USAGE
174             ADD 1 TO NUMBER-INVALID-RECORDS
175             PERFORM 3600-WRITE-INVALID-DATA
176     ELSE
177             PERFORM 3700-WRITE-VALID-DATA.
178     PERFORM 9000-READ-GAS-USAGE.
179
180 2200-WRITE-SUMMARY.
181
182     MOVE NUMBER-INVALID-RECORDS TO NUMBER-INVALID-RECORDS-SL.
183     MOVE SUMMARY-LINE            TO PRINT-LINE.
184     WRITE PRINT-LINE AFTER 2.
185
186 2300-TERMINATE-REPORT.
187
188     CLOSE GAS-USAGE-FILE
189           INVALID-DATA-REPORT
190           VALID-GAS-USAGE-FILE.
191
192 3000-VALIDATE-ACCOUNT-NUMBER.
193
194     IF ACCOUNT-NUMBER-GUR IS NOT NUMERIC
195         MOVE "YES" TO INVALID-ACCOUNT-NUMBER-FLAG.
196
197 3100-VALIDATE-NAME.
198
199     IF NAME-GUR NOT ALPHABETIC
200         MOVE "YES" TO INVALID-NAME-FLAG.
201
202 3200-VALIDATE-PREVIOUS-READING.
203
204     IF PREVIOUS-READING-GUR NOT NUMERIC
205         MOVE "YES" TO INVALID-PREVIOUS-FLAG.
206
```

Program 6b   *(concluded)*

```
207 3300-VALIDATE-PRESENT-READING.
208
209     IF PRESENT-READING-GUR NOT NUMERIC
210         MOVE "YES" TO INVALID-PRESENT-FLAG.
211
212 3400-COMPUTE-AMOUNT-USED.
213
214     IF PREVIOUS-READING-GUR < PRESENT-READING-GUR
215         SUBTRACT PREVIOUS-READING-GUR  FROM PRESENT-READING-GUR
216                                 GIVING AMOUNT-USED
217     ELSE
218         COMPUTE AMOUNT-USED = PRESENT-READING-GUR  + 1000000
219                                 - PREVIOUS-READING-GUR.
220
221 3500-VALIDATE-USAGE.
222
223     IF AMOUNT-USED > UPPER-USAGE-LIMIT
224         MOVE "YES" TO INVALID-USAGE-FLAG.
225
226 3600-WRITE-INVALID-DATA.
227
228     MOVE ACCOUNT-NUMBER-AN-GUR   TO ACCOUNT-NUMBER-DL.
229     MOVE NAME-GUR                TO NAME-DL.
230     MOVE PREVIOUS-READING-AN-GUR TO PREVIOUS-READING-DL.
231     MOVE PRESENT-READING-AN-GUR  TO PRESENT-READING-DL.
232     MOVE AMOUNT-USED             TO USAGE-DL.
233     MOVE DETAIL-LINE             TO PRINT-LINE.
234     WRITE PRINT-LINE AFTER 2.
235     IF INVALID-ACCOUNT-NUMBER
236         WRITE PRINT-LINE FROM MESSAGE-LINE-1 AFTER 1.
237     IF INVALID-NAME
238         WRITE PRINT-LINE FROM MESSAGE-LINE-2 AFTER 1.
239     IF INVALID-PREVIOUS
240         WRITE PRINT-LINE FROM MESSAGE-LINE-3 AFTER 1.
241     IF INVALID-PRESENT
242         WRITE PRINT-LINE FROM MESSAGE-LINE-4 AFTER 1.
243     IF INVALID-USAGE
244         WRITE PRINT-LINE FROM MESSAGE-LINE-5 AFTER 1.
245
246 3700-WRITE-VALID-DATA.
247
248     MOVE GAS-USAGE-RECORD TO VALID-GAS-USAGE-RECORD.
249     WRITE VALID-GAS-USAGE-RECORD.
250
251 9000-READ-GAS-USAGE.
252
253     READ GAS-USAGE-FILE
254         AT END MOVE "YES" TO EOF-FLAG.
```

Figure 6.19   Structure diagram for Program 6b

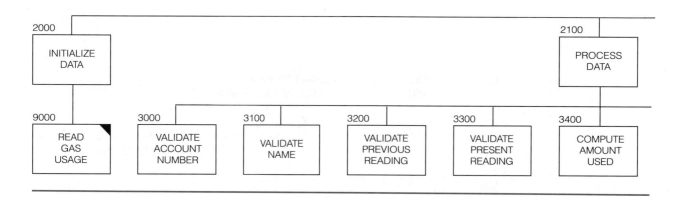

We have also seen that invalid data can be handled in a number of ways. The simplest approach is to create a listing that shows all invalid data records. This listing may not contain any error messages (the least desirable approach), or it may contain error messages designed to help the user determine the type of error contained in the data. We have illustrated two commonly used types of error messages:

- The numeric code in which each digit is associated with a particular type of error. This approach requires minimal space on the report, but it requires that the user be knowledgeable in the meaning of the codes.

- The specific error message describing each error in some detail. This approach is more "user friendly," but it can create voluminous output.

Most data validation programs create a listing of errors, but some go beyond the list to prepare a file containing only valid data. In these cases, the usual procedure is for data processing personnel to take the list of invalid data and attempt to correct the error(s) by examining the source data and resubmitting the record(s) for processing by the system. A simple extension of this concept is for the validation program to create another output file containing the invalid records. This file could be edited to remove the errors and then submitted for processing in the usual fashion.

This chapter has not presented an exhaustive treatment of the subject of data validation. We will return to the topic several times in successive chapters as appropriate COBOL facilities are introduced.

6.11   DEBUG CLINIC

The Case of the Missing Period

One of the most common errors made when using the IF statement is the omission of the period required to terminate the statement. For example, suppose we want to write a program segment to implement the following flowchart:

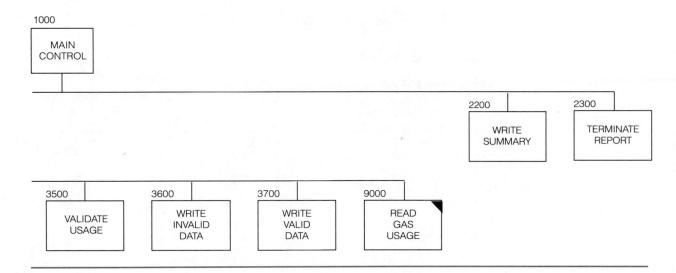

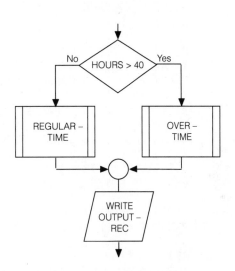

The correct code is

```
IF HOURS > 40
     PERFORM OVER-TIME
ELSE
     PERFORM REGULAR-TIME.
WRITE OUTPUT-REC AFTER 1.
```

However, suppose the program is coded (erroneously) as

```
IF HOURS > 40
     PERFORM OVER-TIME
ELSE
     PERFORM REGULAR-TIME          (note missing period)
WRITE OUTPUT-REC AFTER 1.
```

The result will be to include the WRITE statement as a part of the ELSE clause of the IF statement, as though the flowchart had been written

Figure 6.20 Sample data file and output for Program 6b

Sample Gas Usage File

```
111111JONES JOHN          020000030000
222222SMITH MARY          040000060000
C33333DOE JAMES           000000999999
444444BROWN, CHARLES      200000400000
555555WHITE SUE           A00000500000
666666BLACK SAM           700000B00000
777 77GRAY Dr C           XXXXXXYYYYYY
888888GONZALEZ CARLOS     999000000100
999999JAMES LOIS          999000900000
```

Sample Report

```
           XYZ GAS COMPANY EXCEPTION REPORT

    ACCOUNT     NAME              PREVIOUS   PRESENT      USAGE
    NUMBER                        READING    READING


    C33333    DOE JAMES            000000    999999     999,999
    INVALID ACCOUNT NUMBER
    USAGE AMOUNT IS UNREASONABLE


    444444    BROWN, CHARLES       200000    400000     200,000
    INVALID NAME
    USAGE AMOUNT IS UNREASONABLE


    555555    WHITE SUE            A00000    500000
    PREVIOUS METER READING CONTAINS NON-NUMERIC CHARACTER


    666666    BLACK SAM            700000    B00000
    PRESENT METER READING CONTAINS NON-NUMERIC CHARACTER


    777 77    GRAY Dr C            XXXXXX    YYYYYY
    INVALID ACCOUNT NUMBER
    INVALID NAME
    PREVIOUS METER READING CONTAINS NON-NUMERIC CHARACTER
    PRESENT METER READING CONTAINS NON-NUMERIC CHARACTER


    999999    JAMES LOIS           999000    900000     901,000
    USAGE AMOUNT IS UNREASONABLE

             NUMBER OF INVALID RECORDS    6
```

Sample Valid Gas Usage File

```
111111JONES JOHN          020000030000
222222SMITH MARY          040000060000
888888GONZALEZ CARLOS     999000000100
```

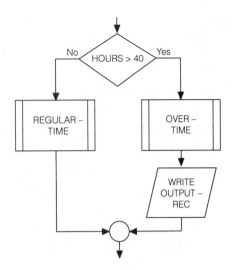

The alignment of the WRITE statement in the same column as the IF and ELSE entries indicates to the reader that the WRITE statement is not a part of the ELSE clause of the IF statement, but the compiler ignores the placement of statements. The period is required to terminate the IF statement.

Conditional and Imperative Statements

A **conditional statement** is a statement which

- contains one or more statements in a clause, and
- selects the action(s) to be taken next depending on the evaluation of some condition.

It is clear that the IF statement is a conditional statement. Other statements also are classed as conditional, including the following:

- any arithmetic statement with the ON SIZE ERROR option
- READ statements with the AT END option

In all of these statements, the action to be taken depends on the evaluation of some condition. In the case of the arithmetic statement with the ON SIZE ERROR option, the statements in the ON SIZE ERROR clause are executed if there is overflow or division by zero; otherwise, execution continues with the next sentence. The statement(s) in the AT END clause of a READ statement are executed at end-of-file; otherwise, the next sentence is executed. Conditional statements are always terminated by a period.

Any statement that is not a conditional statement is an **imperative statement**. Examples of imperative statements include the following:

- arithmetic statements without the clause ON SIZE ERROR
- WRITE statement
- PERFORM statement
- MOVE statement

Imperative statements are terminated either by a period or a COBOL verb signifying the start of another statement.

A single COBOL PROCEDURE DIVISION sentence may be made up of many imperative statements.

─────────── Example ───────────

The following two coding sequences are equivalent:

```
MOVE A TO A-OUT          MOVE A TO A-OUT.
MOVE B TO B-OUT          MOVE B TO B-OUT.
COMPUTE OUT = A + B      COMPUTE OUT = A + B.
WRITE OUT-REC AFTER 1.   WRITE OUT-REC AFTER 1.
```

On the left is a single sentence composed of four imperative statements. On the right are four sentences, each sentence containing a single imperative statement and ending with a period.

Clauses within conditional statements may be made up of any number of imperative statements.

─────────── Example ───────────

```
COMPUTE A = B + C
    ON SIZE ERROR
        MOVE "ERROR IN COMP" TO MSG-OUT
        WRITE OUT-REC FROM ERR-REC AFTER 1
        MOVE 0 TO A.
```

In the example above, the ON SIZE ERROR clause is made up of three imperative statements.

─────────── Example ───────────

```
READ IN-FILE
    AT END
        MOVE 999 TO A
        MOVE "YES" TO EOF-FLAG.
```

In this example the AT END clause is made up of two imperative statements.

Care must be taken that every conditional statement ends with a period. If the period is omitted, succeeding statements will be erroneously included as a part of a clause of the conditional statement.

─────────── Example ───────────

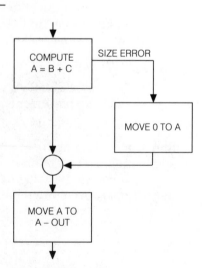

The correct code terminates the conditional COMPUTE statement with a period.

```
COMPUTE A = B + C
    ON SIZE ERROR
        MOVE 0 TO A.
MOVE A TO A-OUT.
```

If the conditional COMPUTE statement is not terminated with a period, as in

```
COMPUTE A = B + C
    ON SIZE ERROR
        MOVE 0 TO A           (note missing period)
MOVE A TO A-OUT.
```

the result is to include the statement MOVE A TO A-OUT as a part of the ON SIZE ERROR clause as though the flowchart had been written like this:

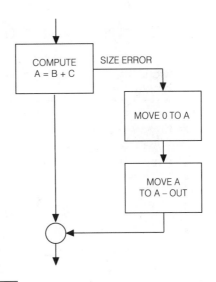

Embedding a conditional statement into a clause of another conditional statement is possible only if the embedded conditional statement is the last one in a clause.

_____ Example _____

Suppose we wish to implement the following flowchart:

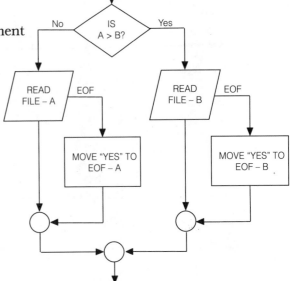

It would be correct to code this procedure as

```
IF A > B
    READ FILE-B AT END MOVE "YES" TO EOF-B
ELSE
    READ FILE-A AT END MOVE "YES" TO EOF-A.
```

The conditional statement READ FILE-B is terminated by ELSE; the conditional statement READ FILE-A and the IF statement itself are terminated by the period.

─────────────────── Example ───────────────────

Suppose we wish to implement the procedure illustrated in Figure 6.21. The best way to code this logic is to write separate paragraphs for READ-FILE-A and READ-FILE-B and PERFORM these paragraphs, as in

```
IF A = B
    PERFORM READ-FILE-A
    PERFORM READ-FILE-B.
```

Figure 6.21   Flowchart of embedded conditional statement example

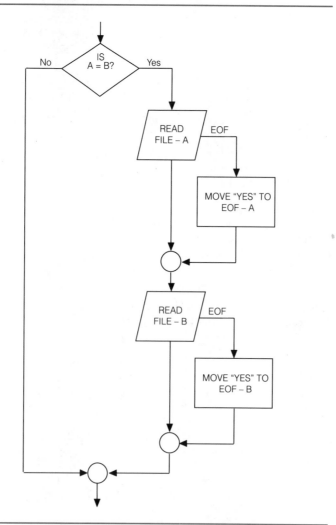

This IF statement has a clause made up of two imperative statements. If one attempts to embed two conditional statements into the IF statement, as in

```
IF A = B
     READ FILE-A AT END MOVE "YES" TO EOF-A
     READ FILE-B AT END MOVE "YES" TO EOF-B.
```

the program would be in error because the READ FILE-B statement would be a part of the AT END clause of the statement READ FILE-A. The above program segment would be executed as though the flowchart read as it does in Figure 6.22. Note that a clause in a conditional statement is made up of statements, *not* sentences. If a programmer tried to salvage the above program segment by placing a period at the end of the first READ statement, as in

```
IF A = B
     READ-FILE-A AT END MOVE "YES" TO EOF-A.
     READ-FILE-B AT END MOVE "YES" TO EOF-B.
```

Figure 6.22   Result of incorrect coding of embedded
                    conditional statement example

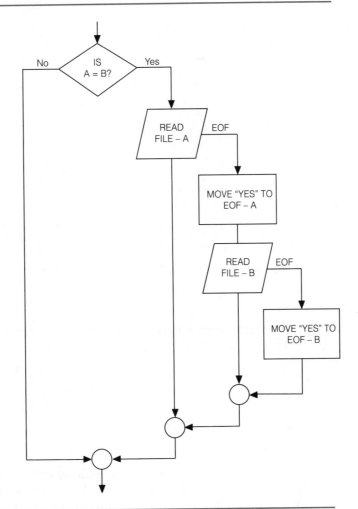

the program would be in error because the added period would terminate not only the READ statement but also the IF statement. The result would be as though the flowchart read as it does in Figure 6.23.

Figure 6.23   Result of misplaced period in coding embedded conditional statement example

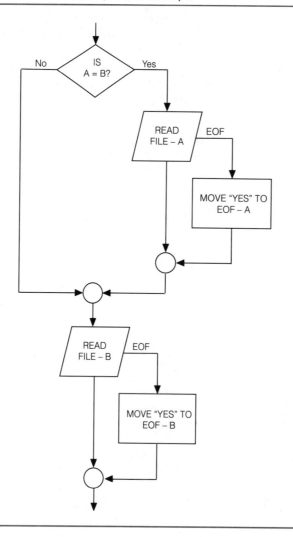

The programmer should break a program into paragraphs to avoid inclusion of conditional statements in a clause of another conditional statement.

6.12 COBOL-85 UPDATE

One of the most significant changes made to the IF statement in COBOL-85 is the inclusion of a scope delimiter END-IF as illustrated in the general syntax shown in Figure 6.24. A minor change is the inclusion of an optional word THEN following the condition. (One restriction on the statement is that the entry NEXT SENTENCE *cannot* be used if END-IF is speci-

Figure 6.24   General form of COBOL-85 IF statement

```
IF condition THEN
          {statement-1...}
          {NEXT SENTENCE }
[ELSE
          {statement-n...}
          {NEXT SENTENCE }]
 [END-IF]
```

fied.) In general, the IF statement in COBOL-85 reads more like the pseudocode version of the statement. The inclusion of the scope delimiter lets the programmer avoid the problems associated with trying to nest an IF statement in another conditional statement. When END-IF is used to terminate the IF statement, it can be used just as an imperative statement is used.

A simple example of an IF statement in COBOL-85 form is shown in Program 6a85, which performs the same function as Program 6a. We have used the loop control approach introduced in the previous chapter. There is one READ statement, which includes the NOT AT END clause to process data read from the file. This processing is conditional; the IF statement specifies the condition and the actions to be taken.

```
IF Year-Hired-PR IS GREATER THAN Year-For-Report
   Add 1 TO Number-Employees
   PERFORM 3000-Write-Detail-Line
END-IF
```

Notice that the END-IF is aligned with the IF, contributing to program readability. Notice also that his statement is embedded in the NOT AT END clause of the READ statement, which is terminated by its own scope delimiter END-READ.

The power of the scope delimiter can be illustrated in the following example: We wish to modify Program 6a85 so that the listing contains all employees, with several asterisks printed at the beginning of the detail line for employees who are recent hires. We will assume that a new field Recent-Hire-Flag-DL has been added to the record for this purpose.

Paragraph 2100-Process-Data can be rewritten to perform this new function as follows:

```
2100-Process-Data.
    READ Personnel-File
        AT END
             MOVE "YES" to Eof-Flag
        NOT AT END
             IF Year-Hired-PR IS GREATER THAN Year-For-Report
                 ADD 1 TO Number-Employees
                 MOVE ALL "*" TO Recent-Hire-Flag-DL
             ELSE
                 MOVE SPACES TO Recent-Hire-Flag-DL
             END-IF
             PERFORM 3000-Write-Detail-Line
    END-READ.
```

Program 6a85

```
  1 IDENTIFICATION DIVISION.
  2
  3 PROGRAM-ID. Recent-Hire-Report-Pro6a85.
  .
  .
  .
102 PROCEDURE DIVISION.
103
104 1000-Main-Control.
105
106     PERFORM 2000-Initialize-Report
107     PERFORM 2100-Process-Data
108             UNTIL Eof-Flag = "YES"
109     PERFORM 2200-Write-Summary-Line
110     PERFORM 2300-Terminate-Report
111     STOP RUN.
112
113 2000-Initialize-Report.
114
115     OPEN INPUT Personnel-File
116          OUTPUT Employee-Report-File
117     MOVE Year-For-Report     TO Year-For-Report-HL
118     WRITE Employee-Report-Record FROM Head-Line   AFTER PAGE
119     WRITE Employee-Report-Record FROM Sub-Head-1 AFTER 2
120     WRITE Employee-Report-Record FROM Sub-Head-2 AFTER 1.
121
122 2100-Process-Data.
123
124     READ Personnel-File
125         AT END
126             MOVE "YES" TO Eof-Flag
127         NOT AT END
128             IF Year-Hired-PR IS GREATER THAN Year-For-Report
129                     ADD 1 TO Number-Employees
130                     PERFORM 3000-Write-Detail-Line
131             END-IF
132     END-READ.
        .
        .
        .
```

One of the perennial problems facing the programmer in COBOL-74 is the implementation of the arithmetic relations "greater than or equal to" and "less than or equal to." The COBOL-74 programmer may use NOT LESS THAN for "greater than or equal to" and NOT GREATER THAN for "less than or equal to." Needless to say this does not make for very readable code because most people must stop to ponder the meaning of a negated condition. To solve this problem, COBOL-85 provides additional relational operators shown in Figure 6.25. It is now possible to express these operations in a much more natural way. For example, if we desire to modify Program 6a85 to include employees hired in 1989 or later, the IF statement could be rewritten as

```
IF Year-Hired-PR IS GREATER THAN OR EQUAL TO Year-For-Report. . .
```

Figure 6.25 Additional relations in COBOL-85

```
IS GREATER THAN OR EQUAL TO
IS >=
IS LESS THAN OR EQUAL TO
IS <=
```

---

or the equivalent

```
IF Year-Hired-PR >= Year-For-Report. . .
```

In the time between the development of COBOL-74 and COBOL-85, computer systems became more adept at handling lowercase as well as uppercase characters. This change in technology is recognized in COBOL-85 in several ways. COBOL-85 programs may be coded in any desired mixture of uppercase and lowercase characters. COBOL-85 has implemented additional classes in the class condition. In addition to NUMERIC and ALPHABETIC, there are ALPHABETIC-UPPER and ALPHABETIC-LOWER. The ALPHABETIC test will be true when a field contains uppercase or lowercase alphabetic characters or space. ALPHABETIC-UPPER will be true when a field contains all uppercase characters or space. ALPHABETIC-LOWER will be true when a field contains all lowercase alphabetic characters or spaces.

You might notice that ALPHABETIC in a COBOL-74 program is equivalent to ALPHABETIC-UPPER in a COBOL-85 program. This may seem like a small point, but it is one bit of evidence of incompatibility between the two standards. That programs behave differently when compiled by the two different compilers has made the COBOL-85 standard quite controversial and, to some extent, has impeded its widespread adoption.

6.13 SELF-TEST EXERCISES

1. Evaluate each of the following conditions based on the following data names:

```
 1 4 5         3 5        B E T A

X PIC S99V9   Y PIC 99    Z PIC X(5)
```

Example:

```
X IS NEGATIVE OR Y > 30
     true          true
            true
```

```
a. X < Y OR Y IS NEGATIVE
b. Z IS ALPHABETIC
c. X IS NUMERIC AND Z IS NOT ALPHABETIC
d. NOT Y IS POSITIVE
e. NOT X IS ZERO OR Y IS NOT NEGATIVE
f. NOT (X > 25 OR Y < 39)
```

    g. `X > Y OR X IS ZERO AND Y > 1`
    h. `X < Y AND (Y < 0 OR X > 30)`

2. Evaluate each of the following conditions:

```
 2                              A B
└─┘                            └─┘ └─┘
 ∧

03 FLDA PIC 9.                 03 FLDB PIC XXX.
   88 ITEM-TYPE-1 VALUE 1.        88 XYZ VALUE "ABC" "AB".
   88 ITEM-TYPE-2 VALUE 2.
   88 ITEM-TYPE-OTHER VALUE 0  3 THRU 9.
```

Example:

```
NOT ITEM-TYPE-1
    └────────┘
        false
└──────────────────┘
          true
```

    a. `ITEM-TYPE-1`
    b. `ITEM-TYPE-1 OR ITEM-TYPE-2`
    c. `XYZ`
    d. `NOT XYZ`
    e. `NOT (ITEM-TYPE-1 OR ITEM-TYPE-2)`
    f. `XYZ AND NOT ITEM-TYPE-1`
    g. `NOT XYZ AND ITEM-TYPE-1 OR NOT ITEM-TYPE-2`
    h. `NOT ITEM-TYPE-OTHER`

3. When possible, write an abbreviated version of each of the following conditions:
    a. `A < B AND A EQUAL C`
    b. `A < B OR C AND A > D`
    c. `A < B AND C < B`
    d. `A IS GREATER THAN B OR A < D`
    e. `A LESS THAN B AND A < C`
    f. `A NOT > B AND A < C AND A NOT = C`

4. Write an IF statement to compute minimum payment defined by

$$\text{minimum payment} = \begin{cases} \text{balance, if balance} \leq \$20 \\ \$20 + 10\% \text{ of (balance} - \$20), \text{ if } \$20 < \text{balance} \leq \$100 \\ \$36 + 20\% \text{ of (balance} - \$100), \text{ if balance} > \$100 \end{cases}$$

5. Write COBOL program segments to implement each of the following flowcharts:

a.

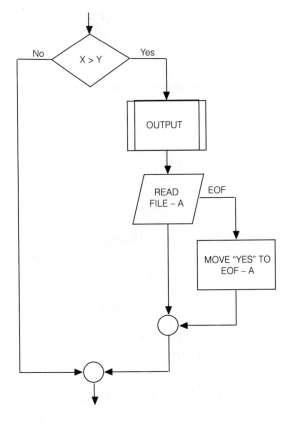

b.

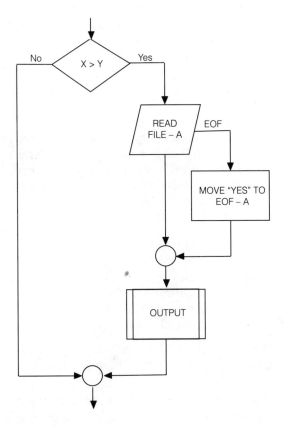

c.

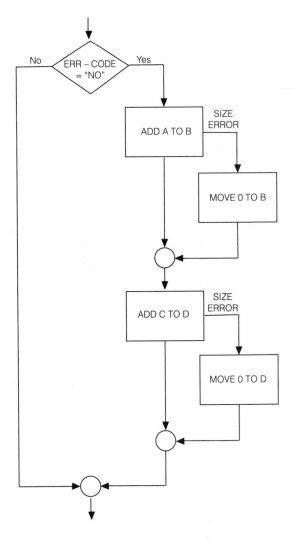

6. Write a data validation routine to check the validity of the following data record:

```
01   DATA-REC.
     03 ACCOUNT-NUM-DR          PIC 9(9).
     03 CUSTOMER-NAME-DR         PIC X(20).
     03 CUSTOMER-ADDRESS-DR.
        05 STREET-ADDRESS-DR     PIC X(15).
        05 CITY-DR               PIC X(8).
        05 STATE-DR              PIC XX.
        05 ZIP-DR                PIC 9(5).
     03 BALANCE-FORWARD-DR       PIC 9999V99.
```

The fields ACCOUNT-NUM-DR, ZIP-DR, and BALANCE-FORWARD-DR must be numeric. The fields CUSTOMER-NAME-DR, CITY-DR, and STATE-DR must be nonblank and contain only alphabetic data. Move "YES" to a field VALIDITY-ERROR if errors are found; otherwise, move "NO" to VALIDITY-ERROR. Why is it not possible to check the validity of STREET-ADDRESS-DR?

7. The PERFORM UNTIL statement is classed as an imperative statement, yet it involves checking a condition and taking alternative actions. Why is the PERFORM UNTIL statement classed as imperative?

8. How could Program 6a be modified to list all women employees born between 1940 and 1960?

9. Translate each of the procedures in Figures 6.21, 6.22, and 6.23 into COBOL, using COBOL-85 syntax.

10. What change was made to the ALPHABETIC test in COBOL-85?

11. Translate each of the flowcharts in Exercise 5 above using COBOL-85 syntax.

6.14 PROGRAMMING EXERCISES

1. The managers of Burgers, Inc., a franchise system of hamburger restaurants, are concerned with the profitability of a number of the company's outlets. They have requested a report showing basic data about each store and with a flag for stores showing profits less than $20,000. The format for the input records is

Positions	Content
1–10	Franchise number
11–25	Location
26–40	Manager's name
41–49	Previous year's profits (S999999V99) (Field could be negative if the store lost money; sign is trailing separate character.)

Print a row of asterisks (e.g., "*****") as a flag for each store with low profits. A printer spacing chart for the required report is shown in Figure 6.26.

2. At ABC Furniture Store, Inc., the manager of the computing center has separately budgeted amounts for computer supplies, office supplies, computer equipment, and office equipment. He needs to keep

Figure 6.26 Printer spacing chart for Exercise 1 Report

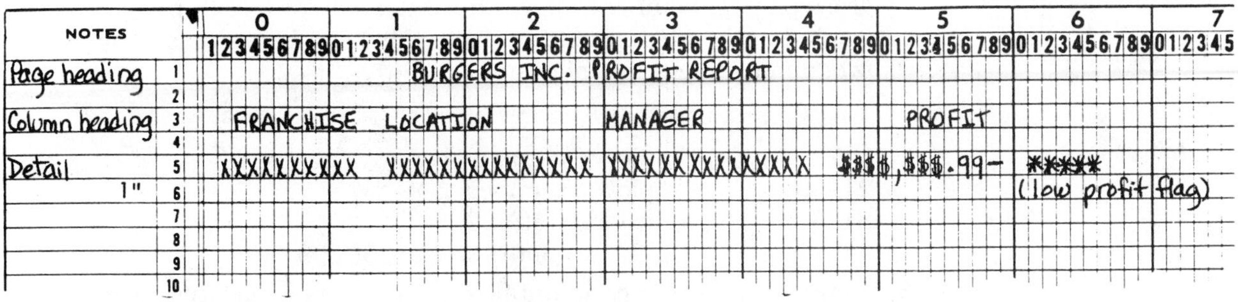

track of his cumulative expenditures in each of these categories. He has created a data file with records in the following format:

Positions	Content
1–6	Date of purchase (*mmddyy*)
7–25	Description of purchase
26–32	Amount (2 decimal places)
33	Account-code
	1 = Computer supplies
	2 = Office supplies
	3 = Computer equipment
	4 = Office equipment

Write a program to list each purchase in an appropriately labeled column. Accumulate and print totals for each account.

3. A bank makes mortgages on homes valued up to $385,000. The down payment schedule is as follows:

3% of the first $45,000
10% of the next $10,000
20% of the remainder

Write a program to accept input records containing an applicant's name and the amount of the loan requested. Output should consist of all input fields and the amount of the down payment required. Reject any application that is for more than $385,000. Also compute the total amounts of loans and down payments. Each record in the file to be processed by this program contains the following:

Positions	Content
1–20	Applicant name
21–26	Home value

4. Using the file described in Program 6b, write a program to compute the amount of the monthly bill. Output should consist of all input data and the amount of the bill based on the following schedule:

$6.00 if amount used is less than 50
$6.00 + .10 × (amount used − 50) if 50 ≤ amount used ≤ 200
$21.00 + .08 × (amount used − 200) if amount used > 200

5. Write a program that could be used to determine a weekly payroll. The input file contains one record per employee with the following fields: employee name, employee number, hourly rate of pay, and

number of hours worked. Have your program list the employee name, employee number, hourly rate of pay, number of hours worked, and gross pay. Remember to pay time and a half for all hours over 40 worked in the week. Each record in the file to be processed by this program contains the following:

Positions	Content
1–20	Employee name
21–29	Employee number
31–34	Hourly rate 99V99
36–39	Number of hours worked 99V99

6. Jones Hardware, Inc., maintains an accounts receivable file with records of the following format:

Positions	Content
1–6	Account number
7–25	Customer name
26–31	Date of last purchase (*mmddyy*)
32–37	Date of last payment (*mmddyy*)
38–44	Balance of account (Sign is trailing separate character, 2 decimal places.)
45–55	Address
56–65	City
66–67	State
68–72	Zip Code

Write a program to produce a report to be used by clerks who will write letters to customers requesting either their continued business for inactive accounts or payment of a past due balance. If the date of last purchase indicates that no purchase has been made in the past three months and the balance either is zero or shows a credit balance, indicate that a letter requesting continued patronage should be written. If the balance of the account is greater than $1 and no payment has been made in the previous two months, indicate a letter requesting payment. If the balance is greater than $100 and no payment has been made in the previous four months, indicate a stronger letter threatening legal action if payment is not forthcoming. For purposes of this program, assume that the current date is 03/30/91.

7. Write a program to list all three-bedroom houses with more than one bath in the price range of $65,000 to $95,000 using the file described in Chapter 4, Exercise 4.

8. Write a program to list all accounts with a past due balance using the file described in Exercise 6 above. Count the number of accounts which have had no payment made in the previous month, the previous two months, the previous three months, and the previous four or more months. Write these counts after processing the entire file.

9. When a house is listed and sold by real estate brokers, the commission is divided among four people: the listing broker (the firm which lists and advertises the house), the listing salesman (the person who secures the listing from the owner), the selling salesman (the person who sells the house), and the selling broker (the firm for whom the selling salesman works).

In Happy Valley, which has six real estate brokers and many salesmen, commissions are divided as follows: When the listing salesman and selling salesman work for the same broker, the commission is divided 25 percent to the listing salesman, 30 percent to the selling salesman, and 45 percent to the broker. When the listing salesman and selling salesman work for different brokers, the commission is divided 25 percent to the listing salesman, 35 percent to the listing broker, 20 percent to the selling salesman, and 20 percent to the selling broker.

Write a program to calculate real estate commissions for the city of Happy Valley. Each record in the file to be processed by this program contains data in the following format:

Positions	Content
1–6	Selling price (999999)
8–9	Commission rate (V99)
11–15	Listing broker ID number
17–21	Listing salesman ID number
23–27	Selling broker ID number
29–33	Selling salesman ID number

10. Modify the program written for Exercise 9 in Chapter 5 (Section 5.12) to produce an amortization schedule for the loan. There should be one line of output for each month's payment showing

Payment number
Payment to interest
Payment to principal
Total monthly payment
New balance

Accumulate and print the total of the interest payments. (The last month's payment may be slightly more or less than the other payments.) For example, for principal of $105,000, interest rate of 17.5 percent, and time of 25 years, the expected output would be similar to

Number	Principal	Interest	Payment	Balance
1	20.16	1531.25	1551.41	104980.00
2	20.45	1530.96	1551.41	104959.00
3	20.75	1530.66	1551.41	104939.00
4	21.05	1530.36	1551.41	104918.00
5	21.36	1530.05	1551.41	104896.00
6	21.67	1529.74	1551.41	104875.00
7	21.99	1529.42	1551.41	104853.00
8	22.31	1529.10	1551.41	104830.00
9	22.64	1528.77	1551.41	104806.00
.				
.				
.				
295	1422.56	128.85	1551.41	7413.10
296	1443.30	108.11	1551.41	5969.80
297	1464.35	87.06	1551.41	4505.45
298	1485.71	65.70	1551.41	3019.74
299	1507.37	44.04	1551.41	1512.37
300	1512.37	22.06	1534.43	0.00

TOTAL INTEREST $360,406.00

11. Write a program to validate the data file described in Exercise 1 above. Check for the following errors:

   Alphabetic character in Franchise number
   Nonalphabetic character in Location
   Nonalphabetic character in Manager's name
   Alphabetic character in Previous year's profits
   Value of profit outside the range − 500,000 to 500,000

   Create a report listing only those records which contain invalid data with suitable error messages.

12. Write a program to validate the data file described in Exercise 2 above. All numeric fields should contain numeric data; all alphanumeric fields should contain alphabetic data. The account code should be in the range 1 to 4. In the date, the month should be in the range 1 to 12, and the day should be in the range 1 to 31. The value of amount should be larger than 1.00. Create a report listing all records in the file with suitable error messages for those records which contain errors.

13. Write a program to validate the data in the file described in Exercise 6 above. Check numeric fields for numeric content and alphanumeric fields except for Address for alphabetic content. Dates should have month values in the range 1 to 12 and day values in the range 1 to 31. In addition to a report listing all invalid data, create two files— one with valid data and a second with invalid data.

7. SEQUENTIAL FILES AND SORTING

Up to this point we have used data files with little regard to the characteristics of the device used or to the various options available to optimize the operation of programs that access the data. This chapter presents a detailed discussion of these very important topics as they relate to the most commonly used types of mass storage: magnetic tape and magnetic disk.

7.1 TAPE CONCEPTS

Data records stored on magnetic tape are separated by an **Inter-Record-Gap (IRG)** as shown in Figure 7.1. The IRG is an unused block of tape that is typically six-tenths of an inch long. When a magnetic tape drive is started, some tape (about three-tenths of an inch) will move past the read/write head before operating speed is reached. When a tape drive is stopped, approximately three-tenths of an inch of tape will move past the read/write head before the tape comes to a stop. The IRG is an allowance for the tape required in both starting and stopping the drive in order to minimize errors in reading and writing data.

Figure 7.1   Inter-Record-Gap for records stored on magnetic tape

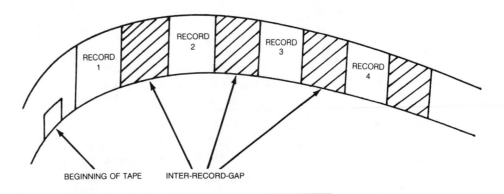

It is often convenient to create physical data records that contain more than one logical data record on the tape. This arrangement is called **blocking**. Two or more logical data records may make up a physical record on the tape. For example, if the blocking factor is three, the data would

Figure 7.2   Blocked records with a label record on magnetic
tape

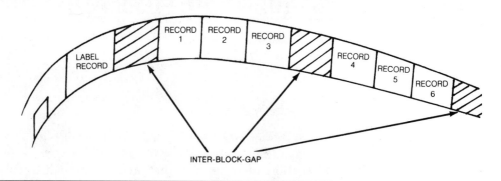

appear on the tape as shown in Figure 7.2. The gap between used portions
of tape is often called an **Inter-Block-Gap (IBG)** to denote the separation of
blocks of data rather than logical records.

The use of blocked records serves to utilize as much tape as possible
and to minimize access time. When writing a program to process a file, the
programmer must know the size of the blocking factor. If a file is being
created by a program, the programmer should choose as large a blocking
factor as possible. When a physical record is read, all of the data contained
on it must be stored in memory; therefore, the maximum size for a blocking factor is limited by the amount of main memory available.

There is a provision for creating a record that will contain identifying
data about the file at the beginning of the tape. This record is called a **label
record** (Fig. 7.2). The label record is created by the operating system when
the file is opened as an output file. When the file is used as an input file,
the operating system will check the content of the label record to verify
that the correct tape has been mounted.

The existence of blocked records and/or label records must be noted
in the FD entry written for the file. The BLOCK clause has the general form:

$$\left[\underline{\text{BLOCK}}\ \text{CONTAINS}\ \text{integer}\ \left\{\begin{array}{l}\text{CHARACTERS}\\ \underline{\text{RECORDS}}\end{array}\right\}\right]$$

The BLOCK clause is used to specify the size of the physical data block. The
LABEL clause has the general form:

$$\underline{\text{LABEL}}\ \left\{\begin{array}{l}\underline{\text{RECORD}}\ \text{IS}\\ \underline{\text{RECORDS}}\ \text{ARE}\end{array}\right\}\ \left\{\begin{array}{l}\underline{\text{OMITTED}}\\ \underline{\text{STANDARD}}\end{array}\right\}$$

This clause is used to specify whether the label record is to be found on
the file. For example, the FD entry for the file illustrated in Figure 7.2
would be

```
FD  DATA-FILE
    BLOCK CONTAINS 3 RECORDS
    LABEL RECORD IS STANDARD
    DATA RECORD IS DATA-RECORD.
```

The programmer does not need to make any modifications to the logic of the program because of the label record and/or blocked records. The operating system performs the required label record creation/checking and deblocks the physical data record into logical records (described in the DATA DIVISION FDs), which are made available to the program for processing one at a time.

The computer requires that you tell it not only which file to use but also what equipment to use to access the file. The SELECT statement is used to associate the file with a physical device. The general form of a SELECT statement is

> SELECT file-name ASSIGN TO system-name.

The form taken by the system-name differs widely among different versions of COBOL. For specific details, the user must check the COBOL manual supplied by the manufacturer of the particular system.

7.2 DISK CONCEPTS

A disk contains one or more recording surfaces. Each surface is organized into **tracks** on which data is recorded. The tracks on a surface may be thought of as a series of concentric circles (Fig. 7.3). There is no industry standard technique for organizing data on the tracks of a disk. One technique that is used on microcomputer floppy disks and hard disks is to divide each track into a series of fixed-length sectors as shown in Figure 7.4. For example, the 5¼″ floppy disk uses sectors of length 512 characters; this disk format uses 40 tracks per side of the disk with 9 sectors per

Figure 7.3   A disk recording surface

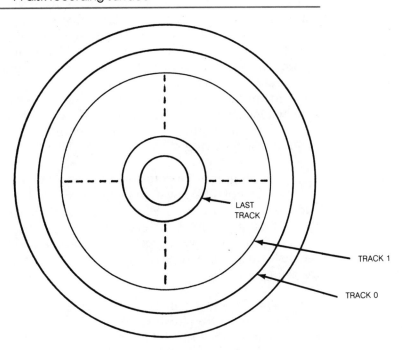

Figure 7.4   A typical track divided into fixed-length sectors

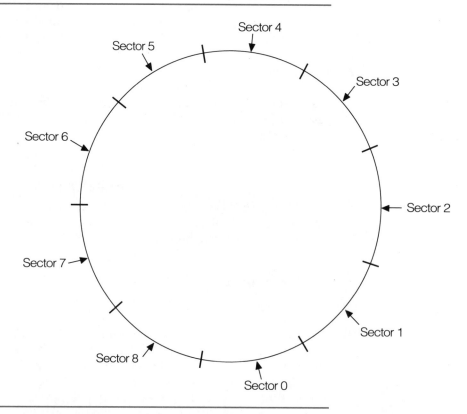

track yielding a total capacity of 2 surfaces $\times$ 40 tracks/surface $\times$ 9 sectors per track $\times$ 512 characters/track = 368,640 characters. There are many variations on this arrangement which yield floppy disk capacities up to 1.44 million characters and hard disk capacities of up to 120 million characters. The capacities of hard disks used with mini- and mainframe computers range upward to 1 billion characters per drive.

It is the task of the operating system to store and retrieve data from the disk; the program is, therefore, shielded from the exact details of how records are stored on the tracks of the disk. From the program's point of view, data is read from and written to the disk one record at a time. In order to optimize access time and utilization of space on the disk, records may be blocked in much the same fashion as on tape files.

A typical sequence of events required to read a record on disk includes the following steps:

1. A program requests a record from a disk file.
2. The operating system (which keeps track of the physical disk address of files and records) instructs the disk drive to read a particular record from a specified surface and track.
3. The disk drive moves its read/write head to the track, and when the disk surface has rotated into position for reading the required record, the data is read.

A similar sequence of events occurs when a record is written onto a disk file. One entire physical record is read/written at a time. The operating system handles the details of (1) accumulating a sufficient number of logical records before writing a physical record and (2) making logical records available to a program one at a time after reading a block of data from the file.

A disk usually contains many files. The operating system maintains a directory of existing files on a disk. This directory contains such information as the location and name of each file. The directory information is the logical equivalent of the label record found on the tape. While the label record is an optional feature for a tape file, the directory information is a required part of creating and accessing a file on disk. Hence, the clause

        LABEL RECORD IS STANDARD

usually *must* be included in the FD for a file found on disk. On some compilers, including the one used to prepare programs for this text, the LABEL RECORD IS STANDARD clause is assumed if the LABEL RECORD clause is omitted from an FD entry. On other compilers, the LABEL RECORD clause must be included in FD entries for all files. The ANSI-74 standard for COBOL indicates that the LABEL RECORD clause is required for all FD entries; the ANSI-85 standard makes the LABEL RECORD clause optional. The user must check specifications for the compiler being used to determine what is required.

Blocking records for a disk file will ensure optimum performance from the computing system when programs accessing that data are executed. Documentation specifying optimum blocking factors for records depending on the record length is usually available.

The nature of magnetic tape requires sequential storage and accessing of the records. However, because of its movable read/write mechanism, a disk has the capability for accessing data stored on any portion of the disk upon demand. This feature figures in a discussion of nonsequential file processing. For the moment, we will be concerned only with the storage of sequential files on disk. When a disk file is accessed sequentially, the operating system locates the first record in the file when the file is opened. Each successive record in the file is then located and read/written as required by the program.

The SELECT entry is used to assign a file to disk. The system-name used for a disk file varies from system to system. The logic required to create and process a sequential file is essentially independent of the device on which the file is stored. For convenience, the discussion that follows will assume that the files will be on disk, but you could make programs work equally well for tape storage simply by changing the SELECT statement.

7.3 THE OPEN STATEMENT

The OPEN statement causes the operating system to make a file available for processing. A file must be opened before any input or output operation can be performed on it. A sequential file can be opened in one of four modes: INPUT, OUTPUT, I-O, and EXTEND (Fig. 7.5).

When a file is opened in INPUT mode, the records from the file are made available to the program one at a time, from first to last. The file must exist on the device specified in the SELECT statement for the file. Two options exist for tape files opened as INPUT mode: WITH NO REWIND and REVERSED. These options are ignored if the file is assigned to a disk. Ordinarily, a tape reel is rewound from the take-up reel onto its original reel and positioned at the first record in the file when the file is opened. The NO REWIND clause can be used when a reel of tape contains multiple files and

Figure 7.5   General form of the OPEN statement

$$
\underline{OPEN} \left\{ \begin{array}{l}
\underline{INPUT} \texttt{ file-name} \\
\underline{OUTPUT} \texttt{ file-name} \\
\underline{I-O} \texttt{ file-name...} \\
\underline{EXTEND} \texttt{ file-name...}
\end{array} \right.
\left[\begin{array}{l}
\underline{REVERSED} \\
\underline{WITH} \; \underline{NO} \; \underline{REWIND}
\end{array} \right]
\left. \begin{array}{l}
\cdots \\
[\underline{WITH} \; \underline{NO} \; \underline{REWIND}] \; \cdots
\end{array} \right\}
$$

you want to process each file in succession. When the first file is closed, the tape must not be rewound; the reel must be left in position for the next file to be opened. The WITH NO REWIND clause would then be used to open the second file. The REVERSED option will cause the file to be positioned at its last record and read in reverse order from last to first. The REVERSED and NO REWIND options are not included in all COBOL compilers.

When a file is opened in OUTPUT mode, the file is assumed to have no data records in it. WRITE statements cause records to be placed in the file sequentially from first to last. If records are already present in the file, they will be destroyed. The WITH NO REWIND clause has the same effect here as it does for the INPUT mode.

When a file is opened in I-O (Input-Output) mode, it is assumed to exist and may be processed by READ and REWRITE statements. The REWRITE statement will cause the content of a record that has been read (and perhaps changed by the processing program) to be rewritten, destroying the content of the original. This mode can be used for disk files only; it is not valid for tape files.

When a file is opened in EXTEND mode, records are written in the file following the last record in the file. When the file is opened, the operating system locates the last record in the file; any record written in the file will follow that record. EXTEND mode may not be implemented on all compilers.

7.4   THE CLOSE STATEMENT

The CLOSE statement terminates processing of a file. The file must be open at the time of execution of a CLOSE statement. After a file has been closed, no further input or output operations may be executed. A general form of the CLOSE statement is shown in Figure 7.6.

When a file is assigned to tape, the NO REWIND clause will prevent the reel of tape from being repositioned to the beginning of the file. Repositioning of the tape reel (rewinding) is performed as part of the CLOSE operation if the NO REWIND clause is omitted.

The LOCK option will prevent the current program (or any subsequent program in the job) from reopening the file. The LOCK option should be invoked if it would be an error for any further processing of the file to take

Figure 7.6   General form of the CLOSE statement

$$
\underline{CLOSE} \texttt{ file-name} \left[\underline{WITH} \left\{ \begin{array}{l} \underline{NO} \; \underline{REWIND} \\ \underline{LOCK} \end{array} \right\} \right] \cdots
$$

place. In some operating systems, the LOCK phrase has the additional function of causing the file to become permanent if the file is being created by this program. For these operating systems, a file will be purged from the disk at the end of the program unless the LOCK option is used.

7.5 MULTIPLE TYPES OF INPUT RECORDS

In many instances there will be more than one type of data record format in a file to be processed. For example, suppose you wish to process a file containing records in the following two formats:

Name and Address Record

Positions	Content
1–9	Identifying number
10–25	Name
26–40	Street address
41–50	City
51–52	State
53–57	Zip Code
58	Record identification code (1)

Time Record

Positions	Content
1–9	Identifying number
10–15	Hours worked (2 decimal places)
16–21	Date
22–57	Blank
58	Record identification code (2)

When a file contains records having different formats, there must be some way for the program to determine which type of record has been read after a READ operation takes place. One way to accomplish this is to place a specific code in a field common to the two records. In the example above, position 58 is used as a record-identification-code field. This field has the value 1 on a name-and-address record and the value 2 on the time record.

It is possible to define the different types of input records in either the FILE section of the DATA DIVISION or the WORKING-STORAGE section of the DATA DIVISION. Description of the records in the FILE section requires that all record descriptions be placed following the FD entry for the file and that the names of the records be included in the DATA RECORDS clause of the FD entry. For example, the following code could be used for the preceding data file:

```
FD   DATA-FILE
     LABEL RECORDS ARE STANDARD
     DATA RECORDS ARE NAME-ADDRESS-RECORD TIME-RECORD.
01   NAME-ADDRESS-RECORD.
     03 ID-NUM-NAR        PIC 9(9).
     03 NAME-NAR          PIC X(16).
     03 STREET-ADR-NAR    PIC X(15).
     03 CITY-NAR          PIC X(10).
     03 STATE-NAR         PIC X(2).
     03 ZIP-NAR           PIC 9(5).
```

```
          03  REC-ID-NAR        PIC 9.
      01  TIME-RECORD.
          03  ID-NUM-TR         PIC 9(9).
          03  HOURS-TR          PIC 9(4)V99.
          03  DATE-TR           PIC 9(6).
          03  FILLER            PIC X(36).
          03  REC-ID-TR         PIC 9.
```

Note that there is only one area in memory allocated for the data record for a given file regardless of the number of data records declared for the file. The data record area for this file may be visualized as

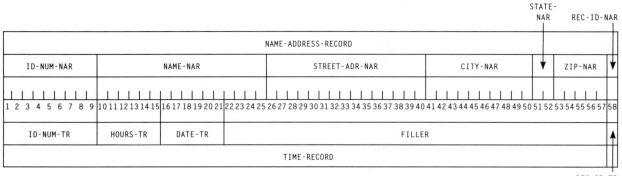

When a file is read, the content of a data record is placed in the memory locations allocated as the data record area for that file. The program may then choose to use any of the descriptions of that record that have been specified. For example, if the record is a name-and-address record, then the fields NAME-NAR, STREET-ADR-NAR, CITY-NAR, and so on, would be processed. However, if the record is a time record, the fields HOURS-TR and DATE-TR would be processed.

The program must decide which of the data descriptions is appropriate for this record. In our example, the decision can be made based on the content of REC-ID-NAR or REC-ID-TR, as these names describe the same field on the record. The following program segment could be used to make this decision:

```
PROCESS-DATA.
    IF REC-ID-NAR = 1
        PERFORM PROCESS-NAME-ADDRESS-RECORD
    ELSE
        PERFORM PROCESS-TIME-RECORD.
    READ DATA-FILE
        AT END MOVE "YES" TO EOF-FLAG.
```

Because there is only one memory area allocated to the data record, the content of all of the fields will change each time a new record is read; data from the new record replaces the data from the previous record. Suppose, for example, that the first record is a name-and-address record and the second record is a time record. The content of the fields NAME-NAR, STREET-ADR-NAR, CITY-NAR, and so forth will change when the second record is read because characters from the second record now occupy the locations in the data record as read. This will cause no inconvenience if the data from the name-and-address record is moved immediately to another location when the program determines that the name-and-address record has been read. In the above example, the content of the paragraph PROCESS-NAME-ADDRESS-RECORD could be as follows:

```
PROCESS-NAME-ADDRESS-RECORD.
      MOVE ID-NUM-NAR       TO ID-NUM-HOLD.
      MOVE NAME-NAR         TO NAME-HOLD.
      MOVE STREET-ADR-NAR   TO STREET-ADR-HOLD.
      MOVE CITY-NAR         TO CITY-HOLD.
      MOVE STATE-NAR        TO STATE-HOLD.
      MOVE ZIP-NAR          TO ZIP-HOLD.
       .
       .
       .
```

The fields with suffix HOLD would, of course, be defined in the WORKING-STORAGE section.

When there are a great many record types, moving fields to different locations can become a nuisance. As an alternative, multiple records may be described in the WORKING-STORAGE section. Using this technique, a minimal description of the record is made in the FILE section; the only field that needs to be specified is the record identification field. Detailed description of the records is given in the WORKING-STORAGE section.

When a record is read, the contents are moved to the appropriate location based on the record identification. For the previous example, this technique could be implemented by the following code:

```
DATA DIVISION.
FILE SECTION.
FD   DATA-FILE
     LABEL RECORDS ARE STANDARD
     DATA RECORD IS DATA-RECORD.
01   DATA-RECORD.
     03 FILLER          PIC X(57).
     03 RECORD-ID       PIC 9.
WORKING-STORAGE SECTION.
       .
       .
       .
01   NAME-ADDRESS-RECORD.
     03 ID-NUM-NAR      PIC 9(9).
     03 NAME-NAR        PIC X(16).
     03 STREET-ADR-NAR PIC X(15).
     03 CITY-NAR        PIC X(10).
     03 STATE-NAR       PIC X(2).
     03 ZIP-NAR         PIC 9(5).
01   TIME-RECORD.
     03 ID-NUM-TR       PIC 9(9).
     03 HOURS-TR        PIC 9(4)V99.
     03 DATE-TR         PIC 9(6).
PROCEDURE DIVISION.
1000-MAIN-CONTROL.
       .
       .
       .
     READ DATA-FILE
         AT END MOVE "YES" TO EOF-FLAG.
```

```
      PERFORM 2010-PROCESS-DATA
          UNTIL EOF-FLAG = "YES".
      .
      .
      .
  2010-PROCESS-DATA.
      IF RECORD-ID = 1
         MOVE DATA-RECORD TO NAME-ADDRESS-RECORD
         PERFORM PROCESS-NAME-ADDRESS-RECORD
      ELSE
         IF RECORD-ID = 2
            MOVE DATA-RECORD TO TIME-RECORD
            PERFORM PROCESS-TIME-RECORD
         ELSE
            PERFORM DATA-RECORD-ERROR.
      READ DATA-FILE
          AT END MOVE "YES" TO EOF-FLAG.
```

One advantage to the preceding method is that the contents of NAME-ADDRESS-RECORD are changed only when a new record of the same type is read. A disadvantage is the necessity of allocating memory locations in addition to the record area required for the file. If records are lengthy and/or there are many different types of records in the file, this excess memory requirement may be a significant factor, particularly in systems with limited memory available.

7.6   INTRODUCTION TO SORTING

A set of data items in either ascending sequence or descending sequence is said to be in **sorted order**. **Sorting** refers to the process of transforming unsorted data items into sorted order. For example, consider the data items

     16, 25, 90, 42, 70

They are neither in ascending sequence (each item smaller than its successor) nor in descending sequence (each item larger than its successor). If the data items were rearranged as

     16, 25, 42, 70, 90

they would be sorted into ascending sequence. If the data items were rearranged as

     90, 70, 42, 25, 16

they would be sorted into descending sequence.

In a data processing situation it is often desirable to have data records in some sequence based on one or more fields within the record. The field used for this sequencing is called the **key field**. For example, consider the following set of data records:

Employee Number	Name		Age	Department
123	DOE	JOHN	32	3
492	SMITH	MARY	40	4
479	JAMES	JOHN	19	4
333	QUE	SUSY	40	2
695	BROWN	JAMES	25	2

This data could be sorted into sequence in a number of different ways. Each of the four fields could be used individually as a key field. If the employee number is chosen as the key field and descending sequence is desired, the resulting set of data would be

	Employee Number	Name		Age	Department
	695	BROWN	JAMES	25	2
	492	SMITH	MARY	40	4
Descending sequence	479	JAMES	JOHN	19	4
	333	QUE	SUSY	40	2
	123	DOE	JOHN	32	3

Using the name as the key field and sorting for ascending sequence would result in

Employee Number		Name		Age	Department
695		BROWN	JAMES	25	2
123	Ascending sequence	DOE	JOHN	32	3
479		JAMES	JOHN	19	4
333		QUE	SUSY	40	2
492		SMITH	MARY	40	4

It is possible to sort a file using more than one key field. For example, we might want a listing of the above data to be grouped by department number. Also, within each department, the data should be listed in ascending sequence based on employee name. In this case, the department number is called the **primary key** (or **major key**) and the name field is the **secondary key** (or **minor key**). The resulting data would be:

Employee Number		Name		Age	Department	
695		BROWN	JAMES	25	2	
333	Ascending	QUE	SUSY	40	2	Ascending
123	sequences	DOE	JOHN	32	3	sequence
479	(three)	JAMES	JOHN	19	4	
492		SMITH	MARY	40	4	

Many other combinations using two or more key fields could conceivably be of value, depending on the logical requirements of the problem being solved.

7.7   FILE SEQUENCE CHECKING

For many types of applications it is imperative that a file be organized in sequence by a key field. Many versions of COBOL have a SORT verb which allows you to resequence a file. The COBOL sort facility is described later in this chapter. Prior to executing a program which depends on a file being in a particular sequence, the user could sort the file or remove out-of-sequence records from the file.

Sorting a file, particularly a large file, is likely to be very time-consuming. It may be advantageous to perform a much simpler sequence check and remove out-of-sequence records from the file. The out-of-sequence records (if any) could be treated as new data and used to update the file by facilities already available in the system. This approach is particularly useful if the probability of finding out-of-sequence records is small. This technique is used in the following program example.

Problem Statement

Data records in the file CUSTOMER-FILE contain the following fields:

Positions	Content
1–9	Account number
10–24	Name
25–34	Street address
35–44	City
45–46	State
47–51	Zip code
52–57	Amount owed (2 decimal places)
58–63	Credit maximum (2 decimal places)
64–69	Date of last payment (mmddyy)
70–80	Unused

The file should be in sequence by account number. Write a program to process this file, placing all properly sequenced records in a file ACCOUNTS-RECEIVABLE-FILE. Create a report as shown in Figure 7.7 showing those records that are out of sequence.

Problem Analysis

This program must process one input file (CUSTOMER-FILE) and produce two output files (ACCOUNTS-RECEIVABLE-FILE and ERROR-FILE). In order to detect an out-of-sequence record, it is necessary to compare the content of the account number on the record just read with the account number of the record last processed. This task will require the use of a holding field (ACCOUNT-NUMBER-HOLD) which will be initialized to the value of the account number of the first record. During the processing of succeeding records, the program must compare the content of account number from the record just read to the content of ACCOUNT-NUMBER-HOLD. If the account number from the record is greater than ACCOUNT-NUMBER-HOLD, the record can be written to ACCOUNTS-RECEIVABLE-FILE and the account number from that record moved to ACCOUNT-NUMBER-HOLD. If the account number from the record is not greater than ACCOUNT-NUMBER-HOLD, then the record is out of sequence and must be written on ERROR-FILE. The report requires two counters: the number of records out of sequence and the number of records in sequence. These counters must be incremented at appropriate points in the processing of each data record. After all

Figure 7.7 Printer spacing chart for Program 7a

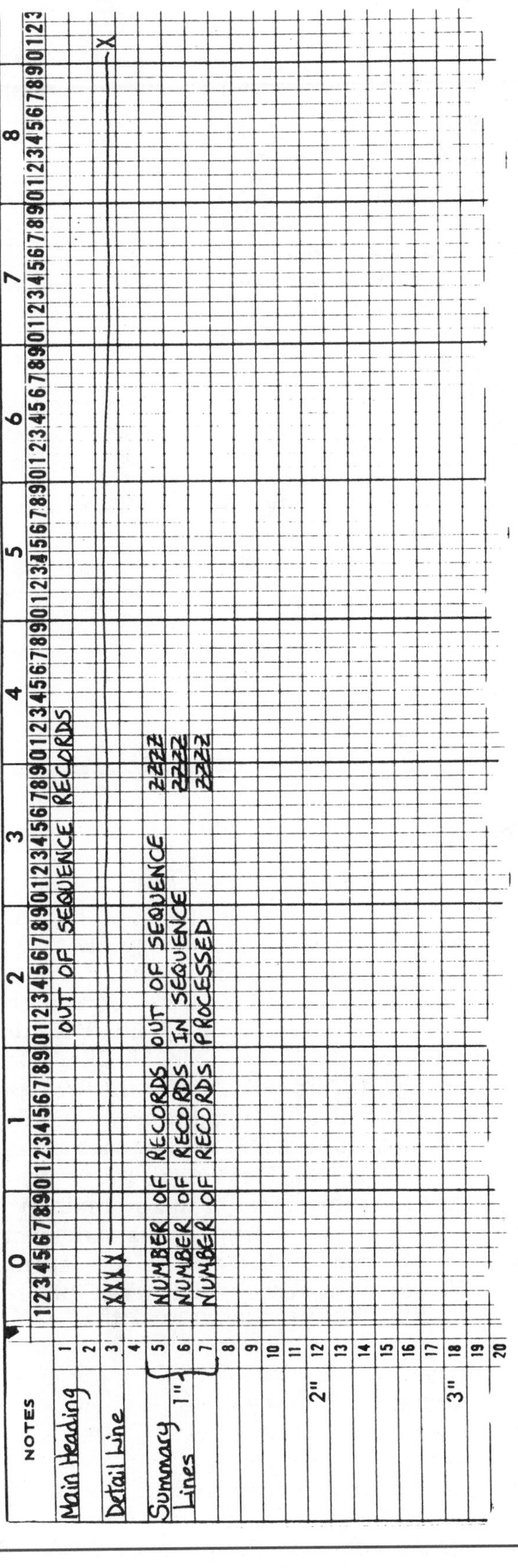

records have been processed, the summary lines can be written. A plan for this program is shown in Figure 7.8.

Figure 7.8   Plan for sequenced file creation program

Main control

    Open files
    Read customer file
    Write accounts receivable record from input record
    Add 1 to records in sequence
    Move customer number from input record to customer number hold
    Read customer file
    Do Process data until end of file
    Write summary files
    Close files
    Stop

Process data

    If account number from input record > account number hold
        Add 1 to records in sequence
        Write accounts receivable record from input record
        Move account number from input record to account number hold
    Else
        Add 1 to records out of sequence
        Write error record from input record
    End if
    Read customer file

Problem Solution

The program that performs this task is shown in Program 7a with the structure diagram for the program shown in Figure 7.9. Sample input and output from the program are shown in Figure 7.10. Note in this program that two records from the input file must be read before entering the processing loop. If the second record were not read, then the value of ACCOUNT-NUMBER-CR and ACCOUNT-NUMBER-HOLD would be equal at line 144 because the value of ACCOUNT-NUMBER-CR would not be replaced by data from a new record. This would cause the first record to be considered out of sequence. Note also the importance of moving the value of ACCOUNT-NUMBER-CR to ACCOUNT-NUMBER-HOLD each time an in-sequence record is processed (see line 146). This causes the value of ACCOUNT-NUMBER-HOLD to store the account number of the preceding valid record each time the program goes through the loop. If this statement were omitted, the effect would be to compare each record to the account number from the first record only, not to the account number of the preceding valid record.

Program 7a

```
 1 IDENTIFICATION DIVISION.
 2
 3 PROGRAM-ID. FILE-CREATION-PRO7A.
 4 AUTHOR. HORN.
 5
 6 ENVIRONMENT DIVISION.
 7
 8 CONFIGURATION SECTION.
 9
10 SOURCE-COMPUTER.
11 OBJECT-COMPUTER.
12
13 INPUT-OUTPUT SECTION.
14
15 FILE-CONTROL.
16
17     SELECT CUSTOMER-FILE ASSIGN TO DISK.
18
19     SELECT ACCOUNTS-RECEIVABLE-FILE ASSIGN TO DISK.
20
21     SELECT ERROR-FILE ASSIGN TO PRINTER.
22
23 DATA DIVISION.
24
25 FILE SECTION.
26
27 FD  CUSTOMER-FILE
28     LABEL RECORDS ARE STANDARD
29     DATA RECORD IS CUSTOMER-RECORD.
30
31 01  CUSTOMER-RECORD.
32     02   ACCOUNT-NUMBER-CR        PIC 9(9).
33     02   NAME-CR                  PIC X(15).
34     02   ADDRESS-CR.
35          03   STREET-CR           PIC X(10).
36          03   CITY-CR             PIC X(10).
37          03   STATE-CR            PIC X(2).
38          03   ZIP-CODE-CR         PIC 9(5).
39     02   AMOUNT-OWED-CR           PIC 9(4)V99.
40     02   CREDIT-MAXIUM-CR         PIC 9(4)V99.
41     02   DATE-OF-LAST-PAYMENT-CR.
42          03   MONTH-CR            PIC 99.
43          03   DAY-CR              PIC 99.
44          03   YEAR-CR             PIC 99.
45     02   FILLER                   PIC X(11).
46
```

Program 7a   *(continued)*

```
47 FD   ACCOUNTS-RECEIVABLE-FILE
48       LABEL RECORDS ARE STANDARD
49       DATA RECORD IS ACCOUNTS-RECEIVABLE-RECORD.
50
51 01   ACCOUNTS-RECEIVABLE-RECORD.
52       02   ACCOUNT-NUMBER-ARR        PIC 9(9).
53       02   NAME-ARR                  PIC X(15).
54       02   ADDRESS-ARR.
55           03   STREET-ARR            PIC X(10).
56           03   CITY-ARR              PIC X(10).
57           03   STATE-ARR             PIC X(2).
58           03   ZIP-CODE-ARR          PIC 9(5).
59       02   AMOUNT-OWED-ARR           PIC 9(4)V99.
60       02   CREDIT-MAXIUM-ARR         PIC 9(4)V99.
61       02   DATE-OF-LAST-PAYMENT-ARR.
62           03   MONTH-ARR             PIC 99.
63           03   DAY-ARR               PIC 99.
64           03   YEAR-ARR              PIC 99.
65       02   FILLER                    PIC X(11).
66
67 FD   ERROR-FILE
68       LABEL RECORDS ARE OMITTED
69       DATA RECORD IS ERROR-RECORD.
70
71 01   ERROR-RECORD              PIC X(132).
72
73 WORKING-STORAGE SECTION.
74
75 01   FLAGS.
76       02 EOF-FLAG                    PIC X(3) VALUE "NO".
77
78 01   HOLD-FIELDS.
79       02 ACCOUNT-NUMBER-HOLD      PIC 9(9) VALUE ZERO.
80
81 01   TOTALS.
82       02 RECORDS-OUT-OF-SEQUENCE  PIC 9(4) VALUE ZERO.
83       02 RECORDS-IN-SEQUENCE      PIC 9(4) VALUE ZERO.
84       02 RECORDS-PROCESSED        PIC 9(4) VALUE ZERO.
85
86 01   MAIN-HEADING.
87       02 FILLER                      PIC X(20) VALUE SPACES.
88       02 FILLER                      PIC X(23) VALUE
89          "OUT OF SEQUENCE RECORDS".
90
91 01   DETAIL-LINE.
92       02 FILLER                      PIC X VALUE SPACE.
93       02 CUSTOMER-DATA-DL            PIC X(80).
94
95 01   SUMMARY-LINE-1.
96       02 FILLER                      PIC X VALUE SPACE.
97       02 FILLER                      PIC X(34) VALUE
98          "NUMBER OF RECORDS OUT OF SEQUENCE".
99       02 FILLER                      PIC X VALUE SPACE.
100      02 OUT-OF-SEQUENCE-SL1         PIC Z(4).
101
```

Program 7a *(continued)*

```
102 01  SUMMARY-LINE-2.
103     02 FILLER                    PIC X VALUE SPACE.
104     02 FILLER                    PIC X(29) VALUE
105        "NUMBER OF RECORDS IN SEQUENCE".
106     02 FILLER                    PIC X(6) VALUE SPACES.
107     02 IN-SEQUENCE-SL2           PIC Z(4).
108
109 01  SUMMARY-LINE-3.
110     02 FILLER                    PIC X VALUE SPACE.
111     02 FILLER                    PIC X(27) VALUE
112        "NUMBER OF RECORDS PROCESSED".
113     02 FILLER                    PIC X(8) VALUE SPACES.
114     02 RECORDS-PROCESSED-SL3     PIC Z(4).
115
116 PROCEDURE DIVISION.
117
118 1000-MAIN-CONTROL.
119
120     PERFORM 2000-INITIALIZE-DATA.
121     PERFORM 2100-PROCESS-DATA
122            UNTIL EOF-FLAG = "YES".
123     PERFORM 2200-WRITE-SUMMARY.
124     PERFORM 2300-TERMINATE-PROGRAM.
125     STOP RUN.
126
127 2000-INITIALIZE-DATA.
128
129     OPEN INPUT CUSTOMER-FILE
130          OUTPUT ACCOUNTS-RECEIVABLE-FILE
131                 ERROR-FILE.
132     WRITE ERROR-RECORD FROM MAIN-HEADING AFTER PAGE.
133     MOVE SPACES TO ERROR-RECORD.
134     WRITE ERROR-RECORD AFTER 1.
135     PERFORM 9000-READ-CUSTOMER-FILE.
136     ADD 1 TO RECORDS-IN-SEQUENCE.
137     MOVE CUSTOMER-RECORD TO ACCOUNTS-RECEIVABLE-RECORD.
138     WRITE ACCOUNTS-RECEIVABLE-RECORD.
139     MOVE ACCOUNT-NUMBER-CR TO ACCOUNT-NUMBER-HOLD.
140     PERFORM 9000-READ-CUSTOMER-FILE.
141
142 2100-PROCESS-DATA.
143
144     IF  ACCOUNT-NUMBER-CR > ACCOUNT-NUMBER-HOLD
145         ADD 1 TO RECORDS-IN-SEQUENCE
146         MOVE ACCOUNT-NUMBER-CR TO ACCOUNT-NUMBER-HOLD
147         WRITE ACCOUNTS-RECEIVABLE-RECORD FROM CUSTOMER-RECORD
148     ELSE
149         ADD 1 TO RECORDS-OUT-OF-SEQUENCE
150         MOVE CUSTOMER-RECORD TO CUSTOMER-DATA-DL
151         WRITE ERROR-RECORD FROM DETAIL-LINE AFTER 1.
152     PERFORM 9000-READ-CUSTOMER-FILE.
153
```

Program 7a   *(concluded)*

```
154 2200-WRITE-SUMMARY.
155
156     ADD RECORDS-OUT-OF-SEQUENCE RECORDS-IN-SEQUENCE
157           GIVING RECORDS-PROCESSED.
158     MOVE RECORDS-OUT-OF-SEQUENCE TO OUT-OF-SEQUENCE-SL1.
159     MOVE RECORDS-IN-SEQUENCE      TO IN-SEQUENCE-SL2.
160     MOVE RECORDS-PROCESSED         TO RECORDS-PROCESSED-SL3.
161     WRITE ERROR-RECORD FROM SUMMARY-LINE-1 AFTER 2.
162     WRITE ERROR-RECORD FROM SUMMARY-LINE-2 AFTER 1.
163     WRITE ERROR-RECORD FROM SUMMARY-LINE-3 AFTER 1.
164
165 2300-TERMINATE-PROGRAM.
166
167     CLOSE CUSTOMER-FILE
168           ACCOUNTS-RECEIVABLE-FILE
169           ERROR-FILE.
170
171 9000-READ-CUSTOMER-FILE.
172
173     READ CUSTOMER-FILE
174           AT END MOVE "YES" TO EOF-FLAG.
```

Figure 7.9   Structure diagram for Program 7a

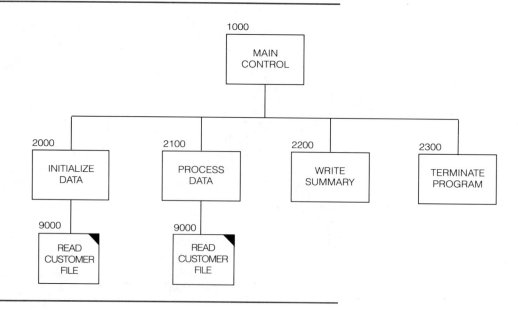

Figure 7.10   Sample execution of Program 7a

Input (CUSTOMER-FILE)

```
111111111JONES JAMES        123 X ST. ELMVILLE   WA12345005000100000010290
222222222SMITH MARY         4 MAIN ST.MAPLE      WA12356000000200000030490
200000000BROWN JAMES        1000 FORD MAPLE      WA12356004000100000041290
333333333WHITE SUE          2 2ND ST. ELMVILLE   WA12345010000100000032390
444444444BLACK SAM          302 1ST AVCENTRAL    WA12367020000100000041290
400000000DOE JOHN           100 10TH  MAPLE      WA12356055000200000050190
300000000DOE JOE            200 ELM STCENTRAL    WA12367060000100000030290
555555555WASHINGTON ABE     10 MAPLE  ELMVILLE   WA12345070000100000050490
```

Output (ACCOUNTS-RECEIVABLE-FILE)

```
111111111JONES JAMES        123 X ST. ELMVILLE   WA12345005000100000010290
222222222SMITH MARY         4 MAIN ST.MAPLE      WA12356000000200000030490
333333333WHITE SUE          2 2ND ST. ELMVILLE   WA12345010000100000032390
444444444BLACK SAM          302 1ST AVCENTRAL    WA12367020000100000041290
555555555WASHINGTON ABE     10 MAPLE  ELMVILLE   WA12345070000100000050490
```

Report (ERROR-FILE)

```
                    OUT OF SEQUENCE RECORDS

200000000BROWN JAMES        1000 FORD MAPLE      WA12356004000100000041290
400000000DOE JOHN           100 10TH  MAPLE      WA12356055000200000050190
300000000DOE JOE            200 ELM STCENTRAL    WA12367060000100000030290

NUMBER OF RECORDS OUT OF SEQUENCE     3
NUMBER OF RECORDS IN SEQUENCE         5
NUMBER OF RECORDS PROCESSED           8
```

7.8   THE SORT WORK-FILE

The COBOL programmer may make use of the COBOL SORT feature in order to sort a file on one or more key fields into any desired sequence. The SORT statement is used in the PROCEDURE DIVISION. It specifies the source of the records to be sorted, the key field(s), the sequencing desired (ascending or descending), the destination for the sorted records, and the name of a **sort work-file** that will be used by the computing system in the performance of the sort. Setting up the sort work-file must be done in the ENVIRONMENT and DATA DIVISIONs in preparation for utilization of the SORT statement in the PROCEDURE DIVISION.

A sequential disk file is required as a sort work-file for utilization of the COBOL SORT command. First, the SORT statement causes records to be read from some source file and copied into the sort work-file. Second, the records are sorted, and third, the records are copied from the sort work-file into some specified destination. Setting up the sort work-file requires a SELECT sentence in the ENVIRONMENT DIVISION for the file in exactly the same manner as for any other file. The description of the file in the DATA DIVISION requires the use of an SD (Sort Description) rather than an FD entry. The general form for an SD entry is shown in Figure 7.11.

The file description used in an SD entry is much the same as in an FD entry. The record described for the sort work-file must contain data-names for any desired key fields.

Figure 7.11   General form of the SD entry

SD   file-name
      [RECORD CONTAINS [integer-1 TO] integer-2 CHARACTERS]

$$\left[\text{DATA} \begin{Bmatrix} \underline{\text{RECORD}} \text{ IS} \\ \underline{\text{RECORDS}} \text{ ARE} \end{Bmatrix} \text{data-name...}\right].$$

Example

Problem Statement

Write a program to sort a file (EMPLOYEE-FILE) that contains data described in Section 7.6. Sort the data into ascending sequence by employee name. The sorted data should be placed in another file (SORTED-EMPLOYEE-FILE).

Problem Analysis

The program will require three files: the two files described in the problem statement and a sort work-file.

Problem Solution

Program 7b performs the desired function. Sample input and output are shown in Figure 7.12. In this case the sort work-file is called SORT-WORK-FILE; however, any suitable name could have been used. Note that the SELECT entry for the sort work-file may vary slightly from the SELECT entry for other files; this requirement is system dependent. The following section describes the SORT statement (lines 64–67) in detail.

7.9   THE SORT STATEMENT

The SORT statement is used in the PROCEDURE DIVISION to activate the sort procedure. A general form for the SORT statement is shown in Figure 7.13. The sort-work-file-name must be specified in an SD entry in the DATA DIVISION. The ON. . . KEY clause gives the programmer the choice of specifying ASCENDING sequence or DESCENDING sequence for the records. The data-name(s) must be defined within the record associated with the sort work-file. If more than one key field is specified, the first field is the primary key and the following fields are secondary keys. The USING clause specifies the source of the data; the GIVING clause specifies the destina-

Program 7b

```
 1 IDENTIFICATION DIVISION.
 2
 3 PROGRAM-ID. EMPLOYEE-SORT1-PRO7B.
 4 AUTHOR. HORN.
 5
 6 ENVIRONMENT DIVISION.
 7
 8 CONFIGURATION SECTION.
 9
10 SOURCE-COMPUTER.
11 OBJECT-COMPUTER.
12
13 INPUT-OUTPUT SECTION.
14
15 FILE-CONTROL.
16
17     SELECT EMPLOYEE-FILE ASSIGN TO DISK.
18
19     SELECT SORT-WORK-FILE ASSIGN TO DISK.
20
21     SELECT SORTED-EMPLOYEE-FILE ASSIGN TO DISK.
22
23
24 DATA DIVISION.
25
26 FILE SECTION.
27
28 FD   EMPLOYEE-FILE
29      LABEL RECORDS ARE STANDARD
30      DATA RECORD IS EMPLOYEE-RECORD.
31
32 01   EMPLOYEE-RECORD.
33         03 EMP-NUM-ER                  PIC 9(9).
34         03 EMP-NAME-ER                 PIC X(20).
35         03 EMP-AGE-ER                  PIC 99.
36         03 EMP-DEPT-ER                 PIC 9.
37         03 FILLER                      PIC X(48).
38
39 SD   SORT-WORK-FILE
40      DATA RECORD IS SORT-WORK-RECORD.
41
42 01   SORT-WORK-RECORD.
43         03 EMP-NUM-SWR                 PIC 9(9).
44         03 EMP-NAME-SWR                PIC X(20).
45         03 EMP-AGE-SWR                 PIC 99.
46         03 EMP-DEPT-SWR                PIC 9.
47         03 FILLER                      PIC X(48).
48
49 FD   SORTED-EMPLOYEE-FILE
50      LABEL RECORDS ARE STANDARD
51      DATA RECORD IS SORTED-EMPLOYEE-RECORD.
52
53 01   SORTED-EMPLOYEE-RECORD.
54         03 EMP-NUM-SER                 PIC 9(9).
55         03 EMP-NAME-SER                PIC X(20).
56         03 EMP-AGE-SER                 PIC 99.
57         03 EMP-DEPT-SER                PIC 9.
58         03 FILLER                      PIC X(48).
59
60 PROCEDURE DIVISION.
61
62 1000-MAIN-CONTROL.
63
64     SORT SORT-WORK-FILE
65         ON ASCENDING KEY EMP-NAME-SWR
66         USING  EMPLOYEE-FILE
67         GIVING SORTED-EMPLOYEE-FILE.
68     STOP RUN.
```

Figure 7.12   Sample execution of Program 7b

Input (EMPLOYEE-FILE)

```
111111111JONES  JAMES          341
100000000SMITH  MARY           202
222222222BLACK  BARRY          201
333333333WHITE  SAM            456
300000000SMITH  JOHN           562
200000000DOE  JOHN             304
```

Output (SORTED-EMPLOYEE-FILE)

```
222222222BLACK  BARRY          201
200000000DOE  JOHN             304
111111111JONES  JAMES          341
300000000SMITH  JOHN           562
100000000SMITH  MARY           242
333333333WHITE  SAM            456
```

Figure 7.13   General form of SORT with USING and GIVING

```
SORT      sort-work-file-name

     ON  { ASCENDING  }  KEY data-name-1...
         { DESCENDING }
    [ON  { ASCENDING  }  KEY data-name-2...]...
         { DESCENDING }
              USING file-name-1...
              GIVING file-name-2
```

tion of the sorted data records. In execution, the SORT command performs the following three functions in sequential order:

1. Reads the file or files specified in the USING clause and places the records in the sort work-file.
2. Sorts the sort work-file on the specified key field(s).
3. Copies the sorted records from the sort work-file into the file specified in the GIVING clause.

For example, the following code could be used to sort the data defined above into alphabetic sequence by name:

```
SORT SORT-WORK-FILE
     ON ASCENDING KEY EMP-NAME-SWR
     USING EMPLOYEE-FILE
     GIVING SORTED-EMPLOYEE-FILE.
```

To sort the records into ascending alphabetic sequence within departments, the following code could be used:

```
SORT SORT-WORK-FILE
      ON ASCENDING KEY EMP-DEPT-SWR EMP-NAME-SWR
      USING SORTED-EMPLOYEE-FILE
      GIVING SORTED-EMPLOYEE-FILE.
```

In this example, the department number is declared to be the primary key, and the employee's name is a secondary key. Here, we have used the same file in the USING *and* GIVING clauses. This means that the original file will be replaced by the new file at the conclusion of the SORT process. You should *never* do this unless a backup of the file is made first. Any system problem that occurs during execution of the SORT could result in your losing some or all of the content of the file.

As many secondary keys as desired may be specified. Furthermore, it is possible to include as many ON . . . KEY clauses as desired. For example, suppose we want to sort the data into descending sequence by age within ascending department number sequence. The arrangement of the data desired is

Employee Number	Name		Age		Department	
333	QUE	SUSY	40		2	
695	BROWN	JAMES	25	Descending	2	
123	DOE	JOHN	53	sequences	3	Ascending
492	SMITH	MARY	40	(three)	4	sequence
497	JAMES	JOHN	19		4	

The required code is

```
SORT SORT-WORK-FILE
      ON ASCENDING KEY EMP-DEPT-SWR
      ON DESCENDING KEY EMP-AGE-SWR
      USING SORTED-EMPLOYEE-FILE
      GIVING SORTED-EMPLOYEE-FILE.
```

The sequence of clauses governs the sequence of keys—primary to secondary.

It is possible to sort more than one file with the same SORT statement. For example, to sort DATA-FILE and NEW-DATA-FILE into ascending sequence by employee number, the following statement could be used:

```
SORT SORT-WORK-FILE
      ON ASCENDING-KEY EMPLOYEE-NUM-SWR
      USING DATA-FILE NEW-DATA-FILE
      GIVING SORTED-EMPLOYEE-FILE.
```

This statement would have the effect of merging the records from the two input files into one output file. This facility can be used to add records to an existing file while preserving the sequencing of the records.

For example, to add the records contained in NEW-DATA-FILE to those contained in SORTED-EMPLOYEE-FILE, the following statement could be used:

```
SORT SORT-WORK-FILE
      ON ASCENDING KEY EMPLOYEE-NUM-SWR
      USING SORTED-EMPLOYEE-FILE NEW-DATA-FILE
      GIVING SORTED-EMPLOYEE-FILE.
```

The new version of SORTED-EMPLOYEE-FILE will contain all of the records from the old version plus all of the records from NEW-DATA-FILE and will be in sequence by employee number.

Sorting Files Containing Multiple Record Types

If it is necessary to sort a file which contains multiple record types, the only fields that can be used as sort keys are fields that have the same position on all records in the file. In writing the description of the sort work-record, the programmer should describe other fields as FILLER. For example, consider DATA-FILE described in Section 7.5. Recall that this file contains two types of records, which we called NAME-ADDRESS-RECORD and TIME-RECORD. These records share two fields—an identifying number (positions 1–9) and a record code (position 58). We could describe the sort work-record for the sort work-file required to sort this file as follows:

```
01  SORT-WORK-RECORD.
    03 ID-NUM-SWR    PIC 9(9).
    03 FILLER        PIC X(48).
    03 REC-ID-SWR    PIC 9.
```

With this description in place, we could sort the file into sequence based on the identifying number of the record code or any combination of the two fields. If we wished to sort the file so that each name and address record would be followed by all related time records, we could write the following:

```
SORT SORT-WORK-FILE
     ON ASCENDING KEY ID-NUM-SWR REC-ID-SWR
     USING DATA-FILE
     GIVING DATA-FILE.
```

7.10 A COMPLETE EXAMPLE

Problem Statement

The procurement system of a company uses a file containing purchase request records. Each record corresponds to an item that must be purchased by the company. Each record contains the following fields:

Positions	Content
1–5	Supplier identification number
6–10	Item number
11–20	Item description
21–25	Item cost (2 decimal places)
26–28	Order quantity
29–80	Unused

Before purchase orders to be sent to the various suppliers can be printed, it is necessary to resequence the file so that all of the requests for a supplier are grouped together. It is also useful to have the records for each supplier in sequence by item number.

Problem Analysis

Two files must be defined in the program: the file containing the data to be sorted (PURCHASE-REQUEST-FILE) and a sort work-file (SORT-FILE). PURCHASE-REQUEST-FILE will be specified in both the USING and the GIVING clauses of the SORT statement. (Remember that it is important that a backup copy of the file be made before sorting in this manner to avoid possible loss of data in the event of system problems.) Two keys will be needed in the ON . . . KEY clause of the SORT statement. The primary key will be the supplier identification number; the secondary key will be the item number. In this way, the new file will have all records for each supplier in a continuous group. Within each group, the records will be in sequence by item number.

Problem Solution

The required program is shown in Program 7c. An alternative way in which the sort work-record could have been described is

```
01   SORT-RECORD.
     03 SUPPLIER-ID-NUMBER-SR    PIC X(5).
     03 ITEM-NUMBER-SR           PIC X(5).
     03 FILLER                   PIC X(70).
```

Only fields that are to be used as key fields in the SORT verb must be described in the sort work-record. Describing other fields does, however, make it easier later to modify the SORT statement to sort on other fields.

7.11 PROCEDURE DIVISION SECTIONS

The SORT feature also provides a means by which a programmer can construct routines for storing the records to be sorted on the sort work-file (an INPUT PROCEDURE) and for copying the sorted data from the sort work-file (an OUTPUT PROCEDURE). The routine to be used in this fashion must be placed in a separate PROCEDURE DIVISION section.

Up to this point the PROCEDURE DIVISION of a program has consisted only of a sequence of paragraphs; no mention has been made of sections in the PROCEDURE DIVISION. It is possible to segment a PROCEDURE DIVISION into named sections, each of which consists of one or more paragraphs. The paragraphs in a section are usually related in some way. For example, they may perform related computations, or they may constitute an input or output routine. It is the latter usage which is important when writing an INPUT PROCEDURE or OUTPUT PROCEDURE for a SORT verb. In order to segment paragraphs of a PROCEDURE DIVISION, each group of paragraphs must be preceded by a section header which has the general form

```
section-name SECTION.
```

For example, suppose a PROCEDURE DIVISION is made up of the paragraphs 1100-MAIN-LOGIC, 2100-INITIALIZATION, 2200-CONTROL, 2300-TERMINATION, 3100 READ-FILE-A, and 3200-READ-FILE-B. The

```
 1 IDENTIFICATION DIVISION.
 2
 3 PROGRAM-ID. PURCH-REQUEST-SORT2-PRO7C.
 4 AUTHOR.
 5
 6 ENVIRONMENT DIVISION.
 7
 8 CONFIGURATION SECTION.
 9
10 SOURCE-COMPUTER.
11 OBJECT-COMPUTER.
12
13 INPUT-OUTPUT SECTION.
14
15 FILE-CONTROL.
16
17     SELECT PURCHASE-REQUEST-FILE ASSIGN TO DISK.
18
19     SELECT SORT-FILE ASSIGN TO DISK.
20
21
22 DATA DIVISION.
23
24 FILE SECTION.
25
26 FD  PURCHASE-REQUEST-FILE
27     LABEL RECORDS ARE STANDARD
28     DATA RECORD IS PURCHASE-REQUEST-RECORD.
29
30 01  PURCHASE-REQUEST-RECORD.
31     03 SUPPLIER-ID-NUMBER-PRR            PIC 9(5).
32     03 ITEM-NUMBER-PRR                   PIC 9(5).
33     03 ITEM-DESCRIPTION-PRR              PIC X(10).
34     03 ITEM-COST-PRR                     PIC 999V99.
35     03 ORDER-QUANTITY-PRR                PIC 9(3).
36     03 FILLER                           PIC X(52).
37
38 SD  SORT-FILE
39     DATA RECORD IS SORT-RECORD.
40
41 01  SORT-RECORD.
42     03 SUPPLIER-ID-NUMBER-SR             PIC 9(5).
43     03 ITEM-NUMBER-SR                    PIC 9(5).
44     03 ITEM-DESCRIPTION-SR               PIC X(10).
45     03 ITEM-COST-SR                      PIC 999V99.
46     03 ORDER-QUANTITY-SR                 PIC 9(3).
47     03 FILLER                           PIC X(52).
48
49 PROCEDURE DIVISION.
50
51 1000-MAIN-CONTROL.
52
53     SORT SORT-FILE
54         ON ASCENDING KEY SUPPLIER-ID-NUMBER-SR
55                          ITEM-NUMBER-SR
56         USING  PURCHASE-REQUEST-FILE
57         GIVING PURCHASE-REQUEST-FILE.
58     STOP RUN.
```

following code divides these paragraphs into three sections: 1000-MAIN, 2000-SECONDARY, and 3000-INPUT-OUTPUT.

```
PROCEDURE DIVISION.
1000-MAIN SECTION.
1100-MAIN-LOGIC.
       .
       .
       .

2000-SECONDARY SECTION.
2100-INITIALIZATION.
       .
       .
       .

2200-CONTROL.
       .
       .
       .

2300-TERMINATION.
       .
       .
       .

3000-INPUT-OUTPUT SECTION.
3100-READ-FILE-A.
       .
       .
       .

3200-READ-FILE-B.
       .
       .
       .
```

Dividing a PROCEDURE DIVISION into sections in no way affects the logic of a program or the way in which statements within a program are executed. For example, a statement in one section may PERFORM a paragraph in another section; after execution of the last statement in the paragraph, control passes back to the PERFORM statement. If, however, a section is referenced in a PERFORM statement, the paragraphs of that section will be executed in succession, and the program will return to the PERFORM statement only after the last statement in the last paragraph of the section has been completed. For example, if the statement

```
PERFORM 3000-INPUT-OUTPUT
```

were executed in the above example, all of the statements in 3100-READ-FILE-A and 3200-READ-FILE-B would be executed in sequence. Only after both paragraphs have been completed will the program return to the statement following the PERFORM.

In the theory of structured programming, a **module** is defined as a procedure that carries out a well-defined task and has a single entry point and single exit. All of our programs thus far have been composed of single paragraph modules. Each paragraph carried out a well-defined function; execution of each paragraph began at its first statement and continued through its last. Dividing a PROCEDURE DIVISION into sections enables us to construct modules consisting of more than one paragraph; the module begins with the first statement of the first paragraph and concludes with the last statement of the last paragraph. It is often advantageous to build multiparagraph modules because each individual paragraph is still usable as a single paragraph module. For example, in the above program, it is still possible to use statements such as PERFORM 3100-READ-FILE-A or PERFORM 3200-READ-FILE-B. In either case, control returns to the PERFORM statement when the paragraph has been completed.

The programmer must exercise caution when writing sections containing several paragraphs. If the entire section is performed, control passes to the next paragraph when the first paragraph of the section is complete, and so on. Only by executing the last statement in the section can the module return control to the performing statement. This usually necessitates the use of the GO TO statement.

7.12 GO TO AND EXIT

The general form of the GO TO statement is shown in Figure 7.14. When the GO TO statement is executed, an immediate branch is made to the specified paragraph or section. Control does not return to the statement following the GO TO at the end of the execution of the paragraph or section as it does when branching takes place via the PERFORM statement. The GO TO statement causes an unconditional branch with *no* provision for return; the PERFORM statement causes an unconditional branch *with* provision for return.

Figure 7.14   General form of the GO TO statement

```
GO TO     {paragraph-name}
          {section-name  }
```

Unstructured programs frequently use GO TO statements. Structured programs also use the GO TO statement in a more restricted and disciplined fashion. A primary usage of the GO TO statement in structured COBOL programming is to transfer control to the last paragraph in a multiparagraph section that has been performed. Typically, the last paragraph contains the single statement EXIT and serves only to return control to the PERFORM statement A typical situation follows:

```
PERFORM 1000-ABC.
        .
        .
        .
1000-ABC SECTION.
1010-PARA-A.
        .
        .
        .
    GO TO 1099-PARA-ABC-EXIT.
1020-PARA-B.
```

Return mechanism is inserted at end of section 1000-ABC by the PERFORM statement.

The first paragraph in the section controls execution of the other paragraphs. At the end of the control paragraph, branch to the last paragraph in the section.

```
        •
        •
        •
1030-PARA-C.
        •
        •
        •
1099-PARA-ABC-EXIT.
                          Return mechanism has been inserted here.
    EXIT. ◄             Execution of this paragraph causes control
                          to return to PERFORM statement.
```

This technique requires that the last paragraph in the section exist, yet there is no work for it to accomplish. COBOL syntax requires that each paragraph have at least one sentence. The EXIT sentence is provided for this contingency. The general form of EXIT is

$$\boxed{\text{EXIT.}}$$

When used, the EXIT sentence must be the *only* sentence in the paragraph. An EXIT statement does not automatically complete a section. The sample code works as described only if the next program statement is a new section name or if the EXIT statement is the very last program statement. Coding an EXIT statement in the middle of a section will *not* cause control to return to the PERFORM statement immediately.

The EXIT sentence is used in paragraphs which are required by COBOL syntax but which otherwise serve no function. When large programs are designed and developed in parts, it is often necessary to include in early versions of the program paragraphs which will be developed later. In order to begin testing the program at early stages of development, programmers frequently include unfinished paragraphs with an EXIT statement as their only content. In this way, the program can be compiled and tested without syntax errors resulting from references to missing paragraphs. Of course, the program will not perform all of its required functions until all dummy paragraphs have been replaced with statements required to perform their designated functions.

7.13 INPUT/OUTPUT PROCEDURES

A complete form of the SORT statement is shown in Figure 7.15. When the INPUT PROCEDURE option is used, the SORT procedure performs the specified INPUT PROCEDURE section prior to sorting the records in the sort work-file. It is the task of the section to store the desired records on the sort work-file. When the OUTPUT PROCEDURE option is used, the SORT procedure performs the specified OUTPUT PROCEDURE section after sorting the records in the sort work-file. The records in the sort work-file are available to the program for further processing in any desired fashion.

When a sort work-file is involved, the RELEASE and RETURN statements are used instead of ordinary WRITE and READ statements. The RELEASE statement has the general form shown in Figure 7.16. The RELEASE statement is used instead of a WRITE statement and causes a record to be written onto the sort work-file.

Figure 7.15   General form of the SORT verb

```
SORT sort-work-file-name

        ON { ASCENDING  } KEY  data-name-1
           { DECENDING  }
       [ON { ASCENDING  } KEY  data-name-2]...
           { DESCENDING }

        { USING        file-name-1...            }
        { INPUT PROCEDURE IS section-name-1      }

        { GIVING       file-name-2               }
        { OUTPUT PROCEDURE IS section-name-2     }
```

Figure 7.16   General form of the RELEASE statement

```
RELEASE sort-record-name [FROM data-name]
```

The RETURN statement has the general form shown in Figure 7.17. The RETURN statement is used instead of a READ statement; it causes a record to be read from a sort work-file. The statements in the AT END clause are executed when the end of the sort work-file is reached.

Figure 7.17   General form of the RETURN statement

```
RETURN sort-file-name RECORD [INTO data-name]
       AT END statement . . .
```

For example, Program 7d could be used to sort the employee data described in Section 7.6. Note that the INPUT PROCEDURE in this program is not completely self-contained (i.e., it performs a paragraph outside the section). Some compilers will not allow this practice. In such systems, an INPUT or OUTPUT PROCEDURE must not transfer control (via GO TO or PERFORM) to a point outside the procedure.

In this example, the SORT verb causes the following sequence of tasks to be executed:

1. The section 2000-CREATE-SORT-WORK-FILE is PERFORMed. At the end of the procedure, control returns to the SORT verb.
2. The file SORT-WORK-FILE is sorted.
3. The content of SORT-WORK-FILE is copied onto SORTED-EMPLOYEE-FILE.

In this example, there seems to be no advantage to using the INPUT PROCEDURE option, because the USING option would have an identical effect. However, note that the logic contained in 2000-CREATE-SORT-WORK-FILE could process the data contained in DATA-RECORD in any desired way. For example, a listing of the data could be produced, fields

Program 7d

```
 1 IDENTIFICATION DIVISION.
 2
 3 PROGRAM-ID. EMPLOYEE-SORT3-PRO7D.
 4 AUTHOR. HORN.
 5
 6 ENVIRONMENT DIVISION.
 7
 8 CONFIGURATION SECTION.
 9
10 SOURCE-COMPUTER.
11 OBJECT-COMPUTER.
12
13 INPUT-OUTPUT SECTION.
14
15 FILE-CONTROL.
16
17     SELECT EMPLOYEE-FILE ASSIGN TO DISK.
18
19     SELECT SORT-WORK-FILE ASSIGN TO DISK.
20
21     SELECT SORTED-EMPLOYEE-FILE ASSIGN TO DISK.
22
23
24 DATA DIVISION.
25
26 FILE SECTION.
27
28 FD  EMPLOYEE-FILE
29     LABEL RECORDS ARE STANDARD
30     DATA RECORD IS EMPLOYEE-RECORD.
31
32 01  EMPLOYEE-RECORD.
33     03 EMP-NUM-ER                   PIC 9(9).
34     03 EMP-NAME-ER                  PIC X(20).
35     03 EMP-AGE-ER                   PIC 99.
36     03 EMP-DEPT-ER                  PIC 9.
37     03 FILLER                       PIC X(48).
38
39 SD  SORT-WORK-FILE
40     DATA RECORD IS SORT-WORK-RECORD.
41
42 01  SORT-WORK-RECORD.
43     03 EMP-NUM-SWR                  PIC 9(9).
44     03 EMP-NAME-SWR                 PIC X(20).
45     03 EMP-AGE-SWR                  PIC 99.
46     03 EMP-DEPT-SWR                 PIC 9.
47     03 FILLER                       PIC X(48).
48
49 FD  SORTED-EMPLOYEE-FILE
50     LABEL RECORDS ARE STANDARD
51     DATA RECORD IS SORTED-EMPLOYEE-RECORD.
52
53 01  SORTED-EMPLOYEE-RECORD.
54     03 EMP-NUM-SER                  PIC 9(9).
55     03 EMP-NAME-SER                 PIC X(20).
56     03 EMP-AGE-SER                  PIC 99.
57     03 EMP-DEPT-SER                 PIC 9.
58     03 FILLER                       PIC X(48).
```

Program 7d   *(concluded)*

```
59
60 WORKING-STORAGE SECTION.
61
62 01  FLAGS.
63     02 EOF-FLAG                        PIC XXX VALUE "NO".
64
65 PROCEDURE DIVISION.
66
67 1000-MAIN SECTION.
68
69 1100-MAIN-CONTROL.
70
71     SORT SORT-WORK-FILE
72         ON ASCENDING KEY EMP-NAME-SWR
73         INPUT PROCEDURE IS 2000-CREATE-SORT-WORK-FILE
74         GIVING SORTED-EMPLOYEE-FILE.
75     STOP RUN.
76
77 2000-CREATE-SORT-WORK-FILE SECTION.
78
79 2100-CREATE-CONTROL.
80
81     OPEN INPUT EMPLOYEE-FILE.
82     PERFORM 9100-READ-EMPLOYEE-FILE.
83     PERFORM 2200-PROCESS-DATA UNTIL EOF-FLAG ="YES".
84     CLOSE EMPLOYEE-FILE.
85     GO TO 2300-EXIT-CREATE.
86
87 2200-PROCESS-DATA.
88
89     RELEASE SORT-WORK-RECORD FROM EMPLOYEE-RECORD.
90     PERFORM 9100-READ-EMPLOYEE-FILE.
91
92 2300-EXIT-CREATE.
93
94     EXIT.
95
96 9000-READ SECTION.
97
98 9100-READ-EMPLOYEE-FILE.
99
100    READ EMPLOYEE-FILE
101        AT END MOVE "YES" TO EOF-FLAG.
```

within the data record could be validated, or any desired computations could be performed.

Suppose you want to print a listing of the records and to sort the records alphabetically by name within descending age sequence. Program 7e could be used. A sample of the execution of this program is shown in Figure 7.18.

In this program, the following sequence of events will occur:

1. The content of SORTED-EMPLOYEE-FILE will be copied onto SORT-WORK-FILE.

2. The SORT-WORK-FILE will be sorted into the prescribed sequence.

Figure 7.18 Sample execution of Program 7e

Input (EMPLOYEE-FILE)

```
111111111JONES JAMES        341
100000000SMITH MARY         202
222222222BLACK BARRY        201
333333333WHITE SAM          456
300000000SMITH JOHN         562
200000000DOE JOHN           304
```

Report (HARDCOPY-FILE)

```
                PERSONNEL REPORT

    NUMBER      NAME              AGE   DEPT.

    300000000   SMITH JOHN        56    2
    333333333   WHITE SAM         45    6
    111111111   JONES JAMES       34    1
    200000000   DOE JOHN          30    4
    222222222   BLACK BARRY       20    1
    100000000   SMITH MARY        20    2
```

---

3. The section 2000-PRINT-REPORT will be executed. At the termination of this procedure, control passes to the statement following the SORT statement.

Of course, it is possible to specify both an INPUT PROCEDURE and an OUTPUT PROCEDURE in a SORT statement. An example of this code would be

```
SORT SORT-WORK-FILE
    ON ASCENDING KEY EMP-NAME-SWR
    INPUT PROCEDURE 2000-CREATE-SORT-WORK-FILE
    OUTPUT PROCEDURE 2100-PRINT-REPORT.
```

Note that in an INPUT/OUTPUT PROCEDURE it is necessary to OPEN the files from which data is to be read or onto which data is to be written, but it is *not* necessary to OPEN the sort work-file. The sort work-file *must not* be opened or closed; these operations are a built-in part of the SORT verb.

7.14 SORT UTILITIES

The task of sorting is fundamental to any data processing system. Most computer installations have utility programs available to perform this task. A utility program is a program designed to perform a specified task (or group of related tasks) on data of any description. In order to use a utility program, the user specifies the exact nature of the data files and the particulars of the task and allows the utility program to do the rest. For example, to use a typical sort utility to perform the simple sort tasks described in Programs 7b and 7c, the user would specify the following:

- name of the input file and the characteristics of its records

- name of the output file and the characteristics of its records
- location and number of the key fields
- nature of the data in the key fields (numeric or alphanumeric)
- desired sequencing

Typically, it is much quicker to write the specifications for the sort utility than to code a COBOL program to perform the same task. More important, the sorting algorithm used by the utility may be more efficient in use of time and/or space than the sort procedure used by COBOL. This is possible because the utility is usually more complex than the routine used to carry out a COBOL SORT. The utility can, therefore, use a more sophisticated sort algorithm which can accomplish the sort process in less time. Also, because the utility is more complex, it is able to make better use of space on the mass storage device than the relatively simpler routine supplied by the COBOL SORT verb.

Most major manufacturers of computers provide sort utilities. Many other companies that specialize in software rather than hardware sell sort utilities. Some of the better-known packages are listed in Figure 7.19. Manufacturers of these packages usually advertise that their software is more efficient or easier to use than other packages, particularly those utilities supplied by the computer manufacturers. A large percentage of commercial data processing computer installations own one or more sort packages produced by independent software companies.

Figure 7.19 Some common sort/merge software packages

Package Name	Supplier	Comments
CA SORT	Computer Associates	IBM mainframes
Autosort-C/CR (Sort Merge Select)	Computer Control Systems, Inc.	CP/M operating system
SORT/1000	Corporate Computer Systems, Inc.	Hewlett-Packard 100
SORT PLUS	Ecosoft, Inc.	Hewlett-Packard 100
FSORT3/VSORT	Evans Griffiths and Hart, Inc.	DEC PDP-11/VAX-11
SORT ROUTINE	Inmark	Perkin Elmer OS
SORT-I-PLUS	Oregon Software, Inc.	DEC VAX
SPEEDSORT/11	Pennington Systems, Inc.	DEC PDP-11
WORDPERFECT SORTER	Satellite Software Inter.	IBM PC/PS 2
FLEX-I-SORT	Bean Computers, Inc.	CP/M & MP/M
INFO-SORT	Info Pros	IBM PC/PS 2
SUPERSORT	Micropro International Corp.	CP/M & MS/DOS
SYNCSORT	Syncsort, Inc.	IBM OS/VS
PRIME	Prime	Primos
SORMER	Sormer Sort	Primos

7.15 DEBUG CLINIC

The SORT verb and multiparagraph sections are very powerful features; however, there are a number of restrictions on their use. Failure to observe these restrictions will result in debugging problems. Some of the most common errors result from failure to observe the following rules:

- *Sort work-files must not be opened or closed.* The SORT verb takes care of opening and closing the sort work-file. The OPEN and CLOSE statements are invalid for sort work-files.

- RETURN *and* RELEASE *rather than* READ *and* WRITE *must be used for a sort work-file.* Use of READ and WRITE verbs for a sort work-file is invalid. Use of RETURN and RELEASE for ordinary files is also invalid.

- *The sort work-file must be defined with an* SD *entry rather than an* FD *entry.* A file defined with an FD entry cannot be used as a sort work-file.

- *An* INPUT/OUTPUT PROCEDURE *cannot contain a* SORT *statement.* The SORT verb causes the execution of a specific routine; this routine cannot be asked to execute itself.

- *A file used in the* USING *or* GIVING *clause must not be open.* A file to be used in USING or GIVING must be closed at the time the SORT statement is executed. Of course, these files may be opened and processed in other parts of the program.

- *A sort work-file must be assigned to disk.* A special designation used in the system name may be used in the ASSIGN entry for a sort work-file. The reader must check local documentation for specific details.

- *In some systems, an* INPUT/OUTPUT PROCEDURE *may not reference a paragraph or section outside the procedure.* INPUT/OUTPUT PRO- CEDUREs must be wholly self-contained sections; there must not be any PERFORM or GO TO statements that address paragraphs or sections external to the section being used to specify the INPUT/OUT- PUT PROCEDURE.

- *Exiting a multiparagraph section must be accomplished by executing its last statement.* When a section is executed either with a PERFORM statement or a SORT statement, the return mechanism is inserted following the last statement of the last paragraph of the section. The GO TO statement is usually used to branch from the controlling paragraph to the last paragraph to effect a return; omission of the GO TO statement will result in the sequential execution of the paragraphs in the section. Omission of the GO TO statement will almost always be an error because the paragraphs which will be executed have already been performed under control of the first paragraph of the section.

- *The* GO TO *statement is used only to branch to the last paragraph of a multiparagraph section.* Unrestricted use of the GO TO statement results in unstructured program modules. This usage of the GO TO statement is necessary to create a single entry/single exit module from a section that is composed of more than one paragraph.

- *A section header is a section-name followed by* SECTION *followed by a period.* A common mistake is to place a hyphen between the section-name and SECTION as in 1000-MAIN-SECTION instead of the correct entry 1000-MAIN SECTION. The compiler will recognize 1000-MAIN-SECTION as a paragraph header instead of a section header.

7.16　COBOL-85 UPDATE

The RETURN statement is very much like the READ statement, so it should come as no surprise that in COBOL-85 the RETURN statement has been enhanced in much the same way as the READ statement. A general form for the COBOL-85 RETURN statement is shown in Figure 7.20. It includes provision for the NOT AT END clause, which will be executed if the end of file is not read, and a scope delimiter END-RETURN.

Figure 7.20　General form of the RETURN statement in COBOL-85

```
RETURN sort-work-file-name RECORD [INTO data-name-1]
    AT END statement-1 . . .
    [NOT AT END statement-n . . .]
[END-RETURN]
```

For example, let us rewrite Program 7e as Program 7e85, taking advantage of the new facilities in COBOL-85. We can gather all of the output procedure into one paragraph by using the in-line PERFORM which repeatedly executes the RETURN statement to read records from the sort work-file. The RETURN statement can use the NOT AT END clause to create and write the detail record in the report. Because the entire section consists of one paragraph, it is unnecessary to use the cumbersome GO TO and EXIT paragraph that was needed before. However, if the section had been composed of multiple paragraphs, the previous technique would still have to be employed. The SORT statement executes the section containing the output (or input) procedure. The return mechanism is placed after the last statement in the section, just as in COBOL-74.

Program 7e

```
 1 IDENTIFICATION DIVISION.
 2
 3 PROGRAM-ID. EMPLOYEE-SORT4-PRO7E.
 4 AUTHOR. HORN.
 5
 6 ENVIRONMENT DIVISION.
 7
 8 CONFIGURATION SECTION.
 9
10 SOURCE-COMPUTER.
11 OBJECT-COMPUTER.
12
13 INPUT-OUTPUT SECTION.
14
15 FILE-CONTROL.
16
17     SELECT SORT-WORK-FILE ASSIGN TO DISK.
18
19     SELECT EMPLOYEE-FILE ASSIGN TO DISK.
20
21     SELECT HARDCOPY-FILE ASSIGN TO PRINTER.
22
23
24 DATA DIVISION.
25
26 FILE SECTION.
27
28 SD  SORT-WORK-FILE
29     DATA RECORD IS SORT-WORK-RECORD.
30
31 01  SORT-WORK-RECORD.
32     03 EMP-NUM-SWR          PIC 9(9).
33     03 EMP-NAME-SWR         PIC X(20).
34     03 EMP-AGE-SWR          PIC 99.
35     03 EMP-DEPT-SWR         PIC 9.
36     03 FILLER              PIC X(48).
37
38 FD  EMPLOYEE-FILE
39     LABEL RECORDS ARE STANDARD
40     DATA RECORD IS EMPLOYEE-RECORD.
41
42 01  EMPLOYEE-RECORD.
43     03 EMP-NUM-ER           PIC 9(9).
44     03 EMP-NAME-ER          PIC X(20).
45     03 EMP-AGE-ER           PIC 99.
46     03 EMP-DEPT-ER          PIC 9.
47     03 FILLER              PIC X(48).
48
49 FD  HARDCOPY-FILE
50     LABEL RECORDS ARE OMITTED
51     DATA RECORD IS HARDCOPY-RECORD.
52
53 01  HARDCOPY-RECORD         PIC X(132).
54
```

```
55 WORKING-STORAGE SECTION.
56
57 01  FLAGS.
58     02 EOF-SWF              PIC XXX VALUE "NO".
59
60 01  PAGE-HEAD.
61     02 FILLER               PIC X(16) VALUE SPACES.
62     02 FILLER               PIC X(16) VALUE "PERSONNEL REPORT".
63
64 01  COLUMN-HEAD.
65     02 FILLER               PIC X(8) VALUE " NUMBER".
66     02 FILLER               PIC X(5) VALUE SPACES.
67     02 FILLER               PIC X(4) VALUE "NAME".
68     02 FILLER               PIC X(18) VALUE SPACES.
69     02 FILLER               PIC X(11) VALUE "AGE   DEPT.".
70
71 01  DETAIL-LINE.
72     02 FILLER               PIC X VALUE SPACE.
73     02 EMP-NUM-DL           PIC 9(9).
74     02 FILLER               PIC XXX VALUE SPACES.
75     02 EMP-NAME-DL          PIC X(20).
76     02 FILLER               PIC XXX VALUE SPACES.
77     02 EMP-AGE-DL           PIC 99.
78     02 FILLER               PIC X(5) VALUE SPACES.
79     02 EMP-DEPT-DL          PIC 9.
80
81 PROCEDURE DIVISION.
82
83 1000-MAIN SECTION.
84
85 1100-MAIN-CONTROL.
86
87     SORT SORT-WORK-FILE
88          ON DESCENDING KEY EMP-AGE-SWR
89          ON ASCENDING  KEY EMP-NAME-SWR
90          USING EMPLOYEE-FILE
91          OUTPUT PROCEDURE IS 2000-PRINT-REPORT.
92     STOP RUN.
93
94 2000-PRINT-REPORT SECTION.
95
96 2100-PRINT-REPORT-CONTROL.
97
98     OPEN OUTPUT HARDCOPY-FILE.
99     WRITE HARDCOPY-RECORD FROM PAGE-HEAD AFTER PAGE.
100    WRITE HARDCOPY-RECORD FROM COLUMN-HEAD AFTER 2.
101    MOVE SPACES TO HARDCOPY-RECORD.
102    WRITE HARDCOPY-RECORD AFTER 1.
103    PERFORM 2900-RETURN-SORT-WORK-FILE.
104    PERFORM 2200-PROCESS-DATA
105         UNTIL EOF-SWF = "YES".
106    CLOSE HARDCOPY-FILE.
107    GO TO 2999-EXIT-PRINT-REPORT.
108
```

Program 7e   *(concluded)*

```
109 2200-PROCESS-DATA.
110
111     MOVE EMP-NUM-SWR      TO EMP-NUM-DL.
112     MOVE EMP-NAME-SWR     TO EMP-NAME-DL.
113     MOVE EMP-AGE-SWR      TO EMP-AGE-DL.
114     MOVE EMP-DEPT-SWR     TO EMP-DEPT-DL.
115     WRITE HARDCOPY-RECORD FROM DETAIL-LINE AFTER 1.
116     PERFORM 2900-RETURN-SORT-WORK-FILE.
117
118 2900-RETURN-SORT-WORK-FILE.
119
120     RETURN SORT-WORK-FILE
121          AT END MOVE "YES" TO EOF-SWF.
122
123 2999-EXIT-PRINT-REPORT.
124
125     EXIT.
```

Program 7e85

```
 1 IDENTIFICATION DIVISION.
 2
 3 PROGRAM-ID. Employee-Sort4-Pro7e85.
 .
 .
 .
79 PROCEDURE DIVISION.
80
81 1000-Main SECTION.
82
83 1100-Main-Control.
84
85     SORT Sort-Work-File
86          ON DESCENDING KEY Emp-Age-SWR
87          ON ASCENDING  KEY Emp-Name-SWR
88          USING Employee-File
89          OUTPUT PROCEDURE IS 2000-Print-Report.
90     STOP RUN.
91
92 2000-Print-Report SECTION.
93
94 2100-Print-Report-Control.
```

Program 7e85   *(concluded)*

```
 95
 96        OPEN OUTPUT Hardcopy-File
 97        WRITE Hardcopy-Record FROM Page-Head AFTER PAGE
 98        WRITE Hardcopy-Record FROM Column-Head AFTER 2
 99        MOVE SPACES TO Hardcopy-Record
100        WRITE Hardcopy-Record AFTER 1
101        PERFORM UNTIL Eof-SWF = "YES"
102            RETURN Sort-Work-File
103              AT END
104                  MOVE "YES"            TO Eof-SWF
105              NOT AT END
106                  MOVE Emp-Num-SWR      TO Emp-Num-DL
107                  MOVE Emp-Name-SWR     TO Emp-Name-DL
108                  MOVE Emp-Age-SWR      TO Emp-Age-DL
109                  MOVE Emp-Dept-SWR     TO Emp-Dept-DL
110                  WRITE Hardcopy-Record FROM Detail-Line AFTER 1
111            END-RETURN
112        END-PERFORM
113        CLOSE Hardcopy-File.
```

7.17   SELF-TEST EXERCISES

1. Draw structure diagrams for Programs 7d and 7e. How will you handle multiparagraph sections? (Structure diagrams should reflect relationships among program modules rather than among paragraphs.)

2. List the actions taken by the SORT statements in lines 53–57 of Program 7c.

3. Fill in the blanks:
   a. A sort work-file is defined in the FILE SECTION by a(n) _____.

   b. A field used to govern the sequence of records in a file is called a(n) _____.

   c. A primary difference between the GO TO and PERFORM statements is _____.

   d. A PROCEDURE DIVISION section is declared by _____.

   e. In structured programming, a procedure that carries out a well-defined task and has a single entry and a single exit and is called a(n) _____.

   f. One permitted use of the GO TO statement is to _____.

   g. The equivalent of READ for a sort work-file is _____.

   h. The equivalent of WRITE for a sort work-file is _____.

   i. The EXIT statement is used as _____.

   j. Two statements that cannot be used in an INPUT/OUTPUT PROCEDURE are _____ and _____.

   k. In order to exit a multiparagraph section, a program must _____.

   l. A sort work-file must be assigned to a(n) _____.

4. Consider the following file descriptions:

```
FILE SECTION.
FD  DATA-FILE
    LABEL RECORDS ARE STANDARD
    DATA RECORD IS DATA-RECORD.
01  DATA-RECORD.
    03 SS-NUM-DR     PIC 9(9).
    03 NAME-DR       PIC X(20).
    03 ST-ADDR-DR    PIC X(20).
    03 CITY-DR       PIC X(10).
    03 STATE-DR      PIC XX.
    03 ZIP-DR        PIC 9(5).
SD  SORT-FILE
    DATA RECORD IS SORT-RECORD.
01  SORT-RECORD.
    03 SS-NUM-SR     PIC 9(9).
    03 NAME-SR       PIC X(20).
    03 ST-ADDR-SR    PIC X(20).
    03 CITY-SR       PIC X(10).
    03 STATE-SR      PIC XX.
    03 ZIP-SR        PIC 9(5).
```

Assume that DATA-FILE is assigned to DISK.

a. Write a SORT statement to sort DATA-FILE into ascending sequence by Social Security number.

b. Write a SORT statement to sort DATA-FILE into sequence by zip code; then, within each zip code, order the records alphabetically by name.

5. Add the following file description to those already given in Exercise 4:

```
FD  NEW-DATA-FILE
    LABEL RECORDS ARE STANDARD
    DATA RECORD IS NEW-DATA-RECORD.
01  NEW-DATA-RECORD.
    03 NAME-NDR      PIC X(20).
    03 SS-NUM-NDR    PIC X(20).
    03 ZIP-NDR       PIC 9(5).
    03 ST-ADDR-NDR   PIC X(20).
    03 CITY-NDR      PIC X(10).
    03 STATE-NDR     PIC XX.
```

Write a SORT statement to sort NEW-DATA-FILE into ascending sequence by state.

6. Write a SORT statement using the files defined in Exercises 4 and 5 to merge the contents of DATA-FILE and NEW-DATA-FILE, placing the resulting file into DATA-FILE in descending sequence by zip code.

7. Write the answers to Exercises 5 and 6 using COBOL-85 syntax.

7.18 PROGRAMMING EXERCISES

1. Consider the file described in Programming Exercise 1 in Chapter 6 (Section 6.14). Write a program to sort the file into sequence by profit. Produce the report outlined in Figure 6.26.
   a. Write this program with `USING` and `GIVING`.
   b. Write this program with `USING` and an `OUTPUT PROCEDURE`.

2. Modify the program you wrote for Exercise 1 above to produce two reports—one for profitable stores and another for unprofitable stores. Hint: Sort the file once using an `INPUT PROCEDURE` that selects only profitable stores for sorting. Then, sort the file again using an `INPUT PROCEDURE` that selects unprofitable stores.

3. Consider the file described in Programming Exercise 1 in Chapter 5 (Section 5.12). Write a program to sort this file into sequence by total sales. Hint: Using an `INPUT PROCEDURE`, read the data and compute the total sales. Add a field for total sales to the sort work-record, and use the total as the sort key. The program should produce the same report as described in Figure 5.11.

4. The records in an employee file contain the employee name, sex, date of birth, and date of hire. Write COBOL programs to produce these required reports:
   a. A list sorted by seniority.
   b. An alphabetic list of all employees over 60 years old.
   c. Separate lists of men and women sorted in alphabetic order.
   d. A list of employees sorted into descending order by seniority (highest seniority first).
   e. Separate lists of men and women sorted into descending order by seniority.

   The layout of the records in this file is as follows:

Positions	Content
1–10	Employee Name
12	Sex (M = male, F = female)
14–19	Date of birth (*mmddyy*)
20–25	Hire date (*mmddyy*)

5. The records of an inventory file contain the following items: product code, description, selling price, cost, and number on hand. Write COBOL programs to
   a. List the items sorted by product code.
   b. List the items that have a markup in excess of 20 percent, sorted by product code.
   c. List the "big ticket" items (selling price greater than $200) sorted by description.

   The layout of the records in this file is as follows:

Positions	Content
1–9	Product code
11–20	Description
22–26	Selling price
28–32	Cost
34–36	Number on hand

8. REPORTS AND CONTROL BREAKS

8.1 REPORT REQUIREMENTS

Businesses require many reports, so it is no surprise that many COBOL programs are written to produce reports that summarize and make available the data in files. These report-writing programs share several features that require special logic. Among these features and requirements are the following:

Feature	Requirement
Headings	Is there a report heading?
	What column headings are required?
	Is a date required?
Page numbers	Are pages to be numbered?
Page totals	Are page totals required for some items?
Subtotals	Are subtotals required for segments of data?
	How many levels of subtotals are required?
Grand totals	What items require grand totals?

In this chapter we will concentrate on program logic necessary to fulfill these requirements.

8.2 REPORT-WRITING TECHNIQUES

When you write a program to generate a report, you will want to give the reader guidance in interpreting the information contained in the report. Usually, you will want to print a heading at the top of every page. Occasionally, a report heading—the company name and the report title, for example—is required on the first page but not on succeeding pages (usually this heading is printed on each page of the report). Including the date in the report heading enables users to determine if the information is recent enough to meet their needs. Generally, there will be column headings on every page to identify the data contained on the lines of the report.

A very useful technique to control the generation of headings is **line counting**. A typical page of computer output contains 64 lines of print, although the number of lines varies greatly among computing systems. (Check the size of the printed page generated on your computer.) The program uses a line counter to keep track of the number of lines of print generated. When a line is written, an appropriate value (1 for single spacing, 2 for double spacing, and so on) is added to the line counter. After each output operation, the value of the line counter is tested against the maximum number of lines allowed on a page. If the page is full, headings are written at the top of a new page, the line counter is reinitialized, and processing proceeds.

Page numbers are often required in reports. The writing of page numbers can be accomplished by the procedure used to print the page headings. A page counter is initialized to value zero. Each time the heading procedure is entered, the page counter is incremented by 1, and this value is moved to the appropriate field on the page heading line.

Page totals are totals of data items occurring on a page. Data items used to accumulate page totals should be reinitialized in the page total procedure. Page totals should be printed when the program detects that a page is full and before page headings for a new page are printed.

Grand totals are printed after all data has been processed. As each record is processed, items are added to appropriate totals. When end-of-file is detected, both page totals (if any) and grand totals should be printed. The last page is usually not a full page of data; therefore, page totals would not have been printed at the usual point in the program.

8.3   DATE, DAY, AND TIME

COBOL provides a mechanism by which the program can access the date maintained by the operating system. This date is commonly used on reports to indicate the date on which the report is produced. A form of the ACCEPT statement is used for this purpose. A general form for this statement is

```
ACCEPT data-name FROM  ⎰ DATE ⎱
                       ⎱ DAY  ⎰
                       ⎰ TIME ⎱
```

The DATE option places the current date in the data-name, the DAY option places the current year and day of the year in data-name, and the TIME option places the current time in data-name. Each of these options will be described in more detail in this section.

The format for the value returned using the DATE option is a six-digit numeric item of the form

yymmdd

The first two digits specify the year, the next two digits specify the month, and the last two digits specify the day. The data item specified by the data-name must be a six-character numeric or alphanumeric field.

──────── Example ────────

Suppose FLDA is defined as PIC 9(6), and suppose that today's date is August 18, 1990. After execution of the statement

```
ACCEPT FLDA FROM DATE
```

the content of FLDA would be

```
9 0 0 8 1 8
```

FLDA PIC 9(6)

In order to access the individual parts of the date, you may wish to define a group data item composed of three two-digit fields. The ACCEPT statement would specify the group item, but the program could then process the individual numeric items as needed.

Example

Suppose DATE-FOR-REPORT is defined as follows

```
01   DATE-FOR-REPORT.
     02 YEAR-DFR    PIC 99.
     02 MONTH-DFR   PIC 99.
     02 DAY-DFR     PIC 99.
```

After execution of the statement

```
ACCEPT DATE-FOR-REPORT FROM DATE
```

the program could then execute the following MOVE statements:

```
MOVE MONTH-DFR TO . . .
MOVE DAY-DFR TO . . .
MOVE YEAR-DFR TO . . .
```

where the destination for the data will be appropriate fields on the heading line for a report. Note that it is usually not appropriate to use the data accessed by the ACCEPT/FROM DATE statement directly because the year is placed first in the string of characters, contrary to the usual date format *mm/dd/yy*.

The ACCEPT/FROM DATE is probably the most often used version of this statement, but the other two options are also used occasionally. The statement ACCEPT/FROM DAY returns a five-digit numeric value of the form

> *yyddd*

where the first two digits (*yy*) represent the year and the next three digits (*ddd*) represent the day of the year (sometimes called the Julian date). In this notation, the number representing January 1 is 001, and the number representing December 31 is 365 (or 366 during leap years); other dates have values between 001 and 365.

Example

Suppose FLDB is defined as PIC 9(5), and suppose the statement

```
ACCEPT FLDB FROM DAY
```

is executed. If the current date is August 18, 1990, the value of FLDB will be

```
9 0 2 3 0
```

FLDB PIC 9(5)

This value indicates that August 18 is the 230th day of the year 1990.

The TIME option of the ACCEPT statement allows the program to access the current value of the system clock. The value returned is eight digits in length, with the value expressed in the form

hhmmssff

where *hh* represents the hour (on a 24-hour clock basis), *mm* represents the minutes, *ss* represents seconds, and *ff* represents fractional parts of seconds. (In some systems that do not maintain the correct time in fractions of a second, the value of *ff* may always be 00.)

─────────────── Example ───────────────

Suppose FLDC is described as PIC 9(8), and suppose the statement

```
ACCEPT FLDC FROM TIME
```

is executed. If the current time is 2:35 P.M., the value returned in FLDC would be

| 1 | 4 | 3 | 5 | 0 | 0 | 0 | 0 |

FLDC PIC 9(8)

The first two digits represent the hour; the time is 2 P.M., so 2 o'clock is hour 14. (Three o'clock is hour 15, 4 o'clock is hour 16, and so forth.) The next two digits represent the minutes—35 in this case. The next four digits represent seconds and fractional parts of a second. During the execution of a program, these values are unlikely to be 0000 as shown above. For example, if the time is 17.58 seconds past 2:35 P.M., the value of FLDC would be

| 1 | 4 | 3 | 5 | 1 | 7 | 5 | 8 |

FLDC PIC 9(8)

You can use the ACCEPT/FROM TIME statement to provide what is technically called a "time stamp" for reports; that is, you can include the time that the report was run (in addition to the date). This information may be of value if several versions of a report are produced during a given day.

8.4 PROGRAM EXAMPLE

Problem Statement

Management of the ABC Company desires a report showing each employee's name, employee number, department, and salary. The report should have appropriate headings on each page, and pages should be numbered. Each page should list the total of the salaries of the employees on that page; the final page should list the total number of employees and the total salaries of all employees. The data for the required report is contained in the file EMPLOYEE-FILE, which contains records in alphabetic sequence for all employees of the company. A printer spacing chart for the required report is shown in Figure 8.1.

Figure 8.1   Printer spacing chart for employee list

NOTES		0	1	2	3	4	5	6	7
		1234567890	1234567890	1234567890	1234567890	1234567890	1234567890	1234567890	1234567890
Major Heading	1	ZZ/ZZ/99		ABC COMPANY EMPLOYEE REPORT					PAGE ZZZ
	2								
Subheading	3	NAME			EMPLOYEE NUMBER		DEPARTMENT		SALARY
	4								
Detail Line	5	X XXXXXXXXXXXXXXXXX			999999999		XXX		$ZZZ,ZZZ
	6								
Summary Line	7				ZZZ9		EMPLOYEES		$$B,$$B,$$B**
	8								
Page Total Line	9						PAGE TOTAL		$$$B,$$B*
	10								
	11								
	12								
	13								
	14								
	15								
	16								
	17								
	18								
	19								
	20								

Problem Analysis

This problem requires the following major report features:

> Report heading at top of each page
> Report date
> Page number
> Column heading on each page
> Page total for salary
> Grand total for salary and number of employees

An appropriate technique to control pagination and page numbers is line counting. This technique requires a field `LINE-COUNT` defined in `WORKING-STORAGE` and initialized to value zero. Additional data items in `WORKING-STORAGE` are required for the page total (`PAGE-TOTAL`), the grand total of salaries (`SALARY-TOTAL`), and the number of employees (`NUMBER-OF-EMPLOYEES`). All of these fields are used as accumulators and, therefore, must be initialized to zero. An additional field is required for the actual page number (`PAGE-COUNT`). This item will be initialized to value 0 and incremented by 1 each time a page heading is written. We will assume that there are 15 lines of print per page, a constant coded into `WORKING-STORAGE` using the data name `LINES-PER-PAGE`. (This practice enables the report to be adapted readily to pages of different length without changing any code in the `PROCEDURE DIVISION`.)

The program must produce page headings before any data has been processed. Thereafter, before any output operation is performed, the content of `LINE-COUNT` is compared to `LINES-PER-PAGE`. If the content of `LINE-COUNT` is greater than `LINES-PER-PAGE`, the page is full of data and new page headings must be printed before the current output can be printed. The page-heading procedure must increment `PAGE-COUNT`, write the page headings, and reinitialize `LINE-COUNT` to the number of lines used in producing the page headings. In this case three lines are used. After output is written, the value of `LINE-COUNT` must be incremented by the number of lines used. A preliminary plan for the desired program showing the technique required for pagination is shown in Figure 8.2.

Figure 8.2   Preliminary plan for employee list program

Main control

    Open files
    Get report date
    Do Write headings
    Read employee file
    Do Process data until end of file
    Close files
    Stop

Process data

    If line count > lines per page
        Do Write headings
    End If
    Write detail line
    Add 1 to line count
    Read employee file

Write headings

    Add 1 to page count
    Write report heading
    Write column heading
    Move 3 to line count

Note that in this preliminary plan there is no provision for page totals or grand totals. Page totals must be written after a page break is detected (i.e., when the program determines that a page is full) and before page headings for a new page are produced. After the page total is written, the accumulator PAGE-TOTAL must be reinitialized to zero for the next page. The processing of each record must include adding the salary to the accumulator's PAGE-TOTAL and SALARY-TOTAL and adding 1 to the counter NUMBER-OF-EMPLOYEES. The revised plan for this program, shown in Figure 8.3, includes the logic required for these features.

Figure 8.3   Final plan for employee list program

Main control

    Open files
    Get report date
    Do Write headings
    Read employee file
    Do Process data until end of file
    Do Write page total
    Write summary line
    Close files
    Stop

Process data

    If line count > lines per page
        Do Write page total
        Do Write headings
    End If
    Add salary to total salary
    Add 1 to number employees
    Add salary to page total
    Write detail line
    Add 1 to line count
    Read employee file

Write headings

    Add 1 to page count
    Write report heading
    Write column heading
    Move 3 to line count

Write page total

    Write page total line
    Move 0 to page total

Problem Solution

The program for this problem is shown in Program 8a; the structure diagram is shown in Figure 8.4. A sample execution of the program is shown in Figure 8.5. Note the way in which the requirements for the report are implemented in the program. The requirement that a heading be produced at the top of each page is handled by performing 9000-WRITE-HEADINGS from 2000-INITIALIZE-REPORT (see line 120) to produce the heading at the top of the first page. Page headings at the top of succeeding pages are produced by checking the value of LINE-COUNT in 2100-PROCESS-DATA (see lines 139–141). When the value of LINE-COUNT exceeds LINES-PER-PAGE, headings are written again. Page numbers are implemented using the counter PAGE-COUNT, which is initialized to zero at line 48 and incremented each time headings are written at line 180. The page totals are implemented using an accumulator PAGE-TOTAL, which is initialized to zero at line 52, incremented at line 165, printed each time a new page heading is produced (see line 193), and reinitialized to zero after it is printed (line 195). The grand totals are implemented using the accumulator SALARY-TOTAL, which is initialized to zero at line 51, and the counter NUMBER-OF-EMPLOYEES, which is initialized to zero at line 50. As each record is processed, the value of SALARY-ER is added to SALARY-TOTAL (line 164) and NUMBER-OF-EMPLOYEES is incremented (line 163). The fields are printed after end-of-file has been reached (see line 150).

The date requirement is handled by defining REPORT-DATE (lines 58-61) as a group item. The value of this item is obtained by the ACCEPT/FROM DATE statement at line 130. Each part of the date is then moved to the appropriate field in MAIN-HEADING at lines 131 through 133 as part of 2000-INITIALIZE-REPORT.

8.5 ADDITIONAL OUTPUT TECHNIQUES

The WRITE statement for the printer has some powerful options that are often useful in writing reports. A general form of the WRITE statement is shown in Figure 8.6.

We have already discussed and illustrated the use of the integer and PAGE options. The use of data-name-2 in the BEFORE/AFTER clause will cause the system to advance a number of lines equal to the value of data-name-2. For example, the statements

```
MOVE 3 TO SPACING-COUNT.
WRITE PRINT-REC AFTER ADVANCING SPACING-COUNT.
```

are equivalent to

```
WRITE PRINT-REC AFTER ADVANCING 3.
```

The use of a data-name in the BEFORE/AFTER clause gives the program considerable flexibility in the spacing of output lines without requiring extra output statements.

The flow of paper through some printers is controlled by a carriage control tape (Fig. 8.7). A carriage control tape is glued into a continuous loop and placed inside the printer mechanism where a special device senses holes punched in various positions of the tape. A carriage control tape is divided into twelve channels. A hole punched in channel 1 typically denotes the top of a page of print; a hole punched in channel 12 denotes

Program 8a

```
 1 IDENTIFICATION DIVISION.
 2
 3 PROGRAM-ID. EMPLOYEE-LIST-PRO8A.
 4 AUTHOR. HORN.
 5
 6 ENVIRONMENT DIVISION.
 7
 8 CONFIGURATION SECTION.
 9
10 SOURCE-COMPUTER.
11 OBJECT-COMPUTER.
12
13 INPUT-OUTPUT SECTION.
14
15 FILE-CONTROL.
16
17     SELECT EMPLOYEE-FILE ASSIGN TO DISK.
18
19     SELECT REPORT-FILE ASSIGN TO PRINTER.
20
21 DATA DIVISION.
22
23 FILE SECTION.
24
25 FD  EMPLOYEE-FILE
26     LABEL RECORDS ARE STANDARD
27     DATA RECORD IS EMPLOYEE-RECORD.
28
29 01  EMPLOYEE-RECORD.
30     02 NAME-ER                PIC X(16).
31     02 EMPLOYEE-NUMBER-ER      PIC 9(9).
32     02 DEPARTMENT-ER           PIC X(3).
33     02 SALARY-ER               PIC 9(6).
34     02 FILLER                  PIC X(46).
35
36 FD  REPORT-FILE
37     LABEL RECORDS ARE OMITTED
38     DATA RECORD IS REPORT-RECORD.
39
40 01  REPORT-RECORD              PIC X(132).
41
42 WORKING-STORAGE SECTION.
43
44 01  CONSTANTS.
45     03 LINES-PER-PAGE          PIC 99 VALUE 15.
46
47 01  ACCUMULATED-TOTALS.
48     03 PAGE-COUNT              PIC 999  VALUE ZERO.
49     03 LINE-COUNT              PIC 999  VALUE ZERO.
50     03 NUMBER-OF-EMPLOYEES     PIC 999  VALUE ZERO.
51     03 SALARY-TOTAL            PIC 9(8) VALUE ZERO.
52     03 PAGE-TOTAL              PIC 9(6) VALUE ZERO.
53
54 01  FLAGS.
55     02 EOF-FLAG                PIC X(3) VALUE "NO".
56        88 END-OF-FILE       VALUE "YES".
57
```

Program 8a *(continued)*

```
58 01   REPORT-DATE.
59       02 YEAR-RD                PIC 99.
60       02 MONTH-RD               PIC 99.
61       02 DAY-RD                 PIC 99.
62
63 01   MAJOR-HEADING.
64       02 FILLER                 PIC X(4)  VALUE SPACES.
65       02 MONTH-MH               PIC ZZ.
66       02 FILLER                 PIC X     VALUE "/".
67       02 DAY-MH                 PIC ZZ.
68       02 FILLER                 PIC X     VALUE "/".
69       02 YEAR-MH                PIC 99.
70       02 FILLER                 PIC X(11) VALUE SPACES.
71       02 FILLER                 PIC X(11) VALUE "ABC COMPANY".
72       02 FILLER                 PIC X     VALUE SPACE.
73       02 FILLER                 PIC X(8)  VALUE "EMPLOYEE".
74       02 FILLER                 PIC X     VALUE SPACE.
75       02 FILLER                 PIC X(6)  VALUE "REPORT".
76       02 FILLER                 PIC X(18) VALUE SPACES.
77       02 FILLER                 PIC X(5)  VALUE "PAGE ".
78       02 PAGE-NUMBER-MH         PIC ZZZ.
79
80 01   SUBHEADING.
81       02 FILLER         PIC X     VALUE SPACES.
82       02 FILLER         PIC X(5)  VALUE "NAME".
83       02 FILLER         PIC X(23) VALUE SPACES.
84       02 FILLER         PIC X(15) VALUE "EMPLOYEE NUMBER".
85       02 FILLER         PIC X(8)  VALUE SPACES.
86       02 FILLER         PIC X(10) VALUE "DEPARTMENT".
87       02 FILLER         PIC X(8)  VALUE SPACES.
88       02 FILLER         PIC X(6)  VALUE "SALARY".
89
90 01   DETAIL-LINE.
91       02 FILLER                 PIC X     VALUE SPACE.
92       02 NAME-DL                PIC X(16).
93       02 FILLER                 PIC X(14) VALUE SPACES.
94       02 EMPLOYEE-NUMBER-DL     PIC 9(9).
95       02 FILLER                 PIC X(15) VALUE SPACES.
96       02 DEPARTMENT-DL          PIC X(3).
97       02 FILLER                 PIC X(10) VALUE SPACES.
98       02 SALARY-DL              PIC $ZZZ,ZZZ.
99
100 01  SUMMARY-LINE.
101      02 FILLER                 PIC X(39) VALUE SPACES.
102      02 NUMBER-OF-EMPLOYEES-SL PIC ZZZ9.
103      02 FILLER                 PIC X(5)  VALUE SPACES.
104      02 FILLER                 PIC X(9)  VALUE "EMPLOYEES".
105      02 FILLER                 PIC X(7)  VALUE SPACES.
106      02 SALARY-TOTAL-SL        PIC $$$,$$$,$$$.
107      02 FILLER                 PIC XX    VALUE "**".
108
109 01  PAGE-TOTAL-LINE.
110      02 FILLER                 PIC X(54) VALUE SPACES.
111      02 FILLER                 PIC X(10) VALUE "PAGE TOTAL".
112      02 FILLER                 PIC X(4)  VALUE SPACES.
113      02 PAGE-TOTAL-PTL         PIC $$$$,$$$.
114      02 FILLER                 PIC X     VALUE "*".
```

```
115
116 PROCEDURE DIVISION.
117
118 1000-MAIN-CONTROL.
119
120     PERFORM 2000-INITIALIZE-REPORT.
121     PERFORM 2100-PROCESS-DATA
122             UNTIL END-OF-FILE.
123     PERFORM 2200-TERMINATE-REPORT.
124     STOP RUN.
125
126 2000-INITIALIZE-REPORT.
127
128     OPEN INPUT EMPLOYEE-FILE
129          OUTPUT REPORT-FILE.
130     ACCEPT REPORT-DATE FROM DATE.
131     MOVE MONTH-RD TO MONTH-MH.
132     MOVE DAY-RD   TO DAY-MH.
133     MOVE YEAR-RD  TO YEAR-MH.
134     PERFORM 9000-WRITE-HEADINGS.
135     PERFORM 9100-READ-EMPLOYEE-FILE.
136
137 2100-PROCESS-DATA.
138
139     IF LINE-COUNT > LINES-PER-PAGE
140         PERFORM 9200-WRITE-PAGE-TOTAL
141         PERFORM 9000-WRITE-HEADINGS.
142     PERFORM 3000-MOVE-INPUT-FIELDS.
143     PERFORM 3100-DO-CALCULATIONS.
144     PERFORM 3200-WRITE-DETAIL-LINE.
145     PERFORM 9100-READ-EMPLOYEE-FILE.
146
147 2200-TERMINATE-REPORT.
148
149     PERFORM 9200-WRITE-PAGE-TOTAL.
150     PERFORM 3300-WRITE-SUMMARY-LINE.
151     CLOSE EMPLOYEE-FILE
152           REPORT-FILE.
153
154 3000-MOVE-INPUT-FIELDS.
155
156     MOVE NAME-ER             TO NAME-DL.
157     MOVE EMPLOYEE-NUMBER-ER TO EMPLOYEE-NUMBER-DL.
158     MOVE SALARY-ER          TO SALARY-DL.
159     MOVE DEPARTMENT-ER      TO DEPARTMENT-DL.
160
161 3100-DO-CALCULATIONS.
162
163     ADD 1 TO NUMBER-OF-EMPLOYEES.
164     ADD SALARY-ER TO SALARY-TOTAL.
165     ADD SALARY-ER TO PAGE-TOTAL.
166
167 3200-WRITE-DETAIL-LINE.
168
169     WRITE REPORT-RECORD FROM DETAIL-LINE AFTER 2 LINES.
170     ADD 2 TO LINE-COUNT.
171
```

Program 8a   *(concluded)*

```
172 3300-WRITE-SUMMARY-LINE.
173
174     MOVE NUMBER-OF-EMPLOYEES     TO NUMBER-OF-EMPLOYEES-SL.
175     MOVE SALARY-TOTAL            TO SALARY-TOTAL-SL.
176     WRITE REPORT-RECORD FROM SUMMARY-LINE AFTER 3 LINES.
177
178 9000-WRITE-HEADINGS.
179
180     ADD 1 TO PAGE-COUNT.
181     MOVE PAGE-COUNT TO PAGE-NUMBER-MH.
182     WRITE REPORT-RECORD FROM MAJOR-HEADING AFTER PAGE.
183     WRITE REPORT-RECORD FROM SUBHEADING AFTER 2 LINES.
184     MOVE 3 TO LINE-COUNT.
185
186 9100-READ-EMPLOYEE-FILE.
187
188     READ EMPLOYEE-FILE
189         AT END MOVE "YES" TO EOF-FLAG.
190
191 9200-WRITE-PAGE-TOTAL.
192
193     MOVE PAGE-TOTAL TO PAGE-TOTAL-PTL.
194     WRITE REPORT-RECORD FROM PAGE-TOTAL-LINE AFTER 2.
195     MOVE 0 TO PAGE-TOTAL.
```

Figure 8.4   Structure diagram for Program 8a

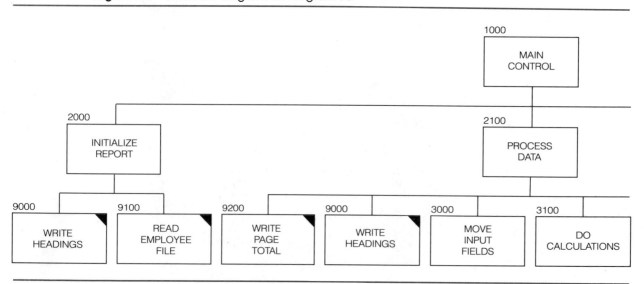

Figure 8.5   Sample execution of Program 8a

```
8/25/90              ABC COMPANY EMPLOYEE REPORT                  PAGE 1

   NAME                     EMPLOYEE NUMBER      DEPARTMENT       SALARY

   JONES JOHN                  77771111             002         $ 40,000
   SMITH MARY                  12222222             002         $ 50,000
   DOE JOHN                    19993333             002         $ 34,000
   BLACK HARVEY                88884444             003         $ 20,000
   WHITE SUE                   15555555             003         $ 45,000
   GREY SAM                    15556666             103         $ 90,000
   GONZALEZ CARLOS             27777777             103         $ 80,000

                                               PAGE TOTAL      $359,000*


8/25/90              ABC COMPANY EMPLOYEE REPORT                  PAGE 2

   NAME                     EMPLOYEE NUMBER      DEPARTMENT       SALARY

   SHEA JOHN                   77770000             111         $ 45,000
   SPADE SAM                   33333333             111         $ 67,000
   CLARK JOHN                  22224444             211         $ 30,000
   HERANDEZ MARIA              55554444             211         $ 80,000
   JONES PATRICIA              45555555             211         $ 50,000

                                               PAGE TOTAL      $272,000*

                                 12 EMPLOYEES                  $631,000**
```

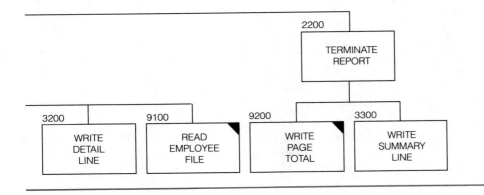

Figure 8.6   General form of the WRITE statement for the printer

```
WRITE record [FROM data-name-1]

 {BEFORE}              {{data-name-2}          [LINE ]
 {     } ADVANCING     {{integer   }           [LINES]
 {AFTER }              {                }
                       {{mnemonic-name}
                       {{PAGE         }
```

the bottom of a page. Typically, other channels are punched to correspond to positions on special preprinted forms (such as checks, invoices, or statements) that will be used for output operations. When the PAGE option is used, the printer begins spacing paper forward until a Channel 1 punch is sensed on the carriage control tape.

By using the mnemonic option in the BEFORE/AFTER clause, the program can execute an advance to any desired channel punch. The mnemonic must be declared in the SPECIAL-NAMES paragraph of the ENVIRONMENT DIVISION. The general form of this paragraph is shown in Figure 8.8.

Figure 8.8   General form of the SPECIAL-NAMES entry

```
SPECIAL-NAMES.
       function-name IS mnemonic-name. . .
```

The purpose of the mnemonic-name is to assign a meaningful name to the technical function to be performed. Mnemonic-names are governed by the same rules as other COBOL data-names; however, mnemonic-names should be as descriptive as possible of the function to be performed. Typical mnemonic-names would be

```
TOP-OF-PAGE
BOTTOM-OF-PAGE
BEGINNING-OF-INVOICE-ITEMS
```

The exact form taken by function-names varies somewhat from one system to another. The following form is quite common:

Function-name	Meaning
C01	Channel 1
C02	Channel 2
C03	Channel 3
.	.
.	.
.	.
C12	Channel 12

For example, to associate the mnemonic TO-TOP-OF-PAGE with a channel 1 punch, TO-BEGINNING-OF-ADDRESS with a channel 3 punch, and TO-

Figure 8.7   Carriage control tape

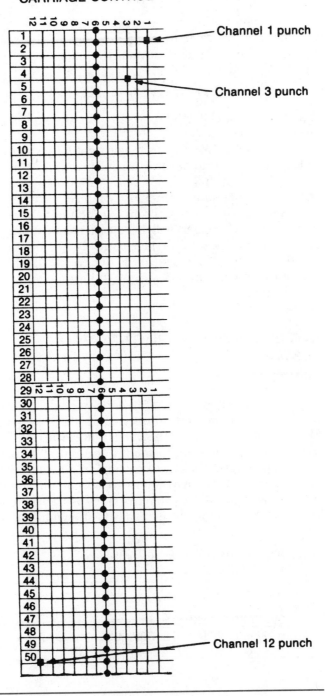

BOTTOM-OF-PAGE with a channel 12 punch, the following SPECIAL-NAMES entry would be used:

```
SPECIAL-NAMES.
    C01 IS TO-TOP-OF-PAGE
    C03 IS TO-BEGINNING-OF-ADDRESS
    C12 IS TO-BOTTOM-OF-PAGE.
```

The following WRITE statement could then be used to write a record at the top of a page:

```
WRITE PRINT-REC AFTER ADVANCING TO-TOP-OF-PAGE.
```

A skip to channel 1 will be executed by the above sentence before writing commences. In order to place a record in the portion of the page designated by the channel 3 punch, the following WRITE statement would be used:

```
WRITE PRINT-REC AFTER ADVANCING TO-BEGINNING-OF-ADDRESS.
```

A skip to channel 3 will be executed by the preceding sentence before writing commences.

WARNING: Don't rush to your computer center to try out this useful output feature. Find out first if your printer has a carriage control tape and if so, what is on that tape. If a program executes a skip to a channel which has no corresponding punch on whatever carriage control tape happens to be mounted when the program is executed, the result may be "run away" paper. That is, paper will be ejected continuously while the printer is searching the specific carriage control tape for the control punch. For this reason, the use of this feature is not encouraged in most student oriented computing environments, although it can be quite valuable to the professional programmer.

8.6 INTERNATIONAL APPLICATIONS FEATURES

Reports must often be generated for use in countries which have different conventions for writing numbers and different symbols for currency. The SPECIAL-NAMES entry of the CONFIGURATION SECTION of the ENVIRONMENT DIVISION can be used to modify the usual symbols used to denote the decimal point and the currency symbol. This feature is useful in data processing applications involving European and other currencies which do not use the symbol "$" for currency and/or the period for the decimal point. The general form for these entries is shown in Figure 8.9.

Figure 8.9 General form of SPECIAL-NAMES entries for international applications

```
SPECIAL-NAMES.
     [CURRENCY SIGN IS literal]
     [DECIMAL-POINT IS COMMA].
```

The DECIMAL-POINT IS COMMA clause causes the role of the comma and the period to be interchanged in specifying PICTUREs in the DATA DIVISION. This is required for certain European countries in which a value such as 12,345,678.90 would be written as 12.345.678,90. If the DECIMAL-POINT IS COMMA clause is used, PICTUREs such as 99.999.999,99 will cause the period to be used to denote groups of digits and the comma to be inserted as a decimal point.

The CURRENCY SIGN IS clause enables the use of the specified literal in the DATA DIVISION instead of the dollar sign. For example, to enable use of the pound sign "£" as a currency symbol the entry

    CURRENCY SIGN IS "£"

would be used. With this entry, PICTURE codes such as

    £££,£££.99 and £Z,ZZZ,ZZZ.99

may be used in the DATA DIVISION. The system will use the specified symbol in exactly the same way as a dollar sign for editing data. The literal used in the CURRENCY SIGN clause may be any single character except 0 through 9, A, B, C, D, L, P, R, S, V, X, Z, *, +, (, −,), /, =, comma, period, quotation mark, semicolon, or space.

8.7 CONTROL BREAKS

Often, subtotals are required for related subsets of data within a report. For example, suppose the data processed by Program 8a has been sorted into order by department number. Program 8b then processes this data and generates a report showing subtotals for each department.

The basic problem encountered in writing such a program is the recognition of changes within a data field called **control breaks**. A control break occurs, for example, when a data record is read for an employee in a department whose number differs from the preceding employee's department number. At this point, the program must produce the totals for the preceding department before processing the current data record. The technique used to detect a break requires a holding location. The content of this location is compared with the key field from the current record when each record is processed. The **key field** is the field used to organize the file; for example, in Program 8b the key field is the department identifier. An example of data showing the location of control breaks is shown in Figure 8.10.

If the two values (content of holding location and key field) are the same, the current record belongs to the same group as the previous record. If the two values differ, the current record belongs to a different group, and a control break is recognized. The control break processing routine, in

Figure 8.10   Control break example

```
JONES JOHN         77771111 002 040000
SMITH MARY         12222222 002 050000
DOE JOHN           19993333 002 034000
BLACK HARVEY       88884444 003 020000
WHITE SUE          15555555 003 045000
GREY SAM           15556666 103 090000
GONZALEZ CARLOS    27777777 103 080000
SHEA JOHN          77770000 111 045000
SPADE SAM          33333333 111 067000
CLARK JOHN         22224444 211 030000
HERNANDEZ MARIA    55554444 211 080000
JONES PATRICIA     45555555 211 050000
```

Control break points

```
 1 IDENTIFICATION DIVISION.
 2
 3 PROGRAM-ID. DEPARTMENT-REPORT-PRO8B.
 4 AUTHOR. HORN.
 5
 6 ENVIRONMENT DIVISION.
 7
 8 CONFIGURATION SECTION.
 9
10 SOURCE-COMPUTER.
11 OBJECT-COMPUTER.
12
13 INPUT-OUTPUT SECTION.
14
15 FILE-CONTROL.
16
17     SELECT EMPLOYEE-FILE ASSIGN TO DISK.
18
19     SELECT REPORT-FILE  ASSIGN TO PRINTER.
20
21 DATA DIVISION.
22
23 FILE SECTION.
24
25 FD   EMPLOYEE-FILE
26      LABEL RECORDS ARE STANDARD
27      DATA RECORD IS EMPLOYEE-RECORD.
28
29 01   EMPLOYEE-RECORD.
30      02 NAME-ER                PIC X(16).
31      02 EMPLOYEE-NUMBER-ER      PIC 9(9).
32      02 DEPARTMENT-ER           PIC X(3).
33      02 SALARY-ER               PIC 9(6).
34      02 FILLER                  PIC X(46).
35
36 FD   REPORT-FILE
37      LABEL RECORDS ARE OMITTED
38      DATA RECORD IS REPORT-RECORD.
39
40 01   REPORT-RECORD             PIC X(132).
41
42 WORKING-STORAGE SECTION.
43
44 01   CONSTANTS.
45      02 LINES-PER-PAGE          PIC 99 VALUE 16.
46
47 01   ACCUMULATED-TOTALS.
48      03 PAGE-COUNT              PIC 999   VALUE ZERO.
49      03 LINE-COUNT              PIC 99    VALUE 17.
50      03 NUMBER-OF-EMPLOYEES     PIC 999   VALUE ZERO.
51      03 SALARY-TOTAL            PIC 9(8)  VALUE ZERO.
52      03 DEPT-TOTAL-SALARY       PIC 9(8)  VALUE ZERO.
53      03 DEPARTMENT-NUMBER-OF-EMPLOYEES PIC 99 VALUE ZERO.
54
55 01   HOLD-FIELD.
56      03 HOLD-DEPARTMENT         PIC X(3) VALUE SPACES.
57
```

Program 8b   *(continued)*

```
58 01   FLAGS.
59       03 EOF-FLAG                    PIC X(3) VALUE "NO".
60          88 END-OF-FILE                 VALUE "YES".
61
62 01   MAJOR-HEADING.
63       02 FILLER                      PIC X(14) VALUE SPACES.
64       02 FILLER                      PIC X(4)  VALUE "ABC ".
65       02 FILLER                      PIC X(8)  VALUE "COMPANY ".
66       02 FILLER                      PIC X(9)  VALUE "EMPLOYEE ".
67       02 FILLER                      PIC X(7)  VALUE "REPORT ".
68       02 FILLER                      PIC X(13) VALUE "BY DEPARTMENT".
69       02 FILLER                      PIC X(14) VALUE SPACES.
70       02 FILLER                      PIC X(5)  VALUE "PAGE ".
71       02 PAGE-COUNTER-MH             PIC ZZZ.
72
73 01   SUBHEADING.
74       02 FILLER                      PIC X     VALUE SPACES.
75       02 FILLER                      PIC X(10) VALUE "DEPARTMENT".
76       02 FILLER                      PIC X(3)  VALUE SPACES.
77       02 FILLER                      PIC X(4)  VALUE "NAME".
78       02 FILLER                      PIC X(24) VALUE SPACES.
79       02 FILLER                      PIC X(15) VALUE
80          "EMPLOYEE NUMBER".
81       02 FILLER                      PIC X(14) VALUE SPACES.
82       02 FILLER                      PIC X(6)  VALUE "SALARY".
83
84 01   DETAIL-LINE.
85       02 FILLER                      PIC X(4)  VALUE SPACES.
86       02 DEPARTMENT-DL               PIC X(3).
87       02 FILLER                      PIC X(7)  VALUE SPACES.
88       02 NAME-DL                     PIC X(16).
89       02 FILLER                      PIC X(14) VALUE SPACES.
90       02 EMPLOYEE-NUMBER-DL          PIC 9(9).
91       02 FILLER                      PIC X(16) VALUE SPACES.
92       02 SALARY-DL                   PIC $ZZZ,ZZZ.
93
94 01   DEPARTMENT-TOTAL-LINE.
95       02 FILLER                      PIC X(25) VALUE SPACES.
96       02 FILLER                      PIC X(16) VALUE
97          "DEPARTMENT TOTAL".
98       02 FILLER                      PIC X(8)  VALUE SPACES.
99       02 NUMBER-OF-EMPLOYEES-DTL PIC Z9.
100      02 FILLER                      PIC X(1) VALUE SPACES.
101      02 FILLER                      PIC X(9) VALUE "EMPLOYEES".
102      02 FILLER                      PIC X(5) VALUE SPACES.
103      02 TOTAL-SALARY-DTL            PIC $$$,$$$,$$$.
104      02 FILLER                      PIC X     VALUE "*".
105
106 01  SUMMARY-LINE.
107      02 FILLER                      PIC X(25) VALUE SPACES.
108      02 FILLER                      PIC X(13) VALUE "COMPANY TOTAL".
109      02 FILLER                      PIC X(9)  VALUE SPACES.
110      02 NUMBER-OF-EMPLOYEES-SL PIC ZZZ9.
111      02 FILLER                      PIC X(1)  VALUE SPACES.
112      02 FILLER                      PIC X(9)  VALUE "EMPLOYEES".
113      02 FILLER                      PIC X(5)  VALUE SPACES.
114      02 SALARY-TOTAL-SL             PIC $$$,$$$,$$$.
115      02 FILLER                      PIC XX    VALUE "**".
```

```
116
117 PROCEDURE DIVISION.
118
119 1000-MAIN-CONTROL.
120
121     PERFORM 2000-INITIALIZE-REPORT.
122     PERFORM 2100-PROCESS-DATA
123             UNTIL END-OF-FILE.
124     PERFORM 2200-TERMINATE-REPORT.
125     STOP RUN.
126
127 2000-INITIALIZE-REPORT.
128
129     OPEN INPUT EMPLOYEE-FILE
130          OUTPUT REPORT-FILE.
131     PERFORM 9000-READ-EMPLOYEE-FILE.
132     MOVE DEPARTMENT-ER TO HOLD-DEPARTMENT.
133
134 2100-PROCESS-DATA.
135
136     IF DEPARTMENT-ER NOT = HOLD-DEPARTMENT
137         PERFORM 9100-DEPARTMENT-BREAK.
138     MOVE NAME-ER            TO NAME-DL.
139     MOVE EMPLOYEE-NUMBER-ER TO EMPLOYEE-NUMBER-DL.
140     MOVE SALARY-ER          TO SALARY-DL.
141     MOVE DEPARTMENT-ER      TO DEPARTMENT-DL.
142     ADD SALARY-ER TO DEPT-TOTAL-SALARY.
143     ADD 1 TO DEPARTMENT-NUMBER-OF-EMPLOYEES.
144     ADD SALARY-ER TO SALARY-TOTAL.
145     ADD 1 TO NUMBER-OF-EMPLOYEES.
146     IF LINE-COUNT > LINES-PER-PAGE
147         PERFORM 9200-WRITE-HEADINGS.
148     WRITE REPORT-RECORD FROM DETAIL-LINE AFTER 1.
149     ADD 1 TO LINE-COUNT.
150     PERFORM 9000-READ-EMPLOYEE-FILE.
151
152 2200-TERMINATE-REPORT.
153
154     PERFORM 9100-DEPARTMENT-BREAK.
155     PERFORM 3000-WRITE-SUMMARY-LINE.
156     CLOSE EMPLOYEE-FILE
157           REPORT-FILE.
158
159 3000-WRITE-SUMMARY-LINE.
160
161     MOVE NUMBER-OF-EMPLOYEES TO NUMBER-OF-EMPLOYEES-SL.
162     MOVE SALARY-TOTAL TO SALARY-TOTAL-SL.
163     WRITE REPORT-RECORD FROM SUMMARY-LINE AFTER 3.
164
165 9000-READ-EMPLOYEE-FILE.
166
167     READ EMPLOYEE-FILE
168         AT END MOVE "YES" TO EOF-FLAG.
169
170 9100-DEPARTMENT-BREAK.
171
172     MOVE DEPARTMENT-NUMBER-OF-EMPLOYEES TO
173         NUMBER-OF-EMPLOYEES-DTL.
```

Program 8b *(concluded)*

```
174        MOVE DEPT-TOTAL-SALARY TO TOTAL-SALARY-DTL.
175        IF LINE-COUNT > LINES-PER-PAGE
176            PERFORM 9200-WRITE-HEADINGS.
177        WRITE REPORT-RECORD FROM DEPARTMENT-TOTAL-LINE AFTER 2.
178        MOVE SPACES TO REPORT-RECORD.
179        WRITE REPORT-RECORD AFTER 1.
180        ADD 3 TO LINE-COUNT.
181        MOVE 0 TO DEPARTMENT-NUMBER-OF-EMPLOYEES.
182        MOVE 0 TO DEPT-TOTAL-SALARY.
183        MOVE DEPARTMENT-ER TO HOLD-DEPARTMENT.
184
185 9200-WRITE-HEADINGS.
186
187        ADD 1 TO PAGE-COUNT.
188        MOVE PAGE-COUNT TO PAGE-COUNTER-MH.
189        WRITE REPORT-RECORD FROM MAJOR-HEADING AFTER PAGE.
190        WRITE REPORT-RECORD FROM SUBHEADING AFTER 2.
191        MOVE 3 TO LINE-COUNT.
```

addition to writing the required totals, must move the key field from the current record to the hold field so that the next control break can be determined. A basic problem occurs in using this scheme for the first record processed, as there is no preceding record with which to compare. This problem is solved by moving the value of the key field to the hold field after the first record is read and before it is processed. Of course, this action should be done only for the first record.

When end-of-file is encountered, a group of data records for the last group will have been processed, but no totals will have been produced for that group. It is therefore necessary to recognize a control break after end-of-file has been reached. This procedure is summarized in the pseudocode shown in Figure 8.11.

Figure 8.11 Generalized procedure for control break program

Main control

    Open files
    Read input file
    Move key field to key field hold
    Do Process data until end of file
    Do Control break
    Close files
    Stop

Process data

    If key field not equal key field hold
        Do Control break
    End If
    Add appropriate data to subtotal
    Do other processing of data
    Write detail record
    Read input file

Figure 8.11 *(concluded)*

Control break

    Write subtotal record
    Move 0 to subtotal
    Move key field to key field hold

8.8 PROGRAM EXAMPLE

Problem Statement

The data file processed by Program 8a has been sorted into sequence by the department identifier. Write a program to list the data records and print the total of salaries and number of employees for each department. The program must also print the grand total of all salaries and the number of employees. Page headings and page numbers are required. The detail lines must be double-spaced. The printer spacing chart for the required report is shown in Figure 8.12.

Problem Analysis

In this problem the key field is the department identifier. All data records for a department will occur in the data file in a continuous group. In order to produce the required department total for salaries and number of employees, we will use a field HOLD-DEPARTMENT, which will be initialized with the content of DEPARTMENT-ER (the key field on the input record). The first step in processing each data record is to compare DEPARTMENT-ER to HOLD-DEPARTMENT. If the two fields are not equal, the department totals that have been accumulated must be written, the accumulators for the department must be reinitialized, and the content of DEPARTMENT-ER must be moved to HOLD-DEPARTMENT. These actions will be grouped together into a procedure that we will call *Department break*.

This program will require accumulators for subtotals of salary and number of employees by department (DEPT-TOTAL-SALARY and DEPARTMENT-NUMBER-OF-EMPLOYEES) and accumulators for the grand total of salaries and number of employees (SALARY-TOTAL and NUMBER-OF-EMPLOYEES).

With these considerations in mind, we can now prepare a preliminary plan for the required program, using the general control break procedure in Figure 8.11 as a model. This preliminary plan is shown in Figure 8.13. The plan does not take into consideration the page headings and page numbers that are required. These requirements will necessitate line counting, so we must define a field LINE-COUNT. An alternate procedure for producing page headings that can be used when page totals are not required is to initialize the line counter to a value indicating that the page is full. In this case, we assume that the page contains 16 lines, so an appropriate initial value of LINE-COUNT would be 17. Using this approach, it is no longer necessary to write page headings as part of the initialization portion of the program. The program simply checks the line counter prior to writing each line of output. If the page is full (LINE-COUNT > 16), the headings are written. Because the value of the line counter has been initialized to indicate a full page, this will cause the headings to be produced prior to writing the first detail line of the report as desired. Thereafter, page headings are written each time the page fills up with data.

Figure 8.12 Printer spacing chart for control break program

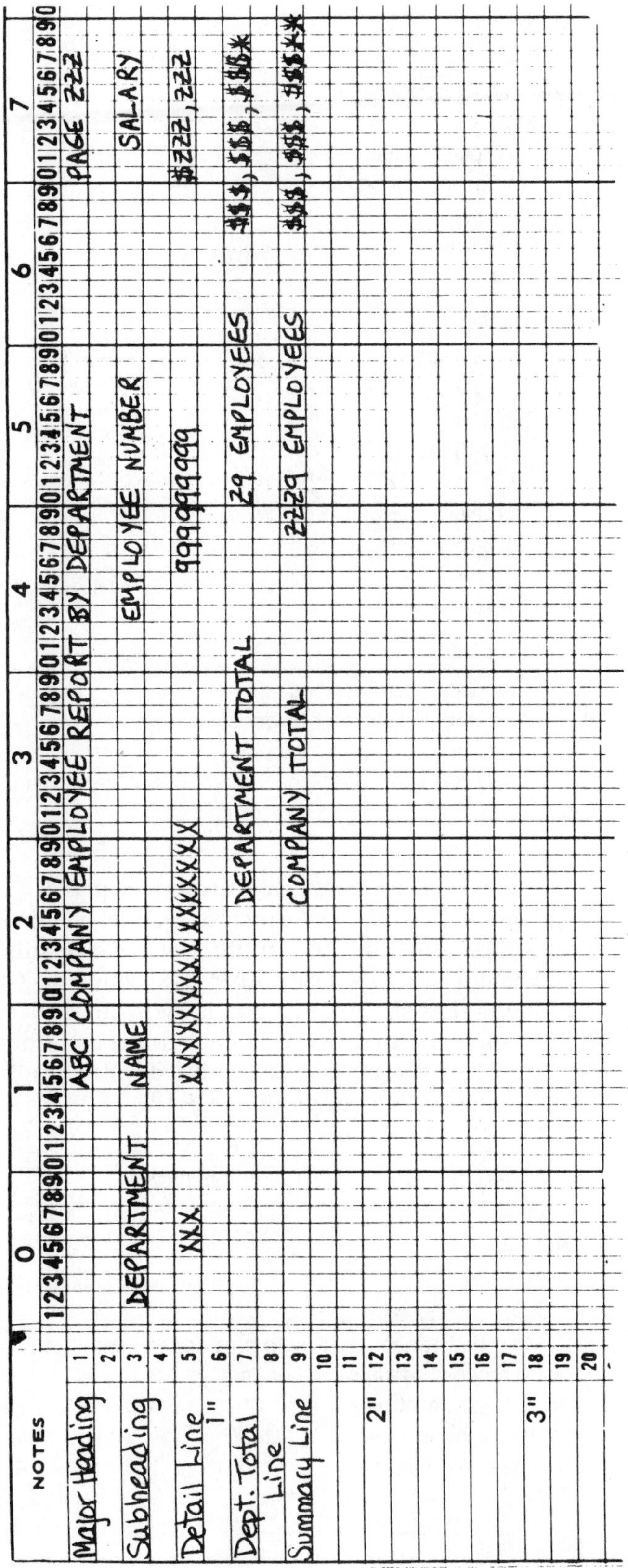

NOTES		0 1234567890	1 1234567890	2 1234567890	3 1234567890	4 1234567890	5 1234567890	6 1234567890	7 1234567890
Major Heading	1		ABC COMPANY EMPLOYEE REPORT BY DEPARTMENT						PAGE ZZZ
	2								
Subheading	3	DEPARTMENT	NAME			EMPLOYEE NUMBER			SALARY
	4								
Detail Line 1"	5	XXX	XXXXXXXXXXXXXXXXXX			999999999			$ZZZ,ZZZ
	6								
Dept. Total Line	7			DEPARTMENT TOTAL		29 EMPLOYEES		$$$,$$$,$$$*	
	8								
Summary Line	9			COMPANY TOTAL		ZZZ9 EMPLOYEES		$$$,$$$,$$$**	
	10								
	11								
2"	12								
	13								
	14								
	15								
	16								
	17								
3"	18								
	19								
	20								

Figure 8.13   Preliminary plan for control break program

Main control

    Open files
    Read employee file
    Move department identifier to hold department
    Do Process data until end-of-file
    Do Department break
    Write summary line
    Close files
    Stop

Process data

    If department identifier not equal hold department
        Do Department break
    End If
    Add 1 to department number of employees
    Add 1 to number of employees
    Add salary to department total salary
    Add salary to salary total
    Write detail line
    Read employee file

Department break

    Write department total line
    Move 0 to department number of employees
    Move 0 to department total salary
    Move department from input record to hold department

It is necessary to check for full page prior to any output; thus, a page-full check should be performed as part of the control break processing as well. This change in the handling of page headings does not affect other requirements of this procedure. The value of the line counter must be incremented each time output is written, and the page number (PAGE-COUNT) must be incremented each time page headings are written. This logic for pagination can now be added to the preliminary plan, resulting in a complete plan shown in Figure 8.14.

Figure 8.14   Completed plan for control break program

Main control

    Open files
    Read employee file
    Move department identifier to hold department
    Do Process data until end of file
    Do Department break
    Write summary line
    Close files
    Stop

Process data

    If department identifier not equal hold department
        Do Department break

Figure 8.14 *(concluded)*

```
        End If
        Add 1 to department number of employees
        Add 1 to number of employees
        Add salary to department total salary
        Add salary to salary total
        If page is full
                Do Write headings
        End If
        Write detail line
        Increment line count
        Read employee file
```

Department break

```
        If page is full
                Do Write headings
        End If
        Write department total line
        Increment line count
        Move 0 to department number of employees
        Move 0 to department total salary
        Move department identifier to hold department
```

Write headings

```
        Add 1 to page count
        Write major heading
        Write column heading
        Initialize line count
```

Problem Solution

The solution to this problem is shown in Program 8b; the structure diagram is shown in Figure 8.15. Output produced by this program for the data in Figure 8.10 is shown in Figure 8.16. The two major concepts illustrated in this program are the detection of control breaks and an alternate way to handle page headings.

Control breaks are detected by using the field HOLD-DEPARTMENT to store the previous value of DEPARTMENT-ER while a new record is read. The value of DEPARTMENT-ER is moved to HOLD-DEPARTMENT as part of the processing of the first record at line 132. The first action taken in processing each record is to compare DEPARTMENT-ER to HOLD-DEPARTMENT (see line 136). When the two fields are not equal, the procedure 9100-DEPARTMENT-BREAK is performed (line 137). This procedure writes the subtotals (line 177), reinitializes the accumulators for the subtotals (lines 181–182), and moves the current value of DEPARTMENT-ER to HOLD-DEPARTMENT (line 183).

Page headings are handled by initializing the value of LINE-COUNT to indicate a full page at line 49. Prior to each output, the program checks for a full page (lines 146 and 175). If the page is full, page headings are written. Because LINE-COUNT indicates that the page is full initially, page headings will be produced in advance of the first detail record. This technique makes it unnecessary to write page headings as part of the initialization procedure.

Figure 8.15   Structure diagram for Program 8b

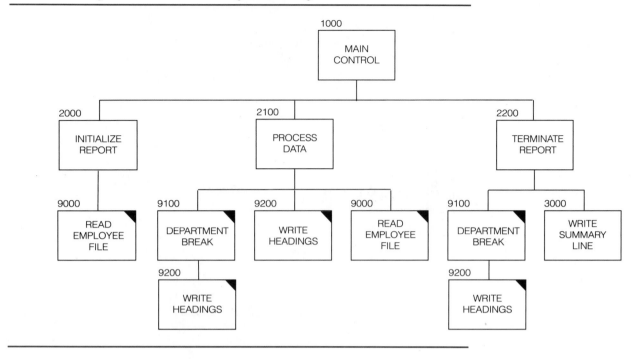

8.9   MULTILEVEL CONTROL BREAKS

Often reports require subtotals for more than one type of subset of the data. For example, suppose the department number of the data processed by Program 8b is coded with the division number of the company as the first digit of the department identifier with the other two digits representing the department within the division. Division totals as well as department totals are produced by Program 8c. This program requires the recognition of two levels of control breaks: a break in department number and a break in division number.

     When two levels of subtotals are required, the file must be in sequence by the major key used as the basis for the largest groups within the file. Records within each major group must be in sequence by the minor key used as the basis for the smaller groups within each major group of data. In the example cited, the major key is the division number, and the minor key is the department number. In processing these records, a change in minor key field values must trigger the production of subtotals for the minor group of records; this change is called a **minor control break**. A change in the major key field values must trigger the production of subtotals for the last minor control group, as well as subtotals for the major subdivision of data. A change in values of the major key field is called a **major control break**. In terms of the division/department data, a change

Figure 8.16   Sample execution of Program 8b

```
              ABC COMPANY EMPLOYEE REPORT BY DEPARTMENT          PAGE   1

DEPARTMENT   NAME                      EMPLOYEE NUMBER          SALARY
   002       JONES JOHN                   77771111           $ 40,000
   002       SMITH MARY                   12222222           $ 50,000
   002       DOE JOHN                     19993333           $ 34,000

                    DEPARTMENT TOTAL      3 EMPLOYEES        $124,000*

   003       BLACK HARVEY                 88884444           $ 20,000
   003       WHITE SUE                    15555555           $ 45,000

                    DEPARTMENT TOTAL      2 EMPLOYEES         $65,000*

   103       GREY SAM                     15556666           $ 90,000
   103       GONZALEZ CARLOS              27777777           $ 80,000

                    DEPARTMENT TOTAL      2 EMPLOYEES        $170,000*



              ABC COMPANY EMPLOYEE REPORT BY DEPARTMENT          PAGE   2

DEPARTMENT   NAME                      EMPLOYEE NUMBER          SALARY
   111       SHEA JOHN                    77770000           $ 45,000
   111       SPADE SAM                    33333333           $ 67,000

                    DEPARTMENT TOTAL      2 EMPLOYEES        $112,000*

   211       CLARK JOHN                   22224444           $ 30,000
   211       HERNANDEZ MARIA              55554444           $ 80,000
   211       JONES PATRICIA               45555555           $ 50,000

                    DEPARTMENT TOTAL      3 EMPLOYEES        $160,000*



                    COMPANY TOTAL        12 EMPLOYEES        $631,000**
```

in department numbers where there is no change in division number must cause the production of totals for a department. A change in division numbers must cause the production of totals for the last department and then the totals for the division. At end-of-file, totals for the minor group, followed by totals for the major group, must be produced. Figure 8.17 shows the location of major and minor control breaks for the data in Figure 8.10.

The recognition of major and minor control breaks requires the use of two hold fields—one for the major key field and one for the minor key field. When the first record is read, both hold fields are initialized. The first step in processing each data record is to check for control breaks. It is imperative that the program check first for the major break and, if a major break has not occurred, check for a minor break. This procedure is summarized in the generalized procedure shown in Figure 8.18.

```
 1 IDENTIFICATION DIVISION.
 2
 3 PROGRAM-ID. DIVISION-DEPT-REPORT-PRO8C.
 4 AUTHOR. HORN.
 5
 6 ENVIRONMENT DIVISION.
 7
 8 CONFIGURATION SECTION.
 9
10 SOURCE-COMPUTER.
11 OBJECT-COMPUTER.
12
13 INPUT-OUTPUT SECTION.
14
15 FILE-CONTROL.
16
17     SELECT EMPLOYEE-FILE ASSIGN TO DISK.
18
19     SELECT REPORT-FILE ASSIGN TO PRINTER.
20
21 DATA DIVISION.
22
23 FILE SECTION.
24
25 FD  EMPLOYEE-FILE
26     LABEL RECORDS ARE STANDARD
27     DATA RECORD IS EMPLOYEE-RECORD.
28
29 01  EMPLOYEE-RECORD.
30     02 NAME-ER                 PIC X(16).
31     02 EMPLOYEE-NUMBER-ER       PIC 9(9).
32     02 DIVISION-ER              PIC X.
33     02 DEPARTMENT-ER            PIC X(2).
34     02 SALARY-ER                PIC 9(6).
35     02 FILLER                   PIC X(45).
36
37 FD  REPORT-FILE
38     LABEL RECORDS ARE OMITTED
39     DATA RECORD IS REPORT-RECORD.
40
41 01  REPORT-RECORD              PIC X(132).
42
43 WORKING-STORAGE SECTION.
44
45 01  CONSTANTS.
46     02 LINES-PER-PAGE           PIC 99 VALUE 26.
47
48 01  COUNTERS.
49     03 PAGE-COUNT               PIC 999 VALUE ZERO.
50     03 LINE-COUNT               PIC 999 VALUE 27.
51        88 PAGE-FULL             VALUE 26 THRU 99.
52
```

Program 8c *(continued)*

```
53 01   ACCUMULATED-TOTALS.
54       03 NUMBER-OF-EMPLOYEES              PIC 999 VALUE ZERO.
55       03 TOTAL-SALARY                     PIC 9(8) VALUE ZERO.
56       03 DEPARTMENT-NUMBER-OF-EMPLOYEES   PIC 99 VALUE ZERO.
57       03 DEPARTMENT-TOTAL-SALARY          PIC 9(8) VALUE ZERO.
58       03 DIVISION-NUMBER-OF-EMPLOYEES     PIC 99 VALUE ZERO.
59       03 DIVISION-TOTAL-SALARY            PIC 9(8) VALUE ZERO.
60
61 01   HOLD-FIELDS.
62       03 HOLD-DEPARTMENT          PIC X(2) VALUE SPACES.
63       03 HOLD-DIVISION            PIC X    VALUE SPACES.
64
65 01   FLAGS.
66       03 EOF-FLAG                 PIC X(3) VALUE "NO".
67          88 END-OF-FILE           VALUE "YES".
68
69 01   MAJOR-HEADING.
70       02 FILLER                   PIC X(14) VALUE SPACES.
71       02 FILLER                   PIC X(3) VALUE "ABC".
72       02 FILLER                   PIC X VALUE SPACES.
73       02 FILLER                   PIC X(7) VALUE "COMPANY".
74       02 FILLER                   PIC X VALUE SPACES.
75       02 FILLER                   PIC X(19) VALUE
76          "DIVISION/DEPARTMENT".
77       02 FILLER                   PIC X VALUE SPACES.
78       02 FILLER                   PIC X(8) VALUE "EMPLOYEE".
79       02 FILLER                   PIC X VALUE SPACES.
80       02 FILLER                   PIC X(6) VALUE "REPORT".
81       02 FILLER                   PIC X(8) VALUE SPACES.
82       02 FILLER                   PIC X(5) VALUE "PAGE ".
83       02 PAGE-COUNTER-MH          PIC ZZZ.
84
85 01   SUBHEADING.
86       02 FILLER                   PIC X VALUE SPACES.
87       02 FILLER                   PIC X(8) VALUE "DIVISION".
88       02 FILLER                   PIC X(11) VALUE " DEPARTMENT".
89       02 FILLER                   PIC X(5) VALUE " NAME".
90       02 FILLER                   PIC X(22) VALUE SPACES.
91       02 FILLER                   PIC X(15) VALUE
92          "EMPLOYEE NUMBER".
93       02 FILLER                   PIC X(9) VALUE SPACES.
94       02 FILLER                   PIC X(6) VALUE "SALARY".
95
96 01   DETAIL-LINE.
97       02 FILLER                   PIC X(4) VALUE SPACES.
98       02 DIVISION-DL              PIC X.
99       02 FILLER                   PIC X(10) VALUE SPACES.
100      02 DEPARTMENT-DL            PIC XX.
101      02 FILLER                   PIC X(4) VALUE SPACES.
102      02 NAME-DL                  PIC X(16).
103      02 FILLER                   PIC X(13) VALUE SPACES.
104      02 EMPLOYEE-NUMBER-DL       PIC 9(9).
105      02 FILLER                   PIC X(10) VALUE SPACES.
106      02 SALARY-DL                PIC $ZZZ,ZZZ.
107
```

Program 8c   *(continued)*

```
108 01   DEPARTMENT-TOTAL-LINE.
109        02 FILLER                  PIC X(13) VALUE SPACES.
110        02 FILLER                  PIC X(13) VALUE
111           "* DEPARTMENT ".
112        02 DEPARTMENT-DTL          PIC XX.
113        02 FILLER                  PIC X(6)  VALUE
114           " TOTAL".
115        02 FILLER                  PIC X(11) VALUE SPACES.
116        02 NUMBER-OF-EMPLOYEES-DTL PIC Z9.
117        02 FILLER                  PIC X(1) VALUE SPACES.
118        02 FILLER                  PIC X(9) VALUE "EMPLOYEES".
119        02 FILLER                  PIC X(9) VALUE SPACES.
120        02 TOTAL-SALARY-DTL        PIC $$$,$$$,$$$.
121        02 FILLER                  PIC X VALUE "*".
122
123 01   DIVISION-TOTAL-LINE.
124        02 FILLER                  PIC X(12) VALUE SPACES.
125        02 FILLER                  PIC X(12) VALUE
126           "** DIVISION ".
127        02 DIVISION-DVTL            PIC X.
128        02 FILLER                  PIC X(6) VALUE " TOTAL".
129        02 FILLER                  PIC X(14) VALUE SPACES.
130        02 NUMBER-OF-EMPLOYEES-DVTL PIC Z9.
131        02 FILLER                  PIC X VALUE SPACES.
132        02 FILLER                  PIC X(9) VALUE "EMPLOYEES".
133        02 FILLER                  PIC X(9) VALUE SPACES.
134        02 TOTAL-SALARY-DVTL       PIC $$$,$$$,$$$.
135        02 FILLER                  PIC XX VALUE "**".
136
137 01   SUMMARY-LINE.
138        02 FILLER                  PIC X(11) VALUE SPACES.
139        02 FILLER                  PIC X(17) VALUE
140           "*** COMPANY TOTAL".
141        02 FILLER                  PIC X(15) VALUE SPACES.
142        02 NUMBER-OF-EMPLOYEES-SL  PIC ZZZ9.
143        02 FILLER                  PIC X VALUE SPACES.
144        02 FILLER                  PIC X(9) VALUE "EMPLOYEES".
145        02 FILLER                  PIC X(9) VALUE SPACES.
146        02 SALARY-TOTAL-SL         PIC $$$,$$$,$$$.
147        02 FILLER                  PIC XXX VALUE "***".
148
149 PROCEDURE DIVISION.
150
151 1000-MAIN-CONTROL.
152
153     PERFORM 2000-INITIALIZE-REPORT.
154     PERFORM 2100-PROCESS-DATA
155            UNTIL END-OF-FILE.
```

Program 8c *(continued)*

```
156        PERFORM 2200-TERMINATE-REPORT.
157        STOP RUN.
158
159 2000-INITIALIZE-REPORT.
160
161        OPEN INPUT EMPLOYEE-FILE
162            OUTPUT REPORT-FILE.
163        PERFORM 9000-READ-EMPLOYEE-FILE.
164        MOVE DEPARTMENT-ER TO HOLD-DEPARTMENT.
165        MOVE DIVISION-ER   TO HOLD-DIVISION.
166
167 2100-PROCESS-DATA.
168
169        IF DIVISION-ER NOT = HOLD-DIVISION
170            PERFORM 9100-DEPARTMENT-BREAK
171            PERFORM 9200-DIVISION-BREAK
172        ELSE
173            IF DEPARTMENT-ER NOT = HOLD-DEPARTMENT
174                PERFORM 9100-DEPARTMENT-BREAK.
175        PERFORM 3000-PROCESS-EMPLOYEE-RECORD.
176        PERFORM 9000-READ-EMPLOYEE-FILE.
177
178 2200-TERMINATE-REPORT.
179
180        PERFORM 9100-DEPARTMENT-BREAK.
181        PERFORM 9200-DIVISION-BREAK.
182        PERFORM 3100-WRITE-SUMMARY-LINE.
183        CLOSE EMPLOYEE-FILE
184            REPORT-FILE.
185
186 3000-PROCESS-EMPLOYEE-RECORD.
187
188        MOVE NAME-ER            TO NAME-DL.
189        MOVE EMPLOYEE-NUMBER-ER TO EMPLOYEE-NUMBER-DL.
190        MOVE SALARY-ER          TO SALARY-DL.
191        MOVE DIVISION-ER        TO DIVISION-DL.
192        MOVE DEPARTMENT-ER      TO DEPARTMENT-DL.
193        ADD SALARY-ER           TO DEPARTMENT-TOTAL-SALARY
194                                   DIVISION-TOTAL-SALARY
195                                   TOTAL-SALARY.
196        ADD 1                   TO DEPARTMENT-NUMBER-OF-EMPLOYEES
197                                   DIVISION-NUMBER-OF-EMPLOYEES
198                                   NUMBER-OF-EMPLOYEES.
199        IF PAGE-FULL
200            PERFORM 9300-WRITE-HEADINGS.
201        WRITE REPORT-RECORD FROM DETAIL-LINE AFTER 1.
202        ADD 1 TO LINE-COUNT.
203
```

Program 8c   *(concluded)*

```
204 3100-WRITE-SUMMARY-LINE.
205
206     MOVE NUMBER-OF-EMPLOYEES TO NUMBER-OF-EMPLOYEES-SL.
207     MOVE TOTAL-SALARY TO SALARY-TOTAL-SL.
208     WRITE REPORT-RECORD FROM SUMMARY-LINE AFTER 1.
209
210 9000-READ-EMPLOYEE-FILE.
211
212     READ EMPLOYEE-FILE
213         AT END MOVE "YES" TO EOF-FLAG.
214
215 9100-DEPARTMENT-BREAK.
216
217     MOVE DEPARTMENT-NUMBER-OF-EMPLOYEES TO
218         NUMBER-OF-EMPLOYEES-DTL.
219     MOVE DEPARTMENT-TOTAL-SALARY TO TOTAL-SALARY-DTL.
220     MOVE HOLD-DEPARTMENT TO DEPARTMENT-DTL.
221     IF PAGE-FULL
222         PERFORM 9300-WRITE-HEADINGS.
223     WRITE REPORT-RECORD FROM DEPARTMENT-TOTAL-LINE AFTER 2.
224     MOVE SPACES TO REPORT-RECORD.
225     WRITE REPORT-RECORD AFTER 1.
226     ADD 3 TO LINE-COUNT.
227     MOVE 0 TO DEPARTMENT-NUMBER-OF-EMPLOYEES
228             DEPARTMENT-TOTAL-SALARY.
229     MOVE DEPARTMENT-ER TO HOLD-DEPARTMENT.
230
231 9200-DIVISION-BREAK.
232
233     MOVE DIVISION-TOTAL-SALARY TO TOTAL-SALARY-DVTL.
234     MOVE DIVISION-NUMBER-OF-EMPLOYEES TO
235         NUMBER-OF-EMPLOYEES-DVTL.
236     MOVE HOLD-DIVISION TO DIVISION-DVTL.
237     IF PAGE-FULL
238         PERFORM 9300-WRITE-HEADINGS.
239     WRITE REPORT-RECORD FROM DIVISION-TOTAL-LINE AFTER 2.
240     MOVE SPACES TO REPORT-RECORD.
241     WRITE REPORT-RECORD AFTER 2.
242     PERFORM 9300-WRITE-HEADINGS.
243     MOVE 0 TO DIVISION-NUMBER-OF-EMPLOYEES
244             DIVISION-TOTAL-SALARY.
245     MOVE DIVISION-ER TO HOLD-DIVISION.
246
247 9300-WRITE-HEADINGS.
248
249     ADD 1 TO PAGE-COUNT.
250     MOVE PAGE-COUNT TO PAGE-COUNTER-MH.
251     WRITE REPORT-RECORD FROM MAJOR-HEADING AFTER PAGE.
252     WRITE REPORT-RECORD FROM SUBHEADING AFTER 2.
253     MOVE SPACES TO REPORT-RECORD.
254     WRITE REPORT-RECORD AFTER 1.
255     MOVE 4 TO LINE-COUNT.
```

Figure 8.17 Two-level control break example

```
JONES JOHN         7777111100 02 040000
SMITH MARY         1222222200 02 050000
DOE JOHN           1999333300 02 034000  ── Minor break
BLACK HARVEY       8888444400 03 020000
WHITE SUE          1555555500 03 045000  ── Minor and Major break
GREY SAM           1555666610 03 090000
GONZALEZ CARLOS    2777777710 03 080000  ── Minor break
SHEA JOHN          7777000011 11 045000
SPADE SAM          3333333311 11 067000  ── Minor and Major break
CLARK JOHN         2222444421 11 030000
HERNANDEZ MARIA    5555444421 11 080000
JONES PATRICIA     4555555521 11 050000  ── Minor and Major break
```

Figure 8.18 Generalized procedure for two-level control break program

Main control

    Open files
    Read input file
    Move major key field to major key field hold
    Move minor key field to minor key field hold
    Do Process data until end of file
    Do Minor control break
    Do Major control break
    Close files
    Stop

Process data

    If major key field not equal major key field hold
        Do Minor control break
        Do Major control break
    Else
        If minor key field not equal minor key field hold
            Do Minor control break
        End If
    End If
    Add appropriate data to subtotals
    Do other processing of data
    Write detail record
    Read input file

Minor control break

    Write minor subtotal record
    Move 0 to minor subtotal
    Move minor key field to minor key field hold

Major control break

    Write major subtotal record
    Move 0 to major subtotal
    Move major key field to major key field hold

The decision structure from the module *Process data* of Figure 8.18 is crucial to the correct detection of control breaks. A flowchart of this portion of the pseudocode follows:

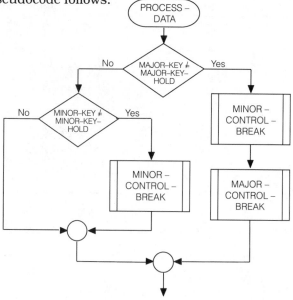

The program must check for a major control break prior to checking for a minor control break; however, when a major control break is found, the minor break processing must be carried out before major break processing.

8.10   PROGRAM EXAMPLE

Problem Statement

Assume that the three-character department identifier in the data processed in Programs 8a and 8b consists of two subfields: The first character represents a division within the company, and the next two characters represent a department within the division. A report is required that will summarize employee data by department and by division with the output for each division beginning on a new page. A printer spacing chart for the required report is shown in Figure 8.19.

Problem Analysis

This problem requires the use of two levels of control breaks: the major break based on the division identifier and the minor break based on the department identifier. The division identifier is the major key; the department identifier is the minor key. We have assumed that the file is in sequence by the three-character field, which has previously been referred to as a *department identifier*. As the division identifier is the leftmost character of the field, the data will be in the proper sequence required for this report. That is, the records for a division will be grouped together, and within each division grouping; the records for each department will occur as a group.

This program will require three sets of counters and accumulators: one set for the final totals (NUMBER-OF-EMPLOYEES and TOTAL-SALARY), another set for the major totals (DIVISION-NUMBER-OF-EMPLOYEES

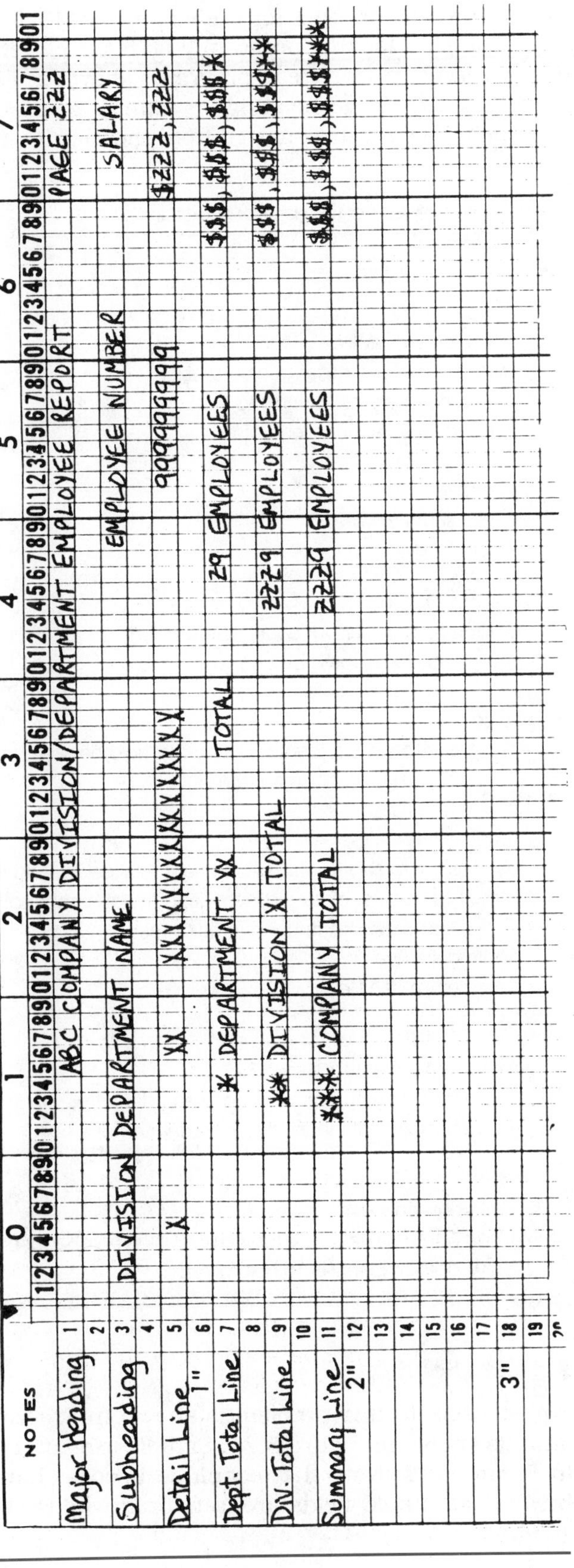

Figure 8.19 Printer spacing chart for two-level control break program

and DIVISION-TOTAL-SALARY), and a third set for the minor totals (DEPARTMENT-NUMBER-OF-EMPLOYEES and DEPARTMENT-TOTAL-SALARY). The program will also require two hold fields: one for the major key (HOLD-DIVISION) and another for the minor key (HOLD-DEPARTMENT).

The plan for this program (Fig. 8.20) closely follows the general plan for two-level control break programs shown in Figure 8.18. The technique to be used for page headings is similar to that used in Program 8b; for simplicity, details are omitted from the plan.

Figure 8.20   Plan for two-level control break program

Main control

    Open files
    Read employee file
    Move division identifier to hold division
    Move department identifier to hold department
    Do Process data until end of file
    Do Department break
    Do Division break
    Write summary line
    Stop

Process data

    If division identifier not equal hold division
        Do Department break
        Do Division break
    Else
        If department identifier not equal hold department
            Do Department break
        End If
    End If
    Add salary to salary total, department total salary, and division total salary
    Add 1 to number of employees, department number of employees,
        and division number of employees
    Write detail line
    Read employee file

Department break

    Write department totals
    Move 0 to department salary total and department number of employees
    Move department identifier to hold department

Division break

    Write division totals
    Move 0 to division salary total and division number of employees
    Move division identifier to hold division

Problem Solution

The solution to this problem is shown in Program 8c; the structure diagram is shown in Figure 8.21. Sample execution of the program is shown in Figure 8.22. Note the technique used to handle two levels of control breaks. Both hold fields are initialized when the first record is read (see

Figure 8.22   Sample execution of Program 8c

```
                    ABC COMPANY DIVISION/DEPARTMENT EMPLOYEE REPORT      PAGE    1

   DIVISION DEPARTMENT NAME                        EMPLOYEE NUMBER        SALARY

      0          02      JONES JOHN                     77771111       $ 40,000
      0          02      SMITH MARY                     12222222       $ 50,000
      0          02      DOE JOHN                       19993333       $ 34,000

                 * DEPARTMENT 02 TOTAL             3 EMPLOYEES          $124,000*

      0          03      BLACK HARVEY                   88884444       $ 20,000
      0          03      WHITE SUE                      15555555       $ 45,000

                 * DEPARTMENT 03 TOTAL             2 EMPLOYEES           $65,000*


              ** DIVISION 0 TOTAL                 5 EMPLOYEES          $189,000**


                    ABC COMPANY DIVISION/DEPARTMENT EMPLOYEE REPORT      PAGE    2

   DIVISION DEPARTMENT NAME                        EMPLOYEE NUMBER        SALARY

      1          03      GREY SAM                       15556666       $ 90,000
      1          03      GONZALEZ CARLOS                27777777       $ 80,000

                 * DEPARTMENT 03 TOTAL             2 EMPLOYEES          $170,000*

      1          11      SHEA JOHN                      77770000       $ 45,000
      1          11      SPADE SAM                      33333333       $ 67,000

                 * DEPARTMENT 11 TOTAL             2 EMPLOYEES          $112,000*


              ** DIVISION 1 TOTAL                 4 EMPLOYEES          $282,000**


                    ABC COMPANY DIVISION/DEPARTMENT EMPLOYEE REPORT      PAGE    3

   DIVISION DEPARTMENT NAME                        EMPLOYEE NUMBER        SALARY

      2          11      CLARK JOHN                     22224444       $ 30,000
      2          11      HERNANDEZ MARIA                55554444       $ 80,000
      2          11      JONES PATRICIA                 45555555       $ 50,000

                 * DEPARTMENT 11 TOTAL             3 EMPLOYEES          $160,000*


              ** DIVISION 2 TOTAL                 3 EMPLOYEES          $160,000**


                    ABC COMPANY DIVISION/DEPARTMENT EMPLOYEE REPORT      PAGE    4

   DIVISION DEPARTMENT NAME                        EMPLOYEE NUMBER        SALARY

              *** COMPANY TOTAL                  12 EMPLOYEES          $631,000***
```

Figure 8.21   Structure diagram for Program 8c

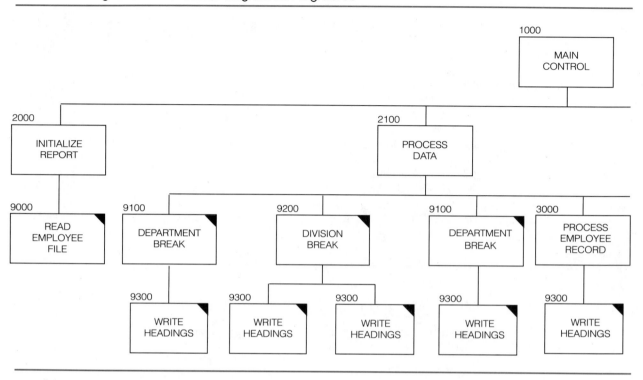

lines 164 and 165). The first step in processing each record is to check for control breaks (lines 169–174):

```
IF DIVISION-ER NOT = HOLD-DIVISION
    PERFORM 9100-DEPARTMENT-BREAK
    PERFORM 9200-DIVISION-BREAK
ELSE
    IF DEPARTMENT-ER NOT = HOLD-DEPARTMENT
        PERFORM 9100-DEPARTMENT-BREAK.
```

It is imperative that the program check for the major break before checking for the minor break because departments in two different divisions might have the same identifier. If there is a break in division identifiers, the program must write the department totals before writing the division totals. Note that the check for a break in department identifiers is made only if there is no break in division identifiers.

Note the sequence of actions taken by the program after end-of-file is detected (lines 180–182):

```
PERFORM 9100-DEPARTMENT-BREAK.
PERFORM 9200-DIVISION-BREAK.
PERFORM 3100-WRITE-SUMMARY-LINE.
```

The sequence in which these actions are taken is important because the line containing the totals for the last department must precede the line for the totals for the last division, and all of these must come before the final totals.

Some programs may require three (or more) levels of totals and therefore require as many levels of control break checks. In the case of three levels, we will call the most important key field the *major key*, the next most important the *intermediate key*, and the least important key field the *minor key*.

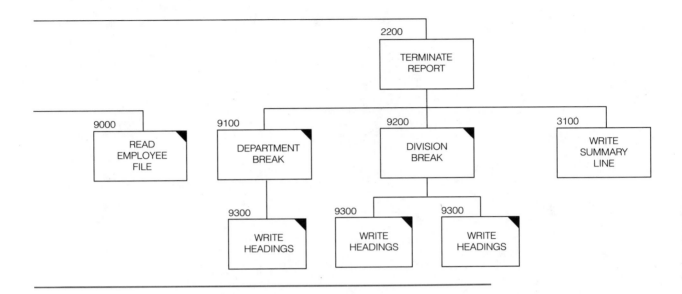

For example, suppose the data file described in Program 8b contained an additional field for plant, and suppose that each plant was organized into divisions and each division was organized into departments. The major key would be the plant identifier, the intermediate key would be the division identifier, and the minor key would be the department identifier. In order to recognize three levels of control breaks, the program will need three hold fields, one for each key. The overall logic for a three-level break program will resemble the two-level break procedure described in Figure 8.20. In this case, however, the first task of the process data module is to check for three conditions as shown in Figure 8.23.

8.11 DEBUG CLINIC

Programs requiring line counting, page numbers, and subtotals are somewhat more complex than programs which have previously been encountered in this text. It is, therefore, not uncommon for programmers to encounter logical errors during the debugging of such programs. The following list presents some of the most common problems and some suggestions as to the possible causes of the problems.

Logical problem	Possible causes
No headings	Page heading paragraph not included
	PERFORM of page heading paragraph omitted

Figure 8.23   Decision structure for three-level control break program

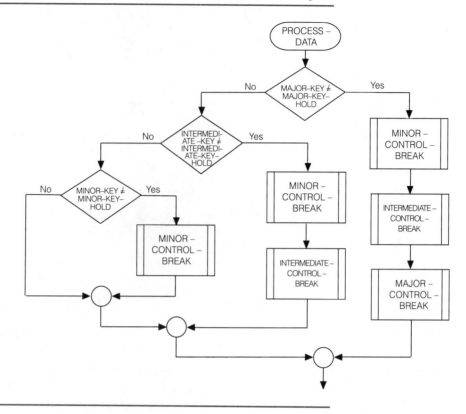

Logical problem	Possible causes
Headings on first page only	PERFORM of page heading paragraph not included in processing of body of report
	Line counter not incremented
Page headings occur on all pages but first	PERFORM of page heading paragraph not included in initialization
	Line counter not initialized properly
Page headings do not occur at top of every physical page of output	Line counter not incremented after each output
	Amount added to line counter not equal to number of lines produced
	Number of lines per page used in program exceeds actual number of lines per page
Page headings occur in the middle of physical pages of output	Computer operator failed to align paper in printer properly
	Skipping to top of a new page not a feature of the printer in use

Logical problem	*Possible causes*
	Skipping to top of a new page has been disallowed (sometimes done to save paper)
Page number is same on all pages	Page counter not incremented in page heading paragraph
Page totals are cumulative	Subtotal field not reinitialized to zero after production of subtotal output
Subtotal with value 0 occurs before first detail output	Hold field not initialized for first input record
Subtotals occur after every detail output line	Hold field not replaced with a new value in the control break routine
No totals at end of report	Program does not perform control break routines as part of termination
A group includes an output line which should be included in the following group	Program checking for control break after detail processing rather than before processing

8.12 A NESTED LOOP APPROACH TO THE CONTROL BREAK PROBLEM

In the programs presented thus far, the basic solution to the control break problem has involved a decision structure. As you have seen, when more than one level of control break must be accommodated, the program requires a nested decision structure. An alternative approach to this problem, favored by some, uses nested loops rather than a nested decision structure.

Consider the problem of recognizing a single-level control break. The highest level task is to process control groups. (A **control group** is a group of records having the same key field value—for example, all the records for employees of one department.) When all control groups have been processed and final totals have been printed, the program is finished. We can summarize this procedure in the following pseudocode:

Main control

    Initialize report
    Read data file
    Do Process control group until end-of-file
    Terminate report
    Stop

The module *Process control group* must, in turn, process each record in the control group until a control break is encountered. When the break is detected, the totals and other processing for the group can be done. This is summarized as follows:

Process control group

    Do Process data until control break
    Write totals
    Initialize hold fields and accumulators

Process data

    Write detail line
    Accumulate totals
    Read data file

In this alternative plan, the details of handling control break detection are the same as before. The major difference in this plan is the use of nested loops—that is, an outer loop which continues until end-of-file and an inner loop which terminates when a control break is encountered.

If two levels of control breaks must be recognized, this alternative plan requires another level of nested loops as shown in the following plan:

Main control

    Initialize report
    Read data file
    Do Process major group until end-of-file
    Terminate report
    Stop

Process major group

    Do Process minor group until major control break
    Write major totals
    Initialize appropriate hold fields and accumulators

Process minor group

    Do Process data until minor control break
    Write minor totals
    Initialize appropriate hold fields and accumulators

Process data

    Write detail line
    Accumulate totals
    Read data file

Program 8d shows an implementation of this alternative approach for a two-level control break problem. Program 8d is functionally equivalent to Program 8c; only the PROCEDURE DIVISION has been rewritten, and the description of EMPLOYEE-RECORD has been modified slightly. Compare the structure diagram of Program 8c (Fig. 8.21) with the structure diagram of Program 8d (shown in Fig. 8.24). The use of nested loops is evident in the presence of an additional level in the structure of Program 8d.

In Program 8d, we have used an alternative approach in detecting end-of-file. Instead of a flag which is set when the end-of-file condition is reached, we have moved HIGH-VALUES to the fields involved in detection of control breaks; these fields are gathered together under the group item RECORD-KEY-ER (see lines 32-34). Recall that HIGH-VALUES is a figurative constant for the largest value that can be contained in a field of a particular data type. Because HIGH-VALUES is different from any value of DIVISION-ER or DEPARTMENT-ER, the required breaks at end-of-file will be triggered automatically.

Program 8d

```
  1 IDENTIFICATION DIVISION.
    .
    .
    .
 29 01   EMPLOYEE-RECORD.
 30      02 NAME-ER                 PIC X(16).
 31      02 EMPLOYEE-NUMBER-ER      PIC 9(9).
 32      02 RECORD-KEY-ER.
 33         03 DIVISION-ER          PIC X.
 34         03 DEPARTMENT-ER        PIC X(2).
 35      02 SALARY-ER               PIC 9(6).
 36      02 FILLER                  PIC X(45).
    .
    .
    .
146 PROCEDURE DIVISION.
147
148 1000-MAIN-CONTROL.
149
150     PERFORM 2000-INITIALIZE-REPORT.
151     PERFORM 2100-PROCESS-ONE-DIVISION
152          UNTIL RECORD-KEY-ER = HIGH-VALUES.
153     PERFORM 2200-TERMINATE-REPORT.
154     STOP RUN.
155
156 2000-INITIALIZE-REPORT.
157
158     OPEN INPUT EMPLOYEE-FILE
159          OUTPUT REPORT-FILE.
160     PERFORM 9000-READ-EMPLOYEE-FILE.
161     MOVE DEPARTMENT-ER TO HOLD-DEPARTMENT.
162     MOVE DIVISION-ER    TO HOLD-DIVISION.
163
164 2100-PROCESS-ONE-DIVISION.
165
166     PERFORM 3000-PROCESS-ONE-DEPARTMENT
167          UNTIL DIVISION-ER NOT = HOLD-DIVISION.
168     ADD DIVISION-TOTAL-SALARY TO
169        TOTAL-SALARY.
170     ADD DIVISION-NUMBER-OF-EMPLOYEES TO
171        NUMBER-OF-EMPLOYEES.
172     MOVE DIVISION-TOTAL-SALARY TO
173        TOTAL-SALARY-DVTL.
174     MOVE DIVISION-NUMBER-OF-EMPLOYEES TO
175        NUMBER-OF-EMPLOYEES-DVTL.
176     MOVE HOLD-DIVISION TO
177        DIVISION-DVTL.
178     IF PAGE-FULL
179        PERFORM 9100-WRITE-HEADINGS.
180     WRITE REPORT-RECORD FROM DIVISION-TOTAL-LINE AFTER 2.
181     MOVE SPACES TO REPORT-RECORD.
182     WRITE REPORT-RECORD AFTER 2.
183     PERFORM 9100-WRITE-HEADINGS.
184     MOVE 0 TO DIVISION-NUMBER-OF-EMPLOYEES
185               DIVISION-TOTAL-SALARY.
186     MOVE DIVISION-ER TO HOLD-DIVISION.
187
```

```
188 2200-TERMINATE-REPORT.
189
190     PERFORM 3100-WRITE-SUMMARY-LINE.
191     CLOSE EMPLOYEE-FILE
192           REPORT-FILE.
193
194 3000-PROCESS-ONE-DEPARTMENT.
195
196     PERFORM 4000-PROCESS-EMPLOYEE-RECORD
197           UNTIL DEPARTMENT-ER NOT = HOLD-DEPARTMENT
198             OR DIVISION-ER   NOT = HOLD-DIVISION.
199     ADD DEPARTMENT-NUMBER-OF-EMPLOYEES TO
200         DIVISION-NUMBER-OF-EMPLOYEES.
201     ADD DEPARTMENT-TOTAL-SALARY TO
202         DIVISION-TOTAL-SALARY.
203     MOVE DEPARTMENT-NUMBER-OF-EMPLOYEES TO
204         NUMBER-OF-EMPLOYEES-DTL.
205     MOVE DEPARTMENT-TOTAL-SALARY TO
206         TOTAL-SALARY-DTL.
207     MOVE HOLD-DEPARTMENT TO
208         DEPARTMENT-DTL.
209     IF PAGE-FULL
210         PERFORM 9100-WRITE-HEADINGS.
211     WRITE REPORT-RECORD FROM DEPARTMENT-TOTAL-LINE AFTER 2.
212     MOVE SPACES TO REPORT-RECORD.
213     WRITE REPORT-RECORD AFTER 1.
214     ADD 3 TO LINE-COUNT.
215     MOVE 0 TO DEPARTMENT-NUMBER-OF-EMPLOYEES
216               DEPARTMENT-TOTAL-SALARY.
217     MOVE DEPARTMENT-ER TO HOLD-DEPARTMENT.
218
219 4000-PROCESS-EMPLOYEE-RECORD.
220
221     MOVE NAME-ER            TO NAME-DL.
222     MOVE EMPLOYEE-NUMBER-ER TO EMPLOYEE-NUMBER-DL.
223     MOVE SALARY-ER          TO SALARY-DL.
224     MOVE DIVISION-ER        TO DIVISION-DL.
225     MOVE DEPARTMENT-ER      TO DEPARTMENT-DL.
226     ADD SALARY-ER           TO DEPARTMENT-TOTAL-SALARY.
227     ADD 1                   TO DEPARTMENT-NUMBER-OF-EMPLOYEES.
228     IF PAGE-FULL
229         PERFORM 9100-WRITE-HEADINGS.
230     WRITE REPORT-RECORD FROM DETAIL-LINE AFTER 1.
231     ADD 1 TO LINE-COUNT.
232     PERFORM 9000-READ-EMPLOYEE-FILE.
233
234 3100-WRITE-SUMMARY-LINE.
235
236     MOVE NUMBER-OF-EMPLOYEES TO
237         NUMBER-OF-EMPLOYEES-SL.
238     MOVE TOTAL-SALARY TO
239         SALARY-TOTAL-SL.
240     WRITE REPORT-RECORD FROM SUMMARY-LINE AFTER 1.
241
```

Program 8d *(concluded)*

```
242 9000-READ-EMPLOYEE-FILE.
243
244     READ EMPLOYEE-FILE
245         AT END MOVE HIGH-VALUES TO RECORD-KEY-ER.
246
247 9100-WRITE-HEADINGS.
248
249     ADD 1 TO PAGE-COUNT.
250     MOVE PAGE-COUNT TO PAGE-COUNTER-MH.
251     WRITE REPORT-RECORD FROM MAJOR-HEADING AFTER PAGE.
252     WRITE REPORT-RECORD FROM SUBHEADING AFTER 2.
253     MOVE SPACES TO REPORT-RECORD.
254     WRITE REPORT-RECORD AFTER 1.
255     MOVE 4 TO LINE-COUNT.
```

Figure 8.24   Structure diagram for Program 8d

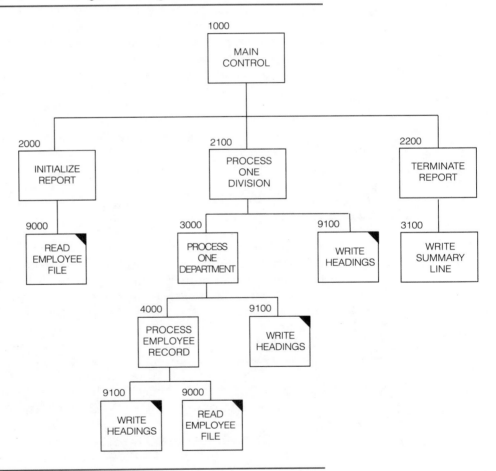

Notice that the detection of a minor control break in the paragraph 3000-PROCESS-ONE-DEPARTMENT requires checking for a change not only in department number (the minor key) but also in division number (the major key) because any change in the major key (a major break) must also trigger a minor break.

Program 8d also illustrates another departure from Programs 8b and 8c. In previous programs, all accumulators were updated during the processing of each detail record. This is convenient because it groups all accumulation in one place in the program; however, it is technically unnecessary. It is possible for the lowest level module to update the accumulators required for the minor control group. When the minor control break is encountered, the minor group accumulators could be used to update the accumulators for the major control group. When a major control break is encountered, the major control group accumulators can be used to update the final totals. This technique is implemented in Program 8d.

Which approach to the control break problem—the nested decision structure or the nested loop structure—is preferable? To a certain extent, the answer to this question is dependent on personal preference since arguments can be made in favor of each approach. In general, decision structures are easier for most people to understand than structures that involve repetition. By this criteria, we might favor the nested decision structure approach. On the other hand, there is a very clear relationship between the nested repetition structure and the problem being solved. Creating the whole report requires processing of each major group; processing each major group requires the processing of all minor groups which constitute the major group, and so on. As a side benefit of this approach, it is unnecessary to recognize minor and major breaks at end-of-file since the required processing is performed as a natural part of the program. Some people maintain that the structure of a program should flow naturally from the problem being solved. By this criteria, we might choose the nested loop approach to the problem. In general, you should choose whichever model you find most natural and easiest to comprehend. (Your instructor may have a preference as well and may insist on one approach over the other.)

8.13   COBOL-85 UPDATE

You have seen the importance of specifying initial values for data items in a variety of circumstances, particularly in relation to counting and accumulation. Unless counters and accumulators start at an appropriate value (usually zero), the program will fail to produce correct totals. Where possible, we have used the VALUE clause in the DATA DIVISION to initialize data items, but sometimes, as in the case of accumulating subtotals, it is necessary to reinitialize a data item during the execution of the program. This is usually accomplished by a statement such as MOVE 0 TO . . . or MOVE SPACES TO . . . . In recognition of the importance of this type of operation, COBOL-85 includes the INITIALIZE statement.

A general form of the INITIALIZE statement is

```
INITIALIZE data-name
```

If data-name is an elementary data item with a numeric or numeric edited type, the INITIALIZE statement will be equivalent to the statement MOVE 0 TO data-name. If data-name is alphabetic or alphanumeric, the INITIALIZE statement is equivalent to MOVE SPACES TO data-name. If data-name is a group item, then numeric or numeric edited elementary items that are subordinated to it will be set to value 0, and alphabetic and alphanumeric items will be set to spaces.

——————— Example ———————

Suppose FldA is a numeric field defined as PIC 9(5)V99. After execution of the statement

        INITIALIZE FldA

the value of FldA will be

        |0,0,0,0,0,0,0,|
                  ^
        FldA PIC 9(5)V99

This is equivalent to the statement MOVE 0 TO FldA.

——————— Example ———————

Suppose FldB is a numeric edited field defined as PIC $ZZZ.99. After execution of

        INITIALIZE FldB

the value of FldB will be

        |$, , , ,.,0,0,|
        FldB PIC $ZZZ.99

This is the equivalent of MOVE 0 TO FldB.

——————— Example ———————

Suppose FldC is an alphanumeric field defined as PIC XXX. After execution of the statement

        INITIALIZE FldC

the value of FldC will be

        |_,_,_,|
        FldC PIC XXX

This is equivalent to MOVE SPACES TO FldC.

——————— Example ———————

Suppose FldD is a group item defined as

        01   FldD.
             03 FldE   PIC 999V99.
             03 FldF   PIC XXX.
             03 FldG   PIC $$$,$$$.99.

After execution of the statement

        INITIALIZE FldD

the content of FldE, FldF, and FldG is

        |0,0,0,0,0,| |_,_,_,| |, , , , , ,$,.,0,0,|
                ^
        FldE PIC 999V99   FldF PIC XXX   FldG PIC $$$,$$$.99.

This is the equivalent of the following MOVE statements:

        MOVE 0 TO FldE FldG
        MOVE SPACES TO FldF.

It is the ability to initialize multiple items with one statement that is likely to be the most useful feature of the `INITIALIZE` statement. For example, in Program 8c, it is necessary to set the fields `DEPARTMENT-NUMBER-OF-EMPLOYEES` and `DEPARTMENT-TOTAL-SALARY` to zero before beginning the processing of a record from a new department. If these fields had been defined as part of a group item such as

```
03 Department-Totals.
   05 Department-Number-Of-Employees    PIC 99 VALUE ZERO.
   05 Department-Total-Salary           PIC 9(8) VALUE ZERO.
```

the `MOVE` statement at lines 227 through 228 of Program 8c could then be written much more compactly as

```
   INITIALIZE Department-Totals.
```

Besides being more compact, the `INITIALIZE` statement makes it possible for a subsequent programmer to add one or more items to `Department-Totals` without locating each point in the program at which these totals are initialized. This should avoid the error of an uninitialized data item in the modified program.

8.14 SELF-TEST EXERCISES

1. Write `DATA DIVISION` entries required to define the following file and its records:

    File-name: `DATA-FILE`

    Record names: `DATA-REC-A`, `DATA-REC-B`

    Record type A:

Positions	Content
1–10	Bid-number
11–20	Project description
21–30	Bid amount
31	Record identification code ("A")

    Record type B:

Positions	Content
1–10	Bid-number
11–20	Disbursement amount
21–30	Disbursement description
31	Record identification code ("B")

2. Write `PROCEDURE DIVISION` entries required to read `DATA-FILE` defined in Exercise 1 above.

3. Write `SPECIAL-NAMES` entries required to substitute the symbol "Q" for the dollar sign. Write a `PICTURE` code to edit a field defined as `9(6)V99`.

4. In Program 8a, the line counter is initialized to value 0. Each output operation increments the counter. Before each output, the counter is tested to see if the page is full. If the page is full, a new page is initiated with headings and page number. Using this scheme, what would happen if the last line in the report fell on the last line of a page? What would happen if there were no records in the file?

5. In Program 8b, an alternative method for handling line counting is used. The line counter is initialized to a value greater than the number of lines on a page. For example, if there are 16 lines on a page, the line counter is defined with initial value 17. The program then tests the line counter for full page before each output operation. Because of the initial value of the line count, page headings will be produced in advance of the first output operation and each time thereafter that the page becomes full. What advantages are there to this scheme? What would happen if (a) there are no records in the file? or (b) the last line of the report falls on the last line of a page? Which method for line counting seems better? Is the method used in Program 8b compatible with page totals? Why or why not?

6. Should the number of lines per page be defined as a data item in WORKING-STORAGE? Why?

7. For Program 8b, suppose we want to include the department number as a part of the output line showing each department total. Which of the following should be moved to the output record: DEPARTMENT-ER or HOLD-DEPARTMENT? Why?

8. Using the procedure shown in Figures 8.18 and 8.22 as guidelines, write a procedure for a three-level control break program.

9. Using a nested loop approach outlined in Section 8.12, rewrite Program 8b.

10. What is likely to be the most useful feature of the COBOL-85 INITIALIZE statement? Why?

8.15 PROGRAMMING EXERCISES

1. Write a program to determine the inventory value of stock items. Input consists of data records containing:

Positions	Content
1–9	Stock number
10–25	Item description
26–30	Quantity
31–35	Unit cost (2 decimal places)

There may be more than one input record per item. For example, baseballs may have been purchased as follows: five baseballs at a unit cost of $2.00 and four baseballs at a unit cost of $2.25. The program should list the quantity, stock number and name, item weighted average, unit cost, and total dollar value of each stock item in appropriately spaced columns. Headings on each page are required, as are page numbers and the current date. Also, write the total value of all items in the inventory.

A printer spacing chart for the desired report is shown in Figure 8.25.

2. The XYZ Wholesale Supply Company has prepared records containing the following items:

Positions	Content
1–4	Department number
6–11	Transaction date (*mmddyy*)
13–17	Amount of order (999V99)

Figure 8.25   Printer spacing chart for Programming Exercise 1

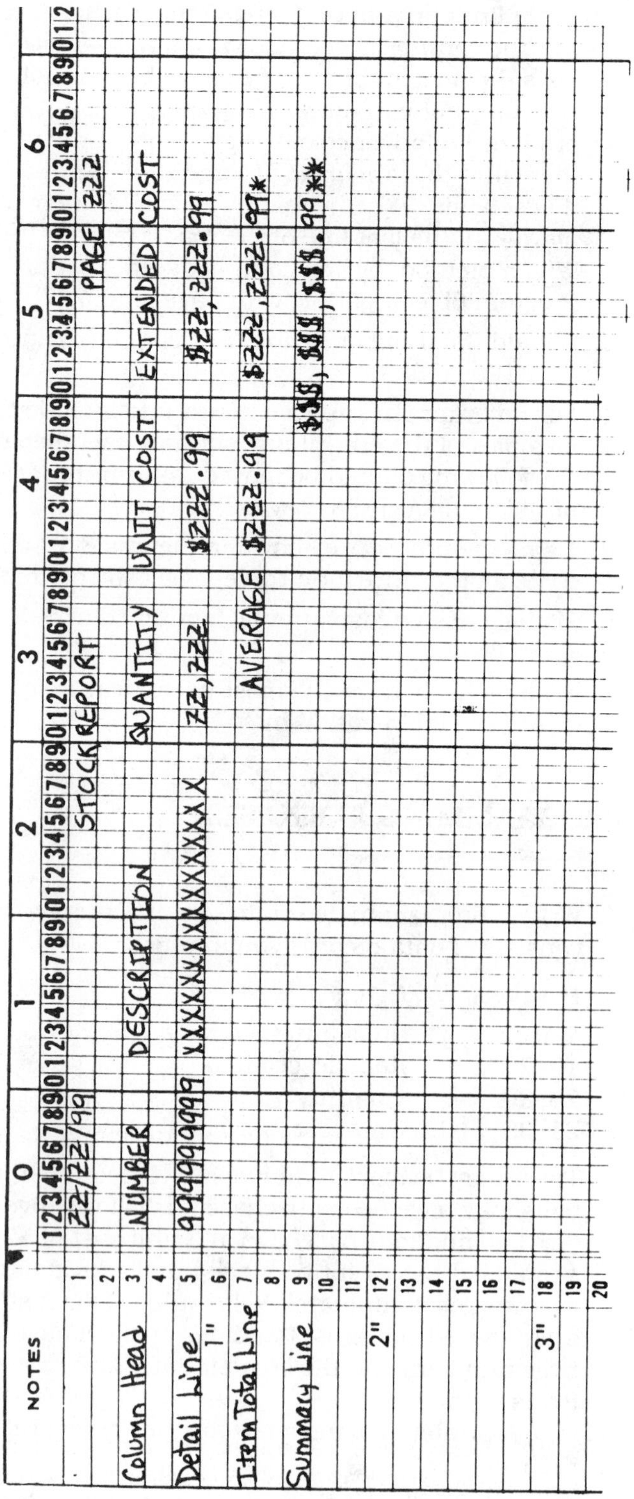

```
                  0         1         2         3         4         5         6
         123456789012345678901234567890123456789012345678901234567890123456789012
NOTES
  1      22/22/99                  STOCK REPORT                    PAGE ZZ2
  2
  3  Column Head  NUMBER   DESCRIPTION      QUANTITY  UNIT COST  EXTENDED COST
  4
  5  Detail Line  99999999 XXXXXXXXXXXXXXXX  ZZ,ZZZ   $Z22.99    $ZZ,ZZZ.99
  6  1"
  7  Item Total Line                AVERAGE  $Z22.99   $ZZZ,Z22.99*
  8
  9  Summary Line                                      $ZZZ,ZZZ.99**
 10
 11
 12  2"
 13
 14
 15
 16
 17
 18  3"
 19
 20
```

Write a program to list each record and produce totals for each department as well as overall totals. List the department number only once for each department's group of records.

3. Modify the program written for Exercise 2 above to produce daily totals within each department. Assume that the data is in sequence by transaction date within each department group.

4. Write a program to alert top management of the XYZ Corporation when sales in its departments are outside certain limits (abnormally high or abnormally low). Input records contain the department number, year, and total sales for that year. You may assume that the records are in ascending sequence by year and that all records for a given department are grouped together (the most recent year is the last record in the department group). If the most recent years sales are more than 10 percent greater than the average for the entire period, then sales are high. If the most recent year's sales are less than 90 percent of the average for the period, then sales are low. Output should be one line per department consisting of department number, most recent year's sales, average sales, and a flag HIGH or LOW if appropriate. Layout for the records is as follows:

Positions	Content
1–4	Department number
6–7	Year
9–15	Sales (99999V99)

5. You have been hired as a programmer for the Harris Hardware Co. Harris makes nuts, bolts, and washers. At the end of each day, a record is prepared for each employee with the following format:

Positions	Content
1–20	Name
21–25	Employee number
27–28	Hours worked
30–33	Rate of pay (99V99)
35–36	Number of dozen stainless steel bolts made
38–39	Number of dozen stainless steel nuts made
41–42	Number of dozen stainless steel washers made
44–45	Number of dozen brass bolts made
47–48	Number of dozen brass nuts made
50–51	Number of dozen brass washers made
53–54	Number of dozen fiber washers made

The cost of production *per item* is as follows:

	Nuts	Bolts	Washers
Stainless Steel	$0.07	$0.07	$0.07
Brass	$0.04	$0.05	$0.02
Fiber	—	—	$0.005

At the end of the week, all records for the week are processed. You may assume that prior to processing, the entire file has been sorted and all the records for each employee are together. There will be one to five records per employee. When each employee's records are processed, write under the appropriate headings the employee's name, employee number, total production by category, total hours worked for the week, and pay for the week, counting any hours worked in one day in excess of eight hours as time and a half. When all records are processed, skip to a new page, and give total production cost for each category as well as grand total cost of production for the week.

6. Sort the data described in Exercise 4 in Chapter 4 (Section 16) into order by zone and selling price. Write a program to list the number of homes in each of the following categories for each zone:

Selling price ≤ $40,000
$40,000 < Selling price ≤ $70,000
$70,000 < Selling price ≤ $95,000
$95,000 < Selling price

7. Sort the data described in Exercise 2 in Chapter 6 (Section 14) into sequence by account code. Write a program to list and summarize expenditures for each account.

9. TABLES AND PERFORM/VARYING

9.1 WHAT IS A TABLE?

A **table** is a sequence of consecutive storage locations (each of which is called an **element**) having a common name. The elements can be accessed using an element name and a specific subscript to point to the particular element to be referenced. For example, suppose we wish to store 75 values representing student grades. One approach would be to create individually named data items to store the values. Another approach would be to create a table and store the values in elements of the table. Such a table might be visualized as

GRADE-TABLE								
GRADE (1)	GRADE (2)	GRADE (3)	GRADE (4)	GRADE (5)	GRADE (6)	GRADE (7)		GRADE (75)
0 4 5	0 9 2	0 7 0	0 9 6	0 5 2	0 9 3	1 0 0		0 8 0

The elements of the table are referenced by a name GRADE and a subscript value enclosed in parentheses.[1] The value of GRADE (1) is 45, the value of GRADE (75) is 80, and so on. The subscript points to a particular value in the table. A subscript must be either a constant or a data-name.[2] When a data-name is used, its value determines the particular element of the table being referenced. The following are valid references:

GRADE (SUB)   The value of SUB at the time of execution will determine which element of GRADE is referenced.

GRADE (35)   The 35th element of GRADE is referenced.

The ability to use a variable as a subscript accounts for the utility of tables. For example, suppose we want to compute the sum of the grades. If the grades had not been stored in a table, a very long computational statement

---

[1] Some compilers require that at least one space must precede a left parenthesis and at least one space or a period followed by at least one space must follow a right parenthesis. Also, a space must not follow a left parenthesis nor precede a right parenthesis. The following table references are invalid for these compilers:
GRADE(1)   No space preceding left parenthesis
GRADE (1)   Space following left parenthesis
GRADE (1)   Space preceding right parenthesis

[2] Some compilers permit any expression to be used as a subscript. For such compilers, the following would be a valid table reference:
GRADE (SUB + 3)   The expression SUB + 3 will be evaluated to determine which element of GRADE is referenced.

(involving 75 different data-names) would have to be used. However, with tables, the sum can be accumulated using the following code:

```
          .
          .
          .
     MOVE 0 TO TOTAL-GRADE.
     MOVE 1 TO SUB.
     PERFORM COMPUTE-SUM UNTIL SUB > 75.
          .
          .
          .
 COMPUTE-SUM.
     ADD GRADE (SUB) TO TOTAL-GRADE.
     ADD 1 TO SUB.
```

At the first repetition of COMPUTE-SUM, the value of SUB will be 1, and the contents of GRADE (1) will be added to TOTAL-GRADE. Then, the value of SUB will become 2, and the contents of GRADE (2) will be added to TOTAL-GRADE, and so on. The process terminates when the value of SUB exceeds 75, at which time all of the grades will have been added into TOTAL-GRADE.

9.2 THE OCCURS CLAUSE

The OCCURS clause is used in the DATA DIVISION to define a table. Figure 9.1 shows a general form for the OCCURS clause. In the OCCURS clause, integer specifies the number of elements to be contained in the table.

Figure 9.1   General Form of the OCCURS clause

```
OCCURS integer TIMES
```

The OCCURS clause cannot be used on an 01 level data item. For example, the following code would create the table for storing 75 grades:

```
01   GRADE-TABLE.
     02 GRADE PIC 999 OCCURS 75 TIMES.
```

The data-name GRADE-TABLE is a group item; it is the overall name for the entire set of 75 data items. The following code would be invalid:

```
01   GRADE   PIC 999 OCCURS 75 TIMES.
```

because of the restriction against using OCCURS with an 01 level item.

A data-name used with an OCCURS clause may be an elementary item, as in the above example, or it may be a group item. For example, suppose we wish to store the names and addresses of 100 people in such a way that one element of the table corresponds to the data being stored about one person. The following code could be used:

```
01   NAME-ADDRESS-TABLE.
     02 NAME-AND-ADDRESS OCCURS 100 TIMES.
        03 NAME    PIC X(20).
        03 ADDRESS PIC X(30).
```

In this case NAME-AND-ADDRESS is a group item; each NAME-AND-ADDRESS is composed of two fields. The data stored for the fifth person then could be referenced by

NAME-AND-ADDRESS (5)

When the OCCURS clause is used on a group item, a subscript may be used not only on the group item name but also on any subordinate field. In the above example it would also be valid to reference

NAME (5)

in order to obtain the name only, and

ADDRESS (5)

in order to obtain the address only. The data structure defined above may be visualized as follows:

NAME-ADDRESS-TABLE					
NAME-AND-ADDRESS (1)		NAME-AND-ADDRESS (2)		NAME-AND-ADDRESS (100)	
NAME (1)	ADDRESS (1)	NAME (2)	ADDRESS (2)	NAME (100)	ADDRESS (100)

Subscripts may be associated only with subordinate parts, not with the overall name of the data structure. For example, NAME-ADDRESS-TABLE (3) would be invalid, since NAME-ADDRESS-TABLE occurs exactly one time; it is a name for $100 \times (20 + 30) = 5000$ characters of data.

An alternative form for storing the above data would be

```
01  ALTERNATE-NAME-ADDRESS-TABLE.
    02 NAME     PIC X(20) OCCURS 100 TIMES.
    02 ADDRESS  PIC X(30) OCCURS 100 TIMES.
```

This structure may be visualized as:

ALTERNATE-NAME-ADDRESS-TABLE						
NAME (1)	NAME (2)	NAME (100)	ADDRESS (1)	ADDRESS (2)	ADDRESS (100)	

In this case, both NAME (5) and ADDRESS (5) would have to be referenced to access all data stored for person number 5. This is less desirable than the other approach if both name and address are desired at the same time.

The subscript used in any reference to an element of a table must have a value in the range one to the size of the table specified in the OCCURS clause. Any reference involving a subscript having a value outside this range will result in a compilation or execution time error message. For example, for the NAME-ADDRESS-TABLE discussed above, the following references would be invalid:

NAME (0)   Zero is not in the range 1 to 100
NAME (101)   101 is too large

Since these subscripts are constants most compilers will flag these statements as errors. If a variable subscript has an invalid value the error message will occur during program execution.

9.3 LOADING AND PROCESSING A TABLE

The OCCURS clause is required to define a table. Data can then be placed into the table. Usually it is not known exactly how many items are to be stored in a table, so the number of elements reserved in the OCCURS clause must be at least as large as the largest number of items anticipated. The program can use a counter to indicate the location into which the item is to be stored and to ensure that the maximum capacity of the table is not exceeded inadvertently. A program segment that could be used to store data in the NAME-ADDRESS-TABLE follows:

```
       .
       .
       .
      MOVE ZERO TO ERROR-FLAG.
      MOVE ZERO TO NUM-ELEMENTS.
      READ INPUT-FILE AT END MOVE "YES" TO EOF-FLAG.
      PERFORM CREATE-TABLE
          UNTIL EOF-FLAG = "YES" OR ERROR-FLAG = 1.
       .
       .
       .

  CREATE-TABLE.
      ADD 1 TO NUM-ELEMENTS.
      IF NUM-ELEMENTS > 100
          MOVE 1 TO ERROR-FLAG
          MOVE 100 TO NUM-ELEMENTS
      ELSE
          MOVE NAME-IR TO NAME (NUM-ELEMENTS)
          MOVE ADDRESS-IR TO ADDRESS (NUM-ELEMENTS)
          READ INPUT-FILE AT END MOVE "YES" TO EOF-FLAG.
```

In the above program segment, the value contained in NUM-ELEMENTS after loading the data into the table reflects the actual number of elements contained in the table. Subsequent processing of the table would use this value for termination. For example, the following code could be used to produce a listing of the elements of NAME-ADDRESS-TABLE:

```
       .
       .
       .
      MOVE ZERO TO TABLE-SUB.
      PERFORM TABLE-OUTPUT
          UNTIL TABLE-SUB = NUM-ELEMENTS.
       .
       .
       .

  TABLE-OUTPUT.
      ADD 1 TO TABLE-SUB.
      MOVE NAME (TABLE-SUB) TO NAME-OR.
      MOVE ADDRESS (TABLE-SUB) TO ADDRESS-OR.
      WRITE OUTPUT-REC FROM NAME-AND-ADDRESS-OUT AFTER 1.
```

Numeric data contained in a table may be processed by any desired arithmetic statement. A subscript must be included to indicate which element of the table is to be operated on. Usually table elements are processed within a loop in order to perform similar operations on some or all of the elements.

――――――― Example ―――――――

A table which represents the total sales for a store for each month in a year is defined in the DATA DIVISION by

```
01  TOTAL-SALES-TABLE.
    03 TOTAL-SALES PIC 9(5)V99 OCCURS 12 TIMES.
```

This table can be visualized as shown:

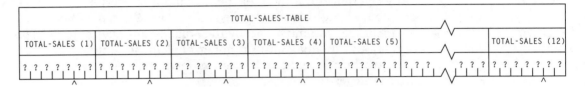

The question marks in the diagram indicate that the initial value in these locations is unknown. This table will be used for accumulation; therefore, it is necessary to start each element at zero. To do this, it is necessary to move zero to TOTAL-SALES (1), TOTAL-SALES (2), and so on. This task can be accomplished by the following program segment:

```
        .
        .
        .
    PERFORM INITIALIZE-TABLE.
        .
        .
        .
INITIALIZE-TABLE.
    MOVE 1 TO SUB.
    PERFORM INITIALIZE-TABLE-ELEMENT
        UNTIL SUB > 12.
INITIALIZE-TABLE-ELEMENT.
    MOVE 0 TO TOTAL-SALES (SUB).
    ADD 1 TO SUB.
```

After the table has been initialized, the table elements can be used as accumulators. If MONTH-NO-IR and SALES-AMOUNT-IR are fields from an input record representing the number of the month and the amount of a sale, then the following program statement would accumulate the total sales by month:

```
ADD SALES-AMOUNT-IR TO TOTAL-SALES (MONTH-NO-IR).
```

In this case MONTH-NO-IR is used as a subscript to pick out the particular element of TOTAL-SALES-TABLE to be operated on.

9.4   OCCURS/DEPENDING ON

In cases where an entire table is not always utilized, it is advantageous to use the DEPENDING ON clause with the OCCURS clause. The DEPENDING ON clause specifies a data-name that will contain the number of table elements used. A general form of the OCCURS/DEPENDING ON clause is given in Figure 9.2.

Figure 9.2   General form of OCCURS/DEPENDING ON statement

```
OCCURS integer-1 TO integer-2 TIMES
DEPENDING ON data-name
```

The content of data-name is treated as the upper limit of the table. Any reference to a table element using a subscript value larger than the content of data-name is treated as invalid. When the DEPENDING ON clause is included, you must specify the smallest number of table elements (integer-1) and the maximum number of elements (integer-2) to be used. It is an error for the content of data-name to be less than integer-1 or greater than integer-2.

Example

Consider the table NAME-ADDRESS-TABLE defined above. An alternate way to create this table would be

```
01   NAME-ADDRESS-TABLE.
     02 NAME-AND-ADDRESS
            OCCURS 1 TO 100 TIMES
            DEPENDING ON NUM-ELEMENTS.
        03 NAME    PIC X(20).
        03 ADDRESS PIC X(30).
```

The data-name NUM-ELEMENTS is used in exactly the same way as before; it stores the location of the last table element in use. Sometimes, the value of data-name is included as an input item rather than calculated by counting.

Example

Each record in a data file contains registration data for a student enrolled at XYZ College. Students may enroll for a maximum of ten courses. A field within the record specifies the number of courses in which the student is enrolled. The following DATA DIVISION entries could be used to define this record:

```
01   STUDENT-RECORD.
     03 STUDENT-NUM-SR PIC 9(9).
     03 STUDENT-NAME-SR PIC X(20).
     .
     .
     .
     03 NUM-COURSES-SR PIC 99.
     03 COURSE-ENROLLMENT-SR
            OCCURS 1 TO 10 TIMES
            DEPENDING ON NUM-COURSES-SR.
        05 COURSE-NUM-SR PIC 9(6).
        05 COURSE-NAME-SR PIC X(20).
```

This data structure can be visualized as shown in Figure 9.3. Note that the use of the DEPENDING ON clause does not affect the actual allocation of

Figure 9.3 Layout of STUDENT-RECORD

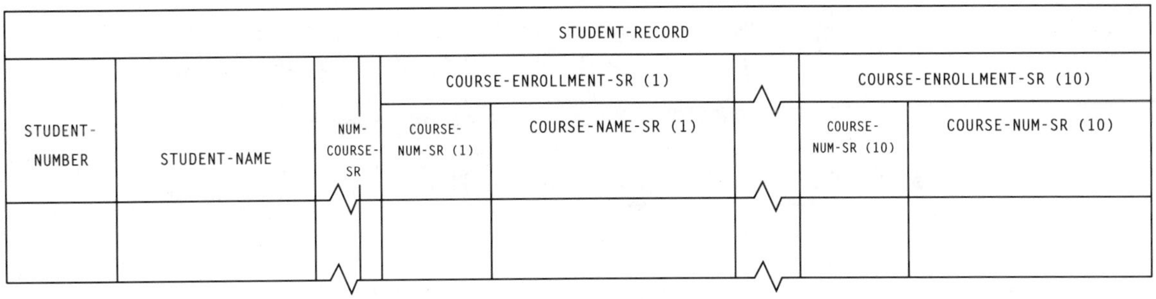

space for the table. In this case, physical memory is allocated for ten table elements.

The advantage in using the DEPENDING ON clause is that the system will automatically check each subscript reference against the actual number of elements in use as opposed to the maximum number of elements allocated. Thus, in the example above, if the value of NUM-COURSES-SR is 4, a reference such as COURSE-NUM-SR (5) would be treated as invalid, even though 5 is less than 10. It is strongly recommended that the programmer use the DEPENDING ON clause for any table that may be only partially used.

9.5 PERFORM WITH THE VARYING OPTION

The PERFORM statement with the VARYING option is used to initialize and increment a counter automatically. For example,

```
PERFORM PARA VARYING SUB FROM 1 BY 1 UNTIL SUB > 10.
```

would cause the data item SUB to have values of 1, 2, 3, . . . , 9, 10 for successive executions of PARA. The execution of this statement proceeds as follows:

1. Move the initial value to the data item (move 1 to SUB in this example).
2. If the condition is *not* met, execute the paragraph; otherwise, go on to the next statement (compare SUB to 10 in this example).
3. After execution of the paragraph, add the increment to the data item (add 1 to SUB in this example).
4. Go to Step 2.

Note that the incrementation of the variable is performed *before* the test is made; therefore, the value of SUB after exit from the loop would be 11, which is the first value of SUB to satisfy the condition. Figure 9.4 illustrates the general form of the PERFORM statement with the VARYING option. In the PERFORM/VARYING, initial-value and increment-value may be either a data-name or a constant.[3]

---

[3] Some compilers will allow any arithmetic expression to be used to specify initial-value and increment-value.

Figure 9.4   General form of PERFORM/VARYING

PERFORM paragraph-name <u>VARYING</u> data-name
<u>FROM</u> initial-value <u>BY</u> increment-value <u>UNTIL</u> condition

Figure 9.5   Flowchart form of PERFORM/VARYING

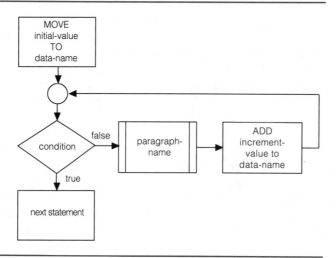

A flowchart of the steps taken automatically in the execution of this version of the PERFORM statement will help you understand how it works (Fig. 9.5). For example, for the statement

PERFORM PARA VARYING SUB FROM 1 BY 1 UNTIL SUB > 10.

the corresponding flowchart would be

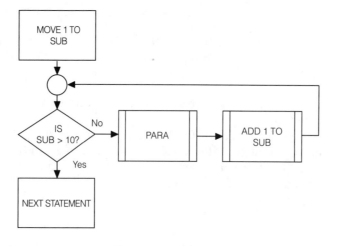

─────────── Example ───────────

PERFORM PARA-A VARYING A FROM 10 BY -1 UNTIL A = 0.

The values of A for successive executions of PARA-A will be 10, 9, 8, . . . , 2, 1. The final value of A is 0, resulting in an exit from the loop.

—————— Example ——————

```
PERFORM PARA-B
    VARYING B FROM 4 BY 0.5 UNTIL B > 6.
```

The values of B for successive executions of PARA-B will be 4, 4.5, 5, 5.5, 6. The final value of B is 6.5, resulting in an exit from the loop.

—————— Example ——————

```
PERFORM PARA-C VARYING C FROM X BY Y
    UNTIL C > 13 OR C + Q > 43.
```

Note that a data-name may be used to specify an initial-value and/or an increment-value. Also, note that the condition may be a complex condition. The results of execution of this statement cannot be determined without knowing values of X, Y, and Q.

—————— Example ——————

```
MOVE 10 TO Y.
PERFORM PARA-X
    VARYING X FROM Y BY 2 UNTIL X > 4.
```

In this example, PARA-X will not be executed because the condition is satisfied by the initial value of X.

The PERFORM statement with the VARYING option is quite useful for manipulating table elements. Compare the following coding examples:

—————— Example ——————

Without PERFORM/VARYING

```
            .
            .
            .
    MOVE 0 TO TOTAL-GRADE.
    MOVE 1 TO SUB.
    PERFORM COMPUTE-SUM UNTIL SUB > 75.
            .
            .
            .
COMPUTE-SUM.
    ADD GRADE (SUB) TO TOTAL-GRADE.
    ADD 1 TO SUB.
```

With PERFORM/VARYING

```
            .
            .
            .
    MOVE 0 TO TOTAL-GRADE.
    PERFORM COMPUTE-SUM
        VARYING SUB FROM 1 BY 1 UNTIL SUB > 75.
```

```
        .
        .
        .
    COMPUTE-SUM.
        ADD GRADE (SUB) TO TOTAL-GRADE.
```

The VARYING option offers a very useful technique for condensing all of the required steps for handling the table subscripting variable into one statement.

──────────── Example ────────────

Without PERFORM/VARYING

```
        .
        .
        .
    PERFORM INITIALIZE-TABLE.
        .
        .
        .
    INITIALIZE-TABLE.
        MOVE 1 TO SUB.
        PERFORM INITIALIZE-TABLE-ELEMENT
            UNTIL SUB > 12.
    INITIALIZE-TABLE-ELEMENT.
        MOVE 0 TO TOTAL-SALES (SUB).
        ADD 1 TO SUB.
```

With PERFORM/VARYING

```
        .
        .
        .
    PERFORM INITIALIZE-TABLE
        VARYING SUB FROM 1 BY 1 UNTIL SUB > 12.
        .
        .
        .
    INITIALIZE-TABLE.
        MOVE 0 TO TOTAL-SALES (SUB).
```

Note the simplicity of the code *with* PERFORM/VARYING compared with the code *without* PERFORM/VARYING.

────────────

When using the PERFORM statement with the VARYING option, take care that the program does not enter an endless loop. The specified condition *must* occur for exiting from the loop; that is, the loop is repeated until the condition is found. For example, the following statement would cause an endless loop:

```
    PERFORM PARA-D VARYING D FROM 1 BY 2 UNTIL D = 4.
```

The values of D will be 1, 3, 5, ... Because D will never have the value 4, the loop will never terminate.

The following statement, while syntactically correct, could cause an infinite loop or other execution time error depending on the values of table Q:

```
PERFORM PARA-E VARYING E FROM 1 BY 1 UNTIL Q (E) = 0.
```

If an element of the array Q has value 0, the loop will terminate; otherwise, an execution time error will result. The above statement is useful for searching for a specified value in a table, but it would be better to write

```
PERFORM PARA-E VARYING E
    FROM 1 BY 1 UNTIL E > NUM-ELEMENTS OR Q (E) = 0.
```

Assuming that NUM-ELEMENTS is the number of elements of the table in use, the above statement will cause an exit when an element of the table Q having value 0 is found or when all the elements of Q have been compared. The search routine now can be written

```
    .
    .
    .
PERFORM PARA-E VARYING E
    FROM 1 BY 1 UNTIL E > NUM-ELEMENTS OR Q (E) = 0.
IF E > NUM-ELEMENTS
    PERFORM ELEMENT-NOT-FOUND
ELSE
    PERFORM ELEMENT-FOUND.
    .
    .
    .
PARA-E.
    EXIT.
```

This procedure assumes that the value of NUM-ELEMENTS is less than the table size. If it is possible for NUM-ELEMENTS to equal the table size, then it is also possible for the value of E to exceed the table size. In this case, the reference to Q (E) will be invalid. This situation would arise when NUM-ELEMENTS is equal to table size or there are no elements in the table with value 0. In light of these considerations, it would be better to write the search routine as follows:

```
    .
    .
    .
MOVE "NO" TO FOUND-FLAG.
PERFORM SEARCH-PROCEDURE
    VARYING E FROM 1 BY 1
    UNTIL E > NUM-ELEMENTS OR FOUND-FLAG = "YES".
IF FOUND-FLAG = "NO"
    PERFORM ELEMENT-NOT-FOUND
ELSE
    PERFORM ELEMENT-FOUND.
    .
    .
    .
SEARCH-PROCEDURE.
    IF Q (E) = 0
        MOVE "YES" TO FOUND-FLAG.
```

9.6 PERFORM WITH THE TIMES OPTION

Another form of the PERFORM statement can be used to execute a paragraph a number of times without varying a specific data-name. Figure 9.6 shows the general form of the PERFORM statement with the TIMES option.

Figure 9.6   General form of PERFORM/TIMES statement

$$\underline{\text{PERFORM}} \text{ paragraph-name} \left\{ \begin{array}{l} \text{data-name} \\ \text{integer} \end{array} \right\} \underline{\text{TIMES}}$$

The number of repetitions is specified using either an integer, as in

```
PERFORM PROCESS 10 TIMES.
```

or a data-name, as in

```
PERFORM PROCESS N TIMES.
```

When a data-name is used, its value determines the number of repetitions. Thus, if the value of N is 10, the preceding two PERFORM statements are equivalent.

───────────── Example ─────────────

A report is designed in such a way that five blank lines are needed at one point during the process of producing the report. The statement

```
PERFORM PRINT-BLANK-LINES 5 TIMES.
```

could be used where the procedure PRINT-BLANK-LINES is defined as

```
PRINT-BLANK-LINES.
    MOVE SPACES TO PRINT-LINE.
    WRITE PRINT-LINE AFTER 1.
```

9.7 PROGRAM EXAMPLE

Problem Statement

As part of its data processing system, the ABC Company maintains a file showing each salesperson and the number of sales made by that person. A report is needed showing a complete listing of the file, and a separate report is needed listing those salespeople with an unacceptably low number of sales. If the number of sales for a particular salesperson is more than four sales less than the average number of sales for all salespeople, the sales performance should be included on the unacceptable list. A printer spacing chart showing the two required reports is shown in Figure 9.7.

Problem Analysis

This problem requires that we pass through the data twice—once to produce the salesperson listing, and a second time to produce the low sales

Figure 9.7   Printer spacing chart for Program 9a

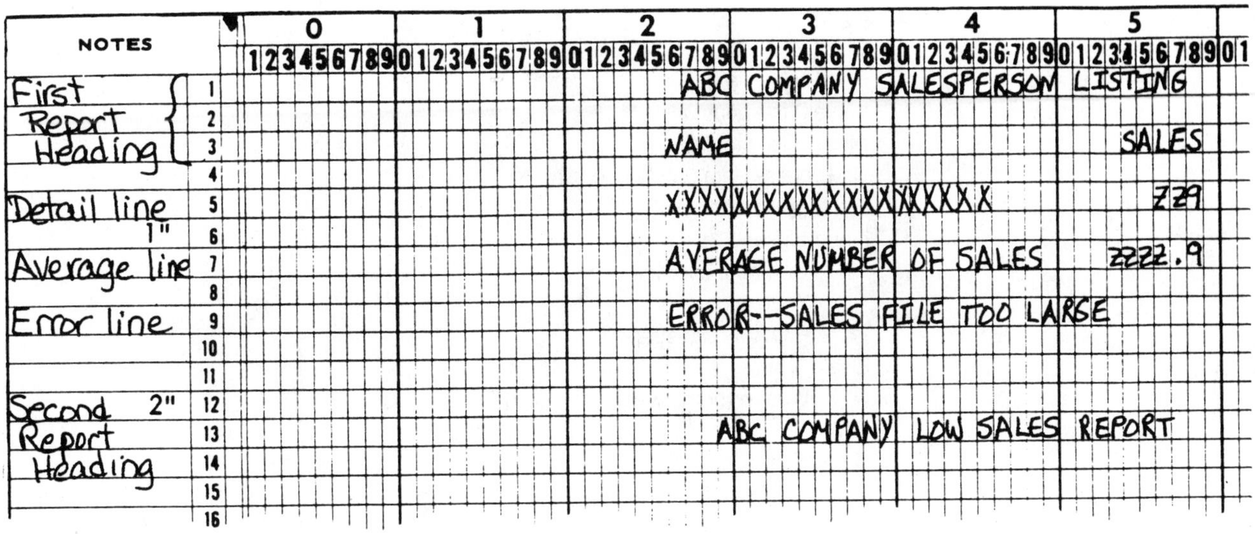

report. A table can be used to store the sales data during the first pass so that it will be unnecessary to process the data from the data file for the second report. Notice that the content of the second report depends on the average of the data contained in the file. During the first pass through the data, we can accumulate the total number of sales and count the number of records. This information is necessary to compute the average. This approach assumes that there is a limited number of salespersons. Let us assume that the company employs no more than 100 people. (If the size of the data file is too large to be loaded into a table in memory, it is necessary to process the file twice to produce the desired reports. The advantage of using the table is speed. It is much more efficient to process data directly from memory than from an external data source such as a disk or tape.)

Because we have assumed that the firm employs no more than 100 salespeople, it will be necessary to confirm that the file contains no more than 100 records to produce valid output. If the file contains too many records, we should print an error message and terminate. We can accomplish this task by checking to see if the end-of-file condition caused the termination of the loop. If it did, the number of records in the file did not exceed the number of elements in the table, and the program can continue to produce the second report. If the loop terminates because 100 records have been processed and the 101st record has been read, then an error condition has occurred because there is no room in the table to store more than 100 records. A plan for the program is shown in Figure 9.8.

Problem Solution

A solution to the problem is shown in Program 9a. The structure diagram for this program is shown in Figure 9.9; sample output is shown in Figure 9.10.

This program makes use of a table to store data read from the file. Note the use of the OCCURS/DEPENDING ON clause in the definition of the table at lines 57 through 61. This clause is not absolutely essential to the program, but it serves as an effective deterrent to attempts to process table

Figure 9.8   Plan for Program 9a (Low Sales Report)

Major logic
    Open files
    Read sales file
    Move 0 to kount
    Move 0 to total sales
    Do Process data until end of file
        or Kount = 100
    If end of file
        Compute average
        Write average
        Print low sales report
    Else
        Write error message
    End if
    Close files
    Stop
Process data
    Write detail line
    Add 1 to kount
    Move data to appropriate table element
    Accumulate total sales
    Read sales file

elements not used to store data from the file. In subsequent portions of the program, if a reference is made to a table element with a subscript value larger than KOUNT, an execution time error would result. Without the OCCURS/DEPENDING ON clause, the program could inadvertently process any one of the 100 elements of the table, whether they stored data or not. This would show up as a logical error in the output produced by the program, but otherwise the execution of the program would continue.

Note that we have assigned data-names to two constants—SALE-LIMIT (value 4) and TABLE-SIZE (value 100) (see lines 53–55). It is quite likely that in the course of the life of the program, someone will want to change one or both of these values. Identifying them with names in the DATA DIVISION aids in locating these parameters and making the change efficiently. Unfortunately, COBOL syntax does not allow you to use TABLE-SIZE in the OCCURS clause in the definition of the table entry, so if this value changed, it would have to be changed twice—once as the value of TABLE-SIZE and again in the OCCURS clause. You could include TABLE-SIZE as an 02 item under the definition of SALESPERSON-INFORMATION-TABLE if desired. This would ensure that all information relevant to the definition of the table is in close proximity in the program. The resulting program segment would appear as follows:

```
01   SALESPERSON-INFORMATION-TABLE.
     02 TABLE-SIZE        PIC 999 VALUE 100.
     02 TABLE-ENTRY-SI    OCCURS 1 TO 100 TIMES
          .               DEPENDING ON KOUNT.
          .
          .
```

Program 9a

_____

```
 1 IDENTIFICATION DIVISION.
 2
 3 PROGRAM-ID. LOW-SALES-PRO9A.
 4 AUTHOR. HORN.
 5
 6 ENVIRONMENT DIVISION.
 7
 8 CONFIGURATION SECTION.
 9
10 SOURCE-COMPUTER.
11 OBJECT-COMPUTER.
12
13 INPUT-OUTPUT SECTION.
14
15 FILE-CONTROL.
16
17     SELECT SALES-FILE ASSIGN TO DISK.
18
19     SELECT REPORT-FILE ASSIGN TO PRINTER.
20
21 DATA DIVISION.
22
23 FILE SECTION.
24
25 FD   SALES-FILE
26      LABEL RECORDS ARE STANDARD
27      DATA RECORD IS SALES-RECORD.
28
29 01   SALES-RECORD.
30      02 NAME-SR              PIC X(20).
31      02 NUMBER-OF-SALES-SR PIC 999.
32      02 FILLER              PIC X(57).
33
34 FD   REPORT-FILE
35      LABEL RECORDS ARE OMITTED
36      DATA RECORD IS REPORT-RECORD.
37
38 01   REPORT-RECORD          PIC X(132).
39
40 WORKING-STORAGE SECTION.
41
42 01   EOF-FLAG              PIC X(3) VALUE "NO".
43      88 END-OF-FILE        VALUE "YES".
44
45 01   SUBSCRIPT.
46      02 SUB                PIC 99 VALUE ZERO.
47
48 01   COMPUTED-AMOUNTS.
49      02 KOUNT              PIC 999      VALUE ZERO.
50      02 TOTAL-SALES        PIC 9(5)     VALUE ZERO.
51      02 AVERAGE            PIC 9(5)V99 VALUE ZERO.
52
53 01   CONSTANTS.
54      02 SALE-LIMIT         PIC 9 VALUE 4.
55      02 TABLE-SIZE         PIC 999 VALUE 100.
56
```

```
57 01   SALESPERSON-INFORMATION-TABLE.
58      02 TABLE-ENTRY-SI OCCURS 1 TO 100 TIMES
59                         DEPENDING ON KOUNT.
60         03 NAME-SI                PIC X(20).
61         03 NUMBER-OF-SALES-SI     PIC 999.
62
63 01   HEAD-LINE-1.
64      02 FILLER       PIC X(26) VALUE SPACES.
65      02 FILLER       PIC X(12) VALUE "ABC COMPANY ".
66      02 FILLER       PIC X(20) VALUE "SALESPERSON LISTING".
67
68 01   HEAD-LINE-2.
69      02 FILLER       PIC X(28) VALUE SPACES.
70      02 FILLER       PIC X(12) VALUE "ABC COMPANY ".
71      02 FILLER       PIC X(17) VALUE "LOW SALES REPORT".
72
73 01   HEAD-LINE-3.
74      02 FILLER       PIC X(25) VALUE SPACES.
75      02 FILLER       PIC X(5) VALUE "NAME".
76      02 FILLER       PIC X(23) VALUE SPACES.
77      02 FILLER       PIC X(11) VALUE "SALES".
78
79 01   AVERAGE-LINE.
80      02 FILLER       PIC X(25) VALUE SPACES.
81      02 FILLER       PIC X(27) VALUE
82         "AVERAGE NUMBER OF SALES ".
83      02 AVERAGE-AL   PIC  ZZZZ.9.
84
85 01   DETAIL-LINE.
86      02 FILLER       PIC X(25) VALUE SPACES.
87      02 NAME-DL      PIC X(20).
88      02 FILLER       PIC X(10) VALUE SPACES.
89      02 NUMBER-OF-SALES-DL        PIC ZZ9.
90
91 01   ERROR-LINE.
92      02 FILLER        PIC X(25) VALUE SPACES.
93      02 FILLER        PIC X(27) VALUE
94         "ERROR-SALES FILE TOO LARGE".
95
96 PROCEDURE DIVISION.
97
98 1000-MAIN-LOGIC.
99
100     PERFORM 2000-INITIALIZE-DATA.
101     PERFORM 2100-PROCESS-DATA
102          UNTIL END-OF-FILE
103             OR KOUNT = TABLE-SIZE.
104     IF   END-OF-FILE
105         PERFORM 2200-COMPUTE-AVERAGE
106         PERFORM 2300-WRITE-AVERAGE
107         PERFORM 2400-PRINT-LOW-SALES-REPORT
108     ELSE
109         PERFORM 2500-WRITE-ERROR.
110     PERFORM 2600-TERMINATE-PROGRAM.
111     STOP RUN.
112
```

Program 9a *(continued)*

```
113 2000-INITIALIZE-DATA.
114
115     OPEN INPUT SALES-FILE
116          OUTPUT REPORT-FILE.
117     PERFORM 3000-WRITE-HEADING.
118     PERFORM 9000-READ-SALES-FILE.
119
120 2100-PROCESS-DATA.
121
122     PERFORM 3100-WRITE-DETAIL.
123     ADD 1 TO KOUNT.
124     MOVE NAME-SR TO NAME-SI (KOUNT).
125     MOVE NUMBER-OF-SALES-SR TO
126          NUMBER-OF-SALES-SI (KOUNT).
127     ADD NUMBER-OF-SALES-SR TO TOTAL-SALES.
128     PERFORM 9000-READ-SALES-FILE.
129
130 2200-COMPUTE-AVERAGE.
131
132     DIVIDE TOTAL-SALES BY KOUNT GIVING AVERAGE.
133
134 2300-WRITE-AVERAGE.
135
136     MOVE AVERAGE TO AVERAGE-AL.
137     WRITE REPORT-RECORD FROM AVERAGE-LINE AFTER 2.
138
139 2400-PRINT-LOW-SALES-REPORT.
140
141     WRITE REPORT-RECORD FROM HEAD-LINE-2 AFTER PAGE.
142     WRITE REPORT-RECORD FROM HEAD-LINE-3 AFTER 2.
143     MOVE SPACES TO REPORT-RECORD.
144     WRITE REPORT-RECORD AFTER 1.
145     PERFORM 3200-WRITE-EXCEPTION
146             VARYING SUB FROM 1 BY 1 UNTIL SUB > KOUNT.
147
148 2500-WRITE-ERROR.
149
150     WRITE REPORT-RECORD FROM ERROR-LINE AFTER 2.
151
152 2600-TERMINATE-PROGRAM.
153
154     CLOSE SALES-FILE
155           REPORT-FILE.
156
157 3000-WRITE-HEADING.
158
159     WRITE REPORT-RECORD FROM HEAD-LINE-1 AFTER PAGE.
160     WRITE REPORT-RECORD FROM HEAD-LINE-3 AFTER 2.
161     MOVE SPACES TO REPORT-RECORD.
162     WRITE REPORT-RECORD AFTER 1.
163
```

Program 9a   (concluded)

```
164 3100-WRITE-DETAIL.
165
166     MOVE NAME-SR TO NAME-DL.
167     MOVE NUMBER-OF-SALES-SR TO
168         NUMBER-OF-SALES-DL.
169     WRITE REPORT-RECORD FROM DETAIL-LINE AFTER 1.
170
171 3200-WRITE-EXCEPTION.
172
173     IF NUMBER-OF-SALES-SI (SUB) < AVERAGE - SALE-LIMIT
174         MOVE NAME-SI (SUB) TO NAME-DL
175         MOVE NUMBER-OF-SALES-SI (SUB) TO
176             NUMBER-OF-SALES-DL
177         WRITE REPORT-RECORD FROM DETAIL-LINE AFTER 1.
178
179 9000-READ-SALES-FILE.
180
181     READ SALES-FILE
182         AT END MOVE "YES" TO EOF-FLAG.
```

Figure 9.9   Structure diagram of Program 9a

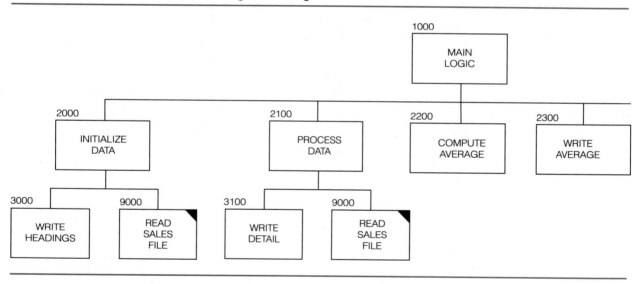

One might be tempted to use the PERFORM/VARYING statement to control the loop used to load the table as in the following:

```
PERFORM 2100-PROCESS-DATA
    VARYING KOUNT FROM 1 BY 1
    UNTIL END-OF-FILE
        OR KOUNT > 100.
```

A problem with this approach is that when the loop terminates, the value of KOUNT is 1 larger than the number of elements in the table because the PERFORM/VARYING statement increases the value of KOUNT before testing. It would be necessary to subtract 1 from the value of KOUNT before proceeding.

You will note that we did use the PERFORM/VARYING statement to control the loop that produces the second report (see lines 145–156). This statement is appropriate in this case since the entire table must be processed using a subscript (SUB) which must vary from 1 to KOUNT.

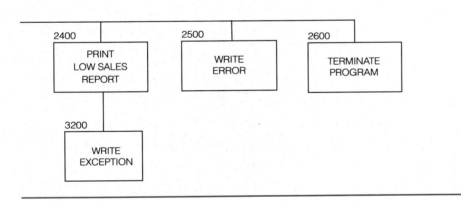

Figure 9.10   Sample output from Program 9a

```
           ABC COMPANY SALESPERSON LISTING

           NAME                        SALES

           JONES, JOHN                   12
           SMITH, HARRY                   1
           DOE, JAMES                     3
           GONZALEZ, JUAN                 4
           BLACK, JAMES                  10
           GREY, JOE                      9
           WHITE, SUE                     4
           MAPLE, MARY                    0
           GREEN, SAM                     1
           QUE, SUSY                      6
           ENGLAND, MERRY                 9
           MCDONALD, RONALD              10
           SPADE, SAM                     9
           MAIN, STREET                  80
           POIROT, HERCULE                7
           SECOND, AVENUE                 9
           BROWN, JOHN                    0
           ORLEANS, NEW                   8
           VIRGINIA, WEST                 7
           CAROLINA, NORTH                7
           DAKOTA, SOUTH                 21
           DAKOTA, NORTH                 22
           NEBRASKA, CENTRAL             23
           YORK, NEW                     24
           BROMLEY, NEW                  25
           RECORD, LAST                  26

           AVERAGE NUMBER OF SALES      12.9



           ABC COMPANY LOW SALES REPORT

           NAME                        SALES

           SMITH, HARRY                   1
           DOE, JAMES                     3
           GONZALEZ, JUAN                 4
           WHITE, SUE                     4
           MAPLE, MARY                    0
           GREEN, SAM                     1
           QUE, SUSY                      6
           POIROT, HERCULE                7
           BROWN, JOHN                    0
           ORLEANS, NEW                   8
           VIRGINIA, WEST                 7
           CAROLINA, NORTH                7
```

9.8 THE REDEFINES CLAUSE

In some instances there is a need to define the same data item with different names and different characteristics. For example, suppose a product classification code contains eight digits, with the first two digits representing the division of the company which manufactures the item. For some purposes, it is useful to use one eight-digit numeric field; for others, it may be useful to have the field broken down into two fields. The REDEFINES clause is used in the DATA DIVISION to accomplish this reclassification.

```
03 PRODUCT-CLASSIFICATION-CODE PIC 9(8).
03 P-C-CODE REDEFINES PRODUCT-CLASSIFICATION-CODE.
   05 DIVISION-PC PIC 9(2).
   05 PRODUCT-PC PIC 9(6).
```

Both PRODUCT-CLASSIFICATION-CODE and P-C-CODE refer to the same eight characters.

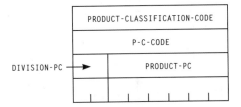

The REDEFINES clause is necessary because of the numeric nature of the data. At first glance, the following code would seem to accomplish the same result:

```
03 PRODUCT-CLASSIFICATION-CODE.
   05 DIVISION-PC PIC 9(2).
   05 PRODUCT-PC  PIC 9(6).
```

However, the PRODUCT-CLASSIFICATION-CODE is a group item; it is, therefore, classed as alphanumeric and cannot be used in computations or numeric edited output.

The general form of the REDEFINES clause is shown in Figure 9.11. The level-number used on the REDEFINES entry must be the same as the level-number on data-name-2 which is being "redefined." The REDEFINES clause may be used on a group item as in the above example or on an elementary item as in the following example:

```
01  XYZ              PIC X(5).
01  ZYW REDEFINES XYZ PIC 9(5).
```

The above coding could be used when you want to reference the same field as both a numeric item and an alphanumeric item.

Figure 9.11 General form of the REDEFINES clause

```
level-number data-name-1 REDEFINES data-name-2
```

The REDEFINES clause is invalid if a data-name with a higher-level number occurs between data-name-1 and data-name-2. For example, the following program segment is invalid:

```
      03 FLDA PIC X(10).
   02 FLDB.
      03 FLDC REDEFINES FLDA. .
```

Data-names with lower-level numbers may occur between data-name-1 and data-name-2. For example, the following code could be used to define a data field as a six-digit numeric field and as three two-digit fields.

```
03 DATE-IN.
   05 MONTH-IN  PIC 99.
   05 DAY-IN    PIC 99.
   05 YEAR-IN   PIC 99.
03 DATE-NUM-IN REDEFINES DATE-IN PIC 9(6).
```

Note that the length of the item named by data-name-1 must exactly equal the length of the item named in data-name-2. In the example above, DATE-IN and DATE-NUM-IN are each six characters in length.

9.9 TABLE LOOK-UP

The REDEFINES clause is often used in the creation of a table of constants to be processed by a program. Consider the following example: XYZ Manufacturing Corporation manufactures five types of widgets.

Code	Description
1	MIDGET
2	REGULAR
3	KING
4	SUPER
5	GIANT

A data record contains an item PRODUCT-CODE having value 1, 2, 3, 4, or 5; a program must output the corresponding verbal description.

One approach to the program is to create a table of constants as follows:

```
DESCRIPTION (1)  | MIDGET  |
DESCRIPTION (2)  | REGULAR |
DESCRIPTION (3)  | KING    |
DESCRIPTION (4)  | SUPER   |
DESCRIPTION (5)  | GIANT   |
```

The following program segment could be used to create this table:

```
01  DESCRIPTION-CONSTANTS.
    02 FILLER PIC X(7) VALUE "MIDGET".
    02 FILLER PIC X(7) VALUE "REGULAR".
    02 FILLER PIC X(7) VALUE "KING".
    02 FILLER PIC X(7) VALUE "SUPER".
    02 FILLER PIC X(7) VALUE "GIANT".
01  DESCRIPTION-TABLE REDEFINES DESCRIPTION-CONSTANTS.
    02 DESCRIPTION PIC X(7) OCCURS 5 TIMES.
```

The data layout created by the above may be visualized as:

DESCRIPTION-CONSTANTS				
DESCRIPTION-TABLE				
DESCRIPTION (1)	DESCRIPTION (2)	DESCRIPTION (3)	DESCRIPTION (4)	DESCRIPTION (5)
M I D G E T	R E G U L A R	K I N G	S U P E R	G I A N T

The data item PRODUCT-CODE from an input record can be used as a subscript to access the appropriate item from the table:

```
MOVE DESCRIPTION (PRODUCT-CODE) TO OUTPUT-DESCRIPTION.
```

If the value of PRODUCT-CODE is 1, 2, 3, 4, or 5, the above code will cause no problems; however, if some other value is contained in PRODUCT-CODE, the reference DESCRIPTION (PRODUCT-CODE) will produce an execution time error. A better statement for accessing the table would be

```
IF PRODUCT-CODE = 0 OR PRODUCT-CODE > 5
    MOVE "INVALID" TO OUTPUT-DESCRIPTION
ELSE
    MOVE DESCRIPTION (PRODUCT-CODE) TO OUTPUT-DESCRIPTION.
```

In this example, the look-up process was exceedingly simple, as there was a one-to-one correspondence between the PRODUCT-CODE and the table element containing the desired data DESCRIPTION (PRODUCT-CODE). If this correspondence does not exist, it may be necessary to search a table to find the desired element. The search may take the form of accessing elements of the table sequentially until the desired element is found, as in the following example: The XYZ Company uses a four-digit inventory code for its five products.

Code	Description
1234	MIDGET
2314	REGULAR
8978	KING
8900	SUPER
7892	GIANT

The numeric data item INV-CODE is contained on an input record. The program must output the corresponding word description.

The following program segment could be used to establish the table of constants:

```
01   INVENTORY-CONSTANTS.
     03 FILLER PIC X(11) VALUE "1234MIDGET".
     03 FILLER PIC X(11) VALUE "2314REGULAR".
     03 FILLER PIC X(11) VALUE "8978KING".
     03 FILLER PIC X(11) VALUE "8900SUPER".
     03 FILLER PIC X(11) VALUE "7892GIANT".
01   INVENTORY-TABLE REDEFINES INVENTORY-CONSTANTS.
     03 INVENTORY-ITEM OCCURS 5 TIMES.
        05 KODE PIC 9(4).
        05 DESCR PIC X(7).
```

The data defined above may be visualized as follows:

INVENTORY-CONSTANTS									
INVENTORY-TABLE									
INVENTORY-ITEM (1)		INVENTORY-ITEM (2)		INVENTORY-ITEM (3)		INVENTORY-ITEM (4)		INVENTORY-ITEM (5)	
KODE (1)	DESCR (1)	KODE (2)	DESCR (2)	KODE (3)	DESCR (3)	KODE (4)	DESCR (4)	KODE (5)	DESCR (5)
1234	MIDGET	2314	REGULAR	8978	KING	8900	SUPER	7892	GIANT

The program must search for an element KODE (SUB), which is equal to INV-CODE. When such an element is found, the value of DESCR (SUB) will contain the desired description. The following program segment could be used:

```
MOVE "NO" TO FOUND-FLAG.
PERFORM SEARCH-PROCEDURE
    VARYING SUB FROM 1 BY 1
        UNTIL SUB > 5 OR FOUND-FLAG = "YES".
IF FOUND-FLAG = "NO"
    MOVE "INVALID" TO OUTPUT-DESCRIPTION
ELSE
    MOVE DESCR (SUB) TO OUTPUT-DESCRIPTION.
    .
    .
    .
SEARCH-PROCEDURE.
    IF KODE (SUB) = INV-CODE
        MOVE "YES" TO FOUND-FLAG.
```

9.10 COUNTING AND ACCUMULATION

Tables may be used for a variety of purposes. In previous examples, tables have been used to store both data and constants. Another usage for a table is in counting.

---- Example ----

A survey has been made of customer arrival times in the XYZ Department Store. One record has been prepared for each arrival, showing in coded form the hour during which the customer arrived. The following code was used in preparing the data records:

Hour	Code
9–10 A.M.	1
10–11 A.M.	2
11–12 A.M.	3
12–1 P.M.	4
1–2 P.M.	5
2–3 P.M.	6
3–4 P.M.	7
4–5 P.M.	8
5–6 P.M.	9

The output desired is a frequency distribution showing the number of customers who arrived during each hour.

A table of nine elements (to be utilized as counters) can be used to accumulate the desired counts. The elements of the table must be initialized to have value 0. This process is complicated somewhat by the fact that the VALUE clause may not be used with an OCCURS clause in the DATA DIVISION; that is, the following program segment is invalid:

```
01   COUNTERS.
     03 KOUNT PIC 99 OCCURS 9 TIMES VALUE 0.
```

One approach to initialization is to use the REDEFINES option as though a table of constants were being created:

```
01   CONSTANTS.
     03 FILLER PIC X(18) VALUE ALL "0".
01   COUNTERS REDEFINES CONSTANTS.
     03 KOUNT PIC 99 OCCURS 9 TIMES.
```

An alternative is to initialize the table in the PROCEDURE DIVISION prior to utilizing the variables for counting. For example,

```
            .
            .
            .
PERFORM INITIALIZE-KOUNT
    VARYING K FROM 1 BY 1 UNTIL K > 9.
            .
            .
            .
INITIALIZE-KOUNT.
    MOVE ZERO TO KOUNT (K).
```

Once the table of counters has been initialized, the process of accumulating the required totals can begin. Suppose the data-name associated with the code on the data record is HOUR-CODE. The contents of this variable can be used to select the element of KOUNT to be incremented. The basic code could be

```
ADD 1 TO KOUNT (HOUR-CODE).
```

If HOUR-CODE has value 1, KOUNT (1) will be incremented; if HOUR-CODE has value 2, 1 will be added to KOUNT (2), and so forth.

Tables may also be used for accumulation. For example, the XYZ Department Store wants to determine which day of the week is, on average, its busiest day. A record for each date in the previous 52 weeks has been prepared with a code 1, 2, 3, ... , 7 showing the day of the week (DAY-CODE) and the amount of sales (SALES-AMOUNT) for that day.

A table containing seven elements can be used to accumulate the desired totals. Each element of the table must be initialized to have value 0; then, as each data record is processed, the value of SALES-AMOUNT is added to the appropriate element of the table, as in the following code:

```
            .
            .
            .
PERFORM INITIALIZATION
    VARYING K FROM 1 BY 1 UNTIL K > 7.
PERFORM READ-AND-PROCESS
    UNTIL END-OF-FILE.
```

```
             .
             .
             .
        INITIALIZATION.
            MOVE 0 TO TOTAL (K).
        READ-AND-PROCESS.
            READ INPUT-FILE
                AT END MOVE "YES" TO EOF-FLAG.
            IF NOT END-OF-FILE
                ADD SALES-AMOUNT TO TOTAL (DAY-CODE).
```

9.11 TWO-LEVEL TABLES

All of the tables with which we have been dealing so far in this chapter have been **one-level tables**—that is, they have been equivalent to linear lists of elements. In some situations, we may need a data structure that is composed of a series of lists. Such a structure is called a **two-level table**. Elements of a two-level table require two subscripts in order to access a particular element. For example, suppose we wish to store grades for four tests for up to 75 students. We could use a data structure such as:

The elements of the table are referenced by the data-name GRADE and two subscripts. The first subscript refers to the student (the row). The second subscript refers to the test number for that student (the column).

Two usages of the OCCURS clause are required to create a two-level table. For example, the data structure could be created with the following DATA DIVISION entries:

```
01  NUM-STUDENTS PIC 99 VALUE 0.
01  GRADE-TABLE.
    02 STUDENT OCCURS 1 TO 75 TIMES
              DEPENDING ON NUM-STUDENTS.
    03 GRADE PIC 999 OCCURS 4 TIMES.
```

An alternate way to visualize this structure is as follows:

Note that the data-name STUDENT may be subscripted. Thus, STUDENT (1) is a reference to all four grades of student number 1. However, STUDENT is a group item and, hence, an alphanumeric field. Any reference to the data-name GRADE must always include two subscripts.

The table could be expanded to store additional data, such as the student's name and average grade. Consider the following code:

```
01   NUM-STUDENTS PIC 99 VALUE 0.
01   STUDENT-DATA-TABLE.
     02 STUDENT OCCURS 1 TO 75 TIMES
                    DEPENDING ON NUM-STUDENTS.
        03 NAME      PIC X(20).
        03 GRADE     PIC 999 OCCURS 4 TIMES.
        03 AVERAGE   PIC 99.
```

The structure created by this program segment can be visualized as

STUDENT-DATA-TABLE																		
STUDENT (1)						STUDENT (2)								STUDENT (75)				
NAME (1)	GRADE (1, 1)	GRADE (1, 2)	GRADE (1, 3)	GRADE (1, 4)	AVERAGE (1)	NAME (2)	GRADE (2, 1)	GRADE (2, 2)	GRADE (2, 3)	GRADE (2, 4)	AVERAGE (2)			NAME (75)	GRADE (75, 1)	GRADE (75, 2)	GRADE (75, 3)	GRADE (75, 4)	AVERAGE (75)

Suppose the data record containing the students' names and grades has the following description:

```
01   DATA-RECORD.
     02 STUDENT-NAME PIC X(20).
     02 STUDENT-GRADE PIC 999 OCCURS 4 TIMES.
```

The following code would be used to input this data and store it into STUDENT-DATA-TABLE:

```
          .
          .
          .
     READ INPUT-FILE INTO DATA-RECORD
          AT END MOVE "YES" TO EOF FLAG.
     PERFORM STORE-AND-READ
          UNTIL END-OF-FILE OR NUM-STUDENTS = 75.
          .
          .
          .
STORE-AND-READ.
     ADD 1 TO NUM-STUDENTS.
     MOVE STUDENT-NAME TO NAME (NUM-STUDENTS).
     PERFORM GRADE-MOVE VARYING SUB FROM 1 BY 1
                    UNTIL SUB > 4.
     READ INPUT-FILE INTO DATA-RECORD
          AT END MOVE "YES" TO EOF-FLAG.
GRADE-MOVE.
     MOVE STUDENT-GRADE (SUB) TO
          GRADE (NUM-STUDENTS, SUB).
```

Assuming that the data has been stored, the following code could be used to compute the averages for each of the students:

```
            .
            .
            .
PERFORM AVERAGE-ROUTINE
    VARYING SUB FROM 1 BY 1 UNTIL SUB > NUM-STUDENTS.
            .
            .
            .
AVERAGE-ROUTINE.
    MOVE ZERO TO SUM-OF-GRADES.
    PERFORM SUMMATION VARYING J FROM 1 BY 1 UNTIL J > 4.
    COMPUTE AVERAGE (SUB) = SUM-OF-GRADES / 4.
SUMMATION.
    ADD GRADE (SUB, J) TO SUM-OF-GRADES.
```

Two-level tables may be used for storing tables of constants which will be used by a program. Consider the example program in the next section.

9.12 PROGRAM EXAMPLE

Problem Statement

The following table shows the wholesale prices of various grades of petroleum products at four refineries:

	Refinery			
	1	2	3	4
Grade 1 Diesel	1.01	1.03	.99	1.05
Grade 2 Regular	.84	.88	.83	.87
Grade 3 Unleaded	.97	.91	.92	.95

The number of gallons purchased, the refinery number, and the number representing the type of fuel have been stored on data records. A program which will look up the appropriate price per gallon and output the total amount of the purchase is needed. The printer spacing chart for the desired report is shown in Figure 9.12.

Problem Analysis

In this problem, the price of gas depends on two factors—the grade and the refinery. Therefore, a two-level table representing the prices of gas by grade (the first level) and refinery (the second level) will be useful. The program will then be able to use the grade number and refinery number from the input record to access the data in the table. In some respects, this problem is very similar to other programs that process a data file to produce a report. A plan for this program is shown in Figure 9.13.

Figure 9.12 Printer spacing chart for Program 9b

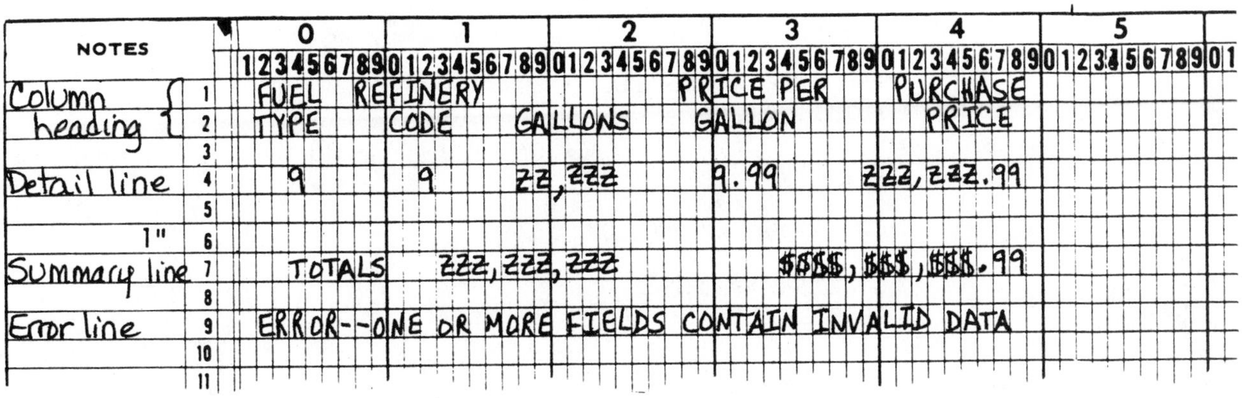

Figure 9.13 Plan for Program 9b

Main control
    Open files
    Read product file
    Do Process data until end of file
    Write summary line
    Close files
    Stop
Process data
    If data is invalid
        Write error message
    Else
        Compute fuel cost by multiplying price from table by gallons
        Accumulate totals
        Write detail line
    End if
    Read product file

Problem Solution

A program for this problem is shown in Program 9b, with the structure diagram for the program shown in Figure 9.14. This program illustrates the use of a two-level table of constants. The table is created at lines 51 through 71, using the REDEFINES clause at line 68 to provide access to the constants created in the preceding data structure (FUEL-PRICE-CONSTANTS defined in lines 51–66). This table can be visualized as follows:

FUEL-PRICE-CONSTANTS											
FUEL-PRICE-TABLE											
DIESEL				REGULAR				UNLEADED			
TYPE-ENTRY-FP (1)				TYPE-ENTRY-FP (2)				TYPE-ENTRY-FP (3)			
PRICE-FP (1, 1)	PRICE-FP (1, 2)	PRICE-FP (1, 3)	PRICE-FP (1, 4)	PRICE-FP (2, 1)	PRICE-FP (2, 2)	PRICE-FP (2, 3)	PRICE-FP (2, 4)	PRICE-FP (3, 1)	PRICE-FP (3, 2)	PRICE-FP (3, 3)	PRICE-FP (3, 4)
1 0 1	1 0 3	0 9 9	1 0 5	0 8 4	0 8 8	0 8 3	0 8 7	0 9 7	0 9 1	0 9 2	0 9 5

Program 9b

```
 1 IDENTIFICATION DIVISION.
 2
 3 PROGRAM-ID. GAS-REPORT-PRO9B.
 4 AUTHOR. HORN.
 5
 6 ENVIRONMENT DIVISION.
 7
 8 CONFIGURATION SECTION.
 9
10 SOURCE-COMPUTER.
11 OBJECT-COMPUTER.
12
13 INPUT-OUTPUT SECTION.
14
15 FILE-CONTROL.
16
17     SELECT PRODUCT-FILE ASSIGN TO DISK.
18
19     SELECT REPORT-FILE ASSIGN TO PRINTER.
20
21 DATA DIVISION.
22
23 FILE SECTION.
24
25 FD   PRODUCT-FILE
26      LABEL RECORDS ARE STANDARD
27      DATA RECORD IS PRODUCT-RECORD.
28
29 01   PRODUCT-RECORD.
30      02 GALLONS-PR              PIC 9(5).
31      02 FUEL-TYPE-PR            PIC 9.
32      02 REFINERY-CODE-PR        PIC 9.
33      02 FILLER                  PIC X(77).
34
35 FD   REPORT-FILE
36      LABEL RECORDS ARE OMITTED
37      DATA RECORD IS PRINT-LINE.
38
39 01   REPORT-RECORD        PIC X(132).
40
41 WORKING-STORAGE SECTION.
42
43 01   FLAGS.
44      02 EOF-FLAG          PIC X(3) VALUE "NO".
45
46 01   TOTALS.
47      02 FUEL-COST              PIC 9(6)V99 VALUE ZERO.
48      02 TOTAL-GALLONS          PIC 9(9)    VALUE ZERO.
49      02 TOTAL-COST             PIC 9(9)V99 VALUE ZERO.
50
```

Program 9b   *(continued)*

```
51 01    FUEL-PRICE-CONSTANTS.
52       02 DIESEL.
53          03 FILLER PIC 9V99 VALUE 1.01.
54          03 FILLER PIC 9V99 VALUE 1.03.
55          03 FILLER PIC 9V99 VALUE 0.99.
56          03 FILLER PIC 9V99 VALUE 1.05.
57       02 REGULAR.
58          03 FILLER PIC 9V99 VALUE 0.84.
59          03 FILLER PIC 9V99 VALUE 0.88.
60          03 FILLER PIC 9V99 VALUE 0.83.
61          03 FILLER PIC 9V99 VALUE 0.87.
62       02 UNLEADED.
63          03 FILLER PIC 9V99 VALUE 0.97.
64          03 FILLER PIC 9V99 VALUE 0.91.
65          03 FILLER PIC 9V99 VALUE 0.92.
66          03 FILLER PIC 9V99 VALUE 0.95.
67
68 01    FUEL-PRICES-TABLE REDEFINES FUEL-PRICE-CONSTANTS.
69       02 TYPE-ENTRY-FP OCCURS 3 TIMES.
70          03 REFINERY-ENTRY-FP OCCURS 4 TIMES.
71             04 PRICE-FP PIC 9V99.
72
73 01    HEADLINE-1.
74       02 FILLER          PIC X VALUE SPACES.
75       02 FILLER          PIC X(14) VALUE "FUEL  REFINERY".
76       02 FILLER          PIC X(12) VALUE SPACES.
77       02 FILLER          PIC X(9) VALUE "PRICE PER".
78       02 FILLER          PIC X(4) VALUE SPACES.
79       02 FILLER          PIC X(8) VALUE "PURCHASE".
80
81 01    HEADLINE-2.
82       02 FILLER          PIC X VALUE SPACES.
83       02 FILLER          PIC X(12) VALUE "TYPE    CODE".
84       02 FILLER          PIC X(5) VALUE SPACES.
85       02 FILLER          PIC X(7) VALUE "GALLONS".
86       02 FILLER          PIC X(3) VALUE SPACES.
87       02 FILLER          PIC X(6) VALUE "GALLON".
88       02 FILLER          PIC X(9) VALUE SPACES.
89       02 FILLER          PIC X(5) VALUE "PRICE".
90
91 01    DETAIL-LINE.
92       02 FILLER                  PIC X(3) VALUE SPACES.
93       02 FUEL-TYPE-DL            PIC 9.
94       02 FILLER                  PIC X(7) VALUE SPACES.
95       02 REFINERY-CODE-DL        PIC 9.
96       02 FILLER                  PIC X(5) VALUE SPACES.
97       02 GALLONS-DL              PIC ZZ,ZZZ.
98       02 FILLER                  PIC X(6) VALUE SPACES.
99       02 PRICE-PER-GALLON-DL     PIC 9.99.
100      02 FILLER                  PIC X(5) VALUE SPACES.
101      02 FUEL-COST-DL            PIC ZZZ,ZZZ.99.
102
103 01   ERROR-LINE.
104      02 FILLER                  PIC X(47) VALUE
105        " ERROR--ONE OR MORE FIELDS CONTAIN INVALID DATA".
106
```

Program 9b   *(continued)*

```
107 01   SUMMARY-LINE.
108      02 FILLER               PIC X(12) VALUE "   TOTALS   ".
109      02 TOTAL-GALLONS-SL     PIC ZZZ,ZZZ,ZZZ.
110      02 FILLER               PIC X VALUE "*".
111      02 FILLER               PIC X(9) VALUE SPACES.
112      02 TOTAL-COST-SL        PIC $$$$,$$$,$$$.99.
113      02 FILLER               PIC X VALUE "*".
114
115 PROCEDURE DIVISION.
116
117 1000-MAIN-CONTROL.
118
119      PERFORM 2000-INITIALIZE-DATA.
120      PERFORM 2100-PROCESS-DATA
121           UNTIL EOF-FLAG = "YES".
122      PERFORM 2200-WRITE-SUMMARY.
123      PERFORM 2300-CLOSE-FILES.
124      STOP RUN.
125
126 2000-INITIALIZE-DATA.
127
128      OPEN INPUT PRODUCT-FILE
129          OUTPUT REPORT-FILE.
130      WRITE REPORT-RECORD FROM HEADLINE-1 AFTER PAGE.
131      WRITE REPORT-RECORD FROM HEADLINE-2 AFTER 1.
132      MOVE SPACES TO REPORT-RECORD.
133      WRITE REPORT-RECORD AFTER 1.
134      PERFORM 9000-READ-PRODUCT-FILE.
135
136 2100-PROCESS-DATA.
137
138      MOVE SPACES TO DETAIL-LINE.
139      MOVE FUEL-TYPE-PR     TO FUEL-TYPE-DL.
140      MOVE REFINERY-CODE-PR TO REFINERY-CODE-DL.
141      MOVE GALLONS-PR       TO GALLONS-DL.
142      IF FUEL-TYPE-PR > 3     OR
143         FUEL-TYPE-PR = 0     OR
144         REFINERY-CODE-PR > 4 OR
145         REFINERY-CODE-PR = 0
146              WRITE REPORT-RECORD FROM DETAIL-LINE AFTER 2
147              WRITE REPORT-RECORD FROM ERROR-LINE AFTER 1
148              MOVE SPACES TO REPORT-RECORD
149              WRITE REPORT-RECORD AFTER 1
150      ELSE
151          MOVE PRICE-FP (FUEL-TYPE-PR, REFINERY-CODE-PR) TO
152               PRICE-PER-GALLON-DL
153          MULTIPLY PRICE-FP (FUEL-TYPE-PR, REFINERY-CODE-PR) BY
154              GALLONS-PR GIVING FUEL-COST
155          MOVE FUEL-COST        TO FUEL-COST-DL
156          ADD  FUEL-COST        TO TOTAL-COST
157          ADD  GALLONS-PR       TO TOTAL-GALLONS
158          WRITE REPORT-RECORD FROM DETAIL-LINE AFTER 1.
159      PERFORM 9000-READ-PRODUCT-FILE.
160
```

Program 9b *(concluded)*

```
161 2200-WRITE-SUMMARY.
162
163     MOVE TOTAL-GALLONS TO TOTAL-GALLONS-SL.
164     MOVE TOTAL-COST    TO TOTAL-COST-SL.
165     WRITE REPORT-RECORD FROM SUMMARY-LINE AFTER 2.
166
167 2300-CLOSE-FILES.
168
169     CLOSE PRODUCT-FILE
170           REPORT-FILE.
171
172 9000-READ-PRODUCT-FILE.
173
174     READ PRODUCT-FILE
175           AT END MOVE "YES" TO EOF-FLAG.
```

Figure 9.14   Structure diagram of Program 9b

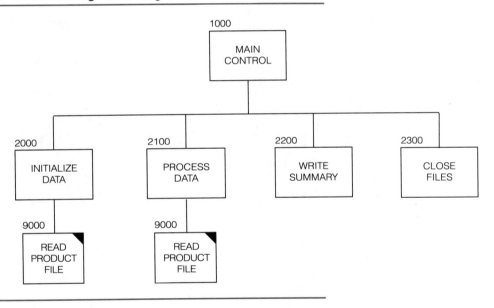

At lines 151 and 153, the program uses data from the table for output and computation. The table reference is

```
...PRICE-FP (FUEL-TYPE-PR, REFINERY-CODE-PR)...
```

The first subscript corresponds to level one of the table (type of fuel), and the second subscript corresponds to level two of the table (refinery).

A potential problem arises if the value of FUEL-TYPE-PR is not in the range 1 to 3 or if the value of REFINERY-CODE-PR is not in the range 1 to 4. If either of these conditions happens, the program will terminate at line 151 with an out-of-range subscript error. In order to avoid this problem, the program checks for valid values in FUEL-TYPE-PR and REFINERY-CODE-PR before using these items as subscripts (see lines 142–149). If either of these fields has values outside the allowable range, an error message is printed on the report. A sample of output produced by the program is shown in Figure 9.15.

Figure 9.15   Sample output from Program 9b

FUEL TYPE	REFINERY CODE	GALLONS	PRICE PER GALLON	PURCHASE PRICE
2	3	100	0.83	83.00
1	4	150	1.05	157.50
3	1	200	0.97	194.00
0	2	300		

ERROR--ONE OR MORE FIELDS CONTAIN INVALID DATA

4	1	300		

ERROR--ONE OR MORE FIELDS CONTAIN INVALID DATA

1	5	200		

ERROR--ONE OR MORE FIELDS CONTAIN INVALID DATA

1	0	200		

ERROR--ONE OR MORE FIELDS CONTAIN INVALID DATA

0	0	200		

ERROR--ONE OR MORE FIELDS CONTAIN INVALID DATA

2	4	200	0.87	174.00
3	3	20,000	0.92	18,400.00
3	4	10,100	0.95	9,595.00
TOTALS		30,750*		$28,603.50*

9.13   THE PERFORM/VARYING/AFTER STATEMENT

Many times, particularly when processing two-dimensional tables, it is necessary to alter two variables over specified ranges. The PERFORM/ VARYING/AFTER statement is an extension of the ideas utilized in PERFORM/VARYING and allows automatic control over two variables in one statement (Fig. 9.16). When one AFTER clause is used, data-name-1 is varied through its range of values for each value of data-name-2 as illustrated in the flowchart shown in Figure 9.17.

Figure 9.16   General form of the PERFORM/VARYING/AFTER statement

```
PERFORM paragraph-name
VARYING data-name-1 FROM initial-value-1 BY increment-value-1 UNTIL condition-1
[AFTER data-name-2 FROM initial-value-2 BY increment-value-2 UNTIL condition-2]
[AFTER data-name-3 FROM initial-value-3 BY increment-value-3 UNTIL condition-3]
```

Figure 9.17 Flowchart of PERFORM/VARYING with one AFTER clause

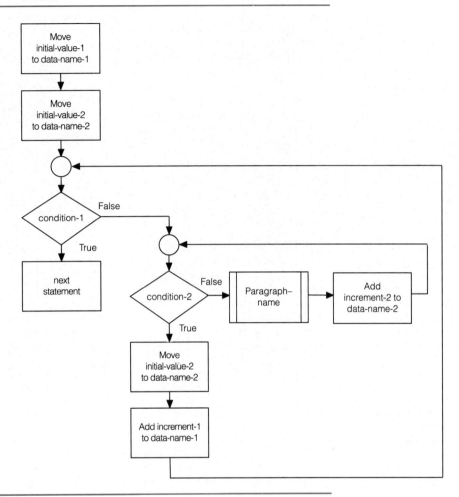

──────── Example ────────

Consider the statement:

```
PERFORM PARA-A
    VARYING X FROM 1 BY 1 UNTIL X > 4
        AFTER Y FROM 1 BY 1 UNTIL Y > 3.
```

PARA-A would be executed $3 \times 4 = 12$ times with the following values of X and Y:

X	1	1	1	2	2	2	3	3	3	4	4	4
Y	1	2	3	1	2	3	1	2	3	1	2	3

For each new value of the first data-name X, the second data-name Y is reinitialized to its starting value and continues to be incremented until the second condition (Y > 3) is satisfied. The flowchart for this statement would be

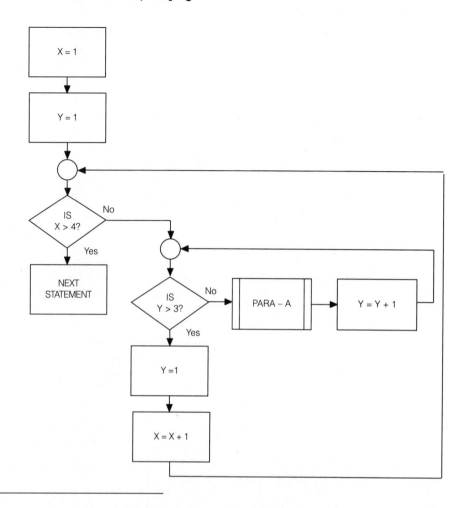

When two AFTER clauses are used, data-name-3 is varied through its range of values for each value of data-name-2, and data-name-2 is varied through its range of values for each value of data-name-1 as shown in Figure 9.18.

──────────── Example ────────────

Consider the statement:

```
PERFORM PARA-B
    VARYING X FROM 1 BY 1 UNTIL X > 3
      AFTER Y FROM 1 BY 1 UNTIL Y > 4
      AFTER Z FROM 1 BY 1 UNTIL Z > 2.
```

PARA-B would be executed $3 \times 4 \times 2 = 24$ times with the following values of X, Y, and Z:

X	1	1	1	1	1	1	1	1	2	2	2	2	2	2	2	2	3	3	3	3	3	3	3	3
Y	1	1	2	2	3	3	4	4	1	1	2	2	3	3	4	4	1	1	2	2	3	3	4	4
Z	1	2	1	2	1	2	1	2	1	2	1	2	1	2	1	2	1	2	1	2	1	2	1	2

──────────── Example ────────────

A file contains production data for each working day at Widgets Mfg., Inc. Each record contains the total number of units produced for each of the five production lines at the factory for a working day. At most, the file con-

Figure 9.18   Flowchart of PERFORM/VARYING with two AFTER clauses

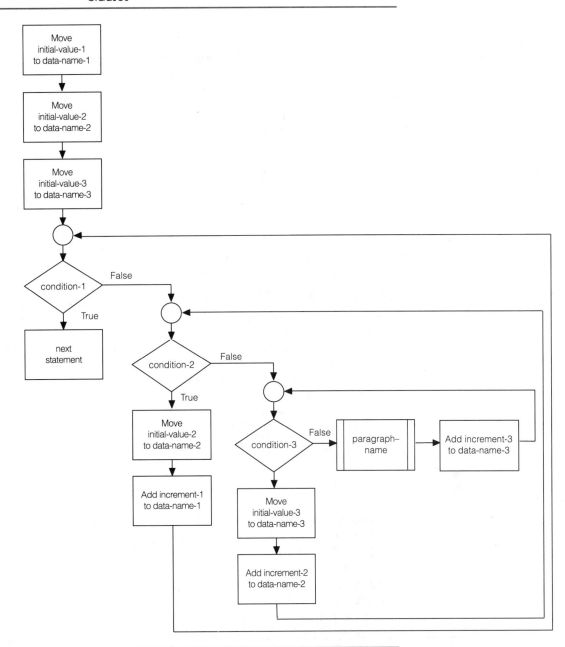

tains one year's data. For a program that will store this data into a table, the following DATA DIVISION entries could be used:

```
01  NUM-DAYS PIC 999 VALUE 0.
01  PRODUCTION-DATA.
    02 DAILY-DATA
           OCCURS 1 TO 366 TIMES.
               DEPENDING ON NUM-DAYS
       03 PRODUCTION PIC 9(5) OCCURS 5 TIMES.
```

Suppose the program has read and stored the data and is required to calculate the average daily production for all production lines. The following program segment could be used:

```
              .
              .
              .
        MOVE 0 TO PRODUCTION-TOTAL.
        PERFORM SUMMATION
            VARYING DAY-SUB
                FROM 1 BY 1 UNTIL DAY-SUB > NUM-DAYS
            AFTER LINE-SUB
                FROM 1 BY 1 UNTIL LINE-SUB > 5.
        COMPUTE AVERAGE-PRODUCTION =
            PRODUCTION-TOTAL / (NUM-DAYS * 5).
              .
              .
              .
    SUMMATION.
        ADD PRODUCTION (DAY-SUB, LINE-SUB)
            TO PRODUCTION-TOTAL.
```

9.14   THREE-LEVEL TABLES

Tables of up to three levels may be created and processed by a COBOL program. A **three-level table** may be visualized as a series of two-level tables. For example, suppose an instructor has five classes and each class contains a maximum of 75 students, each of whom takes five tests. A table to store this data could be defined as

```
01  GRADE-TABLE.
    02 CLASS-ENTRY OCCURS 5 TIMES.
        03 STUDENT-ENTRY OCCURS 75 TIMES.
            04 TEST-ENTRY OCCURS 5 TIMES.
                05 GRADE PIC 999.
```

This structure may be visualized as shown in Figure 9.19.

An alternate way to visualize this table is shown in Figure 9.20. Each CLASS-ENTRY is composed of a table of size 75 × 5; the entire structure contains 5 × 75 × 5 = 1875 elements. References to CLASS-ENTRY require one subscript; references to STUDENT-ENTRY require two subscripts. The first subscript indicates the class, and the second indicates the student within the class. References to TEST-ENTRY and GRADE require three subscripts; the first indicates the class, the second indicates the student, and the third indicates the test.

Note that the order of subscripts from left to right corresponds to the order in which the OCCURS clauses are nested. It would be possible to create storage for this data in a number of different ways. As long as the subscripts used to reference the data correspond to the way in which the structure was created, the same processing steps can be accomplished. For example, suppose the following DATA DIVISION entry is made:

```
01  GRADE-TABLE-ALTERNATE.
    02 TEST-ENTRY OCCURS 5 TIMES.
        03 CLASS-ENTRY OCCURS 5 TIMES.
            04 STUDENT-ENTRY OCCURS 75 TIMES.
                05 GRADE PIC 999.
```

Figure 9.19 Representation of a three-level table

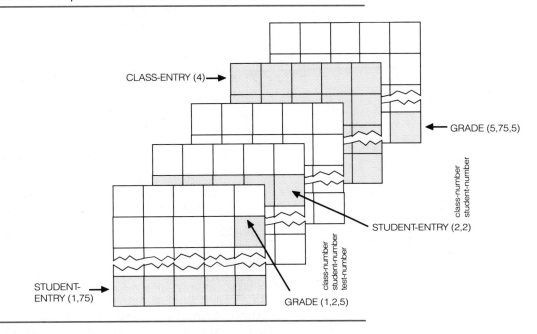

CLASS-ENTRY (4)

GRADE (5,75,5)

class-number
student-number

STUDENT-ENTRY (2,2)

STUDENT-ENTRY (1,75)

class-number
student-number
test-number

GRADE (1,2,5)

Figure 9.20 Alternate representation of a three-level table

GRADE-TABLE																													
CLASS-ENTRY (1)																CLASS-ENTRY (5)													
STUDENT-ENTRY (1, 1)					STUDENT-ENTRY (1, 2)					STUDENT-ENTRY (1, 75)					STUDENT-ENTRY (5, 1)					STUDENT-ENTRY (5, 75)				
TEST-ENTRY (1,1,1)	TEST-ENTRY (1,1,2)	TEST-ENTRY (1,1,3)	TEST-ENTRY (1,1,4)	TEST-ENTRY (1,1,5)	TEST-ENTRY (1,2,1)	TEST-ENTRY (1,2,2)	TEST-ENTRY (1,2,3)	TEST-ENTRY (1,2,4)	TEST-ENTRY (1,2,5)	TEST-ENTRY (1,75,1)	TEST-ENTRY (1,75,2)	TEST-ENTRY (1,75,3)	TEST-ENTRY (1,75,4)	TEST-ENTRY (1,75,5)	TEST-ENTRY (5,1,1)	TEST-ENTRY (5,1,2)	TEST-ENTRY (5,1,3)	TEST-ENTRY (5,1,4)	TEST-ENTRY (5,1,5)	TEST-ENTRY (5,75,1)	TEST-ENTRY (5,75,2)	TEST-ENTRY (5,75,3)	TEST-ENTRY (5,75,4)	TEST-ENTRY (5,75,5)
GRADE (1,1,1)	GRADE (1,1,2)	GRADE (1,1,3)	GRADE (1,1,4)	GRADE (1,1,5)	GRADE (1,2,1)	GRADE (1,2,2)	GRADE (1,2,3)	GRADE (1,2,4)	GRADE (1,2,5)	GRADE (1,75,1)	GRADE (1,75,2)	GRADE (1,75,3)	GRADE (1,75,4)	GRADE (1,75,5)	GRADE (5,1,1)	GRADE (5,1,2)	GRADE (5,1,3)	GRADE (5,1,4)	GRADE (5,1,5)	GRADE (5,75,1)	GRADE (5,75,2)	GRADE (5,75,3)	GRADE (5,75,4)	GRADE (5,75,5)

This structure can be visualized as follows:

GRADE-TABLE-ALTERNATE								
TEST-ENTRY (1)					TEST-ENTRY (5)			
CLASS-ENTRY (1, 1)			CLASS-ENTRY (1, 5)		CLASS-ENTRY (5, 1)			
STUDENT-ENTRY (1, 1, 1)	STUDENT-ENTRY (1, 1, 2)	STUDENT-ENTRY (1, 1, 75)	STUDENT-ENTRY (1, 5, 1)	STUDENT-ENTRY (1, 5, 75)	STUDENT-ENTRY (5, 1, 1)	STUDENT-ENTRY (5, 1, 75)		
GRADE (1, 1, 1)	GRADE (1, 1, 2)	GRADE (1, 1, 75)	GRADE (1, 5, 1)	GRADE (1, 5, 75)	GRADE (5, 1, 1)	GRADE (5, 1, 75)		

Reference to GRADE (4, 1, 2) would mean test number 4, class number 1, and student number 2.

The way in which a table should be created will be governed to some extent by the way data is organized on input and by the type of processing to be performed. For example, suppose it is necessary to include a description of each class, the number of students in each class, and the name of each student in the data structure. The first way in which the data is defined can be modified easily to include this new data as follows:

```
01  GRADE-TABLE-EXTENDED.
    02 CLASS-ENTRY OCCURS 5 TIMES.
        03 CLASS-DESCRIPTION PIC X(20).
        03 NUM-STUDENTS PIC 99.
        03 STUDENT-ENTRY OCCURS 75 TIMES.
            04 STUDENT-NAME PIC X(20).
            04 TEST-ENTRY OCCURS 5 TIMES.
                05 GRADE PIC 999.
```

Trying to modify GRADE-TABLE-ALTERNATE to include the new data would be difficult because it would be necessary to duplicate class and student information for each test.

──────── **Example** ────────

A company assigns a Christmas bonus based on the type of employee (hourly or salaried), years with the company (one to five), and job performance rating (one to four) according to the following tables:

	Hourly						*Salaried*			
	Job Performance						*Job Performance*			
	1	2	3	4			1	2	3	4
1	100	150	200	275		1	200	275	350	425
2	110	160	210	285		2	220	245	375	440
3	140	190	230	295		3	230	305	380	450
4	145	195	235	300		4	240	315	395	465
5	160	200	240	305		5	250	325	400	475

(*Years* labels the rows on the left of each table.)

A data structure to store this data for a program which will look up the appropriate bonus value could be defined as

```
01  BONUS-CONSTANTS.
    02 HOURLY-CONSTANTS.
        03 FILLER PIC X(12) VALUE "100150200275".
        03 FILLER PIC X(12) VALUE "110160210285".
        03 FILLER PIC X(12) VALUE "140190230295".
        03 FILLER PIC X(12) VALUE "145195235300".
        03 FILLER PIC X(12) VALUE "160200240305".
    02 SALARIED-CONSTANTS.
        03 FILLER PIC X(12) VALUE "200275350425".
        03 FILLER PIC X(12) VALUE "220245375440".
        03 FILLER PIC X(12) VALUE "230305380450".
        03 FILLER PIC X(12) VALUE "240315395465".
        03 FILLER PIC X(12) VALUE "250325400475".
01  BONUS-TABLE REDEFINES BONUS-CONSTANTS.
    02 EMPLOYEE-LEVEL-ENTRY OCCURS 2 TIMES.
        03 YEARS-WITH-CO-ENTRY OCCURS 5 TIMES.
            04 JOB-PERFORMANCE-ENTRY OCCURS 4 TIMES.
                05 BONUS-AMOUNT PIC 999.
```

Assume that the data-name EMPLOYEE-LEVEL contains a value 1 if the employee is hourly, and a value 2 if the employee is salaried. Also assume the JOB-PERFORMANCE contains a value 1 to 4 and that YEARS-WITH-CO contains the employee length of service. The following code could be used to compute CHRISTMAS-BONUS:

```
IF YEARS-WITH-CO < 1
    MOVE BONUS-AMOUNT (EMPLOYEE-LEVEL, 1, JOB-PERFORMANCE)
    TO CHRISTMAS-BONUS.
IF YEARS-WITH-CO > 5
    MOVE BONUS-AMOUNT (EMPLOYEE-LEVEL, 5, JOB-PERFORMANCE)
    TO CHRISTMAS-BONUS.
IF YEARS-WITH-CO > 0 AND YEARS-WITH-CO < 6
    MOVE BONUS-AMOUNT (EMPLOYEE-LEVEL, YEARS-WITH-CO,
                            JOB-PERFORMANCE)
    TO CHRISTMAS-BONUS.
```

9.15 DEBUG CLINIC

Errors in utilizing tables most commonly result from problems with out-of-range subscript values. If a subscript expressed as a variable has a value outside the allowable range, an execution time error results. Typically, the program terminates with an error message and perhaps a listing of information which the programmer can use to find the statement causing the problem. Frequently, the programmer has to rerun the program with some diagnostic output to determine the values of appropriate data-names. Diagnostic output need consist only of the values of data-names and perhaps labels to help in evaluating the output produced. For example, suppose the cause of an execution time error has been traced to a statement such as

```
COMPUTE TABL (X, Y) =...
```

It would be useful to know the values of X and Y prior to the error. By inserting code such as the following, the programmer can determine these values:

```
         .
         .
         .
    PERFORM DIAGNOSTIC-OUTPUT.
    COMPUTE TABL (X, Y) =...
         .
         .
         .
DIAGNOSTIC-OUTPUT.
    MOVE X TO X-OUT.
    MOVE Y TO Y-OUT.
    WRITE PRINT-LINE FROM DIAGNOSTIC-LINE AFTER 1.
```

Once the cause of the problem has been found and eliminated, it is necessary to remove all executions of diagnostic output. It is not necessary, however, to remove the actual code from the DATA DIVISION or from the PROCEDURE DIVISION itself unless you want to optimize use of memory. Leaving these elements in a program may make the program easier for some future programmer to debug should maintenance be required on the program.

9.16 DATA REPRESENTATION ON IBM SYSTEMS

In most computing systems, more than one method for representing numeric data internally is used, and methods vary somewhat from system to system. In the discussion that follows, we will restrict ourselves to a description of data representation used on IBM Systems 360/370/43xx/ 30xx/390 and Systems 34, 36, 38, and AS400. These mainframe and minicomputing systems all use the same types of internal data representation.

Although it is usually not absolutely necessary for the COBOL programmer to be aware of the different forms of data representation, in some instances this knowledge enables the programmer to write programs that are more efficient or use less memory or both. This knowledge may also be required to process files produced as output by programs written in languages other than COBOL.

On the IBM systems listed above, the following types of data representation are available:

Zoned decimal
Packed decimal
Binary
Single precision floating point
Double precision floating point

Zoned decimal data representation uses one byte (eight bits) to store each decimal digit. The first four bits for each byte are called the zone for the digit. The codes used are shown in Figure 9.21. Thus, a field containing three digits, having value 370, would be represented as

     | F3 | F7 | F0 |

The zone in the rightmost digit in the field is used to represent the sign.

Figure 9.21   Representation of zoned decimal data

Digit	Binary representation Zone ↓	Hexadecimal representation Zone ↓
1	1111 0001	F1
2	1111 0010	F2
3	1111 0011	F3
4	1111 0100	F4
5	1111 0101	F5
6	1111 0110	F6
7	1111 0111	F7
8	1111 1000	F8
9	1111 1001	F9
0	1111 0000	F0

The following correspondence is used:

Zone	Meaning
F	unsigned (positive value)
C	signed positive
D	signed negative

For example, the value -23 would be represented as

⌞F2⌟D3⌟

Packed decimal data representation uses each byte except the right-most byte in the field to store *two* decimal digits. The rightmost four bits of the rightmost byte are used to store the sign using the codes described above. For example, the value 370 would be represented as

```
                    ┌─ Sign
  ⌞37⌟0F⌟◄──┘
```

Note that the value 370, which requires three bytes when represented in zoned decimal, may be represented in just two bytes in packed decimal. The value of -23 would be represented as

```
                    ┌─ Sign
  ⌞02⌟3D⌟◄──┘
```

In general, values larger than two digits in length occupy fewer bytes when represented in packed rather than in zoned decimal. When computation is performed on zoned decimal data, the data must be transformed into packed decimal form. This transformation, of course, takes a certain amount of time—a consideration which could become significant if many computations are to be performed.

Binary data representation utilizes straight binary numeration to represent values. Either 16, 32, or 64 bits may be used for the data item. For example, the value 370 would be represented in 16 bits as

⌞00000001⌟01110010⌟

Binary data is used for data items such as indexes, which are not used for input or output and which can benefit from the very efficient manner in which the computer hardware performs computations with binary data.

Floating point data representation is similar in many respects to scientific notation. A data item is represented in memory by storing a sequence of significant digits and an exponent representing a power of the base. The following scheme is used:

⌞exponent⌟ fraction ⌟

↑ Assumed position of the decimal point

The value represented is then

$$\text{fraction} \times \text{base}^{\text{exponent}}$$

For example, assuming a base 10 system, the number 37,000,000 might be represented as

⌞08⌟37⌟00⌟00⌟

which would stand for

$$.370000 \times 10^8 = 37{,}000{,}000$$

On IBM Systems, the actual base used is 16. Floating point data may be represented utilizing 32 bits (single precision). A single precision item utilizes the first 8 bits to represent the exponent and the remaining 24 bits to represent the fraction. A double precision item utilizes the first 8 bits for the exponent, just as for a single precision item, but the fraction is now longer (56 bits).

The basic advantage to utilizing floating point data is that values with very large and very small magnitudes may be represented in a fixed space. The primary disadvantage is that only a limited number of significant digits can be represented; for most data values the floating point representation is, therefore, not exact. A COBOL programmer might wish to use floating point data only when evaluating certain formulas that are primarily scientific in nature or when processing a file containing data items stored in this format. For most COBOL business applications, however, *exact* data values (which are provided by zoned decimal, packed decimal, and binary data representations) are necessary.

9.17 THE USAGE CLAUSE

The USAGE clause used in the definition of an elementary data item in the DATA DIVISION specifies the type of data representation to be assumed for this data item. The general form for the USAGE clause is shown in Figure 9.22.

Figure 9.22   General form of the USAGE clause

```
                   ⎧COMPUTATIONAL⎫
                   ⎪COMP         ⎪
USAGE IS           ⎨DISPLAY      ⎬
                   ⎩INDEX        ⎭
```

The details of internal representation of all data types are compiler dependent. DISPLAY is the default type for all numeric fields. Thus the definition

```
03 FLDA PIC 99V9 USAGE IS DISPLAY.
```

is equivalent to

```
03 FLDA PIC 99V9.
```

The type DISPLAY is used primarily for fields contained on input/output records.

A data item that is described as USAGE COMPUTATIONAL (or the equivalent COMP) is a numeric field typically used to store results of computations. Usually a field will be transformed from DISPLAY into COMPUTATIONAL any time an arithmetic operation is performed on the field. (The compiler inserts the instructions required to perform these transformations.) Defining fields used as counters, accumulators, and so on as USAGE COMPUTATIONAL makes the transformation unnecessary, thereby increasing the efficiency of the computer in executing the program.

USAGE type INDEX is used for data items to be used as subscripts for table references. The primary advantage of specifying a data item to have USAGE INDEX is to make table references more efficient. Data items specified as USAGE INDEX may be manipulated only by the PERFORM/VARYING statement and the SET statement.[4] IBM compilers provide additional types of data in the USAGE clause as illustrated in Figure 9.23.

Figure 9.23   USAGE clause for IBM systems

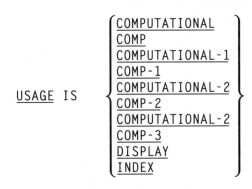

The correspondence between the data items defined in the USAGE clause and the types of data representation used in the computers described in Section 9.16 is shown in Figure 9.24. COMPUTATIONAL-3 data may be specified for fields that are going to be used for computational purposes to reduce the amount of time required to convert from DISPLAY to COMPUTATIONAL-3 and back. For example, counters and accumulators that are used repeatedly in computation may be specified as COMPUTATIONAL-3.

──────── Example ────────

```
03 SUM PIC 9999V99 USAGE COMPUTATIONAL-3.
03 KOUNT PIC 9(5) USAGE COMPUTATIONAL-3.
```

Binary data is required in a COBOL program for subscript values. For example, the value of SUB must be represented in binary when the statement MOVE DATA (SUB) TO DATA-OUT is executed. If a data item used as a subscript is not a binary type item, the COBOL compiler generates code required to make the transformation, but this transformation takes time to perform. COMPUTATIONAL or INDEX data may be specified for fields that will be used as subscripts to reduce the time required to convert from DISPLAY to COMPUTATIONAL for each table reference.

──────── Example ────────

```
01  I PIC 99 USAGE COMPUTATIONAL.
    .
    .
    .
PROCEDURE DIVISION.
```

[4] Detailed coverage of the SET statement is found in Chapter 12, Section 8.

.
.
.

```
MOVE TABLE (I) TO AMOUNT-OUT.
```

The USAGE clause may also be required for describing records in files produced by other programs. For example, suppose we are given the following record description:

Positions	Description
1–16	Name
17–21	Year to date salary (packed decimal)
22–26	Year to date FICA (packed decimal)
27–35	Social Security number

The record description that would be coded into the COBOL program would be

```
01  INPUT-RECORD.
    02 NAME-IR     PIC X(16).
    02 YTD-SAL-IR  PIC 9999999V99 USAGE COMPUTATIONAL-3.
    02 YTD-FICA-IR PIC 9999999V99 USAGE COMPUTATIONAL-3.
    02 SS-NUM-IR   PIC 9(9) USAGE DISPLAY.
```

Note that the field YTD-SAL-IR occupies five bytes in the input record but is given a picture allowing for nine digits. When you use packed decimal data representation, a five-byte field can accommodate a number of this size. The use of USAGE DISPLAY to describe SS-NUM-IR in the above example is for documentation purposes only. This record description would also be used by the program that first created the records in the file.

9.18 COBOL-85 UPDATE

The COBOL-85 standard made changes to the OCCURS clause, data types, and the PERFORM statement. In this section we will cover each of these changes in turn.

In COBOL-74, the maximum allowable nesting of OCCURS clauses and the maximum allowable number of subscripts were three (although many compilers allowed a greater number as a nonstandard feature). In COBOL-85, the maximum allowable nesting of OCCURS clauses and the maximum allowable number of subscripts are increased to seven. Thus, in COBOL-85, it is possible to create a seven-dimensional table. Elements of such a table would be accessed by an expression requiring seven subscripts.

In COBOL-74, the only data types that could be specified in the USAGE clause were COMPUTATIONAL and DISPLAY. Some compilers augmented this list considerably to give the programmer the ability to create programs that would function efficiently on particular machines. In COBOL-85, the list of standard data types is expanded to include BINARY and PACKED-DECIMAL. Binary is equivalent to COMPUTATIONAL; PACKED-DECIMAL is equivalent to COMPUTATIONAL-3 (see Figure 9.24). Most COBOL-85 compilers also support additional nonstandard data types for the reasons cited above.

Figure 9.24 Correspondence between USAGE and data representation for IBM systems

USAGE description	Data representation
DISPLAY	Zoned decimal
COMPUTATIONAL	Binary (no restrictions on manipulation)
COMPUTATIONAL-1	Single precision floating point
COMPUTATIONAL-2	Double precision floating point
COMPUTATIONAL-3	Packed decimal
INDEX	Binary (restrictions on manipulation)

We have seen that a major change in the PERFORM statement in COBOL-85 was the inclusion of the in-line PERFORM and the scope delimiter END-PERFORM. Both versions of the PERFORM statement described in this chapter were similarly augmented. A general form of the PERFORM/ TIMES statement in COBOL-85 is shown below:

```
PERFORM  {data-name}  TIMES
         {integer  }
         statement-1...
END-PERFORM
```

For example, to print N blank lines, the following program segment could be used:

```
MOVE SPACES TO Print-Record
PERFORM N TIMES
     WRITE Print-Record AFTER 1
END-PERFORM
```

A general form of the PERFORM/VARYING statement in COBOL-85 is as follows:

```
PERFORM VARYING data-name-1
     FROM initial-value-1 BY increment-value-1 UNTIL condition-1
    [AFTER data-name-2
     FROM initial-value-2 BY increment-value-2 UNTIL condition-2]  ...
     statement-1...
END-PERFORM
```

In COBOL-74, the maximum number of AFTER clauses is two; in COBOL-85, the maximum number of AFTER clauses is six. This change parallels the increase in number of allowable subscripts. With one PERFORM/VARYING statement, it is possible to vary up to seven variables that might be used as subscripts in processing elements in a seven-dimensional table.

For example, suppose you wish to initialize all elements of a table of 100 elements to have value 0. Suppose further that the table elements are called Table-Element and that Sub is suitably defined. The following program segment could be used:

```
PERFORM VARYING Sub FROM 1 BY 1 UNTIL Sub > 100
     MOVE 0 TO Table-Element (Sub)
END-PERFORM
```

To accomplish a similar operation on a two-dimensional table, you could use one AFTER clause. For example, suppose a two-dimensional table of size 10 by 20 is defined in a program. Suppose further that Table-Element-2 is a table element in the table and that Sub1 and Sub2 are suitably defined. To initialize all elements of the table to zero, we could write

```
PERFORM
    VARYING Sub1 FROM 1 BY 1 UNTIL Sub1 > 10
      AFTER Sub2 FROM 1 BY 1 UNTIL Sub2 > 20
    MOVE 0 TO Table-Element-2 (Sub1, Sub2)
END-PERFORM
```

The in-line version of the PERFORM statement allows you to simplify the structure of a program since it is no longer necessary to create separate paragraphs to carry out simple tasks.

Another change made to the PERFORM/UNTIL statement in COBOL-85 is a provision for changing the location of the test that allows the program to exit the loop. As you have seen, in COBOL-74, the test is always made prior to entering the loop (see Figure 9.5). If the condition is true initially, the next statement is executed immediately without ever executing the paragraph named in the PERFORM statement. (Technically, this form of loop control is called a **pretest** because the test is performed before entering the loop.) This is still the default placement of the test in COBOL-85; however, you can specify WITH TEST BEFORE or WITH TEST AFTER to control the placement of the test. When WITH TEST AFTER is used, the loop control mechanism is called a **posttest form**. Consider, for example, the following program segment:

```
PERFORM Read-Data-File.
PERFORM Process-Data WITH TEST BEFORE
    UNTIL End-Of-File-Flag = "YES".
```

Prior to execution of this statement, it is necessary for the program to establish an appropriate value for the variable End-Of-File. The standard technique for establishing this value has been through the VALUE clause in the DATA DIVISION. Now, consider an alternative version of the statement.

```
PERFORM Process-Data WITH TEST AFTER
    UNTIL End-Of-File-Flag = "YES".
```

It is no longer necessary to establish the initial value of End-Of-File-Flag prior to entering the loop (provided, of course, that the procedure Process-Data accomplishes this task). For example, suppose Process-Data contains the following segment:

```
READ Data-File
    AT END
        MOVE "YES" TO End-Of-File-Flag
    NOT AT END
        MOVE "NO" TO End-Of-File-Flag
            . . .
```

If this is the case, the value of End-Of-File-Flag can be undefined prior to the execution of Process-Data because the test to terminate the loop will be performed after execution of the procedure which takes care of establishing the appropriate value for the controlling variable. The difference between WITH TEST BEFORE and WITH TEST AFTER is summarized in Figure 9.25.

Figure 9.25   Comparison of TEST BEFORE and TEST AFTER

Pretest
```
PERFORM Process-Data WITH TEST BEFORE
    UNTIL End-of-File-Flag = "YES".
```

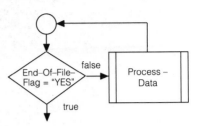

Posttest
```
PERFORM Process-Data WITH TEST AFTER
    UNTIL End-of-File-Flag = "YES".
```

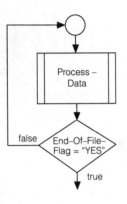

The WITH TEST AFTER clause can be used on any variation of the PER-FORM statement that includes an UNTIL clause as is illustrated in the following examples:

──────────── **Example** ────────────────────

```
PERFORM WITH TEST AFTER
        UNTIL Kount > 10
    ADD 1 TO Kount
END-PERFORM
```

In this program segment, the statement ADD 1 TO Kount will be executed at least once, no matter what the initial value of Kount might be.

──────────── **Example** ────────────────────

```
PERFORM Para-X WITH TEST AFTER
    VARYING Sub FROM 1 BY 1 UNTIL Sub > Num
```

Para-X will be executed at least one time no matter what value is contained in Num. Note the difference between this statement and the alternative (remember WITH TEST BEFORE is the default).

```
PERFORM Para-X
    VARYING Sub FROM 1 BY 1 UNTIL Sub > Num
```

If Num had value 0 in this example, Para-X would not be executed at all since the initial value of Sub will immediately satisfy the terminating condition (1 is greater than 0).

9.19 SELF-TEST EXERCISES

1. The following partial program contains a table giving the description, part number, and price for the inventory of a small retail store. (Only a few items are listed, but the same principles would apply to a complete table or file on a mass storage device.)

```
01    INVENTORY-TABLE.
      03 FILLER PIC X(13) VALUE "AUDIO CABLE".
      03 FILLER PIC X(4) VALUE "1258".
      03 FILLER PIC 99V99 VALUE 4.00.
      03 FILLER PIC X(13) VALUE "EARPHONE".
      03 FILLER PIC X(4) VALUE "1296".
      03 FILLER PIC 99V99 VALUE 37.50.
      03 FILLER PIC X(13) VALUE "MICROPHONE".
      03 FILLER PIC X(4) VALUE "1459".
      03 FILLER PIC 99V99 VALUE 29.75.
      03 FILLER PIC X(13) VALUE "BATTERIES".
      03 FILLER PIC X(4) VALUE "1678".
      03 FILLER PIC 99V99 VALUE 2.35.
      03 FILLER PIC X(13) VALUE "CARRYING CASE".
      03 FILLER PIC X(4) VALUE "1789".
      03 FILLER PIC 99V99 VALUE 13.92.
      03 FILLER PIC X(13) VALUE "**NO MATCH**".
      03 FILLER PIC X(4) VALUE "9999".
      03 FILLER PIC 99V99 VALUE ZERO.
01    PARTS-TABLE REDEFINES INVENTORY-TABLE.
      02 PART OCCURS 6 TIMES.
         03 PART-DESCRIPTION PIC X(13).
         03 PART-NUMBER      PIC X(4).
         03 PART-PRICE       PIC 99V99.
```

a. Write the PROCEDURE DIVISION for a program that could be used to change a price if the part number is known.

b. Given a file with records containing part numbers and quantity ordered, write the PROCEDURE DIVISION for a program that will print billing invoices.

2. Draw a flowchart showing the execution of each of the following:
   a. PERFORM PARA-X
         VARYING J FROM 1 BY 1 UNTIL J > N.
   b. PERFORM PARA-Y
         VARYING L FROM 10 BY −1 UNTIL L = 0.
   c. PERFORM PARA-Z
         VARYING K FROM 1 BY 1 UNTIL K = N
            AFTER M FROM 1 BY 1 UNTIL M = N.
   d. PERFORM PARA-W
         VARYING P FROM 2 BY 2 UNTIL P > N
            AFTER Q FROM 1 BY 3 UNTIL Q > N
            AFTER R FROM 1 BY 1 UNTIL R > N.

3. How many times will the specified paragraph be executed in each part of Exercise 2 if N has value 7? Show the values generated for the variables.

4. a. Consider the program example in Section 9.13 (Widget production data storage). Suppose that an output record is defined as:

```
01  DAILY-OUTPUT.
    03 DAY-DO PIC 999.
    03 DAILY-PRODUCTION-DO OCCURS 5 TIMES.
       05 FILLER PIC X(5).
       05 DAY-PRODUCTION-DO PIC Z(5).
```

Write a PROCEDURE DIVISION program segment to write out the content of the table PRODUCTION-DATA.

b. Write a PROCEDURE DIVISION program segment to compute the average production by line for the table PRODUCTION-DATA.

c. On some days the production lines must be closed because of malfunction of equipment. On these days, production is zero. Write a PROCEDURE DIVISION program segment to compute the number of days in which production is zero for each line.

5. Write a PROCEDURE DIVISION program segment to compute the total of the elements of BONUS-TABLE defined in Section 9.14.

6. Given the array GRADE-TABLE-EXTENDED defined in Section 9.14, write a PROCEDURE DIVISION program segment to compute the class average for each test and class.

7. True/False
   a. Standard COBOL permits use of expressions as subscripts.
   b. The VALUE clause may be used with the OCCURS clause in a DATA DIVISION entry.
   c. The use of the DEPENDING ON clause saves space because only the required amount of storage is allocated.
   d. The REDEFINES clause may be used only on an entry with the same level number as the data-name being redefined.
   e. In the PERFORM/VARYING statement, it is possible that the specified paragraph may never be executed.
   f. The maximum number of subscripts allowed in COBOL-74 is three.

8. For an IBM system, show the internal hexadecimal representation of a field with value +298 defined as:
   a. USAGE DISPLAY
   b. USAGE COMP
   c. USAGE COMP-3
   d. USAGE INDEX

9. What is the maximum number of subscripts allowed in COBOL-85?

10. How many AFTER clauses can be used in a PERFORM/VARYING statement in COBOL-74? In COBOL-85? How is this number related to the maximum number of allowable subscripts?

11. What are two new data types in COBOL-85?

12. Suppose the value of X is 1 and Y is 5. Give the value of each of these variables after execution of each of the following:
    a. PERFORM WITH TEST BEFORE
              UNTIL X < Y
          ADD 1 TO X
       END-PERFORM
    b. PERFORM WITH TEST AFTER
              UNTIL X < Y
          ADD 1 TO X
       END-PERFORM

9.20   PROGRAMMING EXERCISES

1. Records in a file consist of student names and one test grade per student. The layout for each record is as follows:

Positions	Content
1–20	Student name
21–23	Grade

    The program should create two reports—one listing students with grades at or above the average and one listing students with below-average grades. Use the report layout shown in Figure 9.26.

Figure 9.26   Printer spacing chart for Exercise 1

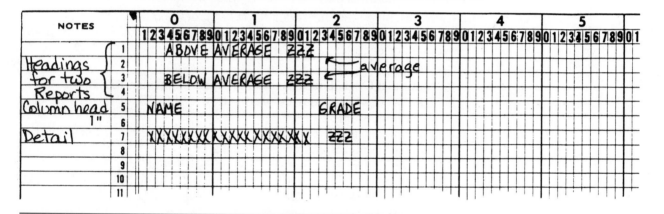

2. Write a program that will list the daily sales of soft drinks to retail dealers under the major headings DEALER, ITEM, QUANTITY, UNIT PRICE, and TOTAL. The QUANTITY and TOTAL columns should be summed for all dealers serviced that day. An input record includes the dealer's name, the type of drink, and the number of cases. Using the OCCURS clause, set up a table of unit costs (constants) in storage for each type of drink. Use these values to compute the total sales for each transaction as it is read. Types of drinks and unit costs are as follows:

Regulars	4.00 per case
Kings	5.00 per case
Cans	4.50 per case

    The record layout is as follows:

Positions	Content
1–20	Dealer name
21	Drink type
	1 = Regular
	2 = King
	3 = can
23–24	Quantity

3. Rewrite the program for Exercise 6 in Chapter 5 (Section 12) using a table to store the digits of the account number.

4. Sales employees of ABC Furniture, Inc., are paid on a commission basis. The commission rate varies from item to item. A commission rate code, which is the last digit in the item stock number, is used to determine the percentage of the wholesale price to be paid as a commission rate.

Rate-code	Commission-rate
1	1.0%
2	3.5%
3	7.0%
4	10.5%
5	12.0%
6	15.75%

Data records containing the following fields are to be processed to produce an employee earnings report:

Positions	Content
1–9	Employee number
11–16	Date of sale (*mmddyy*)
18–22	Retail price (999V99)
24–28	Wholesale price (999V99)
30–38	Stock number

Assume that the records are sorted into sequence by employee number and date. Your program should list each item sold and the associated commission. Subtotals should be written for daily sales and commissions and for each salesperson's total sales and commissions. Final totals of sales and commissions should also be written.

5. Modify the program for Exercise 4 to calculate the average commission rate earned by each salesperson. Average commission rate is calculated by finding the sum of the commissions paid and dividing by the total sales based on wholesale price.

6. Modify the program for Exercise 4 to calculate the profit from each sale, the total profit by salesperson, and the total profits for the period. Profit is computed by subtracting the commission from the markup. Markup is the difference between retail price and wholesale price.

7. Modify the program written for Exercise 4 to produce a report summarizing each salesperson's earnings. Print the report after the body of the existing output. Use tables to store each employee number and appropriate summary data. Assume that no more than 25 salespersons are employed.

8. Modify the program written for Exercise 4 to produce a report summarizing sales by date. Print the report after the existing output. Use a table to accumulate sales for each date. Assume that no more than 31 different dates will be processed by the program.

9. Each record in a data file contains the following fields:

Positions	Content
1	Department number (1 to 9)
3–4	Salesman number (1 to 25)
6–11	Amount of sales (9999V99)

Write a program to compute the total sales for each salesperson and for each department. The data is *not* sorted into sequence by department or salesperson. Assume that employee numbers are not uniquely assigned (e.g., Department 1 may have a Salesperson 1, and Department 2 may have a Salesperson 1, and so forth).

10. Each record in a data file contains the following fields:

Positions	Content
1	Department number (1 to 9)
3–4	Salesperson number (1 to 25)
6–10	Amount of sales for Monday (999V99)
12–16	Amount of sales for Tuesday (999V99)
18–22	Amount of sales for Wednesday (999V99)
24–28	Amount of sales for Thursday (999V99)
30–34	Amount of sales for Friday (999V99)

Write a program to determine which salespersons have total weekly sales more than ten percent above the average weekly sales for all salespersons. Make the same assumptions regarding salesperson numbers as in Exercise 9.

11. Records in a data file contain a date and number of sales for that date. Write a program to produce a bar graph to represent this data. For example,

Date	Sales	
1/1/91	3	***
		***
1/2/91	4	****
		****
1/3/91	0	
1/4/91	7	*******
		*******

Layout for the data record is as follows:

Positions	Content
1–6	Date
8–9	Sales

12. Using the file described in Exercise 11 above, write a program to produce a vertical bar graph. Assume that the data file contains a maximum of seven records. For example:

```
                                        **
                                        **
                                        **
                                        **
                      **                **
    **                **                **
    **                **                **
    **                **                **
  1/1/91            1/2/91    1/3/91   1/4/91
```

13. A file contains the results of a survey conducted by the marketing department of XYZ Corp. Each record contains the following fields:

Positions	Content
1–2	Age of respondent (1 to 99)
4	Brand preference (1, 2, 3, or 4)

Write a program to summarize brand preference by age group. Your output should contain the number of respondents in each age group and the percentage of each age group that preferred each brand. The output should be a table similar to the following:

Age	Number	Brand			
		1	2	3	4
1–10	.	.	.	.	.
11–20	.	.	.	.	.
.	.	.	.	.	.
91–100	.	.	.	.	.

14. Management at XYZ Burger Corporation would like a report showing the average daily sales at each of its 25 branch stores. Each store has an identifying number 1, 2, . . . , 25. Input into your program consists of sales records containing the following data:

Positions	Content
1–3	Store-ID-number
11–16	Date (*mmddyy*)
18–24	Total sales (99999V99)

You may not assume that the data is sorted into any particular order.

15. Compute the overall average daily sales amount and the standard deviation of the average for the program in Exercise 14 above. Flag those stores with average sales that deviate by more than two standard deviations from the overall average. The standard deviation is computed as

$$\sqrt{\frac{\sum_{i=1}^{n} (x_i - \bar{x})^2}{n \cdot (n - 1)}}$$

where x_i represents the data items, $\bar{x}$ represents the average for the data items, and n represents the number of items. In this problem, x_i represents the average daily sales for each store, $\bar{x}$ represents the overall average daily sales amount, and n represents the number of stores.

10. THE STRUCTURED PROGRAMMING ENVIRONMENT

10.1   SYSTEM DESIGN

In a large number of businesses which rely on a data processing system for the timely and cost-effective supply of day-to-day information, the COBOL language and structured programming together form the basis for developing the software required for the system. In addition to the basic software, a data processing system includes provision for the following areas:

- origination and collection of data
- data storage and retrieval mechanisms
- reports and other forms of information that need to be produced
- dissemination of information (who gets what report at what time interval)
- methods for finding and correcting errors in data
- audit trails to assure correct processing of data
- backup plans to assure that the organization can continue to function in the event of computer malfunction or natural disaster
- security systems to prevent unauthorized access to data, information, or programs
- hardware required to accomplish the data processing tasks
- initial and ongoing training of users
- day-to-day operation procedures
- a variety of types of documentation

Unless adequate plans and provisions are made for all of these areas, a data processing system will fail to meet the needs of the organization it is meant to serve.

The job of the programmer is affected in one way or another by decisions made about all these aspects of the system that forms the basic framework in which the programmer works. Programmers are also in a position to make recommendations regarding potential problems that they foresee and that may not have been adequately addressed in the overall plan. To the outside world, unfortunately, any problem in the data processing system is often attributed to the computer or to the programmer, whereas the blame often should be placed on poor planning in one or more of these areas. A good plan will help the data processing system function with few problems and will go far in improving the image of all data processing personnel, including the programming staff, in the eyes of the organization. A positive image is likely to be accompanied by such tangible benefits as job security and financial rewards.

In any medium-sized or large organization, the task of developing a data processing system is carried out by several people, each playing a specific role in the process. Three types of personnel are directly involved:

- systems analyst
- programming manager
- programmer

The job of the **systems analyst** is to build a comprehensive plan for a data processing system and assure that the ultimate system meets specifications. The **programming manager** oversees implementation of the plan and supervises the work of **programmers** who actually code and test the individual programs that constitute the system.

The role of the systems analyst may be likened to that of an architect for a building. The systems analyst, like the architect, is responsible for the conceptual design and plans. Just as the architect oversees the entire building project, the systems analyst exercises general control over the software development effort, particularly during the testing phase when potential problems in the system are eliminated and the system is proved to meet the requirements. The programming manager's job may be compared to that of a general contractor in a building project; both are responsible for implementing the plans once they are made. The role of the programmer may be likened to that of the subcontractor in a building project. Just as the general contractor employs specialized subcontractors to accomplish portions of a project, the programming manager assigns portions of the system to highly specialized programmers.

For the completed system to function properly, the work of each programmer must integrate with that of other programmers assigned to the project. In order for this to be accomplished, very careful plans must be made. Every component of the system must be fully and precisely described so that the programmer responsible for a particular component knows what that part is expected to do. A system that is not adequately and completely planned may result in programs that cannot be integrated into a complete system. When this happens, conflicting programs must be revised so that the desired system can be constructed. This revision, of course, may be expensive and time-consuming and should be avoided whenever possible. Thus, the system design and specifications not only have important implications for the ultimate utility of the system; they are also important in the system development process. A well-thought-out system will work better in the end and is likely to cost less to implement.

Two aspects of the system design are used most directly by the programmer: system flowcharts and program specification statements. They are the basic means by which the designer communicates with the programmers.

10.2   SYSTEM FLOWCHARTING

A **system flowchart** is a schematic representation of the data and processing steps in a data processing system. Unlike program flowcharts, no attempt is made to describe how the processing is to take place. The focus in a system flowchart is on data files (represented by blocks of different shapes, depending on the medium used to store the file), processing steps (represented by rectangles), and the flow of data to and from processing steps (represented by flow lines). A list of the most common system flow-chart symbols is shown in Figure 10.1.

The system flowchart shown in Figure 10.2 represents a system in which data from an on-line device is accepted by a program that generates information printed on the operator's screen and uses the data to update a data file stored on disk. The names used inside the blocks represent file names or program names. These are generally the file and program names used by the operating system for storage of these entities. (Additional examples of system flowcharts are shown later in the chapter in Figures 10.5 and 10.6.)

System flowcharts are useful to the systems analyst, programmers, and users for visualizing the flow of information within a data processing system. They are particularly useful for representing the sequence of processing steps when one step must be accomplished successfully before the next step can begin. Because of their utility, system flowcharts are used for documentation as well as for system design.

10.3 PROGRAM SPECIFICATIONS

The document of greatest importance to the programmer is the **program specification statement,** which is a description of exactly what the program must accomplish. The program specification statement generally includes a description of input and output files and their associated data records, a printer spacing or screen layout chart showing placement of required information, and a description of what the program must accomplish. Depending on the complexity of the task at hand, the program specification statement may or may not include a detailed description of the procedure to be used (in the form of code). This document is the programmer's basic reference for understanding the programming task at hand and designing the required program. Examples of program specification statements are contained in Section 10.4. Clearly, a complete system design and specification document encompasses a great many different considerations essential to the completed system.

Typically, a completed system design for a small system is a book containing several hundred pages. For a large system, the design will resemble a small library. Presented in the following pages is an abbreviated version of a system design for a data processing system for a hypothetical manufacturing company. Because this system is the basis for some of the program examples used in this text, understanding the system will help you appreciate the motivation behind the program examples and will help you visualize how these programs fit with other components of the complete system.

10.4 EXAMPLE OF A COMPLETE SYSTEM

Background

Amalgamated Custom Design, Inc., manufactures customized T-shirts, jackets, hats, and similar items. The company sells primarily to clubs, ath-

Figure 10.1   System flowchart symbols

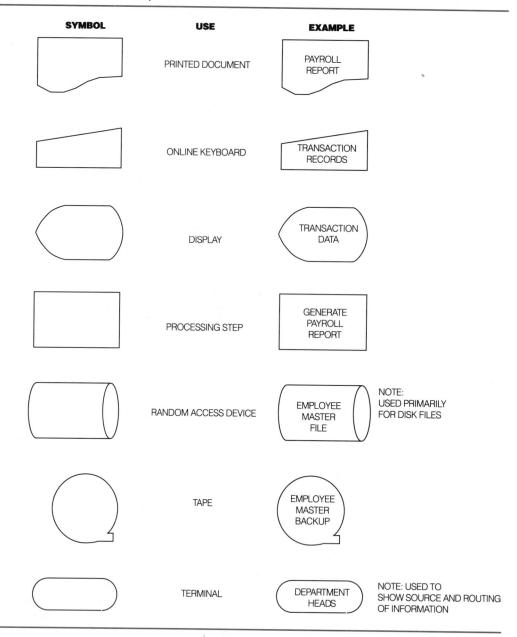

letic teams, schools, and companies which desire custom printing on the products sold by Amalgamated. Amalgamated buys its plain (unprinted) products from a variety of sources. The company's production facilities are set up to process batches of similar items with the same design, such as a batch of jackets all with one design.

As orders are received, they are recorded in the Order Master File. An order is made up of one or more components; an order component corresponds to one line item on an order form for one specific product. An order component is submitted for production when there are sufficient raw materials on hand to manufacture the products required. Any order component that cannot be completed because of lack of sufficient raw materials is placed in a pending state, and appropriate raw material orders are issued. When raw material is received, the pending order component is

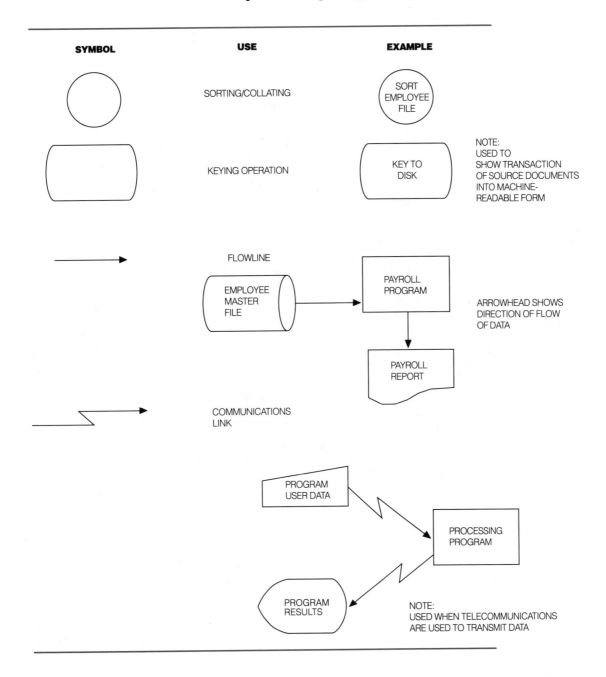

SYMBOL	USE	EXAMPLE

SORTING/COLLATING — SORT EMPLOYEE FILE

KEYING OPERATION — KEY TO DISK

NOTE:
USED TO
SHOW TRANSACTION
OF SOURCE DOCUMENTS
INTO MACHINE-
READABLE FORM

FLOWLINE

EMPLOYEE MASTER FILE → PAYROLL PROGRAM → PAYROLL REPORT

ARROWHEAD SHOWS
DIRECTION OF FLOW
OF DATA

COMMUNICATIONS LINK

PROGRAM USER DATA → PROCESSING PROGRAM → PROGRAM RESULTS

NOTE:
USED WHEN TELECOMMUNICATIONS
ARE USED TO TRANSMIT DATA

then submitted for production. The production supervisor examines each order component record when it is submitted to determine an estimated completion date for the batch of goods ordered. When the batch is completed, it is sent to the warehouse to await shipment. When all components of an order have been completed, shipping orders are issued.

Computing Facilities

Amalgamated owns a small business computing system with both limited on-line and batch capabilities. Terminals are located in the main office and the production facility. The company's data processing system is made up of a mixture of batch and interactive components because of the limited number of terminals, the necessity of maintaining printed records of vari-

Figure 10.2   System flowchart example

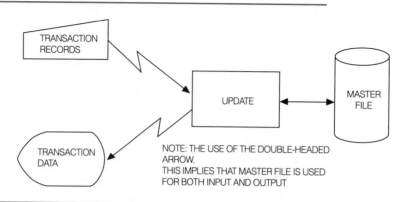

ous types, and the relatively limited capacity of the computing system, which must be utilized efficiently. Batch programs are used for generating management reports, internal and external documents (like production orders, shipping orders, and invoices), and related file updating. Interactive programs are used for data entry and information requests. The interactive programs are executed on demand from the appropriate terminal. During the day, the system is dedicated to these programs. In the evening, the batch portions of the system are processed.

Note that the characteristics of the company's computing system have a significant influence on the design of the data processing system. Under a different set of circumstances, it might be necessary to implement a system that is completely batch or completely interactive. The design described here is typical of that found in small or medium-sized businesses such as Amalgamated.

System Overview

The system is made up of three major subsystems:

- Raw Materials System
- Work in Progress System
- Order Control System

The Raw Materials System is used in submitting orders for production and in accounting for raw materials (unprinted products and other materials used in production). The Raw Materials Master File shows amounts of each raw material on hand, encumbered (needed to complete production orders but not yet used), and on order. The Raw Materials Master File is updated when materials are ordered, used, and received and when a production batch is submitted. The Raw Materials System also makes use of a Supplier Master File which stores details of each supplier and is used in generating orders for supplies.

The Work in Progress System is used in determining the status of production of each batch of products. The Work in Progress Master File is updated when a batch is submitted and scheduled and when production is completed.

The Order Control System is used to control orders from the time they are entered into the system until they are completed and goods are shipped. Orders are entered into the Order Master File when they are received. The system then determines if raw materials are available and either submits the order to the production facility or places the order component in a pending state until sufficient raw materials are available for production. When all order components have been completed, the Order Master File is updated and appropriate shipping orders are generated.

Figure 10.3 shows the states possible for an order from entry through shipping. Figure 10.4 shows the states possible for order components.

Figure 10.3   Status chart of orders

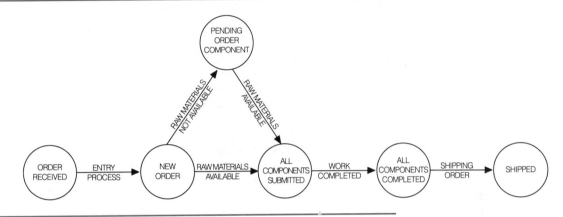

Figure 10.4   Status chart for order components

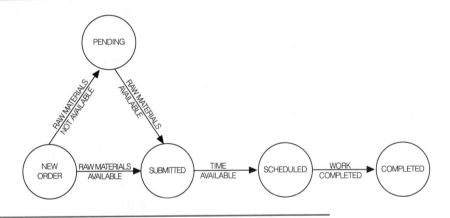

File Specifications

File Name:	Raw Materials Master
Description:	The Raw Materials Master File is used to account for raw materials in stock and on order and to determine whether sufficient stock is on hand to enable production of an order.
Organization:	Indexed; keyed by item number
Record Content:	

• item number	X(5)
• item description	X(10)
• unencumbered on hand	9(3)
• encumbered on hand	9(3)
• on order	9(3)
• item cost	999V99
• minimum order quantity	9(3)
• supplier number	X(5)

File Name:	Order Master File	
Description:	The Order Master File is used to store orders as they are entered and to track orders during the production and shipping process.	
Organization:	Sequential; in sequence by order number	
Record Types:	• Order Master—there is one order master record for each order.	
	• Order Detail—there is one detail record for each component of the order.	

Order Master
Record Content:

- order number — X(5)
- customer number — 9(9)
- customer name — X(20)
- customer address — X(20)
- number of order components — 9(3)
- date of receipt — 9(6)
- shipping date (blank until order is shipped) — 9(6)

Order Detail
Record Content:

- order number — X(5)
- catalog number — X(5)
- quantity — 9(3)
- number of order components — 9(3)
- scheduled completion date — 9(6)
- actual completion date — 9(6)
- raw material requirements — X(5) each
  (from 1 to 5 raw material item numbers)
- batch status—N new order
  - P pending
  - S submitted
  - C completed — X
- customizing instructions — X(15)

File Name:	Work in Progress Master
Description:	The Work in Progress (WIP) Master File is used in scheduling and production of batches of products. A record is placed in the file when the batch is submitted for production. When the production supervisor schedules production for the batch, the file is updated to show estimated completion date. When production is completed, the file is updated again to show date of completion.
Organization:	Relative; randomized placement of records—key field is combined order number and catalog number (batch number)

Record Content:

- order number ⎫ batch number — X(5)
- catalog number ⎭ — X(5)
- quantity — 9(3)
- number of order components — 9(3)
- scheduled completion date (blank if not scheduled) — 9(6)
- actual completion date (blank until completed) — 9(6)
- raw material requirements (from 1 to 5 item numbers) — X(5) each

---

File Name:	Purchase Request File
Description:	The Purchase Request File is used to store purchase requests generated by New Order Processing.
Organization:	Sequential; sorted into sequence by supplier identification number and item number

Record Content:	• supplier ID number	X(5)
	• item number	X(5)
	• item description	X(10)
	• item cost	999V99
	• order quantity	9(3)

File Name:	Supplier Master File	
Description:	The Supplier Master File is used to generate purchase orders. It contains one record for each supplier with whom Amalgamated does business.	
Organization:	Sequential; in order by supplier identification number	
Record Content:	• supplier ID number	X(5)
	• supplier name	X(20)
	• supplier address	X(20)

File Name:	Order Transaction File	
Description:	Stores order transactions resulting from new orders being entered or orders being completed.	
Organization:	Sequential; sorted into sequence by order number	
Record Types:	• Order Master } Content of these records same	
	• Order Detail } as for Order Master File	
	• Component Completion	
	• Order Shipping	

Component Completion Record Content:	• order number	X(5)
	• catalog number	X(5)
	• completion date	9(6)

Order Shipping Record Content:	• order number	X(5)
	• shipping date	9(6)

Program Specifications

Title:	Raw Materials Update
Type:	Interactive
Purpose:	Updates the Raw Materials Master File from transactions regarding receipt and use of raw materials.

Title:	Work in Progress Update
Type:	Interactive/Menu Driven
Purpose:	Updates the Work in Progress Master File and Order Transaction Files. Options on Menu:

- L   List all scheduled batches
- U   List all unscheduled batches
- S   Schedule a batch
- C   Complete a batch (enables updating of WIP Master and places an appropriate record in Order Transaction File)
- A   Add a batch   } used only for error correction and file maintenance;
- D   Delete a batch } records are added to the file as a result of New Order Processing described below

Title:	Order Entry
Type:	Interactive
Purpose:	Validates new order data and adds records to the Order Transaction File.

Title:	Work in Progress Report (Program 10a)
Type:	Batch
Purpose:	Produce report showing status of job components that are in production.

Title:	Order Update
Type:	Batch
Purpose:	Updates Order Master File using records from the Order Transaction File to produce the New Order Master File.

Title:	New Order Processing
Type:	Batch
Purpose:	Processes each component of a new order in the Order Master File. If sufficient raw materials are on hand, the batch is submitted for production (a record is added to the WIP Master and a written order is produced). If sufficient raw materials are not on hand, the batch is placed in a pending state and appropriate purchase request records are added to the Purchase Request File.

Title:	Pending Order Processing
Type:	Batch
Purpose:	Processes all pending order components in the Order Master File. If sufficient raw materials are on hand, the batch is submitted for production (a record is added to the WIP Master and a written order is produced). The Order Master File is updated appropriately.

Title:	Completed Order Processing
Type:	Batch
Purpose:	Generates shipping orders for those orders for which all components have been completed. Adds appropriate record to the Order Transaction File.

Title:	Generate Purchase Orders
Type:	Batch
Purpose:	Summarizes purchase requests by supplier and generates purchase orders.

System Flowcharts

System flowcharts for this system are shown in Figures 10.5 and 10.6.

10.5 SURVEY OF PROGRAM DEVELOPMENT PRACTICES

Programming Team

In very small organizations, the roles of the systems analyst and the programmer may be combined into one job, typically called a **programmer-analyst.** In most organizations, however, system development involves both the systems analyst and the programming staff. A very small system might be assigned to a single programmer for implementation, but most systems require the services of several programmers.

In the past, it was not uncommon for a programming manager to assign specific portions of a system to individual programmers for independent implementation, expecting that the system would function as a whole when each module was completed. Because the work of programmers working alone usually contained inconsistencies when their

Figure 10.5 System flowchart of interactive components

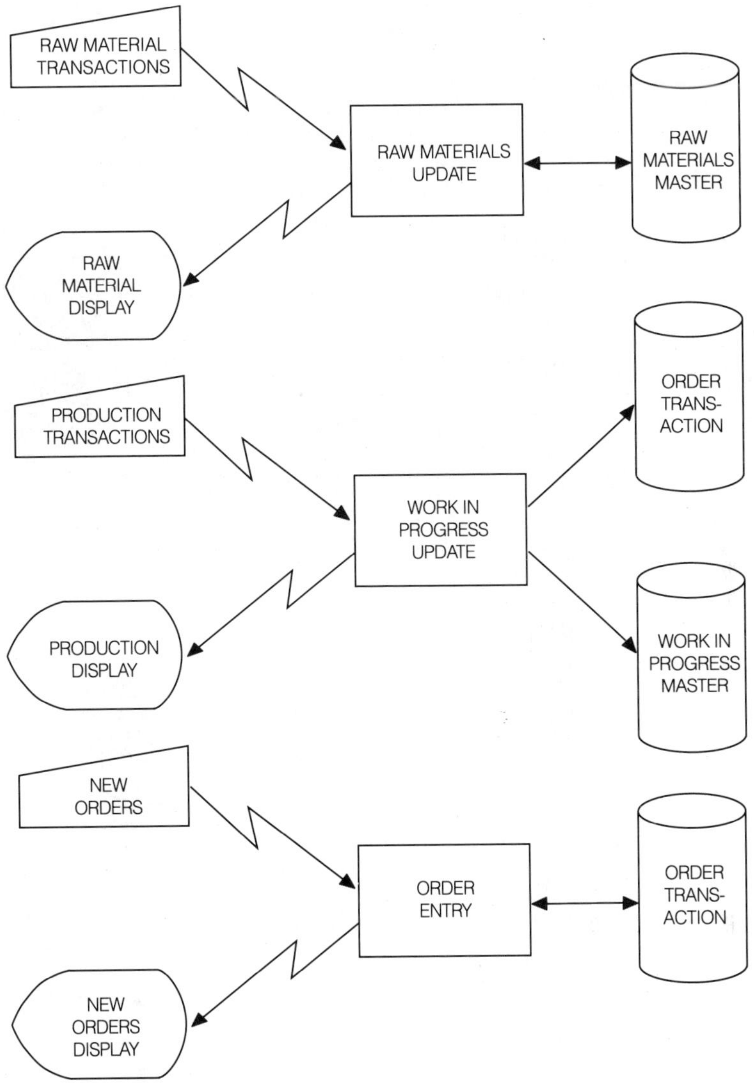

work was combined, this expectation was rarely met, and reworking of one or more components was often a necessity.

Current practice tends toward a closely coordinated team approach to program development. The programming manager assigns responsibility for the project to a team, usually with one member designated as the team leader. The team analyzes the project and collectively decides on a division of labor. Frequent meetings are held to clarify issues as they arise and to ensure coordinated effort. The **programming team** approach has a number of benefits:

- The team is able to capitalize on particular technical strengths of team members.
- The close coordination and review of each other's work ensures that the system will function correctly when finished.
- Team members learn from each other and thereby become better programmers in the long run.

Figure 10.6   System flowchart of batch components

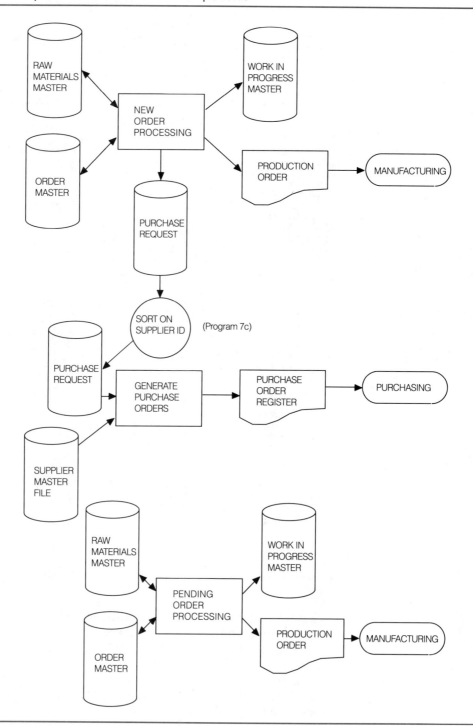

- The team approach is good for morale because team members are able to lend emotional support to each other.

The programming team approach, of course, is not without potential problems:

- The time spent in meetings and coordination may be excessive (and expensive).

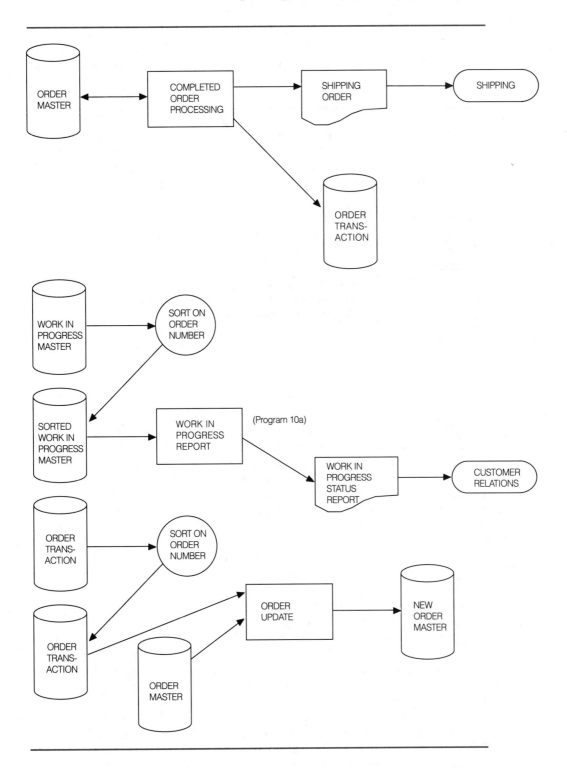

- Team members may disagree on the best way to carry out the task, resulting in the necessity of spending time (and money) to resolve conflicts.
- Personality clashes among team members may be disruptive of the process.

A well-chosen team with appropriate management and support is, however, a very efficient vehicle for implementing a system, and the technique is being used in a growing number of data processing installations today.

Structured Walk-Through

Another practice that lends itself naturally to the team approach is the **structured walk-through.** The idea is to prevent program errors before the program is ever compiled and tested. In installations that use structured walk-throughs, the process usually consists of the following steps:

1. A programmer codes a program.
2. Copies of the program code, together with appropriate documentation (pseudocode or HIPO charts, for example), are distributed to each member of the team.
3. After allowing a suitable time interval (one to two days) for each person to review the program, the team meets as a group.
4. During the meeting, the programmer "walks through" the program, explaining the design and the purpose of each module and, perhaps, tracing the execution sequence for sample data.
5. The team then makes constructive criticism and, as a group, decides whether the program is ready to be compiled and tested or whether modifications need to be made.

This process is carried out while the program is in written form, not after the programmer has invested hours or days in entering the code and compiling the program. The purpose of the technique is to ensure that the program will work correctly the first time it is compiled. Although the technique works well in the programming team approach, it can be used in any environment. It is not necessary that the group members be involved directly with the project to be effective in locating logical errors and design flaws in a program.

A major problem with the structured walk-through technique is that the programmer must be able to accept criticism. Proponents of the method maintain that if programmers do not see a program as an extension of themselves, criticism of the program will not be seen as personal criticism. While this ideal of "ego-less" programming is appealing, most programmers do, in fact, have reasonably strong identification with the programs they construct, and it is natural to resent criticism. Members of the review group must be very careful not to criticize the program but rather make suggestions on how the program can be improved. The distinction between these two ideas is very fine, but it is crucial to the morale of the programmer whose work is being reviewed.

Another potential problem lies in the makeup of the review group. Programmers must not feel that they are on trial or that their supervisor is taking notes that will be used later for evaluation. For this reason, review groups are normally made up of the programmer's peers and exclude supervisory personnel. Also, to avoid the possibility of supervisory review, detailed written minutes of the meetings are not made. The purpose of the technique is to produce better programs, not to evaluate or judge the programmer. If the technique is seen by the programming staff as a means of evaluation, the effect on morale will be negative, and the method could, in the end, be counterproductive.

Data Dictionary

The names assigned to a file and associated records and fields in a given COBOL program are, in general, an arbitrary choice of the programmer. The use of descriptive names to make the program readable and, hence, maintainable, is an important element of structured programming. In any system, there will usually be many programs that process a given file. If every program uses different names for the file and its records and fields, the process of maintaining these programs is complicated unnecessarily. Consider the job of the maintenance programmer assigned to change every program that processes a given file. Even though each program may function correctly in its own right and the names chosen may be descriptive and otherwise acceptable, it will be very confusing and will add a needless measure of complexity to force the maintenance programmer to contend with as many different names as there are programs. A much better approach is to establish a set of data-names for each entity at the outset and require that each program in the system use these data-names. This set of data-names is commonly called a **data dictionary** and should be established before any program code is written. Each programmer working on the project must have access to the dictionary, and someone (usually the programming manager) must assume responsibility for forcing compliance with the use of common data-names. The data dictionary is commonly placed in an on-line system library to facilitate compliance with this standard.

Structured Implementation and Testing

The task of program testing involves verification that the program does indeed perform in accordance with the program specifications. For a simple program (and in most student environments), this task is usually undertaken in the following manner:

1. The programmer codes the program.
2. The program is compiled and corrected until there are no more syntax errors.
3. The programmer creates one or more sample data files. (These may have been provided as part of the assignment in a student environment.)
4. The program is executed.
5. If the output produced is consistent with the output expected from the given sample data, the program is accepted; otherwise, changes are made to the program, and the process is completed.

Although this procedure may be sufficient in some instances, it has many flaws when used with a large or complex program. One of the most glaring problems is that testing of the program does not begin until the entire coding process has been completed. It is well known that the number of errors and the difficulty of the debugging process tend to be related exponentially to the length and complexity of a program. For a large or complex program, the testing process should proceed in parallel with the implementation process; that is, the program should be tested at appropriate stages before all of the program modules are completely coded.

Two somewhat conflicting philosophies exist (both using the general name **structured implementation and testing**), which describe how this parallel testing process should be approached. One alternative is a bottom-up implementation and testing technique. In this technique, the lowest-level functioning modules are coded and tested independently. Then, the next level of controlling modules is coded and tested with the verified low-level modules in place, and so on, proceeding ultimately to the highest level. By using this approach, the potential number and complexity of errors is limited at each stage of the process to the level just added to the program, thereby simplifying the debugging task. Although the bottom-up approach is theoretically sound, some practical problems, including the following, occur when the procedure is strictly adhered to:

- The task of testing functioning modules usually necessitates writing, debugging, and executing complete programs. The task of writing one program suddenly becomes the task of writing many (albeit simpler) programs.

- One will not know if the overall design is sound until the very last stage when all of the subordinate modules have been coded and tested. If there are problems at this top level, it is possible that the entire design will have to be reworked, invalidating much of the work that has gone on before.

An alternative to the bottom-up approach is the top-down approach. In this method, the program is implemented and tested in much the same way as it was designed—from the highest-level control modules to the lowest-level functioning modules. At each stage, modules that are yet to be coded are represented by **program stubs.** In COBOL, this typically means that the paragraph in question is represented by the paragraph name and the EXIT statement, although sometimes temporary output or assignment statements may also be used. Using the top-down approach, the programmer has at each stage a working prototype of the completed program. This technique enables the testing of the overall design first, so that, if changes are necessary, there has been little wasted effort. As with bottom-up testing, the potential number and complexity of errors is limited at each stage in the testing process because the preceding stage has already been verified. On the other hand, it may be impossible to implement a meaningful program without some details supplied by lower-level modules. This is particularly true when a lower-level module passes a control variable to a higher-level module. The higher-level module cannot function correctly without appropriate values for that control data item.

Most programmers tend to use a pragmatic combination of the top-down and bottom-up approaches and vary their technique, depending on the nature of the program at hand. For example, it may be practical to code and test input, output, and certain computational modules separately in a bottom-up approach. At that point, however, it may be advantageous to turn to a top-down approach, using a skeleton structure with the now debugged and tested low-level modules in place.

In any case, programmers working on large or complex programs do not use the student program implementation and testing model outlined earlier. To use such a model would invite potential program debugging problems of great magnitude and complexity. The purpose of structured implementation and testing is to encounter and correct problems a few at a time and in areas of the program that can be readily isolated. Either a top-down or a bottom-up approach, or some combination of the two, will ultimately simplify the testing process and help to ensure a correctly functioning program when the programmer's work is finished.

10.6   PROGRAM EXAMPLE

Problem Statement

Write a program to produce the Work in Progress Report for the Amalgamated Custom Design system described in Section 10.4. The program processes the Sorted Work in Progress Master File, which is a sequential file sorted into order number sequence as shown in the system flowchart of Figure 10.6. Each record in the file contains the following fields:

- Order number
- Catalog number
- Quantity
- Number of order components
- Scheduled completion date (spaces if not yet scheduled)
- Actual completion date (spaces if not yet completed)
- Raw materials required

When a batch is submitted for production, a record is placed in the Work in Progress Master File. When work is begun, the file is updated with a scheduled completion date. When work is completed, the file is updated again to show the actual completion date.

The report must show the status of each order component and contain a summary of the components of each order, as shown in the printer spacing chart in Figure 10.7.

Figure 10.7   Printer spacing chart for Work in Progress Report program

NOTES		0	1	2	3	4	5	6
		1234567890	1234567890	1234567890	1234567890	1234567890	1234567890	12345678
Major heading	1	CUSTOM DESIGN WORK IN PROGRESS					PAGE ZZZ	
	2							
Subhead 1	3	ORDER	CATALOG	QUANTITY		SCHEDULED	ACTUAL	
Subhead 2	4	NUMBER	NUMBER			COMPLETION	COMPLETION	
	5							
Detail line¹"	6	XXXXX	XXXXX	999		99/99/99	99/99/99	
	7							
Summary line	8	NUMBER COMPONENTS: SUBMITTED		ZZ9		IN ORDER	ZZ9	
	9							
	10							
	11							

Problem Analysis

This program will require a control break based on the order number; therefore, a hold field (HOLD-ORDER-NUMBER) will be required. The summary line requires the number of components that have been submitted for production. This value can be calculated by counting each component as it is processed. This will require a counter (NUMBER-COMPONENTS-WIP), which will be set to zero initially and after each control break. The summary line also requires the number of components in the order. This value is contained on each order component record. In order to print this value on the summary line, a hold field (HOLD-COMPONENTS) will be required. This field will be handled essentially the same way as the hold field for the order number. The value of number of components from the first record in the order number group will be moved to the hold field, and, after the summary line is written, the value of number of components from the first record of the new group will be moved to the hold field. Note that the number of components in the order has the same value on each order component record for the order. Pseudocode for the required program is shown in Figure 10.8.

Figure 10.8   Pseudocode for Program 10a

```
Open files
Read data file
Initialize hold fields
Do until end of file
        If new order
                Write order summary
                Increment line count
                Initialize number components
                Initialize hold fields
        End If
        If page is full
                Write headings
                Initialize line count
        End If
        Move data from input record to output record
        Increment number components
        Write detail record
        Increment line count
        Read data file
End Do
Write order summary
Close files
Stop
```

Problem Solution

The required program is shown in Program 10a. Sample output is shown in Figure 10.9, and a structure diagram is shown in Figure 10.10. This program is a control break program with headings similar in many ways to programs described in Chapter 8. Two new features of COBOL are illustrated in this program. The FD entry for WIP-MASTER-FILE is written in a fuller form (see lines 25-30) than has been used in previous programs in this text. A complete general syntax of the FD entry is shown in Figure 10.11.

The RECORD CONTAINS clause specifies the number of characters contained on a record. This clause is optional and is generally used for documentation purposes only, as the length of the record specified for the file in the record description is used by the system as the record length, regardless of the entry in the RECORD CONTAINS clause. The BLOCK CONTAINS clause is used to describe the blocking factor in use when the file was created. One use of the VALUE OF clause is to specify the name of the

Program 10a

```
 1 IDENTIFICATION DIVISION.
 2
 3 PROGRAM-ID. WIP-REPORT-PRO10A.
 4 AUTHOR. HORN.
 5
 6 ENVIRONMENT DIVISION.
 7
 8 CONFIGURATION SECTION.
 9
10 SOURCE-COMPUTER.
11 OBJECT-COMPUTER.
12
13 INPUT-OUTPUT SECTION.
14
15 FILE-CONTROL.
16
17     SELECT WIP-MASTER-FILE ASSIGN TO DISK.
18
19     SELECT REPORT-FILE ASSIGN TO PRINTER.
20
21 DATA DIVISION.
22
23 FILE SECTION.
24
25 FD  WIP-MASTER-FILE
26     BLOCK CONTAINS 1 RECORDS
27     RECORD CONTAINS 80 CHARACTERS
28     LABEL RECORDS ARE STANDARD
29     VALUE OF FILE-ID IS "WIP.DAT"
30     DATA RECORD IS WIP-MASTER-RECORD.
31
32
33 01  WIP-MASTER-RECORD          PIC X(80).
34
35 FD  REPORT-FILE
36     LABEL RECORDS ARE OMITTED
37     DATA RECORD IS REPORT-RECORD.
38
39 01  REPORT-RECORD             PIC X(132).
40
41 WORKING-STORAGE SECTION.
42
43 01  EOF-AND-HOLD-FIELDS.
44     03 EOF-FLAG                PIC XXX VALUE "NO ".
45        88 END-OF-FILE    VALUE "YES".
46     03 HOLD-ORDER-NUMBER       PIC X(5) VALUE SPACES.
47     03 HOLD-COMPONENTS         PIC 999 VALUE ZERO.
48
49 01  COUNTERS.
50     03 PAGE-COUNT              PIC 999 VALUE ZERO.
51     03 NUMBER-COMPONENTS-WIP   PIC 999 VALUE ZERO.
52     03 LINE-COUNT              PIC 999 VALUE 16.
53        88 PAGE-FULL     VALUE 16 THRU 999.
54
```

Program 10a *(continued)*

```
55 01  MAJOR-HEADING.
56      03 FILLER           PIC X(5) VALUE SPACES.
57      03 FILLER           PIC X(29) VALUE
58         "CUSTOM DESIGN WORK IN PROCESS".
59      03 FILLER           PIC X(22) VALUE SPACES.
60      03 FILLER           PIC X(5) VALUE "PAGE ".
61      03 MH-PAGE-COUNTER  PIC ZZZ.
62
63 01  SUBHEAD-1.
64      03 FILLER      PIC X(5) VALUE SPACES.
65      03 FILLER      PIC X(5) VALUE "ORDER".
66      03 FILLER      PIC X(6) VALUE SPACES.
67      03 FILLER      PIC X(7) VALUE "CATALOG".
68      03 FILLER      PIC X(5) VALUE SPACES.
69      03 FILLER      PIC X(8) VALUE "QUANTITY".
70      03 FILLER      PIC X(5) VALUE SPACES.
71      03 FILLER      PIC X(9) VALUE "SCHEDULED".
72      03 FILLER      PIC X(6) VALUE SPACES.
73      03 FILLER      PIC X(6) VALUE "ACTUAL".
74
75 01  SUBHEAD-2.
76      03 FILLER      PIC X(5) VALUE SPACES.
77      03 FILLER      PIC X(6) VALUE "NUMBER".
78      03 FILLER      PIC X(5) VALUE SPACES.
79      03 FILLER      PIC X(6) VALUE "NUMBER".
80      03 FILLER      PIC X(19) VALUE SPACES.
81      03 FILLER      PIC X(10) VALUE "COMPLETION".
82      03 FILLER      PIC X(5) VALUE SPACES.
83      03 FILLER      PIC X(10) VALUE "COMPLETION".
84
85 01  WIP-MASTER-RECORD-WS.
86      03 ORDER-NUMBER-WMR              PIC X(5).
87      03 CATALOG-NUMBER-WMR            PIC X(5).
88      03 QUANTITY-WMR                  PIC 9(3).
89      03 NUMBER-COMPONENTS-WMR         PIC 9(3).
90      03 SCHEDULED-COMPLETION-DATE-WMR PIC 9(6).
91      03 ACTUAL-COMPLETION-DATE-WMR    PIC 9(6).
92      03 RAW-MAT-WMR                   PIC X(5) OCCURS 5 TIMES.
93
94 01  DETAIL-LINE.
95      03 FILLER                    PIC X(5) VALUE SPACES.
96      03 ORDER-NUMBER-DL           PIC X(5).
97      03 FILLER                    PIC X(6) VALUE SPACES.
98      03 CATALOG-NUMBER-DL         PIC X(5).
99      03 FILLER                    PIC X(7) VALUE SPACES.
100     03 QUANTITY-DL               PIC 9(3).
101     03 FILLER                    PIC X(10) VALUE SPACES.
102     03 SCHEDULED-COMPLETION-DATE-DL PIC 99/99/99
103                                   BLANK WHEN ZERO.
104     03 FILLER                    PIC X(7) VALUE SPACES.
105     03 ACTUAL-COMPLETION-DATE-DL PIC 99/99/99
106                                   BLANK WHEN ZERO.
107
```

Program 10α   *(continued)*

```
108 01  CONTROL-BREAK-SUMMARY.
109     03 FILLER                     PIC X(5) VALUE SPACES.
110     03 FILLER                     PIC X(28) VALUE
111        "NUMBER COMPONENTS: SUBMITTED".
112     03 FILLER                     PIC X(5) VALUE SPACES.
113     03 NUMBER-COMPONENTS-WIP-CBS  PIC ZZ9.
114     03 FILLER                     PIC X(5) VALUE SPACES.
115     03 FILLER                     PIC X(8) VALUE "IN ORDER".
116     03 FILLER                     PIC X(5) VALUE SPACES.
117     03 COMPONENTS-IN-ORDER-CBS    PIC ZZZ9.
118
119 PROCEDURE DIVISION.
120
121 1000-MAIN-LOGIC.
122
123     PERFORM 2000-INITIALIZE-DATA.
124     PERFORM 2100-PROCESS-DATA
125            UNTIL END-OF-FILE.
126     PERFORM 9100-ORDER-NUMBER-BREAK.
127     PERFORM 2200-CLOSE-FILES.
128     STOP RUN.
129
130 2000-INITIALIZE-DATA.
131
132     OPEN INPUT WIP-MASTER-FILE
133         OUTPUT REPORT-FILE.
134     PERFORM 9000-READ-WIP-MASTER-FILE.
135     MOVE ORDER-NUMBER-WMR       TO HOLD-ORDER-NUMBER.
136     MOVE NUMBER-COMPONENTS-WMR TO HOLD-COMPONENTS.
137
138 2100-PROCESS-DATA.
139
140     IF ORDER-NUMBER-WMR NOT = HOLD-ORDER-NUMBER
141            PERFORM 9100-ORDER-NUMBER-BREAK.
142     IF PAGE-FULL
143            PERFORM 9200-WRITE-HEADINGS.
144     MOVE ORDER-NUMBER-WMR TO ORDER-NUMBER-DL.
145     MOVE CATALOG-NUMBER-WMR TO CATALOG-NUMBER-DL.
146     MOVE QUANTITY-WMR TO QUANTITY-DL.
147     MOVE SCHEDULED-COMPLETION-DATE-WMR TO
148            SCHEDULED-COMPLETION-DATE-DL.
149     MOVE ACTUAL-COMPLETION-DATE-WMR TO
150            ACTUAL-COMPLETION-DATE-DL.
151     ADD 1 TO NUMBER-COMPONENTS-WIP.
152     MOVE DETAIL-LINE TO REPORT-RECORD.
153     WRITE REPORT-RECORD AFTER 2.
154     ADD 1 TO LINE-COUNT.
155     PERFORM 9000-READ-WIP-MASTER-FILE.
156
157 2200-CLOSE-FILES.
158
159     CLOSE WIP-MASTER-FILE
160            REPORT-FILE.
161
```

Program 10a   *(concluded)*

```
162  9000-READ-WIP-MASTER-FILE.
163
164      READ WIP-MASTER-FILE INTO WIP-MASTER-RECORD-WS
165          AT END MOVE "YES" TO EOF-FLAG.
166
167  9100-ORDER-NUMBER-BREAK.
168
169      MOVE NUMBER-COMPONENTS-WIP TO NUMBER-COMPONENTS-WIP-CBS.
170      MOVE HOLD-COMPONENTS TO COMPONENTS-IN-ORDER-CBS.
171      WRITE REPORT-RECORD FROM CONTROL-BREAK-SUMMARY AFTER 2.
172      ADD 2 TO LINE-COUNT.
173      IF PAGE-FULL
174          PERFORM 9200-WRITE-HEADINGS
175      ELSE
176          MOVE SPACES TO REPORT-RECORD
177          WRITE REPORT-RECORD AFTER 2
178          ADD 2 TO LINE-COUNT.
179      MOVE 0 TO NUMBER-COMPONENTS-WIP.
180      MOVE NUMBER-COMPONENTS-WMR TO HOLD-COMPONENTS.
181      MOVE ORDER-NUMBER-WMR TO HOLD-ORDER-NUMBER.
182
183  9200-WRITE-HEADINGS.
184
185      ADD 1 TO PAGE-COUNT.
186      MOVE PAGE-COUNT TO MH-PAGE-COUNTER.
187      WRITE REPORT-RECORD FROM MAJOR-HEADING AFTER PAGE.
188      WRITE REPORT-RECORD FROM SUBHEAD-1 AFTER 2.
189      WRITE REPORT-RECORD FROM SUBHEAD-2 AFTER 1.
190      MOVE SPACES TO REPORT-RECORD.
191      WRITE REPORT-RECORD AFTER 1.
192      MOVE 5 TO LINE-COUNT.
```

file as it is known to the operating system. The syntax of this statement is dependent on the compiler in use. The general form of this clause is

$$\underline{\text{VALUE}} \ \underline{\text{OF}} \ \text{implementor-name IS} \ \begin{Bmatrix} \text{data-name} \\ \text{literal} \end{Bmatrix}$$

In the system used to compile Program 10a,[1] implementor-name is FILE-ID, and the literal WIP.DAT is used to assign this name to the file WIP-MASTER-FILE. The system you are using may or may not make use of this clause. In many operating systems, the external file name is specified using job control statements. Check the documentation for your system before making use of this feature.[2]

A second new feature of COBOL illustrated in this program is the BLANK WHEN ZERO clause. This is used at lines 103 and 106 to suppress printing of data when the item has value 0. Regardless of the edit picture

---

[1] This program was compiled using Microsoft COBOL 5.0.

[2] RM/COBOL-85 treats the VALUE OF clause as a comment. The external name of a file is associated with the COBOL file name using the SELECT entry (see Appendix H for details).

used to describe a field, if the `BLANK WHEN ZERO` clause is present, spaces will be inserted in the field when the value being moved into the field has value 0.

Figure 10.9 Sample output from Program 10a

```
CUSTOM DESIGN WORK IN PROCESS                          PAGE    1

ORDER        CATALOG      QUANTITY     SCHEDULED       ACTUAL
NUMBER       NUMBER                    COMPLETION      COMPLETION

11111        22222        003          04/25/91

11111        33333        004          04/15/91

11111        44444        002          04/15/91        04/16/91

NUMBER COMPONENTS: SUBMITTED       3      IN ORDER         3

11112        22222        010          05/01/91

NUMBER COMPONENTS: SUBMITTED       1      IN ORDER         1
--------------------------------------------------------------
CUSTOM DESIGN WORK IN PROCESS                          PAGE    2

ORDER        CATALOG      QUANTITY     SCHEDULED       ACTUAL
NUMBER       NUMBER                    COMPLETION      COMPLETION

11113        33333        001          05/01/91

NUMBER COMPONENTS: SUBMITTED       1      IN ORDER         2


11114        22222        003          04/02/91        04/02/91

11114        22223        050

11114        22233        001          05/01/91

NUMBER COMPONENTS: SUBMITTED       3      IN ORDER         3
--------------------------------------------------------------
CUSTOM DESIGN WORK IN PROCESS                          PAGE    3

ORDER        CATALOG      QUANTITY     SCHEDULED       ACTUAL
NUMBER       NUMBER                    COMPLETION      COMPLETION

11115        22222        040          05/01/91        05/02/91

NUMBER COMPONENTS: SUBMITTED       1      IN ORDER         1
```

Figure 10.10   Structure diagram of Program 10a

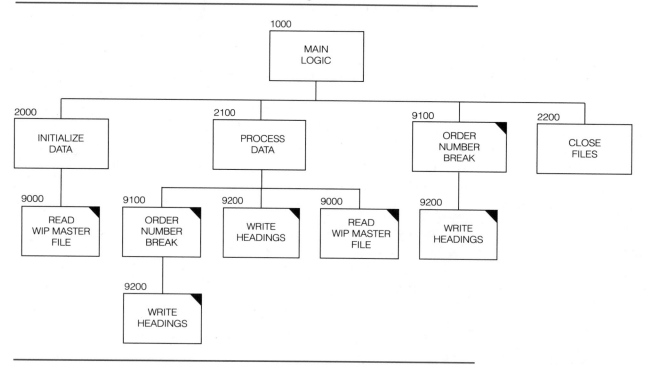

Figure 10.11   General form of the FD entry

```
FD file-name
    [ BLOCK CONTAINS [integer-1 TO] integer-2  {RECORDS   }]
                                               {CHARACTERS}
    [ RECORD CONTAINS [integer-3 TO] integer-4 CHARACTERS]
      LABEL {RECORD IS   } {STANDARD}
            {RECORDS ARE } {OMITTED }
    [ VALUE OF implementor-name-1 IS  {data-name-1}
                                      {literal-1  }
          [ implementor-name-2 IS  {data-name-2}]  ...]
                                   {literal-2  }
    [ DATA {RECORD IS   }  data-name-3 [ data-name-4 ] ...].
           {RECORDS ARE }
```

──────── **Example** ────────

```
MOVE FLDA TO FLDB
 |0|0|0|            |_|_|_|_|_|
      ^
 FLDA PIC 99V9      FLDB PIC 99.9 BLANK WHEN ZERO

 |0|0|1|            |0|0|.|1|
      ^
 FLDA PIC 99V9      FLDB PIC 99.9 BLANK WHEN ZERO
```

10.7 LIBRARIES AND THE COPY STATEMENT

The data dictionary is an important concept when more than one program must be written to process the same data. Adherence to the data-names defined in the data dictionary by all programs processing the same data will greatly enhance the maintainability of the programs in the system.

COBOL contains provisions for the establishment of libraries that can contain COBOL source code. The compiler is then able to insert elements from the library directly into COBOL source programs. The result is the same as if a programmer had written the inserted code. This library facility can be used to implement the data dictionary. If file and record descriptions are placed in the library, a very simple program statement can be used which causes the required statements to be inserted into the program. At that point, all of the data-names will be defined to the standard established for the system.

The mechanism for placing text into a library is dependent on the operating system in use. Refer to the system reference manuals for specific instructions. Some systems maintain only one library (called the "Source Statement Library" in IBM's DOS operating system), whereas others permit the establishment of several libraries, each with a user-defined name. Entries in the library consist of sequences of COBOL code identified by a text-name.

The content of a library entry can be inserted into a COBOL program using the COPY statement. A general form of the COPY statement is shown in Figure 10.12. When the COPY statement is used, the content of the specified text is placed in the COBOL program, replacing the COPY statement itself. On some compilers, the COPY statement is also shown for documentation. The library-name option is used only if the named library feature is part of the operating system in use. The COPY statement may be placed anywhere in the program, although it is most often used in the DATA and, to a lesser extent, the PROCEDURE DIVISIONs. A basic limitation of the COPY statement is that the text inserted in the program cannot contain a COPY statement.

Figure 10.12   General form of the COPY statement

$$\text{COPY text-name} \left[\left\{ \begin{matrix} \underline{\text{IN}} \\ \underline{\text{OF}} \end{matrix} \right\} \text{library-name} \right]$$

For example, let us assume that the following code has been entered into the library AMALGAMATED-PRODUCTION-SYSTEM, using the text-name WORK-IN-PROG-REC-DESC:

```
01  WIP-MASTER-RECORD-WS.
    03 ORDER-NUMBER-WMR                  PIC X(5).
    03 CATALOG-NUMBER-WMR                PIC X(5).
    03 QUANTITY-WMR                      PIC 9(3).
    03 NUMBER-COMPONENTS-WMR             PIC 9(3).
    03 SCHEDULED-COMPLETION-DATE-WMR PIC 9(6).
    03 ACTUAL-COMPLETION-DATE-WMR        PIC 9(6).
    03 RAW-MAT-WMR                       PIC X(5) OCCURS 5 TIMES.
```

In Program 10a, it would be possible to use the statement

```
COPY WORK-IN-PROG-RECORD-DESC OF
     AMALGAMATED-PRODUCTION-SYSTEM.
```

at line 85, omitting lines 86 through 92 from the source program. The result would be indistinguishable from the code shown in Program 10a.[3]

Another possible use for this facility is to place PROCEDURE DIVISION modules in the library. This may reduce the work required when the same procedure is needed by several different programs in the system. The system is easier to maintain if each program uses exactly the same logic to carry out the same procedure. Use of the library can help to ensure this consistency.

One definite advantage of using the library is that if code in any of the library entries must be changed, the change can be made only once. Each of the affected programs can then be recompiled, and the change is propagated throughout the system in a relatively painless fashion. This is certainly a much more efficient method than inserting the new code separately into each affected program. The only disadvantage of this technique is that someone must keep track of which programs are affected and, during the conversion process, which programs have been converted and which have not. One useful technique is to place comment statements specifying a version number in each library entry. These comments are copied harmlessly into each COBOL program. However, it is possible to examine the revision number in the source code to know where that program stands in the revision process.

10.8 STRUCTURED DESIGN AND DOCUMENTATION TECHNIQUES

Documentation is defined as support materials that aid in understanding a program. A primary form of documentation is a listing of the program itself. One of the goals of structured programming is to reduce reliance on other forms of documentation by making the source program as readable and easy to follow as possible. For short programs, this may be sufficient, but for longer or more complex programs, other forms of documentation may be desirable.

Simple programs may be coded as they are being designed by the programmer. The programmer typically is able to visualize the program modules and their relationships without a formal design document. As programs become longer and more complex, it may be necessary to write down the design using one of a variety of techniques. The written design may then be analyzed and rewritten as necessary to produce an optimum program design. Often, several people who must communicate with one another are involved in the design process, making the design document a necessity.

Program design documents, rather than coded programs, are used for this design phase because the design document is less work to produce and, therefore, less work to modify than a complete program. Typically, many details of the complete program are omitted in the design document. The emphasis is on specifying program modules, their functions, and their

---

[3] In RM/COBOL-85, text-name may be expressed as a literal specifying the name of the file which contains the statements to be inserted. For example, if the file-name is "WIPREC.DSC", then the required COPY statement would be COPY "WIPREC.DSC".

relationships. The design is useful not only before but also after a program is written to document the structure of the program. The design documents described in this section are usually included with the program listing and sample input and output as part of the documentation package for a program.

Structure Diagram

Structure diagrams offer a method for exhibiting the hierarchical structure of a program. Each module is represented as a block in the diagram with the module name written in the block. If one module is executed via a `PERFORM` statement from another, a line connecting the two blocks is drawn.

Flowcharting

Program flowcharting is one of the oldest design and documentation techniques. The processing steps and the program flow of control are represented visually, using the standard symbols described in Chapter 1. Program flowcharts are used less than other techniques for program design because they tend to be quite cumbersome and they tend to focus on processing steps rather than on the overall program design. Program flowcharts are useful for visualizing program flow within a module, but they are not very useful for analyzing the relationships among program modules, the fundamental issue in program design.

Data Flow Diagram

A **data flow diagram** is a means for analyzing the sequence of processing steps that will be required to accomplish a particular task, and the data required for each step. Processing steps are represented as a circle with a description of the step placed inside the circle. Arrows connect the circles to show the sequencing of the steps. A description of the data required for that step is placed on the arrow leading to the processing step.

Consider the data flow diagram shown in Figure 10.13, which describes the familiar process of preparing a payroll report from records containing hours, rate of pay, and so forth. Data descriptions do not reflect the physical form of the data (data file, record, or computed value). The

Figure 10.13   Data flow diagram example

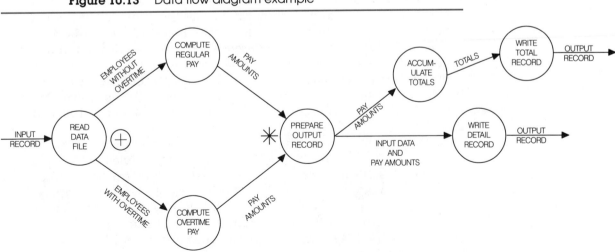

processing steps do not reflect the nature of the program module that will accomplish the required task. The emphasis in a data flow diagram is on the transformations that the data will undergo, not on the logic required to make those transformations.

Two symbols used in data flow diagrams are worthy of special note. The symbol ⊕ indicates that one path or the other in the flow diagram will be taken. In the diagram of Figure 10.13, employees *without* overtime will be processed by "Compute Regular Pay"; employees *with* overtime will be processed by "Compute Overtime Pay." The symbol * indicates that the data from several sources is to be combined in a given processing step. In the diagram of Figure 10.13, amounts calculated from "Compute Regular Pay" and "Compute Overtime Pay" are collected for processing at the step "Prepare Output Record."

Data flow diagrams provide a convenient method for analyzing the processing and data transformations in systems involving manual steps or a number of related computer programs. In using data flow diagrams, it is important to include appropriate amounts of detail. If too little detail is shown, the diagram contributes little to the reader's understanding of the system. If too much detail is shown, the reader is overwhelmed, and again the diagram fails to communicate knowledge of the system in question. Deciding what is appropriate detail is a judgment made with knowledge of the intended audience.

Pseudocode

Pseudocode is a means of describing the processing steps required for accomplishing the goals of a program in an informal language—one that lacks the rigorous syntax of a formal computer language like COBOL. Because the language is informal and the purpose of pseudocode is to communicate the program design and function at a relatively high level, much of the detail required by an actual program may be summarized in the pseudocode. Pseudocode enables the programmer to focus on the algorithms required for the solution of the problem at hand without getting too involved with the details of implementation required in the actual program.

There is no generally agreed upon syntax used for pseudocode. All programmers adopt a style suited to their way of approaching a programming task. Although the syntax is informal, the program must be understandable to another programmer and preferably a nonprogrammer as well. The principle of utilizing only the three basic control structures (sequence, decision, and iteration) must not be violated, but the manner used to describe these structures may vary in any way desired by the programmer. Often a program undergoes various transformations at the pseudocode stage, each transformation yielding a version of the program showing more detail than the previous one. This is the essence of the practice of top-down program design. (See Section 3.2 Top-Down Program Design.) Figure 10.8 illustrates the use of pseudocode in the design of Program 10a.

The pseudocode used in this instance presents a different way of expressing a procedure. In previous examples, modules of the program have been described in the pseudocode. In this figure, the entire procedure has been expressed as one module. Both types of pseudocode are equally valid; the decision as to which to use depends only on the preference of the programmer. When a program is relatively short, the form shown in Figure 10.8 is often used. As programs get more involved, it may be advantageous to segment the pseudocode into modules.

In using pseudocode, the programmer must strike a balance between showing too much detail, which makes the pseudocode as troublesome and unwieldy as the COBOL program, and too little detail, which leaves out significant portions of the program logic. Ideally, the pseudocode is detailed enough to assure that coding of the program will proceed smoothly yet brief enough to afford the reader an overall view of the program's function without becoming enmeshed in detail. This latter characteristic is particularly important when pseudocode is used as a form of documentation.

HIPO

HIPO (*H*ierarchy, *I*nput, *P*rocessing, *O*utput) is a formal technique (generally associated with IBM) for specifying program design. The technique consists of three parts:

1. Hierarchy (H) chart: a structure diagram of essentially the type described earlier in this section. In this context the structure diagram is called a VTOC (*V*isual *T*able *of C*ontents).
2. Input, Processing, Output (IPO): a form used to specify each program module in terms of data required (input), the processing that will take place (processing), and the results (output).
3. Pseudocode for each program module.

IPO specifications and pseudocode for a portion of Program 10a are shown in Figure 10.14. The hierarchy chart for Program 10a is shown in Figure 10.10. These two documents form a complete HIPO documentation of Program 10a.

Many data processing managers require HIPO design and documentation technique as the standard for all programs developed at their installations. The method is well defined and orderly and includes sufficient detail to facilitate coding of a program. Including the hierarchy chart makes it easier for others to understand the overall control structure of the program.

The only problem with using this method is that it generates large amounts of material, much of which is redundant. Critics of this method believe that the time, energy, and money devoted to the religious adherence to these formats could be saved by using less formal methods that convey the same information with a much smaller expenditure of resources.

Nassi-Shneiderman Charts

A **Nassi-Shneiderman chart** (named for Isaac Nassi and Ben Shneiderman) resembles a program flowchart in many respects. Both are graphic representations of the program logic. But, unlike traditional program flowcharts, Nassi-Shneiderman charts can be used only to represent the basic control structures required in structured programming. An example of a Nassi-Shneiderman chart for Program 10a is shown in Figure 10.15. The left-hand margin of the chart is used to record module names. Rectangles in the body of the chart surround pseudocode specifications of the module content. Decisions are shown graphically by splitting the blocks in the body of the chart into two parts, one part representing actions to be taken if the question is answered "yes," the other part if the question is answered "no."

Figure 10.14 IPO specifications for a portion of Program 10a

Author:	Horn		Page 2 of 12
System:	Custom Design Work in Progress		
Name:	2000-INITIALIZATION		

Input	Ref. Process		Output
WIP-MASTER-RECORD	1.	Open Files	HOLD-ORDER-NUMBER
	2.	Read Record from WIP-MASTER	HOLD-COMPONENTS
	3.	Initialize Hold Fields	

Extended Description	Ref.
Input File: WIP-MASTER-FILE Output File: REPORT-FILE	1.
PERFORM 9000-READ-WIP-MASTER-FILE	2.
MOVE ORDER-NUMBER-WMR TO HOLD-ORDER-NUMBER MOVE NUMBER-COMPONENTS-WMR TO HOLD-COMPONENTS	3.

Nassi-Shneiderman charts offer a convenient graphic representation of a program closely related to the structure and form taken by the actual program code. Short programs lend themselves to Nassi-Shneiderman charts more than do long programs. Critics of the charts point out that the graphic portion of the chart really contributes little clarity and that the pseudocode alone is sufficient. A major problem with any graphic form of program documentation is that it does not lend itself to creation or manipulation by electronic means (such as word processors or editors). Any program change requiring a corresponding change in the documentation must be accomplished by hand, which tends to be expensive and opens the possibility of typographical errors.

Figure 10.15   Nassi-Shneiderman chart for Program 10a

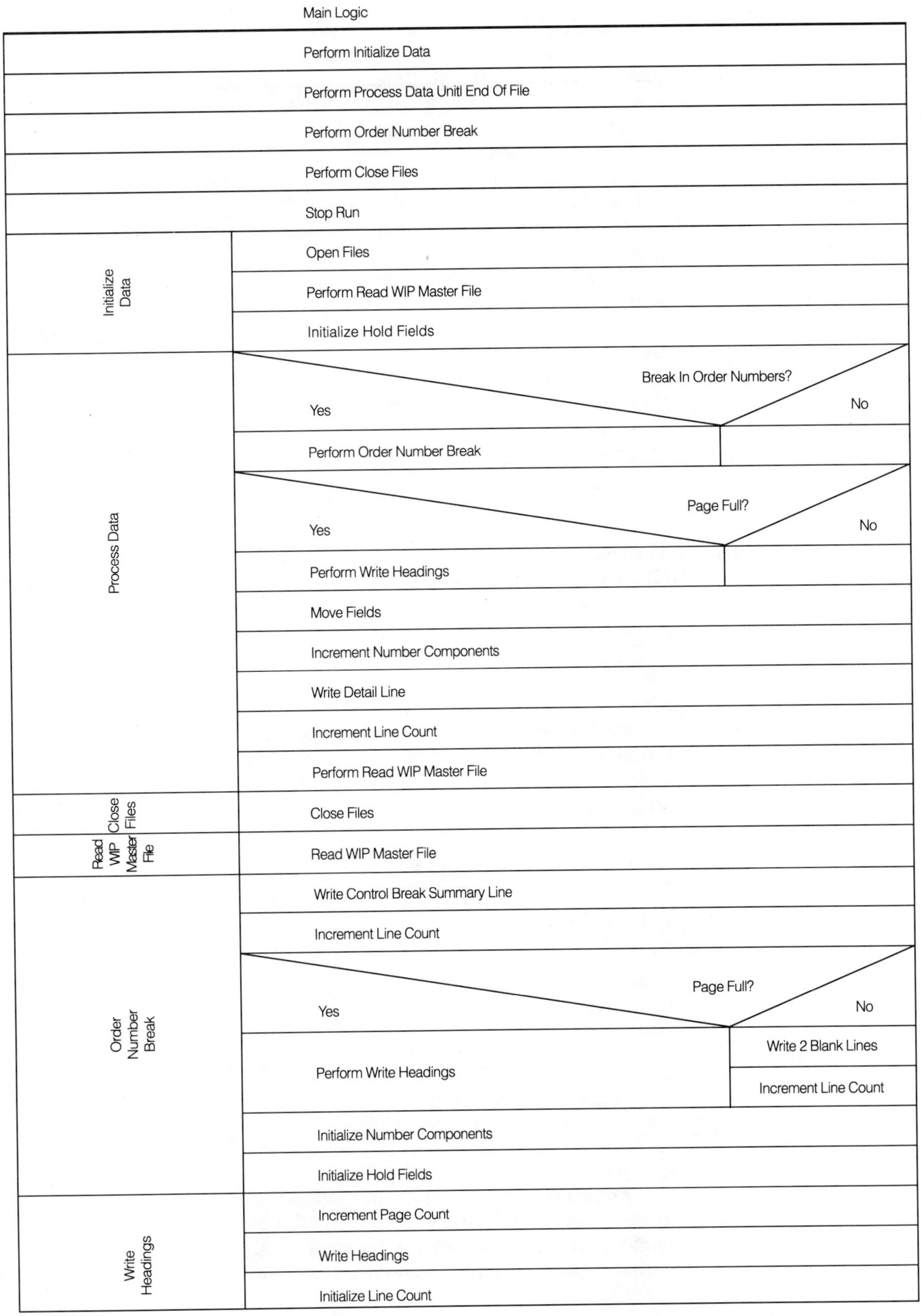

Main Logic
Perform Initialize Data
Perform Process Data Unitl End Of File
Perform Order Number Break
Perform Close Files
Stop Run

Initialize Data	Open Files
	Perform Read WIP Master File
	Initialize Hold Fields

Process Data	Break In Order Numbers?
	Yes / No
	Perform Order Number Break
	Page Full?
	Yes / No
	Perform Write Headings
	Move Fields
	Increment Number Components
	Write Detail Line
	Increment Line Count
	Perform Read WIP Master File

Close Files	Close Files

Read WIP Master File	Read WIP Master File

Order Number Break	Write Control Break Summary Line
	Increment Line Count
	Page Full?
	Yes / No
	Perform Write Headings / Write 2 Blank Lines
	/ Increment Line Count
	Initialize Number Components
	Initialize Hold Fields

Write Headings	Increment Page Count
	Write Headings
	Initialize Line Count

Chapin Charts

Chapin charts (named for their inventor, Ned Chapin) are an alternative form of graphic representation of program logic, representing something of a compromise between traditional program flowcharts and Nassi-Shneiderman charts. Like traditional program flowcharts, each module in a Chapin chart is drawn separately. As in Nassi-Shneiderman charts, the decision structure is represented as a yes/no division beneath the question. Chapin borrowed the oval terminal symbol from traditional program flowcharts and used it to denote the module entry point, program termination, and performance of a module. Like the Nassi-Shneiderman chart, the Chapin chart uses a rectangular grid to surround each program statement. A Chapin chart for Program 10a is shown in Figure 10.16. The advantages and disadvantages of Chapin charts resemble those of Nassi-Shneiderman charts.

At this time, no single form of structured design and documentation technique is universally accepted as the best. In many installations, certain forms have been adopted as local standards; all programs and systems developed at that location must conform to those specifications. Probably the most widely accepted forms are pseudocode and structure diagrams. Other forms are used less often but still find defenders in various segments of the data processing community.

10.9 STRUCTURED PROGRAMMING THEORY: COHESION AND COUPLING

In the past decade, a great deal of theoretical work has been done in structured programming. One widely used concept is that of cohesion. *Cohesion* means what its definition would imply, namely "that which binds together" or "what makes it stick." **Module cohesion** refers to the logical "glue" that binds the parts of the module together. There are several types of cohesion which have been ranked according to their desirability, as shown in Figure 10.17.

Figure 10.17   Levels of module cohesion

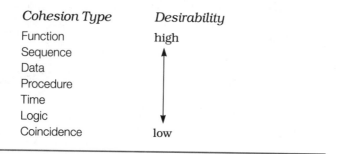

Cohesion Type	Desirability
Function	high
Sequence	↑
Data	
Procedure	
Time	
Logic	↓
Coincidence	low

Functional cohesion is the highest level and most desirable type of cohesion. A module that exhibits strong functional cohesion performs a single, well-defined task, which can generally be described in two or three words. Typical examples of modules exhibiting functional cohesion include

Figure 10.16   Chapin Chart for Program 10a

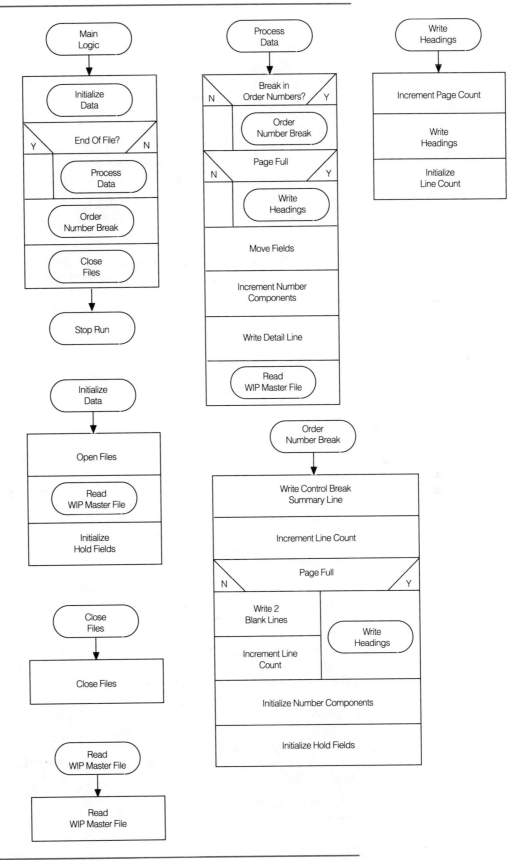

```
CALCULATE-GROSS-PAY
WRITE-HEADING-LINE
VALIDATE-EMPLOYEE-NUMBER
LOOKUP-BONUS-AMOUNT
```

Modules with functional cohesion tend to be homogeneous—all parts of the module contribute materially to the task at hand. They tend to be easy to understand and, therefore, relatively easy to debug and maintain. Functional cohesion is the goal for designing all program modules.

Sequential cohesion implies that the module is made up of elements that must be performed in a designated sequence. Very often the name of the module would (or could) incorporate the word AND, indicating that several tasks are being carried out in sequence. Typical examples include

```
PROCESS-DATA-AND-READ-NEXT-REC
VALIDATE-HRS-COMPUTE-OVERTIME
```

Modules exhibiting sequential cohesion, though less desirable than those exhibiting functional cohesion, may be unavoidable in actual coding of a COBOL program because some programming tasks are essentially sequential in nature.

Data-related cohesion refers to a module that performs several tasks on the same or related data items. For example, a module titled

```
VALIDATE-DATA-RECORD
```

in which each field in the record is validated, exhibits data-related cohesion. Other examples are

```
MOVE-INPUT-DATA-TO-OUTPUT-REC
PROCESS-INPUT-DATA
```

Procedural cohesion refers to a module that relates strongly to the control structure of the program. For example, a module titled LOOP-CONTROL signifies that the main purpose of the module is to enter a loop and continue its execution. Other module names that are indicative of procedural cohesion include

```
CHOOSE-APPROPRIATE-ACTION
LOOP-UNTIL-TERMINATION
```

Modules exhibiting procedural cohesion can result from overreliance on flowcharting as a program design technique. When decisions with regard to modularization are made by arbitrarily partitioning the flowchart using the control structure as the only criterion, the resulting modules are likely to exhibit procedural cohesion. For example, consider the flowchart shown in Figure 10.18. Module 1 and Module 2 as shown would exhibit procedural cohesion. Module 1 is based on a decision structure; Module 2 is based on an iteration structure. It is preferable to partition the program into modules based on the function to be performed by the module rather than on the control structure that happens to be required.

Time-related cohesion implies that the components are related to the time in the execution of the program at which they will be executed. Typical examples include

```
INITIALIZATION-ROUTINE
```

and

```
TERMINATION
```

Figure 10.18   Modular decomposition example

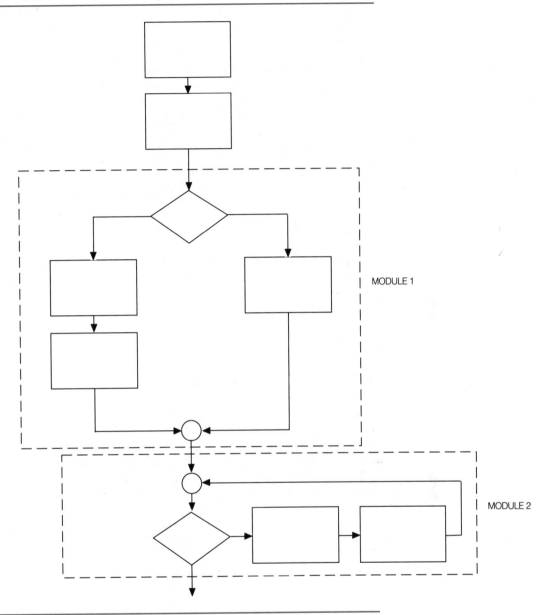

All of the components of INITIALIZATION-ROUTINE must be executed before a processing loop is entered; TERMINATION consists of tasks to be performed after the loop has been completed. Although temporal cohesion ranks relatively low in terms of desirability, modules of this type are, in practice, generally unavoidable in actual coding of structured COBOL programs.

Logical cohesion characterizes a module that consists of a sequence of tasks related in some way but generally spanning several functional areas. For example, a module that reads a data record from each of several files, one that validates data items from several sources, or one that handles error messages from a variety of sources would tend to exhibit logical cohesion. Although the tasks performed by modules such as these are related in some fashion, they are less cohesive than other module types because they are composed of several more specific functions.

The least cohesive type of module exhibits **coincidental cohesion.** This implies that the module contains unrelated tasks that have arbitrarily been grouped together into a module. They result from poor planning or, at times, arbitrary limitations on module size or the number of modules in a program. Modules of this type should be avoided completely in a structured program.

Although functional cohesion is the goal for all program modules and should form the basis for program design, the actual coding of a structured COBOL program will usually result in some modules with a weaker type of cohesion. It is always possible to avoid modules with coincidental cohesion, but it is not always possible to avoid modules with other less desirable forms of cohesion.

A useful exercise is to examine an existing COBOL program and to attempt to categorize the cohesion of each module. This exercise will point out the looseness of the categories described above. It is possible for two persons to classify modules in different ways; the definitions of cohesive types are not specific enough to enable categorizations that can be agreed upon by all. The types of cohesion should be treated as theoretical categories, and the general dictum that in "good" programs the modules should exhibit high levels of cohesion should be treated as a goal in the design and coding phases of the program development cycle.

Module Coupling

The concept of **module coupling** relates to the types of connections that exist among modules. In general, the more one module must "know" about another in order for the interface between them to work properly, the more tightly connected the modules are. In general, the goal is to produce modules that are as loosely coupled as possible. The ideal is to be able to consider a module to be a "black box" that performs its function on demand without requiring that the user be aware of the internal workings of the box. Loosely coupled modules are desirable because they tend to enhance maintainability of the program. The problem with tightly coupled modules is that a change in one module is likely to require changes in other modules to make the program work properly. Often these required changes are obscure and may not be evident until a revised program fails to function properly.

It is possible to identify several types of module coupling, among them the following:

- content coupling
- control coupling
- data coupling

Content coupling, the strongest form of coupling, results when one module refers to the contents of another module. In a COBOL program, content coupling can occur when one paragraph of a multiparagraph module is executed by another module. For example, consider the program segment shown in Figure 10.19. B SECTION contains several paragraphs that are normally treated as a single program module. A reference to any of these paragraphs creates a connection between the modules based on a procedure name defined inside B SECTION. Another way in which content coupling can occur insidiously is when control passes from one module to

Figure 10.19 Example of content coupling

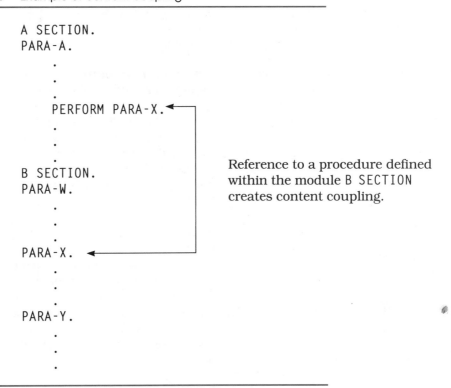

```
A SECTION.
PARA-A.
     .
     .
     .
     PERFORM PARA-X.
     .
     .
     .
B SECTION.
PARA-W.
     .
     .
     .
PARA-X.
     .
     .
     .
PARA-Y.
     .
     .
     .
```

Reference to a procedure defined within the module B SECTION creates content coupling.

another by default. This can happen when, because of a flaw in the control structure, a program allows control to pass from one paragraph to the paragraph that happens to follow it. In general, elimination of most uses of the GO TO statement in structured COBOL has eliminated most of the cases of content coupling between modules, which is quite common in nonstructured programs. Content coupling can and should be avoided in designing and coding a structured COBOL program.

Control coupling is a somewhat weaker form of coupling in which a control variable is passed between two modules. A control variable is one used to determine what action to take in some situation. An end-of-file flag is a common example of a control variable. Its purpose is to record the fact that an end-of-file condition has been encountered and to pass this information to another module, which takes appropriate action. Control coupling connects the module that tests the variable and the module that sets the variable.

Data coupling is a still weaker form of coupling in which modules are connected by access to a common set of data items. Two modules that process the same input record or the same table of constants are connected by data coupling.

In practice, control coupling and data coupling are very common in COBOL programs; content coupling should be avoided. Control coupling should be used only where necessary. The unnecessary use of control variables results in unnecessarily tightly coupled modules, which may cause problems during maintenance.

―――――――――――― Example ――――――――――――

Following is an analysis of the cohesion and coupling among the paragraphs of Program 10a:

Paragraph	Cohesion	Comment
Main Logic	Sequence	This paragraph controls the overall operation of the program; its actions must be performed in strict sequence.
Initialize Data	Time	These tasks must be accomplished at the beginning of the program; hence, the essential relationship is time related. There is also an element of sequential cohesion because the files must be opened before a record can be read, which must be accomplished before data can be moved.
Process Data	Procedure	This module is strongly related to the control structure of the program since it is the paragraph that ensures that the primary loop continues to an appropriate conclusion. There is also an element of sequential cohesion (one record must be processed before the next record is read). However, the sequence is weak because some of the actions could be executed in any order (e.g., the MOVE statements could come before or after the check for a full page).
Close Files Read WIP Master File Write Headings	Function	These modules perform single, well-defined tasks.
Order Number Break	Time	The actions in this module must be accomplished when a break in order numbers is detected. Sequence in the module is weak because many of the actions could be carried out in a different order.

The modules all exhibit data-related coupling because they process a common set of data items. Main Logic is linked to Initialize Data and Process Data by control coupling because of the use of the end-of-file flag that is set in the subordinate module and tested in Main Logic. There is no content coupling in the program.

10.10 SELF-TEST EXERCISES

1. In what way is the programmer's job related to the overall system design?
2. How are the roles of the systems analyst, programming manager, and programmer like those of the architect, contractor, and subcontractor of a building project?
3. Compare the system flowchart and program flowchart. In what ways are they similar; in what ways are they different?

4. In a system flowchart, what is meant by the use of the double-headed arrow?

5. What is the purpose of the program specification statement? What information is usually included?

6. With respect to the Amalgamated Custom Design production system, what motivated the implementation of some portions of the system as interactive systems and other portions as batch? In this system, what general types of programs are interactive and what types are batch?

7. Briefly explain the major advantages and disadvantages of the programming team approach.

8. What is the primary purpose of the structured walk-through? Describe the major disadvantage of the technique.

9. What is "ego-less" programming?

10. What is the primary purpose of the data dictionary concept? How can it be implemented in a COBOL environment?

11. How does structured implementation and testing differ from the usual student implementation and testing technique?

12. Why do most programmers use a combination of top-down and bottom-up techniques for structured implementation and testing?

13. What is a "program stub?"

14. What is the purpose of the COPY statement? What are considerations for its use at your installation?

15. Explain the "black-box" concept of program design.

16. Document a program you have written with each of the following:
   flowchart
   structure diagram
   pseudocode
   Nassi-Shneiderman chart
   Chapin chart

10.11 PROGRAMMING EXERCISES

1. Each record in a file contains a name and a date of birth. The output is to include a detailed listing of the data, the number of people contained in the file, the oldest person's name and date of birth, and the youngest person's name and date of birth. The layout for the records in the file is as follows

Positions	Content
1–20	Name
21–26	Date of birth (*mmddyy*)

The layout for the desired report is shown in Figure 10.20.

2. Each record in a file contains among other items the date of the last time an item was sold, the number of items on hand, the cost per item, and the regular selling price. A store plans to have a sale on slow-moving items. The purpose of the program is to produce a report showing recommended sale prices as follows:

Figure 10.20   Report layout for Exercise 1

If the item has not been sold in the last 30 days, discount is 10%.
If the item has not been sold in the last 60 days, discount is 20%.
If the item has not been sold in the last 90 days, discount is 40%.

Any item that has sold in the last 30 days is not placed on sale. If there is only one of any item left in stock, it is to be discounted 5 percent. Sale prices may not be lower than cost. The layout for the record to be processed by this program is as follows:

Positions	Content
1–9	Stock number
11–25	Description
27–32	Date of last sale (*mmddyy*)
34–38	Cost (999V99)
39–40	Number on hand
42–46	Regular selling price (999V99)

3. Write a program to calculate the depreciation expense and book value for an asset. Depreciation should be calculated using the following three methods:

a. *Straight Line Method*

The amount of depreciation per year is:

$$\frac{\text{cost} - \text{salvage value}}{\text{number of years}}$$

For example, for an asset which cost $22,000 and has a salvage value of $2,000 and a life expectancy of five years, the depreciation amount is

$$(22,000 - 2,000) / 5 = 4,000$$

The new book value is computed by subtracting the depreciation amount from the current book value. The resulting table would be:

Year	Depreciation expense	Book value
1	4,000	18,000
2	4,000	14,000
3	4,000	10,000
4	4,000	6,000
5	4,000	2,000

b. *Sum of Years Digits Method*

The amount of depreciation for the *i*th year is

(cost − salvage value) * P_i

where P_i is a factor computed in the following way:

(1) Compute the following sum:

$S = 1 + 2 + 3 + \ldots + n$ where *n* represents the number of years

(2) Compute $P_i = (n + 1 - i) / S$ for $i = 1, 2, 3, \ldots, n$.

For example, if cost = 22,000 and $n = 5$, we find
$S = 1 + 2 + 3 + 4 + 5 = 15$
and
$P_1 = (5 + 1 - 1) / 15 = 5/15 = 1/3$
$P_2 = (5 + 1 - 2) / 15 = 4/15$

Thus, the depreciation amount for the first year is

(22,000 − 2,000) * 1/3 = 6,667

For the second year the amount is

(22,000 − 2,000) * 4/15 = 5,333

The resulting table would be

Year	Depreciation expense	Book value
1	6,667	15,333
2	5,333	10,000
3	4,000	6,000
4	2,666	3,333
5	1,333	2,000

c. *Declining Balance Method*

The depreciation value is computed by multiplying the old book value by a constant fraction *M*. The value of *M* is defined by

$M = P / n$

where *P* is a proportion chosen by the accountant and *n* represents the number of years. For example, suppose cost = $22,000, $n = 5$, and $P = 150\%$ (there is no salvage value using this method). Then,
$M = 150\% / 5 = 30\%$
depreciation = 22,000 * .30 = 6,600
new book value = 22,000 − 6,600 = 15,400

The resulting table would be

Year	Depreciation expense	Book value
1	6,600	15,400
2	4,620	10,780
3	3,234	7,546
4	2,264	5,282
5	1,585	3,697

The layout of the record to be processed by this program follows:

Positions	Content
1–6	Cost (999999)
8–13	Salvage value (999999)
15–16	Number of years

For the declining balance method use $P = 150\%$.

4. A file contains records pertaining to the amount and analysis of the milk given by cows at a dairy. Each record contains the following items:

Positions	Content
1–9	Cow ID number
11–16	Date (*mmddyy*)
18–20	Amount of milk (999)
22–24	Proportion of butterfat (V999)

Write a program to compute the mean and standard deviation for the amount of butterfat in the milk. The mean is computed by finding the sum of all the observations and dividing by the number of observations:

$$\bar{x} = \frac{\sum x_i}{n}$$

The standard deviation (represented by σ) is computed using the formula

$$\sigma = \sqrt{\frac{\sum (x_i - \bar{x})^2}{n}}$$

Your program should flag for each cow the output which has an average butterfat content greater than $\bar{x} + 2\sigma$ or less than $\bar{x} - 2\sigma$.

5. XYZ Pharmacy, Inc., maintains a system designed to give its customers a statement at the end of each year showing all medicines purchased during the year. Design such a system, making appropriate assumptions regarding what data will be collected and what files will be maintained.

6. An insurance company maintains an automobile accident claim file which has records containing

Positions	Content
1–9	Policy number
11–17	Amount of claim (99999V99)
19–24	Date of accident (*mmddyy*)
26	Sex of driver (M or F)
28–29	Age of driver

Write a program to compute the frequency of claims and average claim amount for each cell of the following table:

Age	M	F
18-21		
22-25		
26-30		
31-35		
36-50		
51-65		
Over 65		

7. Modify the program written for Exercise 6 above to print the proportion of claims computed by dividing the number of claims for drivers in a particular age/sex group by the total number of policy holders in this age/sex group. Assume that your program has access to the master policy file to calculate the required totals for all policy holders.

REFERENCES

Chapin, N., et al. "Structured Programming Simplified." *Computer Decisions* 6, no. 6 (June 1974): 28–31.

Nassi, I., and B. Shneiderman. "Flowchart Techniques for Structured Programming." *ACM SIGPLAN Notices* 8, no. 8 (August 1973): 12–26.

Yourdon, E., and L.L. Constantine. *Structured Design.* Englewood Cliffs, N.J.: Prentice-Hall, 1979.

11. INTERACTIVE PROGRAMS AND CHARACTER STRING MANIPULATION

11.1 INTERACTIVE VS. BATCH ENVIRONMENTS

In many computer systems, the user's primary means of communication with the system is through a computer terminal. The user enters data at the terminal, and the computer responds with appropriate messages. Such systems are referred to as **interactive systems,** as the user and computer system engage in an immediate form of interaction. In other systems, data and programs are prepared in isolation from the computer, using some machine-readable medium. (Punched cards were a prime example, but other machine-readable mediums include off-line optical scanners, written forms, disks, and tapes prepared off line.) When all of the data has been prepared, the data, program, and operating system instructions are submitted for processing. Systems of this type are generally referred to as **batch processing systems.** Data is accumulated over time and processed as a batch rather than immediately as it is collected, as is characteristic of an interactive system.

When using an interactive system for program development the programmer's primary tool is an **editor.** An editor allows the user to create and update files. The first step in developing a COBOL program is to build a file containing the COBOL program statements. The editor usually contains provisions for listing files, adding records to files, changing all or part of existing records, and deleting records from files. The COBOL programmer makes use of this facility to list the program and to add, change, or delete portions of the program. When satisfied with the program, the programmer then enters appropriate operating system instructions to compile the program. If the compilation is successful, the program is executed and output produced by the program is generally directed to either the terminal or an auxiliary printer associated with the terminal. If the compilation is not successful because of syntax errors, the programmer may display the error messages produced by the compiler at the terminal. It is then necessary to use the editor to make necessary revisions to the program. Specific details on use of terminals, operating system instructions, and editor instructions vary greatly from one computing system to another; secure detailed information appropriate to the system available for use before attempting to enter a COBOL program.[1]

Regardless of the type of system used to prepare the program, a processing program may be classed as batch or interactive depending on the mode of usage designed into the program. If the program is designed to

---

[1]RM/CO*, which is supplied with the RM/COBOL-85 compiler, is an example of an interactive editor and program development system. See Appendix H for details.

process data files that are in place at the time the program begins execution, the program may be classed as a batch-oriented program. Such programs can typically be scheduled to run at any time convenient for the computing system and are usually assigned a low priority because response time is not an important factor to the user. On the other hand, if the program is designed to allow the user to enter data and produce responses at a terminal, then the program is primarily interactive in nature. Such programs are typically run by the user when there is data to be processed, or they may run continuously to capture and process data as it occurs. In any case, interactive programs must be assigned a high priority within the system because system response time is a crucial factor in the usability of the software. Remember, the way in which the program is developed has no bearing on the way in which a program processes data. Most program development systems have both interactive and batch components, depending on the needs of the user and the capabilities of the hardware.

11.2 DESIGN AND IMPLEMENTATION OF INTERACTIVE PROGRAMS

In writing a program that is interactive in nature, a programmer must realize that methods of reading data entered at the terminal and writing information to the terminal differ from one system to another. In some systems, the terminal is treated as a data file similar to files assigned to other devices. In such systems, a terminal file is defined in SELECT and FD entries, and the usual READ and WRITE statements are used. In other systems, input from the terminal is handled by the ACCEPT statement, and output to the terminal is produced by the DISPLAY statement. In early implementations of COBOL, which were generally found on batch-oriented systems, the ACCEPT and DISPLAY verbs were used only to communicate with the computer operator. With the advent of interactive systems, ACCEPT and DISPLAY have been adapted not only to perform their original function but also to allow communications with a program user at a terminal. This adaptation is not universal, however. Check the documentation for your system before attempting to use ACCEPT and DISPLAY in the manner outlined below.

The general form of the ACCEPT statement is shown in Figure 11.1. Depending on the system in use, the ACCEPT statement without the FROM option may automatically cause the system to input data from the terminal being used to execute the program. On other systems, it is necessary to define a mnemonic in the SPECIAL-NAMES paragraph of the CONFIGURATION SECTION of the ENVIRONMENT DIVISION to identify the specific device to be used in the operation. For example, an appropriate SPECIAL-NAMES entry could be

```
SPECIAL-NAMES.
     CONSOLE IS OPERATORS-INPUT-DEVICE.
```

Figure 11.1 General form of the ACCEPT statement

```
ACCEPT data-name [ FROM {hardware-name}
                        {mnemonic-name} ]
```

With this mnemonic declared, an appropriate ACCEPT statement would be

```
ACCEPT DATA-IN FROM OPERATORS-INPUT-DEVICE.
```

When an ACCEPT statement is executed, a message may be written at the console, alerting the user that the program is waiting for the user to enter some data.[2] Execution of the program is suspended until the user completes the input operation.

Suppose the data item NUMBER-IN is defined as

```
03 NUMBER-IN PIC 9(4).
```

and the program statement

```
ACCEPT NUMBER-IN.
```

is executed. After displaying an appropriate message, the system will wait until the user enters data at the terminal. The characters entered by the user will be stored in NUMBER-IN, and execution will proceed with the next statement.

It is important that the user enter the data expected by the program. The characters entered by the user are stored in the designated memory location in order from left to right. If too few characters are entered, the remaining rightmost characters may be padded with blanks or zeros, or the system may respond with a message requesting more data. If too many characters are entered, excess characters on the right are ignored.

─────── Example ───────

```
03 NUMBER-IN PIC 9(4).
        .
        .
        .
ACCEPT NUMBER-IN.
```

If the user enters 1234, the value stored in NUMBER-IN will be

```
1 2 3 4
```

If the user enters 12345, the value stored in NUMBER-IN will be

```
1 2 3 4
```

because excess digits on the right are truncated. If the user enters 123, the value stored in NUMBER-IN will be left justified. The rightmost positions may contain invalid data.

```
1 2 3 ?
```
This character is not replaced by the input operation.

Some systems will request that the user enter more data which will be used to fill out the remaining position in NUMBER-IN; other systems will automatically right justify data in a numeric field and left justify data in an alphanumeric field.

─────── Example ───────

```
01  DATA-REC.
    03 NAME-DR PIC X(10).
    03 SS-NUM-DR PIC 9(9).
```

[2]In other systems, the ACCEPT statement causes no output; it is the responsibility of the program to provide a prompt indicating that data must be entered.

.
.
.
```
        ACCEPT DATA-REC.
```

The expected number of characters is 19, the length of the group item DATA-REC. The first 10 characters entered will be stored in NAME-DR; the next 9 characters will be stored in SS-NUM-DR.

The ACCEPT statement may also be used in a batch-oriented computing system to allow the system operator to enter small amounts of data. In such systems, this statement is used only for small amounts of data because of the low speed that is typical of an operator's console and because it takes up the operator's time. It can be useful, however, to allow the operator to enter a data item such as the date for a report or to allow the operator to select among various functions that a program might perform. Also, a program might, for security reasons, ask that the operator's name and time of the run be entered.

Corresponding to the input statement ACCEPT, which allows the user to enter data at a terminal, is the output statement DISPLAY, which causes output at the terminal. The general form of the DISPLAY statement is shown in Figure 11.2.

Figure 11.2   General form of the DISPLAY statement

$$\underline{\text{DISPLAY}} \quad \left\{ \begin{array}{l} \text{literal} \\ \text{data-name} \end{array} \right\} \left[\underline{\text{UPON}} \quad \left\{ \begin{array}{l} \text{hardware-name} \\ \text{mnemonic-name} \end{array} \right\} \right]$$

Any sequence of literals or data items may be written on the terminal using the DISPLAY statement. For example,

```
        DISPLAY WS-DATA.
```

would cause the contents of WS-DATA to be written. The statement

```
        DISPLAY "ENTER REPORT DATE".
```

could be followed by

```
        ACCEPT DATE-IN.
```

The written message produced by the DISPLAY statement serves to guide the operator's response to the item required by the ACCEPT statement.

─────── **Example** ───────

```
        DISPLAY "ENTER NAME AND SOCIAL SECURITY NUMBER"
        ACCEPT DATA-REC.
        DISPLAY "NAME " NAME-DR " SS-NO. " SS-NUM-DR.
```

This example illustrates the use of the DISPLAY statement to prompt the user for the data and echo the input received. Suppose INPUT-REC is defined as in the example above, and the user enters the following data:

```
 J O H N   J O N E S 1 2 3 4 5 6 7 8 9
```

The expected output from the second DISPLAY statement is

```
NAME JOHN JONES SS-NO. 123456789
```

The use of an echo such as this is important to ensure that the data entered by the user is correct and, if not, to give the user a chance to correct the data.

In batch-oriented systems, the DISPLAY statement may be used to direct messages to the system operator's console. It may be used to prompt the operator regarding data requested by an ACCEPT statement. It may also be used to write messages regarding errors or exceptional conditions encountered during the execution of the program.

Typically, error messages regarding data being processed are displayed on the operator's console only on small computing systems that run one program at a time. On larger systems that may execute many programs at one time, error messages are usually written on the printer or on a disk file that is examined after completion of the program.

11.3 PROGRAM EXAMPLE

Problem Statement

Write an interactive program to allow the user to create a file composed of records containing a name, a Social Security number, street address, city, state, zip, and date of birth. Include a provision for the user to check and correct data before it is written to the file.

Problem Analysis

We will assume that the system uses ACCEPT and DISPLAY to communicate with interactive users. The program must include prompts directing the user to enter data. Before data is written to the file, the program must display the data that has been entered and allow the user to verify the correctness of the data. This will be handled by displaying a question and accepting a response from the user. If the response indicates that the data is correct, the record is written on the file; if the response indicates incorrect data, the user enters the data again. This procedure is repeated until an acceptable data record has been entered.

As there is no AT END clause on the ACCEPT statement, there is no "automatic" technique to determine when the end of the file being entered by the user has been reached. This is, of course, a necessary task as the file being created must be closed when all data has been written on it in order for the file to become permanent. The task of determining when there is no more data will be handled by requiring the user to enter the characters "END", "End", or "end" in the name field when all data has been entered. Thus, the procedure used to enter a data record must be repeated until either the name field contains "END", "End", or "end", or a valid record has been entered. A plan for this program is shown in Figure 11.3.

Figure 11.3 Plan for interactive file builder program

Main control
    Get name of file
    Open output file
    Do Get data until answer = "Y" or name = "END"
    Do until name = "END"
        Write data record
        Move "N" to answer
        Do Get data until answer = "Y" or
                      name = "END"
    End Do
    Close file
    Stop
Get data
    Get name
    If name not = "END"
        Get other data
        Write record data on user device
        Get answer
    End if

Problem Solution

A solution to this problem is shown in Program 11a; the structure diagram is shown in Figure 11.4. A sample execution of the program is shown in Figure 11.5. The program creates a file DATA-FILE assigned to disk. The external name of the file to be created is entered by the user (see lines 59–60) before the file is opened for output. The user enters records one field at a time at the terminal (lines 88–99). The program echos the data (lines 103–107) and gives the user the opportunity to reject the data or accept it for entry onto the file (lines 81–84). Note the use of a special value contained in the field NAME-DR used to end the data entry/file building process. When the user enters the characters "END", "End", or "end" as the content of NAME-DR, the program closes the output file, making the data permanent (see lines 52–54). The general approach used in this program is useful for building the data files required for most programming exercises in this text.

11.4 MENU-DRIVEN PROGRAMS

An important aspect of interactive programs is how easy they are to use—their "user friendliness." The program's human interface is its instructions and menus. The program user needs instructions on how to use the program, what data is required, what options are available, what codes to use, and so forth. These instructions are, of course, included in the written documentation (usually called a user's guide), written by the programmer or other member of the data processing staff. It is also very useful to display at least some of these instructions on the screen so that users do not have to rely solely on the written documentation.

    User instructions take a variety of distinct forms. Often one or more screens of information will be displayed when execution of the program is

Program 11a

```
 1 IDENTIFICATION DIVISION.
 2
 3 PROGRAM-ID. FILE-BUILDER-PRO11A.
 4 AUTHOR.
 5
 6 ENVIRONMENT DIVISION.
 7
 8 CONFIGURATION SECTION.
 9
10 SOURCE-COMPUTER.
11 OBJECT-COMPUTER.
12
13 INPUT-OUTPUT SECTION.
14
15 FILE-CONTROL.
16
17     SELECT DATA-FILE ASSIGN TO DISK.
18
19
20 DATA DIVISION.
21
22 FILE SECTION.
23
24 FD   DATA-FILE
25      LABEL RECORDS ARE STANDARD
26      VALUE OF FILE-ID IS FILE-NAME.
27
28 01   DATA-RECORD.
29      03 SS-NUM-DR          PIC 9(9).
30      03 NAME-DR            PIC X(20).
31         88 END-OF-DATA     VALUE "END" "end" "End".
32      03 STREET-ADDRESS-DR  PIC X(15).
33      03 CITY-DR            PIC X(10).
34      03 STATE-DR           PIC XX.
35      03 ZIP-DR             PIC 9(5).
36      03 DOB-DR             PIC 9(6).
37
38 WORKING-STORAGE SECTION.
39
40 01   CONTROL-FIELDS.
41      02 ANSWER             PIC X VALUE "N".
42         88 DATA-OK         VALUE "Y" "y".
43      02 FILE-NAME          PIC X(15) VALUE SPACES.
44
45 PROCEDURE DIVISION.
46
47 1000-MAIN-CONTROL.
48
49     PERFORM 2000-INITIALIZE-PROGRAM.
50     PERFORM 9000-GET-DATA UNTIL
51             DATA-OK OR END-OF-DATA.
52     PERFORM 2100-BUILD-FILE
53             UNTIL END-OF-DATA.
54     PERFORM 2200-CLOSE-FILES.
55     STOP RUN.
56
```

```
57 2000-INITIALIZE-PROGRAM.
58
59     DISPLAY "Enter name of file to be created".
60     ACCEPT FILE-NAME.
61     OPEN OUTPUT DATA-FILE.
62
63 2100-BUILD-FILE.
64
65     WRITE DATA-RECORD.
66     MOVE "N" TO ANSWER.
67     PERFORM 9000-GET-DATA UNTIL
68             DATA-OK OR END-OF-DATA.
69
70 2200-CLOSE-FILES.
71
72     CLOSE DATA-FILE.
73
74 9000-GET-DATA.
75
76     DISPLAY "Enter Name (END to terminate)".
77     ACCEPT NAME-DR.
78     IF NOT END-OF-DATA
79        PERFORM 9100-ENTER-DATA
80        PERFORM 9200-DISPLAY-DATA
81        DISPLAY "Are data correct? (Y/N)"
82        ACCEPT ANSWER
83        IF NOT DATA-OK
84            DISPLAY "Reenter data".
85
86 9100-ENTER-DATA.
87
88     DISPLAY "Enter Social Security Number".
89     ACCEPT SS-NUM-DR.
90     DISPLAY "Enter Street Address".
91     ACCEPT STREET-ADDRESS-DR.
92     DISPLAY "Enter City".
93     ACCEPT CITY-DR.
94     DISPLAY "Enter Two Character State Abbreviation".
95     ACCEPT STATE-DR.
96     DISPLAY "Enter Zip".
97     ACCEPT ZIP-DR.
98     DISPLAY "Enter Date of Birth in form mmddyy".
99     ACCEPT DOB-DR.
100
101 9200-DISPLAY-DATA.
102
103    DISPLAY "Name      : " NAME-DR.
104    DISPLAY "SS #      : " SS-NUM-DR.
105    DISPLAY "Address   : " STREET-ADDRESS-DR.
106    DISPLAY "          " CITY-DR STATE-DR ZIP-DR.
107    DISPLAY "Birth Date: " DOB-DR.
```

Figure 11.4   Structure diagram of Program 11a

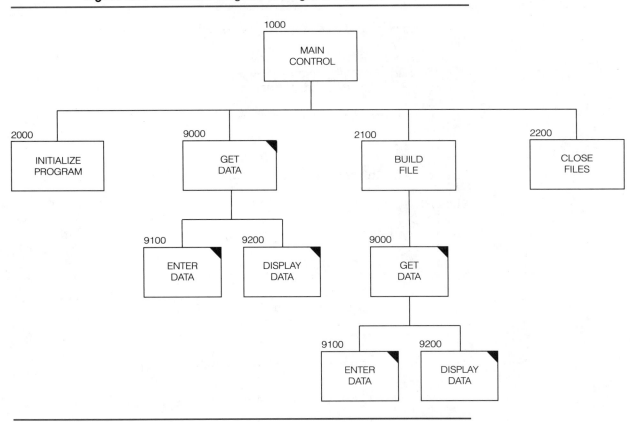

initiated. Line 59 of Program 11a is an example of such initial information generated at the beginning of the program. Prompts may be displayed on the screen when specific data or codes must be entered. Lines 76, 88, 90, and so on of Program 11a are examples of such prompts. A third type of user information is the **menu**. Menus are used when a program allows the user to select certain options. After a menu is displayed, the user enters a code (selected from the menu) that corresponds to the action the user desires to carry out. Menus usually have additional options, including "Help," which causes the program to display information to help the user, and "Quit," which enables the user to terminate the program. The program repeats the menu display/user response/program action sequence until the user selects "Quit."

11.5   PROGRAM EXAMPLE

Problem Statement

Revise Program 11a to allow the user to create DATA-FILE or to list DATA-FILE. Include a menu to allow the user to choose a particular task.

Figure 11.5   Sample execution of Program 11a

```
Enter name of file to be created
PRO11A.DAT
Enter Name (END to terminate)
Joe Jones
Enter Social Security Number
111111111
Enter Street Address
123 Main St.
Enter City
Elmville
Enter Two Character State Abbreviation
MA
Enter Zip
12300
Enter Date of Birth in form mmddyy
012367
Name       : Joe Jones
SS #       : 111111111
Address    : 123 Main St.
             Elmville  MA12300
Birth Date: 012367
Are data correct? (Y/N)
Y
Enter Name (END to terminate)
Mary Smith
Enter Social Security Number
222222222
Enter Street Address
2345 Second Ave.
Enter City
Elmville
Enter Two Character State Abbreviation
MA
Enter Zip
12300
Enter Date of Birth in form mmddyy
051270
Name       : Mary Smith
SS #       : 222222222
Address    : 2345 Second Ave
             Elmville  MA12300
Birth Date: 051270
Are data correct? (Y/N)
y
Enter Name (END to terminate)
END
```

Problem Analysis

A preliminary plan for the program is shown below; this basic plan is shared by all menu-driven programs.

```
Do until quit
    Display menu
    Accept user choice
    Carry out program action
```

End Do
Stop

The required menu will have six options which can be selected in any sequence.

Code	Function
N	Name file
C	Create file
P	Print file (to printer)
L	List file (to screen)
H	Help
Q	Quit

Before working on any file, the user must assign a name to the file; this is the function of the Name file command. The process of creating a file in response to a Create file command will be handled as in Program 11a. Listing or printing the file will employ the logic used any time a sequential file is processed from beginning to end. The Help command will result in a display of information regarding how to use the program. Any invalid choice will result in an error message, and the menu will be displayed again. The program plan can now be written as shown in Figure 11.6.

Figure 11.6 Plan for Program 11b

```
Main control
    Do until quit
        Display menu
        Get Choice
        If Choice is name file
            Do Get file name
        Else if Choice is create
            Do Create file
        Else if Choice is print file
            Do Print file
        Else if Choice is list file
            Do List file
        Else if Choice is help
            Do Write is help
        Else if Choice is invalid
            Do Write error
        End If
    End Do
    Stop
```

Problem Solution

The required program is shown in Program 11b; the structure diagram is shown in Figure 11.7. A sample execution of the program is shown in Figure 11.8. Note that the program segment containing the paragraphs 3300-CREATE-FILE, 9000-GET-DATA, and 9100-ENTER-DATA are virtually identical to paragraphs in Program 11a. In this program, these paragraphs are required to carry out the program action CREATE-FILE. The paragraphs 3500-LIST-FILE and 4100-PROCESS-DATA are required to carry

```
 1 IDENTIFICATION DIVISION.
 2
 3 PROGRAM-ID. ALT-FILE-BUILDER-PRO11B.
 4 AUTHOR. HORN.
 5
 6 ENVIRONMENT DIVISION.
 7
 8 CONFIGURATION SECTION.
 9
10 SOURCE-COMPUTER.
11 OBJECT-COMPUTER.
12
13 INPUT-OUTPUT SECTION.
14
15 FILE-CONTROL.
16
17     SELECT DATA-FILE ASSIGN TO DISK.
18
19
20 DATA DIVISION.
21
22 FILE SECTION.
23
24 FD   DATA-FILE
25      LABEL RECORDS ARE STANDARD
26      VALUE OF FILE-ID IS FILE-NAME.
27
28 01   DATA-RECORD.
29      03 SS-NUM-DR            PIC 9(9).
30      03 NAME-DR              PIC X(20).
31         88 END-OF-DATA       VALUE "END" "end" "End".
32      03 STREET-ADDRESS-DR    PIC X(15).
33      03 CITY-DR              PIC X(10).
34      03 STATE-DR             PIC XX.
35      03 ZIP-DR               PIC 9(5).
36      03 DOB-DR               PIC 9(6).
37
38 WORKING-STORAGE SECTION.
39
40 01   FILE-NAME              PIC X(15) VALUE SPACES.
41
42 01   CONTROL-FIELDS.
43      02 EOF-FLAG             PIC XXX VALUE "NO".
44         88 END-OF-FILE       VALUE "YES".
45      02 ANSWER               PIC X VALUE "N".
46         88 DATA-OK           VALUE "Y" "y".
47      02 COMMAND              PIC X VALUE SPACE.
48         88 NAME-FILE         VALUE "N" "n".
49         88 CREATE-FILE       VALUE "C" "c".
50         88 PRINT-FILE        VALUE "P" "p".
51         88 LIST-FILE         VALUE "L" "l".
52         88 HELP              VALUE "H" "h".
53         88 QUIT              VALUE "Q" "q".
54
```

Program 11b   *(continued)*

```
 55 PROCEDURE DIVISION.
 56
 57 1000-MAIN-CONTROL.
 58
 59     PERFORM 2000-PROCESS-USER-COMMANDS
 60             UNTIL QUIT.
 61     STOP RUN.
 62
 63 2000-PROCESS-USER-COMMANDS.
 64
 65     PERFORM 3000-DISPLAY-MENU.
 66     PERFORM 3100-GET-COMMAND.
 67     IF      NAME-FILE
 68             PERFORM 3200-GET-FILE-NAME
 69     ELSE IF CREATE-FILE
 70             PERFORM 3300-CREATE-FILE
 71     ELSE IF PRINT-FILE
 72             PERFORM 3400-PRINT-FILE
 73     ELSE IF LIST-FILE
 74             PERFORM 3500-LIST-FILE
 75     ELSE IF HELP
 76             PERFORM 3600-WRITE-HELP
 77     ELSE IF QUIT
 78             NEXT SENTENCE
 79     ELSE
 80             PERFORM 3700-WRITE-ERROR.
 81
 82 3000-DISPLAY-MENU.
 83
 84     DISPLAY "Command   Action".
 85     DISPLAY "   N      Name file (Current file " FILE-NAME ")".
 86     DISPLAY "   C      Create file".
 87     DISPLAY "   P      Print file (to printer)".
 88     DISPLAY "   L      List file (to screen)".
 89     DISPLAY "   H      Help".
 90     DISPLAY "   Q      Quit program".
 91
 92 3100-GET-COMMAND.
 93
 94     DISPLAY "Enter Command Code".
 95     ACCEPT COMMAND.
 96
 97 3200-GET-FILE-NAME.
 98
 99     DISPLAY "Enter name of file ".
100     ACCEPT FILE-NAME.
101
```

```
102 3300-CREATE-FILE.
103
104     IF FILE-NAME = SPACES
105         DISPLAY "File has not been named"
106     ELSE
107         DISPLAY "Enter data for file " FILE-NAME
108         DISPLAY "OK to proceed? (Y/N)"
109         ACCEPT ANSWER
110         IF DATA-OK
111             OPEN OUTPUT DATA-FILE
112             MOVE "N" TO ANSWER
113             MOVE SPACES TO NAME-DR
114             PERFORM 9000-GET-DATA UNTIL
115                     DATA-OK OR END-OF-DATA
116             PERFORM 4000-BUILD-FILE
117                     UNTIL END-OF-DATA
118             CLOSE DATA-FILE.
119
120 3400-PRINT-FILE.
121
122     DISPLAY "Command not implemented".
123
124 3500-LIST-FILE.
125
126     IF FILE-NAME = SPACES
127         DISPLAY "File has not been named"
128     ELSE
129         DISPLAY "List content of file " FILE-NAME
130         DISPLAY "OK to proceed? (Y/N)"
131         ACCEPT ANSWER
132         IF DATA-OK
133             OPEN INPUT DATA-FILE
134             MOVE "NO" TO EOF-FLAG
135             PERFORM 9300-READ-DATA-FILE
136             PERFORM 4100-PROCESS-DATA
137                     UNTIL END-OF-FILE
138             CLOSE DATA-FILE.
139
140 3600-WRITE-HELP.
141
142     DISPLAY "Command not implemented".
143
144 3700-WRITE-ERROR.
145
146     DISPLAY "Invalid command code".
147
148 4000-BUILD-FILE.
149
150     WRITE DATA-RECORD.
151     MOVE "N" TO ANSWER.
152     PERFORM 9000-GET-DATA UNTIL
153             DATA-OK OR END-OF-DATA.
154
155 4100-PROCESS-DATA.
156
157     PERFORM 9200-DISPLAY-DATA.
158     PERFORM 9300-READ-DATA-FILE.
```

Program 11b *(concluded)*

```
159
160  9000-GET-DATA.
161
162      DISPLAY "Enter Name (END to terminate)".
163      ACCEPT NAME-DR.
164      IF NOT END-OF-DATA
165          PERFORM 9100-ENTER-DATA
166          PERFORM 9200-DISPLAY-DATA
167          DISPLAY "Are data correct? (Y/N)"
168          ACCEPT ANSWER
169          IF NOT DATA-OK
170              DISPLAY "Reenter data".
171
172  9100-ENTER-DATA.
173
174      DISPLAY "Enter Social Security Number".
175      ACCEPT SS-NUM-DR.
176      DISPLAY "Enter Street Address".
177      ACCEPT STREET-ADDRESS-DR.
178      DISPLAY "Enter City".
179      ACCEPT CITY-DR.
180      DISPLAY "Enter Two Character State Abbreviation".
181      ACCEPT STATE-DR.
182      DISPLAY "Enter ZIP".
183      ACCEPT ZIP-DR.
184      DISPLAY "Enter Date of Birth in form mmddyy".
185      ACCEPT DOB-DR.
186
187  9200-DISPLAY-DATA.
188
189      DISPLAY "Name       : " NAME-DR.
190      DISPLAY "SS #       : " SS-NUM-DR.
191      DISPLAY "Address    : " STREET-ADDRESS-DR.
192      DISPLAY "             " CITY-DR STATE-DR " " ZIP-DR.
193      DISPLAY "Birth Date : " DOB-DR.
194
195  9300-READ-DATA-FILE.
196
197      READ DATA-FILE
198          AT END MOVE "YES" TO EOF-FLAG.
```

out the program action LIST-FILE. One paragraph in the program that is not completely coded is 3600-WRITE-HELP. The content of this paragraph should be chosen with knowledge of the intended user of the program. Inexperienced users generally require more detailed explanations than do more knowledgeable users.

In practice, menus may contain many more choices than the one contained in Program 11b; and, in particularly complex programs, the first action the program takes in response to a particular choice may be to display another menu (called a **submenu**) containing options related to that choice.

In general, the number of choices offered in any menu should be reasonably small and clearly defined so that the user has no difficulty in deciding which action to choose. The art of designing good interactive pro-

Figure 11.7   Structure diagram for Program 11b

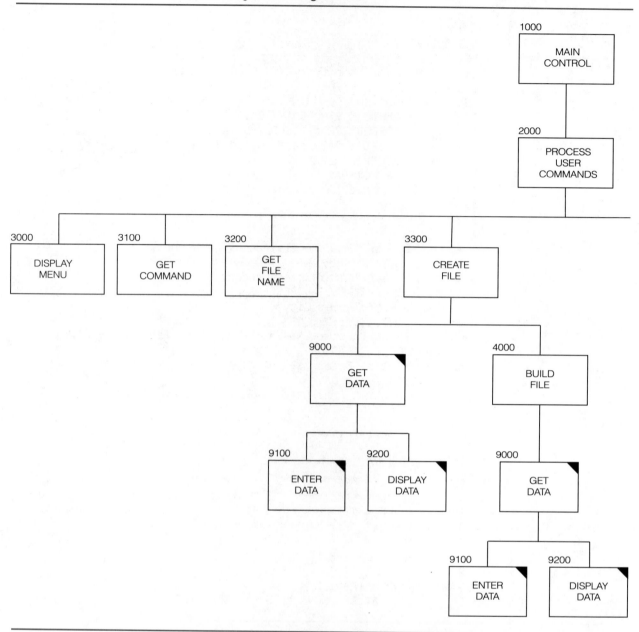

grams requires attention to human psychology as well as to the technical requirements of the task at hand. Very often, as part of the program development process, the menu and instruction portions of programs are field-tested and refined repeatedly, based on the reactions of the test subjects. Careful attention to these details may make the difference between a program that users feel is natural and, therefore, easy to learn and use and one that users find awkward and, hence, difficult to learn and use.

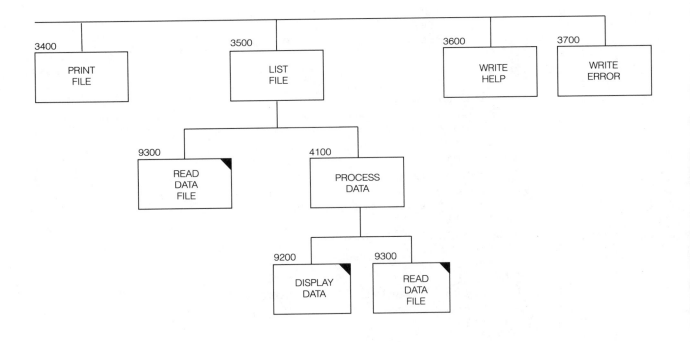

11.6 FORMATTED SCREENS

Interactive program use can be greatly facilitated by the use of formatted screens. A **formatted screen** is one in which certain information is displayed constantly during the time a user is entering data or commands. The ordinary mode of operation for most terminals involves **scrolling**. Text is displayed from top to bottom on the screen. When the screen is full, new text is displayed at the bottom, the top line is removed, and other lines on the screen are moved toward the top. The trouble with this method of using the screen is that important information may be lost when it is scrolled off. (Status information, instructions, previously entered data, and so forth may be needed at all times during an operation.) The solution

Figure 11.8   Sample execution of Program 11b

```
Command   Action
   N        Name file (Current file                        )    ⎫
   C        Create file                                          ⎪
   P        Print file (to printer)                              ⎬  Menu
   L        List file (to screen)                                ⎪
   H        Help                                                 ⎪
   Q        Quit program                                         ⎭
Enter Command Code
n   ◄───────────────────────────────────────── Name command
Enter name of file
PRO11B.DAT                                          Name of file
Command   Action                                         ↓
   N        Name file (Current file PRO11B.DAT       )
   C        Create file
   P        Print file (to printer)
   L        List file (to screen)
   H        Help
   Q        Quit program
Enter Command Code
c   ◄───────────────────────────────────────── Create command
Enter data for file PRO11B.DAT
OK to proceed? (Y/N)
y
Enter Name (END to terminate)
Joe Jones
Enter Social Security Number
111111111
Enter Street Address
123 Main St.
Enter City
Elmville
Enter Two Character State Abbreviation
MA
Enter ZIP
12300
Enter Date of Birth in form mmddyy
012367
Name       : Joe Jones
SS #       : 111111111
Address    : 123 Main St.
             Elmville  MA 12300
Birth Date : 012367
Are data correct? (Y/N)
y
Enter Name (END to terminate)
```

Figure 11.8 *(concluded)*

```
Enter Command Code
l  ←─────────────────────────────────────  List command
List content of file PRO11B.DAT
OK to proceed? (Y/N)
y
Name         : Joe Jones            ⎫
SS #         : 111111111            ⎪
Address      : 123 Main St.         ⎬  File contains 1 record
               Elmville  MA 12300   ⎪
Birth Date : 012367                 ⎭
Command   Action
    N       Name file (Current file PRO11B.DAT    )
    C       Create file
    P       Print file (to printer)
    L       List file (to screen)
    H       Help
    Q       Quit program
Enter Command Code
q  ←─────────────────────────────────────  Quit command
```

to this problem is to change the operation of the terminal to a nonscrolling mode. Required information can then be written at desired locations on the screen and remain there. The screen format may contain provisions for predefining fields into which data is entered. These fields may be highlighted by reverse video or by other means. When the user has finished entering data in one field, the cursor may automatically advance to the next field under program control. In other implementations, the user may control the cursor (by cursor control keys or a mouse) but still be able to enter data only in predefined fields.

Unfortunately, there is no standard method for implementing formatted screens in a COBOL environment. In some systems, the ACCEPT and DISPLAY verbs are enhanced with nonstandard options to control the location and format of data and text being written to the screen or entered at the terminal. In other systems, special control codes are written to the terminal screen using the ordinary READ and WRITE verbs. In still other systems, it is necessary to write a special program to be executed at the terminal to perform the formatting operations; the COBOL program running on the host computer is not involved in the formatting operations at all. Because of this lack of standardization, you must use the manufacturer's reference manuals or other documentation to determine how to format screens on the system you are using.

A great deal of the software for microcomputers depends heavily on formatted screens. For example, the Apple Macintosh[3] makes extensive use of screens displaying menus and featuring fields called **windows** that have a predefined, specific use. Microsoft has developed a similar interface called Windows[4] for MS DOS-based computers. In all likelihood, interactive programs of the future will have to make use of similar features because they contribute significantly to the program's "user friendliness" and to its potential for acceptance and use by people with little experience or training.

[3]Macintosh is a trademark of Apple Computer, Inc.

[4]Windows is a trademark, and Microsoft is a registered trademark of Microsoft Corp.

At the present time, most COBOL compilers do not provide good facilities for screen formatting. The facilities that are provided are specific to the particular compiler: They may be excellent, but they are not standard COBOL. Details of screen format facilities found in RM/COBOL-85 are included in Appendix B. These facilities are similar to those supported by most microcomputer-oriented COBOL systems, but some details will vary.

11.7 THE STRING STATEMENT

There are many instances, particularly in an interactive program, when it is necessary to bring data items that have been defined separately together into one field. An example would be to convert the contents of the two data items defined as

```
03 FIRST-NAME   PIC X(20).
03 LAST-NAME    PIC X(20).
```

into a single string of characters to be contained in a field called NAME with the first and last names separated by a single space. Suppose the content of the data items FIRST-NAME and LAST-NAME are as shown below:

```
| M | A | R | Y |   |   |   |   |   |   |   |   |   |   |   |   |   |   |   |   |
FIRST-NAME PIC X(20)
```

```
| S | M | I | T | H |   |   |   |   |   |   |   |   |   |   |   |   |   |   |   |
LAST-NAME PIC X(20)
```

The desired transformation would be a field with content

```
| M | A | R | Y |   | S | M | I | T | H |   |   |   |   |   |   |   |
NAME PIC X(17)
```

The STRING statement offers the COBOL programmer a very convenient means for performing such transformations. A general form of the STRING statement is shown in Figure 11.9.

Figure 11.9   General form of the STRING statement

$$
\text{STRING} \left\{ \left\{ \begin{matrix} \text{data-name-1} \\ \text{literal-1} \end{matrix} \right\} \ \ldots \ \underline{\text{DELIMITED}} \ \text{BY} \ \left\{ \begin{matrix} \text{data-name-2} \\ \text{literal-2} \\ \underline{\text{SIZE}} \end{matrix} \right\} \right\} \ \ldots
$$

$$
\underline{\text{INTO}} \ \text{data-name-3}
$$
$$
[\text{ON} \ \underline{\text{OVERFLOW}} \ \text{statement}]
$$

The items specified before the DELIMITED phrase are sending fields; the item specified by data-name-3 is the receiving field. Data is transferred from the sending fields to the receiving field as with the alphanumeric MOVE, except that filling the receiving field with blanks is not performed. The DELIMITED BY clause specifies the condition for termination of transfer of characters from the sending field. The content of data-name-2 or literal-2 may be one or more characters. Figurative constants are assumed to be a single character. Transfer of data terminates when the delimiting character pattern is found in the sending field. Specification of SIZE in the DELIMITED BY clause will cause transfer of all characters of the sending item.

─────────── Example ───────────

```
STRING FLD-A FLD-B DELIMITED BY SPACE
       INTO FLD-C.
```

```
A B C D
FLD-A PIC X(8)
```

```
1 2 3   4 5 6 7 8
FLD-B PIC X(10)
```

From FLDA-A   From FLD-B   These characters are not replaced.

```
A B C D 1 2 3 ? ? ?
FLD-C PIC X(10).
```

First the characters ABCD are moved from FLD-A into FLD-C. When the space is encountered in FLD-A, characters from FLD-B are transferred into FLD-C. Transfer of characters from FLD-B terminates after the first three characters because the fourth character is a space. Note that the remaining characters of FLD-C retain their former content. In this example (and others that follow in this chapter), we will use "?" as the content of a field to indicate that its content is not changed by the instruction being illustrated.

It is usually advisable to initialize a receiving field by moving SPACES (or another character as needed) to the field before executing a STRING statement.

─────────── Example ───────────

```
MOVE SPACES TO ITEM-3.
STRING ITEM-1 DELIMITED BY SIZE
       ITEM-2 DELIMITED BY "-"
       INTO ITEM-3.
```

```
A B C
ITEM-1 PIC X(5)
```

```
1 2 - 3 4
ITEM-2 PIC X(5)
```

From ITEM-1   From ITEM-2   This character is not replaced.

```
A B C     1 2
ITEM-3 PIC X(8)
```

All of the characters from ITEM-1 are moved to ITEM-3 because ITEM-1 is delimited by SIZE. The first two characters from ITEM-2 are moved into ITEM-3. Transfer of characters terminates when the delimiting character "-" is encountered in ITEM-2. The remaining character will be a space because ITEM-3 was initialized to SPACES.

──────── Example ────────

```
STRING FIRST-NAME DELIMITED BY SPACE
       " "           DELIMITED BY SIZE
       LAST-NAME DELIMITED BY SPACE
       INTO NAME.
```

```
| M | A | R | Y |   |   |   |   |   |   |   |   |   |   |   |   |   |   |   |   |
```
FIRST-NAME PIC X(20)

```
| S | M | I | T | H |   |   |   |   |   |   |   |   |   |   |   |   |   |   |   |
```
LAST-NAME PIC X(20)

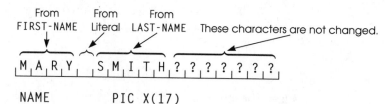

From   From   From
FIRST-NAME   Literal   LAST-NAME   These characters are not changed.

```
| M | A | R | Y |   | S | M | I | T | H | ? | ? | ? | ? | ? | ? | ? |
```

NAME   PIC X(17)

It is the responsibility of the program to make sure that the receiving field contains spaces before execution of this STRING statement because the trailing characters in NAME will not be modified.

──────── Example ────────

```
STRING FLD-C FLD-D DELIMITED BY "AB"
       INTO FLD-E.
```

```
| A | C | B | A | B | A | B |          | B | A | A | B |
```
FLD-C PIC X(7)   FLD-D PIC X(4)

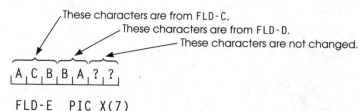

These characters are from FLD-C.
These characters are from FLD-D.
These characters are not changed.

```
| A | C | B | B | A | ? | ? |
```

FLD-E   PIC X(7)

In this example, the delimiting string consists of the two characters "AB". FLD-C contains these two characters in positions 4 and 5, so the first three characters from this field are moved to FLD-E. FLD-D contains these characters in positions 3 and 4 so the first two characters from FLD-D are moved to FLD-E.

If the delimiting character string is not found in a sending field, all of the characters in the field are transferred to the receiving field.

──────── Example ────────

```
STRING    FLD-X "-" FLD-Y DELIMITED BY CHAR
          INTO FLD-Z.
```

```
*
| |
```
CHAR PIC X

```
| A | B | C | D |   |
```
FLD-X PIC X(5)

```
 1 , 2 , * , 3 ,
|__|__|__|__|
FLD-Y PIC X(5)
```

```
  From      From     From
  FLD-X    Literal   FLD-Y    These characters are not changed.
    ↓         ↓        ↓  ↙
  ⏞         ⏞        ⏞
 A , B , C , D ,  - , 1 , 2 , ? , ?
|__|__|__|__|__|__|__|__|__|__|
FLD-Z  PIC X(10)
```

The content of CHAR is used as the delimiting character for FLD-X, FLD-Y, and the literal "-". All characters of FLD-X and the literal "-" are transferred to FLD-Z since neither contains the delimiting character.

Transfer of characters terminates either when all of the characters in the sending fields have been transferred or when there is no more room in the receiving field. The ON OVERFLOW clause can be used to take action in the latter case when the receiving field is full and there are more characters in the sending fields to be transferred.

──────── Example ────────

```
STRING FLD-Q FLD-R DELIMITED BY SIZE
       INTO FLD-S
       ON OVERFLOW PERFORM WRITE-ERROR-MSG.
```

```
 1 , 2 , 3 ,                    A , B , C ,
|__|__|__|                     |__|__|__|
FLD-Q PIC 999                   FLD-R PIC XXX
```

```
From FLD-Q   From FLD-R
    ↓           ↙
  ⏞          ⏞
 1 , 2 , 3 , A ,
|__|__|__|__|
FLD-S  PIC X(4)
```

In this case, FLD-S is too short to contain all characters from the receiving fields, resulting in an overflow situation. The paragraph WRITE-ERROR-MSG would be executed. If the ON OVERFLOW clause had been omitted, the content of FLD-S would be as shown, and the program would continue with the next statement.

11.8 THE UNSTRING STATEMENT

The UNSTRING statement performs the inverse function of the STRING statement. The STRING statement brings many separate items together into one field; the UNSTRING statement enables the program to separate the content of one field into many different items. For example, suppose you want to separate the characters in a field such as

```
 M , A , R , Y ,   , S , M , I , T , H ,   ,   ,   ,   ,   ,   ,   ,
|__|__|__|__|__|__|__|__|__|__|__|__|__|__|__|__|__|
NAME PIC X(17)
```

into two items such as

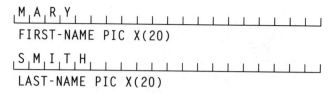

```
M A R Y
```
FIRST-NAME PIC X(20)

```
S M I T H
```
LAST-NAME PIC X(20)

The UNSTRING statement will enable the program to make this transformation. A general form for the UNSTRING statement is shown in Figure 11.10.

Figure 11.10   General form of the UNSTRING statement

UNSTRING data-name-1

$$\left[\underline{\text{DELIMITED}} \text{ BY } [\underline{\text{ALL}}] \left\{ \begin{array}{l} \text{data-name-2} \\ \text{literal} \end{array} \right\} \right]$$

INTO data-name-3...
[ON OVERFLOW statement]

Data-name-1 is the sending field; data-name-3 and those following are receiving fields. When all of these items are alphanumeric, characters are transferred from the sending field to the receiving field(s) from left to right. If the DELIMITED BY clause is omitted, characters are moved into the first receiving field until the field is filled; then, characters are moved into the second receiving field, and so forth. Transfer of characters terminates when all of the characters in the sending field have been transferred or when all of the receiving fields have been filled.

──────── Example ────────

UNSTRING FLD-A INTO FLD-B FLD-C.

```
A B C D E F G H
```
FLD-A PIC X(8)

```
A B C
```
FLD-B PIC X(3)

```
D E F G
```
FLD-C PIC X(4)

The DELIMITED BY clause enables the programmer to specify a character or characters to be used to terminate transfer of data into a receiving field. When the delimiter is found in the sending field, transfer of characters to the receiving field ceases. If other receiving fields are present transfer of characters resumes with the leftmost character following the delimiter.

──────── Example ────────

UNSTRING FLD-E
    DELIMITED BY "-"
    INTO FLD-F, FLD-G, FLD-H.

```
 1 2 3 - 4 5 - 6 7 8 9
FLD-E PIC X(11)

 1 2 3
FLD-F PIC XXX

 4 5
FLD-G PIC XX

 6 7 8 9
FLD-H PIC XXXX
```

Transfer of data into FLD-F ceases when the first "-" is encountered in FLD-E. In like fashion, transfer into FLD-G is terminated by a second "-".

--------- Example ---------

```
UNSTRING NAME
    DELIMITED BY SPACE
    INTO FIRST-NAME LAST-NAME.

 M A R Y   S M I T H
NAME PIC X(17)

 M A R Y
FIRST-NAME PIC X(20)

 S M I T H
LAST-NAME PIC X(20)
```

Note that receiving fields are padded on the right with blanks if the number of characters received is less than the field width.

The discussion of the UNSTRING statement thus far has been restricted to cases where both the sending item and receiving item(s) are alphanumeric. In fact, either the sending item or the receiving item(s) may be numeric. The sending item is always treated in the same way, whether it is described as alphanumeric or numeric; that is, the sending field is treated as a sequence of characters. When a receiving item is described as numeric, the system will treat characters being moved into the field as specifying a value and will complete the operation in the same way as it would in completing a MOVE of numeric data to a numeric receiving field.

--------- Example ---------

```
UNSTRING ITEM-1 DELIMITED BY SPACE INTO ITEM-2 ITEM-3.

 1 2   8
ITEM-1 PIC X(4)

 0 1 2                        0 8
ITEM-2 PIC 999              ITEM-3 PIC 99
```

In this case, since ITEM-2 is a numeric item, the characters "12" moved from ITEM-1 are treated as having value twelve which is represented in a three digit numeric field by "012". Similarly, the character "8" from ITEM-1 is treated as having value eight and is treated as though the statement

```
MOVE 8 TO ITEM-3
```

had been executed.

─────────── Example ───────────

```
UNSTRING ITEM-4 DELIMITED BY "," INTO ITEM-5 ITEM-6.
```

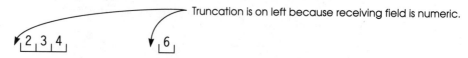

```
ITEM-4 PIC X(7)
```

Truncation is on left because receiving field is numeric.

```
ITEM-5  PIC 999   ITEM-6  PIC 9
```

Note that if the receiving fields are not long enough to receive all of the value being moved to it, truncation will occur on the left in exactly the same way as when a MOVE statement is used to move a value into a numeric field.

If two or more delimiters appear in adjacent positions of the sending field, the affected receiving field will be either blank filled (if an alphanumeric item) or zero filled (if a numeric item).

─────────── Example ───────────

```
UNSTRING INPUT-STRING
    DELIMITED BY ","
    INTO NUM-1, NUM-2, NUM-3.
```

```
1 2 3 , , 4 5
INPUT-STRING PIC X(10)
```

```
1 2 3
NUM-1 PIC 999
```

```
0 0 0
NUM-2 PIC 999
```

```
0 4 5
NUM-3 PIC 999
```

The first occurrence of the comma terminates transfer of characters into NUM-1. The second occurrence of a comma terminates transfer of data into NUM-2. Because no data was transferred and the field is numeric, it is zeroed out. Note that NUM-3 receives data as a numeric item so that the characters "45" are stored as the value forty-five.

If the ALL option is used in the DELIMITED BY clause, all adjacent delimiters are treated as one delimiter.

──────── Example ────────

```
UNSTRING NAME
     DELIMITED BY ALL SPACES
     INTO FIRST-NAME LAST-NAME.
```

```
 J O H N       D O E
```
NAME PIC X(17)

```
 J O H N
```
FIRST-NAME PIC X(20)

```
 D O E
```
LAST-NAME PIC X(20).

The three adjacent spaces in positions 5 through 7 of NAME are treated as one delimiter. Transfer of data into LAST-NAME begins at position 8.

──────────────────────────

The ON OVERFLOW clause can be used to take action when an overflow condition occurs. This happens when there are additional, unexamined characters in the sending field, and all receiving fields have been filled. If an overflow condition occurs and the ON OVERFLOW clause is not included in the statement, execution of the program resumes at the next statement.

──────── Example ────────

```
UNSTRING FLD-A INTO FLD-B FLD-C
     ON OVERFLOW PERFORM WRITE-ERROR-MSG.
```

```
 A B C              A              B
```
FLD-A PIC X(3)   FLD-B PIC X   FLD-C PIC X

Since FLD-A has an additional character which is not examined, an overflow condition results in the execution of WRITE-ERROR-MSG.

──────── Example ────────

```
MOVE "NO" TO ERROR-FLAG
UNSTRING FLD-D
     DELIMITED BY SPACE
     INTO FLD-E FLD-F
     ON OVERFLOW MOVE "YES" TO ERROR-FLAG.
```

```
 A B C D
```
FLD-D PIC X(4)

```
 A B C
```
FLD-E PIC X(3)

```
 ? ? ? ? ?
```
◄──────── This field is not changed by the UNSTRING statement.

FLD-F PIC X(5)

```
 N O
```
ERROR-FLAG PIC XXX.

Since the sending field does not contain an instance of the delimiter, transfer of data into FLD-F cannot begin, and the value of FLD-F remains unchanged. Since all of the characters in FLD-D are "used," overflow does *not* occur, and hence the value of ERROR-FLAG is unchanged.

11.9   THE INSPECT STATEMENT

The INSPECT statement allows a program to process individual characters in a data item by replacing certain characters with other characters. The general form of the INSPECT statement is shown in Figure 11.11. The statement can be used to count characters using the TALLYING option (Format-1), replace characters using the REPLACING option (Format-2), or perform both functions (Format-3). Format-2 of the INSPECT statement will cause some (or all) of the characters in identifier-1 to be replaced. Identifier-5 or literal-3 specifies the character(s) to be replaced. Identifier-6 or literal-4 specifies the replacement character(s).

The LEADING option will cause leftmost occurrences of specified characters to be replaced.

Figure 11.11   General form of the INSPECT statement

Format 1
```
INSPECT identifier-1 TALLYING
  { identifier-2 FOR { { {ALL     }  {identifier-3} } [{BEFORE} INITIAL {identifier-4}] } ... } ...
                        {LEADING  }  {literal-1   }      {AFTER }         {literal-2   }
                        {CHARACTERS}
```

Format 2
```
INSPECT identifier-1 REPLACING
  { CHARACTERS BY {identifier-6} [{BEFORE} INITIAL {identifier-7}]
                  {literal-4   }  {AFTER }         {literal-5   }
  { { {ALL    } {identifier-5} BY {identifier-6} [{BEFORE} INITIAL {identifier-7}] } ... } ...
      {LEADING} {literal-3   }    {literal-4   }   {AFTER }         {literal-5   }
      {FIRST  }
```

Format 3
```
INSPECT identifier-1 TALLYING
  { identifier-2 FOR { { {ALL     }  {identifier-6} } [{BEFORE} INITIAL {identifier-4}] } ... } ...
                        {LEADING  }  {literal-1   }      {AFTER }         {literal-2   }
                        {CHARACTERS}

REPLACING
  { CHARACTERS BY {identifier-6} [{BEFORE} INITIAL {identifier-7}]
                 {literal-4   }   {AFTER }         {literal-5   }
  { { {ALL    } {identifier-5} BY {identifier-6} [{BEFORE} INITIAL {identifier-7}] } ... } ...
      {LEADING} {literal-3   }    {literal-4   }   {AFTER }         {literal-5   }
      {FIRST  }
```

─────── Example ───────

Suppose you wish to insert asterisks in place of leading zeros in a field. The following statement could be used:

    INSPECT DATA-FIELD REPLACING LEADING "0" BY "*".

Before execution

| 0 | 0 | 0 | 4 | 3 | 0 | 5 | 7 |
DATA-FIELD

After execution

| * | * | * | 4 | 3 | 0 | 5 | 7 |
DATA-FIELD

The zero in position 6 is not replaced because it is not a leading zero. If no characters satisfying the condition LEADING "0" had been found, content of the field would not be changed.

─────────────────────────────

The ALL option will cause all occurrences of specified characters to be replaced.

─────── Example ───────

    INSPECT FLD-OUT REPLACING ALL " " BY ",".

Before execution

| 1 | 2 | 3 | | 4 | 5 | | 6 | 7 | 8 | 9 |
FLD-OUT

After execution

| 1 | 2 | 3 | , | 4 | 5 | , | 6 | 7 | 8 | 9 |
FLD-OUT

─────────────────────────────

The FIRST option will replace the first (leftmost) occurrence of a specified character with another character. All other occurrences of the character will be unaffected.

─────── Example ───────

    INSPECT ITEM-A REPLACING FIRST "*" BY "$".

Before execution

| * | * | * | * | 1 | 2 | . | 3 | 0 |
ITEM-A

After execution

| $ | * | * | * | 1 | 2 | . | 3 | 0 |
ITEM-A

─────────────────────────────

The CHARACTERS option is used to specify that all characters in identifier-1 are to be replaced.

─────── Example ───────

```
INSPECT FLD-A REPLACING CHARACTERS BY SPACES.
```

Before Execution

A	B	C	D

FLD-A

After Execution

FLD-A

This statement is equivalent to

```
MOVE SPACES TO FLD-A.
```

Any one of the forms of the INSPECT statement that we have discussed thus far can be extended by adding a BEFORE or AFTER clause to limit the scope of the sequence of characters in identifier-1 that will be replaced. The BEFORE clause will specify that only characters before the first occurrence of a specified character are to be replaced; the AFTER clause will specify that only characters after the first occurrence of a specified character are to be replaced. The word INITIAL can be used in either of these clauses if desired but its only purpose is to clarify the meaning of the phrase.

─────── Example ───────

```
INSPECT FLDA-A REPLACING CHARACTERS BY SPACES
                        AFTER INITIAL "A".
```

Before Execution

D	E	F	A	B	C	A

FLD-A

After Execution

D	E	F	A			

FLD-A

The three characters after the first occurrence of the character "A" are replaced by spaces.

─────── Example ───────

```
INSPECT FLD-A REPLACING ALL "A" BY "–"
                        BEFORE INITIAL SPACE.
```

Before Execution

B	A	A	C			A		B	A

FLD-A

After Execution

B	–	–	C			A		B	A

FLD-A

The first space occurs in position 5 of FLD-A. The two occurrences of the character "A" that precede position 5 (in positions 2 and 3) are replaced by "-".

Format-1 of the INSPECT statement can be used to count occurrences of specific sequences of characters in identifier-1; the value of identifier-1 is not changed. The value computed by the statement is placed in identifier-2 which must be declared in the DATA DIVISION as an elementary numeric item. It is not necessary for the program to initialize this item prior to execution of the statement, since the statement moves the result of the tally operation to this item after execution of the INSPECT statement. This form of the INSPECT statement is similar in many respects to Format-2 of the statement except that the FIRST option does not exist.

The ALL option can be used to count all occurrences of a given character.

--- Example ---

The following statement will count the number of occurrences of the character "E" in the item FLD-B:

```
INSPECT FLD-B TALLYING E-COUNT FOR ALL "E".
```

After Execution

```
 N O W   I S   T H E   T I M E
```
FLD-B PIC X(20)

```
 0 2
```
E-COUNT PIC 99

The value placed in E-COUNT indicates that there are two occurrences of the character "E".

The LEADING option can be used to count the number of occurrences of a character in the initial portion of a sting of characters.

--- Example ---

```
INSPECT FLD-B TALLYING SPACE-COUNT FOR LEADING SPACES
```
After Execution

```
       J O E   J O N E S
```
FLD-B PIC X(20)

```
 0 3
```
SPACE-COUNT PIC 99.
There are three leading spaces in FLD-B.

The CHARACTERS option can be used to count all characters; this option will probably be of greatest use when combined with a BEFORE or AFTER clause because otherwise the value will simply be equal to the field length.

──────── Example ────────

```
INSPECT FLD-B TALLYING CHAR-COUNT FOR CHARACTERS
                AFTER INITIAL "$".
```

After Execution

```
|   |   |   | $ | 9 | 0 | . | 0 | 0 |
FLD-B PIC $$$$$$.99
```

```
| 5 |
CHAR-COUNT PIC 9
```

Note that it is possible to use the INSPECT statement to examine a field of any alphanumeric type including numeric edited fields such as the one in this example.

───────────────────────────────

A Format-3 INSPECT statement enables the programmer to combine a TALLYING option and a REPLACING option in a single statement. Considerations for using this statement are similar to the considerations for using Format-1 and Format-2 statements which it strongly resembles.

──────── Example ────────

```
INSPECT FLD-C TALLYING ZERO-COUNT FOR LEADING ZEROS
                REPLACING LEADING ZEROES BY SPACES.
```

Before Execution

```
| 0 | 0 | 0 | 1 | 2 | 3 |
FLD-C PIC X(6)
```

After Execution

```
|   |   |   | 1 | 2 | 3 |
FLD-C PIC X(6)
```

```
| 0 | 3 |
ZERO-COUNT PIC 99
```

───────────────────────────────

While the condition used for TALLYING and REPLACING may be the same as in the above example, it is not necessary for this to be so. The two portions of the statement are independent and are not necessarily related.

──────── Example ────────

```
INSPECT FLD-C TALLYING A-COUNT FOR ALL "A"
                REPLACING ALL SPACES BY "*".
```

Before Execution

```
| N | O | W |   | I | S |   | T | H | E |   | T | I | M | E |   |   |   |   |   |
FLD-C    PIC X(20)
```

After Execution

```
| N | O | W | * | I | S | * | T | H | E | * | T | I | M | E | * | * | * | * | * |
FLD-C PIC X(20)
```

```
| 0 |
A-COUNT PIC 9
```

Note that it is completely possible that the value of the count can be zero if no characters meeting the required condition are located.

11.10 DATA VALIDATION AND FILE CREATION

One of the primary responsibilities of a system designer is to take steps to help ensure the integrity of the data in the system. There is nothing more frustrating and irritating than a system in which invalid data is difficult or impossible to correct. Surveys of computer users have shown that invalid data is the most common source of user dissatisfaction with data processing systems. To help ensure that invalid data does not enter a system, the data entry program must contain logic to detect invalid data and to allow the data entry person to correct the data before it is stored.

Validity checking may be performed on the characters that make up a field, on the value of the field itself, and on the relationships among the fields within the record. Typically, certain fields can be identified as containing only numeric or alphabetic characters. If the data entered by the user contains characters of an inappropriate type, the data can be rejected as invalid. If the field contains valid characters, it may be possible to perform a range check to determine if the value of the item is inside known boundaries. If the item is too large or too small or otherwise contains an inappropriate value, the data can be rejected. For alphanumeric fields, it is usually important that the data be left justified within the field; that is, the first nonblank character should be in the leftmost position of the field. The program can check the leftmost characters of such fields and reject those with leading spaces.

A collection of otherwise valid data fields may not constitute a valid data record. The data entry person may have inadvertently entered data from parts of two or more separate records or may have made erroneous key strokes in entering the data. Errors of this type are common if the persons's attention is distracted during the data entry process. There are often ways in which a program can check on the consistency among the values contained in fields within a record and reject a record determined to be invalid. A second technique is to display data entered by the user and ask if the record is valid. After reviewing the data, the user may spot errors made in the data entry process. The program should then provide a means for the user to correct individual fields or the entire record.

11.11 PROGRAM EXAMPLE

Problem Statement

Modify Program 11b to perform validation of data as follows:

> Name must be alphabetic and contain no leading spaces
> Social Security number must be numeric
> City must be alphabetic and contain no leading spaces
> State must be alphabetic and contain no leading spaces
> Zip must be numeric
> Date must be numeric; the month and day must be within allowable range; year must be not greater than the current year.

Problem Analysis

The overall structure of the required program is similar to Program 11b. The major differences come in the data entry paragraphs since each of these must perform a data validation function. We can put the INSPECT verb to good use in validating name, city, and state; we simply count leading spaces in the field. If the number of leading spaces is not zero, we know that an error has been made when data was entered into the field. The zip code might contain leading spaces since a zip of 01111 might correctly be entered by the operator as " 1111". We can use the INSPECT verb to replace leading spaces by zeros before checking the field for all numeric characters. Checking the value of year can be accomplished by using the ACCEPT/FROM DATE statement to enter the current date; if the value of year is greater than the value of the current year, the field is in error.

Problem Solution

The required program is shown as Program 11c. One validity flag (VALID-DATA-FLAG) is used for each validation process. The flag is initialized to "NO" prior to each initiation of a data entry process. The data entry is then repeated so long as VALID-DATA-FLAG remains "NO". If the procedure sets the flag to "YES", the data entry process will terminate, and the user will proceed to entering the next field. (See, for example, the procedure used to enter the Social Security number at lines 203–205.) Note that, despite the detailed validation of the content of each field, the program retains the practice of displaying all data for a record so that the user can accept the data or reject it. Remember that the user needs to retain final control over the data that has been entered. The program can check only for obvious errors; more subtle errors can be judged only by the program user.

Summary of Data Validation Techniques

Following is a summary of data validation requirements and techniques found in Program 11c:

- Field must contain one of a specified list of values.
  Command must be one of six characters listed in the menu; 88 level entries include each of these characters (and the lowercase equivalent) in a series of named conditions. If none of the named conditions occurs, an error message is produced.

- Field must be in a specified range of values.
  MONTH-DR and DAY-DR must be in range 1 to 12 and 1 to 31, respectively; named conditions are created containing the list of valid values. YEAR-DR must be in range 0 to current year. The program checks for this condition using a relational condition.

- Field must be alphabetic or numeric.
  The ALPHABETIC and NUMERIC tests are used as appropriate; examples include SS-NUM-AN-DR, NAME-DR, STREET-ADDRESS-DR, and so forth.

- Field must not contain leading spaces.
  The INSPECT verb with the TALLYING option is used to count leading spaces. Examples are NAME-DR, STREET-ADDRESS-DR, CITY-DR, and so forth.

- Leading spaces are okay, but they must be replaced by another character for a field to be valid.

The INSPECT verb with the REPLACING option is used to replace leading characters with other specified characters. An example is the validation of ZIP-DR.

- User must verify correctness of data and choices before program proceeds.

All major operations of Program 11c are preceded by an echo of the operation that is about to take place. The program accepts an answer from the user; if the response is anything other than "Y" or "y", the operation is terminated and control returns to the main menu. After all data has been entered in a record, the content of the record is displayed with a chance for the user to accept the data or reenter the data.

- Program must avoid invalid operations with files.

At the beginning of each major program action, the content of FILE-NAME is tested. If the content is spaces, the operation is aborted; if the content is not spaces, the name of the file is displayed for the user, and the user can continue or abort the operation. (Displaying the name of the file currently being operated on each time the menu is printed helps the user keep track of what is going on; technically, this kind of information is called **status information**.)

11.12 DEBUG CLINIC

As programs become longer and more complex, the job of providing adequate test data becomes more demanding. In fact, it may be necessary to test programs with more than one set of data records to make sure the program will function properly in all sets of circumstances. A common practice is to test each program at least three times: once with no data (that is, with an input file that contains no data records), again with "good" data (data that results in no error conditions), and finally with "bad" data (data that tests the program's ability to handle error conditions). The development of a set of data records that provides a thorough test of the program's logic should be started early in the program development cycle. This task is one that beginning programmers often do not perform adequately because it can be tedious and time-consuming; however, the success or failure of a programming project often hinges as much on thorough testing of the finished product as it does on imaginative program design or meticulous coding. Testing a program is usually divided into two phases:

1. The programmer executes the program using the data designed to verify that the program performs correctly (called **alpha testing**).
2. Representative users test the program with actual data (called **beta testing**).

A program should be thoroughly alpha tested before beta testing begins. Very often, beta testing will reveal errors that went undetected when the programmer tested the program. Placing a program into use before it has been adequately tested will surely be embarrassing for the programmer and perhaps expensive for the organization. The old engineering maxim, "There is never time to do it right but always time to do it over," often applies to programming.

Program 11c

```
 1 IDENTIFICATION DIVISION.
 2
 3 PROGRAM-ID. DATA-VALIDATION-PRO11C.
 .
 .
 .
28 01  DATA-RECORD.
29     03 SS-NUM-AN-DR.
30        05 SS-NUM-DR          PIC 9(9).
31     03 NAME-DR               PIC X(20).
32        88 END-OF-DATA        VALUE "END" "end" "End".
33     03 STREET-ADDRESS-DR     PIC X(15).
34     03 CITY-DR               PIC X(10).
35     03 STATE-DR              PIC XX.
36     03 ZIP-DR                PIC X(5).
37     03 DOB-DR.
38        05 MONTH-DR           PIC 99.
39           88 VALID-MONTH     VALUE 1 THRU 12.
40        05 DAY-DR             PIC 99.
41           88 VALID-DAY       VALUE 1 THRU 31.
42        05 YEAR-DR            PIC 99.
43
44 WORKING-STORAGE SECTION.
45
46 01  FILE-NAME               PIC X(15) VALUE SPACES.
47
48 01  CONTROL-FIELDS.
 .
 .
 .
60     02 VALID-DATA-FLAG      PIC XXX.
61        88 VALID-DATA        VALUE "YES".
62     02 LEADING-SPACES       PIC 99 VALUE 0.
63     02 DATE-CURRENT.
64        03 YEAR-CURRENT      PIC 99.
65        03 FILLER            PIC X(4).
66
67 PROCEDURE DIVISION.
68
69 1000-MAIN-CONTROL.
70
71     ACCEPT DATE-CURRENT FROM DATE.
72     PERFORM 2000-PROCESS-USER-COMMANDS
73           UNTIL QUIT.
74     STOP RUN.
75
```

Program 11c   *(continued)*

```
 76 2000-PROCESS-USER-COMMANDS.
 77
 78     PERFORM 3000-DISPLAY-MENU.
 79     PERFORM 3100-GET-COMMAND.
 80     IF      NAME-FILE
 81                  PERFORM 3200-GET-FILE-NAME
 82     ELSE IF CREATE-FILE
 83                  PERFORM 3300-CREATE-FILE
 84     ELSE IF PRINT-FILE
 85                  PERFORM 3400-PRINT-FILE
 86     ELSE IF LIST-FILE
 87                  PERFORM 3500-LIST-FILE
 88     ELSE IF HELP
 89                  PERFORM 3600-WRITE-HELP
 90     ELSE IF QUIT
 91                  NEXT SENTENCE
 92     ELSE
 93                  PERFORM 3700-WRITE-ERROR.
  .
  .
  .
115 3300-CREATE-FILE.
116
117     IF FILE-NAME = SPACES
118         DISPLAY "File has not been named"
119     ELSE
120         DISPLAY "Enter data for file " FILE-NAME
121         DISPLAY "OK to proceed? (Y/N)"
122         ACCEPT ANSWER
123         IF DATA-OK
124             OPEN OUTPUT DATA-FILE
125             MOVE "N" TO ANSWER
126             MOVE SPACES TO NAME-DR
127             PERFORM 9000-GET-DATA UNTIL
128                     DATA-OK OR END-OF-DATA
129             PERFORM 4000-BUILD-FILE
130                     UNTIL END-OF-DATA
131             CLOSE DATA-FILE.
  .
  .
  .
137 3500-LIST-FILE.
138
139     IF FILE-NAME = SPACES
140         DISPLAY "File has not been named"
141     ELSE
142         DISPLAY "List content of file " FILE-NAME
143         DISPLAY "OK to proceed? (Y/N)"
144         ACCEPT ANSWER
145         IF DATA-OK
146             OPEN INPUT DATA-FILE
147             MOVE "NO" TO EOF-FLAG
148             PERFORM 9300-READ-DATA-FILE
149             PERFORM 4100-PROCESS-DATA
150                     UNTIL END-OF-FILE
151             CLOSE DATA-FILE.
```

Program 11c   *(continued)*

```
          .
          .
          .
161  4000-BUILD-FILE.
162
163      WRITE DATA-RECORD.
164      MOVE "N" TO ANSWER.
165      PERFORM 9000-GET-DATA UNTIL
166              DATA-OK OR END-OF-DATA.
167
168  4100-PROCESS-DATA.
169
170      PERFORM 9200-DISPLAY-DATA.
171      PERFORM 9300-READ-DATA-FILE.
172
173  9000-GET-DATA.
174
175      MOVE "NO" TO VALID-DATA-FLAG.
176      PERFORM 9010-GET-NAME
177              UNTIL VALID-DATA.
178      IF NOT END-OF-DATA
179          PERFORM 9100-ENTER-DATA
180          PERFORM 9200-DISPLAY-DATA
181          DISPLAY "Are data correct? (Y/N)"
182          ACCEPT ANSWER
183          IF NOT DATA-OK
184              DISPLAY "Reenter data".
185
186  9010-GET-NAME.
187
188      DISPLAY "Enter Name (END to terminate)".
189      ACCEPT NAME-DR.
190      IF NAME-DR NOT ALPHABETIC
191          DISPLAY "Name contains invalid character"
192      ELSE
193          MOVE ZERO TO LEADING-SPACES
194          INSPECT NAME-DR TALLYING LEADING-SPACES
195                      FOR LEADING SPACES
196          IF LEADING-SPACES NOT = ZERO
197              DISPLAY "Name is not left justified"
198          ELSE
199              MOVE "YES" TO VALID-DATA-FLAG.
200
```

Program 11c   *(continued)*

```
201 9100-ENTER-DATA.
202
203     MOVE "NO" TO VALID-DATA-FLAG.
204     PERFORM 9400-GET-SS-NUM
205             UNTIL VALID-DATA.
206     MOVE "NO" TO VALID-DATA-FLAG.
207     PERFORM 9500-GET-ST-ADDR
208             UNTIL VALID-DATA.
209     MOVE "NO" TO VALID-DATA-FLAG.
210     PERFORM 9600-GET-CITY
211             UNTIL VALID-DATA.
212     MOVE "NO" TO VALID-DATA-FLAG.
213     PERFORM 9700-GET-ST
214             UNTIL VALID-DATA.
215     MOVE "NO" TO VALID-DATA-FLAG.
216     PERFORM 9800-GET-ZIP
217             UNTIL VALID-DATA.
218     MOVE "NO" TO VALID-DATA-FLAG.
219     PERFORM 9900-GET-DATE
220             UNTIL VALID-DATA.
        .
        .
        .
235 9400-GET-SS-NUM.
236
237     DISPLAY "Enter Social Security Number".
238     ACCEPT SS-NUM-AN-DR.
239     IF SS-NUM-AN-DR NOT NUMERIC
240         DISPLAY "Invalid Social Security Number"
241     ELSE
242         MOVE "YES" TO VALID-DATA-FLAG.
243
244 9500-GET-ST-ADDR.
245
246     DISPLAY "Enter Street Address".
247     ACCEPT STREET-ADDRESS-DR.
248     MOVE ZERO TO LEADING-SPACES.
249     INSPECT STREET-ADDRESS-DR TALLYING LEADING-SPACES
250             FOR LEADING SPACES.
251     IF LEADING-SPACES = ZERO
252         MOVE "YES" TO VALID-DATA-FLAG
253     ELSE
254         DISPLAY "Street Address not left justified".
255
256 9600-GET-CITY.
257
258     DISPLAY "Enter City".
259     ACCEPT CITY-DR.
260     IF CITY-DR NOT ALPHABETIC
261         DISPLAY "Invalid character in name of city"
262     ELSE
263         MOVE ZERO TO LEADING-SPACES
264         INSPECT CITY-DR TALLYING LEADING-SPACES
265                     FOR LEADING SPACES
266         IF LEADING-SPACES NOT = ZERO
267             DISPLAY "City name is not left justified"
268         ELSE
269             MOVE "YES" TO VALID-DATA-FLAG.
```

Program 11c   *(concluded)*

```
270
271 9700-GET-ST.
272
273     DISPLAY "Enter Two Character State Abbreviation".
274     ACCEPT STATE-DR.
275     IF STATE-DR NOT ALPHABETIC
276        DISPLAY "Invalid character in state"
277     ELSE
278        MOVE ZERO TO LEADING-SPACES
279        INSPECT STATE-DR TALLYING LEADING-SPACES
280                       FOR LEADING SPACES
281        IF LEADING-SPACES NOT = ZERO
282            DISPLAY "Invalid abbreviation"
283        ELSE
284            MOVE "YES" TO VALID-DATA-FLAG.
285
286 9800-GET-ZIP.
287
288     DISPLAY "Enter ZIP".
289     ACCEPT ZIP-DR.
290     INSPECT ZIP-DR REPLACING LEADING SPACES BY ZERO.
291     IF ZIP-DR NOT NUMERIC
292         DISPLAY "Invalid ZIP code"
293     ELSE
294         MOVE "YES" TO VALID-DATA-FLAG.
295
296 9900-GET-DATE.
297
298     DISPLAY "Enter Date of Birth in form mmddyy".
299     ACCEPT DOB-DR.
300     INSPECT DOB-DR REPLACING LEADING SPACES BY ZERO.
301     IF DOB-DR NOT NUMERIC
302         DISPLAY "Invalid character in date"
303     ELSE
304        IF NOT VALID-MONTH
305            DISPLAY "Invalid month"
306        ELSE
307            IF NOT VALID-DAY
308                DISPLAY "Invalid day"
309            ELSE
310                IF YEAR-DR > YEAR-CURRENT
311                    DISPLAY "Invalid year"
312                ELSE
313                    MOVE "YES" TO VALID-DATA-FLAG.
```

11.13   COBOL-85 UPDATE

In a COBOL-74 program, the DISPLAY statement always causes the cursor to advance to the beginning of the next line on the screen after writing. The COBOL-85 compiler includes the WITH NO ADVANCING option in the statement that will keep the cursor on the same line positioned after the last character printed on the line. When used, this clause follows all other parts of the statement. If it is omitted, the statement causes the cursor to behave the same as in the COBOL-74 standard. A general form of the DIS-PLAY statement in COBOL-85 is as follows:

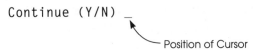

```
DISPLAY  {data-name}  ...  [UPON mnemonic-name] [WITH NO ADVANCING]
         {literal   }
```

This option can be useful when prompting a program user for input. For example, consider the following program segment:

```
DISPLAY "Continue (Y/N) " WITH NO ADVANCING
ACCEPT Answer.
```

During execution of the program, the screen would appear as

```
Continue (Y/N) _
```
                    Position of Cursor

It is usually more natural for a user to enter the response to a prompt on the same line as the prompt as opposed to entering the response on the line below the prompt.

In keeping with changes made in similar conditional statements in the language, the COBOL-85 standard implements two new clauses in the STRING and UNSTRING statements. In each case a NOT ON OVERFLOW clause is permitted following the ON OVERFLOW clause. Also, each statement is supplied with a scope delimiter—END-STRING and END-UNSTRING—making it possible to embed STRING and UNSTRING statements in compound statements. For example, consider the following program segment:

```
UNSTRING Fld-D
    DELIMITED BY SPACE
    INTO Fld-E Fld-F
    ON OVERFLOW
        DISPLAY "Error " Fld-D
    NOT ON OVERFLOW
        DISPLAY Fld-E Fld-F
END-UNSTRING
```

If Fld-D, Fld-E, and Fld-F are defined as follows, then with the content shown for Fld-D, the content of Fld-E and Fld-F will be as shown after execution of the UNSTRING statement.

```
 A   B   C            A                   B
|___|___|___|        |_|                 |_|
Fld-D PIC X(5)       Fld-E PIC X         Fld-F PIC X
```

The system would detect overflow since the sending field contains unexamined characters at the termination of the UNSTRING operation, resulting in the execution of the statement in the ON OVERFLOW clause. At this point, the program will display

```
Error A B C
```

and the program will continue. If the overflow condition had not occurred, the statement in the NOT ON OVERFLOW clause would be executed, and the program will continue.

11.14 SELF-TEST EXERCISES

1. In general terms, distinguish between a batch system and an interactive system.
2. What are some problems not present in a batch program that must be considered in designing an interactive program?
3. How are `ACCEPT` and `DISPLAY` used in a batch system? How can they be used in an interactive system?
4. List three distinct types of user instructions typically supplied by an interactive program.
5. How is a submenu related to a main menu?
6. Why are formatted screens useful in an interactive program?
7. What COBOL verbs are used to communicate with an interactive user in your system?
8. What methods to provide for a formatted screen exist in your system?
9. Given the fields shown below, show the result of each `STRING` statement.

   ```
   | A | B | - | C |
   ITEM-A PIC X(4).

   | 1 | 2 | * | 3 | 4 |
   ITEM-B PIC X(5).

   | A | - | 1 | 2 | * |
   ITEM-C PIC X(5).

   |   |   |   |   |   |   |   |   |   |   |
   ITEM-R PIC X(10) VALUE SPACES.
   ```

   a. STRING ITM-A ITM-B ITM-C
              DELIMITED BY "-"
              INTO ITM-R.
   b. STRING ITEM-B DELIMITED BY "*"
              ITEM-C ITEM-A DELIMITED BY "-"
              INTO ITEM-R.
   c. STRING ITEM-C DELIMITED BY SIZE
              ITEM-A DELIMITED BY "C"
              ITEM-B DELIMITED BY "*"
              INTO ITEM-R.
   d. STRING ITEM-A DELIMITED BY "*"
              ITEM-B DELIMITED BY "-"
              INTO ITEM-R.

10. Given the fields shown below, show the result of each `UNSTRING` statement.

   ```
   | A | B | C | - | D | E | * | 1 | 2 | 3 | - | - | X | Y | * | Z | W |
   FLD-Z PIC X(17)

   |   |   |   |   |
   FLD-A PIC X(4)

   |   |   |   |   |   |
   FLD-B PIC X(5)
   ```

```
|_|_|_|_|_|_|
FLD-C PIC X(6)
a. UNSTRING   FLD-Z
              INTO FLD-A FLD-B FLD-C.
b. UNSTRING   FLD-Z
              DELIMITED BY "*".
              INTO FLD-A, FLD-B FLD-C.
c. UNSTRING   FLD-Z
              DELIMITED BY "-"
              INTO FLD-A FLD-B FLD-C.
d. UNSTRING   FLD-Z
              DELIMITED BY ALL "-"
              INTO FLD-A FLD-B FLD-C.
e. UNSTRING   FLD-Z
              DELIMITED BY "-"
              INTO FLD-A FLD-B.
```

11. A field NAME-IN contains a name in the form

    first-name middle-initial last-name

    where one or more spaces separates each group of characters. The output required is a field NAME-OUT in the form

    last-name, first-name middle-initial

    Write PROCEDURE DIVISION code to transform NAME-IN into NAME-OUT. For example

    ```
    |J|O|H|N| |A| |D|O|E| | | | | | | | | | |
    NAME-IN PIC X(20)
    |D|O|E|,| |J|O|H|N| |A|.| | | | | | | | |
    NAME-OUT PIC X(20)
    ```

12. Write PROCEDURE DIVISION code and any required DATA DIVISION code to transform a nine-digit Social Security number into the form

    ddd-dd-dddd.

13. Show the result of each INSPECT statement

    ```
    |A|B|1|A|B|A|
    ITEM-A PIC X(6)
    ```

    a. INSPECT ITEM-A REPLACING ALL "A" BY "B".
    b. INSPECT ITEM-A REPLACING LEADING "A" BY " ".
    c. INSPECT ITEM-A REPLACING FIRST "B" BY " ".

14. Given the fields shown below, show the result of each UNSTRING statement.

    ```
    |1|2|-|-|3|-|-|4|5|
    ITM-1 PIC X(9)

    |_|_|_|
    ITM-2 PIC 999

    |_|_|
    ITM-3 PIC 99

    |_|
    ITM-4 PIC 9
    ```

```
a. UNSTRING ITM-1
           DELIMITED BY "--"
           INTO ITM-2 ITM-3 ITM-4.
b. UNSTRING ITM-1
           DELIMITED BY "-"
           INTO ITM-2 ITM-3 ITM-4.
c. UNSTRING ITM-1
           DELIMITED BY "-"
           INTO ITM-2 ITM-3 ITM-4
        ON OVERFLOW
           MOVE ZEROES TO ITM-2 ITM-3 ITM-4.
```

15. Show the content of FLD-T after execution of each of the following INSPECT statements assuming the following initial content:

```
 0 0 0 1 0 0 1 1
FLD-T PIC X(8)
```

```
a. INSPECT FLD-T REPLACING
      CHARACTERS BY "*" AFTER INITIAL "0".
b. INSPECT FLD-T REPLACING
      FIRST "0" BY "*" AFTER INITIAL "1".
c. INSPECT FLD-T REPLACING
      ALL "0" BY "*" BEFORE INITIAL "1".
```

16. Show the content of KOUNT after execution of each of the following INSPECT statements. Assume that KOUNT is defined as PIC 99 and that FLD-T is defined as in Exercise 15 above.

```
a. INSPECT FLD-T TALLYING KOUNT
      FOR ALL ZEROES.
b. INSPECT FLD-T TALLYING KOUNT
      FOR ALL ZEROES AFTER INITIAL "1".
c. INSPECT FLD-T TALLYING KOUNT
      FOR LEADING "1".
d. INSPECT FLD-T TALLYING KOUNT
      FOR CHARACTERS AFTER INITIAL "1".
e. INSPECT FLD-T TALLYING KOUNT
      FOR ALL "1" AFTER INITIAL "1".
```

11.15 PROGRAMMING EXERCISES

1. Write an interactive menu-driven program to allow a user to create or list the Supplier Master File used by Amalgamated Custom Design. Your program should validate data placed in the file as appropriate.

2. Modify Program 11a to perform validation of the data entered and to give the user an alternative means of terminating the data entry process. Hint: Give the user a prompt such as "More Data? (Y/N)".

3. The master file for the ABC Automotive Parts Distributors, Inc., inventory system contains the following fields:

Positions	Content
1–6	Part number
7–20	Part description
21–29	Vendor number
30–35	Wholesale price (2 decimal places)
36–42	Retail price (2 decimal places)
43–46	Number on hand

Write an interactive program to allow a user to create this file.

4. Write an interactive program to allow a user to perform any of the following operations, using the master file described in Exercise 3:

- create the file
- list the file on screen
- list the file on printer

5. Write an interactive program that would allow a user to perform any of the following operations, using the master file described in Exercise 3:

- display all relevant information for a part number entered by the user
- display a list of parts supplied by a vendor, where the user enters any desired vendor number

Note that in either case there may be no information to display. Make sure that your program writes appropriate error messages.

6. Write an interactive data entry/data validation program to create a transaction file for an inventory system designed for ABC Automotive Parts Distributors, Inc. Each record in the file contains the following fields:

Positions	Content
1–6	Part number
7	Transaction code
8–13	Transaction date (*mmddyy* format)
14–16	Transaction quantity
17–30	Part description
31–39	Vendor number
40–45	Wholesale price (2 decimal places)
46–52	Retail price (2 decimal places)
53–60	Invoice number

The following are valid transaction codes:

Codes	Meaning
S	Sale
R	Receipt
N	New item
D	Delete item
C	Change in one or more fields

Fields required are dependent on the type of transaction, as shown by the following table:

Field	Transaction Code				
	S	R	N	D	C
Transaction code	√	√	√	√	√
Part number	√	√	√	√	√
Transaction date	√	√	1	1	1
Transaction quantity	√	√			
Part description				√	2
Vendor number				√	2
Wholesale price				√	2
Retail price				√	2
Invoice number	√	√			

Note: √ required
      1 Current date
      2 Field optional

Additional considerations:

- Transaction quantity may be negative.

- Unused fields must be blank on output record.

7. Write a program to produce personalized form letters for use in a promotional scheme for Widgets, Inc. The company is sponsoring a contest which requires that the contestants return the letter to be eligible to win. The format of the letter can be discerned from the following sample letter addressed to John K. Doe, 123 Maple Street, Anywhere, FL 32534. (Screened portions of the letter must be changed for each recipient.)

Widgets, Inc.
1000 Boulevard
Somewhere, FL 10000

John K. Doe
123 Maple Street
Anywhere, FL 32534

Dear John :

How would you like to add $10,000 to the Doe bank account? You could make this deposit to your Anywhere bank by returning this letter to Widgets, Inc., in the enclosed envelope.

Imagine the envy of your neighbors on Maple Street when they learn of your good fortune! Nothing to buy. Enter today.

Yours truly,
Widgets, Inc.

The record layout is as follows:

Positions	Content
1-10	Last name
11-20	First name
21	Middle initial
22-35	Street address
36-45	City
46-47	State
48-52	Zip

12. SEARCH PROCEDURES

12.1 ORIGIN OF TABLE DATA

Data that is to be stored in table form may originate either from within the program itself or from a data file. When table data is relatively stable, it may be useful to create the table by defining constants within the program. For example, a table of the number of days in each month, a list of the names of the days of the week, and a table showing the association between the two-character abbreviations for a state name and the full state name are examples of tables that would normally be created as constants within a program. In the unlikely event that changes must be made in any of these items, the program must be recompiled.

When table data is subject to change, however, it is preferable to store the data in a file and have the program load the data as an initialization step. In this way, changes to the table data can be made without recompiling the program. Tax tables, tables showing associations between product codes and product names or price, and lists of vendors are examples of table data that is usually somewhat volatile and should be loaded from a data file rather than built into a program as constants.

──────────── Example ────────────

Suppose you need to compute the differences in days between two dates. This computation is often needed in banking and other accounting applications. (The existence of leap years complicates matters somewhat, so for the moment, we shall assume that leap years do not exist.) One method for making this computation is to compute the Julian date for each date and then subtract one value from the other. The **Julian date** is defined as the number of days up to and including the specified date from a certain point (the beginning of the year or the beginning of the century). For example, with respect to the beginning of the year, the Julian date for January 1 is 1; February 1 is 32, and December 31 is 365. With respect to the beginning of the century, the Julian date for January 1, 1900, is 1; for January 1, 1992, it is 33,581, which can be computed by $92 \times 365 + 1$. Thus, to compute the difference between two dates such as February 1, 1993, and January 6, 1994, compute the Julian date with respect to the century for each of these dates and subtract. The Julian date for February 1, 1993, is $93 \times 365 + 31 + 1 = 33,977$; the Julian date for January 6, 1994, is $94 \times 365 + 6 = 34,316$; the difference is $34,316 - 33,977 = 339$ days.

To compute the Julian date with respect to the beginning of a year, add the number of days that have elapsed in preceding months and then add the day of the present month. For example, to compute the Julian date of March 6, it is necessary to add the number of days in January (31) and February (28) and then add 6, which represents the number of days up to and including March 6. A table like that shown in Figure 12.1, which contains the total number of days that have accumulated from the beginning of the year to the beginning of each month, will be useful in carrying out this computation.

For example, in computing the Julian date for March 6, the program will access the third element of the table and add 6.

```
DAYS-PREVIOUS-ENTRY (3) + 6 = 59 + 6 = 65.
```

Of course, this computation must be adjusted if the year in question is a leap year. The adjustment is reasonably straightforward, and we will leave leap year consideration as an exercise. Note that in this example the values are constant; barring a change in the calendar, the values will not change, so it is perfectly safe to build them into the program as a table of constants.

──────────── Example ────────────

ABC Hamburger, Inc., is a company that franchises hamburger stands all over the world. Each product sold at an ABC Hamburger location is identified by a three-character code. This code is used in all data reported to the company by franchisees; however, management reports need to have a verbal description of the item rather than the code. Stores generally sell about twenty different items at any given time. From time to time, items are discontinued and new items are introduced.

In any program that must print a description of an item, the use of a table to store the association between the code and the description will be quite useful. Because the table contents do change from time to time, it is much more efficient to load the table contents from a data file. In this way, changes in products do not necessitate recompilations of programs that must refer to the information.

A COBOL program to load this table data is shown in Program 12a. Note the use of the field NUMBER-OF-PRODUCTS. Although this item is not used in the loading process, it will be very important in subsequent uses of the table.

Note also the use of the LOAD-ERROR-FLAG. It is possible that the file may contain more records than were planned for in the design of the table. If the value of SUB is greater than TABLE-SIZE and the end of the file has not been reached, the implication is that the file contains more than TABLE-SIZE records. In this event, the value of LOAD-ERROR-FLAG becomes "YES" (see lines 72–73), and an appropriate error message is printed (lines 58–62).

12.2 DIRECT ACCESS TO TABLE DATA

Occasionally it is possible to create a table that can be accessed by the program directly—that is, by directly specifying the subscript of the desired table element, a technique called **direct access**. This is the case with the table shown in Figure 12.1. The COBOL procedure required to compute the difference between two dates specified in the form of *mmddyy* can be coded as shown in Figure 12.2.

Figure 12.1   The number of days preceding the beginning of
each month

```
01   DAY-CONSTANTS.
     03 FILLER PIC 999 VALUE 0.
     03 FILLER PIC 999 VALUE 31.
     03 FILLER PIC 999 VALUE 59.
     03 FILLER PIC 999 VALUE 90.
     03 FILLER PIC 999 VALUE 120.
     03 FILLER PIC 999 VALUE 151.
     03 FILLER PIC 999 VALUE 181.
     03 FILLER PIC 999 VALUE 212.
     03 FILLER PIC 999 VALUE 243.
     03 FILLER PIC 999 VALUE 273.
     03 FILLER PIC 999 VALUE 304.
     03 FILLER PIC 999 VALUE 334.
01   DAYS-PREVIOUS-TABLE REDEFINES DAY-CONSTANTS.
     03 DAYS-PREVIOUS-ENTRY PIC 999 OCCURS 12 TIMES.
```

Figure 12.2   Date difference computation

```
COMPUTE-DATE-DIFFERENCE.
     COMPUTE JULIAN1 =
         365 * YEAR1 +
         DAYS-PREVIOUS-ENTRY (MONTH1) +
         DAY1.
     COMPUTE JULIAN2 =
         365 * YEAR2 +
         DAYS-PREVIOUS-ENTRY (MONTH2) +
         DAY2.
     COMPUTE DIFFERENCE = JULIAN2 - JULIAN1.
```

The reference DAY-PREVIOUS-ENTRY (MONTH1) constitutes a direct access to the table. The content of the data name MONTH1 represents the position in the table that contains the desired data.

Technically, any table contains two elements: arguments and values. An **argument** is the data item used to access the table; a **value** is the data item associated with the argument in the table. The basic task of accessing data within a table is to locate the value associated with a given argument.

In the example of Figure 12.1, the arguments are 1, 2, 3, . . . , 12; the values are 0, 31, 59, . . . , 334. In Program 12a, the arguments are the product codes, and the values are the product descriptions.

In the example of Figure 12.1, there is a one-to-one correspondence between the argument and the position of the value associated with that argument. The value associated with argument 1 is stored in the first position of the table, the value associated with argument 2 is stored in the second position, and so on. This one-to-one correspondence enables direct access to the table entries and makes the explicit storage of the arguments within the table unnecessary. In Program 12a, the values are such that this direct access technique is not appropriate; the arguments are stored *along with* the values in such a way that the content of the first argument

```
 1 IDENTIFICATION DIVISION.
 2
 3 PROGRAM-ID.  TABLE-LOAD-PRO12A.
 4 AUTHOR. HORN.
 5
 6 ENVIRONMENT DIVISION.
 7
 8 CONFIGURATION SECTION.
 9
10 SOURCE-COMPUTER.
11 OBJECT-COMPUTER.
12
13 INPUT-OUTPUT SECTION.
14
15 FILE-CONTROL.
16
17     SELECT PRODUCT-ID-FILE ASSIGN TO DISK.
18
19
20 DATA DIVISION.
21
22 FILE SECTION.
23
24 FD  PRODUCT-ID-FILE
25     LABEL RECORDS ARE STANDARD.
26
27 01  PRODUCT-ID-RECORD.
28     03 PRODUCT-CODE-PI          PIC XXX.
29     03 PRODUCT-DESCRIPTION-PI    PIC X(20).
30
31 WORKING-STORAGE SECTION.
32
33 01  FLAGS.
34     02 END-OF-PT-FILE-FLAG       PIC XXX VALUE "NO".
35        88 END-OF-PT-FILE         VALUE "YES".
36     02 LOAD-ERROR-FLAG           PIC XXX VALUE "NO".
37        88 LOAD-ERROR             VALUE "YES".
38
39 01  SUBSCRIPTS.
40     02 SUB                       PIC 99 VALUE ZERO.
41
42 01  COUNTERS.
43     02 NUMBER-OF-PRODUCTS        PIC 99 VALUE ZERO.
44
45 01  CONSTANTS.
46     02 TABLE-SIZE                PIC 99 VALUE 40.
47
48 01  PRODUCT-TABLE.
49     03 PRODUCT-ENTRY OCCURS 40 TIMES.
50        05 PRODUCT-CODE-ENTRY        PIC XXX.
51        05 PRODUCT-DESCRIPTION-ENTRY PIC X(20).
52
```

Program 12a   *(concluded)*

```
53 PROCEDURE DIVISION.
54
55 1000-MAIN-CONTROL.
56
57     PERFORM 2000-INITIALIZE-TABLE.
58     IF LOAD-ERROR
59        DISPLAY "TABLE FILE CONTAINS MORE THAN "
60                TABLE-SIZE " RECORDS"
61     ELSE
62        DISPLAY "TABLE CONTAINS " NUMBER-OF-PRODUCTS " RECORDS".
63     STOP RUN.
64
65 2000-INITIALIZE-TABLE.
66
67     OPEN INPUT PRODUCT-ID-FILE.
68     PERFORM 9000-READ-PRODUCT-ID-FILE.
69     PERFORM 3000-LOAD-TABLE
70             VARYING SUB FROM 1 BY 1
71                 UNTIL SUB > TABLE-SIZE OR END-OF-PT-FILE.
72     IF SUB > TABLE-SIZE AND NOT END-OF-PT-FILE
73             MOVE "YES" TO LOAD-ERROR-FLAG.
74     CLOSE PRODUCT-ID-FILE.
75
76 3000-LOAD-TABLE.
77
78     MOVE PRODUCT-ID-RECORD TO PRODUCT-ENTRY (SUB).
79     ADD 1 TO NUMBER-OF-PRODUCTS.
80     PERFORM 9000-READ-PRODUCT-ID-FILE.
81
82 9000-READ-PRODUCT-ID-FILE.
83
84     READ PRODUCT-ID-FILE
85         AT END MOVE "YES" TO END-OF-PT-FILE-FLAG.
```

is associated with the first value, the second argument with the second value, and so on.

We will refer to these stored arguments as **table arguments** to distinguish them from a specific argument which is used to access the table at any given time. This specific argument is called an **actual argument.**

In order to access the data in the table for a given actual argument, it is necessary to find out which table argument matches the data. The location associated with the table argument is the location of the required value. For example, suppose the actual argument value is "3A2", and suppose the third element of the table contains

PRODUCT-CODE-ENTRY (3)	PRODUCT-DESCRIPTION-ENTRY (3)
3 A 2	R E G U L A R H A M B U R G E R

Since the content of PRODUCT-CODE-ENTRY (3) is equal to "3A2", the required value is contained in

    PRODUCT-DESCRIPTION-ENTRY (3)

The process of locating a desired table element when direct access is not possible is called **searching**. Various search techniques are described in the remaining sections of this chapter.

12.3 EXHAUSTIVE AND SEQUENTIAL SEARCHES

The most primitive search technique is the exhaustive search of a table. In an **exhaustive search**, the actual argument is compared to each table argument until either a matching table argument is found or the end of the table is reached.

There are two possible outcomes in any search procedure: The desired element is found, or the desired element is not present in the table. In the case of the exhaustive search procedure, an element is found when a match is made; if the end of the table is reached before a match is made, the element is not present in the table. It is necessary to arrive at a method to communicate the result of a search to the calling procedure. One method is to use a control field with the following three possible values:

```
CONTINUE
FOUND
NOT PRESENT
```

The control field is initialized to have value CONTINUE. The search procedure resets the field to FOUND or NOT PRESENT when appropriate; execution of the search procedure is repeated so long as the value of the control field is CONTINUE. Pseudocode for the exhaustive search procedure using this approach is shown in Figure 12.3.

If the table arguments are in ascending or descending sequence, it is possible to improve on the exhaustive search procedure. Note that the procedure in Figure 12.3 requires that each element of the table be examined

Figure 12.3   Exhaustive search procedure

```
Move "CONTINUE" to search flag
Move 1 to pointer
Do while search flag = "CONTINUE"
        If table argument (pointer) = actual argument
                Move "FOUND" to search flag
        Else
                Add 1 to pointer
                If pointer > table limit
                        Move "NOT PRESENT" to search flag
                End If
        End If
End Do
If search flag = "FOUND"
        Use data in table value (pointer) as appropriate
Else
        Take action appropriate when data is not present in
                table
End If
```

in case an actual argument is not present in the table. If the table arguments are in ascending sequence, it is possible to conclude that the actual argument was not found in the table the first time a table argument of greater value is encountered. Pseudocode for this modification which is called a **sequential search** is shown in Figure 12.4. When this procedure is appropriate, the expected average number of comparisons required to determine that an actual argument is not present is reduced to one-half the number of the elements in the table. The number of repetitions of the loop required to locate an element present in the table does not change.

Figure 12.4   Sequential search of a sequenced table

```
Move "CONTINUE" to search flag
Move 1 to pointer
Do while search flag = "CONTINUE"
        If table argument (pointer) = actual argument
            Move "FOUND" to search flag
        Else
            Add 1 to pointer
            If pointer > table limit
                Move "NOT PRESENT" to search flag
            Else
                If table argument (pointer) > actual argument
                    Move "NOT PRESENT" to search flag
                End If
            End If
        End If
End Do
If search flag = "FOUND"
        Use data in table value (pointer) as appropriate
Else
        Take action appropriate when data is not present in table
End If
```

12.4   PROGRAM EXAMPLE

Problem Statement

Write a program to create a purchase order register for the Amalgamated Custom Design system. Prepared input to the program comes from the PURCHASE-REQUEST-FILE, which contains one record for each item to be purchased. The PURCHASE-REQUEST-RECORD contains the supplier identification number for each item. Other information about the supplier is in the SUPPLIER-MASTER-FILE, which contains one record for each supplier. A printer spacing chart for the required report is shown in Figure 12.5.

Problem Analysis

This program must look up each supplier identification number to determine the supplier name and address for writing a detail line of the required report. In order to facilitate this process, we can load the entire SUPPLIER-MASTER-FILE into a table (assuming, of course, that the file is relatively

Figure 12.5   Printer spacing chart for Program 12b

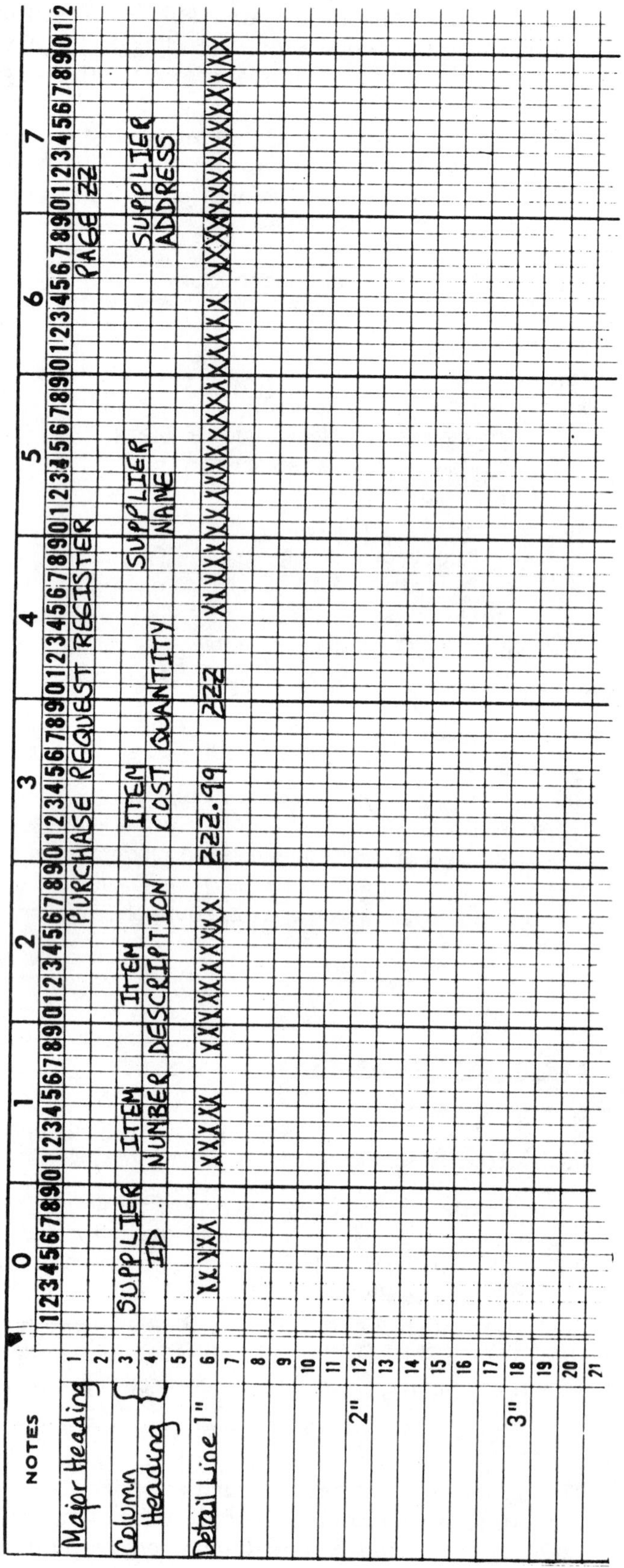

short and enough memory is available). The file is in sequence by supplier identification number, so that the program can use the sequential search of a sequenced table procedure shown in Figure 12.4. A plan for the program is shown in Figure 12.6.

Figure 12.6   Plan for sequential search program

Main control
    Load supplier master file data into table
    Open purchase request file
    Read purchase request file
    Do Process data until end of file
    Close files
    Stop
Process data
    Look up supplier ID number in table
    If found
        Move data to detail line
    Else
        Move error message to detail line
    End If
    Write detail line
    Read purchase request file

Problem Solution

The required program is shown in Program 12b; the structure diagram is shown in Figure 12.7. Sample data for the two files and the report produced by Program 12b are shown in Figure 12.8. The program loads the content of SUPPLIER-MASTER-FILE into SUPPLIER-TABLE (see lines 140–146) before processing any data from PURCHASE-REQUEST-FILE. In this way, the data is readily available as each record in PURCHASE-REQUEST-FILE is processed.

As each PURCHASE-REQUEST-RECORD is processed, the paragraph 3100-SEARCH (see lines 194–205) is used to locate the table argument that is equal to the actual argument SUPPLIER-ID-NUMBER-PRR (from PURCHASE-REQUEST-RECORD). If the value is located, the associated table values are used in creating the required output record (see lines 165–172). If the item is not located, SUPPLIER-NAME-DL and SUPPLIER-ADDRESS-DL are filled with asterisks. The paragraph 3100-SEARCH is a straightforward implementation of the sequential search procedure described in Figure 12.4.

12.5   BINARY SEARCH

The procedure shown in Figure 12.4 makes use of the sequencing of the table arguments in determining that an element is not present, but the procedure makes no use of the sequencing in locating an element that is present. The **binary search** procedure described in this section makes use of the sequential nature of the table to reduce not only the average number of comparisons required to determine that an element is *not* present but

```
 1 IDENTIFICATION DIVISION.
 2
 3 PROGRAM-ID. SEQUENTIAL-SEARCH-PRO12B.
 4 AUTHOR. HORN.
 5
 6 ENVIRONMENT DIVISION.
 7
 8 CONFIGURATION SECTION.
 9
10 SOURCE-COMPUTER.
11 OBJECT-COMPUTER.
12
13 INPUT-OUTPUT SECTION.
14
15 FILE-CONTROL.
16
17     SELECT PURCHASE-REQUEST-FILE ASSIGN TO DISK.
18
19     SELECT SUPPLIER-MASTER-FILE ASSIGN TO DISK.
20
21     SELECT PRINT-FILE ASSIGN TO PRINTER.
22
23
24 DATA DIVISION.
25
26 FILE SECTION.
27
28 FD  PURCHASE-REQUEST-FILE
29     LABEL RECORDS ARE STANDARD.
30
31 01  PURCHASE-REQUEST-RECORD.
32     03 SUPPLIER-ID-NUMBER-PRR          PIC X(5).
33     03 ITEM-NUMBER-PRR                 PIC X(5).
34     03 ITEM-DESCRIPTION-PRR            PIC X(10).
35     03 ITEM-COST-PRR                   PIC 999V99.
36     03 ORDER-QUANTITY-PRR              PIC 999.
37
38 FD  SUPPLIER-MASTER-FILE
39     LABEL RECORDS ARE STANDARD.
40
41 01  SUPPLIER-MASTER-RECORD.
42     03 SUPPLIER-ID-NUMBER-SMR          PIC X(5).
43     03 SUPPLIER-NAME-SMR               PIC X(20).
44     03 SUPPLIER-ADDRESS-SMR            PIC X(15).
45
46 FD  PRINT-FILE
47     LABEL RECORDS ARE OMITTED.
48
49 01  PRINT-RECORD                       PIC X(80).
50
```

Program 12b *(continued)*

```
51 WORKING-STORAGE SECTION.
52
53 01  FLAGS.
54      02 LOAD-ERROR-FLAG          PIC XXX VALUE "NO".
55         88 LOAD-ERROR            VALUE "YES".
56      02 SEARCH-FLAG              PIC X(11) VALUE "CONTINUE".
57         88 CONTINUE-SEARCH       VALUE "CONTINUE".
58         88 NOT-PRESENT           VALUE "NOT PRESENT".
59         88 FOUND                 VALUE "FOUND".
60      02 EOF-FLAG-SMF             PIC XXX VALUE "NO".
61         88 END-OF-SMF            VALUE "YES".
62      02 EOF-FLAG-PRF             PIC XXX VALUE "NO".
63         88 END-OF-PRF            VALUE "YES".
64
65 01  SUBSCRIPTS.
66      02 SUB                      PIC 999 VALUE ZERO.
67
68 01  COUNTERS.
69      02 NUMBER-OF-SUPPLIERS      PIC 999 VALUE ZERO.
70      02 LINE-COUNT               PIC 99 VALUE 16.
71      02 PAGE-NUMBER              PIC 99 VALUE 0.
72
73 01  CONSTANTS.
74      02 TABLE-LIMIT              PIC 999 VALUE 100.
75      02 PAGE-SIZE                PIC 99 VALUE 16.
76
77 01  SUPPLIER-TABLE.
78      03 SUPPLIER-ENTRY OCCURS 1 TO 100 TIMES
79             DEPENDING ON NUMBER-OF-SUPPLIERS.
80         05 SUPPLIER-ID-ENTRY      PIC X(5).
81         05 SUPPLIER-NAME-ENTRY    PIC X(20).
82         05 SUPPLIER-ADDRESS-ENTRY PIC X(15).
83
84 01  MAJOR-HEADING.
85      02 FILLER              PIC X(25) VALUE SPACES.
86      02 FILLER              PIC X(25) VALUE
87         "PURCHASE REQUEST REGISTER".
88      02 FILLER              PIC X(15) VALUE SPACES.
89      02 FILLER              PIC X(5) VALUE "PAGE".
90      02 PAGE-NUMBER-H       PIC ZZ.
91
92 01  COLUMN-HEADING-1.
93      02 FILLER              PIC X VALUE SPACES.
94      02 FILLER              PIC X(30) VALUE
95         "SUPPLIER   ITEM      ITEM".
96      02 FILLER              PIC X(30) VALUE
97         "ITEM          SUPPLIER".
98      02 FILLER              PIC X(20) VALUE
99         "       SUPPLIER".
100
```

Program 12b   *(continued)*

```
101 01   COLUMN-HEADING-2.
102      02 FILLER              PIC X VALUE SPACES.
103      02 FILLER                 PIC X(30) VALUE
104         "   ID     NUMBER DESCRIPTION".
105      02 FILLER                 PIC X(30) VALUE
106         "COST QUANTITY     NAME".
107      02 FILLER               PIC X(20) VALUE
108         "      ADDRESS".
109
110 01   DETAIL-LINE.
111      02 FILLER                    PIC X(3) VALUE SPACES.
112      02 SUPPLIER-ID-NUMBER-DL     PIC X(5).
113      02 FILLER                    PIC XX VALUE SPACES.
114      02 ITEM-NUMBER-DL            PIC X(5).
115      02 FILLER                    PIC XX VALUE SPACES.
116      02 ITEM-DESCRIPTION-DL       PIC X(10).
117      02 FILLER                    PIC XX VALUE SPACES.
118      02 ITEM-COST-DL              PIC ZZZ.99.
119      02 FILLER                    PIC XXX VALUE SPACES.
120      02 ORDER-QUANTITY-DL         PIC ZZZ.
121      02 FILLER                    PIC XXX VALUE SPACES.
122      02 SUPPLIER-NAME-DL          PIC X(20).
123      02 FILLER                    PIC X VALUE SPACES.
124      02 SUPPLIER-ADDRESS-DL       PIC X(15).
125
126 PROCEDURE DIVISION.
127
128 1000-MAIN-CONTROL.
129
130      PERFORM 2000-INITIALIZE-TABLE.
131      IF LOAD-ERROR
132         DISPLAY "SUPPLIER MASTER FILE IS TOO LONG"
133      ELSE
134         PERFORM 2100-INITIALIZE-REPORT
135         PERFORM 2200-PROCESS-DATA
136             UNTIL END-OF-PRF
137         PERFORM 2300-TERMINATE-REPORT.
138      STOP RUN.
139
140 2000-INITIALIZE-TABLE.
141
142      OPEN INPUT SUPPLIER-MASTER-FILE.
143      PERFORM 9000-READ-SM-FILE.
144      PERFORM 3000-LOAD-TABLE UNTIL
145             END-OF-SMF OR LOAD-ERROR.
146      CLOSE SUPPLIER-MASTER-FILE.
147
148 2100-INITIALIZE-REPORT.
149
150      OPEN INPUT PURCHASE-REQUEST-FILE
151             OUTPUT PRINT-FILE.
152      PERFORM 9100-READ-PR-FILE.
153
```

Program 12b   *(continued)*

```
154 2200-PROCESS-DATA.
155
156     MOVE "CONTINUE" TO SEARCH-FLAG.
157     MOVE 1 TO SUB.
158     PERFORM 3100-SEARCH
159         UNTIL FOUND OR NOT-PRESENT.
160     MOVE SUPPLIER-ID-NUMBER-PRR TO SUPPLIER-ID-NUMBER-DL.
161     MOVE ITEM-NUMBER-PRR        TO ITEM-NUMBER-DL.
162     MOVE ITEM-DESCRIPTION-PRR   TO ITEM-DESCRIPTION-DL.
163     MOVE ITEM-COST-PRR          TO ITEM-COST-DL.
164     MOVE ORDER-QUANTITY-PRR     TO ORDER-QUANTITY-DL.
165     IF FOUND
166        MOVE SUPPLIER-NAME-ENTRY (SUB) TO
167             SUPPLIER-NAME-DL
168        MOVE SUPPLIER-ADDRESS-ENTRY (SUB) TO
169             SUPPLIER-ADDRESS-DL
170     ELSE
171        MOVE ALL "*" TO SUPPLIER-NAME-DL
172        MOVE ALL "*" TO SUPPLIER-ADDRESS-DL.
173     IF LINE-COUNT > PAGE-SIZE OR = PAGE-SIZE
174        PERFORM 3200-WRITE-HEADING.
175     WRITE PRINT-RECORD FROM DETAIL-LINE AFTER 2.
176     ADD 2 TO LINE-COUNT.
177     PERFORM 9100-READ-PR-FILE.
178
179 2300-TERMINATE-REPORT.
180
181     CLOSE PURCHASE-REQUEST-FILE
182           PRINT-FILE.
183
184 3000-LOAD-TABLE.
185
186     ADD 1 TO NUMBER-OF-SUPPLIERS.
187     IF NUMBER-OF-SUPPLIERS > TABLE-LIMIT
188        MOVE "YES" TO LOAD-ERROR-FLAG
189     ELSE
190        MOVE SUPPLIER-MASTER-RECORD TO
191             SUPPLIER-ENTRY (NUMBER-OF-SUPPLIERS)
192        PERFORM 9000-READ-SM-FILE.
193
194 3100-SEARCH.
195
196     IF SUPPLIER-ID-ENTRY (SUB) = SUPPLIER-ID-NUMBER-PRR
197        MOVE "FOUND" TO SEARCH-FLAG
198     ELSE
199        ADD 1 TO SUB
200        IF SUB > NUMBER-OF-SUPPLIERS
201           MOVE "NOT PRESENT" TO SEARCH-FLAG
202        ELSE
203           IF SUPPLIER-ID-ENTRY (SUB) > SUPPLIER-ID-NUMBER-PRR
204               MOVE "NOT PRESENT" TO SEARCH-FLAG.
205
```

Program 12b   *(concluded)*

```
206 3200-WRITE-HEADING.
207
208     ADD 1 TO PAGE-NUMBER.
209     MOVE PAGE-NUMBER TO PAGE-NUMBER-H.
210     WRITE PRINT-RECORD FROM MAJOR-HEADING AFTER PAGE.
211     WRITE PRINT-RECORD FROM COLUMN-HEADING-1 AFTER 2.
212     WRITE PRINT-RECORD FROM COLUMN-HEADING-2 AFTER 1.
213     MOVE SPACES TO PRINT-RECORD.
214     WRITE PRINT-RECORD AFTER 1.
215     MOVE 5 TO LINE-COUNT.
216
217 9000-READ-SM-FILE.
218
219     READ SUPPLIER-MASTER-FILE
220         AT END MOVE "YES" TO EOF-FLAG-SMF.
221
222 9100-READ-PR-FILE.
223
224     READ PURCHASE-REQUEST-FILE
225         AT END MOVE "YES" TO EOF-FLAG-PRF.
```

Figure 12.7   Structure diagram for Program 12b

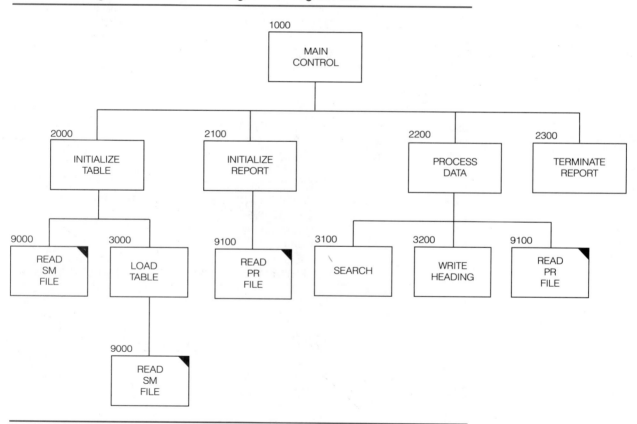

Figure 12.8   Sample execution of Program 12b

SUPPLIER-MASTER-FILE

```
11111WIDGET'S, INC.      NEW YORK, NY
22222ACME                BOSTON, MA
33333INTERNATIONAL SUPPLYLOS ANGELES, CA
34444NATIONAL SALES      LAS VEGAS, NV
```

PURCHASE-REQUEST-FILE

```
1111110000WIDGETS     01000002
3333320000GIDGETS     02200003
2222223000NUTS        00030200
0000545000BOLTS       00023200
3333311111CLOTH       00300020
3333322222WALLPAPER   01000030
2222240000BASKET      20000001
4444430000NAILS       00056004
1111110001GADGETS     00003500
```

PRINT-FILE

```
                  PURCHASE REQUEST REGISTER              PAGE  1

  SUPPLIER  ITEM       ITEM      ITEM                 SUPPLIER          SUPPLIER
     ID    NUMBER  DESCRIPTION   COST QUANTITY          NAME            ADDRESS


   11111   10000   WIDGETS      10.00     2   WIDGET'S, INC.       NEW YORK, NY

   33333   20000   GIDGETS      22.00     3   INTERNATIONAL SUPPLY LOS ANGELES, CA

   22222   23000   NUTS           .30   200   ACME                 BOSTON, MA

   00005   45000   BOLTS          .23   200   ******************** **************

   33333   11111   CLOTH         3.00    20   INTERNATIONAL SUPPLY LOS ANGELES, CA

   33333   22222   WALLPAPER    10.00    30   INTERNATIONAL SUPPLY LOS ANGELES, CA


                  PURCHASE REQUEST REGISTER              PAGE  2

  SUPPLIER  ITEM       ITEM      ITEM                 SUPPLIER          SUPPLIER
     ID    NUMBER  DESCRIPTION   COST QUANTITY          NAME            ADDRESS

   22222   40000   BASKET      200.00     1   ACME                 BOSTON, MA

   44444   30000   NAILS          .56     4   ******************** **************

   11111   10001   GADGETS        .03   500   WIDGET'S, INC.       NEW YORK, NY
```

also the number of comparisons required to locate an element that *is* present in the table.

The idea behind the binary search is employed intuitively by people playing a game in which they have to guess a number. In response to each guess, the player who knows the number responds "higher" or "lower" or "you got it," depending on the value of the target number and the value of the guess. The optimum strategy for players of this game is to begin at the middle of the range. For example, if the range is known to be from 1 to 100, the initial guess would be 50. If the response to this guess is "higher," the player knows that the target value is in the range 51 to 100; if the response is "lower," the target value is in the range 1 to 49. In either case, the next guess should be at the halfway point in the range. With successive guesses, the width of the range containing the unknown value is reduced by one-half until finally the target value is found.

In order to apply this idea to searching for an element in a table, we will need two pointers, HIGH and LOW, which will point to the upper and lower limits of the segment of the table containing the desired value. At each repetition of the search procedure, the midpoint of this range (MID) is computed. (The fraction resulting from the computation MID = (HIGH + LOW)/2 is dropped.) The actual argument is then compared to the table argument at location MID. If the arguments are equal, the search terminates. If the actual argument is less than the table argument at MID, the procedure is repeated with the value of MID replacing the value of HIGH. If the actual argument is greater than the table argument at location MID, the procedure is repeated, with the value of MID replacing the value of LOW. Pseudocode for this procedure is shown in Figure 12.9; examples of the execution of this procedure are shown in Figures 12.10 and 12.11.

Figure 12.9   Binary search procedure

```
Low = 0
High = table limit + 1
Move "CONTINUE" to search flag
Do while search flag = "CONTINUE"
        Mid = (low + high) / 2
        If table argument (mid) = actual argument
            Move "FOUND" to search flag
        Else
            If table argument (mid) < actual argument
                Move mid to low
            Else
                Move mid to high
            End If
            If high − low = 1
                Move "NOT PRESENT" to search flag
            End If
        End If
End Do
If search flag = "FOUND"
        Use data in table value (mid) as appropriate
Else
        Take action appropriate when data is not present in table
End If
```

Figure 12.10 Binary search example for data present in table

Table Argument

(1)	4
(2)	9
(3)	17
(4)	25
(5)	30
(6)	45
(7)	70
(8)	100
(9)	105
(10)	110

Actual Argument

17

Repetition	LOW	Values of HIGH	MID	Comments
1	0	11	5	TABLE-ARGUMENT (5) > 17
2	0	5	2	TABLE-ARGUMENT (2) < 17
3	2	5	3	TABLE-ARGUMENT (3) = 17 Search is completed

Figure 12.11 Binary search example for data not present in table

Table Argument

(1)	4
(2)	9
(3)	17
(4)	25
(5)	30
(6)	45
(7)	70
(8)	100
(9)	105
(10)	110

Actual Argument

104

Repetition	LOW	Values of HIGH	MID	Comments
1	0	11	5	TABLE-ARGUMENT (5) < 104
2	5	11	8	TABLE-ARGUMENT (8) < 104
3	8	11	9	TABLE-ARGUMENT (9) > 104
4	8	9	8	TABLE-ARGUMENT (8) > 104 HIGH – LOW = 1 therefore element is not in table

The maximum number of repetitions required for termination of this procedure is dependent on the size of the table, as shown in Figure 12.12. In general, it can be shown that, in the worst case, the number of repetitions required for termination of a binary search of a table of n elements is the smallest integer greater than $\log_2 n$. For example, if $n = 8$, $\log_2 8 = 3$ (since $2^3 = 8$). The smallest integer greater than 3 is 4; therefore, if $n = 8$, 4 repetitions would be required in the worst possible case for termination of the binary search.

Figure 12.12   Worst case behavior for the binary search

Table Size n	$LOG_2 n$	Maximum Repetitions	Table Size n	$LOG_2 n$	Maximum Repetitions
1	0	1	19	4.24793	5
2	1	2	.	.	.
3	1.58496	2	.	.	.
4	2	3	.	.	.
5	2.32193	3	.	.	.
6	2.58496	3	29	4.85798	5
7	2.80736	3	30	4.90689	5
8	3	4	31	4.9542	5
9	3.16993	4	32	5	6
10	3.32193	4	33	5.04439	6
11	3.45943	4	34	5.08746	6
12	3.58496	4	35	5.12928	6
13	3.70044	4	.	.	.
14	3.80736	4	.	.	.
15	3.90689	4	61	5.93074	6
16	4	5	62	5.9542	6
17	4.08746	5	63	5.97728	6
18	4.16993	5	64	6	7

For a given actual argument, of course, the procedure may terminate in fewer repetitions than the maximum number required. The average behavior will be a little better than the worst case behavior, but not dramatically so, as with the procedure for sequential search of a sequenced table.

―――― Example ――――

Program 12c is the same as Program 12b, except that a binary search rather than a sequential search is implemented. The paragraph 3100-SEARCH of Program 12b is replaced by a straightforward implementation of the binary search procedure of Figure 12.9.

12.6 RANDOMIZED TABLES

Although the binary search technique is very good for sequenced tables, the expected number of comparisons required to locate a desired entry is still greater than 1, which is, of course, the ideal. A carefully constructed **randomized table** makes it possible to approach this ideal, even when the

Program 12c

```
  1 IDENTIFICATION DIVISION.
  2
  3 PROGRAM-ID. BINARY-SEARCH-PRO12C.
  .
  .
  .
 53 01   FLAGS.
 54       02 LOAD-ERROR-FLAG          PIC XXX VALUE "NO".
 55          88 LOAD-ERROR            VALUE "YES".
 56       02 SEARCH-FLAG              PIC X(11) VALUE "CONTINUE".
 57          88 CONTINUE-SEARCH       VALUE "CONTINUE".
 58          88 NOT-PRESENT           VALUE "NOT PRESENT".
 59          88 FOUND                 VALUE "FOUND".
 60       02 EOF-FLAG-SMF             PIC XXX VALUE "NO".
 61          88 END-OF-SMF            VALUE "YES".
 62       02 EOF-FLAG-PRF             PIC XXX VALUE "NO".
 63          88 END-OF-PRF            VALUE "YES".
 64
 65 01   SUBSCRIPTS.
 66       02 SUB                      PIC 999 VALUE ZERO.
 67       02 HI                       PIC 999 VALUE ZERO.
 68       02 LO                       PIC 999 VALUE ZERO.
  .
  .
  .
156 2200-PROCESS-DATA.
157
158       MOVE ZERO TO LO.
159       ADD 1 NUMBER-OF-SUPPLIERS GIVING HI.
160       MOVE "CONTINUE" TO SEARCH-FLAG.
161       PERFORM 3100-SEARCH UNTIL
162              FOUND OR NOT-PRESENT.
  .
  .
  .
197 3100-SEARCH.
198
199       COMPUTE SUB = (LO + HI) / 2.
200       IF SUPPLIER-ID-ENTRY (SUB) = SUPPLIER-ID-NUMBER-PRR
201          MOVE "FOUND" TO SEARCH-FLAG
202       ELSE
203          PERFORM 4000-CONTINUE-SEARCH.
  .
  .
  .
216 4000-CONTINUE-SEARCH.
217
218       IF SUPPLIER-ID-ENTRY (SUB) < SUPPLIER-ID-NUMBER-PRR
219          MOVE SUB TO LO
220       ELSE
221          MOVE SUB TO HI.
222       IF HI - LO = 1
223          MOVE "NOT PRESENT" TO SEARCH-FLAG.
  .
  .
  .
```

nature of the table arguments makes a direct-access technique impossible.

The idea behind a randomized table is to place the table argument and its associated table values in a location computed from the table argument. The computational formula used for this purpose is called a **hash function**. The table arguments and values will generally be scattered throughout the table space in a random fashion. In order to access the table, the hash function is applied to the actual argument. If the actual argument matches the table argument at the computed location, the procedure terminates.

A problem that arises in the implementation of this procedure is the possible existence of two or more table arguments (called **synonyms**) that yield the same location value when the hash function is applied. In the loading process, an instance of this sort is called a **collision**. Collisions are unavoidable because the hash function usually does not yield a one-to-one correspondence between table arguments and table locations. A collision can be handled by placing the table argument in another unused table location determined systematically from the location originally computed. A common technique is to search the table sequentially until an unused table element is found and then to place the table argument and associated value in that location.

The existence of synonyms makes the search procedure somewhat more complicated. If the table argument is not equal to the actual argument at the location "predicted" by the hash function, it is necessary to use the same procedure that was used to handle collisions until either a table argument that matches the actual argument is found or an unused element is found. In the latter instance, we conclude that the desired argument is not present in the table.

In order to optimize access time with a randomized table, it is important to keep the number of synonyms to a minimum. Two considerations are important in this regard: table size and hash function. The table size must be larger than the amount of data to be stored. It has been shown experimentally that the number of collisions begins to increase dramatically when the table is two-thirds full. Even if the table space is quite large, a poorly chosen hash function can reduce the efficiency of this technique. A good hash function must scatter the table elements in a random fashion throughout the table space. A function that tends to favor one area or that results in tight clusters of elements in one or more areas is not desirable.

A great deal of research has been done on hash functions. Although there is no universally "best" function, the following procedure is quite good in a variety of situations. For a table of size n, compute the remainder after dividing the argument by n. The hash function value is the remainder plus 1.

It can be shown that this function results in best performance when n is a prime number. (A **prime number** is one that is divisible only by one and by itself. The first few primes are 2, 3, 5, 7, 11, 13, 17, 19, 23, 29, 31, and so on.) Note that this function always yields values in the range 1, 2, . . . , n since the possible values of the remainders are 0, 1, 2, . . . , $(n - 1)$. For example, suppose the table size is 17, and we want to compute the hash function for argument 45. First, compute the remainder after dividing 45 by 17:

$$
\begin{array}{r}
2 \ r\,11 \\
17\overline{)45} \\
\underline{34} \\
11
\end{array}
$$

Then, add 1 (11 + 1 = 12). Twelve is the hash function value for argument 45.

A procedure for loading data into a randomized table is shown in Figure 12.13. Note that it is necessary for the program to be able to determine whether a table element is in use or not. This can be accomplished by initializing the entire table space to some constant (for example, SPACES or ZEROS) before beginning the loading process. Note also that the table is, in a sense, circular: The element following the last table element is the first one. This is necessary in order to handle collisions with the last element in the table.

Figure 12.13   Loading a randomized table

```
L = hash function (argument)
Move "CONTINUE" to search flag
Move L to initial
Do while search flag = "CONTINUE"
        If table location L is unused
                Move data to table location L
                Move "FINISH" to search flag
        Else
                L = L + 1
                If L > table limit
                    L = 1
                End If
                If L = initial
                        Move "ERROR" to search flag
                End If
        End If
End Do
```

A procedure for searching for data in a randomized table is shown in Figure 12.14. Note that this procedure is quite similar to the loading procedure, with the added facility for locating a TABLE-ARGUMENT equal to an ACTUAL-ARGUMENT.

In both the procedure for loading elements and the procedure for searching for elements in a randomized table, it is necessary to make provision for the possibility that the table may be full. This task is accomplished by initializing a variable to contain the initial value computed for the location of the element. The procedure then proceeds with the search process which may involve examination of successive table elements. If the procedure ever encounters the initial value again, this implies that all of the table elements have been examined and, therefore, the table is full.

—————— Example ——————

Program 12d performs the same functions as Programs 12b and 12c, except that a randomized table is used. The paragraph 2000-INITIALIZE-TABLE of Program 12c is modified to perform two functions: (1) to mark all of the positions of the table as unused by moving spaces to each element and (2) to load data into the table. The paragraph 3000-LOAD-TABLE is an implementation of the procedure shown in Figure 12.13. In this case, the table limit is 97 (a prime number).

Note how Program 12d incorporates the logic required to terminate the loading of the table when the table is full. This task is accomplished by saving the initial value of SUB (in INITIAL-SUB at line 198). Then, after each new value of SUB is computed, it is tested against INITIAL-SUB (see line 237). If the value of SUB ever becomes the same as INITIAL-SUB before a location is found for the table element, the table is full and the procedure must terminate. The paragraph 3100-SEARCH of Program 12c is replaced by a direct implementation of the procedure shown in Figure 12.14. It is not necessary to repeat the process of checking for a full table in searching since the check was made at the time the table was loaded.

Figure 12.14   Searching a randomized table

```
L = hash function (actual argument)
Move "CONTINUE" to search flag
Move L to initial
Do while search flag = "CONTINUE"
        If table argument at location L = actual argument
                Move "FOUND" to search flag
        Else
                If table location L is unused
                        Move "NOT PRESENT" to search flag
                Else
                        L = L + 1
                        If L > table limit
                          L = 1
                        End If
                        If L = initial
                            Move "ERROR" to search flag
                        End If
                End If
        End If
End Do
If search flag = "FOUND"
        Use data from table value (L) as appropriate
Else
        Take action appropriate when data is not present in table
End If
```

12.7   COMPARISON OF TABLE ORGANIZATION AND SEARCH TECHNIQUES

Five table organization and search techniques have been described in this chapter:

- direct access
- exhaustive search
- sequential search of a sequenced table
- binary search
- randomized tables

Program 12d

```
  1 IDENTIFICATION DIVISION.
  2
  3 PROGRAM-ID. RANDOMIZED-TABLE-PRO12D.
    .
    .
    .
 77 01  COMPUTED-VALUES.
 78     02 QUOT                        PIC 999 VALUE ZERO.
    .
    .
    .
146 2000-INITIALIZE-TABLE.
147
148     MOVE SPACES TO SUPPLIER-TABLE.
149     OPEN INPUT SUPPLIER-MASTER-FILE.
150     PERFORM 9000-READ-SM-FILE.
151     PERFORM 3000-LOAD-TABLE UNTIL
152            END-OF-SMF OR LOAD-ERROR.
153     CLOSE SUPPLIER-MASTER-FILE.
    .
    .
    .
161 2200-PROCESS-DATA.
162
163     DIVIDE SUPPLIER-ID-NUMBER-PRR-NUM BY TABLE-LIMIT
164            GIVING QUOT REMAINDER SUB.
165     ADD 1 TO SUB.
166     MOVE "CONTINUE" TO SEARCH-FLAG.
167     PERFORM 3100-SEARCH
168            UNTIL FOUND OR NOT-PRESENT.
    .
    .
    .
193 3000-LOAD-TABLE.
194
195     DIVIDE SUPPLIER-ID-NUMBER-SMR-NUM BY TABLE-LIMIT
196            GIVING QUOT REMAINDER SUB.
197     ADD 1 TO SUB.
198     MOVE SUB TO INITIAL-SUB.
199     MOVE "CONTINUE" TO LOAD-FLAG.
200     PERFORM 4000-LOCATE-ELEMENT
201            UNTIL FINISH OR LOAD-ERROR.
202     IF FINISH
203        MOVE SUPPLIER-MASTER-RECORD TO SUPPLIER-ENTRY (SUB)
204        PERFORM 9000-READ-SM-FILE.
205
206 3100-SEARCH.
207
208     IF SUPPLIER-ID-ENTRY (SUB) = SUPPLIER-ID-NUMBER-PRR
209        MOVE "FOUND" TO SEARCH-FLAG
210     ELSE
211        IF SUPPLIER-ID-ENTRY (SUB) = SPACES
212           MOVE "NOT PRESENT" TO SEARCH-FLAG
213        ELSE
214           ADD 1 TO SUB
215           IF SUB > TABLE-LIMIT
216              MOVE 1 TO SUB.
```

Program 12d   *(concluded)*

```
      .
      .
      .
      .
229 4000-LOCATE-ELEMENT.
230
231     IF SUPPLIER-ID-ENTRY (SUB) = SPACES
232         MOVE "FINISH" TO LOAD-FLAG
233     ELSE
234         ADD 1 TO SUB
235         IF SUB > TABLE-LIMIT
236             MOVE 1 TO SUB.
237     IF NOT FINISH AND SUB = INITIAL-SUB
238         MOVE "ERROR" TO LOAD-FLAG.
      .
      .
      .
      .
```

These methods can be compared in terms of their relative capabilities and efficiency. In general, a programmer should use the most efficient method appropriate for a given program. Figure 12.15 gives a summary of relevant information with respect to each of these methods and can be used to help make the best decision. Figure 12.16 shows a graph of the average behavior expected of the five techniques in determining that an argument is not present in the table.

Analysis of Figures 12.15 and 12.16 leads to the following conclusions:

- The direct access technique is the most efficient and is the method of choice when appropriate.

- If data is sequenced and must remain so, the binary search is the most efficient method in all respects and is the method of choice.

- If sufficient memory is available and fast table access is important, a randomized table is the best method.

- An exhaustive search is the least efficient method and should be used only if no other method is appropriate.

12.8   INDEX VARIABLES AND THE SET STATEMENT

When manipulating tables, it is possible to use any data item with an appropriate value as a subscript; up to now we have handled array references in this way. It is possible, however, to create data items, called **index variables,** with a form that is especially suited for use as a subscript. The advantage is twofold: It typically saves execution time, and it serves as a means of documenting the intended purpose of a variable.

If USAGE INDEX is specified when a data item is defined, then the compiler chooses an appropriate data type for the item and places further restrictions on the way in which the program can manipulate the item. (We will discuss these restrictions shortly.) For example, consider the following DATA DIVISION entry:

Figure 12.15 Comparison of table organization/search techniques for a table of *n* elements

Method	Worst Case Number Repetitions		Expected Average Number of Repetitions		Considerations
	Find an argument	*Argument not present*	*Find an argument*	*Argument not present*	
Direct Access	1	1	1	1	Requires a one-to-one correspondence between table arguments and positions.
Exhaustive Search	n	n	$n/2$	n	Least efficient technique but requires minimum storage and no sequencing of data.
Sequential Search	n	n	$n/2$	$n/2$	Requires sequenced table arguments.
Binary Search	smallest integer greater than $\log_2 n$	smallest integer greater than $\log_2 n$	less than $\log_2 n$	less than $\log_2 n$	Requires sequenced table arguments.
Randomized Table	$n*$	$n*$	close to 1	close to 1	Requires more table space than actual table size. Efficiency depends on fullness and hash function. Sequence of data is destroyed.

* Worst case behavior will result when the table is full.

```
01   INDX PIC 99 USAGE IS INDEX.
```

The data item INDX is declared as data type INDEX.

A second way in which an item can be declared with this data type is by using the INDEXED BY clause when defining a table. For example, consider the table declared in Program 12a. An alternative specification for this table is

```
01   PRODUCT-TABLE.
     03 PRODUCT-ENTRY OCCURS 40 TIMES
                      INDEXED BY TABLE-INDEX.
        05...
```

This program specification is sufficient to declare the variable TABLE-INDEX as a data item with INDEX data type. The restrictions on the items INDX and TABLE-INDEX would be similar. Note that specifying an INDEX-type item in one of these two ways is mutually exclusive. That is, the program either declares the item in the usual fashion as an elementary item with USAGE INDEX, or the item is declared in an INDEXED BY clause. It is incorrect to specify an item in both ways; in fact, the compiler will treat such a specification as an error.

A basic limitation of any item declared with type INDEX is that it cannot be used as the receiving field in any arithmetic statement (ADD, SUBTRACT, MULTIPLY, DIVIDE, or COMPUTE). An item of type INDEX can

Figure 12.16   Expected average number of repetitions in
determining that an argument is not present

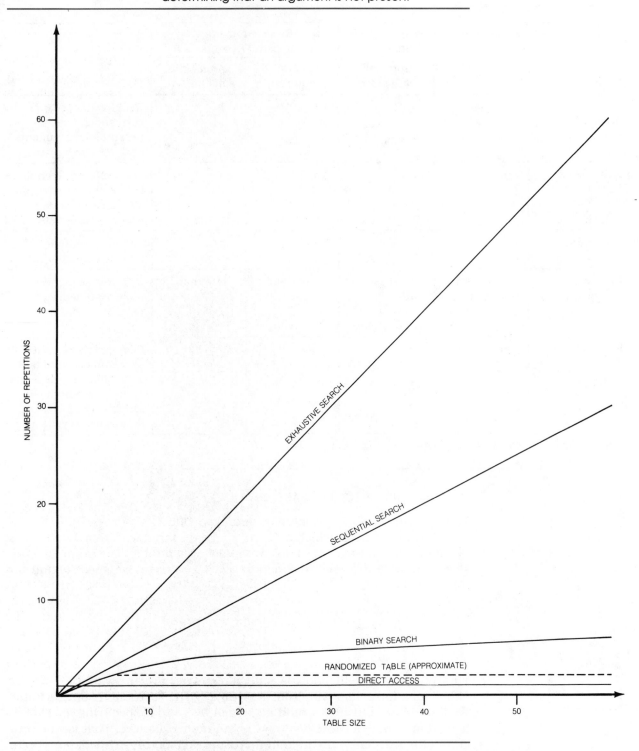

be used as a subscript, which is its intended purpose, or in a condition or
in an arithmetic expression used to compute the value of some other
variable.

Figure 12.17   General form of the SET/TO statement

<u>SET</u> index-name...<u>TO</u> value.

The SET/TO statement is used to establish an initial value for an index variable. A general form of this statement is shown in Figure 12.17. Given the variables INDX and TABLE-INDEX defined above, the following statements would set the value of INDX to 2 and the value of TABLE-INDEX to 1:

```
SET INDX TO 2.
SET TABLE-INDEX TO 1.
```

To change the value of an index variable, the SET/UP/DOWN statement with the general form shown in Figure 12.18 is used. The SET/UP statement increases the value of an index variable by a specified amount; the SET/DOWN statement decreases the index variable in a similar fashion. For example, if INDX and TABLE-INDEX are initialized to 2 and 1 as in the previous example, the following statements would increase TABLE-INDEX by 1 and decrease INDX by 1:

```
SET INDX DOWN BY 1.
SET TABLE-INDEX UP BY 1.
```

After execution of these statements, the value of INDX will be 1, and the value of TABLE-INDEX will be 2.

Figure 12.18   General form of the SET/UP/DOWN statement

$$\underline{SET} \text{ index-name. . .} \left\{ \begin{array}{c} \underline{UP} \text{ BY} \\ \underline{DOWN} \text{ BY} \end{array} \right\} \text{ value.}$$

──────── **Example** ────────

Recall that Program 12a loads the content of a file (PRODUCT-ID-FILE) into a table (PRODUCT-TABLE). Program 12e is a revision of this program but uses an index variable (TABLE-INDEX) and the SET statement to manipulate the index variable. At line 67, the SET/TO statement initializes the value of TABLE-INDEX to 1. After loading an element into the table, the SET/UP statement at line 78 increases the value of TABLE-INDEX by 1.

One might wonder why we chose to initialize TABLE-INDEX to 1 rather than to 0. The reason is a somewhat subtle but nevertheless important restriction placed on an index variable declared by an INDEXED BY clause. The value of such a variable must always be a valid subscript for the table. In the case of Program 12e, the value of TABLE-INDEX must always be in the range 1 to 40. The statement

```
SET TABLE-INDEX TO 0.
```

will be treated as an error. Note that this restriction does not apply to an index variable created by the USAGE clause.

```
 1 IDENTIFICATION DIVISION.
 2
 3 PROGRAM-ID.   TABLE-LOAD-ALT-PRO12E.
 .
 .
 .
45 01  PRODUCT-TABLE.
46     03 PRODUCT-ENTRY OCCURS 40 TIMES
47                      INDEXED BY TABLE-INDEX.
48        05 PRODUCT-CODE-ENTRY        PIC XXX.
49        05 PRODUCT-DESCRIPTION-ENTRY PIC X(20).
 .
 .
63 2000-INITIALIZE-TABLE.
64
65     OPEN INPUT PRODUCT-ID-FILE.
66     PERFORM 9000-READ-PRODUCT-ID-FILE.
67     SET TABLE-INDEX TO 1.
68     PERFORM 3000-LOAD-TABLE
69            UNTIL TABLE-INDEX > TABLE-SIZE OR END-OF-PT-FILE.
70     IF TABLE-INDEX > TABLE-SIZE AND NOT END-OF-PT-FILE
71            MOVE "YES" TO LOAD-ERROR-FLAG.
72     CLOSE PRODUCT-ID-FILE.
73
74 3000-LOAD-TABLE.
75
76     ADD 1 TO NUMBER-OF-PRODUCTS.
77     MOVE PRODUCT-ID-RECORD TO PRODUCT-ENTRY (TABLE-INDEX).
78     SET TABLE-INDEX UP BY 1.
79     PERFORM 9000-READ-PRODUCT-ID-FILE.
 .
 .
 .
```

12.9 SEARCH AND SEARCH ALL

Many versions of COBOL include the SEARCH ALL and SEARCH statements to perform searching. In order to use these statements, you must include the INDEXED and KEY clauses in the OCCURS clause, which is used to define the table. The general form of the OCCURS clause with these options is shown in Figure 12.19.

The data names specified in the KEY clause must be data fields within the table itself. The table must be organized into ASCENDING or DESCEND-ING sequence based on the key fields. The index-name used in the INDEXED clause will be used by the SEARCH statement in its search of the table. The index-name must not be defined elsewhere in the program, since further definition of this index-name will be handled by the compiler automatically.

For example, the following program segment sets up PRODUCT-TABLE defined in Program 12e for application of the SEARCH verb:

Figure 12.19 General form of the OCCURS clause with the KEY
and INDEXED options

$$\underline{\text{OCCURS}} \left\{ \begin{array}{l} \text{integer-1 } \underline{\text{TO}} \text{ integer-2 TIMES } \underline{\text{DEPENDING}} \text{ ON data-name-1} \\ \text{integer-2 } \underline{\text{TIMES}} \end{array} \right\}$$

$$\left[\left\{ \begin{array}{l} \underline{\text{ASCENDING}} \\ \underline{\text{DESCENDING}} \end{array} \right\} \qquad \text{KEY IS data-name-2 . . .} \right]$$

$$[\underline{\text{INDEXED}} \text{ BY index-name}]$$

```
01   PRODUCT-TABLE
     03 PRODUCT-ENTRY OCCURS 40 TIMES
              ASCENDING KEY IS PRODUCT-CODE-ENTRY
              INDEXED BY TABLE-INDEX.
```

The SEARCH ALL statement is used to perform a search of the table
entries until a desired condition has been satisfied. The general form of the
SEARCH ALL statement is shown in Figure 12.20. Although the ANSI specifications for COBOL do not specify the type of procedure to be used in
implementing SEARCH ALL, most compilers use a binary search which is
the most efficient procedure available.

The conditions specified in the WHEN clause are tested for successive
values of the table index. When the condition is satisfied, the statement
following the condition is executed. The condition must test for equality of
the key field to some value or values. If the system searches the entire
table without finding the condition to be satisfied, the statement in the AT
END clause is executed. The programmer need not initialize or modify the
table index variable; the SEARCH ALL statement performs these tasks automatically. For example, the search procedure to locate data in PRODUCT-
TABLE, defined previously, could be coded as follows:

```
SEARCH ALL PRODUCT-ENTRY
      AT END MOVE "INVALID PRODUCT"
          TO PRODUCT-DESCRIPTION
      WHEN PRODUCT-CODE-ENTRY (TABLE-INDEX) = PRODUCT-NO
          MOVE PRODUCT-DESCRIPTION-ENTRY (TABLE-INDEX)
              TO PRODUCT-DESCRIPTION.
```

Figure 12.20 General form of the SEARCH ALL statement

$$\underline{\text{SEARCH}} \ \underline{\text{ALL}} \qquad \text{data-name-1} \quad [\text{AT } \underline{\text{END}} \text{ statement-1}]$$

$$\underline{\text{WHEN}} \left\{ \begin{array}{l} \text{data-name-2} \quad \left\{ \begin{array}{l} \text{IS } \underline{\text{EQUAL}} \text{ TO} \\ \text{IS =} \end{array} \right\} \text{ value-1} \\ \text{condition-name-1} \end{array} \right\}$$

$$\left[\underline{\text{AND}} \left\{ \begin{array}{l} \text{data-name-3} \quad \left\{ \begin{array}{l} \text{IS } \underline{\text{EQUAL}} \text{ TO} \\ \text{IS =} \end{array} \right\} \text{ value-2} \\ \text{condition-name-2} \end{array} \right\} \right] \quad \text{. . .}$$

$$\left\{ \begin{array}{l} \text{statement-2} \\ \underline{\text{NEXT}} \ \underline{\text{SENTENCE}} \end{array} \right\}$$

A flowchart showing how the general SEARCH ALL statement is executed is shown in Figure 12.21, and the SEARCH ALL example above is illustrated in the flowchart shown in Figure 12.22.

It is convenient to use the table index (the variable specified in the INDEXED BY clause) when referencing elements of the table for purposes of placing data in the table or modifying data in the table. However, remember that the index item cannot be modified by the usual arithmetic operation statements used for other COBOL data items.

—————————— Example ——————————

Program 12f performs the same task as Programs 12b through 12d but uses the SEARCH ALL verb instead of a programmer-written search procedure.

Program 12f

```
 1 IDENTIFICATION DIVISION.
 2
 3 PROGRAM-ID. SEARCH-ALL-PRO12F.
 .
 .
 .
73 01  SUPPLIER-TABLE.
74     03 SUPPLIER-ENTRY OCCURS 1 TO 100 TIMES
75            DEPENDING ON NUMBER-OF-SUPPLIERS
76            ASCENDING KEY IS SUPPLIER-ID-ENTRY
77            INDEXED BY INDX.
78        05 SUPPLIER-ID-ENTRY      PIC X(5).
79        05 SUPPLIER-NAME-ENTRY    PIC X(20).
80        05 SUPPLIER-ADDRESS-ENTRY PIC X(15).
 .
 .
 .
152 2200-PROCESS-DATA.
153
154     SEARCH ALL SUPPLIER-ENTRY
155        AT END
156            MOVE "NOT PRESENT" TO SEARCH-FLAG
157        WHEN SUPPLIER-ID-ENTRY (INDX) = SUPPLIER-ID-NUMBER-PRR
158            MOVE "FOUND" TO SEARCH-FLAG.
 .
 .
 .
```

In general, the SEARCH ALL verb results in the simplest program, but remember that SEARCH ALL is valid only when a table is sequential and only when one matching entry is sought. If either of these conditions is not present, then you may use the SEARCH verb (described next), or you may write your own search procedure.

The general form of the SEARCH statement is shown in Figure 12.23. The SEARCH statement is similar in many respects to the SEARCH ALL statement. There is one essential difference, however: The SEARCH ALL statement includes a provision to initialize the index automatically, whereas when using the SEARCH verb, the programmer must initialize the

Figure 12.21   Flowchart of SEARCH ALL

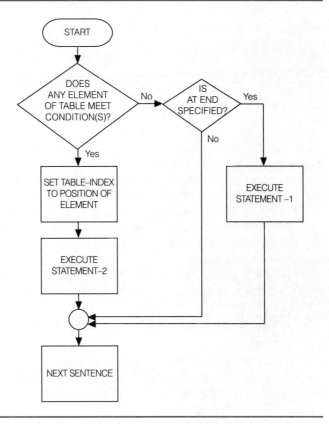

Figure 12.22   Flowchart of SEARCH ALL example

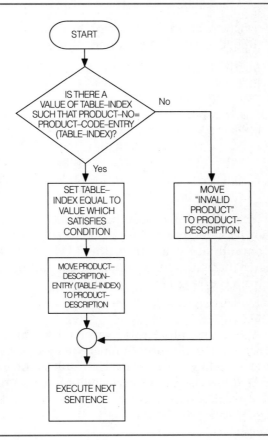

Figure 12.23　　General form of the SEARCH statement

```
SEARCH data-name    [AT END statement-1]
     {WHEN condition-1  {statement-2      }}
                        {NEXT SENTENCE    }} . . .
```

index prior to execution of the SEARCH statement. Another difference between the SEARCH ALL and SEARCH statements is that, in SEARCH statements, conditions may involve inequalities as well as equalities. As with the SEARCH ALL statement, the SEARCH statement provides for automatic incrementing of the index and automatic execution of statements in the AT END clause if the value of the index variable exceeds the number of elements in the table. Figure 12.24 illustrates a flowchart of the execution of the SEARCH statement.

For example, let's use the SEARCH statement to look up the tax deduction permitted by the IRS for a gasoline tax at five cents per gallon (Figure 12.25).

The program segment required to set up the table is

```
01  TAX-TABLE.
    02 TAX-ENTRY OCCURS 18 TIMES
       ASCENDING KEY IS BREAK-MILEAGE
       INDEXED BY TAX-TABLE-INDEX.
       03 LOW-MILEAGE    PIC 9(5).
       03 BREAK-MILEAGE  PIC 9(5).
       03 DEDUCTION-AMT   PIC 9(3).
```

The program segment required to compute the deduction allowed (MILEAGE-DEDUCTION) for the number of miles driven (MILEAGE) is

```
DIVIDE MILEAGE BY 20000 GIVING MULTIPLIER
    REMAINDER LOOK-UP-FACTOR.
SET TAX-TABLE-INDEX TO 1.
SEARCH TAX-ENTRY
    WHEN (LOOK-UP-FACTOR > LOW-MILEAGE (TAX-TABLE-INDEX)
       OR LOOK-UP-FACTOR = LOW-MILEAGE (TAX-TABLE-INDEX))
       AND LOOK-UP-FACTOR < BREAK-MILEAGE (TAX-TABLE-INDEX)
    COMPUTE MILEAGE-DEDUCTION = MULTIPLIER * 83 +
               DEDUCTION-AMOUNT (TAX-TABLE-INDEX).
```

Note that when MILEAGE is less than 20,000, the value of MULTIPLIER will be zero, so the value of MILEAGE-DEDUCTION will be computed as 0 * 83 plus the appropriate value from the TAX-TABLE. When MILEAGE has a value greater than 20,000, an appropriate multiple of 83 will be added to the value from the TAX-TABLE.

―――――――― Example ――――――――

Program 12g is equivalent to Programs 12b through 12d but uses the SEARCH verb instead of a programmer-written procedure. Note the importance of the SET statement at line 154. Unless the index variable is initialized, the SEARCH verb will not perform its function properly.

Figure 12.24   Flowchart of the SEARCH STATEMENT

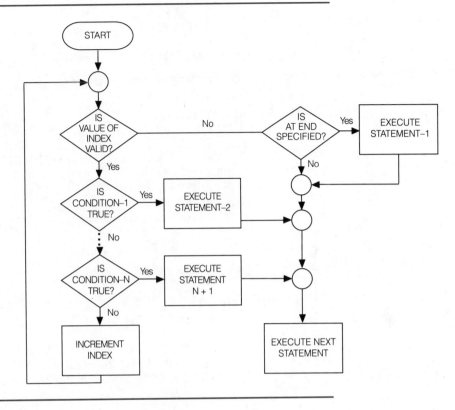

Figure 12.25   Deduction table

Miles Driven	Deduction Amount
Under 3,000	$ 8
3,000 under 4,000	14
4,000 under 5,000	19
5,000 under 6,000	23
6,000 under 7,000	27
7,000 under 8,000	31
8,000 under 9,000	35
9,000 under 10,000	39
10,000 under 11,000 . . .	43
11,000 under 12,000 . . .	48
12,000 under 13,000 . . .	51
13,000 under 14,000 . . .	56
14,000 under 15,000 . . .	60
15,000 under 16,000 . . .	64
16,000 under 17,000 . . .	68
17,000 under 18,000 . . .	72
18,000 under 19,000 . . .	76
19,000 under 20,000 . . .	81
20,000*	83

*For over 20,000 miles, use table amounts for total miles driven. For example, for 25,000 miles, add the deduction for 5,000 to the deduction for 20,000 miles.

Program 12g

```
  1 IDENTIFICATION DIVISION.
  2
  3 PROGRAM-ID. SEARCH-SET-EXAMPLE-PRO12G.
    .
    .
    .
 73 01   SUPPLIER-TABLE.
 74      03 SUPPLIER-ENTRY OCCURS 1 TO 100 TIMES
 75             DEPENDING ON NUMBER-OF-SUPPLIERS
 76             ASCENDING KEY IS SUPPLIER-ID-ENTRY
 77             INDEXED BY INDX.
 78        05 SUPPLIER-ID-ENTRY      PIC X(5).
 79        05 SUPPLIER-NAME-ENTRY    PIC X(20).
 80        05 SUPPLIER-ADDRESS-ENTRY PIC X(15).
    .
    .
    .
152 2200-PROCESS-DATA.
153
154    SET INDX TO 1.
155    SEARCH SUPPLIER-ENTRY
156       AT END
157             MOVE "NOT PRESENT" TO SEARCH-FLAG
158       WHEN SUPPLIER-ID-NUMBER-PRR = SUPPLIER-ID-ENTRY (INDX)
159             MOVE "FOUND" TO SEARCH-FLAG.
    .
    .
    .
```

12.10   DEBUG CLINIC

Some COBOL compilers permit the use of a standard debugging facility that can be of considerable value in providing diagnostic output. When the debug facility is available, the programmer places a D in position 7 of any program line that is a part of the diagnostic procedure. The compiler ordinarily will omit any line coded with a D in position 7 from the compilation process. To include code from such lines in the object program, the clause WITH DEBUGGING MODE must be included in the SOURCE-COMPUTER paragraph of the ENVIRONMENT DIVISION (see Figure 12.26). If this clause is omitted, lines of the program that contain a D in position 7 are treated as comments; they are included in the program listing but are not translated into the object program. If the clause is included, debug lines are translated as a part of the object program. Without the debug facility, it is necessary to remove references to diagnostic output from a program after the program is debugged. Using the debug facility enables the programmer to include or omit diagnostic output from a program by changing only the SOURCE-COMPUTER paragraph.

Figure 12.26   Debug example

```
        Positions
        123456789012 . . .
        Margin A    B
                IDENTIFICATION DIVISION.
                  .
                  .
                  .
                ENVIRONMENT DIVISION.
                CONFIGURATION SECTION.
                SOURCE-COMPUTER. computer-name WITH DEBUGGING MODE.
                  .
                  .
                  .
                DATA DIVISION.
                  .
                  .
                  .
        D01   DIAGNOSTIC-LINE.
        D       03 FILLER PIC X(3) VALUE "X =".
        D       03 X-OUT  PIC 9(5).
        D       03 FILLER PIC X(4) VALUE " Y =".
        D       03 Y-OUT  PIC 9(5).
                  .
                  .
                  .
                PROCEDURE DIVISION.
                  .
                  .
                  .
        D     PERFORM DIAGNOSTIC-OUTPUT.
                COMPUTE TABL (X, Y) = . . .
                  .
                  .
                  .
        DDIAGNOSTIC-OUTPUT.
        D       MOVE X TO X-OUT.
        D       MOVE Y TO Y-OUT.
        D       WRITE PRINT-LINE FROM DIAGNOSTIC-LINE AFTER 1.
                  .
                  .
                  .
```

12.11   COBOL-85 UPDATE

Both versions of the SEARCH verb include one or more imperative statements that are executed when the condition described in the statement is
found, so the SEARCH statement is classified as a conditional statement. As
with other conditional statements, the COBOL-85 standard supplies a

scope delimiter, in this case, END-SEARCH. For example, the SEARCH statement in Program 12g could be written as follows:

```
SEARCH Supplier-Entry
  AT END
        MOVE "NOT PRESENT" TO Search-Flag
  WHEN Supplier-ID-Entry (Indx) = Supplier-ID-Number-PRR
        MOVE "FOUND" TO Search-Flag
END-SEARCH
```

With the END-SEARCH clause in place, the SEARCH statement becomes an imperative statement, which does not need to be terminated by a period.

12.12 SELF-TEST EXERCISES

1. For a year to be a leap year, two conditions must be met:
   a. The year must be divisible by 4.
   b. If the year is divisible by 100, it must also be divisible by 400.

   Modify the program segment of Figure 12.2 to take leap years into consideration.

2. Construct tables similar to those in Figures 12.10 and 12.11, showing the steps involved in locating ACTUAL-ARGUMENTs 115 and 3.

3. A randomized table containing 7 elements is to be formed containing the following data:

   6, 19, 23, 20

   Show the placement of the data in the table. How does the placement change if data is loaded in the following order:

   20, 6, 19, 23

4. For each of the five techniques shown in Figure 12.15, compare the expected average number of repetitions to find that an argument is not present for $n = 10, 50, 100, 500, 1,000, 5,000, 10,000$. Comment on the sequential search and binary search techniques as the value of n increases.

5. Compare the relative advantages and disadvantages of the five table organization and access techniques described in this chapter.

6. Which table organization and access technique would be most appropriate in each of the following situations? Defend your answers.
   a. A table of part numbers and associated unit prices has been established. An inquiry supplies the part number, and the program looks up the unit price. Some numbers are referenced constantly, while others are rarely used.
   b. A 50-element table has been established associating the two-character abbreviation with the state name (sample entry TX TEXAS). The program must supply the full state name in response to the code.
   c. A table associating UPC (Universal Product Code) and a product description and unit price has been established. The table is to be used in an on-line inquiry system such as a supermarket checkout system, in which the optimum response time is a critical factor. The computer contains more than enough memory to accommodate the program and the table.

7. What will happen if the procedure described in Figure 12.14 is used when the table is full?

8. a. Write a COBOL procedure to load a sequenced table from a data file. Relevant DATA DIVISION entries are

```
        SELECT TABLE-FILE ASSIGN TO DISK.
            .
            .
            .
    FD  TABLE-FILE
        LABEL RECORDS ARE STANDARD.
    01  TABLE-RECORD.
        05 TABLE-ARGUMENT-TR  PIC 9(6).
        05 TABLE-VALUE-TR     PIC X(20).
            .
            .
            .
    01  TABLE-DATA.
        05 TABLE-ENTRY OCCURS 1 TO 100 TIMES
                    DEPENDING ON NUM-ENTRY.
            10 TABLE-ARGUMENT PIC 9(6).
            10 TABLE-VALUE    PIC X(20).
    01  NUM-ENTRY PIC 999 VALUE 0.
```

   b. Modify the table definition given above to permit the use of the SEARCH ALL statement, assuming that the table is organized in ascending sequence.

   c. Write a COBOL procedure using a SEARCH ALL statement to locate the TABLE-VALUE corresponding to the content of ACTUAL-ARGUMENT. If the value exists, move it to OUTPUT-VALUE; otherwise, move spaces to OUTPUT-VALUE.

12.13 PROGRAMMING EXERCISES

1. Write a program to load the table of Figure 12.25 from a data file, and process a representative sample of actual mileage values. Write versions of your program using each of the following access techniques:

   sequential search
   binary search
   SEARCH verb
   direct access

   Compare the execution time for each program.

   Note: It may take a fairly large sample data file to be able to observe differences in execution time. If you are unable to see differences in execution time at first, increase the size of the sample data file.

2. Write a program to create a randomized table of 100 different values of your choice for a sequence of table sizes. Keep track of the number of collisions encountered when the size of the table equals 103, 113, 131, 151, 163, 173, 181, 191, 193. What happens to the number of collisions as the table size increases? Is there a point at which the decline becomes pronounced?

3. Write a program for XYZ College's registration system to generate trial schedules for students. Registration records listing section numbers that the student desires are submitted. From 1 to 10 section requests may be included on each record. Each registration record contains the following data:

Positions	Content
1–9	Student number
11–30	Student name
32–61	Section requests (3 digits each)

The program must create a trial schedule, including the following data for each section:

Student name
Student number
Section number
Course number
Course description
Hours
Days
Credits

Two files are available:

Section Master File
Course Master File

Each record in the Section Master File contains the following entries:

Positions	Content
1–3	Section number
5–10	Course number
12–14	Days (e.g., TR or MWF)
16–19	Beginning times (0000 TO 2359; assume 24-hour clock)
21–24	Ending time

The file is in sequence by section number.

Each record in the Course Master File contains:

Positions	Content
1–6	Course number
8–29	Course description
30–31	Credits

The file is in sequence by course number. The program should load each of these files into appropriate tables. For each section in which a student desires enrollment, the program must reference the tables in order to look up the required information.

4. A program is required to produce student grade summary reports. Two files are available:

Course Master File
Student Grade File

The record layout for the Course Master File is the same as described in Exercise 3. The Student Grade File contains grades for each course a student has taken and in sequence by student number. Each record contains:

Positions	Content
1–9	Student number
11–16	Course number
18	Grade
20–30	Term date (e.g., FALL 1991)

Your report should list each course taken, credits and grade. It should also compute and print each student's grade point average (GPA). (Use the scheme employed at your school to compute GPA.) Four versions of this program are required:

a. Use a sequential search of a sequenced table to perform table look-up.
b. Use a binary search to perform table look-up.
c. Use a hash table technique to perform table look-up.
d. Use a SEARCH or SEARCH ALL statement to perform table look-up.

13. SEQUENTIAL FILE MAINTENANCE

13.1 OVERVIEW OF FILE-ORIENTED SYSTEMS

Most data processing systems make extensive use of files for data storage. Indeed, the success or failure of a system may often be traced to the skill with which the files are designed and maintained. The choice of file organization and content is one of the most basic choices to be made in designing a system. Systems are designed around two basic types of files: master and transaction. **Master files,** in general, contain basic data about each entity in the system (a part, a person, an order). **Transaction files** contain data about changes or other activity as they relate to the entities in the system. For example, in a personnel system, the transaction file would store specific data about leaves taken, hours worked, address changes, and so on. Transaction files may be regarded as relatively temporary storage vehicles, whereas a master file may be thought of as relatively permanent storage for summaries of the transactions that have occurred.

File Maintenance

Two basic problems must be solved in any data processing system: file maintenance and information reporting. Reporting information involves access to one or more files that contain data of interest. The program (or other access mechanism) lists, counts, accumulates, selects, computes, and produces the desired information. Most of the COBOL programs you have written thus far have probably been of this type.

The file maintenance task, on the other hand, involves manipulating data stored in the system's files. Programs that perform file maintenance must take into consideration the following types of activities that may need to be performed:

- Addition: Records must be added to the file.
- Deletion: Records must be removed from the file.
- Change: One or more fields within a record must be changed.

Some people distinguish between file maintenance and file updating. **File maintenance** is the periodic, nonroutine process of adding and deleting records and correcting errors by changing fields within records. **File updating** is the routine processing of transactions that cause changes in one or more fields in a record. For purposes of this text, updating will be treated as a specific type of maintenance, that is, changing the content of a field. The logic required to perform this task is the same whether changes are made routinely or nonroutinely.

Both master files and transaction files must be maintained. In maintaining a master file relating to the employees of a company, for example,

517

it is necessary to be able to add records as new employees are hired, remove records when employees leave, and change any item of information contained in any employee's record to reflect changes in the employee's job, place of residence, income tax withholding status, and so on. Transaction files must also be maintained. The most common type of maintenance is to add records to the file, but it may also be necessary to delete a transaction or change an existing transaction if an error is found.

File maintenance may be performed in two distinctly different computing environments: batch and interactive. In a **batch environment,** transactions are accumulated over a period of time and are then used to make changes in appropriate files. In an **interactive environment,** transactions are usually processed immediately to make changes in the relevant files.

In interactive systems, transaction files may not be maintained, or they may be maintained for archival purposes only. Many systems (like the Amalgamated Custom Design system described in Chapter 10) use a mixture of interactive and batch concepts. Some maintenance is performed in an interactive manner (e.g., Raw Materials Master, Work in Progress Master), and other maintenance is performed in a batch mode (e.g., New Order Processing, Order Update).

Backups

Regardless of the type of computing environment, one problem must be confronted in any system design: How can the system recover in the event of user error, equipment malfunction, sabotage, or natural disaster? Detailed plans need to be made for all of these contingencies. One tool that is often used in these plans is the **backup file,** that is, a copy of a file. A backup file may be stored in the same or different medium and at the same or different location. Quite often, levels of backups are maintained. Recently created backups are stored at the computer center site, and older backups are stored in a separate location. Because they are compact and relatively inexpensive, tapes are often used for backups, even when original files are stored on disk.

The goal in planning for system malfunction is to be able to reestablish the system in its former state in a reasonable amount of time (and, it is to be hoped, at reasonable expense). In a batch system, it is usually possible to load the most recently available version of the master files, recreate transaction files for transactions that have occurred since the last time the backup master file was updated, and run appropriate programs to perform the update. In an interactive system, the process of re-creating transactions is made more difficult by the fact that the transactions are entered at keyboards and, often, there is no written record of the transaction. Usually these types of systems keep track of all transactions as they enter the system in a file that may be referred to as a **transaction log.** If something happens to destroy the current version of the master file, the transaction log may be used to remake all the changes that users have made since the backup was created. (The only transactions that are lost in such a system are transactions that have been entered by the user but not yet recorded by the system on the transaction log.)

Backups for both master and transaction files serve other purposes in data processing systems. Not only do they permit recovery in case of emergency, they also provide a record of the status of the system at specified intervals and a permanent record of all data the system has processed. This is very important in establishing an **audit trail** for auditors who must certify that the system is indeed performing its functions correctly. Back-ups of this type are also important to enable programmers to determine the nature and source of errors in the system. They can also be used to test new versions of the system prior to actual implementation.

Access Methods

Files may be accessed sequentially or randomly. In **sequential file access**, records in the file may be processed only in sequential order from first to last. The files you have been working with up until now have been accessed sequentially. Sequential access to data is useful when the entire file must be processed from start to finish. In a batch system, file mainte-nance is often accomplished by sorting the transactions into the same sequence as the master file and processing records alternately from both files, proceeding sequentially from first to last. In **random file access**, records are made available for processing on demand; that is, the program may process any record in the file as needed without having to process other records. Random access files are a very powerful tool, particularly in an interactive computing environment, because changes to the file can be made at the same time that transactions are entered.

Activity

A very important consideration in designing a file maintenance system is the amount of activity that is anticipated. **Activity** may be defined as the ratio of transaction records to master file records in a given time period. For example, suppose a master file contains 100 records and suppose there will be an average of 200 transactions per day to be processed. The activity ratio is $^{200}/_{100} = 2$. In other words, there will be on average twice as many transactions as master file records. In another instance, one might anticipate 50 transactions per day in a system with 100 records in its master file. In this case, the activity ratio is $^{50}/_{100} = .5$; there will be half as many transactions as there are master file records.

The concept of activity is important because it may help in choosing whether to update a file randomly or sequentially. Updating randomly will create a heavier workload on the system than sequential updates because random access takes more time to execute than sequential access. Thus, *other things being equal,* it may be advantageous to use sequential updates in a system when high activity is expected and to use random updates when low activity is expected. "Other things being equal," of course, covers a lot of ground. There are situations in which random access is justified, even when activity is high, because random access makes the changed record immediately available for further processing—a requirement in many interactive systems. Even when immediate updates are desirable, the overhead involved in random access may tax the abilities of a computer system, making immediate updating not feasible for that system.

Volatility

Activity includes transactions of all types—adding, changing, deleting. A related concept, volatility, is concerned only with adding and deleting records. **Volatility** is the ratio of additions and deletions to the number of records in the file. For example, if 50 additions and/or deletions are expected for a file initially containing 100 records, the volatility ratio is $^{50}/_{100} = .5$. A very static file has very few or no additions and deletions and an expected volatility ratio of close to zero.

Volatility affects the choice of file update technique. If random access is being used on a highly volatile file, the size of the file changes quite rapidly as records are added and removed, thereby placing demands on the secondary storage space and the operating system that may adversely affect the performance of the system. Using sequential access for a highly volatile file enables a more systematic, controlled expansion and contraction of the file space and, therefore, places a lesser burden on the computing system resources.

COBOL offers three distinct file organization techniques:

- sequential
- indexed
- relative

Each of these techniques offers advantages and limitations that make the choice of file organization a critical matter in the design of a data processing system. This chapter will cover sequential files, Chapter 14 will treat indexed files, and Chapter 15 will cover relative files.

13.2 ADVANTAGES AND LIMITATIONS OF SEQUENTIAL FILES

A **sequential file** is a file organization technique that enables access to the records in the file from the first record to the second record, and so on to the end of the file. Each READ or WRITE to a sequential file causes the next record in the file to be read or written. Historically, sequential files were the first method used to store data for access by computers. The one-after-the-other access technique was motivated by the magnetic tapes that were used (and, of course, are still used) for data storage.

Because of the physical nature of the tape, sequential storage and access is the only practical technique available. When a disk is used for storage of a sequential file, the sequential access mechanism is managed by the operating system. Insofar as the program is concerned, the physical medium used for storage of a file is immaterial; the important aspect of the file is the capability for sequential access that is enforced when a file is declared to be sequential.

Sequential files are, of course, limited by the fact that only the next record is available for processing. In order to access the fifth record in the file, it is necessary to read the first four, whether or not any processing is to be done on these records. However, sequential file organization does have the following advantages over other file organization techniques when sequential access to the data is required by the program:

- A sequential file can be reassigned from tape to disk, or vice versa, without affecting the logic of the program. Other file organization techniques generally require the random access capabilities of a disk.

- Sequential file organization is usually simpler than other organization techniques and usually does not require the space for tables and directories needed by other file organization techniques.

- Virtually all system software and every programming language have capabilities for handling sequential files; the same is not always true for other file organization techniques.

- Processing time is usually faster with a sequential file than with files organized in other ways. This may become a critical concern with smaller computing systems or when large amounts of data must be stored and processed.

Even though other file organization techniques offer greater flexibility in access techniques, sequential files remain a very useful method for data storage and access.

13.3 REVIEW OF SEQUENTIAL FILE OPEN AND CLOSE

The OPEN statement causes the operating system to make a file available for processing. A file must be opened before any input or output operation can be performed on it. A sequential file can be opened in one of four modes: INPUT, OUTPUT, I-O, and EXTEND (Fig. 13.1).

Figure 13.1   General form of the OPEN statement

$$
\text{OPEN} \left\{
\begin{array}{l}
\underline{\text{INPUT}}\ \text{file-name}\ \left[\left\{\begin{array}{l}\underline{\text{REVERSED}}\\ \text{WITH}\ \underline{\text{NO}}\ \text{REWIND}\end{array}\right\}\right] \cdots \\[2ex]
\underline{\text{OUTPUT}}\ \text{file-name}\ [\text{WITH}\ \underline{\text{NO}}\ \text{REWIND}]\ \cdots \\
\underline{\text{I-O}}\ \text{file-name}\ \cdots \\
\underline{\text{EXTEND}}\ \text{file-name}\ \cdots
\end{array}
\right\}
$$

When a file is opened in INPUT mode, the records from the file are made available to the program one at a time from first to last. The file must exist on the device specified in the SELECT statement for the file. Two options exist for tape files opened in INPUT mode: WITH NO REWIND and REVERSED. Ordinarily, a tape reel is rewound from the take-up reel onto its original reel and positioned at the first record in the file when the file is opened. The WITH NO REWIND clause can be used when a reel of tape contains more than one file and you want to open the second or subsequent files on that tape. When the first file is closed, the tape must not be rewound; the reel must be left in position for the next file to be opened. The REVERSED option will cause the file to be positioned at its last record and to be read in reverse order from last to first. These options are ignored if the file is assigned to a disk. The REVERSED and WITH NO REWIND options are not included in all COBOL compilers.

When a file is opened in OUTPUT mode, the file is assumed to have no data records in it. If records already were present in the file, opening it for OUTPUT would destroy them. WRITE statements cause records to be placed in the file sequentially from first to last. The WITH NO REWIND clause has the same effect in the OUTPUT mode as it does in the INPUT mode.

When a file is opened in I-O (Input-Output) mode, it is assumed to exist and may be processed by READ and REWRITE statements. The REWRITE statement will cause the content of a record that has been read (and perhaps changed by the processing program) to be rewritten, destroying the content of the original. This mode can be used for disk files only; it is not valid for tape files.

When a file is opened in EXTEND mode, the operating system locates the last record in the file; any record written in the file will follow that record. EXTEND mode may not be implemented on all compilers.

The CLOSE statement terminates processing of a file. The file must be open at the time of execution of a CLOSE statement. After a file has been closed, no further input or output operations may be executed. A general form of the CLOSE statement is shown in Figure 13.2.

Figure 13.2   General form of the CLOSE statement

$$\text{CLOSE file-name}\ \left[\ \text{WITH}\ \left\{\begin{array}{l} \underline{\text{NO REWIND}} \\ \underline{\text{LOCK}} \end{array}\right\}\right]\ \dots$$

When a file is assigned to tape, the WITH NO REWIND clause will prevent the reel of tape from being repositioned to the beginning of the file. If the WITH NO REWIND clause is omitted, rewinding is automatically performed as part of the CLOSE operation.

The LOCK option will prevent the current program (or any subsequent program in the job) from reopening the file. The LOCK option should be used if it would be an error for any further processing of the file to take place. In some operating systems, the LOCK phrase has the additional function of causing the file to become permanent if the file is being created by this program. For these operating systems, a file will be purged from the disk at the end of the program unless the LOCK option is used.

13.4   MERGING

Often it is necessary to merge two sequentially organized files of similar data to create one file in proper sequence containing all the data from the original two files. A procedure to perform this task is illustrated in Figure 13.3. Data from TRANSACTION-FILE is to be merged with OLD-MASTER-FILE to create NEW-MASTER-FILE. Both files must be sorted into the same sequence based on the same key field.

In order to maintain sequence in the output file, one record from each of the two input files is read. The record with the smaller key field value is written to the output file, and the next record is read from the appropriate file. This process is repeated until end-of-file is reached on both the TRANS-ACTION-FILE and the OLD-MASTER-FILE.

The key field for each file is used to enable the program to continue processing until end-of-file has been reached on both files. When end-of-file occurs on either of the input files, a high value is moved to the key field for that file. This value is chosen to be the largest value that can be stored in the key field. Processing continues until both key fields have the high value. This method makes it unnecessary to have separate logic within the program to handle the remaining records on one file when end-of-file has been reached on the other.

For example, if end-of-file is reached on the old master file, the value of old master key will become the high value. As this is the largest value that can be contained in the field, all values of transaction key must be less than old master key, which will result in the transaction record being

Figure 13.3   Pseudocode for merge procedure

```
Open files
Read transaction file
      At end move high value to transaction key
Read old master file
      At end move high value to old master key
Do until transaction key = high value and old master key = high value
      If transaction key < old master key
            Write new master record from transaction record
            Read transaction file
                  At end move high value to transaction key
      Else
            Write new master record from old master record
            Read old master file
                  At end move high value to old master key
      End If
End Do
Close files
Stop
```

selected for output each time. When end-of-file is finally reached on TRANSACTION-FILE, the value of transaction key will become the high value, and the procedure will terminate.

Note that it is possible to create a new file with records having key fields with equal values. This condition may or may not be an error, depending on the particular application.

The following modification to the procedure in Figure 13.3 could check for equal values in key fields:

```
Do until transaction key = high value and old master key = high value
      If transaction key = old master key
            Write error message
            Read transaction file
            At end move high value to transaction key
      Else
            .
            .
            .
```

13.5 PROGRAM EXAMPLE

In this chapter all examples will be taken from a billing application that might be part of an accounts receivable system used by a small business. The heart of the system is a master file in which records are identified by a five-character account number. Each record contains the customer name, address, amount owed, credit limit, and date of last payment. We will be writing programs that can be used to maintain this file in a variety of ways.

Problem Statement

Write a program to merge new records into the master file. Assume that both files are in ascending sequence by account number. Reject any new records that have the same account number as an existing record. The program should create a new master file and a report titled "MERGE TRANSACTION REGISTER," listing all transactions. In the report, an error message should precede any transaction that has an account number that duplicates an existing account number. The report should contain a summary of the number of valid and invalid records processed.

Problem Analysis

This program requires two input files (TRANSACTION-FILE and OLD-MASTER-FILE) and two output files (NEW-MASTER-FILE and REPORT-FILE). For simplicity, we will list the content of records in the report without column headings and other niceties that would probably be part of a "real world" report. The procedure required to perform this task was outlined in Figure 13.3.

Problem Solution

The required program is shown as Program 13a. The structure diagram for the program is shown in Figure 13.4; a sample execution is shown in Figure 13.5. To help you focus on the essential logic of the program, we have included only the account number and name in the data files in Figure 13.5.

Figure 13.4   Structure diagram for Program 13a

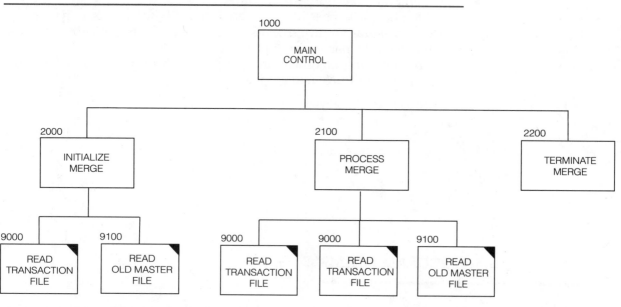

Suspense Files

One modification that can be made to a file update system is to create another output file containing all invalid transactions. This file is usually called a **suspense file** because it contains transactions that are being held temporarily, pending correction of errors. Without this type of file, the only way to correct errors is to rekey invalid transactions as part of a new batch of transactions. With a suspense file, it is possible to edit the content of that file to correct errors and then rerun the update program with the corrected transactions. To keep the examples in this chapter simple and understandable, we have not created suspense files for invalid transactions. It is, however, a relatively simple modification to make. It requires that another file be opened as an output file. Whenever an invalid transaction is encountered, the content of that transaction is written to the new file.

Program 13a

```
 1 IDENTIFICATION DIVISION.
 2
 3 PROGRAM-ID. FILE-MERGING-PRO13A.
 4 AUTHOR. HORN.
 5
 6 ENVIRONMENT DIVISION.
 7
 8 CONFIGURATION SECTION.
 9
10 SOURCE-COMPUTER.
11 OBJECT-COMPUTER.
12
13 INPUT-OUTPUT SECTION.
14
15 FILE-CONTROL.
16
17     SELECT TRANSACTION-FILE ASSIGN TO DISK.
18
19     SELECT OLD-MASTER-FILE ASSIGN TO DISK.
20
21     SELECT NEW-MASTER-FILE ASSIGN TO DISK.
22
23     SELECT REPORT-FILE ASSIGN TO PRINTER.
24
25
26 DATA DIVISION.
27
28 FILE SECTION.
29
30 FD   TRANSACTION-FILE
31      LABEL RECORDS ARE STANDARD
32      DATA RECORD IS TRANSACTION-RECORD.
33
34 01   TRANSACTION-RECORD.
35      03 ACCOUNT-NUMBER-TR        PIC X(5).
36      03 NAME-TR                  PIC X(20).
37      03 ADDRESS-TR.
38         05 STREET-TR             PIC X(15).
39         05 CITY-TR               PIC X(15).
40         05 STATE-TR              PIC XX.
41         05 ZIP-TR                PIC 9(5).
42      03 AMOUNT-OWED-TR           PIC 9(4)V99.
43      03 CREDIT-MAXIMUM-TR        PIC 9(4)V99.
44      03 LAST-PAYMENT-DATE-TR     PIC 9(6).
45
```

Program 13a   *(continued)*

```
46 FD   OLD-MASTER-FILE
47      LABEL RECORDS ARE STANDARD
48      DATA RECORD IS OLD-MASTER-RECORD.
49
50 01   OLD-MASTER-RECORD.
51      03 ACCOUNT-NUMBER-OMR         PIC X(5).
52      03 NAME-OMR                   PIC X(20).
53      03 ADDRESS-OMR.
54         05 STREET-OMR              PIC X(15).
55         05 CITY-OMR                PIC X(15).
56         05 STATE-OMR               PIC XX.
57         05 ZIP-OMR                 PIC 9(5).
58      03 AMOUNT-OWED-OMR            PIC 9(4)V99.
59      03 CREDIT-MAXIMUM-OMR         PIC 9(4)V99.
60      03 LAST-PAYMENT-DATE-OMR      PIC 9(6).
61
62 FD   NEW-MASTER-FILE
63      LABEL RECORDS ARE STANDARD
64      DATA RECORD IS NEW-MASTER-RECORD.
65
66 01   NEW-MASTER-RECORD.
67      03 ACCOUNT-NUMBER-NMR         PIC X(5).
68      03 NAME-NMR                   PIC X(20).
69      03 ADDRESS-NMR.
70         05 STREET-OMR              PIC X(15).
71         05 CITY-NMR                PIC X(15).
72         05 STATE-NMR               PIC XX.
73         05 ZIP-NMR                 PIC 9(5).
74      03 AMOUNT-OWED-NMR            PIC 9(4)V99.
75      03 CREDIT-MAXIMUM-NMR         PIC 9(4)V99.
76      03 LAST-PAYMENT-DATE-NMR      PIC 9(6).
77
78 FD   REPORT-FILE
79      LABEL RECORDS ARE OMITTED
80      DATA RECORD IS REPORT-RECORD.
81
82 01   REPORT-RECORD                 PIC X(80).
83
84 WORKING-STORAGE SECTION.
85
86 01   COUNTERS.
87      02 TRANS-PROCESSED            PIC 9(4) VALUE ZERO.
88      02 TRANS-NOT-PROCESSED        PIC 9(4) VALUE ZERO.
89
90 01   HEADING-LINE.
91      02 FILLER                     PIC X(26) VALUE
92         "MERGE TRANSACTION REGISTER".
93
94 01   SUMMARY-LINE-1.
95      02 FILLER                     PIC X(29) VALUE
96         "    Transactions processed : ".
97      02 TRANS-PROCESSED-SL         PIC ZZZ9.
98
99 01   SUMMARY-LINE-2.
100     02 FILLER                     PIC X(29) VALUE
101        "Transactions not processed : ".
102     02 TRANS-NOT-PROCESSED-SL     PIC ZZZ9.
```

Program 13a *(continued)*

```
103
104 01  DUPLICATE-ERROR-LINE.
105     02 FILLER                      PIC X(52) VALUE
106         "Duplicate Acct. No. in following transaction".
107
108 PROCEDURE DIVISION.
109
110 1000-MAIN-CONTROL.
111
112     PERFORM 2000-INITIALIZE-MERGE.
113     PERFORM 2100-PROCESS-MERGE
114             UNTIL ACCOUNT-NUMBER-TR = HIGH-VALUES
115                 AND ACCOUNT-NUMBER-OMR = HIGH-VALUES.
116     PERFORM 2200-TERMINATE-MERGE.
117     STOP RUN.
118
119 2000-INITIALIZE-MERGE.
120
121     OPEN INPUT OLD-MASTER-FILE
122               TRANSACTION-FILE
123         OUTPUT NEW-MASTER-FILE
124               REPORT-FILE.
125     PERFORM 9000-READ-TRANSACTION-FILE.
126     PERFORM 9100-READ-OLD-MASTER-FILE.
127     WRITE REPORT-RECORD FROM HEADING-LINE AFTER PAGE.
128     MOVE SPACES TO REPORT-RECORD.
129     WRITE REPORT-RECORD AFTER 1.
130
131 2100-PROCESS-MERGE.
132
133     IF ACCOUNT-NUMBER-TR = ACCOUNT-NUMBER-OMR
134         WRITE REPORT-RECORD FROM DUPLICATE-ERROR-LINE AFTER 1
135         WRITE REPORT-RECORD FROM TRANSACTION-RECORD AFTER 1
136         ADD 1 TO TRANS-NOT-PROCESSED
137         PERFORM 9000-READ-TRANSACTION-FILE
138     ELSE
139         IF ACCOUNT-NUMBER-TR < ACCOUNT-NUMBER-OMR
140             WRITE NEW-MASTER-RECORD FROM TRANSACTION-RECORD
141             ADD 1 TO TRANS-PROCESSED
142             WRITE REPORT-RECORD FROM TRANSACTION-RECORD AFTER 1
143             PERFORM 9000-READ-TRANSACTION-FILE
144         ELSE
145             WRITE NEW-MASTER-RECORD FROM OLD-MASTER-RECORD
146             PERFORM 9100-READ-OLD-MASTER-FILE.
147
148 2200-TERMINATE-MERGE.
149
150     MOVE TRANS-PROCESSED TO TRANS-PROCESSED-SL.
151     WRITE REPORT-RECORD FROM SUMMARY-LINE-1 AFTER 2.
152     MOVE TRANS-NOT-PROCESSED TO TRANS-NOT-PROCESSED-SL.
153     WRITE REPORT-RECORD FROM SUMMARY-LINE-2 AFTER 1.
154     CLOSE TRANSACTION-FILE
155             OLD-MASTER-FILE
156             NEW-MASTER-FILE
157             REPORT-FILE.
158
```

Program 13a   *(concluded)*

```
159 9000-READ-TRANSACTION-FILE.
160
161     MOVE SPACES TO TRANSACTION-RECORD.
162     READ TRANSACTION-FILE
163         AT END MOVE HIGH-VALUES TO ACCOUNT-NUMBER-TR.
164
165 9100-READ-OLD-MASTER-FILE.
166
167     MOVE SPACES TO OLD-MASTER-RECORD.
168     READ OLD-MASTER-FILE
169         AT END MOVE HIGH-VALUES TO ACCOUNT-NUMBER-OMR.
```

Figure 13.5   Sample execution of Program 13a

OLD-MASTER-FILE

```
11111JOE JONES
22222MARY SMITH
44444SUE WHITE
77777SAM SPADE
```

TRANSACTION-FILE

```
00111SID BLACK
55555JOHN WHITE
66666JOAN JONES
77777JOE GREEN
77778JACK SPRATT
88889LYNN BROWN
```

NEW-MASTER-FILE

```
00111SID BLACK
11111JOE JONES
22222MARY SMITH
44444SUE WHITE
55555JOHN WHITE
66666JOAN JONES
77777SAM SPADE
77778JACK SPRATT
88889LYNN BROWN
```

REPORT-FILE

```
MERGE TRANSACTION REGISTER

00111SID BLACK
55555JOHN WHITE
66666JOAN JONES
Duplicate Acct. No. in following transaction
77777JOE GREEN
77778JACK SPRATT
88889LYNN BROWN

    Transactions processed :    5
Transactions not processed :    1
```

13.6   CHANGE

Records stored in a file will need to be changed (updated) from time to time. One approach to file updating is to submit change transactions in essentially the same format as the records to be updated, but to have blanks in fields that do not require changes and new data in all fields that do require change. It is desirable for the program that performs the update function to accept any number of changes for a given record; the changes may all be placed on the same change transaction or on different change transactions.

The logic required to perform the update function can be treated as an extension of the procedure outlined in Figure 13.3. The procedure would be rewritten as shown in Figure 13.6. The update procedure would scan the transaction record for nonblank fields. The content of each non-blank field would replace the appropriate field in the old master record. After the update procedure is executed, the next transaction record is read. The updated old master record is written onto the new file only when a transaction record containing a larger key field has been read.

Another approach to transaction processing makes use of a code in the transaction record that will be used by the program to determine what action to take. The transaction code option affects only the update procedure itself; the logic of Figure 13.6 remains unchanged.

Figure 13.6   Pseudocode for file updating (change transactions only)

```
Open files
Read transaction file
        At end move high value to transaction key
Read old master file
        At end move high value to old master key
Do until transaction key = high value and old master key = high value
        If transaction key < old master key
                Write error message
                Read transaction file
                        At end move high value to transaction key
        Else
                If transaction key = old master key
                        Do Update procedure
                        Read transaction file
                                At end move high value to old master key
                Else
                        Write new master record from old master record
                        Read old master file
                                At end move high value to old master key
                End If
        End If
End Do
Close files
Stop
```

Example

Program 13b uses an "update by replacement" scheme in which a transaction record completely replaces a master file record with the same key to change records in the master file used in Program 13a. A sample execution of this program is shown in Figure 13.7. Note that multiple changes for a given record can be submitted. (See, for example, the changes made to the record with account number 33333.) When this happens, the last change record is the one that becomes part of the new master file. Also note that an out-of-sequence record in the transaction file will be treated as an error since there is no way for such a record to be matched in the old master file.

```
  1 IDENTIFICATION DIVISION.
  2
  3 PROGRAM-ID. UPDATE-BY-REPLACEMENT-PRO13B.
  .
  .
  .
108 PROCEDURE DIVISION.
109
110 1000-MAIN-CONTROL.
111
112     PERFORM 2000-INITIALIZE-REPLACE.
113     PERFORM 2100-PROCESS-REPLACE
114           UNTIL ACCOUNT-NUMBER-TR = HIGH-VALUES
115              AND ACCOUNT-NUMBER-OMR = HIGH-VALUES.
116     PERFORM 2200-TERMINATE-REPLACE.
117     STOP RUN.
118
119 2000-INITIALIZE-REPLACE.
120
121     OPEN INPUT OLD-MASTER-FILE
122                TRANSACTION-FILE
123          OUTPUT NEW-MASTER-FILE
124                 REPORT-FILE.
125     PERFORM 9000-READ-TRANSACTION-FILE.
126     PERFORM 9100-READ-OLD-MASTER-FILE.
127     WRITE REPORT-RECORD FROM HEADING-LINE AFTER PAGE.
128     MOVE SPACES TO REPORT-RECORD.
129     WRITE REPORT-RECORD AFTER 1.
130
131 2100-PROCESS-REPLACE.
132
133     IF ACCOUNT-NUMBER-TR < ACCOUNT-NUMBER-OMR
134        WRITE REPORT-RECORD FROM ERROR-LINE AFTER 1
135        WRITE REPORT-RECORD FROM TRANSACTION-RECORD AFTER 1
136        ADD 1 TO TRANS-NOT-PROCESSED
137        PERFORM 9000-READ-TRANSACTION-FILE
138     ELSE IF ACCOUNT-NUMBER-TR = ACCOUNT-NUMBER-OMR
139        MOVE TRANSACTION-RECORD TO OLD-MASTER-RECORD
140        WRITE REPORT-RECORD FROM TRANSACTION-RECORD AFTER 1
141        ADD 1 TO TRANS-PROCESSED
142        PERFORM 9000-READ-TRANSACTION-FILE
143     ELSE
144        WRITE NEW-MASTER-RECORD FROM OLD-MASTER-RECORD
145        PERFORM 9100-READ-OLD-MASTER-FILE.
146
147 2200-TERMINATE-REPLACE.
148
149     MOVE TRANS-PROCESSED TO TRANS-PROCESSED-SL.
150     MOVE TRANS-NOT-PROCESSED TO TRANS-NOT-PROCESSED-SL.
151     WRITE REPORT-RECORD FROM SUMMARY-LINE-1 AFTER 2.
152     WRITE REPORT-RECORD FROM SUMMARY-LINE-2 AFTER 1.
153     CLOSE TRANSACTION-FILE
154           OLD-MASTER-FILE
155           NEW-MASTER-FILE
156           REPORT-FILE.
  .
  .
  .
```

Figure 13.7 Sample execution of Program 13b

```
OLD-MASTER-FILE          TRANSACTION-FILE          NEW-MASTER-FILE
11111JOE JONES           22222MARY BROWN           11111JOE JONES
22222MARY SMITH          22223SARAH SMITH          22222MARY BROWN
33333SUE BLACK           33333BETTY DOE            33333BETTY ROE
44444SAM SPADE           33333BETTY ROE            44444SAM SPADE
                         55555JOHN WHITE
                         88889LYNN BROWN
                         00000JOHN DOE
```

```
REPORT-FILE

CHANGE TRANSACTION REGISTER

22222MARY BROWN
 Following transaction not processed :
22223SARAH SMITH
33333BETTY DOE
33333BETTY ROE
 Following transaction not processed :
55555JOHN WHITE
 Following transaction not processed :
88889LYNN BROWN
 Following transaction not processed :
00000JOHN DOE

      Transactions processed :      3
  Transactions not processed :      4
```

13.7 DELETE

It is often necessary to delete unneeded records from a file. For a personnel file, the employee may have quit or been fired; for an inventory file, the item may no longer be stocked. When an entirely new file is being produced, a record is deleted simply by not writing that record onto the new master file.

For example, suppose a transaction file consists of records to be deleted from a master file. Pseudocode for a program that will delete these records by creating a new master file is shown in Figure 13.8. A record is deleted by skipping over both the transaction record and the matching old master record; this is accomplished by reading the next record from each of these files and not writing the matching old master record to the new master file. Note that if the value of the transaction key field is less than the old master key field, then that transaction must be an error. In this case, it is impossible to find in the old master file a record that will match the transaction, as the file is assumed to be in ascending sequence and all subsequent key field values will be even larger.

Figure 13.8   Pseudocode for record deletion

```
Open files
Read transaction file
    At end move high value to transaction key
Read old master file
    At end move high value to old master key
Do until transaction key = high value and old master key = high value
    If transaction key = old master key
        Read old master file
            At end move high value to old master key
        Read transaction file
            At end move high value to transaction key
    Else
        If transaction key > old master key
            Write new master record from old master record
            Read old master file
                At end move high value to old master key
        Else
            Write error message
            Read transaction file
                At end move high value to transaction key
        End If
    End If
End Do
Close files
Stop
```

───────── Example ─────────

Program 13c deletes records from the master file used in Programs 13a and 13b. The records in the transaction file contain only the account number of the record to be deleted. When a transaction record account number matches a master file account number, the program reads both a new transaction and a new master file record (see lines 133–137). Figure 13.9 shows a sample execution of the program in which two records (account numbers 22222 and 44444) are deleted from the master file. Other transactions are in error because they do not match a master file record. Note that a duplicate delete transaction is treated as an error since the first one causes the program to advance to the next master file record.

13.8   COMPLETE FILE MAINTENANCE PROCESS

The procedures in Figures 13.3, 13.6, and 13.8 are suitable when the transaction file contains only one type of transaction—add, change, or delete. In most instances, it is desirable to be able to perform all three types of transactions using one procedure. In the most general case, it is possible that records may be added and that one or more fields may be changed and then deleted in the same batch of transactions. The procedure shown in Figure 13.10 can be used for this purpose. There are two

Program 13c

```
  1 IDENTIFICATION DIVISION.
  2
  3 PROGRAM-ID. UPDATE-BY-DELETE-PRO13C.
    .
    .
    .
108 PROCEDURE DIVISION.
109
110 1000-MAIN-CONTROL.
111
112     PERFORM 2000-INITIALIZE-DELETE.
113     PERFORM 2100-PROCESS-DELETE
114             UNTIL ACCOUNT-NUMBER-TR = HIGH-VALUES
115                AND ACCOUNT-NUMBER-OMR = HIGH-VALUES.
116     PERFORM 2200-TERMINATE-DELETE.
117     STOP RUN.
118
119 2000-INITIALIZE-DELETE.
120
121     OPEN INPUT OLD-MASTER-FILE
122                TRANSACTION-FILE
123          OUTPUT NEW-MASTER-FILE
124                 REPORT-FILE.
125     PERFORM 9000-READ-TRANSACTION-FILE.
126     PERFORM 9100-READ-OLD-MASTER-FILE.
127     WRITE REPORT-RECORD FROM HEADING-LINE AFTER PAGE.
128     MOVE SPACES TO REPORT-RECORD.
129     WRITE REPORT-RECORD AFTER 1.
130
131 2100-PROCESS-DELETE.
132
133     IF ACCOUNT-NUMBER-TR = ACCOUNT-NUMBER-OMR
134         WRITE REPORT-RECORD FROM TRANSACTION-RECORD AFTER 1
135         ADD 1 TO TRANS-PROCESSED
136         PERFORM 9000-READ-TRANSACTION-FILE
137         PERFORM 9100-READ-OLD-MASTER-FILE
138     ELSE IF ACCOUNT-NUMBER-TR > ACCOUNT-NUMBER-OMR
139         WRITE NEW-MASTER-RECORD FROM OLD-MASTER-RECORD
140         PERFORM 9100-READ-OLD-MASTER-FILE
141     ELSE
142         WRITE REPORT-RECORD FROM ERROR-LINE AFTER 1
143         WRITE REPORT-RECORD FROM TRANSACTION-RECORD AFTER 1
144         ADD 1 TO TRANS-NOT-PROCESSED
145         PERFORM 9000-READ-TRANSACTION-FILE.
146
147 2200-TERMINATE-DELETE.
148
149     MOVE TRANS-PROCESSED TO TRANS-PROCESSED-SL.
150     MOVE TRANS-NOT-PROCESSED TO TRANS-NOT-PROCESSED-SL.
151     WRITE REPORT-RECORD FROM SUMMARY-LINE-1 AFTER 2.
152     WRITE REPORT-RECORD FROM SUMMARY-LINE-2 AFTER 1.
153     CLOSE TRANSACTION-FILE
154           OLD-MASTER-FILE
155           NEW-MASTER-FILE
156           REPORT-FILE.
    .
    .
    .
```

Figure 13.9   *Sample execution of Program 13c*

OLD-MASTER-FILE

```
11111JOE JONES
22222MARY SMITH
33333SUE BLACK
44444SAM SPADE
```

TRANSACTION-FILE

```
22222
22223
11111
44444
44444
99999
```

NEW-MASTER-FILE

```
11111JOE JONES
33333SUE BLACK
```

REPORT-FILE

```
DELETE TRANSACTION REGISTER

22222
 Following transaction not processed :
22223
 Following transaction not processed :
11111
44444
 Following transaction not processed :
44444
 Following transaction not processed :
99999

        Transactions processed :    2
Transactions not processed :    4
```

---

major differences between the procedure in Figure 13.8 and the procedure in Figure 13.10:

- Data either from the old master file or, for new records, from the transaction file is moved to the new master record when the record is read. All changes are then made to the new master record. When a break is found in the transactions, the new master record is written.

- A flag *(read flag)* is used to determine if it is appropriate to read the next record from the old master file. When a record is added, data from the transaction record is moved to the new master record, and the read flag is set to NO. The current old master file record remains the next record from that file to be processed. When it is appropriate to get the next old master file record for processing, read flag is tested. If its value is NO, reading the next record from the old master file is bypassed.

The procedure in Figure 13.10 makes use of the key fields for end-of-file detection in the same way as in previous procedures; the details are omitted from the pseudocode for clarity.

The procedure of Figure 13.10 makes use of the **Case structure,** which can be very useful in describing such complex procedures. The Case structure is appropriate when exactly one condition of a series of possibilities will hold. The general form of the Case structure and some alternate ways to represent the same logic is shown in Figure 13.11.

The Case structure is not one of the fundamental structures required for structured programming because exactly the same function can be achieved by using nested IF/ELSE statements. The Case structure is,

Figure 13.10 Pseudocode for complete file maintenance procedure

```
Open files
Read transaction file
Read old master file
Move "YES" to read flag
Move old master record to new master record
Do until transaction key = high value and new master key = high value
      If transaction key < new master key
            Write new master record
            If read flag = "YES"
                  Read old master file
            End If
            Move old master record to new master record
            Move "YES" to read flag
      Else
            If transaction key = new master key
                  Case
                        Transaction is add
                              Write error message 1
                              Read transaction file
                        Transaction is delete
                              Read transaction file
                              If read flag = "YES"
                                    Read old master file
                              End If
                              Move old master record to new master record
                              Move "YES" to read flag
                        Transaction is change
                              Do update procedure
                              Read transaction file
                  End case
            Else
                  Case
                        Transaction is add
                              Move transaction record to new master record
                              Move "NO" to read flag
                        Transaction is delete
                              Write error message 2
                        Transaction is change
                              Write error message 3
                  End Case
                  Read transaction file
            End If
      End If
End Do
Close files
Stop
```

Figure 13.11   General form of the Case structure

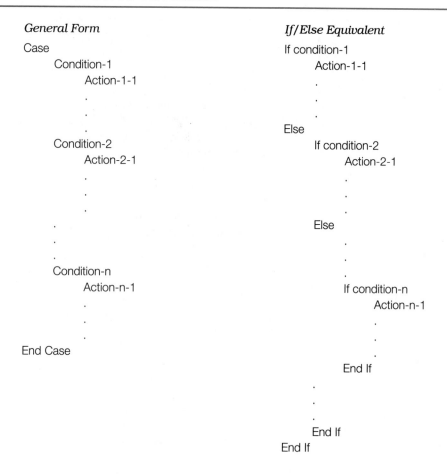

General Form

```
Case
        Condition-1
            Action-1-1
            .
            .
            .
        Condition-2
            Action-2-1
            .
            .
            .
        Condition-n
            Action-n-1
            .
            .
End Case
```

If/Else Equivalent

```
If condition-1
        Action-1-1
        .
        .
        .
Else
        If condition-2
            Action-2-1
            .
            .
            .
        Else
            .
            .
            .
            If condition-n
                Action-n-1
                .
                .
                .
            End If
            .
            .
            .
        End If
End If
```

however, a convenient means of representing the concept of selection among a variety of mutually exclusive alternatives.

Implementation of the Case structure in COBOL-74 requires nested IF/ELSE statements. The standard for COBOL-85 contains an EVALUATE statement that can be used to implement the Case structure in a very straightforward way. (See Section 13.14 for details.)

────────────── Example ──────────────

Program 13d makes use of the procedure shown in Figure 13.10 to perform all three maintenance functions on the master file used in Programs 13a through 13c. The structure diagram for this program is shown in Figure 13.12. The transaction file has been revised to make use of a transaction code in position 1 of each record. Three codes are implemented:

    A = Add a record
    C = Change a record
    D = Delete a record

All changes are made to the record in the new master record area. No record is written to the new master file until there has been a break in account numbers; that is, all transactions that match the record in the new master record area are processed before the new master record is

Flowchart Equivalent

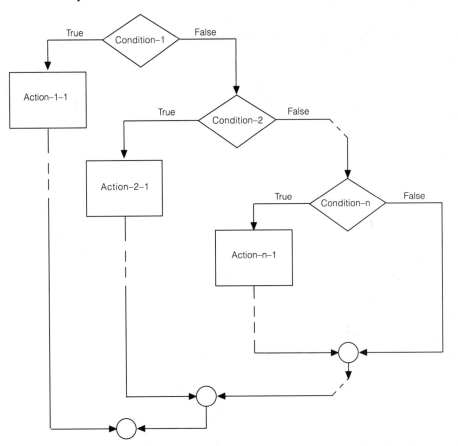

written. This feature is useful because it enables the program to process multiple update transactions on the master file in one processing cycle. An example of this can be seen in the sample execution shown in Figure 13.13. Note that the record with account number 44445 is added, changed, and deleted all in one batch of transactions. It is, however, imperative that the transaction records be sorted into ascending sequence with the transaction code as the secondary key. That is, for a given account number, all Add transaction(s) must precede Change transaction(s), which must all precede Delete transaction(s). If this is not the case, then the transaction that is out of sequence will be treated as an error. Note that for a single account number, the program will process exactly one Add transaction (assuming that the record is *not* matched in the master file), multiple Change transactions (if the account number is matched in the master file), but only one Delete transaction (assuming that the transaction is matched in the master file).

Perhaps the most interesting and potentially confusing feature of this program is the use of a flag to govern the program's action in reading a record from the old master file. When there is a break in account numbers, the program is usually required to read the next record from the old master file and move it to the new master file record area in preparation for output to the new master file. The only exception comes when a record is added to the file by way of an Add transaction. In this case, it is necessary to hold the old master record in abeyance while the program processes the new record and any related transactions. When an Add transaction is processed, READ-FLAG is set to NO (see line 203). The program continues as usual. When the next break occurs, 9100-READ-OLD-MASTER is performed (line 170) in conjunction with writing the new master file. The procedure 9100-READ-OLD-MASTER checks the content of READ-FLAG (line 222) before actually reading the next record from the old master file. Only if READ-FLAG is set to YES is the next record read from the file. Whether or not a record is read, the procedure sets READ-FLAG to YES so that the next record will be read from the old master file the next time the procedure is executed.

Program 13d

```
 1 IDENTIFICATION DIVISION.
 2
 3 PROGRAM-ID. UPDATE-PRO13D.
 .
 .
 .
26 DATA DIVISION.
27
28 FILE SECTION.
29
30 FD  TRANSACTION-FILE
31     LABEL RECORDS ARE STANDARD
32     DATA RECORD IS TRANSACTION-RECORD.
33
34 01  TRANSACTION-RECORD.
35     02 TRANSACTION-CODE        PIC X.
36        88 ADD-RECORD           VALUE "A".
37        88 CHANGE-RECORD        VALUE "C".
38        88 DELETE-RECORD        VALUE "D".
39     02 TRANSACTION-DATA.
40        03 ACCOUNT-NUMBER-TR      PIC X(5).
41        03 NAME-TR                PIC X(20).
42        03 ADDRESS-TR.
43           05 STREET-TR           PIC X(15).
44           05 CITY-TR             PIC X(15).
45           05 STATE-TR            PIC XX.
46           05 ZIP-TR              PIC 9(5).
47        03 AMOUNT-OWED-TR         PIC 9(4)V99.
48        03 CREDIT-MAXIMUM-TR      PIC 9(4)V99.
49        03 LAST-PAYMENT-DATE-TR   PIC 9(6).
 .
 .
 .
89 WORKING-STORAGE SECTION.
90
91 01  COUNTERS.
92     02 TRANS-PROCESSED        PIC 9(4) VALUE ZERO.
93     02 TRANS-NOT-PROCESSED    PIC 9(4) VALUE ZERO.
94
95 01  FLAGS.
96     02 READ-FLAG              PIC XXX VALUE "YES".
97
```

Program 13d *(continued)*

```
 98 01  HEADING-LINE.
 99     02 FILLER                 PIC X(27) VALUE
100        "UPDATE TRANSACTION REGISTER".
101
102 01  ERROR-LINES.
103     02 NO-MATCH-LINE.
104        03 FILLER              PIC X(80) VALUE
105           " Following transaction is unmatched".
106     02 INVALID-CODE-LINE.
107        03 FILLER              PIC X(80) VALUE
108           " Following transaction has invalid code".
109     02 DUPLICATE-ERROR-LINE.
110        03 FILLER              PIC X(80) VALUE
111           " Following transaction has duplicate key".
112
113 01  SUMMARY-LINE-1.
114     02 FILLER                 PIC X(29) VALUE
115        "    Transactions processed : ".
116     02 TRANS-PROCESSED-SL     PIC ZZZ9.
117
118 01  SUMMARY-LINE-2.
119     02 FILLER                 PIC X(29) VALUE
120        "Transactions not processed : ".
121     02 TRANS-NOT-PROCESSED-SL  PIC ZZZ9.
122
123 PROCEDURE DIVISION.
124
125 1000-MAIN-CONTROL.
126
127     PERFORM 2000-INITIALIZE-UPDATE.
128     PERFORM 2100-PROCESS-UPDATE
129            UNTIL ACCOUNT-NUMBER-TR = HIGH-VALUES
130              AND ACCOUNT-NUMBER-NMR = HIGH-VALUES.
131     PERFORM 2200-TERMINATE-UPDATE.
132     STOP RUN.
133
134 2000-INITIALIZE-UPDATE.
135
136     OPEN INPUT OLD-MASTER-FILE
137               TRANSACTION-FILE
138         OUTPUT NEW-MASTER-FILE
139               REPORT-FILE.
140     PERFORM 9000-READ-TRANSACTION-FILE.
141     PERFORM 9100-READ-OLD-MASTER-FILE.
142     MOVE OLD-MASTER-RECORD TO NEW-MASTER-RECORD.
143     WRITE REPORT-RECORD FROM HEADING-LINE AFTER PAGE.
144     MOVE SPACES TO REPORT-RECORD.
145     WRITE REPORT-RECORD AFTER 1.
146
147 2100-PROCESS-UPDATE.
148
149     IF ACCOUNT-NUMBER-TR > ACCOUNT-NUMBER-NMR
150         PERFORM 3000-WRITE-NEW-MASTER
151     ELSE IF ACCOUNT-NUMBER-TR = ACCOUNT-NUMBER-NMR
152         PERFORM 3100-PROCESS-MATCH-CASE
153     ELSE
154         PERFORM 3200-PROCESS-ADD.
155
```

```
156 2200-TERMINATE-UPDATE.
157
158     MOVE TRANS-PROCESSED TO TRANS-PROCESSED-SL.
159     MOVE TRANS-NOT-PROCESSED TO TRANS-NOT-PROCESSED-SL.
160     WRITE REPORT-RECORD FROM SUMMARY-LINE-1 AFTER 2.
161     WRITE REPORT-RECORD FROM SUMMARY-LINE-2 AFTER 1.
162     CLOSE TRANSACTION-FILE
163           OLD-MASTER-FILE
164           NEW-MASTER-FILE
165           REPORT-FILE.
166
167 3000-WRITE-NEW-MASTER.
168
169     WRITE NEW-MASTER-RECORD.
170     PERFORM 9100-READ-OLD-MASTER-FILE.
171     MOVE OLD-MASTER-RECORD TO NEW-MASTER-RECORD.
172
173 3100-PROCESS-MATCH-CASE.
174
175     IF ADD-RECORD
176         WRITE REPORT-RECORD FROM DUPLICATE-ERROR-LINE AFTER 1
177         WRITE REPORT-RECORD FROM TRANSACTION-RECORD AFTER 1
178         ADD 1 TO TRANS-NOT-PROCESSED
179         PERFORM 9000-READ-TRANSACTION-FILE
180     ELSE IF DELETE-RECORD
181         WRITE REPORT-RECORD FROM TRANSACTION-RECORD AFTER 1
182         ADD 1 TO TRANS-PROCESSED
183         PERFORM 9000-READ-TRANSACTION-FILE
184         PERFORM 9100-READ-OLD-MASTER-FILE
185         MOVE OLD-MASTER-RECORD TO NEW-MASTER-RECORD
186     ELSE IF CHANGE-RECORD
187         WRITE REPORT-RECORD FROM TRANSACTION-RECORD AFTER 1
188         ADD 1 TO TRANS-PROCESSED
189         MOVE TRANSACTION-DATA TO NEW-MASTER-RECORD
190         PERFORM 9000-READ-TRANSACTION-FILE
191     ELSE
192         WRITE REPORT-RECORD FROM INVALID-CODE-LINE AFTER 1
193         WRITE REPORT-RECORD FROM TRANSACTION-RECORD AFTER 1
194         ADD 1 TO TRANS-NOT-PROCESSED
195         PERFORM 9000-READ-TRANSACTION-FILE.
196
197 3200-PROCESS-ADD.
198
199     IF ADD-RECORD
200         MOVE TRANSACTION-DATA TO NEW-MASTER-RECORD
201         WRITE REPORT-RECORD FROM TRANSACTION-RECORD AFTER 1
202         ADD 1 TO TRANS-PROCESSED
203         MOVE "NO" TO READ-FLAG
204     ELSE IF DELETE-RECORD OR CHANGE-RECORD
205         WRITE REPORT-RECORD FROM NO-MATCH-LINE AFTER 1
206         WRITE REPORT-RECORD FROM TRANSACTION-RECORD AFTER 1
207         ADD 1 TO TRANS-NOT-PROCESSED
208     ELSE
209         WRITE REPORT-RECORD FROM INVALID-CODE-LINE AFTER 1
210         WRITE REPORT-RECORD FROM TRANSACTION-RECORD AFTER 1
211         ADD 1 TO TRANS-NOT-PROCESSED.
212     PERFORM 9000-READ-TRANSACTION-FILE.
213
```

Program 13d *(concluded)*

```
214  9000-READ-TRANSACTION-FILE.
215
216      MOVE SPACES TO TRANSACTION-RECORD.
217      READ TRANSACTION-FILE
218          AT END MOVE HIGH-VALUES TO ACCOUNT-NUMBER-TR.
219
220  9100-READ-OLD-MASTER-FILE.
221
222      IF READ-FLAG = "YES"
223          MOVE SPACES TO OLD-MASTER-RECORD
224          READ OLD-MASTER-FILE
225              AT END MOVE HIGH-VALUES TO ACCOUNT-NUMBER-OMR.
226      MOVE "YES" TO READ-FLAG.
```

13.9 ADDING RECORDS WITH EXTEND

To add records to an existing disk or tape file without having to create a separate, completely new file, it is possible to open the file in EXTEND mode. For example, to add records to a file MASTER-FILE, you would use

```
OPEN EXTEND MASTER-FILE.
```

EXTEND mode causes the operating system to locate the last record in the file and place any additional records to be written in the file following that record.[1]

If a file opened in EXTEND mode does not exist, the effect of EXTEND is the same as opening the file in OUTPUT mode: The file is created and records are placed in the file in sequential order.

In using EXTEND mode, you cannot merge the new records with the existing records in the file. Therefore, the file MASTER-FILE may not be in proper sequence in this case, and it may be necessary to sort the file using either a system utility program or the COBOL SORT facility (see Chapter 7) in order to perform any further processing of the file.

——— Example ———

Program 13e shows the use of EXTEND mode to add records to the master file referenced in Programs 13a through 13d. Previously, we have always generated a new master file. In this case, the old master file becomes the new master file on completion of the program. In the sample execution shown in Figure 13.14, the old master file contained four records before execution of the program. The transaction file contained three records which were appended to the master file, yielding a file with seven records. Since this program changes the file in place, there is no automatic backup of the master file as there is in all of the procedures we have examined in this chapter. Because of this characteristic, it would be wise to make a copy of the master file before execution of Program 13e. In this way, if something goes wrong, you will be able to recover the data in its former state.

[1]In some systems, a tape may be used to store multiple files. EXTEND mode would be valid only for the last file on the tape since adding records to a file earlier in the tape will destroy the integrity of the file which follows.

Figure 13.12   Structure diagram for Program 13d

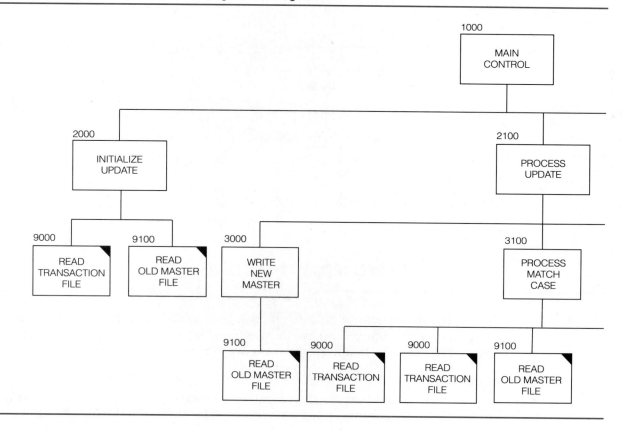

Figure 13.13   Sample execution of Program 13d

OLD-MASTER-FILE
```
11111JOE JONES
22222MARY SMITH
33333SUE BLACK
44444SAM SPADE
```

TRANSACTION-FILE
```
D11111
A11112CAROL ROBERTS
C11112CAROL ROBERT
C22222MARY R. SMITH
A22222MARY DOE
D22223
d22223
c33333
A44444JOE DOE
A44445JOSH WHITE
C44445JOSHUA WHITE
D44445
A99998J. SEYMORE
C99998JAN SEYMORE
C99998JANE SEYMORE
```

NEW-MASTER-FILE
```
11112CAROL ROBERT
22222MARY R. SMITH
33333SUE BLACK
44444SAM SPADE
99998JANE SEYMORE
```

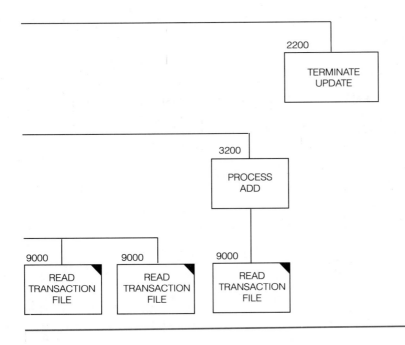

REPORT-FILE

```
UPDATE TRANSACTION REGISTER

D11111
A11112CAROL ROBERTS
C11112CAROL ROBERT
C22222MARY R. SMITH
 Following transaction has duplicate key
A22222MARY DOE
 Following transaction is unmatched
D22223
 Following transaction has invalid code
d22223
 Following transaction has invalid code
c33333
 Following transaction has duplicate key
A44444JOE DOE
A44445JOSH WHITE
C44445JOSHUA WHITE
D44445
A99998J. SEYMORE
C99998JAN SEYMORE
C99998JANE SEYMORE


    Transactions processed :    10
 Transactions not processed :     5
```

```
 1 IDENTIFICATION DIVISION.
 2
 3 PROGRAM-ID. EXTEND-EXAMPLE-PRO13E.
 4 AUTHOR. HORN.
 .
 .
 .
15 FILE-CONTROL.
16
17     SELECT MASTER-FILE ASSIGN TO DISK.
18
19     SELECT TRANSACTION-FILE ASSIGN TO DISK.
20
21     SELECT REPORT-FILE ASSIGN TO PRINTER.
 .
 .
 .
84 PROCEDURE DIVISION.
85
86 1000-MAIN-CONTROL.
87
88     PERFORM 2000-INITIALIZE-EXTEND.
89     PERFORM 2100-PROCESS-TRANSACTIONS
90             UNTIL END-OF-FILE.
91     PERFORM 2200-TERMINATE-EXTEND.
92     STOP RUN.
93
94 2000-INITIALIZE-EXTEND.
95
96     OPEN EXTEND MASTER-FILE
97          INPUT TRANSACTION-FILE
98         OUTPUT REPORT-FILE.
99     PERFORM 9000-READ-TRANSACTION-FILE.
100    WRITE REPORT-RECORD FROM HEADING-LINE AFTER PAGE.
101    MOVE SPACES TO REPORT-RECORD.
102    WRITE REPORT-RECORD AFTER 1.
103
104 2100-PROCESS-TRANSACTIONS.
105
106    WRITE MASTER-RECORD FROM TRANSACTION-RECORD.
107    ADD 1 TO TRANS-PROCESSED.
108    WRITE REPORT-RECORD FROM TRANSACTION-RECORD AFTER 1.
109    PERFORM 9000-READ-TRANSACTION-FILE.
110
111 2200-TERMINATE-EXTEND.
112
113    MOVE TRANS-PROCESSED TO TRANS-PROCESSED-SL.
114    WRITE REPORT-RECORD FROM SUMMARY-LINE AFTER 2.
115    CLOSE TRANSACTION-FILE
116          MASTER-FILE
117          REPORT-FILE.
118
119 9000-READ-TRANSACTION-FILE.
120
121    MOVE SPACES TO TRANSACTION-RECORD.
122    READ TRANSACTION-FILE
123         AT END MOVE "YES" TO EOF-FLAG.
```

Figure 13.14   Sample execution of Program 13e

MASTER-FILE	TRANSACTION-FILE	MASTER-FILE
Before		*After*
11111JOE JONES	77777JIM JONES	11111JOE JONES
22222MARY SMITH	88888JOSHUA WHITE	22222MARY SMITH
33333SUE BLACK	99998JANE SEYMORE	33333SUE BLACK
44444SAM SPADE		44444SAM SPADE
		77777JIM JONES
		88888JOSHUA WHITE
		99998JANE SEYMORE

13.10   UPDATING A SEQUENTIAL FILE IN PLACE

As noted earlier, it is not possible to change existing data in a tape file; a completely new file must be produced each time an update operation is performed. Files that are stored on mass storage, however, may be updated in place. In fact, new records can be added to the file, and existing records can be changed or even deleted without requiring that an entirely new file be created.

Adding records to an existing file is accomplished using EXTEND mode. Changing existing records and deleting records are accomplished by opening the file in I-0 mode and using the REWRITE statement. When the file is opened in I-0 mode, as in

```
OPEN I-O MASTER-FILE.
```

records may be read from the file using READ and written on the file using REWRITE. The REWRITE statement can be used only after a READ operation. It causes the record that was read to be rewritten onto the file; the new copy of the record replaces the old one. The general form of the REWRITE statement is shown in Figure 13.15.

Figure 13.15   General form of the REWRITE statement

```
REWRITE record-name [FROM data-name]
```

For example, in order to rewrite a record onto MASTER-FILE, the statement

```
REWRITE MASTER-RECORD.
```

can be used. The REWRITE statement may be executed only once for a given record; it will replace the last record read from the file.[2]

The basic procedure used to change an existing record in a file is to make changes to the record based on transactions. After all transactions

---

[2]The actual restriction is that the last input/output statement executed for the file must be a successfully completed READ statement. After a REWRITE is executed, the last input/output statement for the file will be REWRITE, so no further use of REWRITE for this particular record is permitted.

regarding a particular record are processed, the changed record is rewritten onto the file using the REWRITE statement. This approach is used in the procedure shown in Figure 13.16.

In order to delete records from a file, it is necessary to add a deletion code to the record. When the deletion code has a predetermined value, the record is considered to have been deleted; if the code has any other value, the record is considered to be active. The routine that reads records from the file must bypass all deleted records. Records from the file are read until either a nondeleted record is found or the end-of-file is reached.

Pseudocode for the procedure to read a record from MASTER-FILE is as follows:

> *Read master file procedure*
> > Read master file
> > Do until end of file or active record
> > > Read master file
> > End Do

This method for deleting records has some advantages over physically removing records from a file. The record remains in the file and is, therefore, accessible by any program processing the file. A report showing all

Figure 13.16   Pseudocode for in-place maintenance of a sequential file

```
Open files
Read transaction file
Do read master file procedure
Do until end of transaction file
        Case
                Transaction key = master key
                        Case
                                Transaction is change
                                        Do Update procedure
                                        Read transaction file
                                Transaction is delete
                                        Move "DELETE" to deletion code
                                        Rewrite master record
                                        Read transaction file
                                        Do Read master file procedure
                        End Case
                Transaction key < master key
                        Write error message: "Invalid transaction"
                        Read transaction file
                Transaction key > master key
                        Rewrite master record
                        Do Read master file procedure
        End Case
End Do
Close files
Stop
```

Note: All changes are made to the master record before it is rewritten onto the master file. This procedure will accommodate multiple change transactions for one master record.

deleted records can be produced at any time. A record can be changed back to active status by changing the value of the deletion code. However, there are some disadvantages. Eventually, the file may become full of deleted records, causing the file to take up too much space on the disk. Because any program processing the file must read (and ignore) deleted records as well as active records, the performance of the computing system for programs processing the file may be degraded. When a file becomes full of deleted records, it is necessary to create a second file that contains only active records and omits those that have been deleted. A backup of the old version of the file can be maintained (perhaps on tape) should it be necessary to access any of the records in the original version of the file.

--------------------- Example ---------------------

Program 13f is a revision of Program 13b which processes change transactions against the master file used in the examples in this chapter. Recall that Program 13b created a new master file; Program 13f will update the master file in place. The master file is opened in I-0 mode (line 102), and records are read from the file in sequence as before. However, when a transaction that matches a master record is processed, the content of the transaction record is moved to the master record (line 114). When a break in account numbers is encountered, the current copy of the master record is written back into the file using the REWRITE statement (see line 124). Note that the record may or may not have been changed at this point. If it has not been changed, then the program replaces the record with an image of itself. The program can be made slightly more efficient by setting a flag when a change is encountered and by rewriting the master file record only when the flag indicates that this is necessary.

As with Program 13e, this program makes changes directly to the master file so the importance of a backup of the master file cannot be overstated. An interruption of the execution of this program could leave the master file in a corrupted state, making it impossible for programs to have further access to it.

13.11   THE MERGE STATEMENT

The process of merging two sets of data, each of which is already in sequence, has been described in Section 13.4. The COBOL sort facility has a MERGE statement available to perform this task. The general form of the MERGE statement is shown in Figure 13.17. Many of the considerations regarding use of the SORT statement are also true for the MERGE statement. For example, the MERGE statement requires the use of a sort work-file, which is used the same way in the MERGE as in the SORT. In fact, MERGE is actually a version of the SORT, with some restrictions in its syntax. The major differences are as follows:

- The verb MERGE replaces the verb SORT.
- The USING clause must be included; there is no provision for an INPUT PROCEDURE.
- At least two files must be listed in the USING clause. More can be named, if desired.

```
  1 IDENTIFICATION DIVISION.
  2
  3 PROGRAM-ID. UPDATE-IN-PLACE-PRO13F.
  .
  .
  .
 90 PROCEDURE DIVISION.
 91
 92 1000-MAIN-CONTROL.
 93
 94     PERFORM 2000-INITIALIZE-UPDATE.
 95     PERFORM 2100-PROCESS-TRANSACTIONS
 96             UNTIL ACCOUNT-NUMBER-TR = HIGH-VALUES.
 97     PERFORM 2200-TERMINATE-UPDATE.
 98     STOP RUN.
 99
100 2000-INITIALIZE-UPDATE.
101
102     OPEN I-O MASTER-FILE
103        INPUT TRANSACTION-FILE
104       OUTPUT REPORT-FILE.
105     PERFORM 9000-READ-TRANSACTION-FILE.
106     PERFORM 9100-READ-MASTER-FILE.
107     WRITE REPORT-RECORD FROM HEADING-LINE AFTER PAGE.
108     MOVE SPACES TO REPORT-RECORD.
109     WRITE REPORT-RECORD AFTER 1.
110
111 2100-PROCESS-TRANSACTIONS.
112
113     IF ACCOUNT-NUMBER-TR = ACCOUNT-NUMBER-MR
114         MOVE TRANSACTION-RECORD TO MASTER-RECORD
115         ADD 1 TO TRANS-PROCESSED
116         WRITE REPORT-RECORD FROM TRANSACTION-RECORD AFTER 1
117         PERFORM 9000-READ-TRANSACTION-FILE
118     ELSE IF ACCOUNT-NUMBER-TR < ACCOUNT-NUMBER-MR
119         WRITE REPORT-RECORD FROM ERROR-LINE AFTER 1
120         WRITE REPORT-RECORD FROM TRANSACTION-RECORD AFTER 1
121         ADD 1 TO TRANS-NOT-PROCESSED
122         PERFORM 9000-READ-TRANSACTION-FILE
123       ELSE
124          REWRITE MASTER-RECORD
125          PERFORM 9100-READ-MASTER-FILE.
126
127 2200-TERMINATE-UPDATE.
128
129     MOVE TRANS-PROCESSED TO TRANS-PROCESSED-SL
130     MOVE TRANS-NOT-PROCESSED TO TRANS-NOT-PROCESSED-SL.
131     WRITE REPORT-RECORD FROM SUMMARY-LINE-1 AFTER 2.
132     WRITE REPORT-RECORD FROM SUMMARY-LINE-2 AFTER 1.
133     CLOSE TRANSACTION-FILE
134           MASTER-FILE
135           REPORT-FILE.
  .
  .
  .
```

Figure 13.17   General form of the MERGE statement

MERGE sort-file-name ON $\left\{ \begin{array}{l} \underline{ASCENDING} \\ \underline{DESCENDING} \end{array} \right\}$ KEY data-name-1 [data-name-2] . . .

$\left[\text{ON} \left\{ \begin{array}{l} \underline{ASCENDING} \\ \underline{DESCENDING} \end{array} \right\} \text{KEY data-name-3 [data-name-4] . . .} \right]$ . . .

USING file-name-1 file-name-2 [file-name-3] . . .

$\left\{ \begin{array}{l} \underline{OUTPUT}\ \underline{PROCEDURE}\ \text{IS section-name-1} \\ \underline{GIVING}\ \text{file-name-4} \end{array} \right\}$

──────── Example ────────

Suppose that two files called DATA-FILE-A and DATA-FILE-B are in ascending sequence. The key field in each case is an account number. Suppose further that a sort work-file called SORT-WORK has been declared and that the sort work-record has been given an appropriate description. If the content of DATA-FILE-A is to be merged with DATA-FILE-B, creating a new file called DATA-FILE-C, the following program segment could be used:

```
MERGE SORT-WORK
     ON ASCENDING KEY ACCOUNT-NUM-SWR
     USING DATA-FILE-A DATA-FILE-B
     GIVING DATA-FILE-C.
```

If DATA-FILE-B were to be merged into DATA-FILE-A, the following code could be used:

```
MERGE SORT-WORK
     ON ASCENDING KEY ACCOUNT-NUM-SWR
     USING DATA-FILE-A DATA-FILE-B
     GIVING DATA-FILE-A.
```

In this example, there is a danger that DATA-FILE-A might be corrupted if a problem occurs during execution of the program. Creating a backup of DATA-FILE-A before running this program is imperative.

The MERGE procedure assumes that its input files are in the required sequence. If either of the files is out of sequence, the procedure will terminate execution of the program with an appropriate error message.

It should be noted that the SORT verb could be substituted for MERGE in the preceding example with little effect on the outcome; the only difference would be that the SORT procedure would not terminate if records that were out of sequence were encountered. What, then, is the advantage of using MERGE rather than SORT? If it is known that existing files are in sequence, MERGE may be preferable to SORT because MERGE tends to be faster than SORT and uses less mass storage space for work areas. The amount of execution time and mass storage space required for execution of a SORT statement is not insignificant. Because of the assumptions about the sequencing of the data, MERGE should be executed in much less time (and with the least possible use of work areas) than SORT, even for the same data files.

Program 13g uses the MERGE statement to perform the same task as in Program 13a. One disadvantage of the MERGE statement is that it is not possible to create a transaction register as we did in Program 13a. Out-of-sequence transactions will cause an execution time error. Transactions with duplicate key field values will be merged into the output file.

Program 13g

```
  1 IDENTIFICATION DIVISION.
  2
  3 PROGRAM-ID. MERGE-EXAMPLE-PRO13G.
  .
  .
  .
 15 FILE-CONTROL.
 16
 17     SELECT TRANSACTION-FILE ASSIGN TO DISK.
 18
 19     SELECT OLD-MASTER-FILE ASSIGN TO DISK.
 20
 21     SELECT NEW-MASTER-FILE ASSIGN TO DISK.
 22
 23     SELECT SORT-WORK-FILE ASSIGN TO DISK.
  .
  .
  .
 78 SD   SORT-WORK-FILE
 79      DATA RECORD IS SORT-WORK-RECORD.
 80
 81 01   SORT-WORK-RECORD.
 82      03 ACCOUNT-NUMBER-SWR        PIC X(5).
 83      03 NAME-SWR                  PIC X(20).
 84      03 ADDRESS-SWR.
 85         05 STREET-OMR             PIC X(15).
 86         05 CITY-SWR               PIC X(15).
 87         05 STATE-SWR              PIC XX.
 88         05 ZIP-SWR                PIC 9(5).
 89      03 AMOUNT-OWED-SWR           PIC 9(4)V99.
 90      03 CREDIT-MAXIMUM-SWR        PIC 9(4)V99.
 91      03 LAST-PAYMENT-DATE-SWR     PIC 9(6).
 92
 93 PROCEDURE DIVISION.
 94
 95 1000-MAIN-CONTROL.
 96
 97     MERGE SORT-WORK-FILE
 98         ON ASCENDING KEY ACCOUNT-NUMBER-SWR
 99         USING OLD-MASTER-FILE TRANSACTION-FILE
100         GIVING NEW-MASTER-FILE.
```

13.12   DEBUG CLINIC

When writing programs dealing extensively with files, the programmer may be confronted with system error messages produced during execution of the program if an error is made. Failing to open the file prior to an input or output operation, attempting an input operation on a file opened in output mode, and attempting a REWRITE operation when a file is not opened in I-0 mode are a few examples of errors that will produce execution time error messages and cause termination of the program.

COBOL provides a way for the programmer to monitor the results of all input/output verbs. To make use of this facility, a FILE STATUS clause is added to the SELECT entry as shown in Figure 13.18. The data-name declared as a FILE STATUS item is automatically updated to show the result of each input/output operation related to the file. The FILE STATUS item must be two characters in length and must be defined in the DATA DIVISION. For example, to define a FILE STATUS item for MASTER-FILE, the SELECT entry could be written as

```
SELECT MASTER-FILE
     ASSIGN TO DISK
     FILE STATUS IS MASTER-STATUS.
```

The field MASTER-STATUS could be defined in WORKING-STORAGE as

```
01   MASTER-STATUS.
     02 M-STATUS-1 PIC 9.
     02 M-STATUS-2 PIC 9.
```

Defining the FILE STATUS item as a group item subdivided into two fields, each of length 1, is useful because each digit of the FILE STATUS item is a code with a specified meaning (Fig. 13.19).

Figure 13.18   General form of the SELECT entry for sequential files

```
SELECT file-name
     ASSIGN TO system-name
     [FILE STATUS IS data-name].
```

Figure 13.19   Meaning of FILE STATUS codes for sequential files

Status-key 1	Status-key 2	Meaning
0	0	Successful completion
1	0	At end
3	0	Permanent error
3	4	Boundary violation
9	-	Differs among compilers

For example, if the value of MASTER-STATUS was "00" after an OPEN, READ, or WRITE statement, the file was opened or a record was read or written without incident. If the value of MASTER-STATUS was "10" after a READ, the end-of-file was encountered. The meaning of other settings of the FILE STATUS item may differ among systems; check with your COBOL system manual. The FILE STATUS item can be processed by a program as any other item. For example, it can be tested as in

```
IF MASTER-STATUS NOT = "00" ...
```

Or, the FILE STATUS item can be made a part of diagnostic output as in

```
READ MASTER-FILE
    AT END MOVE "YES" TO EOF-FLAG.
MOVE MASTER-STATUS TO M-STATUS-OUT.
WRITE OUTPUT-LINE FROM DIAGNOSTIC-LINE AFTER 1.
```

The use of the FILE STATUS item in diagnostic output is particularly helpful in debugging programs when system error messages are not specific enough to enable you to determine the cause of the problem.

13.13 APPLICATIONS OF SEQUENTIAL FILES

Although there are many limitations to the use of sequential file organization in data processing systems, this technique remains useful in several situations. If the file will be stored on and processed from tape, sequential organization is the only available choice. In batch-oriented systems, master files and transaction files may be given sequential organization when random access is not needed by the logic of the system design. Note that it is usually necessary to sort sequential files into sequence before they can be processed. A transaction file must be in sequence using the same key field as the related master file before maintenance is performed. In interactive systems, sequential files are appropriate for transaction log files (containing records of all transactions entered by users), which are maintained for re-creation of the master file in case of system problems. Sequential files are also useful for backups of active files regardless of the organization of the active file. The program that re-creates the active file can also re-create the appropriate file organization.

Sequential file organization is not appropriate when a file must be completely maintained interactively. (If only Change and Delete transactions are needed, sequential organization may be used.) Sequential files are not appropriate when random access to data is needed. Even when random access is not needed by any component of the system but programs require access to the records in the file in different sequences (necessitating repeated sorting of the file), other file organization techniques should be considered.

Because sequential file organization is simple and flexible, it is the method of choice in many situations; however, each system must be evaluated carefully. Overreliance on sequentially organized files may lead to systems that spend too much time in sorting and are inflexible and cumbersome.

13.14 COBOL-85 UPDATE

One very interesting new statement in COBOL-85 is the EVALUATE statement, which can be particularly useful in implementing the Case structure. The EVALUATE statement is quite complex because many forms of it can be used. We will concentrate on two of the simpler forms that can be extended with various options if desired. You may refer to the COBOL-85 reference manual for further details.

Perhaps the simplest form of the EVALUATE statement is the following:

```
EVALUATE condition
    WHEN TRUE
        statement-1 . . .
    WHEN FALSE
        statement-2 . . .
[END-EVALUATE]
```

When the condition is true, the first sequence of statements will be executed; when the condition is false, the second sequence of statements will be executed. END-EVALUATE is a scope delimiter which is optional; if it is included, the EVALUATE statement is an imperative statement that can be embedded in larger imperative statements. This form of the EVALUATE statement is equivalent to the IF statement with an ELSE clause. For example, the following two coding segments are equivalent:

```
EVALUATE X > Y              IF X > Y
    WHEN TRUE
        MOVE X TO Big          MOVE X TO Big
    WHEN FALSE             ELSE
        MOVE Y TO Big          MOVE Y TO Big
END-EVALUATE              END-IF
```

A second and potentially more useful form of the EVALUATE statement allows the program to make a multiple selection.

```
EVALUATE TRUE
    WHEN condition-1
        statement-1 . . .
    [WHEN condition-2
        statement-2 . . .]
            .
            .
            .
    [WHEN condition-n
        statement-n . . .]
    [WHEN OTHER
        statement-m . . .]
[END-EVALUATE]
```

If condition-1 is true, the sequence of statements beginning with statement-1 will be executed; if condition-2 is true, the sequence of statements beginning with statement-2 will be executed, and so forth. If none of the conditions *1* through *n* are true, then the statements in the OTHER clause will be executed. The OTHER clause is optional; if it is omitted and none of the conditions are true, then none of the statements will be executed. The conditions are checked in the order specified. Thus, if it is possible that both condition-1 and condition-2 are true, only the statements following condition-1 will be executed. When one of the conditions is found to be true and the statements are executed, control is passed to the next sentence or to the statement following END-EVALUATE if that clause is included.

—————— Example ——————

Consider the following program segment:

```
IF X > Y
    MOVE "Big" TO X-Status
ELSE
    IF X < Y
        MOVE "Small" TO X-Status
    ELSE
        MOVE "Equal" TO X-Status
    END-IF
END-IF
```

This can be coded using the EVALUATE statement as follows:

```
EVALUATE TRUE
    WHEN X > Y
        MOVE "Big" TO X-Status
    WHEN X < Y
        MOVE "Small" TO X-Status
    WHEN X = Y
        MOVE "Equal" TO X-Status
END-EVALUATE
```

As an alternative, the last condition could be expressed as

```
WHEN OTHER
    MOVE "Equal" TO X-Status
```

—————— Example ——————

Recall that we expressed the procedure for the complete maintenance of a sequential file in terms of a Case structure as shown in Figure 13.10. Program 13d made use of the IF statement to implement this procedure. Program 13d85 is equivalent to Program 13d but makes use of the EVALUATE statement to select among the alternative courses of action. By using END-EVALUATE to terminate each EVALUATE statement, we are able to nest the EVALUATE statements so that much of the logic of the program is expressed in the paragraph 2100-Process-Update. (You will recall that in the similar paragraph in Program 13d, the paragraph 2100-PROCESS-UPDATE used several subordinate modules to complete the selection process.)

The advantage to the EVALUATE statement is that it is natural—that is, easier to read and comprehend—and has a less mathematical/logical "flavor" than the IF statement. This tends to make a program easier to read and comprehend and thus easier to maintain and less prone to logical errors. Compare Programs 13d and 13d85. Which program do you find more natural? If you choose Program 13d85, then the designers of COBOL-85 had people like you in mind when they added the statement to the language. If you choose Program 13d, then you can continue to use the traditional IF/ELSE statement to implement a selection structure if you wish (that is, unless the style manual adopted in your installation requires use of EVALUATE).

Program 13d85

```
  1 IDENTIFICATION DIVISION.
  2
  3 PROGRAM-ID. Evaluate-Example-Pro13d85.
  .
  .
  .
115 PROCEDURE DIVISION.
116
117 1000-Main-Control.
118
119     PERFORM 2000-Initialize-Update
120     PERFORM 2100-Process-Update
121             UNTIL Account-Number-TR = HIGH-VALUES
122               AND Account-Number-NMR = HIGH-VALUES
123     PERFORM 2200-Terminate-Update
124     STOP RUN.
125
126 2000-Initialize-Update.
127
128     OPEN INPUT Old-Master-File
129               Transaction-File
130          OUTPUT New-Master-File
131               Report-File
132     PERFORM 9000-Read-Transaction-File
133     PERFORM 9100-Read-Old-Master-File
134     MOVE Old-Master-Record TO New-Master-Record
135     WRITE Report-Record
136           FROM Heading-Line AFTER PAGE
137     MOVE SPACES TO Report-Record
138     WRITE Report-Record AFTER 1.
139
```

```
140 2100-Process-Update.
141
142     EVALUATE TRUE
143       WHEN Account-Number-TR > Account-Number-NMR
144         WRITE New-Master-Record
145         PERFORM 9100-Read-Old-Master-File
146         MOVE Old-Master-Record TO New-Master-Record
147       WHEN Account-Number-TR = Account-Number-NMR
148         EVALUATE TRUE
149           WHEN Add-Record
150             WRITE Report-Record
151                   FROM Duplicate-Error-Line AFTER 1
152             WRITE Report-Record
153                   FROM Transaction-Record AFTER 1
154             ADD 1 TO Trans-Not-Processed
155             PERFORM 9000-Read-Transaction-File
156           WHEN Delete-Record
157             WRITE Report-Record
158                   FROM Transaction-Record AFTER 1
159             ADD 1 TO Trans-Processed
160             PERFORM 9000-Read-Transaction-File
161             PERFORM 9100-Read-Old-Master-File
162             MOVE Old-Master-Record TO New-Master-Record
163           WHEN Change-Record
164             WRITE Report-Record
165                   FROM Transaction-Record AFTER 1
166             ADD 1 TO Trans-Processed
167             MOVE Transaction-Data TO New-Master-Record
168             PERFORM 9000-Read-Transaction-File
169           WHEN OTHER
170             WRITE Report-Record
171                   FROM Invalid-Code-Line AFTER 1
172             WRITE Report-Record
173                   FROM Transaction-Record AFTER 1
174             ADD 1 TO Trans-Not-Processed
175             PERFORM 9000-Read-Transaction-File
176         END-EVALUATE
177       WHEN OTHER
178         EVALUATE TRUE
179           WHEN Add-Record
180             MOVE Transaction-Data TO New-Master-Record
181             WRITE Report-Record
182                   FROM Transaction-Record AFTER 1
183             ADD 1 TO Trans-Processed
184             MOVE "NO" TO Read-Flag
185           WHEN Delete-Record OR Change-Record
186             WRITE Report-Record
187                   FROM No-Match-Line AFTER 1
188             WRITE Report-Record
189                   FROM Transaction-Record AFTER 1
190             ADD 1 TO Trans-Not-Processed
191           WHEN OTHER
192             WRITE Report-Record
193                   FROM Invalid-Code-Line AFTER 1
194             WRITE Report-Record
195                   FROM Transaction-Record AFTER 1
196             ADD 1 TO Trans-Not-Processed
197         END-EVALUATE
198         PERFORM 9000-Read-Transaction-File
199     END-EVALUATE.
```

Program 13d85   (concluded)

```
200
201 2200-Terminate-Update.
202
203     MOVE Trans-Processed TO Trans-Processed-SL.
204     MOVE Trans-Not-Processed TO Trans-Not-Processed-SL.
205     WRITE Report-Record FROM Summary-Line-1 AFTER 2.
206     WRITE Report-Record FROM Summary-Line-2 AFTER 1.
207     CLOSE Transaction-File
208           Old-Master-File
209           New-Master-File
210           Report-File.
             .
             .
             .
```

13.15   SELF-TEST EXERCISES

1. What input/output statements are valid when a sequential file is opened as INPUT, OUTPUT, I-O, and EXTEND?

2. Define each of the following terms:
   a. rewind
   b. key field
   c. audit trail
   d. file status
   e. backup file
   f. activity
   g. volatility

3. Are there any circumstances in which placement of a large value, such as 99999, in a key field when end-of-file is reached would be invalid? How would the method be modified if the key field were alphanumeric?

4. Write the pseudocode for a program required to merge three files, FILE-A, FILE-B, FILE-C, with respective record key fields KEY-A, KEY-B, KEY-C. The output file is NEW-FILE.

5. What are two types of file access methods supported in COBOL? What are the advantages and disadvantages of each method?

6. How does the expected activity in a system affect the choice of file update technique?

7. How does the expected volatility in a file affect the choice of file update technique?

8. Is it possible for the volatility ratio to exceed the activity ratio? Why or why not?

9. Describe two distinct approaches to entering change records. What are the advantages and limitations of each?

10. Under what circumstances should a sequential file be used in a system? When would a sequential file be inappropriate?

11. Why are backup files often given sequential organization?

12. What are the main differences between batch and interactive file-update procedures?

13. What are the primary limitations on updating a sequential file in place? When is this technique appropriate?

14. In the procedure in Figure 13.10, what purpose is served by the item "read flag"?

15. In Program 13d, suppose the transaction file is sorted with the transaction codes appearing in Delete, Add, Change sequence. What implication would this have for the types of operations that the user could perform on the master file?

13.16   PROGRAMMING EXERCISES

1. Write a program to maintain the `TABLE-FILE` used in programming Exercise 6 in Chapter 12 (Section 13). The program should allow the user to perform the following functions:

Function	Transaction Code
Add a course	A
Change department number	CD
Change course name	CN
Change number credits	CC
Delete course	D

    The program should process the old `TABLE-FILE` and a `TRANSACTION-FILE` to produce a `NEW-TABLE-FILE`.

2. Write a program to create a student master file for ABC College. Each record should contain the following fields:

    Student number
    Name
    Address
    Major (2 character code)
    Date of first enrollment (*mmddyy*)
    Date of last enrollment (*mmddyy*)
    Credit hours currently enrolled
    Cumulative GPA

3. Write a program to process a transaction file containing records for new students. Your program should process the master file created in Exercise 2 and create a new master file.

4. Write a program that uses a transaction file to maintain the student master file created in Exercise 2. Records in the transaction file have the same layout as records in the master file with the addition of a transaction code.

Function	Transaction Code
New student	NS
Change name	CN
Change address	CA
Change major	CM
Change date of first enrollment	CF
Change date of last enrollment	CL

Change credit hours completed   CC
Change credit hours currently enrolled   CE
Change GPA   CG
Delete student   DS

5. A student grade file contains records, in sequence by student number, with the following fields:

Student number
Section number
Course number
Credit hours
Grade (A, B, C, D, F, or W)

Write a program to process the student grade file to update fields of the master student file created in Exercise 2. Use an update-in-place technique.

6. Write a program to update a master file with records defined as follows:

Picture	Description
X(5)	Store identifier
X(3)	Department identifier
9(9)	Customer number
9(6)	Date of sale (mmddyy)
99	Quantity
9(9)	Inventory number of item sold
9999V99	Wholesale price/item
9999V99	Retail price/item
XX	Status code: Paid by cash (CA)
	Paid by VISA (VS)
	Paid by MasterCard (MC)
	Credit purchase (CR)
X	Tax code: Sale is taxable (T)
	Sale is nontaxable (N)

14. INDEXED FILES

14.1 ADVANTAGES AND LIMITATIONS OF INDEXED FILES

The only way to access records stored in a sequential file is one after another—that is, sequentially. **Sequential access** always means the processing of each record in a file from first to last, one after the other. Although this step-by-step process may be suitable for many purposes, there are some applications in which the computer must access records randomly. For example, it may be desirable to update a file *without* having the transactions sorted into sequential order. As each transaction is processed, the associated master file record must be read; in order to do this, the master file must be read randomly. **Random access** is the ability to access any record regardless of its position in the file and without accessing previous records. A type of file organization technique that permits random access is **indexed organization,** available to COBOL programmers in most computer systems.

An indexed file is a sequential file similar in many ways to those discussed in Chapter 13. In fact, an indexed file can be used in place of any sequential file, if desired. However, indexed files give us a very powerful added capability—the ability to process records from the file randomly. In random processing, the program specifies a value, and the READ statement immediately returns the record from the file that has a key field with that value. Records may not only be read from the file but may also be changed and placed directly back into the file. Unlike the technique used in sequential processing, using random processing, records may be deleted from or added to the file without the program having to create an entirely new file.

In a sense, storing records in an indexed file is like storing pages in a looseleaf notebook with an external tab on each page showing the topic of information on that page. The user can retrieve information from the notebook at will by using the appropriate tab. In a similar way, a program can retrieve any desired record from an indexed file by specifying the key field value. The user of the looseleaf notebook can retrieve any page, make changes, and reinsert it into the notebook. In much the same way, a program can perform similar operations on data records contained in an indexed file. The notebook user has the option of throwing pages away at will; in a similar way, records can be deleted from an indexed file.

The implementation of indexed files differs in many details among various computing systems. Typically, however, the system maintains at least one index, a table of pointers to records within the file. To access a record, the system looks up the key field value in the index and uses the pointer (which may be the actual physical address of the record) to read the desired record from the file. In some systems, more than one index is maintained requiring the look-up operation to proceed from a master index through one or more subindexes to find the record in the file. These indexes may be stored in the computer's memory or as part of the disk file itself. Using the looseleaf notebook analogy, the index corresponds roughly to the tabs on each page; it gives the system the ability to access records on demand.

Records within an indexed file generally are stored in sequential order to permit rapid and efficient sequential retrieval of the records. Thus, when the file is created initially, the records stored in the file should be in sequential order in order to maximize the efficiency of the data retrieval process. All required indexes are built by the operating system at the time the file is created. Adding records to and deleting records from the file are done in ways that do not destroy the capability of the system to access the file sequentially. This is because typically there will be associated with the file an **overflow area,** a disk area into which added records are placed. In order to maintain the sequential nature of the file, appropriate pointers are constructed to indicate the sequential position within the file for added records. Deleted records generally are removed from the file by setting a code rather than by physically removing the data.

If a great many records have been added to or deleted from an indexed file, the overflow area may be filled up entirely with the new records, while the deleted records still are occupying physical space within the file. At this point, it becomes necessary to reorganize the file by physically removing the deleted records and inserting the added records into their appropriate physical position. This operation typically is provided for by an operating system utility program designed for this task. (Utility programs are provided for the user as a part of the operating system.)

The primary advantage of indexed files is the provision for both sequential and random access to data. Indexed files also enable in-place file maintenance, including add, change, and delete—a facility not available for sequential files. On the other hand, there are some disadvantages that must be considered. Indexed files must be assigned to a mass storage device (typically disk) with random access capabilities; this precludes use of magnetic tape for an indexed file. Sequential files, on the other hand, may be assigned to any mass storage device (disk or tape). There is considerable system overhead in the storage space required for an indexed file. As noted above, indexes and an overflow area must be allocated, in addition to space for data. This overhead reduces the amount of data that can be stored on a given device. Sequential files, on the other hand, require little additional storage other than actual data areas. The sequential processing time for an indexed file tends to be slower than for a sequential file. This is particularly true when the file has been updated with many new records that have been placed in overflow areas. The operating system takes care of locating desired records in the file, but many disk access operations may be required. Access time for a sequential file, on the other hand, tends to be as fast as possible, usually requiring only one disk access for reading each block of data. In some systems, indexed files require periodic reorganization to clear out overflow areas and purge the file of deleted records; this operation is not required for sequential files. Indexed files are not universally supported in all programming languages and other system software. Thus, an indexed file created by a COBOL program may not be available for processing by a program written in another programming language or by a file management utility program. Sequential files, on the other hand, may usually be processed by programs written in any language and by any system utility.

When choosing a file organization technique for a file in a given system, the systems analyst or programmer must carefully weigh the relative merits of all available options for file organization. Random access and in-place maintenance capabilities are not achieved without cost.

14.2 FILE CREATION

To create an indexed file, the SELECT sentence for that file should contain entries shown in Figure 14.1. The ACCESS clause specifies SEQUENTIAL, as the records placed in the file will be in sequential order. The ORGANIZATION clause specifies the type of file organization, in this case, INDEXED. (If the ORGANIZATION clause were omitted, the file would be assumed to have standard sequential organization.) The RECORD KEY clause specifies the name of the field within the record defined for the file that will be used for creating and accessing the file. Since sequential access is specified, the records must be in ascending sequence based on the value contained in this key field; this restriction applies only to sequential access. There must not be any records with the same key field value; this is a fundamental restriction on indexed files and is applicable for all access modes. For example, to create a file PRODUCT-MASTER-FILE as an indexed file with record key PRODUCT-ID, the following SELECT could be used:

```
SELECT PRODUCT-MASTER-FILE ASSIGN TO DISK
       ORGANIZATION IS INDEXED
       ACCESS IS SEQUENTIAL
       RECORD KEY IS PRODUCT-ID.
```

Figure 14.1   SELECT entry for sequential access to an indexed file

```
SELECT file-name ASSIGN TO system-name
       ORGANIZATION IS INDEXED
       ACCESS IS SEQUENTIAL
       RECORD KEY IS data-name.
```

The WRITE statement for an indexed file must be of the form shown in Figure 14.2. The statement in the INVALID KEY clause is executed when an attempt is made to write a record to the file that has an invalid key field value. Since the indexed file is created using sequential access, the INVALID KEY condition will be encountered when the key fields of the records are not in ascending sequence. In all access modes, the INVALID

Figure 14.2   WRITE statement for indexed file

```
WRITE record-name [FROM data-name]
      [INVALID KEY statement]
```

KEY condition will be true when an attempt is made to place two records with the same key field value into the file. For example, given the indexed PRODUCT-MASTER-FILE in the example above, a suitable WRITE statement would be

```
WRITE PRODUCT-MASTER-RECORD
    INVALID KEY
        MOVE "RECORD OUT OF SEQUENCE OR DUPLICATED"
            TO ERROR-MESSAGE
        WRITE REPORT-RECORD
            FROM ERROR-MESSAGE AFTER 1
        WRITE REPORT-RECORD
            FROM PRODUCT-MASTER-RECORD AFTER 1.
```

—————— Example ——————

In this chapter we will illustrate indexed files using a master file that could be part of a personnel system. Each record in the file will contain the following fields:

> Name
> Social Security number
> Address (street, city, state, zip)
> Birth date

The file will be indexed using the Social Security number as the record key. (It would not be appropriate to use Name as the record key because people often use different versions of their name and sometimes change their name entirely. Also, two different people may have the same name. The Social Security number is a unique identifier which does not change and, therefore, is a very good record key for this file.)

The programs we will write will be interactive, menu-driven programs. This is not a requirement for processing indexed files; indexed files are equally useful in batch-oriented systems. However, because indexed files can be updated in place, they are well suited to an interactive environment and can be used where sequential files are inappropriate. The interactive nature of this system also allows us to illustrate programs with levels of menus—a concept not previously covered.

Problem Statement

Write a program to allow the user to create an indexed file with records containing the data described above. The program should be interactive and menu driven. The user should have the following menu options:

> Name the file
> Create a file
> List a file to the screen
> Print a file to the printer
> Secure help information
> Quit the program

Problem Analysis

The user must name the output file before performing any other functions of the program, but we wish to make the program flexible enough to deal with several different files of the same format. To accomplish this, we will list "Name the file" as a menu option, and once a file is named, display that name each time the menu is written to remind the user of which file is currently "active." We should also check to make sure that the file has been named prior to executing any command such as "Create" or "List" since these commands would be invalid unless a file name has been entered. (An alternative to this approach would be to begin the program with a default file name which would be used unless the user changed the name via the Name command.)

The program will process the indexed file sequentially either as an output file (for the Create command) or as an input file (for the List and Print commands). Since random access is not required for this program, the `SELECT` entry will contain the clauses

`ORGANIZATION IS INDEXED`	(required for all `INDEXED` files)
`ACCESS IS SEQUENTIAL`	(indicates sequential input and output only)

The `WRITE/INVALID KEY` statement will be used to write records to the file. The `INVALID KEY` clause will be executed when an attempt is made to write a record with a record key value that is not greater than the previous record written to the file. The `READ/AT END` statement will be used to read records from the file in the same way as for a sequential file.

Problem Solution

A partial solution to this problem is shown as Program 14a. In this program, two of the command options are not implemented (see the program stubs in paragraphs `3500-PRINT-FILE` at lines 139–141 and `3600-WRITE-HELP` at lines 143–145); however, the other commands, including Name file, Create file, and List file, are completed. (You can finish the program as an exercise if desired.) The structure diagram for the program is shown in Figure 14.3. Notice that the structure diagram reflects the menu structure of the program. The paragraph `1000-MAIN-CONTROL` controls `2000-PROCESS-USER-COMMANDS`; this creates a loop which terminates when the Quit program command is given. The paragraph `2000-PROCESS-USER-COMMANDS` controls the display of the menu, accepting the user's commands and selecting the appropriate program module to execute each command.

A sample execution of Program 14a is shown in Figures 14.4a–c. Figure 14.4a shows the initial menu presentation with the Current file showing all spaces. After the Name file command is executed, the Current file field shows the name of the file being created or processed. Note that the program verifies each command entered by the user. For example, after the Create command, the program responds with a description of what the command will accomplish (`Enter data for file . . .`) and a prompt (`OK to proceed? (Y/N)`). If the user enters N, the execution of the command is aborted. This feature is important in interactive menu-driven programs. The user can "get into trouble" fairly easily by giving unintended commands. The program should allow the user to back out of a command gracefully.

Figure 14.4b shows what happens when an out-of-sequence record is entered by a user. The error message is produced by the program when an attempt is made to write the record to the file (see lines 153–155). It is appropriate to remind the user that the data will not be written to the file. Figure 14.4c shows the use of the List command to list the file to the screen. The sample file created in this session contains three records. This data will be used as the basis for subsequent examples in this chapter.

```
 1 IDENTIFICATION DIVISION.
 2
 3 PROGRAM-ID. INDEXED-FILE-CREATE-PRO14A.
 4 AUTHOR. HORN.
 5
 6 ENVIRONMENT DIVISION.
 7
 8 CONFIGURATION SECTION.
 9
10 SOURCE-COMPUTER.
11 OBJECT-COMPUTER.
12
13 INPUT-OUTPUT SECTION.
14
15 FILE-CONTROL.
16
17     SELECT DATA-FILE ASSIGN TO DISK
18             ORGANIZATION IS INDEXED
19             ACCESS IS SEQUENTIAL
20             RECORD KEY IS SS-NUM-DR.
21
22 DATA DIVISION.
23
24 FILE SECTION.
25
26 FD  DATA-FILE
27     LABEL RECORDS ARE STANDARD
28     VALUE OF FILE-ID IS FILE-NAME.
29
30 01  DATA-RECORD.
31     03 SS-NUM-DR          PIC X(9).
32     03 NAME-DR            PIC X(20).
33        88 END-OF-DATA     VALUE "END" "end" "End".
34     03 STREET-ADDRESS-DR  PIC X(15).
35     03 CITY-DR            PIC X(10).
36     03 STATE-DR           PIC XX.
37     03 ZIP-DR             PIC 9(5).
38     03 DOB-DR             PIC 9(6).
39
40 WORKING-STORAGE SECTION.
41
42 01  FILE-NAME             PIC X(15) VALUE SPACES.
43
44 01  CONTROL-FIELDS.
45     02 EOF-FLAG           PIC XXX VALUE "NO".
46        88 END-OF-FILE     VALUE "YES".
47     02 ANSWER             PIC X VALUE "N".
48        88 DATA-OK         VALUE "Y" "y".
49     02 COMMAND            PIC X VALUE SPACE.
50        88 NAME-FILE       VALUE "N" "n".
51        88 CREATE-FILE     VALUE "C" "c".
52        88 PRINT-FILE      VALUE "P" "p".
53        88 LIST-FILE       VALUE "L" "l".
54        88 HELP            VALUE "H" "h".
55        88 QUIT            VALUE "Q" "q".
56        88 VALID-COMMAND   VALUE "N" "n" "C" "c"
57                                 "P" "p" "L" "l"
58                                 "H" "h" "Q" "q".
```

```
59
60 PROCEDURE DIVISION.
61
62 1000-MAIN-CONTROL.
63
64     PERFORM 2000-PROCESS-USER-COMMANDS
65             UNTIL QUIT.
66     STOP RUN.
67
68 2000-PROCESS-USER-COMMANDS.
69
70     PERFORM 3000-DISPLAY-MENU.
71     PERFORM 3100-GET-COMMAND.
72     IF      NAME-FILE
73             PERFORM 3200-GET-FILE-NAME
74     ELSE IF CREATE-FILE
75             PERFORM 3300-CREATE-FILE
76     ELSE IF LIST-FILE
77             PERFORM 3400-LIST-FILE
78     ELSE IF PRINT-FILE
79             PERFORM 3500-PRINT-FILE
80     ELSE IF HELP
81             PERFORM 3600-WRITE-HELP
82     ELSE IF NOT VALID-COMMAND
83             PERFORM 3700-WRITE-ERROR.
84
85 3000-DISPLAY-MENU.
86
87     DISPLAY "Command  Action".
88     DISPLAY "   N     Name file (Current file " FILE-NAME ")".
89     DISPLAY "   C     Create file".
90     DISPLAY "   L     List file to screen".
91     DISPLAY "   P     Print file to printer".
92     DISPLAY "   H     Help".
93     DISPLAY "   Q     Quit program".
94
95 3100-GET-COMMAND.
96
97     DISPLAY "Enter Command Code".
98     ACCEPT COMMAND.
99
100 3200-GET-FILE-NAME.
101
102     DISPLAY "Enter name of file ".
103     ACCEPT FILE-NAME.
104
```

```
105  3300-CREATE-FILE.
106
107      IF FILE-NAME = SPACES
108         DISPLAY "File has not been named"
109      ELSE
110         DISPLAY "Enter data for file " FILE-NAME
111         DISPLAY "OK to proceed? (Y/N)"
112         ACCEPT ANSWER
113         IF DATA-OK
114            OPEN OUTPUT DATA-FILE
115            MOVE "N" TO ANSWER
116            MOVE SPACES TO NAME-DR
117            PERFORM 9000-GET-DATA
118                    UNTIL DATA-OK OR END-OF-DATA
119            PERFORM 4000-BUILD-FILE
120                    UNTIL END-OF-DATA
121            CLOSE DATA-FILE.
122
123  3400-LIST-FILE.
124
125      IF FILE-NAME = SPACES
126         DISPLAY "File has not been named"
127      ELSE
128         DISPLAY "List content of file " FILE-NAME
129         DISPLAY "OK to proceed? (Y/N)"
130         ACCEPT ANSWER
131         IF DATA-OK
132            OPEN INPUT DATA-FILE
133            MOVE "NO" TO EOF-FLAG
134            PERFORM 9300-READ-DATA-FILE
135            PERFORM 4100-PROCESS-DATA
136                    UNTIL END-OF-FILE
137            CLOSE DATA-FILE.
138
139  3500-PRINT-FILE.
140
141      DISPLAY "Command not implemented".
142
143  3600-WRITE-HELP.
144
145      DISPLAY "Command not implemented".
146
147  3700-WRITE-ERROR.
148
149      DISPLAY "Invalid command code".
150
151  4000-BUILD-FILE.
152
153      WRITE DATA-RECORD INVALID KEY
154            DISPLAY "Record out of sequence or duplicated"
155            DISPLAY "Record not placed in file " FILE-NAME.
156      MOVE "N" TO ANSWER.
157      PERFORM 9000-GET-DATA UNTIL
158            DATA-OK OR END-OF-DATA.
159
```

Program 14a *(concluded)*

```
160 4100-PROCESS-DATA.
161
162     PERFORM 9200-DISPLAY-DATA.
163     PERFORM 9300-READ-DATA-FILE.
164
165 9000-GET-DATA.
166
167     DISPLAY "Enter Name (END to terminate)".
168     ACCEPT NAME-DR.
169     IF NOT END-OF-DATA
170        PERFORM 9100-ENTER-DATA
171        PERFORM 9200-DISPLAY-DATA
172        DISPLAY "Are data correct? (Y/N)"
173        ACCEPT ANSWER
174        IF NOT DATA-OK
175           DISPLAY "Reenter data".
176
177 9100-ENTER-DATA.
178
179     DISPLAY "Enter Social Security Number".
180     ACCEPT SS-NUM-DR.
181     DISPLAY "Enter Street Address".
182     ACCEPT STREET-ADDRESS-DR.
183     DISPLAY "Enter City".
184     ACCEPT CITY-DR.
185     DISPLAY "Enter Two Character State Abbreviation".
186     ACCEPT STATE-DR.
187     DISPLAY "Enter ZIP".
188     ACCEPT ZIP-DR.
189     DISPLAY "Enter Date of Birth in form mmddyy".
190     ACCEPT DOB-DR.
191
192 9200-DISPLAY-DATA.
193
194     DISPLAY "Name       : " NAME-DR.
195     DISPLAY "SS #       : " SS-NUM-DR.
196     DISPLAY "Address    : " STREET-ADDRESS-DR.
197     DISPLAY "             " CITY-DR STATE-DR " " ZIP-DR.
198     DISPLAY "Birth Date : " DOB-DR.
199
200 9300-READ-DATA-FILE.
201
202     READ DATA-FILE AT END
203           MOVE "YES" TO EOF-FLAG.
```

Figure 14.3   Structure diagram of Program 14a

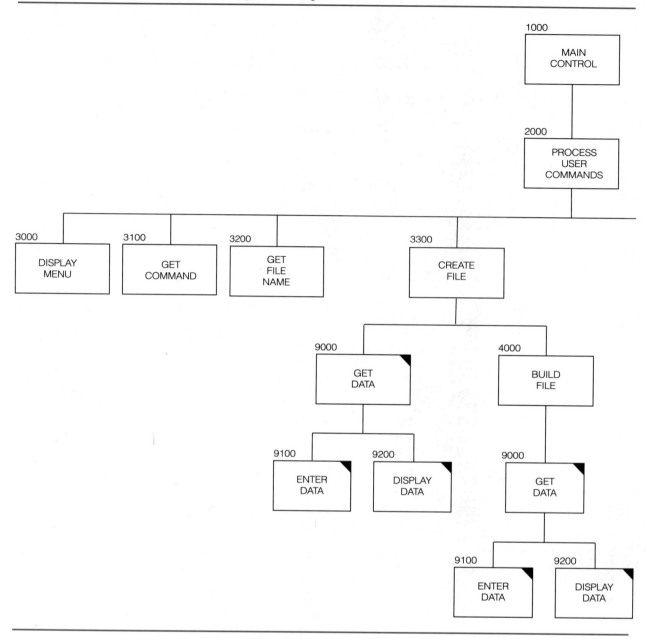

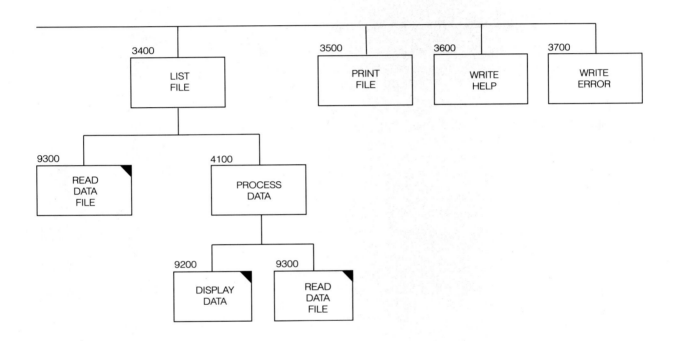

Figure 14.4a   Execution of Program 14a

No active file when   Command Action
program begins execution   N   Name file (Current file
                               C   Create file
                               L   List file to screen
                               P   Print file to printer
                               H   Help
                               Q   Quit program
                            Enter Command Code
Name command   N

                            Enter name of file
Name of file   PRO14.DAT

                            Command Action
                               N   Name file (Current file PRO14.DAT
                               C   Create file
                               L   List file to screen
                               P   Print file to printer
                               H   Help
                               Q   Quit program
                            Enter Command Code
Create command   C

                            Enter data for file PRO14.DAT
                            OK to proceed? (Y/N)
Command verification   Y

                          ⎧ Enter Name (END to terminate)
                          ⎪ JOE JONES
                          ⎪
                          ⎪ Enter Social Security Number
                          ⎪ 11111111111
                          ⎪
                          ⎪ Enter Street Address
                          ⎪ 123 X ST.
                          ⎪
Data for one record   ⎨ Enter City
                          ⎪ ELM CITY
                          ⎪
                          ⎪ Enter Two Character State Abbreviation
                          ⎪ AL
                          ⎪
                          ⎪ Enter ZIP
                          ⎪ 12300
                          ⎪
                          ⎪ Enter Date of Birth in form mmddyy
                          ⎩ 010368

                          ⎧ Name   : JOE JONES
                          ⎪ SS #   : 111111111
Content of the record   ⎨ Address   : 123 X ST.
                          ⎪   ELM CITY AL 12300
                          ⎩ Birth Date : 010368
                            Are data correct? (Y/N)
Verification of correctness Y

Figure 14.4b   Execution of Program 14a

A second record

```
Name        : MARY SMITH
SS #        : 100000000
Address     : 5900 MAIN ST
              ELM CITY   AL 12300
Birth Date : 062370
Are data correct? (Y/N)
Y
```

Error message; when creating an indexed file, the records must be in ascending sequence.

```
Record out of sequence or duplicated
Record not placed in file PRO14.DAT
Enter Name (END to terminate)
MARY SMITH

Enter Social Security Number
222222222

Enter Street Address
5900 MAIN ST

Enter City
ELM CITY

Enter Two Character State Abbreviation
AL

Enter ZIP
12300

Enter Date of Birth in form mmddyy
062370
```

Corrected record; this record will be accepted since its key field value is greater than the key field value in the first record.

```
Name        : MARY SMITH
SS #        : 222222222
Address     : 5900 MAIN ST
              ELM CITY   AL 12300
Birth Date : 062370
Are data correct? (Y/N)
Y
```

Figure 14.4c   Execution of Program 14a

| Terminate data entry | ```
Enter Name (END to terminate)
END
``` |
| | ```
Command  Action
    N       Name file (Current file PRO14.DAT      )
    C       Create file
    L       List file to screen
    P       Print file to printer
    H       Help
    Q       Quit program
Enter Command Code
``` |
| List command | ```
L
``` |
| | ```
List content of file PRO14.DAT
OK to proceed? (Y/N)
Y
``` |
| Content of PRO14. DAT (3 records) | ```
Name       : JOE JONES
SS #       : 111111111
Address    : 123 X ST.
             ELM CITY  AL 12300
Birth Date : 010368
Name       : MARY SMITH
SS #       : 222222222
Address    : 5900 MAIN ST
             ELM CITY  AL 12300
Birth Date : 062370
Name       : SUE BROWN
SS #       : 333333333
Address    : 1200 2ND AVE
             OAKTOWN   AL 12301
Birth Date : 071256
``` |
| | ```
Command  Action
    N       Name file (Current file PRO14.DAT      )
    C       Create file
    L       List file to screen
    P       Print file to printer
    H       Help
    Q       Quit program
Enter Command Code
``` |
| Quit command | ```
Q
``` |

14.3   RANDOM ACCESS TO DATA RECORDS

When an indexed file is used as an input file in a program, the records may be accessed either sequentially or randomly. Sequential accessing of records in an indexed file is like processing a sequential file. Records are read from the beginning to the end of the file. The READ statement must include an AT END clause to specify the action to be taken when end-of-file is found. Sequential processing of an indexed file and the creation of an indexed file use the same SELECT entry. For example, Program 14a uses the READ/AT END statement to read records from the indexed file (see lines 200–203).
```

Figure 14.5   SELECT entry for random access to an indexed file

```
SELECT file-name ASSIGN TO system-name
       ORGANIZATION IS INDEXED
       ACCESS IS RANDOM
       RECORD KEY IS data-name.
```

Note that except for the SELECT entry, Program 14a is similar to a program for processing a sequential file. To get the computer to read records from an indexed file in random sequence, you must use the SELECT entry shown in Figure 14.5.

When the ACCESS clause specifies RANDOM, the records will be read only on demand rather than sequentially. As with sequential processing, the RECORD KEY clause specifies the field that has been used as the basis for organizing the file. In order to access a record from the file, the program must place a value in the field specified as the RECORD KEY and then execute a READ statement of the form shown in Figure 14.6. If such a record exists, the data is returned to the program and processing continues normally. If such a record does not exist or if the record has been deleted, an INVALID KEY condition will be detected and reported. The general form for a READ statement for randomly accessing a file is shown in Figure 14.6. If an INVALID KEY condition is detected, the statement in the INVALID KEY clause will be executed.

For example, consider Program 14b described in detail in Section 14.6. In this program the data file is described in the SELECT entry as

```
ORGANIZATION IS INDEXED
ACCESS IS RANDOM
```

With this access mode, a READ statement must specify the INVALID KEY clause to handle the possibility that the required record might not be present in the file. For example, consider the READ statement at lines 172 through 173:

```
READ DATA-FILE
     INVALID KEY MOVE "YES" TO ERROR-FLAG.
```

Immediately prior to this statement, the user has entered the value of the record key for the record to be read from the file:

```
DISPLAY "Enter SS Number of record to be changed".
ACCEPT SS-NUM-DR.
```

The next statement initializes ERROR-FLAG to "NO". After execution of the READ statement, either the required record will have been read from the file (ERROR-FLAG will continue to have value "NO"), or the record was not present in the file (and ERROR-FLAG will have value "YES" since the INVALID KEY clause on the READ statement will be executed).

Figure 14.6   General form of the READ statement for random access to an indexed file

```
READ file-name [INTO data-name]
     [INVALID KEY statement]
```

The importance of the interconnection of the record key and the random access READ statement cannot be overemphasized. When reading a file randomly, the current value of the record key governs which record will be read. If a record exists with that key field value, the record is read from the file and placed in memory; if no record is found in the file that matches the current value of the record key, then the INVALID KEY condition is recognized, and the statement(s) in that clause are executed.

The WRITE statement used when an indexed file is in random access mode has the same format as that used when the file is in sequential mode; that is, the statement includes an INVALID KEY clause. When used in sequential access mode, the INVALID KEY condition will occur when an attempt is made to write a record with a key field value that is equal to or less than the key field value of the record previously written to the file. However, when the WRITE statement is used with random access mode, the INVALID KEY condition will be recognized only if an attempt is made to write a record with the same key field value as a previously existing record. It is not necessary to write records to the file sequentially. For example, consider the WRITE statement at lines 156 through 158 in Program 14b:

```
WRITE DATA-RECORD
      INVALID KEY DISPLAY "Record exists"
                  DISPLAY "New data not entered into file".
```

The program has just accepted data for a new record from the user. If the key field value already exists in the file, the record will not be written; instead, the INVALID KEY clause will be executed, and the error messages will be written.

14.4　MAINTAINING AN INDEXED FILE

When maintenance is performed on a sequential file, it is necessary to create an entirely new file with the changes inserted at appropriate points. Indexed files may be maintained in place; records may be added, changed, or deleted in an existing file without having to create a new file. Moreover, because an indexed file can be accessed randomly, the transaction records do not have to be in any particular sequence. As each transaction record is read, the appropriate master file record will be read, the changes will be made to it, and the record will be rewritten onto the master file.

The SELECT sentence for an indexed file to be updated randomly will be the same as for a file to be processed randomly. A file to be updated will be processed as both an input file (when a record is read from the file) and an output file (when the updated record is written onto the file). For this reason, the file must be opened in I-O mode. The same READ statement used to access data from a file randomly is also used when the file is opened in I-O mode. The INVALID KEY clause must be present. The statement required to rewrite the changed record onto the file has the form shown in Figure 14.7.

In order to use the REWRITE statement, a record must first have been accessed via a READ statement. The key field value of the record to be written is compared against the key field value of the last record read from the file. If the two key field values are not equal, then the INVALID KEY condition is true. Therefore, it is important that the program does not modify the key field value between the point at which the record is read and the

Figure 14.7   General form of the REWRITE statement for an
indexed file

<u>REWRITE</u> record-name [<u>FROM</u> data-name]
   [<u>INVALID</u> KEY statement]

---

point at which it is rewritten onto the file. Program 14b illustrates the
updating process. In this program, the REWRITE verb is used for transactions that involve changing values for existing fields in the master file (lines
183–184):

REWRITE DATA-RECORD
     INVALID KEY DISPLAY "Internal logic error".

The INVALID KEY clause will be executed only if the content of the key field
has changed between the time a record was read and the point at which
the REWRITE statement is executed. The purpose of this error message,
which, if everything is done properly, will never be printed, is primarily to
warn the programmer during testing that the key field value has changed.

14.5   ADDING AND DELETING RECORDS

In order to add records to an indexed file or to delete records from an
indexed file, ACCESS must be random, and the file must be opened in I-O
mode. The WRITE statement shown in Figure 14.2 is used to write new
records in the file. Remember that the INVALID KEY condition occurs when
an attempt is made to write a record with a key field that duplicates the
key field of a record already present in the file. The DELETE statement,
which has the general form shown in Figure 14.8, is used to delete records
from an indexed file.

Figure 14.8   General form of the DELETE statement

<u>DELETE</u> file-name RECORD
   [<u>INVALID</u> KEY statement]

If the file is being processed in sequential access mode, the DELETE
statement will cause deletion of the last record read from the file. The
INVALID KEY clause cannot be specified in this case.

If the file is being processed in random access mode, the content of
the record key is used to determine the record to be deleted from the file.
The INVALID KEY condition occurs if the file does not contain a record with
a record key equal to that contained in the record key field.

In order for the records to be deleted from a file, the file must be
opened in I-O mode, as deletion actually causes the system to read the file
(to determine if a record exists) and to write a new value into a code field
to indicate that the record is deleted.

14.6   A COMPLETE MAINTENANCE EXAMPLE

Problem Statement

Write a program to allow the user to perform maintenance functions—add, change, and delete—on the indexed personnel file used in Program 14a. The program should be interactive and menu driven.

Problem Analysis

The design of any program of this nature should begin with the menu structure. We will need a main menu similar to that used in Program 14a. Let us use the following items in the main menu:

> Name a file
> Update a file
> Secure help
> Quit the program

Updating the file will have a number of options. Let us use another menu, technically called a submenu, to allow the user to choose from among the different types of operations that are available:

> New record (to add a record to the file)
> Delete a record
> Change an existing record
> Quit the update

Figure 14.9   Menu structure of Program 14b

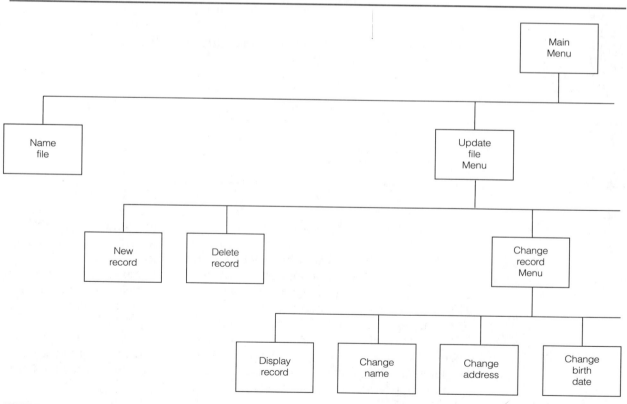

Adding or deleting a record is fairly straightforward, but changing a record involves many possible activities. After the record key value of the record to be changed has been entered, the user will need to select which field(s) are to be changed. It would be helpful to allow the user to display the current content of the record at any point in the process to verify the correctness of the data. Finally, it would be a nice touch to allow the user to discard the changes that have been entered if need be. We will use the following submenu for changing a record:

Display the record
Change the name
Change the address
Change the birth date
Quit changes with save
Quit changes and discard (no save)

It is useful to view the menu structure as a tree rooted at the main menu as shown in Figure 14.9. You will find that the structure of the program follows the structure of the menu tree quite closely, so having the menu structure clearly laid out early in the design process is a big advantage.

Problem Solution

A partial solution to this program is shown in Program 14b. (As with Program 14a, some procedures are not fully implemented.) In order to conserve space, only relevant portions of this program are reprinted here; portions that are omitted are substantially similar to portions of Program 14a.

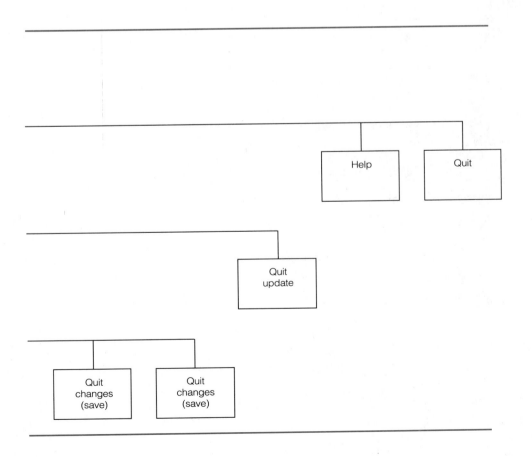

Program 14b

```
 1 IDENTIFICATION DIVISION.
 2
 3 PROGRAM-ID. INDEXED-FILE-UPDATE-PRO14B.
 .
 .
 .
15 FILE-CONTROL.
16
17     SELECT DATA-FILE ASSIGN TO DISK
18             ORGANIZATION IS INDEXED
19             ACCESS IS RANDOM
20             RECORD KEY IS SS-NUM-DR.
 .
 .
 .
43 01  CONTROL-FIELDS.
44     02 ANSWER                PIC X VALUE "N".
45         88 DATA-OK           VALUE "Y" "y".
46     02 ERROR-FLAG            PIC XXX VALUE "NO".
47     02 COMMAND               PIC X VALUE SPACE.
48         88 NAME-FILE         VALUE "N" "n".
49         88 UPDATE-FILE       VALUE "U" "u".
50         88 HELP              VALUE "H" "h".
51         88 QUIT              VALUE "Q" "q".
52         88 VALID-COMMAND     VALUE "N" "n" "U" "u"
53                                    "H" "h" "Q" "q".
54     02 UPDATE-COMMAND        PIC X VALUE SPACE.
55         88 NEW-RECORD        VALUE "N" "n".
56         88 DELETE-RECORD     VALUE "D" "d".
57         88 CHANGE-RECORD     VALUE "C" "c".
58         88 QUIT-UPDATE       VALUE "Q" "q".
59         88 VALID-UPDATE      VALUE "N" "n" "C" "c"
60                                    "D" "d" "Q" "q".
61     02 CHANGE-COMMAND        PIC X VALUE SPACE.
62         88 DISPLAY-RECORD    VALUE "D" "d".
63         88 CHANGE-NAME       VALUE "N" "n".
64         88 CHANGE-ADDRESS    VALUE "A" "a".
65         88 CHANGE-BIRTH-DATE VALUE "B" "b".
66         88 QUIT-CHANGES      VALUE "Q" "q".
67         88 VALID-CHANGE      VALUE "D" "d" "N" "n"
68                                    "A" "a" "B" "b" "Q" "q".
69 PROCEDURE DIVISION.
70
71 1000-MAIN-CONTROL.
72
73     PERFORM 2000-PROCESS-USER-COMMANDS
74             UNTIL QUIT.
75     STOP RUN.
76
```

Program 14b *(continued)*

```
77  2000-PROCESS-USER-COMMANDS.
78
79       PERFORM 3000-DISPLAY-MENU.
80       PERFORM 3100-GET-COMMAND.
81       IF      NAME-FILE
82               PERFORM 3200-GET-FILE-NAME
83       ELSE IF UPDATE-FILE
84               PERFORM 3300-UPDATE-FILE
85       ELSE IF HELP
86               PERFORM 3400-WRITE-HELP
87       ELSE IF NOT VALID-COMMAND
88               PERFORM 3500-WRITE-ERROR.
         .
         .
         .
109 3300-UPDATE-FILE.
110
111      IF FILE-NAME = SPACES
112          DISPLAY "File has not been named"
113      ELSE
114          DISPLAY "Update file " FILE-NAME
115          DISPLAY "OK to proceed? (Y/N)"
116          ACCEPT ANSWER
117          IF DATA-OK
118              OPEN I-O DATA-FILE
119              MOVE SPACES TO UPDATE-COMMAND
120              PERFORM 4000-UPDATE-FILE
121                      UNTIL QUIT-UPDATE
122              CLOSE DATA-FILE.
         .
         .
         .
132 4000-UPDATE-FILE.
133
134      DISPLAY "Update Menu (Current File " FILE-NAME ")".
135      DISPLAY "Command Action".
136      DISPLAY "   N    New record".
137      DISPLAY "   D    Delete record".
138      DISPLAY "   C    Change record".
139      DISPLAY "   Q    Quit update".
140      DISPLAY "Enter update command"
141      ACCEPT UPDATE-COMMAND.
142      IF NEW-RECORD
143          PERFORM 5000-WRITE-NEW-RECORD
144      ELSE IF DELETE-RECORD
145          PERFORM 5100-DELETE-RECORD
146      ELSE IF CHANGE-RECORD
147          PERFORM 5200-CHANGE-RECORD
148      ELSE IF NOT VALID-UPDATE
149          DISPLAY "Invalid update code".
150
```

Program 14b   *(continued)*

```
151 5000-WRITE-NEW-RECORD.
152
153     MOVE "N" TO ANSWER.
154     PERFORM 9000-GET-DATA
155             UNTIL DATA-OK.
156     WRITE DATA-RECORD
157         INVALID KEY DISPLAY "Record exists"
158                    DISPLAY "New data not entered into file".
159
160 5100-DELETE-RECORD.
161
162     DISPLAY "Enter SS Number of record to be deleted".
163     ACCEPT SS-NUM-DR.
164     DELETE DATA-FILE RECORD
165         INVALID KEY DISPLAY "Record not present in file".
166
167 5200-CHANGE-RECORD.
168
169     DISPLAY "Enter SS Number of record to be changed".
170     ACCEPT SS-NUM-DR.
171     MOVE "NO" TO ERROR-FLAG.
172     READ DATA-FILE
173         INVALID KEY MOVE "YES" TO ERROR-FLAG.
174     IF ERROR-FLAG = "YES"
175        DISPLAY "Record does not exist in file"
176     ELSE
177         MOVE SPACE TO CHANGE-COMMAND
178         PERFORM 6000-GET-CHANGES
179                 UNTIL QUIT-CHANGES.
180     IF ERROR-FLAG = "NO"
181        IF CHANGE-COMMAND = "Q"
182           DISPLAY "Changes being copied to file"
183           REWRITE DATA-RECORD
184                   INVALID KEY DISPLAY "Internal logic error".
185     IF ERROR-FLAG = "NO"
186        IF CHANGE-COMMAND = "q"
187           DISPLAY "Changes discarded".
188
189 6000-GET-CHANGES.
190
191     DISPLAY "Change Menu (Current Record " SS-NUM-DR ")".
192     DISPLAY "Command Action".
193     DISPLAY "   D     Display record".
194     DISPLAY "   N     Change name".
195     DISPLAY "   A     Change address".
196     DISPLAY "   B     Change date of birth".
197     DISPLAY "   Q     Quit changes: write changed record".
198     DISPLAY "   q     Quit changes: do not write changed record".
199     DISPLAY "Enter change command"
200     ACCEPT CHANGE-COMMAND.
```

Program 14b   *(concluded)*

```
201        IF DISPLAY-RECORD
202             PERFORM 9200-DISPLAY-DATA
203        ELSE IF CHANGE-NAME
204             DISPLAY "Enter new name"
205             ACCEPT NAME-DR
206        ELSE IF CHANGE-ADDRESS
207             DISPLAY "Enter new Street Address"
208             ACCEPT STREET-ADDRESS-DR
209             DISPLAY "Enter new City"
210             ACCEPT CITY-DR
211             DISPLAY "Enter new Two Character State Abbreviation"
212             ACCEPT STATE-DR
213             DISPLAY "Enter new ZIP"
214             ACCEPT ZIP-DR
215        ELSE IF CHANGE-BIRTH-DATE
216             DISPLAY "Enter new Date of Birth in form mmddyy"
217             ACCEPT DOB-DR
218        ELSE IF NOT VALID-CHANGE
219             DISPLAY "Invalid change code".
                        .
                        .
                        .
```

Since random access to the file is required, the SELECT entry for DATA-FILE specifies

```
ORGANIZATION IS INDEXED
ACCESS IS RANDOM
```

The file is opened in I-0 mode (line 118) to enable all operations that are required in the complete maintenance process.

This program illustrates the use of input/output statements for a random-access indexed file. The WRITE statement at lines 156 through 158 is used to add a record to the file. Note the use of the INVALID KEY clause to write an error message regarding duplicate records. The DELETE statement at lines 164 and 165 is used to remove a record from the file. Again note the use of the INVALID KEY clause to display an error message if the specified record is not present in the file. The REWRITE statement (lines 183–184) is used to write changes that the user has made to an existing record. The INVALID KEY clause is used to alert the user to a programming error, namely, that the content of the record key is different from that on the record last read from the file. The READ statement (lines 172–173) is used to read a specified record from the file; the INVALID KEY clause is executed when the record is not present in the file.

Figures 14.10a–d illustrate a sample execution of Program 14b using the data file created by Program 14a as shown in Figure 14.4c. Figure 14.10a shows the main menu with current file already set to PRO14.DAT (accomplished by the Name file command). We wish to add a record with key field value 222000000 so we issue the Update command and, from the Update submenu, the New record command. This allows us to enter the data and verify its correctness. At this point, the record is added to the file.

Figure 14.10b illustrates use of the Delete record command—first the error message that occurs when an attempt is made to delete a record that is not present and then to delete a record that exists (record 222222222).

Figure 14.10α   Execution of Program 14b

```
                        Main Menu
                     Command  Action
Current file            N       Name file (Current file PRO14.DAT        )
                        U       Update file
                        H       Help
                        Q       Quit program
                     Enter command
Update command       U


                     Update file PRO14.DAT
                     OK to proceed? (Y/N)
                     Y


                     Update Menu (Current File PRO14.DAT           )
                     Command Action
                        N     New record
                        D     Delete record
                        C     Change record
                        Q     Quit update
                     Enter update command
New record command   N

                     Enter Name
                     SAM SPADE

                     Enter Social Security Number
                     222000000

                     Enter Street Address
                     345 FIRST AVE

                     Enter City
                     OAKTOWN

Data for new record  Enter Two Character State Abbreviation
                     AL

                     Enter ZIP
                     12301

                     Enter Date of Birth in form mmddyy
                     012356

                     Name       : SAM SPADE
                     SS #       : 222000000
                     Address    : 345 FIRST AVE
                                  OAKTOWN    AL 12301
                     Birth Date : 012356
                     Are data correct? (Y/N)
Verification of correctness  Y
```

Figure 14.10b   Execution of Program 14b

```
                          Update Menu (Current File PRO14.DAT        )
                          Command Action
                              N    New record
                              D    Delete record
                              C    Change record
                              Q    Quit update
                          Enter update command
Delete record command     D

Record key of record      Enter SS Number of record to be deleted
to be deleted             123456789

Error message; record     Record not present in file
not in file               Update Menu (Current File PRO14.DAT        )
                          Command Action
                              N    New record
                              D    Delete record
                              C    Change record
                              Q    Quit update
                          Enter update command
Delete record command     D

                          Enter SS Number of record to be deleted
This record will be deleted  222222222
```

Figure 14.10c   Execution of Program 14b

```
                          Update Menu (Current File PRO14.DAT        )
                          Command Action
                              N    New record
                              D    Delete record
                              C    Change record
                              Q    Quit update
                          Enter update command
Change record command     C

Record to be              Enter SS Number of record to be changed
changed                   333333333

Current record key;       Change Menu (Current Record 333333333)
all changes will pertain  Command Action
to this record                D    Display record
                              N    Change name
                              A    Change address
                              B    Change date of birth
                              Q    Quit changes: write changed record
                              q    Quit changes: do not write changed record
                          Enter change command
Display record command    D

                         ⎧ Name        : SUE BROWN
                         ⎪ SS #        : 333333333
Current content of record ⎨ Address     : 1200 2ND AVE
                         ⎪              OAKTOWN    AL 12301
                         ⎩ Birth Date : 071256
```

Figure 14.10d   Execution of Program 14b

Change name

```
Enter change command
N
```

New name; change is
made in memory,
not on disk

```
Enter new name
S. BROWN

Change Menu (Current Record 333333333)
Command Action
     D      Display record
     N      Change name
     A      Change address
     B      Change date of birth
     Q      Quit changes: write changed record
     q      Quit changes: do not write changed record
Enter change command
Q
```

Quit changes and make
them permanent; "q"
command would
terminate without
writing new record

```
Changes being copied to file
Update Menu (Current File PRO14.DAT          )
Command Action
     N      New record
     D      Delete record
     C      Change record
     Q      Quit update
Enter update command
Q
```

Quit update command

```
     Main Menu
Command   Action
     N        Name file (Current file PRO14.DAT          )
     U        Update file
     H        Help
     Q        Quit program
Enter command
Q
```

Quit program

Figure 14.11   Content of file PRO14.DAT after update

```
Name       : JOE JONES
SS #       : 111111111
Address    : 123 X ST.
             ELM CITY   AL 12300
Birth Date : 010368
```

New record

Record 222222222
was deleted

New name

```
Name       : SAM SPADE
SS #       : 222000000
Address    : 345 FIRST AVE
             OAKTOWN     AL 12301
Birth Date : 012356
Name       : S. BROWN
SS #       : 333333333
Address    : 1200 2ND AVE
             OAKTOWN     AL 12301
Birth Date : 071256
```

Figure 14.10c shows the process of changing a record using the Change record command. The user is first prompted for the record key of the record to be changed. This record key is displayed as the Current Record in the Change Menu. (This reminds the user which record is being changed.) We wish to examine the current content of the record so the Display record command is used. Figure 14.10d shows the process of changing the name in the Current Record. Note the presence of two quit commands. Using the command Q, the program will exit the changes and, using the REWRITE statement, will make the changes part of the file; the command q will also exit the Change submenu, but the changes will not be made part of the file.

The content of the file after this session is shown in Figure 14.11.

An Alternative Solution

Program 14c shows an alternative solution to this problem, which allows not only the options listed above but also the functions performed by Program 14a. The main menu for this program is shown in Figure 14.12. The major feature of Program 14c is the use of two SELECT entries for two files—DATA-FILE with random access and NEW-DATA-FILE with sequential access. The program chooses from these two files the one which meets its needs to perform the operations required to execute a given command. For example, when creating a new file in response to the Create a new file command, the program opens NEW-DATA-FILE. This allows sequential access to the file. A similar choice would be made for List a file and Print a file commands since these also need sequential access to the file. To update the file, however, DATA-FILE would be used since these operations require random access. (It is not a logical inconsistency to use two different SELECTs to describe what may physically be the same file during the execution of the program. The SELECT entry specifies only how the file is organized and what type of access is permitted; this organization/access can be applied to any appropriate file of the user's choice.)

14.7   DYNAMIC ACCESS

In addition to sequential and random access methods discussed previously, COBOL permits dynamic access to an indexed file. **Dynamic access** allows both sequential access and random access to the same file by the

---

Figure 14.12   Main menu for Program 14c

```
     Main Menu
     Command   Action
        N         Name file (Current file PRO14.DAT        )
        C         Create a new file
        U         Update an existing file
        L         List a file (to screen)
        P         Print a file (to printer)
        H         Help
        Q         Quit program
     Enter command
```

```
  1 IDENTIFICATION DIVISION.
  2
  3 PROGRAM-ID. INDEXED-FILE-UPDATE-PRO14C.
  .
  .
  .
 15 FILE-CONTROL.
 16
 17     SELECT DATA-FILE ASSIGN TO DISK
 18             ORGANIZATION IS INDEXED
 19             ACCESS IS RANDOM
 20             RECORD KEY IS SS-NUM-DR.
 21     SELECT NEW-DATA-FILE ASSIGN TO DISK
 22             ORGANIZATION IS INDEXED
 23             ACCESS IS SEQUENTIAL
 24             RECORD KEY IS SS-NUM-NDR.
  .
  .
  .
 92 PROCEDURE DIVISION.
 93
 94 1000-MAIN-CONTROL.
 95
 96     PERFORM 2000-PROCESS-USER-COMMANDS
 97                 UNTIL QUIT.
 98     STOP RUN.
 99
100 2000-PROCESS-USER-COMMANDS.
101
102     PERFORM 3000-DISPLAY-MENU.
103     PERFORM 3100-GET-COMMAND.
104     IF     NAME-FILE
105             PERFORM 3200-GET-FILE-NAME
106     ELSE IF CREATE-FILE
107             PERFORM 3300-NEW-FILE
108     ELSE IF UPDATE-FILE
109             PERFORM 3400-UPDATE-FILE
110     ELSE IF LIST-FILE
111             PERFORM 3500-LIST-FILE
112     ELSE IF PRINT-FILE
113             PERFORM 3600-PRINT-FILE
114     ELSE IF HELP
115             PERFORM 3700-WRITE-HELP
116     ELSE IF NOT VALID-COMMAND
117             PERFORM 3800-WRITE-ERROR.
118
```

Program 14c   *(concluded)*

```
119 3000-DISPLAY-MENU.
120
121     DISPLAY "   Main Menu".
122     DISPLAY "Command   Action".
123     DISPLAY "   N      Name file (Current file " FILE-NAME ")".
124     DISPLAY "   C      Create a new file".
125     DISPLAY "   U      Update an existing file".
126     DISPLAY "   L      List a file (to screen)".
127     DISPLAY "   P      Print a file (to printer)".
128     DISPLAY "   H      Help".
129     DISPLAY "   Q      Quit program".
      .
      .
      .
141 3300-NEW-FILE.
142
143     IF FILE-NAME = SPACES
144         DISPLAY "File has not been named"
145     ELSE
146         DISPLAY "Create new file " FILE-NAME
147         DISPLAY "OK to proceed: (Y/N)"
148         ACCEPT ANSWER
149         IF DATA-OK
150             OPEN OUTPUT NEW-DATA-FILE
151             MOVE "Y" TO ANSWER
152             PERFORM 4000-CREATE-FILE
153                     UNTIL NOT DATA-OK
154             CLOSE NEW-DATA-FILE.
      .
      .
      .
199 4000-CREATE-FILE.
200
201     MOVE "N" TO ANSWER.
202     PERFORM 9000-GET-DATA
203             UNTIL DATA-OK.
204     WRITE NEW-DATA-RECORD FROM DATA-RECORD
205         INVALID KEY DISPLAY "Record out of sequence"
206                     DISPLAY "Data discarded".
207     DISPLAY "More data? (Y/N)".
208     ACCEPT ANSWER.
      .
      .
      .
```

program. The general form of the SELECT entry for dynamic access is shown in Figure 14.13.

When an indexed file is accessed dynamically and opened in either INPUT or I-O mode, records are read sequentially from the file using the Format-1 READ statement with the NEXT RECORD option, as shown in Figure 14.14. In order to read records randomly from a file, a Format-2 READ statement is required.

When a Format-1 READ statement is executed, the next available record is read from the file; if the file has just been opened, then the first record is read. When a Format-2 READ statement is executed, the value

Figure 14.13   General form of the SELECT entry for dynamic access to an indexed file

---

```
SELECT file-name ASSIGN TO system-name
       ORGANIZATION IS INDEXED
       ACCESS MODE IS DYNAMIC
       RECORD KEY IS data-name.
```

---

contained in the key field specified for the file is used to determine the record to be read. If a Format-1 READ statement is executed after a Format-2 statement, the record immediately following the record by the Format-2 statement will be read. This feature can be used to continue the processing of an indexed file in a sequential manner after reading a specified record.

For example, suppose we want to process all the records in the DATA-FILE described in Program 14b, beginning with record number 111111111. The SELECT statement would be written as

```
SELECT DATA-FILE
    ASSIGN TO DISK
    ORGANIZATION IS INDEXED
    ACCESS IS DYNAMIC
    RECORD KEY IS SS-NUM-DR.
```

The program would initially execute a procedure similar to the following:

```
MOVE "111111111" TO SS-NUM-DR.
MOVE "YES" TO RECORD-PRESENT-FLAG.
READ DATA-FILE
    INVALID KEY MOVE "NO" TO RECORD-PRESENT-FLAG.
```

This procedure will read the required record if it is present in the file. Then, a procedure like the following could process the remainder of the records in the file:

```
MOVE "NO" TO EOF-FLAG.
IF RECORD-PRESENT-FLAG = "YES"
    PERFORM PROCESS-DATA UNTIL EOF-FLAG = "YES".
PROCESS-DATA.
    PERFORM PROCESS-RECORD.
    READ DATA-FILE NEXT RECORD
        AT END MOVE "YES" TO EOF-FLAG.
```

Figure 14.14   General form of READ statements

Format-1   (for sequential access)

```
READ file-name [NEXT] RECORD
    [INTO data-name]
    [AT END statement]
```

Format-2   (for random access)

```
READ file-name RECORD
    [INTO data-name]
    [KEY IS data-name]
    [INVALID KEY statement]
```

In this example, a Format-1 READ statement is used for sequential access to the data after the Format-2 READ statement has read the initial record. Note that the NEXT clause is required when both Format-1 and Format-2 READ statements are present.

Figure 14.15   General form of the START statement

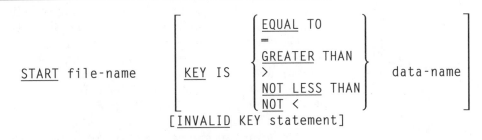

Some versions of COBOL support the START statement, which can be used to begin processing of an indexed file accessed in dynamic mode at a specified record. The general form of the START statement is shown in Figure 14.15. The START statement will cause subsequent access to the file to begin with a record whose key field value satisfies the relation specified in the KEY IS clause. The data-name specified in the KEY IS clause will normally be the RECORD KEY field specified for the file. For example, suppose INVENTORY-FILE has been established as an indexed file with key field INVENTORY-NUMBER-IR, with length 4. In order to begin processing this file with the record *following* the record with inventory number equal to 5000, the following could be used:

```
MOVE "5000" TO INVENTORY-NUMBER-IR.
START INVENTORY-FILE KEY > INVENTORY-NUMBER-IR
    INVALID KEY PERFORM 3000-ERROR.
```

The INVALID KEY condition will result if there is no record in the file satisfying the condition (i.e., no record with key field value greater than 5000).

If the KEY IS clause is omitted, the current content of the RECORD KEY is used for comparison, and the "equal to" relation is assumed. For example, to begin the processing of the file with record 5000, either of the following two coding sequences could be used:

```
MOVE "5000" TO INVENTORY-NUMBER-IR.
START INVENTORY-FILE
    KEY IS EQUAL TO INVENTORY-NUMBER-IR
    INVALID KEY PERFORM 3000-ERROR.
```

or

```
MOVE "5000" TO INVENTORY-NUMBER-IR.
START INVENTORY-FILE
    INVALID KEY PERFORM 3000-ERROR.
```

The NOT LESS THAN option is useful to begin processing of a file at a specified record if it exists or, if it does not, at the next record. For example, to begin the processing of INVENTORY-FILE at record 5000, or if record 5000 is not in the file with the first record with key field greater than 5000, the following code could be used:

```
MOVE "5000" TO INVENTORY-NUMBER-IR.
START INVENTORY-FILE
     KEY NOT LESS THAN INVENTORY-NUMBER-IR
     INVALID KEY PERFORM 3000-ERROR.
```

──────────── Example ────────────

Program 14c accomplishes the task of obtaining both sequential and random access to the same file by using two SELECTs and two FD entries for the file. When a file is opened using only the sequential access description, sequential access statements are allowed; when a file is opened using the random access description only random access statements are allowed. This approach is acceptable under certain circumstances, but it has the disadvantage of not offering both random and sequential access alternately to the same file.

Program 14d makes use of the DYNAMIC access method for the file to enable both sequential and random access to the file as needed. The file is described in the SELECT entry (lines 17–20) as

```
ORGANIZATION IS INDEXED
ACCESS IS DYNAMIC
```

The most striking difference between this program and other variations we have written comes when the program needs sequential access to carry out the List file command. To accomplish this task, the file is opened for INPUT mode (line 139). To begin reading at the beginning of the file, we use the START statement with the record key field set to LOW VALUES (see lines 140–142). The procedure which reads DATA-FILE must use the Format-1 READ statement (lines 287–288):

```
READ DATA-FILE NEXT RECORD
     AT END . . .
```

In this case, the clause NEXT RECORD is not optional as it usually is in a sequential READ statement. In fact, it is this clause that enables the compiler to determine that the program is to perform a sequential READ rather than a random READ.

14.8 DEBUG CLINIC

One of the most difficult aspects of programming with indexed files is the close relationships among the access method, open mode, and input/output statements that can be used to process a file. Many difficult debugging problems can be traced to mistakes made in this area. An indexed file may be accessed by three methods (SEQUENTIAL, RANDOM, and DYNAMIC) and opened in three modes (INPUT, OUTPUT, I-O). The combination of access method and open mode governs the types of input/output statements that may be used.

Sequential Access

INPUT mode permits the statements READ (Format-1) and START to be used. This combination is used to read all or part of a file sequentially.

Program 14d

```
 1 IDENTIFICATION DIVISION.
 2
 3 PROGRAM-ID. INDEXED-FILE-UPDATE-PRO14D.
 .
 .
 .
15 FILE-CONTROL.
16
17     SELECT DATA-FILE ASSIGN TO DISK
18            ORGANIZATION IS INDEXED
19            ACCESS IS DYNAMIC
20            RECORD KEY IS SS-NUM-DR.
 .
 .
 .
72 PROCEDURE DIVISION.
73
74 1000-MAIN-CONTROL.
75
76     PERFORM 2000-PROCESS-USER-COMMANDS
77            UNTIL QUIT.
78     STOP RUN.
79
80 2000-PROCESS-USER-COMMANDS.
81
82     PERFORM 3000-DISPLAY-MENU.
83     PERFORM 3100-GET-COMMAND.
84     IF     NAME-FILE
85            PERFORM 3200-GET-FILE-NAME
86     ELSE IF UPDATE-FILE
87            PERFORM 3300-UPDATE-FILE
88     ELSE IF LIST-FILE
89            PERFORM 3400-LIST-FILE
90     ELSE IF HELP
91            PERFORM 3500-WRITE-HELP
92     ELSE IF NOT VALID-COMMAND
93            PERFORM 3600-WRITE-ERROR.
94
95 3000-DISPLAY-MENU.
96
97     DISPLAY "   Main Menu".
98     DISPLAY "Command  Action".
99     DISPLAY "   N     Name file (Current file " FILE-NAME ")".
100    DISPLAY "   U     Update file".
101    DISPLAY "   L     List file".
102    DISPLAY "   H     Help".
103    DISPLAY "   Q     Quit program".
 .
 .
 .
```

Program 14d   *(concluded)*

```
130 3400-LIST-FILE.
131
132     IF FILE-NAME = SPACES
133         DISPLAY "File has not been named"
134     ELSE
135         DISPLAY "List file " FILE-NAME
136         DISPLAY "OK to proceed? (Y/N)"
137         ACCEPT ANSWER
138         IF DATA-OK
139             OPEN INPUT DATA-FILE
140             MOVE LOW-VALUES TO SS-NUM-DR
141             START DATA-FILE
142                  KEY NOT LESS THAN SS-NUM-DR
143             MOVE "NO" TO EOF-FLAG
144             PERFORM 9300-READ-DATA-FILE
145             PERFORM 4100-PROCESS-DATA-FILE
146                  UNTIL END-OF-FILE
147             CLOSE DATA-FILE.
           .
           .
           .
285 9300-READ-DATA-FILE.
286
287     READ DATA-FILE NEXT RECORD
288             AT END MOVE "YES" TO EOF-FLAG.
```

OUTPUT mode permits only the WRITE statement. This combination is usually used to create an indexed file.

I-0 mode permits use of READ (Format-1), REWRITE, START, and DELETE statements. This combination is used for sequentially updating an indexed file. Note that new records cannot be added because the WRITE statement cannot be used.

Random Access

INPUT mode permits only the Format-2 READ statement. This combination is used to access data records in the file randomly; no changes to the file can be made.

OUTPUT mode permits only the WRITE statement. This combination is used to add records to a file randomly.

I-0 mode permits the use of the READ (Format-2), WRITE, REWRITE, START, and DELETE statements. This combination is used to perform random maintenance of an indexed file; it permits addition, deletion, and changing of records.

Dynamic Access

INPUT mode permits the Format-1 READ for sequential access, the Format-2 READ for random access, and the START statement. This combination is used to process sequential segments of an indexed file.

OUTPUT mode permits only the WRITE statement. This combination can be used only to add records to an indexed file; dynamic access always implies that the file is in existence.

I-0 mode permits the use of Format-1 READ (for sequential access), Format-2 READ (for random access), WRITE, REWRITE, START, and DELETE statements. This combination allows the program the greatest possible flexibility in processing an indexed file.

Choosing the Best Combination

In general, a programmer should choose that combination of access method and open mode that permits only the type of operation on a file required by the particular program. This practice will result in fewer potential errors in the long run, and it is in keeping with the principle that restricting operations on a file to the minimum required to perform a given task enhances the overall security of the data processing system.

Figure 14.16   Relationship among access method, open mode, and input/output statements for indexed and relative files

Access Method	Open Mode	READ (1)	READ (2)	WRITE	REWRITE	START	DELETE
Sequential	INPUT	X				X	
	OUTPUT			X			
	I-0	X			X	X	X
Random	INPUT		X				
	OUTPUT			X			
	I-0		X	X	X		X
Dynamic	INPUT	X	X			X	
	OUTPUT			X			
	I-0	X	X	X	X	X	X

Note: READ (1) represents the sequential READ statement (NEXT RECORD).
READ (2) represents random READ.

Figure 14.16 presents a summary of these relationships. You may wish to refer to this figure as you plan a program involving indexed files. For example, from the table you can determine that if an indexed file is specified to have RANDOM access and is open in I-0 mode, the Format-2 READ statement (random access read), the WRITE, the REWRITE, and the DELETE statements are permitted.

14.9   MULTIPLE RECORD KEYS

In our previous discussion of indexed files, we have included only one record key (called the **prime key**). All access to the file was governed by the content of that field. When the file is first created, it is possible to specify alternate record key fields to provide other ways to access data in the file. The record keys declared when the file is created define all the record keys that can be used by other programs needing access to that file.

For example, the prime key for the file mentioned in Section 14.7 is INVENTORY-NUMBER-IR. By placing an appropriate value in this field, the program is able to read the corresponding record from the file. But suppose the record associated with a particular part description must be accessed. To enable the program to access the desired record, the part description field must be declared to be an ALTERNATE KEY by including the appropriate clause in the SELECT sentence. The general form of the SELECT entry for indexed files is shown in Figure 14.17.

The ALTERNATE KEY clause provides a major option: If duplicate values of the alternate key are permitted, the WITH DUPLICATES clause is included. If each record in the file must have a unique value in the alternate key field (in the same way as each record must have a unique value in the prime key field), the clause is omitted. For example, to permit access to the file INVENTORY-FILE by both inventory number and part description, the SELECT entry could be written as

```
SELECT INVENTORY-FILE
    ASSIGN TO DISK
    ORGANIZATION IS INDEXED
    ACCESS IS DYNAMIC
    RECORD KEY IS INVENTORY-NUMBER-IR
    ALTERNATE RECORD KEY IS PART-DESCRIPTION-IR WITH
        DUPLICATES.
```

This example assumes that more than one record may have the same part description. More than one alternate record key is permitted on most COBOL systems. For example, the following SELECT would provide access by part supplier as well as inventory number and part description.

```
SELECT INVENTORY-FILE
    ASSIGN TO DISK
    ORGANIZATION IS INDEXED
    ACCESS IS DYNAMIC
    RECORD KEY IS INVENTORY-NUMBER-IR
    ALTERNATE RECORD KEY IS PART-DESCRIPTION-IR WITH
        DUPLICATES
    ALTERNATE RECORD KEY IS PART-SUPPLIER-IR WITH
        DUPLICATES.
```

In the two SELECT entries above, the WITH DUPLICATES clause was included for each alternate key because this is the most common situation in data organization: There is a single, unique identifying number or name associated with a record and other nonunique numbers or names associated with the record, as well.

Often, all records associated with a given nonunique identifier need to be found. In this example, a list of all inventory items supplied by a given supplier or all inventory items with a given description could be produced. To accomplish this, a START statement is used to locate the first desired record and sequential READs to locate the remainder. Because this method of access is required, DYNAMIC access must be specified in the SELECT entry, as shown in the above examples.

For example, the following program segment could be used to list all parts supplied by "ABC SUPPLY":

```
LIST-BY-SUPPLIER.
    MOVE "ABC SUPPLY" TO PART-SUPPLIER-IR.
    MOVE "CONTINUE" TO LIST-FLAG.
```

```
          START INVENTORY-FILE
              KEY = PART-SUPPLIER-IR
              INVALID KEY
                  MOVE "FINISH" TO LIST-FLAG.
          IF LIST-FLAG = "FINISH"
              DISPLAY "NO RECORDS FOR ABC SUPPLY".
          PERFORM READ-LIST
              UNTIL LIST-FLAG = "FINISH".
      READ-LIST.
          READ INVENTORY-FILE NEXT RECORD
              AT END MOVE "FINISH" TO LIST-FLAG.
          IF LIST-FLAG NOT = "FINISH" AND PART-SUPPLIER-IR =
              "ABC SUPPLY"
                  DISPLAY INVENTORY-RECORD
          ELSE
                  MOVE "FINISH" TO LIST-FLAG.
```

The START statement establishes a **key of reference** to be used in subsequent sequential READ statements. The first READ statement reads the record located by the START statement; subsequent repetitions of the READ statement read other records in sequence, using the established key of reference. Because of the START statement in this example, the key of reference is PART-SUPPLIER-IR, and the records will be returned in sequence based on this field rather than on the actual physical sequence of the records in the file. In this context, "NEXT RECORD" should be construed as the record following in the sequence of data records as if the file were sorted on this key. In previous examples, the key of reference has always been the prime key; now we are able to specify other fields as well.

──────────── Example ────────────

Write a program segment to list all inventory items whose part descriptions begin with WASHER. (This type of processing would be particularly valuable in an interactive environment where the user is not quite sure of the part desired and wishes to examine some likely alternatives.)

```
      LIST-PARTS-BY-NAME.
          MOVE "WASHER" TO TEST-VALUE.
          INSPECT TEST-VALUE REPLACING ALL " " BY HIGH-VALUE.
          MOVE "WASHER" TO PART-DESCRIPTION-IR.
          START INVENTORY-FILE
              KEY IS NOT LESS THAN PART-DESCRIPTION-IR
              INVALID KEY
                  MOVE "FINISH" TO LIST-FLAG.
          IF LIST-FLAG = "FINISH"
              DISPLAY "NO RECORDS IN FILE".
          PERFORM READ-LIST
              UNTIL LIST-FLAG = "FINISH".
      READ-LIST.
          READ INVENTORY-FILE NEXT RECORD
              AT END MOVE "FINISH" TO LIST-FLAG.
          IF LIST-FLAG NOT = "FINISH" AND PART-DESCRIPTION-IR
                  < TEST-VALUE
              DISPLAY INVENTORY-RECORD
          ELSE
              MOVE "FINISH" TO LIST-FLAG.
```

In this example, all records with part description fields having values ranging from "WASHER" to "WASHERZZZ . . . Z" will be DISPLAYed.

It is also possible to access a file randomly, using either the prime key, as we have done previously, or any of the alternate keys. This is accomplished by using a Format-2 READ statement including the KEY IS clause (see Fig. 14.14). If the KEY IS clause is omitted, the content of the prime key is used to access the file. By specifying one of the alternate keys as the data-name in the KEY IS clause, the record corresponding to that key field value will be read. If there is more than one record in the file with the same key field value (remember that duplicates may be allowed for alternate record keys), the record read will be the first record encountered in the file with the specified key field value.

For example, suppose we wish to read the first record associated with the supplier "ABC SUPPLY" from the file INVENTORY-FILE described above. This can be accomplished by the following statements:

```
MOVE "ABC SUPPLY" TO PART-SUPPLIER-IR.
READ INVENTORY-FILE
    KEY IS PART-SUPPLIER-IR
    INVALID KEY
        PERFORM SUPPLIER-NOT-FOUND.
```

Execution of a Format-2 READ statement sets the key of reference in much the same way as a START statement. If the file is open in DYNAMIC mode, subsequent Format-1 READ statements would access the next record based on the key of reference (PART-SUPPLIER-IR in this example). Using this feature, it is possible to rewrite the routine to list all records associated with the supplier, "ABC SUPPLY", as follows:

```
LIST-BY-SUPPLIER-2.
    MOVE "ABC SUPPLY" TO PART-SUPPLIER-IR.
    MOVE "CONTINUE" TO LIST-FLAG.
    READ INVENTORY-FILE
        KEY IS PART-SUPPLIER-IR
        INVALID KEY
            MOVE "FINISH" TO LIST-FLAG.
    IF LIST-FLAG = "FINISH"
        DISPLAY "NO RECORDS FOR ABC SUPPLY".
    PERFORM LIST-READ
        UNTIL LIST-FLAG = "FINISH".
LIST-READ.
    DISPLAY INVENTORY-RECORD.
    READ INVENTORY-FILE NEXT RECORD
        AT END
            MOVE "FINISH" TO LIST-FLAG.
    IF LIST-FLAG NOT = "FINISH" AND PART-SUPPLIER-IR NOT
        = "ABC SUPPLY"
            MOVE "FINISH" TO LIST-FLAG.
```

14.10 FILE STATUS AND DECLARATIVES

The use of a FILE STATUS item can help ease the task of debugging a program which processes an indexed file. The FILE STATUS item is updated automatically after each input/output operation. The value contained in the item shows the status of the input/output operation. In order to make use of a FILE STATUS item, you must include a FILE STATUS entry in the SELECT sentence for the file, as shown in Figure 14.17.

Figure 14.17   General form of SELECT entry for indexed files

```
SELECT file-name

   ASSIGN TO system-name

      ORGANIZATION IS INDEXED

   ┌                      ┌ SEQUENTIAL ┐ ┐
   │ ACCESS MODE IS       │ RANDOM     │ │
   │                      │ DYNAMIC    │ │
   └                      └            ┘ ┘

      RECORD KEY IS data-name-1

      [ALTERNATE RECORD KEY IS data-name-2 [WITH DUPLICATES]] . . .

      [FILE STATUS IS data-name-3].
```

A FILE STATUS item must be defined as a two-character field in WORKING-STORAGE. The meaning ascribed to each possible setting of the FILE STATUS item is shown in Figure 14.18.

There are two ways in which these codes can be of importance to the programmer. Perhaps the most common use is in interpreting system error messages when a program terminates abnormally. For example, a program that is creating an indexed file with sequential access mode will ter-

Figure 14.18   Meaning of a FILE STATUS item for indexed input/output

First Character	Second Character	Meaning
0	0	Successful Completion
0	2	Successful Completion, Duplicate Key
1	0	At End
2	1	Sequence Error
2	2	Duplicate Key
2	3	No Record Found
2	4	Boundary Violation
3	0	Permanent Error
9	—	Implementor Defined

minate if a sequence error is encountered in the data being written to the file. The error message produced may include a reference to the file status value, which, in this case, would be 21.

A second way in which the file status item can be used is for the program to assume control of error conditions relating to a file processing statement. This is possible by the inclusion of a DECLARATIVES SECTION and appropriate USE statements that serve to "trap" the ordinary error-handling procedure and give control of the process back to the program.

If a DECLARATIVES section is to be used, it must precede all other components of the PROCEDURE DIVISION. A general form for coding a DECLARATIVES section is shown in Figure 14.19. The DECLARATIVES section begins with a header

DECLARATIVES.

and ends with

END DECLARATIVES.

Figure 14.19   General form of PROCEDURE DIVISION with a DECLARATIVES section

```
PROCEDURE DIVISION.
DECLARATIVES.
section-name SECTION.
    declarative-sentence.
[ paragraph-name.          ]
[     sentence . . .       ]      . . .
END DECLARATIVES.
[section-name SECTION.]
[ paragraph-name.          ]
[     sentence . . .       ]      . . .
```

The DECLARATIVES must contain at least one named SECTION. Following the section header is a declarative-sentence that begins with USE; this sentence determines when the procedure being specified will be executed. (Readers familiar with the Report Writer will recall that DECLARATIVES are useful for intervening in the "normal" sequence of events in that context as well.) Following the declarative-sentence may be one or more paragraphs containing COBOL code; these paragraphs are, however, optional. A typical general form for the USE statement as related to input/output operations is shown in Figure 14.20.

If an appropriate DECLARATIVES section is included in a program, exceptional conditions such as end-of-file or a sequence error will cause execution of the DECLARATIVES section code. If this code permits or if the

Figure 14.20   General form of the USE statement

$$\underline{USE} \ \underline{AFTER} \ STANDARD \ \begin{Bmatrix} \underline{EXCEPTION} \\ \underline{ERROR} \end{Bmatrix} \ \underline{PROCEDURE} \ ON \ file\text{-}name \ . \ . \ .$$

Note: EXCEPTION and ERROR have the same meaning and effect.

DECLARATIVES section contains no executable code, control returns to the statement following the input/output statement that caused the original exceptional condition. At this point the program can test the file status item and take whatever action may be appropriate under the circumstances. For example, suppose the file INVENTORY-FILE is defined as follows:

```
SELECT INVENTORY-FILE
    ASSIGN TO DISK
    ORGANIZATION IS INDEXED
    ACCESS IS SEQUENTIAL
    RECORD KEY IS INVENTORY-NUMBER-IR
    FILE STATUS IS INV-STATUS.
```

A PROCEDURE DIVISION and relevant INPUT/OUTPUT statements for a program that will create this file are shown below:

```
PROCEDURE DIVISION.
DECLARATIVES.
ERROR-TRAP SECTION.
    USE AFTER ERROR PROCEDURE ON INVENTORY-FILE.
END DECLARATIVES.
1000-MAIN-CONTROL.
    .
    .
    .

    OPEN OUTPUT INVENTORY-FILE.
    IF INV-STATUS NOT = "00"
        DISPLAY "ERROR IN OPENING INVENTORY-FILE"
        DISPLAY "STATUS = " INV-STATUS
        PERFORM 9000-TERMINATION.
    .
    .
    .

2000-PROCESS-DATA.
    WRITE INVENTORY-RECORD.
    IF INV-STATUS = "00" OR INV-STATUS = "02"
        NEXT SENTENCE
    ELSE
        DISPLAY "ERROR IN WRITING INVENTORY-FILE"
        DISPLAY "STATUS = " INV-STATUS
        PERFORM 9000-TERMINATION.
    .
    .
    .
```

When using declaratives to trap errors for a file, it is not necessary to include an INVALID KEY clause on any input/output statement addressing that file. This technique does, however, place an added burden on the program to take appropriate action when error conditions do occur. If the program does not handle the conditions correctly, errors that are quite difficult to diagnose will result. On a more positive note, this technique can make systems appear to be more user friendly by shielding the user from the more esoteric system-produced error messages. This technique is highly recommended for interactive systems because, in many instances, the user can take corrective action in the event of exceptional conditions; otherwise, the program would usually be terminated by the operating system.

─────── Example ───────

Program 14e is a revision of Program 14a, but it makes use of DECLARA-TIVES and FILE STATUS items to handle exceptional conditions after input/output operations. A portion of the SELECT entry for the file is as follows (lines 19–21):

```
ACCESS IS SEQUENTIAL
RECORD KEY IS SS-NUM-DR
FILE STATUS IS DATA-FILE-STATUS.
```

The item DATA-FILE-STATUS is defined in WORKING-STORAGE as PIC XX (line 45). The DECLARATIVES entry is the first entry in the PROCEDURE DIVISION. It contains one SECTION which contains one sentence

```
USE AFTER STANDARD ERROR PROCEDURE ON DATA-FILE.
```

After each input/output statement in the program, the value of DATA-FILE-STATUS is available and can be checked as needed. For example, after the WRITE statement at line 178, the program can test to make sure that the record was written correctly (lines 179–183):

```
IF DATA-FILE-STATUS = "21" OR "22"
    DISPLAY "Record out of sequence or duplicated".
IF DATA-FILE-STATUS NOT = "00"
    DISPLAY "Record not placed in file " FILE-NAME
             " ERROR code : " DATA-FILE-STATUS.
```

Note that when DECLARATIVES are utilized, the INVALID KEY clause is no longer necessary on a WRITE statement such as that at line 178 in Program 14e.

DECLARATIVES offer a very powerful tool for the COBOL program to be as user friendly as may be desired. The only burden is on the programmer to make sure that all exceptional conditions are handled by the program rather than by the operating system.

14.11 APPLICATIONS OF INDEXED FILES

Indexed files are very useful in designing a system when

- random access to the data is required,
- sequential access to the data is required or desirable, and
- complete in-place maintenance capabilities (add, change, delete) are required.

The choice of key fields is critical when an indexed file is designed. If multiple access paths are desired, the specification of multiple record keys should be considered. In an extreme situation, every field within the record could be declared as a key field. The general problem with multiple key fields and the basic reason that this facility should be used judiciously is the overhead required by alternate key fields. Additional space must be reserved for the pointers that permit access by alternate keys. Speed of access may also be critical, particularly in smaller systems. For example, in most systems, an indexed file is maintained in physical sequence based on the prime key, yielding very efficient sequential access to the data. (Only records that have been added are not physically located in the proper

Program 14e

```
 1 IDENTIFICATION DIVISION.
 2
 3 PROGRAM-ID. DECLARATIVES-EXAMPLE-PRO14E.
 .
 .
 .
17     SELECT DATA-FILE ASSIGN TO DISK
18             ORGANIZATION IS INDEXED
19             ACCESS IS SEQUENTIAL
20             RECORD KEY IS SS-NUM-DR
21             FILE STATUS IS DATA-FILE-STATUS.
 .
 .
 .
41 WORKING-STORAGE SECTION.
42
43 01  FILE-NAME              PIC X(15) VALUE SPACES.
44
45 01  DATA-FILE-STATUS      PIC XX.
 .
 .
 .
62 PROCEDURE DIVISION.
63
64 DECLARATIVES.
65
66 ERROR-TRAP SECTION.
67
68     USE AFTER STANDARD ERROR PROCEDURE ON DATA-FILE.
69
70 END DECLARATIVES.
71
72 1000-MAIN-CONTROL.
73
74     PERFORM 2000-PROCESS-USER-COMMANDS
75             UNTIL QUIT.
76     STOP RUN.
 .
 .
 .
```

```
115 3300-CREATE-FILE.
116
117     IF FILE-NAME = SPACES
118        DISPLAY "File has not been named"
119     ELSE
120        DISPLAY "Enter data for file " FILE-NAME
121        DISPLAY "OK to proceed? (Y/N)"
122        ACCEPT ANSWER
123        IF DATA-OK
124           OPEN OUTPUT DATA-FILE
125           IF DATA-FILE-STATUS NOT = "00"
126              DISPLAY "Error in opening file " FILE-NAME
127                      " Error code : " DATA-FILE-STATUS
128           ELSE
129              MOVE "N" TO ANSWER
130              MOVE SPACES TO NAME-DR
131              PERFORM 9000-GET-DATA
132                      UNTIL DATA-OK OR END-OF-DATA
133              PERFORM 4000-BUILD-FILE
134                      UNTIL END-OF-DATA
135              CLOSE DATA-FILE
136              IF DATA-FILE-STATUS NOT = "00"
137                 DISPLAY "Error in closing file " FILE-NAME
138                         " Error code : "  DATA-FILE-STATUS.
139
140 3400-LIST-FILE.
141
142     IF FILE-NAME = SPACES
143        DISPLAY "File has not been named"
144     ELSE
145        DISPLAY "List content of file " FILE-NAME
146        DISPLAY "OK to proceed? (Y/N)"
147        ACCEPT ANSWER
148        IF DATA-OK
149           OPEN INPUT DATA-FILE
150           IF DATA-FILE-STATUS NOT = "00"
151              DISPLAY "Error in opening file " FILE-NAME
152                      " Error code : " DATA-FILE-STATUS
153              DISPLAY "Check to see that file is present"
154           ELSE
155              MOVE "NO" TO EOF-FLAG
156              PERFORM 9300-READ-DATA-FILE
157              PERFORM 4100-PROCESS-DATA
158                      UNTIL END-OF-FILE
159              CLOSE DATA-FILE
160              IF DATA-FILE-STATUS NOT = "00"
161                 DISPLAY "Error in closing file " FILE-NAME
162                         " Error code : " DATA-FILE-STATUS.
      .
      .
      .
```

Program 14e *(concluded)*

```
176 4000-BUILD-FILE.
177
178     WRITE DATA-RECORD.
179     IF DATA-FILE-STATUS = "21" OR "22"
180         DISPLAY "Record out of sequence or duplicated".
181     IF DATA-FILE-STATUS NOT = "00"
182         DISPLAY "Record not placed in file " FILE-NAME
183                 " Error code : " DATA-FILE-STATUS.
184     MOVE "N" TO ANSWER.
185     PERFORM 9000-GET-DATA UNTIL
186         DATA-OK OR END-OF-DATA.
          .
          .
          .
228 9300-READ-DATA-FILE.
229
230     READ DATA-FILE.
231     IF DATA-FILE-STATUS = "10"
232         MOVE "YES" TO EOF-FLAG
233     ELSE IF DATA-FILE-STATUS NOT = "00"
234         DISPLAY "Error in reading file " FILE-NAME
235                 " Error code : "  DATA-FILE-STATUS.
```

sequence.) Attempting to gain sequential access by any of the alternate keys requires the system to read records in other than the physical sequence. This is likely to be much more time-consuming than the corresponding operation using the prime key.

When considering indexed organization for a file, the systems analyst should be aware of the activity and volatility expected for the file. Recall that activity refers to the relative frequency of file access operations, and volatility is related to the occurrence of record additions and deletions. Activity is an important consideration because, in general, random access to a file requires more system resources than does sequential access. A large indexed file with high activity may take much more of the system's capacity than is necessary or feasible. In such situations, it may be advisable or necessary, because of system constraints, to revise the system design to maintain the file as a sequential file. Generally, this is possible, but it will require sorting files to use them and may rule out interactive transaction processing for the file.

The expected volatility of a file is an important consideration because additions are usually placed in an overflow area and deleted records are flagged as deleted but still occupy space in the system. As the number of record additions increases, the amount of time required to access records in the file increases as well. As noted earlier, it is necessary in some systems to reorganize the file periodically to physically remove deleted records and to merge new records into the file in physical sequence.

If the file is highly volatile, and especially if it is also large, these considerations place a burden on the system's resources, which may preclude use of an indexed file. In this case, it may be necessary to redesign the system and use sequential organization and sequential maintenance techniques (or a relative file), placing less of a burden on the system.

In any system permitting in-place maintenance of files, constructing transaction logs, and making backups for relevant files is especially important. Sources of problems that may affect the integrity of data in the system are myriad and impossible to control completely. When problems that destroy the integrity of a data file arise, it is necessary to re-create the data based on the backup file and the transaction log. In some large systems, this will be taken care of by the operating system, but in most systems this function must be designed into each application system. For example, in Program 14b, every transaction that has an effect on the indexed master file should be written on a transaction log file. In this way, by running a program that processes the transactions contained in the transaction log file against the backup version of the master file, an up-to-date version of the master file can be re-created.

Indexed files are very powerful and permit great latitude in the design of a data processing system. In addition to considering the logical needs of the system being designed, however, it is important for the systems analyst to consider

- the expected activity
- the expected volatility
- the need to create backups and transaction logs
- the need to process the file by other systems that may not support indexed files
- the need for periodic reorganization of indexed files (in some systems)
- the storage capacity of the disk or other available random-access storage device
- the capacity of the computing system vis-à-vis the requirements for processing indexed files

In some instances, these system considerations will make alternate choices for file organization techniques mandatory.

14.12 COBOL-85 UPDATE

The major change made in COBOL-85 to the statements described in this chapter was the inclusion of scope delimiters for each of the statements and a NOT INVALID KEY clause for each statement that has an INVALID KEY clause. The general form for each of these statements in COBOL-85 is as follows:

```
DELETE file-name RECORD
    [INVALID KEY statement-1]
    [NOT INVALID KEY statement-2]
[END-DELETE]
```

Format-1 READ (sequential)

```
READ file-name [NEXT] RECORD [INTO data-name]
    AT END statement-1
    [NOT AT END statement-2]
[END-READ]
```

Format-2 READ (random)

```
READ file-name RECORD [INTO data-name]
    [KEY IS data-name]
    [INVALID KEY statement-1]
    [NOT INVALID KEY statement-2]
[END-READ]
```

```
WRITE record-name [FROM data-name]
    [INVALID KEY statement-1]
    [NOT INVALID KEY statement-2]
[END-WRITE]
```

```
REWRITE record-name [FROM data-name]
    [INVALID KEY statement-1]
    [NOT INVALID KEY statement-2]
[END-REWRITE]
```

```
START file-name  [ KEY IS  { EQUAL TO               }  data-name ]
                           { =                       }
                           { GREATER THAN            }
                           { >                       }
                           { NOT LESS THAN           }
                           { NOT <                   }
                           { GREATER THAN OR EQUAL TO }
                           { >=                      }
        [INVALID KEY statement . . .
        [NOT INVALID KEY statement . . .]
[END-START]
```

You will also note a new relationship that can be used in the START statement (GREATER THAN OR EQUAL TO and the equivalent > =).

The inclusion of a NOT INVALID KEY clause can make some program
segments more straightforward and easy to understand. For example, consider the following rewrite of paragraph 5200-CHANGE-RECORD from Program 14b (lines 167–188):

```
5200-Change-Record.
    DISPLAY "Enter SS number of record to be changed"
    ACCEPT SS-Num-DR
    READ Data-File
        INVALID KEY
            DISPLAY "Record does not exist in file"
        NOT INVALID KEY
            MOVE SPACE TO Change-Command
            PERFORM 6000-Get-Changes UNTIL Quit-Changes
            EVALUATE TRUE
                WHEN Change-Command = "Q"
                    DISPLAY "Changes being copied to file"
                    REWRITE Data-Record
                        INVALID KEY
                            DISPLAY "Internal logic error"
                    END-REWRITE
                WHEN Change-Command = "q"
                    DISPLAY "Changes discarded"
            END-EVALUATE
    END-READ.
```

Compare this program segment with the equivalent one in Program 14b. The COBOL-85 coding is shorter, easier to read, and, therefore, easier to debug and maintain.

14.13   SELF-TEST EXERCISES

1. What combination of access method and open mode would be best for the indexed file described in each of the following operations:
   a. creating an indexed file
   b. processing a sequentially organized file of transactions to update an indexed file
   c. deleting records randomly from an indexed file
   d. reading data randomly from an indexed file
   e. adding records randomly to an indexed file
   f. sequentially listing a portion of the records in an indexed file
   g. maintaining (add/delete/change) an indexed file

2. Distinguish between the WRITE and REWRITE statements. What purpose is served by each?

3. Distinguish between the Format-1 READ and Format-2 READ statements. What purpose is served by each?

4. Can an indexed file be created under dynamic access? Explain. Can an indexed file be created under random access? Why is sequential access recommended when an indexed file is being created?

5. Write a program segment to begin sequential processing of an indexed file, beginning with the record with key-field value "200" or the next available record.

6. A Format-2 READ statement for an indexed file has resulted in a FILE STATUS item value 23. Were the statements in the INVALID KEY clause of the statement executed? Why or why not?

7. An indexed file containing inventory data must be created from a sequential file. The IDENTIFICATION, ENVIRONMENT, and DATA

DIVISIONs are given below. Write the PROCEDURE DIVISION to create the indexed file, and produce a listing of the file.

```
IDENTIFICATION DIVISION.
PROGRAM-ID.  EXERCISE 7.
AUTHOR. YOUR NAME.
ENVIRONMENT DIVISION.
CONFIGURATION SECTION.
SOURCE-COMPUTER.
OBJECT-COMPUTER.
INPUT-OUTPUT SECTION.
FILE-CONTROL.
     SELECT INPUT-FILE ASSIGN TO DISK.
     SELECT INVENTORY-FILE ASSIGN TO DISK
          ORGANIZATION IS INDEXED
          ACCESS IS SEQUENTIAL
          RECORD KEY IS INVENTORY-NUMBER-IRR.
     SELECT PRINT ASSIGN TO PRINTER.
DATA DIVISION.
FILE SECTION.
FD  INPUT-FILE
     LABEL RECORDS ARE STANDARD
     DATA RECORD IS INPUT-RECORD.
01   INPUT-RECORD.
     02 INVENTORY-NUMBER-IR      PIC X(5).
     02 DESCRIPTION-IR           PIC X(20).
     02 QUANTITY-ON-HAND-IR      PIC 9(5).
     02 REORDER-POINT-IR         PIC 9(5).
     02 REORDER-AMOUNT-IR        PIC 9(5).
     02 UNIT-SELLING-PRICE-IR    PIC 9(4)V99.
     02 UNIT-COST-PRICE-IR       PIC 9(4)V99.
FD  INVENTORY-FILE
     LABEL RECORDS ARE STANDARD
     DATA RECORD IS INVENTORY-RECORD.
01   INVENTORY-RECORD.
     02 INVENTORY-NUMBER-IRR     PIC X(5).
     02 DESCRIPTION-IRR          PIC X(20).
     02 QUANTITY-ON-HAND-IRR     PIC 9(5).
     02 REORDER-POINT-IRR        PIC 9(5).
     02 REORDER-AMOUNT-IRR       PIC 9(5).
     02 UNIT-SELLING-PRICE-IRR   PIC 9(4)V99.
     02 UNIT-COST-PRICE-IRR      PIC 9(4)V99.
FD  PRINT
     LABEL RECORDS ARE OMITTED
     DATA RECORD IS PRINT-LINE.
01   PRINT-LINE                  PIC  X(132).
WORKING-STORAGE SECTION.
01   FLAGS.
     03  EOF-FLAG               PIC XXX VALUE "NO".
```

8. Write the PROCEDURE DIVISION to create a listing of the file INVENTORY-FILE created in Exercise 7.

9. A transaction file contains sales records for the inventory system described in Exercise 7. Each record in the file contains an inventory number and the number of parts sold. A program is required to

update the file INVENTORY-MASTER based on the sales data. The IDENTIFICATION, ENVIRONMENT, and DATA DIVISIONs for the program are given below. Write the PROCEDURE DIVISION.

```
IDENTIFICATION DIVISION.
PROGRAM-ID. EXERCISE 9.
AUTHOR. YOUR NAME.
ENVIRONMENT DIVISION.
CONFIGURATION SECTION.
SOURCE-COMPUTER.
OBJECT-COMPUTER.
INPUT-OUTPUT SECTION.
FILE-CONTROL.
    SELECT SALES-FILE ASSIGN TO DISK.
    SELECT INVENTORY-FILE ASSIGN TO DISK
        ORGANIZATION IS INDEXED
        ACCESS IS RANDOM
        RECORD KEY IS INVENTORY-NUMBER-IRR.
    SELECT PRINT ASSIGN TO PRINTER.
DATA DIVISION.
FILE SECTION.
FD  SALES-FILE
    LABEL RECORDS ARE STANDARD
    DATA RECORD IS SALES-RECORD.
01  SALES-RECORD.
    02 INVENTORY-NUMBER-SR       PIC X(5).
    02 NUMBER-SOLD-SR            PIC 999.
FD  INVENTORY-FILE
    LABEL RECORDS ARE STANDARD
    DATA RECORD IS INVENTORY-RECORD.
01  INVENTORY-RECORD.
    02 INVENTORY-NUMBER-IRR      PIC X(5).
    02 DESCRIPTION-IRR           PIC X(20).
    02 QUANTITY-ON-HAND-IRR      PIC 9(5).
    02 REORDER-POINT-IRR         PIC 9(5).
    02 REORDER-AMOUNT-IRR        PIC 9(5).
    02 UNIT-SELLING-PRICE-IRR    PIC 9(4)V99.
    02 UNIT-COST-PRICE-IRR       PIC 9(4)V99.
FD  PRINT
    LABEL RECORDS ARE OMITTED
    DATA RECORD IS PRINT-LINE.
01  PRINT-LINE                   PIC X(132).
WORKING-STORAGE SECTION.
01  FLAGS.
    03 EOF-FLAG                  PIC XXX VALUE "NO".
```

10. Write the SELECT entry and PROCEDURE DIVISION for a program that would process all records in INVENTORY-FILE (described in Exercise 9) that follow the record with inventory number "05000".

11. Write the PROCEDURE DIVISION for a program to maintain the file INVENTORY-FILE described above. The transaction file contains records in essentially the same format as the records in the master file, with the addition of a transaction code. The program should process each transaction, taking appropriate action on records in the master file. The following transaction codes are used:

Code	Meaning
CD	change description
CQ	change quantity on hand
CP	change reorder point
CA	change reorder amount
CS	change unit selling price
CC	change unit cost
AQ	add to quantity on hand
SQ	subtract from quantity on hand
AR	add record to file
DR	delete record from file

The IDENTIFICATION, ENVIRONMENT, and DATA DIVISIONs are shown below.

```
IDENTIFICATION DIVISION.
PROGRAM-ID. EXERCISE 11.
AUTHOR. YOUR NAME.
ENVIRONMENT DIVISION.
CONFIGURATION SECTION.
SOURCE-COMPUTER.
OBJECT-COMPUTER.
INPUT-OUTPUT SECTION.
FILE-CONTROL.
    SELECT TRANSACTIONS ASSIGN TO DISK.
    SELECT INVENTORY-FILE ASSIGN TO DISK
        ORGANIZATION IS INDEXED
        ACCESS IS RANDOM
        RECORD KEY IS INVENTORY-NUMBER-IR.
    SELECT PRINT ASSIGN TO PRINTER.
DATA DIVISION.
FILE SECTION.
FD   TRANSACTIONS
     LABEL RECORDS ARE STANDARD
     DATA RECORD IS TRANSACTION-RECORD.
01   TRANSACTION-RECORD.
     03 INVENTORY-NUMBER-TR           PIC X(5).
     03 DESCRIPTION-TR                PIC X(20).
     03 QUANTITY-ON-HAND-TR           PIC 9(5).
     03 REORDER-POINT-TR              PIC 9(5).
     03 REORDER-AMOUNT-TR             PIC 9(5).
     03 UNIT-SELLING-PRICE-TR         PIC 9(4)V99.
     03 UNIT-COST-PRICE-TR            PIC 9(4)V99.
     03 TRANSACTION-CODE-TR           PIC XX.
        88 CHANGE-DESCRIPTION         VALUE "CD".
        88 CHANGE-QUANTITY-ON-HAND    VALUE "CQ".
        88 CHANGE-REORDER-POINT       VALUE "CP".
        88 CHARGE-REORDER-AMOUNT      VALUE "CA".
        88 CHANGE-UNIT-SELLING-PRICE  VALUE "CS".
        88 CHANGE-UNIT-COST           VALUE "CC".
        88 ADD-TO-QTY-ON-HAND         VALUE "AQ".
        88 SUBTRACT-FROM-QTY-ON-HAND  VALUE "SQ".
        88 ADD-RECORD                 VALUE "AR".
        88 DELETE-RECORD              VALUE "DR".
        88 VALID-TRANSACTION-CODE     VALUE
           "CD"   "CQ"   "CP"   "CA"   "CS"
           "CC"   "AQ"   "SQ"   "AR"   "DR".
```

```
FD   INVENTORY-FILE
     LABEL RECORDS ARE STANDARD
     DATA RECORD IS INVENTORY-RECORD.
01   INVENTORY-RECORD.
     03  INVENTORY-NUMBER-IR          PIC X(5).
     03  DESCRIPTION-IR               PIC X(20).
     03  QUANTITY-ON-HAND-IR          PIC 9(5).
     03  REORDER-POINT-IR             PIC 9(5).
     03  REORDER-AMOUNT-IR            PIC 9(4)V99.
     03  UNIT-SELLING-PRICE-IR        PIC 9(4)V99.
     03  UNIT-COST-PRICE-IR           PIC 9(4)V99.
FD   PRINT
     LABEL RECORDS ARE OMITTED
     DATA RECORD IS PRINT-RECORD.
01   PRINT-RECORD                     PIC X(132).
WORKING-STORAGE SECTION.
01   FLAGS.
     03  EOF-FLAG                     PIC X(3) VALUE "NO".
         88  END-OF-TRANSACTIONS      VALUE "YES".
     03  RECORD-FOUND-FLAG            PIC X(3) VALUE "YES".
         88  RECORD-FOUND             VALUE "YES".
```

12. A personnel file, which will be accessed by employee Social Security number (prime key), employee name, department number, and zip code (alternate keys) is to be created as an indexed file. Write the SELECT entry for the program that will create the file.

13. For the personnel file of Exercise 12, write the SELECT entry and a PROCEDURE DIVISION for a program that will create a listing of all employees in Department 3.

14. Consider the procedure to delete a record in Program 14b. What will happen if the user enters the Social Security number of a record that is present in the file but that is different from the one the user intended to enter? How could the program help to prevent the user from making this error?

14.14   PROGRAMMING EXERCISES

1. Write a program to create an indexed file with records in the following format:

Picture	Description
X(5)	Store identifier
X(3)	Department identifier
9(6)V99	Year-to-date total cash sales
9(6)V99	Year-to-date total VISA sales
9(6)V99	Year-to-date total MasterCard sales
9(6)V99	Year-to-date total credit sales
9(6)V99	Year-to-date total taxable sales
9(6)V99	Year-to-date total nontaxable sales
9(6)V99	Year-to-date total wholesale costs
9(6)V99	Year-to-date total retail sales

Use the eight-character field containing the store identifier and the department identifier as the key field for the file.

2. Write a program to use the data file described below to update the file created in Exercise 1.

Picture	Description
X(5)	Store identifier
X(3)	Department identifier
9(9)	Customer number
9(6)	Date of sale (*mmddyy*)
99	Quantity
9(9)	Inventory number of item sold
9999V99	Wholesale cost/item
9999V99	Retail price/item
XX	Status code: paid by cash (CA)
	paid by VISA (VS)
	paid by MasterCard (MC)
	credit purchase (CR)
X	Tax code: Sale is taxable (T)
	Sale is nontaxable (N)

3. Write a program to create a report summarizing the data contained in the file created in Exercise 1. Include totals for each store and for the entire company.

4. Write a program to produce a report listing those departments showing a zero or negative profit margin. For purposes of this report, profit margin is defined as the difference between total wholesale costs and total retail sales.

5. XYZ College requires a student records system. At the heart of the system will be a Student Master File. The file will be indexed using the student Social Security number as the prime key. Each record in the Student Master File will contain the following fields:

> Student Social Security number
> Name
> Address
> Declared major (2-character code)
> Birth date
> Sex code
> Credit hours completed
> Grade point average
> Credit hours in progress
> Date of first registration
> Date of last registration

Write a program to create the Student Master File with data of your choosing.

6. Write a program to maintain the Student Master File created in Exercise 5. Include provisions to:

> Add a new student
> Delete a student
> Change any field

7. Write an interactive program to process registration information for XYZ College. The program must update appropriate fields in the Student Master File record for each student registering for a course and must create a sequential file REGISTRATION-DETAIL containing one

record for each course registration. (If a student registers for 2 courses, REGISTRATION-DETAIL will contain 2 records.) Each REGISTRATION-DETAIL record should contain the following fields:

> Course number
> Section number
> Student Social Security number
> Registration date
> Credit hours
> Grade (blank until course is completed)

8. Assume that the file REGISTRATION-DETAIL has been updated with grades at the end of the term and is in sequence by student Social Security number. Write a program to update the Student Master File.

9. Modify the program written for Exercise 5 to allow access to records by declared major. Write an interactive program to allow a user to enter a major and to secure a listing of all students with that declared major.

10. Write a program to purge inactive student records from the Student Master File described in Exercise 5. Students are classified as inactive if they have not registered for courses in the previous five years. Any record removed from the Student Master File should be added to a sequential Inactive Student File.

11. The following problems relate to Exercise 1 in Chapter 13 (Section 16):

    a. Write a program to transform TABLE-FILE into an indexed file.
    b. Revise the program to update the indexed TABLE-FILE.

15. RELATIVE FILES

15.1 CAPABILITIES OF RELATIVE FILES

Random access to data is a very powerful tool for designing data processing systems. As we have seen in Chapter 14, the random access feature of indexed files opens up possibilities that do not exist with sequential files alone. COBOL systems provide another file type that supports random access—relative files. A **relative file** is a sequence of records that can be accessed by specifying a record number. A program can access the first record or the fifteenth record or the eighth record or, indeed, any record within the file by specifying the number of the desired record and executing an appropriate input or output statement. The operating system takes care of locating the record within the file (for READ and START), placing the record in the file (for WRITE or REWRITE), or deleting a record (for DELETE).

In many respects, a relative file resembles a table. In both cases, access to the content is gained by specifying the location of the desired element in the structure. Of course, a relative file is physically located in mass storage, whereas a table is located in memory. Because of this difference, the access speed is dramatically different (it may differ by a factor of 1000 or more). This difference in speed must be considered when deciding whether a table or a relative file is to be used in a particular application. If sufficient memory is available, a table is much more efficient, but if the amount of data exceeds memory size, a relative file offers essentially the same capabilities except for speed.

For situations in which the key field for a file is restricted, a relative file can enable very efficient direct access to records within a data file. For example, suppose an organization uses three-digit employee numbers. It would be possible to use the employee number as the address of the employee record within the data file. Thus, employee 203 would be placed in the 203rd record in the file. Because there are 999 possible employee numbers, the file would potentially need to contain space for 999 records. This method is analogous to the direct table look-up method described in Chapter 12.

15.2 PROCESSING RELATIVE FILES SEQUENTIALLY

The general form of the SELECT entry for a relative file is shown in Figure 15.1. Note that the ACCESS MODE may be SEQUENTIAL, RANDOM, or DYNAMIC, as needed. SEQUENTIAL access implies that records are to be

Figure 15.1   General form of the SELECT entry for a relative file

```
SELECT file-name
ASSIGN TO system-name
  ORGANIZATION IS RELATIVE
 [                      ⎧ SEQUENTIAL  [RELATIVE KEY IS data-name-1] ⎤
 [ ACCESS MODE IS ⎨ RANDOM  ⎬                                      ⎥
 [                      ⎩ DYNAMIC ⎭  RELATIVE KEY IS data-name-1    ⎦
[FILE STATUS IS data-name-2].
```

written in consecutive record number order or read in ascending (but not necessarily consecutive) record number order. As with indexed files, RANDOM access implies that the program will specify the desired record before an input/output statement, and DYNAMIC access implies that random and sequential access statements are permitted for the file.

The mechanism for specifying the record to be read or written is contained in the RELATIVE KEY clause. The data-name specified here must contain the record number of the desired record before a random access input/output statement can be executed. This data-name must be defined as an unsigned integer by the program, typically as a WORKING-STORAGE item.

For ACCESS IS SEQUENTIAL, the RELATIVE KEY clause is optional. If the file is being created, the clause can be omitted; the records will automatically be stored consecutively, starting with record 1. The clause can also be omitted if records are to be read sequentially. The only time a RELATIVE KEY clause is needed for SEQUENTIAL access is when a START statement will be used in the program. Then, the desired record number is placed in the relative key field prior to execution of the START statement. We shall say more about the RELATIVE KEY clause in the following sections. A SELECT entry for a program that would sequentially create a relative file with consecutive records starting with record number 1 is

```
SELECT file-name
    ASSIGN TO system-name
    ORGANIZATION IS RELATIVE
    ACCESS IS SEQUENTIAL.
```

The ACCESS clause in this case is actually optional; if the ACCESS clause is omitted, SEQUENTIAL access is assumed.

The general form for input/output statements for sequential access to a relative file is shown in Figure 15.2. A sequential-access relative file may be opened in INPUT, OUTPUT, or I-0 mode. If the file is being created, it would be opened as OUTPUT. The only valid input/output statement for an OUTPUT file is WRITE. The same method is used to secure a sequential listing of all files, whether sequential, indexed, or relative—by opening the file as INPUT and using the sequential READ statement. Opening the file in I-0 mode will enable all input/output statements except WRITE.

Note that the WRITE statement must include the INVALID KEY clause unless a USE procedure for the file has been specified (see Chapter 14, Section 10). The invalid key condition will be true only when an attempt is made to write beyond the physical limits of a file.

If a RELATIVE KEY clause is specified in the SELECT entry and if the ACCESS IS SEQUENTIAL, then the value of the relative key field will be updated as a result of each execution of a WRITE statement. Thus, the

Figure 15.2 Sequential-access input/output statements for relative files

```
READ file-name [NEXT] RECORD [INTO data-name] [AT END statement]
WRITE record-name [FROM data-name] [INVALID KEY statement]

      ⎧ INPUT file-name . . .  ⎫
OPEN  ⎨ OUTPUT file-name . . . ⎬  . . .
      ⎩ I-O file-name . . .    ⎭
```

value contained in the relative key field will always be the number of the record just written—for example, 1 after the first record, 2 after the second record, and so on.

The sequential READ statement for a relative file has the same considerations as sequential READs for other file types. The NEXT clause is required only for sequential access when the access mode is DYNAMIC.

─────────── Example ───────────

In this chapter we will use the same file system used in the previous chapter as the basis for our examples. Because indexed and relative files are quite closely related, much of the program logic for the programs in Chapter 14 can be carried forward when the file organization is changed to relative. We will focus primarily on those areas where the programs differ.

Program 15a is a revision of Program 14a with the file organization changed from INDEXED to RELATIVE. The program enables the user to create or list a file interactively using the same menu as in Program 14a. Note that the only difference between the programs lies in the SELECT statement. The relevant clauses in Program 15a are (lines 18–19)

```
ORGANIZATION IS RELATIVE
ACCESS IS SEQUENTIAL.
```

Because the program writes consecutive records (it will first write record 1, then record 2, and so forth), random access is not needed, thus it is not necessary to specify a RELATIVE KEY for the file.

15.3 MAINTENANCE PROCEDURES— RANDOM ACCESS

Random access to a relative file is possible if ACCESS IS RANDOM or ACCESS IS DYNAMIC is included in the SELECT entry for the file. The clause ACCESS IS DYNAMIC will permit both sequential and random access to the file.

The general form for input/output statements required for random access to a relative file is shown in Figure 15.3. The READ statement is valid if the file is opened in INPUT or I-O mode. In order to read a record randomly, the program must place the number of the desired record into the relative key field defined in the SELECT entry for the file. The READ statement will then access that record in the file. If there is no record associated with the address contained in the relative key field, the INVALID KEY condition exists. The INVALID KEY clause is required unless appropriate DECLARATIVES and USE entries are provided.

Program 15a

```
 1 IDENTIFICATION DIVISION.
 2
 3 PROGRAM-ID. RELATIVE-FILE-CREATE-PRO15A.
 .
 .
 .
15 FILE-CONTROL.
16
17     SELECT DATA-FILE ASSIGN TO DISK
18             ORGANIZATION IS RELATIVE
19             ACCESS IS SEQUENTIAL.
 .
 .
 .
59 PROCEDURE DIVISION.
60
61 1000-MAIN-CONTROL.
62
63     PERFORM 2000-PROCESS-USER-COMMANDS
64             UNTIL QUIT.
65     STOP RUN.
66
67 2000-PROCESS-USER-COMMANDS.
68
69     PERFORM 3000-DISPLAY-MENU.
70     PERFORM 3100-GET-COMMAND.
71     IF      NAME-FILE
72             PERFORM 3200-GET-FILE-NAME
73     ELSE IF CREATE-FILE
74             PERFORM 3300-CREATE-FILE
75     ELSE IF LIST-FILE
76             PERFORM 3400-LIST-FILE
77     ELSE IF PRINT-FILE
78             PERFORM 3500-PRINT-FILE
79     ELSE IF HELP
80             PERFORM 3600-WRITE-HELP
81     ELSE IF NOT VALID-COMMAND
82             PERFORM 3700-WRITE-ERROR.
83
84 3000-DISPLAY-MENU.
85
86     DISPLAY "Command  Action".
87     DISPLAY "   N     Name file (Current file " FILE-NAME ")".
88     DISPLAY "   C     Create file".
89     DISPLAY "   L     List file to screen".
90     DISPLAY "   P     Print file to printer".
91     DISPLAY "   H     Help".
92     DISPLAY "   Q     Quit program".
 .
 .
 .
```

Program 15a   *(concluded)*

```
150 4000-BUILD-FILE.
151
152     WRITE DATA-RECORD.
153     MOVE "N" TO ANSWER.
154     PERFORM 9000-GET-DATA
155             UNTIL DATA-OK OR END-OF-DATA.
        .
        .
        .
197 9300-READ-DATA-FILE.
198
199     READ DATA-FILE
200             AT END MOVE "YES" TO EOF-FLAG.
```

Figure 15.3   General form for relative file random-access input/
output statements

READ file-name RECORD [INTO data-name] [INVALID KEY statement]

REWRITE record-name [FROM data-name] [INVALID KEY statement]

OPEN { INPUT file-name . . .
OUTPUT file-name . . . } . . .
I-O file-name . . .

WRITE record-name [FROM data-name] [INVALID KEY statement]

DELETE file-name RECORD [INVALID KEY statement]

START file-name [KEY { IS EQUAL TO
IS =
IS GREATER THAN
IS >
IS NOT LESS THAN
IS NOT < } data-name]
[INVALID KEY statement]

——— Example ———

Suppose a file has been defined by the following SELECT entry:

```
SELECT DATA-MASTER
    ASSIGN TO DISK
    ORGANIZATION IS RELATIVE
    ACCESS IS RANDOM
    RELATIVE KEY IS DATA-ADDRESS.
```

Assuming that the file is open in INPUT or I-O mode, the following program
segment could be used to read the fourth record from the file:

```
MOVE 4 TO DATA-ADDRESS.
READ DATA-MASTER
    INVALID KEY PERFORM ERROR-EXIT.
```

Remember that the relative key field must be defined in the DATA DIVI-SION as an unsigned integer. In this example, an appropriate definition would be

```
01  DATA-ADDRESS   PIC 999.
```

The length of the field must, of course, be governed by the total number of records in the file.

The REWRITE statement is used to replace the content of a record whose record number is specified in the relative key field. The file must be open in I-0 mode to permit execution of the REWRITE statement. The reason for this is that, in executing the REWRITE, the system first reads the file to determine whether the record exists. If it does, then the new content is written into the appropriate position within the file. If the desired record does not exist, the INVALID KEY condition occurs, and the statement in the INVALID KEY clause is executed. The INVALID KEY clause is required unless appropriate DECLARATIVES/USE entries for the file have been included.

──────────── Example ────────────

Suppose the content of the 23rd record of the file DATA-MASTER must be changed. Assuming that the file is open in I-0 mode, the following program segment could be used:

```
MOVE NEW-DATA TO DATA-MASTER-RECORD.
MOVE 23 TO DATA-ADDRESS.
REWRITE DATA-MASTER-RECORD
    INVALID KEY PERFORM ERROR-EXIT-2.
```

This code could, of course, be rewritten using the FROM option as follows:

```
MOVE 23 TO DATA-ADDRESS.
REWRITE DATA-MASTER-RECORD FROM NEW-DATA
    INVALID KEY PERFORM ERROR-EXIT-2.
```

The WRITE statement is also permitted in random access to a relative file. The WRITE statement can be used to add records to a file; the number of the record must be placed in the relative key field prior to execution of the WRITE. If a record with that number does not exist, it will be added to the file; if a record does exist, an INVALID KEY condition results.

──────────── Example ────────────

Suppose we wish to add record number 65 to the file DATA-MASTER. The following program segment could be used:

```
MOVE 65 TO DATA-ADDRESS.
WRITE DATA-MASTER-RECORD
    INVALID KEY PERFORM ERROR-EXIT-3.
```

If record number 65 already exists, the INVALID KEY condition will be true, and the file will be unchanged. The existence of record number 65 does *not* imply that record 64 or any other record exists in the file. The system permits "holes" in a relative file.[1] Records are simply identified by record number when written into the file and when read from the file.

Records can be added into the midst of a relative file, or they can be appended to the end of the file. For example, suppose the largest record number in a relative file is 100. Ten records with relative keys 101 through 110 need to be added to the file. The following program segment could be used:

```
MOVE 100 TO RELATIVE-KEY.
PERFORM WRITE-PROCESS 10 TIMES.
       .
       .
       .
WRITE-PROCESS.
    ADD 1 TO RELATIVE-KEY.
    READ NEW-DATA-FILE AT END MOVE "YES" TO EOF.
    WRITE DATA-RECORD FROM NEW-DATA-RECORD
        INVALID KEY PERFORM ERROR-EXIT-4.
```

The INVALID KEY condition occurs if the file already contains a record that has the number found in the relative key field.

The DELETE statement may be used to remove records from a relative file. For example, if record number 4 needed to be removed from a relative file, the following program segment could be used:

```
MOVE 4 TO RELATIVE-KEY.
DELETE DATA-FILE RECORD
    INVALID KEY PERFORM ERROR-EXIT-5.
```

The INVALID KEY condition exists if a record with the appropriate address is not found in the file. In this example (with consecutive relative key values), the INVALID KEY condition could be true only if the file contained only three records or if record 4 had been deleted. Note that the DELETE statement does *not* cause a change in the record number of remaining records in the file. In this example, the record that was previously number 5 will remain record number 5.

The START statement is useful to begin sequential processing of a relative file at any desired point. The data-name used in the statement must be the relative key for the file. If the KEY clause is omitted, the IS EQUAL TO phrase is implied. For example, in order to begin processing a relative file DATA-FILE with the fourth record, the following procedure could be used:

```
MOVE 4 TO RELATIVE-KEY.
START DATA-FILE KEY IS = RELATIVE-KEY
    INVALID KEY
        PERFORM ERROR-EXIT.
```

[1] In some implementations of relative files, these "holes" actually take up space on the mass storage device, even though they are not used to store data. For example, a file containing one record with record number 100 may take up the same amount of space whether records 1 through 99 are present or not. Implementation is, however, system dependent; check the documentation of your system for details.

The INVALID KEY condition is true if no record exists in the file meeting the prescribed condition (if, for example, record 4 had been deleted). The file must be open in INPUT or I-0 mode. Access mode must be SEQUENTIAL or DYNAMIC.

─────────── Example ───────────

A COBOL relative file could be useful for storing a table that contains too many elements to store in memory. Recall that a relative file bears a strong resemblance to a table; the relative key takes the place of a subscript as the method of specifying the desired element. Suppose, for example, we wish to use a relative file to store a table in which the table arguments are in ascending sequence. The program could search the file sequentially (using ACCESS IS SEQUENTIAL and sequential READ), or the more efficient binary search procedure could be used (using ACCESS IS RANDOM and random READ). In the latter case, the relative key value would be computed before each READ in the same way that the subscript for the table entry was computed for a binary search.

Random Access Example

Program 15b, which is equivalent to Program 14b, can be used to maintain the relative file created by Program 15a. Maintaining the file involves adding, deleting, and changing records in the file; hence random access is required, and the SELECT entry must specify a RELATIVE KEY (lines 18–20):

```
ORGANIZATION IS RELATIVE
ACCESS IS RANDOM
RELATIVE KEY IS RECORD-NUMBER.
```

The data item RECORD-NUMBER is defined in WORKING-STORAGE as PIC 999. All access to the file will require an appropriate value to be placed in this item first.

Consider, for example, the program segment used to add a record to the file (paragraph 5000-WRITE-NEW-RECORD, lines 154–168). The first action required of the user is to enter the value of RECORD-NUMBER. The program then reads the file using a random read. If the record does not exist, the program can move forward; if the record does exist, then the user has entered an invalid record number.

In the program segment used to change a record (5200-CHANGE-RECORD), the record number is first entered by the user (lines 179–180), and then the program reads the record from the file. If the record exists, the process moves forward; if the record does not exist, then an error message is written (see lines 181–189).

The importance of the record number is emphasized to the user by displaying the record number along with the data (see the paragraph 9200-DISPLAY-DATA at lines 262–269) and in the Change menu (see lines 201–202).

Program 15b

```
 1 IDENTIFICATION DIVISION.
 2
 3 PROGRAM-ID. RELATIVE-FILE-UPDATE-PRO15B.
 .
 .
 .
15 FILE-CONTROL.
16
17     SELECT DATA-FILE ASSIGN TO DISK
18             ORGANIZATION IS RELATIVE
19             ACCESS IS RANDOM
20             RELATIVE KEY IS RECORD-NUMBER.
 .
 .
 .
39 WORKING-STORAGE SECTION.
40
41 01  FILE-NAME               PIC X(15) VALUE SPACES.
42
43 01  RECORD-NUMBER           PIC 999 VALUE ZERO.
 .
 .
 .
63     02 CHANGE-COMMAND       PIC X VALUE SPACE.
64        88 DISPLAY-RECORD     VALUE "D" "d".
65        88 CHANGE-SS-NUM      VALUE "S" "s".
66        88 CHANGE-NAME        VALUE "N" "n".
67        88 CHANGE-ADDRESS     VALUE "A" "a".
68        88 CHANGE-BIRTH-DATE  VALUE "B" "b".
69        88 QUIT-CHANGES       VALUE "Q" "q".
70        88 VALID-CHANGE       VALUE "D" "d" "S" "s" "N" "n"
71                                    "A" "a" "B" "b" "Q" "q".
72 PROCEDURE DIVISION.
73
74 1000-MAIN-CONTROL.
75
76     PERFORM 2000-PROCESS-USER-COMMANDS
77             UNTIL QUIT.
78     STOP RUN.
79
80 2000-PROCESS-USER-COMMANDS.
81
82     PERFORM 3000-DISPLAY-MENU.
83     PERFORM 3100-GET-COMMAND.
84     IF      NAME-FILE
85             PERFORM 3200-GET-FILE-NAME
86     ELSE IF UPDATE-FILE
87             PERFORM 3300-UPDATE-FILE
88     ELSE IF HELP
89             PERFORM 3400-WRITE-HELP
90     ELSE IF NOT VALID-COMMAND
91             PERFORM 3500-WRITE-ERROR.
92
```

Program 15b   *(continued)*

```
 93 3000-DISPLAY-MENU.
 94
 95     DISPLAY "   Main Menu".
 96     DISPLAY "Command  Action".
 97     DISPLAY "   N      Name file (Current file " FILE-NAME ")".
 98     DISPLAY "   U      Update file".
 99     DISPLAY "   H      Help".
100     DISPLAY "   Q      Quit program".
  .
  .
  .
112 3300-UPDATE-FILE.
113
114     IF FILE-NAME = SPACES
115        DISPLAY "File has not been named"
116     ELSE
117         DISPLAY "Update file " FILE-NAME
118         DISPLAY "OK to proceed? (Y/N)"
119         ACCEPT ANSWER
120         IF DATA-OK
121             OPEN I-O DATA-FILE
122             MOVE SPACES TO UPDATE-COMMAND
123             PERFORM 4000-UPDATE-RECORD
124                     UNTIL QUIT-UPDATE
125             CLOSE DATA-FILE.
  .
  .
  .
135 4000-UPDATE-RECORD.
136
137     DISPLAY "Update Menu (Current File " FILE-NAME ")".
138     DISPLAY "Command Action".
139     DISPLAY "   N    New record".
140     DISPLAY "   D    Delete record".
141     DISPLAY "   C    Change record".
142     DISPLAY "   Q    Quit update".
143     DISPLAY "Enter update command"
144     ACCEPT UPDATE-COMMAND.
145     IF NEW-RECORD
146         PERFORM 5000-WRITE-NEW-RECORD
147     ELSE IF DELETE-RECORD
148         PERFORM 5100-DELETE-RECORD
149     ELSE IF CHANGE-RECORD
150         PERFORM 5200-CHANGE-RECORD
151     ELSE IF NOT VALID-UPDATE
152         DISPLAY "Invalid update code".
153
```

Program 15b *(continued)*

```
154 5000-WRITE-NEW-RECORD.
155
156     DISPLAY "Enter record number for new record".
157     ACCEPT RECORD-NUMBER.
158     MOVE "YES" TO ERROR-FLAG.
159     READ DATA-FILE
160         INVALID KEY MOVE "NO" TO ERROR-FLAG.
161     IF ERROR-FLAG = "YES"
162         DISPLAY "Record exists"
163     ELSE
164         MOVE "N" TO ANSWER
165         PERFORM 9000-GET-DATA
166             UNTIL DATA-OK
167         WRITE DATA-RECORD
168             INVALID KEY DISPLAY "Internal logic error".
169
170 5100-DELETE-RECORD.
171
172     DISPLAY "Enter record number of record to be deleted".
173     ACCEPT RECORD-NUMBER.
174     DELETE DATA-FILE RECORD
175         INVALID KEY DISPLAY "Record not present in file".
176
177 5200-CHANGE-RECORD.
178
179     DISPLAY "Enter record number of record to be changed".
180     ACCEPT RECORD-NUMBER.
181     MOVE "NO" TO ERROR-FLAG.
182     READ DATA-FILE
183         INVALID KEY MOVE "YES" TO ERROR-FLAG.
184     IF ERROR-FLAG = "YES"
185         DISPLAY "Record does not exist in file"
186     ELSE
187         MOVE SPACE TO CHANGE-COMMAND
188         PERFORM 6000-GET-CHANGES
189             UNTIL QUIT-CHANGES.
190     IF ERROR-FLAG = "NO"
191         IF CHANGE-COMMAND = "Q"
192             DISPLAY "Changes being copied to file"
193             REWRITE DATA-RECORD
194                 INVALID KEY DISPLAY "Internal logic error".
195     IF ERROR-FLAG = "NO"
196         IF CHANGE-COMMAND = "q"
197             DISPLAY "Changes discarded".
198
```

```
199 6000-GET-CHANGES.
200
201     DISPLAY "Change Menu (Current Record Number "
202                        RECORD-NUMBER ")".
203     DISPLAY "Command Action".
204     DISPLAY "  D    Display record".
205     DISPLAY "  S    Change social security number".
206     DISPLAY "  N    Change name".
207     DISPLAY "  A    Change address".
208     DISPLAY "  B    Change date of birth".
209     DISPLAY "  Q    Quit changes: write changed record".
210     DISPLAY "  q    Quit changes: do not write changed record".
211     DISPLAY "Enter change command"
212     ACCEPT CHANGE-COMMAND.
213     IF DISPLAY-RECORD
214            PERFORM 9200-DISPLAY-DATA
215     ELSE IF CHANGE-SS-NUM
216            DISPLAY "Enter new social security number"
217            ACCEPT SS-NUM-DR
218     ELSE IF CHANGE-NAME
219            DISPLAY "Enter new name"
220            ACCEPT NAME-DR
221     ELSE IF CHANGE-ADDRESS
222            DISPLAY "Enter new Street Address"
223            ACCEPT STREET-ADDRESS-DR
224            DISPLAY "Enter new City"
225            ACCEPT CITY-DR
226            DISPLAY "Enter new Two Character State Abbreviation"
227            ACCEPT STATE-DR
228            DISPLAY "Enter new ZIP"
229            ACCEPT ZIP-DR
230     ELSE IF CHANGE-BIRTH-DATE
231            DISPLAY "Enter new Date of Birth in form mmddyy"
232            ACCEPT DOB-DR
233     ELSE IF NOT VALID-CHANGE
234            DISPLAY "Invalid change code".
235
236 9000-GET-DATA.
237
238     PERFORM 9100-ENTER-DATA.
239     PERFORM 9200-DISPLAY-DATA.
240     DISPLAY "Are data correct? (Y/N)".
241     ACCEPT ANSWER.
242     IF NOT DATA-OK
243        DISPLAY "Reenter data".
      .
      .
      .
262 9200-DISPLAY-DATA.
263
264     DISPLAY "Record #   : " RECORD-NUMBER.
265     DISPLAY "Name       : " NAME-DR.
266     DISPLAY "SS #       : " SS-NUM-DR.
267     DISPLAY "Address    : " STREET-ADDRESS-DR.
268     DISPLAY "             " CITY-DR STATE-DR " " ZIP-DR.
269     DISPLAY "Birth Date : " DOB-DR.
```

Dynamic Access Example

Program 15c, a revision of program 14d, makes use of DYNAMIC access to enable the program user to maintain the file (using random-access input/output statements) or to list the file (using sequential input/output statements). The SELECT entry specifies DYNAMIC access (lines 18–20):

```
ORGANIZATION IS RELATIVE
ACCESS IS DYNAMIC
RELATIVE KEY IS RECORD-NUMBER.
```

The maintenance procedures in this program are similar to those in Program 15b. The most interesting part of the program lies in the paragraph 3400-LIST-FILE, which is devoted to listing the file sequentially. We begin by opening the file in INPUT mode (line 142). The sequential read statement (which specifies NEXT RECORD) at line 301 reads each record in the file in turn. As was the case with INDEXED files with DYNAMIC access, the NEXT RECORD clause on the READ statement is imperative to denote a sequential rather than a random read.

15.4 DIRECT AND RANDOMIZED RELATIVE FILES

You have probably been wondering why anyone would use relative file organization for data storage since it is necessary for the program user to know the record number for each record in the file; whereas with indexed access, we can use one of the naturally occurring data fields (the RECORD KEY) to access data in the file. In fact, indexed file organization makes much more sense than relative organization in the example we have presented thus far. It is unreasonable to ask the user to know the record number of a record in the file if that record number is unrelated to any data within the record. In this section, we will present a technique for organizing a relative file in such a way that the program can compute the record number from some field within the record and use that number to place the record in or read a record from the file.

Consider a file in which the key field is quite short—for example, three digits. Perhaps the file contains records with data about the employees of a small company, and the key field is the employee number. We could use a relative file with the employee number as the relative key. For example, the record for employee number 100 would be stored in the 100th record in the file. Let us call this method **direct relative file organization**. Usually, however, key-field values are not this small. An employee number is typically the employee Social Security number—a nine-digit number. An attempt to use the direct method described above would require a file containing one billion records, which would far exceed the capacity of any mass storage device currently available. Moreover, only the records associated with actual employees would be used; the vast majority would contain no data. The direct access afforded by this method is very powerful, but the direct relative file organization method will not work except in very restricted circumstances.

Relative files can still be very useful, however, if the records are randomly placed in the file. This method is similar to the randomized table method presented in Chapter 12, in which a record's address is determined using a hash function. We will call this method **randomized relative file organization**.

```
 1 IDENTIFICATION DIVISION.
 2
 3 PROGRAM-ID. RELATIVE-FILE-UPDATE-PRO15C.
 .
 .
 .
16
17     SELECT DATA-FILE ASSIGN TO DISK
18             ORGANIZATION IS RELATIVE
19             ACCESS IS DYNAMIC
20             RELATIVE KEY IS RECORD-NUMBER.
 .
 .
 .
39 WORKING-STORAGE SECTION.
40
41 01   FILE-NAME              PIC X(15) VALUE SPACES.
42
43 01   RECORD-NUMBER          PIC 999 VALUE ZERO.
 .
 .
 .
75 PROCEDURE DIVISION.
76
77 1000-MAIN-CONTROL.
78
79     PERFORM 2000-PROCESS-USER-COMMANDS
80             UNTIL QUIT.
81     STOP RUN.
82
83 2000-PROCESS-USER-COMMANDS.
84
85     PERFORM 3000-DISPLAY-MENU.
86     PERFORM 3100-GET-COMMAND.
87     IF      NAME-FILE
88             PERFORM 3200-GET-FILE-NAME
89     ELSE IF UPDATE-FILE
90             PERFORM 3300-UPDATE-FILE
91     ELSE IF LIST-FILE
92             PERFORM 3400-LIST-FILE
93     ELSE IF HELP
94             PERFORM 3500-WRITE-HELP
95     ELSE IF NOT VALID-COMMAND
96             PERFORM 3600-WRITE-ERROR.
97
```

Program 15c   *(concluded)*

```
 98 3000-DISPLAY-MENU.
 99
100     DISPLAY "   Main Menu".
101     DISPLAY "Command  Action".
102     DISPLAY "   N      Name file (Current file " FILE-NAME ")".
103     DISPLAY "   U      Update file".
104     DISPLAY "   L      List file".
105     DISPLAY "   H      Help".
106     DISPLAY "   Q      Quit program".
      .
      .
133 3400-LIST-FILE.
134
135     IF FILE-NAME = SPACES
136         DISPLAY "File has not been named"
137     ELSE
138         DISPLAY "List file " FILE-NAME
139         DISPLAY "OK to proceed? (Y/N)"
140         ACCEPT ANSWER
141         IF DATA-OK
142            OPEN INPUT DATA-FILE
143            MOVE "NO" TO EOF-FLAG
144            PERFORM 9300-READ-DATA-FILE
145            PERFORM 4100-PROCESS-DATA-FILE
146                  UNTIL END-OF-FILE
147            CLOSE DATA-FILE.
      .
      .
299 9300-READ-DATA-FILE.
300
301     READ DATA-FILE NEXT RECORD
302         AT END MOVE "YES" TO EOF-FLAG.
```

A hash function is used to compute an address based on the record key. A very common hash function is the division/remainder method: divide the key-field value by the number of records in the file. Take the remainder and add 1. For example, if the file contained space for 59 records, the record address for the record with key-field value 203 would be computed as follows:

$$\begin{array}{r} 3 \\ 59\overline{)203} \\ \underline{177} \\ 26 \end{array}$$

The record address is $26 + 1 = 27$.

Of course, this method can result in **synonyms**—records that have different key fields yielding the same address. One method of handling synonyms is to examine following records until an unused record is located (when loading data) or until the desired record is located (when searching for data). Finding a used position while searching for a place to put data is called a **collision**.

As with the randomized table technique, this method has been shown to work best when the file size is a prime number. When the file is more than two-thirds full, the number of collisions tends to rise dramatically. This results in a severe degradation in the performance of the program because multiple reads must be executed to locate a single record. Within these constraints, the randomized placement of records in a relative file offers a good alternative to indexed files for many applications that require random-access to data.

One method for applying this randomization technique involves writing an initial program to create a relative file completely filled with records containing null values. That is, all fields in all records are initialized to spaces or zeros, as appropriate. Once the file has been created and filled with "dummy" records, a second program loads actual data into the file using a randomization technique; this second program uses random access to rewrite appropriate records, thereby filling those records with actual data.

Example

Program 15d is used to create an initial version of a randomized relative file that can be used for random access to the data we have been using in this chapter. The number of records in the file (7 records in this example) is fixed at the time of initialization (see line 42). All fields in the initial version of the file have value spaces (see lines 104–106).

By first filling the file with dummy records, the necessary logic to locate and update records later is somewhat simplified because a REWRITE statement is then used for all adds, changes, and deletions.

The procedure for placing records in such a randomized file is described in pseudocode in Figure 15.4. The procedure begins by calculating the expected address using the appropriate hash function. The corresponding record is read from the file. If the record contains no data (that is, it is a dummy record), the program can REWRITE the record with actual data. If, on the other hand, the record contains data, a collision has occurred; the procedure then increments the address by one, and the process is repeated. Remember that the file is essentially circular: The record following the last one in the file is the first one, so if the address becomes larger than the file size, it is reset to one.

Pseudocode for a procedure to change the content of existing records is shown in Figure 15.5. We assume that transaction data is available to update a master record. The procedure for locating a master record terminates when the key field from the master record just read matches the transaction key. If a dummy record is read before the desired master record is located, the desired master record is not present in the file. If the record that is read is neither the desired record nor a dummy record, the address is incremented so the next record can be read. The procedure terminates when either the desired record is found or when it is determined that the record being sought is not present, at which time appropriate action is taken. If the matching record is found, changes are made to the appropriate fields in the master record, and the master record is rewritten to the file.

Deleting records from a randomized relative file is accomplished by performing a logical deletion rather than a physical deletion. To accomplish this, it is necessary to include a code within the record marking it as

Program 15d

```
 1 IDENTIFICATION DIVISION.
 2
 3 PROGRAM-ID. RANDOM-FILE-INITIALIZE-PRO15D.
 .
 .
 .
15 FILE-CONTROL.
16
17     SELECT DATA-FILE ASSIGN TO DISK
18             ORGANIZATION IS RELATIVE
19             ACCESS IS SEQUENTIAL.
 .
 .
 .
38 WORKING-STORAGE SECTION.
39
40 01  FILE-PARAMETERS.
41     02 FILE-NAME          PIC X(15) VALUE SPACES.
42     02 FILE-SIZE          PIC 99 VALUE 7.
43
44 01  CONTROL-FIELDS.
45     02 ANSWER             PIC X VALUE "N".
46        88 DATA-OK          VALUE "Y" "y".
47     02 COMMAND            PIC X VALUE SPACE.
48        88 NAME-FILE        VALUE "N" "n".
49        88 INITIALIZE-FILE  VALUE "I" "i".
50        88 HELP             VALUE "H" "h".
51        88 QUIT             VALUE "Q" "q".
52        88 VALID-COMMAND    VALUE "N" "n" "I" "i"
53                                  "H" "h" "Q" "q".
54
55 PROCEDURE DIVISION.
56
57 1000-MAIN-CONTROL.
58
59     PERFORM 2000-PROCESS-USER-COMMANDS
60             UNTIL QUIT.
61     STOP RUN.
62
63 2000-PROCESS-USER-COMMANDS.
64
65     PERFORM 3000-DISPLAY-MENU.
66     PERFORM 3100-GET-COMMAND.
67     IF      NAME-FILE
68             PERFORM 3200-GET-FILE-NAME
69     ELSE IF INITIALIZE-FILE
70             PERFORM 3300-INITIALIZE-FILE
71     ELSE IF HELP
72             PERFORM 3400-WRITE-HELP
73     ELSE IF NOT VALID-COMMAND
74             PERFORM 3500-WRITE-ERROR.
75
```

Program 15d   *(concluded)*

```
 76 3000-DISPLAY-MENU.
 77
 78     DISPLAY "Command   Action".
 79     DISPLAY "   N       Name file (Current file " FILE-NAME ")".
 80     DISPLAY "   I       Initialize file".
 81     DISPLAY "   H       Help".
 82     DISPLAY "   Q       Quit program".
    .
    .
    .
 94 3300-INITIALIZE-FILE.
 95
 96     IF FILE-NAME = SPACES
 97         DISPLAY "File has not been named"
 98     ELSE
 99         DISPLAY "Initialize file " FILE-NAME
100         DISPLAY "OK to proceed? (Y/N)"
101         ACCEPT ANSWER
102         IF DATA-OK
103             OPEN OUTPUT DATA-FILE
104             MOVE SPACES TO DATA-RECORD
105             PERFORM 4000-BUILD-FILE
106                     FILE-SIZE TIMES
107             CLOSE DATA-FILE.
    .
    .
    .
117 4000-BUILD-FILE.
118
119     WRITE DATA-RECORD.
```

Figure 15.4   Adding records to a randomized file

```
Record number = hash function (key field)
Move "CONTINUE" to found flag
Do while found flag = "CONTINUE"
      Read data file
      If record contains actual data
            Add 1 to record number
            If record number > file size
                  Move 1 to record number
            End If
      Else
            Move "FINISH" to found flag
      End If
End Do
Move actual data to data file record
Rewrite data file record
```

Figure 15.5 Changing a record in a randomized file

```
Record number = hash function (transaction key)
Move "CONTINUE" to found flag
Do while found flag = "CONTINUE"
      Read data file
      If record does not contain actual data
            Move "NOT PRESENT" to found flag
      Else
            If key field = transaction key
                  Move "FOUND" to found flag
            Else
                  Add 1 to record number
                  If record address > file size
                        Move 1 to record number
                  End If
            End If
      End If
End Do
If found flag = "FOUND"
      Move transaction data to appropriate fields in data record
      Rewrite data record
Else
      Take action appropriate for invalid transaction
End If
```

active or deleted. Deleting a record, then, requires only that the deletion code be changed for that record. All programs that access the file must check the deletion code field to determine whether the record is active before making use of the data. However, a deleted record is still considered to be "in use" for purposes of searching the file to locate a record. A deleted record can also be reused for a new data record if needed. A procedure for deleting records is shown in Figure 15.6. Note that this procedure is essentially similar to the one required to change a record. Deleting a record becomes a specialized type of change.

Consider the problem of clearing a randomized file of deleted records. As the number of logically deleted records increases, the performance of the system degrades because the number of collisions increases during each file access. At some point, it will become advantageous to make a new version of the file with all deleted records omitted. In order to perform this function, a program will be needed to read each record from the old file (sequentially) and place each active (nondeleted) record in its appropriate position in the new file. Pseudocode for this procedure is shown in Figure 15.7. Note that this same procedure would be required to increase the physical size of a randomized file since the placement of the record in the file depends on the file size.

 Example

Program 15e shows the use of the procedures just outlined to maintain the randomized relative file initialized in Program 15d. Program 15e is essentially similar to Program 14b; the primary main menu options are to name and update the file. The update menu allows two options: to add a new

Figure 15.6   Deleting records from a randomized file

```
Record number = hash function (transaction key)
Move "CONTINUE" to found flag
Do while found flag = "CONTINUE"
      Read data file
      If record does not contain actual data
            Move "NOT PRESENT" to found flag
      Else
            If key field = transaction key
                  Move "FOUND" to found flag
            Else
                  Add 1 to record number
                  If record address > file size
                        Move 1 to record number
                  End If
            End If
      End If
End Do
If found flag = "FOUND"
      Reset deletion code field
      Rewrite data record
Else
      Take action appropriate for invalid transaction
End If
```

record or to change an existing record. (The task of implementing record deletion is left as an exercise for the reader.)

At the heart of each of the procedures that accomplish the update tasks is locating the position of a record in the file. Program 15e follows the randomization and search procedures outlined in Figures 15.4 and 15.5 with one added feature. It is possible that the file may be full of actual (nondummy) records. The very simple procedures we have used up to now would not detect a full file; in fact, it is possible for either of these procedures to enter an infinite loop when confronted with a file in which every record is in use for actual data.

In Program 15e, both the add and change procedures make use of the procedure 9300-LOCATE-RECORD to determine the position of a desired record in the file. This procedure returns an item SEARCH-FLAG which has one of the following values:

YES   if record is found in the file
NO   if record is not found in the file
FULL   if the file is full

If the value of SEARCH-FLAG is "YES", then the content of RECORD-NUMBER points to the record that corresponds to value of TRANSACTION-SS-NUM.

Each update procedure takes different actions based on the value of SEARCH-FLAG. For example, the procedure 5000-WRITE-NEW-RECORD (lines 158–173) displays an error message if the value of SEARCH-FLAG is either "YES" (the record already exists) or "FULL" (there is no more room in the file). If the value of SEARCH-FILE is "NO", then the content of the relative key RECORD-NUMBER points to a record in the file that is unused and is the proper location for the data associated with this data. In this

Figure 15.7   Removing deleted records from a randomized file

```
Open files
Read next record from data file
Do while not end of data file
    If active record
            Record number = hash function (record key)
            Move "CONTINUE" to found flag
            Do while found flag = "CONTINUE"
                    Read new data file
                    If new data record does not contain actual data
                            Move "FINISH" to found flag
                    Else
                            Add 1 to record number
                            If record number greater than file size
                                    Move 1 to record number
                            End If
                    End If
            End Do
            Move data record to new data record
            Rewrite new data record
    End If
    Read next record from data file
End Do
Close files
Stop
```

Notes: Data file is accessed sequentially. New data file is accessed randomly.

case, the program proceeds to allow the user to enter the new data and uses the REWRITE statement to add the record to the file. In the case of the procedure 5100-CHANGE-RECORD (lines 175–195), if the value of SEARCH-FLAG is "FULL" or "NO", an error message is written. If the value is "YES", then the record has been located, and the user can proceed to enter desired changes. After all changes have been entered and the user has chosen to make the changes permanent, the REWRITE statement is used to replace the old record with the new one (lines 191–192).

Consider now the procedure 9300-LOCATE-RECORD (lines 262–273). Its first task is to use the hash function to compute the initial value of RECORD-NUMBER (lines 264–265). (The DISPLAY statements at lines 267 through 269 are coded as comments in the program; it is interesting to remove the asterisk and watch the values of the various variables as they are computed during the execution of the program.) The task of detecting a full file is accomplished by retaining the initial value of RECORD-NUMBER in RECORD-NUMBER-HOLD (line 270). Then, in the procedure 9400-GET-RECORD (lines 275–286), if the new value of RECORD-NUMBER ever equals RECORD-NUMBER-HOLD, then the system has cycled through the entire file and has not found the desired record or a dummy record. In other words, the file is full, and "FULL" becomes the value of SEARCH-FLAG at that point (see lines 285–286). If the desired record is located (SS-NUM-DR is equal to TRANSACTION-SS), the value of SEARCH-FLAG is set to "YES" (line 280); if a

```
 1 IDENTIFICATION DIVISION.
 2
 3 PROGRAM-ID. RANDOMIZED-FILE-UPDATE-PRO15E.
 .
 .
 .
15 FILE-CONTROL.
16
17     SELECT DATA-FILE ASSIGN TO DISK
18             ORGANIZATION IS RELATIVE
19             ACCESS IS RANDOM
20             RELATIVE KEY IS RECORD-NUMBER.
 .
 .
39 WORKING-STORAGE SECTION.
40
41 01   FILE-PARAMETERS.
42      02 FILE-NAME          PIC X(15) VALUE SPACES.
43      02 FILE-SIZE          PIC 99 VALUE 7.
44
45 01   RECORD-PARAMETERS.
46      02 RECORD-NUMBER      PIC 99 VALUE ZERO.
47      02 RECORD-NUMBER-HOLD PIC 99 VALUE ZERO.
48      02 QUOTIENT           PIC 9(9) VALUE ZERO.
49
50 01   CONTROL-FIELDS.
51      02 ANSWER             PIC X VALUE "N".
52         88 DATA-OK         VALUE "Y" "y".
53      02 SEARCH-FLAG        PIC X(8) VALUE "CONTINUE".
54      02 COMMAND            PIC X VALUE SPACE.
55         88 NAME-FILE       VALUE "N" "n".
56         88 UPDATE-FILE     VALUE "U" "u".
57         88 HELP            VALUE "H" "h".
58         88 QUIT            VALUE "Q" "q".
59         88 VALID-COMMAND   VALUE "N" "n" "U" "u"
60                                  "H" "h" "Q" "q".
61      02 UPDATE-COMMAND     PIC X VALUE SPACE.
62         88 NEW-RECORD      VALUE "N" "n".
63         88 CHANGE-RECORD   VALUE "C" "c".
64         88 QUIT-UPDATE     VALUE "Q" "q".
65         88 VALID-UPDATE    VALUE "N" "n" "C" "c"
66                                  "Q" "q".
67      02 CHANGE-COMMAND     PIC X VALUE SPACE.
68         88 DISPLAY-RECORD  VALUE "D" "d".
69         88 CHANGE-NAME     VALUE "N" "n".
70         88 CHANGE-ADDRESS  VALUE "A" "a".
71         88 CHANGE-BIRTH-DATE VALUE "B" "b".
72         88 QUIT-CHANGES    VALUE "Q" "q".
73         88 VALID-CHANGE    VALUE "D" "d" "N" "n"
74                                  "A" "a" "B" "b" "Q" "q".
75
```

Program 15e   *(continued)*

```
 76 01   TRANSACTION-SS.
 77      03 TRANSACTION-SS-NUM    PIC 9(9).
 78
 79 PROCEDURE DIVISION.
 80
 81 1000-MAIN-CONTROL.
 82
 83      PERFORM 2000-PROCESS-USER-COMMANDS
 84              UNTIL QUIT.
 85      STOP RUN.
 86
 87 2000-PROCESS-USER-COMMANDS.
 88
 89      PERFORM 3000-DISPLAY-MENU.
 90      PERFORM 3100-GET-COMMAND.
 91      IF      NAME-FILE
 92              PERFORM 3200-GET-FILE-NAME
 93      ELSE IF UPDATE-FILE
 94              PERFORM 3300-UPDATE-FILE
 95      ELSE IF HELP
 96              PERFORM 3400-WRITE-HELP
 97      ELSE IF NOT VALID-COMMAND
 98              PERFORM 3500-WRITE-ERROR.
 99
100 3000-DISPLAY-MENU.
101
102      DISPLAY "    Main Menu".
103      DISPLAY "Command   Action".
104      DISPLAY "   N      Name file (Current file " FILE-NAME ")".
105      DISPLAY "   U      Update file".
106      DISPLAY "   H      Help".
107      DISPLAY "   Q      Quit program".
      .
      .
      .
119 3300-UPDATE-FILE.
120
121      IF FILE-NAME = SPACES
122          DISPLAY "File has not been named"
123      ELSE
124          DISPLAY "Update file " FILE-NAME
125          DISPLAY "OK to proceed? (Y/N)"
126          ACCEPT ANSWER
127          IF DATA-OK
128              OPEN I-O DATA-FILE
129              MOVE SPACES TO UPDATE-COMMAND
130              PERFORM 4000-UPDATE-FILE
131                      UNTIL QUIT-UPDATE
132              CLOSE DATA-FILE.
      .
      .
      .
```

```
142 4000-UPDATE-FILE.
143
144     DISPLAY "Update Menu (Current File " FILE-NAME ")".
145     DISPLAY "Command Action".
146     DISPLAY "  N    New record".
147     DISPLAY "  C    Change record".
148     DISPLAY "  Q    Quit update".
149     DISPLAY "Enter update command"
150     ACCEPT UPDATE-COMMAND.
151     IF   NEW-RECORD
152             PERFORM 5000-WRITE-NEW-RECORD
153     ELSE IF CHANGE-RECORD
154             PERFORM 5100-CHANGE-RECORD
155     ELSE IF NOT VALID-UPDATE
156             DISPLAY "Invalid update code".
157
158 5000-WRITE-NEW-RECORD.
159
160     DISPLAY "Enter Social Security Number for new record".
161     ACCEPT TRANSACTION-SS.
162     PERFORM 9300-LOCATE-RECORD.
163     IF   SEARCH-FLAG = "YES"
164             DISPLAY "Record exists in file"
165     ELSE IF SEARCH-FLAG = "FULL"
166             DISPLAY "File is full"
167     ELSE
168             MOVE "N" TO ANSWER
169             PERFORM 9000-GET-DATA
170                     UNTIL DATA-OK
171             MOVE TRANSACTION-SS TO SS-NUM-DR
172             REWRITE DATA-RECORD
173                 INVALID KEY DISPLAY "Internal logic error 5000".
174
175 5100-CHANGE-RECORD.
176
177     DISPLAY
178     "Enter Social Security Number of record to be changed".
179     ACCEPT TRANSACTION-SS.
180     PERFORM 9300-LOCATE-RECORD.
181     IF SEARCH-FLAG = "NO" OR "FULL"
182         DISPLAY "Record does not exist in file"
183     ELSE
184        MOVE SPACE TO CHANGE-COMMAND
185        PERFORM 6000-GET-CHANGES
186                UNTIL QUIT-CHANGES.
187     IF SEARCH-FLAG = "YES"
188        IF CHANGE-COMMAND = "Q"
189             DISPLAY "Changes being copied to file"
190             MOVE TRANSACTION-SS TO SS-NUM-DR
191             REWRITE DATA-RECORD
192                  INVALID KEY DISPLAY "Internal logic error 5100".
193     IF SEARCH-FLAG = "YES"
194        IF CHANGE-COMMAND = "q"
195             DISPLAY "Changes discarded".
196
```

Program 15e   *(concluded)*

```
      .
      .
      .
254 9200-DISPLAY-DATA.
255
256     DISPLAY "Name      : " NAME-DR.
257     DISPLAY "SS #      : " TRANSACTION-SS.
258     DISPLAY "Address   : " STREET-ADDRESS-DR.
259     DISPLAY "          " CITY-DR STATE-DR " " ZIP-DR.
260     DISPLAY "Birth Date : " DOB-DR.
261
262 9300-LOCATE-RECORD.
263
264     DIVIDE TRANSACTION-SS-NUM BY FILE-SIZE GIVING QUOTIENT
265                              REMAINDER RECORD-NUMBER.
266     ADD 1 TO RECORD-NUMBER.
267*    DISPLAY "TSN" TRANSACTION-SS-NUM.
268*    DISPLAY "RN" RECORD-NUMBER.
269*    DISPLAY "Q" QUOTIENT.
270     MOVE RECORD-NUMBER TO RECORD-NUMBER-HOLD.
271     MOVE "CONTINUE" TO SEARCH-FLAG.
272     PERFORM 9400-GET-RECORD
273             UNTIL SEARCH-FLAG NOT = "CONTINUE".
274
275 9400-GET-RECORD.
276
277     READ DATA-FILE
278         INVALID KEY DISPLAY "Internal logic error 9400".
279     IF   SS-NUM-DR = TRANSACTION-SS
280         MOVE "YES" TO SEARCH-FLAG
281     ELSE IF SS-NUM-DR = SPACES
282             MOVE "NO" TO SEARCH-FLAG
283     ELSE
284         PERFORM 9500-COMPUTE-NEXT-RECORD
285         IF RECORD-NUMBER = RECORD-NUMBER-HOLD
286             MOVE "FULL" TO SEARCH-FLAG.
287
288 9500-COMPUTE-NEXT-RECORD.
289
290     ADD 1 TO RECORD-NUMBER.
291     IF RECORD-NUMBER > FILE-SIZE
292         MOVE 1 TO RECORD-NUMBER.
```

dummy record is located (SS-NUM-DR is equal to SPACES), the value of
SEARCH-FLAG is set to "NO" (line 282). If none of the conditions is encountered, the value of RECORD-NUMBER is advanced to point to the next record
in the file (see 9500-COMPUTE-NEXT-RECORD at lines 288–292). This procedure retains the notion of a circular file; if the value of RECORD-NUMBER
is greater than FILE-SIZE, the value of RECORD-NUMBER is reset to one
(line 292).

15.5 DEBUG CLINIC

Associated with each relative file is a two-character file status item that contains information about the status of an input/output operation. The program can gain access to this item if the FILE STATUS clause is included in the SELECT entry for the file. Definitions of possible settings of the file status item are shown in Figure 15.8. The potential use of the file status item is similar in relative, indexed, and sequential files.

Figure 15.8   FILE STATUS item settings for relative files

Setting	Meaning
00	Successful completion
10	End of file
22	Duplicate key
23	No record found
24	Boundary violation
30	Permanent error
9x	Implementor defined (see local documentation)

As with indexed files, the input/output statements that are permitted for relative files depend on the combination of access declaration (RANDOM, SEQUENTIAL, or DYNAMIC) and open mode (INPUT, OUTPUT, or I-O). The permitted statements are exactly the same as for indexed files which are summarized in Figure 14.15. Debugging problems in programs utilizing relative files can often be traced to inappropriate use of input or output statements in a particular context. For example, in dealing with a relative file that uses the dummy record method outlined in Section 15.4, it would be inappropriate to use the WRITE statement to add a record to the file. (Remember that the file was filled with dummy records during the file initialization; thereafter, all operations are accomplished by changing the content of the existing records using REWRITE.)

15.6 COMPARISON WITH OTHER FILE TYPES

The choice of file organization and content is a very crucial decision in the design of a data processing system. The choice must be made only after careful consideration of both the present and potential future needs of the user and the capabilities and limitations of the various file organization techniques. When random access is needed for a file, there is often a choice of indexed or relative files. In general, an indexed file should be chosen if both random and sequential access to data in sequence are required and the key field cannot be used as a record address. Indexed files have some drawbacks. Access speed is often fairly slow, since many mass storage operations may be required for one record to be read. A direct relative file is a good choice if the key field can be used as a record address. A randomized relative file is a good choice if the key field cannot be used directly as a record address and if access to the data in ascending (or descending) sequence is not needed. In both cases, the number of mass storage operations is reduced to one for direct access to a relative file, or close to one, on the average, for a randomized relative file. For storage and access to table data in mass storage rather than in memory, a relative file is the method of choice, as it permits easy implementation of any desired search procedure and easy methods for performing file maintenance. In general, the choice of a relative file over an indexed file may make the program more efficient in execution time. Both relative and indexed files demand extra space on the mass storage medium, and both types of files must be assigned to a device capable of random access. If space is at a premium or if tape must be used for file storage, the only type of file organization available is sequential.

Relative files are quite often underutilized in data processing systems because they are comparatively new. (This implementation was first described in the ANSI 74 Standard.) Their capabilities are not fully understood by many practicing programmers and analysts. If properly used, relative files can contribute to data processing systems' efficiency not possible with other file organization techniques.

15.7 COBOL-85 UPDATE

All of the input and output statements used for relative files are also used for indexed files. Therefore, the COBOL-85 statements related to indexed files covered in Chapter 14, Section 12 are the same for relative files. There are three major changes:

- Inclusion of NOT INVALID KEY clause for READ, WRITE, REWRITE, DELETE, and START.
- Addition of scope delimiter for each statement (END-READ, END-WRITE, and so forth).
- Additional conditions in the START verb.

Refer to Section 14.12 for complete descriptions of each of these changes.

15.8 SELF-TEST EXERCISES

1. Write pseudocode for a program to list all deleted records in a randomized relative file DATA-FILE.
2. How would a system be designed to warn an operator or systems programmer when a randomized relative file should be reorganized?
3. Can the DELETE verb be used to remove records from a randomized relative file? Why?
4. How are new records added to a randomized relative file? Can the random WRITE be used for this purpose?
5. Revise the procedures of Figures 15.4 and 15.5 to take into account deleted records.
6. How could a relative file be used to store table data? What would be the most efficient search procedure for this technique?
7. Why would a programmer or analyst choose relative organization for a file?
8. List the major disadvantages of relative files.

9. Each record in a relative file contains the fields TABLE-ARGUMENT and TABLE-VALUE. Using a binary search, write pseudocode for a procedure to locate the value associated with ACTUAL-ARGUMENT.

15.9 PROGRAMMING EXERCISES

1. Revise Programs 15d and 15e to take into account deleted records.

2. Write a program to remove all deleted records from the file created in Exercise 1 above. Use the procedure outlined in Figure 15.7 as a guide.

3. Consider the table shown in Figure 12.1. Write a program to transform a sequential file containing that data into a relative file. Then, write a program to access the data from this relative file to convert dates entered in the form *mmddyy* into the equivalent Julian date.

4. Write a program to transform a sequential file containing the data shown in Figure 12.25 into a relative file. Write a program to process a representative sample of actual mileage values using a binary search strategy to locate the deduction amount from the relative file. (Compare this exercise with Exercise 1 in Chapter 12, Section 13.)

5. Consider the Student Master File described in Exercise 2 in Chapter 13 (Section 16). Assume that the maximum number of students to be processed is 57. Write a program to create an initial version of this file as a randomized relative file. Then, write a program to maintain this file using the codes given in Exercise 4 in Chapter 13 (Section 16).

6. Using randomized relative file organization, write programs required for Exercise 6 in Chapter 13 (Section 16). Assume a maximum file size of 13 stores.

7. Modify Program 15c to allow the user also to create a new file. You will need to

   • Add a new valid option ("C" or "c") to create the file and include this option on the main menu display.

   • Add an ELSE IF in paragraph 2000 to check for the create option and perform a create procedure.

   • Add a create procedure that checks for a file name, asks if it is okay to proceed, and, if so, executes just two commands: OPEN OUTPUT DATA-FILE and CLOSE DATA-FILE.

   Now the user can use the update menu to add records to the file. Notice that it is not imperative that a direct relative file be created with records in sequential order (but it is more efficient in terms of execution speed, if this is so).

16. SUBPROGRAMS

16.1 THE SUBPROGRAM CONCEPT

A **subprogram** is a program that is executed by another program. Subprograms cannot be executed on their own; they must be combined with a **calling program** that exercises control of the execution sequence by calling for the execution of subprograms as needed. Subprograms are typically compiled separately from the calling program; hence, the overall structure of a COBOL subprogram will resemble any other program in many respects. For example, a subprogram is organized into four DIVISIONs, as is a calling program; the syntax used to specify entries in each DIVISION is, in general, the same for all programs. Each program unit (calling program or subprogram) typically requires a separate execution of the COBOL compiler, although some compilers will accept multiple program units during one execution.

After a subprogram is compiled, it is typically stored in a library where it is accessible to any program that needs to execute the procedure contained in the subprogram. Some operating systems execute a linking function prior to creating and storing an executable program. **Linking** means that the calling program and any required subprograms are located and assigned memory locations that do not conflict. Typically these are contiguous, as shown in Figure 16.1, but this is not necessarily the case. Also, the linking function resolves addressing references from one program unit to another, so that when a reference in the calling program to a subprogram is made during execution, the correct address is in place. The completely linked program forms an executable set of program units, called a **load module.** The load module is usually stored in a library and is ready for immediate execution. Other operating systems determine the location for referenced subprograms during the execution process. That is, when the calling program references a subprogram, the operating system searches the library of subprograms. If the subprogram is available, memory space is found for the subprogram, and addressing conflicts are resolved. Check with local documentation to determine which type of system you are using.[1]

Subprograms are likely to be written for tasks that are needed by more than one program. The procedure is written, compiled, and debugged only once. It can then be made available to all programs requiring that that task be performed. For example, suppose a payroll system is being developed. The analyst identifies several programs in the system that will need

---

[1] RM/COBOL-85 and most other microcomputer-oriented COBOL program development systems load the subprogram during execution of the calling program.

Figure 16.1   Linking example

After Compilation
Program units exist as separate modules.

After Linking
Program units have been relocated and assigned nonconflicting memory locations.

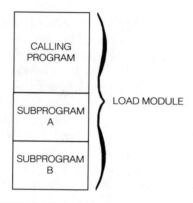

to compute federal withholding tax. Rather than reproduce the required logic in each program, it would be advantageous to develop a subprogram to carry out this task.

Subprograms are also useful to enhance the maintainability of a system. For example, if the rules for computing federal withholding tax change (which they do from time to time), it is sufficient to rewrite the subprogram and then, if needed, relink the program units to create an updated run unit. In systems that load subprograms during execution time, it is sufficient to change only the subprogram. The revised version of the procedure will then be made available to the programs automatically.

16.2   WRITING SUBPROGRAMS

Communication of data is usually required between a calling program and a subprogram. The subprogram carries out its operations using data supplied to it by the calling program and/or returns values to the calling program.

A subprogram has three distinct features that are not found in other programs:

- A LINKAGE SECTION in the DATA DIVISION in which descriptions of the data that will be passed between the calling program and the subprogram are placed.

- A USING clause on the PROCEDURE DIVISION entry in which specific items to be passed between the calling program and subprogram are listed.
- An EXIT PROGRAM statement which serves to return control from the subprogram to the calling program.

The placement of the LINKAGE SECTION in the DATA DIVISION is shown in Figure 16.2. (This figure also shows the placement of the REPORT SECTION which is used in conjunction with the Report Writer facility and which is described in Appendix A.) The LINKAGE SECTION contains data descriptions of items listed in the CALL statement (in the calling program) and the USING clause (in the subprogram). These data items are described in the LINKAGE SECTION using essentially the same syntax as for items in the WORKING-STORAGE SECTION with the following exception: In the LINKAGE SECTION, the VALUE clause can be used only for 88-level items because the value of data items being described is defined in the calling program or computed in the subprogram.

Figure 16.2   General form of the DATA DIVISION with LINKAGE and REPORT SECTIONs

```
DATA DIVISION.
     ┌                          ┐
     │ FILE SECTION.            │
     │ file-section-entry...    │
     └                          ┘
     ┌                              ┐
     │ WORKING-STORAGE SECTION.     │
     │ record-description-entry...  │
     └                              ┘
     ┌                              ┐
     │ LINKAGE SECTION.             │
     │ record-description-entry...  │
     └                              ┘
     ┌                          ┐
     │ REPORT SECTION.          │
     │ report-section-entry...  │
     └                          ┘
```

No space is actually allocated for items defined in the LINKAGE SECTION. The data-names defined here enable the subprogram to reference data actually defined in the calling program. The LINKAGE SECTION may contain a sequence of elementary data items or record descriptions (group data items), as necessary. The length of each item must match the length defined for the associated data item in the calling program.

The general form of the PROCEDURE DIVISION entry with a USING clause is shown in Figure 16.3. The data-names included in the list must be defined in the LINKAGE SECTION of the subprogram as 01-level or 77-

Figure 16.3   General form of the PROCEDURE DIVISION entry with a USING clause

```
PROCEDURE DIVISION [USING data-name...].
```

level items.[2] The USING clause is necessary to pass data between the calling program and the subprogram.

The general form of the EXIT PROGRAM statement is shown in Figure 16.4. When the EXIT PROGRAM statement is executed, control returns to the calling program. EXIT PROGRAM must not be combined with any other statement and must be the only sentence in a paragraph.

Figure 16.4   General form of the EXIT PROGRAM statement

```
paragraph-name.
    EXIT PROGRAM.
```

Example

Programs often require dates in the form

month-name day, year

rather than the year, month, day form provided by the operating system when an ACCEPT/FROM DATE statement is executed.

The statement ACCEPT DATE-IN FROM DATE will return a six-digit numeric value in DATE-IN in the form *yymmdd*. Thus, August 6, 1992, would be returned as

```
Year  Month  Day
 9 2   0 8   0 6
01  DATE-IN.
    03  YEAR-IN    PIC 99.
    03  MONTH-IN   PIC 99.
    03  DAY-IN     PIC 99.
```

Although the logic required to transform this data into the desired form is relatively straightforward and can easily be reproduced in any program, the need for making this transformation occurs in many programs. Therefore, writing a subprogram to do this task would be very beneficial.

Program 16a is a subprogram to carry out this transformation. In this example, the LINKAGE SECTION contains only one entry—DATE-STRING—but, in general, a LINKAGE SECTION can contain any number of entries. Note the USING clause in the PROCEDURE DIVISION entry (lines 49–50). The content of DATE-STRING will be passed back to the calling program when the EXIT PROGRAM statement is executed. In this example, control passes from 1000-MAIN-CONTROL to 9000-EXIT-PROGRAM automatically. This is acceptable in this context, but in reality it is a form of content coupling that should be avoided, if possible, in a structured program (see Chapter 10, Section 9). If there were other paragraphs in the subprogram, they should follow the EXIT-PROGRAM paragraph so that control would pass directly from MAIN-CONTROL to EXIT-PROGRAM.

Another option is to place the statement GO TO 9000-EXIT-PROGRAM as the last statement in 1000-MAIN-CONTROL in order to transfer control

---

[2] A 77-level item can be included only in WORKING-STORAGE. It must be an elementary data item. In the past, it was common to use 77-level items as subscripts, counters, accumulators, and so on. Present COBOL standards usually preclude the use of 77-level items although they continue to be supported by the compiler. Future standards for COBOL will probably not support 77-level items.

Program 16a

```
 1 IDENTIFICATION DIVISION.
 2
 3 PROGRAM-ID. DATETRAN-PRO16A.
 4 AUTHOR. HORN.
 5
 6 ENVIRONMENT DIVISION.
 7
 8 CONFIGURATION SECTION.
 9
10 SOURCE-COMPUTER.
11 OBJECT-COMPUTER.
12
13 DATA DIVISION.
14
15 WORKING-STORAGE SECTION.
16
17 01   MONTH-NAME-CONSTANTS.
18      03 FILLER PIC X(10) VALUE "January ".
19      03 FILLER PIC X(10) VALUE "February ".
20      03 FILLER PIC X(10) VALUE "March ".
21      03 FILLER PIC X(10) VALUE "April ".
22      03 FILLER PIC X(10) VALUE "May ".
23      03 FILLER PIC X(10) VALUE "June ".
24      03 FILLER PIC X(10) VALUE "July ".
25      03 FILLER PIC X(10) VALUE "August ".
26      03 FILLER PIC X(10) VALUE "September ".
27      03 FILLER PIC X(10) VALUE "October ".
28      03 FILLER PIC X(10) VALUE "November ".
29      03 FILLER PIC X(10) VALUE "December ".
30
31 01   MONTH-NAME-TABLE REDEFINES MONTH-NAME-CONSTANTS.
32      03 MONTH-NAME   PIC X(10) OCCURS 12 TIMES.
33
34 01   DATE-IN.
35      03 YEAR-IN    PIC 99.
36      03 MONTH-IN   PIC 99.
37      03 DAY-IN     PIC 99.
38
39 01   CALCULATED-VALUES.
40      03 YEAR-NUMBER    PIC 9999.
41      03 DAY-NUMBER     PIC ZZ.
42
43 01 CENTURY          PIC 9999 VALUE 1900.
44
45 LINKAGE SECTION.
46
47 01   DATE-STRING      PIC X(20).
48
```

Program 16a   *(concluded)*

```
49 PROCEDURE DIVISION
50     USING DATE-STRING.
51
52 1000-MAIN-CONTROL.
53
54     ACCEPT DATE-IN FROM DATE.
55     MOVE DAY-IN TO DAY-NUMBER.
56     ADD CENTURY YEAR-IN GIVING YEAR-NUMBER.
57     MOVE SPACES TO DATE-STRING.
58     STRING
59        MONTH-NAME (MONTH-IN) DELIMITED BY SPACE
60        " " DAY-NUMBER ", " YEAR-NUMBER DELIMITED BY SIZE
61        INTO DATE-STRING.
62
63 9000-EXIT-PROGRAM.
64
65     EXIT PROGRAM.
```

to the EXIT PROGRAM sentence. It would *not* be appropriate to PERFORM the paragraph 9000-EXIT-PROGRAM since the PERFORM statement always implies that control will return to the statement following the PERFORM, which will not happen in this case.

16.3   THE CALL STATEMENT

The CALL statement, which has the general form shown in Figure 16.5, is used to execute a subprogram. The CALL statement includes the name of the subprogram as a literal. The mechanism for establishing the name of a subprogram is system dependent. In some systems, the name is taken from the subprogram's PROGRAM-ID entry. In other systems (including RM/COBOL-85 and other microcomputer-based COBOL compilers), the name of the subprogram is the name of the file which contains the subprogram's object code. The CALL statement also includes a list of data items that are passed to the subprogram. It is imperative that the items in this list match the number, sequence, and size of items specified in the subprogram's USING clause and defined in the subprogram's LINKAGE SECTION.

Figure 16.5   General form of the CALL statement

```
CALL "program-name" [USING data-name...]
```

For example, to execute the date translation subprogram shown in Program 16a, the statement

```
CALL "PRO16A" USING ALPHANUMERIC-DATE.
```

could be used. ("PRO16A" is the name of the file containing the subprogram.) The item ALPHANUMERIC-DATE must be defined in the calling program so that it is consistent with the definition of the corresponding item in the subprogram. It is not necessary that the list of items in the CALL statement be 01-level or 77-level items, but this is permitted if appropriate. Thus, a description such as

```
01  ALPHANUMERIC-DATE  PIC X(20).
```

would suffice for this CALL. A complete program illustrating this concept is shown in Program 16b.

A subprogram can be executed as many times as desired from a calling program with the same or a different list of items in the statement. It is also possible for a subprogram to CALL another subprogram: The CALL statement is valid in any program module. In no case, however, may a subprogram call itself or call another subprogram that would result in its execution.

In systems that load subprograms during execution, the CALL statement may be able to use a data-name in place of the literal containing the subprogram name. For example, in such systems the following statements would be valid:

```
MOVE "PRO16A" TO SUBPROG-NAME.
CALL SUBPROG-NAME USING ALPHANUMERIC-DATE.
```

This option is not available on systems that create a complete load module before the program is executed since the content of the data-name used in the CALL statement is not defined prior to execution.

Program 16b

```
 1 IDENTIFICATION DIVISION.
 2
 3 PROGRAM-ID. DATETEST-PRO16B.
 4 AUTHOR. HORN.
 5
 6 ENVIRONMENT DIVISION.
 7
 8 CONFIGURATION SECTION.
 9
10 SOURCE-COMPUTER.
11 OBJECT-COMPUTER.
12
13 DATA DIVISION.
14
15 WORKING-STORAGE SECTION.
16
17 01  ALPHANUMERIC-DATE        PIC X(20).
18
19 PROCEDURE DIVISION.
20
21 1000-MAIN-CONTROL.
22
23     CALL "PRO16A" USING ALPHANUMERIC-DATE.
24     DISPLAY ALPHANUMERIC-DATE.
25     STOP RUN.
```

16.4 PROGRAM EXAMPLE

In Chapter 12, a program that produced a Purchase Request Register as part of the Amalgamated Custom Design data processing system was developed. Program 12b utilizes a sequential search procedure to locate data (name and address) for suppliers in a table that was loaded from a file (SUPPLIER-MASTER-FILE). In Program 16d, a revision of Program 12b, the load procedure is carried out in a subprogram rather than in an internal procedure. The subprogram, which is called PRO16C, is shown in Program 16c.

In Program 16d, the subprogram is invoked by the CALL statement at lines 120 through 122. Three arguments are passed to the subprogram:

```
NUMBER-OF-SUPPLIERS
LOAD-ERROR-FLAG
SUPPLIER-TABLE
```

In Program 16c, all the arguments are defined in the LINKAGE SECTION and listed in the USING clause of the PROCEDURE DIVISION entry. In these two programs, the same data names have been used in both the calling program and the subprogram. Although this practice aids in readability, it is not required by COBOL syntax. Each program is compiled separately. The only communication between the two programs is via the list of data items in the USING clauses. Note that the sequence of items and the description of the items match exactly in the two programs. This *is* a requirement. If each item does not match its counterpart or if the descriptions of the items are not the same, the results of executing the program unit are unpredictable and, in all likelihood, will result in a system error message of some type; certainly the results of the execution will be invalid.

16.5 IMPLICATIONS FOR PROGRAM DEVELOPMENT

Subprograms are an important tool in system development. An obvious benefit is that programmers can develop subprograms for procedures that will be needed by several different programs in the system. Writing and testing the subprograms need only be carried out one time, thereby saving the time and effort that would otherwise be required to incorporate the procedure into each program in which it is required.

Subprograms are also useful in developing large programs (even when the procedure may be needed only once in the entire system) because subprograms can be developed, coded, compiled, and tested independently of other program units. Thus, it is often possible to break up a large program into a series of semi-independent subprograms. Testing a subprogram with data usually requires that a calling program (sometimes called a **main program**) be written to pass data to the subprogram and to receive and interpret the output of the subprogram, but such developmental programs are relatively easy to write. Of course, they are ultimately discarded when the subprograms are combined into a complete working program. One advantage of this "bottom-up" program development approach is that the debugging and testing tasks are carried out in incremental steps. If the specifications for each of the subprograms have been correctly written and if each subprogram has been thoroughly tested to verify that

Program 16c

```
 1 IDENTIFICATION DIVISION.
 2
 3 PROGRAM-ID.  TABLE-LOAD-SUBPROGRAM-PRO16C.
 .
 .
 .
14 FILE-CONTROL.
15      SELECT SUPPLIER-MASTER-FILE ASSIGN TO DISK
16           "SUPMAST.DAT" ORGANIZATION IS LINE SEQUENTIAL.
17
18 DATA DIVISION.
19
20 FILE SECTION.
21
22 FD   SUPPLIER-MASTER-FILE
23      LABEL RECORDS ARE STANDARD.
24
25 01   SUPPLIER-MASTER-RECORD.
26      03 SUPPLIER-ID-SMR          PIC X(5).
27      03 SUPPLIER-NAME-SMR        PIC X(20).
28      03 SUPPLIER-ADDRESS-SMR     PIC X(15).
29
30 WORKING-STORAGE SECTION.
31
32 01   FLAGS.
33      02 EOF-FLAG                 PIC XXX VALUE "NO".
34         88 END-OF-FILE           VALUE "YES".
35
36 01   SUBSCRIPTS.
37      02 SUB                      PIC 99 VALUE ZERO.
38
39 01   CONSTANTS.
40      02 TABLE-SIZE               PIC 999 VALUE 100.
41
42 LINKAGE SECTION.
43
44 01   NUMBER-OF-SUPPLIERS         PIC 999.
45
46 01   LOAD-ERROR-FLAG             PIC XXX.
47      88 LOAD-ERROR               VALUE "YES".
48
49 01   SUPPLIER-TABLE.
50      03 SUPPLIER-ENTRY OCCURS 1 TO 100 TIMES
51           DEPENDING ON NUMBER-OF-SUPPLIERS.
52         05 SUPPLIER-ID-ENTRY       PIC X(5).
53         05 SUPPLIER-NAME-ENTRY      PIC X(20).
54         05 SUPPLIER-ADDRESS-ENTRY   PIC X(15).
55
```

```
56 PROCEDURE DIVISION
57     USING NUMBER-OF-SUPPLIERS
58             LOAD-ERROR-FLAG
59             SUPPLIER-TABLE.
60
61 1000-MAIN-CONTROL.
62
63     PERFORM 2000-INITIALIZE-TABLE.
64     IF LOAD-ERROR
65        DISPLAY "SUPPLIER MASTER FILE CONTAINS MORE THAN "
66                 TABLE-SIZE " RECORDS"
67     ELSE
68         DISPLAY "SUPPLIER MASTER FILE CONTAINS "
69                 NUMBER-OF-SUPPLIERS " RECORDS".
70     GO TO 9100-EXIT-PROGRAM.
71
72 2000-INITIALIZE-TABLE.
73
74     OPEN INPUT SUPPLIER-MASTER-FILE.
75     MOVE "NO" TO LOAD-ERROR-FLAG.
76     MOVE ZERO TO NUMBER-OF-SUPPLIERS.
77     PERFORM 9000-READ-SUPPLIER-MASTER-FILE.
78     PERFORM 3000-LOAD-TABLE
79             VARYING SUB FROM 1 BY 1
80                 UNTIL SUB > TABLE-SIZE
81                     OR END-OF-FILE.
82     IF SUB > TABLE-SIZE AND NOT END-OF-FILE
83         MOVE "YES" TO LOAD-ERROR-FLAG.
84     CLOSE SUPPLIER-MASTER-FILE.
85
86 3000-LOAD-TABLE.
87
88     MOVE SUPPLIER-MASTER-RECORD TO SUPPLIER-ENTRY (SUB).
89     ADD 1 TO NUMBER-OF-SUPPLIERS.
90     PERFORM 9000-READ-SUPPLIER-MASTER-FILE.
91
92 9000-READ-SUPPLIER-MASTER-FILE.
93
94     READ SUPPLIER-MASTER-FILE
95         AT END MOVE "YES" TO EOF-FLAG.
96
97 9100-EXIT-PROGRAM.
98
99     EXIT PROGRAM.
```

Program 16d

```
 1 IDENTIFICATION DIVISION.
 2
 3 PROGRAM-ID. SEQ-SRCH-W-SUBR-PRO16D.
 4 AUTHOR.
 5
 6 ENVIRONMENT DIVISION.
 7
 8 CONFIGURATION SECTION.
 9
10 SOURCE-COMPUTER.
11 OBJECT-COMPUTER.
12
13 INPUT-OUTPUT SECTION.
14
15 FILE-CONTROL.
16
17     SELECT PURCHASE-REQUEST-FILE ASSIGN TO DISK.
18
19     SELECT PRINT-FILE ASSIGN TO PRINTER.
20
21
22 DATA DIVISION.
23
24 FILE SECTION.
25
26 FD  PURCHASE-REQUEST-FILE
27     LABEL RECORDS ARE STANDARD.
28
29 01  PURCHASE-REQUEST-RECORD.
30     03 SUPPLIER-ID-NUMBER-PRR        PIC X(5).
31     03 ITEM-NUMBER-PRR               PIC X(5).
32     03 ITEM-DESCRIPTION-PRR          PIC X(10).
33     03 ITEM-COST-PRR                 PIC 999V99.
34     03 ORDER-QUANTITY-PRR            PIC 999.
35
36 FD  PRINT-FILE
37     LABEL RECORDS ARE OMITTED.
38
39 01  PRINT-RECORD                     PIC X(80).
40
41 WORKING-STORAGE SECTION.
42
43 01  FLAGS.
44     02 SEARCH-FLAG               PIC X(11) VALUE "CONTINUE".
45        88 CONTINUE-SEARCH        VALUE "CONTINUE".
46        88 NOT-PRESENT            VALUE "NOT PRESENT".
47        88 FOUND                  VALUE "FOUND".
48     02 EOF-FLAG-PRF              PIC XXX VALUE "NO".
49        88 END-OF-PRF             VALUE "YES".
50
51 01  SUBSCRIPTS.
52     02 SUB                       PIC 999 VALUE ZERO.
53
```

```
 54 01  COUNTERS.
 55        02 LINE-COUNT              PIC 99 VALUE 16.
 56        02 PAGE-NUM                PIC 99 VALUE 0.
 57
 58 01  CONSTANTS.
 59        02 TABLE-LIMIT              PIC 999 VALUE 100.
 60        02 PAGE-SIZE                PIC 99 VALUE 16.
 61
 62 01  MAJOR-HEADING.
 63        02 FILLER          PIC X(25) VALUE SPACES.
 64        02 FILLER          PIC X(25) VALUE
 65                           "PURCHASE REQUEST REGISTER".
 66        02 FILLER          PIC X(15) VALUE SPACES.
 67        02 FILLER          PIC X(5) VALUE "PAGE".
 68        02 PAGE-NUM-H      PIC ZZ.
 69
 70 01  COLUMN-HEADING-1.
 71        02 FILLER          PIC X VALUE SPACES.
 72        02 FILLER          PIC X(30) VALUE
 73             "SUPPLIER  ITEM      ITEM".
 74        02 FILLER          PIC X(30) VALUE
 75             "ITEM             SUPPLIER".
 76        02 FILLER          PIC X(20) VALUE
 77            "        SUPPLIER".
 78
 79 01  COLUMN-HEADING-2.
 80        02 FILLER          PIC X VALUE SPACES.
 81        02 FILLER          PIC X(30) VALUE
 82            "  ID    NUMBER DESCRIPTION".
 83        02 FILLER          PIC X(30) VALUE
 84            "COST QUANTITY     NAME".
 85        02 FILLER          PIC X(20) VALUE
 86            "        ADDRESS".
 87
 88 01  DETAIL-LINE.
 89        02 FILLER                  PIC X(3) VALUE SPACES.
 90        02 SUPPLIER-ID-NUMBER-DL   PIC X(5).
 91        02 FILLER                  PIC XX VALUE SPACES.
 92        02 ITEM-NUMBER-DL          PIC X(5).
 93        02 FILLER                  PIC XX VALUE SPACES.
 94        02 ITEM-DESCRIPTION-DL     PIC X(10).
 95        02 FILLER                  PIC XX VALUE SPACES.
 96        02 ITEM-COST-DL            PIC ZZZ.99.
 97        02 FILLER                  PIC XXX VALUE SPACES.
 98        02 ORDER-QUANTITY-DL       PIC ZZZ.
 99        02 FILLER                  PIC XXX VALUE SPACES.
100        02 SUPPLIER-NAME-DL        PIC X(20).
101        02 FILLER                  PIC X VALUE SPACES.
102        02 SUPPLIER-ADDRESS-DL     PIC X(15).
103
104 01  NUMBER-OF-SUPPLIERS          PIC 999.
105
106 01  LOAD-ERROR-FLAG              PIC XXX.
107        88 LOAD-ERROR              VALUE "YES".
108
```

Program 16d *(continued)*

```
109 01   SUPPLIER-TABLE.
110      03 SUPPLIER-ENTRY OCCURS 1 TO 100 TIMES
111            DEPENDING ON NUMBER-OF-SUPPLIERS.
112         05 SUPPLIER-ID-ENTRY      PIC X(5).
113         05 SUPPLIER-NAME-ENTRY    PIC X(20).
114         05 SUPPLIER-ADDRESS-ENTRY PIC X(15).
115
116 PROCEDURE DIVISION.
117
118 1000-MAIN-CONTROL.
119
120     CALL "PRO16C" USING NUMBER-OF-SUPPLIERS
121                         LOAD-ERROR-FLAG
122                         SUPPLIER-TABLE.
123     IF NOT LOAD-ERROR
124        PERFORM 2000-INITIALIZE-REPORT
125        PERFORM 2100-PROCESS-DATA
126            UNTIL END-OF-PRF
127        PERFORM 2200-TERMINATE-REPORT.
128     STOP RUN.
129
130 2000-INITIALIZE-REPORT.
131
132     OPEN INPUT PURCHASE-REQUEST-FILE
133          OUTPUT PRINT-FILE.
134     PERFORM 9000-READ-PR-FILE.
135
136 2100-PROCESS-DATA.
137
138     MOVE "CONTINUE" TO SEARCH-FLAG.
139     MOVE 1 TO SUB.
140     PERFORM 3000-SEARCH
141         UNTIL FOUND OR NOT-PRESENT.
142     MOVE SUPPLIER-ID-NUMBER-PRR TO SUPPLIER-ID-NUMBER-DL.
143     MOVE ITEM-NUMBER-PRR        TO ITEM-NUMBER-DL.
144     MOVE ITEM-DESCRIPTION-PRR   TO ITEM-DESCRIPTION-DL.
145     MOVE ITEM-COST-PRR          TO ITEM-COST-DL.
146     MOVE ORDER-QUANTITY-PRR     TO ORDER-QUANTITY-DL.
147     IF FOUND
148        MOVE SUPPLIER-NAME-ENTRY (SUB) TO
149             SUPPLIER-NAME-DL
150        MOVE SUPPLIER-ADDRESS-ENTRY (SUB) TO
151             SUPPLIER-ADDRESS-DL
152     ELSE
153        MOVE ALL "*" TO SUPPLIER-NAME-DL
154        MOVE ALL "*" TO SUPPLIER-ADDRESS-DL.
155     IF LINE-COUNT > PAGE-SIZE OR = PAGE-SIZE
156        PERFORM 3100-WRITE-HEADING.
157     WRITE PRINT-RECORD FROM DETAIL-LINE AFTER 2.
158     ADD 2 TO LINE-COUNT.
159     PERFORM 9000-READ-PR-FILE.
160
```

Program 16d   *(concluded)*

```
161 2200-TERMINATE-REPORT.
162
163     CLOSE PURCHASE-REQUEST-FILE
164           PRINT-FILE.
165
166 3000-SEARCH.
167
168     IF SUPPLIER-ID-ENTRY (SUB) = SUPPLIER-ID-NUMBER-PRR
169        MOVE "FOUND" TO SEARCH-FLAG
170     ELSE
171        ADD 1 TO SUB
172        IF SUB > NUMBER-OF-SUPPLIERS
173           MOVE "NOT PRESENT" TO SEARCH-FLAG
174        ELSE
175           IF SUPPLIER-ID-ENTRY (SUB) > SUPPLIER-ID-NUMBER-PRR
176              MOVE "NOT PRESENT" TO SEARCH-FLAG.
177
178 3100-WRITE-HEADING.
179
180     ADD 1 TO PAGE-NUM.
181     MOVE PAGE-NUM TO PAGE-NUM-H.
182     WRITE PRINT-RECORD FROM MAJOR-HEADING AFTER PAGE.
183     WRITE PRINT-RECORD FROM COLUMN-HEADING-1 AFTER 2.
184     WRITE PRINT-RECORD FROM COLUMN-HEADING-2 AFTER 1.
185     MOVE SPACES TO PRINT-RECORD.
186     WRITE PRINT-RECORD AFTER 1.
187     MOVE 5 TO LINE-COUNT.
188
189 9000-READ-PR-FILE.
190
191     READ PURCHASE-REQUEST-FILE
192           AT END MOVE "YES" TO EOF-FLAG-PRF.
```

it performs the functions defined for it in the specifications, the task of combining the subprograms into a whole program is greatly simplified. After this kind of testing, problems that may become evident can usually be traced to the main program, which controls execution of the subprograms because the logic in the subprograms has already been tested.

There are also some quite pragmatic benefits from this approach to program development. Once the subprogram specifications have been written, different programmers may proceed with coding and testing concurrently, reducing the time period required for developing the program. The load placed on the computing system is reduced somewhat because many small compilations, instead of a smaller number of large ones, will be performed over a period of time. These benefits are not gained without some cost, however. The total number of hours of programmer effort required to complete a project may increase because of the need to write specifications for subprograms, the need to write developmental main programs to test each subprogram, and the need to coordinate the efforts of several programmers working on the same project. Some of this time may, of course, be recouped when the entire program is finally assembled for testing. If all has gone well, the final product should be relatively bug-free and require a minimum amount of time for testing and implementation.

16.6 SELF-TEST EXERCISES

1. Define the following terms:
   a. subprogram
   b. calling program
   c. program unit
   d. load module
   e. linking

2. Describe two ways in which program units are converted into executable programs.

3. What are three features found in subprograms that are not found in other programs?

4. What restriction is placed on data items defined in the LINKAGE SECTION?

5. What restrictions are placed on items listed in a PROCEDURE DIVISION USING clause?

6. Where is the name of a subprogram defined?

7. What are some advantages of subprograms for program development and maintenance?

8. How is linking handled on your system?

9. Is it possible for a subprogram to execute another subprogram? What restrictions are there in this regard?

10. Write a subprogram to accept a date in the form *mmddyy*, and convert it to the Julian date equivalent. Recall that the Julian date is the number of days elapsed from a fixed point, usually the beginning of a year or the beginning of the century. Thus, using the beginning of the year as the basis, the Julian date for January 1 is 1, for February 1 is 32, and for December 31 is 365 or 366 (depending on whether it is a leap year).

11. Write a subprogram to accept one data item, FULL-NAME, which contains a string of characters in the form

    last-name first-name middle-initial

    and returns three items
    LAST-NAME, FIRST-NAME, MIDDLE-INITIAL

    For example, if the content of FULL-NAME is

    ```
    |D|O|E| |J|O|H|N| |E| | | | | | | | | | |
    ```
    FULL-NAME PIC X(20)

    the required items would be

    ```
    |D|O|E| | | | | | | |
    ```
    LAST-NAME PIC X(10)

    ```
    |J|O|H|N| | | | | | |
    ```
    FIRST-NAME PIC X(10)

    ```
    |E|
    ```
    MIDDLE-INITIAL PIC X

°16.7   PROGRAMMING EXERCISES

1. The statement

   ```
   ACCEPT data-name FROM TIME
   ```

   places an eight-digit numeric value into the Specified data-name. The value is composed of hours (2 digits), minutes (2 digits), seconds (2 digits), and hundredths of a second (2 digits). Hours are expressed on a 24-hour-clock basis such as

12-hour-clock time	Value of TIME
1:30 A.M.	01300000
12:00 P.M.	12000000
2:56 P.M.	14560000

   Write and test a subprogram to convert the value of time and return to the calling program a string of characters like those shown above. Round off the value of minutes to the nearest minute.

2. Consider the order file described in Exercise 2 in Chapter 8 (Section 15). A program needs to summarize this data by department and by date; that is, two reports will be generated, a Department Report in which data is summarized by department identifier and a Daily Summary Report in which data is summarized by date. Write the program, using subprograms where possible to simplify the program development task.

3. Revise the program written for Exercise 1 in Chapter 12 (Section 13), using subprograms to carry out the search procedures.

4. Revise the program written for Exercise 4 in Chapter 7 (Section 18), using a subprogram to produce the required lists.

5. Modify Program 14c by adding a subprogram to carry out the Print file command.

A. REPORT WRITER

The report writer module allows the programmer to specify report features, including headings, subtotals, and final totals, without writing the detailed PROCEDURE DIVISION logic required to produce these elements. The required PROCEDURE DIVISION logic is generated by the COBOL compiler; the programmer is freed from the tedious task of coding and debugging routines for the line counting, page numbering, data movement, and control breaks. The report writer is not available in RM/COBOL-85 and some other COBOL compilers; the reader should check locally available documentation before attempting to write programs using report writer. The programs in this section were compiled and tested using Microsoft COBOL 3.0.

The report writer contains facilities to generate the following report elements automatically:

1. Report heading: produced automatically once at the beginning of the report.
2. Page heading: produced automatically at the beginning of each page.
3. Detail line: produced under the control of the program; as many different types of detail lines as required may be specified.
4. Control heading: produced automatically, once at the beginning of processing of each control group.
5. Control footing: produced automatically at the end of processing each control group.
6. Page footing: produced automatically at the end of each page.
7. Report footing: produced automatically at the end of the report.

Additionally, the report writer contains facilities for generating subtotals, line and page counts, output lines without MOVE or WRITE statements, and a variety of other features to facilitate the programmer's task in writing report-type programs. The report writer does not assume the complete task of controlling the program; the program must still open files, control the processing of records, and close files upon completion of processing. The report writer also includes three additional and very powerful PROCEDURE DIVISION verbs:

1. INITIATE, used to begin the production of the report;
2. GENERATE, used to produce detail, control break, and page-related lines; and
3. TERMINATE, used to end the production of the report.

Use of these verbs causes the "automatic" features of the report writer module to be carried out during execution of the program.

A.1　PROGRAM EXAMPLE

Program 8a of Chapter 8 is rewritten using the report writer and is shown as Program Aa. Comparison of programs 8a and Aa will reveal major differences in the DATA and PROCEDURE DIVISIONs. The report produced by this program makes use of the following elements:

- Page heading
- Detail line
- Page footing (page totals)
- Control footing (final totals)

A sample of the report produced by Program Aa is shown in Figure A.1. Let us examine the program required to produce this report.

Figure A.1　Sample report

```
                    ABC COMPANY EMPLOYEE REPORT              PAGE   1     ⎫
  NAME              EMPLOYEE NUMBER            DEPARTMENT       SALARY     ⎬ Page Heading
                                                                          ⎭
  JONES  JOHN       11111111                     002        $ 40,000      ⎫
                                                                          │
  SMITH  MARY       12222222                     002        $ 50,000      │
                                                                          │
  DOE  JOHN         13333333                     002        $ 34,000      ⎬ Detail
                                                                          │
  BLACK  HARVEY     14444444                     003        $ 20,000      │
                                                                          │
  WHITE  SUE        15555555                     003        $ 45,000      ⎭
                                              PAGE  TOTAL   $189,000*      ⎬ Page Footing

                    ABC COMPANY EMPLOYEE REPORT              PAGE   2     ⎫
  NAME              EMPLOYEE NUMBER            DEPARTMENT       SALARY     ⎬ Page Heading
                                                                          ⎭
  GREY  SAM         16666666                     103        $ 90,000      ⎫
                                                                          │
  GONZALEZ  CARLOS  27777777                     103        $ 80,000      │
                                                                          │
  SHEA  JOHN        30000000                     111        $ 45,000      ⎬ Detail
                                                                          │
  SPADE  SAM        33333333                     111        $ 67,000      │
                                                                          │
  CLARK  JOHN       34444444                     211        $ 30,000      ⎭
                                              PAGE  TOTAL   $312,000*      ⎬ Page Footing

                    ABC COMPANY EMPLOYEE REPORT              PAGE   3     ⎫
  NAME              EMPLOYEE NUMBER            DEPARTMENT       SALARY     ⎬ Page Heading
  HERNANDEZ  MARIA  44444444                     211        $ 80,000      ⎫ Detail
  JONES  PATRICIA   45555555                     211        $ 50,000      ⎭
                            12      EMPLOYEES              $631,000**      ⎬ Control Footing
                                                                            Final



                                              PAGE  TOTAL   $130,000*      ⎬ Page Footing
```

```
 1 IDENTIFICATION DIVISION.
 2
 3 PROGRAM-ID. LIST-REPORT-WRITER-PROAA.
 4 AUTHOR. HORN.
 5
 6 ENVIRONMENT DIVISION.
 7
 8 CONFIGURATION SECTION.
 9
10 SOURCE-COMPUTER.
11 OBJECT-COMPUTER.
12
13 INPUT-OUTPUT SECTION.
14
15 FILE-CONTROL.
16
17     SELECT EMPLOYEE-FILE ASSIGN TO DISK.
18
19     SELECT REPORT-FILE ASSIGN TO PRINTER.
20
21 DATA DIVISION.
22
23 FILE SECTION.
24
25 FD  EMPLOYEE-FILE
26     LABEL RECORDS ARE STANDARD
27     DATA RECORD IS EMPLOYEE-RECORD.
28
29 01  EMPLOYEE-RECORD.
30     02 NAME-ER                PIC X(16).
31     02 EMPLOYEE-NUMBER-ER      PIC 9(9).
32     02 DEPARTMENT-ER           PIC X(3).
33     02 SALARY-ER               PIC 9(6).
34     02 FILLER                  PIC X(46).
35
36 FD  REPORT-FILE
37     LABEL RECORDS ARE OMITTED
38     REPORT IS EMPLOYEE-REPORT.
39
40 WORKING-STORAGE SECTION.
41
42 01  ACCUMULATED-TOTALS.
43     03 NUMBER-OF-EMPLOYEES     PIC 999  VALUE ZERO.
44     03 PAGE-TOTAL              PIC 9(6) VALUE ZERO.
45
46 01  FLAGS.
47     02 EOF-FLAG                PIC X(3) VALUE "NO".
48        88 END-OF-FILE          VALUE "YES".
49
50 REPORT SECTION.
51 RD  EMPLOYEE-REPORT
52         CONTROL IS FINAL
53         PAGE LIMIT IS 17 LINES
54         FIRST DETAIL 5
55         LAST DETAIL 13.
56
57 01  MAJOR-HEADING
```

```
58                   TYPE IS PAGE HEADING.
59        02 LINE NUMBER IS 1.
60           03 COLUMN 24           PIC X(11) VALUE "ABC COMPANY".
61           03 COLUMN 36           PIC X(8)  VALUE "EMPLOYEE".
62           03 COLUMN 45           PIC X(6)  VALUE "REPORT".
63           03 COLUMN 69           PIC X(4)  VALUE "PAGE".
64           03 COLUMN 74           PIC ZZZ   SOURCE IS PAGE-COUNTER.
65
66        02 LINE NUMBER IS PLUS 2.
67           03 COLUMN 2            PIC X(5)  VALUE "NAME".
68           03 COLUMN 19           PIC X(15) VALUE "EMPLOYEE NUMBER".
69           03 COLUMN 53           PIC X(10) VALUE "DEPARTMENT".
70           03 COLUMN 72           PIC X(6)  VALUE "SALARY".
71
72 01   TYPE IS PAGE FOOTING
73           LINE NUMBER IS 15.
74      02 COLUMN 55      PIC X(10) VALUE "PAGE TOTAL".
75      02 PAGE-TOTAL-PTL
76           COLUMN 69   PIC $$$$,$$$ SOURCE IS PAGE-TOTAL.
77      02 COLUMN 77      PIC X     VALUE "*".
78
79 01   DETAIL-LINE
80          TYPE IS DETAIL
81          LINE NUMBER IS PLUS 2.
82      02 COLUMN 2     PIC X(16) SOURCE IS NAME-ER.
83      02 COLUMN 18    PIC 9(9)  SOURCE IS EMPLOYEE-NUMBER-ER.
84      02 COLUMN 56    PIC X(3)  SOURCE IS DEPARTMENT-ER.
85      02 COLUMN 69    PIC $ZZZ,ZZZ SOURCE IS SALARY-ER.
86
87 01   TYPE IS CONTROL FOOTING FINAL
88          LINE NUMBER IS PLUS 2.
89      02 COLUMN 40    PIC ZZZ9 SOURCE IS NUMBER-OF-EMPLOYEES.
90      02 COLUMN 49    PIC X(9)  VALUE "EMPLOYEES".
91      02 COLUMN 66    PIC $$$,$$$,$$$ SUM SALARY-ER.
92      02 COLUMN 77    PIC XX    VALUE "**".
93
94 PROCEDURE DIVISION.
95
96 DECLARATIVES.
97
98 0000-END-OF-PAGE SECTION.
99
100    USE BEFORE REPORTING MAJOR-HEADING.
101
102 0100-INITIALIZE-PAGE-TOTAL.
103
104    MOVE ZERO TO PAGE-TOTAL.
105
106 END DECLARATIVES.
107
108 1000-MAIN-CONTROL.
109
110    PERFORM 2000-INITIALIZE-REPORT.
111    PERFORM 2100-PROCESS-DATA
112           UNTIL END-OF-FILE.
113    PERFORM 2200-TERMINATE-REPORT.
114    STOP RUN.
```

Program Aa   (concluded)

```
115
116 2000-INITIALIZE-REPORT.
117
118     OPEN INPUT EMPLOYEE-FILE
119         OUTPUT REPORT-FILE.
120     INITIATE EMPLOYEE-REPORT.
121     PERFORM 9000-READ-EMPLOYEE-FILE.
122
123 2100-PROCESS-DATA.
124
125     ADD 1 TO NUMBER-OF-EMPLOYEES.
126     GENERATE DETAIL-LINE.
127     ADD SALARY-ER TO PAGE-TOTAL.
128     PERFORM 9000-READ-EMPLOYEE-FILE.
129
130 2200-TERMINATE-REPORT.
131
132     TERMINATE EMPLOYEE-REPORT.
133     CLOSE EMPLOYEE-FILE
134         REPORT-FILE.
135
136 9000-READ-EMPLOYEE-FILE.
137
138     READ EMPLOYEE-FILE
139         AT END MOVE "YES" TO EOF-FLAG.
```

The program involves two files—EMPLOYEE-FILE and REPORT-FILE—defined in SELECT statements (lines 17–19) and in FD entries (lines 25–38). The FD entry for REPORT-FILE (lines 36–38) makes use of the REPORT clause:

```
FD  REPORT-FILE
    LABEL RECORDS ARE OMITTED
    REPORT IS EMPLOYEE-REPORT.
```

The REPORT clause specifies the report name and serves to link the file to the RD entry of the REPORT SECTION which follows.

The WORKING-STORAGE SECTION of the DATA DIVISION (lines 40–48) contains far fewer entries in Program Aa as compared with Program 8a. The specification of an end-of-file flag is still required (lines 47–48). (Recall that the reading and processing of files are still controlled by the program in the usual way.) Also required are accumulators that are not under automatic control of the report writer logic. In this case, accumulators PAGE-TOTAL and NUMBER-OF-EMPLOYEES must be defined (lines 43–44). (Note that it is not actually necessary to initialize PAGE-TOTAL to zero, as this task will be accomplished within the PROCEDURE DIVISION.) The accumulator for the final total is defined later and will be handled as part of the automatic functions provided by report writer.

The REPORT SECTION of the DATA DIVISION is used to give an overall description of the report (the RD entry at lines 51–55) and to describe the different types of lines to be included in the report (as 01 entries following the RD entry at lines 57–87). The overall syntax of the REPORT SECTION is similar to that of the FILE SECTION with the RD entry taking the place of the FD entry and line descriptions taking the place of record descriptions.

The RD entry at lines 51–55 contains the report name and numerous clauses specifying information pertaining to the entire report as follows:

```
RD   EMPLOYEE-REPORT
          CONTROL IS FINAL
          PAGE LIMIT IS 17 LINES
          FIRST DETAIL 5
          LAST DETAIL 13.
```

The report name (EMPLOYEE-REPORT) must match the name specified in the REPORT clause of the FD entry of the associated file. The CONTROL clause specifies the level(s) of control breaks to be recognized in the report. CONTROL IS FINAL specifies that the only control break desired is to be the end of the report. If other levels of subtotals had been desired, the names of the control fields would be specified here. (A more complete discussion of this feature is presented in Section A.3.) The PAGE LIMIT clause specifies the total number of lines on a report page. The FIRST DETAIL and LAST DETAIL clauses specify the line number for the first and last detail lines, respectively.

The entries following the RD entry specify the lines of the report and differentiate them by type. The first 01 entry (lines 57–58) specifies the page heading as follows:

```
01   MAJOR-HEADING
     TYPE IS PAGE-HEADING.
```

The entries which follow (lines 59–70) specify the contents of the page headings:

```
02 LINE NUMBER IS 1.
   03   COLUMN 24   PIC X(11)   VALUE "ABC COMPANY".
   03   COLUMN 36   PIC X(8)    VALUE "EMPLOYEE".
   03   COLUMN 45   PIC X(6)    VALUE "REPORT".
   03   COLUMN 69   PIC X(4)    VALUE "PAGE".
   03   COLUMN 74   PIC ZZZ     SOURCE IS PAGE-COUNTER.

02 LINE NUMBER IS PLUS 2.
   03   COLUMN 2    PIC X(5)    VALUE "NAME".
   03   COLUMN 19   PIC X(15)   VALUE "EMPLOYEE NUMBER".
   03   COLUMN 53   PIC X(10)   VALUE "DEPARTMENT".
   03   COLUMN 72   PIC X(6)    VALUE "SALARY".
```

Note that most entries in the REPORT SECTION do not have to have a data-name associated with them; even the data-name FILLER is not required. Note also the use of the LINE NUMBER and COLUMN clauses. The LINE NUMBER clause specifies the line number on the page for the placement of the line; the COLUMN clause specifies the column number in the line for the placement of the item being described. Compare the above specifications for the heading line to the specification of essentially the same lines of output in Program 8a.

Note the use of the SOURCE IS clause in the last 03 entry in the description of the page heading. The SOURCE IS clause takes the place of a MOVE instruction. When this line of output is generated, the content of the field designated in the SOURCE IS clause is moved automatically to the specified area on the output record; it is not necessary to designate a data-name for the receiving field. Note that in this case, the field designated in the SOURCE IS clause is PAGE-COUNTER which is a field automatically defined and incremented by the report writer.

The next series of entries specifies the page footing (lines 72–77).

```
01   TYPE IS PAGE FOOTING
         LINE NUMBER IS 15.
     02 COLUMN 55       PIC X(10)      VALUE "PAGE TOTAL".
     02 PAGE-TOTAL-PTL
            COLUMN 69   PIC $$$$,$$$  SOURCE IS PAGE-TOTAL.
     02 COLUMN 77       PIC X          VALUE "*".
```

This line will automatically be produced when a page is full and before the page headings are printed on the next page.

The next series of entries specifies the detail line of the report (lines 79–85).

```
01   DETAIL-LINE
         TYPE IS DETAIL
         LINE NUMBER IS PLUS 2.
     02 COLUMN 2     PIC X(16)     SOURCE IS NAME-ER.
     02 COLUMN 18    PIC 9(9)      SOURCE IS EMPLOYEE-NUMBER-ER.
     02 COLUMN 56    PIC X(3)      SOURCE IS DEPARTMENT-ER.
     02 COLUMN 69    PIC $ZZZ,ZZZ  SOURCE IS SALARY-ER.
```

The data-name for a type DETAIL line is not optional as with other lines because it is necessary to reference this line by name from the PROCEDURE DIVISION. (The GENERATE statement must include a data-name.) Note the use of the clause

```
LINE NUMBER IS PLUS 2
```

in the definition of the detail line. This entry specifies where the next detail line is to be placed (in this case double spacing is specified). Recall that the position of the first detail line is specified in the RD entry.

The last series of entries in the REPORT SECTION defines the line containing final totals (lines 87–92):

```
01   TYPE IS CONTROL FOOTING FINAL
         LINE NUMBER IS PLUS 2
     02 COLUMN 40    PIC ZZZ9 SOURCE IS NUMBER-OF-EMPLOYEES.
     02 COLUMN 49    PIC X(9) VALUE "EMPLOYEES".
     02 COLUMN 66    PIC $$$,$$$,$$$ SUM SALARY-ER.
     02 COLUMN 77    PIC XX   VALUE "**".
```

Note the use of the SUM clause in the next to last 02 entry for this line. This clause causes the sum of the values of the specified field to be computed automatically, and, when the line is generated, the value of the sum is moved to the designated receiving area in the output record. Only lines of type CONTROL FOOTING can contain an element specified with the SUM clause. (One might inquire why this line is declared to be type CONTROL FOOTING rather than type REPORT FOOTING as both are produced one time at the end of the report. The necessity of including a SUM clause governs the choice of line types.)

Comparison of the PROCEDURE DIVISION of Programs 8a and Aa will reveal the extent of the programming effort saved by use of the report writer features. Note the absence of routine MOVE statements, manipulation of the PAGE-COUNTER and LINE-COUNTER, and the WRITE statements. All of this logic will be generated by report writer.

In Program Aa, it is necessary to include DECLARATIVES prior to the description of the program logic. DECLARATIVES are generally used to specify actions that are to be performed automatically by the program when certain conditions are encountered. In this case, a DECLARATIVES procedure is required to zero out the field PAGE-TOTAL for each new page. The DECLARATIVES specifications from lines 96–106 are shown below:

```
DECLARATIVES.
0000-END-OF-PAGE SECTION.
    USE BEFORE REPORTING MAJOR-HEADING.
0100-INITIALIZE-PAGE-TOTAL.
    MOVE ZERO TO PAGE-TOTAL.
END DECLARATIVES.
```

DECLARATIVES are terminated by the sentence END DECLARATIVES and are composed of any number of SECTIONs. The SECTION header indicates when the procedure described in that SECTION is to be executed. The USE statement gives the relevant condition. In this case,

```
USE BEFORE REPORTING MAJOR-HEADING.
```

means that the procedure is to be executed automatically prior to producing the line MAJOR-HEADING. (Any named line from the report could be included in a USE specification.) Note that if the DECLARATIVES procedure had been omitted, the page total would have become a running total. There is no other way in the program to zero out this field because production of the line is controlled "automatically" by report writer.

The main portion of the PROCEDURE DIVISION logic resembles that of any other COBOL program as shown below:

```
1000-MAIN-CONTROL.
    PERFORM 2000-INITIALIZE-REPORT.
    PERFORM 2100-PROCESS-DATA
            UNTIL END-OF-FILE.
    PERFORM 2200-TERMINATE-REPORT.
    STOP RUN.
2000-INITIALIZE-REPORT.
    OPEN INPUT EMPLOYEE-FILE
         OUTPUT REPORT-FILE.
    INITIATE EMPLOYEE-REPORT.
    PERFORM 9000-READ-EMPLOYEE-FILE.
2100-PROCESS-DATA.
    ADD 1 TO NUMBER-OF-EMPLOYEES.
    GENERATE DETAIL-LINE.
    ADD SALARY-ER TO PAGE-TOTAL.
    PERFORM 9000-READ-EMPLOYEE-FILE.
2200-TERMINATE-REPORT.
    TERMINATE EMPLOYEE-REPORT.
    CLOSE EMPLOYEE-FILE
          REPORT-FILE.
9000-READ-EMPLOYEE-FILE.
    READ EMPLOYEE-FILE
         AT END MOVE "YES" TO EOF-FLAG.
```

The paragraph 1000-MAIN-CONTROL controls execution of other paragraphs as in any structured program. The paragraph 2000-INITIALIZE-REPORT serves to OPEN the required files, INITIATE the report, and cause the first record to be read. As a result of the INITIATE verb,

- All accumulators automatically controlled by report writer are set to zero (in this program, such an accumulator used to compute the sum of the values is SALARY-ER).

- PAGE-COUNTER is set to 1.
- LINE-COUNTER is set to O (LINE-COUNTER is an automatically allocated and controlled data-name similar to PAGE-COUNTER).

The paragraph 2100-PROCESS-DATA causes processing of the data record just read, the production of the relevant report lines (via the GENERATE statement), and the reading of the next record. In this case, processing the data-record entails incrementing the accumulator NUMBER-OF-EMPLOYEES and adding SALARY-ER to PAGE-TOTAL. (Recall that the SUM clause can be used only in conjunction with CONTROL FOOTING lines; hence, accumulating PAGE-TOTAL must be accomplished "manually.") The effect of the GENERATE statement is dependent on the current stage of program execution. The first execution of the GENERATE statement in this program causes the following actions to take place:

1. Execute DECLARATIVES procedure.
2. Produce MAJOR-HEADING.
3. Produce DETAIL-LINE.
4. Increment LINE-COUNTER.

Subsequent executions of the GENERATE statement in this program cause the following actions to take place:

1. If LINE-COUNTER > last detail line number,
      Produce page footing
      Execute DECLARATIVES procedure
      Increment PAGE-COUNTER
      Produce MAJOR-HEADING
      Initialize LINE-COUNTER
2. Produce DETAIL-LINE
3. Increment LINE-COUNTER

The paragraph 2200-TERMINATE-REPORT is executed after all records from the file EMPLOYEE-FILE have been processed. The paragraph terminates production of the report (via the TERMINATE statement), closes the files, and stops execution of the program. The TERMINATE statement causes CONTROL FOOTING FINAL type lines to be produced, followed by production of PAGE FOOTING lines and REPORT FOOTING lines, if any (in this example there were no REPORT FOOTING lines).

A.2 GENERAL FORMS

Complete explanation of all facets of report writer is beyond the scope of this appendix. General forms of all elements of ANSI-74 COBOL, including report writer, are shown in Appendix C. The COBOL-85 forms (which also include specifications for report writers) are in Appendix D. Descriptions of some of the more useful features of report writer follow.

The REPORT SECTION

The general form of the REPORT SECTION is shown in Figure A.2. Of particular importance is the CONTROL clause of the RD entry. In this entry, a list of data-names that form the basis for detection of control breaks and the

Figure A.2   General form of the REPORT SECTION entry

```
REPORT SECTION.
RD   report-name
     [{CONTROL IS  } {data-name-1 ...                    }]
     [{CONTROLS ARE} {FINAL      [data-name-1] ...       }]

     [     [{LIMIT IS   }             {LINE }]]
     [PAGE [{LIMITS ARE } integer-1   {LINES}]]
     [HEADING integer-2]
     [FIRST DETAIL integer-3]
     [LAST DETAIL integer-4]
     [FOOTING integer-5].
report-group-description-entry....
```

generation of subtotals is specified. For example, in order to produce subtotals for departments in Program Aa, the RD entry would be

```
RD   DEPARTMENT-REPORT
     CONTROL IS DEPARTMENT-ER
         .
         .
         .
```

In order to produce both department subtotals and final totals, the RD
entry would be (see Program Ab):

```
RD   DEPARTMENT-REPORT
     CONTROLS ARE FINAL
             DEPARTMENT-ER
         .
         .
         .
```

The order of the list of data-names in the CONTROL clause determines
the relative ordering of control breaks from highest to lowest level. Lower-
level breaks occur more frequently than higher-level breaks. For example,
in order to produce both department and division subtotals as well as
grand totals as in Program 8c, the following RD entry would be used:

```
RD   DIVISION-REPORT
     CONTROLS ARE FINAL
             DIVISION-ER
             DEPARTMENT-ER
         .
         .
         .
```

The Report Group Description

The general form of the 01 level report group description is shown in Figure A.3. Following the RD entry, 01 level descriptors are required to specify
the various elements of the report. Of particular importance is the CON-
TROL FOOTING entry, which is used to generate control breaks for each of
the control fields specified in the CONTROL clause of the RD entry. For

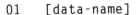

Figure A.3 General form of 01 entry for report writer

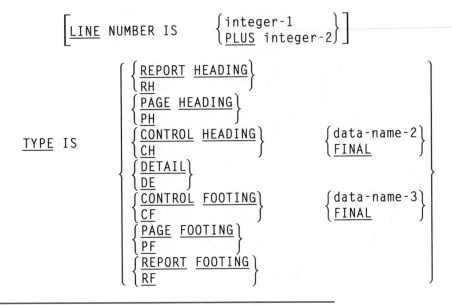

```
01   [data-name]
```

example, to generate department subtotals for the report of Program Aa, an 01 entry such as the following would be required:

```
01   LINE NUMBER IS PLUS 2
     TYPE IS CONTROL FOOTING DEPARTMENT-ER.
```

Each level of control break requires a separate 01 level report group description entry. The content of the line is produced when a change in the control field is encountered.

The general forms of subordinate report group descriptions are shown in Figure A.4. Format 1-type descriptions may be used to create multiple report lines of a particular type. Format 2-type descriptions are used to specify elementary items for a line.

The GROUP INDICATE clause can be used only on specification of lines of type DETAIL. When the clause is present, the content of the field is printed for the first record of each control group and for the first record at the top of a new page.

The SUM clause causes the automatic accumulation of the sum of specified data items. The clause can be used only in the specification of lines of type CONTROL FOOTING. The value of the accumulator is reset to zero each time the content is printed; hence, this feature is well suited to the automatic generation of subtotals as shown in Program Ab.

A.3 CONTROL BREAK EXAMPLE

Program Ab uses report writer to produce essentially the same report as that of Program 8b. The output consists of a detailed listing of the input file with totals for each department as well as final totals. Report writer elements found in Program Ab include multiple-line page headings, detail

```
 1 IDENTIFICATION DIVISION.
 2
 3 PROGRAM-ID. CTRL-BRK-REPT-WRITER-PROAB.
 4 AUTHOR. HORN.
 5
 6 ENVIRONMENT DIVISION.
 7
 8 CONFIGURATION SECTION.
 9
10 SOURCE-COMPUTER.
11 OBJECT-COMPUTER.
12
13 INPUT-OUTPUT SECTION.
14
15 FILE-CONTROL.
16
17     SELECT EMPLOYEE-FILE ASSIGN TO DISK.
18
19     SELECT REPORT-FILE ASSIGN TO PRINTER.
20
21 DATA DIVISION.
22
23 FILE SECTION.
24
25 FD  EMPLOYEE-FILE
26     LABEL RECORDS ARE STANDARD
27     DATA RECORD IS EMPLOYEE-RECORD.
28
29 01  EMPLOYEE-RECORD.
30     02 NAME-ER                 PIC X(16).
31     02 EMPLOYEE-NUMBER-ER       PIC 9(9).
32     02 DEPARTMENT-ER            PIC X(3).
33     02 SALARY-ER                PIC 9(6).
34     02 FILLER                   PIC X(46).
35
36 FD  REPORT-FILE
37     LABEL RECORDS ARE OMITTED
38     REPORT IS EMPLOYEE-REPORT.
39
40 WORKING-STORAGE SECTION.
41
42 01  ACCUMULATED-TOTALS.
43     03 TOTAL-NUMBER-OF-EMPLOYEES     PIC 999 VALUE ZERO.
44     03 DEPT-NUMBER-OF-EMPLOYEES      PIC 999 VALUE ZERO.
45
46 01  FLAGS.
47     02 EOF-FLAG                 PIC X(3) VALUE "NO".
48        88 END-OF-FILE           VALUE "YES".
49
50 REPORT SECTION.
51 RD  EMPLOYEE-REPORT
52         CONTROLS ARE FINAL
53                     DEPARTMENT-ER
54         PAGE LIMIT IS 17 LINES
55         FIRST DETAIL 5
56         LAST DETAIL 13.
57
58 01  TYPE IS PAGE HEADING.
```

Program Ab   (continued)

```
59       02 LINE NUMBER IS 1.
60          03 COLUMN 24          PIC X(11) VALUE "ABC COMPANY".
61          03 COLUMN 36          PIC X(8)  VALUE "EMPLOYEE".
62          03 COLUMN 45          PIC X(6)  VALUE "REPORT".
63          03 COLUMN 69          PIC X(4)  VALUE "PAGE".
64          03 COLUMN 74          PIC ZZZ   SOURCE IS PAGE-COUNTER.
65
66       02 LINE NUMBER IS PLUS 2.
67          03 COLUMN 2           PIC X(5)  VALUE "NAME".
68          03 COLUMN 19          PIC X(15) VALUE "EMPLOYEE NUMBER".
69          03 COLUMN 53          PIC X(10) VALUE "DEPARTMENT".
70          03 COLUMN 72          PIC X(6)  VALUE "SALARY".
71
72 01   DETAIL-LINE
73          TYPE IS DETAIL
74          LINE NUMBER IS PLUS 1.
75       02 COLUMN 2    PIC X(16) SOURCE IS NAME-ER.
76       02 COLUMN 18   PIC 9(9)  SOURCE IS EMPLOYEE-NUMBER-ER.
77       02 COLUMN 56   PIC X(3)  SOURCE IS DEPARTMENT-ER.
78       02 COLUMN 69   PIC $ZZZ,ZZZ SOURCE IS SALARY-ER.
79
80 01   DEPARTMENT-HEADING-LINE
81          TYPE IS CONTROL HEADING DEPARTMENT-ER
82          LINE NUMBER IS PLUS 1.
83       02 COLUMN 1    PIC X VALUE SPACE.
84
85 01   DEPARTMENT-SUMMARY-LINE
86          TYPE IS CONTROL FOOTING DEPARTMENT-ER
87          LINE NUMBER IS PLUS 2.
88       02 COLUMN 40   PIC ZZZ9 SOURCE IS
89                              DEPT-NUMBER-OF-EMPLOYEES.
90       02 COLUMN 49   PIC X(9)  VALUE "EMPLOYEES".
91       02 COLUMN 66   PIC $$$,$$$,$$$ SUM SALARY-ER.
92       02 COLUMN 77   PIC XX    VALUE "*".
93
94 01   TYPE IS CONTROL FOOTING FINAL
95          LINE NUMBER IS PLUS 2.
96       02 COLUMN 40   PIC ZZZ9 SOURCE IS
97                              TOTAL-NUMBER-OF-EMPLOYEES.
98       02 COLUMN 49   PIC X(9)  VALUE "EMPLOYEES".
99       02 COLUMN 66   PIC $$$,$$$,$$$ SUM SALARY-ER.
100      02 COLUMN 77   PIC XX    VALUE "**".
101
102 PROCEDURE DIVISION.
103
104 DECLARATIVES.
105
106 0000-END-OF-PAGE SECTION.
107
108     USE BEFORE REPORTING DEPARTMENT-HEADING-LINE.
109
110 0100-INITIALIZE-DEPT-EMPLOYEES.
111
112     MOVE ZERO TO DEPT-NUMBER-OF-EMPLOYEES.
113
114 END DECLARATIVES.
115
116 1000-MAIN-CONTROL.
```

Program Ab   *(concluded)*

```
117
118        PERFORM 2000-INITIALIZE-REPORT.
119        PERFORM 2100-PROCESS-DATA
120               UNTIL END-OF-FILE.
121        PERFORM 2200-TERMINATE-REPORT.
122        STOP RUN.
123
124 2000-INITIALIZE-REPORT.
125
126        OPEN INPUT EMPLOYEE-FILE
127             OUTPUT REPORT-FILE.
128        INITIATE EMPLOYEE-REPORT.
129        PERFORM 9000-READ-EMPLOYEE-FILE.
130
131 2100-PROCESS-DATA.
132
133        GENERATE DETAIL-LINE.
134        ADD 1 TO TOTAL-NUMBER-OF-EMPLOYEES.
135        ADD 1 TO DEPT-NUMBER-OF-EMPLOYEES.
136        PERFORM 9000-READ-EMPLOYEE-FILE.
137
138 2200-TERMINATE-REPORT.
139
140        TERMINATE EMPLOYEE-REPORT.
141        CLOSE EMPLOYEE-FILE
142              REPORT-FILE.
143
144 9000-READ-EMPLOYEE-FILE.
145
146        READ EMPLOYEE-FILE
147             AT END MOVE "YES" TO EOF-FLAG.
```

Figure A.4   General form for subordinate group descriptions for report writer

Format 1

level-number   [data-number-1]

$$\left[\underline{\text{LINE}} \text{ NUMBER IS} \quad \left\{ \begin{array}{l} \text{integer-1} \\ \underline{\text{PLUS}} \text{ integer-2} \end{array} \right\} \right]$$

Format 2

level-number   [data-name-1]
                [GROUP INDICATE]
                [COLUMN NUMBER IS integer-1]

$$\left\{ \begin{array}{l} \underline{\text{PICTURE}} \\ \underline{\text{PIC}} \end{array} \right\} \qquad \text{IS picture-codes}$$

$$\left\{ \begin{array}{l} \underline{\text{SOURCE}} \text{ IS data-name-2} \\ \underline{\text{VALUE}} \text{ IS literal} \\ \underline{\text{SUM}} \text{ data-name-3 ...} \end{array} \right\}$$

Figure A.5 Sample report with one control group

```
                  ABC COMPANY EMPLOYEE REPORT              PAGE    1  }  Page Heading
     NAME            EMPLOYEE NUMBER              DEPARTMENT      SALARY  }  Control Heading

     JONES  JOHN       11111111                      002      $ 40,000  }
     SMITH  MARY       12222222                      002      $ 50,000  }  Detail
     DOE  JOHN         13333333                      002      $ 34,000  }
                                                                       }  Control Footing
                                  3      EMPLOYEES         $124,000*    }
                                                                       }  Control Heading
     BLACK  HARVEY     14444444                      003      $ 20,000  }  Detail
     WHITE  SUE        15555555                      003      $ 45,000  }
```

```
                  ABC COMPANY EMPLOYEE REPORT              PAGE    2  }  Page Heading
     NAME            EMPLOYEE NUMBER              DEPARTMENT      SALARY  }
                                                                       }  Control Footing
                                  2      EMPLOYEES          $65,000*    }
                                                                       }  Control Heading
     GREY  SAM         16666666                      103      $ 90,000  }  Detail
     GONZALEZ  CARLOS  27777777                      103      $ 80,000  }
                                                                       }  Control Footing
                                  2      EMPLOYEES         $170,000*    }
                                                                       }  Control Heading
     SHEA  JOHN        30000000                      111      $ 45,000  }  Detail
     SPADE  SAM        33333333                      111      $ 67,000  }
```

```
                  ABC COMPANY EMPLOYEE REPORT              PAGE    3  }  Page Heading
     NAME            EMPLOYEE NUMBER              DEPARTMENT      SALARY  }
                                                                       }  Control Footing
                                  2      EMPLOYEES         $112,000*    }
                                                                       }  Control Heading
     CLARK  JOHN       34444444                      211      $ 30,000  }
     HERNANDEZ  MARIA  44444444                      211      $ 80,000  }  Detail
     JONES  PATRICIA   45555555                      211      $ 50,000  }
                                                                       }  Control Footing
                                  3      EMPLOYEES         $160,000*    }
                                                                       }  Control Footing
                                 12      EMPLOYEES         $631,000**   }  Final
```

lines, control headings based on department number, control footings based on department number, and control footing final. These elements are illustrated in the sample report shown in Figure A.5.

As with Program Aa, most of the desired output can be handled "automatically" by features of report writer. However, the process of counting elements of each control group makes the use of DECLARATIVES necessary to zero out the counter DEPT-NUMBER-OF-EMPLOYEES. The appropriate time to perform this task would normally be after the value of the field has been printed and before the processing of the next record begins. Unfortunately, the USE statement contains only the option BEFORE REPORTING; there is no direct way to cause the desired action after the control footing line as been produced. The problem is solved by introducing a line of type CONTROL HEADING into the report. Lines of this type are produced automatically at the beginning of processing each control group. In our case, the timing of the production of the line is more important than the content of the line (which is merely a sequence of spaces). We use DECLARATIVES to execute a procedure prior to production of this line. In the procedure, we zero out the counter, thus forcing the counter to be reset to zero at the beginning of processing each control group. When the GEN-ERATE statement (line 133) is executed, the following actions take place:

1. If LINE-COUNTER > last detail line number
   Increment PAGE-COUNTER
   Produce page headings
   Initialize LINE-COUNTER
2. If control break has occurred
   Produce DEPARTMENT-SUMMARY-LINE
   Zero out salary accumulator on this line
   Execute DECLARATIVES procedure
   Produce DEPARTMENT-HEADING-LINE
   Increment LINE-COUNTER
3. Produce DETAIL-LINE
4. Add SALARY-ER to appropriate accumulators
5. Increment LINE-COUNTER

Because of the timing of the production of DEPARTMENT-HEADING-LINE, we are able to use the BEFORE REPORTING feature of the USE statement to cause the desired actions to be taken at the appropriate time—after the totals have been produced and before the next record has been processed.

Careful analysis of the examples and explanations in this appendix should enable the reader to get started using report writer. A useful exercise would be to rewrite any program from Chapter 8 using report writer. Report writer has a great many restrictions, which the programmer may inadvertently violate in initial programming efforts. If problems are encountered, the COBOL reference manual for the user's system should be consulted.

B. MICROCOMPUTER SCREEN HANDLING

In a microcomputer environment, most software is interactive in nature. The basic means of communication between the computer and the user is the keyboard and the computer screen. Because of this reliance on the screen to display information to the user, most microcomputer-oriented COBOL compilers feature nonstandard facilities for screen management. In this section, we present a few of these features that are commonly found in microcomputer-oriented compilers, but you should be forewarned. There are no standards in this area, and the features described here may or may not be implemented on the compiler you are using. (The material in this chapter is based on the RM/COBOL-85 compiler; if you are using another microcomputer-oriented compiler such as Microsoft COBOL, consult the compiler reference materials for the specific implementation of these features. The mechanics for handling screens in a mini- or mainframe environment may differ dramatically from the techniques described in this appendix. Your instructor or locally available reference materials can supply details.)

B.1 ENHANCED ACCEPT AND DISPLAY

The most common means for facilitating screen management is to add enhancements to the ACCEPT and DISPLAY verbs. Figures B.1 and B.2 show a few of the enhancements of these verbs that are available on the RM/COBOL-85 compiler.

Ordinary ACCEPT and DISPLAY statements use the next available line on the screen for the input or output operation. As the screen fills up, data is scrolled off at the top, and new operations take place at the bottom of the screen. Enhanced ACCEPT and DISPLAY verbs usually allow you to specify the position on the screen for the input or output to begin. This is done by specifying LINE and POSITION numbers. A typical screen is divided into 25 lines and 80 columns as shown in Figure B.3. The character position in the upper left corner is LINE 1 POSITION 1. When the ACCEPT or DISPLAY statement specifies the position for the operation, other parts of the screen are not affected.

In order to make effective use of this feature, it is necessary to think in terms of designing a series of screens for your programs. Using a form much like a printer spacing chart, you should lay out labels and areas for data entry in an attractive and consistent fashion. Then, using the screen design, you are able to write the appropriate ACCEPT and DISPLAY statements in a program.

Figure B.1   Enhanced form of ACCEPT

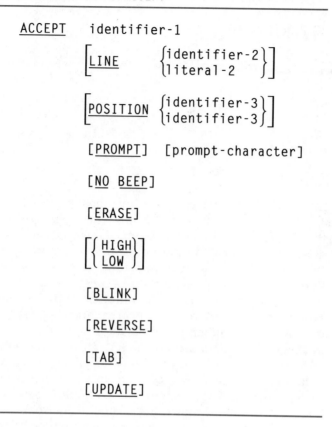

```
ACCEPT    identifier-1
          ⎡LINE      ⎧identifier-2⎫⎤
          ⎣          ⎩literal-2   ⎭⎦

          ⎡POSITION  ⎧identifier-3⎫⎤
          ⎣          ⎩identifier-3⎭⎦

          [PROMPT]   [prompt-character]

          [NO BEEP]

          [ERASE]

          ⎡⎧HIGH⎫⎤
          ⎣⎩LOW ⎭⎦

          [BLINK]

          [REVERSE]

          [TAB]

          [UPDATE]
```

Figure B.2   Enhanced form of DISPLAY

```
DISPLAY      ⎧identifier-1⎫
             ⎩literal-1   ⎭

             ⎡LINE      ⎧identifier-2⎫⎤
             ⎣          ⎩literal-2   ⎭⎦

             ⎡POSITION  ⎧identifier-3⎫⎤
             ⎣          ⎩literal-3   ⎭⎦

             [BEEP]

             [ERASE]

             ⎡⎧HIGH⎫⎤
             ⎣⎩LOW ⎭⎦

             [BLINK]

             [REVERSE]
```

Figure B.3   Typical microcomputer screen terminology

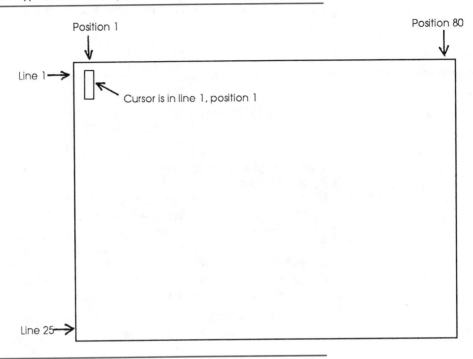

In addition to the ability to specify the screen location for an input or output operation, the enhanced ACCEPT and DISPLAY statements allow you to specify a variety of special effects using additional clauses. Note that you can specify any desired combination of special effects by including as many of the options as needed. Many of the options, including BLINK, HIGH, LOW, ERASE, and REVERSE, are common to the two statements; other options are appropriate only on one of the statements.

The BLINK option will cause the data being displayed or typed to flash on and off rapidly. The HIGH option will cause data being displayed or typed to be brighter than normal; the LOW option will cause data to be displayed at ordinary intensity. (The default setting for the RM/COBOL-85 compiler is HIGH.)

The REVERSE option will cause data being displayed to be written in black on a field of a lighter color. For example, the following statement will cause a field equal in length to the number of characters entered by the user to be highlighted at the appropriate position on the computer screen when the statement is executed:

```
ACCEPT ANSWER
       LINE 10
       POSITION 20
       REVERSE.
```

The REVERSE option is extremely useful in designing screens for data entry because it gives the user a visual clue to separate elements on the screen into two classes. For example, when displaying a data record to the user, you might use reverse video for those portions of the screen which represent data and normal video for labels.

The ERASE option on either statement causes the screen to be blanked out before the data being displayed is written on the screen or before the data entry operation is performed. This option is useful to begin displaying a new screen of information. For example, consider the following program segment:

```
DISPLAY "More data (Y/N)"
          LINE 1 POSITION 1
          HIGH
          ERASE.
ACCEPT MORE-DATA
          LINE 1 POSITION 20
          REVERSE.
```

This program segment will first erase the screen (because of the ERASE option on the DISPLAY statement) and then display the prompt "More data (Y/N)" in bright characters on line 1. When data is entered, the field for MORE-DATA will be displayed in reverse video at position 20 on line 1.

One option that is available only on the ACCEPT statement is PROMPT. This clause allows the program to specify the character that is to be displayed in the field before the user enters data. If the character is omitted, the default character is the underscore. For example, suppose that FLD-X is four characters in width. The statement

```
ACCEPT FLD-X
          LINE 10 POSITION 20
          PROMPT.
```

will cause four underscore characters to be displayed beginning at position 20 on line 10. The cursor is placed in position 20; as the user enters data, the underscore character is replaced. If the backspace key is used to delete a character, the underscore character returns.

When a user completes entering characters in a field, the system generates a sound called a "BEEP." The NO BEEP option will cause no sound to be emitted by the computer when the data entry process is completed. For example, the following statement would allow the user to enter a value for data item ANSWER at position 20 on line 10 and would, in addition, cause the sound to be omitted:

```
ACCEPT ANSWER
          LINE 10
          POSITION 20
          NO BEEP.
```

A very useful option available on the ACCEPT statement is UPDATE. If this option is used, the current content of the field being entered is displayed. The cursor is placed at the leftmost character in the field, and the user can change characters in the field as desired. Characters not changed by the user remain in the field unchanged. For example, suppose the current content of FLD-X is "ABCD". Execution of the statement

```
ACCEPT FLD-X
          LINE 30
          POSITION 10
          UPDATE.
```

will cause the characters ABCD to be displayed at position 10 of line 30; the cursor would be positioned over the A for the user to make changes in the field.

Normally, the data entry process initiated by an ACCEPT statement is terminated either when all characters in the field have been typed or when

Figure B.4   Summary of ACCEPT and DISPLAY options for RM/
COBOL-85

Option	Description	ACCEPT	DISPLAY
LINE	Specify the line number for input or output operation.	yes	yes
POSITION	Specify the position (column) for an input or output operation.	yes	yes
ERASE	Erase screen before beginning input or output operation.	yes	yes
HIGH	Characters displayed in high intensity (default setting).	yes	yes
LOW	Characters displayed in low intensity.	yes	yes
BLINK	Characters flash on and off rapidly.	yes	yes
REVERSE	Characters displayed on a light background.	yes	yes
BEEP	Make a "beep" sound when characters are displayed.	no	yes
NO BEEP	Suppress the "beep" sound when input operation is completed.	yes	no
PROMPT	Display the specified character in the field (default if character omitted in the underscore).	yes	no
UPDATE	Display the current content of the data item.	yes	no
TAB	Terminate date entry only by Enter key.	yes	no

the user presses the Enter key. This can present a problem if the user inadvertently types the last character in the field only to discover that a mistake has been made and the field needs to be corrected. (Correction by using the arrow keys and/or the backspace key is no problem during the data entry process but impossible once the process has been completed.) The TAB option on the ACCEPT statement has the effect of forcing the user to use the Enter key to terminate the data entry process. The data entry process is not terminated simply by entering all of the characters in the field. This gives the user a chance to review the field and to edit it, if desired, before terminating the data entry process for that field.

Figure B.4 summarizes the options for RM/COBOL-85 ACCEPT and DISPLAY statements discussed in this section.

B.2 PROGRAM EXAMPLE

Program Ba is a revision of Program 11a which allows a user to create a data file interactively.[1] Three basic screens are used in the program. The first is a simple file name screen shown in Figure B.5. This screen allows the user to enter the name of the file to be created by the program. This screen is handled by the paragraph 2000-INITIALIZE-PROGRAM (lines 59–65). The DISPLAY statement uses the ERASE option to erase the screen so that only the prompt appears on the screen. The ACCEPT statement uses the PROMPT option to make the field visible as a series of underscore characters.

[1]The program listing for Program Ba is adapted from the listing produced by the RM/COBOL-85 compiler. The six-digit numbers in the left-hand margin represent addresses of object code and are not part of the program.

Figure B.5   File name screen in Program Ba

Enter name of file to be created   PROBA.DAT_____

Program Ba

```
 1                        IDENTIFICATION DIVISION.
 2
 3                        PROGRAM-ID. FILE-BUILDER-PROBA.
 .
 .
 .
45                        PROCEDURE DIVISION.
46
47     000002             1000-MAIN-CONTROL.
48
49     000005                 PERFORM 2000-INITIALIZE-PROGRAM.
50     000008                 PERFORM 9000-GET-DATA UNTIL
51                                    DATA-OK OR END-OF-DATA.
52     000035                 PERFORM 2100-BUILD-FILE
53                                    UNTIL END-OF-DATA.
54     000048                 PERFORM 2200-CLOSE-FILES.
55     000051                 STOP RUN.
56
57     000054             2000-INITIALIZE-PROGRAM.
58
59     000057                 DISPLAY "Enter name of file to be created"
60                                    LINE 1 POSITION 1
61                                    ERASE.
62     000070                 ACCEPT FILE-NAME
63                                    LINE 1 POSITION 40
64                                    UPDATE
65                                    PROMPT.
66     000084                 OPEN OUTPUT DATA-FILE.
67
68     000094             2100-BUILD-FILE.
69
70     000097                 WRITE DATA-RECORD.
71     000104                 MOVE "N" TO ANSWER.
72     000110                 MOVE SPACES TO DATA-RECORD.
73     000116                 PERFORM 9000-GET-DATA UNTIL
74                                    DATA-OK OR END-OF-DATA.
75
76     000145             2200-CLOSE-FILES.
77
78     000148                 CLOSE DATA-FILE.
79
80     000157             9000-GET-DATA.
81
82     000160                 DISPLAY "Enter Name (END to terminate)"
83                                    LINE 1 POSITION 1
84                                    ERASE.
85     000173                 ACCEPT NAME-DR
86                                    LINE 1 POSITION 40
87                                    PROMPT
88                                    UPDATE.
```

```
 89    000187                IF NOT END-OF-DATA
 90                               PERFORM 9100-ENTER-DATA
 91                               PERFORM 9200-DISPLAY-DATA
 92                               DISPLAY "Are data correct? (Y/N)"
 93                                    LINE 24 POSITION 1
 94                                    BLINK
 95                               MOVE "Y" TO ANSWER
 96                               ACCEPT ANSWER
 97                                    LINE 24 POSITION 25
 98                                    PROMPT
 99                                    UPDATE
100                               IF NOT DATA-OK
101                                 DISPLAY "Reenter data; press <Enter> to
continue"
102                                      LINE 25 POSITION 1
103                                      REVERSE
104                                 MOVE SPACE TO ANSWER
105                                 ACCEPT ANSWER
106                                      LINE 25 POSITION 60
107                                      UPDATE
108                                      TAB.
109
110 ·  000286                9100-ENTER-DATA.
111
112    000289                DISPLAY "Name :"
113                                  LINE 1 POSITION 1
114                                  LOW
115                                  ERASE.
116    000302                DISPLAY NAME-DR
117                                  LINE 1 POSITION 40
118                                  LOW.
119    000315                DISPLAY "Enter Social Security Number"
120                                  LINE 2 POSITION 1
121                                  LOW.
122    000328                ACCEPT SS-NUM-DR
123                                  LINE 2 POSITION 40
124                                  PROMPT
125                                  UPDATE.
126    000342                DISPLAY "Enter Street Address"
127                                  LINE 3 POSITION 1
128                                  LOW.
129    000355                ACCEPT STREET-ADDRESS-DR
130                                  LINE 3 POSITION 40
131                                  PROMPT
132                                  UPDATE.
133    000369                DISPLAY "Enter City"
134                                  LINE 4 POSITION 1
135                                  LOW.
136    000382                ACCEPT CITY-DR
137                                  LINE 4 POSITION 40
138                                  PROMPT
139                                  UPDATE.
140    000396                DISPLAY "Enter Two Character State Abbreviation"
141                                  LINE 5 POSITION 1
142                                  LOW.
```

```
143    000409              ACCEPT STATE-DR
144                                LINE 5 POSITION 40
145                                PROMPT
146                                UPDATE.
147    000423              DISPLAY "Enter Zip"
148                                LINE 6 POSITION 1
149                                LOW.
150    000436              ACCEPT ZIP-DR
151                                LINE 6 POSITION 40
152                                PROMPT
153                                UPDATE.
154    000450              DISPLAY "Enter Date of Birth in form mmddyy"
155                                LINE 7 POSITION 1
156                                LOW.
157    000463              ACCEPT DOB-DR
158                                LINE 7 POSITION 40
159                                PROMPT
160                                UPDATE.
161
162    000479          9200-DISPLAY-DATA.
163
164    000482              DISPLAY "Name      : "
165                                LINE 1 POSITION 1
166                                ERASE
167                                LOW.
168    000495              DISPLAY  NAME-DR
169                                LINE 1 POSITION 13
170                                LOW
171                                REVERSE.
172    000509              DISPLAY "SS #      : "
173                                LINE 2 POSITION 1
174                                LOW.
175    000522              DISPLAY SS-NUM-DR
176                                LINE 2 POSITION 13
177                                LOW
178                                REVERSE.
179    000536              DISPLAY "Address   : "
180                                LINE 3 POSITION 1
181                                LOW.
182    000549              DISPLAY STREET-ADDRESS-DR
183                                LINE 3 POSITION 13
184                                LOW
185                                REVERSE.
186    000563              DISPLAY CITY-DR
187                                LINE 4 POSITION 13
188                                LOW
189                                REVERSE.
190    000577              DISPLAY STATE-DR
191                                LINE 4 POSITION 24
192                                LOW
193                                REVERSE.
194    000591              DISPLAY ZIP-DR
195                                LINE 4 POSITION 27
196                                LOW
197                                REVERSE.
```

Program Ba	*(concluded)*	

```
198    000605              DISPLAY "Birth Date: "
199                                LINE 5 POSITION 1
200                                LOW.
201    000618              DISPLAY DOB-DR
202                                LINE 5 POSITION 13
203                                LOW
204                                REVERSE.
```

Figure B.6   Data entry screen for Program Ba

```
Name  :                                         JOE JONES
Enter Social Security Number                    111111111
Enter Street Address                            123 X ST
Enter City                                      OAK CITY
Enter Two Character State Abbreviation AL
Enter Zip                                       12300
Enter Date of Birth in form mmddyy             011267
```

Figure B.7   Data verification screen in Program Ba

```
Name      : JOE JONES
SS #      : 111111111
Address   : 123 X ST.
            OAK CITY    AL 12300
Birth Date: 011267 ◄ —————— Data display is highlighted.
```

Flashes on and off. ———►
Brighter than normal.   `Are data correct? (Y/N) Y`

The second major screen is the data entry screen shown in Figure B.6. This screen is for the user to enter the data for the various fields in a record. It is handled in the program by the paragraphs 9000-GET-DATA and 9100-ENTER-DATA (lines 80–161). The screen is erased by the ERASE option on the initial DISPLAY statement (lines 82–84). PROMPT is used for each of the fields in the ACCEPT statements in 9100-ENTER-DATA.

The third major screen is the data verification screen shown in Figure B.7. This screen displays the data that has just been entered by the user (using the REVERSE option) and then prompts the user to verify correctness of the data. This screen is handled by 9000-GET-DATA and 9200-DISPLAY-DATA. The BLINK option is used on the prompt at the bottom of the screen to call the user's attention to the message (see lines 92–94). If the user responds that the data is not okay, the message "Reenter data; press <Enter> to continue" is displayed on line 25. The ACCEPT statement at lines 105–108 uses the TAB option. This statement serves to halt the system so that the program user can read the message just displayed and forces the user to respond with the Enter key to continue.

C. GENERAL FORM OF COBOL-74 ELEMENTS

GENERAL FORMAT FOR IDENTIFICATION DIVISION

IDENTIFICATION DIVISION.

PROGRAM-ID. program-name.

[AUTHOR. [comment-entry] ...]

[INSTALLATION. [comment-entry] ...]

[DATE-WRITTEN. [comment-entry] ...]

[DATE-COMPILED. [comment-entry] ...]

[SECURITY. [comment-entry] ...]

GENERAL FORMAT FOR ENVIRONMENT DIVISION

ENVIRONMENT DIVISION.

CONFIGURATION SECTION.

SOURCE-COMPUTER.   computer-name [WITH DEBUGGING MODE] .

OBJECT-COMPUTER.   computer-name

$$\left[, \text{MEMORY SIZE integer} \left\{ \begin{array}{l} \text{WORDS} \\ \text{CHARACTERS} \\ \text{MODULES} \end{array} \right\} \right]$$

[, PROGRAM COLLATING SEQUENCE IS alphabet-name]

$$\left[,\ \underline{\text{SEGMENT-LIMIT}}\ \underline{\text{IS}}\ \text{segment-number}\right]\ \ .$$

$$\left[\underline{\text{SPECIAL-NAMES}}.\ \ \left[,\ \text{implementor-name}\right.\right.$$

$$\left\{\begin{array}{l}\underline{\text{IS}}\ \text{mnemonic-name}\ \left[,\ \underline{\text{ON}}\ \text{STATUS}\ \underline{\text{IS}}\ \text{condition-name-1}\ \left[,\ \underline{\text{OFF}}\ \text{STATUS}\ \underline{\text{IS}}\ \text{condition-name-2}\right]\right]\\ \underline{\text{IS}}\ \text{mnemonic-name}\ \left[,\ \underline{\text{OFF}}\ \text{STATUS}\ \underline{\text{IS}}\ \text{condition-name-2}\ \left[,\ \underline{\text{ON}}\ \text{STATUS}\ \underline{\text{IS}}\ \text{condition-name-1}\right]\right]\\ \underline{\text{ON}}\ \text{STATUS}\ \underline{\text{IS}}\ \text{condition-name-1}\ \left[,\ \underline{\text{OFF}}\ \text{STATUS}\ \underline{\text{IS}}\ \text{condition-name-2}\right]\\ \underline{\text{OFF}}\ \text{STATUS}\ \underline{\text{IS}}\ \text{condition-name-2}\ \left[,\ \underline{\text{ON}}\ \text{STATUS}\ \underline{\text{IS}}\ \text{condition-name-1}\right]\end{array}\right\}\ \cdots$$

$$\left[,\ \text{alphabet-name}\ \text{IS}\ \left\{\begin{array}{l}\underline{\text{STANDARD-1}}\\ \underline{\text{NATIVE}}\\ \text{implementor-name}\\ \text{literal-1}\left[\begin{array}{l}\left\{\dfrac{\underline{\text{THROUGH}}}{\underline{\text{THRU}}}\right\}\ \text{literal-2}\\ \underline{\text{ALSO}}\ \text{literal-3}\ \left[,\ \underline{\text{ALSO}}\ \text{literal-4}\right]\cdots\end{array}\right]\\ \left[\text{literal-5}\left[\begin{array}{l}\left\{\dfrac{\underline{\text{THROUGH}}}{\underline{\text{THRU}}}\right\}\ \text{literal-6}\\ \underline{\text{ALSO}}\ \text{literal-7}\ \left[,\ \underline{\text{ALSO}}\ \text{literal-8}\right]\cdots\end{array}\right]\right]\cdots\end{array}\right\}\cdots\right]$$

$$\left[,\ \underline{\text{CURRENCY}}\ \text{SIGN}\ \underline{\text{IS}}\ \text{literal-9}\right]$$

$$\left[,\ \underline{\text{DECIMAL-POINT}}\ \underline{\text{IS}}\ \underline{\text{COMMA}}\right]\ \ .\ \ \Big]$$

GENERAL FORMAT FOR ENVIRONMENT DIVISION

$$\left[\underline{\text{INPUT-OUTPUT}}\ \underline{\text{SECTION}}.\right.$$

$$\underline{\text{FILE-CONTROL}}.$$

$$\left\{\text{file-control-entry}\right\}\ \cdots$$

$$\left[\underline{\text{I-O-CONTROL}}.\right.$$

$$\left[;\ \underline{\text{RERUN}}\ \left[\underline{\text{ON}}\ \left\{\begin{array}{l}\text{file-name-1}\\ \text{implementor-name}\end{array}\right\}\right]\right.$$

$$\left.\underline{\text{EVERY}}\ \left\{\begin{array}{l}\left\{\begin{array}{l}\left[\underline{\text{END}}\ \text{OF}\right]\ \left\{\dfrac{\underline{\text{REEL}}}{\underline{\text{UNIT}}}\right\}\\ \text{integer-1}\ \underline{\text{RECORDS}}\end{array}\right\}\ \text{OF file-name-2}\\ \text{integer-2}\ \underline{\text{CLOCK-UNITS}}\\ \text{condition-name}\end{array}\right\}\right]\ \cdots$$

$$\left[;\ \underline{\text{SAME}}\ \left[\begin{array}{l}\text{RECORD}\\ \underline{\text{SORT}}\\ \underline{\text{SORT-MERGE}}\end{array}\right]\ \text{AREA FOR file-name-3}\ \left\{,\ \text{file-name-4}\right\}\ \cdots\right]\ \cdots$$

$$\left[;\ \underline{\text{MULTIPLE}}\ \underline{\text{FILE}}\ \text{TAPE CONTAINS file-name-5}\ \left[\underline{\text{POSITION}}\ \text{integer-3}\right]\right.$$

$$\left.\left[,\ \text{file-name-6}\ \left[\underline{\text{POSITION}}\ \text{integer-4}\right]\right]\ \cdots\ \right]\ \cdots\ \ .\Big]\Big]$$

GENERAL FORMAT FOR FILE CONTROL ENTRY

FORMAT 1:

SELECT [OPTIONAL] file-name

    ASSIGN TO implementor-name-1 [, implementor-name-2] ...

    [; RESERVE integer-1 $\begin{bmatrix} \text{AREA} \\ \text{AREAS} \end{bmatrix}$]

    [; ORGANIZATION IS SEQUENTIAL]

    [; ACCESS MODE IS SEQUENTIAL]

    [; FILE STATUS IS data-name-1] .

FORMAT 2:

SELECT file-name

    ASSIGN TO implementor-name-1 [, implementor-name-2] ...

    [; RESERVE integer-1 $\begin{bmatrix} \text{AREA} \\ \text{AREAS} \end{bmatrix}$]

    ; ORGANIZATION IS RELATIVE

    $\left[; \text{ACCESS MODE IS} \left\{ \begin{array}{l} \underline{\text{SEQUENTIAL}} \quad [, \underline{\text{RELATIVE}} \text{ KEY IS data-name-1}] \\ \left\{ \begin{array}{l} \underline{\text{RANDOM}} \\ \underline{\text{DYNAMIC}} \end{array} \right\} \quad , \underline{\text{RELATIVE}} \text{ KEY IS data-name-1} \end{array} \right\} \right]$

    [; FILE STATUS IS data-name-2] .

FORMAT 3:

SELECT file-name

    ASSIGN TO implementor-name-1 [, implementor-name-2] ...

    [; RESERVE integer-1 $\begin{bmatrix} \text{AREA} \\ \text{AREAS} \end{bmatrix}$]

    ; ORGANIZATION IS INDEXED

    $\left[; \text{ACCESS MODE IS} \left\{ \begin{array}{l} \underline{\text{SEQUENTIAL}} \\ \underline{\text{RANDOM}} \\ \underline{\text{DYNAMIC}} \end{array} \right\} \right]$

    ; RECORD KEY IS data-name-1

    [; ALTERNATE RECORD KEY IS data-name-2 [WITH DUPLICATES]] ...

    [; FILE STATUS IS data-name-3] .

FORMAT 4:

SELECT file-name ASSIGN TO implementor-name-1 [, implementor-name-2] ...

GENERAL FORMAT FOR DATA DIVISION

DATA DIVISION.

[FILE SECTION.

[FD file-name

  [; BLOCK CONTAINS [integer-1 TO] integer-2 $\left\{ \begin{array}{l} \text{RECORDS} \\ \text{CHARACTERS} \end{array} \right\}$]

  [; RECORD CONTAINS [integer-3 TO] integer-4 CHARACTERS]

  ; LABEL $\left\{ \begin{array}{l} \text{RECORD IS} \\ \text{RECORDS ARE} \end{array} \right\}$ $\left\{ \begin{array}{l} \text{STANDARD} \\ \text{OMITTED} \end{array} \right\}$

  [; VALUE OF implementor-name-1 IS $\left\{ \begin{array}{l} \text{data-name-1} \\ \text{literal-1} \end{array} \right\}$

   [, implementor-name-2 IS $\left\{ \begin{array}{l} \text{data-name-2} \\ \text{literal-2} \end{array} \right\}$] ...]

  [; DATA $\left\{ \begin{array}{l} \text{RECORD IS} \\ \text{RECORDS ARE} \end{array} \right\}$ data-name-3 [, data-name-4] ...]

  [; LINAGE IS $\left\{ \begin{array}{l} \text{data-name-5} \\ \text{integer-5} \end{array} \right\}$ LINES [, WITH FOOTING AT $\left\{ \begin{array}{l} \text{data-name-6} \\ \text{integer-6} \end{array} \right\}$]

   [, LINES AT TOP $\left\{ \begin{array}{l} \text{data-name-7} \\ \text{integer-7} \end{array} \right\}$] [, LINES AT BOTTOM $\left\{ \begin{array}{l} \text{data-name-8} \\ \text{integer-8} \end{array} \right\}$]]

  [; CODE-SET IS alphabet-name]

  [; $\left\{ \begin{array}{l} \text{REPORT IS} \\ \text{REPORTS ARE} \end{array} \right\}$ report-name-1 [, report-name-2] ...] .

[record-description-entry] ...] ...

[SD file-name

  [; RECORD CONTAINS [integer-1 TO] integer-2 CHARACTERS]

  [; DATA $\left\{ \begin{array}{l} \text{RECORD IS} \\ \text{RECORDS ARE} \end{array} \right\}$ data-name-1 [, data-name-2] ...] .

{record-description-entry} ...] ...]

$$\left[\begin{array}{l} \underline{\text{WORKING-STORAGE}}\ \underline{\text{SECTION}}. \\ \left[\begin{array}{l} \text{77-level-description-entry} \\ \text{record-description-entry} \end{array}\right]\ \dots \end{array}\right]$$

$$\left[\begin{array}{l} \underline{\text{LINKAGE}}\ \underline{\text{SECTION}}. \\ \left[\begin{array}{l} \text{77-level-description-entry} \\ \text{record-description-entry} \end{array}\right]\ \dots \end{array}\right]$$

$$\left[\begin{array}{l} \underline{\text{COMMUNICATION}}\ \underline{\text{SECTION}}. \\ [\text{communication-description-entry} \\ [\text{record-description-entry}]\ \dots\ ]\ \dots\ \end{array}\right]$$

$$\left[\underline{\text{REPORT}}\ \underline{\text{SECTION}}. \right.$$

$$\left[\underline{\text{RD}}\ \text{report-name}\right.$$

$$\left[;\ \underline{\text{CODE}}\ \text{literal-1}\right]$$

$$\left[;\ \left\{\begin{array}{l} \underline{\text{CONTROL}}\ \text{IS} \\ \underline{\text{CONTROLS}}\ \text{ARE} \end{array}\right\}\ \left\{\begin{array}{l} \text{data-name-1}\ [,\ \text{data-name-2}]\ \dots \\ \underline{\text{FINAL}}\ [,\ \text{data-name-1}\ [,\ \text{data-name-2}]\ \dots] \end{array}\right\}\right]$$

$$\left[;\ \underline{\text{PAGE}}\ \left[\begin{array}{l} \underline{\text{LIMIT}}\ \text{IS} \\ \underline{\text{LIMITS}}\ \text{ARE} \end{array}\right]\ \text{integer-1}\ \left[\begin{array}{l} \underline{\text{LINE}} \\ \underline{\text{LINES}} \end{array}\right]\ [,\ \underline{\text{HEADING}}\ \text{integer-2}\right.$$

$$\left[,\ \underline{\text{FIRST}}\ \underline{\text{DETAIL}}\ \text{integer-3}\right]\ \left[,\ \underline{\text{LAST}}\ \underline{\text{DETAIL}}\ \text{integer-4}\right]$$

$$\left[,\ \underline{\text{FOOTING}}\ \text{integer-5}\ ]\ \right].$$

$$\left. \{\text{report-group-description-entry}\ \}\ \dots\ ]\ \dots\ \right]$$

GENERAL FORMAT FOR DATA DESCRIPTION ENTRY

FORMAT 1:

level-number $\begin{Bmatrix} \text{data-name-1} \\ \underline{\text{FILLER}} \end{Bmatrix}$

$\Big[\text{; } \underline{\text{REDEFINES}}\text{ data-name-2}\Big]$

$\left[\text{; } \begin{Bmatrix} \underline{\text{PICTURE}} \\ \underline{\text{PIC}} \end{Bmatrix} \text{ IS character-string}\right]$

$\left[\text{; } \Big[\underline{\text{USAGE}}\text{ IS}\Big] \begin{Bmatrix} \underline{\text{COMPUTATIONAL}} \\ \underline{\text{COMP}} \\ \underline{\text{DISPLAY}} \\ \underline{\text{INDEX}} \end{Bmatrix}\right]$

$\left[\text{; } \Big[\underline{\text{SIGN}}\text{ IS}\Big] \begin{Bmatrix} \underline{\text{LEADING}} \\ \underline{\text{TRAILING}} \end{Bmatrix} \Big[\underline{\text{SEPARATE}}\text{ CHARACTER}\Big]\right]$

$\Bigg[\text{; } \underline{\text{OCCURS}} \begin{Bmatrix} \text{integer-1 } \underline{\text{TO}}\text{ integer-2 TIMES } \underline{\text{DEPENDING}}\text{ ON data-name-3} \\ \text{integer-2 } \underline{\text{TIMES}} \end{Bmatrix}$

$\left[\begin{Bmatrix} \underline{\text{ASCENDING}} \\ \underline{\text{DESCENDING}} \end{Bmatrix} \text{ KEY IS data-name-4 } \Big[\text{, data-name-5}\Big] \text{ ... }\right] \text{ ...}$

$\left.\Big[\underline{\text{INDEXED}}\text{ BY index-name-1 } \Big[\text{, index-name-2}\Big] \text{ ... }\Big]\right]$

$\left[\text{; } \begin{Bmatrix} \underline{\text{SYNCHRONIZED}} \\ \underline{\text{SYNC}} \end{Bmatrix} \begin{bmatrix} \underline{\text{LEFT}} \\ \underline{\text{RIGHT}} \end{bmatrix}\right]$

$\left[\text{; } \begin{Bmatrix} \underline{\text{JUSTIFIED}} \\ \underline{\text{JUST}} \end{Bmatrix} \text{ RIGHT}\right]$

$\Big[\text{; } \underline{\text{BLANK}}\text{ WHEN } \underline{\text{ZERO}}\Big]$

$\Big[\text{; } \underline{\text{VALUE}}\text{ IS literal}\Big]$.

FORMAT 2:

66 data-name-1; $\underline{\text{RENAMES}}$ data-name-2 $\left[\begin{Bmatrix} \underline{\text{THROUGH}} \\ \underline{\text{THRU}} \end{Bmatrix} \text{ data-name-3}\right]$

FORMAT 3:

88 condition-name; $\begin{Bmatrix} \underline{\text{VALUE}}\text{ IS} \\ \underline{\text{VALUES}}\text{ ARE} \end{Bmatrix}$ literal-1 $\left[\begin{Bmatrix} \underline{\text{THROUGH}} \\ \underline{\text{THRU}} \end{Bmatrix} \text{ literal-2}\right]$

$\left[\text{, literal-3 } \left[\begin{Bmatrix} \underline{\text{THROUGH}} \\ \underline{\text{THRU}} \end{Bmatrix} \text{ literal-4}\right]\right] \text{ ... }$.

GENERAL FORMAT FOR COMMUNICATION DESCRIPTION ENTRY

FORMAT 1:

CD cd-name;

FOR [INITIAL] INPUT

$$
\left[
\begin{array}{l}
[; \text{SYMBOLIC } \underline{\text{QUEUE}} \text{ IS data-name-1}] \\
\qquad [; \text{SYMBOLIC } \underline{\text{SUB-QUEUE-1}} \text{ IS data-name-2}] \\
\qquad [; \text{SYMBOLIC } \underline{\text{SUB-QUEUE-2}} \text{ IS data-name-3}] \\
\qquad [; \text{SYMBOLIC } \underline{\text{SUB-QUEUE-3}} \text{ IS data-name-4}] \\
\qquad [; \underline{\text{MESSAGE}} \ \underline{\text{DATE}} \text{ IS data-name-5}] \\
\qquad [; \underline{\text{MESSAGE}} \ \underline{\text{TIME}} \text{ IS data-name-6}] \\
\qquad [; \text{SYMBOLIC } \underline{\text{SOURCE}} \text{ IS data-name-7}] \\
\qquad [; \underline{\text{TEXT}} \ \underline{\text{LENGTH}} \text{ IS data-name-8}] \\
\qquad [; \underline{\text{END}} \ \underline{\text{KEY}} \text{ IS data-name-9}] \\
\qquad [; \underline{\text{STATUS}} \ \underline{\text{KEY}} \text{ IS data-name-10}] \\
\qquad [; \underline{\text{MESSAGE}} \ \underline{\text{COUNT}} \text{ IS data-name-11}] \\
[\text{data-name-1, data-name-2, ..., data-name-11}]
\end{array}
\right]
$$

FORMAT 2:

CD cd-name; FOR OUTPUT

[; DESTINATION COUNT IS data-name-1]

[; TEXT LENGTH IS data-name-2]

[; STATUS KEY IS data-name-3]

[; DESTINATION TABLE OCCURS integer-2 TIMES

    [; INDEXED BY index-name-1 [, index-name-2]...]]

[; ERROR KEY IS data-name-4]

[; SYMBOLIC DESTINATION IS data-name-5] .

<u>GENERAL FORMAT FOR REPORT GROUP DESCRIPTION ENTRY</u>

<u>FORMAT 1</u>:

01 [data-name-1]

    $\left[\text{; } \underline{\text{LINE}} \text{ NUMBER IS } \left\{ \begin{array}{l} \text{integer-1 } \left[\text{ON } \underline{\text{NEXT}} \underline{\text{PAGE}} \right] \\ \underline{\text{PLUS}} \text{ integer-2} \end{array} \right\} \right]$

    $\left[\text{; } \underline{\text{NEXT}} \underline{\text{GROUP}} \text{ IS } \left\{ \begin{array}{l} \text{integer-3} \\ \underline{\text{PLUS}} \text{ integer-4} \\ \underline{\text{NEXT}} \underline{\text{PAGE}} \end{array} \right\} \right]$

    $\text{; } \underline{\text{TYPE}} \text{ IS } \left\{ \begin{array}{l} \left\{ \begin{array}{l} \underline{\text{REPORT}} \underline{\text{HEADING}} \\ \underline{\text{RH}} \end{array} \right\} \\ \left\{ \begin{array}{l} \underline{\text{PAGE}} \text{ HEADING} \\ \underline{\text{PH}} \end{array} \right\} \\ \left\{ \begin{array}{l} \underline{\text{CONTROL}} \underline{\text{HEADING}} \\ \underline{\text{CH}} \end{array} \right\} \left\{ \begin{array}{l} \text{data-name-2} \\ \underline{\text{FINAL}} \end{array} \right\} \\ \left\{ \begin{array}{l} \underline{\text{DETAIL}} \\ \underline{\text{DE}} \end{array} \right\} \\ \left\{ \begin{array}{l} \underline{\text{CONTROL}} \underline{\text{FOOTING}} \\ \underline{\text{CF}} \end{array} \right\} \left\{ \begin{array}{l} \text{data-name-3} \\ \underline{\text{FINAL}} \end{array} \right\} \\ \left\{ \begin{array}{l} \underline{\text{PAGE}} \underline{\text{FOOTING}} \\ \underline{\text{PF}} \end{array} \right\} \\ \left\{ \begin{array}{l} \underline{\text{REPORT}} \underline{\text{FOOTING}} \\ \underline{\text{RF}} \end{array} \right\} \end{array} \right\}$

    $\left[\text{; } \left[\underline{\text{USAGE}} \text{ IS} \right] \underline{\text{DISPLAY}} \right] \text{ .}$

<u>FORMAT 2</u>:

level-number [data-name-1]

    $\left[\text{; } \underline{\text{LINE}} \text{ NUMBER IS } \left\{ \begin{array}{l} \text{integer-1 } \left[\text{ON } \underline{\text{NEXT}} \underline{\text{PAGE}} \right] \\ \underline{\text{PLUS}} \text{ integer-2} \end{array} \right\} \right]$

    $\left[\text{; } \left[\underline{\text{USAGE}} \text{ IS} \right] \underline{\text{DISPLAY}} \right] \text{ .}$

<u>FORMAT 3</u>:

level-number [data-name-1]

    $\left[\text{; } \underline{\text{BLANK}} \text{ WHEN } \underline{\text{ZERO}} \right]$

    $\left[\text{; } \underline{\text{GROUP}} \text{ INDICATE} \right]$

    $\left[\text{; } \left\{ \begin{array}{l} \underline{\text{JUSTIFIED}} \\ \underline{\text{JUST}} \end{array} \right\} \text{ RIGHT} \right]$

    $\left[\text{; } \underline{\text{LINE}} \text{ NUMBER IS } \left\{ \begin{array}{l} \text{integer-1 } \left[\text{ON } \underline{\text{NEXT}} \underline{\text{PAGE}} \right] \\ \underline{\text{PLUS}} \text{ integer-2} \end{array} \right\} \right]$

$$\left[; \underline{\text{COLUMN}} \text{ NUMBER IS integer-3}\right]$$

$$; \left\{\begin{array}{l}\underline{\text{PICTURE}}\\\underline{\text{PIC}}\end{array}\right\} \text{ IS character-string}$$

$$\left\{\begin{array}{l}; \underline{\text{SOURCE}} \text{ IS identifier-1}\\\\; \underline{\text{VALUE}} \text{ IS literal}\\\\\{; \underline{\text{SUM}} \text{ identifier-2 } [, \text{ identifier-3}] \ldots\\\\\quad\left[\underline{\text{UPON}} \text{ data-name-2 } [, \text{ data-name-3}] \ldots\right]\} \ldots\\\\\quad\left[\underline{\text{RESET}} \text{ ON } \left\{\begin{array}{l}\text{data-name-4}\\\underline{\text{FINAL}}\end{array}\right\}\right]\end{array}\right\}$$

$$\left[; \left[\underline{\text{USAGE}} \text{ IS}\right] \underline{\text{DISPLAY}}\right].$$

GENERAL FORMAT FOR PROCEDURE DIVISION

FORMAT 1:

$\underline{\text{PROCEDURE}} \underline{\text{DIVISION}} \left[\underline{\text{USING}} \text{ data-name-1 } [, \text{ data-name-2}] \ldots\right].$

$\left[\underline{\text{DECLARATIVES}}.\right.$

$\{$section-name $\underline{\text{SECTION}}$ [segment-number] . declarative-sentence

$[$paragraph-name. [sentence] $\ldots] \ldots\} \ldots$

$\underline{\text{END}} \underline{\text{DECLARATIVES}}.\left.\right]$

$\{$section-name $\underline{\text{SECTION}}$ [segment-number] .

$[$paragraph-name. [sentence] $\ldots] \ldots\} \ldots$

FORMAT 2:

$\underline{\text{PROCEDURE}} \underline{\text{DIVISION}} \left[\underline{\text{USING}} \text{ data-name-1 } [, \text{ data-name-2}] \ldots\right].$

$\{$paragraph-name. [sentence] $\ldots\} \ldots$

GENERAL FORMAT FOR VERBS

ACCEPT identifier [FROM mnemonic-name]

ACCEPT identifier FROM $\begin{Bmatrix} \text{DATE} \\ \text{DAY} \\ \text{TIME} \end{Bmatrix}$

ACCEPT cd-name MESSAGE COUNT

ADD $\begin{Bmatrix} \text{identifier-1} \\ \text{literal-1} \end{Bmatrix}$ [, identifier-2] ... TO identifier-m [ROUNDED]

     [, identifier-n [ROUNDED]] ... [; ON SIZE ERROR imperative-statement]

ADD $\begin{Bmatrix} \text{identifier-1} \\ \text{literal-1} \end{Bmatrix}$, $\begin{Bmatrix} \text{identifier-2} \\ \text{literal-2} \end{Bmatrix}$ [, identifier-3] ...

     GIVING identifier-m [ROUNDED] [, identifier-n [ROUNDED]] ...

     [; ON SIZE ERROR imperative-statement]

ADD $\begin{Bmatrix} \text{CORRESPONDING} \\ \text{CORR} \end{Bmatrix}$ identifier-1 TO identifier-2 [ROUNDED]

     [; ON SIZE ERROR imperative-statement]

ALTER procedure-name-1 TO [PROCEED TO] procedure-name-2

     [, procedure-name-3 TO [PROCEED TO] procedure-name-4] ...

CALL $\begin{Bmatrix} \text{identifier-1} \\ \text{literal-1} \end{Bmatrix}$ [USING data-name-1 [, data-name-2] ...]

     [; ON OVERFLOW imperative-statement]

CANCEL $\begin{Bmatrix} \text{identifier-1} \\ \text{literal-1} \end{Bmatrix}$ [, identifier-2] ...

CLOSE file-name-1 $\left[\begin{matrix} \begin{Bmatrix} \text{REEL} \\ \text{UNIT} \end{Bmatrix} \begin{bmatrix} \text{WITH NO REWIND} \\ \text{FOR REMOVAL} \end{bmatrix} \\ \text{WITH} \begin{Bmatrix} \text{NO REWIND} \\ \text{LOCK} \end{Bmatrix} \end{matrix} \right]$

$\left[, \text{file-name-2} \left[\begin{matrix} \begin{Bmatrix} \text{REEL} \\ \text{UNIT} \end{Bmatrix} \begin{bmatrix} \text{WITH NO REWIND} \\ \text{FOR REMOVAL} \end{bmatrix} \\ \text{WITH} \begin{Bmatrix} \text{NO REWIND} \\ \text{LOCK} \end{Bmatrix} \end{matrix} \right] \right]$ ...

CLOSE file-name-1 [WITH LOCK] [, file-name-2 [WITH LOCK]] ...

COMPUTE identifier-1 [ROUNDED] [, identifier-2 [ROUNDED]] ...

  = arithmetic-expression [; ON SIZE ERROR imperative-statement]

DELETE file-name RECORD [; INVALID KEY imperative-statement]

DISABLE $\begin{Bmatrix} \text{INPUT} \ [\text{TERMINAL}] \\ \text{OUTPUT} \end{Bmatrix}$ cd-name WITH KEY $\begin{Bmatrix} \text{identifier-1} \\ \text{literal-1} \end{Bmatrix}$

DISPLAY $\begin{Bmatrix} \text{identifier-1} \\ \text{literal-1} \end{Bmatrix}$ $\begin{bmatrix} \text{, identifier-2} \\ \text{, literal-2} \end{bmatrix}$ ... [UPON mnemonic-name]

DIVIDE $\begin{Bmatrix} \text{identifier-1} \\ \text{literal-1} \end{Bmatrix}$ INTO identifier-2 [ROUNDED]

  [, identifier-3 [ROUNDED]] ... [; ON SIZE ERROR imperative-statement]

DIVIDE $\begin{Bmatrix} \text{identifier-1} \\ \text{literal-1} \end{Bmatrix}$ INTO $\begin{Bmatrix} \text{identifier-2} \\ \text{literal-2} \end{Bmatrix}$ GIVING identifier-3 [ROUNDED]

  [, identifier-4 [ROUNDED]] ... [; ON SIZE ERROR imperative-statement]

DIVIDE $\begin{Bmatrix} \text{identifier-1} \\ \text{literal-1} \end{Bmatrix}$ BY $\begin{Bmatrix} \text{identifier-2} \\ \text{literal-2} \end{Bmatrix}$ GIVING identifier-3 [ROUNDED]

  [, identifier-4 [ROUNDED]] ... [; ON SIZE ERROR imperative-statement]

DIVIDE $\begin{Bmatrix} \text{identifier-1} \\ \text{literal-1} \end{Bmatrix}$ INTO $\begin{Bmatrix} \text{identifier-2} \\ \text{literal-2} \end{Bmatrix}$ GIVING identifier-3 [ROUNDED]

  REMAINDER identifier-4 [; ON SIZE ERROR imperative-statement]

DIVIDE $\begin{Bmatrix} \text{identifier-1} \\ \text{literal-1} \end{Bmatrix}$ BY $\begin{Bmatrix} \text{identifier-2} \\ \text{literal-2} \end{Bmatrix}$ GIVING identifier-3 [ROUNDED]

  REMAINDER identifier-4 [; ON SIZE ERROR imperative-statement]

ENABLE $\begin{Bmatrix} \text{INPUT} \ [\text{TERMINAL}] \\ \text{OUTPUT} \end{Bmatrix}$ cd-name WITH KEY $\begin{Bmatrix} \text{identifier-1} \\ \text{literal-1} \end{Bmatrix}$

ENTER language-name [routine-name] .

EXIT [PROGRAM] .

GENERATE $\begin{Bmatrix} \text{data-name} \\ \text{report-name} \end{Bmatrix}$

GO TO [procedure-name-1]

GO TO procedure-name-1 [, procedure-name-2] ... , procedure-name-n

  DEPENDING ON identifier

IF condition; $\begin{Bmatrix} \text{statement-1} \\ \text{NEXT SENTENCE} \end{Bmatrix}$ $\begin{Bmatrix} \text{; ELSE statement-2} \\ \text{; ELSE NEXT SENTENCE} \end{Bmatrix}$

INITIATE report-name-1 [, report-name-2] ...

INSPECT identifier-1 TALLYING

$$\left\{ \text{, identifier-2 } \underline{\text{FOR}} \left\{ \text{, } \left\{ \begin{matrix} \underline{\text{ALL}} \\ \underline{\text{LEADING}} \\ \underline{\text{CHARACTERS}} \end{matrix} \right\} \left\{ \begin{matrix} \text{identifier-3} \\ \text{literal-1} \end{matrix} \right\} \left[\left\{ \begin{matrix} \underline{\text{BEFORE}} \\ \underline{\text{AFTER}} \end{matrix} \right\} \text{ INITIAL } \left\{ \begin{matrix} \text{identifier-4} \\ \text{literal-2} \end{matrix} \right\} \right] \right\} \cdots \right\} \cdots$$

INSPECT identifier-1 REPLACING

$$\left\{ \begin{matrix} \underline{\text{CHARACTERS}} \ \underline{\text{BY}} \left\{ \begin{matrix} \text{identifier-6} \\ \text{literal-4} \end{matrix} \right\} \left[\left\{ \begin{matrix} \underline{\text{BEFORE}} \\ \underline{\text{AFTER}} \end{matrix} \right\} \text{ INITIAL } \left\{ \begin{matrix} \text{identifier-7} \\ \text{literal-5} \end{matrix} \right\} \right] \\ \left\{ \text{, } \left\{ \begin{matrix} \underline{\text{ALL}} \\ \underline{\text{LEADING}} \\ \underline{\text{FIRST}} \end{matrix} \right\} \left\{ \text{, } \left\{ \begin{matrix} \text{identifier-5} \\ \text{literal-3} \end{matrix} \right\} \underline{\text{BY}} \left\{ \begin{matrix} \text{identifier-6} \\ \text{literal-4} \end{matrix} \right\} \left[\left\{ \begin{matrix} \underline{\text{BEFORE}} \\ \underline{\text{AFTER}} \end{matrix} \right\} \text{ INITIAL } \left\{ \begin{matrix} \text{identifier-7} \\ \text{literal-5} \end{matrix} \right\} \right] \right\} \cdots \right\} \cdots \end{matrix} \right\}$$

INSPECT identifier-1 TALLYING

$$\left\{ \text{, identifier-2 } \underline{\text{FOR}} \left\{ \text{, } \left\{ \begin{matrix} \underline{\text{ALL}} \\ \underline{\text{LEADING}} \\ \underline{\text{CHARACTERS}} \end{matrix} \right\} \left\{ \begin{matrix} \text{identifier-3} \\ \text{literal-1} \end{matrix} \right\} \left[\left\{ \begin{matrix} \underline{\text{BEFORE}} \\ \underline{\text{AFTER}} \end{matrix} \right\} \text{ INITIAL } \left\{ \begin{matrix} \text{identifier-4} \\ \text{literal-2} \end{matrix} \right\} \right] \right\} \cdots \right\} \cdots$$

REPLACING

$$\left\{ \begin{matrix} \underline{\text{CHARACTERS}} \ \underline{\text{BY}} \left\{ \begin{matrix} \text{identifier-6} \\ \text{literal-4} \end{matrix} \right\} \left[\left\{ \begin{matrix} \underline{\text{BEFORE}} \\ \underline{\text{AFTER}} \end{matrix} \right\} \text{ INITIAL } \left\{ \begin{matrix} \text{identifier-7} \\ \text{literal-5} \end{matrix} \right\} \right] \\ \left\{ \text{, } \left\{ \begin{matrix} \underline{\text{ALL}} \\ \underline{\text{LEADING}} \\ \underline{\text{FIRST}} \end{matrix} \right\} \left\{ \text{, } \left\{ \begin{matrix} \text{identifier-5} \\ \text{literal-3} \end{matrix} \right\} \underline{\text{BY}} \left\{ \begin{matrix} \text{identifier-6} \\ \text{literal-4} \end{matrix} \right\} \left[\left\{ \begin{matrix} \underline{\text{BEFORE}} \\ \underline{\text{AFTER}} \end{matrix} \right\} \text{ INITIAL } \left\{ \begin{matrix} \text{identifier-7} \\ \text{literal-5} \end{matrix} \right\} \right] \right\} \cdots \right\} \cdots \end{matrix} \right\}$$

$\underline{\text{MERGE}}$ file-name-1 ON $\left\{ \begin{matrix} \underline{\text{ASCENDING}} \\ \underline{\text{DESCENDING}} \end{matrix} \right\}$ KEY data-name-1 $\left[\text{, data-name-2} \right]$ ...

$\left[\text{ON} \left\{ \begin{matrix} \underline{\text{ASCENDING}} \\ \underline{\text{DESCENDING}} \end{matrix} \right\} \text{ KEY data-name-3 } \left[\text{, data-name-4} \right] \cdots \right]$ ...

$\left[\text{COLLATING } \underline{\text{SEQUENCE}} \text{ IS alphabet-name} \right]$

$\underline{\text{USING}}$ file-name-2, file-name-3 $\left[\text{, file-name-4} \right]$ ...

$\left\{ \begin{matrix} \underline{\text{OUTPUT}} \ \underline{\text{PROCEDURE}} \text{ IS section-name-1} \left[\left\{ \begin{matrix} \underline{\text{THROUGH}} \\ \underline{\text{THRU}} \end{matrix} \right\} \text{ section-name-2} \right] \\ \underline{\text{GIVING}} \text{ file-name-5} \end{matrix} \right\}$

$\underline{\text{MOVE}}$ $\left\{ \begin{matrix} \text{identifier-1} \\ \text{literal} \end{matrix} \right\}$ $\underline{\text{TO}}$ identifier-2 $\left[\text{, identifier-3} \right]$ ...

$\underline{\text{MOVE}}$ $\left\{ \begin{matrix} \underline{\text{CORRESPONDING}} \\ \underline{\text{CORR}} \end{matrix} \right\}$ identifier-1 $\underline{\text{TO}}$ identifier-2

$\underline{\text{MULTIPLY}}$ $\left\{ \begin{matrix} \text{identifier-1} \\ \text{literal-1} \end{matrix} \right\}$ $\underline{\text{BY}}$ identifier-2 $\left[\underline{\text{ROUNDED}} \right]$

$\left[\text{, identifier-3} \left[\underline{\text{ROUNDED}} \right] \right]$ ... $\left[\text{; ON } \underline{\text{SIZE}} \ \underline{\text{ERROR}} \text{ imperative-statement} \right]$

MULTIPLY $\begin{Bmatrix} \text{identifier-1} \\ \text{literal-1} \end{Bmatrix}$ BY $\begin{Bmatrix} \text{identifier-2} \\ \text{literal-2} \end{Bmatrix}$ GIVING identifier-3 [ROUNDED]

[, identifier-4 [ROUNDED]] ... [; ON SIZE ERROR imperative-statement]

OPEN $\begin{Bmatrix} \underline{\text{INPUT}} \text{ file-name-1} \left[\begin{matrix} \text{REVERSED} \\ \text{WITH NO REWIND} \end{matrix} \right] \left[, \text{ file-name-2} \left[\begin{matrix} \text{REVERSED} \\ \text{WITH NO REWIND} \end{matrix} \right] \right] ... \\ \underline{\text{OUTPUT}} \text{ file-name-3} [\text{WITH NO REWIND}] [, \text{ file-name-4} [\text{WITH NO REWIND}]] ... \\ \underline{\text{I-O}} \text{ file-name-5} [, \text{ file-name-6}] ... \\ \underline{\text{EXTEND}} \text{ file-name-7} [, \text{ file-name-8}] ... \end{Bmatrix}$ ...

OPEN $\begin{Bmatrix} \underline{\text{INPUT}} \text{ file-name-1} [, \text{ file-name-2}] ... \\ \underline{\text{OUTPUT}} \text{ file-name-3} [, \text{ file-name-4}] ... \\ \underline{\text{I-O}} \text{ file-name-5} [, \text{ file-name-6}] ... \end{Bmatrix}$ ...

PERFORM procedure-name-1 $\left[\begin{Bmatrix} \text{THROUGH} \\ \text{THRU} \end{Bmatrix} \text{ procedure-name-2} \right]$

PERFORM procedure-name-1 $\left[\begin{Bmatrix} \text{THROUGH} \\ \text{THRU} \end{Bmatrix} \text{ procedure-name-2} \right] \begin{Bmatrix} \text{identifier-1} \\ \text{integer-1} \end{Bmatrix}$ TIMES

PERFORM procedure-name-1 $\left[\begin{Bmatrix} \text{THROUGH} \\ \text{THRU} \end{Bmatrix} \text{ procedure-name-2} \right]$ UNTIL condition-1

PERFORM procedure-name-1 $\left[\begin{Bmatrix} \text{THROUGH} \\ \text{THRU} \end{Bmatrix} \text{ procedure-name-2} \right]$

VARYING $\begin{Bmatrix} \text{identifier-2} \\ \text{index-name-1} \end{Bmatrix}$ FROM $\begin{Bmatrix} \text{identifier-3} \\ \text{index-name-2} \\ \text{literal-1} \end{Bmatrix}$

BY $\begin{Bmatrix} \text{identifier-4} \\ \text{literal-3} \end{Bmatrix}$ UNTIL condition-1

$\left[\text{AFTER} \begin{Bmatrix} \text{identifier-5} \\ \text{index-name-3} \end{Bmatrix} \text{FROM} \begin{Bmatrix} \text{identifier-6} \\ \text{index-name-4} \\ \text{literal-3} \end{Bmatrix} \right.$

BY $\begin{Bmatrix} \text{identifier-7} \\ \text{literal-4} \end{Bmatrix}$ UNTIL condition-2

$\left[\text{AFTER} \begin{Bmatrix} \text{identifier-8} \\ \text{index-name-5} \end{Bmatrix} \text{FROM} \begin{Bmatrix} \text{identifier-9} \\ \text{index-name-6} \\ \text{literal-5} \end{Bmatrix} \right.$

BY $\begin{Bmatrix} \text{identifier-10} \\ \text{literal-6} \end{Bmatrix}$ UNTIL condition-3 $\left. \vphantom{\begin{matrix} a \\ b \end{matrix}} \right] \right]$

READ file-name RECORD [INTO identifier] [; AT END imperative-statement]

READ file-name [NEXT] RECORD [INTO identifier]

[; AT END imperative-statement]

<u>READ</u> file-name RECORD $\left[\,\underline{\text{INTO}}\,\text{ identifier}\,\right]$ $\left[\,;\,\underline{\text{INVALID}}\,\text{ KEY imperative-statement}\,\right]$

<u>READ</u> file-name RECORD $\left[\,\underline{\text{INTO}}\,\text{ identifier}\,\right]$

  $\left[\,;\,\underline{\text{KEY}}\,\text{ IS data-name}\,\right]$

  $\left[\,;\,\underline{\text{INVALID}}\,\text{ KEY imperative-statement}\,\right]$

<u>RECEIVE</u> cd-name $\left\{\begin{array}{l}\underline{\text{MESSAGE}}\\\underline{\text{SEGMENT}}\end{array}\right\}$ <u>INTO</u> identifier-1 $\left[\,;\,\underline{\text{NO}}\,\underline{\text{DATA}}\,\text{ imperative-statement}\,\right]$

<u>RELEASE</u> record-name $\left[\,\underline{\text{FROM}}\,\text{ identifier}\,\right]$

<u>RETURN</u> file-name RECORD $\left[\,\underline{\text{INTO}}\,\text{ identifier}\,\right]$; AT <u>END</u> imperative-statement

<u>REWRITE</u> record-name $\left[\,\underline{\text{FROM}}\,\text{ identifier}\,\right]$

<u>REWRITE</u> record-name $\left[\,\underline{\text{FROM}}\,\text{ identifier}\,\right]$ $\left[\,;\,\underline{\text{INVALID}}\,\text{ KEY imperative-statement}\,\right]$

<u>SEARCH</u> identifier-1 $\left[\,\underline{\text{VARYING}}\,\left\{\begin{array}{l}\text{identifier-2}\\\text{index-name-1}\end{array}\right\}\right]$ $\left[\,;\,\text{AT }\underline{\text{END}}\text{ imperative-statement-1}\,\right]$

  ; <u>WHEN</u> condition-1 $\left\{\begin{array}{l}\text{imperative-statement-2}\\\underline{\text{NEXT}}\,\underline{\text{SENTENCE}}\end{array}\right\}$

  $\left[\,;\,\underline{\text{WHEN}}\,\text{ condition-2}\,\left\{\begin{array}{l}\text{imperative-statement-3}\\\underline{\text{NEXT}}\,\underline{\text{SENTENCE}}\end{array}\right\}\right]$ ...

<u>SEARCH</u> <u>ALL</u> identifier-1 $\left[\,;\,\text{AT }\underline{\text{END}}\text{ imperative-statement-1}\,\right]$

  ; <u>WHEN</u> $\left\{\begin{array}{l}\text{data-name-1}\,\left\{\begin{array}{l}\text{IS }\underline{\text{EQUAL}}\text{ TO}\\\text{IS }=\end{array}\right\}\,\left\{\begin{array}{l}\text{identifier-3}\\\text{literal-1}\\\text{arithmetic-expression-1}\end{array}\right\}\\\text{condition-name-1}\end{array}\right\}$

  $\left[\,\underline{\text{AND}}\,\left\{\begin{array}{l}\text{data-name-2}\,\left\{\begin{array}{l}\text{IS }\underline{\text{EQUAL}}\text{ TO}\\\text{IS }=\end{array}\right\}\,\left\{\begin{array}{l}\text{identifier-4}\\\text{literal-2}\\\text{arithmetic-expression-2}\end{array}\right\}\\\text{condition-name-2}\end{array}\right\}\right]$ ...

  $\left\{\begin{array}{l}\text{imperative-statement-2}\\\underline{\text{NEXT}}\,\underline{\text{SENTENCE}}\end{array}\right\}$

<u>SEND</u> cd-name <u>FROM</u> identifier-1

<u>SEND</u> cd-name $\left[\,\underline{\text{FROM}}\,\text{ identifier-1}\,\right]$ $\left\{\begin{array}{l}\text{WITH identifier-2}\\\text{WITH }\underline{\text{ESI}}\\\text{WITH }\underline{\text{EMI}}\\\text{WITH }\underline{\text{EGI}}\end{array}\right\}$

$\left[\,\left\{\begin{array}{l}\underline{\text{BEFORE}}\\\underline{\text{AFTER}}\end{array}\right\}\,\text{ADVANCING}\,\left\{\begin{array}{l}\left\{\left\{\begin{array}{l}\text{identifier-3}\\\text{integer}\end{array}\right\}\,\left[\begin{array}{l}\text{LINE}\\\text{LINES}\end{array}\right]\right\}\\\left\{\begin{array}{l}\text{mnemonic-name}\\\underline{\text{PAGE}}\end{array}\right\}\end{array}\right\}\right]$

$$\underline{\text{SET}} \quad \left\{ \begin{array}{l} \text{identifier-1} \quad [\text{, identifier-2}] \quad \dots \\ \text{index-name-1} \quad [\text{, index-name-2}] \quad \dots \end{array} \right\} \quad \underline{\text{TO}} \quad \left\{ \begin{array}{l} \text{identifier-3} \\ \text{index-name-3} \\ \text{integer-1} \end{array} \right\}$$

$$\underline{\text{SET}} \quad \text{index-name-4} \quad [\text{, index-name-5}] \quad \dots \quad \left\{ \begin{array}{l} \underline{\text{UP BY}} \\ \underline{\text{DOWN BY}} \end{array} \right\} \quad \left\{ \begin{array}{l} \text{identifier-4} \\ \text{integer-2} \end{array} \right\}$$

$$\underline{\text{SORT}} \quad \text{file-name-1 ON} \quad \left\{ \begin{array}{l} \underline{\text{ASCENDING}} \\ \underline{\text{DESCENDING}} \end{array} \right\} \quad \text{KEY data-name-1} \quad [\text{, data-name-2}] \quad \dots$$

$$\left[\text{ON} \quad \left\{ \begin{array}{l} \underline{\text{ASCENDING}} \\ \underline{\text{DESCENDING}} \end{array} \right\} \quad \text{KEY data-name-3} \quad [\text{, data-name-4}] \quad \dots \right] \quad \dots$$

$$\left[\text{COLLATING} \quad \underline{\text{SEQUENCE}} \text{ IS alphabet-name} \right]$$

$$\left\{ \begin{array}{l} \underline{\text{INPUT}} \ \underline{\text{PROCEDURE}} \text{ IS section-name-1} \left[\left\{ \begin{array}{l} \underline{\text{THROUGH}} \\ \underline{\text{THRU}} \end{array} \right\} \text{ section-name-2} \right] \\ \underline{\text{USING}} \text{ file-name-2} \quad [\text{, file-name-3}] \quad \dots \end{array} \right\}$$

$$\left\{ \begin{array}{l} \underline{\text{OUTPUT}} \ \underline{\text{PROCEDURE}} \text{ IS section-name-3} \left[\left\{ \begin{array}{l} \underline{\text{THROUGH}} \\ \underline{\text{THRU}} \end{array} \right\} \text{ section-name-4} \right] \\ \underline{\text{GIVING}} \text{ file-name-4} \end{array} \right\}$$

$$\underline{\text{START}} \quad \text{file-name} \left[\underline{\text{KEY}} \quad \left\{ \begin{array}{l} \text{IS } \underline{\text{EQUAL}} \text{ TO} \\ \text{IS } = \\ \text{IS } \underline{\text{GREATER}} \text{ THAN} \\ \text{IS } > \\ \text{IS } \underline{\text{NOT}} \ \underline{\text{LESS}} \text{ THAN} \\ \text{IS } \underline{\text{NOT}} < \end{array} \right\} \quad \text{data-name} \right]$$

$$\left[\text{; } \underline{\text{INVALID}} \text{ KEY imperative-statement} \right]$$

$$\underline{\text{STOP}} \quad \left\{ \begin{array}{l} \underline{\text{RUN}} \\ \text{literal} \end{array} \right\}$$

$$\underline{\text{STRING}} \quad \left\{ \begin{array}{l} \text{identifier-1} \\ \text{literal-1} \end{array} \right\} \quad \left[\begin{array}{l} \text{, identifier-2} \\ \text{, literal-2} \end{array} \right] \quad \dots \quad \underline{\text{DELIMITED}} \text{ BY} \quad \left\{ \begin{array}{l} \text{identifier-3} \\ \text{literal-3} \\ \underline{\text{SIZE}} \end{array} \right\}$$

$$\left[\text{, } \left\{ \begin{array}{l} \text{identifier-4} \\ \text{literal-4} \end{array} \right\} \quad \left[\begin{array}{l} \text{, identifier-5} \\ \text{, literal-5} \end{array} \right] \quad \dots \quad \underline{\text{DELIMITED}} \text{ BY} \quad \left\{ \begin{array}{l} \text{identifier-6} \\ \text{literal-6} \\ \underline{\text{SIZE}} \end{array} \right\} \right] \quad \dots$$

$$\underline{\text{INTO}} \text{ identifier-7} \left[\text{WITH } \underline{\text{POINTER}} \text{ identifier-8} \right]$$

$$\left[\text{; ON } \underline{\text{OVERFLOW}} \text{ imperative-statement} \right]$$

$$\underline{\text{SUBTRACT}} \quad \left\{ \begin{array}{l} \text{identifier-1} \\ \text{literal-1} \end{array} \right\} \quad \left[\begin{array}{l} \text{, identifier-2} \\ \text{, literal-2} \end{array} \right] \quad \dots \quad \underline{\text{FROM}} \text{ identifier-m} \left[\underline{\text{ROUNDED}} \right]$$

$$\left[\text{, identifier-n} \left[\underline{\text{ROUNDED}} \right] \right] \quad \dots \quad \left[\text{; ON } \underline{\text{SIZE}} \ \underline{\text{ERROR}} \text{ imperative-statement} \right]$$

$$\underline{\text{SUBTRACT}} \left\{ \begin{array}{l} \text{identifier-1} \\ \text{literal-1} \end{array} \right\} \left[\begin{array}{l} \text{, identifier-2} \\ \text{, literal-2} \end{array} \right] \cdots \underline{\text{FROM}} \left\{ \begin{array}{l} \text{identifier-m} \\ \text{literal-m} \end{array} \right\}$$

$$\underline{\text{GIVING}} \text{ identifier-n} \left[\underline{\text{ROUNDED}} \right] \left[\text{, identifier-o} \left[\underline{\text{ROUNDED}} \right] \right] \cdots$$

$$\left[; \text{ ON } \underline{\text{SIZE}} \ \underline{\text{ERROR}} \text{ imperative-statement} \right]$$

$$\underline{\text{SUBTRACT}} \left\{ \begin{array}{l} \underline{\text{CORRESPONDING}} \\ \underline{\text{CORR}} \end{array} \right\} \text{ identifier-1} \ \underline{\text{FROM}} \text{ identifier-2} \left[\underline{\text{ROUNDED}} \right]$$

$$\left[; \text{ ON } \underline{\text{SIZE}} \ \underline{\text{ERROR}} \text{ imperative-statement} \right]$$

$\underline{\text{SUPPRESS}}$ PRINTING

$\underline{\text{TERMINATE}}$ report-name-1 $\left[\text{, report-name-2} \right] \cdots$

$\underline{\text{UNSTRING}}$ identifier-1

$$\left[\underline{\text{DELIMITED}} \text{ BY } \left[\underline{\text{ALL}} \right] \left\{ \begin{array}{l} \text{identifier-2} \\ \text{literal-1} \end{array} \right\} \left[\text{, } \underline{\text{OR}} \left[\underline{\text{ALL}} \right] \left\{ \begin{array}{l} \text{identifier-3} \\ \text{literal-2} \end{array} \right\} \right] \cdots \right]$$

$$\underline{\text{INTO}} \text{ identifier-4} \left[\text{, } \underline{\text{DELIMITER}} \text{ IN identifier-5} \right] \left[\text{, } \underline{\text{COUNT}} \text{ IN identifier-6} \right]$$

$$\left[\text{, identifier-7} \left[\text{, } \underline{\text{DELIMITER}} \text{ IN identifier-8} \right] \left[\text{, } \underline{\text{COUNT}} \text{ IN identifier-9} \right] \right] \cdots$$

$$\left[\text{WITH } \underline{\text{POINTER}} \text{ identifier-10} \right] \left[\underline{\text{TALLYING}} \text{ IN identifier-11} \right]$$

$$\left[; \text{ ON } \underline{\text{OVERFLOW}} \text{ imperative-statement} \right]$$

$$\underline{\text{USE}} \ \underline{\text{AFTER}} \text{ STANDARD} \left\{ \begin{array}{l} \underline{\text{EXCEPTION}} \\ \underline{\text{ERROR}} \end{array} \right\} \underline{\text{PROCEDURE}} \text{ ON} \left\{ \begin{array}{l} \text{file-name-1} \left[\text{, file-name-2} \right] \cdots \\ \underline{\text{INPUT}} \\ \underline{\text{OUTPUT}} \\ \underline{\text{I-O}} \\ \underline{\text{EXTEND}} \end{array} \right\}.$$

$$\underline{\text{USE}} \ \underline{\text{AFTER}} \text{ STANDARD} \left\{ \begin{array}{l} \underline{\text{EXCEPTION}} \\ \underline{\text{ERROR}} \end{array} \right\} \underline{\text{PROCEDURE}} \text{ ON} \left\{ \begin{array}{l} \text{file-name-1} \left[\text{, file-name-2} \right] \cdots \\ \underline{\text{INPUT}} \\ \underline{\text{OUTPUT}} \\ \underline{\text{I-O}} \end{array} \right\}.$$

$\underline{\text{USE}} \ \underline{\text{BEFORE}} \ \underline{\text{REPORTING}}$ identifier.

$$\underline{\text{USE}} \text{ FOR } \underline{\text{DEBUGGING}} \text{ ON} \left\{ \begin{array}{l} \text{cd-name-1} \\ \left[\underline{\text{ALL}} \text{ REFERENCES OF} \right] \text{ identifier-1} \\ \text{file-name-1} \\ \text{procedure-name-1} \\ \underline{\text{ALL}} \ \underline{\text{PROCEDURES}} \end{array} \right\}$$

$$\left[\text{, } \begin{array}{l} \text{cd-name-2} \\ \left[\underline{\text{ALL}} \text{ REFERENCES OF} \right] \text{ identifier-2} \\ \text{file-name-2} \\ \text{procedure-name-2} \\ \underline{\text{ALL}} \ \underline{\text{PROCEDURES}} \end{array} \right] \cdots .$$

WRITE record-name [FROM identifier-1]

$$\left[\left\{ {BEFORE \atop AFTER} \right\} \text{ADVANCING} \left\{ {\left\{ {identifier-2 \atop integer} \right\} \left[{LINE \atop LINES} \right] \atop \left\{ mnemonic-name \atop PAGE \right\}} \right\} \right]$$

$$\left[; AT \left\{ {END-OF-PAGE \atop EOP} \right\} \text{imperative-statement} \right]$$

WRITE record-name [FROM identifier] [; INVALID KEY imperative-statement]

GENERAL FORMAT FOR CONDITIONS

RELATION CONDITION:

$$\left\{ {identifier-1 \atop literal-1 \atop arithmetic-expression-1 \atop index-name-1} \right\} \left\{ {IS [NOT] \underline{GREATER} THAN \atop IS [NOT] \underline{LESS} THAN \atop IS [NOT] \underline{EQUAL} TO \atop IS [NOT] > \atop IS [NOT] < \atop IS [NOT] =} \right\} \left\{ {identifier-2 \atop literal-2 \atop arithmetic-expression-2 \atop index-name-2} \right\}$$

CLASS CONDITION:

identifier IS [NOT] $\left\{ {NUMERIC \atop ALPHABETIC} \right\}$

SIGN CONDITION:

arithmetic-expression IS [NOT] $\left\{ {POSITIVE \atop NEGATIVE \atop ZERO} \right\}$

CONDITION-NAME CONDITION:

condition-name

SWITCH-STATUS CONDITION:

condition-name

NEGATED SIMPLE CONDITION:

NOT simple-condition

COMBINED CONDITION:

$$\text{condition} \ \left\{ \left\{ \frac{\text{AND}}{\text{OR}} \right\} \ \text{condition} \right\} \ \dots$$

ABBREVIATED COMBINED RELATION CONDITION:

$$\text{relation-condition} \ \left\{ \left\{ \frac{\text{AND}}{\text{OR}} \right\} \ [\underline{\text{NOT}}] \ \big[\text{relational-operator} \big] \ \text{object} \right\} \ \dots$$

MISCELLANEOUS FORMATS

QUALIFICATION:

$$\left\{ \begin{matrix} \text{data-name-1} \\ \text{condition-name} \end{matrix} \right\} \ \left[\left\{ \frac{\text{OF}}{\text{IN}} \right\} \ \text{data-name-2} \right] \ \dots$$

$$\text{paragraph-name} \ \left[\left\{ \frac{\text{OF}}{\text{IN}} \right\} \ \text{section-name} \right]$$

$$\text{text-name} \ \left[\left\{ \frac{\text{OF}}{\text{IN}} \right\} \ \text{library-name} \right]$$

SUBSCRIPTING:

$$\left\{ \begin{matrix} \text{data-name} \\ \text{condition-name} \end{matrix} \right\} \ (\text{subscript-1} \ [, \ \text{subscript-2} \ [, \ \text{subscript-3}]] \ )$$

INDEXING:

$$\left\{ \begin{matrix} \text{data-name} \\ \text{condition-name} \end{matrix} \right\} \ \left(\ \left\{ \begin{matrix} \text{index-name-1} \ [\{\pm\} \ \text{literal-2}] \\ \text{literal-1} \end{matrix} \right\} \right.$$

$$\left[, \ \left\{ \begin{matrix} \text{index-name-2} \ [\{\pm\} \ \text{literal-4}] \\ \text{literal-3} \end{matrix} \right\} \left[, \ \left\{ \begin{matrix} \text{index-name-3} \ [\{\pm\} \ \text{literal-6}] \\ \text{literal-5} \end{matrix} \right\} \right] \right] \ )$$

IDENTIFIER: FORMAT 1

$$\text{data-name-1} \ \left[\left\{ \frac{\text{OF}}{\text{IN}} \right\} \ \text{data-name-2} \right] \ \dots \ \Big[(\text{subscript-1} \ [, \ \text{subscript-2}$$

$$[, \ \text{subscript-3}] \ ] \ ) \Big]$$

D. GENERAL FORM OF COBOL-85 ELEMENTS

GENERAL FORMAT FOR IDENTIFICATION DIVISION

IDENTIFICATION DIVISION.

PROGRAM-ID. program-name $\left[\text{IS} \left\{ \left| \begin{matrix} \underline{\text{COMMON}} \\ \underline{\text{INITIAL}} \end{matrix} \right| \right\} \text{PROGRAM} \right]$.

[AUTHOR. [comment-entry] ...]

[INSTALLATION. [comment-entry] ...]

[DATE-WRITTEN. [comment-entry] ...]

[DATE-COMPILED. [comment-entry] ...]

[SECURITY. [comment-entry] ...]

GENERAL FORMAT FOR ENVIRONMENT DIVISION

[ENVIRONMENT DIVISION.

[CONFIGURATION SECTION.

[SOURCE-COMPUTER. [computer-name [WITH DEBUGGING MODE].]]

[OBJECT-COMPUTER. [computer-name

$$\left[\underline{\text{MEMORY}} \text{ SIZE integer-1} \left\{ \begin{matrix} \underline{\text{WORDS}} \\ \underline{\text{CHARACTERS}} \\ \underline{\text{MODULES}} \end{matrix} \right\} \right]$$

[PROGRAM COLLATING SEQUENCE IS alphabet-name-1]

[SEGMENT-LIMIT IS segment-number].]]

```
[SPECIAL-NAMES.  [[ implementor-name-1

         ⎧ IS mnemonic-name-1 [ON STATUS IS condition-name-1 [OFF STATUS IS condition-name-2]] ⎫
         ⎪ IS mnemonic-name-2 [OFF STATUS IS condition-name-2 [ON STATUS IS condition-name-1]] ⎪ ...
         ⎨ ON STATUS IS condition-name-1 [OFF STATUS IS condition-name-2]                       ⎬
         ⎩ OFF STATUS IS condition-name-2 [ON STATUS IS condition-name-1]                       ⎭

    [ALPHABET alphabet-name-1 IS

              ⎧ STANDARD-1                                         ⎫
              ⎪ STANDARD-2                                         ⎪
              ⎪ NATIVE                                             ⎪
              ⎨ implementor-name-2                                 ⎬ ...
              ⎪           ⎡ ⎧THROUGH⎫              ⎤                ⎪
              ⎪ ⎧         ⎢ ⎨       ⎬  literal-2   ⎥ ⎫              ⎪
              ⎩ ⎨literal-1⎢ ⎩THRU   ⎭              ⎥ ⎬ ...          ⎭
                ⎩         ⎣ {ALSO literal-3} ...   ⎦ ⎭

    ⎡ SYMBOLIC CHARACTERS ⎧ ⎧ {symbolic-character-1} ... ⎧IS ⎫ {integer-1} ... ⎫ ...
    ⎢                     ⎨ ⎨                            ⎩ARE⎭                  ⎬
    ⎢       [IN alphabet-name-2] ⎭ ⎦ ...
                                       ⎭

    ⎡                          ⎧          ⎡ ⎧THROUGH⎫           ⎤ ⎫     ⎤
    ⎢ CLASS class-name-1 IS    ⎨ literal-4⎢ ⎨       ⎬ literal-5 ⎥ ⎬ ... ⎥ ...
    ⎣                          ⎩          ⎣ ⎩THRU   ⎭           ⎦ ⎭     ⎦
    [CURRENCY SIGN IS literal-6]

    [DECIMAL-POINT IS COMMA].]]]

[INPUT-OUTPUT SECTION.

FILE-CONTROL.

    {file-control-entry} ...

[I-O-CONTROL.

  ⎡ ⎡                                            ⎧ ⎧ [END OF] ⎧REEL⎫ ⎫                    ⎫ ⎤
  ⎢ ⎢        ⎡    ⎧file-name-1          ⎫ ⎤      ⎪ ⎨          ⎩UNIT⎭ ⎬ OF file-name-2     ⎪ ⎥ ...
  ⎢ ⎢ RERUN  ⎢ ON ⎨                     ⎬ ⎥ EVERY⎨ ⎩ integer-1 RECORDS ⎭                  ⎬ ⎥
  ⎢ ⎣        ⎣    ⎩implementor-name-1   ⎭ ⎦      ⎪ integer-2 CLOCK-UNITS                   ⎪ ⎥
  ⎢                                             ⎩ condition-name-1                        ⎭ ⎦

  ⎡       ⎡ RECORD     ⎤                                         ⎤
  ⎢ SAME  ⎢ SORT       ⎥ AREA FOR file-name-3 {file-name-4} ... ⎥ ...
  ⎣       ⎣ SORT-MERGE ⎦                                         ⎦

  [MULTIPLE FILE TAPE CONTAINS  {file-name-5 [POSITION integer-3]} ... ] ... .]]]]
```

GENERAL FORMAT FOR FILE CONTROL ENTRY

SEQUENTIAL FILE:

SELECT [OPTIONAL] file-name-1

   ASSIGN TO $\begin{Bmatrix} \text{implementor-name-1} \\ \text{literal-1} \end{Bmatrix}$ ...

   $\left[\underline{\text{RESERVE}} \text{ integer-1} \begin{bmatrix} \text{AREA} \\ \text{AREAS} \end{bmatrix} \right]$

   [[ORGANIZATION IS] SEQUENTIAL]

   $\left[\underline{\text{PADDING}} \text{ CHARACTER IS } \begin{Bmatrix} \text{data-name-1} \\ \text{literal-2} \end{Bmatrix} \right]$

   $\left[\underline{\text{RECORD}} \underline{\text{ DELIMITER}} \text{ IS } \begin{Bmatrix} \underline{\text{STANDARD-1}} \\ \text{implementor-name-2} \end{Bmatrix} \right]$

   [ACCESS MODE IS SEQUENTIAL]

   [FILE STATUS IS data-name-2].

RELATIVE FILE:

SELECT [OPTIONAL] file-name-1

   ASSIGN TO $\begin{Bmatrix} \text{implementor-name-1} \\ \text{literal-1} \end{Bmatrix}$ ...

   $\left[\underline{\text{RESERVE}} \text{ integer-1} \begin{bmatrix} \text{AREA} \\ \text{AREAS} \end{bmatrix} \right]$

   [ORGANIZATION IS] RELATIVE

   $\left[\underline{\text{ACCESS}} \text{ MODE IS } \begin{Bmatrix} \underline{\text{SEQUENTIAL}} & [\underline{\text{RELATIVE}} \text{ KEY IS data-name-1}] \\ \begin{Bmatrix} \underline{\text{RANDOM}} \\ \underline{\text{DYNAMIC}} \end{Bmatrix} & \underline{\text{RELATIVE}} \text{ KEY IS data-name-1} \end{Bmatrix} \right]$

   [FILE STATUS IS data-name-2].

<u>INDEXED FILE</u>:

<u>SELECT</u> [<u>OPTIONAL</u>] file-name-1

    <u>ASSIGN</u> TO $\begin{Bmatrix} \text{implementor-name-1} \\ \text{literal-1} \end{Bmatrix}$ ...

    $\left[\underline{\text{RESERVE}} \text{ integer-1} \begin{bmatrix} \text{AREA} \\ \text{AREAS} \end{bmatrix} \right]$

    [<u>ORGANIZATION</u> IS] <u>INDEXED</u>

    $\left[\underline{\text{ACCESS}} \text{ MODE IS} \begin{Bmatrix} \underline{\text{SEQUENTIAL}} \\ \underline{\text{RANDOM}} \\ \underline{\text{DYNAMIC}} \end{Bmatrix} \right]$

    <u>RECORD</u> KEY IS data-name-1

    [<u>ALTERNATE</u> <u>RECORD</u> KEY IS data-name-2 [WITH <u>DUPLICATES</u>]] ...

    [FILE <u>STATUS</u> IS data-name-3].

<u>SORT OR MERGE FILE</u>:

<u>SELECT</u> file-name-1 <u>ASSIGN</u> TO $\begin{Bmatrix} \text{implementor-name-1} \\ \text{literal-1} \end{Bmatrix}$ ... .

<u>REPORT FILE</u>:

<u>SELECT</u> [<u>OPTIONAL</u>] file-name-1

    <u>ASSIGN</u> TO $\begin{Bmatrix} \text{implementor-name-1} \\ \text{literal-1} \end{Bmatrix}$ ...

    $\left[\underline{\text{RESERVE}} \text{ integer-1} \begin{bmatrix} \text{AREA} \\ \text{AREAS} \end{bmatrix} \right]$

    [[<u>ORGANIZATION</u> IS] <u>SEQUENTIAL</u>]]

    $\left[\underline{\text{PADDING}} \text{ CHARACTER IS} \begin{Bmatrix} \text{data-name-1} \\ \text{literal-2} \end{Bmatrix} \right]$

    $\left[\underline{\text{RECORD}} \text{ } \underline{\text{DELIMITER}} \text{ IS} \begin{Bmatrix} \underline{\text{STANDARD-1}} \\ \text{implementor-name-2} \end{Bmatrix} \right]$

    [<u>ACCESS</u> MODE IS <u>SEQUENTIAL</u>]

    [FILE <u>STATUS</u> IS data-name-2].

GENERAL FORMAT FOR DATA DIVISION

[DATA DIVISION.

[FILE SECTION.

$$\begin{bmatrix} \text{file-description-entry \{record-description-entry\} ...} \\ \text{sort-merge-file-description-entry \{record-description-entry\} ...} \\ \text{report-file-description-entry} \end{bmatrix} ...$$

[WORKING-STORAGE SECTION.

$$\begin{bmatrix} \text{77-level-description-entry} \\ \text{record-description-entry} \end{bmatrix} ...$$

[LINKAGE SECTION.

$$\begin{bmatrix} \text{77-level-description-entry} \\ \text{record-description-entry} \end{bmatrix} ...$$

[COMMUNICATION SECTION.

[communication-description-entry [record-description-entry] ...] ...]

[REPORT SECTION.

[report-description-entry {report-group-description-entry} ...] ...]]

<u>GENERAL FORMAT FOR FILE DESCRIPTION ENTRY</u>

<u>SEQUENTIAL FILE</u>:

<u>FD</u>   file-name-1

   [IS <u>EXTERNAL</u>]

   [IS <u>GLOBAL</u>]

$$\left[\underline{BLOCK} \text{ CONTAINS } [\text{integer-1 } \underline{TO}] \quad \text{integer-2} \left\{ \begin{array}{l} \underline{RECORDS} \\ \underline{CHARACTERS} \end{array} \right\} \right]$$

$$\left[\underline{RECORD} \left\{ \begin{array}{l} \text{CONTAINS integer-3 CHARACTERS} \\ \text{IS } \underline{VARYING} \text{ IN SIZE } [[\text{FROM integer-4}] \ [\underline{TO} \text{ integer-5}] \text{ CHARACTERS}] \\ \qquad [\underline{DEPENDING} \text{ ON data-name-1}] \\ \text{CONTAINS integer-6 } \underline{TO} \text{ integer-7 CHARACTERS} \end{array} \right\} \right]$$

$$\left[\underline{LABEL} \left\{ \begin{array}{l} \underline{RECORD} \text{ IS} \\ \underline{RECORDS} \text{ ARE} \end{array} \right\} \left\{ \begin{array}{l} \underline{STANDARD} \\ \underline{OMITTED} \end{array} \right\} \right]$$

$$\left[\underline{VALUE} \ \underline{OF} \left\{ \text{implementor-name-1 IS } \left\{ \begin{array}{l} \text{data-name-2} \\ \text{literal-1} \end{array} \right\} \right\} \cdots \right]$$

$$\left[\underline{DATA} \left\{ \begin{array}{l} \underline{RECORD} \text{ IS} \\ \underline{RECORDS} \text{ ARE} \end{array} \right\} \ \{\text{data-name-3}\} \ \cdots \right]$$

$$\left[\underline{LINAGE} \text{ IS } \left\{ \begin{array}{l} \text{data-name-4} \\ \text{integer-8} \end{array} \right\} \text{ LINES } \left[\text{WITH } \underline{FOOTING} \text{ AT } \left\{ \begin{array}{l} \text{data-name-5} \\ \text{integer-9} \end{array} \right\} \right] \right.$$

$$\left. \left[\text{LINES AT } \underline{TOP} \left\{ \begin{array}{l} \text{data-name-6} \\ \text{integer-10} \end{array} \right\} \right] \left[\text{LINES AT } \underline{BOTTOM} \left\{ \begin{array}{l} \text{data-name-7} \\ \text{integer-11} \end{array} \right\} \right] \right]$$

[<u>CODE-SET</u> IS alphabet-name-1].

RELATIVE FILE:

FD   file-name-1

   [IS EXTERNAL]

   [IS GLOBAL]

   $\left[\text{BLOCK CONTAINS [integer-1 TO] integer-2} \left\{\begin{array}{l}\text{RECORDS}\\\text{CHARACTERS}\end{array}\right\}\right]$

   $\left[\text{RECORD} \left\{\begin{array}{l}\text{CONTAINS integer-3 CHARACTERS}\\\text{IS VARYING IN SIZE [[FROM integer-4] [TO integer-5] CHARACTERS]}\\\quad\text{[DEPENDING ON data-name-1]}\\\text{CONTAINS integer-6 TO integer-7 CHARACTERS}\end{array}\right\}\right]$

   $\left[\text{LABEL} \left\{\begin{array}{l}\text{RECORD IS}\\\text{RECORDS ARE}\end{array}\right\} \left\{\begin{array}{l}\text{STANDARD}\\\text{OMITTED}\end{array}\right\}\right]$

   $\left[\text{VALUE OF} \left\{\text{implementor-name-1 IS} \left\{\begin{array}{l}\text{data-name-2}\\\text{literal-1}\end{array}\right\}\right\} \ldots\right]$

   $\left[\text{DATA} \left\{\begin{array}{l}\text{RECORD IS}\\\text{RECORDS ARE}\end{array}\right\} \{\text{data-name-3}\} \ldots\right].$

INDEXED FILE:

FD   file-name-1

   [IS EXTERNAL]

   [IS GLOBAL]

   $\left[\text{BLOCK CONTAINS [integer-1 TO] integer-2} \left\{\begin{array}{l}\text{RECORDS}\\\text{CHARACTERS}\end{array}\right\}\right]$

   $\left[\text{RECORD} \left\{\begin{array}{l}\text{CONTAINS integer-3 CHARACTERS}\\\text{IS VARYING IN SIZE [[FROM integer-4] [TO integer-5] CHARACTERS]}\\\quad\text{[DEPENDING ON data-name-1]}\\\text{CONTAINS integer-6 TO integer-7 CHARACTERS}\end{array}\right\}\right]$

   $\left[\text{LABEL} \left\{\begin{array}{l}\text{RECORD IS}\\\text{RECORDS ARE}\end{array}\right\} \left\{\begin{array}{l}\text{STANDARD}\\\text{OMITTED}\end{array}\right\}\right]$

   $\left[\text{VALUE OF} \left\{\text{implementor-name-1 IS} \left\{\begin{array}{l}\text{data-name-2}\\\text{literal-1}\end{array}\right\}\right\} \ldots\right]$

   $\left[\text{DATA} \left\{\begin{array}{l}\text{RECORD IS}\\\text{RECORDS ARE}\end{array}\right\} \{\text{data-name-3}\} \ldots\right].$

SORT-MERGE FILE:

SD   file-name-1

$$
\left[\underline{RECORD}\ \left\{ \begin{array}{l} \text{CONTAINS integer-1 CHARACTERS} \\ \text{IS } \underline{VARYING} \text{ IN SIZE [[FROM integer-2] [}\underline{TO}\text{ integer-3] CHARACTERS]} \\ \qquad \text{[}\underline{DEPENDING}\text{ ON data-name-1]} \\ \text{CONTAINS integer-4 } \underline{TO}\text{ integer-5 CHARACTERS} \end{array} \right\} \right]
$$

$$
\left[\underline{DATA}\ \left\{ \begin{array}{l} \underline{RECORD}\text{ IS} \\ \underline{RECORDS}\text{ ARE} \end{array} \right\}\ \{\text{data-name-2}\}\ \ldots \right]\ .
$$

REPORT FILE:

FD   file-name-1

[IS EXTERNAL]

[IS GLOBAL]

$$
\left[\underline{BLOCK}\text{ CONTAINS [integer-1 }\underline{TO}\text{] integer-2 } \left\{ \begin{array}{l} \underline{RECORDS} \\ \text{CHARACTERS} \end{array} \right\} \right]
$$

$$
\left[\underline{RECORD}\ \left\{ \begin{array}{l} \text{CONTAINS integer-3 CHARACTERS} \\ \text{CONTAINS integer-4 } \underline{TO}\text{ integer-5 CHARACTERS} \end{array} \right\} \right]
$$

$$
\left[\underline{LABEL}\ \left\{ \begin{array}{l} \underline{RECORD}\text{ IS} \\ \underline{RECORDS}\text{ ARE} \end{array} \right\}\ \left\{ \begin{array}{l} \underline{STANDARD} \\ \underline{OMITTED} \end{array} \right\} \right]
$$

$$
\left[\underline{VALUE}\ \underline{OF}\ \left\{ \text{implementor-name-1 IS } \left\{ \begin{array}{l} \text{data-name-1} \\ \text{literal-1} \end{array} \right\} \right\}\ \ldots \right]
$$

[CODE-SET IS alphabet-name-1]

$$
\left\{ \begin{array}{l} \underline{REPORT}\text{ IS} \\ \underline{REPORTS}\text{ ARE} \end{array} \right\}\ \{\text{report-name-1}\}\ \ldots\ \ .
$$

GENERAL FORMAT FOR DATA DESCRIPTION ENTRY

FORMAT 1:

level-number $\begin{bmatrix} \text{data-name-1} \\ \text{FILLER} \end{bmatrix}$

[REDEFINES data-name-2]

[IS EXTERNAL]

[IS GLOBAL]

$\left[\begin{Bmatrix} \text{PICTURE} \\ \text{PIC} \end{Bmatrix} \text{ IS character-string} \right]$

$\left[\text{[USAGE IS]} \begin{Bmatrix} \text{BINARY} \\ \text{COMPUTATIONAL} \\ \text{COMP} \\ \text{DISPLAY} \\ \text{INDEX} \\ \text{PACKED-DECIMAL} \end{Bmatrix} \right]$

$\left[\text{[SIGN IS]} \begin{Bmatrix} \text{LEADING} \\ \text{TRAILING} \end{Bmatrix} \text{[SEPARATE CHARACTER]} \right]$

$\begin{bmatrix} \text{OCCURS integer-2 TIMES} \\ \qquad \left[\begin{Bmatrix} \text{ASCENDING} \\ \text{DESCENDING} \end{Bmatrix} \text{KEY IS } \{\text{data-name-3}\} \dots \right] \dots \\ \qquad \text{[INDEXED BY } \{\text{index-name-1}\} \dots] \\ \text{OCCURS integer-1 TO integer-2 TIMES DEPENDING ON data-name-4} \\ \qquad \left[\begin{Bmatrix} \text{ASCENDING} \\ \text{DESCENDING} \end{Bmatrix} \text{KEY IS } \{\text{data-name-3}\} \dots \right] \dots \\ \qquad \text{[INDEXED BY } \{\text{index-name-1}\} \dots] \end{bmatrix}$

$\left[\begin{Bmatrix} \text{SYNCHRONIZED} \\ \text{SYNC} \end{Bmatrix} \begin{bmatrix} \text{LEFT} \\ \text{RIGHT} \end{bmatrix} \right]$

$\left[\begin{Bmatrix} \text{JUSTIFIED} \\ \text{JUST} \end{Bmatrix} \text{RIGHT} \right]$

[BLANK WHEN ZERO]

[VALUE IS literal-1].

FORMAT 2:

66 data-name-1 <u>RENAMES</u> data-name-2 $\left[\begin{Bmatrix} \underline{THROUGH} \\ \underline{THRU} \end{Bmatrix} \text{data-name-3} \right]$.

FORMAT 3:

88 condition-name-1 $\begin{Bmatrix} \underline{VALUE} \text{ IS} \\ \underline{VALUES} \text{ ARE} \end{Bmatrix}$ $\begin{Bmatrix} \text{literal-1} \left[\begin{Bmatrix} \underline{THROUGH} \\ \underline{THRU} \end{Bmatrix} \text{literal-2} \right] \end{Bmatrix}$ ... .

GENERAL FORMAT FOR COMMUNICATION DESCRIPTION ENTRY

FORMAT 1:

<u>CD</u> cd-name-1

FOR [<u>INITIAL</u>] <u>INPUT</u>

$$
\left[
\begin{array}{l}
\text{[[SYMBOLIC } \underline{QUEUE} \text{ IS data-name-1]} \\
\quad \text{[SYMBOLIC } \underline{SUB\text{-}QUEUE\text{-}1} \text{ IS data-name-2]} \\
\quad \text{[SYMBOLIC } \underline{SUB\text{-}QUEUE\text{-}2} \text{ IS data-name-3]} \\
\quad \text{[SYMBOLIC } \underline{SUB\text{-}QUEUE\text{-}3} \text{ IS data-name-4]} \\
\quad \text{[}\underline{MESSAGE} \text{ } \underline{DATE} \text{ IS data-name-5]} \\
\quad \text{[}\underline{MESSAGE} \text{ } \underline{TIME} \text{ IS data-name-6]} \\
\quad \text{[SYMBOLIC } \underline{SOURCE} \text{ IS data-name-7]} \\
\quad \text{[}\underline{TEXT} \text{ } \underline{LENGTH} \text{ IS data-name-8]} \\
\quad \text{[}\underline{END} \text{ } \underline{KEY} \text{ IS data-name-9]} \\
\quad \text{[}\underline{STATUS} \text{ } \underline{KEY} \text{ IS data-name-10]} \\
\quad \text{[}\underline{MESSAGE} \text{ } \underline{COUNT} \text{ IS data-name-11]]} \\
\text{[data-name-1, data-name-2, data-name-3,} \\
\quad \text{data-name-4, data-name-5, data-name-6,} \\
\quad \text{data-name-7, data-name-8, data-name-9,} \\
\quad \text{data-name-10, data-name-11]}
\end{array}
\right]
$$

FORMAT 2:

CD   cd-name-1 FOR OUTPUT

    [DESTINATION COUNT IS data-name-1]

    [TEXT LENGTH IS data-name-2]

    [STATUS KEY IS data-name-3]

    [DESTINATION TABLE OCCURS integer-1 TIMES

        [INDEXED BY {index-name-1} ...]]

    [ERROR KEY IS data-name-4]

    [SYMBOLIC DESTINATION IS data-name-5].

FORMAT 3:

CD   cd-name-1

$$
\text{FOR } [\underline{\text{INITIAL}}] \ \underline{\text{I-O}}
\begin{bmatrix}
[[\text{MESSAGE DATE IS data-name-1}] \\
\quad [\text{MESSAGE TIME IS data-name-2}] \\
\quad [\text{SYMBOLIC TERMINAL IS data-name-3}] \\
\quad [\text{TEXT LENGTH IS data-name-4}] \\
\quad [\text{END KEY IS data-name-5}] \\
\quad [\text{STATUS KEY IS data-name-6}]] \\
[\text{data-name-1, data-name-2, data-name-3,} \\
\quad \text{data-name-4, data-name-5, data-name-6}]
\end{bmatrix}
$$

GENERAL FORMAT FOR REPORT DESCRIPTION ENTRY

RD report-name-1

   [IS GLOBAL]

   [CODE literal-1]

$$\left[\left\{ \begin{array}{l} \underline{CONTROL} \ IS \\ \underline{CONTROLS} \ ARE \end{array} \right\} \quad \left\{ \begin{array}{l} \{data\text{-}name\text{-}1\} \ ... \\ \underline{FINAL} \ [data\text{-}name\text{-}1] \ ... \end{array} \right\} \right]$$

$$\left[\underline{PAGE} \left[\begin{array}{l} LIMIT \ IS \\ LIMITS \ ARE \end{array} \right] integer\text{-}1 \left[\begin{array}{l} LINE \\ LINES \end{array} \right] [\underline{HEADING} \ integer\text{-}2] \right.$$

$$[\underline{FIRST} \ \underline{DETAIL} \ integer\text{-}3] \quad [\underline{LAST} \ \underline{DETAIL} \ integer\text{-}4]$$

$$\left. [\underline{FOOTING} \ integer\text{-}5] \right] .$$

GENERAL FORMAT FOR REPORT GROUP DESCRIPTION ENTRY

FORMAT 1:

01 [data-name-1]

$$\left[\underline{LINE} \ NUMBER \ IS \ \left\{ \begin{array}{l} integer\text{-}1 \ [ON \ \underline{NEXT} \ \underline{PAGE}] \\ \underline{PLUS} \ integer\text{-}2 \end{array} \right\} \right]$$

$$\left[\underline{NEXT} \ \underline{GROUP} \ IS \ \left\{ \begin{array}{l} integer\text{-}3 \\ \underline{PLUS} \ integer\text{-}4 \\ \underline{NEXT} \ \underline{PAGE} \end{array} \right\} \right]$$

$$\underline{TYPE} \ IS \ \left\{ \begin{array}{l} \left\{ \begin{array}{l} \underline{REPORT} \ \underline{HEADING} \\ \underline{RH} \end{array} \right\} \\ \left\{ \begin{array}{l} \underline{PAGE} \ \underline{HEADING} \\ \underline{PH} \end{array} \right\} \\ \left\{ \begin{array}{l} \underline{CONTROL} \ \underline{HEADING} \\ \underline{CH} \end{array} \right\} \left\{ \begin{array}{l} data\text{-}name\text{-}2 \\ \underline{FINAL} \end{array} \right\} \\ \left\{ \begin{array}{l} \underline{DETAIL} \\ \underline{DE} \end{array} \right\} \\ \left\{ \begin{array}{l} \underline{CONTROL} \ \underline{FOOTING} \\ \underline{CF} \end{array} \right\} \left\{ \begin{array}{l} data\text{-}name\text{-}3 \\ \underline{FINAL} \end{array} \right\} \\ \left\{ \begin{array}{l} \underline{PAGE} \ \underline{FOOTING} \\ \underline{PF} \end{array} \right\} \\ \left\{ \begin{array}{l} \underline{REPORT} \ \underline{FOOTING} \\ \underline{RF} \end{array} \right\} \end{array} \right\}$$

   [[USAGE IS] DISPLAY].

GENERAL FORMAT FOR REPORT GROUP DESCRIPTION ENTRY

FORMAT 2:

level-number [data-name-1]

$$\left[\text{\underline{LINE} NUMBER IS} \left\{ \begin{array}{l} \text{integer-1 [ON \underline{NEXT} \underline{PAGE}]} \\ \text{\underline{PLUS} Integer-2} \end{array} \right\} \right]$$

[[USAGE IS] DISPLAY].

FORMAT 3:

level-number [data-name-1]

$$\left\{ \begin{array}{l} \text{\underline{PICTURE}} \\ \text{\underline{PIC}} \end{array} \right\} \text{ IS character-string}$$

[[USAGE IS] DISPLAY]

$$\left[\text{[\underline{SIGN} IS]} \left\{ \begin{array}{l} \text{\underline{LEADING}} \\ \text{\underline{TRAILING}} \end{array} \right\} \text{\underline{SEPARATE} CHARACTER} \right]$$

$$\left[\left\{ \begin{array}{l} \text{\underline{JUSTIFIED}} \\ \text{\underline{JUST}} \end{array} \right\} \text{ RIGHT} \right]$$

[BLANK WHEN ZERO]

$$\left[\text{\underline{LINE} NUMBER IS} \left\{ \begin{array}{l} \text{integer-1 [ON \underline{NEXT} \underline{PAGE}]} \\ \text{\underline{PLUS} integer-2} \end{array} \right\} \right]$$

[COLUMN NUMBER IS integer-3]

$$\left\{ \begin{array}{l} \text{\underline{SOURCE} IS identifier-1} \\[1ex] \text{\underline{VALUE} IS literal-1} \\[1ex] \text{\{\underline{SUM} \{identifier-2\} ... [\underline{UPON} \{data-name-2\} ...]\} ...} \\[1ex] \quad \left[\text{\underline{RESET} ON} \left\{ \begin{array}{l} \text{data-name-3} \\ \text{\underline{FINAL}} \end{array} \right\} \right] \end{array} \right\}$$

[GROUP INDICATE].

GENERAL FORMAT FOR PROCEDURE DIVISION

FORMAT 1:

[PROCEDURE DIVISION [USING {data-name-1} ...].

[DECLARATIVES.

{section-name SECTION [segment-number].

    USE statement.

[paragraph-name.

    [sentence] ...] ... } ...

END DECLARATIVES.]

{section-name SECTION [segment-number].

[paragraph-name.

    [sentence] ...] ... } ...]

FORMAT 2:

[PROCEDURE DIVISION [USING {data-name-1} ...].

{paragraph-name.

    [sentence] ... } ...]

GENERAL FORMAT FOR COBOL VERBS

ACCEPT identifier-1 [FROM mnemonic-name-1]

ACCEPT identifier-2 FROM $\left\{ \begin{array}{l} \text{DATE} \\ \text{DAY} \\ \text{DAY-OF-WEEK} \\ \text{TIME} \end{array} \right\}$

ACCEPT cd-name-1 MESSAGE COUNT

ADD $\left\{ \begin{array}{l} \text{identifier-1} \\ \text{literal-1} \end{array} \right\}$ ... TO {identifier-2 [ROUNDED]} ...

   [ON SIZE ERROR imperative-statement-1]

   [NOT ON SIZE ERROR imperative-statement-2]

   [END-ADD]

ADD $\left\{ \begin{array}{l} \text{identifier-1} \\ \text{literal-1} \end{array} \right\}$ ... TO $\left\{ \begin{array}{l} \text{identifier-2} \\ \text{literal-2} \end{array} \right\}$

   GIVING {identifier-3 [ROUNDED]} ...

   [ON SIZE ERROR imperative-statement-1]

   [NOT ON SIZE ERROR imperative-statement-2]

   [END-ADD]

ADD $\left\{ \begin{array}{l} \text{CORRESPONDING} \\ \text{CORR} \end{array} \right\}$ identifier-1 TO identifier-2 [ROUNDED]

   [ON SIZE ERROR imperative-statement-1]

   [NOT ON SIZE ERROR imperative-statement-2]

   [END-ADD]

ALTER {procedure-name-1 TO [PROCEED TO] procedure-name-2} ...

CALL $\left\{ \begin{array}{l} \text{identifier-1} \\ \text{literal-1} \end{array} \right\}$ $\left[\text{USING} \left\{ \begin{array}{l} \text{[BY REFERENCE] \{identifier-2\} ...} \\ \text{BY CONTENT \{identifier-2\} ...} \end{array} \right\} ... \right]$

   [ON OVERFLOW imperative-statement-1]

   [END-CALL]

CALL {identifier-1} [USING {[BY REFERENCE] {identifier-2} ...} ...]
      {literal-1   }   {BY CONTENT   {identifier-2} ... }

    [ON EXCEPTION imperative-statement-1]

    [NOT ON EXCEPTION imperative-statement-2]

    [END-CALL]

CANCEL {identifier-1} ...
        {literal-1   }

SW CLOSE {file-name-1 [{REEL} [FOR REMOVAL]   ]} ...
          {   [{UNIT}   ]}
          {   [WITH {NO REWIND}   ]}
          {   [{LOCK   }   ]}

RI CLOSE {file-name-1 [WITH LOCK]} ...

COMPUTE {identifier-1 [ROUNDED]} ... = arithmetic-expression-1

    [ON SIZE ERROR imperative-statement-1]

    [NOT ON SIZE ERROR imperative-statement-2]

    [END-COMPUTE]

CONTINUE

DELETE file-name-1 RECORD

    [INVALID KEY imperative-statement-1]

    [NOT INVALID KEY imperative-statement-2]

    [END-DELETE]

DISABLE {INPUT [TERMINAL]} cd-name-1 [WITH KEY {identifier-1}]
         {I-O TERMINAL   }   {literal-1   }
         {OUTPUT   }

DISPLAY $\begin{Bmatrix} \text{identifier-1} \\ \text{literal-1} \end{Bmatrix}$ ...   [<u>UPON</u> mnemonic-name-1]   [WITH <u>NO</u> <u>ADVANCING</u>]

<u>DIVIDE</u> $\begin{Bmatrix} \text{identifier-1} \\ \text{literal-1} \end{Bmatrix}$ <u>INTO</u> {identifier-2 [<u>ROUNDED</u>]} ...

    [ON <u>SIZE</u> <u>ERROR</u> imperative-statement-1]

    [<u>NOT</u> ON <u>SIZE</u> <u>ERROR</u> imperative-statement-2]

    [<u>END-DIVIDE</u>]

<u>DIVIDE</u> $\begin{Bmatrix} \text{identifier-1} \\ \text{literal-1} \end{Bmatrix}$ <u>INTO</u> $\begin{Bmatrix} \text{identifier-2} \\ \text{literal-2} \end{Bmatrix}$

    <u>GIVING</u>   {identifier-3 [<u>ROUNDED</u>]} ...

    [ON <u>SIZE</u> <u>ERROR</u> imperative-statement-1]

    [<u>NOT</u> ON <u>SIZE</u> <u>ERROR</u> imperative-statement-2]

    [<u>END-DIVIDE</u>]

<u>DIVIDE</u> $\begin{Bmatrix} \text{identifier-1} \\ \text{literal-1} \end{Bmatrix}$ <u>BY</u> $\begin{Bmatrix} \text{identifier-2} \\ \text{literal-2} \end{Bmatrix}$

    <u>GIVING</u>   {identifier-3 [<u>ROUNDED</u>]} ...

    [ON <u>SIZE</u> <u>ERROR</u> imperative-statement-1]

    [<u>NOT</u> ON <u>SIZE</u> <u>ERROR</u> imperative-statement-2]

    [<u>END-DIVIDE</u>]

<u>DIVIDE</u> $\begin{Bmatrix} \text{identifier-1} \\ \text{literal-1} \end{Bmatrix}$ <u>INTO</u> $\begin{Bmatrix} \text{identifier-2} \\ \text{literal-2} \end{Bmatrix}$ <u>GIVING</u> identifier-3 [<u>ROUNDED</u>]

    <u>REMAINDER</u> identifier-4

    [ON <u>SIZE</u> <u>ERROR</u> imperative-statement-1]

    [<u>NOT</u> ON <u>SIZE</u> <u>ERROR</u> imperative-statement-2]

    [<u>END-DIVIDE</u>]

DIVIDE $\begin{Bmatrix} \text{identifier-1} \\ \text{literal-1} \end{Bmatrix}$ BY $\begin{Bmatrix} \text{identifier-2} \\ \text{literal-2} \end{Bmatrix}$ GIVING identifier-3 [ROUNDED]

    REMAINDER identifier-4

    [ON SIZE ERROR imperative-statement-1]

    [NOT ON SIZE ERROR imperative-statement-2]

    [END-DIVIDE]

ENABLE $\begin{Bmatrix} \text{INPUT [TERMINAL]} \\ \text{I-O TERMINAL} \\ \text{OUTPUT} \end{Bmatrix}$ cd-name-1 $\left[\text{WITH KEY} \begin{Bmatrix} \text{identifier-1} \\ \text{literal-1} \end{Bmatrix}\right]$

ENTER language-name-1 [routine-name-1].

EVALUATE $\begin{Bmatrix} \text{identifier-1} \\ \text{literal-1} \\ \text{expression-1} \\ \text{TRUE} \\ \text{FALSE} \end{Bmatrix}$ $\left[\text{ALSO} \begin{Bmatrix} \text{identifier-2} \\ \text{literal-2} \\ \text{expression-2} \\ \text{TRUE} \\ \text{FALSE} \end{Bmatrix}\right]$ ...

  {{WHEN

$\begin{Bmatrix} \text{ANY} \\ \text{condition-1} \\ \text{TRUE} \\ \text{FALSE} \\ \text{[NOT]} \begin{Bmatrix} \text{identifier-3} \\ \text{literal-3} \\ \text{arithmetic-expression-1} \end{Bmatrix} \left[\begin{Bmatrix} \text{THROUGH} \\ \text{THRU} \end{Bmatrix} \begin{Bmatrix} \text{identifier-4} \\ \text{literal-4} \\ \text{arithmetic-expression-2} \end{Bmatrix}\right] \end{Bmatrix}$

  [ALSO

$\begin{Bmatrix} \text{ANY} \\ \text{condition-2} \\ \text{TRUE} \\ \text{FALSE} \\ \text{[NOT]} \begin{Bmatrix} \text{identifier-5} \\ \text{literal-5} \\ \text{arithmetic-expression-3} \end{Bmatrix} \left[\begin{Bmatrix} \text{THROUGH} \\ \text{THRU} \end{Bmatrix} \begin{Bmatrix} \text{identifier-6} \\ \text{literal-6} \\ \text{arithmetic-expression-4} \end{Bmatrix}\right] \end{Bmatrix}$] ... } ...

  imperative-statement-1} ...

  [WHEN OTHER imperative-statement-2]

  [END-EVALUATE]

<u>EXIT</u>

<u>EXIT</u> <u>PROGRAM</u>

<u>GENERATE</u> $\begin{Bmatrix} \text{data-name-1} \\ \text{report-name-1} \end{Bmatrix}$

<u>GO</u> TO [procedure-name-1]

<u>GO</u> TO {procedure-name-1} ...   <u>DEPENDING</u> ON identifier-1

<u>IF</u> condition-1 THEN $\begin{Bmatrix} \{\text{statement-1}\} \\ \underline{\text{NEXT}} \ \underline{\text{SENTENCE}} \end{Bmatrix} \cdots$ $\begin{Bmatrix} \underline{\text{ELSE}} \ \{\text{statement-2}\} \ \cdots \ [\underline{\text{END-IF}}] \\ \underline{\text{ELSE}} \ \underline{\text{NEXT}} \ \underline{\text{SENTENCE}} \\ \underline{\text{END-IF}} \end{Bmatrix}$

<u>INITIALIZE</u> {identifier-1} ...

$$\left[\underline{\text{REPLACING}} \ \left\{ \begin{Bmatrix} \underline{\text{ALPHABETIC}} \\ \underline{\text{ALPHANUMERIC}} \\ \underline{\text{NUMERIC}} \\ \underline{\text{ALPHANUMERIC-EDITED}} \\ \underline{\text{NUMERIC-EDITED}} \end{Bmatrix} \text{DATA} \ \underline{\text{BY}} \ \begin{Bmatrix} \text{identifier-2} \\ \text{literal-1} \end{Bmatrix} \right\} \cdots \right]$$

<u>INITIATE</u> {report-name-1} ...

<u>INSPECT</u> identifier-1 <u>TALLYING</u>

$$\left\{ \begin{Bmatrix} \text{identifier-2} \ \underline{\text{FOR}} \ \begin{Bmatrix} \underline{\text{CHARACTERS}} \ \left[\begin{Bmatrix} \underline{\text{BEFORE}} \\ \text{AFTER} \end{Bmatrix} \text{INITIAL} \begin{Bmatrix} \text{identifier-4} \\ \text{literal-2} \end{Bmatrix} \right] \cdots \\ \begin{Bmatrix} \underline{\text{ALL}} \\ \underline{\text{LEADING}} \end{Bmatrix} \begin{Bmatrix} \text{identifier-3} \\ \text{literal-1} \end{Bmatrix} \left[\begin{Bmatrix} \underline{\text{BEFORE}} \\ \underline{\text{AFTER}} \end{Bmatrix} \text{INITIAL} \begin{Bmatrix} \text{identifier-4} \\ \text{literal-2} \end{Bmatrix} \right] \cdots \end{Bmatrix} \cdots \end{Bmatrix} \cdots \right\} \cdots$$

<u>INSPECT</u> identifier-1 <u>REPLACING</u>

$$\left\{ \begin{Bmatrix} \underline{\text{CHARACTERS}} \ \underline{\text{BY}} \begin{Bmatrix} \text{identifier-5} \\ \text{literal-3} \end{Bmatrix} \left[\begin{Bmatrix} \underline{\text{BEFORE}} \\ \underline{\text{AFTER}} \end{Bmatrix} \text{INITIAL} \begin{Bmatrix} \text{identifier-4} \\ \text{literal-2} \end{Bmatrix} \right] \cdots \\ \begin{Bmatrix} \underline{\text{ALL}} \\ \underline{\text{LEADING}} \\ \underline{\text{FIRST}} \end{Bmatrix} \begin{Bmatrix} \text{identifier-3} \\ \text{literal-1} \end{Bmatrix} \underline{\text{BY}} \begin{Bmatrix} \text{identifier-5} \\ \text{literal-3} \end{Bmatrix} \left[\begin{Bmatrix} \underline{\text{BEFORE}} \\ \underline{\text{AFTER}} \end{Bmatrix} \text{INITIAL} \begin{Bmatrix} \text{identifier-4} \\ \text{literal-2} \end{Bmatrix} \right] \cdots \end{Bmatrix} \cdots \right\} \cdots$$

INSPECT identifier-1 TALLYING

$$\left\{ \begin{array}{l} \text{identifier-2 } \underline{\text{FOR}} \left\{ \begin{array}{l} \underline{\text{CHARACTERS}} \left[\left\{ \begin{array}{l} \underline{\text{BEFORE}} \\ \underline{\text{AFTER}} \end{array} \right\} \text{INITIAL} \left\{ \begin{array}{l} \text{identifier-4} \\ \text{literal-2} \end{array} \right\} \right] \dots \\ \left\{ \begin{array}{l} \underline{\text{ALL}} \\ \underline{\text{LEADING}} \end{array} \right\} \left\{ \begin{array}{l} \text{identifier-3} \\ \text{literal-1} \end{array} \right\} \left[\left\{ \begin{array}{l} \underline{\text{BEFORE}} \\ \underline{\text{AFTER}} \end{array} \right\} \text{INITIAL} \left\{ \begin{array}{l} \text{identifier-4} \\ \text{literal-2} \end{array} \right\} \right] \dots \right\} \dots \end{array} \right\} \dots$$

REPLACING

$$\left\{ \begin{array}{l} \underline{\text{CHARACTERS}} \; \underline{\text{BY}} \left\{ \begin{array}{l} \text{identifier-5} \\ \text{literal-3} \end{array} \right\} \left[\left\{ \begin{array}{l} \underline{\text{BEFORE}} \\ \underline{\text{AFTER}} \end{array} \right\} \text{INITIAL} \left\{ \begin{array}{l} \text{identifier-4} \\ \text{literal-2} \end{array} \right\} \right] \dots \\ \left\{ \begin{array}{l} \underline{\text{ALL}} \\ \underline{\text{LEADING}} \\ \underline{\text{FIRST}} \end{array} \right\} \left\{ \begin{array}{l} \text{identifier-3} \\ \text{literal-1} \end{array} \right\} \underline{\text{BY}} \left\{ \begin{array}{l} \text{identifier-5} \\ \text{literal-3} \end{array} \right\} \left[\left\{ \begin{array}{l} \underline{\text{BEFORE}} \\ \underline{\text{AFTER}} \end{array} \right\} \text{INITIAL} \left\{ \begin{array}{l} \text{identifier-4} \\ \text{literal-2} \end{array} \right\} \right] \dots \right\} \dots \end{array} \right\} \dots$$

INSPECT identifier-1 $\underline{\text{CONVERTING}}$ $\left\{ \begin{array}{l} \text{identifier-6} \\ \text{literal-4} \end{array} \right\}$ $\underline{\text{TO}}$ $\left\{ \begin{array}{l} \text{identifier-7} \\ \text{literal-5} \end{array} \right\}$

$\left[\left\{ \begin{array}{l} \underline{\text{BEFORE}} \\ \underline{\text{AFTER}} \end{array} \right\} \text{INITIAL} \left\{ \begin{array}{l} \text{identifier-4} \\ \text{literal-2} \end{array} \right\} \right] \dots$

$\underline{\text{MERGE}}$ file-name-1 $\left\{ \text{ON} \left\{ \begin{array}{l} \underline{\text{ASCENDING}} \\ \underline{\text{DESCENDING}} \end{array} \right\} \text{KEY} \; \{\text{data-name-1}\} \dots \right\} \dots$

[COLLATING $\underline{\text{SEQUENCE}}$ IS alphabet-name-1]

$\underline{\text{USING}}$ file-name-2 {file-name-3} ...

$\left\{ \begin{array}{l} \underline{\text{OUTPUT}} \; \underline{\text{PROCEDURE}} \; \text{IS procedure-name-1} \left[\left\{ \begin{array}{l} \underline{\text{THROUGH}} \\ \underline{\text{THRU}} \end{array} \right\} \text{procedure-name-2} \right] \\ \underline{\text{GIVING}} \; \{\text{file-name-4}\} \dots \end{array} \right\}$

$\underline{\text{MOVE}}$ $\left\{ \begin{array}{l} \text{identifier-1} \\ \text{literal-1} \end{array} \right\}$ $\underline{\text{TO}}$ {identifier-2} ...

$\underline{\text{MOVE}}$ $\left\{ \begin{array}{l} \underline{\text{CORRESPONDING}} \\ \underline{\text{CORR}} \end{array} \right\}$ identifier-1 $\underline{\text{TO}}$ identifier-2

$\underline{\text{MULTIPLY}}$ $\left\{ \begin{array}{l} \text{identifier-1} \\ \text{literal-1} \end{array} \right\}$ $\underline{\text{BY}}$ {identifier-2 [$\underline{\text{ROUNDED}}$]} ...

[ON $\underline{\text{SIZE}}$ $\underline{\text{ERROR}}$ imperative-statement-1]

[$\underline{\text{NOT}}$ ON $\underline{\text{SIZE}}$ $\underline{\text{ERROR}}$ imperative-statement-2]

[$\underline{\text{END-MULTIPLY}}$]

MULTIPLY $\begin{Bmatrix} \text{identifier-1} \\ \text{literal-1} \end{Bmatrix}$ BY $\begin{Bmatrix} \text{identifier-2} \\ \text{literal-2} \end{Bmatrix}$

GIVING {identifier-3 [ROUNDED]} ...

[ON SIZE ERROR imperative-statement-1]

[NOT ON SIZE ERROR imperative-statement-2]

[END-MULTIPLY]

S OPEN $\begin{Bmatrix} \underline{\text{INPUT}} \quad \{\text{file-name-1} \begin{bmatrix} \underline{\text{REVERSED}} \\ \text{WITH } \underline{\text{NO}} \text{ REWIND} \end{bmatrix}\} \cdots \\ \underline{\text{OUTPUT}} \ \{\text{file-name-2} \ [\text{WITH } \underline{\text{NO}} \text{ REWIND}]\} \cdots \\ \underline{\text{I-O}} \ \{\text{file-name-3}\} \cdots \\ \underline{\text{EXTEND}} \ \{\text{file-name-4}\} \cdots \end{Bmatrix} \cdots$

RI OPEN $\begin{Bmatrix} \underline{\text{INPUT}} \ \{\text{file-name-1}\} \cdots \\ \underline{\text{OUTPUT}} \ \{\text{file-name-2}\} \cdots \\ \underline{\text{I-O}} \ \{\text{file-name-3}\} \cdots \\ \underline{\text{EXTEND}} \ \{\text{file-name-4}\} \cdots \end{Bmatrix} \cdots$

W OPEN $\begin{Bmatrix} \underline{\text{OUTPUT}} \ \{\text{file-name-1} \ [\text{WITH } \underline{\text{NO}} \text{ REWIND}]\} \cdots \\ \underline{\text{EXTEND}} \ \{\text{file-name-2}\} \cdots \end{Bmatrix} \cdots$

PERFORM $\left[\text{procedure-name-1} \left[\begin{Bmatrix} \underline{\text{THROUGH}} \\ \underline{\text{THRU}} \end{Bmatrix} \text{procedure-name-2}\right]\right]$

[imperative-statement-1 END-PERFORM]

PERFORM $\left[\text{procedure-name-1} \left[\begin{Bmatrix} \underline{\text{THROUGH}} \\ \underline{\text{THRU}} \end{Bmatrix} \text{procedure-name-2}\right]\right]$

$\begin{Bmatrix} \text{identifier-1} \\ \text{integer-1} \end{Bmatrix}$ TIMES [imperative-statement-1 END-PERFORM]

PERFORM $\left[\text{procedure-name-1} \left[\begin{Bmatrix} \underline{\text{THROUGH}} \\ \underline{\text{THRU}} \end{Bmatrix} \text{procedure-name-2}\right]\right]$

$\left[\text{WITH } \underline{\text{TEST}} \ \begin{Bmatrix} \underline{\text{BEFORE}} \\ \underline{\text{AFTER}} \end{Bmatrix}\right]$ UNTIL condition-1

[imperative-statement-1 END-PERFORM]

PERFORM $\left[\text{procedure-name-1} \left[\begin{Bmatrix}\underline{\text{THROUGH}}\\\underline{\text{THRU}}\end{Bmatrix} \text{procedure-name-2}\right]\right]$

$\left[\text{WITH } \underline{\text{TEST}} \begin{Bmatrix}\underline{\text{BEFORE}}\\\underline{\text{AFTER}}\end{Bmatrix}\right]$

$\underline{\text{VARYING}} \begin{Bmatrix}\text{identifier-2}\\\text{index-name-1}\end{Bmatrix} \underline{\text{FROM}} \begin{Bmatrix}\text{identifier-3}\\\text{index-name-2}\\\text{literal-1}\end{Bmatrix}$

$\underline{\text{BY}} \begin{Bmatrix}\text{identifier-4}\\\text{literal-2}\end{Bmatrix} \underline{\text{UNTIL}} \text{ condition-1}$

$\left[\underline{\text{AFTER}} \begin{Bmatrix}\text{identifier-5}\\\text{literal-3}\end{Bmatrix} \underline{\text{FROM}} \begin{Bmatrix}\text{identifier-6}\\\text{index-name-4}\\\text{literal-3}\end{Bmatrix}\right.$

$\left.\underline{\text{BY}} \begin{Bmatrix}\text{identifier-7}\\\text{literal-4}\end{Bmatrix} \underline{\text{UNTIL}} \text{ condition-2}\right] \dots$

[imperative-statement-1 <u>END-PERFORM</u>]

<u>PURGE</u> cd-name-1

SRI <u>READ</u> file-name-1 [<u>NEXT</u>] RECORD [<u>INTO</u> identifier-1]

[AT <u>END</u> imperative-statement-1]

[<u>NOT</u> AT <u>END</u> imperative-statement-2]

[<u>END-READ</u>]

R <u>READ</u> file-name-1 RECORD [<u>INTO</u> identifier-1]

[<u>INVALID</u> KEY imperative-statement-3]

[<u>NOT</u> <u>INVALID</u> KEY imperative-statement-4]

[<u>END-READ</u>]

I READ file-name-1 RECORD   [INTO identifier-1]

    [KEY IS data-name-1]

    [INVALID KEY imperative-statement-3]

    [NOT INVALID KEY imperative-statement-4]

    [END-READ]

RECEIVE cd-name-1 $\begin{Bmatrix} \text{MESSAGE} \\ \text{SEGMENT} \end{Bmatrix}$ INTO identifier-1

    [NO DATA imperative-statement-1]

    [WITH DATA imperative-statement-2]

    [END-RECEIVE]

RELEASE record-name-1   [FROM identifier-1]

RETURN file-name-1 RECORD   [INTO identifier-1]

    AT END imperative-statement-1

    [NOT AT END imperative-statement-2]

    [END-RETURN]

S REWRITE record-name-1   [FROM identifier-1]

RI REWRITE record-name-1   [FROM identifier-1]

    [INVALID KEY imperative-statement-1]

    [NOT INVALID KEY imperative-statement-2]

    [END-REWRITE]

```
SEARCH identifier-1 [ VARYING {identifier-2 }]
                               {index-name-1}

    [AT END imperative-statement-1]

    {WHEN condition-1 {imperative-statement-2}} ...
    {                 {NEXT SENTENCE          }}

    [END-SEARCH]


SEARCH ALL identifier-1 [AT END imperative-statement-1]

    WHEN {data-name-1 {IS EQUAL TO} {identifier-3            }}
         {            {IS =       } {literal-1               }}
         {                          {arithmetic-expression-1 }}
         {condition-name-1

         [      {data-name-2 {IS EQUAL TO} {identifier-4            }}]
         [ AND  {            {IS =       } {literal-2               }}] ...
         [      {                          {arithmetic-expression-2 }}]
         [      {condition-name-2                                    ]

    {imperative-statement-2}
    {NEXT SENTENCE         }

    [END-SEARCH]


SEND cd-name-1 FROM identifier-1


SEND cd-name-1 [FROM identifier-1] {WITH identifier-2}
                                   {WITH ESI         }
                                   {WITH EMI         }
                                   {WITH EGI         }

    [{BEFORE}          {{identifier-3} [LINE ]}]
    [{AFTER } ADVANCING {{integer-1   } [LINES]}]
    [                   {{mnemonic-name-1}     }]
    [                   {{PAGE           }     }]

    [REPLACING LINE]


SET {index-name-1} ... TO {index-name-2}
    {identifier-1 }        {identifier-2}
                           {integer-1   }
```

SET {index-name-3} ... $\left\{\begin{matrix} \underline{UP} \ \underline{BY} \\ \underline{DOWN} \ \underline{BY} \end{matrix}\right\}$ $\left\{\begin{matrix} identifier-3 \\ integer-2 \end{matrix}\right\}$

SET $\left\{ \{mnemonic-name-1\} \ ... \ \underline{TO} \ \left\{\begin{matrix} \underline{ON} \\ \underline{OFF} \end{matrix}\right\} \right\}$ ...

SET {condition-name-1} ... $\underline{TO}$ $\underline{TRUE}$

$\underline{SORT}$ file-name-1 $\left\{ ON \ \left\{\begin{matrix} \underline{ASCENDING} \\ \underline{DESCENDING} \end{matrix}\right\} \ KEY \ \{data-name-1\} \ ... \right\}$ ...

[WITH $\underline{DUPLICATES}$ IN ORDER]

[COLLATING $\underline{SEQUENCE}$ IS alphabet-name-1]

$\left\{\begin{matrix} \underline{INPUT} \ \underline{PROCEDURE} \ IS \ procedure-name-1 \ \left[\left\{\begin{matrix} \underline{THROUGH} \\ \underline{THRU} \end{matrix}\right\} \ procedure-name-2\right] \\ \underline{USING} \ \{file-name-2\} \ ... \end{matrix}\right\}$

$\left\{\begin{matrix} \underline{OUTPUT} \ \underline{PROCEDURE} \ IS \ procedure-name-3 \ \left[\left\{\begin{matrix} \underline{THROUGH} \\ \underline{THRU} \end{matrix}\right\} \ procedure-name-4\right] \\ \underline{GIVING} \ \{file-name-3\} \ ... \end{matrix}\right\}$

$\underline{START}$ file-name-1 $\left[\underline{KEY} \ \left\{\begin{matrix} IS \ \underline{EQUAL} \ TO \\ IS \ = \\ IS \ \underline{GREATER} \ THAN \\ IS \ > \\ IS \ \underline{NOT} \ \underline{LESS} \ THAN \\ IS \ \underline{NOT} \ < \\ IS \ \underline{GREATER} \ THAN \ \underline{OR} \ \underline{EQUAL} \ TO \\ IS \ >= \end{matrix}\right\} \ data-name-1 \right]$

[$\underline{INVALID}$ KEY imperative-statement-1]

[$\underline{NOT}$ $\underline{INVALID}$ KEY imperative-statement-2]

[$\underline{END-START}$]

$\underline{STOP}$ $\left\{\begin{matrix} \underline{RUN} \\ literal-1 \end{matrix}\right\}$

STRING $\left\{ \begin{Bmatrix} \text{identifier-1} \\ \text{literal-1} \end{Bmatrix} \right. \dots$ DELIMITED BY $\left. \begin{Bmatrix} \text{identifier-2} \\ \text{literal-2} \\ \underline{\text{SIZE}} \end{Bmatrix} \right\} \dots$

INTO identifier-3

[WITH POINTER identifier-4]

[ON OVERFLOW imperative-statement-1]

[NOT ON OVERFLOW imperative-statement-2]

[END-STRING]

SUBTRACT $\begin{Bmatrix} \text{identifier-1} \\ \text{literal-1} \end{Bmatrix} \dots$ FROM {identifier-3 [ROUNDED]} ...

[ON SIZE ERROR imperative-statement-1]

[NOT ON SIZE ERROR imperative-statement-2]

[END-SUBTRACT]

SUBTRACT $\begin{Bmatrix} \text{identifier-1} \\ \text{literal-1} \end{Bmatrix} \dots$ FROM $\begin{Bmatrix} \text{identifier-2} \\ \text{literal-2} \end{Bmatrix}$

GIVING {identifier-3 [ROUNDED]} ...

[ON SIZE ERROR imperative-statement-1]

[NOT ON SIZE ERROR imperative-statement-2]

[END-SUBTRACT]

SUBTRACT $\begin{Bmatrix} \underline{\text{CORRESPONDING}} \\ \underline{\text{CORR}} \end{Bmatrix}$ identifier-1 FROM identifier-2 [ROUNDED]

[ON SIZE ERROR imperative-statement-1]

[NOT ON SIZE ERROR imperative-statement-2]

[END-SUBTRACT]

SUPPRESS PRINTING

TERMINATE {report-name-1} ...

UNSTRING identifier-1

$$\left[\underline{DELIMITED} \ BY \ [\underline{ALL}] \ \begin{Bmatrix} identifier\text{-}2 \\ literal\text{-}1 \end{Bmatrix} \ \left[\underline{OR} \ [\underline{ALL}] \ \begin{Bmatrix} identifier\text{-}3 \\ literal\text{-}2 \end{Bmatrix} \right] \ \ldots \right]$$

INTO {identifier-4 [DELIMITER IN identifier-5] [COUNT IN identifier-6]} ...

[WITH POINTER identifier-7]

[TALLYING IN identifier-8]

[ON OVERFLOW imperative-statement-1]

[NOT ON OVERFLOW imperative-statement-2]

[END-UNSTRING]

$$SRI \ \ \underline{USE} \ [\underline{GLOBAL}] \ \underline{AFTER} \ STANDARD \ \begin{Bmatrix} \underline{EXCEPTION} \\ \underline{ERROR} \end{Bmatrix} \ \underline{PROCEDURE} \ ON \ \begin{Bmatrix} \{file\text{-}name\text{-}1\} \ \ldots \\ \underline{INPUT} \\ \underline{OUTPUT} \\ \underline{I\text{-}O} \\ \underline{EXTEND} \end{Bmatrix}$$

$$W \ \ \underline{USE} \ \underline{AFTER} \ \underline{STANDARD} \ \begin{Bmatrix} \underline{EXCEPTION} \\ \underline{ERROR} \end{Bmatrix} \ \underline{PROCEDURE} \ ON \ \begin{Bmatrix} \{file\text{-}name\text{-}1\} \ \ldots \\ \underline{OUTPUT} \\ \underline{EXTEND} \end{Bmatrix}$$

USE [GLOBAL] BEFORE REPORTING identifier-1

$$\underline{USE} \ FOR \ \underline{DEBUGGING} \ ON \ \begin{Bmatrix} cd\text{-}name\text{-}1 \\ [\underline{ALL} \ REFERENCES \ OF] \ identifier\text{-}1 \\ file\text{-}name\text{-}1 \\ procedure\text{-}name\text{-}1 \\ \underline{ALL} \ \underline{PROCEDURES} \end{Bmatrix} \ \ldots$$

S WRITE record-name-1 [FROM identifier-1]

$$\left[\left\{{BEFORE \atop AFTER}\right\} \quad ADVANCING \quad \left\{{identifier\text{-}2 \atop integer\text{-}1} \atop {mnemonic\text{-}name\text{-}1 \atop PAGE}\right\} \left[{LINE \atop LINES}\right]\right]$$

$$\left[AT \quad \left\{{END\text{-}OF\text{-}PAGE \atop EOP}\right\} \quad imperative\text{-}statement\text{-}1\right]$$

$$\left[NOT \ AT \quad \left\{{END\text{-}OF\text{-}PAGE \atop EOP}\right\} \quad imperative\text{-}statement\text{-}2\right]$$

[END-WRITE]

RI WRITE record-name-1   [FROM identifier-1]

    [INVALID KEY imperative-statement-1]

    [NOT INVALID KEY imperative-statement-2]

    [END-WRITE]

GENERAL FORMAT FOR COPY AND REPLACE STATEMENTS

$$COPY \ text\text{-}name\text{-}1 \quad \left[\left\{{OF \atop IN}\right\} \ library\text{-}name\text{-}1\right]$$

$$\left[REPLACING \left\{{==pseudo\text{-}text\text{-}1== \atop identifier\text{-}1 \atop literal\text{-}1 \atop word\text{-}1}\right\} \ BY \ \left\{{==pseudo\text{-}text\text{-}2== \atop identifier\text{-}2 \atop literal\text{-}2 \atop word\text{-}2}\right\} \ \ldots\right]$$

REPLACE   {==pseudo-text-1==   BY   ==pseudo-text-2==} ...

REPLACE OFF

GENERAL FORMAT FOR CONDITIONS

RELATION CONDITION:

$$
\begin{Bmatrix} \text{identifier-1} \\ \text{literal-1} \\ \text{arithmetic-expression-1} \\ \text{index-name-1} \end{Bmatrix}
\begin{Bmatrix}
\text{IS [\underline{NOT}] \underline{GREATER} THAN} \\
\text{IS [\underline{NOT}] >} \\
\text{IS [\underline{NOT}] \underline{LESS} THAN} \\
\text{IS [\underline{NOT}] <} \\
\text{IS [\underline{NOT}] \underline{EQUAL} TO} \\
\text{IS [\underline{NOT}] =} \\
\text{IS \underline{GREATER} THAN \underline{OR} \underline{EQUAL} TO} \\
\text{IS >=} \\
\text{IS \underline{LESS} THAN \underline{OR} \underline{EQUAL} TO} \\
\text{IS <=}
\end{Bmatrix}
\begin{Bmatrix} \text{identifier-2} \\ \text{literal-2} \\ \text{arithmetic-expression-2} \\ \text{index-name-2} \end{Bmatrix}
$$

CLASS CONDITION:

$$
\text{identifier-1 IS [\underline{NOT}]}
\begin{Bmatrix}
\text{\underline{NUMERIC}} \\
\text{\underline{ALPHABETIC}} \\
\text{\underline{ALPHABETIC-LOWER}} \\
\text{\underline{ALPHABETIC-UPPER}} \\
\text{class-name-1}
\end{Bmatrix}
$$

CONDITION-NAME CONDITION:

condition-name-1

SWITCH-STATUS CONDITION:

condition-name-1

SIGN CONDITION:

$$
\text{arithmetic-expression-1 IS [\underline{NOT}]}
\begin{Bmatrix}
\text{\underline{POSITIVE}} \\
\text{\underline{NEGATIVE}} \\
\text{\underline{ZERO}}
\end{Bmatrix}
$$

NEGATED CONDITION:

<u>NOT</u> condition-1

COMBINED CONDITION:

$$\text{condition-1} \left\{ \left\{ \begin{array}{c} \underline{AND} \\ \underline{OR} \end{array} \right\} \text{condition-2} \right\} \dots$$

ABBREVIATED COMBINED RELATION CONDITION:

$$\text{relation-condition} \left\{ \left\{ \begin{array}{c} \underline{AND} \\ \underline{OR} \end{array} \right\} \; [\underline{NOT}] \quad [\text{relational-operator}] \quad \text{object} \right\} \dots$$

GENERAL FORMAT FOR QUALIFICATION

FORMAT 1:

$$\left\{ \begin{array}{l} \text{data-name-1} \\ \text{condition-name-1} \end{array} \right\} \left\{ \begin{array}{l} \left\{ \left\{ \begin{array}{c} \underline{IN} \\ \underline{OF} \end{array} \right\} \text{data-name-2} \right\} \dots \left[\left\{ \begin{array}{c} \underline{IN} \\ \underline{OF} \end{array} \right\} \left\{ \begin{array}{l} \text{file-name-1} \\ \text{cd-name-1} \end{array} \right\} \right] \\ \left\{ \begin{array}{c} \underline{IN} \\ \underline{OF} \end{array} \right\} \left\{ \begin{array}{l} \text{file-name-1} \\ \text{cd-name-1} \end{array} \right\} \end{array} \right\}$$

FORMAT 2:

$$\text{paragraph-name-1} \left\{ \begin{array}{c} \underline{IN} \\ \underline{OF} \end{array} \right\} \text{section-name-1}$$

FORMAT 3:

$$\text{text-name-1} \left\{ \begin{array}{c} \underline{IN} \\ \underline{OF} \end{array} \right\} \text{library-name-1}$$

FORMAT 4:

$$\underline{\text{LINAGE-COUNTER}} \left\{ \begin{array}{c} \underline{IN} \\ \underline{OF} \end{array} \right\} \text{file-name-2}$$

FORMAT 5:

$$\left\{ \begin{array}{l} \underline{\text{PAGE-COUNTER}} \\ \underline{\text{LINE-COUNTER}} \end{array} \right\} \left\{ \begin{array}{c} \underline{IN} \\ \underline{OF} \end{array} \right\} \text{report-name-1}$$

FORMAT 6:

$$\text{data-name-3} \left\{ \begin{array}{l} \left\{ \begin{array}{l} \underline{IN} \\ \underline{OF} \end{array} \right\} \text{data-name-4} \left[\left\{ \begin{array}{l} \underline{IN} \\ \underline{OF} \end{array} \right\} \text{report-name-2} \right] \\ \left\{ \begin{array}{l} \underline{IN} \\ \underline{OF} \end{array} \right\} \text{report-name-2} \end{array} \right\}$$

MISCELLANEOUS FORMATS

SUBSCRIPTING:

$$\left\{ \begin{array}{l} \text{condition-name-1} \\ \text{data-name-1} \end{array} \right\} \quad \left(\left\{ \begin{array}{l} \text{integer-1} \\ \text{data-name-2 } [\{\pm\} \text{ integer-2}] \\ \text{index-name-1 } [\{\pm\} \text{ integer-3}] \end{array} \right\} \ldots \right)$$

REFERENCE MODIFICATION:

data-name-1 (leftmost-character-position: [length])

IDENTIFIER:

$$\text{data-name-1} \left[\left\{ \begin{array}{l} \underline{IN} \\ \underline{OF} \end{array} \right\} \text{data-name-2} \right] \ldots \left[\left\{ \begin{array}{l} \underline{IN} \\ \underline{OF} \end{array} \right\} \left\{ \begin{array}{l} \text{cd-name-1} \\ \text{file-name-1} \\ \text{report-name-1} \end{array} \right\} \right]$$

[({subscript} ...)]   [(leftmost-character-position: [length])]

GENERAL FORMAT FOR NESTED SOURCE PROGRAMS

<u>IDENTIFICATION DIVISION</u>.

<u>PROGRAM-ID</u>. program-name-1 [IS <u>INITIAL</u> PROGRAM].

[<u>ENVIRONMENT DIVISION</u>. environment-division-content]

[<u>DATA DIVISION</u>. data-division-content]

[<u>PROCEDURE DIVISION</u>. procedure-division-content]

[[nested-source-program] ...

<u>END PROGRAM</u> program-name-1.]

GENERAL FORMAT FOR NESTED-SOURCE-PROGRAM

IDENTIFICATION DIVISION.

PROGRAM-ID.   program-name-2 $\left[\text{IS} \left\{\left|\begin{array}{c}\underline{\text{COMMON}}\\ \underline{\text{INITIAL}}\end{array}\right|\right\} \text{PROGRAM}\right]$.

[ENVIRONMENT DIVISION. environment-division-content]

[DATA DIVISION. data-division-content]

[PROCEDURE DIVISION. procedure-division-content]

[nested-source-program] ...

END PROGRAM program-name-2.

GENERAL FORMAT FOR A SEQUENCE OF SOURCE PROGRAMS

{IDENTIFICATION DIVISION.

 PROGRAM-ID. program-name-3 [IS INITIAL PROGRAM].

[ENVIRONMENT DIVISION. environment-division-content]

[DATA DIVISION. data-division-content]

[PROCEDURE DIVISION. procedure-division-content]

[nested-source-program] ...

 END PROGRAM program-name-3.} ...

 IDENTIFICATION DIVISION.

 PROGRAM-ID. program-name-4 [IS INITIAL PROGRAM].

[ENVIRONMENT DIVISION. environment-division-content]

[DATA DIVISION. data-division-content]

[PROCEDURE DIVISION. procedure-division-content]

[[nested-source-program] ...

 END PROGRAM program-name-4.]

E. PERSONNEL SYSTEM

E.1 BACKGROUND

The ABC Company uses a computer-based system to perform most functions related to payroll and personnel accounting. At the heart of this system is a file called the "Personnel Master File," which contains one record for each current employee. The layout for the records in this file is shown in Figure E.1. The programming exercises in this appendix all relate to this file. Figure E.2 contains a sample data set that you may use to test programs you write. Your instructor will tell you what you must do to make use of this data on your system.

Figure E.1   Record layout for Personnel Master File

Record Positions	Descriptions	PIC
1–9	Employee Social Security number	9(9)
10–30	Employee name	
	10–19 Last name	X(10)
	20–29 First name	X(10)
	30 Middle initial	X
31–36	Date hired (*mmddyy*)	9(6)
37–41	Cost center	9(5)
42	Pay type	X
	S = Salary	
	H = Hourly/full-time	
	P = Hourly/part-time	
43	Marital status	X
	M = Married	
	S = Single	
44–49	Pay amount	9(4)V99
	Pay type S: Biweekly amount	
	Pay type H/P: Hourly amount	
50–51	Number dependents	99
52–58	Year-to-date gross pay	9(5)V99
59–65	Year-to-date federal income tax	9(5)V99
66–71	Year-to-date Social Security tax	9(4)V99
72–77	Year-to-date state income tax	9(4)V99

Figure E.2   Sample data for personnel system programming exercises

Employee Social Security Number	Last Name	First Name	M.I.	Date Hired	Cost Center	Pay Type	M.S.	Pay Amount	Number Dependents	Y.T.D. Gross Pay	Y.T.D. Federal Income Tax	Y.T.D. Social Security Tax	Y.T.D. State Income Tax
100000000	SMITH	LEE	A	031490	04000	S	M	100000	02	0400000	0080000	032000	005332
111111111	BARKLEY	WALTER	I	050281	07000	S	M	087500	03	0350000	0070000	028000	004666
200000000	CARR	BONNIE	S	120579	05000	H	S	001875	01	0600000	0120000	048000	007998
222222222	DREW	VIRGINIA	R	030185	00001	H	M	001563	03	0500000	0100000	040000	006665
300000000	BOMAR	CHARLES	B	070783	03000	S	S	150000	02	0600000	0120000	048000	007998
333333333	JACKSON	RAMONE	M	100588	03000	P	M	001000	02	0090000	0090000	072000	000000
400000000	MOYER	JAMES	E	040185	06000	H	M	001250	04	0400000	0080000	032000	005332
400000004	ROWE	ROBERTA	T	050690	03001	S	S	150000	01	0600000	0120000	048000	007998
444444444	KAY	RONALD	A	011589	07000	S	S	001250	01	0400000	0080000	032000	005332
500000000	MCGEE	CALVIN	S	053091	03000	P	M	000800	05	0100000	0005000	008000	001333
500000005	MILLER	DAVID	L	061588	00001	H	M	001563	03	0500000	0100000	040000	006665
555555555	PATTERSON	JOHN	J	110190	05000	S	M	125000	02	0500000	0100000	040000	006665
566666666	ROBINSON	ANDREW	R	090190	03001	P	S	000750	02	0030000	0003000	002400	000000
577777777	GREY	HELEN	S	071591	00001	P	M	000800	02	0050000	0005000	004000	000000
588888888	BEECH	STEVEN	A	080184	06000	S	S	050000	01	0200000	0040000	016000	002666
599999999	JORDAN	JOHN	R	030783	05000	S	S	075000	01	0300000	0060000	024000	003998
600000000	LEWIS	EUNICE	A	080184	07000	S	M	100000	03	0400000	0080000	032000	005332
600000006	MCBRIDE	LEE	S	020189	04000	H	M	001250	03	0400000	0080000	032000	005332
611111111	PETERSON	GARRY	J	060188	00001	H	S	001719	02	0550000	0110000	044000	007332
622222222	RICH	RICHARD	K	121591	06000	P	S	000800	01	0060000	0006000	004800	000000
633333333	TURNER	LAURIE	R	081590	03000	S	M	075000	03	0300000	0060000	024000	003999
666666666	WADE	MARY	M	090188	03001	S	M	087500	02	0650000	0070000	028000	004666
699999999	WILLIAMS	SONJA	C	051591	07000	H	M	001578	02	0505000	0101000	040400	006732
700000000	TODD	DOUGLAS	R	070189	04000	H	M	001906	04	0610000	0130000	048800	008131
711111111	ROSE	PETER	M	071590	03000	S	S	110000	01	0440000	0088000	035200	005865
722222222	MCGRAW	STEPHEN	T	100187	00001	P	M	000800	02	0060000	0006000	004800	000000
744444444	DYE	WILLIAM	J	100190	06000	S	M	100000	02	0400000	0080000	032000	005332
755555555	BARNES	ARTHUR	R	010185	03001	H	M	000969	03	0310000	0062000	024800	004132
766666666	ALEXANDER	JOSEPH	J	041590	07000	P	S	000800	01	0110000	0022000	008800	001466
777777777	BISHOP	RICHARD	R	050682	03000	S	M	062500	03	0250000	0050000	020000	003333
788888888	CARROLL	ANNE	B	091591	00001	S	M	082500	02	0330000	0066000	026400	004398

E.2   PROGRAMMING EXERCISES

Note: The chapter reference in parentheses after each exercise indicates the background required to write the program.

1. Write a program to produce a report showing the Social Security number, name, and cost center for each employee. Include appropriate headings as shown on the printer spacing chart illustrated in Figure E.3. (Chapter 2)

2. Write a program to produce a report showing detail of year-to-date pay for all employees, including totals for gross pay, federal income tax, Social Security tax, and state income tax as shown in Figure E.4. (Chapter 3)

3. Write a program to produce a detailed listing of the Personnel Master

File. Use appropriate labels and editing for each field as shown in Figure E.5. (Chapter 4)

4. Modify the program written for Exercise 2 to compute and print each employee's net income (gross pay minus all withholding amounts). (Chapter 5)

5. Write a program to compute and print the annual bonus amount due each employee based on the following rules:
   - Salaried employees receive 5% of their annual income, not to exceed $2000.
   - Full-time hourly employees receive one week's pay (40 hours).
   - Part-time hourly employees receive no bonus.

   Include totals as shown in the printer layout of Figure E.6. (Chapter 6)

6. Write a program to validate the records contained in the Personnel Master File using the following guidelines:

   Numeric Fields

   All numeric fields must contain numeric data:
   > Employee Social Security number
   > Date hired (the date-hired field must contain a valid date: month must be in the range 1 to 12; day must be in the range of 1 to 31)
   > Cost center (valid cost centers are shown in Exercise 9)
   > Pay amount
   > Number dependents
   > All year-to-date fields

   Alphabetic Fields

   > Employee name (must contain alphabetic characters; must not contain all spaces)
   > Pay type (only S, H, and P are valid)
   > Marital status (only M and S are valid)

   Your program should list any record found to contain invalid data with an appropriate error message. Additional sample data that can be used to test this program is shown in Figure E.7. (Chapter 6)

7. Write a program to sort the Personnel Master File into ascending sequence by cost center. Records within each cost center group must be in ascending sequence by employee name. (Chapter 7)

8. Write a program to process the file created in Exercise 7 to produce a summary of personnel expenditures by cost center. Use the printer spacing chart shown in Figure E.8. (Chapter 8)

9. Modify the program you wrote for Exercise 8 to produce a separate report for each cost center. The heading of each report should contain the cost center identification as in the following table:

Cost Center	Identification
00001	Administration
03000	Manufacturing plant A
03001	Manufacturing plant B
04000	Purchasing
05000	Accounting
06000	Shipping
07000	Advertising

   Set up the table shown above as a table of constants in your program. (Chapter 9)

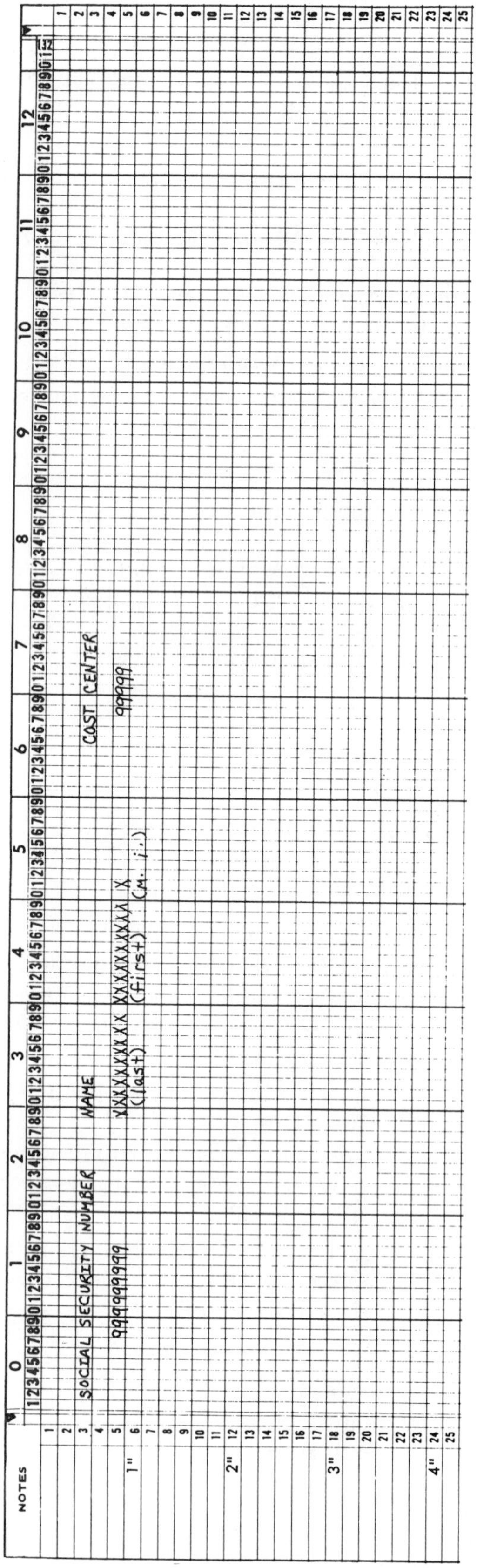

Figure E.3   Printer spacing chart for Exercise 1

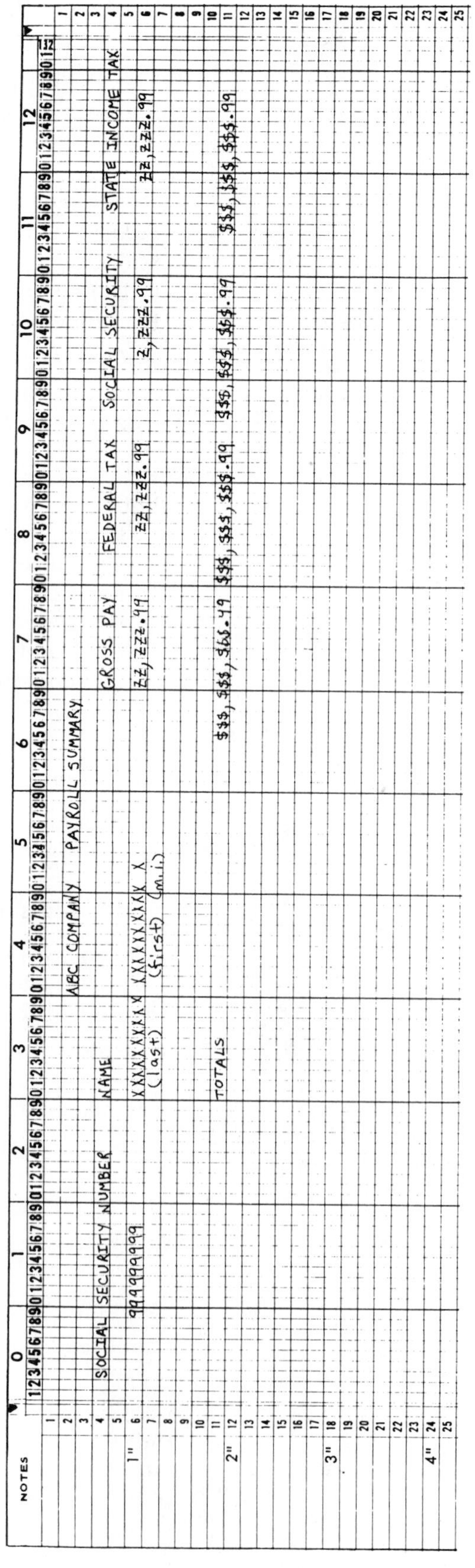

Figure E.4   Printer spacing chart for Exercise 2

Figure E.5 Printer spacing chart for Exercise 3

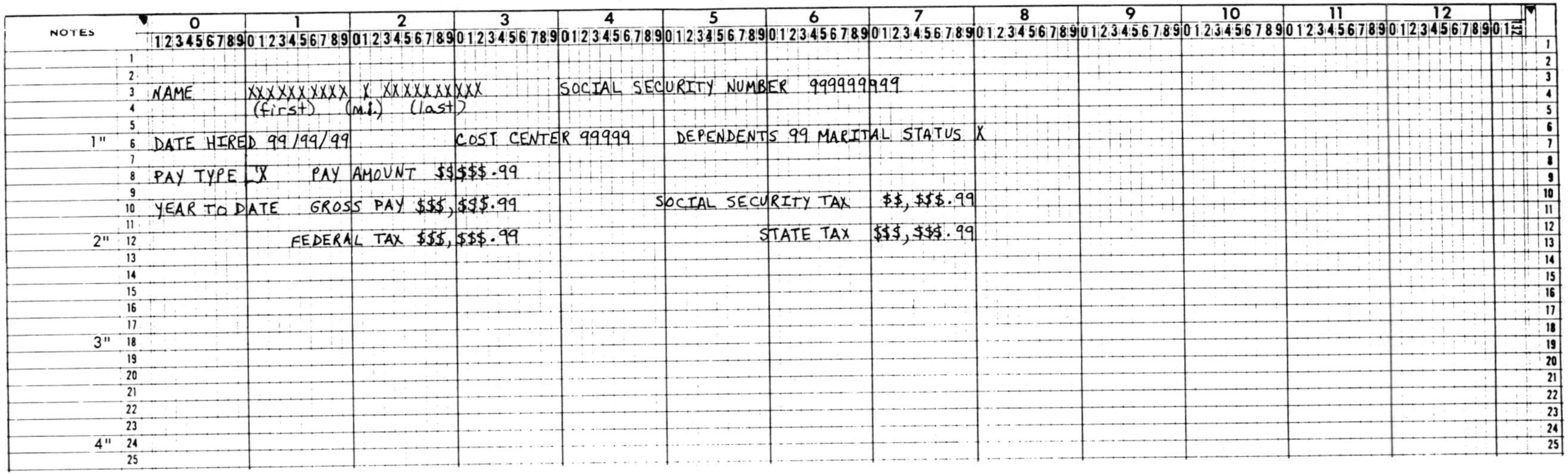

Figure E.6 Printer spacing chart for Exercise 5

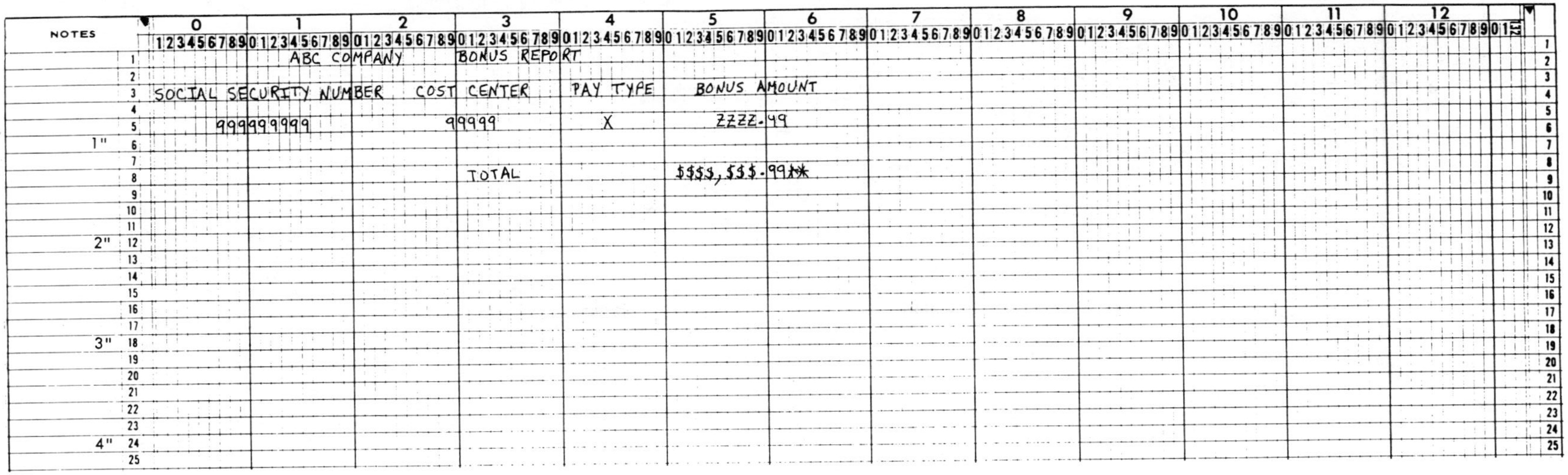

Figure E.7 Additional data to test data validation program

Employee Social Security Number	Last Name	First Name	M.I.	Date Hired	Cost Center	Pay Type	M.S.	Pay Amount	Number Dependents	Y.T.D. Gross Pay	Y.T.D. Federal Income Tax	Y.T.D. Social Security Tax	Y.T.D. State Income Tax	Comment
11111	JONES	JOHN	D	010291	0100	0	SM	0900000	3	0000000	00000000	00000000	00000000	Nonnumeric Social Security number
200000002	MOORE	MARY	M	010391	0200	0	MH	0010000	1	0000000	00000000	00000000	00000000	Invalid pay type and marital status
800000000	MORTON	WILLIAM3RD	A	010391	0500	0	HM	0008500	2	0000000	00000000	00000000	00000000	Nonalphabetic first name
300000003	WARD	MARGRET	S	013391	0400	0	SS	1100000	0	0000000	00000000	00000000	00000000	Invalid date hired
400000044	KNOTT	DANIEL	W	010491	0C00	0	PM	0006000	3	0000000	00000000	00000000	00000000	Nonnumeric cost center
500000055	HALL	CHARLES	C	010591	0400	0	SM	0000000	2					Nonnumeric data in Y.T.D. amounts
600000066	HAND	NANCY	R	000591			SM	0200000	0	0000000	00000000	00000000		Invalid date hired, nonnumeric cost center and state income tax
700000077	DALE	CHIP	R	010391	1 0000		SM	1200000	3	0000000	00000000	00000000	00000000	Invalid cost center
800000088	BOOTH	MARIE	R	010391	00001		S0	0100000	2	0000000	00000000	00000000	00000000	Invalid pay type
800000888	SPRINGER	DAN	S	010391	0000		QS	0100000						Invalid cost center, marital status, nonnumeric data in pay amount, number dependents, Y.T.D. amounts

Figure E.8 Printer spacing chart for Exercise 8

F. SALES ACCOUNTING SYSTEM

F.1 BACKGROUND

The ABC Company uses a computer-based system for entering sales information for products which are sold in its stores to both wholesale and retail customers. At the heart of this system is the Sales Detail File which contains one record for each sale. The record layout for this file is shown in Figure F.1. The programming exercises in this appendix make use of this file. Figure F.2 contains sample data which you may use to test your programs. Your instructor will tell you what you must do to make use of this data on your system.

F.2 PROGRAMMING EXERCISES

Note: The chapter reference in parentheses after each exercise indicates the background required to write the program.
1. Write a program to produce a report showing the item number, item description, retail price, wholesale price, type of sale, and quantity for each record in the Sales Detail File. Use the printer spacing chart shown in Figure F.3. (Chapter 2)
2. Modify the program written for Exercise 1 to include the total number of items sold. This output should follow the body of the report. (Chapter 3)
3. Write a program to produce a detailed listing of each record in the Sales Detail File. Use appropriate labels and editing for each field as shown in Figure F.4. (Chapter 4)
4. Write a program to produce a report showing the item number, item description, type of sale, price per item, quantity, and amount of sale. The price per item should be the wholesale list price for a type W sale; for a type R sale, the price per item should be the retail list price. Include totals as shown in the printer spacing chart illustrated in Figure F.5. (Chapter 5)
5. Write a program to generate an invoice for each record in the Sales Detail File. The amount of sale must be computed as described in Exercise 4 above. Retail sales should have sales tax computed; wholesale sales are not subject to sales tax. Sales which are to be shipped by UPS should have a shipping charge of 1% of the amount of sale for each item; sales which are shipped by parcel post have a shipping

Figure F.1   Record layout for sales detail file

Positions	Content	PIC
1–9	Item number	9(9)
10–19	Item description	X(10)
20–25	Retail list price (each)	9(4)V99
26–31	Wholesale list price (each)	9(4)V99
32–34	Quantity	999
35	Type of sale	X
	W = Wholesale	
	R = Retail	
36–38	Sales tax rate	V999
39–43	Salesperson identifier	9(5)
44–45	Store number	99
46–54	Customer account number	9(9)
55–60	Date of sale (*mmddyy*)	9(6)
61	Billing code	X
	C = Cash	
	R = Credit	
62	Shipping code	X
	C = Customer pickup	
	U = UPS	
	P = Parcel post	

charge of 1 1/2% of the amount of sale. Use the printer spacing chart shown in Figure F.6. (Chapter 6)

6. Write a program to validate records in the Sales Detail File using the following guidelines:

Numeric fields

All numeric fields must contain numeric data.
> Item number
> Retail list price
> Wholesale list price
> Quantity
> Sales tax rate
> Salesperson identifier
> Store number (only store numbers 01, 02, 04, and 14 are valid)
> Customer account number
> Date of sale (must contain a valid date: month must be in the range of 1 to 12; day must be in the range of 1 to 31)

Alphabetic fields

> Type of sale (only W and R are valid)
> Billing code (only C and R are valid)
> Shipping code (only C, U, and P are valid)

The item description field may contain alphabetic and/or numeric characters but must not contain all spaces. Your program must list any record found to contain invalid data with an appropriate error message. Additional sample data that can be used to test this program is shown in Figure F.7. (Chapter 6)

7. Write a program to sort the Sales Detail File into ascending sequence by store number. Records within each store group should be in ascending sequence by salesperson number. (Chapter 7)

8. Write a program to process the file created in Exercise 7 to produce a summary of sales by store and salesperson. Use the printer spacing chart shown in Figure F.8. (Chapter 8)

9. Modify the program you wrote for Exercise 8 to produce a separate report for each store. The heading of each report should contain the store identifier as shown in the following table:

Store Number	Identifier
01	Main
02	Mall
04	Suburb A
14	Suburb B

Set up the table shown above as a table of constants in your program. (Chapter 9)

Figure F.2   Sample data for sales accounting system programming exercises

Item Number	Item Description	Retail List Price	Wholesale List Price	Quantity	Type	Sales Tax Rate	Salesperson Identifier	Store Number	Customer Account Number	Date of Sale	Billing Code	Shipping Code
111111111	SECR CHAIR	007900	006000	001	W	050	00002	01	0000010000	011391	C	C
222222222	EXEC CHAIR	012950	009998	003	R	050	00003	01	0000099990	011391	R	U
300000000	L DESK	032500	029900	001	R	050	00011	04	0000010000	011391	R	P
300000003	EXEC DESK	044900	042195	002	W	050	00012	02	0000020000	011391	C	C
222222222	EXEC CHAIR	012950	009998	002	W	050	00002	01	0000030000	011391	C	C
300000003	EXEC DESK	044900	042195	001	R	050	00002	04	0000099990	011391	R	U
100000000	DESK LAMP	003500	002895	004	R	050	00011	14	0000088880	011491	R	U
400000000	CREDENZA	031900	029190	001	R	050	00011	04	0000077770	011491	R	P
222222222	EXEC CHAIR	012950	009998	001	W	050	00003	01	0000010000	011491	C	U
300000000	L DESK	032500	029900	002	W	050	00003	01	0000010000	011491	C	U
111111111	SECR CHAIR	007900	006000	004	R	050	00013	02	0000077770	011491	R	P
111111222	SECR CHAIR	009900	007000	003	W	050	00012	02	0000066660	011591	R	P
222222333	EXEC CHAIR	015900	013090	001	R	050	00002	01	0000030000	011591	C	C
300000333	RECPT DESK	041900	038990	001	W	050	00011	14	0000077770	011591	R	U
111111111	SECR CHAIR	007900	006000	002	R	050	00012	02	0000020000	011591	C	C
111111222	SECR CHAIR	009900	007000	001	R	050	00012	02	0000020000	011591	C	C
400000004	CREDENZA	035900	033195	001	R	050	00013	02	0000020000	011591	C	C
500000000	BOOK SHELF	013900	011990	004	W	050	00011	14	0000030000	011591	C	C
500000005	BOOK SHELF	014900	012995	006	W	050	00002	04	0000077770	011591	R	U
300000003	EXEC DESK	044900	042195	002	W	050	00002	04	0000099990	011591	R	U
222222444	EXEC CHAIR	019800	014990	002	R	050	00003	61	0000088880	011591	R	U
111111111	SECR CHAIR	007900	006000	001	R	055	00011	14	0000010000	011691	R	P
500000000	BOOK SHELF	013900	011990	001	W	055	00012	02	0000088880	011691	R	P
222222222	EXEC CHAIR	012950	009998	002	R	055	00011	04	0000099990	011691	C	U
300000333	RECPT DESK	041900	038990	002	R	055	00011	14	0000010000	011691	R	P
300000003	EXEC DESK	044900	042195	001	W	055	00012	02	0000020000	011691	C	U
222222222	EXEC CHAIR	012950	009998	001	W	055	00013	02	0000020000	011691	C	C
100000000	DESK LAMP	003500	002895	002	W	055	00011	04	0000060000	011691	R	U
300000000	L DESK	032500	029900	002	R	055	00011	14	0000070000	011691	C	C
300000003	EXEC DESK	044900	042195	003	W	055	00002	01	0000080000	011691	R	P
100000000	DESK LAMP	003500	002895	001	R	055	00012	02	0000020000	011691	C	C

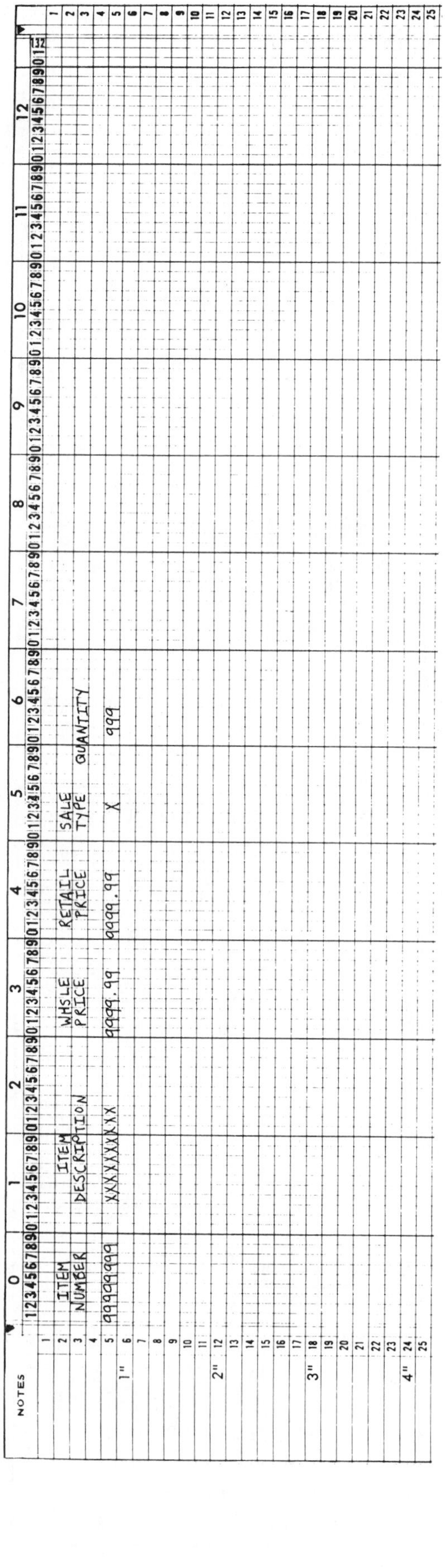
NOTES
ITEM NUMBER
ITEM DESCRIPTION
WHSLE PRICE
RETAIL PRICE
SALE TYPE
QUANTITY
999999999
XXXXXXXXXXXX
9999.99
9999.99
X
999

Figure F.3 Printer spacing chart for Exercise 1

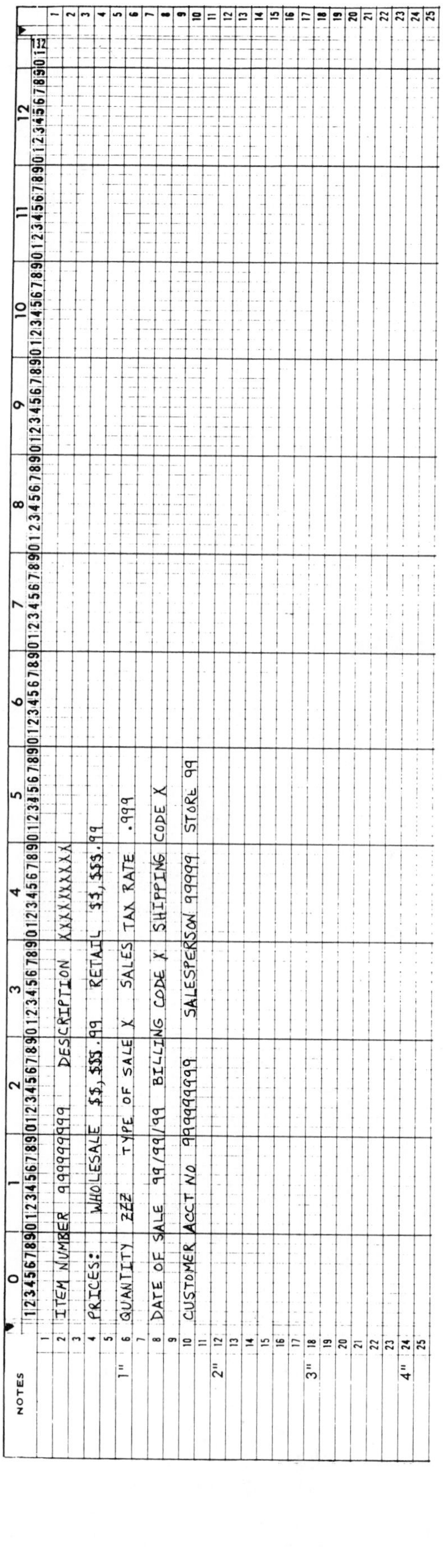
NOTES
ITEM NUMBER 999999999 DESCRIPTION XXXXXXXXXXX
PRICES: WHOLESALE $$,$$$.99 RETAIL $$,$$$.99
QUANTITY ZZZ TYPE OF SALE X SALES TAX RATE .999
DATE OF SALE 99/99/99 BILLING CODE X SHIPPING CODE X
CUSTOMER ACCT NO 999999999 SALESPERSON 99999 STORE 99

Figure F.4 Printer spacing chart for Exercise 3

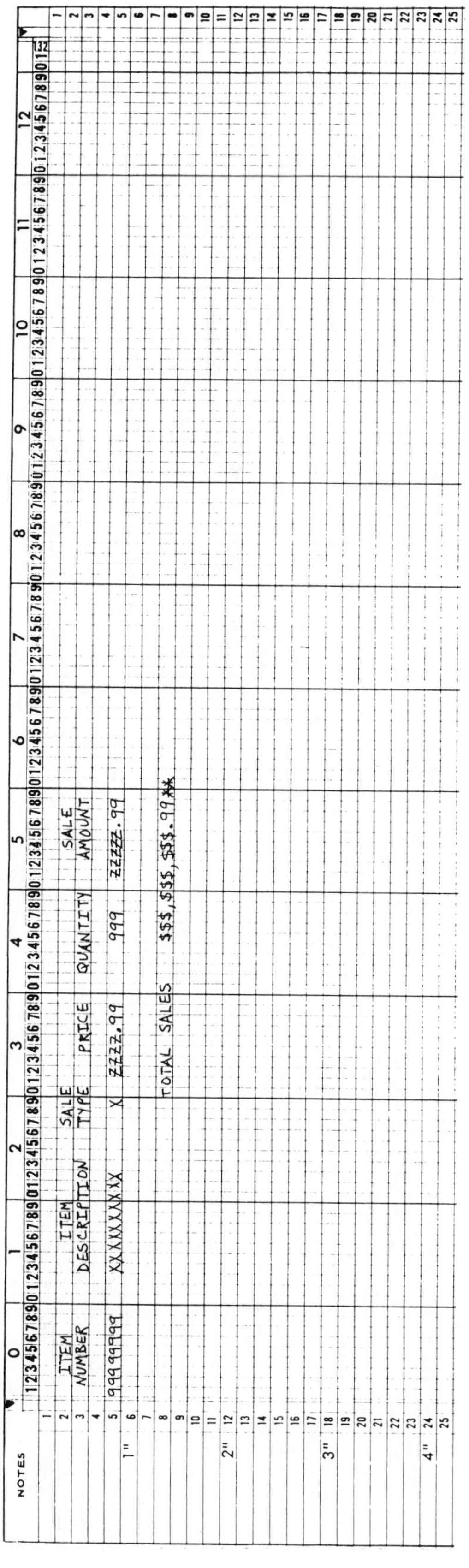

Figure F.5   Printer spacing chart for Exercise 4

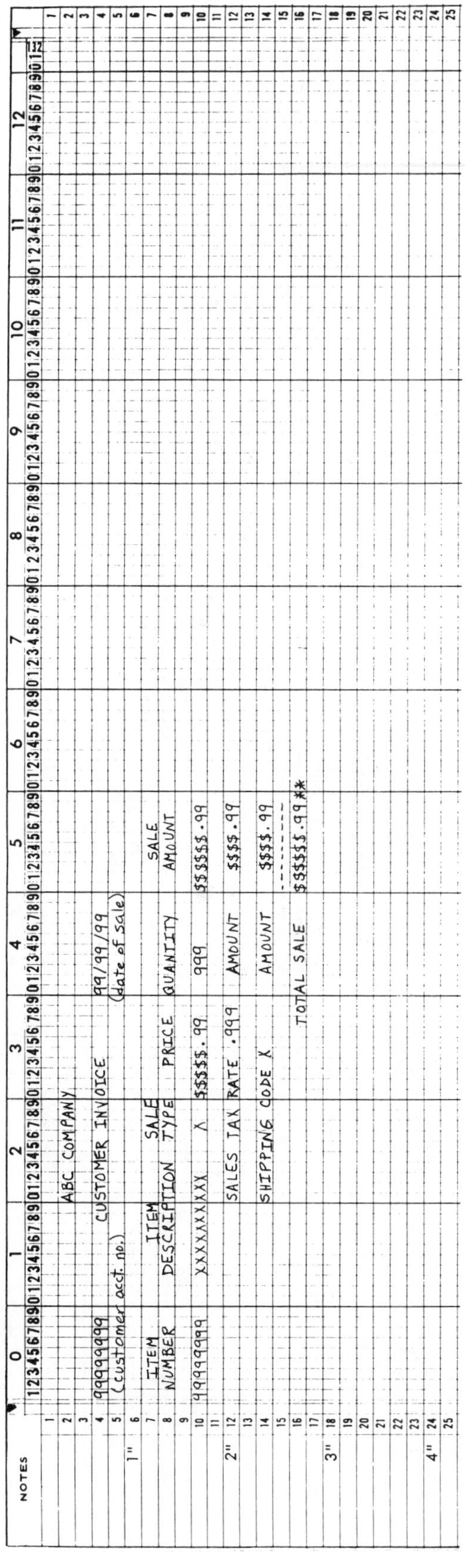

NOTES														
	0	1	2	3	4	5	6	7	8	9	10	11	12	
1														
2	ITEM	ITEM	SALE				SALE							
3	NUMBER	DESCRIPTION	TYPE	PRICE	QUANTITY		AMOUNT							
4														
5	99999999	XXXXXXXXXX	X	ZZZZ.99	999		ZZZZZ.99							
6														
7														
8				TOTAL SALES		$$$,$$$,$$$.99**									

Figure F.6   Printer spacing chart for Exercise 5

NOTES														
	0	1	2	3	4	5	6	7	8	9	10	11	12	
1														
2			ABC COMPANY											
3														
4	99999999		CUSTOMER INVOICE		99/99/99									
5	(customer acct. no.)				(date of sale)									
6														
7	ITEM	ITEM	SALE				SALE							
8	NUMBER	DESCRIPTION	TYPE	PRICE	QUANTITY		AMOUNT							
9														
10	99999999	XXXXXXXXXXX	X	$$$$$.99	999		$$$$$$.99							
11														
12			SALES TAX RATE .999		AMOUNT		$$$$.99							
13														
14			SHIPPING CODE X		AMOUNT		$$$$.99							
15							----------							
16				TOTAL SALE		$$$$$$.99**								

Figure F.7 Additional data for data validation program

Item Number	Item Description	Retail List Price	Wholesale List Price	Quantity	Type	Sales Tax Rate	Salesperson Identifier	Customer Account Number	Store Number	Date of Sale	Billing Code	Shipping Code	Comment
111111	SECR CHAIR	007900	006000	002	W	055	00002	04000	04000	011791	C	P	Nonnumeric item number
222222222		12950	9998	001	R	055	00001	10000	05000	011791	R	C	Missing item description, nonnumeric prices
300000000	L DESK	032500	029900	00013	02		00000	5555		011791	C	C	Invalid quantity, type and sales tax rate
300000000	L DESK	032500	029900	001	R	055				011791	R	C	Invalid salesperson id, store number, cust. acct. no.
300000003	EXEC DESK	044900	042195	001	W	055	00002	01000	01111	11791	R	C	Invalid date of sale
222222222	EXEC CHAIR	012900	009998	001	W	055	00002	01000	01110	011791			Invalid billing and shipping codes
A1111111		007900	006000	1	0	055	00000	B15	00000	1110	011791	C	U	Missing item description, nonnumeric quantity, invalid store number

Figure F.8 Printer spacing chart for Exercise 8

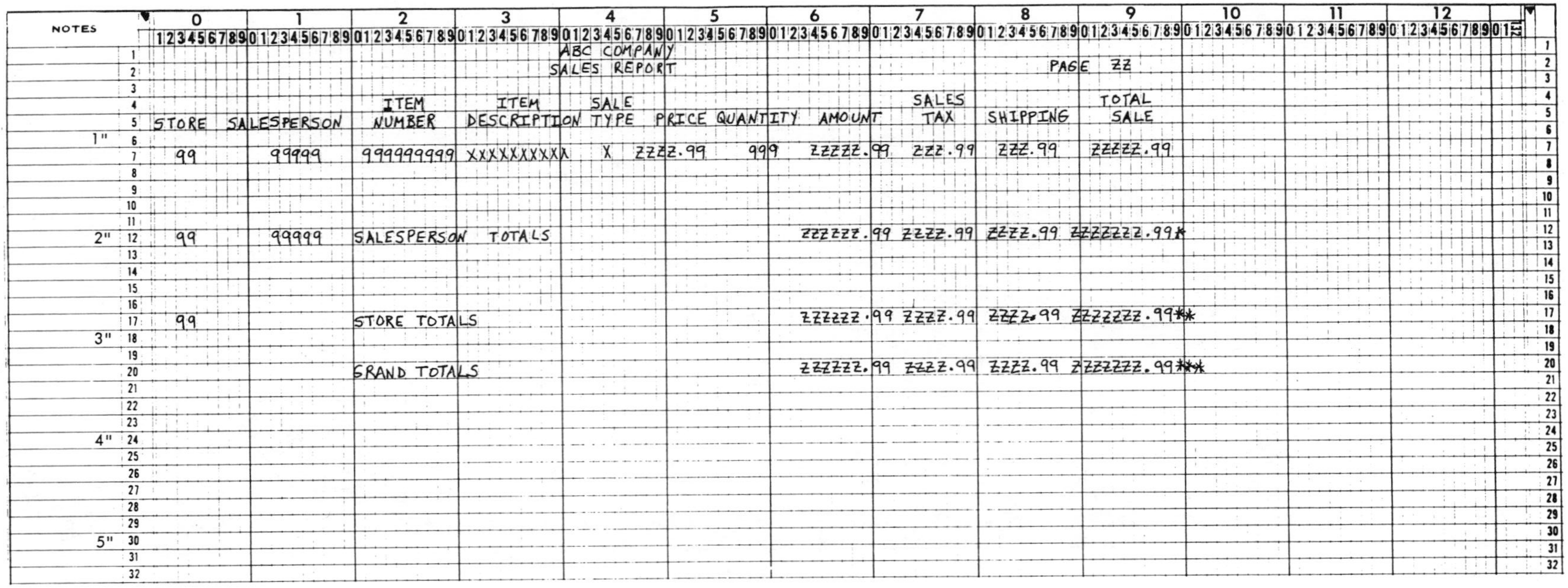

G. SUBSCRIPTION SYSTEM

G.1 BACKGROUND

Amalgamated Publishing, Inc., publishes several specialized magazines and distributes them by mail to subscribers. The management wishes to implement a subscription system that would make use of the company's small business computer. The computer is currently used for accounting and payroll; it has both batch and interactive capabilities.

The purpose of the system is to keep track of subscribers—which magazines a subscriber is taking, the expiration date for each subscription, the amounts paid, and the amounts owed. The system is also used to determine, for the production department, the number of magazines of each type to print and, for the mailing department, to produce the mailing labels. Because the company advertises heavily on TV and has a toll-free number for subscribers, the subscription-entry portion of the system is to be interactive. (Mail-in subscriptions either accompanied or not accompanied by payment must also be processed.) Most other portions of the system will be batch oriented.

The company publishes the following magazines on a monthly basis:

Name	Code
Everyone's Computer	EC
You and Your Garden	YG
Suburban Family Life	SF
Farmer's Guide	FG

From time to time new magazines are added to the list and, rarely, magazines are dropped. The system should be designed to handle a maximum of ten titles. Some subscribers take more than one magazine.

Each subscriber is assigned a 17-character identifier, made up of

Positions	Content
1–5	Zip code
6–11	First 6 characters of street address (with any spaces removed)
12–15	First 4 characters of last name
16–17	Magazine code

―――――― Example ――――――

John Jones, 123 Maple Street, Anywhere, CA 00576, who subscribes to *You and Your Garden*, would have as his identifier:

```
        Zip Code      Address    Last Name  Magazine
       ┌────────┐   ┌───────┐   ┌───────┐  ┌──┐
        0 0 5 7 6   1 2 3 M A P  J O N E Y  G
```

The purpose of this identifier is to facilitate retrieval of data as well as production of mailing labels and required reports.

G.2 THE SYSTEM

Two files make up the heart of the system: Magazine Master File and Subscription Master File. The Magazine Master File is a sequential file containing one record for each magazine published by the company. Each record contains the following fields:

Positions	Content	PIC
1–2	Magazine code	X(2)
3–20	Magazine title	X(18)
21–24	Subscription rate 6 mo.	99V99
25–28	Subscription rate 12 mo.	99V99
29–32	Subscription rate 24 mo.	99V99
33–36	Extra production quantity	9999

The Subscription Master File is an indexed file and contains one record for each subscription. Each record contains the following fields:

Positions	Content	PIC
1–17	Subscription identifier	X(17)
18–30	Subscriber name	X(13)
31–45	Street address	X(15)
46–54	City	X(9)
55–56	State	X(2)
57–60	Subscription date (mmyy)	9(4)
61–64	Expiration date (mmyy)	9(4)
65–68	Subscription amount	99V99
69	New subscription flag	X
70–71	Account age	99
72–77	Date of last payment (mmddyy)	9(6)
78–81	Total amount paid	99V99
82	Payment type:	9
	0 = No payment received	
	1 = Check	
	2 = VISA	
	3 = MasterCard	
	4 = Returned check	

The system is divided into five subsystems:

- Magazine Master File Maintenance
- Subscription Master File Maintenance
- Billing and Payment Accounting
- Production and Shipping
- Management Information

Each of the subsystems is described in more detail below.

Magazine Master File Maintenance

A program is needed to perform file maintenance operations—add, change, and delete—on the Magazine Master File. Because the file is sequential and not all of the operations can be made in place, this program will be batch oriented. The system flowchart for this subsystem is shown in Figure G.1.

Subscription Master File Maintenance

An interactive program is needed to perform file maintenance operations—add, change, and delete—on the Subscription Master File. This program would be used routinely by personnel who take phoned-in subscriptions and by others who process mailed-in subscriptions and answer inquiries from subscribers. The system flowchart for this portion of the subscription system is shown in Figure G.2.

Billing and Payment Accounting

After an unpaid subscription is entered into the system, a bill is sent to the subscriber. This is accomplished in the system by periodically running a program that will generate bills for new subscribers. This program will scan the Subscription Master File for accounts showing a balance due as determined by the Amount paid and Subscription amount fields; when a bill is produced, the program will add 1 to Account age. This program also produces past-due notices when appropriate.

When payment is received from a subscriber, the appropriate master file record must be updated. Occasionally, subscribers' checks are returned; the master file record must be modified accordingly. Payment accounting will be accomplished using an interactive program. The system flowchart for the billing and payment accounting subsystem is shown in Figure G.3.

Figure G.1   Magazine master file maintenance subsystem

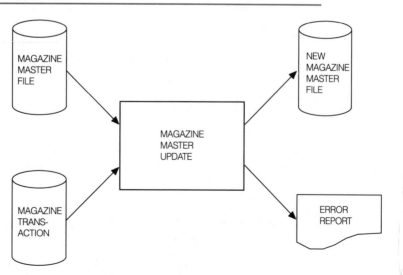

Figure G.2   Subscription master file maintenance subsystem

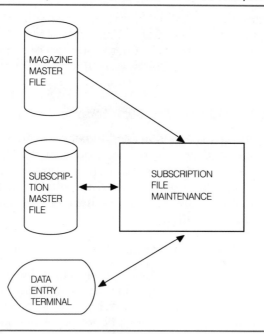

Figure G.3   Billing and payment accounting subsystem

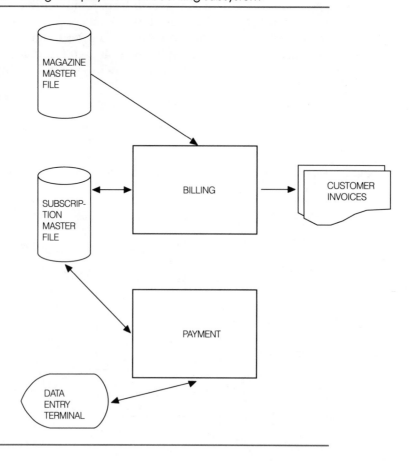

Production and Shipping

Amalgamated Publishing contracts with a local printer to print its magazines each month. The printed magazines are returned to Amalgamated's shipping department, which attaches mailing labels.

Because the subscriber base is growing rapidly, the quantities produced must be updated monthly. The subscription system must have a program that determines the number of subscribers for each magazine. The program should add an extra number for waste, free copies, internal use, and promotion.

Mailing labels are a very important product of the subscription system. The labels must be produced for each magazine in zip-code order to comply with post office regulations. In order to do this, the subscription master file must be sorted into the required sequence before mailing labels are printed. A system flowchart for the production and shipping subsystem is shown in Figure G.4.

Figure G.4   Production and shipping subsystem

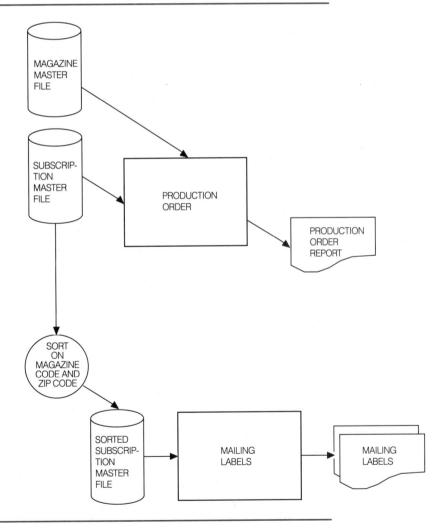

Management Information

Management of Amalgamated Publishing requires various reports that are used to monitor the ongoing operation of the company. Among the required reports are:

- Subscription Activity Report: This report lists new subscribers for each magazine by length of subscription. The report is produced as a batch job and is routinely run once a month to summarize data for that month.
- Aged Accounts Receivable Report: This report lists each account with a balance due and summarizes the data according to the time elapsed since receiving a payment of the account. This report is produced as a batch job once a month.

A system flowchart for this subsystem is shown in Figure G.5.

G.3 PROGRAMMING EXERCISES

1. Write a program to perform the Magazine Master Update described in Figure G.1. The record layout for the Magazine Transaction File is as follows:

Positions	Content	PIC
1–2	Magazine code	X(2)
3–20	Magazine title	X(18)
21–24	Subscription rate 6 mo.	99V99
25–28	Subscription rate 12 mo.	99V99
29–32	Subscription rate 24 mo.	99V99
33–36	Extra production	9999
37	Transaction code	X
	A = Add record to file	
	C = Change content of a field	
	D = Delete record from file	

Figure G.5 Management information subsystem

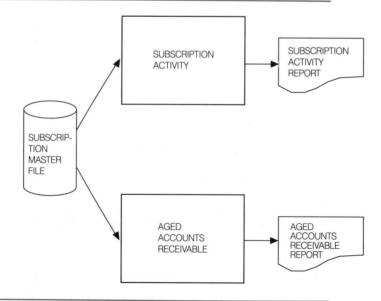

For change transactions, only fields that do not contain spaces should be changed.

Your program should permit multiple transaction types for a given record (i.e., add, change, and delete for one magazine in a cycle should be permitted if the transaction records are in this sequence) and multiple change records for one magazine. Be sure to test your program with sufficient invalid transactions and sequences of transactions and to exercise all error messages contained in the program.

2. Write a program to perform the Subscription File Maintenance function described in Figure G.2. The following transaction codes should be implemented:

   D Display content of a record for a given subscriber.
   L List all records in Subscriber Master File.
   A Add a subscription.
   K Delete a subscription.
   C Change address.
   E Extend expiration date for subscription.

Notes:

   a. In order to access a record for the subscriber or add a new record to the file, all parts of the subscriber identifier must be entered. Recall that the identifier is comprised of the zip code, street address, last name, and magazine code.
   b. The program should load the content of the Magazine Master File into a table and look up data regarding subscription costs from that table.
   c. When a subscription is added to the file, the New subscription flag is set to "Y", and the subscription date should be the current month and year. The expiration date should be computed from the subscription term chosen by the subscriber. The subscription amount should be copied from the table described in Note b above. Positions 69 to 80 should be zeros when the record is first written into the file if payment is not received with the order. If payment is received, then the content of these fields should reflect the date, type, and amount of payment.
   d. When a change of address transaction is processed, it is necessary to delete the old record and add a new record with a new subscriber identifier. Positions 57 to 80 of the new record should be copied directly from the old record.
   e. In order to extend the expiration date for a subscription, the term of the subscription should be added to the old expiration date. The subscription amount and other fields should be treated as for a new record. Do not permit a subscription that has a balance due to be extended.
   f. The transaction code L should permit a display of records either at the terminal or on a printed copy.

3. Write a program to perform the billing function described in Figure G.3. Only one invoice should be sent to a given subscriber, no matter how many magazines the reader subscribes to. Each entry on the invoice should list the subscription date, the expiration date, the magazine name (in full), the subscription amount, the amount paid, and the balance due. (For an existing subscription, the balance due is the difference between the subscription amount and the total amount paid. For a new unpaid subscription, the balance due is the subscription amount.) For an item included in an invoice, add 1 to

the billing code in the subscription record. (This field is used to determine how long the account has had an outstanding balance.) Each invoice should contain the customer's name, address, and totals in an appropriate format.

Notes:

a. Only new subscriptions and subscriptions for which there is an outstanding balance should be included in an invoice. Paid customers should not receive an invoice.

b. Your program should load the content of the Magazine Master File into a table and look up the full magazine name for an invoice entry as required.

4. Write a program to perform the payment function described in Figure G.3. The program must be interactive and allow the following types of transactions:

    D Display a subscription record.

    P Payment; update a record to reflect payment on account.

    R Returned check; update a record as appropriate.

Notes:

a. A payment transaction should cause the amount paid to be added to the total amount paid. The date of the last payment should be changed to the current date, and the payment type field should be updated as appropriate. The Account age field should be reset to zero.

b. A returned check transaction should cause the amount of the check to be deducted from the total amount paid, and the Account age field should be incremented by 1. The payment type field should be changed to "4."

5. Write a program to perform the production order function described in Figure G.4. The production order report should list the full name of each magazine, the actual number of subscribers, the number of copies to be added, and the total production to be ordered.

Note:

The content of the Magazine Master File should be loaded into a table and used as a reference to determine the full name of the magazine and added production amount.

6. Write a program to perform the sort function described in Figure G.4. Your program should transform the indexed Subscription Master File into the sequential sorted Subscription Master File, which contains records only for nonexpired subscriptions and which is in sequence by magazine code (primary key) and zip code (secondary key).

7. Write a program to perform the mailing labels function described in Figure G.4. The mailing label should contain the name, full address, subscription identifier, and subscription expiration date.

Note:

If you have access to actual fanfold mailing labels (and can construct an appropriate carriage control tape for your printer if required), this exercise can be made quite realistic.

8. Write a program to perform the subscription activity function described in Figure G.5. The required report should list all new subscriptions entered during the current month and should produce

totals for each magazine, as well as grand totals of appropriate fields. This program should set the New subscription flag to "N".

Note:

Try to put yourself in the manager's position as you design this report. Include as much detail as desired.

9. Write a program to perform the Aged Accounts Receivable function described in Figure G.5. The report should list each account that has a balance due and should show whether the account is current (less than 30 days old), 30 to 60 days old, or over 90 days old. Relevant totals should be produced for each magazine and for all magazines. (See Note for Exercise 8.)

10. Modify the organization of the Magazine Master File to a randomized relative file. Write a Magazine Master Update program that is interactive rather than batch, as in Exercise 1. Revise other programs in the system as required to process the file in its new form, including Subscription File Maintenance, Billing, and Production Order.

H. USING RM/COBOL-85

H.1 OVERVIEW

RM/COBOL-85 is a compiler and program development system developed by Ryan McFarland Corporation. The compiler features an enhanced version of COBOL-85. The system also contains a project manager and editor called RM/CO* (pronounced "R M COSTAR") which may be used in conjunction with the compiler if desired.

The software that is available to adopters of this text is an educational form of RM/COBOL-85 (Version 04.10.06). It incorporates most of the features of the commercial software with the following major exceptions:

- Programs are limited to 800 lines of code.
- Utilities are not included.
- Report Writer is not supported.

There are five files that make up the educational software package:

- RMCOBOL.EXE
- RMCOBOL.OVL
- RMCOSTAR.EXE
- RMCOSTAR.HLP
- RUNCOBOL.EXE

RMCOBOL.EXE and RMCOBOL.OVL constitute the RM/COBOL-85 compiler; RMCOSTAR.EXE and RMCOSTAR.HLP contain the project manager and editor system; RUNCOBOL.EXE is the RM/COBOL-85 run time interpreter. In most educational computing labs, these files will have been copied to a hard disk; the student will store files on a floppy disk (usually in drive A). This software can also be used on systems that do not have a hard disk; if this is your situation, your instructor will provide detailed instructions.

Creating and testing a program in this system is a four-step process:

1. Create the COBOL source program using RM/CO* or any other editor that can generate an ASCII file. (If you are using a word processor, make sure that you save the file as an ASCII file; the compiler cannot process a file in a word processor format. Using word processors to edit programs is not recommended, however.) Give the program file a name of your choice, but use the extension .CBL. (The compiler expects all COBOL source programs to have a name with the extension .CBL.)

2. Create a sample data file if appropriate. It is a good idea to use the extension .DAT for data files, but you can use any name of your choice. Save this file as an ASCII file.

3. Use the compiler to translate the COBOL program into a low-level language that can be executed by the program RUNCOBOL; this file is given the extension .COB. The compiler checks for syntax errors; if any are found, they are displayed on the screen and no .COB file is created. The compiler may generate a program listing if desired; this file will have the extension .LST. This will be an ASCII file that you can examine and/ or print using your editor or RM/CO*.

4. Use RUNCOBOL to execute the program. At this time, the code in your .COB file will be interpreted, and your data file will be processed to produce your output. In the programs in this text, we have reassigned all printer files to a disk file with the extension .RPT, which is short for "RePorT." When the program has been executed, you can use your editor or RM/CO* to examine this file and produce a printed copy of it if desired.

This process is summarized in Figure H.1. Note that the compiler keeps the same basic file name that you supply (including drive designation and path) for all of the files that it creates. It is a good idea for you to use the same basic file name with different extensions for the data file you create (.DAT) and the report file that your program creates (.RPT). When you finish, you will typically have the following files present on your data disk:

- *file-name*.CBL   Your COBOL source program
- *file-name*.COB   The output from the compiler
- *file-name*.LST   Your program listing (optional)
- *file-name*.DAT   The data file that your program will process
- *file-name*.RPT   The output from your program

All of these files, except the .COB file, are ASCII files that can be processed through RM/CO* or another editor. You are responsible for creating the .CBL and .DAT files using RM/CO* or another editor. The compiler creates the .LST and .COB files; your program creates the .RPT file.

H.2 COMPILING PROGRAMS

For hard-disk based systems, it is best to copy the RM/COBOL-85 programs to a subdirectory (perhaps called RM) on the hard disk. The AUTO-EXEC.BAT file should have a line in it such as the following:

```
SET PATH=C:RM;%PATH%
```

Use the subdirectory in which the RM/COBOL-85 programs are located in place of "RM."[1] In most educational computing labs, this will have been done for the student. If this SET PATH statement is not a part of the AUTO-EXEC.BAT file, the user can type it at the DOS prompt before changing the default drive to drive A.

To begin a session with RM/COBOL-85, boot the system and insert a disk in drive A. At the DOS prompt, type A:. This sets the default drive to

---

[1] If students will be using an editor other than RM/CO*, a similar provision should be made for that editor.

Figure H.1 The program development process using RM/
COBOL-85

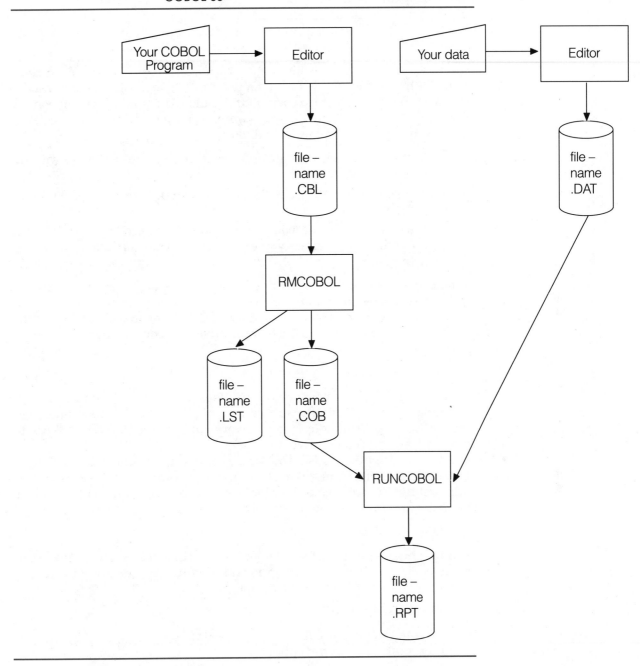

A so that all files that you create with your editor, the COBOL compiler, and your program will be placed on the disk in drive A. You still have access to the COBOL compiler and the editor because the SET PATH statement will cause the system to examine these subdirectories for files that are not located on the default disk drive.

In this section, we will assume that the .CBL and .DAT files that are needed for a particular project have been created and are located on a disk in drive A. Section H.6 covers the details of creating files using RM/CO*.

In order to compile a program, you will use a DOS command of the following form:

```
RMCOBOL file-name [option-list]
```

The file-name is the DOS file name of the .CBL file. (You do not include .CBL with the file-name because the COBOL compiler automatically assumes that this is the extension for the file.) The option-list can contain any one of several options, or you can omit options entirely. Some of the options that you will find most useful are

- L which causes the compiler to create a program-listing file with the extension .LST.
- P which causes the compiler to send the program-listing file to the printer.
- Y which causes the compiler to include a symbol table with the .COB file. This enables you to display the value of data items during debugging.

If more than one option is included, the options are separated from one another by a space or comma.

For example, suppose the file PRO2B.CBL is located on a disk in drive A. Assuming that drive A is the default drive, the command to compile the program would be

```
RMCOBOL PRO2B
```

If syntax errors are found, they will be displayed on the screen followed by a summary of errors. If no syntax errors are found, the error summary will appear on the screen indicating no errors, and the file PRO2B.COB will be produced and stored on drive A.

If there are numerous errors or if you wish to use the debugging facility which is described in following sections, you will need to secure a program listing. To produce a disk file containing this listing with the same file name and the .LST extension, you would use the L option:

```
RMCOBOL PRO2B L
```

If you wished to print the listing to the printer instead of placing the listing in a disk file, you will use the P option. Make sure that the printer is turned on and is on line before using this option.

```
RMCOBOL PRO2B P
```

If you wanted to print the listing and place a copy of it in the .LST file, you could use both the L and P options:

```
RMCOBOL PRO2B L P
```

It is usually better to use the L option when you compile; then use an editor to examine the .LST file and print it out if desired. Using the P option will make the compilation process much slower and may result in producing unneeded printouts which are a waste of both paper and time.

In order to make effective use of the debug facility, you will need to have the compiler include a copy of the symbol table with the .COB file. (The symbol table is a list of data-names defined in the program together with the memory address associated with that data item.) In order to do this, you will compile the program using the Y option:

```
RMCOBOL PRO2B Y
```

Probably the most often used options will be L and Y to secure an .LST file and include the symbol table for debugging purposes; therefore, the recommended form of the command is

```
RMCOBOL file-name L Y
```

Figure H.2 shows the content of the .LST file produced by using the command

```
RMCOBOL PRO2B L Y
```

Figure H.2   Program listing for Program 2b

Source file is
PRO2B.CBL

Date and time of compilation

```
RM/COBOL-85 (Version 4.10.06) For DOS 2.00+    05/29/91  21:11:47 Page 1
Source File: PRO2B                              Options: L Y
```

Compile options

```
LINE   DEBUG    PG/LN  A...B......2.........3.........4.........5.........6.........7..ID....8

  1                     IDENTIFICATION DIVISION.
  2
  3                     PROGRAM-ID. CUSTOMER-LIST-PRO2B.
  4                     AUTHOR. HORN.
  5
  6                     ENVIRONMENT DIVISION.
  7
  8                     CONFIGURATION SECTION.
  9
 10                     SOURCE-COMPUTER.
 11                     OBJECT-COMPUTER.
 12
 13                     INPUT-OUTPUT SECTION.
 14
 15                     FILE-CONTROL.
 16
 17                         SELECT ACCOUNT-FILE ASSIGN TO DISK
 18                             "PRO2B.DAT" ORGANIZATION IS LINE SEQUENTIAL.
 19                         SELECT REPORT-FILE ASSIGN TO PRINTER
 20                             "PRO2B.RPT".
 21                     DATA DIVISION.
 22
 23                     FILE SECTION.
 24
 25                     FD  ACCOUNT-FILE
 26                         LABEL RECORDS ARE STANDARD
 27                         DATA RECORD IS ACCOUNT-RECORD.
 28
 29                     01  ACCOUNT-RECORD.
 30                         02 ACCOUNT-NUMBER-AR      PIC 9(9).
 31                         02 LAST-NAME-AR           PIC X(10).
 32                         02 FIRST-NAME-AR          PIC X(10).
 33                         02 MIDDLE-INITIAL-AR      PIC X.
 34                         02 FILLER                 PIC X(54).
 35
 36                     FD  REPORT-FILE
 37                         LABEL RECORDS ARE OMITTED
 38                         DATA RECORD IS REPORT-RECORD.
 39
 40                     01  REPORT-RECORD.
 41                         02 FILLER                 PIC X(11).
 42                         02 ACCOUNT-NUMBER-RR      PIC 9(9).
 43                         02 FILLER                 PIC X(10).
 44                         02 FIRST-NAME-RR          PIC X(10).
 45                         02 FILLER                 PIC X.
```

Program name (Do not confuse program name with the name of the source file.)

Input file is PRO2B.DAT on default disk drive.

Output file is PRO2B.RPT on default disk drive.

Program listing for
    Program 2b *(continued)*

```
RM/COBOL-85 (Version 4.10.06) For DOS 2.00+   05/29/91  21:11:47 Page 2
Source File: PRO2B                 Options: L Y

LINE   DEBUG     PG/LN  A...B......2.........3.........4.........5.........6.........7..ID....8
  46                           02 MIDDLE-INITIAL-RR      PIC X.
  47                           02 FILLER                 PIC X.
  48                           02 LAST-NAME-RR            PIC X(10).
  49                           02 FILLER                 PIC X(79).
  50
  51                     WORKING-STORAGE SECTION.
  52
  53                     01  FLAGS.
  54                           02  EOF-FLAG       PIC X(3)  VALUE "NO".
  55
  56                     PROCEDURE DIVISION.
  57
  58     000002         1000-MAIN-CONTROL.
  59
  60     000005             OPEN INPUT ACCOUNT-FILE
  61                             OUTPUT REPORT-FILE.
  62     000018             MOVE SPACES TO REPORT-RECORD.
  63     000024             READ ACCOUNT-FILE
  64                             AT END MOVE "YES" TO EOF-FLAG.
  65     000040             PERFORM 2000-PROCESS-DATA
  66                             UNTIL EOF-FLAG = "YES".
  67     000054             CLOSE ACCOUNT-FILE
  68                                 REPORT-FILE.
  69     000067             STOP RUN.
  70
  71     000070         2000-PROCESS-DATA.
  72
  73     000073             MOVE ACCOUNT-NUMBER-AR     TO ACCOUNT-NUMBER-RR.
  74     000080             MOVE FIRST-NAME-AR         TO FIRST-NAME-RR.
  75     000087             MOVE MIDDLE-INITIAL-AR     TO MIDDLE-INITIAL-RR.
  76     000094             MOVE LAST-NAME-AR          TO LAST-NAME-RR.
  77     000101             WRITE REPORT-RECORD AFTER ADVANCING 1 LINE.
  78     000113             READ ACCOUNT-FILE
  79                             AT END MOVE "YES" TO EOF-FLAG.
```

Header is reproduced on each page of listing.

Grid shows Margin A, Margin B, and other columns in source statements.

These numbers show the address of machine code in the .COB file.

Line number is needed to use the debug facility of RUNCOBOL.

**Program listing for
    Program 2b**   *(concluded)*

```
RM/COBOL-85 (Version 4.10.06) For DOS 2.00+    05/29/91  21:11:47 Page 3
Source File: PRO2B                    Options: L Y

PROGRAM SUMMARY STATISTICS
CUSTOMER-LIST-PRO2B  ◄——————— Program name from PROGRAM-ID entry


READ ONLY SIZE =                     470 (X"000001D6") BYTES

READ/WRITE SIZE =                    524 (X"0000020C") BYTES

OVERLAYABLE SEGMENT SIZE =             0 (X"00000000") BYTES

TOTAL GENERATED OBJECT SIZE =        994 (X"000003E2") BYTES      79 LINES

        0 ERRORS          0 WARNINGS    FOR PROGRAM CUSTOMER-LIST-PRO2B



OBJECT VERSION LEVEL =    2

OPTIONS IN EFFECT:
    Y - SYMBOL TABLE OUTPUT TO OBJECT FILE
```

Summary information about.COB file

Compilation summary (A similar message is written on the screen at the conclusion of the compilation.)

In order to print out this file, it is necessary to set most printers to compressed print mode because each line in the file is longer than 80 characters. (If the file is printed using ordinary noncompressed mode, portions of each line may be truncated.) Examine the listing carefully; you will note that it is made up of three pages. The first two pages contain the source code, and the last page contains a summary of the compilation and the object code that was generated. Each page of the listing has a heading showing the version of the compiler that was used, the name of the source file, the date and time, the page number, and the options in effect for this compilation. Note that the program name specified in the PROGRAM-ID entry is used at several points in the program listing. Do not confuse this name with the name of the file which contains the program. The file-name is used on all DOS commands; the program name is used by RMCOBOL and RUNCOBOL in some of the output that these programs produce. Note that beneath the page header in the source code listing is a grid that shows the position of characters in the COBOL statements. Margins A and B, as well as position 72 (labeled ID), are shown. Remember that COBOL statements must be coded between Margin A and position 72; positions 73 through 80 are used for an identification sequence and are not translated by the compiler.

The example shown in Figure H.2 has no syntax errors present. Unfortunately, syntax errors often occur at the initial stages in preparing a program. The compiler prints error messages on the screen during compilation as each syntax error is encountered. If only one or two errors are present, the programmer may be able to correct the program based on this information. If more errors are found, then it is best to examine the .LST file in which error messages will be printed along with the source statements that caused the problem.

Program 2d described in Chapter 2 has a variety of syntax errors. A portion of the .LST file for this program is shown in Figure H.3. RM/COBOL-85 recognizes two levels of errors—W for Warning and E for Error.

Figure H.3   Example of diagnostics—.LST file for Program 2d

```
RM/COBOL-85 (Version 4.10.06) For DOS 2.00+   05/29/91  23:39:07 Page 2
Source File: PRO2D                      Options: L

  LINE   DEBUG     PG/LN  A...B......2........3........4........5........6.........7..ID.....8
BALANCE-PRO2D

    52                          02 FILLER                X(11)    VALUE "NEW BALANCE".
                                                         $        $
*****    1) E 137: DATA DESCRIPTION SYNTAX (SCAN SUPPRESSED) *E*E*E*E*E*E*E*E*E*E*E*E*E*E*E
*****    2) I   5: SCAN RESUME *I*I*I*I*I*I*I*I*I*I*I*I*I*I*I*I*I*I*I*I*I*I*I*I*I*I*I*I*I*I*I

    53
    54                          01  DETAIL-LINE.
                                $
*****    1) E 254: GROUP LEVEL *E*E*E*E*E*E*E*E*E*E*E*E*E*E*E*E*E*E*E*E*E*E*E*E*E*E*E*E*E*E
*****LAST DIAGNOSTIC AT LINE:      52

    55                          02 FILLER           PIC X(5)     VALUE SPACES.
    56                          02 OLD-BALANCE-DL    PIC 9999.99.
    57                          02 FILLER           PIC X(11)    VALUE SPACES.
    58                          02 DEPOSIT-AMOUNT-DL PIC 9(4).99.
    59                          02 FILLER           PIC X(7)     VALUE SPACES
    60                          02 NEW-BALANCE-DL    PIC 9(4).99.
                                $
*****    1) E 319: PERIOD SPACE REQUIRED *E*E*E*E*E*E*E*E*E*E*E*E*E*E*E*E*E*E*E*E*E*E*E*E
*****LAST DIAGNOSTIC AT LINE:      54

    61
    62                          PROCEDURE DIVISION.
    63
    64      000002              1000-MAIN-CONTROL.
    65
    66      000005              OPEN INPUT ACCOUNT-FILE
                                $
*****    1) W  60: VERB IN AREA A*W*W*W*W*W*W*W*W*W*W*W*W*W*W*W*W*W*W*W*W*W*W*W*W*W*W*W*W*W
*****LAST DIAGNOSTIC AT LINE:      60

    67                                  OUTPUT REPORT-FILE.
    68      000018              MOVE HEAD-LINE TO REPORT-RECORD.
                                     $                    $
*****    1) E 260: IDENTIFIER INVALID (SCAN SUPPRESSED)*E*E*E*E*E*E*E*E*E*E*E*E*E*E*E*E*E*E
*****    2) I   5: SCAN RESUME *I*I*I*I*I*I*I*I*I*I*I*I*I*I*I*I*I*I*I*I*I*I*I*I*I*I*I*I*I*I*I
*****LAST DIAGNOSTIC AT LINE:      66

    69      000021              WRITE REPORT-RECORD AFTER ADVANCING PAGE.
    70      000030              READ ACCOUNT-FILE
    71                              AT END MOVE "YES" TO EOF-FLAG.
    72      000046              PERFORM 2000-CREATE-REPORT
    73                                  UNTIL EOF-FLAG = "YES".
    74      000060              CLOSE ACCOUNT-FILE
    75                                  REPORT-FILE.
    76      000073              STOP RUN.
    77
    78      000076              2000-CREATE-REPRT.
    79
    80      000079              MOVE OLD-BALANCE-AR TO OLD-BALANCE-DL.
    81      000084              MOVE DEPOSIT-AMOUNT-AR TO DEPOSIT-AMOUNT-DL.
    82      000089              ADD OLD-BALANCE-AR DEPOSIT-AMOUNT-AR GIVING NEW-BALANCE-DL.
    83      000096              MOVE DETAIL-LINE TO REPORT-RECORD.
    84      000104              WRITE REPORT-RECORD AFTER ADVANCING 1 LINES.
    85      000116              READ ACCOUNT-FILE
    86                              AT END MOVE "YES" TO EOF-FLAG.
    87
```

Figure H.3   *(concluded)*

```
RM/COBOL-85 (Version 4.10.06) For DOS 2.00+    05/29/91  23:39:07 Page 3
Source File: PRO2D                          Options: L

SUMMARY DIAGNOSTICS
BALANCE-PRO2D


E 315: PERFORM ENTRY UNDEFINED*E*E*E*E*E*E*E*E*E*E*E*E:  2000-CREATE-REPORT
I   3: AT LINE NUMBER *I*I*I*I*I*I*I*I*I*I*I*I*I*I*I:        72

RM/COBOL-85 (Version 4.10.06) For DOS 2.00+    05/29/91  23:39:07 Page 4
Source File: PRO2D                          Options: L

PROGRAM SUMMARY STATISTICS
BALANCE-PRO2D


READ ONLY SIZE =                      510 (X"000001FE") BYTES

READ/WRITE SIZE =                     600 (X"00000258") BYTES

OVERLAYABLE SEGMENT SIZE =              0 (X"00000000") BYTES

TOTAL GENERATED OBJECT SIZE =        1110 (X"00000456") BYTES       87 LINES

     5 ERRORS          1 WARNING    FOR PROGRAM BALANCE-PRO2D

LAST DIAGNOSTIC AT LINE:   68



OBJECT VERSION LEVEL =   2
```

W-level errors are flagged on the program listing with an appropriate message, but the compilation process continues. If a program contained only W-level errors, a .COB file will be produced. E-level errors are more serious; the presence of one such error will result in no .COB file being produced. For example, in the listing shown in Figure H.3, there is one W-level error at line 66. (The OPEN verb should begin in Margin B rather than in Margin A.) This program also has five E-level errors. Four of these are flagged in the body of the program (lines 52, 54, 60, and 68). The fifth error comes from misspelling the paragraph name at line 78; this error is listed in the compilation summary. (Compare this listing with the listing of Program 2d, in Chapter 2, which was produced by the Microsoft COBOL compiler.)

An RM/COBOL-85 syntax error message is made up of four parts:

- A message number, such as 1 or 2, which refers to the $ printed beneath the line of preceding line of code. Message number 1 refers to the character marked by the first $; message number 2 refers to the character marked by the second $, and so forth.

- A one-character code (I, E, or W), which represents the message level. I-level messages are for information only, W-level messages are warnings, and E-level messages are errors that result in no .COB file being produced.

- A message number, which can be used to reference more information about the error in Appendix A of *RM/COBOL-85 User's Guide for DOS Systems*.

- A brief description of the error.

The remainder of the line is filled with characters designed to draw your attention to the error.

When the compiler encounters an element in a program that it cannot translate, it takes two actions: an appropriate error message is produced and the translation process, called **scanning**, is terminated. The compiler then proceeds with its examination of the program to locate the next part of the program that represents a valid COBOL program element. Some E-level errors have the additional information `"SCAN SUPPRESSED"` attached to them. Later in the program, an I-level message shows `"SCAN RESUME"`. All parts of the program between the point marked `"SCAN SUPPRESSED"` and the element marked `"SCAN RESUME"` have been ignored by the compiler. For example, in Figure H.3, line 68 has two error messages attached to it. The first error, marked under `"HEAD-LINE"`, indicates that this identifier is invalid and that scanning stopped at this point. The second message indicates that the scan resumed at the end of the line of code.

H.3 RUNNING PROGRAMS

The RM/COBOL-85 compiler generates a file with the extension .COB, which contains machine-level code translated from the COBOL source program. This file can be executed only by using the program RUNCOBOL. This program acts as an interpreter to execute the code in the .COB file.

The general syntax for invoking RUNCOBOL is

```
RUNCOBOL file-name [option-list]
```

You do not use the extension .COB on the file-name because RUNCOBOL automatically assumes that this is the extension that will be present. The option-list is omitted if it is not needed. (More information on available options is found in Section H.5.)

For example, to execute program PRO2B, type

```
RUNCOBOL PRO2B
```

The screen shown in Figure H.4 is displayed when the program RUNCOBOL is loaded.

The educational version or RUNCOBOL distributed with this text is slightly different from the commercial version of the software. The educational version automatically places the user in the debug mode. In this mode, you can choose to execute the program, step through the program one line at a time, display the content of data items, or perform other operations useful in removing errors from a program.[2] In debug mode, immediately after the informational screen, the user is presented with a prompt in the following form:

```
ST line-number program-name C?_
```

In this prompt, ST is a code meaning STep, line-number is the line number of the first executable statement in the program, program-name is the

---

[2] In the commercial version of RUNCOBOL, the user must choose to enter this mode by using the D option in the RUNCOBOL invocation statement.

Figure H.4   Use of RUNCOBOL to execute Program 2b

```
A:\>runcobol pro2b

RM/COBOL-85 Runtime (Version 4.10.06) for DOS 2.00+.  Configured for 001 user.
Educational Version - Restricted Usage
(c) Copyright 1985, 1989 by Ryan McFarland Corp. All rights reserved.
Registration Number: CZ-0000-01141-01
```

name of the program taken from the PROGRAM-ID entry, and C? is a prompt indicating that the system is expecting a command. The cursor is shown as an underscore character. You type a command and press Enter. To execute the program, use the command R which means "Resume execution." When you enter this command, the program is executed until either an error condition occurs or a STOP RUN statement is encountered. In either case, an appropriate message is printed, and the system presents a prompt in the following form:

$$\left\{\begin{matrix} \text{SR} \\ \text{ER} \end{matrix}\right\} \text{ line-number program-name C?\_}$$

In this prompt, SR is a code meaning Stop Run, and ER is a code meaning ERror. The remaining elements have the same meaning as in the prompt described above. The appropriate command to enter at this point is Q which means Quit. This will return you to the operating system prompt. The complete set of commands for the execution of Program 2b is shown in Figure H.5.

Figure H.5   Commands required to execute Program 2b

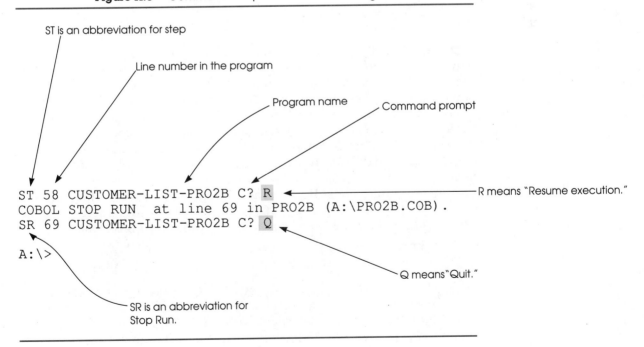

In summary, executing a program involves the following steps:

1. At the operating system prompt type RUNCOBOL file-name.
2. Enter the command R at the first prompt presented by RUNCOBOL. (R is short for "Resume execution".)
3. Enter the command Q at the second prompt presented by RUNCOBOL. (Q is short for "Quit".)

More information on using the debug facility is presented in Section H.5.

H.4 FILE CONSIDERATIONS

Most microcomputer-oriented COBOL compilers including RM/COBOL-85 feature two enhancements of the COBOL standard that facilitate the processing of files in a microcomputing environment. Both of these enhancements relate directly to the SELECT entry.

- A nonstandard file type called LINE SEQUENTIAL is available. This file type is quite similar in many respects to the standard type SEQUENTIAL, but LINE SEQUENTIAL files can be created and edited by most program editors including RM/CO*. This file type is sometimes called an ASCII file or a Text file.
- The program can specify the external-file-name (that is, the DOS file name) associated with the file in the SELECT entry as either a literal or a data item that will contain the file name.

A general form for the SELECT entry for file type LINE SEQUENTIAL is shown below:

```
SELECT file-name ASSIGN TO DISK [external-file-name]
       ORGANIZATION IS LINE SEQUENTIAL.
```

In this statement, external-file-name can be specified as a literal or a data-name; if it is omitted, the first eight characters of file-name will be used as the external-file-name. If a data-name is used to specify the external-file-name, then that data-name must be defined in WORKING-STORAGE as an alphanumeric data item, and it must conform to all of the conventions for DOS file names including drive and path specifications if appropriate. The ORGANIZATION IS clause may also be omitted. If it is omitted, the default file type is SEQUENTIAL, to which RM/COBOL-85 also refers as BINARY SEQUENTIAL.

For example, consider Program 2b shown in Figure H.2. The file ACCOUNT-FILE is a LINE SEQUENTIAL file with external-name "PRO2B.DAT". The SELECT entry at lines 17 through 18 is as follows:

```
SELECT ACCOUNT-FILE ASSIGN TO DISK
       "PRO2B.DAT" ORGANIZATION IS LINE SEQUENTIAL.
```

When ACCOUNT-FILE is opened, the system will locate the file "PRO2B.DAT" on the default disk drive and make its content available to the program.

An alternative way to specify the external-file-name of a file is to use a data-name in the SELECT entry. For example, suppose the SELECT entry has been coded as

```
SELECT ACCOUNT-FILE ASSIGN TO DISK
       FILE-NAME ORGANIZATION IS LINE SEQUENTIAL.
```

The data item FILE-NAME must be declared as a field type alphanumeric in WORKING-STORAGE; an appropriate definition would be

```
01   FILE-NAME PIC X(12).
```

Prior to opening this file, the program must establish a value for FILE-NAME. This can be done in a variety of ways, but the most useful way is to allow the user to enter the name of the file at the keyboard. The following program segment would allow the user to enter the external-name of the file prior to the program opening the file for processing:

```
DISPLAY "Enter name of file".
ACCEPT FILE-NAME.
OPEN INPUT ACCOUNT-FILE.
```

This procedure is used extensively in the interactive programs in this text beginning in Chapter 10.

A third, though generally less desirable, alternative is to allow the system to use the first eight characters of file-name as the external-file-name. For example, suppose the SELECT statement is coded as follows:

```
SELECT ACCOUNT-FILE ASSIGN TO DISK
       ORGANIZATION IS LINE SEQUENTIAL.
```

The default external-file-name would be "ACCOUNT-" which constitutes the first eight characters of file-name. (Recall that DOS file names are up to eight characters in length, followed by the optional three-character extension and may be preceded by drive and path specifications.)

It is appropriate at this point to consider the differences between file type LINE SEQUENTIAL and type SEQUENTIAL. The ANSI standard for COBOL recognizes only three file types: SEQUENTIAL, INDEXED, and RELATIVE. In the RM/COBOL-85 implementation (and in most other microcomputer-based COBOL compilers), the type SEQUENTIAL refers to a data set in which each record is fixed in length and in which there is no special character separating one record from another. The standard format for a file created by an editor includes two characters—a carriage return (CR) and a line feed (LF)—at the end of each line of text which corresponds to a record in the file. These characters are inserted in the file when the user presses the Enter key on the keyboard. Thus, the lines (i.e., records) are of potentially varying length and have two additional characters that act as delimiters. In order for a COBOL program to process such a file, it is necessary for the compiler to be informed of the exact format of the data; this is accomplished by using the file type LINE SEQUENTIAL.

In most of the program listings in this text, we have omitted the specification of the external-file-name and the declaration of the file type unless it is INDEXED or RELATIVE. The reason for doing this is to make the programs generic so that the user can adapt the programs to a wide variety of computing environments. (Users of mini- and mainframe-based COBOL compilers generally do not have files of type LINE SEQUENTIAL.) The files that are contained on the disk that accompanies this text have appropriate declarations of the external-file-name and the file type.

There is one characteristic of the RM/COBOL-85 implementation that is potentially troublesome. When a record is read from a LINE SEQUENTIAL file, it is placed in the area of memory reserved for the record associated with the file. Only the number of characters that are physically contained in the record are placed in memory; the system does not clear the record area prior to reading a new record. If all records in the file have exactly the same length, which is often the case, this presents no problems. However, if a long record is followed by a shorter record, the record area will contain characters from a preceding long record when the shorter record is read. For example, suppose a LINE SEQUENTIAL file contains the following two records:

```
| A | B | C | CR | LF |
```

```
| 1 | 2 | CR | LF |
```

CR and LF refer to two characters that delimit records in LINE SEQUENTIAL files. When the first record is read, the record area will contain

```
| A | B | C |
```

as it should. The second record contains only two actual data characters. When it is read, the record area will contain

```
| 1 | 2 | C |
```

The third character is "left over" from the preceding record. To solve this problem, it is necessary for the program to clear the record area by moving spaces to the record prior to reading a record from a LINE SEQUENTIAL file.

The following program segment will solve the problem for a file DATA-FILE with record DATA-RECORD:

```
MOVE SPACES TO DATA-RECORD.
READ DATA-FILE AT END . . .
```

Remember, this is a problem only when records in a LINE SEQUENTIAL file have different lengths. For most of the programs in this text, each record contains the same number of characters so this additional step is not required. This is also a characteristic of RM/COBOL-85; other microcomputer-oriented compilers, such as Microsoft COBOL, appear to clear the record area prior to reading and, therefore, this problem does not occur.

For the most part, LINE SEQUENTIAL files can be used interchangeably with SEQUENTIAL files in COBOL programs. A major exception is in the SORT and MERGE statements. These statements process only SEQUENTIAL files and will not function correctly if the file is on type LINE SEQUENTIAL. The disk that accompanies this text contains a utility program, "LSEQ2SEQ.CBL", that will read a LINE SEQUENTIAL file with records up to 80 characters in length and will create an equivalent SEQUENTIAL file with 80-character records. If you wish to write a program using SORT or MERGE to process a LINE SEQUENTIAL file, you will need to use this utility program (or a version of it that will create records of length other than 80) to transform your file into a SEQUENTIAL file and have the program process the SEQUENTIAL copy of the file.

Files that are assigned to PRINTER are automatically of type LINE SEQUENTIAL. Printer files can be reassigned to another file by specifying an external-file-name for the printer as shown in the following general form:

```
SELECT file-name ASSIGN TO PRINTER [external-file-name].
```

For example, in Program 2b, which is shown in Figure H.2, the file REPORT-FILE is assigned to a disk file called "PRO2B.RPT" by the SELECT entry at lines 19–20:

```
SELECT REPORT-FILE ASSIGN TO PRINTER
    "PRO2B.RPT".
```

The operating system contains some file names for standard devices that can be useful occasionally. Two of these are "PRN", which is assigned to the printer, and "CON", which is assigned to the console, that is, the keyboard and screen of a microcomputer. For example, you might wish to direct the output of a printer file to the screen of the computer. To do this for Program 2b, you could change the SELECT statement to

```
SELECT REPORT-FILE ASSIGN TO PRINTER
    "CON".
```

Of course, if the program produces more than 25 lines of output, the lines will scroll off the screen too fast for you to be able to read them.

One technique that is often useful allows the user to choose, at the time of execution of the program, where the output is to be directed. This can be done by using a data-name such as REPORT-FILE-NAME in the SELECT entry as the external-file-name:

```
SELECT REPORT-FILE ASSIGN TO PRINTER
    REPORT-FILE-NAME.
```

The data-name REPORT-FILE-NAME must be defined as an alphanumeric item in WORKING-STORAGE by an entry such as the following:

```
01  REPORT-FILE-NAME PIC X(12).
```

The program then allows the user to enter the external name for REPORT-FILE by a program segment such as the following:

```
DISPLAY "Enter destination for report".
DISPLAY "  CON   for screen output".
DISPLAY "  PRN   for printed output".
DISPLAY "Other Name for disk output".
ACCEPT REPORT-FILE-NAME.
OPEN OUTPUT REPORT-FILE.
```

As indicated by the information displayed to the user, entering "CON" as the external-file-name will result in the output being directed to the screen; entering "PRN" will direct the output to the printer; entering any other sequence of characters will cause the program to create an ASCII file with that name on the default disk drive, or another disk if a suitable drive designator and path are included.

In the program listings reproduced in this text, we have omitted the external-file-name for printer files. However, in the files on the disk that accompanies this text, we have assigned all print files to a disk file with the same basic file name as the program file but with the file extension .RPT. (Thus, the output from Program 2b is directed to a file PRO2B.RPT.) This enables you to compile and execute the program whether or not you have an actual printer attached to your computer. It also saves paper and speeds the execution of the program as compared with actually printing the report each time the program is executed. You can use your editor or RM/CO* to review (and even edit the content of the file) and produce a printed copy if desired.

H.5 USING THE DEBUG FACILITY

One difference between the commercial version of RM/COBOL-85 and the educational version is that RUNCOBOL automatically places the user in debug mode. We have discussed two commands that you can enter while in this mode—R, which is short for "Resume execution," and Q, which is short for "Quit." In this section we will describe other commands that you can issue. These commands will give you a great deal of control over the execution of your program and can be extremely useful in the debugging process.

The debug prompt line is of the following general form:

```
[cd] line-number program-name C?_
```

In this prompt, cd is a code indicating the condition that caused the program to halt. The possible values of cd are shown in the following table:

Code	Program is halted because of
BP	Break point
DT	Data trap
ER	Execution time ERror
SR	Execution of a STOP RUN statement
ST	Program STepping is active

In some prompts, the code is omitted; in these cases, the prompt is equivalent to one with the code ST. The value of line-number is the number of the line in the source program that is the next one to be executed. Program-name is taken from the PROGRAM-ID entry. The entry "C?" is a command prompt which is followed by a cursor represented by an underscore. When this statement is presented, you can enter one of the commands shown in the following table:

Command	Meaning
R	Resume execution
Q	Quit execution; return to DOS as if STOP RUN has been executed
E	End debugging session; program continues execution
S	Step; execute the current instruction and stop at the next instruction
D	Display content of a specified data item
B	Set break point—line number at which program is to stop execution
C	Clear break points
T	Specify name of data item to be used as a trap; execution will stop when value of this item changes
U	Untrap; clear one or all traps

In the following sections, we will discuss each of these commands in more detail.[3]

The Step command is useful to "Step" through the program one statement at a time. When you issue the Step command, RUNCOBOL will exe-

---

[3] This is not an exhaustive list of available debug commands but rather the commands that are most likely to be useful to students. A complete discussion of using the debug facility is contained in Chapter 4 of *RM/COBOL-85 User's Guide for DOS Systems.*

Figure H.6   Using Step, Display, and Break point commands

```
ST 58 CUSTOMER-LIST-PRO2B C? S  ⎫
ST 60 CUSTOMER-LIST-PRO2B C? S  ⎬  The Step command allows RUNCOBOL to
ST 62 CUSTOMER-LIST-PRO2B C? S  ⎬  execute statements one at a time.
ST 63 CUSTOMER-LIST-PRO2B C? S  ⎭
ST 65 CUSTOMER-LIST-PRO2B C? D ACCOUNT-RECORD  ◄── The Display command allows you
8 GRP   111111111JONES      JAMES      A                to examine specified data items.
80 GRP
65 CUSTOMER-LIST-PRO2B C? D EOF-FLAG
236 ANS   NO
65 CUSTOMER-LIST-PRO2B C? B 77  ◄───────── The Breakpoint command sets a line number
65 CUSTOMER-LIST-PRO2B C? R                    at which execution will halt.
BP 77 CUSTOMER-LIST-PRO2B C? D REPORT-RECORD
100 GRP              111111111        JAMES       A JONES
170 GRP
77 CUSTOMER-LIST-PRO2B C? C  ◄───────── The clear command removes all
77 CUSTOMER-LIST-PRO2B C?                    break points.
```

cute the statement at the current line as indicated in the debug prompt and then present you with another prompt showing the line number of the next statement to be executed. For example, Figure H.6 shows the use of the Step command to execute the first few statements in Program 2b. The initial debug prompt shows that the first executable statement in the program is at line 58, which corresponds to the paragraph header of the first paragraph in the program as shown in Figure H.2. Issuing the Step command yields the second prompt showing line 60 as the next statement to be executed. This is the OPEN statement that is placed on two lines of code. Issuing the Step command once again shows that the next statement to be executed is at line 62, and so forth. You can use the Step command to follow the execution path of the program—the sequence in which the program statements are being executed. This is useful to trace the flow of control within the program.

If you have compiled the program using the "Y" option (which, you will remember, causes the compiler to include a copy of the symbol table with the .COB file), then you can examine the content of data items by using the Display command. You specify the name of the data item following the D command; RUNCOBOL will respond with output of the following form:

```
loc  type    value
```

In this output, loc refers to an offset within the data segment of the program (essentially a machine-level address for the data item); type refers to a three- or four-character code showing the data type of the item as shown in Figure H.7; value represents the current content of the specified data item. Up to 72 characters will be displayed on one line; if the item is longer, an additional line of output will be generated in the same format to display additional characters. For example, at the fifth line of output in the debug session for Program 2b (shown in Figure H.6), the command

```
D ACCOUNT-RECORD
```

is given. The system responds with two lines showing the 80 characters that make up ACCOUNT-RECORD. The second line of output appears blank

Figure H.7　Data Type Codes

ABS	Alphabetic	NLC	Numeric display signed (leading combined)
ABSE	Alphabetic edited	NLS	Numeric display signed (leading separate)
ANS	Alphanumeric		
ANSE	Alphanumeric edited	NPP	Packed unsigned
GRP	Group	NPS	Packed signed
HEX	Hexadecimal	NPU	Packed unsigned
IXN	Index-name	NSE	Numeric edited
NBS	Binary signed	NSU	Numeric display unsigned
NBU	Binary unsigned or index data item	NTC	Numeric display signed (trailing combined)
NCS	Numeric unpacked signed	NTS	Numeric display signed (trailing separate)
NCU	Numeric unpacked unsigned		

because ACCOUNT-RECORD contains spaces in these positions. The code "GRP" printed on each line of output indicates that ACCOUNT-RECORD is a group item. The next command is

```
D EOF-FLAG
```

The response indicates that this is an alphanumeric item (type code ANS) and that its value is "NO".

Remember that you *must* compile the program with the "Y" option to use the Display command. If the program were compiled without that option and you attempt to use the Display command, an appropriate error message will be displayed by RUNCOBOL.

A break point is a line in a program at which execution is temporarily suspended. You will find that stepping through a program one statement at a time can be extremely tedious. Often you know approximately where a problem lies; you can then set a break point at that statement and, using Resume execution, have RUNCOBOL execute statements automatically until the break point is reached. At that point a prompt with the code BP is presented, and you can proceed to step through the program one statement at a time or examine selected data items using the Display command. For example, in the debugging session illustrated in Figure H.6, a break point is set at line 77 using the command

```
B  77
```

Line 77 was chosen because it is the WRITE statement; all of the data items that make up the output record should be in place in the record at that time. Then the Resume execution command is given. The next debug prompt is

```
BP  77  . . .
```

Figure H.8   Using Trap and End commands

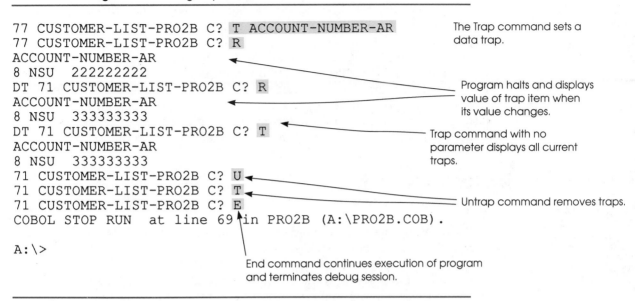

```
77 CUSTOMER-LIST-PRO2B C? T ACCOUNT-NUMBER-AR          The Trap command sets a
77 CUSTOMER-LIST-PRO2B C? R                            data trap.
ACCOUNT-NUMBER-AR
8 NSU  222222222
DT 71 CUSTOMER-LIST-PRO2B C? R                         Program halts and displays
ACCOUNT-NUMBER-AR                                      value of trap item when
8 NSU  333333333                                       its value changes.
DT 71 CUSTOMER-LIST-PRO2B C? T
ACCOUNT-NUMBER-AR                                      Trap command with no
8 NSU  333333333                                       parameter displays all current
71 CUSTOMER-LIST-PRO2B C? U                            traps.
71 CUSTOMER-LIST-PRO2B C? T
71 CUSTOMER-LIST-PRO2B C? E                            Untrap command removes traps.
COBOL STOP RUN  at line 69 in PRO2B (A:\PRO2B.COB).

A:\>
                                                       End command continues execution of program
                                                       and terminates debug session.
```

This indicates that the program is halted at line 77 because a break point has been reached. At his point, a Display command is used to display REPORT-RECORD; you could have displayed any other data items of interest as well.

If you use the Resume execution after a break point halt, the program will continue execution until the specified break point is reached again. If you no longer need a break point, you can clear all break points by using the Clear command which is the last command shown in Figure H.6. You can clear specific break points by using a command of the form

C [line-number]

For example, to clear the break point set at line 77, use the command

C 77

Using the Clear command with no line-number will clear all break points that you have previously set.

Another available strategy that can be useful on occasion is to set a data trap. This allows the program to halt when the value of selected data item(s) changes. You specify in the Trap command the name of the desired data item and then use Resume execution to continue execution in a normal fashion; when the data item changes value, the program will display the new value and then halt. For example, Figure H.8 shows a continuation of the debugging session of Program 2b. The first command is to set a trap for ACCOUNT-NUMBER-AR. The program resumes execution and then halts again at line 71. Another Resume execution command is given, and the program halts again at line 71. Note that line 71 is the paragraph header for the paragraph 2000-PROCESS-DATA. The content of ACCOUNT-NUMBER-AR changed as a result of the READ statement at line 78; the PER-FORM statement at line 65 sent control to line 71.

The Untrap command can be used to clear one or all traps. If used with a data-name, it clears that particular trap; if used without a data-name, as shown in Figure H.8, all traps are cleared. Note that we have followed the Untrap command by a Trap command with no parameters; if any traps were set, their values would be listed. Since the Untrap command has cleared all traps, the Trap command causes no output to be produced.

The End and Quit commands offer alternative ways to terminate a session with RUNCOBOL. The Quit command acts as a `STOP RUN` statement; the program is terminated and control returns to DOS. The End command ends the debugging session but allows the program execution to proceed normally until it terminates of its own accord. The End command is illustrated in Figure H.8 as the last debug command given.

H.6 USING RM/CO*

RM/CO* is a system provided by Ryan McFarland to facilitate the program development process. This software includes: (1) a project manager that allows you to specify a group of related files that can be treated as one unit for many purposes and (2) a full screen text editor that can be used to create COBOL programs and other ASCII files. In this section we will discuss the overall concepts underlying this system and describe some of the facilities that are likely to be of most use in a student program development environment. (More detail about this system can be found in Ryan McFarland's publication *RM/CO* For DOS User's Guide*.) Throughout the discussion, we assume that the two files that are related to RM/CO* (RMCOSTAR.EXE and RMCOSTAR.HLP) have been installed in the same directory as the compiler and that the appropriate path, as described in Section H.2, has been established.

The following diagram shows a conceptual overview of RM/CO*.

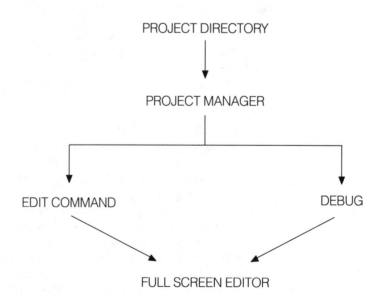

At the topmost level is a "Project Directory." This portion of the system will display all existing projects on the default drive by name and will give the user the opportunity to create new projects if needed. A **project** is defined to be a group of files. Each project is assigned a name; the system creates a file with the project name and the extension .CPJ (COBOL ProJect) on the default disk drive.

After defining a project by name, the user enters the "Project Manager." This portion of the system allows you to add files to or remove files from the project. This portion also keeps track of changes that may have been made to files in the system and lets you determine whether or not programs have been compiled. You can use the Project Manager to invoke the compiler and the run time system as well.

The Project Manager allows you to enter the Edit subsystem to create or edit files that make up the project. The entry point into the Edit subsystem is called "Edit Command." This portion of the system allows you to perform operations such as importing text into the file and printing.

From Edit Command you can enter the "Full Screen Editor." This portion of the software allows you to enter text into the file and perform various editing functions. When you edit an existing file, the system creates a "Change file" containing the new version of the file; it does not change the existing file immediately. You must choose to "Update" the file using a command issued to the Project Manager. (The system creates the Change file using the extension .Cnn where nn is 00 for the first Change file, 01 for the second Change file, and so forth.)

As noted above, the Project Manager allows you to compile and run programs. A unique feature of running programs through RM/CO* is that in debug mode, which is the default mode for RUNCOBOL, the system will display the source code as you step through the program. Not only will you be told the line number of the statement that is to be executed, but you will also have the actual line of source code highlighted on the screen. You can leave debug mode and use the Full Screen Editor to make changes in the file if desired. The changes that you make will have no effect on the current .COB file. However, this is a handy way to correct errors that become evident during the execution of the program, and it allows you to examine the DATA DIVISION so that you don't have to have a printed copy of the program at hand to refer to specific data names during the debugging process.

The design of the screens that you must use to interact with the various parts of RM/CO* follows a consistent pattern. Screens are divided into four parts as illustrated in Figure H.9:

- The top line is displayed in highlighted form and is called the **Status Line.** It lists information regarding the status of your project or file.

- Following the Status Line is the **Information Block.** In this area you will see a list of your files (when working with the Project Manager) or the text of your file (when working with the editing subsystem).

- Beneath the Information Block is the **Menu Area.** This area displays commands that are available at the current state of the system. The first letter of each available command is highlighted, or the appropriate key is highlighted followed by the command. To select the command, press the highlighted key. In most cases, one entire command will be highlighted; you can select this command simply by pressing Enter. If a command is listed but its first letter is not highlighted, then that command is not available, given the current state of the system.

- The last line on the screen is a highlighted line call the **Message Line.** This line displays information regarding actions taken by the system, prompts for the user, and occasionally prompts for entry of a limited amount of text.

Figure H.9   Beginning RM/CO* screen

Status line ——→
Information Block ——→
Menu Area
Message Line ——→

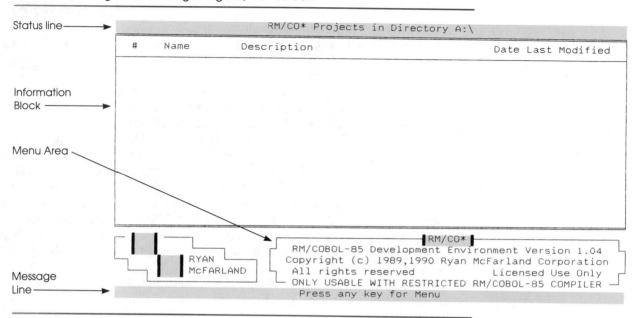

To illustrate the basic screens that you can expect in working with RM/CO*, let us create a simple project and then compile and execute a program using this system.

To enter RM/CO*, type RMCOSTAR at the DOS prompt. The initial screen shown in Figure H.9 is displayed. Note that the Status Line indicates that the default drive is drive A, and the Message Line tells you to press any key to continue. The next screen is the Project Directory screen shown in Figure H.10. We have used the New Project command to create a project called "CH2" and, in response to prompts, have given it the description "Programs for Chapter 2." You can choose any name and description that you wish for a project. Remember that RM/CO* creates a file with the project name and the extension .CPJ on the default disk. In this case, you would find a file called CH2.CPJ on drive A. Pressing the Enter key lets you enter the project which initially will contain no files. After using the Add Member command to add files, the screen will appear as shown in Figure H.11. The commands that you can use at this point are summarized in Figure H.12. Most of the commands are self-explanatory; however, one very important point is not displayed on the screen. When adding a file to the project, the name of .CBL files should be entered *without* the file extension. The Project Manager will automatically add the extension .CBL for you. To add a file of any other type to the project, type the entire file name including the extension. For example, we typed "PRO2B.DAT" to enter the data file into the project.

The Project Manager screen is divided into seven columns:

1. The column headed by "#" lists the file number for reference purposes. The files are automatically listed in alphabetical sequence.

2. The column headed "Member Name" is the file name.

3. The next column headed "U" will display "*" if the file has been changed but not updated. (Remember that using the editor to make changes to a file does not automatically update the file; in order to make

Figure H.10   Project Directory screen

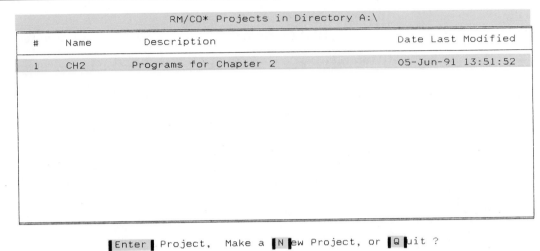

```
                   RM/CO* Projects in Directory A:\

  #     Name       Description                      Date Last Modified

  1     CH2        Programs for Chapter 2           05-Jun-91 13:51:52
```

```
 Enter  Project,  Make a  N ew Project, or  Q uit ?
```

```
Project "CH2" created
```

Figure H.11   Project Manager screen

```
CH2: 2 Members          |          |          |          |   Run   | 06/05 13:53

  #    Member Name    U  Last Edit: Lines  C  Last Comp:   Err Wng   Options

  1    PRO2B.CBL          06/04 22:50   79     06/04 22:51   0   0    LY
  2    PRO2B.DAT
```

```
                         ┌── Project Commands ──┐
  A dd Member      O ptions        U pdate               S yntax-Check
  D rop Member     Q uit Project   V iew Status/File     C ompile
  Enter  Member                    X ecute OS Command    R un
```

```
1 Member added
```

the change permanent you must use the Update command. The presence of "*" in this column is a reminder that there is a change file present for this file.)

4. The column headed "Last Edit: Lines" displays the date the last time the file was edited and the number of lines in the file.

5. The column headed "C" will display "*" if the file as been changed but not recompiled.

6. The column headed "Last Comp: Err Wng" displays the date of the last compile and the number of errors and the number of warnings in that compile.

Figure H.12   Summary of Project Manager commands

Command	Definition
ADD MEMBER	Add one or more members to a project
COMPILE	Compile RM/COBOL-85 source files
DROP MEMBER	Remove the highlighted member from the project
ENTER MEMBER	Invoke the Editor or Library Browser
OPTIONS	Select RM/COBOL-85 and RM/CO* options
QUIT PROJECT	Save and leave the current project and return to the Project Directory
RUN	Execute the program
SYNTAX-CHECK	Syntax-check your source code
UPDATE	Update changed source files
VIEW STATUS/FILE	View the status of the current file, or a file outside RM/CO*
XECUTE OS COMMAND	Execute an operating system command

7. The last column headed "Options" shows the options in effect on the last compile. You can set these options by using the Options command. This command will list all options and allow you to set options for one file or for all .CBL files in the project.

To enter the Edit Command subsystem from the Project Manager, use the arrow key to highlight the file that you wish to edit, and press Enter. PRO2B.CBL was selected in this way, resulting in the screen shown in Figure H.13. A summary of the available edit commands is shown in Figure H.14. Note that the Escape key is used to exit the edit subsystem and to return to the Project Manager; the Enter key is used to enter the Full Screen Editor.

The basic screen for the Full Screen Editor is shown in Figure H.15. The cursor is shown as a blinking underscore and will be placed in the information block. The position of the cursor on the screen is shown in the upper right corner of the status line. (In this case, the cursor is placed in line 2, position 8.) For .CBL files, the cursor is always positioned in Margin A (position 8). The Tab key is set for 4 positions, so pressing the Tab key will move the cursor from Margin A to Margin B. (If you are editing files of other types, the cursor will be placed in position 1 instead of position 8.) You type text as you would with any other word processor or editor. Edit commands are given by pressing Alt and another key as summarized in Figure H.16. Pressing Escape will return you to the Edit Command Screen. From there, press Escape another time to return to the Project Manager.

Remember that the Project Manager will allow you to compile and execute programs directly. A third option is to check for syntax. This is less time consuming than a full compile but does not produce a .COB program even if there are no errors.

Figure H.13   Edit Command screen

```
CH2: PRO2B.CBL          | SOURCE  |        |        |        |        |  01,08
0001          IDENTIFICATION DIVISION.
0002
0003          PROGRAM-ID. CUSTOMER-LIST-PRO2B.
0004          AUTHOR. HORN.
0005
0006          ENVIRONMENT DIVISION.
0007
0008          CONFIGURATION SECTION.
0009
0010          SOURCE-COMPUTER.
0011          OBJECT-COMPUTER.
0012
0013          INPUT-OUTPUT SECTION.
0014
0015          FILE-CONTROL.
0016
0017              SELECT ACCOUNT-FILE ASSIGN TO DISK
```

```
┌──────────────── Edit Commands ────────────────┐  ┌─── Screens ───┐
│ D isplay   I mp/Export   O ptions   U ndo      │  │ F9   Debug        │
│ E dit      L ast         P rint     V iew      │  │ F10  Run Screen   │
│ F ind      N ext         S ubstitute X ecute OS│  │ Esc  Quit Edit    │
└────────────────────────────────────────────────┘  └───────────────────┘
```

Figure H.14   Summary of Edit Commands

Command	Definition
DISPLAY	Select the display mode
EDIT	Use the Full Screen Editor
FIND	Find a string, line number, or other target
IMPORT/EXPORT	Export a marked block, or Import an entire file
LAST	Locate the previous error, warning, or program unit
NEXT	Locate the next error, warning, or program unit
OPTIONS	Display and change options
PRINT	Print all or part of a file
SUBSTITUTE	Replace a string with another
UNDO	Undo the last or all changes made to the file
VIEW	View the status of the current file, another file, or Key Stroke Macros
XECUTE OS	Invoke the operating system

Figure H.15   The Full Screen editor

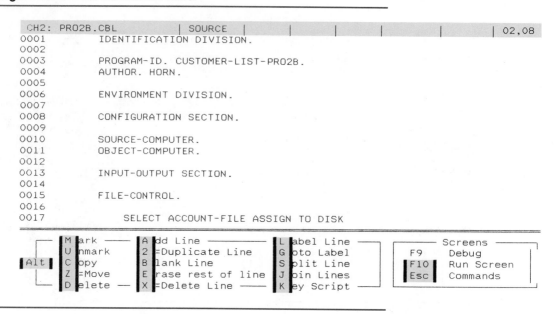

When running a program using the Project Manager, you have available the source text as shown in Figure H.17, which shows the execution of Program 2b. A highlighted bar is placed on the program statement that is to be executed next. In this case, line 58 is highlighted. When you enter debug commands, such as Step, the bar will move to show the next statement to be executed.

You can edit the file as you debug it by moving the arrow key or by pressing F9. Figure H.18 shows the display after line 77 in the file has been modified. The old program text is displayed with a horizontal line drawn through it (the line is red on color displays); the new text is listed above the old. Remember that making changes to the file at this time does not affect the .COB file or the original source file. To implement the changes, you would need to use the Project Manager Update command and then recompile the program. After exiting from the debug session illustrated in Figure H.18, the Project Manager screen appears as in Figure H.19. The "*" in the "U" column indicates that the file needs to be updated; the "*" in the "C" column indicates that the file has been changed since it was last compiled.

H.7   RUN TIME ERROR MESSAGES

In this section we present a partial listing of RM/COBOL-85 error messages that may occur during the execution of the program. This information is taken directly from Appendix B of *RM/COBOL-85 User's Guide for DOS Systems* published by Ryan McFarland (1988) and is reproduced here by permission from Liant Software.

Figure H.16   Summary of available functions in the Full screen
editor

Function	Definition	Key Stroke
ADD LINE	Insert a blank line in your file	Alt-A or F2
BLANK LINE	Replace the line on which the cursor sits with a blank line	Alt-B or F5
COPY BLOCK	Copy a marked block	Alt-C
DELETE BLOCK	Delete a marked block	Alt-D
DELETE LINE	Delete a single line	Alt-X
DUPLICATE LINE	Copy a single line	Alt-2
ERASE TO END OF LINE	Erase the line from the current cursor position to the end of the line	Alt-E or F6
GOTO LINE	Go to a line labeled with the LABEL LINE Function	Alt-G
JOIN LINES	Join two lines	Alt-J
KEY SCRIPT	Create and name a keystroke macro	Alt-K
LABEL LINE	Assign a single key label to a line of code	Alt-L
MARK BLOCK	Select a block of text	Alt-M
MOVE BLOCK	Move as marked block of code	Alt-Z
SPLIT LINE	Split line of code into two lines	Alt-S
UNMARK BLOCK	Unmark a previously marked block	Alt-U
HELP	Display Help panel	Alt-H or F1

Error Message Format

The different types of messages use the same general format:

```
COBOL type error code at line number in
        prog-id compiled date time
```

type is one of the following types of messages:

- data reference
- procedure
- input-output
- internal
- traceback
- operator requested termination
- sort-merge
- message control
- configuration
- initialization

Figure H.17   Debugging with RM/CO*

```
CH2: PRO2B.CBL          | LISTING |      |      |      |         | 01,01
0054              02  EOF-FLAG       PIC X(3)  VALUE "NO".
0055
0056          PROCEDURE DIVISION.
0057
0058          1000-MAIN-CONTROL.
0059
0060              OPEN INPUT ACCOUNT-FILE
0061                   OUTPUT REPORT-FILE.
0062              MOVE SPACES TO REPORT-RECORD.
0063              READ ACCOUNT-FILE
0064                  AT END MOVE "YES" TO EOF-FLAG.
0065              PERFORM 2000-PROCESS-DATA
0066                    UNTIL EOF-FLAG = "YES".
0067              CLOSE ACCOUNT-FILE
0068                   REPORT-FILE.
0069              STOP RUN.
0070
```

```
ST 58 CUSTOMER-LIST-PRO2B C?
At line 58 in Program CUSTOMER-LIST-PRO2B Keys: [F9]=Edit [F10]=Show Run
```

Figure H.18   Editing in RM/CO* debug mode

```
CH2: PRO2B.CBL          | LISTING |      |      |      |         | 01,01
0067              CLOSE ACCOUNT-FILE
0068                   REPORT-FILE.
0069              STOP RUN.
0070
0071          2000-PROCESS-DATA.
0072
0073              MOVE ACCOUNT-NUMBER-AR     TO ACCOUNT-NUMBER-RR.
0074              MOVE FIRST-NAME-AR         TO FIRST-NAME-RR.
0075              MOVE MIDDLE-INITIAL-AR     TO MIDDLE-INITIAL-RR.
0076              MOVE LAST-NAME-AR          TO LAST-NAME-RR.
                  WRITE REPORT-RECORD AFTER ADVANCING 2 LINES.
0077———————————WRITE—REPORT-RECORD—AFTER—ADVANCING—1—LINE.———————
0078              READ ACCOUNT-FILE
0079                  AT END MOVE "YES" TO EOF-FLAG.
READ ONLY SIZE =                    470 (X"000001D6") BYTES
READ/WRITE SIZE =                   524 (X"0000020C") BYTES
OVERLAYABLE SEGMENT SIZE =            0 (X"00000000") BYTES
```

```
ST 74 CUSTOMER-LIST-PRO2B C? s
ST 75 CUSTOMER-LIST-PRO2B C? s
ST 76 CUSTOMER-LIST-PRO2B C? s
ST 77 CUSTOMER-LIST-PRO2B C? s
ST 78 CUSTOMER-LIST-PRO2B C?
At line 78 in Program CUSTOMER-LIST-PRO2B Keys: [F9]=Edit [F10]=Show Run
```

code is the first two digits of the error numbers listed in this appendix.

number identifies a particular line in the PROCEDURE DIVISION of the source program. It is the line in which the statement being referred to starts, and it can be looked up in the leftmost column (labeled LINE) on the source listing produced by the compiler. If a question mark appears in this position, the following *prog-id* field refers to a machine language subprogram or a valid line number has not been established following an Interactive Debug R (Resume) Command.

Figure H.19   Project Manager screen after changing a file

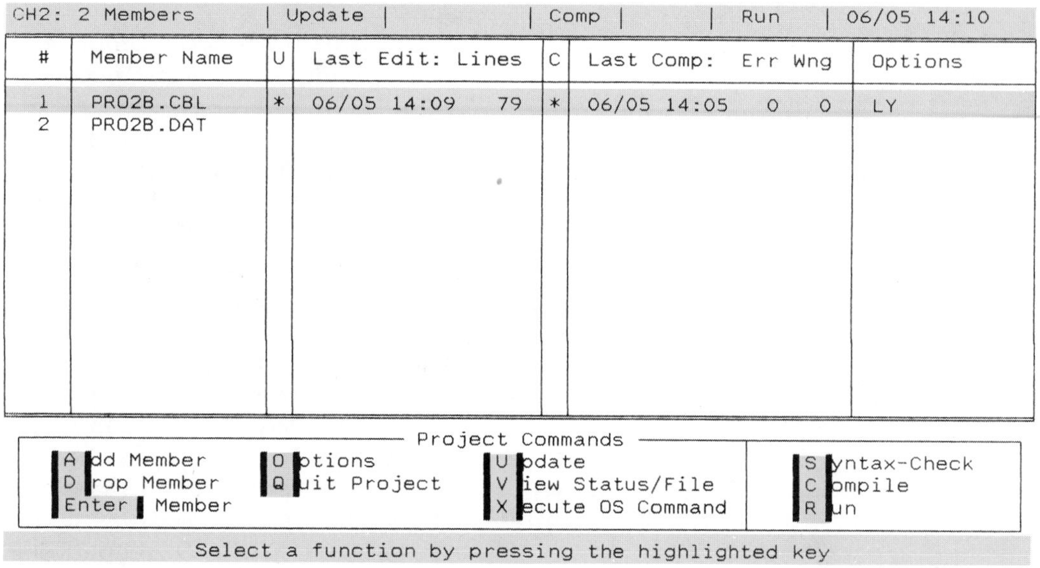

```
CH2: 2 Members       | Update |            | Comp |      | Run  | 06/05 14:10
┌───┬──────────────┬─┬─────────────────┬─┬────────────┬──────────┬──────────┐
│ # │ Member Name  │U│ Last Edit: Lines│C│ Last Comp: │ Err Wng  │ Options  │
├───┼──────────────┼─┼─────────────────┼─┼────────────┼──────────┼──────────┤
│ 1 │ PRO2B.CBL    │*│ 06/05 14:09  79 │*│ 06/05 14:05│  0    0  │ LY       │
│ 2 │ PRO2B.DAT    │ │                 │ │            │          │          │
│   │              │ │                 │ │            │          │          │
│   │              │ │                 │ │            │          │          │
│   │              │ │                 │ │            │          │          │
│   │              │ │                 │ │            │          │          │
│   │              │ │                 │ │            │          │          │
│   │              │ │                 │ │            │          │          │
└───┴──────────────┴─┴─────────────────┴─┴────────────┴──────────┴──────────┘
                         ── Project Commands ──
┌─────────────────────┬─────────────────────┬───────────────────┬────────────┐
│ A dd Member         │ O ptions            │ U pdate           │ S yntax-Check│
│ D rop Member        │ Q uit Project       │ V iew Status/File │ C ompile   │
│ Enter  Member       │                     │ X ecute OS Command│ R un       │
└─────────────────────┴─────────────────────┴───────────────────┴────────────┘
       Select a function by pressing the highlighted key
```

prog-id identifies the program interrupted in order to produce this message. It has the following format:

> *program-name*   *(pathname.ext)*

program-name is taken from the PROGRAM-ID paragraph of the source program.

pathname.ext is the fully qualified DOS pathname of the object library in which the object program resides.

date and *time* are the date and time the program was compiled; they correspond exactly to the date and time printed on the program listing.

Data Reference Errors

Data reference errors include invalid data types, improper data definitions, improper data values, and illegal subscripting.

Number	Description
101	There is a reference to a LINKAGE SECTION data item for which no corresponding operand exists because:
	1. There are more data items specified in the PROCEDURE DIVISION header than are specified in the USING phrase of the CALL statement in the calling program.
	2. The PROCEDURE DIVISION header in the first (or main) program in the run unit specifies more than one data item.
102	There is a range error on a variable-length group reference.

103   An identifier or literal referenced in an `INSPECT CON-VERTING` statement is illegal for one of the following reasons:

1. The source translation template (identifier-6 or literal-4) contains multiple occurrences of the same value.
2. The source translation template (identifier-6 or literal-4) does not have the same length as the destination translation template (identifier-7 or literal-5).
3. The destination translation template (literal-5) is figurative and its length is not one.

104   A reference to a data item is illegal for one of the following reasons:

1. The computed composite subscript value for a subscripted reference has a value which is negative, zero, or exceeds the maximum value for the referenced item.
2. There is a reference to a `LINKAGE SECTION` data item whose description specifies more characters than are present in the corresponding operand in the `USING` phrase of the `CALL` statement.
3. There is a reference to a `LINKAGE SECTION` data item in the first (or main) program in the run unit whose description specifies more characters than are supplied by the A Runtime Command Option.

105   A subscript calculation overflowed or underflowed.

106   An index-name value indicates more than 65535 occurrences.

Procedure Errors

Procedure errors include improper program structure or invalid calls.

Number	Description
201	A `CANCEL` statement has attempted to cancel a program which is still active; that is, a program which has called, directly or indirectly, the program attempting the cancel.
202	The program-name on a `CALL` statement has a value which is equal to spaces.
203	The program-name on the Runtime Command or `CALL` statement does not match any of the `PROGRAM-ID` names in any library but does match a valid RM/COBOL-85 library object filename. The call-by-filename technique is valid only for single-program object files.
204	The program-name on the Runtime Command or `CALL` statement does not match any of the `PROGRAM-ID` names in any library and does not match a valid RM/COBOL-85 object filename or machine language (.EXE) file. Note that an object program with a higher object version number than the runtime version number is not considered a valid program.
205	A `CALL` statement has attempted to call a program which is still active; that is, a program which has called, directly or indirectly, the program attempting the call in error.

Number	Description
207	There is not enough memory to load the program from the Runtime Command or the CALL statement, or to build the in-memory library structures indicated in the Runtime Command, or to reserve memory for the ACCEPT and DISPLAY buffers. This may be caused by memory fragmentation resulting from the dynamics of CALL and CANCEL operations and file I/O, or it may mean the requested program is too large for the available memory.
208	The ALTER statement has an undefined section or paragraph name.
209	The GO TO statement was not altered before execution of the statement was attempted.
210	The PERFORM statement attempts to perform an undefined section or paragraph.
211	An E level compilation error has been encountered.
213	The RM/COBOL-85 object library file specified in the Runtime Command cannot be found.
214	The RM/COBOL-85 object library file specified in the Runtime Command does not contain a valid object program.
215	A PERFORM statement in an independent segment has performed a section or paragraph in a fixed segment which performed a section or paragraph in a different independent segment.

Input/Output Errors

Input/output errors occur during file access. The format is:

```
COBOL I/O error number on COBOL-filename
        file external-file-name
```

The numerically ordered list presented below shows the values that can appear as *number* in the I/O error messages, and a description of each error. The I/O error number has the form:

```
mm, nn
```

mm is a two-digit decimal number indicating the general class of error that occurred. It is also the value stored into the FILE STATUS data item if such an item has been specified for the associated file. Thus, this value is available to the program.

nn is a two-digit code that provides more specific information on the nature of the error. This value is available to the program only if you call the subprogram C$RERR.

The phrase "1985 mode" indicates that the error message description applies to 85-standard COBOL only. The phrase "1974 mode" indicates that the error message description applies to 74-standard COBOL only. Messages not marked with either phrase indicate that the description applies to both 85- and 74-standard COBOL.

Number	*Description*
00	The operation was successful.
02	The operation was successful and a duplicate key was detected.
04, 05	The record read from the file is shorter than the minimum record length. (1985 mode)
04, 06	The record read from the file is longer than the record area. (1985 mode)
05	An OPEN operation was successful and the optional file was not present. If the open mode is I-O or EXTEND, the file has been created. A DELETE FILE statement was successful and the file was not present. (1985 mode)
07	The operation was successful. If the operation was a CLOSE statement with a NO REWIND, REEL, UNIT, or FOR REMOVAL clause, or if the operation was an OPEN statement with the NO REWIND clause, the referenced file is not on a unit/reel medium. (1985 mode)
10	An attempt was made to read past the end of file.
14	A sequential READ statement was attempted for a relative file and the number of significant digits in the relative record number is larger than the size of the relative key data item. (1985 mode)
21	Invalid prime key sequence.
22	The new record value attempts to duplicate an indexed file key which prohibits duplicates, or a relative record number that already exists.
23	The specified record does not exist.
24	There is insufficient disk space for the operation.
24, 01	A sequential WRITE statement was attempted for a relative file and the number of significant digits in the relative record number is larger than the size of the relative key data item. (1985 mode)
30, *nn*	I/O error *nn* occurred, where *nn* may depend on the device or machine on which the file resides. In general, this is the decimal error number from a DOS function call. See the *DOS Reference Manual* for detailed information on these errors. On DOS 2.*n* systems, displayed error codes 19 through 31 correspond to INT 24H error codes 0 through 12. A Procedure Division statement which explicitly or implicitly causes an overlay to be loaded may receive this error if the RM/COBOL-85 object file cannot be read when the statement is executed.
34	There is insufficient disk space for the operation.
35	The file is not available because the external filename could not be found. The DOS path or file may not exist or the name may be misspelled. Specifying a pathname or filename that is not a valid DOS name or that is longer than DOS allows also results in this error. (1985 mode)
37, 01	The file must be mass storage. The unit-name specified for the file was DISC, DISK, or RANDOM, but the external filename identifies a nondisk or nonfile. (1985 mode)

Number	Description
37, 07	The OPEN or DELETE FILE operation is invalid on the read-only file. An open mode of OUTPUT, EXTEND, or I-O was attempted on a read-only file. 1985 mode)
38	An OPEN or DELETE FILE operation failed because the filename was previously closed WITH LOCK. (1985 mode)
39, 01	The file organization specified for the filename does not match the actual file organization of the external file. (1985 mode)
39, 02	The minimum record length specified in the RECORD CONTAINS clause or implied by the record descriptions of the filename does not match the actual minimum record length of the external file. (1985 mode)
39, 03	The maximum record length specified in the RECORD CONTAINS clause or implied by the record descriptions of the filename does not match the actual maximum record length of the external file. (1985 mode)
39, 04	The minimum block length specified in the BLOCK CONTAINS clause for the filename does not match the actual minimum block size of the external file. (1985 mode)
39, 05	The maximum block length specified in the BLOCK CONTAINS clause for the filename does not match the actual maximum block size of the external file. (1985 mode)
39, 06	The record delimiting technique, LINE or BINARY SEQUENTIAL, specified for the filename does not match the actual record delimiting technique of the external file. (1985 mode)
39, 07	The CODE-SET specified for the filename does not match the actual character code of the external file. (1985 mode)
39, 08	The COLLATING SEQUENCE specified for the indexed file does not match the actual collating sequence of the external file.(1985 mode)
39, 09	The record type attribute, fixed or variable, specified in the RECORD CONTAINS clause or implied by the record descriptions of the filename does not match the record type attribute of the external file. (1985 mode)
41, 01 or 02	A duplicate open was rejected by a system which does not allow the external file to be opened twice. (1985 mode)
41, 03	A DELETE FILE was rejected because the file was in an open mode. (1985 mode)
42	A CLOSE operation was attempted on an unopened file. (1985 mode)
43	A DELETE or REWRITE operation was attempted on a file declared to be ACCESS MODE SEQUENTIAL, and the last operation on the file was not a successful READ operation. (1985 mode)
44, 03	The length of the record area specified in the WRITE, REWRITE, or RELEASE statement is less than the minimum record length of the file. (1985 mode) This error will also occur if the number of keys specified does not match the actual number of keys in the external file. (1985 mode)

Number	*Description*
44, 04	The length of the record area specified in the WRITE, REWRITE, or RELEASE statement is greater than the maximum record length of the file. (1985 mode)
44, 07	A REWRITE statement attempted to change the length of a record in a sequential organization file. (1985 mode)
46	No file position is currently defined. A READ or READ NEXT operation was attempted, but the last READ, READ NEXT, or START operation was unsuccessful or returned an at end condition. (1985 mode)
47, 01	The requested operation conflicts with the open mode of the file. A START or READ operation is attempted on a file that is not open in the INPUT or I-O mode. (1985 mode)
47, 02	A READ or START operation was attempted on an unopened file. (1985 mode)
48, 01	The requested operation conflicts with the open mode of the file. A WRITE operation is attempted on a file that is not open in the OUTPUT or EXTEND mode. (1985 mode)
48, 02	A WRITE operation was attempted on an unopened file. (1985 mode)
49, 01	The requested operation conflicts with the open mode of the file. A DELETE or REWRITE operation is attempted on a file that is not open in the I-O mode. (1985 mode)
49, 02	A DELETE or REWRITE operation was attempted on an unopened file. (1985 mode)
90, 01	The requested operation conflicts with the open mode of the file. A START or READ operation is attempted on a file that is not open in the INPUT or I-O mode. A WRITE operation is attempted on a file that is not open in the OUTPUT or EXTEND mode. A DELETE or REWRITE operation is attempted on a file that is not open in the I-O mode. (1974 mode)
90, 02	A DELETE or REWRITE operation was attempted on a file declared to be ACCESS MODE SEQUENTIAL, and the last operation on the file was not a successful READ operation. (1974 mode)
90, 03	The requested operation conflicts with the media type. A READ or OPEN INPUT operation was attempted on a file with a unit-name of OUTPUT, PRINT, or PRINTER. A WRITE, OPEN OUTPUT, or EXTEND operation was attempted on a file with a unit-name of CARD-READER or INPUT. A DELETE, REWRITE, START, or OPEN I-O operation was attempted on a file with a unit-name other than DISC, DISK, or RANDOM.
90, 04	The requested operation conflicts with the defined organization. A DELETE or START operation was attempted on an ORGANIZATION SEQUENTIAL file.
90, 05	A file truncate operation conflicts with other users. An OPEN OUTPUT operation was attempted on an external filename that is already open.
90, 07	The OPEN or DELETE FILE operation is invalid on a read-only file. An open mode of OUTPUT, EXTEND, or I-O was attempted on a read-only file. (1974 mode)
91	A CLOSE operation was attempted on an unopened file. (1974 mode)

Number	Description
Number	*Description*
91, 02	A READ, START, WRITE, DELETE, or REWRITE operation was attempted on an unopened file. (1974 mode)
92, 01 or 02	A duplicate open was rejected by a system which does not allow the external file to be opened twice. (1974 mode)
92, 03	A DELETE FILE was rejected because the file was in an open mode. (1974 mode)
93, 02	An open was rejected because file lock conflicts with another user. An OPEN WITH LOCK was attempted on a file which is already open, or an OPEN without lock was attempted and the file is already open WITH LOCK.
93, 03	An OPEN or DELETE FILE operation failed because the filename was previously closed WITH LOCK. (1974 mode)
93, 04	The file could not be opened because another file in the same SAME AREA clause is currently open.
93, 05	The file could not be opened because another file in the same MULTIPLE FILE TAPE clause is already open.
94, 01	The file organization specified for the filename does not match the actual file organization of the external file. (1974 mode)
94, 02	The minimum record length specified in the RECORD CONTAINS clause or implied by the record descriptions of the filename does not match the actual minimum record length of the external file. (1974 mode)
94, 03	The maximum record length specified in the RECORD CONTAINS clause or implied by the record descriptions of the filename does not match the actual maximum record length of the external file. (1974 mode)
94, 04	The minimum block length specified in the BLOCK CONTAINS clause for the filename does not match the actual minimum block size of the external file. (1974 mode)
94, 05	The maximum block length specified in the BLOCK CONTAINS clause for the filename does not match the actual maximum block size of the external file. (1974 mode)
94, 06	The record delimiting technique, LINE or BINARY SEQUENTIAL, specified for the filename does not match the actual record delimiting technique of the external file. (1974 mode)
94, 07	The CODE-SET specified for the filename does not match the actual character code of the external file. (1974 mode)
94, 08	The COLLATING SEQUENCE specified for the indexed file does not match the actual collating sequence of the external file. (1974 mode)
94, 09	The record type attribute, fixed or variable, specified in the RECORD CONTAINS clause or implied by the record descriptions of the filename does not match the record type attribute of the external file. (1974 mode)
94, 20	The file is not available because the external filename could not be found. The DOS path or file may not exist or the name may be misspelled. Specifying a pathname or filename that is not a valid DOS name or that is longer than DOS allows also results in this error. (1974 mode)

Number	Description

Number   *Description*

94, 21   The file organization specified is invalid or unsupported, or the requested open operation is illegal on the specified organization.

94, 22   The minimum record length is invalid. The minimum record length specified in the RECORD CONTAINS clause for the filename exceeds the maximum record length.

94, 23   The maximum record length is invalid. The maximum record length specified in the RECORD CONTAINS clause of the filename exceeds 65280.

94, 24   The minimum block size is invalid. The minimum block size specified in the BLOCK CONTAINS clause of the filename exceeds the maximum block size.

94, 25   The maximum block size is invalid. The maximum block size specified in the BLOCK CONTAINS clause of the filename is too large.

For indexed organization files, the computed block size is also a function of the maximum record size. In general, if the BLOCK CONTAINS clause is omitted, the runtime support system will default to the valid block size that is a multiple of the disk sector size. For files with a very large record size, specifying BLOCK CONTAINS 1 RECORDS will yield the minimum possible block size.

94, 26   The record delimiter is invalid. A record delimiting technique other than LINE or BINARY was specified.

94, 27   The CODE-SET specified is invalid or unsupported.

94, 28   The COLLATING SEQUENCE specified for an indexed file is invalid or unsupported.

94, 29   The record type attribute, fixed or variable, specified for the filename is unsupported.

94, 61   There is insufficient disk space to create a file.

94, 62   There are invalid linage parameters. One or more linage parameters could be negative or greater than 32767, either LINAGE or FOOTING equals zero, or FOOTING is greater than LINAGE.

95, 01   The file must be mass storage. The unit-name specified for the file was DISC, DISK, or RANDOM, but the external filename identifies a nondisk or file. (1974 mode)

96   No file position is currently defined. A READ or READ NEXT operation was attempted, but the last READ, READ NEXT, or START operation was unsuccessful or returned an at end condition. (1974 mode)

97, 01   One or more characters in the record are illegal in a line sequential file.

97, 02   One or more characters could not be translated from the native character set to the external code-set.

97, 03   The length of the record area specified in the WRITE, REWRITE, or RELEASE statement is less than the minimum record length of the file. (1974 mode)

97, 04   The length of the record area specified in the WRITE, REWRITE, or RELEASE statement is greater than the maximum record length of the file. (1974 mode)

97, 05   The record read from the file is shorter than the minimum record length.

Number	Description
97, 06	The record read from the file is longer than the record area.
97, 07	A REWRITE statement attempted to change the length of a record in a sequential organization file. (1974 mode)
97, 08	LINAGE parameter values error. One or more LINAGE parameters are negative or greater than 32767, LINAGE equals zero, FOOTING equals zero, or FOOTING is greater than LINAGE.
97, 09	The LINAGE TO LINE value is outside page body.

Sort-Merge Errors

Sort-Merge errors include errors processing a SORT or MERGE statement.

Number	Description
301	There was insufficient memory available to initiate a sort or merge process.
302	Fewer than three intermediate files were available to begin a SORT statement. The sort procedure cannot begin unless it is able to create at least three intermediate files.
303	A record read from a MERGE file or SORT USING file was not long enough to include all the keys.
304	Too many out of sequence records were passed to the sort process. Use the B Runtime Command Operation to increase the memory available to sort; or divide the records to be sorted into several files, sort the several files, and merge the resulting files.
305	A SORT or MERGE statement was attempted while a sort or merge process was already active.
306	A RELEASE or RETURN statement was attempted and no sort or merge was active.
307	A RELEASE or RETURN statement was attempted for a sort or merge description other than the one currently being sorted or merged.
308	A RELEASE statement was attempted in an OUTPUT PROCEDURE, or a RETURN statement was attempted in an INPUT PROCEDURE.
309	A RETURN statement was attempted in an OUTPUT PROCEDURE after the at end condition was returned on the sort or merge file.
310	An application I/O statement was attempted on a file currently opened as a sort or merge USING or GIVING file.

GLOSSARY

INTRODUCTION

The terms in this section are defined in accordance with their meaning in COBOL and may not have the same meaning in other languages. Terms marked with an asterisk are standard definitions adapted from the ANSI COBOL-85 Standard document.

* **Abbreviated combined relation condition.** The combined condition that results from the explicit omission of a common subject or a common subject and common relational operator in a consecutive sequence of relation conditions.
* **Access mode.** The manner in which records are to be operated upon within a file.
  Accumulation. Programming technique used to compute sums by adding values into a running total.
  Accumulator. Data item used to maintain a running total.
  Activity. The ratio of all transactions to the size of the file being maintained.
  Actual argument. Item for which associated information from a table is sought.
* **Actual decimal point.** The physical representation, using the decimal point characters period (.) or comma (,), of the decimal point position in a data item.
  Address. Number associated with each memory location.
* **Alphabetic character.** A letter or a space character.
* **Alphabet-name.** A user-defined word, in the SPECIAL-NAMES paragraph of the Environment Division, that assigns a name to a specific character set and/or collating sequence.
* **Alphanumeric character.** Any character in the computer's character set.
  Alphanumeric edited field. A field described with picture codes appropriate for editing alphanumeric items.
  Alphanumeric field. Any nonnumeric field.
  Alpha testing. Program testing performed by programmers and other personnel who developed a program.
* **Alternate record key.** A key, other than the prime record key, whose contents identify a record within an indexed file.

Application software.   Software designed to perform tasks related to processing specific types of data to meet the information needs of computer users.

Argument.   Parameter; a value which determines the behavior of a system, such as a search procedure.

* Arithmetic expression.   An identifier of a numeric elementary item, a numeric literal, such identifiers and literals separated by arithmetic operators, two arithmetic expressions separated by an arithmetic operator, or an arithmetic expression enclosed in parentheses.

Arithmetic/Logic unit.   Unit of the computer that performs arithmetic and logical operations on data.

* Arithmetic operation.   The process caused by the execution of an arithmetic statement or the evaluation of an arithmetic expression that results in a mathematically correct solution to the arguments presented.

* Arithmetic operator.   A single character or fixed two-character combination that belongs to the following set:

Character	Meaning
+	addition
−	subtraction
*	multiplication
/	division
**	exponentiation

* Arithmetic statement.   A statement that causes an arithmetic operation to be executed. The arithmetic statements are the ADD, COMPUTE, DIVIDE, MULTIPLY, and SUBTRACT statements.

* Ascending key.   A key upon the values of which data is ordered, starting with the lowest value of key up to the highest value of key, in accordance with the rules for comparing data items.

* Assumed decimal point.   A decimal point position which does not involve the existence of an actual character in a data item. The assumed decimal point has logical meaning with no physical representation.

* At end condition.   A condition caused

1. during the execution of a READ statement for a sequentially accessed file when no next logical record exists in the file or when the number of significant digits in the relative record number is larger than the size of the relative key data item or when an optional input file is not present.

2. during the execution of a RETURN statement when no next logical record exists for the associated sort or merge file.

3. during the execution of a SEARCH statement when the search operation terminates without satisfying the condition specified in any of the associated WHEN phrases.

Audit trail.   Records maintained to ensure that all processing of data is carried out correctly.

Backup file.   Copy of a file.

Batch computing.   Type of computing system in which data is accumulated over a period of time before being submitted to a computer for processing.

Batch environment. *See* Batch processing system.

Batch processing system. Type of data processing system in which data accumulates for a period of time before being submitted to the computer for processing.

Beta testing. Program testing performed by actual users of a program.

Binary. Base-2 data representation.

Binary search. Search procedure in which the table is divided into successively smaller segments until either the actual argument is matched or the length of the segment becomes one.

Block. In a program flowchart, a geometric symbol designed to show the type of action being described.

* **Block.** A physical unit of data that is normally composed of one or more logical records. For mass storage files, a block may contain a portion of a logical record. The size of a block has no direct relation to the size of the file within which the block is contained or to the size of the logical record(s) that are either contained within the block or overlap the block. The term is synonymous with physical record.

Blocking. Technique for combining multiple logical records to create a physical record.

Body. Multiple lines containing detailed data and information in a report.

* **Body group.** Generic name for a report group of TYPE DETAIL, CONTROL HEADING, or CONTROL FOOTING.

* **Bottom margin.** An empty area that follows the page body.

* **Called program.** A program that is the object of a CALL statement, combined at object time with the calling program, to produce a run unit.

* **Calling program.** A program which executes a CALL to another program.

Case structure. Pseudocode form for describing multiple selection structure.

Cathode ray tube (CRT). Technology used in computer display devices.

* **Cd-name.** A user-defined word that names an MCS interface area described in a communication description entry within the Communication Section of the Data Division.

Central processing unit (CPU). The Control and Arithmetic/Logic units.

Chapin chart. Schematic diagram used for program design.

* **Character.** The basic indivisible unit of the language.

* **Character position.** A character position is the amount of physical storage required to store a single, standard, data format character whose usage is DISPLAY. Further characteristics of the physical storage are defined by the implementor.

* **Character-string.** A sequence of contiguous characters that forms a COBOL word, a literal, a PICTURE character-string, or a comment-entry.

* **Class condition.** The proposition, for which a truth value can be determined, that the content of an item is wholly alphabetic or wholly numeric or consists exclusively of those characters listed in the definition of a class-name.

* **Class-name.** A user-defined word defined in the SPECIAL-NAMES paragraph of the Environment Division that assigns a name to the propo-

sition, for which a truth value can be defined, that the content of a data item consists exclusively of those characters listed in the definition of the class-name.

* Clause. A clause is an ordered set of consecutive COBOL character-strings whose purpose is to specify an attribute of an entry.

COBOL. Acronym for Common Business Oriented Language.

* COBOL character set. The complete COBOL character set consists of the following characters:

Character	Meaning
0, 1, . . . , 9	digit
A, B, . . . , Z	uppercase letter
a, b, . . . , z	lowercase letter
	space (blank)
+	plus sign
−	minus sign
*	asterisk
/	slash (solidus)
=	equal sign
$	currency sign
,	comma (decimal point)
;	semicolon
.	period (decimal point, full stop)
"	quotation mark
(	left parenthesis
)	right parenthesis
>	greater than symbol
<	less than symbol
:	colon

Note 1: In cases where an implementation does not provide all of the COBOL character set to be graphically represented, substitute graphics may be specified by the implementor to replace the characters not represented. The COBOL character set graphics are a subset of American National Standard X3.4-1977, Code for Information Interchange. With the exception of "$", they are also a subset of the graphics defined for the International Reference Version of International Standard ISO 646-1973, 7-Bit Coded Character Set for Information Processing Interchange.

Note 2: When the computer character set includes lowercase letters, they may be used in character-strings. Except when used in nonnumeric literals and some PICTURE symbols, each lowercase letter is equivalent to the corresponding uppercase letter.

COBOL reserved words. Words that have a predefined meaning to the COBOL compiler. The list of reserved words is reproduced on the inside covers of this text.

* COBOL word. A character-string of not more than 30 characters which forms a user-defined word, a system-name, or a reserved word.

Cohesion. *See* Module cohesion.

Coincidental cohesion. The parts of a module are unrelated.

* Collating sequence. The sequence in which the characters that are acceptable to a computer are ordered for purposes of sorting, merging, and comparing, and for processing indexed files sequentially.

Collision. Event in which a new value cannot be placed at the designated location in a randomized table or file because a previously placed item is in the desired position.

* **Column.** A character position within a print line. The columns are numbered from 1, by 1, starting at the leftmost character position of the print line and extending to the rightmost position of the print line.

Column heading. One or more lines of output printed beneath page headings used to identify the data contained in a report.

* **Combined condition.** A condition that is the result of connecting two or more conditions with the AND or the OR logical operator.

* **Comment-entry.** An entry in the Identification Division that may be any combination of characters from the computer's character set.

* **Comment line.** A source program line represented by an asterisk (*) in the indicator area of the line and any characters from the computer's character set in area A and area B of that line. The comment line serves only for documentation in a program. A special form of comment line represented by a slash (/) in the indicator area of the line and any characters from the computer's character set in area A and area B of that line cause page ejection prior to printing the comment.

* **Common program.** A program which, despite being directly contained within another program, may be called from any program directly or indirectly contained in that other program.

* **Communication description entry.** An entry in the Communication Section of the Data Division that is composed of the level indicator CD, followed by a cd-name, and then by a set of clauses as required. It describes the interface between the message control system (MCS) and the COBOL program.

* **Communication device.** A mechanism (hardware or hardware/ software) capable of sending data to a queue and/or receiving data from a queue. This mechanism may be a computer or a peripheral device. One or more programs containing communication description entries and residing within the same computer define one or more of these mechanisms.

* **Communication section.** The section of the Data Division that describes the interface areas between the message control system (MCS) and the program, composed of one or more communication description entries.

Compiler. A program designed to transform a high-level language program into machine language.

* **Compiler directing statement.** A statement, beginning with a compiler directing verb, that causes the compiler to take a specific action during compilation. The compiler directing statements are the COPY, ENTER, REPLACE, and USE statements.

* **Compile time.** The time at which a COBOL source program is translated by a COBOL compiler to a COBOL object program.

* **Complex condition.** A condition in which one or more logical operators act upon one or more conditions.

* **Computer-name.** A system-name that identifies the computer on which the program is to be compiled or run.

Computer terminal. Device used by a computer user to send information to and receive information from a computer.

* **Condition.** A status of a program at execution time for which a truth value can be determined. Where the term "condition" (condition-1, condition-2, and so forth) appears in these language specifications in or in reference to "condition" (condition-1, condition-2, and so forth) of a general format, it is a conditional expression consisting of either a simple condition optionally parenthesized or a combined condition consisting of the syntactically correct combination of simple conditions, logical operators, and parentheses for which a truth value can be determined.

* **Conditional expression.** A simple condition or a complex condition specified in an EVALUATE, IF, PERFORM, or SEARCH statement.

* **Conditional phrase.** A conditional phrase specifies the action to be taken upon determination of the truth value of a condition resulting from the execution of a conditional statement.

* **Conditional statement.** A conditional statement specifies that the truth value of a condition is to be determined and that the subsequent action of the object program is dependent on this truth value.

* **Conditional variable.** A data item, of which one or more values have a condition-name assigned to it.

* **Condition-name.** A user-defined word that assigns a name to a subset of values that a conditional variable may assume; or a user-defined word assigned to a status of an implementor-defined switch or device. When "condition-name" is used in the general formats, it represents a unique data item reference consisting of a syntactically correct combination of a condition-name together with qualifiers and subscripts, as required for uniqueness of reference.

* **Condition-name condition.** The proposition, for which a truth value can be determined, that the value of a conditional variable is a member of the set of values attributed to a condition-name associated with the conditional variable.

* **Configuration section.** A section of the Environment Division that describes overall specifications of source and object programs.

* **Contiguous items.** Items that are described by consecutive entries in the Data Division and that bear a definite hierarchical relationship to each other.

Content coupling. Modules are related because one must be aware of the content of the other.

* **Control break.** A change in the value of a data item that is referenced in the CONTROL clause. More generally, a change in the value of a data item that is used to control the hierarchical structure of a report.

* **Control break level.** The relative position within a control hierarchy at which the most major control break occurred.

Control coupling. Modules are related because one passes a control variable to the other.

* **Control data item.** A data item, a change in whose content may produce a control break.

* **Control data-name.** A data-name that appears in a CONTROL clause and refers to a control data item.

* **Control footing.** A report group that is presented at the end of the control group of which it is a member.

* **Control group.** A set of body groups that is presented for a given value of a control data item or of FINAL. Each control group may begin with a control heading, end with a control footing, and contain detail report groups.

* **Control heading.** A report group that is presented at the beginning of the control group of which it is a member.

* **Control hierarchy.** A designated sequence of report subdivisions defined by the positional order of FINAL and the data-names within a CONTROL clause.

Control unit. Unit of the computer that carries out each program instruction.

* **Counter.** A data item used for storing numbers or number representations in a manner that permits these numbers to be increased or decreased by the value of another number, or to be changed or reset to zero or to an arbitrary positive or negative value.

Counting. Programming technique in which a constant (usually 1) is added to a data item each time some condition is satisfied.

Coupling. *See* Module coupling.

CPU. *See* Central Processing Unit.

CRT. *See* Cathode Ray Tube.

* **Currency sign.** The character "$" of the COBOL character set.

* **Currency symbol.** The character defined by the CURRENCY SIGN clause in the SPECIAL-NAMES paragraph. If no CURRENCY SIGN clause is present in a COBOL source program, the currency symbol is identical to the currency sign.

* **Current record.** In file processing, the record which is available in the record area associated with a file.

* **Current record pointer.** A conceptual entity that is used in the selection of the next record.

* **Current volume pointer.** A conceptual entity that points to the current volume of a sequential file.

Data. Symbols that represent some event or idea.

Data base. Group of related files, together with software, designed to enable users to store and retrieve data across file boundaries.

* **Data clause.** A clause, appearing in a data description entry in the Data Division of a COBOL program, that provides information describing a particular attribute of a data item.

Data coupling. Modules are related because they process the same set of data items.

* **Data description entry.** An entry in the Data Division of a COBOL program that is composed of a level-number followed by a data-name, if required, and then followed by a set of data clauses, as required.

Data dictionary. List of data names, file names, and other items that programmers are required to use in all programs in a given data processing system.

Data Division. Division of a COBOL program in which the programmer describes the records associated with files and other data items that the program will process.

Data field.   Group of related characters.

Data flow diagram.   Schematic representation of the flow of data from one processing step to another.

* **Data item.**   A unit of data (excluding literals) defined by the COBOL program.

* **Data-name.**   A user-defined word that names a data item described in a data description entry. When used in the general formats, "data-name" represents a word which must not be reference-modified, subscripted, or qualified unless specifically permitted by the rules of the format.

Data-related cohesion.   Parts of a module are related because they process the same data.

Debugging.   Process of removing syntax and logical errors from a program.

* **Debugging line.**   A debugging line is any line with a D in the indicator area of the line.

* **Debugging section.**   A debugging section is a section that contains a USE FOR DEBUGGING statement.

Decision structure.   Program structure used to select between two alternative courses of action; also called If/Then/Else structure.

* **Declaratives.**   A set of one or more special purpose sections, written at the beginning of the Procedure Division, the first of which is preceded by the key word DECLARATIVES, and the last of which is followed by the key words END DECLARATIVES. A declarative is composed of a section header, followed by a USE compiler-directing sentence and then by a set of zero, one, or more associated paragraphs.

* **Declarative sentence.**   A compiler-directing sentence consisting of a single USE statement terminated by the separator period.

* **De-edit.**   The logical removal of all editing characters from a numeric edited data item in order to determine that item's unedited numeric value.

De-editing.   Capability found in COBOL-85 to transform a numeric-edited field into a numeric field.

* **Delimited scope statement.**   Any statement which includes its explicit scope terminator.

* **Delimiter.**   A character or a sequence of contiguous characters that identifies the end of a string of characters and separates that string of characters from the following string of characters. A delimiter is not part of the string of characters that it delimits.

* **Descending key.**   A key upon the values of which data is ordered, starting with the highest value of key down to the lowest value of key, in accordance with the rules for comparing data items.

* **Destination.**   The symbolic identification of the receiver of a transmission from a queue.

* **Digit position.**   A digit position is the amount of physical storage required to store a single digit. This amount may vary depending on the usage specified in the data description entry that defines the data item. If the data description entry specifies that usage is DISPLAY, then a digit position is synonymous with a character position. Further characteristics of the physical storage are defined by the implementor.

Direct access. Mode of access to a table or file in which the data is retrieved in one step.

Direct relative file. Relative file in which the program accesses the desired record by specifying the record number.

Disk drive. Device used to read and write a disk.

* **Division.** A set of zero, one, or more sections of paragraphs, called the division body, that are formed and combined in accordance with a specific set of rules. Each division consists of the division header and the related division body. There are four divisions in a COBOL program: Identification, Environment, Data, and Procedure.

* **Division header.** A combination of words, followed by a separator period, that indicates the beginning of a division. The division headers in a COBOL program are

```
IDENTIFICATION DIVISION.
ENVIRONMENT DIVISION.
DATA DIVISION.
PROCEDURE DIVISION [USING {data-name-1} . . . ] .
```

Documentation. Material supplied with a program to explain the function, use, and design of the software.

* **Dynamic access.** An access mode in which specific logical records can be obtained from or placed into a mass storage file in a nonsequential manner and obtained from a file in a sequential manner during the scope of the same OPEN statement.

Edited field. Any field described with picture codes composed of editing characters.

* **Editing character.** A single character or a fixed two-character combination belonging to the following set:

Character	Meaning
B	space
0	zero
+	plus
−	minus
CR	credit
DB	debit
Z	zero suppress
*	check protect
$	currency sign
,	comma (decimal point)
.	period (decimal point)
/	slash (solidus)

Editor. Software designed to enable the user to create a text file for a program or data.

Element. *See* Table element.

* **Elementary item.** A data item that is described as not being further logically subdivided.

* **End of Procedure Division.** The physical position in a COBOL source program after which no further procedures appear.

* **End program header.** A combination of words, followed by a separator period, that indicates the end of a COBOL source program. The end program header is

```
END PROGRAM program-name.
```

* **Entry.** Any descriptive set of consecutive clauses terminated by a separator period and written in the Identification Division, Environment Division, or Data Division of a COBOL program.

* **Environment clause.** A clause that appears as part of an Environment Division entry.

Environment Division. Division of a COBOL program in which the programmer describes the computing environment in which the program will function.

* **Execution time.** The time at which an object program is executed. The term is synonymous with object time.

Exhaustive search. Search procedure in which each table argument is compared with the actual argument.

* **Explicit scope terminator.** A reserved word which terminates the scope of a particular Procedure Division statement.

* **Expression.** An arithmetic or conditional expression.

* **Extend mode.** The state of a file after execution of an OPEN statement with the EXTEND phrase specified for that file and before the execution of a CLOSE statement without the REEL or UNIT phrase for that file.

* **External data.** The data described in a program as external data items and external file connectors.

* **External data item.** A data item which is described as part of an external record in one or more programs of a run unit and which itself may be referenced from any program in which it is described.

* **External data record.** A logical record which is described in one or more programs of a run unit and whose constituent data items may be referenced from any program in which they are described.

* **External file connector.** A file connector which is accessible to one or more object programs in the run unit.

External file name. Name of a file as known to the operating system.

* **External switch.** A hardware or software device, defined and named by the implementor, which is used to indicate that one of two alternate states exists.

Field. *See* Data field.

* **Figurative constant.** A compiler generated value referenced through the use of certain reserved words.

* **File.** A collection of logical records.

* **File attribute conflict condition.** An unsuccessful attempt has been made to execute an input-output operation on a file, and the file attributes, as specified for that file in the program, do not match the fixed attributes for that file.

* **File clause.** A clause that appears as part of any of the following Data Division entries: file description entry (FD entry) and sort-merge file description entry (SD entry).

* **File connector.** A storage area which contains information about a file and is used as the linkage between a file-name and a physical file and between a file-name and its associated record area.

* **FILE-CONTROL.** The name of an Environment Division paragraph in which the data files for a given source program are declared.

* **File control entry.** A SELECT clause and all its subordinate clauses which declare the relevant physical attributes of a file.

* **File description entry.** An entry in the File Section of the Data Division that is composed of the level indicator FD, followed by a file-name, and then followed by a set of file clauses as required.

File maintenance. Adding, changing, and deleting records in a file.

* **File-name.** A user-defined word that names a file connector described in a file description entry or a sort-merge file description entry within the File Section of the Data Division.

* **File organization.** The permanent logical file structure established at the time that a file is created.

* **File position indicator.** A conceptual entity that contains the value of the current key within the key of reference for an indexed file, the record number of the current record for a sequential file, or the relative record number of the current record for a relative file; or that indicates that no next logical record exists, that the number of significant digits in the relative record number is larger than the size of the relative key data item, that an optional input file is not present, that the at end condition already exists, or that no valid next record has been established.

* **File section.** The section of the Data Division that contains file description entries and sort-merge file description entries together with their associated record descriptions.

File updating. Changing the content of records in a file.

* **Fixed file attributes.** Information about a file which is established when a file is created and cannot subsequently be changed during the existence of the file. These attributes include the organization of the file (sequential, relative, or indexed), the prime record key, the alternate record keys, the code set, the minimum and maximum record size, the record type (fixed or variable), the collating sequence of the keys for indexed files, the blocking factor, the padding character, and the record delimiter.

* **Fixed length record.** A record associated with a file whose file description or sort-merge description entry requires that all records contain the same number of character positions.

Floating point. Type of data representation in which data is presented as a mantissa containing significant digits and an exponent representing the magnitude of the number.

Floppy disk. Type of magnetic disk used in microcomputer systems, also called a diskette.

* **Footing area.** The position of the page body adjacent to the bottom margin.

* **Format.** A specific arrangement of a set of data.

Formatted screen. Display of labels, highlighting, and status information designed to help a computer user.

Functional cohesion. All parts of a module are directly related to a specific, well-defined function.

* **Global name.** A name which is declared in only one program but which may be referenced from that program and from any program con-

tained within that program. Condition-names, data-names, file-names, record-names, report-names, and some special registers may be global names.

* Group item. A data item that is composed of subordinate data items.

Hard copy. Printed output from a computer system.

Hard disk. Magnetic disk storage medium used on all types of computers.

Hardware. Computer equipment.

Hardware costs. Costs associated with physical components of a computing system.

Hash function. Function used to compute an address for a data item.

High-level language. A computer language designed to facilitate the creation of programs in terms relatively familiar to computer users.

* High order end. The leftmost character of a string of characters.

HIPO. Formal technique for designing a program. HIPO is an acronym for Hierarchy, Input, Processing, Output.

IBG. *See* Inter-Block-Gap.

Identification Division. Division of a COBOL program in which the programmer specifies the program name, the author's name, and other documentary information.

* Identifier. A syntactically correct combination of a data-name, with its qualifiers, subscripts, and reference modifiers, as required for uniqueness of reference, that names a data item. The rules for "identifier" associated with the general formats may, however, specifically prohibit qualification, subscripting, or reference modification.

* Imperative statement. A statement that either begins with an imperative verb and specifies an unconditional action to be taken or is a conditional statement that is delimited by its explicit scope terminator (delimited scope statement). An imperative statement may consist of a sequence of imperative statements.

* Implementor-name. A system-name that refers to a particular feature available on that implementor's computing system.

* Implicit scope terminator. A separator period which terminates the scope of any preceding unterminated statement or a phrase of a statement which by its occurrence indicates the end of the scope of any statement contained within the preceding phrase.

* Index. A computer storage position or register, the content of which represents the identification of a particular element in a table.

* Index data item. A data item in which the values associated with an index-name can be stored in a form specified by the implementor.

* Indexed file. A file with indexed organization.

* Indexed organization. The permanent logical file structure in which each record is identified by the value of one or more keys within that record.

* Index-name. A user-defined word that names an index associated with a specific table.

Index variable. A variable declared as in the INDEXED BY clause or USAGE INDEX.

Infinite loop. Continuous execution of a program segment with no possibility for termination.

Information. Meaning attached to data.

Information block. In RM/CO*, the information block displays the project directory, the project manager, and the edit screens.

* **Initial program.** A program that is placed into an initial state every time the program is called in a run unit.

* **Initial state.** The state of a program when it is first called in a run unit.

* **Input file.** A file that is opened in the input mode.

* **Input mode.** The state of a file after execution of an OPEN statement, with the INPUT phrase specified, for that file and before the execution of a CLOSE statement without the REEL or UNIT phrase for that file.

* **Input-output file.** A file that is opened in the I-O mode.

* **Input-output section.** The section of the Environment Division that names the files and the external media required by an object program and which provides information required for transmission and handling of data during execution of the object program.

* **Input-output statement.** A statement that causes files to be processed by performing operations upon individual records or upon the file as a unit. The input-output statements are: ACCEPT (with the identifier phrase), CLOSE, DELETE, DISABLE, DISPLAY, ENABLE, OPEN, PURGE, READ, RECEIVE, REWRITE, SEND, SET (with the TO ON or TO OFF phrase), START, and WRITE.

* **Input procedure.** A set of statements to which control is given during the execution of a SORT statement for the purpose of controlling the release of specified records to be sorted.

Input unit. Unit of a computer that transfers data from the outside world into the memory of the computer.

* **Integer.** A numeric literal or a numeric data item that does not include any digit position to the right of the assumed decimal point. When the term "integer" appears in general formats, integer must not be a numeric data item and must not be signed nor zero unless explicitly allowed by the rules of that format.

Interactive computing. Type of computing system in which the computer and the user engage in a dialogue with the computer responding to user commands as they are given.

Interactive environment. *See* Interactive computing.

Interactive systems. Computer systems in which the user is in immediate contact with the computer. The computer usually processes data immediately as it is entered by the user.

Inter-Block-Gap (IBG). Space between blocks of data, especially on magnetic tape.

* **Internal data.** The data described in a program excluding all external data items and external file connectors. Items described in the Linkage Section of a program are treated as internal data.

* **Internal data item.** A data item which is described in one program in a run unit. An internal data item may have a global name.

* **Internal file connector.** A file connector which is accessible to only one object program in the run unit.

Inter-Record-Gap (IRG). Unused space between records, especially on magnetic tape.

* **Intra-record data structure.** The entire collection of groups and elementary items from a logical record which is defined by a contiguous subset of the data description entries which describe that record. These data description entries include all entries whose level-number is greater than the level-number of the first data description entry describing the intra-record data structure.

* **Invalid key condition.** A condition, at object time, caused when a specific value of the key associated with an indexed or relative file is determined to be invalid.

* `I-O-CONTROL`. The name of an Environment Division paragraph in which object program requirements for rerun points, sharing of the same areas by several data files, and multiple file storage on a single input-output device are specified.

* `I-O-CONTROL` **entry.** An entry in the `I-O-CONTROL` paragraph of the Environment Division that contains clauses which provide information required for the transmission and handling of data on named files during the execution of a program.

* **I-O mode.** The state of a file after execution of an `OPEN` statement with the `I-O` phrase specified for that file and before the execution of a `CLOSE` statement without the `REEL` or `UNIT` phrase for that file.

* **I-O status.** A conceptual entity which contains the two-character value indicating the resulting status of an input-output operation. This value is made available to the program through the use of the `FILE STATUS` clause in the file control entry for the file.

IRG. *See* Inter-Record-Gap.

Iteration structure. Program structure used to control the repetition of a series of program statements.

Julian date. Sequence number associated with a date from some fixed point, such as the beginning of the year, the decade, or the century.

* **Key.** A data item which identifies the location of a record, or a set of data items which serves to identify the ordering of data.

Key field. Field used as the basis for organizing or accessing a file.

* **Key of reference.** The key, either prime or alternate, currently being used to access records within an indexed file.

* **Key word.** A reserved word whose presence is required when the format in which the word appears is used in a source program.

Label record. Record at the beginning of a file which specifies the name and other information about the file.

* **Language-name.** A system-name that specifies a particular programming language.

* **Letter.** A character belonging to one of the following two sets: (1) uppercase letters: A, B, C, D, E, F, G, H, I, J, K, L, M, N, O, P, Q, R, S, T, U, V, W, X, Y, Z; or (2) lowercase letters: a, b, c, d, e, f, g, h, i, j, k, l, m, n, o, p, q, r, s, t, u, v, w, x, y, z.

* **Level indicator.** Two alphabetic characters that identify a specific type of file or a position in a hierarchy. The level indicators in the Data Division are CD, FD, RD, and SD.

* **Level-number.** A user-defined word, expressed as a one- or two-digit number, which indicates the hierarchical position of a data item or the special properties of a data description entry. Level-numbers in the range 1 through 49 indicate the position of a data item in the hierarchical structure of a logical record. Level-numbers in the range 1 through 9 may be written either as a single digit or as a zero followed by a significant digit. Level-numbers 66, 77, and 88 identify special properties of a data description entry.

* **Library-name.** A user-defined word that names a COBOL library that is to be used by the compiler for a given source program compilation.

* **Library text.** A sequence of text words, comment lines, the separator space, or the separator pseudo-text delimiter in a COBOL library.

* **LINAGE-COUNTER.** A special register whose value points to the current position within the page body.

* **Line.** A division of a page representing one row of horizontal character positions. Each character position of a report line is aligned vertically beneath the corresponding character position of the report line above it. Report lines are numbered from 1, by 1, starting at the top of the page. The term is synonymous with report line.

Line counting. Programming technique used to control the number of lines placed on a page and to trigger the production of page headings at appropriate points.

* **Line number.** An integer that denotes the vertical position of a report line on a page.

* **Linkage section.** The section in the Data Division of the called program that describes data items available from the calling program. These data items may be referred to by both the calling and the called program.

Linking. Process of assembling separately compiled program units to create an executable program.

* **Literal.** A character-string whose value is implied by the ordered set of characters comprising the string.

Load module. Executable program made up of one or more separately compiled program units.

Logical cohesion. Module performs the same task, such as reading or writing, but otherwise spans more than one functional area.

Logical error. Error found when a program does not perform the function for which it was intended.

* **Logical operator.** One of the reserved words AND, OR, or NOT. In the formation of a condition, either AND or OR or both can be used as logical connectives. NOT can be used for logical negation.

* **Logical page.** A conceptual entity consisting of the top margin, the page body, and the bottom margin.

* **Logical record.** The most inclusive data item. The level-number for a record is 01. A record may be either an elementary item or a group item. The term is synonymous with record.

Log off. *See* Sign off.

Log on. *See* Sign on.

* **Low order end.** The rightmost character of a string of characters.

Machine language. A numerical computer language designed for a specific processor.

Magnetic tape drive. Device used to read and write magnetic tapes.

Main program. Program that is capable of being executed. Each load module is made up of one main program and zero or more subprograms.

Major control break. Control break triggered by a change in the major key field.

Major key. *See* Primary key.

* **Mass storage.** A storage medium in which data may be organized and maintained in both a sequential and nonsequential manner.

* **Mass storage control system (MSCS).** An input-output control system that directs or controls the processing of mass storage files.

* **Mass storage file.** A collection of records that is assigned to a mass storage medium.

Master file. A file storing relatively permanent summarized information about entities in a data processing system.

* **MCS.** Message control system; a communication control system that supports the processing of messages.

Memory unit. Unit of the computer that stores program and data during the execution of a program.

Menu. List of commands that a user can enter.

Menu area. In RM/CO*, the menu area shows available commands.

* **Merge file.** A collection of records to be merged by a MERGE statement. The merge file is created by and can be used only by the merge function.

* **Message.** Data associated with an end of message indicator or an end of group indicator.

* **Message control system (MCS).** A communication control system that supports the processing of messages.

* **Message count.** The count of the number of complete messages that exist in the designated queue of messages.

* **Message indicators.** EGI (end of group indicator), EMI (end of message indicator), and ESI (end of segment indicator) are conceptual indications that serve to notify the message control system that a specific condition exists (end of group, end of message, end of segment). Within the hierarchy of EGI, EMI, and ESI, an EGI is conceptually equivalent to an ESI, EMI, and EGI. An EMI is conceptually equivalent to an ESI and EMI. Thus, a segment may be terminated by an ESI, EMI, or EGI. A message may be terminated by an EMI or EGI.

Message line. In RM/CO*, the message line reports information and prompts for input.

* **Message segment.** Data that forms a logical subdivision of a message, normally associated with an end of segment indicator.

Microcomputer. Computer based on a microprocessor.

Microprocessor. Central processing unit contained on an integrated circuit.

Minor control break. Control break triggered by a change in a secondary key field.

Minor key. *See* Secondary key.

* **Mnemonic-name.** A user-defined word that is associated in the Environment Division with a specific implementor-name.

Module. *See* Program module.

Module cohesion. The logical "glue" that binds parts of a module together.

Module coupling. Types of connections that exist between modules.

* **MSCS.** Mass storage control system; an input-output control system that directs or controls the processing of mass storage files.

Multiuser system. Computer system that can serve several different users at a time.

Nassi-Schneiderman chart. Schematic diagram used for program design.

* **Native character set.** The implementor-defined character set associated with the computer specified in the OBJECT-COMPUTER paragraph.

* **Native collating sequence.** The implementor-defined collating sequence associated with the computer specified in the OBJECT-COMPUTER paragraph.

* **Negated combined condition.** The NOT logical operator immediately followed by a parenthesized combined condition.

* **Negated simple condition.** The NOT logical operator immediately followed by a simple condition.

Nested. Contained within; for example, when an IF statement is contained within the scope of another IF statement, the IF statements are said to be "nested."

* **Next executable sentence.** The next sentence to which control will be transferred after execution of the current statement is complete.

* **Next executable statement.** The next statement to which control will be transferred after execution of the current statement is complete.

* **Next record.** The record which logically follows the current record of a file.

* **Noncontiguous item.** Elementary items, in the Working-Storage and Linkage Sections, which bear no hierarchic relation to other data items.

* **Nonnumeric item.** A data item whose description permits its content to be composed of any combination of characters taken from the computer's character set. Certain categories of nonnumeric items may be formed from more restricted character sets.

* **Nonnumeric literal.** A literal bounded by quotation marks. The string of characters may include any character in the computer's character set.

* **Numeric character.** A character that belongs to the following set of digits: 0, 1, 2, 3, 4, 5, 6, 7, 8, 9.

Numeric edited field. A field made up of editing characters appropriate for editing numeric data.

Numeric field. *See* Numeric item.

* **Numeric item.**   A data item whose description restricts its content to a value represented by characters chosen from the digits 0 through 9; if signed, the item may also contain a "+", "−", or other representation of an operational sign.

* **Numeric literal.**   A literal composed of one or more numeric characters that may contain either a decimal point or an algebraic sign or both. The decimal point must not be the rightmost character. The algebraic sign, if present, must be the leftmost character.

* OBJECT-COMPUTER.   The name of an Environment Division paragraph in which the computer environment, within which the object program is executed, is described.

* **Object computer entry.**   An entry in the OBJECT-COMPUTER paragraph of the Environment Division which contains clauses which describe the computer environment in which the object program is to be executed.

* **Object of entry.**   A set of operands and reserved words, within a Data Division entry of a COBOL program, that immediately follows the subject of the entry.

* **Object program.**   A set or group of executable machine language instructions and other material designed to interact with data to provide problem solutions. In this context, an object program is generally the machine language result of the operation of a COBOL compiler on a source program. Where there is no danger of ambiguity, the word "program" alone may be used in place of the phrase "object program."

* **Object time.**   The time at which an object program is executed. The term is synonymous with execution time.

* **Obsolete element.**   A COBOL language element in Standard COBOL that is to be deleted from the next revision of Standard COBOL.

Off line.   Not in direct communication with a computer.

One-level table.   Table created with one OCCURS clause and accessed with one subscript.

On line.   In direct communication with the computer.

* **Open mode.**   The state of a file after execution of an OPEN statement for that file and before the execution of a CLOSE statement without the REEL or UNIT phrase for that file. The particular open mode is specified in the OPEN statement as either INPUT, OUTPUT, I-O, or EXTEND.

* **Operand.**   Whereas the general definition of operand is "that component which is operated upon," for the purposes of this publication, any lowercase word (or words) that appears in a statement or entry format may be considered to be an operand and, as such, is an implied reference to the data indicated by the operand.

* **Operational sign.**   An algebraic sign, associated with a numeric data item or a numeric literal, to indicate whether its value is positive or negative.

* **Optional file.**   A file which is declared as being not necessarily present each time the object program is executed. The object program causes an interrogation for the presence or absence of the file.

* **Optional word.** A reserved word that is included in a specific format only to improve the readability of the language and whose presence is optional to the user when the format in which the word appears is used in a source program.

* **Output file.** A file that is opened in either the output mode or the extend mode.

* **Output mode.** The state of a file after execution of an OPEN statement with the OUTPUT or EXTEND phrase specified for that file and before the execution of a CLOSE statement without the REEL or UNIT phrase for that file.

* **Output procedure.** A set of statements to which control is given during execution of a SORT statement after the sort function is completed or during execution of a MERGE statement after the merge function reaches a point at which it can select the next record in merged order when requested.

Output unit. Unit of the computer that copies information from the memory of the computer to some external medium.

Overflow area. Area on disk in which some operating systems place records added to an indexed file.

Packed decimal. Type of data representation in which two decimal digits are stored in all bytes except the rightmost one which is used to store a digit and the sign of the item.

* **Padding character.** An alphanumeric character used to fill the unused character positions in a physical record.

* **Page.** A vertical division of a report representing a physical separation of report data, the separation being based on internal reporting requirements and/or external characteristics of the reporting medium.

* **Page body.** That part of the logical page in which lines can be written and/or spaced.

* **Page footing.** A report group that is presented at the end of a report page as determined by the report writer control system.

* **Page heading.** A report group that is presented at the beginning of a report page as determined by the report writer control system.

Page heading. One or more lines of output printed at the top of each page of a report.

* **Paragraph.** In the Procedure Division, a paragraph-name followed by a separator period and by zero, one, or more sentences. In the Identification and Environment Divisions, a paragraph header followed by zero, one, or more entries.

* **Paragraph header.** A reserved word, followed by the separator period, that indicates the beginning of a paragraph in the Identification and Environment Divisions.
  The permissible paragraph headers in the Identification Division are
    PROGRAM-ID.
    AUTHOR.
    INSTALLATION.
    DATE-WRITTEN.
    DATE-COMPILED.
    SECURITY.

The permissible paragraph headers in the Environment Division are
```
SOURCE-COMPUTER.
OBJECT-COMPUTER.
SPECIAL-NAMES.
FILE-CONTROL.
I-O-CONTROL.
```

* **Paragraph-name.** A user-defined word that identifies and begins a paragraph in the Procedure Division.

* **Phrase.** A phrase is an ordered set of one or more consecutive COBOL character-strings that form a portion of a COBOL procedural statement or COBOL clause.

* **Physical page.** A device-dependent concept defined by the implementor.

* **Physical record.** The term is synonymous with block.

Picture. Clause used to describe elementary items.

Picture codes. Characters such as 9, Z, X, and so forth, used in picture clauses.

Posttest. Type of loop control statement in which the exit test is made after execution of the body of the loop.

Pretest. Type of loop control statement in which the exit test is made before the execution of the body of the loop.

Primary key. Most important key when multiple keys are used in organizing or accessing data.

Prime key. Key used to organize an indexed file.

Prime number. A number that is divisible only by one and itself.

* **Prime record key.** A key whose contents uniquely identify a record within an indexed file.

* **Printable group.** A report group that contains at least one print line.

* **Printable item.** A data item, the extent and contents of which are specified by an elementary report entry. This elementary report entry contains a COLUMN NUMBER clause, a PICTURE clause, and a SOURCE, SUM, or VALUE clause.

Printer spacing chart. Form used to design printed reports.

Procedural cohesion. A module is based on a specific program structure, such as selection or iteration.

* **Procedure.** A paragraph or group of logically successive paragraphs or a section or group of logically successive sections within the Procedure Division.

* **Procedure branching statement.** A statement that causes the explicit transfer of control to a statement other than the next executable statement in the sequence in which the statements are written in the source program. The procedure branching statements are ALTER, CALL, EXIT, EXIT PROGRAM, GO TO, MERGE (with the OUTPUT PROCEDURE phrase), PERFORM, and SORT (with the INPUT PROCEDURE or OUTPUT PROCEDURE phrase).

Procedure Division. Division of a COBOL program in which the programmer defines how data is to be processed and how information is to be produced.

* **Procedure-name.** A user-defined word which is used to name a paragraph or section in the Procedure Division. It consists of a paragraph-name (which may be qualified) or a section-name.

Program. Set of instructions that can be executed by a computer.

Program flowchart. Schematic diagram of a program showing statements contained in variously shaped blocks and the flow of control indicated by lines connecting the blocks.

* Program identification entry. An entry in the PROGRAM-ID paragraph of the Identification Division which contains clauses that specify the program-name and assign selected program attributes to the program.

Programmer. Person who designs, codes, and tests programs.

Programmer-analyst. Person who performs the functions of both programmer and systems analyst.

Programmer-defined entry. An entry, such as a data-name or file-name, that can be any valid sequence of characters.

Programming manager. Person who manages a programming project.

Programming team. Technique for organizing the work of a programming staff whereby a group of programmers assumes collective control and responsibility for some or all of the system.

Program module. A block of code with a well-defined purpose and a single entry point and a single exit point.

* Program-name. In the Identification Division and the end program header, a user-defined word that identifies a COBOL source program.

Program specification statement. Description of the data to be processed and the information required to be produced by a program.

Program stub. Incomplete portions of a program typically consisting of a paragraph name and the EXIT statement.

Project. In RM/CO*, a project is made up of related program and data files.

Pseudocode. Informal language used in the design of a program.

* Pseudo-text. A sequence of text words, comment lines, or the separator space in a source program or COBOL library bounded by, but not including, pseudo-text delimiters.

* Pseudo-text delimiter. Two contiguous equal sign (=) characters used to delimit pseudo-text.

* Punctuation character. A character that belongs to the following set:

Character	Meaning
,	comma
;	semicolon
:	colon
.	period (full stop)
"	quotation mark
(	left parenthesis
)	right parenthesis
	space (blank)
=	equal sign

* Qualified data-name. An identifier that is composed of a data-name, followed by one or more sets of either of the connectives OF and IN, followed by a data-name qualifier.

* **Qualifier.**

>   1. A data-name or a name associated with a level indicator which is used in a reference either together with another data-name which is the name of an item that is subordinate to the qualifier or together with a condition-name.

>   2. A section-name which is used in a reference together with a paragraph-name specified in that section.

>   3. A library-name which is used in a reference together with a text-name associated with that library.

* **Queue.** A logical collection of messages awaiting transmission or processing.

* **Queue name.** A symbolic name that indicates to the message control system the logical path by which a message or a portion of a completed message may be accessible in a queue.

* **Random access.** An access mode in which the program-specified value of a key data item identifies the logical record that is obtained from, deleted from, or placed into a relative or indexed file.

Random file access. File access type in which records are processed on demand.

Randomized relative file. Relative file organization in which records are scattered at random throughout the file by means of a hash function.

Randomized table. Type of table organization in which data is scattered in a random fashion by use of a hash function.

Record. Group of related fields.

* **Record.** The most inclusive data item. The level-number for a record is 01. A record may be either an elementary item or a group item. The term is synonymous with logical record.

* **Record area.** A storage area allocated for the purpose of processing the record described in a record description entry in the File Section of the Data Division. In the File Section, the current number of character positions in the record area is determined by the explicit or implicit RECORD clause.

* **Record description.** The total set of data description entries associated with a particular record. The term is synonymous with record description entry.

* **Record description entry.** The total set of data description entries associated with a particular record. The term is synonymous with record description.

* **Record key.** A key whose contents identify a record within an indexed file. Within an indexed file, a record key is either the prime record key or an alternate record key.

* **Record-name.** A user-defined word that names a record described in a record description entry in the Data Division of a COBOL program.

* **Record number.** The ordinal number of a record in the file whose organization is sequential.

* **Reel.** A discrete portion of a storage medium, the dimensions of which are determined by each implementor, that contains part of a file, all of a file, or any number of files. The term is synonymous with both unit and volume.

* **Reference format.** A format that provides a standard method for describing COBOL source programs.

* **Reference modifier.** The leftmost character position and length used to establish and reference a data item.

* **Relation.** The term is synonymous with relational operator.

* **Relational operator.** A reserved word, a relation character, a group of consecutive reserved words, or a group of consecutive reserved words and relation characters used in the construction of a relation condition. The permissible operators and their meanings are

Relational Operator	Meaning
IS [NOT] GREATER THAN	greater than or not greater than
IS [NOT] >	
IS [NOT] LESS THAN	less than or not less than
IS [NOT] <	
IS [NOT] EQUAL TO	equal to or not equal to
IS [NOT] =	
IS GREATER THAN OR EQUAL TO	greater than or equal to
IS >=	
IS LESS THAN OR EQUAL TO	less than or equal to
IS <=	

* **Relation character.** A character that belongs to the following set:

Character	Meaning
>	greater than
<	less than
=	equal to

* **Relation condition.** The proposition, for which a truth value can be determined, that the value of an arithmetic expression, data item, nonnumeric literal, or index-name has a specific relationship to the value of another arithmetic expression, data item, nonnumeric literal, or index-name.

* **Relative file.** A file with relative organization.

* **Relative key.** A key whose contents identify a logical record in a relative file.

* **Relative organization.** The permanent logical file structure in which each record is uniquely identified by an integer value greater than zero, which specifies the record's logical ordinal position in the file.

* **Relative record number.** The ordinal number of a record in a file whose organization is relative. This number is treated as a numeric literal which is an integer.

* **Report clause.** A clause in the Report Section of the Data Division that appears in a report description entry or a report group description entry.

* **Report description entry.** An entry in the Report Section of the Data Division that is composed of the level indicator RD, followed by the report-name, followed by a set of report clauses as required.

* **Report file.** An output file whose file description entry contains a REPORT clause. The contents of a report file consist of records that are written under control of the report writer control system.

* **Report footing.** A report group that is presented only at the end of a report.

* **Report group.** In the Report Section of the Data Division, an 01 level-number entry and its subordinate entries.

* **Report group description entry.** An entry in the Report Section of the Data Division that is composed of the level-number 01, an optional data-name, a TYPE clause, and an optional set of report clauses.

* **Report heading.** A report group that is presented only at the beginning of a report.

* **Report line.** A division of a page representing one row of horizontal character positions. Each character position of a report line is aligned vertically beneath the corresponding character position of the report line above it. Report lines are numbered from 1, by 1, starting at the top of the page.

* **Report-name.** A user-defined word that names a report described in a report description entry within the Report Section of the Data Division.

* **Report section.** The section of the Data Division that contains zero, one, or more report description entries and their associated report group description entries.

* **Report writer control system (RWCS).** An object time control system, provided by the implementor, that accomplishes the construction of reports.

* **Report writer logical record.** A record that consists of the report writer print line and associated control information necessary for its selection and vertical positioning.

* **Reserved word.** A COBOL word specified in the list of words which may be used in a COBOL source program but which must not appear in the program as user-defined words or system-names.

* **Resource.** A facility or service, controlled by the operating system, that can be used by an executing program.

* **Resultant identifier.** A user-defined data item that is to contain the result of an arithmetic operation.

* **Routine-name.** A user-defined word that identifies a procedure written in a language other than COBOL.

* **Run unit.** One or more object programs which interact with one another and which function, at object time, as an entity to provide problem solutions.

* **RWCS.** Report writer control system; an object time control system, provided by the implementor, that accomplishes the construction of reports.

Scanning. Process by which RM/COBOL-85 determines the meaning of COBOL source code.

Scope delimiter. Reserved word used to terminate a conditional statement.

Scrolling. Process in which lines on a computer screen appear at the bottom of the screen and disappear at the top.

Searching. Process of locating a table argument that matches an actual argument.

Secondary key. Less important key when multiple keys are used in organizing or accessing data.

* **Section.** A set of zero, one, or more paragraphs or entries, called a section body, the first of which is preceded by a section header. Each section consists of the section header and the related section body.

* **Section header.** A combination of words followed by a separator period that indicates the beginning of a section in the Environment, Data, and Procedure Divisions. In the Environment and Data Divisions, a section header is composed of reserved words followed by a separator period.

  The permissible section headers in the Environment Division are
      CONFIGURATION SECTION.
      INPUT-OUTPUT SECTION.
  The permissible section headers in the Data Division are
      FILE SECTION.
      WORKING-STORAGE SECTION.
      LINKAGE SECTION.
      COMMUNICATION SECTION.
      REPORT SECTION.
  In the Procedure Division, a section header is composed of a section-name, followed by the reserved word SECTION, followed by a segment-number (optional), followed by a separator period.

* **Section-name.** A user-defined word which names a section in the Procedure Division.

* **Segment-number.** A user-defined word which classifies sections in the Procedure Division for purposes of segmentation. Segment-numbers may contain only the characters "0", "1", . . . , "9". A segment-number may be expressed as either a one- or two-digit number.

* **Sentence.** A sequence of one or more statements, the last of which is terminated by a separator period.

* **Separately compiled program.** A program which, together with its contained programs, is compiled separately from all other programs.

* **Separator.** A character or two contiguous characters used to delimit character-strings.

Sequence structure. Fundamental program structure in which actions are carried out in sequence.

* **Sequential access.** An access mode in which logical records are obtained from or placed into a file in a consecutive predecessor-to-successor logical record sequence determined by the order of records in the file.

Sequential cohesion. Parts of a module are related because they must be carried out in a prescribed sequence.

* **Sequential file.** A file with sequential organization.

Sequential file access. Access type in which records are processed, one after the other, from start to finish.

* **Sequential organization.** The permanent logical file structure in which a record is identified by a predecessor-successor relationship established when the record is placed into the file.

Sequential search. Search procedure in which a sequenced list of actual arguments is compared sequentially to the actual argument until either a match is made or the table argument is larger than the actual argument.

* **77-level-description-entry.** A data description entry that describes a noncontiguous data item with the level-number 77.

* **Sign condition.** The proposition, for which a truth value can be determined, that the algebraic value of a data item or an arithmetic expression is either less than, greater than, or equal to zero.

Sign off. Process of terminating a computing session in a multiuser computing system.

Sign on. Process of identifying oneself to gain access to a multiuser computing system.

* **Simple condition.** Any single condition chosen from the following set:

    relation condition
    class condition
    condition-name condition
    switch-status condition
    sign condition
    (simple-condition)

Single-user system. Computer system that can be used by only one person at a time.

Software. Computer programs.

Sorted order. Ascending or descending sequence.

* **Sort file.** A collection of records to be sorted by a SORT statement. The sort file is created and can be used by the sort function only.

Sorting. Process of changing the order of data.

* **Sort-merge file description entry.** An entry in the File Section of the Data Division that is composed of the level indicator SD, followed by a file-name, and then followed by a set of file clauses as required.

Sort work-file. *See* Sort file.

* **Source.** The symbolic identification of the originator of a transmission to a queue.

* **SOURCE-COMPUTER.** The name of an Environment Division paragraph in which the computer environment, within which the source program is compiled, is described.

* **Source computer entry.** An entry in the SOURCE-COMPUTER paragraph of the Environment Division which contains clauses that describe the computer environment in which the source program is to be compiled.

* **Source item.** An identifier designated by a SOURCE clause that provides the value of a printable item.

* **Source program.** Although it is recognized that a source program may be represented by other forms and symbols, in this document, it always refers to a syntactically correct set of COBOL statements. A COBOL source program commences with an Identification Division, a COPY statement, or a REPLACE statement. A COBOL source program is terminated by the end program header, if specified, or by the absence of additional source program lines.

Source program. Program written in a high-level language.

* **Special character.** A character that belongs to the following set:

Character	Meaning
+	plus sign
–	minus sign
*	asterisk
/	slash (solidus)

=	equal sign
$	currency sign
,	comma (decimal point)
;	semicolon
.	period (decimal point, full stop)
"	quotation mark
(	left parenthesis
)	right parenthesis
>	greater than symbol
<	less than symbol
:	colon

* **Special character word.** A reserved word which is an arithmetic operator or a relation character.

* **SPECIAL-NAMES.** The name of an Environment Division paragraph in which implementor-names are related to user-specified mnemonic names.

* **Special names entry.** An entry in the SPECIAL-NAMES paragraph of the Environment Division which provides means for specifying the currency sign, choosing the decimal point, specifying symbolic characters, relating implementor-names to user-specified mnemonic-names, relating alphabet-names to character sets or collating sequences, and relating class-names to sets of characters.

* **Special registers.** Certain compiler-generated storage areas whose primary use is to store information produced in conjunction with the use of specific COBOL features.

* **Standard data format.** The concept used in describing data in a COBOL Data Division under which the characteristics or properties of the data are expressed in a form oriented to the appearance of the data on the printed page of infinite length and breadth, rather than in a form oriented to the manner in which the data is stored internally in the computer or on a particular medium.

* **Statement.** A syntactically valid combination of words, literals, and separators, beginning with a verb, written in a COBOL source program.

Status information. In RM/CO*, status information is displayed in the status line.

Status line. In RM/CO*, the status line is displayed at the top of the screen and shows the status of the project.

Structure. Patterns in the relationship of program statements.

Structure diagram. Schematic diagram in which modules are represented by blocks, and the relationship among modules is represented by lines connecting the blocks.

Structured implementation and testing. Systematic process of coding and testing a program in parts using either a bottom-up or top-down approach.

Structured programming. Programming technique which restricts the program structures that may be used and emphasizes modularity, top-down program design, program readability, and other practices that enhance program maintainability.

Structured walk-through. Technique whereby a programming staff performs a detailed analysis of the logic and structure of a program to ensure that the program is correct.

* Subject of entry.   An operand or reserved word that appears immediately following the level indicator or the level-number in the Data Division entry.

Submenu.   List of commands that are subordinate to a menu item at a higher level in the menu hierarchy.

* Subprogram.   A program which is the object of a CALL statement combined at object time with the calling program to produce a run unit. The term is synonymous with called program.

* Sub-queue.   A logical hierarchical division of a queue.

* Subscript.   An occurrence number represented by either an integer; a data-name, optionally followed by an integer with the operator "+" or "–"; or an index-name, optionally followed by an integer with the operator "+" or "–", which identifies a particular element in a table.

* Subscripted data-name.   An identifier that is composed of a data-name, followed by one or more subscripts enclosed in parentheses.

* Sum counter.   A signed numeric data item established by a SUM clause in the Report Section of the Data Division. The sum counter is used by the report writer control system to contain the result of designated summing operations that take place during production of a report.

Summary line(s).   One or more lines printed at the end of a report and containing summary information about data in the report.

Suspense file.   A file that stores records that cannot be processed by a file maintenance program.

Switch.   Data item used to communicate the occurrence of some event from one part of a program to another.

* Switch-status condition.   The proposition, for which a truth value can be determined, that an implementor-defined switch, capable of being set to an "on" or "off" status, has been set to a specific status.

* Symbolic-character.   A user-defined word that specifies a user-defined figurative constant.

Synonym.   Two values which yield the same hash function value.

Syntax error.   Error in the construction of a program that makes it impossible for the compiler to translate the program.

System flowchart.   Schematic diagram showing flow of data and processing steps in a data processing system.

* System-name.   A COBOL word which is used to communicate with the operating environment.

Systems analyst.   Person who analyzes and designs data processing systems.

System software.   Software designed to perform tasks related to control and use of a computer system.

* Table.   A set of logically consecutive items of data that are defined in the Data Division of a COBOL program by means of the OCCURS clause.

Table argument.   List of items in a table that will be used to compare with the actual argument.

* Table element.   A data item that belongs to the set of repeated items comprising a table.

* Terminal.   The originator of a transmission to a queue or the receiver of a transmission from a queue.

* **Text-name.** A user-defined word which identifies library text.

* **Text word.** A character or a sequence of contiguous characters between margin A and margin R in a COBOL library, in a source program, or in pseudo-text which is

  1. a separator, except for space, a pseudo-text delimiter, and the opening and closing delimiters for nonnumeric literals. The right parenthesis and left parenthesis characters, regardless of context within the library, source program, or pseudo-text, are always considered text words.

  2. a literal, including, in the case of nonnumeric literals, the opening quotation mark and the closing quotation mark which bound the literal.

  3. any other sequence of contiguous COBOL characters, except comment lines and the word COPY, bounded by separators, which is neither a separator nor a literal.

Three-level table. Table created with three OCCURS clauses and accessed with three subscripts.

Time-related cohesion. Parts of a module are related because they must be carried out at a specific time, such as at the beginning or end of a program.

Timesharing. Technique of sharing the computer with several different users.

Top-down program design. Design process in which stepwise refinement design is used to successively redefine portions of a program at progressively lower levels of detail.

* **Top margin.** An empty area which precedes the page body.

Tracks. Concentric circles on which data is recorded on a disk.

Transaction file. A file containing information about activities that have occurred in a data processing system.

Transaction log. File containing the details of each transaction processed by a system.

Truncation. Cut off; characters or digits may be lost or truncated when an item of one length is moved to an item of a different length.

* **Truth value.** The representation of the result of the evaluation of a condition in terms of one of two values: true or false.

Two-level table. Table created with two OCCURS clauses and accessed with two subscripts.

* **Unary operator.** A plus (+) or a minus (–) sign which precedes a variable or a left parenthesis in an arithmetic expression and which has the effect of multiplying the expression by +1 or –1 respectively.

* **Unit.** A discrete portion of a storage medium, the dimensions of which are determined by each implementor, that contains part of a file, all of a file, or any number of files. The term is synonymous with both reel and volume.

Unit. Logical component of a digital computer. The units of a computer are Input, Output, Control, Memory, and Arithmetic/Logic.

* **Unsuccessful execution.** The attempted execution of a statement that does not result in the execution of all the operations specified by that statement. The unsuccessful execution of a statement does not affect any data referenced by that statement but may affect status indicators.

* **User-defined word.** A COBOL word that must be supplied by the user to satisfy the format of a clause or statement.

Value. The content of a data item or particular table element.

* **Variable.** A data item whose value may be changed by execution of the object program. A variable used in an arithmetic-expression must be a numeric elementary item.

* **Variable length record.** A record associated with a file whose file description or sort-merge description entry permits records to contain a varying number of character positions.

* **Variable occurrence data item.** A variable occurrence data item is a table element which is repeated a variable number of times. Such an item must contain an `OCCURS DEPENDING ON` clause in its data description entry or be subordinate to such an item.

* **Verb.** A word that expresses an action to be taken by a COBOL compiler or object program.

Volatility. The ratio of Add and Delete transactions to the size of the file being maintained.

* **Volume.** A discrete portion of a storage medium, the dimensions of which are determined by each implementor, that contains part of a file, all of a file, or any number of files. The term is synonymous with both reel and unit.

Window. Technique for organizing information on a screen in which related items are displayed with a surrounding border.

* **Word.** A character-string of not more than 30 characters which forms a user-defined word, a system-name, or a reserved word.

* **Working-storage section.** The section of the Data Division that describes working storage data items, composed of either noncontiguous items or working storage records or both.

Zoned decimal. Type of data representation in which each byte is used to store one decimal digit.

Chapter 1

1. 1. u 2. m 3. s 4. q 5. v 6. f 7. h 8. l 9. n 10. e 11. x 12. p 13. i 14. w
   15. t 16. k 17. g 18. y 19. b 20. o 21. a 22. j 23. c 24. r 25. d 26. z

2. 1. e 2. d 3. f 4. c 5. a 6. b

3.

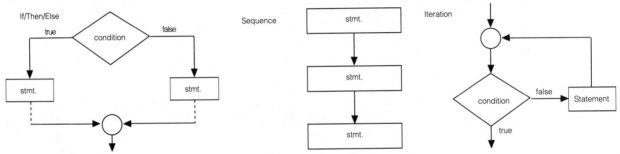

4. See Section 1.9

5. See Section 1.4.

6. Answers will vary.

7. A printer spacing chart is used to show the layout of a printed report.

Chapter 2

1. 1. j 2. n 3. e 4. s 5. m 6. r 7. y 8. i 9. f 10. g 11. t 12. a 13. x 14. z
   15. d 16. p 17. h 18. l 19. w 20. b 21. q 22. u 23. o 24. v 25. k 26. c

2.
```
   IDENTIFICATION DIVISION.
   PROGRAM-ID. BALANCE-PRO2C.
   AUTHOR. YOUR NAME.
   INSTALLATION.  YOUR COLLEGE.
   DATE-WRITTEN.  1/1/91.
   DATE-COMPILED.
   SECURITY.  NONE.
```

3.

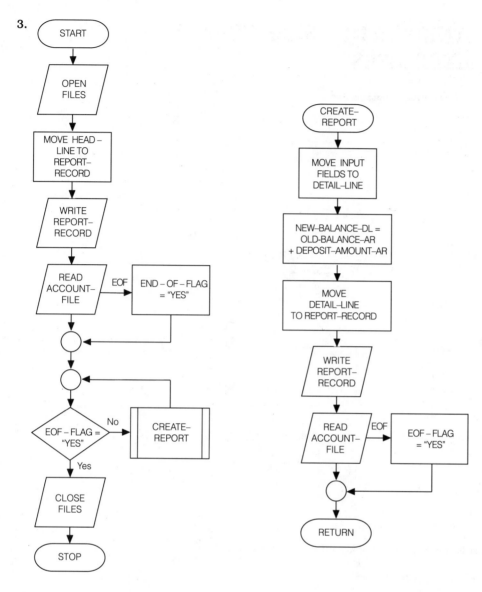

4. Division headers, section headers, paragraph names, FD entries, 01 entries.

5. a. valid b. invalid, no alphabetic character c. invalid, embedded space
   d. invalid, ends with a " – " e. invalid, too long f. invalid, embedded space

6. 1. d 2. a, i 3. i 4. k 5. b, i 6. e 7. c 8. i 9. e 10. f 11. h 12. g, i 13. j
   14. j 15. i 16. i 17. c, i

7.
```
01   NAME-ADDR-REC.
     02   CUSTOMER-NAME-NAR     PIC X(20).
     02   STREET-ADDRESS-NAR    PIC X(15).
     02   CITY-NAR              PIC X(10).
     02   STATE-NAR             PIC XX.
     02   ZIP-NAR               PIC 9(5).
     02   FILLER                PIC X(28).
```

8.

Where defined in DATA DIVISION

Type of Item	FILE SECTION		WORKING-STORAGE SECTION		
	Used for Input	*Used for Output*	*Used for Input*	*Used for Control*	*Used for Output*
File	ACCOUNT-FILE	REPORT-FILE			
Record	ACCOUNT-RECORD	REPORT-RECORD			HEAD-LINE DETAIL-LINE
Field	OLD-BALANCE-AR DEPOSIT-AMOUNT-AR			EOF-FLAG FLAGS	OLD-BALANCE-DL DEPOSIT-AMOUNT-DL NEW-BALANCE-DL

9. Answers will vary.

10. See Section 2.12.

Chapter 3

1. A switch is a data item that can contain one of the two values—1 or 0, "yes" or "no," "on" or "off." Switches are used as communication links between paragraphs of a program.

2. An accumulator is a data item which is used to store a running total. Typically, a sequence of values is added to the accumulator one at a time. Accumulators are used to compute totals.

3. A counter is an accumulator into which a constant, such as 1, is added.

4. Change line 6 to

```
PERFORM 2100-BUILD-FILE
    UNTIL EOF-FLAG = "YES".
```

Add the following at line 20:

```
PERFORM 9000-READ-OLD-FILE.
```

5. Numbers in paragraph names help the reader to locate paragraphs and to understand the level of the paragraph in the structure of the program. They are required by style, not by COBOL syntax.

6.

READ-DATA-FILE	acceptable
ANSWER	unacceptable; suggest COMPUTE-ANSWER
DO-COMPUTATIONS	acceptable
DATA-MOVEMENT	unacceptable; suggest MOVE-DATA
ZZYZX	unacceptable; not enough information to make a suggested improvement

7. A structure diagram shows the hierarchical relationships of program modules. Structure diagrams are used to help people understand program structure.

8.
```
1000-MAIN-CONTROL.
    PERFORM 2000-INITIALIZE-PROGRAM.
    PERFORM 2100-PROCESS-DATA
            UNTIL EOF-FLAG = "YES".
    PERFORM 2200-TERMINATE-PROGRAM.
    STOP RUN.
2000-INITIALIZE-PROGRAM.
    OPEN INPUT ACCOUNT-FILE
         OUTPUT REPORT-FILE.
    PERFORM 3000-WRITE-HEADINGS.
    PERFORM 9000-READ-ACCOUNT-FILE.
```

```
2100-PROCESS-DATA.
    PERFORM 3100-COMPUTE-NEW-BALANCE.
    PERFORM 3200-WRITE-DETAIL-LINE.
    PERFORM 9000-READ-ACCOUNT-FILE.
2200-TERMINATE-PROGRAM.
    CLOSE ACCOUNT-FILE
        REPORT-FILE.
3000-WRITE-HEADINGS.
    MOVE HEAD-LINE TO REPORT-RECORD.
    WRITE REPORT-RECORD AFTER ADVANCING PAGE.
3100-COMPUTE-NEW-BALANCE.
    ADD OLD-BALANCE-AR DEPOSIT-AMOUNT-AR GIVING NEW-BALANCE-DL.
3200-WRITE-DETAIL-LINE.
    MOVE OLD-BALANCE-AR TO OLD-BALANCE-DL.
    MOVE DEPOSIT-AMOUNT-AR TO DEPOSIT-AMOUNT-DL.
    MOVE DETAIL-LINE TO REPORT-RECORD.
    WRITE REPORT-RECORD AFTER ADVANCING 1 LINE.
9000-READ-ACCOUNT-FILE.
    READ ACCOUNT-FILE
        AT END MOVE "YES" TO EOF-FLAG.
```

Control Paragraphs: 1000, 2000, 2100
Operational Paragraphs: 2200, 3000, 3100, 3200, 9000
Structure Diagram:

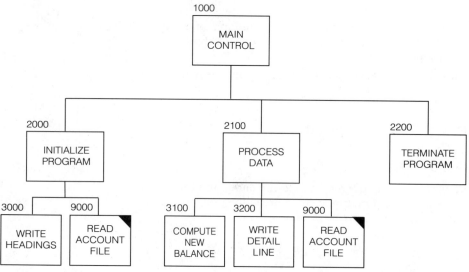

9.

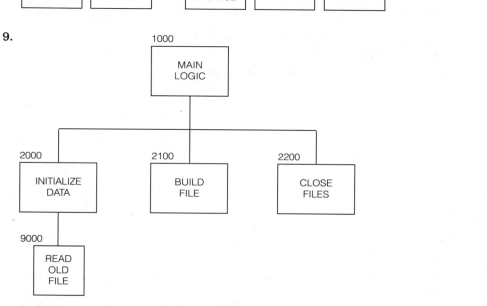

10. An imperative statement has no clause whose execution is dependent on a condition. A PERFORM statement is imperative; a READ statement with an AT END clause is conditional because the execution of the AT END clause is dependent on detection of the end of the file.

11. A scope delimiter terminates a statement. In COBOL-74, the period is the basic scope delimiter. Scope delimiters of the form END-statement were added in COBOL-85.

12. An in-line PERFORM statement contains the statements to be executed within the body of the statement itself. Use of the in-line PERFORM statement simplifies the structure of the program since fewer separate paragraphs are necessary.

Chapter 4

1. a. FD   SALES-FILE
          LABEL RECORDS ARE STANDARD
          DATA RECORD IS SALES-RECORD.
   b. OPEN INPUT SALES-FILE.
   c. READ SALES-FILE
          AT END MOVE "YES" TO EOF-FLAG.
   d. CLOSE SALES-FILE.

2. a. FD   PAYROLL-FILE
          LABEL RECORDS ARE OMITTED
          DATA RECORD IS PAYROLL-RECORD.
   b. OPEN OUTPUT PAYROLL-FILE.
   c. WRITE PAYROLL-RECORD AFTER 1.
   d. CLOSE PAYROLL-FILE.

3. a.
```
0 0 1 2 3^

  1 2 3^

0 0 0 0 0 1 2 3^

1 2 3 4 5 0 0^

0 1 2 3 4 5 0^

  1
```
   b.
```
      1 2 3

    $ 1 2 3 . 4 5

  * 1 2 3 . 4
```
   c.
```
4 3 2 1

4 3

      4 3 2 1

2 1
```
   d.
```
      - 1 2 . 3 4

      - 1 2 . 3 4

        1 2 . 3 4 C R

$       1 2 . 3 4   D B
```
   e.
```
0 0 0 1^

+       1 . 2 3

        1 . 2 3

        1 . 2 3
```
   f.
```
$ 3 4 5 6 . 7 8

1 2 3 4 5 6 . 7 8 0 0

2 3 , 4 5 6 . 7
```
   g.
```
0 1 2 3 4

0 1 2 3

0 1 0 2 3 0 4

0 1   2 3 4
```
   h.
```
  3 / 1 1 / 8 2
```

4.

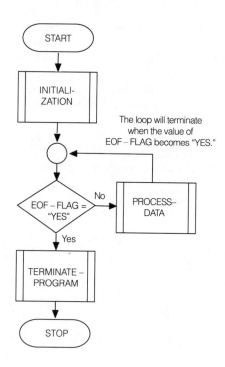

The loop will terminate when the value of EOF – FLAG becomes "YES."

5. Page heading
Column heading
Detail line
Total line

6.

	Receiving field			
	Alphanumeric	*Numeric*	*Numeric edited*	*Alphanumeric edited*
Alphanumeric	permitted	not permitted	not permitted	permitted
Numeric	permitted	permitted	permitted	permitted
Numeric edited	permitted	not permitted	not permitted	not permitted
Alphanumeric edited	permitted	not permitted	not permitted	not permitted

Sending field

7. Qualification is using IN or OF to show subordination of one data item to another. Qualification is required to provide unique references when an identifier is defined more than once in the DATA DIVISION.

8. The advantage of MOVE CORRESPONDING is that it can simplify statements in the PROCEDURE DIVISION. The disadvantage is that it requires defining the same identifier more than once which then necessitates use of qualification which, in turn, can contribute to wordiness in the PROCEDURE DIVISION.

9. De-editing is the ability to move an edited field into a numeric field. This operation may be useful when making modifications to an existing COBOL program.

Chapter 5

1. a. ADD A TO B.
   or
   ADD A B GIVING A.
   or
   COMPUTE A = B + A.

   b. SUBTRACT EXPENSE FROM INCOME GIVING BALANCE.
   or
   COMPUTE BALANCE = INCOME − EXPENSE.

   c. MULTIPLY D BY A.
   or
   MULTIPLY A BY D GIVING A.
   or
   COMPUTE A = A * D.

   d. DIVIDE SALES BY 12 GIVING MONTHLY-AVERAGE.
   or
   DIVIDE 12 INTO SALES GIVING MONTHLY-AVERAGE.
   or
   COMPUTE MONTHLY-AVERAGE = SALES / 12.

   e. COMPUTE VOLUME = 4 / 3 * 3.14159 * R ** 2.

   f. COMPUTE I = P * R * T.

   g. MULTIPLY B BY 0.25 GIVING A
   or
   COMPUTE A = B * 0.25.

   h. COMPUTE A = P * (1 + R) ** N.

2. a. | 0 | 7 |
      C PIC 99

   b. | 1 | 3 |
      B PIC 99

   c. | 1 | 3 | 4̄ |
      B PIC S999

   d. | 0 | 0 | 1̄ | | 0 | 0 |
      A PIC S99V9   D PIC S99

   e. | 0 | 2 | 7̄ |
      A PIC S999

   f. | 0 | 0 |
      A PIC V99
      Note: SIZE ERROR because of overflow

   g. | 0 | 0 | 0 |
      A PIC 99V9
      Note: SIZE ERROR because of division by 0

   h. | 3 | 3 |
      C PIC 99
      Note: loss of sign on result

   i. | 0 | 2 | 0̄ |
      B PIC S99V9

3. Control Paragraphs: 1000, 2100
   Operational Paragraphs: 2000, 2200, 3000, 3100, 9000

4. a. The use of group data items such as COMPUTED-AMOUNTS increases the readability of the program.
   b. The use of the VALUE clause for a numeric data item such as WITH-AMT makes the program easier to debug and maintain. Since the value of WITH-AMT is computed by the program, the VALUE clause is not required for initialization of the item.
   c. The placement of constants such as FICA-FACTOR in WORKING-STORAGE makes the program easier to maintain.
   d. The ROUNDED option will ensure that the employee's pay is rounded to the nearest penny.

5. COMPUTE JULIAN-DATE = (M − 1) * 29.7 + D
  Note: This formula is only approximate since not all months have 29.7 days. In some applications, the year is also important. The Julian date for the century or decade can be approximated by

  COMPUTE JULIAN-DATE = Y * 365.25 + (M − 1) * 29.7 + D

where Y represents the year in four-digit or two-digit form.

6. See Section 5.10.

7. R will receive the result.

8. Structure diagram of Program 5a85.

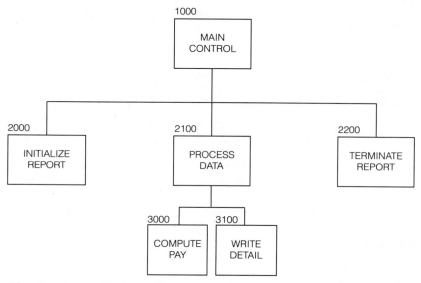

The structure of Program 5a is more complex than that of Program 5a85.

Chapter 6

1. a. X < Y OR Y IS NEGATIVE
     true   false
         true

   b. Z IS ALPHABETIC
        true

   c. X IS NUMERIC AND Z IS NOT ALPHABETIC
        true   false
              false

   d. NOT Y IS POSITIVE
           true
        false

   e. NOT X IS ZERO OR Y IS NOT NEGATIVE
        false   true
           true
              true

   f. NOT (X > 25 OR Y < 39)
          false   true
              true
             false

   g. X > Y OR X IS ZERO AND Y > 1
      false   false   true
                     false
           false

   h. X < Y AND (Y < 0 OR X > 30)
      true   false   false
                    false
           false

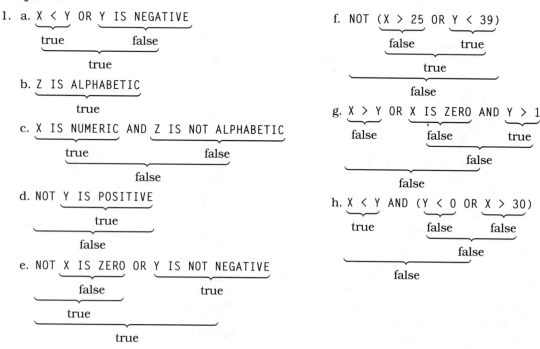

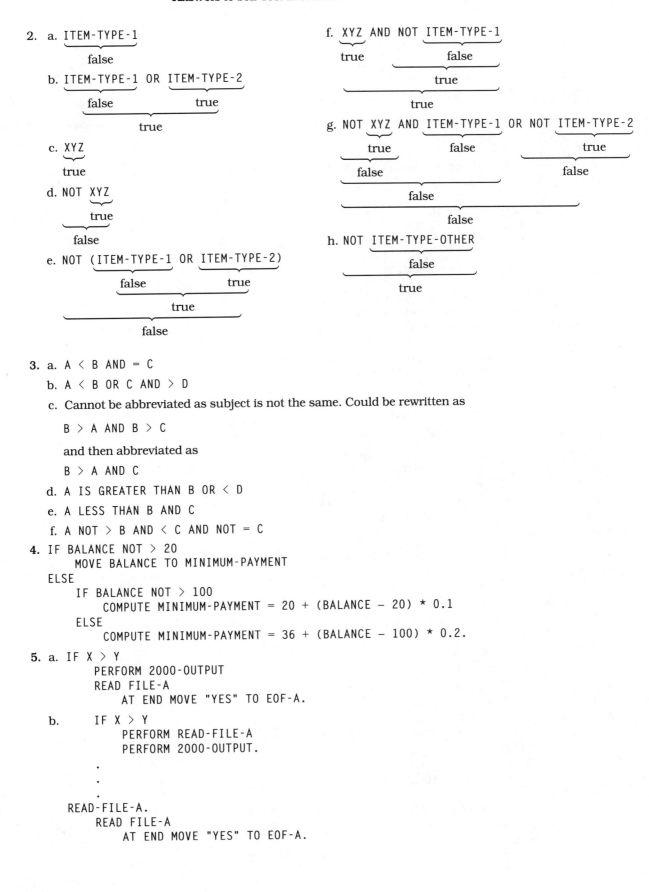

2. a. ITEM-TYPE-1
  false

b. ITEM-TYPE-1 OR ITEM-TYPE-2
  false   true
      true

c. XYZ
  true

d. NOT XYZ
      true
  false

e. NOT (ITEM-TYPE-1 OR ITEM-TYPE-2)
      false   true
          true
      false

f. XYZ AND NOT ITEM-TYPE-1
  true   false
      true
      true

g. NOT XYZ AND ITEM-TYPE-1 OR NOT ITEM-TYPE-2
      true   false   true
      false   false
          false
              false

h. NOT ITEM-TYPE-OTHER
      false
      true

3. a. A < B AND = C

b. A < B OR C AND > D

c. Cannot be abbreviated as subject is not the same. Could be rewritten as

  B > A AND B > C

  and then abbreviated as

  B > A AND C

d. A IS GREATER THAN B OR < D

e. A LESS THAN B AND C

f. A NOT > B AND < C AND NOT = C

4. IF BALANCE NOT > 20
      MOVE BALANCE TO MINIMUM-PAYMENT
  ELSE
      IF BALANCE NOT > 100
          COMPUTE MINIMUM-PAYMENT = 20 + (BALANCE − 20) * 0.1
      ELSE
          COMPUTE MINIMUM-PAYMENT = 36 + (BALANCE − 100) * 0.2.

5. a. IF X > Y
          PERFORM 2000-OUTPUT
          READ FILE-A
              AT END MOVE "YES" TO EOF-A.

b.   IF X > Y
              PERFORM READ-FILE-A
              PERFORM 2000-OUTPUT.

          .
          .
          .
      READ-FILE-A.
          READ FILE-A
              AT END MOVE "YES" TO EOF-A.

```
c.      IF ERR-CODE = "NO"
            PERFORM COMPUTATIONS.
              .
              .
              .
      COMPUTATIONS.
          ADD A TO B ON SIZE ERROR MOVE 0 TO B.
          ADD C TO D ON SIZE ERROR MOVE 0 TO D.
```

```
6. VALIDATE-DATA.
      MOVE "NO" TO VALIDITY-ERROR.
      IF ACCOUNT-NUM-DR NOT NUMERIC
          OR
          ZIP-DR NOT NUMERIC
          OR
          BALANCE-FORWARD-DR NOT NUMERIC
              MOVE "YES" TO VALIDITY-ERROR.
      IF CUSTOMER-NAME-DR = SPACES
          OR
          CUSTOMER-NAME-DR NOT ALPHABETIC
              MOVE "YES" TO VALIDITY-ERROR.
      IF CITY-DR = SPACES
          OR
          CITY-DR NOT ALPHABETIC
              MOVE "YES" TO VALIDITY-ERROR.
      IF STATE-DR = SPACES
          OR
          STATE-DR NOT ALPHABETIC
              MOVE "YES" TO VALIDITY-ERROR.
```

It is not possible to check the field STREET-ADDRESS-DR since it may legitimately contain both alphabetic and numeric characters as well as other characters such as ".", "#", and so on.

7. The PERFORM/UNTIL does not have a clause consisting of one or more statements, so it is not a conditional statement.

8. Modify line 133 as follows:

```
IF YEAR-HIRED-PR > 40 AND YEAR-HIRED-PR < 60 AND SEX-PR = "F"
```

9. Figure 6.21:

```
    IF A = B
        READ File-A
            AT END MOVE "YES" TO Eof-A
        END-READ
        READ File-B
            AT END MOVE "YES" TO Eof-B
        END-READ
    END-IF
```

Figure 6.22:

```
  IF A = B
      READ File-A
          AT END
              MOVE "YES" TO Eof-A
              READ File-B
                  AT END MOVE "YES" TO Eof-B
              END-READ
      END-READ
  END-IF
```

Figure 6.23:

```
IF A = B
    READ File-A
        AT END MOVE "YES" TO Eof-A
    END-READ
END-IF
READ File-B
    AT END MOVE "YES" TO Eof-B
END-READ
```

10. The ALPHABETIC test in COBOL-85 recognizes lowercase characters as alphabetic.

11. a.
```
IF X > Y
    PERFORM Output
    READ File-A
        AT END MOVE "YES" TO Eof-A
    END-READ
END-IF
```

   b.
```
IF X > Y
    READ File-A
        AT END MOVE "YES" TO Eof-A
    END-READ
    PERFORM Output
END-IF
```

   c.
```
IF Err-Code = "NO"
    ADD A TO B
        ON SIZE ERROR MOVE ZERO TO B
    END-ADD
    ADD C TO D
            ON SIZE ERROR MOVE ZERO TO D
    END-ADD
END-IF
```

Chapter 7

1. Program 7d:

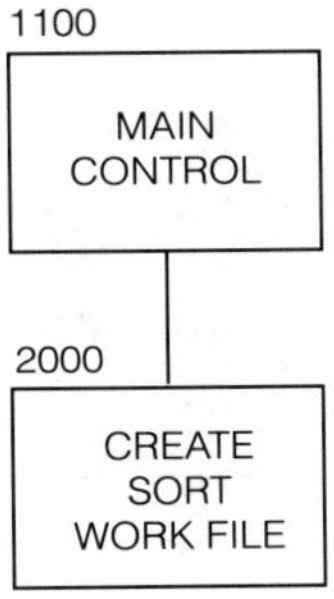

Program 7e:

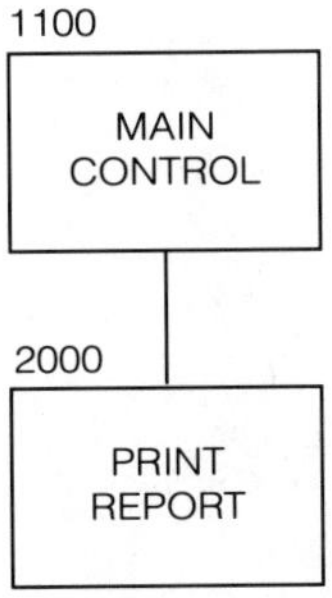

Multiparagraph sections are treated as one program module and represented by one block in a structure diagram.

2. 1. Records from PURCHASE-REQUEST-FILE are copied into SORT-FILE.
    2. Records in SORT-FILE are sorted.
    3. Records from SORT-FILE are copied into PURCHASE-REQUEST-FILE.

3. a. SD entry.
    b. Key field.
    c. The PERFORM contains provision for returning after execution of the paragraph or section; GO TO does not.
    d. Section header which has the form section-name SECTION.
    e. Module.
    f. Branch to the last paragraph in a multiparagraph section.
    g. RETURN
    h. RELEASE
    i. The only statement in a paragraph.
    j. SORT and PERFORM a paragraph outside the procedure.
    k. Execute the last statement in the section.
    l. Disk.

4. a.
```
SORT  SORT-FILE
     ON ASCENDING KEY SS-NUM-SR
     USING DATA-FILE
     GIVING DATA-FILE.
```

    b.
```
SORT  SORT-FILE
     ON ASCENDING KEY ZIP-SR NAME-SR
     USING DATA-FILE
     GIVING DATA-FILE.
```

5.
```
     SORT  SORT-FILE
          ON ASCENDING KEY STATE-SR
          INPUT PROCEDURE IS 2000-BUILD-FILE
          GIVING DATA-FILE.

          .
          .
          .

2000-BUILD-FILE SECTION.
2100-BUILD-FILE-CONTROL.
     MOVE "NO" TO EOF-FLAG.
     OPEN INPUT NEW-DATA-FILE.
     READ NEW-DATA-FILE
          AT END MOVE "YES" TO EOF-FLAG.
     PERFORM 2300-RELEASE-READ
          UNTIL EOF-FLAG = "YES".
     CLOSE NEW-DATA-FILE.
     GO TO 2900-BUILD-FILE-EXIT.
2300-RELEASE-READ.
     MOVE  SS-NUM-NDR TO SS-NUM-SR.
     MOVE  NAME-NDR TO NAME-SR.
     MOVE  ST-ADDR-NDR TO ST-ADDR-SR.
     MOVE  CITY-NDR TO CITY-SR.
     MOVE  STATE-NDR TO STATE-SR.
     MOVE  ZIP-NDR TO ZIP-SR.
     RELEASE SORT-RECORD.
     READ NEW-DATA-FILE
          AT END MOVE "YES" TO EOF-FLAG.
2900-BUILD-FILE-EXIT.
     EXIT.
```

```
6.      SORT  SORT-FILE
            ON DESCENDING KEY ZIP-SR
            INPUT PROCEDURE IS 2000-BUILD-FILE
            GIVING DATA-FILE.

            .
            .
            .
    2000-BUILD-FILE SECTION.
    2100-BUILD-FILE-CONTROL.
        MOVE "NO" TO EOF-FLAG.
        OPEN INPUT DATA-FILE.
        READ DATA-FILE
            AT END MOVE "YES" TO EOF-FLAG.
        PERFORM 2200-COPY-DATA-FILE
            UNTIL EOF-FLAG = "YES".
        CLOSE DATA-FILE.
        MOVE "NO" TO EOF-FLAG.
        OPEN INPUT NEW-DATA-FILE.
        READ NEW-DATA-FILE
            AT END MOVE "YES" TO EOF-FLAG.
        PERFORM 2210-COPY-NEW-DATA-FILE
            UNTIL EOF-FLAG = "YES".
        CLOSE NEW-DATA-FILE.
        GO TO 2290-BUILD-FILE-EXIT.
    2200-COPY-DATA-FILE
        RELEASE SORT-RECORD FROM DATA-RECORD.
        READ DATA-FILE
            AT END MOVE "YES" TO EOF-FLAG.
    2210-COPY-NEW-DATA-FILE.
        MOVE   SS-NUM-NDR TO SS-NUM-SR
        MOVE   NAME-NDR TO NAME-SR.
        MOVE   ST-ADDR-NDR TO ST ADDR-SR.
        MOVE   CITY-NDR TO CITY-SR.
        MOVE   STATE-NDR TO STATE-SR.
        MOVE   ZIP-NDR TO ZIP-SR.
        RELEASE SORT-RECORD.
        READ NEW-DATA-FILE
            AT END MOVE "YES" TO EOF-FLAG.
    2290-BUILD-FILE-EXIT.
        EXIT.
```

7. Exercise 5:

```
    2000-Build-File SECTION.
    2100-Build-File-Control.
        MOVE "NO" TO Eof-Flag
        OPEN INPUT New-Data-File
        PERFORM UNTIL Eof-Flag = "YES"
            READ New-Data-File
                AT END
                    MOVE "YES" TO Eof-Flag
                NOT AT END
                    MOVE SS-Num-NDR TO SS-Num-SR

                    .
                    .
                    .
                    RELEASE Sort-Record
            END-READ
        END-PERFORM
        CLOSE New-Data-File.
```

Exercise 6:

```
2000-Build-File SECTION.
2100-Build-File-Control.
    MOVE "NO" TO Eof-Flag
    OPEN INPUT New-Data-File
    PERFORM UNTIL Eof-Flag = "YES"
        READ Data-File
            AT END
                MOVE "YES" TO Eof-Flag
            NOT AT END
                RELEASE Sort-Record FROM Data-Record
        END-READ
    END-PERFORM
    CLOSE Data-File
    MOVE "NO" TO Eof-Flag
    OPEN INPUT New-Data-File
    PERFORM UNTIL Eof-Flag = "YES"
        READ New-Data-File
            AT END
                MOVE "YES" TO Eof-Flag
            NOT AT END
                MOVE SS-Num-NDR TO SS-Num-SR
                .
                .
                .
                RELEASE Sort-Record
        END-READ
    END-PERFORM
    CLOSE New-Data-File.
```

Chapter 8

```
1. FD   DATA-FILE
        LABEL RECORDS ARE STANDARD
        DATA RECORDS ARE DATA-REC-A DATA-REC-B.
   01   DATA-REC-A.
        03 BID-NUMBER-DRA   PIC 9(10).
        03 PROJ-DESC-DRA    PIC X(10).
        03 BID-AMT-DRA      PIC 9(8)V99.
        03 REC-ID           PIC X.
   01   DATA-REC-B.
        03 BID-NUMBER-DRB   PIC 9(10).
        03 DISP-AMT-DRB     PIC 9(8)V99.
        03 DISP-DESC-DRB    PIC X(10).
        03 FILLER           PIC X.
2. READ DATA-FILE
        AT END MOVE "YES" TO EOF-CODE.
   .
   .
   .
   IF  REC-ID = "A"
       PERFORM PROCESS-REC-TYPE-A
   ELSE
       IF REC-ID = "B"
           PERFORM PROCESS-REC-TYPE-B
       ELSE
           PERFORM ERROR-IN-REC-ID.
3. SPECIAL-NAMES.
       CURRENCY SIGN IS "Q".
   QQQQ,QQQ.99
```

4. Program 8a produces a correctly formatted report, no matter where the last line of the report falls. If there were no records in the file, a page containing only page headings and final totals, which would all be zero, would be produced.

5. If there are no records in the file, a page containing only page headings and final totals, which would all be zero, would be produced. If the last line of the report falls on the last line of a page, the report would terminate. Because no special initialization steps to produce page headings on the first page are needed, the method of Program 8b is recommended. This method is not compatible with page totals because it would cause a superfluous page total output at the beginning of the program.

6. The number of lines per page should always be defined as a data item in `WORKING-STORAGE` to facilitate later revision of the program.

7. The value of `HOLD-DEPARTMENT` should be written. The value of `DEPARTMENT-ER` is the new department number; the total being produced is for the old department number contained in `HOLD-DEPARTMENT`.

8.
```
PROCESS-DATA.
    IF MAJOR-KEY NOT = MAJOR-KEY-HOLD
        PERFORM MINOR-BREAK
        PERFORM INTERMEDIATE-BREAK
        PERFORM MAJOR-BREAK
    ELSE
        IF INTERMEDIATE-KEY NOT = INTERMEDIATE-KEY-HOLD
            PERFORM MINOR-BREAK
            PERFORM INTERMEDIATE-BREAK
        ELSE
            IF MINOR-KEY NOT = MINOR-KEY-HOLD
                PERFORM MINOR-BREAK.
```

9. Nested loop version of Program 8b:
```
1000-MAIN-CONTROL.
    PERFORM 2000-INITIALIZE-REPORT.
    PERFORM 2100-PROCESS-ONE-DEPARTMENT
            UNTIL DEPARTMENT-ER = HIGH-VALUES.
    PERFORM 2200-TERMINATE-REPORT.
    STOP RUN.
2200-INITIALIZE-REPORT.
    OPEN INPUT EMPLOYEE-FILE OUTPUT REPORT-FILE.
    PERFORM 9000-READ-EMPLOYEE-FILE.
    MOVE DEPARTMENT-ER TO HOLD-DEPARTMENT.
2100-PROCESS-ONE-DEPARTMENT.
    PERFORM 3100-PROCESS-DATA
            UNTIL DEPARTMENT-ER NOT = HOLD-DEPARTMENT.
    ADD DEPARTMENT-NUMBER-OF-EMPLOYEES TO NUMBER-OF-EMPLOYEES.
    ADD DEPT-TOTAL-SALARY TO SALARY-TOTAL.
    PERFORM 9100-DEPARTMENT-BREAK.
2200-TERMINATE-REPORT
    PERFORM 3000-WRITE-SUMMARY-LINE.
    CLOSE EMPLOYEE-FILE REPORT-FILE.
3000-WRITE-SUMMARY-LINE.
    .
    .
    .
```

```
3100-PROCESS-DATA.
    MOVE NAME-ER TO NAME-DL.
        .
        .
        .
    ADD SALARY-ER TO DEPT-TOTAL-SALARY.
    ADD 1 TO DEPARTMENT-NUMBER-OF-EMPLOYEES.
    IF LINE-COUNT > LINES-PER-PAGE
        PERFORM 9200-WRITE-HEADINGS.
    WRITE REPORT-RECORD FROM DETAIL-LINE AFTER 1.
    PERFORM 9000-READ-EMPLOYEE-FILE.
9000-READ-EMPLOYEE-FILE.
    READ EMPLOYEE-FILE.
        AT END MOVE HIGH-VALUES TO DEPARTMENT-ER.
9100-DEPARTMENT-BREAK.
        .
        .
        .
9200-WRITE-HEADINGS.
        .
        .
        .
```

10. The ability to initialize multiple items with one statement is likely to be the most useful feature of the INITIALIZE verb.

Chapter 9

1. a.
```
    PERFORM SEARCH-TABLE
        VARYING SUB FROM 1 BY 1 UNTIL
            PART-NUMBER (SUB) = "9999" OR
            PART-NUMBER (SUB) = KNOWN-PART-NUMBER.
    IF PART-NUMBER (SUB) NOT = "9999"
        MOVE NEW-PRICE TO PART-PRICE (SUB).
        .
        .
        .
    SEARCH-TABLE.
        EXIT.
```

b. After a search procedure such as that included in part "a" above, include:
```
    IF PART-NUMBER (SUB) NOT = "9999"
        MOVE PART-DESCRIPTION (SUB) TO DESCRIPTION-OUT
        MOVE NUMBER-ORDERED TO NUMBER-ORDERED-OUT
        MOVE KNOWN-PART-NUMBER TO PART-NUMBER-OUT
        MULTIPLY NUMBER-SOLD BY PART-PRICE (SUB)
            GIVING INVOICE-AMT-OUT
        WRITE OUT-LINE FROM DETAIL-LINE AFTER 1
    ELSE
        PERFORM ERROR-ROUTINE.
```

2. a.

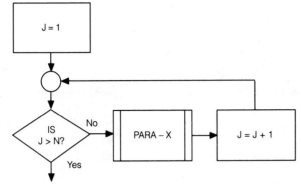

b.

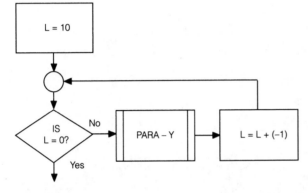

c.

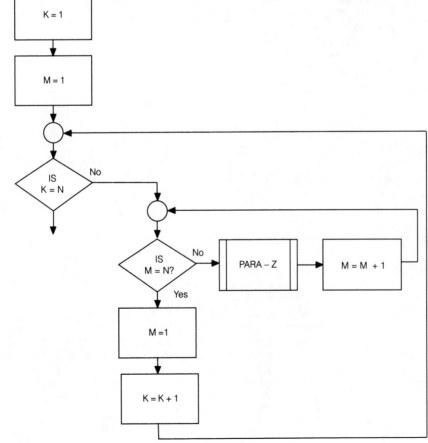

d.

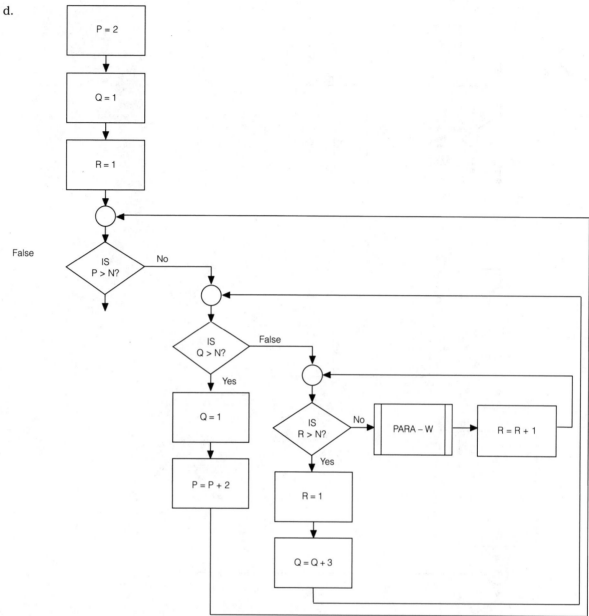

3. a. J | 1 2 3 4 5 6 7   **7 times**

   b. L | 10 9 8 7 6 5 4 3 2 1   **10 times**

   c. K | 1 1 1 1 1 1 2 2 ... 2 3 ... 3 4 ... 4 5 ... 5 6 ... 6   **36 times**

      M | 1 2 3 4 5 6 1 2 ... 6 1 ... 6 1 ... 6 1 ... 6 1 ... 6

   d. P | 2 2 ... 2 2 2 ... 2 2 2 ... 2 4 ... 4 4 ... 4 4 ... 4 6 ... 6 6 ... 6 6 ... 6   **63 times**

      Q | 1 1 ... 1 4 4 ... 4 7 7 ... 7 1 ... 1 4 ... 4 7 ... 7 1 ... 1 4 ... 4 7 ... 7

      R | 1 2 ... 7 1 2 ... 7 1 2 ... 7 1 ... 7 1 ... 7 1 ... 7 1 ... 7 1 ... 7 1 ... 7

4. a.
```
PRODUCTION-OUTPUT.
     MOVE SPACES TO DAILY-OUTPUT.
     PERFORM DETAIL-OUTPUT
          VARYING D FROM 1 BY 1 UNTIL D > NUM-DAYS.
DETAIL-OUTPUT.
     PERFORM DATA-MOVE
          VARYING L FROM 1 BY 1 UNTIL L > 5.
     MOVE D TO DAY-DO.
     WRITE OUTPUT-LINE FROM DAILY-OUTPUT AFTER 1.
DATA-MOVE.
     MOVE PRODUCTION (D, L) TO
          DAY-PRODUCTION-DO (L).
```

   b. Assume the table AV-PROD is defined as:

```
01   CONSTANTS.
     02   FILLER PIC X(30) VALUE ALL "0".
01   AV-PROD REDEFINES CONSTANTS.
     02   PRODUCTION-BY-LINE  PIC 9(6) OCCURS 5 TIMES.
```
   PROCEDURE DIVISION code required:
```
     PERFORM SUMMATION
          VARYING SUB-1 FROM 1 BY 1 UNTIL SUB-1 > NUM-DAYS
               AFTER SUB-2 FROM 1 BY 1 UNTIL SUB-2 > 5.
     PERFORM COMPUTE-AVERAGES
          VARYING SUB FROM 1 BY 1 UNTIL SUB > 5.
          .
          .
          .

SUMMATION.
     ADD PRODUCTION (SUB-1, SUB-2) TO
          PRODUCTION-BY-LINE (SUB-2).
COMPUTE-AVERAGES.
     DIVIDE NUM-DAYS INTO PRODUCTION-BY-LINE (SUB).
```

   c. Assume the table DAYS-DOWN is defined as:

```
01   CONSTANTS-2.
     02   FILLER PIC X(15) VALUE ALL "0".
01   DAYS-DOWN REDEFINES CONSTANTS-2.
     02 DAYS-DOWN-BY-LINE OCCURS PIC 999 OCCURS 5 TIMES.
```
   PROCEDURE DIVISION code required:
```
     PERFORM COUNT-ROUTINE
          VARYING SUB-1 FROM 1 BY 1 UNTIL SUB-1 > NUM-DAYS
               AFTER SUB-2 FROM 1 BY 1 UNTIL SUB-2 > 5.
     COUNT-ROUTINE.
          IF PRODUCTION (SUB-1, SUB-2) = 0
               ADD 1 TO DAYS-DOWN-BY-LINE (SUB-2).
```

5.
```
     MOVE 0 TO SUM-OF-ELEMENTS.
     PERFORM SUMMATION
          VARYING SUB-1 FROM 1 BY 1 UNTIL SUB-1 > 2
          AFTER VARYING SUB-2 FROM 1 BY 1 UNTIL SUB-2 > 5
          AFTER VARYING SUB-3 FROM 1 BY 1 UNTIL SUB-3 > 4.
          .
          .
          .

SUMMATION.
     ADD BONUS-AMOUNT (SUB-1, SUB-2, SUB-3) TO
          SUM-OF-ELEMENTS.
```

6. Assume the table AV-BY-TEST-CLASS is defined as:

```
01  CONSTANTS-3 PIC X(125) VALUE ALL ZEROS.
01  AV-BY-TEST-CLASS REDEFINES CONSTANTS-3.
    02  CLASS-ENTRY OCCURS 5 TIMES.
        03  TEST-ENTRY OCCURS 5 TIMES.
            04  AVERAGE PIC 9(5).
```

PROCEDURE DIVISION code required would be:

```
PERFORM SUMMATION
    VARYING SUB-1 FROM 1 BY 1 UNTIL SUB-1 > 5
        AFTER SUB-2 FROM 1 BY 1 UNTIL SUB-2 >
                NUM-STUDENTS (SUB-1)
        AFTER SUB-3 FROM 1 BY 1 UNTIL SUB-3 > 5.
PERFORM COMPUTE-AVERAGES
    VARYING SUB-1 FROM 1 BY 1 UNTIL SUB-1 > 5
        AFTER SUB-2 FROM 1 BY 1 UNTIL SUB-2 > 5.

        .
        .
        .

SUMMATION.
    ADD GRADE (SUB-1, SUB-2, SUB-3) TO
        AVERAGE (SUB-1, SUB-3).
COMPUTE-AVERAGES.
    DIVIDE NUM-STUDENTS (SUB-1) INTO
        AVERAGE (SUB-1, SUB-2).
```

7. a. F b. F c. F d. T e. T f. T

8. a. |F2|F9|C8|

   b. |01|2A|

   c. |29|8C|

   d. |01|2A|

9. The maximum number of subscripts in COBOL-85 is seven.

10. The maximum number of AFTER clauses in COBOL-74 is two; in COBOL-85, the maximum is six. These maximums are one less than the maximum number of subscripts in each case.

11. Two new data types in COBOL-85 are BINARY and PACKED-DECIMAL.

12. a. X = 1, Y = 5
    b. X = 2, Y = 5

Chapter 10

1. Programmers may be able to contribute to system design because they may be able to foresee problems that others have overlooked. The programmer's work is defined and constrained by the elements of the system design, however.

2. The systems analyst, like an architect, is responsible for the planning and design of the system. The programming manager, like a general contractor, is responsible for implementation of the system. The programmer, like a subcontractor, is responsible for implementation of specific portions of the system.

3. Both the system and the program flowcharts are schematic representations. The major components of the system flowchart are the data files and the processing programs; in a program flowchart, the major components are the processing steps within a specific program.

4. In a system flowchart, the double-headed arrow is used to signify that a file is used as both an input and an output file by the processing program.

5. The program specification statement is used to communicate the requirements for each program in a system. It usually includes a description of the input and output files, layouts for input and output records, and a description of the processing required of the program.

6. Because the company's computer was capable of handling a limited amount of interactive computing, some portions of the system were interactive, whereas report generation is batch. In general, data acquisition and validation are interactive, whereas report generation is batch.

7. A major advantage to the team approach is that the close coordination among team members helps to ensure that all portions of the system will mesh correctly. A major disadvantage is the time required for the team's meetings and other coordination efforts.

8. The primary purpose of the structured walk-through is to eliminate programming errors before programs are compiled or tested. A major disadvantage is the potential for harming the morale of the programmer whose work is reviewed.

9. "Ego-less" programming refers to the disengagement between the programmer and the program that must take place so that a programmer does not perceive criticism of a program as criticism of the programmer.

10. The data dictionary concept implies that all programs in a system will use the same data names for the same files, records, and fields. The COBOL source statement library can be used to make data descriptions available to each program that must reference the elements.

11. Structured implementation and testing implies that coding and testing are carried out alternately, as opposed to the more primitive techniques of coding a program completely before beginning to test it.

12. In carrying out structured implementation and testing, strict adherence to a bottom-up approach often results in too much work, and strict adherence to a top-down approach may not be useful because of the logic of the program. Most programmers use a combination of the two techniques.

13. A "program stub" is a dummy procedure that will later be replaced by the real thing.

14. The COPY statement allows insertion of code from a library into a program. Considerations for use will vary from one installation to another.

15. In a programming context, the term "black box" implies that each program module should perform its function in a way that does not require other program modules to have knowledge of the inner workings of the module.

16. Answers to this exercise will vary greatly.

Chapter 11

1. In general, a batch system processes data after it has accumulated over a period of time, whereas an interactive system processes data as it occurs.

2. In designing an interactive program, the programmer must pay close attention to user communications to make sure that users understand what they are expected to do and that they know how to do it.

3. In a batch system, ACCEPT and DISPLAY are used to handle communication with the system operator. In an interactive system, they are used for the same purpose and may also be used to allow communication with the program user.

4. Instructions may be provided in the form of initial instructions, prompts, or menus. Another form of user instructions in many systems comes from the help option found on many menus.

5. A submenu gives the user options that relate to the choice made in the main menu.

6. Formatted screens contribute greatly to a program's user friendliness.

7. The answer is system dependent.

8. The answer is system dependent.

9. **a.**
```
| A | B | 1 | 2 | * | 3 | 4 | A |   |   |   |
       ITM-R
```
   c.
```
| A | - | 1 | 2 | * | A | B | - | 1 | 2 |
       ITM-R
```
   b.
```
| 1 | 2 | A | A | B |   |   |   |   |   |   |
       ITM-R
```
   d.
```
| A | B | - | C | 1 | 2 | * | 3 | 4 |   |
       ITM-R
```

10. **a.**
```
| A | B | C | - |
     FLD-A
| D | E | * | 1 | 2 |
     FLD-B
| 3 | - | - | X | Y | * |
     FLD-C
```
   c.
```
| A | B | C |   |
     FLD-A
| D | E | * | 1 | 2 |
     FLD-B
|   |   |   |   |   |   |
     FLD-C
```
   e.
```
| A | B | C |   |
     FLD-A
| D | E | * | 1 | 2 |
     FLD-B
```
   b.
```
| A | B | C | - |
     FLD-A
| 1 | 2 | 3 | - | - |
     FLD-B
| Z | W |   |   |   |   |
     FLD-C
```
   d.
```
| A | B | C |   |
     FLD-A
| D | E | * | 1 | 2 |
     FLD-B
| X | Y | * | Z | W |   |
     FLD-C
```

11.
```
UNSTRING NAME-IN
      DELIMITED BY ALL SPACES
      INTO FIRST-NAME
           MIDDLE-INITIAL
           LAST-NAME.
MOVE SPACES TO NAME-OUT.
STRING LAST-NAME     DELIMITED BY SPACE
       ", "          DELIMITED BY SIZE
       FIRST-NAME    DELIMITED BY SPACE
       " "           DELIMITED BY SIZE
       LAST-NAME     DELIMITED BY SPACE
      INTO NAME-OUT.
```

12. Assume the following DATA DIVISION entries:
```
01   FIRST     PIC 999.
01   SECOND    PIC 99.
01   THIRD     PIC 9999.
UNSTRING SS-NUM
    INTO FIRST SECOND THIRD.
STRING FIRST, "-", SECOND, "-", THIRD
    DELIMITED BY SIZE
    INTO SS-NUM-OUT.
```

or

Assume the following DATA DIVISION entry:
```
03  SS-NUM-OUT  PIC 999B99B9999.
MOVE SS-NUM TO SS-NUM-OUT.
INSPECT SS-NUM-OUT REPLACING ALL " " BY "-".
```

13. a. | B | B | 1 | B | B | B |

b. | | B | 1 | A | B | A |

c. | A | | 1 | A | B | A |

14. a. | 0 | 1 | 2 | | 0 | 3 | | 5 |

     ITM-2   ITM-3   ITM-4

b. | 0 | 1 | 2 | | 0 | 0 | | 3 |

     ITM-2   ITM-3   ITM-4

c. | 0 | 0 | 0 | | 0 | 0 | | 0 |

     ITM-2   ITM-3   ITM-4

Note: Overflow occurs

15. a. | 0 | * | * | * | * | * | * |

     FLD-T

b. | 0 | 0 | 0 | 1 | * | 0 | 1 | 1 |

     FLD-T

c. | * | * | * | 1 | 0 | 0 | 1 | 1 |

     FLD-T

16. a. KOUNT = 5
   b. KOUNT = 2
   c. KOUNT = 0
   d. KOUNT = 4
   e. KOUNT = 2

Chapter 12

1.
```
COMPUTE-DATE-DIFFERENCE.
    DIVIDE YEAR1 BY 4 GIVING Q1 REMAINDER R1.
    COMPUTE JULIAN1 =
        365.25 * YEAR1 +
        DAYS-PREVIOUS-ENTRY (MONTH1) +
        DAY1.
    IF R1 = 0 AND MONTH1 > 2
        ADD 1 TO JULIAN1.
    DIVIDE YEAR2 BY 4 GIVING Q2 REMAINDER R2.
    COMPUTE JULIAN2=
        365.25 * YEAR2 +
        DAYS-PREVIOUS-ENTRY (MONTH2) +
        DAY2.
    IF R2 = 0 AND MONTH2 > 2
        ADD 1 TO JULIAN2.
    SUBTRACT JULIAN1 FROM JULIAN2
        GIVING DIFFERENCE.
```

Note: The second condition regarding leap years is not incorporated into this procedure because only the last two digits of the year are available.

2.

	TABLE-ARGUMENT
(1)	4
(2)	9
(3)	17
(4)	25
(5)	30
(6)	45
(7)	70
(8)	100
(9)	105
(10)	110

ACTUAL-ARGUMENT

115

Values of

Repetition	LOW	HIGH	MID	Comments
1	0	11	5	TABLE-ARGUMENT (5) < 115
2	5	11	8	TABLE-ARGUMENT (8) < 115
3	8	11	9	TABLE-ARGUMENT (9) < 115
4	9	11	10	TABLE-ARGUMENT (10) < 115
	10	11		HIGH − LOW = 1; therefore, element is not in table.

ACTUAL-ARGUMENT

3

Values of

Repetition	LOW	HIGH	MID	Comments
1	0	11	5	TABLE-ARGUMENT (5) > 3
2	0	5	2	TABLE-ARGUMENT (2) > 3
3	0	2	1	TABLE-ARGUMENT (1) > 3
	0	1		HIGH − LOW = 1; therefore, element is not in table.

3.

Data	Hash function value
6	7
19	6
23	3
20	7

TABLE

(1)	20
(2)	
(3)	23
(4)	
(5)	
(6)	19
(7)	6

Note: Position 7 is already occupied; therefore, position 1 is used for 20.

Data	Hash function value
20	7
6	7
19	6
23	3

TABLE

(1)	6
(2)	
(3)	23
(4)	
(5)	
(6)	19
(7)	20

Note: Positions of items 20 and 6 in the table are interchanged.

4.

	Table Size						
Technique	10	50	100	500	1000	5000	10000
Direct Access	1	1	1	1	1	1	1
Exhaustive Search	10	50	100	500	1000	5000	10000
Sequential Search	5	25	50	250	500	2500	5000
Binary Search	less than 4	less than 6	less than 7	less than 9	less than 10	less than 13	less than 14
Randomized Table	approx. 1	approx. 1	approx. 1	approx. 1	approx. 1	approx. 1	approx. 1

Note: The difference between a sequential search and a binary search become much more pronounced as the table size increases.

5. See Section 12.7.

6. a. An exhaustive search in which the most frequently used values are placed at the beginning of the table would be best if space does not permit a randomized table.

b. A sequenced table with a binary search, or if space permits, a randomized table.

c. A randomized table would provide optimum response time and, since space is not a problem, would be the best solution.

7. The value of search flag will be "ERROR".

8. a.
```
LOAD-ROUTINE.
    MOVE "YES" TO MORE-DATA.
    OPEN INPUT TABLE-FILE.
    READ TABLE-FILE
        AT END MOVE "NO" TO MORE-DATA.
    PERFORM MOVE-READ
        UNTIL MORE-DATA = "NO".
    CLOSE TABLE-FILE.
MOVE-READ.
    ADD 1 TO NUM-ENTRY.
    MOVE TABLE-RECORD TO
        TABLE-ENTRY (NUM-ENTRY).
    READ TABLE-FILE
        AT END MOVE "NO" TO MORE-DATA.
```

```
b. 01  TABLE-DATA.
      05  TABLE-ENTRY  OCCURS 1 TO 100 TIMES
                DEPENDING ON NUM-ENTRY
                ASCENDING KEY IS TABLE-ARGUMENT
                INDEXED BY INDX.
          10  TABLE-ARGUMENT   PIC 9(6).
          10  TABLE-VALUE      PIC X(20).
c. SEARCH ALL TABLE-ENTRY
      AT END MOVE SPACES TO OUTPUT-VALUE
      WHEN ACTUAL-ARGUMENT = TABLE-ARGUMENT (INDX)
          MOVE TABLE-VALUE (INDX) TO OUTPUT-VALUE.
```

Chapter 13

1.

	Mode			
	INPUT	OUTPUT	I/O	EXTEND
Valid Input/Output Statements	READ	WRITE	READ REWRITE	WRITE

2. a. rewind: a tape file is repositioned to its beginning.

b. key field: a field used as the basis for organizing a file.

c. audit trail: maintenance of complete records to enable an auditor to retrace and verify actions taken by a data processing system.

d. file status: a two-character field declared in the SELECT entry and updated automatically after each input/output operation related to a file.

e. backup: a copy of a file maintained in case of error.

f. activity: the ratio of transaction records to master file records.

g. volatility: the ratio of add and delete transaction records to master file records.

3. If a key field can legitimately have a value like 99999 (for example, this value was actually assigned as an account number), the method used in this chapter would have to be modified. It is possible to use other fields, each of which is one digit wider than the key field for the file. Each time a record is read, the key field is moved to its corresponding other field. At end-of-file, the large value is moved to the other field. Only the other fields are compared when determining action to be taken on a record. In this way, an actual key-field value like 99999 will be less than another key-field terminal value like 999999, resulting in appropriate processing for the record. For an alphanumeric key field, HIGH VALUES can be used to signify end-of-file.

4. Open files
Read FILE-A
Read FILE-B
Read FILE-C
Do until KEY-A = high value and KEY-B = high value and KEY-C = high value
    If KEY-A ≤ KEY-B and KEY-A ≤ KEY-C
        Write new record from FILE-A record
        Read FILE-A
    Else
        If KEY-B ≤ KEY-A and KEY-B ≤ KEY-C
            Write new record from FILE-B record
            Read FILE-B
        Else
            Write new record from FILE-C record
            Read FILE-C
        End If

```
        End If
   End Do
   Close files
   Stop
```

5. COBOL provides for sequential and random access to data files. Sequential access is simple, and there is the least possible system overhead when this method is used. However, sequential access makes possible only next record access to the file. Random access provides for access to records on demand; however, there is an added burden of complexity and system overhead.

6. If activity is expected to be high, interactive file updating may place a large burden on a data processing system.

7. If volatility is high, the process of adding and deleting records on demand may place stress on the resources of the computing system.

8. Since add and delete transactions are a subset of all transactions, it is not possible for the volatility ratio to exceed the activity ratio.

9. Change records may be entered in the same format as master file records with unaffected fields left blank, or change records may contain a transaction code specifying the field to be changed. The first method is relatively easy to implement but places a considerable burden on the data entry function, since each field must be placed in exactly the right location. The second method places a somewhat greater burden on the processing program but is simpler to use by data entry personnel.

10. A sequential file is appropriate in batch-oriented file maintenance, when next record access is all that is required, or for backups, logs, and other system files, and when tape is to be used as the storage medium for the file. A sequential file would not be appropriate in interactive file maintenance or when records must be accessed on demand.

11. Because backup files are used only to re-create active files, it is usually unnecessary to maintain the indexed or relative file organization. When the active file is re-created, the software can copy the backup into a file with appropriate organization.

12. In a batch-update procedure, all transactions are collected in a single file which is sorted and then used to update the master file. In an interactive update procedure, the master file is updated dynamically as each transaction record is entered.

13. Updating a sequential file in place necessitates the use of a flag in each record to mark deleted records. Records can be added to the end of the file but cannot be merged between existing records. This technique is appropriate when master file records need only to be changed or deleted.

14. In the procedure of Figure 13.10, the item read flag is used to determine whether or not a record must be read from the old master file.

15. With transactions in Delete, Add, Change sequence, it will be possible to delete a record in the master file, add a new record with the same key field value, and then process changes against the new master file record. It would no longer be possible to add, change, and delete a record during the same maintenance cycle.

Chapter 14

1. a. `SEQUENTIAL/OUTPUT`
   b. `SEQUENTIAL/I-O`
   c. `RANDOM/I-O`
   d. `RANDOM/INPUT`
   e. `RANDOM/OUTPUT`
   f. `SEQUENTIAL/INPUT`
   g. `DYNAMIC/I-O`

2. The WRITE statement is used to add records to a file; the REWRITE statement is used to change an existing record.

3. Format-1 READ may include the NEXT RECORD clause and is used to read records sequentially. Format-2 READ includes an INVALID KEY clause and is used to read records randomly.

4. An indexed file can be created under the sequential or random access methods but not dynamic access; dynamic access always implies that the file exists. Sequential access is used to place the records in physical sequence corresponding to the logical sequence; this serves to optimize system performance when sequential retrieval of the data is carried out.

5. START I-S-FILE KEY NOT < "200".

6. The statements in the INVALID KEY clause will be executed, since FILE STATUS value "23" indicates that no record with the specified key-field value was found.

7.
```
PROCEDURE DIVISION.
1000-MAJOR-LOGIC.
    PERFORM 2000-INITIALIZATION.
    PERFORM 2100-CONTROL UNTIL EOF-FLAG = "YES".
    PERFORM 2200-RE-INITIALIZE.
    PERFORM 2300-LIST-READ UNTIL EOF-FLAG = "YES".
    PERFORM 2400-TERMINATION.
    STOP RUN.
2000-INITIALIZATION.
    OPEN INPUT INPUT-FILE
        OUTPUT INVENTORY-FILE.
    READ INPUT-FILE AT END MOVE "YES" TO EOF-FLAG.
2100-CONTROL.
    MOVE INPUT-RECORD TO INVENTORY-RECORD.
    WRITE INVENTORY-RECORD
        INVALID KEY
            PERFORM 3000-ERROR.
    READ INPUT-FILE AT END MOVE "YES" TO EOF-FLAG.
2200-RE-INITIALIZE.
    CLOSE INPUT-FILE
        INVENTORY-FILE.
    OPEN INPUT INVENTORY-FILE
        OUTPUT PRINT.
    MOVE "NO" TO EOF-FLAG.
    READ INVENTORY-FILE
        AT END
            MOVE "YES" TO EOF-FLAG.
2300-LIST-READ.
    MOVE INVENTORY-RECORD TO PRINT-LINE.
    WRITE PRINT-LINE AFTER 2.
    READ INVENTORY-FILE
        AT END MOVE "YES" TO EOF-FLAG.
2400-TERMINATION.
    CLOSE INVENTORY-FILE
        PRINT.
3000-ERROR.
    EXIT.
```

```
8. PROCEDURE DIVISION.
   1000-MAIN-LOGIC.
       OPEN INPUT INVENTORY-FILE
           OUTPUT PRINT.
       READ INVENTORY-FILE AT END MOVE "YES" TO EOF-FLAG.
       PERFORM 2000-PROCESS-DATA UNTIL EOF-FLAG = "YES".
       CLOSE INVENTORY-FILE PRINT.
       STOP RUN.
   2000-PROCESS-DATA.
       WRITE PRINT-LINE FROM INVENTORY-RECORD AFTER 1.
       READ INVENTORY-FILE AT END MOVE "YES" TO EOF-FLAG.
9. PROCEDURE DIVISION.
   1000-MAIN-LOGIC.
       PERFORM 2000-INITIALIZATION.
       PERFORM 2100-UPDATE UNTIL EOF-FLAG = "YES".
       PERFORM 2200-TERMINATION.
       STOP RUN.
   2000-INITIALIZATION.
       OPEN INPUT SALES-FILE
           I-O INVENTORY-FILE
           OUTPUT PRINT.
       READ SALES-FILE AT END MOVE "YES" TO EOF-FLAG.
   2100-UPDATE.
       MOVE INVENTORY-NUMBER-SR TO INVENTORY-NUMBER-IRR.
       READ INVENTORY-FILE
           INVALID KEY
               PERFORM 3000-ERROR.
       SUBTRACT NUMBER-SOLD-SR FROM QUANTITY-ON-HAND-IRR.
       REWRITE INVENTORY-RECORD
           INVALID KEY
               PERFORM 3100-ERROR-RECOVERY.
       READ SALES-FILE AT END MOVE "YES" TO EOF-FLAG.
   2200-TERMINATION.
       CLOSE INVENTORY-FILE PRINT SALES-FILE.
   3000-ERROR.
       EXIT.
   3100-ERROR-RECOVERY.
       EXIT.
10.    SELECT INVENTORY-FILE ASSIGN TO DISK
           ACCESS IS DYNAMIC
           ORGANIZATION IS INDEXED
           RECORD KEY IS INVENTORY-NUMBER-IRR.

           .
           .
           .

   PROCEDURE DIVISION.
   1000-MAIN-LOGIC.
       OPEN INPUT INVENTORY-FILE.
       MOVE "05000" TO INVENTORY-NUMBER-IRR.
       READ INVENTORY-FILE
           INVALID-KEY PERFORM 3000-ERROR.
       READ INVENTORY-FILE NEXT RECORD
           AT END MOVE "YES" TO EOF-FLAG.
       PERFORM 2000-PROCESS-DATA
           UNTIL EOF-FLAG = "YES".
       CLOSE INVENTORY-FILE.
       STOP RUN.
```

```
    2000-PROCESS-DATA.
        .
        .
        .
        READ INVENTORY-FILE NEXT RECORD
            AT END MOVE "YES" TO EOF-FLAG.
    3000-ERROR.
        EXIT.
11. PROCEDURE DIVISION.
    1000-MAJOR-LOGIC.
        PERFORM 2000-INITIALIZATION.
        PERFORM 2100-PROCESS-DATA UNTIL END-OF-TRANSACTIONS.
        PERFORM 2200-TERMINATION.
        STOP RUN.
    2000-INITIALIZATION.
        OPEN INPUT TRANSACTIONS
            I-O INVENTORY-FILE
            OUTPUT PRINT.
        READ TRANSACTIONS AT END MOVE "YES" TO EOF-FLAG.
    2100-PROCESS-DATA.
        IF NOT VALID-TRANSACTION-CODE
            PERFORM 3000-ERROR-IN-TRANS-CODE
        ELSE
            IF ADD-RECORD
                PERFORM 3100-ADD-RECORD-TO-FILE
            ELSE
                IF DELETE-RECORD
                    PERFORM 3200-DELETE-RECORD-FROM-FILE
                ELSE
                    PERFORM 3300-UPDATE-RECORD.
        READ TRANSACTIONS AT END MOVE "YES" TO EOF-FLAG.
    2200-TERMINATION.
        CLOSE TRANSACTIONS INVENTORY-FILE PRINT.
    3000-ERROR-IN-TRANS-CODE.
        EXIT.
    3100-ADD-RECORD-TO-FILE.
        MOVE TRANSACTION-RECORD TO INVENTORY-RECORD.
        WRITE INVENTORY-RECORD
            INVALID KEY PERFORM 9000-ERROR-IN-ADD.
    3200-DELETE-RECORD-FROM-FILE.
        MOVE INVENTORY-NUMBER-TR TO INVENTORY-NUMBER-IR.
        DELETE INVENTORY-RECORD
            INVALID KEY PERFORM 9100-ERROR-IN-DELETE.
    3300-UPDATE-RECORD.
        MOVE INVENTORY-NUMBER-TR TO INVENTORY-NUMBER-IR.
        MOVE "YES" TO RECORD-FOUND-FLAG.
        READ INVENTORY-FILE
            INVALID KEY MOVE "NO" TO RECORD-FOUND-FLAG.
        IF RECORD-FOUND
            PERFORM 4000-CHANGE-FIELD
        ELSE
            PERFORM 9200-ERROR-IN-UPDATE.
    4000-CHANGE-FIELD.
        IF CHANGE-DESCRIPTION
            MOVE DESCRIPTION-TR TO DESCRIPTION-IR.
        IF CHANGE-QUANTITY-ON-HAND
            MOVE QUANTITY-ON-HAND-TR TO QUANTITY-ON-HAND-IR.
        IF CHANGE-REORDER-POINT
            MOVE REORDER-POINT-TR TO REORDER-POINT-IR.
```

```
      IF CHANGE-REORDER-AMOUNT
          MOVE REORDER AMOUNT-TR TO REORDER-AMOUNT-IR.
      IF CHANGE-UNIT-SELLING-PRICE
          MOVE UNIT-SELLING-PRICE-TR TO UNIT-SELLING-PRICE-IR.
      IF ADD-TO-QTY-ON-HAND
          ADD QUANTITY-ON-HAND-TR TO QUANTITY-ON-HAND-IR.
      IF SUBTRACT-FROM-QTY-ON-HAND
          SUBTRACT QUANTITY-ON-HAND-TR FROM QUANTITY-ON-HAND-IR.
      REWRITE INVENTORY-RECORD
          INVALID KEY PERFORM 9300-ERROR-IN-PROGRAM.
  9000-ERROR-IN-ADD.
      EXIT.
  9100-ERROR-IN-DELETE.
      EXIT.
  9200-ERROR-IN-UPDATE.
      EXIT.
  9300-ERROR-IN-PROGRAM.
      EXIT.
```

12. ```
    SELECT PERSONNEL-FILE
        ASSIGN TO DISK
        ORGANIZATION IS INDEXED
        ACCESS IS SEQUENTIAL
        RECORD KEY IS SS-NO-PR
        ALTERNATE RECORD KEY IS
            EMPLOYEE-NAME-PR WITH DUPLICATES
        ALTERNATE RECORD KEY IS
            DEPARTMENT-NUMBER-PR WITH DUPLICATES
        ALTERNATE RECORD KEY IS
            ZIP-CODE-PR WITH DUPLICATES.
    ```

13. SELECT entry is the same as for Exercise 12 above, except ACCESS IS DYNAMIC.
    ```
    PROCEDURE DIVISION.
    1000-MAIN-CONTROL.
        OPEN INPUT INVENTORY-FILE.
        MOVE "3" TO DEPARTMENT-NUMBER-PR.
        START PERSONNEL-FILE
            KEY IS EQUAL TO DEPARTMENT-NUMBER-PR
          INVALID KEY
            DISPLAY "NO EMPLOYEES IN DEPT. 3"
            CLOSE PERSONNEL-FILE
            STOP RUN.
        READ PERSONNEL-FILE NEXT RECORD
            AT END MOVE "YES" TO END-OF-DATA.
        PERFORM 2000-PROCESS-DATA
            UNTIL END-OF-DATA = "YES"
                OR DEPARTMENT-NUMBER-PR NOT = "3".
        CLOSE PERSONNEL-FILE.
        STOP RUN.
    2000-PROCESS-DATA.
        WRITE PRINT-RECORD FROM
                PERSONNEL-RECORD AFTER 1.
        READ PERSONNEL-FILE NEXT RECORD
            AT END MOVE "YES" TO END-OF-DATA.
    ```

14. The record with the given Social Security number will be deleted. The program could read the record, display its content, and then ask the user to verify that this is indeed the record to be deleted.
    ```

Chapter 15

1. File access: Sequential
   Open Mode: Input

   Open files
   Read data file
   Do while not end of file
       If deleted record
           Move data file record to output record
           Write output record
       End If
       Read data file
   End Do
   Close files
   Stop

2. Each time a program that accesses the file is run, the program could compute the ratio of total number of collisions to the number of file accesses required in the execution of the program. This value, along with a time stamp and possibly other information, should be added to a log file. Periodically, the operator or systems programmer could examine the content of the log file. If the ratios are increasing over time, there is an indication that it is possibly time to reorganize the file.

3. The DELETE verb cannot be used to remove records without modifying the procedure for adding records to the file because the removed record creates a logical "hole" in the file. If this location were needed for another record, a random READ would result in an INVALID KEY condition, and the REWRITE verb would be invalid if the record did not already exist.

4. New records are added by seeking an unused record and rewriting that record with new information. The random WRITE creates a new record in the file and cannot be used if there is an existing record at that location.

5. *Revision of Figure 15.4*

   Record address = hash function (key field)
   Move "CONTINUE" to found flag
   Do while found flag = "CONTINUE"
       Read data file
       If active record
           Add 1 to record-address
           If record-address > file size
               Move 1 to record-address
           End If
       Else
           Move "FINISH" to found flag
       End If
   End Do
   Move actual data to data file record
   Rewrite data file record

   Revision of Figure 15.5

   Record-address = hash function (transaction key)
   Move "CONTINUE" to found flag
   Do while found flag = "CONTINUE"
       Read data file
       If record does not contain data
           Move "NOT PRESENT" to found flag
       Else
           If record is active and key field = transaction key
               Move "FOUND" to found flag

```
                Else
                        Add 1 to record-address
                        If record-address > file size
                                Move 1 to record-address
                        End If
                End If
        End If
    End Do
    If found flag = "FOUND"
            Move transaction date to appropriate fields in data record
            Rewrite data record
    Else
            Take action appropriate for invalid transaction
    End If
```

6. A relative file can be used to store table data by using the table argument as the key field. Look-up can be accomplished using the START verb to locate the record that has the desired relationship with the actual argument.

7. A relative file may be chosen for efficiency of execution time.

8. For a relative file, space must usually be reserved to store records with all possible valid keys, whether or not those records exist. Thus a relative file may require excessive space in mass storage.

9.
```
Low = 0
High = table size + 1
Move "CONTINUE" to search flag
Do while search flag = "CONTINUE"
        Record address = (low + high) / 2
        Read relative file
        If table-argument = actual argument
                Move "FOUND" to search flag
        Else
                If table argument > actual argument
                        Move record address to low
                Else
                        Move record-address to high
                End If
                If high − low = 1
                        Move "NOT PRESENT" to search flag
                End If
        End If
End Do
If search flag = "FOUND"
        Use table-value as appropriate
Else
        Take action appropriate when data is not present in the table
End If
```

Chapter 16

1. a. A *subprogram* is a program that is executed by another program. A subprogram is sometimes referred to as a "called" program.
   b. A *calling program* is a program that executes another program. A calling program is sometimes referred to as a "main" program.
   c. A *program unit* is a subprogram or a main program.
   d. A *load module* is a set of program units ready for execution.
   e. *Linking* is a process of relocating program units and resolving address references.

2. Program modules may be linked before or during execution. RM/COBOL-85 carries out this process during the execution of the program at the time that the subprogram is called.

3. Three features found in subprograms, but not in other programs, are:
   - LINKAGE SECTION.
   - PROCEDURE DIVISION USING . . .
   - EXIT PROGRAM.

4. The VALUE clause can be used only in conjunction with an 88-level item in the LINKAGE SECTION.

5. Items listed in a PROCEDURE DIVISION USING clause must be defined in the LINKAGE SECTION as 01-level or 77-level items.

6. The name of a subprogram is usually defined in the PROGRAM-ID entry. In RM/COBOL-85, the subprogram name is the name of the .COB file containing the subprogram.

7. Subroutines aid program development by: (1) enabling many programmers to work on a project simultaneously, (2) enabling significant portions of a program to be tested independently of other parts, (3) simplifying the debugging task at each stage of program development, and (4) saving time if the procedure can be used by another program. Subroutines aid program maintenance by simplifying the propagation of any change in a routine common to several programs in the system.

8. Answers will vary. The student should ascertain the details of creating subprograms and load modules from local documentation. RM/COBOL-85 carries out the process during program execution at the time the subprogram is called and loaded into memory.

9. A subprogram can execute another subprogram. However, a subprogram cannot execute itself or another subprogram that would cause an execution of the calling subprogram.

10.
```
    IDENTIFICATION DIVISION.

    PROGRAM-ID. JULIAN.
    *REMARKS.  CONVERT MMDDYY TO JULIAN DATE.
    *          ANSWER TO EXERCISE 11 SECTION 16.6.

    ENVIRONMENT DIVISION.

    CONFIGURATION SECTION.

    SOURCE-COMPUTER.
    OBJECT-COMPUTER.

    DATA DIVISION.

    WORKING-STORAGE SECTION.

    01   REFERENCE-CONSTANTS.
         03   FILLER   PIC 999 VALUE 0.
         03   FILLER   PIC 999 VALUE 31.
         03   FILLER   PIC 999 VALUE 59.
         03   FILLER   PIC 999 VALUE 90.
         03   FILLER   PIC 999 VALUE 120.
         03   FILLER   PIC 999 VALUE 151.
         03   FILLER   PIC 999 VALUE 181.
         03   FILLER   PIC 999 VALUE 212.
         03   FILLER   PIC 999 VALUE 243.
         03   FILLER   PIC 999 VALUE 273.
         03   FILLER   PIC 999 VALUE 304.
         03   FILLER   PIC 999 VALUE 334.
    01   REFERENCE-TABLE REDEFINES REFERENCE-CONSTANTS.
         03   DAYS-ELAPSED  PIC 999 OCCURS 12 TIMES.
    01   QUOT             PIC 99.
    01   REM              PIC 99.
```

```
LINKAGE SECTION.

01   DATE-IN.
     03  MONTH-IN      PIC 99.
     03  DAY-IN        PIC 99.
     03  YEAR-IN       PIC 99.
01   JULIAN-DATE    PIC 999.

PROCEDURE DIVISION
     USING DATE-IN, JULIAN-DATE.

1000-MAIN.

     COMPUTE JULIAN-DATE = DAYS-ELAPSED (MONTH-IN) + DAY-IN.
     DIVIDE YEAR-IN BY 4 GIVING QUOT REMAINDER REM.
     IF REM = 0 AND MONTH-IN > 2
         ADD 1 TO JULIAN-DATE.

2000-EXIT.

     EXIT PROGRAM.
```

11.
```
IDENTIFICATION DIVISION.

PROGRAM-ID. NAMECONV.

*REMARKS. CONVERTS NAME STRING TO SEPARATE FIELDS.
*          ANSWER TO EXERCISE 12 SECTION 16.6.

ENVIRONMENT DIVISION.

CONFIGURATION SECTION.

SOURCE-COMPUTER.
OBJECT-COMPUTER.

DATA DIVISION.

LINKAGE-SECTION.

01   FULL-NAME       PIC X(20).
01   LAST-NAME       PIC X(10).
01   FIRST-NAME      PIC X(10).
01   MIDDLE-INITIAL  PIC X.

PROCEDURE DIVISION

        USING FULL-NAME, LAST-NAME, FIRST-NAME,
            MIDDLE-INITIAL.

1000-MAIN.

     UNSTRING FULL-NAME DELIMITED BY ALL SPACES
        INTO LAST-NAME, FIRST-NAME, MIDDLE-INITIAL.

1100-EXIT.

     EXIT PROGRAM.
```

INDEX